ENCYCLOPEDIA OF CONTEMPORARY LATIN AMERICAN AND CARIBBEAN CULTURES

ENCYCLOPEDIA OF CONTEMPORARY LATIN AMERICAN AND CARIBBEAN CULTURES

Volume 2: E–N

Edited by
Daniel Balderston, Mike Gonzalez
and Ana M. López

London and New York

First published 2000
by Routledge
11 New Fetter Lane, London EC4P 4EE

Simultaneously published in the USA and Canada
by Routledge
29 West 35th Street, New York, NY 10001

Routledge is an imprint of the Taylor & Francis Group

© 2000 Routledge

Typeset in Baskerville by Taylor & Francis Books Ltd
Printed and bound in Great Britain by TJ International Ltd,
Padstow, Cornwall

All rights reserved. No part of this book may be reprinted or reproduced
or utilized in any form or by any electronic, mechanical, or other means,
now known or hereafter invented, including photocopying and recording,
or in any information storage or retrieval system, without permission in
writing from the publishers.

British Library Cataloguing in Publication Data
A catalogue record for this book is available from the British Library

Library of Congress Cataloging in Publication Data
Encyclopedia of contemporary Latin American and Caribbean cultures/
edited by Daniel Balderston, Mike Gonzalez and Ana M. López.
p. cm
Includes bibliographical references and index.
1. Latin America–Encyclopedias. 2. Caribbean Area–Encyclopedias.
I. Balderston, Daniel, 1952- II. Gonzalez, Mike. III. López, Ana M.
F1406 .E515 2000
972.9003–dc21   00–032303

ISBN 0–415–13188–X (set)
ISBN 0415–22971–5 (vol 1)
ISBN 0415–22972–3 (vol 2)
ISBN 0415–22973–1 (vol 3)

Contents

Volume 1

Editorial team	vii
List of contributors	ix
Introduction	xix
How to use this encyclopedia	xxiii
Acknowledgements	xxv
Thematic entry list	xxvi
Decades	1
Entries A–D	30

Volume 2

Entries E–N	501

Volume 3

Entries O–Z	1063
Bibliography	1625
Index	1627

earthquakes

With the exception of Brazil and parts of some other countries, earthquakes form part of the life and historical memory of Latin America and the Caribbean. Their devastating effects have particularly affected Mexico, Central America and the Andean Region because of their proximity to the Pacific Ring of Fire, an area of major tectonic activity which releases 80 per cent of the total seismic energy affecting the earth's surface.

In the Caribbean, major earthquakes seem to occur every 100 years. In Mexico and Central America, where the centres of population sit exactly on the fault lines, earthquakes cause huge devastation approximately once every thirty years, and serious damage at least annually. Cities like Guatemala and San Salvador have had to be rebuilt several times, and Managua was almost completely destroyed in 1931 and 1972. Mexico City, previously protected by its marshy subsoil, was very badly damaged and suffered enormous loss of life in the 1985 earthquake. The Andean countries have also been the victim of periodic earthquakes and their coasts often struck by the tidal waves they cause. The 1960 earthquake in Chile reached the highest point ever on the Richter scale; in 1970 Peru was left with a toll of 66,000 dead, among the highest number of deaths registered anywhere in the world.

The panic that accompanies an earthquake and the desolation that follows it have been frequent themes of popular songs as well as poetry, novels and films. Guadalupe Chávez's 'Corrido de los temblores' (Ballad of the Earthquakes) was written in 1931; *Ancash-31*, a volume of poems by Peruvian writers edited by Jesús Cabel appeared in 1976. The 1985 earthquake in Mexico City inspired a number of books including Elena **Poniatowska**'s *Nada, nadie* (Nothing, Nobody) (1988) and Carlos Elizondo's *Septiembre 19: en el umbral del infierno* (September 19th, on the Threshold of Hell) (1986). Pedro Joaquín **Chamorro**'s *Richter 7* (1976) was a response to the Nicaraguan experience. In the cinema, Mari Carmen de Lara's *No les pedimos un viaje a la luna* (We are not Asking for the Moon) (1986) analyses the impact of the 1985 earthquake on Mexico City women garment workers.

Futher reading

Cabel, J. (1973) *Literatura del sismo; reportaje a Ancash, por Cabel*, Lima: Librería-Editorial J. Mejía Baca.

Fernández, M. (1990) *Ciudad rota : la ciudad de México después del sismo*, Mexico: Universidad Nacional Autonóma de México, Instituto de Investigaciones Estéticas.

Hernandez Parker, L. (1960) *Catástrofe en el paraíso; reportaje al Sur de Chile y 61 fotografías del sismo mayor de la historia*, Santiago, Chile: Editorial del Pacífico.

Pacheco, C. (1986) *Zona de desastre*, Mexico, DF: Ediciones Océano.

Sevilla, B.S. (1995) *Participación y catástrofe: Mendoza, una comunidad afectada por el sismo : vulnerabilidad y reacciones ante una situación límite*, Mendoza: EDIUNC.

LUIS L. ESPARZA

East Indians

From 1838, a new slave trade in the English colonies in the Caribbean brought labourers from India to work the sugar plantations. To distinguish them from the indigenous and other inhabitants of the West Indies, these new immigrants became known as 'East Indians' or, later, 'Indo-Caribbeans'. Despite gruelling work, harsh conditions, racial prejudice and political hostility, these communities survived to become a distinct component of the cultural life not only of Guyana and Trinidad, where they are the majority, but of the whole Caribbean. Cheddi **Jagan**, Hasan Ali and the **Naipauls** have joined the list of Caribbean celebrities, and *roti* and **doubles** have crossed the world to the accompaniment of **chutney** music.

LUIS L. ESPARZA

eating out

For the majority of Latin Americans and Caribbeans eating out actually means buying food from a cart or vendor on the street and eating it there while standing, leaning or sometimes crouching. Throughout the region, there are vendors of sandwiches or filled pastries, grilled meat, cotton candy, glazed peanuts, fruit and fruit juices on every street corner. These vendors often find themselves in conflict with the police and municipal authorities who in the name of hygiene try to control these vendors or to remove them to designated areas. This is really more about social control than about hygiene, although issues of **public health** are real enough. The **cholera** outbreak of 1990 almost certainly spread through the sale of ***ceviche*** on the streets of Lima and Guayaquil. Some foods that are often sold in this way include *tacos* and *tamales* in Mexico, *pupusas* in Central America (see **corn and corncakes**), *empanadas* in Chile and Argentina, *anticuchos* (roasted organ meats) in Peru, *roti* and **doubles** in Trinidad, *pastéis* (filled fried pastries) in Brazil. In coastal areas, beach stalls will sell fresh fish or shellfish. What is interesting about this phenomenon is that both the vendors and their customers belong to the same social class. Other venues that cater to the popular classes are the informal and economical restaurants called by various names, including *cocina económica* (cheap kitchen) or *comedor popular* (people's diner), often located in or near municipal markets.

Many of the same foods are available in a very different setting in *restaurantes típicos* (traditional restaurants), serving national cuisine to a middle-class clientele. While it is to be hoped that the hygiene questions that alarm the authorities with regard to street food are absent from these establishments, this is regrettably not always the case. Restaurants specializing in roast meat are called *churrascaria* in Brazil, *parrilla* in Argentina and *churrasquería* elsewhere. International cuisine available in middle-class restaurants rarely strays from pizza, pasta and Chinese food (called *chifa* in Peru). Vegetarian restaurants, which increased in number from the 1980s onwards, offer salad bars and a variety of prepared food, often at a cheap fixed price; the fancier ones tend to be associated with **New Age** groups or **green activism**.

The bulk of eating out is done in restaurants that offer varieties of the local cuisine or in one of the proliferating chains of **fast food** restaurants, often franchised by USA-based corporations (Wendy's, McDonald's, Denny's, Kentucky Fried Chicken and now even Taco Bell), though these will sometimes adapt to some extent to local conditions, adding spices, condiments or chili peppers. There are also restaurants associated with immigrant groups (primarily Spanish and Portuguese, but also Hungarian, Middle Eastern, Eastern European, etc.) (see **immigration to Latin America**), where eating reaffirms ethnic identification.

For those who can afford it, there are exclusive and luxurious restaurants serving French (and other European) cuisine, Japanese food (particularly in Brazil) or more elaborate versions of the local cuisine. The distinguishing features of these restaurants are often valet parking, numerous attendants and waiters (usually male), live music and a dress code. These establishments are often located in the more luxurious hotels or social clubs.

Further reading

Babb, F. (1998) *Between Field and Cooking Pot: The*

Political Economy of Marketwomen in Peru, Austin: University of Texas Press.

Barros, C. and Buenrostro, M. (1996) *Itacate*, Mexico City: Grijalbo.

Kennedy, D. (1972) *The Cuisines of Mexico*, New York: Harper & Row.

Lambert Ortiz, E. (1980) *The Book of Latin American Cooking*, New York: Vintage.

MIKE GONZALEZ AND DANIEL BALDERSTON

Echevarría, Nicolas

b. 1947, Tepic, Mexico

Film-maker

An important documentary film-maker, Echevarría achieved international recognition for his film *Cabeza de Vaca* (1990). He studied composition with Carlos **Chávez** in 1969 and co-founded the composition group Quanta with Mario **Lavista** in 1970. He is also an enthusiastic painter, and has published and illustrated his own storyboards.

In 1972 Echevarría joined the Millennium Film Workshop in New York, a well-known cradle of underground film-makers. Returning to Mexico, he embarked on a series of documentaries about indigenous peoples, giving voice to marginal groups and representing their religious, artistic and cultural expressions. For Echevarría, this kind of film-making was a mystical experience that also gave access to the magic of Indian worlds. His first experimental film, *Judea, Semana Santa entre las coras* (Judeah, Holy Week among the Coras) (1973), showed that vision at its best. *Hikura Tame, peregrinación del peyote* (**Peyote** Pilgrimage) (1975) drew on all the wisdom of indigenous culture. *Hay hombres que respiran luz* (Some Men Breathe Light) (1976) followed the presidential campaign of Luis **Echeverría**; he returned to indigenous themes in *Tesquinada, semana santa tarahumara* (Holy Week with the Tarahumara) (1979) and *El niño Fidencio, el taumaturgo de Espinazo* (The Child Fidencio, the Magician of Espinazo) (1981). *Maria Sabina, mujer y espíritu* (Maria **Sabina**, Woman and Spirit) (1978) offered an exceptional insight into the mystical world of the deceased religious figure whose powers of healing through mushrooms made her such a central figure in Mexican popular culture.

A commission from **Televisa** to make a television film of *Las trampas de la fe* (The Pitfalls of Faith) by Octavio **Paz** challenged Echevarría to make the transition from documentary to fiction, and to enter the world of literature, religion and women in a different historical epoch, the colonial period. Several cultural documentaries and series for television followed.

Cabeza de Vaca, his first full-length film, was completed in 1990 after nearly ten years of arguments, frustrations and disappointment. In this work, Echevarría achieved the masterly recreation of a magical, fictional world using documentary techniques, a project that would certainly have failed had the director approached it through traditional fictional narrative forms.

Further reading

García, G. and Cavia, J.F. (1997) *Nuevo cine mexicano*, Mexico: Clío.

PATRICIA TORRES SAN MARTÍN

Echeverría Alvarez, Luis

b. 1922, Mexico City, Mexico

Politician

Echeverría was a President of Mexico whose populist (see **populism**) administration (1970–1976) featured growing state intervention in the economy. Secretary of the Interior during the massacre of student protesters in **Tlatelolco** in 1968, Echeverría met with widespread opposition both before and during his presidency. His conflicts with the private sector culminated toward the end of his term, when he nationalized farmland and devalued the currency for the first time in decades. His administration incorporated leftist opposition groups and cultural workers into the governing party, but by the end of his term Echeverría was largely discredited. After serving as Mexico's ambassador to UNESCO and Australia he retired from public life.

JUAN CARLOS GAMBOA

Ecker, Enrique Eduardo

b. 1887, Curaçao, Netherlands Antilles;
d. 1966, Cleveland, USA

Scientist

The author of widely published research on numerous aspects of bacteriology and immunology, Ecker was the co-author, with Howard J. Karsner, of the standard work *The Principles of Immunology* (1921). He studied medicine in Chicago, specializing in hygiene, anatomy and bacteriology. After 1918 he was affiliated with Western Reserve University, Cleveland, where he became a professor in 1942.

AART G. BROEK

ECLA *see* SELA

economic miracle

The 'economic miracle' (*milagre brasileiro*) is the name given to the boom in the Brazilian economy from 1968 to 1973, which saw unparalleled annual growth rates of 11 per cent and established Brazil as a major producer and exporter of manufactured goods. Fuelled by cheap oil (see **oil in Latin America**) and a massive influx of multinational capital investment, the miracle years saw Brazil's total exports increase from less than US$3 billion to just under US$10 billion. A fast-growing and affluent middle-class led consumer demand for products from key manufacturing sectors, automobiles and electronic household goods, and provided the technical and managerial personnel for the new factories, the financial system and the state apparatus.

The consumer boom was not shared equally, however. The costs of industrializing agriculture were borne by the thousands of unskilled rural workers, forced to seek employment in the cities, while in the urban sector the real value of the minimum wage fell by about 25 per cent between 1968 and 1973. It was not coincidental that these years were also the most repressive of the military dictatorship installed in 1964. The so-called '*coup within the coup*' of 1968 brought an intensified crackdown on political and trade union opposition and the annulment of civil rights for many thousands through a ruthlessly efficient apparatus of terrorism, **censorship**, imprisonment and torture.

The suppression of working-class organization, beginning with the armed crushing of a factory strike and occupation in Osasco, on the outskirts of São Paulo, guaranteed the conditions for the militarized state and its multinational investors to maximize their profits. The already distorted distribution of income between rich and poor was dramatically exacerbated. The richest 10 per cent saw their share of the cake rise from 41.28 per cent to 51.15 per cent between 1960 and 1970, while the proportion of total income received by the poorest half of the population fell from 15.87 to 10.49 per cent.

The regime's propaganda of social consensus around the 'miracle' did not go unchallenged, despite its efforts to censor any cultural expressions of dissent. The nightmarish contradictions of the boom were subjected to a carnivalesque, parodic treatment by the film-makers, musicians and artists of the experimental **Tropicália** movement. Songwriter Chico **Buarque**, in compositions like 'Construção' (Building Site), dramatized the tragic consequences of the construction boom for internal immigrant workers.

In 1974, euphoria gave way to crisis and open disaffection among the regime's supporters, as international oil prices quadrupled and struck at the foundations of the boom. Growth in GDP fell catastrophically from 14 per cent in 1973 to 5.6 per cent in 1975, throwing the balance of payments into long-standing deficit and raising the foreign debt to US $12 billion by 1974. In the short term this led to a renewed hardline response to the crisis, but the collapse of the political consensus around the spectacle of economic success ultimately forced the regime to accommodate to the growing demands of a broad-based opposition movement and to embark on the democratic 'transition' known as *abertura*.

Further reading

Baer, W. (1989) *The Brazilian Economy: Growth and Development*, London: Praeger.

Kucinski, B. (1982) *Brazil: State and Struggle*, London: Latin American Bureau.

DAVID TREECE

Ecopetrol

Ecopetrol (Empresa Colombiana de Petróleos) is the Colombian national oil company, created in 1948, to supervise the oil industry. It operates in Barrancabermeja (Department of Santander), and the regions of the Magdalena Valley and the Llanos. Ecopetrol has signed contracts of cooperation to exploit oil on Colombian soil with foreign oil companies.

MIGUEL A. CARDINALE

ecotourism

Ecotourism, also referred to as 'green', 'soft-path', 'alternative', 'academic', 'adventure', or 'responsible' **tourism**, emerged in the late 1970s as one of several touristic practices posed as alternative to the mass and **luxury tourism** scenarios, which were increasingly criticized for their ecologically and culturally unsustainable practices. Partially a product of the emergent ideology of sustainable development, these 'alternative' tourisms were posited as consistent with natural and social values, respecting natural resources and allowing both hosts and guests to enjoy a more mutually positive interaction.

However, the degree to which ecotourism has been uncritically accepted and endorsed is problematic. Unlike mass tourism scenarios, in which the tourist economy is extremely focused and segregated, alternative tourism scenarios do generally create more points of econonomic and cultural leakage. Research suggests that though these alternative tourism practices may have a less intense effect upon local ecosystems than mass tourism, social contact between indigenous groups and tourists tends to be much more intensive in alternative tourism situations. The nature of this contact and the implicit power relations invested therein merit further examination. Language-learning tourism, for example, which is becoming extremely popular in Mexico and Central America, creates particularly intensive contact scenarios between hosts and guests. Students are usually housed with local families, participating in community development projects as part of the curricula aimed to maximize intercultural contact.

Many ecotourist enterprises capitalize on the increasing global concern with disappearing cultures and ecosystems, marketing a pristine, authentic, exotic 'other' to European and North American consumers in scenarios which, although given a postmodern world-beat face-lift, still resemble the primitivist kitsch exoticism which sent hordes of tiki-lounge travellers limbo-ing their way from Havana to Rio in the 1950s. However, many such scenarios do indeed represent efforts to increase understanding between hosts and guests while gaining capital to preserve local environments and cultures. Also, though ecotourist schemes tend to create more points of acculturative leakage, these host–guest interactions often instigate a social identity crisis in the host community, actually causing the reaffirmation and increased cohesion of a particular ethnic group.

Ecotourism scenarios are more often locally controlled than mass tourism scenarios. Indigenous groups have initiated ecotouristic enterprises with their respective governments in order to generate income to protect and maintain their lands, controlling and managing the projects themselves with widely varying degrees of success. Costa Rica, probably the most famous ecotourist destination in Latin America, offers a university degree programme in ecotourism, supporting local control of this industry. However, many ecotourist sites in this same country, conceived with very little planning, have become just as vulnerable to external pressures as mass tourism sites, suffering the economic, natural, and cultural consequences of myopic over-development. Ecotourism has, in fact, become one of the largest industries in Latin America, experiencing an enormous growth in the 1980s from Mexico to Tierra del Fuego.

Further reading

Boullon, R.C. (1993) *Ecoturismo: sistemas naturales y urbanos*, Buenos Aires, Argentina: Librerías Turísticas.

Diagnostico do desenvolvimento do ecoturismo no Pantanal brasileiro (1994) Programa de Estudos e Pesquisas nos Vales Amazonicos. Belem: A Superintendencia.

Harvey, J. (1995) *Ecoturismo en el Ecuador: trayectorias y desafios*, Quito: PROBONA, Programa Regional de Bosques Nativos Andinos: Intercooperation.

—— (1999) *Ecoturismo y desarrollo sostenible en Republica Dominicana, el Caribe y el mundo*, Santo Domingo: Ediciones Fundación Cienca y Arte.

Smith, R. (1996) *Manual de ecoturismo: para guias y comunidades indígenas de la Amazonia ecuatoriana*, Quito, Ecuador: Abya-Yala.

Wunder, S. (1996) *Ecoturismo, ingresos locales y conservación: el caso de Cuyabeno*, Ecuador. Quito: Unión Mundial para la Naturaleza, Oficina Regional para America del Sur.

JOHN HARVEY

Ecuador

The equator crosses the South American continent, passing through the Ecuadorean **Galapagos Islands** as well as Ecuador's beaches, snow-capped mountains and verdant tropical forest. Border conflicts (see **borders**) marred relations between Ecuador and neighbouring Peru through the 1980s and 1990s, despite many years of negotiations, but a peace treaty was signed in 1998.

The second smallest republic in the continent (283,520 square miles), Ecuador boasts wide diversity in geographical setting, ethnic populations and cultural expression. One half of the Ecuadorean people live in a tropical coastal region west of the Andean mountain chain; African-Ecuadoreans (7 per cent of the population) are found in Esmeraldas. In the mountainous Andes, **Quichua**-speaking Indians maintain their traditional way of life in small villages which nestle in the valleys between the sprawling modern cities. Native peoples are also found in the tropical forest to the east of the Andes; the lowland Quichua, Cofán, Shuar and Huaorani peoples live along the rivers and in the interior of the forest. Ecuadorean census figures report that 40 per cent of the population is Indian, 40 per cent **mestizo** (mixed blood), and 10 per cent of European descent, with another 10 per cent of Black or Asian origin.

Much of Ecuadorean literature reflects the economic and social realities of the multicultural nation. The **Guayaquil Group**, formed in the 1930s to narrate the plight of the coastal inhabitants, and the work of Jorge **Icaza**, particularly his *indigenista* novel *Huasipungo* (The Villagers) (1934), continue to influence Ecuadorean writers. Nelson **Estupiñán Bass**'s *Cuando los guayacanes florecían* (When the Guayacan Trees Bloomed) (1954) depicts the folkloric rhythms and lyrics of the African Ecuadorean population on the coast, as does Antonio Preciado's poetry. Jorge Enrique **Adoum**'s narrative, poetry and essays explore the complex personal and international stature of an Ecuador which is no longer provincial and isolated. His innovative novel *Entre Marx y una mujer desnuda* (Between Marx and a Naked Woman) (1976) wrestles with problems of narrative form as well as depicting the drama of intellectual introspection. Eliécer **Cárdenas**'s *Polvo y ceniza* (Dust and Ashes) (1979) recounts the deeds of a legendary bandit who battles the landowners in southern Ecuador. *La linares* (The Linares Woman) (1975) by Iván **Egüez** depicts the heady world of politics where a beautiful woman brings down a President. Literary references and folkloric memory celebrate political events such as the kidnapping of President León Febres Cordero, the election of President Abdalá Bucaram, known as 'El Loco' (The Crazy One) by a slim margin (1996), and the eventual ousting of Bucaram for reasons of 'mental incapacity' by the military. For several days in 1997, Rosalía Arteaga assumed the presidency amidst much commentary, as she was the first female head of state, but she was soon replaced by Fabián Alarcón.

Women writers also address the cultural constructs of nation. Most notable is the literary group Mujeres del Atico (Women From the Attic), who maintain a literary salon and publish editorial pieces in the Guayaquil newspaper *El Telégrafo* . Internationally recognized for her novels is Alicia **Yánez Cossío**, author of *La cofradía del mullo de vestido de la virgen Pipona* (The Religious Brotherhood of the Shell Garment of the Virgin Pipona) (1985); her novels blend a controlled **magical realism** and Catholic lore with the sharp irony and wit reflective of the region. One of the more notable innovations in the literary scene is the publication of two books of poetry in Quichua by the Otavalan Indian Ariruma Kowii, *Mutsuctsurini* (1988) and *Taisik* (1993).

Literary themes are often repeated in cinema, photography, theatre, dance and art. *Cumandá*, the 'foundational novel' of Ecuador, has been filmed for television and boasted high viewer ratings. *La Tigra* (The Tigress), a short story by José de la **Cuadra**, has received critical acclaim for the sultry acting in the film. Adoum's *Entre Marx y una mujer desnuda* was adapted to the screen by Camilo Luzuriaga (1995). Bolivian film-maker Jorge **Sanjinés** collaborated with the Central University in *Lluschi caymanta/Fuera de aquí* (Get Out of Here!) (1977) which highlights problems of land ownership. *Icemen of Chimborazo* (1980), by Gustavo Guayasamín, details the poverty of those peasants who ascend a mountain to cut ice and sell it in their village. Similarly, *In Time of Women* (1980) by Mónica Vasquez depicts the desolation of a small town where many men with few economic possibilities emigrate to the United States, leaving women and families behind.

Ecuadorean writers and artists receive support and exhibition space in the national and regional branches of the **Casa de la Cultura Ecuatoriana** (the Ecuadorean National Endowment for the Arts), a government agency founded by Benjamín **Carrión** in 1941. As in most Latin American countries, film-making in Ecuador has been curtailed by lack of government subsidies. However, under Ulises Estrella, the Ecuadorean Cinemateca (Film Foundation) of the Casa de la Cultura screens vintage and contemporary films and has diligently set about restoring Ecuador's rich collection of early twentieth-century films.

Indigenous figures with massive hands and intense expression are featured in the artistic production of Oswaldo **Guayasamín**, whose works are elegantly displayed in a museum in Quito and in a mural for the National Congress. Eduardo **Kingman** is credited with early depictions of the Indian; Osvaldo **Viteri**'s oil canvases display cloth figurines and weavings, a tactile entry into Andean folkways. In music, traditional indigenous melodies for rituals and festivals predominate in the disks produced by Nanda Mañachi, Los Huayanay, Los Corazas, Los Jatari, the folklore group Peguche and Zig Zag. Jesús Fichamba won a Spanish prize for his song, 'La Pinta, La Niña y la Santa María' (Christopher Columbus's ships) in which he recognizes his indigenous Otavalan origins.

The political, sociological and ethnic themes of Ecuadorean cultural production attest to the richness of a nation deemed 'una sociedad pluricultural' (a multicultural society) in essays, **graffiti**, street theatre and orchestral compositions, as well as the medium of film and prose. The most powerful testimony to that national reality, however, has been the eruption into national political life of the organizations of indigenous peoples (see **CONAIE**) from 1990 onwards and their definitive presence in the National Constituent Assembly of 1997 (see **indigenous movements**).

In 1999 these organizations joined trade movements and other protesting groups in a mass resistance movement that overthrew the Mahnad government, which had proposed the 'dollarization' of the economy. The withdrawal of the indigenous organizations from its successor government early in 2000 presaged a new wave of activity against the impact of neoliberal economic policies.

Further reading

Hurtado, O. (1980) *Political Power in Ecuador*, Albuquerque, NM: University of New Mexico Press.

Martz, J.D. (1972) *Ecuador: Conflicting Political Culture and the Quest for Progress*, Chapel Hill, NC: University of North Carolina Press.

Miller, T. (1986) *The Panama Hat Trail: A Journey from South America*, New York: Marrow Press.

REGINA HARRISON

Ecury, Nydia Maria Enrica

b. 1926, Aruba

Actor, director and poet

Ecury moved to Curaçao in the 1950s, where she translated plays by Paso, Williams, Genet and Shakespeare into the creole **Papiamentu**. She is an actress and director, as well as the author of various collections of poetry, including the 1984 bilingual edition of *Kantika pa Mama Tera/Songs for Mother Earth*. Ecury has been strongly opposed to the consolidation of female stereotypes and to the relegation of women to the periphery of public life. She has been a performing artist of Papiamentu poetry at numerous literary festivals both inside and outside the Caribbean.

AART G. BROEK

Edgell, Zee

b. 1940, Belize City, Belize

Novelist and activist

The foremost writer of Belize, Edgell's first novel *Beka Lamb* (1982) is autobiographical and relates the problems of a young **creole** girl maturing into adulthood to the growing pains of a country struggling for independence. After travelling widely abroad, she became Director of the Women's Bureau in the new country of Belize (1981). Out of this experience came her second novel, *In Times like These* (1991). Presently a professor at Kent State University, Edgell's most recent novel, based on a historical incident, is *The Festival of San Joachim*, in which she examines domestic abuse and the **mestizo** community in Belize.

GAY WILENTZ

Ediciones de la Banda Oriental

Heber Raviolo, Alcides Abella and other members of the editorial staff of a periodical called *Tribuna Universitaria* founded the Uruguayan publishing house Ediciones de la Banda Oriental in 1961. Raviolo is still general editor and series editor for 'Lectores de la Banda Oriental' (Readers of the Banda Oriental), a monthly collection started in 1978 for subscribers. Ediciones began by publishing two books, and is now one of the leading national publishers in the fields of literature, history and social sciences. They publish authors such as Tomás de **Mattos**, Idea **Vilariño** and Hector Galmés.

VICTORIA RUÉTALO

Editora Abril

One of the largest media conglomerates in Latin America, Editora Abril was founded in 1950 by Victor Civita with the publication of a Portuguese version of the comic, *Donald Duck* (see **comics**). The company grew steadily through the 1950s and 1960s, fuelled, at first, by the success of *Capricho* (1952), a teen magazine with the largest circulation of any magazine in Latin America in the 1950s, *Quatro rodas* (1960), which exploited the boom in road building and auto ownership, and *Contigo* (1963), a women's magazine with popular *fotonovela* supplements (see ***fotonovelas***). It also introduced the ever-influential ***Veja*** (1968) and, since 1975, the Portuguese version of *Playboy*. In the 1980s and 1990s, the company diversified aggressively, moving into international publications markets and other media such as home video, TV channels, cable TV services (TVA, the first in the nation since 1991), direct-to-home satellite television (see **satellite and cable television and telecommunication**), CDs and CD-ROMs, direct marketing and on-line services (Universo Online). Its revenues as of 1998 were estimated at $1.5 billion.

ANA M. LÓPEZ

Editorial Nueva Nicaragua

Created by governmental decree in 1981, Editorial Nueva Nicaragua (ENN) was the most prominent Sandinista (see **Sandinista Revolution**) publishing institution. Led by Sergio **Ramírez**, the series Biblioteca Popular Sandinista published the works of the Nicaraguan authors as well as books about Nicaragua produced abroad. ENN in fact began in 1960, when Carlos **Fonseca Amador** and other Sandinista leaders organized a modest press. In spite of the 1980s economic embargo, ENN had published over 157 titles by 1987, and established the Nueva Nicaragua prize for Latin American narrative. Luis Rocha serves as the editor of ENN in the late 1990s, when it was no longer financed by the government.

ESTEBAN E. LOUSTAUNAU AND ILEANA RODRIGUEZ

EDUCA

The Central American University Press, EDUCA (Editorial Universitaria Centroamericana), is one of the most important publishing houses in Central America. Located in San José, Costa Rica, it was established by the Confederation of Central American Universities. Throughout the political turmoil that the different Central American nations endured during the 1970s and 1980s, many of the writers and intellectuals identified with the left had to flee their countries. Costa Rica remained a safe place of refuge for these intellectuals, while EDUCA published and distributed their works.

BEATRIZ CORTEZ

education

Education in Latin America has been characterized over the past three decades by both gleaming progress and dismal retreat. With a discourse hauntingly reminiscent of the 'modernization' theories and 'human capital' approaches of the 1960s and 1970s, education is once again being called upon to serve as the panacea which will increase national productivity, strengthen democratic values and institutions, close the gaps between the rich and the poor, and contribute to solving the many challenges facing Latin American countries. Education has also proven to be an arena in which political, economic and cultural contradictions and conflicts are manifested. It is an area which often highlights the precarious relationship between the ends and means of development, the changing role of the state, and the ways in which public policy is made. In order to present an overview of education in Latin America, it is necessary to briefly review past gains and current deficiencies, fundamental problems and policy issues, new actors in the educational policy-making field, and challenges for the future.

During the 1950s and 1960s, the pace of educational development in Latin America was astounding: between 1960 and 1970, the indices of growth for higher education were 247.9 per cent; and for secondary and primary education, 258 per cent and 167.5 per cent, respectively. New sectors of the population had more access to schooling, which was generally considered to be one of the most effective means of social mobility. While most countries in the region currently enjoy universal gross primary enrolments, the statistics regarding grade repetitions, or percentage of age cohort reaching a certain grade, or the number of years of school life expectancy, are much more problematic. For example, the percentage of first graders repeating in 1990 varied from approximately 20 per cent in Chile and Venezuela to approximately 30 per cent in Argentina, Colombia, Mexico and Peru to more than 50 per cent in Brazil and Nicaragua. Latin America also has one of the lowest rate of school completion in the world, with only 54 per cent of students who enter first grade reaching grade four, and only four countries with primary completion rates higher than 75 per cent. In terms of gross secondary enrolments, countries can be divided into three groups. Argentina, Chile and Uruguay form the first group, with rates of 70 per cent or over. The second group, with rates of between 45 per cent and 67 per cent, includes Colombia, Costa Rica, Ecuador, Mexico, Panama and Peru. The third is made up of Bolivia, Brazil, El Salvador, Guatemala, Honduras, Nicaragua, Paraguay and Venezuela, with rates of between 23 per cent and 42 per cent.

However, in the 1980s, while enrolments continued to grow, the rate of growth of educational expenditures, adjusted for inflation, diminished. Between 1975 and 1980, total expenditures on education increased in all countries in the region, and between 1980 and 1993, public expenditures on education as a percentage of GNP also increased slightly from 3.9 per cent to 4.6 per cent. However, evidence from the 1980s shows that total expenditures in real terms diminished in many countries, and it is imperative to point out that the 1980s were a period of slow economic growth in the region. Thus, educational expenditures have only slightly kept up, if at all, with their pre-crisis levels.

These troubling educational indicators, among others, point to several fundamental problems and inequalities. First, equality, quality and relevance of educational provision in the region continue to be crucial issues. However, Latin American governments do not have or do not choose to allocate the necessary financial resources to deal with these issues, especially given their political sensitivity. Second, schooling in Latin America is segregated by class, with the poor attending public schools and middle and upper classes attending private schools (except in the case of higher education, which is often the opposite). Brazil provides a particularly striking example of this situation. Third, although the estimated net enrolment rate in pre-school education has increased from 2.4 per cent in 1960 to 17.4 per cent in 1992, with few exceptions, the important pre-school experience is not widely available for the majority of poor children. Fourth, in terms of rural inequalities, children in the rural areas of Latin America are at a great disadvantage vis-à-vis children in urban areas. This is reflected in the differences which are seen in the percentage of children who do not complete their primary education, the percentage of children who must repeat a grade in the first two years of school, and the percentage who live in extreme poverty. Fifth, Stromquist (1996) points out that it is crucial to consider gender differences, particularly in regard to disparities in illiteracy rates, access and retention in rural versus urban areas, and inequalities among different racial and ethnic groups. She also calls attention to the context of textbooks and classroom practices. Sixth, multiethnic and multilingual issues, particularly in Mexico, Guatemala, Peru, Bolivia and elsewhere, still need to be addressed. Finally, school reform agendas have been launched simultaneously in many Latin American countries, resulting in a deep restructuring that goes beyond the mere improvement of the efficiency of existing systems. This restructuring aims at the transformation of purposes, assumptions and methods of school systems, and it tends to focus on competency testing, school and teacher certification, and national standards.

Given this brief outline of some of the most fundamental educational problems in Latin America, it is important to consider the actors who participate in the formulation and implementation of educational policy. While there are many traditional actors, such as ministries of education, parents, teachers, community organizations and so on, the roles of teachers' unions and international organizations have expanded considerably in the past decades and thus merit attention.

Teachers, as state employees, are important actors who fulfil a leading role in the state. As such, many of them think of themselves as the main public education employees responsible for the transmission of a nation's collective values to its children. For many years, teachers' unions had a strong influence on state educational policies, with corporatist patterns of decision making in which central unions became active partners in designing and implementing policies. However, since the 1980s school reform agendas throughout Latin America are being implemented at times of serious financial retrenchment in public spending. Trying to reduce expenses of financially overburdened school systems and attempting to make them more cost-effective often involves layoffs and substitution of lower paid instructional personnel for fully trained, more expensive teachers. This situation, along with recent initiatives for alternative school finance, has placed teachers' organizations at the centre of disputes on educational policy and practice. It has also led to an unstable consensus between teachers' unions and the state, and new areas of conflict in the interaction between teachers, teachers' organizations and the state are developing.

International organizations (financial, bilateral, multilateral and NGOs) are actively involved in financing and planning for education in Latin America. Although international influences on education in the region are not new, beginning in the 1960s there was a qualitative change in the way influence was exerted, namely, the appearance of loans (in contrast to grants) for education from powerful international financial organizations. The case of the World Bank and the **Inter-American Development Bank** provide interesting examples. The World Bank was the first international financier to make loans for education projects, and it has become the largest financier of education projects in developing countries, including Latin America. It has also become the leader in research and in the general policy debates surrounding education and development, particularly since the 1990 Jomtien Conference on Education for All. For example, World Bank lending for primary education in Latin America increased from an average of US $20 million per year in 1985–90 to a projected US $500 million per year in 1991–5.

Changes in the relationships between the economy (trends towards de-industrialization and export-oriented models in the context of globalization), politics (a growing neo-conservative rhetoric regarding diminishing the welfare roles of the state, a withdrawal of public investment, and shrinking public employment) and education (the new impetus towards privatization and user fees, decentralization, and vouchers), challenge previous notions about the role of education in development, citizenship building and democracy. Furthermore, a central concern continues to be about the role of the state in the social pact that articulates Latin American democracies. Prevailing notions of the state held by policy makers and researchers influence the dominant research agenda, the analysis of educational problems and policy prescriptions. **Neoliberalism** and its market-based policies have diminished the involvement and commitment of the state in financing educational development. New conflicts are arising, and these involve contentious views of what democratic governance of societies and schools should be, including notions of power, participation, representation and democratic decision making. Perhaps it is safe to argue that the notions of globalization and neoliberalism in Latin American education have transformed the debates surrounding the politics of education, thus increasing the challenges to emancipatory goals and practices.

See also: conscientization; Freire, Paulo; literacy; popular education; higher education

Further reading

ECLAC Social Panorama (1996), Santiago: ECLAC.
Plank, D. (1994) 'Public Purpose and Private Interest in Brazilian Education', in C.A. Torres (ed.), Education and Social Change in Latin America, Australia: James Nicholas Publishers, 145–54.
Puryear, J. (1997) Education in Latin America: Problems and Challenges, Santiago: PREAL.
Reimers, F. (1991) 'The Impact of Economic Stabilization and Adjustment on Education in Latin America', Comparative Education Review May: 319–52.
Scheifelbein, E. (1995) 'Education Reform in Latin America and the Caribbean: An Agenda for Action', The Major Project of Education in Latin America and the Caribbean 37, Santiago: UNESCO.
Stromquist, N. (1996) Gender and Democracy in Education in Latin America, New York: Council on Foreign Relations.
Torres, C.A. and Puiggrós, A. (1997) Latin American Education: Comparative Perspectives, Boulder, CO: Westview Press.
UNESCO Statistical Yearbook, various years, Paris: UNESCO.
Wolff, L., Schiefelbien, E. and Valenzuela, J. (1994). Improving the Quality of Primary Education in Latin America and the Caribbean, Washington, DC: World Bank.

CARLOS ALBERTO TORRES AND JULIE THOMPSON

Edwards, Jorge

b. 1931, Santiago, Chile

Writer

Edwards started his writing career in 1952 with the publication of a collection of short stories entitled El patio (The Backyard). Against the background of the simple situations of everyday life, the child protagonists obliquely experience the authoritarian regime of the adults, their lack of communication and the ineffectiveness of the bourgeois system. Although Gente de la ciudad (City People) (1961) and Las máscaras (Masks) (1967) present bureaucrats and urban adults leading an empty and pedestrian life, the same tensions created by the social and economic regimes are still present. Edwards has been defined as an author of few themes and multiple elaborations on the conflict between conventionalized roles and defeated masks.

After completing his law studies at the University of Chile and Princeton University, Edwards went into diplomacy. In 1970, Salvador **Allende** sent him to Cuba from where, after three months and for no explicit reason, he was expelled. This experience led him to write *Persona non grata* (1973), a testimonial account of the economic difficulties of the Cuban Revolution (see **revolutions**) and the problems of a political power which represses independent artistic creation and jails writers such as Heberto **Padilla**.

His novels *Los convidados de piedra* (The Stone Visitors) (1978), *El museo de cera* (The Wax Museum) (1981) and *La mujer imaginaria* (The Imaginary Woman) (1985) are, in a sense, a chronicle of the decadence and rearticulation of oligarchic power in Chile. The narrator is a *voyeur* who, with distance and irony, envelops the characters' voices and perspectives. Within this frame, past and present merge in a temporal line where each period retroactively sheds light onto the present. Thus, in *Los convidados de piedra*, although the plot centres on the bourgeois ritual of a birthday celebration for an aristocrat, time extends back to 1890, the critical year preceding the Revolution of 1891, and the subsequent regeneration of the oligarchy. According to Edwards's ideology, Chilean history has been dominated by the anachronistic power of colonial aristocracy, a concept symbolized by the Marquis de Villa-Rica, who detained social change by sculpturing reality into wax.

In 1971, Edwards worked with Pablo **Neruda** as cultural attaché in Paris, and his memoirs of Neruda entitled *Adiós, Poeta...* (Farewell, Poet...) (1990) won the III Comillas Prize sponsored by Tusquets Editores in 1990. He was awarded the National Prize for Literature in Chile in 1995.

Further reading

Moody, M. (1985) 'Chile and *El museo de cera*', *Chasqui* 14(3): 37–42

Otero, J. (1990) 'Subjetividad y mito como modos narrativos en *Persona non grata*', *Confluencia* 5(2): 47–53.

Rodríguez, M.A. (1988) '*La mujer imaginaria*: Una reflexión de Jorge Edwards sobre la historia chilena reciente', *Revista de Filología* 4: 225–39.

Rojas Piña, B. (1992) '*El anfitrión* de Jorge Edwards: Reescritura de mitos en el contexto de la dictadura y el exilio chilenos', *Chasqui* 21(1): 77–91.

—— (1994) 'El narrador en *El museo de cera* de Jorge Edwards', *Acta Literaria* 19: 69–85.

LUCÍA GUERRA

Edwards Bello, Joaquín

b. 1887, Valparaíso, Chile; d. 1968, Santiago, Chile

Writer and journalist

A keen observer of Latin American culture, Edwards's chronicles, travel diaries and memoirs offer valuable insights on all aspects, from politics to fashion. As an aristocrat who despised the values of his social class, he presents in his novels *El inútil* (The Loser) (1910) and *El roto* (The Down and Out) (1920), a morbid microcosm of poverty, denouncing the injustices of the Chilean rich in the 1920s. Esmeraldo is a countertext of the *roto*, the national symbol which reconstructs men from the lower classes as brave, strong and adventurous.

LUCÍA GUERRA

Egas, Camilo

b. 1899, Quito, Ecuador; d. 1962, New York City

Painter

A leading figure in Ecuadoran ***indigenismo***, Egas (born Camilo Alejandro Egas Silva) sought to dramatize the sufferings of the country's native peoples, and of working people elsewhere. He studied and exhibited in Europe in the 1920s, was art director of National Theatre in 1926, then moved to New York where he lived from 1927 to his death. He taught at the New School in New York for many years, directing its painting department from 1935 onwards, and painted a mural, *Festival*, there in 1932. In New York, he became friendly with the Mexican muralists, especially **Orozco**, and later with visiting surrealists. The **Casa de la Cultura Ecuatoriana** has significant holdings of his work.

DANIEL BALDERSTON

Egüez, Iván

b. 1944, Ecuador

Writer

Egüez was at the forefront of every aspect of the cultural scene in Ecuador, from the creation of avant-garde publications to the establishment of his own publishing house, Abrapalabra. In his own work, his command of technique, psychological insight, and unique use and manipulation of language are outstanding as well as his biting humour, experimentation, and incursions into the world of the sensual. His major publications are *La Linares* (The Linares Woman) (1976), *El poder del gran señor* (The Grand Lord's Power) (1985) and *Historias leves* (Light Stories) (1994).

HUMBERTO E. ROBLES

Eguren, José María

b. 1874, Lima, Peru; d. 1942, Lima

Poet and plastic artist

Eguren lived a secluded life due to poor health, and his need to rest for long periods of time allowed him to become a voracious reader. His main influences were the English Pre-Raphaelites and the French Symbolists. His poetry, collected in *Poesías* (1929), relies on a symbolic system of suggestions, impressions and correspondences that link the perceptions of the real world to the imaginary. He evokes dreamlike, misty atmospheres through subdued and nuanced colours. He also wrote poetic prose and essays collected in 1959 under the title *Motivos estéticos* (Esthetic Motifs).

MAGDALENA GARCÍA PINTO

Ehlers, Freddy

b. 1945, Quito, Ecuador

Journalist and politician

Director from 1990 of the weekly cultural programme *La televisión*, in 1996 Ehlers became the presidential candidate for the Nuevo País (New Country) coalition, which included **CONAIE** (the Ecuadorean organization of indigenous peoples), the social democratic Izquierda Democrática (Democratic Left) and the Marxist Socialista-Frente Amplio (Socialist-Broad Front). He was an outsider who exposed the cracks in the political system of the country and presented arguments for plurinationalism and ecological awareness. The coalition was subsequently disbanded, but Ehlers himself clearly has a promising political future.

RAÚL VALLEJO

Eichelbaum, Samuel

b. 1894, Domínguez, Entre Ríos, Argentina; d. 1967, Buenos Aires, Argentina

Writer and dramatist

Eichelbaum's plays accurately reflect his self-portrait as 'a maniac of introspection'. He is best remembered for *Un guapo del 900* (A Turn-of-the-Century Tough Guy) (1940), a commercial success which also earned him Argentina's National and Municipal Prizes. *Un guapo del 900* profiles a figure who 'cultivates courage' and whose sense of honour and justice confronts established political and legal interests. In his over thirty plays, mostly centred on the middle class, intellectual curiosity crafted his characters. The balance he struck between recognizable Argentine characters and individual idiosyncracies served to redirect his country's theatre away from strictly realistic scenarios.

SAÚL SOSNOWSKI

Eiriz, Antonia

b. 1929, Havana, Cuba; d. 1995, Miami, USA

Painter

One of the Los Once group formed in the 1950s, Eiriz's first individual exhibition in 1964 included key works like *Una tribuna para la paz* (A Tribune for Peace) and the controversial *La **anunciación*** (The Annunciation); with its iconography of violence, anguish and mutilations. She influenced a new generation of artists through her classes at the National Art School (1965–9) and her work in local craft workshops. She returned to painting and drawing in the 1990s, exhibiting with great success in the USA. She lived in Miami from 1993 until her death.

WILFREDO CANCIO ISLA

ejido

A grant of land to communities and municipalities in medieval Spain, it was then established in America for indigenous communities in the new centres of population. During the Mexican Revolution (see **revolutions**), the rebellious communities of the centre and south of the country reclaimed the lands to which they had been given title during the colonial period. The first agrarian reformers of the revolution called for the redistribution of *latifundio* land into *ejidos*. It then become institutionalized in law as an inalienable social and economic form, until the reform of Article 27 of the Mexican Constitution in 1991, by the neoliberal (see **neoliberalism**) regime of Carlos **Salinas de Gortari** placed *ejido* land back in circulation.

VICTOR MARTÍNEZ ESCAMILLA

El Salvador

The smallest country in mainland Latin America, El Salvador's 8,260 square miles embrace a population of just over 5 million, of whom around 25 per cent live in the capital San Salvador. Its twentieth-century history has been framed by two key moments – 1932 and 1980–1 – but shaped largely by its dependence on a single export commodity – coffee – and by its location in an area of strategic interest to the USA.

The expansion of coffee lands in the 1880s drove many indigenous communities off the land they had held communally, and turned that land from the cultivation of food crops or the more traditional exports like indigo to coffee production. The dominant 'fourteen families' (a phrase still used to designate the small core of families holding political and economic power, though the number is no longer precise) controlled the coffee trade, and what development there was in the early part of the century – railroad construction, the first electricity plant, roads – was designed to facilitate coffee exports. The Meléndez-Quiñonez regime (1913–27) ensured that their interests would continue to prevail. The extreme poverty in which many rural labourers lived, and the concentration of power throughout the early part of the century, go some way to explaining what came to be known as 'la Matanza' (the massacre) – the response of the State to the attempted insurrection of 1932. The Crash of 1929 was followed by a catastrophic decline in living standards in El Salvador's vulnerable single-product economy. The growth of trade union and socialist organizations in the late 1920s produced a major figure in Farabundo **Martí** (who had fought with **Sandino** in Nicaragua); it seemed inevitable that he was to lead the popular insurrection. Announced for early January 1932, Martí realized that the movement was unprepared and postponed the date of the rising; in the interim he was arrested and the army moved to crush the movement. At least 20,000 were killed in the repression that followed, ordered by the man who would be president (with brief interruptions) from 1931 to 1944 – Hernández Martínez.

Hernández Martínez's regime was the first in a series of military regimes that continued virtually uninterrupted for five decades – sometimes elected in carefully controlled elections, sometimes self-appointed by military *coup*. Until the late 1940s, the economy of El Salvador continued to depend almost exclusively on coffee. A modernizing thrust, beginning in the 1950s, was hastened in the early 1960s by new foreign capital investment, which fostered the industrial development without social upheaval supported by the **Alliance for Progress**. Industry's share of GNP rose from 20 to nearly 41 per cent in the decade, and the industrial working class virtually doubled – all this under a series of repressive regimes. The tensions exploded in 1969, when the so-called 'football war' expressed the rivalry of two military regimes, one of which (El Salvador) appeared to be stealing a march on the other (Honduras). Within a few years, it effectively signed the end of the nascent **Central American Common Market**. Tens of thousands of Salvadorans were driven out of Honduras, where they had been living, in some cases, for many years, and back into the overcrowded conditions of the Salvadoran countryside.

Internal pressures grew in the countryside and in the city, where trade unions in the capital's 'free-trade zones' were growing more combative. The social tensions were met with the usual repression – as a British parliamentary delegation reported in 1977. The first guerrilla organizations (see **guerrillas**) arose in El Salvador in the early 1970s: the ERP (1971) was led by the poet Roque **Dalton**, until he was killed in an internal dispute by his own comrades; the veteran communist trade union (see **trade unions**) leader Salvador **Cayetano Carpio** launched his own FPL (Popular Liberation Forces) in 1970. As the social crisis deepened through the late 1970s, civil resistance and trade union struggle ran in parallel with the construction of revolutionary organizations.

Observers of Central America anticipated that the first explosion in Central America would probably occur in El Salvador; instead it came in Nicaragua in July 1979. The urban insurrection of January 1980 was, in a way, Salvador's attempted revolution, led by the organizations of the Salvadoran left combined in the **FMLN** (Frente Farabundo Martí de Liberación Nacional). It was driven back into the countryside where it continued for another ten years of war and strife. The murder of Archbishop **Romero**, orchestrated by the leader of the right in the military, Roberto **D'Abuisson**, signalled the level of violence that would follow. This was also an indicator of the influence of **liberation theology** within and outside the church and the hostility to it that eventually resulted in the murder of eight people at the Jesuit university, **UCA**, in 1989. The level of US military aid to the country during the decade rose constantly until the peace process, culminating in 1989, officially ended the ten years of violence. Sadly, it ushered El Salvador into a peace framed by the aggressive policies of **structural adjustment** that then prevailed across the whole region – the majority of Salvadorans could expect little in the way of material improvements, even after the years of war.

These circumstances have dramatically shaped El Salvador's cultural life. The stories of **Salarué**, like his *Cuentos de barro* (1932), provide a tableau of peasant life in El Salvador; the extraordinary poetry of Claudia Lars, by contrast, was unknown until very recently, though it spans much of the century. Francisco Gavidia (1865–1955) really represents a generation of poets influenced by Darío, whereas Pedro Geoffroy Rivas (1908–79) points forward to the Círculo Literario Universitario of the mid-1950s, which included Roque **Dalton**, Roberto Armijo (1937–97), Hugo Lindo and Manlio **Argueta**. Argueta is perhaps better known for his imaginative novel, *Un día en la vida* (One Day of Life) (1980).

The outstanding figures of contemporary Salvadoran literature are Roque Dalton and Claribel **Alegría**. Dalton was a poet, political leader, novelist and writer of two key books for an understanding of El Salvador's past – his poetic history, *Las historias secretas de Pulgarcito* (Secret Lives of Tom Thumb) and his reworking of the extraordinary life story of *Miguel Mármol* (1972). Alegría has lived for many years in Nicaragua, yet much of her poetry and prose is rooted in the experience of El Salvador; *Cenizas de Izalco* (Ashes of Izalco) (1966), written with her partner, Darwin Flakoll, explores the lived experience of La Matanza.

In the context of civil war through the 1980s, cultural activity was either conducted in exile or in the 'liberated territories' under FMLN control, where the necessity for local communication produced exciting developments in **radio**, like Radio Rebelde, and in adult education, conducted by the liberation forces themselves. There was also an active film and video workshop, linked to the political organizations.

In music, the domination of US commercial music in the cities, and of Mexican music in the countryside was to some extent countered by the rediscovery of popular culture in the liberated areas – Yolacamba-Ita, for example, introduced the small, waist-held **marimba** and rediscovered the indigenous and mestizo roots of Salvadoran music.

Further reading

Dalton, R. (1972) *Miguel Mármol*, San José: Editorial Universitaria Centroamericana.

Didion, J. (1983) *Salvador*, London: Chatto & Windus.

Dunkerley, J. (1988) *Power in the Isthmus: A Political History of Modern Central America*, London: Verso.

Pearce, J. (1986) *The Promised Land: Peasant Rebellion in Chalatenango*, London: Latin America Bureau.

MIKE GONZALEZ

Electra Garrigó

Electra Garrigó is a play written in 1941 by Virgilio **Piñera** and presented for the first time by the Prometeo group in 1948 under the direction of Francisco Morín. The play translates classical tragedy into a Cuban context, desanctifies mythological characters and develops a parody full of comic reference and verbal brilliance. Clytemnestra's death occurs when she eats a huge papaya, and the ancient chorus is replaced by a typical **Guantanamera**. This piece inaugurates modern theatre in Cuba and introduces a new way of conceiving scenic space. The work itself is a penetrating exploration of what elements comprise Cuban identity.

WILFREDO CANCIO ISLA

Elite

Venezuelan magazine and publishing house established in 1924. In the mid-1930s, after the disappearance of Juan Vicente **Gómez** from the political scene, and under the directorship of Carlos Eduardo Frías, *Elite* was central among a group of magazines (*Arquero* (1932), *El ingenioso hidalgo* (1935) and *Gaceta de América* (1935)) that provided the space for intense debates and polemics among intellectuals of the avant-garde. The background to these debates about art was mostly political, specifically intellectual and cultural policies. *Elite* sought a nationalist and Americanist stance that would provide what they called a 'most attentive index of Venezuelan art movements among Indo-American literature'.

JACINTO FOMBONA

Elizondo, Salvador

b. 1932, Mexico City

Writer

Elizondo's highly reflective narrative texts, essays and contributions to literary, film and cultural journals and radio programmes mark him out as one of the leading authors of his generation. His first and most celebrated novel, *Farabeuf* (1965), has often been associated with the French *nouveau roman* and deals mainly with time, eroticism and the act of writing. His deep reflections on these subjects became a trade mark. His texts are always constructed with utmost rigour and irony. He received the Xavier Villaurrutia Prize (1965) and the Mexican National Prize for Letters (1990).

JUAN PELLICER

Ellis, Zoila

b. 1957, Dangriga, Belize

Writer and environmental lawyer

One of an emerging literary community in Belize, whose foremost writer is also a woman (Zee **Edgell**), Ellis grew up in the Garifuna (see **Garinagu**) community, a group tied closely to its African roots. Her collection of short stories, *On Heroes, Lizards, and Passions* (1980), explores the lives of Belizeans, with their passions and inter-ethnic prejudices, at home and in the United States. In addition to her short stories, Ellis has also published poetry in the **CAFRA** collection, *Creation Fire* (1990) edited by Ramabai **Espinet**. With degrees in law and development studies, Ellis works as development consultant and environmental lawyer while continuing her writing.

GAY WILENTZ

Elomar (Elomar Figueira de Melo)

b. 1937, Vitória da Conquista, Bahia, Brazil

Musician

Known as the 'príncipe das catingas' (prince of the scrublands), Elomar is one of the great singer-songwriters of the Bahian ***sertão***. He first gained recognition in 1973 with the recording *Das Barrancas do Rio Gavião* (From the Canyons of the Gaviao River). Rooted in the traditions of Iberian troubadours and minstrels, his music often makes use of Arabic scales and medieval modes which were brought to Brazil by Portuguese peasants during the colonial period. His song lyrics draw from the poetic traditions of the rural northeast, including *cantoria* (song-challenge), *romance* (sung narrative verse) and *cordel* literature. He has recorded several albums, including acclaimed collaborations with Geraldo **Azevedo**, Xangai, and Vital Farias.

CHRISTOPHER DUNN

Elpidio Valdés

A popular Cuban cartoon character created by Juan Padrón, Elpidio Valdés is a young rebel soldier (*mambí*) in the army fighting for independence at the end of the nineteenth century. He first appeared in the weekly *Pionero* in 1970, and in the same year appeared in two short films, *Una aventura de Elpidio Valdés* (An Elpidio Valdes Adventure) and *Elpidio Valdés contra el tren militar* (Elpidio Against the Military Train). Padron's historical research was so thorough that he became historical adviser to several other films. The first full-length cartoon, *Elpidio Valdés* (1979), was followed by *Elpidio Valdés contra dólar y cañón* (Elpidio Against the Dollar and the Cannon) (1983).

See also: animation; comics

JOSÉ ANTONIO EVORA

Eltit, Diamela

b. 1949, Santiago, Chile

Writer and performance artist

One of Chile's most talented contemporary writers, Eltit, together with poet Raúl **Zurita** and the visual artist Lotty **Rosenfeld**, was a member of the performance art group **CADA**, which staged art events critical of political and social realities under the military regime of Augusto **Pinochet**. Eltit has also published several novels, including *Lumpérica* (1983), *Por la patria* (For the Fatherland) (1986), *El cuarto mundo* (The Fourth World) (1988), *Vaca sagrada* (Sacred Cow) (1991) and *Los vigilantes* (The Vigilantes) (1995). She has also published a testimonial work, *El padre mío* (My Father) (1989), and collaborated with photographer Paz **Errázuriz** on the book *El infarto del alma* (The Soul's Heart Attack) (1994). Eltit's work has been described as poetic and experimental in its approach to themes like women and the body, tyranny, violence, rebellion and writing. Her writings problematize the Spanish language and the Chilean dialect, and use them in inventive, non-representational and non-referential ways. Her novels combine genres such as poetry, drama and narrative, and incorporate practices from the literary vanguard, the **neo-baroque**, psychoanalysis and film. *Lumpérica* and *Por la patria* exploit multiple art forms (painting, **video art**, **performance art**) and literary forms (poem, narrative, dramatic text) and connect writing and visual expression.

El cuarto mundo and *Los vigilantes* challenge traditional concepts of the family and social institutions modelled on the patriarchal family. The fragmentation produced by the multiple narrative voices of her texts – both rational and coherent and irrational and unconscious – is one technique for subverting structures of domination and established order. Characters use multiple systems of expression, including conscious and unconscious voices, the language of the body, and writing. In *Los vigilantes* the creative process is the protagonist's only means of salvation from a repressive and violent world. Writing becomes the sole way she can order and give meaning to her existence. Through her style and subject matter,

Eltit engages readers in a complex exploration of the violent struggle for representation on the social, sexual and cultural margins of Latin America.

Eltit won a Guggenheim fellowship in 1985. In 1992–3 she was cultural attaché at the Chilean embassy in Mexico. She often lectures at US universities.

Further reading

Brito, E. (1990) *Campos minados: literatura post-golpe en Chile*, Santiago: Cuarto Propio.

Lértora, J.C. (ed.) (1993) *Una poética de literatura menor*, Santiago: Cuarto Propio.

AMALIA PEREIRA

Emar, Juan

b. 1893, Santiago, Chile; d. 1964, Santiago

Writer

Juan Emar (Alvaro Yáñez Bianchi) was the intellectual power behind the Chilean avant-garde movements of the early 1920s. He is one of the innovative forces behind the new narrative, texts which interrogate language and expose its inadequacies in communicating a reality. His texts suggest but never explain, enunciating the impossibility of narration, derealizing the nominal world, questioning reality and its logic. His works include *Ayer, Un año y Miltín* (Yesterday, One Year and Miltin) (1934–5), *Diez* (Ten) (1937) and *Umbral* (Threshold) (1977).

ELIANA ORTEGA

Embrafilme

The Brazilian state film company Embrafilme was originally formed in 1969 to distribute Brazilian films abroad and aid producers. Its first products were ***pornochanchada*** films exploiting the guaranteed market for national films. After hostile reactions to their poor quality and Embrafilme's lack of direction, the enterprise extended its activities into distribution, exhibition and professional training and was joined by members of **Cinema Novo**. National audiences doubled from 30 million to 60 million, and Embrafilme supported high quality films like **Diegues**'s *Bye Bye Brasil* (1980). It was abolished in 1990 by President **Collor**, who accused it of corporatism; this served only to deepen the crisis of Brazilian cinema.

ISMAIL XAVIER AND THE USP GROUP

En el corazón de junio

Luis **Gusman**'s novel *En el corazón de junio* (At the Heart of June) won the 1983 Boris Vian Prize. The author's obsessions are evidenced in a plot in which Joyce co-exists with events in Argentine history like the bombings of the Plaza de Mayo, and a recent recipient of a heart transplant imagines his destiny in the fictions he reads while convalescing. Less fragmented and more measured than his previous novels, this is one of Gusman's most balanced works and certainly one of the best Argentine novels of the last twenty years.

DANIEL LINK

En rojo

One result of Puerto Rico's post-1950s floundering commonwealth relationship to the United States was a wave of pro-independence parties with their own organs. Like its sponsor, the Movimiento Pro Independencia (Pro-Independence Movement, later the Puerto Rican Socialist Party), the newspaper ***Claridad*** (Clarity) was founded in 1957. Its cultural supplement, *En rojo* (In Red), became an important cultural voice during the 1970s. Since then, *En rojo* has provided a cultural forum complementing the independentist political debate by *Claridad*. For example, like other important Puerto Rican writers, Luis Rafael **Sánchez** has regularly contributed essays (see **essay**) championing vernacular Puerto Rican culture's resistance to the virtual colonization of the island by the United States.

JOHN D. PERIVOLARIS

encuentros feministas

A series of continent-wide feminist conferences aimed at mobilizing and organizing Latin American feminist activists across boundaries of geography, education, ethnicity and class. The first 'Encuentro Feminista Latinoamericano y del Caribe' was held in 1981 in Bogotá, Colombia. Succeeding *encuentros* have taken place in Peru, Brazil, Mexico, Argentina, El Salvador and Chile. The eighth conference was held in the Dominican Republic in 1998. The first 'Encuentro de Lesbianas Feministas' was held in 1987, in conjunction with the fourth conference in Mexico. Organizers from the *encuentros* also participated in 1995's World Conference on Women in Beijing, China. The gatherings have sometimes been plagued by discord grounded in the heterogeneity and unequal power relations of the region, but have remained an important focal point of feminist organizing.

CAROL J. WALLACE

Engels, Christiaan Joseph Hendrikus

b. 1907, Rotterdam, The Netherlands; 1980, Curaçao, Netherlands Antilles

Writer, painter and musician

Engels established his medical practice on Curaçao in 1937, and there began to write a poetry of free association, characterized by its idiosyncratic syntax and personalized imagery. He was publisher and editor of the literary magazine *De **Stoep***. His later prose and essays dealt with the pre-Columbian indigenous continental and island cultures. He was also founder of the Curaçao Museum, a centre of artistic activities and exhibitions in the 1950s and 1960s. He also turned to painting and music. As a composer and pianist, he was a member of the Curaçao Philharmonic Orchestra.

AART G. BROEK

Engels-Boskaljon, Lucila

b. 1920, Curaçao; d. 1993, Curaçao

Painter

Lucila Engels started painting during the Second World War after her husband Chris **Engels** did, but soon she overshadowed him in ability. Her style is a colourful and romantic expressionism. Although oil painting was her main interest, she also made mosaics and wall paintings. She had important exhibitions in Amsterdam, Caracas and New York, and participated in the Bienales of São Paulo in 1955 and 1967 (see **Bienale de São Paulo**). Many children on the island received their first drawing lessons from her.

NEL CASIMIRI

English-based creoles

The English-based creoles of the Caribbean are scattered across the territories from the Bahamas in the north to Guyana in the south and from Belize in Central America to Guyana and Suriname in the southwest. Of the English-based creoles of the region, only a few (Jamaican and Guyanese in particular) have been the subject of in-depth linguistic investigation.

There are clear historical links between various subsets of the English-based creoles of the region, derived from the movement of peoples from territory to territory. It has been argued that there is little mutual intelligibility across English-based creoles; however, this has not been clearly established and there is little linguistic evidence beyond some low level aspects of the sound system to justify this claim.

As is the case with all the creoles of the region, these languages demonstrate a low level of inflectional morphology, even lower than is the case for English itself. Of the English-based creoles of the Caribbean, Jamaican, Guyanese, Samaraccan, Sranan Tongo and Ndjuka (the creoles of Suriname) are the only ones to have been subjected to detailed linguistic analysis. Each of these creoles shows some influence of languages other than the main lexical input languages. Samaraccan is viewed as a creole with significant retentions from Portuguese. All the Suriname creoles manifest some influence from Dutch in their lexicon. In other territories a few lexical inputs have been made from indigenous languages as well.

Where, as in the case of Jamaica and Guyana, the creole exists in a social context in which English is the prestige language, there has developed what has been termed a dialect continuum. Some linguists believe that such continua develop out of the continuing power structure within the societies in which the desire to acquire English leads to gradual approximation of English forms. Other linguists point out that such apparent approximation is essentially a matter of form and that the content remains essentially creole in its conceptualization. Though the notion of such continua enjoys considerable popularity, it is not accepted by a significant but growing minority of creolists.

See also: creole languages; Dutch-based creoles; French-based creoles

Further reading

Alleyne, M.C. (1980) *Comparative Afro-American: An Historical Comparative Study of English-based Afro-American Dialects of the New World*.

Balutansky, K.M. (ed.) (1998) *Caribbean Creolization: Reflections on the Cultural Dynamics of Language, Literature and Identity*, Gainesville, FL: University of Florida Press.

Taylor, D.M. (1977) *Languages of the West Indies*, Baltimore: Johns Hopkins University Press.

IAN ROBERTSON

English in Central America

It might come as a great surprise to English-speakers, especially those of the United States, whose own vocabulary has been quite receptive to loans from Latin American Spanish, that their language is also spoken by a small minority (numbering some 270,000 in the 1980s) in several Central American countries. English and Spanish have coexisted, often uneasily, in the New World since the sixteenth century, becoming the national languages of many of the Western Hemisphere's new republics in the nineteenth, and enjoying status as two of the world's major languages late in the twentieth. Political acquisitions, economic realities and historical migratory patterns have ensured, however, that national language is only a relative term in much of the New World, especially given the presence of both Spanish-speaking minority communities in North America and English-speaking ones in Central America.

English is spoken in a variety of dialects ranging from **English-based creoles** to regional variations of Standard English along much of the Caribbean coast of Central America from Belize (where it is the official language) to Panama, constituting the first language of numerous communities in officially Spanish-speaking Honduras (Bay Islands), Nicaragua (Bluefields, Pearl Lagoon), Costa Rica (Puerto Limón) and Panama (Panama City, Colón, Bocas del Toro), and serving as a *lingua franca* among various ethnic groups in the region. The language first gained a foothold on the Miskito Coast of Nicaragua in the 1630s. It was supplemented the length of the Central American Caribbean coast by further English colonization, especially in British Honduras (later **Belize**), and successive waves of nineteenth- and early twentieth-century immigration from Jamaica and Barbados which provided the labour force for US banana (see **bananas**) and **rubber** plantations as well as railroad and canal construction projects. The long isolation of the Caribbean coastal regions from the Spanish-speaking Pacific coast and central highlands and the largely African and indigenous ethnic backgrounds of the English-speaking minorities historically have prevented their linguistic and cultural Hispanicization. However, with the withdrawal of the US fruit conglomerates in the 1930s, the United States's return of the Panama **Canal Zone**, and the various attempts of the Central American governments to assimilate their Caribbean coastal regions, in many of these communities English is the first language of citizens who view the increasing bilingualism of their communities as a distinct economic advantage.

Further reading

Holm, J. (ed.) (1983) *Central American English*, Heidelberg: Groos.

SCOTT A. COOPER

Enigma of Arrival, The

In *The Enigma of Arrival* (1987) V.S. **Naipaul** breaks new ground in his continuing exploration of the dilemmas of the post-colonial writer. Proustian and symbolic, the novel probes the meaning of time, decay and renewal through circular reflections in which Naipaul's own thinly fictionalized life is viewed by an alter ego or implicated in parallel biographies. Embodying Naipaul's own quest to understand his life through writing, the novel becomes a meditation on the nature of art itself.

Divided into two halves and five parts, the novel takes its title from a surrealist painting by de Chirico, named by Apollinaire, which reflects the mystery of stasis and movement. Returning to the wharf to rejoin his ship, the traveller finds 'There was no mast above the walls of the wharf. No ship. His journey – his life's journey – had been made.' The first section, 'Jack's Garden' is set in Wiltshire, Naipaul's home for much of his life in England. Here he becomes familiarized with the landscape and natives of this most English of landscapes. In 'Ivy', the focus moves from the life of the labourer (Jack) to the squirearchy. The owner of the manor refuses to have the ivy removed because he likes it, a motif of a refusal to change. Naipaul perceives that England's past culture relates to his own roots in rural India, where a feudal system also held within it the principle of decay. Yet his new awareness of history leads him forward from a vision of loss to one of recurring patterns within cultural change.

Opening the second half of the novel, 'The Journey' relates a dual passage, Naipaul's physical voyage to Europe, and the writings through which he had journeyed towards understanding the permanent realities beneath transience. In the penultimate chapter, 'Rooks', the author juxtaposes his own life in writing with the unfulfilled career and early death of Alan, an English alter ego. He finds he cannot make his own cultural connection between life and writing until he finally confronts his Indian roots in Trinidad. This is intimated in the epilogue, 'The Ceremony of Farewell', where the author returns to Trinidad for his sister's death and cremation, and the Hindu belief in reincarnation hints at Naipaul's final 'arrival' at his awareness of cultural continuity. As the book ends, he hurries away to begin writing it. A slow, poetic, suggestive work, the final meaning of the book eludes any synopsis and remains, as the title indicates, an 'enigma'.

Further reading

Jussawalla, F. (ed.) (1997) *Conversations with V.S. Naipaul*, Literary Conversations Series, University Press of Mississippi.

Mustafa, F. (1995) *V.S. Naipaul*, Cambridge Studies in African and Caribbean Literature 4, Cambridge University Press.

Phillips, C. (ed.) (1999) *Extravagant Strangers: A Literature of Belonging*, New York: Vintage Books.

Theroux, P. (1998) *Sir Vidia's Shadow: A Friendship across Five Continents*, Boston: Houghton Mifflin Co.

LOUIS JAMES

Enríquez, Carlos

b. 1901, Zulueta, Cuba; d. 1957, Havana

Painter and writer

A key figure in the renewal of Cuban painting, he returned from a brief period of study in Pennsylvania to join the artistic movement that was breaking with the academic tradition in art. He participated in the Exposición de Arte Nuevo in 1927 and the journal, *Avance*, organized his first solo exhibition in 1930. Until then his style was expressionist, but with an erotic charge that often provoked scandal. His work in the 1930s, by contrast, explored and reinterpreted the great themes of the Cuban tradition – *Rey de los campos de Cuba* (The King of the Cuban Fields) (1935), *El rapto de las mulatas* (The Kidnapping of the Mulattas) (1938) and *La arlequina* (1946) all won national prizes. His landscapes, peasant figures and nudes are represented in transparent colours that achieve an explosion of dynamic sensuality. In 1939, Enríquez published his first novel, *Tilín García*, before moving to his house in the country outside Havana, where he later died of alcoholism. Two more novels were published posthumously in 1960: *La feria de Guaicanama* (Guaicanama Fair) and *La vuelta de Chencho* (Chencho's Return).

WILFREDO CANCIO ISLA

Enríquez, Manuel

b. 1926, Ocotlán, Jalisco, Mexico; d. 1994, Mexico City

Composer, musician

An outstanding violinist, Enríquez attended New York's Juilliard School, where he also studied composition. Director of the Mexican Conservatorio Nacional (1972–3), in 1977 he became director of the composition workshop at Mexico's Centro Nacional de Información y Documentacion Musical. His early compositions, like Concerto No. 1 for Violin and Orchestra (1954) show the influence of Hindemith. From 1964 on, Enríquez worked with dodecaphonic music, as in his *Reflexiones Para Violín Solo* and *Tres Formas Concertantes* (Three Concerted Forms), for violin, cello, clarinet, bassoon, horn and percussion. Although Enríquez wrote less for piano than for strings, his piano works include outstanding pieces such as A Lápiz (In Pencil) (1967) and Con ánimo (Soulfully) (1973).

EDUARDO GUÍZAR-ALVAREZ

Ensayo

Ensayo is an association for the study and production of theatre formed in Lima in 1983 by Jorge **Guerra**, Alberto Isola and Luis Peirano. Although the majority of its members came from the theatre department of the Catholic University, their work involved actors and actresses from other backgrounds and other generations. Between 1983 and 1986, Ensayo produced twenty-three plays by Peruvian, Latin American and world dramatists and presented them in Lima and throughout Peru.

The group participated in international theatre festivals in Delphi, Miami and Havana, where it was awarded a prize.

CÉSAR SALAS

Entenado, El

El entenado (The Witness) (1983), by Juan José **Saer**, relates the story of the only survivor of the Solís expedition to the Río de la Plata (River Plate) and his capture by the Charrúa Indians. The experience of living with them for several years transforms the cabin boy and his attitudes. One of the novel's central passages is an anthropophagic banquet, which provides an opportunity for a discussion about otherness. *El entenado* gives access in its turn to Jean de Léry's *Journey to the Land of Brazil, Also Called America*, Montaigne's essay 'On Cannibals' and Oswald de **Andrade**'s *Manifesto antropófago*.

MARÍA JULIA DAROQUI

Envío

Envío is the journal of the Central American Historical Institute (IHCA), one of the research centres of the Jesuit-owned Universidad Centroamericana (**UCA**), based in Managua. An interdisciplinary journal dedicated to the analysis of the social realities of Central America, it has published extensively on **agrarian reform**, electoral politics and political parties. Its emphasis is on socioeconomic and political analysis from a democratic perspective, but without compromising either the facts or its position in favour of the poor. *Envío* publishes ten issues each year.

ESTEBAN LOUSTAUNAU AND ILEANA RODRÍGUEZ

environmental issues

The environment in Latin America is beset by a series of dire threats, but there is little agreement on which issues are most important. Popular concern from outside the region has focused almost entirely on the destruction of the **rainforest**, especially the Amazon (see **Amazonia**). As the cynical Brazilian saying has it, concern for the Amazon rainforest seems to be directly proportional to one's distance from it. Common local concerns are over more immediate hazards to human health such as sewage treatment and urban air and water pollution (see **water resources in Latin America**).

The acuteness of these urban environmental problems is reflected in emergencies leading to driving bans and the closure of factories on high pollution inversion days in Mexico City, São Paulo, Santiago, Bogotá and Caracas. Comparative urban air pollution data is not available outside these cities, but estimates of per capita emissions of carbon dioxide show that Trinidad, Venezuela, Suriname, Mexico and Argentina are the largest emitters in Latin America relative to their populations.

The recent **cholera** epidemic which affected Peru, Ecuador, Colombia and Brazil drew attention to the fact that in the 1990s sewage treatment and safe drinking water are still the exception rather than the norm in the region. For example in São Paulo – the continent's most powerful industrial centre with over fifteen million people and over a quarter of Brazil's entire gross national product – more than 80 per cent of the population lacks sewage treatment. That is, while 64 per cent of São Paulo households have sewage pipes, about 85 per cent of waste water goes untreated. The situation is similar or worse in most other Latin American cities: across the region, 20–80 per cent of national populations officially lacked sewage treatment in 1990.

Many chemicals banned long ago in the USA and Europe continue to be used in the region, some exported from these countries themselves or produced by foreign-owned firms in Latin America. Poor training and equipment for handling toxic chemicals account for dangerous exposures to humans and the environment in industry and agriculture throughout the region, especially in export agriculture and in assembly and chemical factories such as in the *maquiladora* belt along the US–Mexico border (see ***maquiladoras***).

Land degradation is severe, especially of marginally arid and hilly farming and grazing lands. The Sonoran, Patagonian and Atacama deserts are at risk of spreading with continued unsustainable land use, and the northeast of Brazil is in a severe and extended drought already well documented in literature (**Ramos**'s ***Vidas secas***) and film (**Rocha**'s ***Deus e o diabo na terra do sol***). Most countries have over half of their land classified as disturbed by human action. Recent reports are that 40 per cent of the land in Central America and Mexico has had its productivity reduced by erosion: this is true for 77 per cent of El Salvador. This is widely cited as an underlying reason for the 'Soccer War' of 1969 between Honduras and El Salvador. Coastal pollution and the destruction of mangroves and reefs are less well-known problems which carry critical ramifications for their ecology and for Latin American fishing and **tourism** industries.

Finally, deforestation and other habitat loss has wiped out about 70 per cent of Central America's rainforests and almost 93 per cent of Brazil's Atlantic Coast forest. Most Caribbean nations were totally deforested centuries ago, but small remnant forests in Trinidad, Jamaica, Haiti and the Dominican Republic are disappearing rapidly. Costa Rica and Paraguay also have high national deforestation rates. Meanwhile, some areas of the rainforest were until recently considered relatively 'safe' against deforestation, due to their size or inaccessibility. The most recent estimates for the Amazon region (both in Brazil and in the other eight countries which contain Amazon forests) show continuing deforestation, but that about 80–90 per cent remains uncleared overall. As South and East Asian countries deplete their supplies of lumber, they have been turning increasingly to the Americas. Reports are now coming out of the Guyanas (Suriname, French Guiana and Guyana) of huge lumber concessions to Korean, Indonesian and Malaysian companies. Timber deals involving exports have also been reported in Nicaragua, Panama, Honduras, Guatemala, Belize and Peru. Assuming that five million species inhabit the tropical moist forests of the world (the majority of which are in Latin America), E.O. Wilson estimated in 1988 that 17,500 species are being driven to extinction each year by deforestation. Four nations in Latin America have been called centres of 'megadiversity': Mexico, Brazil, Colombia and Panama.

War, poverty and the increasing concentration of landholdings have combined to drive refugees and profiteers into the region's remaining wildlands to farm, lumber, grow and smuggle coca, drill for oil (see **oil in Latin America**) and pan for gold. Indigenous populations have suffered these incursions in the forms of disease, degraded environments and cultural loss. Because of people's desperation and the difficulty of policing, areas officially 'protected' in national, indigenous or extractive reserves are often nothing but 'paper parks'. A graphic example is the fact that fifteen years after their establishment, Brazil still has not 'delimited' most of its indigenous reserves in the Amazon (that is, completed surveys and official processing of land titling and regularization). On average, about 8 per cent of the land in Latin American countries is now officially 'protected' in **national parks** and other reserved areas. National variation is great, however: while Belize, Costa Rica, the Dominican Republic, Panama, Chile, Venezuela and Ecuador have over 10 per cent of their land in protected areas, Jamaica, Uruguay, Haiti, Guyana and El Salvador each have less than 1 per cent.

Tracing the roots of all these environmental problems in Latin America is difficult but important. First, Latin America's incorporation into the world economic system was essentially in the role of peripheral reserve for the extraction of natural resources. As such, the region's mineral and agricultural resources have been devastated for centuries by colonial and later neo-colonial powers. While a few parts of the region were settled in earnest, others were considered only temporary stopping places from which to make one's fortune and return to a homeland elsewhere. Patterns of trade have always been unfavourable to the region, and the removal of its resources has left precious little by way of an integrated social infrastructure which can absorb the impacts of subsequent waves of capital expansion, extraction and contraction. Concern was seldom paid to the sustainability of production under such conditions.

Twentieth-century efforts by Latin American states to integrate their national territories and substitute imports (see **import substitution industrialization**) with locally-made products were precisely attempts to break some of the negative patterns of extractive areas. To gather enough capital to fund these efforts, many countries adopted government-led strategies and borrowed heavily from overseas. Large loans from foreign banks and multilateral agencies such as the IMF and the World Bank often went to fund development megaprojects. One dramatic example of the relation between megaprojects and debt was the massive Itaipú dam between Brazil and Paraguay, which cost Brazil US $20 billion, one-fifth of its foreign debt at the time. Megaprojects have also included airports, highways, industries, mining, colonization and ranching programmes, as well as many combined export projects with objectives such as opening bottlenecks in national infrastructure or heavy industry by the construction of oil refineries, pipelines, steel mills and mines.

This debt-supported economic development had some success for a time, but as interest rates soared in the late 1970s, several Latin American countries found themselves in economic crisis. The persistence of widespread poverty worsened by this pressure of debt service payments made countries even more in need of quick commodities to export and raise cash. Many critics and environmentalists in Latin America have therefore connected the 'debt crisis' with damage to the region's environment.

The megaprojects were easy to begin but – because weak governments had extreme difficulty enforcing environmental regulations, creating environmental and social calamities – they often spun out of control. This is especially true outside the official projects' boundaries. For example, in Brazil the Carajás railroad and its buffer zone were carefully reseeded and protected. However, just outside that area there has been a flood of land clearing and contamination in ranches, farms and gold mines. Many megaprojects have had devastating environmental consequences, and some were heavily critiqued by locals as providing only questionable benefits for human welfare. Many outside-financed megaprojects were said to have benefited mainly political elites and well-connected government subcontracting companies.

The complexity of environmental enforcement for such megaprojects is shown by the Brazilian case. Environmental impact analysis was formally adopted by Brazil in 1986, but the biggest projects with the greatest potential environmental impacts are government-directed, and the government exempts itself from preparing environmental impact statements. Strong political pressure from environmentalists has been necessary for any impact analyses to be carried out and credibly done. Since 1980, however, large numbers of home-grown and foreign-supported environmental movements have appeared in Latin America.

See also: green activism

Further reading

Barkin, D. (1995) 'Wealth, Poverty, and Sustainable Development', working paper, Lincoln Institute, March 1995.

Collinson, H. (ed.) (1996) *Green Guerrillas: Environmental Conflicts and Initiatives in Latin America and the Caribbean*, London: Latin America Bureau/Monthly Review Press.

Dinerstein, E. et. al. (1995) *A Conservation Assessment of the Terrestrial Ecoregions of Latin America and the Caribbean*, Washington, DC: World Wildlife Fund and the World Bank.

Faber, D. (1993) *Environment Under Fire: Imperialism and the Ecological Crisis in Central America*, New York: Monthly Review Press.

Hajek, E. (1991) *La situación ambiental en América Latina: algunos estudios de casos*, Buenos Aires: CIEDLA (Centro Interdisciplinário de Estúdios sobre Desarrollo Latinoamericano).

Hecht, S. and Cockburn, A. (1990) *The Fate of the Forest: Developers, Destroyers and Defenders of the Amazon*, New York: Harper Perennial.

Mendes, C. (1989) *Fight for the Forest*, London: Latin America Bureau.

Muñoz, H. and Robin, R. (eds) (1993) *Difficult Liaison: Trade and the Environment in the Americas*, New Brunswick, NJ: Transaction Press.

J. TIMMONS ROBERTS

Epoca, La

La Epoca is a Chilean Christian Democrat newspaper influenced by the Catholic Church. Founded in 1987, after the official **censorship** imposed during the **Pinochet** military government had ended, it was the first national daily paper to inform about the dictatorship's **human rights** abuses and to lobby openly for a return to political freedom. It won the support of the proponents of democracy and gained international recognition. After the military regime ended and the centre–left Democratic Coalition came to power, *La Epoca*'s style and content became less confrontational. The paper's first director was Emilio Filippi; Carlos Aldunate was director in the late 1990s.

AMALIA PEREIRA

EPS

In 1979, Nicaragua's revolutionary government replaced Somoza's (see **Somoza dynasty**) National Guard with a new military force. The Sandinista Ministry of Defense was divided into the Sandinista Popular Army, or Ejército Popular Sandinista (EPS), which concentrated primarily on military activities; the Sandinista Popular Militia (MPS) which served as an army reserve; and the Sandinista Police (PS), dedicated to domestic law enforcement. In response to US threats, the Sandinistas increased the country's defensive capabilities and the EPS rose from 13,000–18,000 to 60,000–75,000 through the 1980s. After the electoral defeat of the Sandinistas in 1990, the EPS was depoliticized and transformed into a national army, though it remained under the overall command of Humberto Ortega until 1994.

ANUPAMA MANDE AND ILEANA RODRÍGUEZ

Errázuriz, Paz

b. 1945, Santiago, Chile

Photographer

Errázuriz's black and white photographs document the marginals of Chilean society: transvestites, circus performers, the elderly, mental hospital patients and the last living members of Chile's southernmost indigenous group, the Alacalufe. Her photos of the twenty-eight surviving Alacalufes were shown in a 1995 solo exhibit at Santiago's Fine Arts Museum. Errázuriz began photographing professionally in the 1970s, and has exhibited since 1980. She has published *La manzana de Adán* (Adam's Apple) (1990) with photographs of Chilean transvestites, in collaboration with journalist Claudia Donoso, and *El infarto del alma* (The Soul's Breakdown) (1994) with photographs of couples living in a mental hospital and text by Diamela **Eltit**.

AMALIA PEREIRA

Escalona, Rafael

b. 1929, Patillal, Colombia

Popular composer

In his **vallenato** songs, most in the variation called *paseo*, Escalona chronicles popular episodes of personal and local daily life in a vast region of northern Colombia comprising the departments of César, Guajira and Magdalena. His most popular songs include 'La casa en el aire' (The House in the Clouds) and 'La vieja Sara' (Old Sarah). Carlos **Vives**, the Colombian singer, made Escalona's song 'La gota fría' (It Rained on Your Parade) a hit throughout the Hispanic world.

MIGUEL A. CARDINALE

Escambray *see* Grupo Escambray

escena de avanzada

Escena de avanzada is a term coined by the Franco-Chilean critic Nelly **Richard** to encompass a variety of activities in several media during the dictatorship of Augusto **Pinochet**, especially the years from 1977 to the mid-1980s. The most significant artist of the group is Eugenio **Dittborn**. Some of the other members, such as Lotty **Rosenfeld** and Diamela **Eltit**, were also members of the **CADA** group. The *avanzada* was an anti-establishment group of **intellectuals** concerned with finding a critical expression against authoritarianism without engaging in direct political agitation.

GABRIEL PEREZ-BARREIRO

Escobar, Sixto

b. 1913, Barceloneta, Puerto Rico; d. 1982, San Juan, Puerto Rico

Boxer

One of the first Puerto Ricans to achieve international sporting fame, Escobar started professional boxing in 1931 and became a national hero when he defeated Baby Casanova in Montréal for the world bantamweight title. He lost his title in 1937, but regained it a year later. He remained undefeated in 1949. Completing his army service in 1945, he lived in New York and mentored aspiring boxers. He returned to Puerto Rico in the 1960s and worked for the state-supported sports agency. San Juan's oldest stadium honours his name.

VíCTOR F. TORRES ORTIZ

Escobar Gaviria, Pablo

b. 1949, El Tablazo, Antioquia, Colombia; d. 1993, Medellín, Colombia

Drug dealer

Escobar began as a small-time smuggler, ultimately rising to the head of the drug trafficking (see **drugs in Latin America**) network known as the Medellín **cartel**. Responsible for murders, kidnappings and unbridled corruption in protecting his trade and resisting extradition, he waged war on the Colombian state as head of the 'Extraditables'. Yet those who benefited from his largesse viewed him as a modern Robin Hood. In June 1991 he surrendered conditionally to the government and moved his operation to a self-designed prison in Envigado nicknamed 'The Cathedral'. Thirteen months later he simply walked out, to live on the run until his death in a government ambush.

KAREN BRACKEN

Escoffery, Gloria Blanche

b. 1923, Gayle, Jamaica

Painter and writer

Escoffery explains a fierce attachment to her birthplace as a result of 'the nationalist fervor emanating from the Manleys and affecting young people of my generation'. During the 1950s, she contributed poetry to the BBC's ***Caribbean Voices*** and was a critic for the programme. She was a regular contributor to ***Bim*** and other literary journals, and her poems appeared in several anthologies. In the 1980s she worked as a regular columnist for ***The Daily Gleaner*** and was art critic for the ***Jamaica Journal***. The 1988 collection *Loggerhead* revived interest in her poetry.

SANDRA COURTMAN

Escorel, Eduardo

b. 1945, São Paulo, Brazil

Film-maker

Escorel was an active member of the **Cinema Novo** group in Brazil and a close collaborator of director Joaquim Pedro de **Andrade**, with whom he worked on ***Macunaíma*** (1969) and *Os inconfidentes* (The Rebels) (1971), among others. He edited films by Glauber **Rocha** (***Terra em transe*** (Land in Anguish) (1967)), Leon **Hirszman** and Eduardo **Coutinho**. His own films include the short *Chico Antonio, herói com caráter* (Chico Antonio, a Hero with Character) (1983) and the full-length features *Ato de violência* (Act of Violence) (1979) and *O cavalinho azul* (The Blue Pony) (1984). He has also made television documentaries.

ISMAIL XAVIER AND THE USP GROUP

Escrava Isaura, A

A Escrava Isaura is a *telenovela* adapted by Gilberto Braga from a novel by Bernardo Guimarães and broadcast by TV **Globo** in 1976–7. A period piece, it tells the story of the slave Isaura, a young mulatta who becomes the object of a white landowner's passion; she decides to flee the plantation where she lives, but during a ball she is unmasked, captured and imprisoned. The series was extremely successful, and shown in over thirty countries; it brought international stardom to Lucélia Santos, who played the leading character, and helped solidify TV Globo's international distribution networks.

ANTONIO CARLOS MARTINS VAZ

Escudero, Gonzalo

b. 1903, Quito, Ecuador; d. 1971, Brussels, Belgium

Poet

Among the leaders of the avant-garde in Ecuador, Escudero's early *modernista* (see **modernismo, Spanish American**) poetry evolved in a metaphorical direction under the influence of futurism, cubism and surrealism (see **surrealism in Latin American art**). His later works turned towards **existentialism** and the Spanish classics in search of serenity and harmony. *Poesía* (Poetry) (1965) is a compendium of his poems. He also wrote one of the few examples of avant-garde drama in Ecuador, the surrealist-inspired *Paralelograma* (Parallelogram) (1936). His *Justicia para el Ecuador* (Justice for Ecuador) (1968) is a plea for understanding of Ecuador's position on the border disputes with Peru.

HUMBERTO E. ROBLES

Escuela de Cine Documental de Santa Fe

Founded in 1956 by Dr Angela Romera Vera of the National University of El Litoral, the Escuela de Cine Documental de Santa Fe was the first Argentine university centre officially devoted to the study of film. Its director, Fernando **Birri**, insisted that the school should provide not just a technical education but also a social one. Thus the curriculum was divided into three sections – theory, workshop and production – and encouraged documentary and investigative journalism. In 1958, the school produced its first short films, including *Tire dié* (Throw Me a Dime) and three years later the internationally acclaimed *Los inundados* (The Flood Victims), directed by Fernando Birri.

DIANA PALADINO

Escuela de Tres Mundos

Escuela de Tres Mundos is an international film and television school founded in 1986 at San Antonio de los Baños, 35 kilometres south of Havana, under the auspices of the Fundación del Nuevo Cine Latinoamericano (**New Latin American Cinema** Foundation) headed by Gabriel **García Márquez**. Its three-year courses, devised by Argentine director Fernando **Birri**, embrace every aspect of film-making, including scriptwriting, direction, cinematography and production. It also provides specialized workshops and master classes given by experienced film-makers including George Lucas, Francis Ford Coppola and Robert Redford. Students from Third World countries attend courses free, hence its name. The economic crisis in Cuba has meant that more recently courses have been taught almost entirely by Cubans. The school now also offers paid seminars to international film professionals.

JOSÉ ANTONIO EVORA

Escuela Internacional de Teatro de América Latina y el Caribe

This itinerant school (abbreviated as EITALC) has its roots in the III Encuentro de Teatristas de America Latina y el Caribe (Third Meeting of Theatre Workers of Latin America and the Caribbean) held in 1987, in Havana, organized by **Casa de las Américas**. At that time, CELCIT, through its director Luis Molina López, suggested to the Cuban Ministry of Culture that Cuba house a centre for the study of Latin American Theatre that would contribute to the development of Latin American *teatristas* based on a fertile interchange of the diverse creative processes that configure the rich panorama of theatre in the continent. As stated in its constitution of 28 April 1988, the school's work would be inspired by 'the defence and the search for our Latin American and Caribbean identity and by the ideals of liberation and sovereignty of our people'. The Argentine playwright Osvaldo **Dragún** was elected as Director of the School, which held its first workshop in Machurrucutu, Cuba, in 1989. Even though the school is technically housed in Cuba, it is in fact an itinerant enterprise that has held workshops in different countries led by key personalities of the Latin American stage.

The workshops are attended by representatives of many Latin American and Caribbean countries, which converge at the time of the workshops to learn from each other as much as from the leaders of the official *talleres* (workshops) organized by the school.

MARINA PIANCA

Espacio Escultórico

In the 1950s, Mexico's Universidad Nacional Autónoma (**UNAM**) was built over an immense lava flow known as the 'Pedregal' in the south of Mexico City. Much of the terrain, unsuitable for construction, was left wild. In 1977 the university commissioned six sculptors (Helen Escobedo, Manuel Felguérez, Mathias **Goeritz**, Hersúa, **Sebastián** and Federico Silva) to create a work for the open landscape. Working in collaboration, the artists placed sixty-four large isosceles triangles of concrete around a circle of exposed lava, measuring 120 metres in diameter. Four portal-like openings are oriented to the north, south, east, and west. Resembling at once an amphitheatre (for which it has been used), the nearby circular pyramid of Cuicuilco and a space-age launching pad, the Espacio Escultórico (completed in 1979) is a compelling confrontation between nature and geometry.

JAMES OLES

Espectador, El

The second most important Colombian newspaper after **El Tiempo**, *El Espectador* has maintained a consistently liberal position since its foundation. Famous for the consistently high standard of its journalism, Gabriel **García Márquez** learned his trade there. It was the first to expose Colombian drug baron Pablo **Escobar**, in 1982, and to investigate the murky business activities of the Grupo Grancolombiano financial and industrial complex. In the 1980s several of its journalists were murdered, among them its editor Guillermo Cano; UNESCO's World Press Freedom Award was instituted in his memory. Shortly after his death, a bomb placed by the Medellín drug cartel blew up the newspaper's offices, obliging its owners to seek international loans for its relaunch. *El Espectador* has been forced to close on several occasions because of political or economic pressures. In 1996 it changed format and its circulation rose 10 per cent. In 1997 the Bavaria group bought 70 per cent of its shares, which until then had been owned exclusively by the Cano family. Its Sunday literary supplement is considered the most important in Colombia. Its website is www.elespectador.com.

WILFREDO CANCIO ISLA

Espinet, Ramabai

b. 1948, Princes Town, Trinidad and Tobago

Writer

An Indo-Trinidadian-Canadian poet, fiction writer, academic and activist in the women's movement, Espinet is best known for her anthology of poetry *Nuclear Seasons* (1991). Her writing addresses the specificities of Indo-Caribbean culture, indentureship, and the experiences of women of the Indian diaspora. Her poetry and her collaborative experimental poetry/dance/performance piece 'Indian Robber Talk' synthesize elements of Indian, Indo-Caribbean and Afro-Caribbean folk traditions to develop a hybrid Caribbean feminist (see **feminism**) aesthetics sensitive to cultural diversity. With the support of the Caribbean Association for Feminist Research and Action, in 1990 Espinet edited *Creation Fire*, an anthology of poetry by 121 contemporary women from throughout the Caribbean. The anthology is significant for gathering the individual creative expressions of both well-known and unpublished women poets, creating a public archive and a collective context for the poetry.

SHALINI PURI

Espino, Héctor

b. 1943, Chihuahua, Mexico; d. 1997, Monterrey, Mexico

Baseball player

First baseman and powerful homerun hitter, Espino was nicknamed Superman because of his strength. He hit 772 home runs – still a record for a Mexican – and had a 336 career batting average. He made his debut in 1962 for the Sultanes de Monterrey. In 1964 he signed for the St. Louis Cardinals but played only one season in the US Major League, returning to Mexico where he played for various teams before retiring with the Sultanes in 1984. His shirt number, 21, was retired from the Mexican League in his honour. In 1976 he won the Caribbean Series with the Naranjeros de Hermosillo.

ERIC WEIL

Espínola, Francisco

b. 1901, San José, Uruguay; d. 1973, Montevideo, Uruguay

Writer

Espínola was a skilled **short-story** writer. His inventive and witty stories of *Raza ciega* (Blind Race) (1926) and *El rapto y otros cuentos* (The Kidnapping and Other Stories) (1950) are rooted in the popular culture of the River Plate region. He wrote theatre criticism for several newspapers, and his own play *La fuga en el espejo* (Escape into the Mirror) was produced in 1937. His gifts as a storyteller brought him fame as a radio and television performer, and he received the National Literature Prize in 1961. His unpublished articles and stories were collected in several volumes published in 1984–5.

CELINA MANZONI

Espínola, Lourdes

b. 1954, Asunción, Paraguay

Writer

Although a dentist by profession, Espínola has written poetry from an early age. She followed her first book *Visión del Arcángel en once puertas* (Vision of the Archangel in Eleven Doors) (1973) with others which have won two international literary prizes, among them *Almenas del silencio* (Parapets of Silence), *Ser mujer y otras desventuras* (Being a Woman and Other Misadventures), a bilingual English–Spanish edition, *Tímpano y silencio* (Harmonica and Silence), and *Partidas y regresos* (Departures and Returns), with a prologue by Augusto **Roa Bastos**. Her *La estrategia del caracol* (The Snail's Strategy) was adapted for cinema by Sergio **Cabrera**.

TERESA MÉNDEZ-FAITH

Espinosa, Germán

b. 1938, Cartagena, Colombia

Novelist and poet

Los cortejos del diablo (The Retinues of the Devil) (1970), a novel which portrays the persecutions of the Inquisition in Cartagena, is Espinosa's masterwork. He is also the author of collections of short stories, including *La noche de la trapa* (The Night of the Trappist) (1965) and *Los doce infiernos* (Twelve Infernos) (1974).

MIGUEL A. CARDINALE

Espinosa, Victoria

b. 1922, Santurce, Puerto Rico

Theatre director and actress

Espinosa was a driving force in theatre in Puerto Rico for several decades and a mentor for generations of actors. She trained at the University of Puerto Rico, where she began teaching in 1949, establishing a children's and high school theatre programme and initiating a prominent stage career as a challenging, offbeat director. Her stage credits include many of García Lorca's plays, among them the world premiere of *El público*. From 1985 to 1989 she directed the Oficina de Fomento Teatral.

ViCTOR F. TORRES

espiritismo *see* New Age

esquerda festiva

The *esquerda festiva* (festive left) was an urban social group of students, professors, journalists, artists and other liberal professionals who created and consumed protest culture marked by an irreverent, festive atmosphere after the 1964 military *coup* in Brazil. The movement was frustrated with the reformist orthodoxy of the Brazilian Communist Party (PCB), and was inspired by international counterculture and Latin American **guerrilla movements**. In Rio de Janeiro, it was also known as the *Geração Paissandu*, in reference to the fashionable movie theatre where young leftists met.

CHRISTOPHER DUNN

Esquivel, Laura

b. 1949, Mexico City

Novelist

Esquivel is best known as the author of **Como agua para chocolate**: *Novela de mensuales con recetas* (Like Water for Chocolate: A Novel in Monthly Instalments) (1989), a best-selling novel which has sold over 300,000 copies in Spanish and more than a million in English, and was made into a hit movie of the same title directed by Alfonso **Arau**. Her second novel, *La ley del amor* (The Law of Love) (1996), is set in the Mexico City of 2200 and its protagonist is an astroanalyst whose patients' psychological problems are caused by acts they committed in previous lives. This New Age, multimedia novel is marketed with a CD including opera arias by Puccini, **salsa** music and **comics**.

CYNTHIA STEELE

essay

Latin America has produced a rich body of creative and critical essays, particularly works that reinterpret social representations, symbols, metaphors and concepts and show the relationship between intellectuals and the social ethos. Some authors, like **Arciniegas**, have taken its origin back to the very moment of the discovery and conquest of America; others, like Arturo Andrés **Roig**, have found the origins of the Latin American essay in romanticism and journalistic practices linked to the circulation of new ideas in the eighteenth and nineteenth centuries. For writers like José Guilherme **Merquior**, by contrast, it is *modernismo* (see ***modernismo*, Spanish American**) and the emergence of a layer of **intellectuals** that explain this origin.

The essay, in its contemporary form, is clearly linked to the world of books, newspapers, intellectuals and to the maturing of the conditions for the emergence of a public that Eduardo Nicol described as 'la generalidad de los cultos' (cultured people in general). The century opened with the essays of José Martí, Rubén Darío, Manuel González Prada and José Enrique Rodó, and the Ateneo de la Juventud generation in Mexico. For these writers, positivist universalism had entered into a profound crisis, and they turned instead to an exploration of Iberoamerica's relations with the Latin and Anglo Saxon worlds.

The theme of 'civilization versus barbarism', first addressed in the nineteenth century by Sarmiento and in subsequent writings by Alcides **Arguedas** and Euclides da Cunha among others, which shared a negative vision of *mestizaje* and the rural world, were now overtaken by a new current of ideas. One group of writers developed the Shakespearean symbolism of **Caliban** and Ariel first from a Latinist point of view (in Darío and Rodó) and later from a frankly anti-colonialist perspective in the work of Roberto **Fernández Retamar** and Leopoldo **Zea**. Other writers sought out the specificity of Latin American experience, like **Lezama Lima** in *La expresión americana* (American Expression) and Alejo **Carpentier** with his idea of '*lo real maravilloso*'.

In the 1940s, Latin Americanist thought that stressed a unity of origin and destiny re-emerged with Pedro **Henríquez Ureña**, Alfonso **Reyes** and Germán Arciniegas; it reopened questions about the relations between Latin America and Spain and between Latin America and the United States, and became increasingly concerned with the tension between the local and the universal (Jorge Cuesta, Jorge Luis **Borges**, Octavio **Paz** and Carlos **Fuentes** are examples). Essayists like Ezequiel **Martínez Estrada**, José Carlos **Mariátegui**, Guillermo **Francovich** and the Octavio Paz of *El **laberinto** de la soledad* (The Labyrinth of Solitude) (1950) share a concern to explore national characteristics; others, like Arturo **Uslar Pietri**, Mariano **Picón Salas**, Luis Alberto **Sánchez** and Germán Arciniegas continued to develop the Latin Americanist current set in train by the Mexican José **Vasconcelos** and reflected in journals like ***Repertorio Americano*** and ***Cuadernos Americanos***.

Avant-garde aesthetic ideas opened new directions in the essay (César **Vallejo**, Luis **Cardoza y Aragón**, Aimé Césaire, Miguel Angel **Asturias** and Lezama Lima). Today, Latin American critical writing appears in synchrony with developments elsewhere in the world. It increasingly shares common frontiers with poetry and narrative (Cuesta, Borges, Ernesto **Sabato**, Paz, Fuentes), with philosophy (where the influence of José Ortega y Gasset and José **Gaos** on the relationship between ideas and circumstance particularly influenced Leopoldo Zea), or thinkers like Francisco Romero, Adolfo Sánchez Vázquez, Eduardo Nicol and Luis **Villoro**), with the ***crónica*** (Elena Poniatowska, Carlos **Monsiváis**) , with anthropology (Fernando **Ortiz**, Gilberto **Freyre**, Darcy

Ribeiro), with the exploration of popular culture and the impact of mass media (Beatriz **Sarlo**, Néstor **García Canclini**), with social science, education and history (José Luis **Romero**, Gregorio **Weinberg**, Enrique Krauze and Roger **Bartra**), with economics (José Medina Echavarría, Daniel Cosío Villegas, Jesús Silva Herzog, Raúl **Prebisch**) and with literary criticism (Enrique **Anderson Imbert**, Angel **Rama**, Antonio **Cornejo Polar**, Antonio **Candido**, Julio **Ortega**, Juan José **Saer**, Roberto **Schwarz**). The works of Alfonso Reyes, Jorge Luis Borges, Julio **Cortázar**, Octavio Paz, Mario **Vargas Llosa** and Tomás Segovia will continue to represent the essay at the frontiers of its possibilities.

See also: arielismo

Further reading

Levy, K.L. and Ellis, K. (1970) *El ensayo y la crítica literaria en Iberoamérica*, Toronto: University of Toronto/Instituto Internacional de Literatura Iberoamericana.

Oviedo, J.M. (1990) *Breve historia del ensayo hispanoamericano*, Madrid: Alianza Editorial.

Skirius, J. (1981) *El ensayo latinoamericano*, Mexico City: Fondo de Cultura Económica.

Stabb, M.S (1967) *In Quest of Identity: Patterns in the Spanish American Essay of Ideas 1890–1960*, Chapel Hill, NC: University of North Carolina Press.

LILIANA WEINBERG

Estado de São Paulo, O

A daily newspaper created in 1875 by a group of São Paulo Republicans, *O Estado de São Paulo* sold 2,000 copies in a city of 25,000. It changed its name with the declaration of the Republic in 1889, and in 1891 Julio de Mesquita (see **Mesquita** family) became its editor. Its circulation rose to 30,000, and during the First World War it campaigned against militarism. The São Paulo revolution of 1924 closed the paper and imprisoned its editor. His son Julio Mesquita Filho took over the editorship after his father's death and continued the paper's editorial line. In 1969 he ceded his post to his son, who modernized the paper's format. It is now considered one of Brazil's most conservative newspapers.

ANTONIO CARLOS MARTINS VAZ

Estado Novo

The name Estado Novo is given to the Brazilian governmental period between 1937 and 1945, following Getulio **Vargas**'s *coup d'état*, characterized by the centralization of power in the executive and increased state intervention. A state of emergency was declared, increasing still further the powers of the president, and the institutions of public order, including the infamous secret police, specializing in torture and assassination, came under armed forces control. A Departamento de Imprensa e Propaganda (**DIP**) exercised ideological control over the mass media. The victory of democracy in 1945, however, strengthened the movement for redemocratization, which was incompatible with Vargas's continuation in power, and he was deposed by the armed forces.

ANTONIO CARLOS MARTINS VAZ

estancia

The term *estancia* designates the extensive cattle and sheep ranches of the Argentine and Uruguayan *pampas* (great plains) (see **pampa**) and Patagonia, which have provided export wealth from colonial times to the present. The concentration of prime fattening pastures in the hands of a relatively small number of owners led to a concentration of power and wealth and impeded the distribution of land to immigrants. The cosmopolitan owners of large *estancias* formed the core of high society, while their **gaucho** (cowboy) employees figure centrally in the region's folklore.

See also: fazenda; hacienda; plantation

THOMAS EDSALL

Estévez, Abilio

b. 1954, Havana, Cuba

Writer

Estévez' play *La verdadera culpa de Juan Clemente Zenea* (Juan Clemente Zenea's Real Guilt) won the UNEAC drama prize in 1984 and is considered one of the most important works of contemporary Cuban theatre. His other theatrical pieces include *Perla marina* (Deep-Sea Pearl) (1993), *Santa Cecilia* (1994) and *La noche* (The Night) (world premiere in 1996), which won the 1994 Tirso de Molina prize. He has written short stories, published in *Juego con Gloria* (A Game with Glory) (1987), a volume of poetry, *Manual de las tentaciones* (The Handbook of Temptations) (1989), and a successful novel, *Tuyo es el reino* (Thine is the Kingdom) (1997).

WILFREDO CANCIO ISLA

Estigarribia, José Félix

b. 1888, Caraguatay, Paraguay; d. 1940, Altos, Paraguay

Soldier and statesman

Remembered chiefly as the architect of his country's triumph over Bolivia in the 1932–5 **Chaco War**, Estigarribia's brilliant overall strategy and devastating use of guerrilla tactics (see **guerrillas**) accomplished what few expected: international recognition of Paraguay's claim to the Chaco region. Estigarribia capitalized on his image as a war hero to win the nation's presidency in 1939, but his term ended prematurely with his death in an airplane accident. While in office he promoted the 1940 Constitution, which sought to strengthen the executive branch. His early death ensured that his almost mythic status would remain untouched.

TRACY K. LEWIS

Estorino, Abelardo

b. 1925, Unión de Reyes, Cuba

Playwright and theatre director

A major figure in the new Cuban theatre movement of the 1960s, Estorino's *El robo del cochino* (The Stolen Pig) (1961) and *La casa vieja* (The Old House) (1964) offer vivid and critical insights into the reality of Cuban family life and social behaviour. Other works in the same vein include *Los mangos de Caín* (Cain's Mangos) (1964), *Ni un sí ni un no* (Neither Yes nor No) (1979), *Morir del evento* (1983) and *Parece blanca* (She Looks White) (1994). As a director, he has worked primarily with **Teatro Estudio**.

WILFREDO CANCIO ISLA

Estrada (Velasco), Julio

b. 1943, Mexico City

Composer and critic

A pupil of Carlos **Chávez** in Mexico, Estrada studied in Europe with Messiaen (1965–8) and Stockhausen (1968) among others. He introduced into Mexico the works of Takemitsu, Xenakis, Legeti and Cage. A research scholar at the Instituto de Investigaciones Estéticas at the Universidad Nacional Autónoma de México (**UNAM**) since 1976, he has published widely on the musicology and ethnomusicology of Mexico. As a composer he uses aleatory techniques with particular success in his *Música de Ficción* (Fictional Music) (1971–2). Outstanding compositions include *Memorias* (1971), for keyboard instruments; *Fuga en Cuatro Dimensiones* (Fugue in Four Dimensions) (1974), which uses his concept of 'grupo finito' (finite group) and 'Canto alterno' (1978), for solo cello.

EDUARDO GUÍZAR-ALVAREZ

estridentismo

Estridentismo was the first clearly defined Mexican vanguardist group, whose suggestive designation and aggressive manifestoes revealed an initial influence of European futurism and dadaism. Its central figure was Manuel **Maples Arce**, who wrote most of the early 1920s manifesto broadsides (for example, 'Actual No. 1', from 1921, and 'Manifesto No. 2', from 1923) and was the motivating force behind the combative literary journals *Irradiador* (1923) and *Horizonte* (1926–7), the principal group publications. Other group members were the poets Germán **List Arzubide** and Luis Quintanilla and prose writers Arqueles Vela, Xavier Icaza and Salvador Gallardo.

MERLIN H. FORSTER

Estupiñán Bass, Nelson

b. 1912, Súa, Esmeralda, Ecuador

Writer

A poet inspired by the Afro-Ecuadorean culture of his native province of Esmeraldas, Estupiñán Bass's early work in particular is framed by the philosophy of *negrismo*, and characterized by its use of popular rhythms and forms. *Las tres carabelas* (Three Caravelles) (1973) gathers together his poetry, short stories and theatre.

The African community of Esmeraldas was ostensibly established when seventeen men and women from a wrecked Spanish ship escaped into the jungle in 1553 and created an 'Indo-African-Ecuadorean community'. The community grew with the addition of new members from the wreck of a slave ship in 1600 and escaped slaves from surrounding plantations. The population expanded again in the nineteenth century as a result of booms in rubber and gold. Yet two centuries earlier, Esmeraldas was already referred to as 'the black Republic'. The failure of a series of expeditions to dominate the area allowed the growth of interactions among whites, blacks and Indians reflected in poetry combining literary forms and rhythms derived from the Spanish tradition with African elements; the result is a dynamic and unique culture.

Estupiñán Bass also wrote novels set in this cultural space, the first of which was *Cuando los guayacanes florecían* (When the Guayacanes were in Bloom) (1954). Other novels, like *Senderos brillantes* (Bright Paths) (1974) belonged within the political novel tradition of the 1930s, though the writer introduced new narrative techniques. *Las puertas del verano* (Gates of Summer) (1978) and *Bajo el cielo nublado* (Under a Cloudy Sky) (1981) belong to the same genre, though some critics have located the latter within a magical realist tradition (see **magical realism**). *El crepúsculo* (Dusk) (1992) is a thriller.

In all his work, Estupiñán Bass brings to a long tradition of social protest writing the additional element of an attack on racism. The protagonist of *El último río* (The Last River) (1966), for example, adopts what Frantz **Fanon** called a 'white mask', rejecting his origins and denying his roots. His impotence and ultimate madness express the insoluble contradiction between oppressor and oppressed, black and white incarnated in a single character. One critic has described the novel as 'the first black novel of Ecuador', superior even to Adalberto **Ortiz**'s *Juyungo* (1943).

See also: black cultures

Further reading

Richards, H.J. (1997) '*El crepúsculo* de Nelson Estupiñán Bass, crisol de técnicas narrativas', in *Cultura: Revista del Banco Central del Ecuador* 1, Quito.

CELINA MANZONI

ethnicity

Ethnicity refers to a cultural identity based in a concept of common descent and shared history. In some parts of Latin America, ethnicity has been identified with '**race**'. After its revolution, Mexico adopted an ideology of *la raza* (the race), a hybrid of the European/Castilian stock and the indigenous peoples forming a new, robust populace that together would forge a new nation. Some indigenous groups in Mexico have internalized this model. Juan Ramón Bastarrechea, former president of the Academy of the Maya Language (of Yucatán, Campeche and Quintana Roo), at an international linguistics conference in 1993, stated that all Yucatec Maya are **mestizo**. This perception is not shared by all indigenous groups of Mexico. The

Tzeltals, Tzotzils and Tojolab'als (Mayan groups of highland Chiapas) consider themselves Indians (see **Indian**), rather than mestizo, identifying the latter term with the State and a nation-building strategy. Prior to the 1994 Zapatista uprising (see **Zapatistas**), members of these highland groups had begun to self-identify as *indio*, rather than *indígena*, as a token of conscientization. The Zapatista conflict in Chiapas has been defined as an ethnic confrontation, where the opposing ethnic groups are not understood to refer to particular indigenous communities and their associated languages, but to the autochthonous inhabitants as a whole versus a non-indigenous, neo-colonial national hegemonic group. While this armed conflict is the most blatant rejection of the homogenization of ethnicity in Mexico, official government policies have been retailored to fit a pluri-ethnic nation. Since the early 1980s, the Mexican government has recognized the integrity of indigenous communities and local identities. It finances bilingual/bicultural programmes for indigenous communities. Emphasis has shifted from glorification of hybridization to acceptance of heterogeneity.

As the concept of 'race' has been invalidated by the scientific community, discussions of identity shifted to the construct of 'ethnicity' or the 'ethnic group'. Rather than being defined phenotypically, ethnic groups are defined by a shared descent, often from a mythological ancestor. They reproduce themselves biologically and generally are constituted by rich networks of intercommunication, interchange and interaction. Ethnic groups, unlike nations or states, need not have institutionalized power structures or governments. Indigenous groups are the ethnic groups, *par excellence*, in Latin America. Often these groups define themselves, not only by shared ancestry and descent, but also in opposition to a hegemonic group of mixed European or European and indigenous ascendancy. In much of Latin America, indigenous languages (see **indigenous languages of highland South America**; **indigenous languages of lowland South America**) have served as markers of the separate groups. However, many indigenous peoples have ceased to speak their languages, opting instead for the official languages of the nations they inhabit. Despite the **language loss**, most continue to self-identify as indigenous.

Where access to non-traditional jobs, Western education and political influence have allowed integration of indigenous peoples into the 'national' economies and power structures, the continuance of separate identities surprised national planners. In parts of Ecuador, notably Otovalo, new-found indigenous economic prosperity of the late 1990s has brought about a resurgence in Kichwa (**Quechua** or Quichua) language use. Kichwa language songs are played over public loudspeakers in the squares. Signs in Kichwa are proliferating. Ethnic identity has not been swept away on the crest of commercial success. Joshua Fishman writing in 1985 found that ethnic revivals and language revitalizations were doomed to be short-lived. However, by 1991 he was documenting successful strategies for language maintenance and associated cultural continuity. The 1990s witnessed fragmentation of European and Near Eastern countries along ethnic lines. In Latin America accommodation has been made to indigenous peoples. In Nicaragua, autonomous regions were created, with an indigenous Congress, independent of the 'national' Congress. In Panama, Kuna areas are managed locally and the national government prohibits the copying and/or wholesaling of Kuna handicrafts. Indigenous groups, as opposed to European or Asian ethnicities, are often recognized in Latin American constitutions as social entities to be protected – cultures that have contributed to the national heritage. In Guatemala, the 1985 constitution notes that Mayan languages (see **Mexican and Central American indigenous languages**) and groups are part of the 'cultural' patrimony. Mexico, Costa Rica, Colombia, Peru, Bolivia and Paraguay give explicit constitutional protection to the indigenous languages *per se*. In Guatemala, Point Three of the Peace Accords, signed in March of 1995, dealt with 'Identity and Rights of Indigenous Peoples'. **FUNAI** (Fundacao Nacional do Indio) in Brazil has been working since the 1960s to ensure the Indians rights, especially those to land, but also to health care and education.

Many non-indigenous ethnic groups also exist in Latin America. These are typically identified by country of origin. Chinese immigrants had a large impact on colonial Mexico. Middle Eastern groups form an integral part of the mercantile class of

Central America. German immigrants helped implement the coffee boom in Central America. Italians, Spaniards and Germans settled in Buenos Aires and surrounding areas of Argentina; social clubs and business organizations celebrate their European ethnic heritage, while affirming their national identity as Argentines. Africans brought to the Caribbean and to the eastern coasts of Central and South America have forged vibrant cultures, most without specific links to a language or local culture in Africa, but sharing an ideology of African descent, shared New World experiences and unifying cultural practices, including religious rituals and cosmologies.

Ethnicity as a basis for social identity competes with other structuring mechanisms, notably religion, occupation, local residence, social **class** and political organization. When these constructs pattern isomorphically with ethnicity a strong basis for social mobilization can be found. Where one of the rival structures predominates, ethnicity may be little more than a social emblem, a basis for celebrating feast days or celebrating a shared history.

Further reading

Asociación para el Avance de las Ciencias Sociales en Guatemala (1996) *De la etnia a la nación: la discusión sobre la identidad nacional, base necesaria en la construcción de la paz y la democracia en Guatemala*, Guatemala: AVANCSO.

Barth, F. (1969) *Ethnic Groups and Boundaries*, Boston: Little, Brown & Company.

Fishman, J.A. (1991) *Reversing Language Shift: Theoretical and Empirical Foundations of Assistance to Threatened Languages*, Clevedon: Multilingual Matters.

—— (1985) *The Rise and Fall of the Ethnic Revival: Perspectives on Language and Ethnicity*, Berlin: Mouton de Gruyter.

JUDITH M. MAXWELL

ethnographic film

A most perplexing form of cinema that defies easy categorization, occupying a position equally marginal to **documentary** film and the discipline of **anthropology**. In a sense, all film footage can be considered 'anthropological', to the degree that it displays information about the culture of the maker and the culture of human subjects. Yet the term ethnographic is typically applied only to documentary or semi-documentary films that focus on the representation of cultures exotic to the West. Thus, the bulk of what is considered ethnographic filmmaking has taken place in those countries/regions with large indigenous populations, often lensed by foreigners attempting to record their exotic 'otherness'.

In Peru, a group of photographers (including Manuel and Víctor Chambi, sons of the legendary photographer Martín **Chambi**) in Cusco founded the Cine Club Cusco and sponsored a series of short films that were the first depictions of the Peruvian Andes filmed by people of the region and not from Lima or abroad. *Kukuli* (1961), directed by Luis Figueroa, was their most ambitious project; although reflecting an indigenist aesthetic, it presented a dazzling vision of indigenous reality. Their feature *Jarawi*, co-directed by Eulogio **Nishiyama** and Figueroa in 1966, unfortunately marked the end of their activities, although Figueroa filmed other works addressing peasant themes – like *Los perros hambrientos* (The Starving Dogs) (1976) and *Yawar fiesta* (1986).

Bolivian film-makers have often used the cinema to explore the problems and contradictions of its majority **Quechua** and **Aymara** indigenous populations. Although it would be difficult to call them 'ethnographies', many of these films were often received as such by audiences, especially the work of Jorge Ruiz, called by John Grierson in 1958 'one of the six more important documentary film-makers in the world'. His short *Vuelve Sebastiana* (Sebastiana Returns) (1953), a semi-documentary account of the indigenous Chipayas communities on the altiplano, transcended the merely descriptive through a fictional narrative. He employed a similar approach for the feature, *La vertiente* (The Watershed) (1958), combining a melodramatic subplot with a documentary about the efforts of the Rurenabaque community (in Bolivia's tropical region) to install fresh water facilities. The subsequent work of Jorge **Sanjinés** and **Grupo Ukamau** followed a similar, albeit more politicized, trajectory consonant with the goals of the **New Latin American Cinema**.

In Colombia, the work of Marta **Rodríguez** and Jorge **Silva** was notable in the 1960s and 1970s, especially their mid-length ***Chircales*** (Brickmakers) (1967–72), a film produced only after a six-month investigation of the community by a trained anthropologist (Rodríguez) and thus a rare example of ethnographic research on film. Although not purely ethnographic, Ciro Durán's *Gamín* (1978), a ***sobreprecio*** production, is also notable as an insightful record/analysis of street children in Bogotá. Reymundo Gleyzer and Jorge **Prelorán** in Argentina also produced an important group of films generally considered ethnographic, although they could just as easily be classified as social documentaries in a testimonial style (see ***testimonio***). Especially significant were Prelorán's *Ocurrido en Hualfín* (It Happened in Hualfín) (1969) and *Hermógenes Cayo* (1975).

In Brazil, the cycle of nineteen films produced by Thomas Farkas and his group of documentarists in the 1960s and 1970s was similarly inspired by an ethnographic ethos and attempted to analyse the life and culture of the northeast, albeit often from a marked sociological perspective. Works like *Loucora e cultura* (Madness and Culture) (1972) by Antonio Manuel and *Di* (1977) by Glauber **Rocha** changed the terms of traditional ethnographic film-making, since they used the medium not to deal with peoples considered primitive, but with those social groups to which the film-makers-cum-anthropologists themselves belonged.

Since the 1980s and through the 1990s, ethnographic film-makers have shifted over to video, a move that enabled not only greater flexibility, but a crucial syntactic shift, in which the subjects themselves are also often empowered to look through the camera eye to construct their own audio-visual reality. Exemplary in this vein has been the work of Vincent Carrelli and his group in Brazil. In *The Spirit of TV* (1990) they documented the Waiapi Indians' first contact with the modern technologies of video and television, while in *Video Cannibalism* (1994) they introduced the Euanuene tribe to video in order to inform them about the outside world and to capture on tape what they wanted to share about their culture with others.

Further reading

Burton, J. (1990) *The Social Documentary in Latin America*, Pittsburgh: University of Pittsburgh Press.

Colombres, A. (1985) *Cine, antopología y colonialismo*, Buenos Aires: Editora del Sol.

ANA M. LÓPEZ

ethnomusicology

Ethnomusicology has been defined in terms of: 1) its study object; that is, any music outside of European-derived classical music; and 2) its anthropological methodology and theoretical orientation. Both features distinguish the field from musicology. Ethnomusicological research in Latin America and the Caribbean has suffered from the fact that only fairly recently has the second definition of the field begun to be developed.

The first records of musical practices come from *cronistas*, missionaries, travellers and others, and date almost from the first days of European contact. The first publications on music, dating in various parts of the continent from the latter part of the 1800s, tended to come from amateur folklorists whose compilations of data included song texts and descriptions of musical events. A growing concern with documenting the national patrimony and the advent of recording equipment helped to promote studies directed exclusively at music. These studies were often conceived as national music histories and/or collections of folk customs (the term ethnomusicology gained worldwide currency in the mid-1950s). Examples of these attempted overviews of national music include those by Vicente T. Mendoza (Mexico), Maria de Barratta (El Salvador), Fernando **Ortiz** (Cuba), Andrés Pardo Tovar (Colombia), Segundo Luis Moreno (Ecuador), Manuel Dannemann (Chile), Carlos Vega (Argentina) and Oneyda Alvarenga (Brazil), among others. These works contain valuable documentation, but many suffer from a tendency to analyse music in terms of European classical conventions and a failure to acknowledge their researcher's 'outsider' status. While Latin American researchers have focused on traditions within their own national borders, their position in the educated elite has meant that the cultural distance between them and the tradition bearers they study has often been as great as that experienced by other ethnomusicologists doing field-work outside their native country.

The most important single research centre during the 1960s and 1970s was INIDEF, the Instituto Interamericano de Etnomusicología y Folklore (now FUNDEF – Fundación de Ethnomusicología y Folklore), based in Caracas and directed by the Argentinean Isabel **Aretz** and (now deceased) Venezuelan Luis Felipe Ramón y Rivera. Short, six-month courses, funded by UNESCO, offered limited training to students from throughout the continent. A search for origins and unchanged retentions, especially of European forms, is a characteristic that has only recently begun to be overcome by a deeper appreciation of the inherent dynamism of expressive culture. The last two decades have seen qualitative advances in the application of contemporary anthropological and ethnomusicological theory, and a corresponding move from limited descriptive to interpretative ethnographic methodologies, especially in Mexico, Brazil and the Southern Cone.

Further reading

Aretz, I. (1991) *Historia de la etnomusicología en América Latina: Desde la época precolombina hasta nuestros días*, Caracas: Ediciones FUNDEF–CONAC-OEA.

—— (1977) *América Latina en su música*, Mexico City: Siglo XXI.

Béhague, G. (ed.) (1991) 'Reflections on the Ideological History of Latin American Ethnomusicology', in *Comparative Musicology and Anthropology of Music*, eds B. Nettl and P. Bohlman, pp. 56–68, Chicago: University of Chicago.

Manuel, P. (1988) *Popular Musics of the Non-Western World: An Introductory Survey*, New York: Oxford University Press.

T.M. SCRUGGS

EUDEBA

The University of Buenos Aires Publishing House (EUDEBA) was founded in 1958 as a mixed public-private enterprise. Under Boris Spivakow's direction it played a key role, translating hitherto unknown works into Spanish, publishing the work of local authors and contributing to the **Boom** of the decade. EUDEBA was taken over when the university was occupied by the military government in 1966, and Spivakow then formed the **Centro Editor de América Latina** (CEAL). With the return of democracy in 1973, EUDEBA briefly flowered under Arturo **Jauretche** until the state took control of it for the second time in 1975.

PABLO KREIMER

Eulálio, Alexandre

b. 1932, Rio de Janeiro, Brazil; d. 1988, São Paulo, Brazil

Literary critic

One of the most curious, encylopedic and sensitive minds of his generation, Eulálio only began university teaching in 1979. Before that he was a journalist, editor of the *Revista do Livro*, and a diplomat in Venice. His work is enormously varied: it consists mostly of essays, many of which were published posthumously as *Livro involuntário* (Involuntary Book) (1993). He had a special interest in the city of Diamantina, Minas Gerais, where his family was from, and in the plastic arts. His only book was on the Swiss poet Blaise Cendrars' journey to Brazil in the 1920s.

JOHN GLEDSON

evil eye

The term 'evil eye' refers to damage of many kinds, attributed in ancient belief to the malicious, though not necessarily intentional, effect of the look of some people. It has a range of symptoms, including apathy, sleepiness, loss of appetite, constipation and trembling. Treatments include amulets, massage, spells and other magical formulas. Therapeutic treatment cannot be delivered arbitrarily, but only on particular occasions, like Christmas Eve. Horns are particularly effective amulets. Another cure involves an official practitioner who stares for hours at the victim of the evil eye until the curse is broken. If one glance can cause the evil eye, it is reasoned, then another must be able to eliminate it.

JULIO SCHVARTZMAN

Excélsior

Mexican daily newspaper founded in 1916, it is a newspaper of conventional appearance. In 1968, under Julio **Scherer García**'s editorship, it began to acquire a considerable reputation for independent reporting of a high standard. In 1976, after a series of critical reports on the presidency of Luis **Echeverría**, government pressure forced Scherer to resign, and many of the newspaper's best contributors resigned with him and went on to found *Proceso*, a weekly that soon won a high reputation for independent in-depth journalism. *Excélsior* continues to publish in the same format, with dense print and few photographs. Its website is www.excelsior.com.mx. Its print run is approximately 85,000.

WILFREDO CANCIO ISLA

Excos

Excos is one of the most innovative bands currently making popular **maroon music** in Suriname. The members are Ndyuka maroons, who migrated from their traditional villages in the interior rainforest to the capital of Paramaribo. Their songs reflect the multidimensional experience of young maroon migrants, referencing both the historical struggles of their ancestors and the rigours of life on the modern urban periphery. Although proficient in a cosmopolitan variety of Afro-Caribbean genres, the Excos excel at ragga-kaseko, a vital new fusion of Jamaican **dancehall** music and Surinamese kaseko and kawina that they helped to create in the early 1990s.

KEN BILBY

exile

Exile has been a recurring theme in Latin American culture, particularly since on the one hand economic pressures have driven large sections of the population to migrate, within or outside the country, in search of work, and on the other political oppression has forced many **intellectuals**, artists and politicians to flee their country.

The decades of the 1970s and 1980s, for example, found many Latin Americans living in countries where a different language was spoken; these were those who had survived Argentina's 'dirty war' or who had escaped death in Chile after the 1973 military *coup* led by **Pinochet**. The hardening of authoritarian military rule in Brazil after 1968 drove artists like Caetano **Veloso** and Chico **Buarque** out of the country – both lived in Britain for over two years – while many of Chile's leading musicians of the **Popular Unity** period – like **Inti-Illimani** and **Quilapayún** – were to spend nearly two decades in Europe. Indeed, the Uruguayan writer Mario **Benedetti**, himself an exile, described the curious phenomenon of *desexilio* – the return after a long period to a country often changed and sometimes determined to forget the events that produced repression and persecution in the first place. A number of films have dealt, too, with the experience of prolonged exile – among them *Tangos: el exilio de Gardel* (1985).

The departure, forced and otherwise, of many intellectuals from Cuba in the wake of the 1959 revolution (see **revolutions**) led also to a Cuban literature in exile, which addressed the issue from many perspectives, and by no means all of them from a conservative anti-**Castro** posture. Many gay writers and artists, Reinaldo **Arenas** among them, focused on their experience of homophobia in Castro's Cuba.

An earlier generation of artists had also experienced exile in other forms – the Mexican muralists (see **muralism**), for example, worked outside Mexico in the early 1930s. In her *Las genealogías*, Margo **Glantz** describes an earlier community of exiles living in Mexico City; in a slightly different way, the culture of exile influenced Latin America very directly when a generation of progressive Spanish intellectuals arrived in the region, particularly in Mexico, at the end of the

Spanish Civil War (see **Spanish Civil War, impact of**). The group included philosopher José **Gaos**, writer Max Aub and many more, and their influence was significant. Leon Trotsky, a leader of the Russian Revolution, found his last of many exiles in Mexico City; his embattled house in the district of Coyoacán is an austere place, but it was not able to save him from assassination at the hand of a Stalinist agent in 1940. A poignant visit by a group of Argentine exiles in the Mexican capital is the subject of Tununa Mercado's story 'Visita guiada', in *En estado de memoria* (1990).

There are also other kinds of exile: internal exile (or *destierro*) was a device often used by military regimes to neutralize and isolate their political opponents – it is the subject of several films, among them *La frontera* (The Frontier) (Larraín, 1991) and ***Tiempo de revancha*** (Time of Revenge) (Aristaraín, 1981), as well as Ricardo **Piglia**'s novel, ***Respiración artificial*** (1980). The protagonist of *Verónico Cruz* (directed by Miguel Pereira) is also dismissed to a remote corner of Argentina. If many of those who leave their homes or their countries are driven by economic necessity rather than direct political persecution, it is no less a disruptive and alienating experience for them. Unsurprisingly they leave fewer individual records; yet the Mexican migrant workers, or the Central American exiles fleeing to the towns and later across borders are, in every sense, exiles. (See also *El norte*, directed by Gregory Nava, for example.)

Of the many songs written about exile, perhaps Patricio **Manns**'s wonderful Cuando me acuerdo de mi país (When I Remember My Country) is the most representative in its ability to combine the sense of loss and privation with the sustaining power of memory – 'Cuando me acuerdo de mi país/me siento un volcán' (When I remember my country/I am a volcano).

Further reading

Kaminsky, A. (1999) *After Exile: Writing the Latin American Diaspora*, Minneapolis: University of Minnesota Press

MIKE GONZALEZ

existentialism

French philosophical and literary movement that had a great impact on Latin American writing in the 1950s and 1960s. After the split between its two principal figures, Jean Paul Sartre and Albert Camus, their Latin American followers also took separate paths for a time: Camus was one of Victoria **Ocampo**'s heroes and was featured in *Sur*, while Sartre influenced León **Rozitchner** and others in the ***Contorno*** group, as well as the young **Vargas Llosa**. Other writers close to existentialism's central concerns – alienation, the search for meaning, the need for ethical and political engagement – included Juan Carlos **Onetti** and Virgilio **Piñera**, though this may be somewhat coincidental as they were interested in these issues before the works of Camus and Sartre were much known outside of France. A figure who has adhered to the tenets of existentialism since his early days, and who now at century's end perhaps deserves the title of the Last Existentialist, faithful to these ideas long after they passed out of fashion, is Ernesto **Sabato**.

DANIEL BALDERSTON

experimental film

Latin America does not really have a long-standing tradition of experimental or avant-garde film-making, given that film-makers were, until the 1950s, primarily preoccupied with establishing national cinemas on an industrial basis and, afterwards, with the politically *engagé* practices of the **New Latin American Cinema**. Yet, throughout the last century and especially since the 1980s, there have also been 'other' cinema practices: distributed erratically or not at all, often produced by visual artists or amateurs rather than film-makers, and frequently ignored by the film archives and museums that define the boundaries of 'national' cinemas.

Perhaps the most extraordinary example of experimental film-making in Latin America was Mário **Peixoto**'s ***Limite*** (The Limit) (1930). Influenced by French avant-garde film-makers of the 1920s, Peixoto mercilessly pushed at the limits of narrative film-making with a visual elegance and flair that few have been able to match. Unfortunately, *Limite* was a unique experiment: Peixoto never completed another film and no other contemporary film-maker took up the challenge of his experimentation; with the coming of sound, other constraints and demands took precedence.

In the cultural renaissance of post-revolutionary 1920s and 1930s Mexico, a self-conscious vanguard of artists experimented with film, although they are all known for their work in other fields: photographer Emilio Amero, caricaturist Marius de Zayas, Miguel and Rosa **Covarrubias**, Manuel and Lola **Alvarez Bravo** and Adolfo Best Maugard. Lola Alvarez Bravo's experiments with the medium include footage of Frida **Kahlo**, apparently for a longer film project that was never completed. Manuel Alvarez Bravo also tried his hand at film-making: in 1934 he took a camera to Tehuantepec to film the local Indian women's elegant movements while walking. Adolfo Best Maugard was a minor painter, less remarkable for his work than for his extraordinarily influential art education primer, *Método de dibujo* (Drawing Method) (1923). His one feature film, *La mancha de sangre* (The Bloodstain) (1937), only recently rediscovered and restored, was a peculiar mixture of melodrama (reminiscent of the later *Cabaretera* genre (see **Cabaretera films**)) and formal experimentation and surrealism, at times echoing the work of still photographer Man Ray.

The growth of film culture in the 1950s also led several groups to try their hand at film-making with new experimental approaches. A notable experience was that of a group of friends in Barranquilla, Colombia, which included writers Alvaro Cepeda Samudio and Gabriel **García Márquez**, the painter Enrique **Grau** and photographer Nereo López. At times humorous, often poetic and oblique, their film, *La langosta azul* (The Blue Lobster) (1954) is both symbolic and realist, an unusual combination of documentary footage and surrealism.

In the 1960s, the spirit of renovation was especially explored in an experimental vein by a group of film-makers in Mexico, many linked to the new film magazine (see **film magazines**), *Nuevo Cine* (launched in 1961) and stimulated by the first and second Concurso de Cine Experimental (Experimental Film Competitions) established by the industry in 1965 and 1967. Although many of the films submitted to the competition were simply unusual narratives and hardly 'experimental', Ruben Gámez's *La fórmula secreta* (The Secret Formula) (1965), awarded the first prize in the first Concurso, was an iconoclastic revelation: 'an irrational essay unified only by the author's unique voice full of surreal moments and provocative scenarios related to intellectual debates about the Mexican national character' (González and Lerner).

Amidst the politicization and radicalism of the new cinemas and the New Latin American Cinema, several film-makers carved out a space for complex artistic experimentation, especially as new formats and more portable and inexpensive technologies like Super 8 mm became available. Perhaps the most sustained has been Diego Risquez in Venezuela, whose trilogy of films about the conquest, especially *Bolívar: sinfonía tropical* (Bolivar, a Tropical Symphony) (1980), were shot in Super 8 and later blown up to 35 mm. With stunningly rich and complex visual images, Risquez's films eschew all dialogue yet present a coherent and critical reinterpretation of Venezuelan history. Following a similar aesthetic paradigm, Paul **Leduc** in Mexico has also abandoned dialogue – though not narrative – to concentrate exclusively on music, especially in his *Barroco* (1989), structured like a concerto with four movements, and *Latino Bar* (1991). In Brazil, the work of Artur **Omar** has been of great significance and has had international repercussions.

Since the 1970s, but especially throughout the 1980s, film-makers have exploited new technologies – not only Super 8 but video and, more recently, digital media for audio-visual experimentation. Especially notable is the work of Sergio García in Mexico, the unheralded theorist of a free form, psychedelic 'fourth cinema' (after **Solanas** and Getino's ***tercer cine***). Many film-makers – Rafael Cordiki, for example – turned to video in the 1980s 'out of [economic] desperation'. Pola Weiss, also a performance artist, was Mexico's video pioneer; following in her footsteps with powerful feminist pieces was artist Silvia Gruner. Ximena Cuevas is perhaps the most prolific and hard-hitting contemporary video artist. Her collagist videos often irreverently take on the symbols of Mexicanness and performances of gender, most notably in her work with Jesusa **Rodríguez** (*Víctimas del pecado neo-liberal* (Victims of the Neoliberal Sin) (1995)) and performance artist Astrid **Hadad** (*Corazón sangrante* (Bleeding Heart) (1993)).

See also: video art

Further reading

González, R. and Lerner, J.M. (1998) *Experimental Cinema*, Santa Monica, CA: Smart Art Press

ANA M. LÓPEZ

experimental theatre

An important aspect of the experimental theatre movement is the aversion to traditional methods of representing political oppression. The construction of this model is the result of a century that discouraged free expressionism and promoted **censorship**. In 1920 almost all theatrical repertoires in Latin American had adopted the Spanish genre tradition, which included romantic melodramas, musicals and repetitive realism. In experimental theatre, artists play with new ways of acting, new forms of costume and lighting, and new ideas about scenography. The formal stage is absent and the theatrical space is arranged to fit each particular play.

Visual artists, composers and dancers now work together. The originating dates of experimental theatre vary from country to country but represent, for some, a method of expression defining national character, and, for others, a way to simply reproduce some of Europe's avant-garde work. In Mexico in 1928, Gabriel Fernandez Ledesma wrote an article in the magazine *¡30-30!* suggesting 'the creation of a theatre that is rooted in collective problems and popular traditions as a mechanism of national identity'. In 1945 in Venezuela, the Grupo Nuevo theatre company was established to analyse social problems and make theatre available to the general public. In 1953, the Teatro Arena (see **Arena Theatre Group**), in São Paulo challenged European theatrical traditions and opted to create a Brazilian Theatre dedicated to social and political change. TEC, the **Teatro Experimental de Cali**, Colombia (Experimental Theatre of Cali) was founded in 1955 and was the point of departure for a rapid growth of private, experimental and university theatre groups. In 1960 it became more openly political and was one of the first Latin American theatre groups to explore the possibilities of collective creation, a form of dramatic social commentary. In Mexico, the Teatro Estudio (Studio Theatre), formed in Guadalajara in 1982, was a group providing workshops in scenography and acting. The Centro de Experimentación Teatral (CET) (The Center for Experimental Theatre), created in 1978 by the Theatre Department of Mexico City's **INBA**, provided an opportunity for students to work in an experimental theatre company. Both the Teatro Experimental Popular (Popular Experimental Theatre), founded in 1976, and Jornadas de Teatro en la Calle (Street Theatre Days), active until the mid-1980s in the Dominican Republic, were experimental centres that promoted social action. In Buenos Aires, the **Teatro Abierto** (Open Theatre), founded 1980, was a collaboration between actors and directors that encouraged experimentation. Their first cycle in 1981 was interrupted when the Teatro Picadero mysteriously burned down but the project continued immediately in the Teatro Tabarís. In Cuba, the Estudio Teatral de Santa Clara, an actors' collective, set out to develop a unique vision of contemporary Cuban identity. Since 1986, Teatro Buendía, consisting largely of art school graduates, has been in the vanguard of Cuban theatre.

Further reading

Antología del teatro Hispanoamericano del siglo XX, tomo I (1979), Ottawa: GIROL Book.

Instituto Nacional de Bellas Artes (1985) *50 Años de teatro*, Mexico: Secretaría de Educación Pública.

The World Encyclopedia of Contemporary Theatre, Volume 2, Americas (1996) London: Routledge.

ISABEL BARBUZZA

expresión americana, La

An essay collection published in 1957 by the Cuban writer José **Lezama Lima**, *La expresión americana* is a seminal contribution to the debate on Latin American identity, and a brief yet startlingly original cultural history of Latin America. Lezama proposes a theory of interpretation which allows for American culture to translate or transfigure inherited cultural elements, thus creating new forms in dialogue with a different, shaping landscape. The first and quintessential Latin American artistic movement, the American Baroque, is an expression of this landscape; it is also a hybrid cultural expression, product of a dialogue between African, indigenous New World and European cultures.

BEN A. HELLER

expressionism

Expressionism arose in Germany with Die Brücke, founded in 1905 by Heckel, Kirchner and Schmidt Rottluff, and continued through the Blaue Reiter group, founded in 1911 and including Kandinsky and Marc. Their paintings and drawings defined the 'expressionist style': arbitrary space and colour, clear brushstrokes, dramatic gestures, deformations, tensions in the composition and high contrasts, all of which served to express the artist's emotions and/or to move the spectator. Between the wars, the German New Objectivity movement (including Grosz, Beckman and Dix) employed similiar artistic means with an openly sociopolitical content. Expressionism re-emerged after the war as a stylistic element in the work of several different artists and artistic currents; in American abstract expressionism, for example, and European informalism. An important link between German expressionism and Latin American art was Lasar **Segall**, who was active in the expressionist groups, particularly in Dresden; he visited Brazil several times before settling there definitively in 1923.

In Latin America, the influence of expressionism is particularly clear among the politically committed graphic artists (see **graphic art**) of the 1930s and 1940s. In the 1960s, after the boom in depersonalized and universalist geometric abstraction, the expressionist style was again recuperated by figurative artists working within a historico-philosophical framework. This was the era of repressive military dictatorships which forced many artists into exile in Europe and the USA, creating a possibility of interchange with the informalist and neo-figurative movements. The Argentinians Luis Felipe **Noé**, Ernesto Deira, Jorge de la **Vega** and Rómulo Macció organized a movement called Nueva Figuración (see **otra figuración**), whose purpose was to return to the figurative image of man in relationship to other human beings and the world of things. In Venezuela, in the midst of a boom in **kinetic art**, Jacobo **Borges** also opted for an expressionist figurative art to satirize and condemn the reign of Rómulo **Betancourt** in series like 'Ha comenzado el espectáculo' (The Show Has Begun) or in the recreations of the works of David, the favoured artist of Napoleon, emblem of unrestrained power. The Mexican José Luis **Cuevas**, through sharp calligraphic line drawings, created monsters that speak of his obsessions: illness, flesh, prostitution and despotism. In Chile, after the military *coup* of 1973, José **Balmes**, Eduardo Martínez Bonati and Guillermo **Núñez**, who had turned to abstraction, returned to figurative work with a strong element of protest; monstrous, twisted bodies broken and torn at the torturers' hands, invade their work.

Further reading

Bayon, D. (1991) *Aventura plástica de Hispanoamérica*, Mexico City: Fondo de Cultura Económica.

Castedo, L. (1988) *Historia del arte iberoamericano*, Madrid: Alianza Editorial.

Lucie-Smith, E. (1993) *Latin American Art of the 20th Century*, London: Thames and Hudson.

Sullivan, E. (1992) *Artistas latinoamericanos del siglo XX*, New York: Museum of Modern Art.

MARÍA ALBA BOVISIO

F

Fabini, Eduardo

b. 1883, Lavalleja, Uruguay; d. 1950, Montevideo, Uruguay

Composer

Founder of the Uruguayan Conservatoire (1907) and of the Asociación de Música de Cámara (Chamber Music Association) of Uruguay in 1910, Fabini studied in Montevideo and later in Brussels, where he specialized in composition. His work employs impressionistic techniques in adapting themes from Uruguayan folk music. Outstanding among his works are the symphonic poems *Campo* (Countryside) (1929) and *La isla de los ceibos* (Island of the Ceiba trees) (1925), his ballets *Mburucuyá* (1932) and *Mañana de Reyes* (Morning of Epiphany) (1937) as well as choral works and pieces for piano and **guitar**.

MARCO MAGGI

Fabulosos Cadillacs, Los

Los Fabulosos Cadillacs are a very popular Argentine rock band formed in 1985 by eight friends brought together by a common interest in the Jamaican **ska** rhythm utilized by several British groups, whose black suit and hats they adopted. **Reggae** was soon added to ska, and their musical style continued to broaden to include a wide gamut of rhythmic forms, including **tango**, **salsa**, **merengue** and **bolero**, all in their own boisterous rock style. They were awarded a Grammy for best performance by an alternative Latin Rock group in 1998. Their albums include *Bares y Fondas* (Bars and Inns) (1986), *Sopa de Caracol* (Snail Soup) (1991), *Rey Azúcar* (King Sugar) (1995) and *La Marcha del Golazo Solitario* (The March of the Spectacular Solo Goal) (1999).

EDUARDO GUÍZAR-ALVAREZ

Facio, Sara

b. 1932, Buenos Aires, Argentina

Photographer

Facio is one of the most influential contemporary Argentine photographers, for the breadth of her photographic interests as for her actual photography, which has been widely published in newspapers and collections such as *Buenos Aires, Buenos Aires* (with Alicia **D'Amico**, 1968) and *Hasta aquí* (Up to Here) with Mario **Benedetti** (1974). In 1979, she and fellow photographers María Cristina Orive and Alicia D'Amico founded La Azotea publishing house to disseminate historical and contemporary work. Her major exhibitions have travelled the Americas and Europe.

AMANDA HOPKINSON

Fagoth, Stedman

b. 1953, San Esquipulas (Río Coco), Nicaragua

Political leader

Fagoth was leader of **MISURASATA** in the 1980s, allied with the **contras**, and with US aid he mobilized Miskitus (see **Miskitus**) against the Sandinistas (see **Sandinista Revolution**). He was arrested in 1981, but the Sandinistas freed Fagoth when he promised to emigrate to Bulgaria. Instead, he mobilized 3,000 Miskitus and fled to Honduras to broadcast counter-revolutionary propaganda. Peace negotiations between the Miskitus and the Sandinistas did not begin until 1984, when the government granted autonomy to the Atlantic Coast. In 1987, Fagoth returned to create a new Miskitu organization which won the majority of Miskitu votes in 1990, and led to the appointment of Brooklyn **Rivera** as adviser to the Chamorro government.

ANUPAMA MANDE AND ILEANA RODRÍGUEZ

fairs and markets

On the threshold of the twenty-first century it seems odd that markets and fairs should still figure so large in the life of Latin America. Global consumption patterns have brought shopping malls to most Latin American cities, and with them the usual logos and shop fronts that make the shopping centre into a kind of everyplace that could be easily and imperceptibly transported to any comparable city. The traditional function of the market – as a place of exchange of goods, gifts and information between relatively disconnected communities – might easily seem redundant in an age of instant and constant communication.

That it is not is testimony not to one thing but to many. First, it remains the case that a very significant number of Latin Americans – despite the globalization thesis – remain permanently excluded from the glass-covered shopping streets. They may go to some lengths to create an atmosphere of openness; the interior design of the shopping mall may often incorporate fountains, terraces and imitation squares; but they remain gated and selective. Thus there will almost invariably be a bustling parallel market outside the building.

There are also designated market areas still extant in most cities – in many countries they are State-subsidized buildings with some basic facilities provided where local people can buy their basic necessities at a cheaper price. However, there are still fairs in most Latin American countries where local farmers can bring goods for direct sale. On the streets of most Bolivian and Peruvian towns and cities there is a bewildering variety of stalls and stands selling food, handmade goods and manufactured goods. The paradox is that these genuinely popular markets crowding the pavements will sell a large proportion of cheap factory-made items – clothes, plastic items, cooking utensils and electronic goods – many of which will carry a Made in Taiwan or the Philippines label. Yet the sellers, particularly in the Andean region, will often themselves be wearing at least some traditional costume.

Despite the origin of the goods, the traditional function of the market still holds – as a place of meeting and exchange of information, greetings, news and opinion.

In every Latin American country there are markets that do correspond to the anticipated image of a traditional market, selling **crafts** and artisanal goods. Ironically, there is a high likelihood that the majority of customers will be foreign tourists seeking 'authentic' ethnic products, often produced in a semi-industrial way by rural or provincial collectives.

Yet even in huge cities like São Paulo there are street markets set up on particular days of the week in different neighbourhoods, and middle-class people prefer to buy produce there because it is cheaper and better. Markets are never merely places of purchase or consumption; they are often protected spaces, refuges for the marginal, as well as sources of cheap goods. The eclecticism of what is on offer may indicate quite contrary things – either the decline of traditional production or its adaptation to the complex realities of a culture full of contradictions.

Further reading

Babb, F. (1998) *Between Field and Cooking Pot: the Political Economy of Market Women in Peru*, Austin: University of Texas Press.

MIKE GONZALEZ

Falcón, Ada

b. 1905, Buenos Aires, Argentina; date of death unknown, Córdoba, Argentina

Singer

Although she never achieved the fame of singers like Tita **Merello** or Olinda Bazán, Falcón belonged to that group of women who developed their own particular style. 'La joyita argentina' (the little Argentine jewel), as she was known in the theatre, sang **tango** in dramatic style in a deep mezzo voice. Her best known interpretation is 'Tres esperanzas' (Three Hopes), which she sang with the Francisco **Canaro** orchestra. Although she appeared on stage and in film, she retired at the height of her fame to a convent in Córdoba.

LUIS GUSMAN

Fallas, Carlos Luis

b. 1909, Alajuela, Costa Rica; d. 1966, San José, Costa Rica

Writer

One of Latin America's most important social realist writers, Fallas's novel *Mamita Yunai* (1941) describes the life and conditions of workers on Costa Rica's banana plantations. As a young man he worked on the United Fruit Company's plantations on his country's Atlantic coast, became a union organizer and joined the Communist party. In 1934 he was among the leaders of a national banana workers' strike, an experience that provided the core material for his most famous novel. The novel was rejected by the judges of the 1941 Farrar Rinehart prize (eventually won by Ciro **Alegría**), presumably on the grounds that it was too explicitly propagandistic. Nonetheless, it was widely read and imitated by other 'proletarian writers' in subsequent years. Through the last twenty years of his life, Fallas was centrally involved in national politics and in a struggle with José Figueres for recognition of the communist party, of which he was a leading member. He continued to write, but without repeating the success of his first work.

MIKE GONZALEZ

Fals Borda, Orlando

b. 1925, Barranquilla, Colombia

Sociologist

Fals Borda's works reflect his concern for how social change takes form and how the ruling elite respond to those changes in Colombia. *La Violencia en Colombia* (La Violencia in Colombia) (1962), which he wrote together with Germán Guzmán and Eduardo Umaña Luna, attempts to understand the traumatic consequences of that period of Colombian history. In his book *Historia doble de la Costa, 1979–1986* (Colombian North Coast, 1979–1986: A Twofold History), Fals Borda reflects his interest in applying a research methodology that articulates the study of social reality with political practice for social change.

MIGUEL A. CARDINALE

Falú, Eduardo Yamil

b. 1923, Salta, Argentina

Musician

A self-taught guitarist, Falú began his career on radio as a member of Los Troperos. He worked closely with the reciter Rodolfo Alvarez and the Salta poet César Perdiguero. His songs 'Canción de luna y cosecha' (Song of Moon and Harvest) and 'Tabacalera' (Tobacco Field) contained social commentary at a time when most songs – with the exception of the work of Atahualpa **Yupanqui** – limited themselves to discussing love or landscape. He made his first appearance in Buenos Aires in 1945, where he remained, appearing regularly on radio and in concert. In the 1940s, folk music was favoured by the wealthier classes and limited to exclusive clubs, but in the 1950s the majority of

Falú's work and the most important folk music and tango singers of the time were recorded on the Teca label. In 1962 he was contracted by Radio El Mundo and presented a successful season at the Presidente Alvear Theatre in the capital. He went on to sign with Radio Splendid. The duo Falú and Jaime Dávalos (guitar and charango) opened new directions in folk music, making famous popular classics like 'Tonada de un viejo amor' (Tonada of an Old Love), 'Trago de zambas' (Zambas for Drinkers) 'Resolanas' and others.

In 1954 Falú travelled to the USA and in 1958 to the Soviet Union, where he gave eighteen concerts. In the same year he cut his first album outside Argentina, in France. From 1960 he toured throughout the world, often sharing the stage with his son Juan José and the flamenco guitarist Paco Peña. He wrote and played the 'Suite Argentina' for guitar and strings, with the Camerata Bariloche and conceived the 'Romance de la muerte de Juan Lavalle' (Ballad for the Death of Lavalle) based on Ernesto **Sabato**'s novel *Sobre héroes y tumbas* (On Heroes and Tombs). This composition for guitar, narrator and voice was recorded on the Phillips label, with Sabato himself as narrator and Falú as both guitarist and singer, and frequently presented in theatres across Argentina. Falú became President of the Argentine Society of Authors and Composers. His music always sought out new and unorthodox directions, untrammelled by academic restraints on technique; his arrangements introduced a range of innovative harmonies while remaining within the framework of Argentine popular music.

Further reading

Sabato, E.R. (1974) *Eduardo Falú*, Madrid: Ediciones Júcar.

CLAUDIA TORRE

Familia Burrón

Familia Burrón is one of the longest running and best-loved Mexican comic book series, written by Gabriel **Vargas** and published weekly since at least 1953. The comic focuses on a working-class urban family headed by don Regino Burrón, a staid, dependable barber, and Borola Tacuche, an idealist willing to take on any cause and undaunted by her repeated failures. The comic addresses a wide range of current social issues, and Vargas's seemingly inexhaustible reserves of popular speech and humour have influenced three generations of Mexican writers, including Carlos **Monsiváis**, Sergio **Pitol** and Juan Villoro.

CYNTHIA STEELE

family

In Latin America, as in other parts of the world, the family is a socio-legal concept that often has diverse manifestations. Legally and historically, it has been defined as a heterosexual household sanctioned by the State and/or the Roman Catholic Church. This union was the legal transmitter of property and status, and is idealized as the most appropriate social unit. Governed by the father or husband, families were supposed to be the basic organization of society, one that remained intact regardless of political circumstances.

At the same time that laws outlined the privileges that pertained to legal families, they clearly explained the social costs borne by families who challenged social conventions. Children born as the result of incest, adultery, common-law relationships and unions with priests or nuns all suffered legal and social discrimination throughout their lives. They could not inherit their parents' property as equals to legal heirs and, in some cases, were banned from inheritance. At the same time fathers and mothers did not always have the same rights to govern these children. The pain that such discrimination caused was revealed in the life of Evita **Perón**. These stigmas were eliminated by legal reforms in many countries during the twentieth century.

Legal reforms were imperative because, traditionally, most couples in Latin America never married because of the economic and social costs of marriage. Furthermore, the impact of conquest, miscegenation, slavery, rape and wars – added to the unwillingness or inability of both men and women to conform to these patterns – have led to great variety within the Latin American family. The formation of same-sex relations also led to non-reproductive family units.

The stereotype of the Latin American patriarchal family was popularized by Brazilian sociologist Gilberto **Freyre**. He based his model on the patriarchal culture that emerged from the slave-based sugar plantation economy in Brazil. In his classic work, ***Casa grande e senzala*** (The Master and the Slaves) (1933), Freyre depicted the patriarch as a man with almost unlimited power over his family and slaves. Despite this popular image of the head of Latin American families, popular culture has also recognized that mothers have also wielded important powers through their relationships with their children and relatives, as well as with their spouses. Supposedly submissive and docile, mothers such as the one personified in **Puenzo**'s *La historia oficial* (The Official Story) (1984) can summon remarkable fortitude. Fathers, traditionally the breadwinners, have not always been able to provide for their families. As seen in Héctor Babenco's ***Pixote a lei do mais fraco***, some Brazilian children are left to fend for themselves, while Maria Carolina de **Jesus**'s *Quarto do despejo* (Child of the Dark) (1960), the autobiography of a poor Afro-Brazilian woman from São Paulo, depicted a barely literate mother who took care of her children without the aid of their fathers.

Freyre also popularized the concept of *machismo* (see **machismo, Mexican**), or the cult of male hypersexuality, which enabled men and boys to exercise a double sexual standard not available to their wives or sisters. While males had access to all women, wives were supposed to be chaste. Nevertheless, ***Dona Flor e seus dois maridos*** (Dona Flor and Her Two Husbands), the famous novel by Jorge **Amado**, suggests that women can have more sexual options than imagined in the traditional family, one reaffirmed by Maria Carolina de Jesus. The lyrics of Argentine tangos (see **tango**) often lamented the unfaithfulness of women.

Gay and lesbian couples are struggling for legal recognition in Latin America as elsewhere, though not with the success gained in parts of Europe in the last few years. Annick Prieur's study *Mema's House* (1998) depicts in a very moving way the attempts by a group of young drag queens, under the tutelage of Mema, an older queen, to form an alternative family of mothers and daughters. Jaime Humberto **Hermosillo**'s ***Doña Herlinda y su hijo*** (1984) turns on a widow's desire to secure her only son's happiness by welcoming into her house the son's male lover, while at the same time securing him a measure of social respectability by having him marry and father a son.

The recent film, *Estação do Brasil* (Central Station) (1998), starring Fernanda **Montenegro** (who years before had memorably played the motherly prostitute in *Pixote*) suggests that families are invented, not born. Change – due to migration and **urbanization**, divorce and the growing recognition (and sometimes acceptance) of diverse sexual and social practices – is having an impact on the shape and nature of the Latin American family.

Further reading

Balderston, D. and Guy, D.J. (eds) (1997) *Sex and Sexuality in Latin America*, New York: New York University Press.

Lavrin, A. (ed.) (1989) *Sexuality and Marriage in Colonial Latin America*, Lincoln: University of Nebraska Press.

Melhuus, M. and Stølen, K.A. (eds) (1996) *Machos, Mistresses, Madonnas: Contesting the Power of Latin American Gender Imagery*, London: Verso.

Parker, R.G. (1991) *Bodies and Pleasures: Sexual Culture in Contemporary Brazil*, Boston: Beacon Press.

Prieur, A. (1998) *Mema's House, Mexico City: On Transvestites, Queens, and Machos*, Chicago: University of Chicago Press.

DONNA J. GUY AND DANIEL BALDERSTON

Fangio, Juan Manuel

b. 1911, Balcarce, Argentina; d. 1995, Balcarce

Racing car driver

Classified by many as the greatest Argentine sportsman of all time, Fangio began his racing career in 1938, driving the Grand Prix circuit from 1948 to 1958 where he ran fifty-one races, held twenty-eight pole positions, captured twenty-four victories and won five World Championships (1951, 1954–7). Competitors found him fearless and uncompromising, yet helpful and never mean or deliberately dangerous. A true national hero, he inspired in Argentines a sense of identity, pride and success. A Centro Tecnológico-Cultural and Museo del Automovilismo bearing his name opened in Balcarce in 1986.

JOSEPH ARBENA

Fanon, Frantz

b. 1925, Fort-de-France, Martinique; d. 1961, Bethesda, Maryland

Philosopher, revolutionary and psychiatrist

At times a cry of anguish and at times a militant call to arms, Fanon's life and writings reflect the conflicts and contradictions of colonial subjectivity. And they call forth an era, a moment in modern history when the struggle for Third World liberation was perceived in the realm of the possible. Fanon grew up in Martinique, and was educated there and later in France. He served in the French army during the Second World War, and afterwards studied medicine and psychiatry at the University of Lyon. In 1952 he published *Peau noire, masques blancs* (Black Skin, White Masks), a psychoanalytic study of racism and the alienation of the black man in the face of dominant white culture. Shortly after the publication of *Peau noire*, Fanon took up a post as head of the psychiatry unit in the Blida-Joinville Hospital in Algeria. In 1954, the Algerian Revolution broke out and the young psychiatrist joined the revolt against the French. In 1961, following his experiences in Algeria, he published his best-known book, *Les damnés de la terre* (The Wretched of the Earth), which advocated armed revolution against colonial oppression in the Third World. Fanon died of leukemia that same year, at the age of 36.

Fanon's writings also include two other books of social and political commentary: the 1959 *L'An V de la révolution algérienne* (Studies in a Dying Colonialism) and *Pour la révolution africaine* (Toward the African Revolution), published posthumously in 1964.

Further reading

Gates, H.L., Jr (1991) 'Critical Fanonism', *Critical Inquiry* 17(Spring): 457–70.
Gendzier, I.L. (1973) *Frantz Fanon: A Critical Study*, New York: Grove.
Gordon, L.R (ed.) (1996) *Fanon: A Critical Reader*, Oxford: Blackwell.

CATHERINE DEN TANDT

fantastic literature

Though most famously associated with **Borges**, **Bioy Casares** and **Cortázar**, fantastic literature has much earlier roots in Latin America. The Argentine writer and scientist Eduardo Ladislao Holmberg (1852–1937), influenced by E.T.A. Hoffmann, wrote Gothic stories that play on a tension between scientific and spiritual thinking. Leopoldo **Lugones**, in the stories of *Las fuerzas extrañas* (The Strange Forces) (1906), also reflects an interest in the occult; this collection includes the famous stories 'La lluvia de fuego' (The Rain of Fire), 'Yzur' and 'Los caballos de Abdera' (The Horses of Abdera). Alfonso **Reyes**, Horacio **Quiroga**, Manuel Peyrou and Santiago Dabove were other practitioners of the fantastic.

Without doubt, though, the modern tradition of the fantastic in Latin America begins with a bang in 1940 with the publication of the ***Antología de la literatura fantástica*** by Borges, Bioy Casares and Silvina **Ocampo**. In tandem with Bioy's novel *La invención de Morel* (Morel's Invention) (1940), which appeared with a preface by Borges, and the Borges stories that culminated in ***Ficciones*** (1944), the anthology set out to show Latin American writers, and the reading public, that a distinct literature distant from the dominant social realist tradition was possible. The Borges story 'Tlön, Uqbar, Orbis Tertius' was the boldest Latin American work included in the first edition of the anthology, and it was celebrated by Bioy in the preface as an example of a new literary genre. The second edition of the anthology, published in 1965, included works by Cortázar, **Murena**, **Wilcock**, **Garro** and **Bianco**.

Julio Cortázar was, after Borges, the most important Latin American practitioner and theorist of the fantastic. His 'Sentimiento de lo fantástico' (The Feeling of the Fantastic) in *La vuelta al día en ochenta mundos* (Around the Day in Eighty Worlds) (1967), and the comments on the fantastic in 'Del cuento breve y sus alrededores' (On the Short Story and Environs) in *Ultimo round* (Last Round) (1969), focused on the psychological effects of the fantastic (following Poe, whose work Cortázar had translated) instead of focusing on the formal structures that had interested Borges and Bioy Casares.

The tradition of the fantastic in Spanish America has been studied by Ana María **Barrenechea** and Oscar **Hahn**; the Brazilian tradition, particularly the work of Murilo **Rubião**, has been studied by Jorge **Schwartz**. The fantastic, particularly the form cultivated in Argentina, is sometimes confused with so-called **magical realism** (and with **Carpentier**'s *real maravilloso*), but at least in general terms the Argentine version was more controlled and cerebral, while **García Márquez** and his successors preferred flashier effects.

Further reading

Hahn, O. (1978) *El cuento fantástico hispanoamericano en el siglo XIX*, Mexico City: Premiá.

—— (1990) *El cuento fantástico hispanoamericano en el siglo XX*, Santiago: Editorial Universitaria.

König, I. (1984) *La formación de la narrativa fantástica hispanoamericana en la época moderna*, Frankfurt: Peter Lang.

Wheelock, C. (1980) 'Fantastic Symbolism in the Spanish American Short Story', *Hispanic Review* 48: 415–34.

DANIEL BALDERSTON

Farias, Roberto

b. 1932, Nova Friburgo, Rio de Janeiro, Brazil

Film-maker

Founder of the film production company R.F. Farias and co-director of DiFilm, the **Cinema Novo** distributor, Farias directed **Embrafilme** (1974–8) in one of its most prolific periods. An assistant with **Atlântida** in the 1950s, his first film as director in 1957 was a **chanchada**. He worked in several genres: *Asalto ao trem pagador* (Great Train Robbery) (1962) was a social thriller, *Selva trágica* (Tragic Forest) (1964) was a social protest film and the closest to **Cinema Novo**, while the political thriller *Pra frente Brasil* (Forward Brazil) (1981) confronted the dictatorship. He also directed naive musicals starring pop singer Roberto **Carlos** and comedies with Os **Trapalhões**.

ISMAIL XAVIER AND THE USP GROUP

Fariña, Soledad

b. 1943, Antofagasta, Chile

Poet

Fariña's writing insistently explores a series of unanswerable questions: how to express a sexuality denied, how to recuperate a pre-Columbian culture long suppressed, and how to discover the Latin American dimension of language. She has published three volumes of poetry: *El primer libro* (The First Book) (1985), *Albricia* (Good News) (1988) and *En amarillo oscuro* (In Dark Yellow) (1994), which has been widely studied and translated. She graduated in political science from the University of Chile, and in philosophy and letters from the University of Stockholm.

ELIANA ORTEGA

Faro a Colón

The Faro a Colón (Columbus Lighthouse) is a cross-shaped monument in Santo Domingo, capital of the Dominican Republic. The concrete structure – 800 feet long and 150 feet tall – projects a cross of light into the sky, and cost US $250 million. It holds Christopher Columbus's supposed remains, and was built as part of the celebrations of the Quinto Centenario (see **Columbian quincentenary**) to commemorate the Spanish Conqueror's arrival at Hispaniola. Although a lighthouse had been discussed since the 1800s, the project began during Rafael Leonidas **Trujillo**'s dictatorship; President Joaquín **Balaguer** completed it more as a tribute to himself than to Columbus.

FERNANDO VALERIO-HOLGUÍN

fascism in Latin America

Fascism is an emotive term that is often used to describe political formations that employ extreme violence and torture as a method of social control, and who employ the State to crush all forms of democratic participation and all attempts by the victims to organize. In that sense, the label can easily apply to a series of authoritarian regimes across the region and throughout the century. The Brazilian military regime (1964–86) employed torture and terror in a systematic way; so too did the Chilean military dictatorship (1973–89) under **Pinochet**, and the Argentine military junta (1976–83; see **Proceso de Reorganización Nacional**) whose invention of the transitive verb 'to disappear' is one of its more sinister legacies, especially since it appears to have been applied not only to their political enemies, but even to their enemies' small children. The Uruguayan military (1973–85), behind the blanket of silence they imposed, employed all forms of repression. The history of the military regimes of Central America is one of arbitrary and terrible cruelty – particularly in the aftermath of the Guatemalan *coup* against **Arbenz** in 1954. The examples are legion and endlessly repeated. Yet, in and of itself, savage brutality, repression and the regular and organized use of violence do not constitute fascism.

There were, of course, a number of groups that actively supported Nazi Germany and fascist Italy until 1945 in Latin America, and who wore the usual brown or blue shirt insignias of those ideologies. In Brazil, the authoritarian concepts of F.J. de Oliveira Vianna (1885–1951) found an enthusiastic successor in Plínio Salgado, founder of the Integralista party in 1932, an enthusiastic disciple of Mussolini whose ideas married with the prevailing ideology of Getúlio **Vargas**'s **Estado Novo**. In Argentina, where events in Italy were always closely followed, enthusiasm for Mussolini's corporate State was expressed by high Church dignitaries, but also by younger military officers, like Juan Domingo **Perón**, who was profoundly influenced by Italian corporatism. Enthusiastic support for fascist ideas came too from less predictable quarters: Leopoldo **Lugones**'s flirtation with socialism ended abruptly when he delivered his famous 'La hora de la espada' (Hour of the Sword) speech in 1924 in support of authoritarian governance. Those thoughts were echoed by Manuel **Gálvez** in Argentina and in Chile by A. Edwards Vives.

It is equally well-established that high-ranking Nazis were helped to escape after the Second World War by a sort of underground railroad that took them to Paraguay, Bolivia and Chile, where sympathetic dictatorships were willing to harbour them. Some established communities like Colonia Dignidad in Chile; others, like Barbie and Mengele, were given official responsibilities in those countries. By and large, however, these individuals did not produce movements around themselves, though their continuing liberty has fascinated decades of pulp-fiction readers and excited small bands of resurgent European fascists from time to time. This serves to illustrate an important question in the discussion of fascism.

Fascism is, in its original phase, a mass movement, mobilizing a section of the population that is fearful for its survival – usually the *petit bourgeois* of small businessmen or functionaries – in support of the State and against those it perceives to be the source of the threat – the working class. In the longer run, this movement's demands for control and authority serve the interests of powerful groups in society who, at a particular juncture, choose not to express directly their long-term interest in a disarmed working class and an authoritarian system of social control. At a later stage, as was the case in Germany and Italy, those powerful corporations will resume control directly or through pliable representatives. The final factor in the equation is an ideology that can bind these different segments together – perhaps extreme nationalism, perhaps anti-Semitism, perhaps another racist ideology.

It is true that the Argentine military regime established under **Videla** in 1976 was overtly anti-Semitic, and that it fostered militant, quasi-military groups driven by that ideology. In Guatemala in the late 1970s, several leading politicians expressed genocidal intentions towards the indigenous population. But in other cases – Chile and Brazil are examples – extremely repressive regimes employing torture enjoy the active support of the USA and other democracies for those methods of rule. In such cases, they should be seen not as states of exception, but as the last recourse of any capitalist State threatened by real or imaginary enemies. After all, Chile was once celebrated as a historic democracy and later it was fêted for its 'miraculous' economic performance; its characteristic violence was normalized, as Armand Mattelart has pointed out, by the judicious allocation of cartoon characters' names to each military operation.

Further reading

Bethell, L. (ed.) (1996) *Ideas and Ideologies in 20th century Latin America*, Cambridge: Cambridge University Press.

Potash, R. (1984) *Perón y el GOU*, Buenos Aires: Sudamericana.

MIKE GONZALEZ

fast food

Fast food is not an invention of the twentieth century, nor of the USA; in the pre-Hispanic era there were stalls in the markets where people could eat. Today the market continues to be an eating place for the poorer sections of the population. The food they serve may not be 'fast' of course – it may have required many hours of preparation, yet it is instantly available and ready to eat for the consumer.

While the multinational food chains were conspicuous almost everywhere in Latin America at the end of the twentieth century – McDonald's, Denny's, Wendy's, Pizza Hut and so on – they were not the only fast food available. In parks, at bus and train stations and terminals, along busy streets, there are still a staggering number of street sellers dispensing 'instant' food for the traveller. It may range from **coffee**, coca tea or *mate*, to fruit juice stands hooked perilously to the overhead power-lines, to sellers of corncakes (see **corn and corncakes**) of various kinds with various fillings in Mexico and Central America, to the buckets with steaming *tamales*. It is noticeable that the consumers range widely in social origin and appearance; taco sellers outside government offices will often be surrounded by customers in suits.

Typical of Brazilian street corners are stands offering Bahian food, where *baianas*, dressed in gauzy white, stand next to steaming cauldrons of **dendé oil** and serve up *acarajás* (see **acarajá**) and other delicacies. At snack bars in all major cities, passers-by sidle up to the counters to quickly consume *salgadinhos* (savouries) like *empadas* (meat, chicken or seafood pastries); croquettes of all sorts, like *bolinhos de bacalhau* (salt cod) or *coxinhas* (chicken); or small dishes of *carne seca* (jerked beef) with *farinha* (**manioc** meal). All are typically washed down with small glasses of ice cold *choppes* (draft beer) or natural fruit juices. Some stands specialize in 'ethnic' foods, featuring Middle Eastern snacks (*esfigas* and *kibbes*) or Japanese noodle dishes.

Fast food is undoubtedly a phenomenon of urban growth, of a work-force travelling very long distances to work, and of the imposition of a US and Northern European working day. It is also part of the process of globalization where eating and eating habits have themselves become internationalized (see **eating out**). The paradox, however, is that the archetypal, original fast food (the hamburger) now competes with versions of other foods in their 'faster' varieties – *sushi*, instant noodles and the 'Taco Bell' chains that reflect the spread of Hispanic food throughout the USA. In the opposite direction, the hamburger and its close relatives have penetrated to the south, but in many cases have undergone a sort of 'hybridization', acquiring chilli pepper, spices and other local additives as they go.

In fact, regional chains often compete with the US franchises: in Brazil, the Big Boy chain of hamburgers is more popular than McDonald's, and since the mid-1990s the phenomenon of 'food by the kilo' restaurants (customers load up their plates from a wide assortment of hot and cold foods, and are charged a set rate per kilo at the cash register) have made a serious dent in the typical business of fast-food places, offering slightly more comfort and better foods with the same speed of service at reasonable prices.

MIKE GONZALEZ

Favio, Leonardo

b. 1938, Mendoza, Argentina

Actor, singer and film-maker

Favio (born Fuad Jorge Jury) began his career as a film director as part of the **Generación del 60** (Sixties Generation) with *Crónica de un niño solo* (Chronicle of a Lonely Child) (1964), the first of a group of black-and-white films. The film, in which Favio appeared, recounts the difficult life of a boy from a poor family and is narrated from the child's point of view, requiring an innovative formal approach (particularly in the camera work) which evidenced the director's debt to Italian neo-realism (in the selection of a shanty town (see **shanty towns and slums**) as a privileged space) and the French new wave.

El romance del Aniceto y la Francisca (Ballad of Aniceto and Francisca) (1965) and *El dependiente* (The Shop Assistant) (1967) followed. *Juan Moreira* (1972) began a second phase characterized by the use of colour. Based on a nineteenth-century Argentine literary classic, it was a great box office success. The marginalized but irrepressible Moreira dies because he refuses to surrender to the forces of order; this was read as a metaphor for the complex political history of Argentina (military government, armed resistance, trade union and student struggles, the imminent return of **Perón**). In this new phase, Favio recuperated a series of popular icons and stressed the importance of myth, a new concept in Argentine cinema. Further successes followed, including *Nazareno Cruz y el lobo* (Nazareno Cruz and the Wolf) (1974) and *Soñar, soñar* (Dream, Dream) (1976), starring world champion boxer Carlos **Monzón**. The military dictatorship of 1976 silenced and exiled Favio, who was clearly identified with **Peronism**.

Favio returned to the screen in 1993 with *Gatica, el mono* (**Gatica**, the Monkey), based on the life of a famous Argentine boxer of the 1940s and 1950s. Favio draws a parallel between the boxer's rise and subsequent decline and the political biography of Argentina, and particularly of Peronism; it combines fictional images of El Mono's life with newsreel footage. The film is a testimony to the heroism of an Argentine people expressed in the 17th of October, the victories of Gatica, Perón and Evita (see **Perón, María Eva Duarte de**). Perón's embrace with Gatica at Luna Park shows the central role of spectacle and artifice in the lives of both men. In the late 1990s, Favio began working on a film about the events of October 17th and on another on Che **Guevara**.

Futher reading

Oubiña, D. and Aguilar, G.M. (1993) *El cine de Leonardo Favio*, Buenos Aires: Nuevo Extremo.

DIEGO BENTIVEGNA

fazenda

Fazenda is a term used to refer to a large estate in Brazil. It is the Portuguese equivalent of the Spanish term **hacienda**, which is used throughout Spanish-speaking Latin America. However, in Brazil plantations (see **plantation**) are also often referred to as *fazendas*, while in Spanish America the term *plantación* (plantations) is used.

See also: agrarian reform; *latifundio*

CRISTÓBAL KAY

Federación de Mujeres Cubanas

The Federación de Mujeres Cubanas (FMC) is a women's organization founded in August 1960 and presided over since then by revolutionary excombatant Vilma Espín. It is structured from the local delegation level, through municipal, provincial and national blocks, culminating in a national decision-making congress. Its objectives include the incorporation of women into active national life, hence its concentration on health and education campaigns and on the political mobilization of women. Its independent character, however, is questionable; it has been a political and propaganda instrument of the socialist state from its foundation. While over 80 per cent of Cuban women are FMC members, its activities and influence are in permanent decline.

WILFREDO CANCIO ISLA

feeling

Feeling is a Cuban song style whose name suggests the influence of the North American romantic ballad, but whose style owed much more to traditional Cuban trova. Key compositions included 'Hasta mañana, vida mía' (Until Tomorrow My Love) (1945) by Rosendo Ruiz and 'Contigo en la distancia' (With You in the Distance) (1946) and 'Delirio' (Madness) (1948), both by César **Portillo de la Luz**. Its principal performers usually sang to a guitar accompaniment; most came from poor backgrounds and had little or no academic training; hence the importance of arrangers like Bebo Valdés, Nino Rivera and Pedro Justiz (Peruchín). The songs were often spoken rather than sung, though later artists like Elena **Burke** were virtuoso singers.

JOSÉ ANTONIO EVORA

feijoada

Now considered the 'national' dish of Brazil, the *feijoada*'s current, almost ceremonial status – the *de rigueur* Saturday lunch menu for chic *cariocas* (Rio de Janeiro) at the even more elegant Copacabana Palace Hotel, for example – belies its humble origins as a hotchpotch of beans and leftover meat fragments used for seasoning rather than eating, typically produced by slaves for their own consumption. Today's *feijoada completa* is a luxurious, albeit heavy, dish, a brilliant parody of which is invoked in Joaquim Pedro de **Andrade**'s *Macunaíma* (1969). The standard ingredients are **beans** (usually black, although in the northeast *mulatinho* (pinto) beans are typical), *carne seca* (jerked beef), bacon, tongue, cured meats, and pork ears, feet and tails. Vegetables such as kale and pumpkin are also typically included. For table presentation, the cooked meats are separated from the beans, then sliced and arranged on a platter with the tongue in the centre. Sliced oranges are passed around with the beans as well as sliced onions, hot pepper sauce, rice and *farinha* (**manioc** meal). To aid digestion, a few ounces of **cachaça** are highly recommended.

ANA M. LÓPEZ

Feijóo, Samuel

b. 1914, San Juan de los Yeras, Cuba; d. 1992, Santa Clara, Cuba

Writer, artist and ethnologist

Director of the Department of Folklore Studies at Cuba's Central University of Las Villas, Feijóo's research into the traditions and customs of rural Cuba was fundamental. His published work included *El girasol sediento* (The Thirsty Sunflower) (1963) and *Poeta en el paisaje* (Poet in the Landscape) (1966) and a popular novel *Juan Quinquin en Pueblo Mocho* (1964), later filmed by Julio **García Espinosa**. Self-taught, he contributed regularly to journals including **Carteles** and **Orígenes**; in 1958 he became director of his university's publishing house and editor of its journal *Islas*.

WILFREDO CANCIO ISLA

Feldman, Simón

b. 1922, Buenos Aires, Argentina

Film-maker

Abandoning a promising career as a painter, Feldman opted for the cinema. After making short films, his directing debut was *El negocio* (The Big Business) (1959). His next film, *Los de la mesa diez* (The People on Table Ten) (1960) confirmed his place as one of the key figures of the **Generación del 60**. In the years that followed, he made only shorts. In 1985 he was appointed Director of CERC (Centro Experimental de Realización Cinematográfica – Experimental Film Centre). He has also published several books on cinema.

DIANA PALADINO

Felipe, Liliana

b. 1954, Córdoba, Argentina

Performance artist

Felipe describes herself as 'composer, cabaret artist and gardener'. A member of the Divas group, in 1991 she co-founded, with Jesusa **Rodríguez**, *El Hábito*, a theatrical space of great creative freedom which gave new impetus to Mexican musical theatre and cabaret. Her brilliant, usually one-woman shows go beyond humour and social criticism; they include *Lilith, el segundo fracaso de Dios* (Lilith, God's Second Failure), *Santa Chichilia* and *La Tabaquería* (The Tobacconist's), based on the hononymous poem by Fernando Pessoa. She also set to music Laura **Esquivel**'s 'interactive' novel *La ley del amor* (The Power of Love) (1997).

TITO VASCONCELOS

Félix, María

b. 1904, Alamos, Sonora, Mexico

Actress

Performing in more than forty-five Mexican and European films, María Félix (María de los Angeles Félix Guereña) was one of the brightest stars of the Mexican cinema's 'Golden Age'. Better known for her stardom than her acting, Félix's personal life and physical beauty were fetishized by the public and by her peers: she was painted by artists such as Diego **Rivera**, Leonora **Carrington**, and Jean Cocteau; Agustín **Lara** wrote songs for his 'María Bonita'; poems about her beauty were composed by Efraín **Huerta** and Renato Leduc; Dior designed her gowns.

As **Doña Bárbara** in Fernando de Fuentes's screen adaptation of Rómulo **Gallegos**'s novel, Félix became one of the primary figures in Mexican cinema and earned her lifelong nickname, 'La Doña'. But it was in *La Mujer sin alma* (The Woman Without a Soul) (1943) that Félix concretized the archetypal woman with whom she would be identified throughout her career – a strong woman, driven by love, whose independence and sexual appetite challenge the code of Mexican *machismo* (see **machismo, Mexican**).

Félix's films often played on her celebrity; the appeal of *El rapto* (The Rapture) (1953), for example, lay in the recent marriage of its co-stars, Félix and Jorge **Negrete**, and in the fact that it was completed shortly before Negrete's death. Her renown as a femme fatale is evident in the titles of her films: *Doña Diabla* (Mrs. Devil) (1949), *La mujer de todos* (Everybody's Woman) (1946), *La mujer sin alma* (The Woman without a Soul), and *La devoradora* (The Devourer) (1946).

Félix's characters' consumption of men is balanced by the fetishism of Félix as a celebrity. In the context of Mexican *machismo*, Félix's beauty threatened social convention and stability because as one of her suitors says in *Doña Diabla*, 'A beautiful woman can't be the property of just one man'. Félix herself tried to fight the stereotype of a beautiful trophy and in later films acted roles typically considered to be masculine. Thus, in a series of lush homages to the Mexican Revolution – *La cucaracha* (1958), *Juana Gallo* (1960), *La bandida* (1962), *La Valentina* (1965) and *La generala* (The Lady General) (1970) – she plays strong but beautiful women who fight for their country and their position.

Like many screen representations of women in the era, Félix's strong women were nearly always subjugated at the end. Thus, the challenge to *machismo* ends in a reaffirmation of male superiority. Her characters begin as strong, independent women who eventually concede to follow their man obediently. Indeed, Félix's attempts to counteract the representation of Mexican women as docile, stupid and obedient ultimately reinforced the stereotype.

'María bonita' embodied the Mexican woman as no other actress has since. She once remarked, 'Don't call me a legend, because it sounds like past tense'. Yet, as a star and a celebrity, María Félix is in fact one of the greatest legends of the Mexican cinema's finest moments.

Further reading

Barajas Sandoval, C. (1993) *Una mujer llamada María Felix: historia no autorizada*, Mexico City: Edamex.

Burdin, H. (1982) *Mexicaine: María Félix*, Paris: Editions Encre.

Félix, M. (1993) *María Félix: todas mis guerras*, Mexico: Espejo de Obsidiana.

—— (1997) *Raya en el agua* with prologue by Octavio Paz, Mexico: Imprenta Madero.

Taibo, P.I. (1991) *La doña*, Mexico: Planeta.

ILENE S. GOLDMAN

Fem

Fem, the first contemporary feminist (see **feminism**) journal in Latin America, was founded in Mexico City in 1976 by a collective of intellectual women journalists, including Elena **Poniatowska** and Alaíde **Foppa**, a leading Guatemalan feminist who was **disappeared** by the Guatemalan army in 1980. The magazine, which appears three times a year, aims at a broad audience of Mexican women and covers a wide range of political, social and cultural issues.

CYNTHIA STEELE

Feminaria

Feminaria, a semi-annual feminist journal of theory, criticism and literature, is a pioneer publication on women's issues. Founded in Buenos Aires in 1988, and directed by Lea **Fletcher**, its editorial board (Fletcher, Diana **Bellessi**, Alicia Genzano, Jutta Marx, and Diana Maffia) receives contributions internationally, with translation directed by Márgara Averbach and frequent cartoons by Diana Raznovich. Most issues include six sections: essays on social and cultural theory and criticism, annotated and/or specialized bibliography, art, humour, notes and interviews, and 'Feminaria literaria' which combines creative and critical works.

GWEN KIRKPATRICK

femininity

The repertoires from which Latin American femininity can be assembled will necessarily vary with region, class and race. **Quechua** notions of femininity will not concur with those of the white educated elites of Buenos Aires or the black poor living in the *favelas* of Rio de Janeiro. Nevertheless, there are some generally recognized, albeit contested, prototypical representations of femininity, many drawing their ideology and normative underpinnings from the Catholic Church.

Because femininity is meaningful by association and by contrast, to be feminine is generally acknowledged as *not* to be masculine. If the ability to penetrate essentially distinguishes men from women, then the ability to have children – to become mothers – distinguishes women from men. Thus, both motherhood and penetration are significant cultural phenomena underpinning articulations of femininity. This is reflected in the differing grounds for evaluation of men and women.

Whereas women appear to be primarily classified as either decent or not decent, men are classified along a continuum, relative to each other, as either more or less manly. Hence **masculinity** can be continually contested in ways femininity cannot. Moreover, what robs a man of his masculinity more than anything else is an inscribed femininity. Femininity (in women) seems to be a non-issue: for a woman it is not her femininity that is at stake, but her virtue. Female virtue is often associated with values of chastity, passivity, presence and self-sacrifice, and is symbolically expressed through notions of virginity (as the Mexican cinema brilliantly remarked in the *Cabaretera* genre – see ***Cabaretera* films**). Conversely, the lack of female virtue is tied to promiscuity, to being active. These moral attributes are not unequivocal, but contextually determined. Nevertheless, they feed off a dominant imagery which includes the myths of the Virgin of Guadalupe (see **Virgins, miraculous**) and La Malinche, two prominent symbols of purity and treachery.

This configuration reflects a pervasive gender ideology grounded in notions of complementarity and essential differences between the sexes, which is articulated through a moral code where notions of honour and shame (or in the Caribbean, notions of respectability and reputation) are tied to particular gender-specific perceptions of sexuality.

These perceptions underpin sexual divisions of labour; they also tie notions of femininity to morality.

It may appear that the very persona of the transvestite subverts and blurs the distinctions between femininity and masculinity. Nevertheless, it is the grounding of attributes of gender in essentialist notions that creates the ambiguities that arise in their wake, and thereby the multiple meanings of femininity evidenced in local discourses. Notions of femininity are necessarily contingent, depending upon articulations of same-sex as well as cross-sex relations; they can only be grasped within the terms set by these relations.

Further reading

Balderston, D. and Guy, D. (1997) *Sex and Sexuality in Latin America*, New York: New York University Press.

Kulick, D. (1998) *Travesti: Sex, Gender and Culture among Brazilian Transgendered Prostitutes*, Chicago: University of Chicago Press.

Melhuus, M. and Stølen, K.A. (eds) (1996) *Machos, Mistresses, Madonnas: Contesting the Power of Latin American Gender Imagery*, London: Verso.

Montecino, S. (1993) *Madres y huachos. Alegorias del mestizaje chileno*, Santiago: Cuarto Propio/Ediciones CEDEM.

MARIT MELHUUS

feminism

There is a long tradition of feminist thinking and writing in Latin America. Sor Juana Inés de la Cruz (1651–95) wrote her famous response to the Bishop of Puebla in 1690, contesting his attempts to censor her writing and thinking. Much later, her compatriot Rosario **Castellanos** was to invoke Sor Juana in 'Meditación en el umbral' (Meditation on the Threshold), a poem that marks both the presence of women writers and feminist thinking in Latin American letters as well as their marginalization in modern Latin American intellectual history. In the 1980s and 1990s, following the growth of the women's movement (see **women's movements**) and the development of academic feminism, Latin American women writers (see **women's writing**) experienced a **Boom** of their own, moving into anthologies and college curricula with great success.

However, the term 'feminist' remains problematic in the Latin American context, along with the question of feminist theory. Although she tells women's stories in her 1981 collection *Virgenes y mártires* (Virgins and Martyrs), co-authored with Carmen **Lugo Filippi**, Puerto Rican author Ana Lydia **Vega** has always rejected the term as one that corresponds to North American and Anglo versions of gendered identity. Typically, Anglo feminism is seen as privileging gender over other categories of struggle, whereas Latin American feminists have insisted on the need to foreground gender along with other battles for social and political justice, such as **class** and struggles for national liberation. This discomfort with feminism has caused some confusion and dismay for North American and European feminists, especially when feminist theory is seen as complicit with an elite intellectual tradition that has rarely made space for Latin American experiences. Nonetheless, feminism and feminist struggles have marked the social and political landscape of recent Latin American history, as is evident in movements such as the **Madres de Plaza de Mayo** in Argentina, the proliferation of *testimonios* (see ***testimonio***) giving voice to women's experiences with poverty and political repression, the *guerrilleras* in Nicaragua, El Salvador, Uruguay and elsewhere, as well as continuing historical and artistic explorations of gender in more academic contexts.

Further reading

Castillo, D. (1992) *Talking Back: Towards a Latin American Feminist Literary Criticism*, Ithaca, NY: Cornell University Press.

González, P.E. and Ortega, E. (eds) (1985) *La sartén por el mango. Encuentro de escritoras latinoamericanas*, Río Piedras: Huracán.

Kaminsky, A. (1993) *Reading the Body Politic: Feminist Criticism and Latin American Women Writers*, Minneapolis: University of Minnesota Press.

Mohanty, C.T., Russo, A. and Torres, L. (eds)

(1991) *Third World Women and the Politics of Feminism*, Bloomington: Indiana University Press.

CATHERINE DEN TANDT

feminist liberation theology

In recent years, a growing number of Latin American female theologians have aimed at creating a coherent dialogue between **liberation theology** and feminist concerns, in theology and in other areas. Theologians such as María Pilar **Aquino**, Ana María Bidegain, Ivone **Gebara** and Elsa **Tamez** endorse the central presuppositions of liberation theology and criticize it for not taking into account sexism and the specific problems of poor women.

Supported by theoretical models of feminist criticism, Latin American feminist liberation theology critiques contemporary models of civilization, social organization and the church based on principles of exclusion, hierarchy and antagonism. This theology also offers a critique of the androcentric conceptual frameworks of the dominant theological discourses, including liberation theology itself. Latin American feminist liberation theologians seek to interpret the experience of faith from the point of view of the impoverished and marginalized women of their continent. In dialogue with feminist theologies in other regions, especially in Africa and Asia, Latin American feminist theology has been developed both by Catholic and Protestant women. These theologians take up the concept of *la vida cotidiana* (everyday life) as the critical corrective of liberation theology from the point of view of poor women, which makes it possible to discuss such issues as violence against women, **family**, the Virgin Mary and her meaning to women, women's marginalization within the churches, and reproduction.

Until recently, issues of reproductive ethics have mostly been interpreted by secular feminists. Since theological underpinnings and Catholic moral codes are so central for issues of reproduction in the Latin American context, feminist liberation theologians are in the important position of being able to enter into dialogue both with the religious tradition and the feminist movements. However, in order to accomplish this task, they may have to distance themselves from some of the presuppositions of traditional liberation theology.

Further reading

Aquino, M.P. (1992) *Our Cry for Life: Feminist Theology from Latin America*, New York: Orbis Books.

Gebara, I. and Bingemer, M.C. (1989) *Mary: Mother of God, Mother of the Poor*, New York: Orbis Books.

King, U. (ed.) (1994) *Feminist Theology from the Third World: A Reader*, London and New York: SPCK/Orbis Books.

Tamez, E. (ed.) (1986) *Las mujeres toman la palabra*, San José: Editorial DEI.

Vuola, E. (1997) *Limits of Liberation: Praxis as Method in Latin American Liberation Theology and Feminist Theology*, Helsinki: The Finnish Academy of Science and Letters.

ELINA VUOLA

Ferguson, Amos

b. 1920, Exuma Island, Bahamas

Visual artist

Ferguson was employed as a farmer and an assistant in his father's carpentry shop before moving to Nassau. He began to paint houses, but says he cannot remember when he started to paint pictures; it just happened. He came to international attention in the mid-1980s. He uses house paints, claims to be divinely inspired, and is deeply religious. He sees the islands of the Bahamas as part of god's divine plan. Despite having travelled to many countries, he believes it is his duty only to paint the islands whose folklore, history and characters and personalities have been his inspiration.

KEITH JARDIM

Feria del Libro, La

The Montevideo Feria del Libro y el Grabado (Book and Illustration Fair) was founded in 1959 to promote national culture in dance, music, literature and visual arts. Its founder, poet Nancy Bacelo, remains its driving force. It begins annually in December with an open-air exhibition of books, engravings and crafts, and since the 1960s has also promoted a literary competition whose winners have included Walter de Ayala, Hugo **Achugar**, Silvia Riestra and others, and which contributed to a publishing movement which produced imprints like Alfa, **Arca** and **Ediciones de la Banda Oriental**. It continued through the military dictatorship (1973–85), providing a rare focus for cultural resistance.

NORAH GIRALDI DEI CAS

Feria, Teatro de la

Formed in 1977 by two ex-members of the **ICTUS** group, Jaime Vadell and José Manuel Salcedo, Teatro de la Feria's works were acts of collective creation. It set out to build on popular cultural expression to produce a national-popular aesthetics that combined humour and a response to immediate issues. It created a company for each work, using both professional and non-professional performers. Its most important works were *Hojas de Parra* (Parra Leaves) (1977), based on texts by the poet Nicanor **Parra**, *Bienaventurados los pobres* (Blessed are the Poor), *Una pena y un cariño* (Sorrow and Tenderness) and *La república de Jauja* (The Republic of Milk and Honey).

CAROLA OYARZÚN

Ferland, Barbara

b. 1919, Spanish Town, Jamaica

Poet and songwriter

A member of a circle of young writers and artists, including Derek **Walcott** and V.S. **Naipaul**, Ferland became a contributor to the BBC's ***Caribbean Voices***. As a songwriter, she collaborated with Louise **Bennett** on a collection of Jamaican folk songs and wrote songs for the first all-Jamaican pantomime, *Busha Bluebeard* (1949). Ferland's song 'Evening-Time' is still used as Radio Jamaica's signature tune. Her poetry, sharpened to knifepoint, was published in anthologies and in the journals ***Bim*** and *Focus*. She received the Sir Robert Barker Prize for Lyric Poetry (1952) and in 1994 published the collection *Without Shoes I Must Run*.

SANDRA COURTMAN

Fernandes, Florestan

b. 1922, São Paulo, Brazil; d. 1995, São Paulo

Sociologist and politician

The father of contemporary Brazilian critical **sociology**, Fernandes was dismissed from his position at the University of São Paulo in 1969 and exiled from Brazil until 1977. Fernandes defines Brazilian society in work that sets out to reconcile Marxist dialectics with functionalism and Weberian methodology in an often original and highly polemical way. Much of his originality comes from his analyses of race relations and his denial that these relations have ever been cordial, as in his *The Negro in Brazilian Society* (1969). His students have included Fernando Henrique **Cardoso**, Octávio Ianni and Luis Bresser Pereira.

SUSAN CANTY QUINLAN

Fernandes, Millor

b. 1924, Rio de Janeiro, Brazil

Graphic artist

Fernandes's first drawing appeared in *O Jornal* when he was eleven. Throughout the 1940s, his satirical drawings appeared in Brazil's most important magazines. Their political content often brought him into conflict with the censors, particularly when the military came to power in 1964. A founder of the satirical magazine ***O pasquim***, he also wrote a number of theatre pieces, including *Liberdade, Liberdade*, which was banned across the nation in 1966. He drew for

Veja, *IstoÉ* and later in the *Jornal do Brasil*, where he began to use computer graphics.

ANTONIO CARLOS MARTINS VAZ

Fernández, Emilio ('El Indio')

b. 1904, El Hondo, Sabinas Coahuila, Mexico; d. 1986, Mexico City

Film-maker

In the 1940s and 1950s, his name was synonymous with the national cinema; his monumental films created a Mexican 'look', provided tremendous impetus to the star system and received numerous international awards that put the Mexican (and Latin American) cinema(s) on the international cinematographic map.

After participating in some battles during the Mexican Revolution (see **revolutions**), Fernández headed north to Hollywood and worked in the Hispanic cinema (see **Hispanic cinema in Hollywood**) as an extra, secondary actor and even as a dancer (notably in *Flying Down to Rio*, which starred his compatriot, the already famous Dolores **Del Rio**). Upon his return to Mexico in the early 1930s, he began working as an actor; his dark indigenous good looks (the reason why he was dubbed 'Indio') served him as well as the star of *Janitzio* (Carlos Novarro) (1934), an indigenist (see *indigenismo*) film that inspired many of his later works. He began directing in 1941 with *La isla de la pasión* (The Island of Passion), but his career did not take off until he gathered the production team with whom he would make some of Mexico's most significant films: cinematographer Gabriel **Figueroa**, screenwriter Maurico **Magdaleno**, and the actors Pedro **Armendáriz** and the recently returned Dolores Del Rio (with whom he also had a passionate relationship). Their first films together – *Flor silvestre* (Wild Flower) (1943), but especially the much-awarded **María Candelaria** (1943) – established many of the parameters of his subsequent work: amidst a luscious landscape of cotton candy clouds and monumental *magueys*, proud indigenous characters battled against prejudices and cultural misunderstandings, and provided a gloriously exalted vision of the nation. Although they were charged with folkloricism and excessive nationalism, the beauty and lyricism of these films were undeniable. Fernández's most creative period was between 1943 and 1950, with hit after hit like *Bugambilia* (Bougainvillaea) (1944), *La perla* (The Pearl) (1945), *Enamorada* (In Love) (1945) and *Río Escondido* (Hidden River) (1947) (the latter two also among María **Félix**'s best films). *Pueblerina* (Town Girl) (1948) and *Víctimas del pecado* (Victims of Sin) (1950) were among his best ever; the former was a sublime indigenous love story narrated with intense lyricism, the latter an exemplary *Cabaretera* melodrama (see **Cabaretera films**) set in dark, mysterious and claustrophobic night-clubs. His career waned through the 1950s, however, coinciding with a general decline in the Mexican industry. With few opportunities to direct, he fell back to acting and appeared, typically as an indigenous 'bad guy', in innumerable films like Ismael Rodríguez's *La cucaracha* (The Roach) (1958). His efforts to recapture some of his earlier glory by making second and even third versions of some of his films were, with perhaps the exception of *Pueblito* (Little Town) (1961), thoroughly unsuccessful.

Further reading

García Riera, E. (1987) *Emilio Fernández*, Guadalajara: CIEC.

Tuñón, J. (1995) 'Emilio Fernández: A look behind the bars', in P.A. Paranaguá (ed.) *Mexican Cinema*, London: BFI, pp. 179–92.

—— (1988) *En su propio espejo* (Entrevista con Emilio 'El Indio' Fernández), Mexico City: Universidad Autónoma Metropolitana/Ixtapalapa.

ANA M. LÓPEZ

Fernández, Macedonio

b.1874, Buenos Aires, Argentina; d. 1952, Buenos Aires

Writer

One of Argentina's outstanding writers, Fernández' reputation is partly attributable to **Borges**, for whom he was simply an intellectual, and partly due to his well-known distaste for editing Fernández' works. Both are false. Borges' views are disproved by Fernández' rich body of work – stories, poems, novels, letters, essays which he called his 'papers' (*papeles*). His *Museo de la novela de la Eterna* (Museum of the Novel of the Eternal), posthumously published in 1967, is the expression of an avant-garde which does not distract itself with unrealizable Utopias but sees the novel itself as the distraction rendered Utopia. Fernandez constructs all his work in opposition to the aesthetics of **Lugones**, which is why the **ultraísta** movement of the 1920s adopted him as an emblematic progenitor. He was a fine poet and author of one of the most beautiful erotic poems in Spanish, 'Elena Bellamuerte', an extraordinary thinker hostile to all systems of thought, and a humorist of genius.

ENRIQUE FOFFANI

Fernández, Oscar Lorenzo

b. 1897, Rio de Janeiro, Brazil; d. 1948, Rio de Janeiro

Composer and conductor

Fernández is an outstanding representative of Brazilian musical nationalism. He founded the Conservatorio Brasileiro in 1936, and the Brazilian Academy of Music (with **Villa-Lobos**) in 1945. His early compositions were romantic and impressionist, later evolving into the nationalism of his opera *Malazarte* (1931–3), which included the classic piece *Batuque*. Among his important orchestral works are *Suite sinfônica* (1925) and *Variações sinfônicas* (Symphonic Variations) (1948). His songs include 'Canção sertaneja' (Song of the Northeast) (1924) and 'Berceuse da Onda' (1928, with text by Cecília **Meireles**).

ALFONSO PADILLA

Fernández, Pablo Armando

b. 1930, Central Delicias, Holguín, Cuba

Writer

An outstanding exponent of the Cuban school of 'conversational poetry', Fernández worked and lived in the USA until 1959, when he returned to Cuba. He was a leading figure in **Lunes de Revolución** and an editor of the journal **Casa de las Américas**. He wrote several volumes of poetry, and his novel *Los niños se despiden* (The Children Say Farewell) won the 1968 Casa de las Américas prize for fiction. He subsequently published two more novels and a volume of short stories *El talismán y otras evocaciones* (The Talisman and Other Evocations) (1994).

WILFREDO CANCIO ISLA

Fernández de Lewis, Piri

b. 1925, San Juan, Puerto Rico

Theatre director and educator

Fernández de Lewis (Carmen Pilar Fernández) was a leading figure in Puerto Rico's cultural life for several decades, an outspoken advocate of the island's sovereignty, and faculty member of the University of Puerto Rico where she promoted Afro-Caribbean literature. Among other positions, she served as President of the **Ateneo Puertorriqueño** (1961–5) and as Chairperson of the Theater Advisory Board of the Institute of Puerto Rican Culture (1956–71). Her many endeavours promoting the theatre in Puerto Rico include her work as an actress, playwright and stage director.

VÍCTOR F. TORRES

Fernández Retamar, Roberto

b. 1930, Havana, Cuba

Writer

A poet and essayist, Fernández Retamar has played a key role in the cultural institutions of the Cuban Revolution, and is regarded by many as one of the main cultural influences in post-revolutionary Cuba. Books of essays like **Caliban** (1971) and *Para una teoría de la literatura latinoamericana* (Towards a Theory of Latin American Literature) (1975) were polemical interventions in debates with other Latin American **intellectuals** in which the issues in dispute were political rather than simply aesthetic. His directorship of the journal, *Casa de las Américas*, since 1965, and of the institution since 1986, has made him in some sense the official spokesperson for Cuban cultural policy.

As a poet he is regarded as one of the most important exponents of the school of 'conversational poetry', which included Fayad Jamís, Pablo Armando **Fernández** and Heberto **Padilla** among others, though the relationship that many of his contemporaries had with the Fidel **Castro** regime was often highly problematic. One of the younger poets associated with the **Orígenes** group, Retamar's first volume of poetry, *Elegía como un himno* (Elegy like a Hymn), was published in 1950. There followed *En su lugar poesía* (In its Place, Poetry) (1961), *Con las mismas manos* (With the Same Hands) (1962) and *Que veremos arder* (We'll Watch it Burn) (1970). His *Juana y otros poemas personales* (Juana and Other Personal Poems) (1980) won the Ruben Darío Latin American Poetry Prize and *Aquí* (Here) (1994) was awarded the Pérez Bonalde Poetry Prize. Retamar is also well known for his research on the work of the nineteenth-century poet and politician, José Martí, developed through numerous talks, articles and anthologies as well as his own *Introducción a José Martí* (Introduction to José Martí) (1978).

Further reading

Benedetti, M. (1971) 'Fernández Retamar: Poesía desde el cráter', in *Crítica cómplice*, Havana: Instituto del Libro.

Fernández Retamar, R. (1962) *Con las mismas manos 1949–62*, Havana: Unión.

Pogolotti, G. (1963) 'La poesía de Fernández Retamar', *Unión* 2(5/6): 111–17.

Vitier, C. (1952) 'Roberto Fernández Retamar', in *Cincuenta años de poesía Cubana (1902–1952)*, Havana: Ministerio de Educación.

WILFREDO CANCIO ISLA

Fernández Spencer, Antonio

b. 1922, Santo Domingo, Dominican Republic; d. 1995, Santo Domingo

Poet

Poet, literary critic, professor, and diplomat, Fernández Spencer first published his poems in *Poesía Sorprendida* (Poetry Surprised) in 1944 and later founded the poetry journal *Entre las soledades* (Amid Loneliness). Fernández studied in Spain, where he won prizes for *Bajo la luz del día* (In the Daylight) (1953) and *Diario del mundo* (World Diary) (1970). After returning to Santo Domingo, Fernández Spencer founded the Colección Arquero (Archer Collection). His poetry is influenced by the mysticism of the Spanish poets such as Santa Teresa de Jesús and San Juan de la Cruz.

FERNANDO VALERIO-HOLGUÍN

Fernández Violante, Marcela

b. 1941, Mexico City

Film-maker

Fernández Violante has made more films than any other Mexican woman director (three shorts and six full-length features). A graduate of Mexico's first film school, CUEC, she directed the documentary *Frida* **Kahlo** (1971). Her first commercial film, *De todos modos Juan te llamas* (In Any Case Juan's Your Name) (1974–5), was set during the Cristero Wars (see **Cristero War**); her second, *Cananea* (1976), during the Mexican Revolution (see **revolutions**). *Misterio* (Mystery) (1978), a powerful narrative, was based on a Vicente **Leñero** novel. In the Mexico of **Salinas**, the protagonists of her *Golpe de suerte* (Stroke of Luck) (1991) faced 'the wreckage of modernity'.

PATRICIA TORRES SAN MARTÍN

Ferrari, León

b. 1920, Buenos Aires, Argentina

Visual artist

Ferrari's 1965 montage *Homage to Vietnam* showed Jesus Christ crucified on a US bomber. In 1997, his reproductions of classical visions of the Apocalypse left at the mercy of passing pigeons was an example of meta-eschatology. Between the two projects, Ferrari's artistic trajectory has transformed the pictorial into the conceptual, and literature has become a bare image. Politics, religion, art; Ferrari has driven back the boundaries in each of them to produce a libertarian critique of the history of representation.

JULIO SCHVARTZMAN

Ferré, Luis A.

b. 1904, Ponce, Puerto Rico

Politician, engineer and philanthropist

Luis Ferré is probably best known for his work as leader of a Puerto Rican pro-statehood movement. A former piano student at the New England Music Conservatory and engineering graduate of MIT, he is co-owner of an important group of industries that includes Puerto Rico Cement Inc. Convinced of the greatness of US democracy, after his return to Puerto Rico in 1925 Ferré became active in the island's politics. Among his many political activities, Ferré collaborated in the writing of Puerto Rico's Constitution (1952) and, after his party refused to participate, organized a movement of United Statehooders during the 1967 plebiscite. Out of this movement, Ferré founded the Partido Nuevo Progresista (New Progressive Party), which led to the establishment of a bipartisan system in Puerto Rican politics.

In 1968, Ferré was elected governor of Puerto Rico. Ferré credits himself with the construction of the Centro de Bellas Artes (Performing Arts Centre) and a principal highway connecting San Juan to Ponce, both of which bear his name. After losing the 1972 elections, Ferré continued helping the PNP and, in 1980, was elected president of the Senate. Although he has not run for any governmental position since 1984, he has remained an active leader of the pro-statehood movement, supporting the party's candidates and presiding over the national division of the Republican Party.

Luis Ferré is also a distinguished philanthropist, through the Luis A. Ferré Foundation. His contributions to Puerto Rican culture include the foundation of Ponce's first public library in 1937, the co-founding of Ponce's Catholic University and, most importantly, the creation of the Ponce Museum of Art, established in 1959, which houses the only collection of fine art in the Caribbean to rival Havana's Museum of Fine Arts. In 1945, Ferré bought the newspaper *El Día*, selling it to his son in 1970. It eventually became Puerto Rico's leading newspaper, and is now called ***El Nuevo Día***.

Ferré's contributions to Puerto Rican politics and culture have earned him numerous awards and honorary degrees. In 1992 he published his memoirs, narrated by his daughter, the writer Rosario **Ferré**.

Further reading

Ferré, R. (1992) *Memorias de Ponce. Autobiografía de Luis A. Ferré*, Bogotá: Norma.

ROBERTO CARLOS ORTIZ

Ferré, Rosario

b. 1938, Ponce, Puerto Rico

Writer

A controversial and prolific feminist (see **feminism**) writer, Ferré was born into a wealthy family and was educated mostly in the United States. She began her literary career in the late 1960s, when she founded an illustrated literary magazine, ***Zona de carga y descarga***, with other young writers like Manuel **Ramos Otero**, as an outlet for their controversial stories. Her first book, *Papeles de Pandora* (Pandora's Papers) (1976), is a collection of experimental short stories incorporating elements from popular culture, and deliberately contrasting upper- and lower-class worlds. These stories revolve around women from different social stations who face love, marital bondage and sexuality. Among the most acclaimed pieces are 'Cuando las mujeres quieren a los hombres' (When Women Love Men), and 'La muñeca menor' (The Youngest Doll). Her second work, *Sitio a Eros* (Eros under Siege) (1980) is a collection of essays on distinguished women writers like Virginia Woolf, Jean **Rhys**, Sylvia Plath, Julia de **Burgos** and Tina Modotti. One essay addresses the importance of journal or diary writing for women.

Fábulas de la garza desangrada (Fables of the Bleeding Heron) (1982) is a book of long poems of remarkable figural beauty. Her main concern is the process of subverting the figuration of classical and contemporary feminine myths, including Julia de **Burgos**, the Puerto Rican poet much admired by Ferré, and many writers from this Caribbean island. Her other works include *Maldito amor* (Sweet Diamond Dust) (1986), a novel that reconstructs the wealthy life and the demise of the Puerto Rican landowning class. It is the story of three generations marking three crucial periods in Puerto Rico's history: the arrival of US capital, the decline of traditional agriculture and the development of a new industrial urban culture. The theme of the Latin American **family** and the problem of **class** is explored in most of Ferré's fiction to date.

In addition, she has written essays on Julio **Cortázar**, on Spanish classics including Sor Juana Inés de la Cruz, and Felisberto **Hernández**. In the 1990s, she published a short story entitled *Las dos Venecias* (The Two Venices) (1992), and *The House in the Lagoon* (1995) in English. As well as several volumes of children's books which draw on oriental fables, Germanic fairy tales and American Indian legends, she also helped her politician father, Luis **Ferré**, to write his memoirs. She published another novel in 1999, *Eccentric Neighborhoods*.

Further reading

García Pinto, M. (1991) 'Interview with Rosario Ferré', in *Women Writers of Latin America: Intimate Histories*, Austin, TX: University of Texas Press.

Fernández Olmos, M. (1990) 'Rosario Ferré', in D. Marting (ed.) *Contemporary Women Authors of Latin America: A Bio-Bibliographical Source Book*, New York: Greenwood Press.

MAGDALENA GARCÍA PINTO

Ferrer, Horacio

b. 1933, Montevideo, Uruguay

Tango lyricist, poet and musician

One of the authors of the new **tango** avant-garde of the 1950s, Ferrer was associated with the two tango legends of the second half of the century, Aníbal **Troilo** and Astor **Piazzola**. Along with Piazzola, he created a new style of tango represented first in the tango opera *María de Buenos Aires*, and then in the *Baladas* and *Preludios*. His tangos stimulated paintings by many of the most famous Argentine and Uruguayan artists of the period, including the series painted by Antonio **Berni** depicting the life of Juanito Laguna. He is also known for his extensive encyclopedia *El libro del tango* (1960).

FLORENCIA GARRAMUÑO

Ferrer, Lupita

b. 1949, Mexico

Actress

Ferrer is a Venezuelan actress born in Mexico, famous for her roles in television soap operas (***telenovelas***). She studied theatre with Horacio Peterson, but achieved national and international success on television. Her first starring role was in *Esmeralda* which, with *Lucecita*, was the most famous television soap opera of the sixties. But her fame was the result of the films she made in Mexico with **Cantinflas** (Mario Moreno) and of the soap opera *Cristal* (Glass), which drew a vast Spanish-speaking audience at the end of the 1980s. She then went on to appear in a series of television soaps made for the Hispanic community of the United States.

JORGE ROMERO LEÓN

Ferrer, Pedro Luis

b. 1952, Yaguajay, Cuba

Musician

A composer, guitarist and singer, Ferrer's songs refer back to the ***trova tradicional***, with its provocative lyrics and its son rhythms, and in particular to Nico **Saquito**, in whose musical tradition Ferrer locates his own work. His songs often describe with caustic irony the contradictions of daily life in Cuba, with the result that his music is rarely played by the mass media, all of which are State-controlled. In 1981 he formed his own group, with whom he has recorded a number of albums including *Pedro Luis Ferrer* (1999).

WILFREDO CANCIO ISLA

Ferrer, Renée

b. 1944, Asunción, Paraguay

Writer

Ferrer is one of the most prolific writers of her generation and has won various prestigious national and international prizes. *La voz que me fue dada [Poesía 1965–1995]* (The Voice That Was Given to Me [Poetry 1965–1995]) is a sort of personal poetic anthology. Her narrative works include *Los nudos del silencio* (The Knots of Silence) (1988), her first novel, and *Desde el encendido corazón del monte* (From the Burning Heart of the Woodland) (1994), a book of ecological tales which won the First Prize of UNESCO and the Fundación del Libro in the 1995 Feria del Libro (Book Fair) of Buenos Aires. She is also the author of several books of poems and stories for children.

TERESA MÉNDEZ-FAITH

Ferreyra, José Agustín

b. 1889, Buenos Aires, Argentina; d. 1943, Buenos Aires

Film-maker and tango lyricist

Ferreyra was of Argentine silent cinema's most prolific directors. Although some of his films developed gaucho themes, such as *De vuelta al pago* (Back to the Homestead) (1919), he is best remembered for his **tango melodramas** such as *Una noche de garufa* (A Night on the Town) (1915). In 1931 he made the first talkie, *Muñequitas porteñas* (Buenos Aires Girls), and later directed a trilogy of films which conquered the Latin American market and made Libertad **Lamarque** into its first major female star: *Ayúdame a vivir* (Help Me to Live) (1936), *Besos brujos* (Bewitched Kisses) (1937) and *La ley que olvidaron* (The Law They Forgot) (1938).

DIANA PALADINO

Festival Internacional del Nuevo Cine Latinoamericano

Film festival organized by **ICAIC**, the Cuban Film Institute, every December in Havana since 1979. Intended to serve as a meeting ground for Latin American film-makers and for the films of the **New Latin American Cinema**, the festival has featured and given awards to the most significant films of the movement as well as showcasing a wide variety of international cinema series. Over the years it has also developed a film market, MECLA, as well as additional special sections, such as video/TV and children's audiovisual production. Lasting as long as 18 or 19 days (before the economic constraints of Cuba's special period forced cutbacks), the festival grew to encompass much more than film screenings, becoming a veritable carnival of cultural activities. Alongside film programming throughout principal and neighbourhood theatres of Havana (and touring series throughout the provinces), the festival has also included art exhibits (most notably the extraordinary work of film poster designers – see **poster art**), musical performances, theatre productions, and even nightly outdoor dance parties typically featuring the best of Cuba's contemporary musicians (like Los **Van Van**). For almost three weeks, Havana becomes film-obsessed.

At first a celebration of the achievements of film-makers who had often worked in isolation from each other throughout the continent, the festival appeared at a time when the very nature of the

New Latin American cinema had begun to change due to political and economic exigencies. In fact, one could say that by 1979 the New Latin American Cinema had already splintered into discrete national cinemas bounded by contextual constraints: Brazilian **Cinema Novo** had turned into **Embrafilme**, a state agency funded by the military government; the Chilean new cinema of Unidad Popular (see **Popular Unity**) disappeared with **Pinochet**'s 1973 *coup*; Argentina's ***tercer cine*** was in exile in Paris; the ICAIC cinema had become an official national cinema. Thus, paradoxically, the festival was created to celebrate the achievements of a movement that was already waning and would instead mark its institutionalization.

Nevertheless, the festival has been very important for the growing international visibility of Latin American film and video/TV. Its prestigious prizes, the '**Corales**', have been awarded by prominent international juries to the most important films of the last two decades in the categories fiction, documentary, script, acting, animation, and film poster design. Additionally, the festival also awards other prizes such as the Saúl Yelín award granted by the Comité de Cineastas de América Latina (Latin American film-makers' committee).

Further reading

Toledo, T. (1990) *10 Años del nuevo cine latinoamericano*, Madrid: Verdoux SL.

ANA M. LÓPEZ

Ficciones

A famous collection of short stories by Jorge Luis **Borges**, published in 1944. The first half of the book first appeared as *El jardín de senderos que se bifurcan* (The Garden of Forking Paths) (1941–2) and included the extraordinary and innovative stories 'Pierre Menard, autor del Quijote' (Pierre Menard, Author of Don Quixote) (1939), and 'Tlön, Uqbar, Orbis Tertius' (1940), both of which appeared first in the journal ***Sur***, as well as the innovative work of **crime fiction** that gave the volume its name. In 1944 a second half was added, entitled 'Artificios' (Artifices), which included the stories 'Funes el memorioso' (Funes the Memorious), 'La forma de la espada' (The Shape of the Sword), 'La muerte y la brújula' (Death and the Compass) and 'El milagro secreto' (The Secret Miracle). (Additional stories were added to the second edition of *Ficciones* in 1956.)

Ficciones was a title that implied an aesthetic programme for Borges, including the elements of a highly self-conscious fiction (including a dizzying degree of fictions within fictions), a distancing from the social realist style that dominated the period, and the cultivation of seemingly minor genres like crime fiction, **science fiction** and the fantastic (see **fantastic literature**). The programme was outlined by Adolfo **Bioy Casares** in his 1940 preface to the ***Antología de la literatura fantástica*** (Anthology of Fantastic Literature), in which Bioy notes that Borges has just created a new kind of fantastic literature in his story 'Tlön, Uqbar, Orbis Tertius', and in Borges's 1940 preface to Bioy's *La invención de Morel* (Morel's Invention), which expresses a preference for plot over character. In Borges's own case, this permitted a radically new kind of fiction, first realized fully in 'Pierre Menard', in which a French symbolist poet rewrites – word for word – certain passages of Cervantes's *Don Quixote*, an event whose full implications must be divined by the reader.

Borges's use of the term *ficciones* was probably derived from John Dewey's division (in his library classification system) of literature into fiction and non-fiction; the English substrate adheres to the word, which acquired the status of a neologism in Spanish, closely associated with Borges's practice. Ironically, though, the stories of *Ficciones* are profoundly involved with the 'non-fictional' realms of philosophy, history and politics. Borges's stories have dazzled readers for decades, have been the focus of a vast amount of critical work, and have revolutionized the practice of the short story.

Further reading

Balderston, D. (1993) *Out of Context: Historical Reference and the Representation of Reality in Borges*, Durham: Duke University Press.

Shaw, D.L. (1990) 'Jorge Luis Borges: Ficciones' in

Landmarks in Modern Latin American Fiction, London: Routledge.

DANIEL BALDERSTON

Fierro, Enrique

b. 1942, Montevideo, Uruguay

Writer

A prolific poet, Fierro has published twenty-five books of poems; *De la invención* (About Invention) (1964) was his first. His poetry, representative of the vitality of recent Uruguayan poetry, is constructed on a system of references that reveal his vast cultural and literary knowledge, marked by a skilful use of humour and irony. He directed the National Library of Montevideo, and since 1989 has taught at the University of Texas at Austin. He is married to the poet Ida **Vitale**.

MAGDALENA GARCÍA PINTO

fiesta

Festivals have characterized Latin American life for centuries and played a pivotal role during the Pre-Columbian and colonial periods. For example, the Mexica, Inca and Maya defined their relationship to the supernatural through a complex system of rituals. Through private and public ceremonies, indigenous peoples sought to interpret and control their environment; the elite bolstered their prestige and legitimacy by claiming that they were intermediaries to the gods and ritual and religious experts. The arrival of Europeans introduced new religious and secular festivals that built upon native traditions and aided evangelization and acculturation of subjugated peoples. These same fiestas, however, allowed the conquered and enslaved to express not only religious devotion but resistance. This led to the creation of syncretic religious belief systems that drew upon European and native or African traditions and cosmologies. Today fiestas celebrate national pride, ethnicity, religious fervour, solidarity; they confirm and strengthen a sense of community, as they did centuries ago. Religious celebrations continue to mark the major stages of life for many Latin Americans, and include baptisms, marriages and funerals. Of particular importance for young women is the *quinceañera* or debut at age fifteen that hails the advent of womanhood with formal parties.

Private ceremonies very often coincide with very public large-scale rituals. For example, the dearly departed are not merely mourned at their death but are also commemorated during Todos los Muertos (**Day of the Dead**) in Mexico, Guatemala and the Andean world. Pilgrimages and processions still seek intervention from saints, and celebrations such as those to the Virgin of Guadalupe (see **Virgins, miraculous**) or Copacabana attract thousands. Celebrations dedicated to patron saints and Easter week continue to play an important role in traditional indigenous communities such as the Tarahumara and the Chamula in Mexico. Popular festivals such as **carnival** are celebrated in some manner everywhere in Latin America, but carnival in Rio de Janeiro is the largest and most famous event internationally. National holidays include parades, feasts and vacations from work and include independence day celebrations, the Día de la Raza, the commemoration of important battles (for example, 5 de mayo in Mexico), and International Workers Day on May 1. Other public fiestas spotlight Latin American culture like the International **Merengue** Festival in the Dominican Republic or the Entrada del Gran Poder in La Paz, Bolivia. Although the latter is ostensibly a religious procession in honour of the Christ of great power, the parade spotlights indigenous and African contributions to Bolivian history and culture through the performances of different dance groups.

Further reading

Bastien, J. (1985) *Mountain of the Condor: Metaphor and Ritual in an Andean Ayllu*, Prospect Heights, IL: Waveland Press.

Beezley, W., Martin, C. and French, W. (eds) (1994) *Rituals of Rule, Rituals of Resistance: Public Celebrations and Popular Culture in Mexico*, Wilmington, DE: Scholarly Resources.

Matta, R. da (1991) *Carnivals, Rogues, and Heroes: An Interpretation of the Brazilian Dilemma*, trans. John

Drury, Notre Dame, IN: University of Notre Dame.

LINDA A. CURCIO-NAGY

Figari, Pedro

b. 1861, Montevideo, Uruguay; d. 1938, Montevideo

Painter

Famous for the lyricism, strength of colours and dynamic movement of his art, Figari dedicated himself fully to painting later in life after a prominent career as lawyer, judge, journalist (he founded the newspaper *El Diario*), teacher, and politician. His writings on poetry, education, law and aesthetics led to his appointment as director of Uruguay's School of Fine Arts and Crafts in 1915, where he set in motion radical reforms. In 1921 he moved to Buenos Aires and dedicated himself to painting and to the defence of modern art, as one of the founders of Los Amigos del Arte in 1924. He lived in Paris from 1925 to1933, when he returned to Montevideo, remaining there until his death.

Because of his art's strong regionalist focus, he is often labelled a nativist or vernacular painter. Colonial buildings, local street bands, popular dances, *pampa* scenes, and especially Uruguay's Afro-Latin population are represented in his work, with little intrusion of the technological modernity fascinating to many artists of his time. As described in 1930 by **Borges**, his work represents 'a remorse, a reproach of things abandoned without the intercession of a farewell', an act of remembering the disappearance of a past world now committed to modernization. In his oil painting on cardboard Figari used some of the techniques of the impressionists and pointillist style to achieve the luminosity so notable in his works, even in nocturnal scenes, and flattened out his scenes by abandoning traditional perspectivism, influenced partially by Bonnard and Vuillard. But he also employed freely applied intense colour, smudged paint, and sketched rather than carefully drew figures to capture the dynamism of the beings and landscapes he represented. His paintings pay particular attention to social gatherings and ritual events, most notably the scenes of **Candomblé** weekly gatherings and dances of slave descendants, as in *African Nostalgia* and *Cambacuá*. Some scenes juxtapose the legacy of African traditions with white creole cultural practices, such as dance and dress. Figari focused on groups and scenes (gauchos, Afro-Latins, provincial life, the countryside) which he saw as more directly related to nature and uncontaminated by social hierarchy and modernity. His landscapes capture the vast distances of the River Plate *pampas*, with their ombu trees, horses, and cattle as if in a dream sequence. Like his Argentine contemporary **Xul Solar**, Figari was a Utopian theorist as well as an artist. In Paris he published *Historia Kiria* (1930), a Utopian critique and satire of contemporary society and its pessimism, wars, racism, and the excesses of 'civilization' over nature.

Although distinguished as a writer and thinker, Figari's primary legacy are his paintings and their role in establishing a new Latin American (specifically River Plate) consciousness. His emphasis on primal, natural forces and the energy and expansiveness of those he considered its most authentic inhabitants is part of an aesthetic and cultural movement which sought to reassert the specificities of local experience through memory. With nostalgia and humour, his work forms part of the visual, literary, and musical movements which incorporated techniques of modern art in the service of regional and national memory.

GWEN KIRKPATRICK

Figueredo, Ignacio

b. 1899, Cunaviche, Venezuela; d. 1995, San Fernando de Apure, Venezuela

Musician and composer

A prolific composer, Figueredo, known as 'El Indio', was steeped in Venezuelan popular music from childhood. He learned the songs of the rural interior where he grew up so that he could accompany his father singing at village festivals and dances and, as a teenager, taught himself the **harp**, a popular traditional instrument. Professional musicians saw him playing in 1948 and, impressed by his virtuosity, invited him to play at a major event in Caracas. He soon became well-known throughout Venezuela, through concert performances and **radio** and **television** appearances, and toured the country widely from the 1950s onwards.

MARK DINNEEN

Figueres Ferrer, José

b. 1906, San Ramón, Costa Rica; d. 1990, Curridabat, Costa Rica

Politician

Figueres Ferrer is the most important Costa Rican politician this century. In 1948 his citizens' army waged a six-week 'war of national liberation' against a president whom he accused of electoral fraud. He declared himself President, abolished the armed forces, imposed a 10 per cent wealth tax and nationalized the banks, reforms later institutionalized in a new social democratic constitution. Figueres returned as president in 1953 and 1970. An initial supporter of the Cuban Revolution (see **revolutions**), Figueres broke with **Castro** and became a firm ally of the USA. He was later accused of receiving **CIA** support and accepting money from the corrupt financier, Robert Vesco.

PHILIP O'BRIEN

Figueroa, Elías

b. 1946, Villa Alemana, Chile

Soccer player

Figueroa was the most renowned Chilean football (soccer) player in Latin America and Europe in the 1970s and early 1980s. Known by the nickname 'Don Elías', Figueroa won acclaim for his defensive skills. He played for the Uruguayan team Peñarol until the 1970s, and then joined Brazilian team International of Porto Alegre. At this time, the European press elected him the best player in the world. He first appeared in the Chilean national team in 1965 and played continually until 1982, for most of that time as captain. Since retiring, Figueroa has been a soccer coach, a newspaper columnist, a television soccer commentator and a businessman.

LUIS E. CÁRCAMO-HUECHANTE

Figueroa, Gabriel

b. 1908, Mexico City; d. 1997, Mexico City

Cinematographer

One of the most widely recognized cinematographers in the world, Figueroa's many international awards included prizes at Brussels for *Enamorada* (Beloved) (1947), at Venice and Locarno in the same year for *La perla* (The Pearl) and **María Candelaria** respectively, at Karlovy Vary and Madrid for *Pueblerina* (Country Girl) (1950), and the prize for best black and white photography at Cannes in 1960 for *Macario*.

An orphan at sixteen, Figueroa worked to finance his studies in fine art at the San Carlos Academy and in music at the National Conservatory of Mexico. His life unfolded, as his teacher put it, 'between the sacrifices of the worker and the privileges of the artist'. A pupil of another great cinematographer, Alex Phillips, Figueroa was sent by the **CLASA** company to Hollywood, where he learned camera techniques with Gregg Toland, cinematographer for Orson Welles's classic *Citizen Kane*. In Mexico, he debuted as assistant to Jack Draper on Fernando de **Fuentes**'s ¡*Vámonos con Pancho Villa!* (Let's Go with Villa!) before filming alone on de Fuentes's *Allá en el Rancho Grande* (Out There on Rancho Grande) (1936), which won the prize for best photography at Venice – the first international prize ever awarded to a Mexican film. By the time he worked on Chano Urueta's *La noche de los mayas* (Night of the Mayas) (1939), Figueroa had found his own style: sensitively and dramatically lit interiors, sharply contrasted black and white, and landscapes of great plasticity. It was Figueroa's aesthetic, inspired by painting, and particularly the work of the Mexican muralists (see **muralism**), that created a recognizable Mexican visual identity on film.

In his fifty-year career, he worked with the finest directors, among them Alejandro **Galindo**, Julio **Bracho**, Benito **Alazraki** and Ismael **Rodríguez**. But it was his work with Emilio 'El Indio' **Fernández** and Luis **Buñuel** that brought him most recognition. With Fernández he created the images in which Mexico came to recognize itself, while with Buñuel, in films like *Los olvidados* (The Forgotten Ones) (1950), *Nazarín* (1958) and *El ángel exterminador* (Exterminating Angel) (1962), he painted a bizarre and shifting world. He also worked with foreign directors like John Ford (*The Fugitive*, 1947), John Huston (*Night of the Iguana*, 1963, and *Under the Volcano*, 1983) to mention only a few. Figueroa was also a key figure in the Mexican trade union movement, and a founder member of the Film Workers Union (**STPC**).

Further reading

Isaac, A. (1993) *Conversaciones con Gabriel Figueroa*, Guadalajara: Ed. Universidad de Guadalajara.

Ramírez Berg, C. (1993) 'The cinematic invention of Mexico: the poetics and politics of the Fernández–Figueroa style', in *The Mexican Cinema Project*, Los Angeles: UCLA, pp.13–25.

PATRICIA TORRES SAN MARTÍN

Figueroa, John J.M.

b. 1920, Kingston, Jamaica; d. 1998, London, England

Poet

James T. Livingston has called John Figueroa 'perhaps the most classical of West Indian poets'. Long a believer in an eclectic approach to art, Figueroa agreed with Terence that 'nothing human is alien to me'. His poetry collections are *Blue Mountain Peak* (1943), *Love Leaps Here* (1962) and *Ignoring Hurts* (1976). Figueroa taught at London University and was a professor of education at the **University of the West Indies** from 1957–73. He also held academic posts in Nigeria and in various British institutions. He has published many essays on educational and literary topics, and edited the first substantial anthology of Caribbean poetry, *Caribbean Voices*.

KEITH JARDIM

Figueroa, Luis

b. 1928, Cusco, Peru

Film director

A member of the so-called 'Cusco school', a group of film-makers who in the 1950s and 1960s made a series of important ethnographic documentaries (see **ethnographic film**). Figueroa made his first full length feature in 1961, codirecting (with Eulogio **Nishiyama** and César Villanueva) *Kukuli* (1961), the first ever Peruvian film in **Quechua**, which recreated an indigenous legend. He later made short films and the features *Los perros hambrientos* (Hungry Dogs) (1976) and *Yawar fiesta* (1986), adaptations of eponymous novels by Ciro **Alegría** and José María **Arguedas** respectively.

CESAR SALAS

Figuerola, Enrique

b. 1938, Santiago de Cuba

Athlete

Figuerola was the first Cuban (and one of the first ever) to run 100 metres in ten seconds – at Budapest on 17 June 1967. In equalling the world record, Figuerola reached the high point of a distinguished athletic career which included silver medals at the 1964 Tokyo Olympics (100 metres) and Mexico 1968 (in the 4 × 100 metres relay), bronze at the Pan-American Games in Chicago 1959 and gold in the 1963 Pan-American Games at São Paulo. He won at the **Central American and Caribbean Games** in 1966 and retired from athletics in 1969.

WILFREDO CANCIO ISLA

Filho, Adonias

b. 1915, Itajuípe, Bahia; d. 1990, Ilhéus, Bahia

Writer

Adonias Aguiar Filho grew up in the *cacau* region in southern Bahia, where several of his narratives are set (for example, *Corpo vivo* (Living Body) (1962)). His fiction melds the social concerns of the regionalist novel (see ***regionalismo***) with psychological and existential introspection. Many of his characters are caught in a blind struggle against destiny in a nightmarish, seemingly godless world where they must rely only on their own instincts. Narratives such as *O forte* (The Fortress) (1965) and the short stories of *Léguas da promissão* (The Leagues of Promise) (1968) are written in a densely poetic, elliptical style that juxtaposes multiple levels of time and space.

RANDAL JOHNSON

Filho, Daniel

b. 1937, Rio de Janeiro, Brazil

Actor and director

Filho appeared in ***telenovelas*** for the pioneer station TV Tupy and hosted TV Excelsior's programme *Time Square* before joining TV **Globo** in 1966 to direct its soap operas. In the 1970s he was instrumental in reviving Globo's dramas, creating with writer Janet **Clair** successes including *Selva de Pedra* (Stone jungle) and *Pecado Capital* (Mortal Sin). In 1978 the very modern *Dancing Days*, starring Sonia **Braga**, created a huge national following. In 1985 he became director of Globo's production company Central Globo de Producao. He published his autobiography *Antes que me esquecam* (Before They Forget Me), and is rumoured to be next to assume the direction of TV Globo.

ANTONIO CARLOS MARTINS VAZ

Filhos de Gandhi

The oldest existing ***afoxé*** in Salvador, the Filhos de Gandhi (Sons of Gandhi) was founded in 1949 by a group of Afro-Brazilian stevedores inspired by the pacifist anti-colonialism of Mahatma Gandhi. Members tend to be devotees of the Afro-Brazilian religion **Candomblé**, and dress in white to honour Oxalá, the *orixá* of peace (see ***orixás***). They promote their beliefs during civic and religious festivals with secularized versions of **Yoruba** liturgical chants accompanied by a percussion ensemble which plays the lilting *ijexá* rhythm. The Filhos de Gandhi was an important precursor to recent Afro-Brazilian cultural affirmation.

CHRISTOPHER DUNN

Filloy, Juan

b. 1894, Córdoba, Argentina; d. 2000, Córdoba

Writer

Trained as a lawyer, Filloy privately published several works in the 1930s for a very limited public. When some of them were republished by Paidos, including *¡Estafen!* (1932) and *Op Oloop* (1934), Filloy became the great 'discovery' of the time, though **Cortázar** had already referred to him in ***Rayuela***. He is recognized as a great master of parody and illusive realism. The new interest in his work led other important works to be republished, among them *La Potra* (1973), *Vil-y-vil* (1975) and *La purga* (1992). Filloy is a particularly skilful coiner of palindromes, some of them in a satirical vein. His long silence as a writer is explained by the fact that he became a judge in 1968.

ENRIQUE FOFFANI

film criticism and scholarship

Although the Latin American periodical press have commented amply on the cinema since its introduction in the late 1890s and the phenomenon has attracted the attention of notable intellectuals (ranging from José Carlos **Mariáte-**

gui and Mário de **Andrade** to Rómulo **Gallegos**, Horacio **Quiroga** and Vinicius de Morais), specialized film writing did not appear until the publication of market-oriented **film magazines** in the mid- to late 1920s. Although focused on film, however, these early publications were essentially fan magazines and were mostly concerned with Hollywood films (see **Hollywood's impact on Latin American cinema**) and stars rather than with film criticism *per se*. Even when they championed national film-makers or films, like ***Cinearte***'s endorsement of the work of Humberto **Mauro** in Brazil, for example, they eschewed intellectual considerations in favour of lighter fare. Criticism proper and film historiography do not begin to appear until the late 1940s and 1950s, alongside the development of film culture exemplified by **cine clubs**, **cinematheques**, **film festivals** and the entry of film into universities. In fact, the first generation of Latin American film critics emerge directly from the cine club movements, with notable examples like Paulo Emílio Salles **Gomes** in Brazil and José Manuel Valdés Rodríguez in Cuba. In Mexico, a new generation of critics appeared, among them Emilio **García Riera**, Carlos **Fuentes**, Eduardo Lizalde, José Miguel **García Ascot** (who later published the influential journal, *Nuestro Cine* (1961–2)), Carlos **Monsiváis**, Gabriel Ramírez, Tomas Pérez Turrent and Jorge Ayala Blanco. Meanwhile, in Colombia, Gabriel **García Márquez** wrote influential film chronicles in 1954–5. Books of film criticism and aesthetics also begin to appear in the late 1940s: for example, Julian de Ajuria's *El cinematógrafo, espejo del mundo* was published in Buenos Aires in 1946. However, the first book-length historical assessments of national cinemas were, in 1959, with Alex **Viany**'s *Introdução ao cinema Brasileiro* and Domingo di Núbila's two-volume *Historia del cine argentino*.

Stimulated by the achievements of new national cinemas and the rise of the **New Latin American Cinema** movement, film writing and scholarship mushroomed in the 1960s. In many instances, publications endorsed the radical work of new film-makers and their manifestos, like **Rocha**'s 'An **aesthetics of hunger**,' or Julio **García Espinosa**'s '*Por un **cine imperfecto***' (For an imperfect cinema). Other publications promoted the scholarly study of the medium. Notable among these is García Riera's monumental documentary history, *Historia documental del cine mexicano* (1969–76) and Jorge Miguel Couselo's critical study of silent-film pioneer José Agustín **Ferreyra**. Since then, and often sponsored by national film institutes and/or cinematheques, film scholarship of national cinemas has flourished. The research and publications sponsored by **Embrafilme** in the 1980s were of great significance and brought to light the notable critical voice of Ismail Xavier, among others. Other important contemporary Brazilian film scholars are Jean Claude Bernardet, Maria Rita Galvão and Lucia Nagib. In Mexico, the film department at the Universidad de Guadalajara directed by García Riera is a veritable film 'think tank' and has published the work of new critics like Eduardo de la Vega Alfaro and Patricia Torres San Martín. Also notable is the work of historian Aurelio de los Reyes, who almost single-handedly has researched the history of silent Mexican cinema. In Argentina, many scholars are based at the University of Buenos Aires – including Claudio España, David Oubiña and Diana Paladino – although many others work without institutional affiliations, like Sergio Wolf, or are based in the cinematheque, like César Maranghello and Alejandra Portela.

As of the late 1990s, almost every national cinema has received a book-length historical analysis, no matter how slim, and many monographs of individual film directors have also been published. Curiously, however, there has been little comparative or pan-Latin American scholarship; almost without exception all film scholarship with a pan-national focus has been published either in the USA or in France.

Further reading

Bedoya, R. (1992) *Cien años de cine en el Perú*, Lima: Universidad de Lima.

Bernardet, J.C. (1967) *Brasil em tempo de cinema*, Rio de Janeiro: Civilização Brasileira.

Couselo, J.M. (1969) *El negro Ferreyra, un cine por instinto*, Buenos Aires: Freeland.

Di Núbila, Domingo (1959) *Historia del cine Argentino*, Buenos Aires: Cruz de Malta.

España, C. (1984) *Medio siglo de cine: Argentina Sono Film*, Buenos Aires: Abril.

García Riera, Emilio (1969–78) *Historia documental del cine Mexicano*, Mexico City: Era.

Paranaguá, P.A. (1984) *Cinema na América Latina*, Porto Alegre: L. & P.M. Editores.

Viany, A (1959) *Introdução ao cinema Brasileiro*, Rio de Janeiro: INL.

ANA M. LÓPEZ

film distribution

Although less glamorous than film production and invisible in comparison to **film exhibition**, distribution is the most crucial – and profitable – sector of the film business. Because of its seeming transparency, however, distribution has also been the most neglected sector in Latin America; foreign companies, especially Hollywood ones, have dominated Latin American distribution, and national or regional distributors have rarely thrived.

At first exhibition and distribution were typically carried out by the same entrepreneurs and their firms, some establishing regional circuits encompassing neighbouring countries. Thus, in the silent period, the Di Domenico family was established in Colombia, but their distribution network followed the sea trade routes north, through Venezuela and Central America into Panama (where other family members ran a subsidiary). Similarly Max Glucksmann, an Argentine pioneer, set up subsidiaries in Uruguay, Paraguay and Chile, and during the First World War opened an office in New York to distribute US films throughout South America.

Their efforts, however, were ineffectual against Hollywood's increasing interest in Latin American markets after the First World War. Given the disruptions caused by war in Europe and their own efficient domestic structure, the Hollywood majors sought new markets – for additional profits, but also to displace the previous centrality of European films in the continent. Beginning in 1916 (Buenos Aires, Rio de Janeiro, Havana) and through the 1930s, the majors established subsidiaries in Latin American capitals and even in cities of the interior. Trade weeklies designed to increase business were published in the US in Spanish: *Cine mundial* (1916–38), the *Mensajero Paramount* (in the 1920s) and *Cinelandia* (1927–48). By the 1930s, and despite the proportionally slight marketing disruptions caused by the coming of sound (see **Hispanic cinema in Hollywood**), the majors had a firm foothold on Latin American distribution that they have retained ever since.

This distribution network at one time even included secondary, 'amateur' formats: during the Second World War, at the height of the 'Good Neighbour Policy', a US government-sponsored agency even established an extensive 16 mm distribution network for newsreels and 'educational' films (see **Hollywood's impact on Latin American cinema**). Some nations attempted to compete via State-run distribution companies; Mexico's were the most efficient. As the State moved towards nationalizing the industry in the 1940s, it created Pelmex in 1945 for international distribution, Azteca (1945) to distribute to Spanish-language theatres in the USA (there were then approximately 600) and Películas Nacionales (1947) for domestic distribution. In 1954 all three companies were put under the control of the State agency for the cinema, the Banco Nacional Cinematográfico. Pelmex, in fact, became a substantial international distributor, operating in more than twenty countries. Yet, this nationalizing impetus resulted in an isolationist anti-innovative attitude within the industry that froze the national cinema for more than twenty years and did not, in fact, change the dominance of US films, still profitably distributed by the majors (between 57 and 70 per cent of all films exhibited in Mexico in this period were from the USA). Neither was the industry able to significantly penetrate US markets beyond the limited Spanish-language one. Even the great success of **Cantinflas** was not a help; his films were represented internationally by Columbia Pictures. A similar thing happened to the **Vera Cruz Studios** in Brazil. The studio had negotiated a contract with Columbia for international distribution and, although they had a big hit on their hands (*O cangaceiro*, 1954) that could have solved some of the company's financial problems, Columbia reaped the profits.

In the 1960s and 1970s, several alternative distributors appeared, specializing in the products of the **New Latin American Cinema** and the new international connections established through **film festivals** and other cultural film events. Of special significance was Walter **Achugar**'s Renascimiento Films in Montevideo, which distributed films from all over Latin America, including Brazilian **Cinema Novo**, Cuban cinema and other 'new' cinemas. The Cuban film institute, **ICAIC**, had complete control over national and international distribution after 1959; the domestic market was a captive one, but the foreign one proved more elusive and ICAIC rarely managed to place its films beyond festival and *cinemateca* (see **cinematheques**) circuits.

By the 1980s, with the consolidation of the international art market circuit, some Latin American producers were able to obtain international distribution. For example, Brazil's State film agency, **Embrafilme**, counting upon protective legislation enforcing national exhibition, also managed to break into international circuits with films like Bruno **Barreto**'s ***Dona Flor e seus dois maridos*** (1976) and Héctor **Babenco**'s ***Pixote*** (1981). In the USA, mid-sized distributors appeared to service this new market and specialized in foreign films (New Yorker Films, for example). As the potential profitability of international art house distribution became apparent, however, it created a curious situation: the potential for two levels of national film-making, one ostensibly geared to national consumption (inexpensive films that could recoup costs with limited national distribution; often quota quickies) and one with international art market aspirations. No film crystallized this phenomenon better than Mexico's ***Como agua para chocolate*** (Like Water for Chocolate, Alfonso **Arau**) (1991). As the importance of national distribution has continued to decrease through the 1990s and the economics of production deteriorate, being picked up by a US distributor is now what all Latin American producers dream of. After all, despite all its previous achievements, no other ICAIC films has ever had the repercussions of **Gutiérrez Alea**'s ***Fresa y chocolate*** (Strawberry and Chocolate) (1993), successfully marketed internationally by Miramax Films.

Further reading

King, J. (1990) *Magical Reels*, London: Verso.
Paranaguá, P.A. (1996) 'América Latina busca su imagen', in *Historia general del cine*, Vol X, Madrid: Cátedra.

ANA M. LÓPEZ

film exhibition

The crucial final link in the film business – exhibition – completes the production cycle and brings the 'product' to consumers; box-office receipts are the fuel of film-production. Controlling film theatres – either via direct ownership or block booking practices – has been the key to sustaining studio-based production.

In Latin America, film exhibition was, at first, the only indigenous aspect of a phenomenon that was first and foremost an import. In the silent cinema period (see **silent film**), entertainment entrepreneurs exhibited the new medium in already-established venues, ranging from legitimate theatres to open-air sites like the *carpas* in Mexico City (see ***carpa***). They were instrumental in securing the legitimacy of the medium. In many instances, such as that of the Di Doménico chain based in Colombia, entire families staked their fortunes on the medium and established local and/or regional empires; the Di Doménicos' business extended from Colombia to Central America, for example.

However, movie theatre ownership quickly became a precarious business, dependent on the quality and appeal of the available product. As Hollywood films became dominant internationally circa the First World War, Latin American exhibitors had to negotiate contracts with the local subsidiaries of the US studios in order to survive. Thus, for example, Francisco Serrador in Brazil developed his vast intrastate exhibition chain in the 1910s and 1920s based upon his exclusive contracts with foreign film distributors; Serrador created the **Cinelândia** entertainment district in the heart of Rio de Janeiro and built luxurious movie palaces while also continuing to invest in smaller neighbourhood theatres.

Sound – circa 1927 – was a watershed: retrofitting existing theatres for sound was financed by local entrepreneurs in collaboration with US firms. Luis Severiano Ribeiro, another Brazilian theatre owner, built and updated his extensive chain of neighbourhood and elegant downtown theatres with capital from Metro Goldwyn Mayer. In the 1940s, his association with the local production company, **Atlântida** – a rare example of Latin American vertical integration – was what guaranteed the popularity and viability of the *chanchada* genre that the studio specialized in.

Historically, theatre owners have preferred imports because of their greater box-office potential; this has positioned them as arch-enemies of national cinemas. Cinema protection laws typically include screen quota provisions, requiring all theatres to screen national films for set periods. These quotas have sometimes been effective, generating, for example, important work in **short films** in the 1970s; more often, they have led to 'quota quickies', as in the compilation films in Mexico in the 1950s and 1960s, and the *sobreprecio* cinema in Colombia in the 1980s.

With the growth of television and the even more recent boom in home video, film exhibition suffered dramatic losses in the 1980s. Even in Cuba, where **ICAIC** has a *de facto* vertical monopoly, the number of theatres declined markedly and film attendance decreased. Throughout the continent, film theatres closed and existing installations were allowed to decline; the neighbourhood theatres were the first to disappear. However, beginning in the 1990s, there have been efforts to modernize the exhibition infrastructure, especially in large urban centres like São Paulo, where luxurious stadium-type theatres are beginning to appear. The classic movie palaces of the 1940s and 1950s have also begun to be valued and restored, for example the Cinema São Luiz in Fortaleza (Brazil).

ANA M. LÓPEZ

film festivals

A thoroughly modern phenomenon, film festivals provide a forum for the recognition of artistic achievement as well as for marketing and **film distribution**. Latin American films have had an international impact since film festivals were inaugurated. At the Venice Film Festival (the first, founded in 1932), Gabriel **Figueroa**'s cinematography for *Allá en el rancho grande* won the Mexican cinema's first international award in 1938. However, film festivals only began to acquire their contemporary significance after the Second World War, when Cannes was founded and festivals began to proliferate throughout Europe. Again, the Mexican cinema shone early on, winning an award at Cannes for *María Candelaria* in 1946. Argentina's first international festival award was an honourable mention at Venice for Hugo **Del Carril**'s *Las aguas bajan turbias* (Muddy Waters) in 1952. In 1953, Brazil obtained its first international award at Cannes with the **Vera Cruz Studios** production, *O cangaceiro* (The Bandit).

Festivals must be distinguished from film competitions, which take place in a different context, such as the 'Oscars' awarded by the US Academy of Motion Picture Arts and Sciences. However, the Oscars do have an award for foreign films and a number of Latin American films have been nominated for this category, ranging from Luis César **Amadori**'s *Dios se lo pague* (God Will Repay You) in 1947 to, most recently, Walter Salles Jr's *Central do Brasil* (Central Station) in 1999; Luis **Puenzo**'s *La historia oficial* (The Official Story) won the best foreign-film Oscar in 1985. Other prestigious international awards include the respected New York Critics' prize; when awarded to the Cuban film *Memorias del subdesarrollo* (Memories of Underdevelopment) in 1974 it unleashed a gargantuan polemic. In Latin America, the Mexican '**Arieles**', awarded annually by the Mexican Academy of the Cinematographic Arts since 1946, are similar to the Oscars.

In Latin America, film festivals appeared alongside the growth of film culture in the late 1940s and 1950s (**cine clubs**, **film magazines**, etc.). The first film festivals, like the Mar del Plata festival (since 1954), were geared towards European production, with one major exception, the **documentary** and experimental-film festival hosted in Montevideo by **SODRE** in 1954. The filmmakers of the emerging new cinemas (later, the **New Latin American Cinema**) first met in

Europe, at the Sestri Levante (Italy) festival of 1962. After another encounter at another festival in Uruguay organized by the Cine Club Marcha, they also gathered at the momentous 1967 **Viña del Mar Festival**, where the new movement was made official (and ratified in subsequent festivals in Viña, Mérida and Caracas throughout the 1970s). The films of the movement have also been widely recognized and awarded at all international festivals.

Since then, festivals have appeared in almost every country in Latin America. Beyond awarding prizes, these festivals serve multiple functions. A central one is to provide an international marketplace where producers and distributors can exchange ideas, see films and sign contracts. Co-production deals (see **co-productions**), for example, are often born in festivals, like the **Festival Internacional del Nuevo Cine Latinoamericano** in Havana (since 1979). Festivals also provide a unique space for the introduction of new films and movements. Sometimes, they are also sites for artistic and political contention: the 1998 edition of the Mar del Plata festival, for example, was threatened by a boycott protesting the state of the Argentine film industry.

Since the 1980s, a number of festivals have emerged that focus upon Latino, Spanish or Latin American films, most notably in Brussels, Chicago (Latino filmfest), Biarritz and Gramado (Brazil). Festivals that award prizes are regulated by the FIAPF (Fédération Internationale des Associations de Producteurs de Films). Between 1984 and its last edition in 1990, FestRio in Brazil was the only FIAPF Class A prize-awarding event in Latin America. Since its rebirth in 1996 after a sixteen-year hiatus, the Mar del Plata festival has now assumed that place.

ANA M. LÓPEZ

film magazines

Specialized film magazines appeared in Latin America around the 1920s, as a result of the expansion of the Latin American film market and its penetration by Hollywood films circa the First World War. Thus, the earliest film publications were primarily geared to imports, promoting the films and stars as symbols of cosmopolitan modernity (see **cultural theory**). Notable examples include *Cinearte* (published in Rio de Janeiro, 1926–42), *La semana cinematográfica* (Lima, 1926–82), *Ecran* (Santiago de Chile, 1930–71) and *Imparcial film* (Buenos Aires, 1918–39). By the 1930s and 1940s many of these publications were also including considerations of the other 'new' popular entertainment medium, **radio**, for example *Sintonía* (Buenos Aires, 1933–56) and *Radiolandia* (Mexico City, 1934–46).

Magazines devoted to film criticism (see **film criticism and scholarship**) emerged in the 1940s–50s, alongside the growth of film culture and **cine clubs**, although *O fan*, published in Rio de Janeiro by the cine club Chaplin (1928–30), was a notable predecessor. Important magazines of this era included *Revista do cinema* (Belo Horizonte, 1954–7), *Gente de cine* (Buenos Aires, 1951–7), *Cine club* (Montevideo, 1948–53) and *Séptimo arte* (Mexico, 1957–62). A second boom occurred alongside the general spirit of renewal and revolution of the late 1950s and through the 1960s that evolved into the **New Latin American Cinema**. In magazines like *Nuevo cine* (Mexico, 1961–2) and *Tiempo de cine* (Buenos Aires, 1960–8) a new generation of critics and often would-be film-makers debated alternative models of film production and new revolutionary aesthetics, especially the merits of Italian Neorealism. *Cine cubano* published in Cuba by **ICAIC** since 1960 was perhaps the most consistent in postulating and promoting the aesthetics and unity of the new movement, although *Hablemos de cine* (Lima, 1962–84), *Filme cultura* (Rio de Janeiro, 1966–88), *Cine al día* (Caracas, 1967–83) and *Ojo al cine* (Cali, 1974–6) were also significant.

Specialized film publication suffered in the wake of the military dictatorships and repression of the 1970s. However, in the 1980s and 1990s, new publications continued to establish a firm foundation for film criticism, among them, for example, *Dicine* (Mexico, 1983), *Encuadre* (Caracas, 1984),

Pantalla (Mexico, 1985), *Kinetoscopio* (Medellín, 1990), *El amante cine* (Buenos Aires, 1991), *La gran ilusión* (Lima, 1993) and *Cinemais* (Rio de Janeiro, 1996). There is a world of a difference between these recent publications and the old magazines focused on the star system, echoing a similar change in how the cinema is now approached throughout the continent.

ANA M. LÓPEZ

Fina estampa

A Peruvian 'vals' or **waltz** composed in 1956 by singer and composer Chabuca **Granda**, it describes the *fina estampa* (high style) of a Lima society gentleman. The polyrhythmic Peruvian 'vals', unlike its European parent, uses guitar, denoting Spanish influence, and percussion, derived from black culture. The 'vals' is thus representative of urban culture as opposed to Peru's rural music of indigenous origins. Chabuca Granda's own interpretation, accompanied by the Mariachi Vargas de Tecalitlán and violins, remains the best of many recorded versions. Brazilian singer Caetano **Veloso**'s orchestral arrangement became enormously popular throughout Latin America in the 1990s.

ALEJANDRA LAERA

Finot, Enrique

b. 1891, Santa Cruz, Bolivia; d. 1952, La Paz, Bolivia

Writer and historian

Professor of drawing and cartography, Finot was Director of the Escuela Modelo in La Paz and over thirty years also held a series of diplomatic posts in Latin America. He was involved in negotiations both before (1931) and after (1934) the **Chaco War** between Bolivia and Paraguay. He was editor of two newspapers – *El Liberal* and *El Oriente* – and was a member of the Argentine, Venezuelan and Bolivian Academy of History. His best-known writings include *Nueva historia de Bolivia* (New History of Bolivia) (1946) and *Historia de la literatura boliviana* (History of Bolivian Literature) (1964).

XIMENA MEDINACELI

Fioravanti, José

b. 1896, Buenos Aires, Argentina; d. 1977, Buenos Aires

Sculptor

Fioravanti's most celebrated works are public sculptures celebrating Argentina's most prestigious presidents: the monuments to Nicolás Avellaneda (1936), Roque Saenz Peña (1936) and Simón Bolívar (1942). His statues have an architectural dimension which complements their heroic quality. Self-taught, he sold one piece on his first trip to Europe in 1924. He exhibited his work in 1927 in Buenos Aires, then lived in Paris for six years. In 1935 he was appointed Professor of Sculpture at Buenos Aires' School of Fine Arts, and was awarded the Gran Premio del Salón Nacional.

MAGDALENA GARCÍA PINTO

Firmenich, Mario

b. 1947, Buenos Aires

Guerrilla leader

A right-wing Catholic nationalist of Croatian descent, Firmenich emerged in the late 1960s as spokesman and leader of the **Montoneros**, a pro-Perón leftist political and guerrilla group. Active in many of the Montoneros's most spectacular actions, Firmenich helped to lead the largest guerrilla army in Latin American history. He went into exile when the movement was brutally repressed, returning to Buenos Aires in 1991 when Carlos **Menem** pardoned both guerrillas and military. His roots in ultraconservative and Catholic movements and military connections suggest that he may have been a military informer during his years with the Montoneros.

THOMAS EDSALL

Firpo, Luis Alberto

b. 1896, Junín, Argentina; d. 1960, Buenos Aires, Argentina

Boxer

Argentine heavyweight champion of the 1920s, Firpo was called the 'Wild Bull of the *Pampas*' due to his formidable size and strength and a fighting style characterized by wild milling punches. He fought numerous bouts against US boxing legends such as Jack Dempsey in 1923. His status as Argentina's first internationally famous sportsman symbolized for many the nation's arrival as a world power, although he never won the world heavyweight title. He invested his winnings in ranching and died a wealthy man, with a life-sized statue in **Recoleta** cemetery.

THOMAS EDSALL

Fittipaldi, Emerson

b. 1946, São Paulo, Brazil

Racing driver

Formula One driver who competed in 144 world championship Grand Prix races, won 14 of them and took the world title in 1972 driving a Lotus-Ford and again in 1974 in a McLaren-Ford. In 1984 he switched to Indy cars in the USA and won 22 more races, including the famous Indianapolis 500 on two occasions. Now retired and with residences in both Brazil and the USA, he has business interests in orange plantations, men's sportswear and car accessories as well as a recent venture into cigar manufacture.

ERIC WEIL

FLACSO

FLACSO (Facultad Latinoamericana de las Ciencias Sociales – Latin American Faculty of Social Sciences) was founded in 1957, as a result of a UNESCO initiative, to promote the social sciences throughout Latin America. Fourteen countries are currently members of the Faculty, and its representatives make up the Faculty's governing General Assembly; its General Secretariat has been housed since 1979 in Costa Rica. Its activities are organized through a series of programmes of research, teaching, technical co-operation and university extension. It was instrumental in its early years in promoting and supporting the teaching of social sciences in Latin American universities and in the creation of independent social science institutes, like the Instituto Di tella in Buenos Aires. Prominent figures who have been associated with FLACSO include Fernando Henrique **Cardoso**, José Joaquín **Brunner** and Norbert Lechner. The Santiago, Chile centre was important in the development of **dependency theory**.

MIKE GONZALEZ

Fletcher, Lea

b. 1946, Panama Canal Zone

Writer, journalist and literary historian

In 1988 Fletcher founded ***Feminaria***, an independent semi-annual feminist journal of theory, criticism, and literature, and in 1992 founded Feminaria Editora. *Feminaria* has been an important voice in Latin America for its focus on women's issues and writings and is distinguished particularly by its emphasis on historical investigation of women's writings, particularly in Argentina. Her work as editor and writer has been complemented by her leadership as co-organizer of women's conferences, both national and international (1992, 1996, 2000). Author and editor of several books (*Modernismo. Sus cuentistas olvidados en la Argentina* (Forgotten Modernist Short Story Writers in Argentina) (1986), *Una mujer llamada Herminia* (A Woman Called Herminia) (1987), *Mujeres y cultura en* *la Argentina del siglo XIX* (Women and Culture in Nineteenth-Century Argentina) (1994), she has also published numerous articles on women's writing and feminist theory, and has established essential bibliographies.

GWEN KIRKPATRICK

Flor silvestre

Flor silvestre (Wild Flower) was the third film by Emilio 'El Indio' **Fernández**, one of Mexico's most prolific film-makers. In 1943, *Flor silvestre* brought together the team that stayed with him for several films: cinematographer Gabriel **Figueroa**, actors Dolores **Del Rio** and Pedro **Armendáriz** and scriptwriter Mauricio **Magdaleno**. Set during the Mexican Revolution (see **revolutions**), in *Flor silvestre* Esperanza, a peasant's daughter, secretly marries José Luis, the landowner's son who is then disinherited; he is later shot by bandits while attempting to protect his wife and child. The film exemplifies Fernández's sentimental vision of agricultural society, where tragedy is the key to the narrative.

PATRICIA TORRES SAN MARTÍN

Flores, Angel

b. 1900, Barceloneta, Puerto Rico; d. 1994, New York, USA

Critic

A prolific critic of Hispanic literature, Flores's career spans several decades and the breadth of his knowledge several centuries and two continents. Flores taught and wrote in several US institutions, including Rutgers University and Cornell. He published criticism on Spanish Golden Age literature, and edited numerous anthologies of Spanish and Latin American literature from the Middle Ages to Pablo **Neruda**. Flores also translated works of Hispanic literature, including Pablo Neruda's 1935 *Residencia en la tierra* (Residence on Earth) (1946) and Esteban Echeverría's 1871 *El matadero* (The Slaughter House) (1959).

CATHERINE DEN TANDT

Flores, Celedonio

b. 1896, Buenos Aires, Argentina; d. 1947, Buenos Aires

Songwriter

Flores's songs are chronicles of port life, written in **lunfardo** and ranging in subject matter from the reflective to urban protest and rebellion. Flores came from **sainete** theatre, but was influenced by *modernista* (see ***modernismo***), Spanish American poets Amado Nervo and Rubén Darío. His best known tangos, 'Atenti, pebeta' (Hang On, Girl), 'Cuando me entrés a fallar' (If You Let Me Down), '**Mano a mano**' (Hand to Hand), were memorably sung by Rosita **Quiroga**, Carlos **Gardel** (who immortalized his 'El bulín de la calle Ayacucho' (The Bar on Ayacucho Street)) and Edmundo **Rivero**.

LUIS GUSMAN

Flores, Pedro

b. 1894, Naguabo, Puerto Rico; d. 1979, San Juan, Puerto Rico

Musician and composer

One of the great composers of Latin American popular music, Flores worked in New York, Cuba, Mexico and Puerto Rico. He was a prolific writer of boleros (see **bolero**) and guarachas (see **guaracha**), among them 'Bajo un palmar' (Under a Palm Tree), 'Linda' (Pretty Woman), 'Borinquen', 'Azucenas' (Lilies), 'Súplica' (Begging You), 'Esperanza inútil' (Futile Hope), 'Amor perdido' (Lost Love) and 'Se vende una casita' (A House for Sale). His songs were recorded by **Toña la Negra**, Marco Antonio Muniz and Daniel **Santos**, among others.

JUAN CARLOS QUINTERO HERENCIA

Flores Galindo, Alberto

b. 1949, Lima, Peru; d. 1990, Lima

Historian

Flores Galindo was an outstanding contemporary Latin American historian and analyst of the social, economic and cultural history of the Andean area. His books develop some of the initial concerns set forth by José Carlos **Mariátegui**, expressed in the 1920s, about the importance and the role of the Indian and **mestizo** population of Peru within a modern and national state. His first book, *Los mineros de la Cerro de Pasco* (The Mine Workers of the Cerro de Pasco [Copper Corporation]) (1976) discussed the social transformation produced by the presence of a US corporation in the central Andes. His second book, *Arequipa y el sur andino: ensayo de historia regional, siglos XVIII-XIX* (Arequipa and the Andean South: An Essay on Regional History, Eighteenth and Nineteenth Centuries) (1977) examines the formation of a regional oligarchy in debate with the thesis of economic dependency (see **dependency theory**). Later came *Apogeo y crisis de la república aristocrática* (Apogee and Crisis of the Aristocratic Republic) (1980) in collaboration with Manuel Burga, a thorough analysis of the period 1870–1920 and the dynamics between popular classes and the Peruvian landowning oligarchy. *La agonía de Mariátegui* (The Dying Mariátegui) (1980) is a study of the originality of the first Latin American Marxist and his differences with the Comintern (the second edition, of 1989, proposes a more constructive understanding of his pre-Marxist period). *Aristocracia y plebe* (Aristocracy and Plebs) (1983), initially his doctoral dissertation at the University of Paris, deals with Lima's vic500al society.

However, his major contribution is *Buscando un inca: identidad y utopía en los Andes* (Looking for an Inca: Identity and Utopia in the Andes) (1986). It won the **Casa de las Américas** prize in Cuba that same year. The book constitutes 'the biography of an idea', as Flores Galindo defines his reconstruction of the ideological motivation for several peasant rebellions during the colonial and postcolonial periods in the Andes. The return of an idealized Incan state and the transformation of the historical past as a tool for a social and economic redemption in the future is what constitutes the core of this study. Despite his early death, Flores Galindo remains one of the most influential thinkers among scholars who work on the Andean area. He was a professor at the Catholic University of Peru and founder of 'Sur', a research institution devoted to the study of socialist (see **socialism**) interpretations of Peruvian society.

JOSÉ ANTONIO MAZZOTTI

Floria, Carlos Alberto

b. 1929, Buenos Aires

Political analyst

Mainly interested in Argentine political history, Floria co-authored *Historia de los argentinos* (History of the Argentines) (1992) with Cesar A. García Belsunce. He also writes about political theory, Latin American and international political subjects. Floria was a Consultant Member of the Pontifical Justitia et Pax Council and member of the editorial board of **Criterio**, a liberal Catholic journal. Eisenhower Fellow (1966), he was Minister of Education in the province of Buenos Aires (1962–1963). Since 1996 he has been the Argentine Ambassador to UNESCO.

FERNANDO RABOSSI

Florida

Running from **Avenida de Mayo** to Plaza San Martín in Buenos Aires, Florida became a thriving commercial centre and a promenade for the wealthy new residents of the area in the early twentieth century. In the 1920s Florida became associated with writers working on the avant-garde journal **Martín Fierro**. In the 1960s, it was the site of the **Instituto Di Tella**, a private gallery and theatrical space devoted to incorporating European aesthetic trends into Argentine culture. Although still lined with shops, Florida lost its association with elite culture as the Instituto Di Tella closed down, the middle and upper classes moved to the suburbs, and large shopping malls appeared in the 1980s.

See also: Boedo vs Florida

LAURA PODALSKY

Florit, Eugenio

b. 1903, Madrid, Spain; d. 1999, Miami, Florida, USA

Writer

An outstanding lyric poet of his generation, Florit lived in Cuba from the age of fourteen. A member of the **Revista de avance** group, he moved to New York in 1940 but collaborated with the Cuban **Orígenes** group and wrote for its magazine. He also co-edited *Revista Hispánica Moderna* in New York with Federico de **Onís** and Angel del Río. His many works, from *Trópico* (1930) to *A pesar de todo* (Despite Everything) (1987), present a poetry of existential concerns, marked by a sense of man's essential solitude and characterized by serenity and rich language.

WILFREDO CANCIO ISLA

FMLN

The FMLN (Frente Farabundo Martí de Liberación Nacional – Farabundo **Martí** National Liberation Front) was formed in 1980 when the five main guerrilla organizations of El Salvador agreed to unite under a single command. The FPL (Popular Liberationary Army), RN (National Resistance), PCS (Salvadorean Communist Party) and the PRTC (Central American Workers' Party) had all been active on both political and military fronts through the political crises of the 1970s (with the exception of the Communist Party, which only reluctantly developed an armed strategy during 1979). The huge demonstrations in San Salvador in January 1980 suggested that the Nicaraguan Revolution might precipitate a rising tide of revolutionary struggle throughout Central America. Right-wing forces began to mobilize pre-emptive action; the assassination of Archbishop **Romero** in May 1980 and the US government's growing hostility to Nicaragua were a warning of things to come. By the time the FMLN launched its so-called 'final offensive' early in 1981, the military was well prepared and armed with new US weaponry. The armed confrontation continued throughout the decade, however, until 1990, when the political wing of the FMLN negotiated a peace agreement.

MIKE GONZALEZ

foco

The term belongs to the theory and practice of guerrilla warfare (see **guerrillas**) presented in Che **Guevara**'s 1963 manual of the same name. Guevara argues that the insurrectionary struggle need not wait for appropriate objective conditions to exist – the guerrilla *foco*, an active cell or unit by its very existence, can become a focus for discontent, and the core of a future revolutionary army. In Latin America it would of necessity be rural and built largely in inaccessible mountain or rainforest locations. In Brazil and Uruguay, *foco* theory was adapted (by Carlos **Marighela** and Raúl **Sendic**) to urban conditions. By the late 1960s Guevara was dead and few *focos* survived sustained military counter-guerrilla strategies.

MIKE GONZALEZ

Folha de São Paulo

Beginning as an evening newspaper in 1921, the morning version of the *Folha de São Paulo* was launched in 1925, and an early evening edition began publication in the 1940s. All three editions were merged in 1960 into the *Folha de São Paulo*. In 1962, Octavio Frias de Oliveira and Carlos Caldeira Filho (who remained until 1992) won majority control of the paper.

In 1984 the newspaper adopted an editorial line which it called the 'Folha Project', the establishment of a non-party, pluralist and critical journalistic ethos. It became a defender of representative democracy and the market economy, and encouraged discussion of social problems. In August 1994 the *Atlas geografico mundial folha/New York Times* was the first of a series of free educational and cultural supplements. In December 1995 it opened a modern printing works capable of producing the paper entirely in-house. The editorial pages of the newspaper have included outstanding personalities from the political, cultural and economic fields writing from a variety of ideological positions, like ex-President José Sarney, ex-guerrilla and federal deputy Fernando **Gabeira**, entrepreneur Ermirio de Moraes and ex-minister Roberto **Campos**.

Folha was the first newspaper in Brazil to offer thematic supplements on cultural matters, particularly cinema, music and literature, and to have a readers' representative on the editorial board, the ombudsman, a journalist enjoying the protection of the labour laws and with a specific contract with the company to offer criticisms of the newspaper itself. The polemical writing of its leader writers is one of its characteristics; and it often promotes seminars and debates on a wide variety of topics.

Apart from *Folha*, the parent company also distributes other printed and electronic materials. The Folha Agency, besides maintaining a network of correspondents in twelve states, sells and distributes materials produced by the company. It oversees more than 150 communications media in Brazil, including Datafolha, an important public opinion research institute working for a variety of organizations but principally looking at population distribution during periods of electoral campaigning, and the Online University, in association with the Grupo Abril (which runs the magazine ***Veja***), which allows access to the Internet from Brazil.

Further reading

Silva, C.E.L. da (1988) *Mil dias: os bastidores da revolução em um grande jornal*, São Paulo: Trajectória Cultural.

ANTONIO CARLOS VAZ

folheto

In Brazil, the cheaply produced chapbooks or pamphlets of the popular poetry widely known as ***literatura de cordel*** are commonly referred to as *folhetos*. When this literature was at its most popular, in the 1940s and 1950s, there were dozens of print shops of varying size throughout Northeast Brazil producing thousands of *folhetos* daily. It was a very dynamic system of mass communication. In recent decades the number produced has declined significantly, but it continues to survive as a form of popular expression in parts of Brazil, including the Northeast, constantly adapting to meet new circumstances.

MARK DINNEEN

folk dance

A direct corollary of the rich **folk music** heritage in Latin America, almost every traditional community in the continent practised some form of folk dancing. Folk dances are typically performed for the pleasure of the participants and do not require an audience, therefore overlapping somewhat with tribal dances – defined as **dancing** originally from African tribes, often associated with syncretic religious practices like **Santería** and **Candomblé** – and some types of social dancing. Furthermore, when a traditional folk dance is performed onstage in a formal concert, its steps and patterns may be those of folk dance, but it has been removed from the context of folk culture.

Many communities have preserved and continue to practise their folk dances into the twentieth century, especially in areas with rich indigenous traditions like the Bolivian **altiplano**. Reflecting a mixture of Native American and Spanish elements, Masaya folk dances in Nicaragua – especially 'Las Inditas' and 'Toro Guaco' in which dancers representing Spanish conquistadors and indigenous peoples mock each other – draw from both traditions.

Typically, folk dances are open to the entire community and do not have to be formally taught, as everyone grows up with them. Meant for general participation, folk dances tend to be composed of fairly simple body movements in short patterns than can be repeated over and over. However, participation in some folk dances is limited according to gender, age or status. The Mexican *concheros*, for example, are a secret dance group and the only ones allowed to perform their dances. Clothing is often a very important part of folk dances, such as the full skirts, handkerchiefs and capes of the **cueca**, a Chilean couple dance, or the wide-brimmed sombrero of the Mexican hat dance.

Since mid-century, however, **urbanization**, **internal migration** and the advent of mass media have stimulated popular dance styles at the expense of traditional folk dances, which have become performative and symbolic rather than community-based. Thus, for example, in Venezuela, the joropo, which was originally a folk dance associated with the figure of the *llanero*, the cowboy from the plains, has become the national dance. More spectacularly, the Brazilian **samba** or batuque, as an expression of Afro-Brazilian community life, was originally a highly syncopated group circle dance before becoming urbanized, mass-mediated and the 'national' rhythm.

Organizations and dance troupes have also been set up to preserve and promote traditional folk dances. The **Ballet Folklórico de México**, for example, an internationally known Mexico City ensemble, works to preserve authentic Mexican folk dances while also integrating classical music into their choreographies.

Further reading

Lekis, L. (1958) *Folk Dances of Latin America*, New York: Scarecrow Press.

ANA M. LÓPEZ

folk medicine

Folk medicine is the diagnosis and treatment of illness using traditional methods and remedies rooted in the knowledge and belief systems of a people with respect to the causes and origins of disease. Traditional remedies are most often prepared from the leaves, flowers, roots or bark of plants, but animal products, such as ground bone or the secretions of poisonous amphibians and insects, may also be used. Knowledge of the therapeutic properties and uses of traditional medicines is generally the province of the local *curandero* (Portuguese *curandeiro*), or shaman (see **shamanism**).

Practitioners of folk medicine frequently attribute illness wholly or in part to acts of witchcraft or to the influence of malign or offended spirits. In addition to observing a sufferer's physical and psychological symptoms, then, in making a diagnosis and formulating an appropriate treatment, the *curandero* also seeks to discern the underlying spiritual factors which give rise to the ailment. In doing so, he or she may resort to the use of hallucinogens such as **yage** (*ayahuasca*) or other drugs to heighten awareness of the spiritual realm. Treatment entails not only the alleviation of physical suffering, but also remediation of the underlying spiritual cause of the infirmity by counteracting evil spells, appeasing offended spirits or otherwise restoring spiritual harmony.

Folk remedies have led to the development of many modern medicines, some of the better known of which are quinine from chinchona bark, digitalis (a heart stimulant) from the foxglove plant and salicylates, precursors of aspirin, from willow bark. Even curare, the infamous jungle poison, has therapeutic uses. Interest in the discovery and development of new medicines from folk cures and other plant and animal essences remains high. Many pharmaceutical companies maintain active research and development programmes to investigate the therapeutic properties of previously unknown or untested biological substances.

Further reading

Balick, M.J. (1996) *Plants, People and Culture: The Science of Ethnobotany*, New York: Scientific American Library.

Balladelli, P.P. (1988) *Entre lo mágico y lo natural: la medicina indígena*, Quito: Ediciones Abya-Yala.

Fernandez, B. (1990) *Medicine Woman: The Herbal Tradition of Belize*, Belize City: National Library Service.

Frisancho Piñeda, D. (1988) *Medicina indígena y popular*, Lima: Editorial Los Andes.

ROGER L. PARKS

folk music

'Folk music' is a slippery concept because of the ambiguity of who constitutes the 'folk', since nationalisms often privilege one group among many. Many discussions of Latin American music associate the concept of 'folk music' with the music that derives in the last instance from that of Spain and Portugal, thus excluding indigenous and African-influenced music (see **African influences on Latin American music**) from the 'folk', as well as those kinds of music (including **waltz**, schottische, mazurka, quadrille, etc.) that came to the region with other immigrant groups (see **immigration to Latin America**). Nevertheless, the Iberian presence in much Latin American music is strong.

The German romantic concept of 'folklore' was important for many collectors of the traditional songs and dances of rural Latin America, and in Argentina today '*folclor*' is used to describe all of the traditional rural music of the country (including the **zamba**, the **chamamé**, the **vidalita** and numerous other forms). Atahualpa **Yupanqui** in Argentina and Violeta **Parra** in Chile, like the Lomaxes in the USA, travelled around rural areas and small towns collecting old songs, and their collections served as the basis for their subsequent careers as composers and singers. Researchers in Mexico have compiled extensive books of the copla popular, derived in large measure from Spanish sources, which in turn influenced musical forms from the **corrido** to the **bolero**.

Collections such as the *Cancionero noble de Colombia*, films such as the *Argentinísima* series, recordings of blind singers in the Brazilian northeast and market violinists in Peru all hark back to the romantic idea of an authentic folk culture. Music, of course, is anything but static, and jumps across national borders with ease, but cultural nationalists (see **cultural nationalism**) would often not have it so.

DANIEL BALDERSTON

Folkloristas, Los

One of Latin America's most popular musical ensembles, the seven-member Mexican group Los Folkloristas, was founded in 1966 to preserve and record the traditional music of Mexico and Latin America. With some 100 instruments in their collection, they have recorded more than thirty albums performing music from over a dozen different countries, including pre-Columbian America. They contributed to the soundtrack for the award-winning films *El Norte* and *My Family*. In 1992, they received the INDIE award in World Music from the National Association of Record Distributors for their recording *Mexico*, and in June, 1996, they were honoured with a special concert given at the Palacio de Bellas Artes in Mexico City, to celebrate their thirtieth anniversary. Their work with singer Amparo **Ochoa** was particularly important.

EDUARDO GUÍZAR-ALVAREZ

Fondo de Cultura Económica

The Fondo de Cultura Económica (FCE) has been the cornerstone of twentieth-century Mexican publishing. Founded in 1934 by Daniel Cosío Villegas and Eduardo Villaseñor with subsidies from government offices and private investments, the FCE has vigorously promoted Latin American culture. Through Spanish translations, the FCE made available important titles in history, anthropology and the social sciences. In the 1950s it became a major institution for Mexican literature and culture with two new collections: 'Letras Mexicanas' introduced new writers and 'Colección Popular' promoted reading with inexpensive paperbacks. At the same time, FCE began publishing the complete works of canonical figures such as Alfonso **Reyes**.

Under Daniel Cosío Villegas's direction from 1934 to 1948, the FCE took advantage of the expertise of **intellectuals** exiled during and after the **Spanish Civil War** of 1936–9. Former FCE employees later founded other publishing houses. Joaquín Díez-Canedo left the FCE and founded

Joaquín Mortiz because he wanted to create a strictly literary publishing house, but Arnaldo **Orfila Reynal**'s tenure marked an important and radical change at FCE. As director from 1948 to 1965, Orfila Reynal modernized the company's literary profile while the **Boom** in the Spanish American novel was emerging. In 1965, after publishing a Spanish translation of Oscar Lewis's *The Children of Sánchez*, he was dismissed from the FCE. He later went on to form **Siglo XXI**. State intervention in the FCE has created managerial tensions since then. The 1982 Mexican debt crisis profoundly affected the publishing industry, and further exacerbated financial constraints at the FCE. Although FCE has remained a key Mexican publisher in the 1980s and 1990s, institutional histories by Víctor Díaz Arciniega have underscored the difficult mission of a cultural firm that must respond to governmental guidelines, remain financially solvent, and also strive to maintain independent criteria for judging cultural values.

Further reading

Díaz Arciniega, V. (1994) *Historia de la casa: Fondo de Cultura Económica (1934–1994)*, Mexico City: Fondo de Cultura Económica.

Zaid, G. (ed.) (1985) *Daniel Cosío Villegas: imprenta y vida pública*, Mexico City: Fondo de Cultura Económica.

DANNY J. ANDERSON

Fondo Nacional de las Artes

Fondo Nacional de las Artes (National Fund of the Arts) is an Argentine government institution created in 1958 which sponsors the arts, literature and cultural activities such as graphic design, architecture, publishing and folklore. It focuses primarily on giving financial support to artistic projects and educational travel, granting fellowships and loans to individuals and institutions. It organizes contests in different artistic fields, and has an annual award, the Gran Premio Fondo Nacional de las Artes, in recognition of an outstanding artistic career.

FERNANDO J. ROSENBERG

Fons, Jorge

b. 1939, Tuxpan, Mexico

Film-maker

Fons was one of the group of directors who renewed the 1960s' Mexican cinema. *Nosotros* (We), a powerful drama, was his contribution to *Tú, yo, nosotros* (You, I, We) (1971). *Caridad*, part of *Fe, experanza y caridad* (Faith, Hope and Charity) (1973), is a moving critical, popular film and perhaps his best work. After *Los albañiles* (The Construction Workers) (1976), based on Vicente **Leñero**'s play, Fons produced nothing until *Rojo amanecer* (Red Dawn) in 1989. *El callejón de los milagros* (The Street of Miracles) (1994) was widely praised for its combination of stylistic and narrative innovation with elements of classic Mexican film.

PATRICIA TORRES SAN MARTÍN

Fonseca, Carlos

b. 1936, Matagalpa, Nicaragua; d. 1976, North Zelaya, District of Ziuica, Nicaragua

Political activist

Founder in 1963 of Nicaragua's Frente Sandinista de Liberación Final (**FSLN**), together with Tomás **Borge** and Silvio Mayorga, Fonseca was also the main theorist of the group. He became involved in the resistance to the dictatorship of the Somozas (see **Somoza dynasty**) while a student of law at the University of León. It was there that he and a small circle of friends studied the experience of Augusto **Sandino**, leader of the Nicaraguan resistance to US occupation in the early 1930s, as well as some of the writings of Karl Marx. The Cuban Revolution convinced Fonseca, like many others of his generation, of the inevitability of armed struggle. After early setbacks, the FSLN began to grow in the early 1970s, but there were internal disagreements. Fonseca returned to Nicaragua in 1976, after a period in Cuba, to attempt to resolve the dispute and was caught in an ambush laid by Somoza's National Guard and killed. In 1979, his body was exhumed and reburied in the Plaza of the Revolution in Managua.

MIKE GONZALEZ

Fonseca, Gonzalo

b. 1922, Montevideo, Uruguay; d. 1997, Seravezza, Italy

Visual artist

Linked to **Taller Torres García** until 1949, he moved to Paris in 1953 and later to New York in 1958. In 1968 he designed and built a concrete tower for the XIX Olympic Games in Mexico. He has exhibited in the Jewish museum of New York (1971), the Vokesund Sculpture Museum in Denmark (1985), the Tetriakov Gallery in Moscow (1988) and the Venice Biennale in 1990. He divided his time between New York and his workshop in Seravezza, Italy.

MARCO MAGGI

Fonseca, Rubem

b. 1925, Juiz de Fora, Minas Gerais, Brazil

Writer

One of Brazil's most eminent living writers, and arguably one of the masters of the **short story** in the continent, Fonseca focuses on raw and often painful aspects of reality, though his writing sometimes has a playful and humorous quality even as it deals with very brutal and sordid events. A splendid example of this tendency is his story, 'A matéria do sonho' (The Stuff of Dreams), in *Lúcia McCartney* (1969), narrated by a solitary young man whose fantasy life has been taken in hand by a social worker who has provided him with an inflatable sex doll; the humour in the story is provided by the lists of the narrator's readings, which range wildly through high and low culture,

and by the contrast between his earnest efforts at self-improvement and the equally earnest, but somehow more misguided, efforts to 'solve' the alleged problem of his solitude. The stories of *Feliz ano novo* (Happy New Year) (1975) and *O cobrador* (The Collector) (1979) consolidated his reputation as one of Brazil's foremost writers, while taking an acid, violent look at the fractured worlds of the rich and the poor. Several of his subsequent books have been highly regarded novels. *A grande arte* (High Art) (1983) is an accomplished thriller, interspersed with instructions on the use of firearms. *Bufo & Spallanzani* (1985) is based on the life of an eighteenth-century Italian biologist, while *Vastas emoções e pensamentos imperfeitos* (Vast Emotions and Imperfect Thoughts) works with the life story of the Russian writer, Isaac Babel (1894–1941). *Agosto* (August) (1990) is an eloquent examination of the moment in Brazilian history marked by the suicide of Getúlio **Vargas**. Some of Fonseca's work has been translated into Spanish and English, but his powerful writing is not yet as well known outside Brazil as it deserves to be.

Further reading

Ballantyne, Christopher J. (1986) 'The rhetoric of violence in Rubem Fonseca', in *Luso-Brazilian Review* 23(2): 1–20.

Silva, Deonisio da (1996) *Rubem Fonseca: Proibido e consagrado*, Rio de Janeiro: Relume-Dumara.

Xavier, Elódia (1987) 'Rubem Fonseca: O conto depurado', in *O conto Brasileiro e sua trajetória*, Rio de Janeiro: Padrão, pp. 119–32.

DANIEL BALDERSTON

Fontana, Lucio

b. 1899, Rosario, Argentina; d. 1968, Comabbio, Italy

Sculptor

Fontana is usually considered more an Italian than an Argentine artist, and most of his innovative work was done in Italy in the 1950s. From 1939 to 1947 he lived in Buenos Aires, where he taught at the Altamira Academy. In 1946 he and his students published the *Manifiesto Blanco* (White Manifesto) which was a precursor of the 'spacialist' ideas he would develop in Italy. While in Argentina he had some contact with the **Arte Madí** artists and with Emilio **Pettoruti**.

GABRIEL PEREZ-BARREIRO

Fontanarrosa, Roberto

b. 1944, Rosario, Argentina

Cartoonist and writer

Distinguished by an acute philosophical and sociological understanding framed by humour, Fontanarrosa has published twenty volumes of the famous comic strip ***Inodoro Pereyra*** and eleven of the strip *Boogie, el Aceitoso* (Greasy Boogie). *Fontanarrosa y la política* (Fontanarrosa and Politics), *Fontanarrosa y el sexo* (Fontanarrosa and Sex) and *Fontanarrosa contra la cultura* (Fontanarrosa Against Culture) are selections from his comic strips. He has published seven books of short stories, and three novels: *Best seller* (1981), *El área 18* (1982) and *La gansada* (1989). He currently contributes to ***Clarín*** (Argentina), ***El Tiempo*** (Colombia), *La República* (Uruguay) and ***Proceso*** (Mexico).

LAURA SIRI

food and drink

It is difficult to define 'a' Latin American or Caribbean diet, for the simple reason that there is a great diversity within many of the countries as well as between them. There are, however, certain staples that recur across frontiers, defining regional food: for example, the highland areas of the Andean countries, where the **potato** originated and remains central in numerous different forms and varieties; corn (maize) (see **corn and corncakes**), the staple of Mexico, Central America and northern South America, particularly in a great variety of corncakes (*tortillas*, *arepas*, *pupusas*, etc.), but also cooked and eaten on the cob, as well as fermented as ***chicha***; **manioc** (cassava), the main source of carbohydrate in **Amazonia**; and the ubiquitous bean (see **beans**) (Brazilian *feijoada* is one of the many varieties of boiled, stewed and mashed beans), usually paired with rice in the Caribbean, Central America and Brazil. Other areas of the continent, however, have diets based primarily on meat, notably Argentina (see **meat in Argentina**), Uruguay and southern Brazil. Fish is consumed along rivers and seacoasts; the richest fishing grounds are in Peru and Chile, with famous shellfish dishes in Chile and ***ceviche*** in Peru and Ecuador. Although the stereotype holds that Latin American and Caribbean cooking is spicy, particularly with extracts and seeds of the capsicum chile pepper, there are actually several countries where the food is quite bland.

National dishes often reflect the cultural origins of their populations, and serve as symbols of the national 'mix'. Thus, ***sancocho*** or *sancoche* defines parts of the Caribbean, **doubles** and ***roti*** have clear roots in ethnically diverse Trinidad, **pepperpot** combines all the ingredients of Guyanese society and *curanto*, with origins in southern Chile, is now identified as the dish of the whole nation. The *asado* (roast meat), with its almost tribal rituals of consumption, belongs to the **Southern Cone** countries. Pastries filled with meat (*empanadas*) are important in Chile and Argentina, whereas flavoured dough cooked in banana leaves (or corn husks) is favoured farther north in dishes like the Mexican *tamal*, the Caribbean pastrie or *pastel* and the Brazilian *pastel*.

Besides the banana (see **bananas**), tropical America's emblematic export, and the mango, the papaya and the starfruit, there are hundreds of other tropical fruits, many of them unknown outside their country of origin. Many of these are used in juices (often prepared and consumed in the street), preserves and locally made ice creams, which are enormously popular almost everywhere in the continent.

Besides fruit juices, there is huge consumption of soft drinks throughout the continent, most produced by multinational franchises, though sometimes these compete with local alternatives like Inka Cola in Peru, *guaraná* in Brazil and Tropicola in Cuba. The popularity of canned soft drinks is at least partly attributable to the unreliable quality of drinking water in many places, even in major urban areas.

Alcoholic drinks include the fine wine of

Argentina and Chile, and excellent beer, brewed locally in Bolivia and Jamaica, for instance, and produced on a huge industrial scale in Brazil, Argentina and Mexico. Distilled liquors include **tequila and *mezcal*** in Mexico, **rum** throughout the Caribbean, *pisco* in Peru and Chile, ***cachaça*** in Brazil, and numerous other variants on the idea of *aguardiente* throughout the region. Famous mixed drinks include the Cuba Libre and *mojito* in Cuba, *pisco sour* in Peru and Chile, *daiquirí* in the Caribbean, margarita in Mexico and *caipirinha* in Brazil. Alcoholic beverages that are produced and consumed on a more local scale include *pulque* in Mexico and *chicha* in the Andean countries.

See also: Armando Scannone; Laura Esquivel; *Como agua para chocolate*; coffee; sugar; *vatapá*; meals and mealtimes; restaurants; fast food; Mexican cuisine; Nitza Villapol

Further reading

Kennedy, Diane (1972) *The Cuisines of Mexico*, New York: Harper & Row.

Lambert Ortiz, Elisabeth (1980) *The Book of Latin American Cooking*, New York: Vintage.

DANIEL BALDERSTON AND MIKE GONZALEZ

football

Football was brought to Latin America before 1920 by a combination of British settlers, European immigrants and the sons of local exiles who had played the game on educational visits to the old world. It was a modern, urban phenomenon, with the growth in its popularity particularly marked in the expanding cities such as Buenos Aires, Montevideo, Rio de Janeiro, São Paulo and Santiago. Football was one of the factors promoting social intercourse in new migrant communities. Most of the great football clubs of Argentina, Brazil and Uruguay had been established by 1914, together with competitive leagues and international matches. The first regional football organization was established not in Europe but in South America, the Confederación Sudamericana de Fútbol (1916), which has organized the South American Championships since then.

Apart from a few footballing traveller's tales, Europeans were unprepared for the level of skill reached by South American footballers and were astonished by the victory of Uruguay in the 1924 Olympic Tournament. Uruguay beat Argentina in the 1928 final, and defeated their local rivals again in the first **World Cup** in 1930. An unforeseen consequence of these triumphs was a transfer of the best players to Europe, tempted by riches unavailable at home, where open professionalism had replaced the 'shamateurism' of 'tips' in the 1930s. Blacks and poor whites found in football, as in popular music, an opportunity to win fame and fortune. Big crowds flocked to the top matches, which were given near saturation coverage in newspapers, radio, and later television.

During the second half of the century, football became synonymous with Brazil, winner of four World titles (1958, 1962, 1970 and 1994). It was the style of these victories, particularly in 1970, when much of the world saw the match on colour television, which led to the widespread adoption of Brazil as everyone's second favourite team. **Pelé** became the best-known Brazilian, and some Brazilian commentators likened the third World Cup win to Neil Armstrong's walk on the moon. Even critics of successive dictatorial regimes were no longer ashamed to be patriots.

Football was something that Brazil did well. Argentina was not far behind, with World Cup victories in 1978 and 1986. Their greatest star was Diego **Maradona**, who went from traditional rags to riches, particularly when he became the uncrowned King of Naples after leading the team to their first Italian championships in 1987 and 1990. South Americans played an important role in the administration of world football, none more so than the Brazilian millionaire João **Havelange**, President of FIFA (Federation of International Football Associations) from 1974 to 1998.

Football was imported by the elites from Europe, but then returned as a South American export to the old world. In Latin America, football is a passion which cuts across class boundaries, providing excitement, meaning and identity. But as football becomes not merely commercial but a profit-making business, the domestic game in Argentina and Brazil struggles under the weight of too many uncompetitive matches, decreasing crowds, loss of stars and lack of investment. It does not fill empty bellies or provide many jobs. Like patriotism, it is not enough.

Further reading

Archetti, E. (1994) 'Argentina and the World Cup: In Search of National Identity', in J. Sugden and A. Tomlinson (eds), *Hosts and Champions: Soccer Cultures, National Identities and the USA World Cup*, Aldershot: Arena.

Caldas, W. (1990) *O pontapé inicial: memória do futebol brasileiro*, Rio de Janeiro.

Lever, J. (1983) *Soccer Madness*, Chicago: University of Chicago Press.

Mason, T. (1995) *Passion of the People? Football in South America*, London: Verso.

TONY MASON

Foppa, Alaíde

b. 1914, Barcelona; d. 1980, Guatemala

Writer

Foppa grew up in Italy, married Guatemalan politician Mario Solórzano, and adopted Guatemalan citizenship. Exiled in Mexico after the 1954 *coup*, she developed a feminist radio programme in the late 1970s for the **UNAM**, which highlighted the oppression of Mayan women. Foppa published her first collection of feminist poems there in 1970, *Elogio de mi cuerpo* (Eulogy of My Body), and helped to edit the journal **Fem**. Her poetry is intensely lyrical, not always overtly political, and not as strident as the poems of some of the younger women poets. Kidnapped and presumably murdered upon her return to Guatemala in 1980, she is a symbol of women's participation in Guatemalan resistance.

MARC ZIMMERMAN

Forde, A.N.

b. 1923, Barbados

Writer

A multi-faceted writer, Forde has published a one act play, *The Passing Cloud* (1966), a poetry collection, *Canes by the Roadside* (1951), and edited the anthology *Talk of the Tamarinds* (1971). He is well known as a teacher, and has had his work broadcast on the BBC. When the Barbados literary magazine **Bim** was in its heyday, he was one of its editors, contributing stories, poems and essays to it and other journals. His riveting poetic short story, 'Sunday with a Difference', is included in the anthology *From the Green Antilles* (1966).

KEITH JARDIM

Formell, Juan

b. 1942, Havana, Cuba

Musician and composer

Formell was founder and leader of Cuba's most famous contemporary musical group, Los **Van Van**. He played bass with several bands before joining **Orquesta Revé** in 1968. In 1970, when Formell formed Los Van Van, the influence of the Beatles and other British and US rock groups was at its height (because of its isolation, they had come late to Cuba). His band introduced more modern arrangements and sounds into traditional Cuban music. The most highly regarded Cuban composer of popular music both inside and outside the country, Formell's songs often comment on the realities of daily life on the island.

JOSÉ ANTONIO EVORA

Forner, Raquel

b. 1902, Buenos Aires, Argentina; d. 1988, Buenos Aires

Painter

Raquel Forner was one of Argentina's most significant women artists. She studied in Buenos

Aires then travelled to Europe, where she lived from 1929–32. Back in Argentina, she founded the first free art courses with Alfredo **Guterro**. Her work of the 1930s and 1940s is realist and socially concerned, while from the 1950s it is more abstract and poetic, with astronauts as regular subjects.

GABRIEL PEREZ-BARREIRO

Fornes, Rosita

b. 1923, New York, USA

Singer and actress

While still an adolescent, Rosita Fornes (Rosalía Palet Bonavia) appeared on the popular radio show *La Corte Suprema del Arte* (The Supreme Court of Art). Ernesto **Lecuona**, the great Cuban composer, then invited her to join his zarzuela and operetta company when she was only seventeen. Her fine lyrical soprano voice brought immediate recognition and her repertoire came to include popular songs by some of Cuba's most important composers. She has also appeared in some fifteen films produced in Mexico and Cuba. Born in New York during a short visit by her parents, she grew up in Cuba, where she still lives.

JOSÉ ANTONIO EVORA

Fornet, Ambrosio

b. 1932, Bayamo, Oriente, Cuba

Writer

Narrator, essayist and editor, Fornet headed the Arte y Literatura publisher, part of the Cuban National Publishers and later of the National Book Institute, between 1964 and 1971. Educated in the United States and Spain, he was the Cuban delegate to the International PEN Conference at Abidjan, Ivory Coast in 1967; the following year he was secretary of Commission III at the Havana Cultural Congress. His writings have appeared in ***Carteles***, ***Lunes de revolución***, ***Casa de las Américas***, ***Unión*** and ***Revolución y cultura***, as well as in several anthologies and his own volumes of stories and essays.

JOSÉ ANTONIO EVORA

forro

Brazilian music/dance style from the Northeast, traditionally played in trio with accordion, triangle and marching drum. Forro can also include other instruments but, like Louisiana zydeco, remains accordion-led. It is also an umbrella term for other musical styles (xote, xaxado, maxixe and **frevo**). Accordionist and singer Luiz **Gonzaga** popularized the rhythm which is now emblematic of cities like Recife. Many believe the word **forro** derives from the English words 'for all,' having become popular during the early twentieth-century construction boom, when multinational corporations would host parties 'for all'. However, Brazilian dictionaries register forro as a reduced form of *forrobodo* (hop dance, or noisy party).

MARÍA JOSÉ SOMERLATE BARBOSA

Forti, Liber

b. 1917, Tucumán, Argentina

Theatre promoter

Until the age of six, Forti lived in the little town of Tupiza, in Bolivia's Potosí province. Returning to his birthplace in Argentina, he worked in his father's printing shop and began a lifelong project, the dissemination of Bolivian theatre. He founded the magazine ***Nuevos horizontes*** and organized a series of drama courses throughout Bolivia, reaching even its most remote areas. Those who attended became teachers in their turn. The annual 'Teatro de los Barrios' Festival was dedicated to Forti in 1996.

J.M. DE LA VEGA RODRÍGUEZ

Fortunato, René

b. 1959, Santo Domingo, Dominican Republic

Film-maker

Film critic Fortunato studied social communication at the Universidad Autónoma de Santo Domingo. In 1985 he made his first documentary *Tras las huellas de Palau* (In Search of Palau), a tribute to Dominican photography pioneer Francisco Arturo Palau. His most celebrated work is *Abril: la trinchera del honor* (April: The Trench of Honor) (1988), which analyzes the 1965 April War. Subsequently, he made the documentary series *Trujillo: El poder del Jefe* (**Trujillo**: The Power of the Chief) (1991) about the dictatorship. Fortunato's works have won awards in international film festivals.

FERNANDO VALERIO-HOLGUÍN

fotonovelas

A genre of photo-based narratives of great popularity throughout Latin America, the *fotonovela* evolved from retellings of film stories using stills from movies. The most typical *fotonovela* tells a love story using black and white photographs adorned with balloon captions for the dialogue; typical titles are *Cariño mío* (My Sweetheart), *Amores juveniles* (Young Loves), *Cita de lujo* (Luxury Date) and *Historias de mujer* (Female Stories). A close relative of the *telenovela* (see **telenovelas**), it shares with it a marked melodramatic proclivity and popularity among lower-class urban women. However, the form has also been appropriated for telling other kinds of stories: several subgenres are aimed specifically at men, for example the adventure stories (the *fotoaventura*), masked wrestler tales (like the Mexican **Santo**) or explicit pornography. Within the last decade, the *fotonovela* format has also been used by national and international health organizations in informational campaigns and has proved quite effective in **AIDS** education efforts throughout the continent. Furthermore, the *fotonovela* format has also been adopted by artists seeking alternatives to the static, single-image paradigm of traditional photography and who are trying to connect with the *fotonovela*'s refreshingly accessible and entertaining rendering of human relations.

The *fotonovela* was initiated by large French and Italian publishers before World War Two and gained wide distribution in Latin America (and North Africa) in the 1950s. By the 1970s, although imports were still significant, the bulk of production had shifted to indigenous publishers like Bloch Editores and **Editora Abril** in Brazil. Mexican-produced *fotonovelas* have the widest distribution; many are photographed in Mexico (featuring up-and-coming TV actors) but printed in Miami or Los Angeles. A typical run of a single issue can be anywhere between 100,000 and 400,000, but the actual readership is much larger: purchased issues are passed on among family members and friends, and most working-class neighbourhoods also have a rental 'library' where issues can be circulated for years. Despite their great profitability, *fotonovelas* are scorned by publishers as 'pot boilers', necessary only to sustain their more legitimate activities (like women's magazines, which often contain a *fotonovela* insert).

Like many popular, mass-mediated, fiction genres, part of the pleasure derived from the *fotonovela* stems from its inherent escapism: it offers self-contained worlds in which disaffections stemming from the injustices of daily life can be channelled and where readers find imaginary solutions. In so doing, the genre also offers a powerful tool for mediating the complexities of everyday urban life.

Further reading

Bulter Flora, C. and Flora, J. (1978) 'The fotonovelas as a tool for class and cultural domination', *Latin American Perspectives* 5(1), winter.

Flores, R.D. (1995) *Fotonovela Argentina: Heredera del melodrama*, Buenos Aires: Asociación Argentina de Editores de Revistas.

Levy Reed, J. (1998) 'The Fotonovela', special issue of *Camerawork: A Journal of Photographic Arts* 25(2), fall/winter.

ANA M. LÓPEZ

Franceschi, Gustavo

b. 1871, Corsica; d. 1957, Buenos Aires, Argentina

Cleric, editor, sociologist and philosopher

Franceschi was an ultra-conservative priest who played a crucial role in the development and course of Argentina's Catholic nationalist movement. As a conservative activist, lecturer and author, Franceschi was the intellectual representative of the influential but minority right-wing Catholic movement still influential in Argentine theology and politics. He was ordained in 1902, and taught philosophy at the Catholic University of Buenos Aires and sociology and Catholic social thought at the primary seminary. He wrote a noted column and edited the conservative Catholic review **Criterio** from 1933 until his death.

THOMAS EDSALL

Francia, Aldo

b. 1923, Valparaíso, Chile

Film-maker and physician

Part of the **New Latin American Cinema** movement of the 1960s, and associated with the **Viña del Mar Festival**, Francia began to make short films after obtaining his medical degree. His later films were characterized by their critical approach to official history and their exploration of questions of social reality and national identity. Francia produced two features: *Valparaíso, mi amor* (Valparaíso, My Love) (1969), and *Ya no basta con rezar* (Praying is No Longer Enough) (1972). The third part of a projected trilogy was never completed because of post-1973 censorship; Francia has since abandoned film-making and continues to practice medicine.

LUIS E. CÁRCAMO-HUECHANTE

Franco, Siron

b. 1947, Goiás Velho, Brazil

Painter and installation artist

Born into a poor family in the centre-west state of Goiás, Franco's background would suggest little in the way of artistic training. His first self-taught experiments date from the late 1950s, when he informally joined an open air studio. By the early 1960s he was able to make some money from society portraits and minor graphic design commissions. In 1968, he entered and won a prize at the Bahia Bienal, which gave him the encouragement to attempt a career as an artist. Franco's first works in an independent style date from 1970, in which machines and men are combined in fantastic combinations. By 1973, his works show more of an engagement with the painterly material, and also an interest in the grotesque and the deformed. These early works show similar concerns to the Mexican artist José Luis **Cuevas** and also to his fellow Goiás artist Ana María **Pacheco**. Favourite subjects include corrupt businessmen, politicians and soldiers. In the mid-1970s he used this now characteristic figurative style in a series called *Fabulas de horror* (Horror Fables). This series launched him as a successful artist. Franco won two important travel prizes, the first (1973) to Mexico, where he saw Cuevas's works, and the second to Madrid (1976). In 1980 he began his most important series to date, called *Semelhantes* (Likenesses). These works show a bold and loose sense of colour, which was to become a major interest. The *Semelhantes* combined interests in ecology, politics, sex and the darker side of human existence. By the late 1980s, he had developed a series of paintings based on animal pelts which show an increasing concern with ecology and also with the abstract textural qualities of paint.

A nuclear accident in Goiânia (where the artist now lived away from the dominant Rio–São Paulo cultural centres) in 1987 launched a turning point in his work. The desire to record the horrors of the accident coincided with a period of intense public activity. A series of paintings inspired by the accident mark a more serious and committed attitude to his work as a painter and as a social agitator. Following the nuclear accident Siron became increasingly interested in installation art, and made a series of provocative public works, usually self-commissioned. His painting became increasingly abstract and complex, with a series of 'magical object' paintings in the 1990s. By this time he had become a national figure in Brazil for his social activities and his international success as a painter.

Further reading

Ades, D. (1995), *Siron Franco: Figures and Likenesses*, Rio de Janeiro: Index.

GABRIEL PEREZ-BARREIRO

Francovich, Guillermo

b. 1901, Sucre, Bolivia; d. 1990, Rio de Janeiro, Brazil

Philosopher

A central figure in the history of ideas in Bolivia, Francovich's key works include *La filosofía en Bolivia* (Philosophy in Bolivia) (1945) and *El pensamiento boliviano en el siglo XX* (Twentieth Century Bolivian Thought) (1956). His philosophical essays, like *Filósofos brasileños* (Brazilian Philosophers) (1939), attempted to recuperate the Latin American intellectual tradition. He was also a playwright, and in his seventies produced a volume on *El estructuralismo* (Structuralism) (1973) and its reception in Latin America. Francovich was also a diplomat, and for ten years was Director of the Regional Centre of UNESCO in Havana, Cuba.

ISABEL BASTOS

Frank, André Gunder

b. 1929, Berlin, Germany

Political economist

Frank shot to fame in the late 1960s with his thesis of 'the development of underdevelopment', which argues that the underdeveloped countries made a major contribution to the **development** of today's developed countries which, at the same time, were responsible for the underdevelopment of Latin America, Asia and Africa. Linked to this thesis is his argument that Latin America became capitalist with the Spanish and Portuguese conquest in the sixteenth century. These propositions had a major influence on **dependency theory** and on mode of production debates.

The significance of Frank's intervention was mainly political. In arguing that capitalism was the cause of Latin America's underdevelopment and responsible for its continuation, he challenged the orthodox Latin American **communist parties**, who proclaimed that Latin America was still largely feudal and that the popular forces should therefore support the national bourgeoisie in fulfilling its revolutionary task of completing the transition from feudalism to capitalism. This bourgeoisie would in turn facilitate the growth of the proletariat. According to Frank, the Latin American bourgeoisie was only perpetuating the development of underdevelopment and therefore, following the example of the Cuban Revolution (see **revolutions**), capitalism had to be overthrown because only socialism could eliminate underdevelopment.

Frank emigrated with his family in 1933, from Nazi Germany to the USA. Educated in the USA, in 1957 he received a Ph.D. in economics from the University of Chicago. He visited Cuba in 1960 soon after the revolution, which had a lasting influence on him. From 1962 to 1973 he spent most of his time in Latin America, teaching at universities in Mexico, Brazil and Chile. This was a particularly creative period for Latin American social scientists who were inspired by, and often participated in, the social and political upheavals of the time. He was able to observe at close hand the events during **Allende**'s ill-fated 'Chilean road to socialism' (1970–3) as a researcher at the University of Chile's Center for Socio-Economic Studies (CESO), the hotbed of dependency theory in Latin America.

Frank was politically committed to national liberation and socialist revolution. He regarded the dilemma facing Latin America as lying between 'capitalist underdevelopment or socialist revolution', as appeared in the sub-title of his essay, 'Who is the Immediate Enemy?', first published in the Cuban journal *Pensamiento Crítico* (1968), in which he advanced the following thesis: 'The immediate enemy of national liberation in Latin America tactically is the native bourgeoisie.... This is so – in Asia and Africa included – notwithstanding that strategically the principal enemy undoubtedly is imperialism.' He has published more than a dozen books and hundreds of articles in the past two decades. He continues to be an internationally renowned figure, but the peak of his fame was in the 1960s and 1970s.

See also: Faletto, Enzo; Cardoso, Fernando Henrique

Further reading

Chew, S.C. and Denemark, R.A. (eds) (1996) *The Underdevelopment of Development*, Thousand Oaks, CA: Sage Publications.

Frank, A.G. (1967) *Capitalism and Underdevelopment in Latin America*, New York: Monthly Review Press.

CRISTÓBAL KAY

Franqui, Carlos

b. 1921, Cifuentes, Cuba

Writer and journalist

Of working-class origins, Franqui joined the struggle against the dictatorship of Fulgencio **Batista** at an early age, and suffered imprisonment and exile as a result. In 1955 he created *Revolución*, the underground journal of the 26th of July Movement led by Fidel **Castro**. In 1958 he joined the armed struggle in the Sierra Maestra and became director of the rebel radio station, Radio Rebelde. In 1959, with the victory of the Cuban Revolution, he became editor of *Revolución* and was the inspiration behind its cultural supplement, ***Lunes de revolución***, until 1963, when he was dismissed. In 1968 he assisted in the organization of the Cultural Congress in Havana, and shortly thereafter went into exile in Italy. In 1993 he moved to Puerto Rico. His publications include *El libro de los doce* (The Book of the Twelve) (1966), about the development of the guerrilla war in Cuba, *Retrato de familia con Fidel* (Family Portrait with Fidel) (1981) and *Vida, aventura y desastres de un hombre llamado Fidel* (The Life, Adventures and Disasters of a Man Called Fidel) (1988). In he founded and has since edited *Carta de Cuba*, a bulletin publishing reports from independent Cuban journalists.

WILFREDO CANCIO ISLA

Fray, Manuel Antonio

b. 1897, Curaçao; d. 1967, Curaçao

Novelist

Fray (also spelled Fraai) was one of a small group of authors who, in the decades before the Second World War, were the first to write in the creole **Papiamentu**. In his youth Fray was a seaman, and he travelled widely throughout the Caribbean before settling on his native island and becoming a civil servant. At first he strongly defended Roman Catholicism in his thesis novels and lengthy articles for local newspapers. His later prose writing was less pronouncedly Roman Catholic, but it retained a strong didactic tone.

AART G. BROEK

Frei Montalva, Eduardo

b.1910, Santiago, Chile; d. 1982, Santiago

Politician

As candidate for the Christian Democratic Party, Frei was elected President of Chile for the term 1964–70, a time of political confrontation between sectors from the right, left and centre. Important events that occurred during his government included educational reforms, extensive **agrarian reform**, and nationalization of the Electric Company and of a controlling percentage of copper mining, which at the time generated over 80 per cent of national income. The author of numerous political and moralistic works, Frei was married to María Ruiz Tagle and had seven children, including Eduardo **Frei Ruiz Tagle**.

AMALIA PEREIRA

Frei Ruiz Tagle, Eduardo

b. 1942, Santiago, Chile

Politician

Son of ex-President Eduardo **Frei Montalva**, Frei was elected President of Chile for the term 1994–2000 as the Christian Democrat representative of the centre-left Coalition for Democracy. He is the second president of the transition to democracy initiated with the end of **Pinochet**'s dictatorship in 1990. Because of Frei's support for free market economics and the country's political stability, Chile reached record levels of foreign investment and gross domestic product grew at a 7 per cent annual rate during his presidency. However, in March of 1995, the Coalition government did not win the Congressional majority required to reform the old Consitution, which restricts certain political liberties, and the government was much criticized for its attempts to block the extradition of Pinochet from the UK to Spain in 1998.

AMALIA PEREIRA

Freire, Paulo

b. 1921, Recife, Brazil; d. 1997, São Paulo, Brazil

Educator

With the publication in 1970 of his seminal work *Pedagogia do Oprimido* (Pedagogy of the Oppressed), Paulo Freire achieved worldwide acclaim as one of the most important educational thinkers of modern times. From his work in the early 1960s with marginalized groups in northeastern Brazil he concluded that, politically, **education** could never remain neutral: traditional education promoted the values of the dominant classes, ignored the real-life knowledge and experience of the 'oppressed', and maintained a social order in which the oppressed came to blame themselves, not the oppressors, for their destitution. He argued for an education which would 'liberate' rather than 'domesticate', which would enable people to both understand the structures of oppression and try to do something about them. Only the oppressed themselves can bring about their own liberation – it cannot be done by revolutionary vanguards – and education should contribute to this 'empowerment'. Freire's greatest contribution is to have developed a pedagogical method which helps educators do this, with the 'Freirian method' of teaching **literacy** gaining particular renown.

Freire was first jailed then exiled after the Brazilian *coup* of 1964 and worked most notably in Chile and Guinea Bissau before returning to Brazil in 1980. Some of his ideas have been co-opted by less radical educationists, his politics were criticized from both left and right and there has been constant discussion of his relevance to a 'first world' context. He remains a key figure in Latin American **popular education**.

Freire used the term 'banking education' to describe a process in which educators are seen as bearers of truth who 'deposit' their knowledge in the learner's empty mind. This process 'dehumanizes', claimed Freire, as it puts no value on the knowledge which people already have. Denied the chance to examine and articulate their own view of the world, the oppressed are thus encouraged to be passive 'objects' while the oppressors become the 'subjects' of history. Though Freire's initial target is the oppressor, he was equally critical of revolutionaries who practise 'banking education', albeit with a different 'truth' to deposit.

In Freire's view, an education committed to the oppressed should liberate people to become 'subjects' of change. It should value what people already know about the world and should be based on dialogue between educators and students in which each group learns from the other. It should challenge students to analyse their own reality more deeply, a process which itself will lead to an awareness of the structures of oppression and which Freire called '*conscientização*' (**conscientization**, or consciousness-raising). The educator's role is not to provide solutions but to pose problems, ask questions and help learners look objectively at their own everyday experience. In Freirian classes (or 'culture circles'), for example, learners would typically analyse and discuss photographs that reflected important issues in their lives. Crucially, the educator will encourage the group to consider what action they might take to change their reality, action which, if taken, will then be the subject of analysis. With the aim of helping the oppressed to change the world, education should be an ongoing process of action, reflection and action, an idea that has come to form an integral part of popular education throughout Latin America.

Freire was probably most famous for his literacy work. He argued that in itself, literacy was of no use to the oppressed unless it helped them understand the world better (what he called 'reading the world') in order to be able to change it. In the Freirian method, instead of dealing with letters and sounds, the teaching of literacy should focus from the start on whole words (or even phrases) representing aspects of the learners' experience which are likely to generate discussion ('landowners', 'migration', 'refugee', for example). Coincidentally, these words should also generate the different sounds which have to be learned and in Portuguese or Spanish this can be done with as few as fifteen words. (In teaching literacy to refugees in Latin America, for example, the word 're-fu-gi-a-do' would be 'generative' in both senses used by Freire.) By encouraging learners to write about their reality from an early stage, the process seeks to develop skills of literacy and social analysis side by side. It has generally proved an effective way to teach literacy.

Freire's intellectual inspiration came from a wide variety of sources, such as classical philosophy, **liberation theology** and Che **Guevara**. He was often described as an eclectic thinker who discovered nothing new but whose genius lay in having synthesized great ideas into an identifiable educational practice. His eclecticism can give rise to different interpretations, however, and in practice it is possible to be selective about aspects of Freire's work: his literacy method, for example, has been co-opted by reactionary educators who ignore the political vision on which it is based. Seen as too political by the right, he is accused by Marxists of vagueness in his discussion of oppression and of overemphasizing the importance of cultural, as opposed to economic, domination.

On returning to Brazil from exile, Freire joined the **PT** or Workers Party and became Secretary of Education in São Paulo from January 1989 until May 1991. In 1992 he published *Pedagogia da Esperança* (Pedagogy of Hope), in which he responds to more than twenty years of review and critique of *Pedagogy of the Oppressed*. He also claimed to have become more radical as he grew older, and he optimistically addressed the challenges facing liberatory education at the end of the 1990s.

Further reading

Freire, P. (1978) *Pedagogy in Process*, London: Writers and Readers Publishing Cooperative.
—— (1994) *Pedagogy of Hope*, New York: Continuum.
—— (1996) *Pedagogy of the Oppressed*, London: Penguin.
Taylor, P.V. (1993) *Texts of Paulo Freire*, Buckingham: Open University Press.
Youngman, F. (1986) *Adult Education and Socialist Pedagogy*, London: Routledge.

LIAM KANE

French, Stanley

b. 1937, Castries, St Lucia

Playwright

Stanley French is the most outstanding St Lucian playwright after Derek and Roderick **Walcott**. Educated in St Lucia and England, French is a civil engineer. He writes in the realistic mode and often examines the predicaments of colonial and neo-colonial subjects. His plays explore Christianity in the Caribbean, the conflict between tradition and modernity, between the political elite/leaders and the general citizenry and the nature of the language continuum in St. Lucia. His plays include *The Rape of Fair Helen* (1983), *No Pain, No Play* (1972), *Under a Sky of Incense* (1981), *Ballad of a Man and Dog* (1970) and *The Light and the Dark* (1970).

FUNSO AIYEJINA

French Antilles

The French Overseas Departments in the Caribbean are the islands of Guadeloupe and Martinique and the mainland territory of French Guyana in South America. Along with Haiti and

Quebec, they represent the oldest areas of French settlement in the Americas. They share with the Caribbean a history of plantation slavery based upon uprooted Africans working on sugar estates. Unlike Haiti and other Caribbean neighbours, these colonies are not independent but chose to become French departments in 1946, consequently cementing a historical bond with France and benefiting from an artificially high standard of living.

These Departments are as different from each other as they are from the rest of the region. Guadeloupe is the larger of the two islands, both of which are volcanic, with populations approximating 400,000. Because of their special relationship with France, many Guadeloupeans and Martinicans live in France where the French West Indian community in Paris is known as 'the third island'. In contrast to Martinique which is more French, and has an influential white creole or *beke* class and light-skinned middle class, Guadeloupe has always been more politically volatile with a predominantly black population and significant East Indian minority. With only a third of the population of the island Departments and a relatively large land mass, French Guyana is the least developed of the Departments with an extremely diverse population. What these Departments all have in common, however, is their transformation from traditional agricultural societies to tertiarized, consumer economies since the 1960s. This has meant the decline of local productivity, massive Europeanization and the threat of cultural extinction.

Marked by French education and intellectual traditions, these societies have made major contributions to Caribbean literature. Martinique stands out as the island of intellectuals as opposed to Guadeloupe, with a significant but small number of women writers, and French Guyana, which has only a handful of writers with international reputations. Writers like Aimé **Césaire**, Frantz **Fanon**, Edouard **Glissant** and Patrick **Chamoiseau** have produced various theories of cultural difference that led to movements such as ***négritude***, Antillanité and **Créolité**. The Departments have also made significant contributions to popular culture through music, including **zouk**, which can be traced back to earlier musical forms like the **béguine** and the mazurka, and rhythmic traditions like the bel air and gwo-ka. The most popular exponent of zouk is the group **Kassav'**, which in the spirit of the Creolité movement sings only in creole and has dominated French West Indian music since 1979.

Further reading

Burton, R. and Reno, F. (ed.) (1995) *French and West Indian: Martinique, Guadeloupe and French Guyana Today*, London: Macmillan.

J. MICHAEL DASH

French-based creoles

Because French-based creoles rely essentially on French for their lexical terms, there is a popular misconception that these languages derive from French. As is the case with the other creole languages, those with a French-based lexicon developed in territories where French was the dominant language, including Trinidad and Grenada, where the French were the socially and numerically dominant linguistic group even though the area was under the political control of others. The French-lexicon creoles boast more speakers than any other group of creoles, though they are concentrated in the southern half of the Caribbean region.

The French lexicon creoles of the region are spoken in the French Departments of Guadeloupe, Martinique and Cayenne, as well as in former French colonies such as Haiti; they are also the main language of the majority of the population in the officially English-speaking territories of Dominica and St Lucia. In Trinidad and Grenada, there are still small pockets of French-lexicon creole communities, though they have had no history of being French territories.

On the basis of their morphosyntactic structure, the French-lexicon creoles of the region have been divided into Greater and Lesser Antillean varieties. They are mutually intelligible despite obvious but minor phonological, morphological and syntactic differences between them. In fact, the French lexicon creoles of the Caribbean are also intelligible on the Indian ocean islands of Mauritius and Réunion and in Louisiana in the United States.

See also: creole languages; Haitian creole

Further reading

Byrne, F. and Huebner, T. (eds) (1991) *Development and Structure of Creole languages*, John Benjamins.

Balutanus, K.M. (ed.) *Caribbean Creolization: Reflections on the Cultural Dynamics of Language, Literature and Identity*, Gainesville, FL: University of Florida Press.

Holm, J.A. (1988) *Pidgins and Creoles*, 2 vols, Cambridge: Cambridge University Press.

IAN ROBERTSON

French Guyana

Considered Latin America's most isolated state, French Guyana (capital: Cayenne) is the only French-speaking outpost on the continent. Despite its underdevelopment, it enjoys a high standard of living because of its status as an Overseas Department. French Guyanese identity as a penal colony (Devil's Island) is adversely affected not only by its inauspicious beginnings and haphazard development, but also by the problem of illegal immigration from neighbouring states, especially Haiti, and by the powerful presence of the European Space Programme at Kourou. The sense of marginalization is reinforced by the fact that the Department's most important writers, like René **Maran** and León **Damas**, have chosen to live outside their native land.

J. MICHAEL DASH

Frente Amplio

In response to imperialistic practices and economic deterioration, this 'broad front' coalition party, led by Zelmar Michelini, arose on 5 February 1971 in Montevideo to unite Uruguay's traditional left. With the 1973 *coup* d'état, the Frente was outlawed. In 1984, when it was once again legalized, Líber Seregni was declared the party's leader. In 1989 the Frente Amplio won in Montevideo, electing the Socialist Tabaré Vázquez to the municipal administration. Ironically, the diversity once celebrated within the party grew into opposition and tension, causing dissension during its rule.

VICTORIA RUÉTALO

Frente Homosexual de Acción Revolucionaria

Frente Homosexual de Acción Revolucionaria (Revolutionary Homosexual Action Front) (FHAR) was the first militant Mexican gay organization founded in the late 1970s, alongside the Grupo Lambda de Liberación Homosexual and Oikabeth. FHAR was inspired by socialist and anarchist ideology, but remained largely male and, at times, misogynist. Its policy was confrontational and short-lived. It ceased to exist in the mid-1980s, only to be succeeded by smaller initiatives (Guerrilla Gay, Círculo Cultural Gay, Grupo Homosexual de Acción Revolucionaria and the Colectivo Sol) founded by ex-FHAR members and focusing on the organization of gay and lesbian archives as well as on support and education about **AIDS**.

PATRICIA TORRES SAN MARTÍN

Frente Negra Brasileira

The Frente Negra Brasileira (Black Brazilian Front) was founded in the wake of the 1930 Revolution by Afro-Brazilian leaders of São Paulo who had been associated with the newspaper *O Clarim d'Alvorada* and the Palmares Civic Center in the late 1920s. Emphasizing moral uplift, education, self-determination and political activism, it attracted working and middle-class Afro-Brazilians. Supporting Getulio **Vargas**'s nationalist government and praising its support for native workers over European immigrant labour, the front and its official paper *A voz da raça* (The Voice of the Race) became increasingly dominated by right-wing xenophobic ideologues.

CHRISTOPHER DUNN

Fresa y chocolate

Fresa y chocolate (Strawberry and Chocolate) (1993) was the eleventh feature film by Tomás **Gutiérrez Alea**, and the first that he co-directed with Juan Carlos **Tabío** (the other was *Guantanamera* (1995)). Based on the story 'El lobo, el bosque y el hombre nuevo' (The Wolf, the Forest and the New Man) by Senel **Paz**, who also wrote the screenplay, it is the story of the meeting between David, a young university student and militant communist, and Diego, a homosexual, in an ice cream parlour in central Havana. The friendship that develops undermines David's prejudices, homophobia and political dogmatism; his understanding of what it means to be Cuban changes as a result of his conversations with Diego. Gutiérrez Alea frequently repeated Paz's declaration that the theme was not homosexuality but intolerance. The film had a tremendous impact within and outside Cuba, where it played a key role in attempting to address discrimination against gays in Cuba. It is the only Cuban film ever nominated (in 1995) for an Oscar.

JOSÉ ANTONIO EVORA

Fresnedo Siri, Román

b. 1903, Salto, Uruguay; d. 1975

Architect

Fresnedo Siri was the designer of more than one hundred projects in Uruguay including the Auditorium of **SODRE**, the Palacio de la Luz, the Varig Tower and more than fifteen buildings in the health sector. A graduate of Columbia University's Planning and Housing department (1941), in 1961 he won first prize in an international competition to design the headquarters of the Organización Panamericana de Salud (Panamerican Health Organization) in Washington, and in 1971 for the same organization's headquarters in **Brasília**.

MARCO MAGGI

frevo

The frevo is a fast and frenetic dance rhythm originally from the northeastern state of Pernambuco. Its name is derived from *ferver*, which means to boil. Captain José Lourenço da Silva of the Pernambuco Military Brigade Band is often credited with inventing the rhythm in 1909 by increasing the tempo and syncopation of the polka-marcha. Within a decade it had become the premiere rhythm of the Recife **carnival** and was exported to Salvador in 1950 by the creators of the **trio elétrico**. Its popularity began to wane in the 1980s with the advent of **samba-reggae** and **axé** music.

CHRISTOPHER DUNN

Freyre, Gilberto

b. 1900, Recife, Brazil; d. 1987, Recife

Social historian and writer

Freyre's extensive work embraces anthropology, sociology, literature and, most notably, social history. He came to prominence in 1926 when he launched the Northeast Regionalist Movement in Recife with the aim of promoting and protecting the cultural traditions of the region, which Freyre saw as threatened by economic modernization and the emergence of mass culture and eclipsed by the urban dynamism of Rio de Janeiro and São Paulo. The movement called for action to preserve the traditions of the northeast and to research regional customs and folklore. It revealed the conservative approach to culture that characterized Freyre's later work, but it also stimulated intellectual and artistic activity in the northeast, including the production of regionalist literature by authors like José Lins do **Rego** (see **regionalism**).

Although in his major works Freyre addressed questions of national cultural formation, his primary concern for the northeast is evident in much of his writing. The key issues and themes that would dominate his later work were established in ***Casa grande e senzala*** (The Masters and the Slaves), published in 1933, which is one of the most influential and widely read Brazilian twentieth-century texts. It is an innovative work, which combines new methods of anthropological and sociological investigation which Freyre assimilated while studying in the USA with a clear and fluid literary style influenced by **Brazilian modernism**. It also presented a positive and optimistic evaluation of Brazil's cultural development, countering the negative interpretations rooted in late nineteenth-century determinist theories. Freyre argued that the adaptability and tolerance of the Portuguese and the dynamic process of miscegenation had created a distinct and unified national culture with considerable potential. For some, Freyre's work seeks to create a mythical cultural homogeneity for Brazil, while others argue that his theories on the positive achievements of Portuguese colonialism serve to justify it. Nonetheless, no one has made a greater contribution to the study of Brazilian social history, for which his texts are still essential reading.

Further reading

Freyre, G. (1963) *The Mansions and the Shanties: The Making of Modern Brasil*, New York: Knopf.
—— (1956) *The Masters and the Slaves: A Study in the Development of Brazilian Civilization*, New York: Knopf.
Andrade, M. (1995) *Gilberto Freyre: pensamento e acao/ organizacao e apresentacao*, Recife: Editoro Massangana.
Coutinho, E. (1994) *Gilberto Freyre*, Rio de Janeiro: Agir.
Piñeiro Iñiguez, C. (1999) *Sueños paralelos: Gilberto Freyre y el lusotropicalismo: identidad, cultura y política en Brasil y Portugal*, Buenos Aires: Nuevohacer.

MARK DINNEEN

Frida, naturaleza viva

Frida, naturaleza viva (Frida, Moving Life) was the third documentary by Paul **Leduc**, one of Mexico's most talented directors of the 1970s and 1980s, which was both an aesthetic achievement and a commercial success. The 1984 film follows the tormented life of the Mexican painter Frida **Kahlo** in a creative interplay of spaces and times, a collage of images beautifully photographed by Angel Goded. It is a visual tribute with a minimum of dialogue and a finely detailed soundtrack. As usual with Leduc, photography and atmosphere are the key elements, as well as, in this case, the extraordinary performance of Ofelia **Medina** as Kahlo.

PATRICIA TORRES SAN MARTÍN

Friedemann, Nina S. de

b. 1935, Santafé de Bogotá, Colombia

Anthropologist

Since 1965, Friedemann has concentrated her research mainly among Afro-Colombian communities. She has also studied extensively the celebration of **carnival** in different Colombian communities with special emphasis on Afro-Colombian contributions. She founded the journal *América Negra* magazine. Her writings include *Lengua y sociedad en el Palenque de San Basilio* (Language and Society in San Basilio Palenque) (1983), *Carnaval en Barranquilla* (Carnival in Barranquilla) (1985), and *Ma NGombe, guerreros y ganaderos en Palenque* (Ma NGombe, Warriors and Cattle Raisers in Palenque) (1987).

MIGUEL A. CARDINALE

Frómeta, Billo

b. 1915, Santo Domingo, Dominican Republic; d. 1988, Caracas, Venezuela

Musician

Frómeta (Luis María Frómeta Pereyra) arrived in Venezuela in 1937 as musical director of Billo's Happy Boys, renamed Billo's Caracas Boys in 1940. It became the most popular dance band in the country until the death of its founder and director. Singers of national and international stature performed with the band at different times, including Manolo Monterrey, Cheo García, Felipe Parela, Memo Morales and José Luis **Rodríguez** El Puma. He arranged many of the most popular Caribbean songs, but Caracas was always his favourite musical subject. His successes included 'Ariel', 'El profesor Rirúa', 'Yolanda', 'Oye Isidoro', 'Vicente chico' and 'Bella Caracas' (Beautiful Caracas).

JORGE ROMERO LEÓN

frontera *see* borders

FSLN

The Frente Sandinista de Liberación Nacional (FSLN) was founded in 1961 by Carlos **Fonseca Amador**, Silvio Mayorga and Tomás **Borge**, with the purpose of overthrowing the Somoza dictatorship (see **Somoza dynasty**). It adopted the name Sandinista (see **Sandinista Revolution**) two years later. The organization was modelled on Fidel **Castro**'s 26th of July Movement, and believed that **guerrilla warfare** was the only way to implement political change. From 1962 until the mid-1970s the FSLN grew slowly, operating clandestinely as a single guerrilla (*foco*) group in the mountainous jungles of central Nicaragua. The FSLN's first attempt at guerrilla warfare in 1963 ended with their defeat at El Chaparral by Somoza's National Guard. In 1967 Fonseca led the guerrillas against the National Guard in the mountains of Matagalpa and was defeated at Pancasan.

In the 1970s, the failure of most guerrilla fronts led Latin American revolutionaries to reassess their strategies. The electoral victory of the Unidad Popular (**Popular Unity** Coalition) in Chile in 1970 led all Latin American guerrilla groups, including the FSLN, to rethink their military and political tactics. Consequently, the FSLN suffered an internal schism and split into three factions: the Proletarians, who aimed at building a Leninist revolutionary party; the Prolonged People's War (GPP), which followed the original rural *foco* strategy; and the Insurrectional Tendency (**Terceristas**), who advocated immediate urban and rural insurrection and a tactical alliance with all anti-Somoza forces, including the bourgeoisie. The FSLN grew rapidly in late 1978 and early 1979, leading a maximum of some 5,000 troops for the final offensive against Somoza in June and July 1979 which united the three factions of the FSLN.

Because of its military leadership and its role in organizing the final opposition coalition, the FSLN was the major voice in the new government that took power in July 1979. A five-person Government Junta of National Reconstruction was established, consisting of two Conservatives, one pro-Sandinista intellectual and two FSLN guerrilla veterans. From 1979 to 1990, the FSLN promoted a mixed economy with heavy participation by the private sector, political pluralism featuring inter-class dialogue and efforts to institutionalize input and feedback from all sectors, and ambitious social programmes based on grassroots voluntarism. It maintained good diplomatic and economic relations with as many nations as possible, regardless of ideology. The failure of many of their economic programmes was largely due to the contra war (see **contras**) and other US-orchestrated destabilization programmes. In 1990, the FSLN finally lost the elections to Violeta **Chamorro** and the **UNO**, a US-sponsored opposition coalition.

Further reading

Borge, T. *et al.* (1982) *Sandinistas Speak*, New York: Pathfinder.
Hodges, D. (1986) *Intellectual Foundations of the Nicaraguan Revolution*, Austin: University of Texas Press.
Walker, T. (ed.) (1985) *Nicaragua: The First Five Years*, New York: Praeger.

ANUPAMA MANDE AND ILEANA RODRÍGUEZ

Fuad, Jorge Jury *see* Favio, Leonardo

Fuentes, Carlos

b. 1928, Panama City

Writer

Fuentes is one of the leading Hispanic American literary figures of the twentieth century, associated with the so-called **Boom** of the 1960s. His numerous works include novels and short stories as well as plays and essays. Because of his eloquence and his deep understanding of the present and past reality of Latin America, he has come to be regarded, mainly in the USA, as a sort of spokesman for the sub-continent.

The son of a Mexican diplomat, Fuentes was born in Panama City and lived in Quito, Montevideo and Rio de Janeiro before attending primary school in Washington, DC. He went to secondary school in Santiago, Buenos Aires and Mexico City. He studied law at the Institut des Hautes Études Internationales in Geneva (1950) and at the National University of Mexico, **UNAM** (1951). He was the secretary to the Mexican delegation to the International Law Commission of the United Nations in Geneva (1951) and Director of Cultural Affairs at the Mexican Ministry of Foreign Affairs (1957). His literary awards have included the Xavier Villaurrutia Prize (1975), the Rómulo Gallegos Prize (1977), the Mexican National Prize for Letters (1984) and the Cervantes Prize (1987).

His main contribution to Hispanic-American literature may be found among his narrative texts as well as in his essays. Conscious of the traditions born out of his special background that includes the heritages of Hispanic, English and French cultures and literatures, his writings are rooted in Cervantes and Quevedo, in Shakespeare and Joyce, in Flaubert and Balzac as well as in Dostoevsky and Thomas Mann.

Los días enmascarados (Masked Days), a collection of six short stories, marked his literary debut in 1954. 'Chac Mool', the first story, is now regarded as a small masterpiece of the fantastic genre. His first novel, *La región más transparente* (Where the Air is Clear) (1958), is a portrait of Mexico in the 1950s, particularly of Mexico City and its multi-levelled middle class where Fuentes belongs. Its experimental character regarding language and new novelistic forms was acclaimed as the breakthrough of a most promising young narrative talent. But it was *La muerte de Artemio Cruz* (The Death of Artemio Cruz) (1962) that established its author as a first-class novelist. Many regard this novel as his masterpiece. It is the story of the social and economic rise – and corruption – of a man who participated in the Mexican Revolution (see **revolutions**); it can be read as the history of the corruption of the revolution. This novel's remarkably dynamic narrative includes, among other devices, interior monologues, juxtaposing of narrative points of view, masterful handling of time as well as first, second and third-person narration, all within the memory of the dying protagonist. All this is done with extremely realistic language. It projects ethical meaning through a most accomplished aesthetic virtuosity.

Aura (1962) and *Cumpleaños* (Birthday) (1970) are two short novels related by their intertextuality and by their common themes: identity and time. The story in the novel *Cambio de piel* (A Change of Skin) (1967) takes place in Cholula, a pre-Hispanic religious centre, in the 1960s. It has been suggested that the central role played by history in *Aura* and the tense co-existence of Cholula's past with the characters present in *Cambio de Piel* paved the way towards Fuentes' most ambitious project: the rewriting of Hispanic history in his monumental novel *Terra Nostra* (1975).

The novel *Cristóbal Nonato* (Christopher Unborn) (1987), represents a chaotic and apocalyptic portrait of Mexico at the end of the twentieth century. This text's most outstanding acomplishment might be the pyrotechnical nature of its language based on hallucinating plays of words sustained throughout the text by different means: witty puns, double meanings – above all related to sexual power – creative blendings of Spanish and English words producing new meanings, and so on.

As an essayist, Fuentes has also produced brilliant texts. Within the field of literary criticism, *La nueva novela hispanoamericana* (The New Hispanic American Novel) (1969), and *Valiente mundo nuevo* (Brave New World) (1990) study the historic context and significance of modern Hispanic American novelists. *Myself With Others* (1981) is a collection of short essays that also includes autobiographical information. In order to mark the **Columbian quincentenary** of the European discovery of America, he published *El espejo enterrado* (The Buried Mirror) (1992). It is a didactic description, with eloquent commentary, of the development of Hispanic culture from the Middle Ages until today, both in the Iberian peninsula and in the Americas. He has also made a **television** series under the same title.

Fuentes's literary texts reveal the privileged point of view of a Mexican who grew up both in his country and abroad, a Mexican who can look at his own country from the United States and France – where he seems to feel at home – as well as from his familiar Argentina and Chile. This heightened perspective is an asset as well as a handicap; at times, Mexico is rendered picturesque and even touristy in his writings. However, Fuentes is consistently sympathetic to progressive causes in Latin America.

Further reading

Faris, W.B. (1983) *Carlos Fuentes*, New York: Ungar.

Fuentes, C. (1985–9) *Obras completas*, Mexico: Aguilar.

Hernandez de Lopez, A.M. (1988) *La obra de Carlos Fuentes, una visión múltiple*, Madrid: Pliegos.

Van Delden, M. (1998) *Carlos Fuentes, Mexico and Modernity*, Liverpool: Liverpool University Press.

JUAN PELLICER

Fuentes, Fernando de

b. 1894, Veracruz, Mexico; d. 1958, Mexico City

Film-maker

The most important figure in the Mexican cinema of the 1930s, Fuentes was a skilled technician and a man of broad culture. He published his first poems at the age of twenty, then went on to manage the Olimpia cinema in Mexico City. With the advent of sound he joined Antonio Moreno as second assistant on **Santa** (1931); his own directing career began in 1932. He produced thirty-three feature films, often initiating the genres that became characteristic of early Mexican cinema; his trilogy *El prisionero trece* (Prisoner no.13), *El compadre Mendoza* (My Kinsman Mendoza) in 1933 and *Vámonos con Pancho Villa* (Let's Go with **Villa**) in 1935 initiated the melodrama of the Mexican revolution (see **revolutions**); *La Calandria* (1933), the comedy of manners; *El tigre de Yautepec* (The Tiger of Yautepec) (1933), the historical drama; *Cruz Diablo* (Devil's Cross) (1934), the cloak and dagger adventure; *El fantasma del convento* (Ghost in the Convent) (1934), the horror film; and *La familia Dressel* (The Dressel Family) (1935), the family drama.

Allá en el Rancho Grande (Out There on Rancho Grande) (1936) was a major box office success and gave the emerging Mexican cinema a generic formula – the *comedia ranchera* (see **rancheras, comedias**) – which brought it fame and prestige. The failure of *Vámonos con Pancho Villa* the previous year convinced Fuentes to move in a commercial direction, and as a result his subsequent films were significantly inferior in quality, despite the artistic aspirations of films like **Doña Bárbara** (1943) or *Crimen y castigo* (Crime and Punishment) (1950).

Fuentes's most significant contribution was 'the cinema of the revolution', which represented a time of barbarism when the emotional ties between people were broken and corruption became a system of government. *El compadre Mendoza*, his major work, is the key work of 1930s Mexican cinema. It is a tragedy exploring the contradictions of the revolutionary period and their individual consequences; treachery, opportunism, confusion. Sadly, his incisive and very modern vision was not followed up in subsequent films of the Revolution, which became merely folkloric.

Further reading

Luna, A. de (1984) *La batalla y su sombra: La revolución en el cine mexicano*, Mexico City: UNAM.

García Riera, E. (1984) *Fernando de Fuentes (1894–1958)*, Mexico City: Ed. Cineteca Nacional.

PATRICIA TORRES SAN MARTÍN

Fuguet, Alberto

b. 1964, Santiago, Chile

Writer

Fuguet is the author of the short story collection *Sobredosis* (Overdose) (1990), and the novels *Mala Onda* (Bad Vibes) (1991), *Por Favor Rebobinar* (Please Rewind) (1994) and *Tinta Roja* (Red Ink) (1997). From 1993–5 he was literary editor of the youth supplement **Zona de Contacto** published weekly by *El Mercurio*, Chile's largest newspaper. Narrating in a realistic style the decadent pastimes of upper-class urban teenagers, *Sobredosis* and *Mala Onda* were best sellers and raised controversy in Chilean literary circles. In particular, *Mala Onda*, the great moral novel of the 1980s, repudiates Chile's social climate during the **Pinochet** dictatorship.

AMALIA PEREIRA

Fujimori, Alberto

b. 1938, Lima, Peru

Politician

Fujimori was elected president of Peru in 1990. The son of Japanese immigrants, he won the election over Mario **Vargas Llosa**. His unpredicted victory took the political establishment by surprise. After an initial period allied to the left, Fujimori's government carried through neoliberal (see **neoliberalism**) **structural adjustment** policies. In April 1992 he performed a 'self-*coup*', closing down the parliament and the courts, and has since then consolidated an authoritarian order. In September 1992 his troops captured **Sendero Luminoso**'s leader Abimael **Guzmán**. Fujimori's slogans have been 'A President Like You' and 'Work and Technology'. In 1995 he was elected for a second five-year term, and at the time of writing is running for a third.

MAARIA SEPPÄNEN

FUNAI

The Fundação Nacional do Indio (FUNAI, or National Indian Foundation) is the institution responsible for the Indian policy of the Brazilian government, created in 1967 to replace the Serviço de Proteção ao Indio (Indian Protection Service). FUNAI's function, among others, is to guarantee Indian rights, define and recognize their lands and offer them medical and educational assistance. In general, it acts with institutions like the Instituto Brasileiro do Meio Ambiente e dos Recursos Naturais (IBAMA, or Brazilian Institute for the Environment and Natural Resources), the Instituto Brasileiro de Colonização e Reforma Agraria (Brazilian Institute of Colonization and Agrarian Reform), universities, NGOs and representatives of the indigenous peoples themselves.

VIVALDO SANTOS

FUNARTE

Created in 1975 as a department of the Brazilian Ministry of Culture, the role of FUNARTE (Fundação Nacional de Arte, National Art Foundation) is to encourage and support the production and development of artistic activities throughout Brazil. Based in Rio de Janeiro, it is particularly recognized for its work in the fields of photography, music, graphic arts, folklore and dance. It sponsors the National Prize for Art, and supports the Édison **Carneiro** Folklore Museum and several theatres and galleries throughout the country. In 1990, FUNARTE disappeared when its functions were transferred to the Brazilian Institute of Art and Culture (IBAC). In 1994, IBAC was replaced by a new FUNARTE.

ANTONIO CARLOS VAZ

funding for scientific research

The institutionalization of scientific research in Latin America occurs primarily, varying between individual countries, between 1900 and the 1930s. But the practice of **science** was largely restricted to the children of the economic elites who were able to fund their own research. In the 1940s, scientific research began to be recognized as a professional activity. The University Reform Movement (*la Reforma*) of 1918 had a crucial role in calling attention to the issue of university research, and the countries of the southern cone began to provide full-time salaried research posts as the middle classes gained access to the universities.

In the 1950s, and partly due to the involvement of international organisms like UNESCO, National Research Councils like **CONICET** in Argentina and the Conselho Nacional de Pesquisa in Brazil were established to promote research. The 1960s brought two new concerns into scientific thinking; the need to plan scientific research, and the conviction that such research had a role in the processes of **development**, as suggested by the so-called 'linear model of innovation'; basic science to applied science to technological innovation. Consequently, resources for research became relatively abundant in the 1960s and 1970s, with differing emphases in each country. The financing of research into information sciences in Brazil and nuclear physics in Argentina were outstanding examples.

In the 1980s, the situation began to deteriorate as a consequence of the **debt crisis** experienced by all the countries of the region and the imposition of tax adjustment policies which implied, in general, severe cutbacks in the budget for scientific research. The situation was further aggravated by another characteristic of the Latin American countries; the lack of private funds for research and development. In Europe, for example, private spending represents an average of 50 per cent of the total, whereas in Latin America it rarely goes beyond 20 per cent, so that the major responsibility for funding scientific research has fallen on the public purse.

Further reading

Amadeo, E. (1975) *Consejos nacionales de ciencia y tecnología: éxitos y fracasos del primer decenio*, in *Desarrollo Económico*.

Houssay, B. (1989) *Escritos y discursos*, Buenos Aires: EUDEBA.

RICYT (1996) *Indicadores Latinoamericanos de Ciencia y Tecnología*, Buenos Aires: Universidad Nacional de Quilmes.

Salomon, J.J., Sagasti, F. and Sachs, C. (1994) *The Uncertain Quest: Science, Technology and Development*, Tokyo: United Nations University.

PABLO KREIMER

funk

Funk is a musical phenomenon initially associated with the Zona Norte (North Zone) suburbs of Greater Rio de Janeiro, where in hundreds of clubs, predominantly black youths dance to imported US soul and hip hop recordings played by specialist DJs. In the early 1970s, the 'bailes da pesada' (mean, heavy dances) became the most significant expression of urban black youth identity. Ignored by the recording industry and commercial radio until the mid-1980s, the *bailes funk* gained some notoriety for their alleged association with racialized gang violence. Although dancers preferred US artists, a homegrown funk and soul industry emerged around pioneer Tim Maia, his brother Ed Motta and Sandra de Sá.

DAVID TREECE

Furtado, Celso

b. 1920, Pombal, Paraíba, Brazil

Economist

Furtado is of the main contributors to the influential structuralist perspective in development economics (see **development**). From 1949 to 1957 he worked with the United Nations Economic Commission for Latin America (ECLA) in Chile, and in 1958 became director of the National Economic Development Bank for the Northeast Region, one of the poorest areas of Brazil. During 1962 and 1963 he was Minister of Planning. Following the military coup of 1964, he left Brazil and later became Director of the Institute of Advanced Studies for Latin America at the University of Paris. With the return to democracy in Brazil he served as Minister for Culture from 1985 to 1988.

CRISTÓBAL KAY

Futoransky, Luisa

b. 1939, Buenos Aires, Argentina

Writer

The piercing, deconstructing humour of Futoransky's novels (for which she has been called a female Woody Allen) combines in her poetry with a lyrical but pitiless vision of loneliness in an alien world. A poet and a novelist, she lived in Japan and China before moving to Paris in 1981. She has published six volumes of poetry and the novels *Son cuentos chinos* (Those Are Chinese Tales) (1983), *De Pe a Pa (o de Pekín a París)* (From Peking to Paris) (1986), and *Urracas* (Magpies) (1992). She won the order of Chevalier des Arts et Lettres of France, and a Guggenheim Fellowship in 1991.

FLORINDA F. GOLDBERG

Fuzis, Os

A key work of the Brazilian **Cinema Novo**, *Os Fuzis* (The Guns) (1963) addresses the themes of hunger and social injustice, Messianism and the conflict between order and rebellion. The film follows a group of soldiers sent to a small town in the Brazilian Northeast during a drought to protect the local store from a hungry crowd gathered in the town square. Director Ruy **Guerra** is primarily concerned to address the basic conflict within Cinema Novo between the intellectual (see **intellectuals**), urban universe of the narrative (represented by the newly arrived soldiers) and a peasant world portrayed in a documentary style which does nothing to make them more transparent.

ISMAIL XAVIER AND THE USP GROUP

G

Gabeira, Fernando

b. 1941, Juiz de Fora, Minas Gerais, Brazil

Author, political activist and legislator

Gabeira came to fame as part of the group who kidnapped the American ambassador in 1969, during the most repressive period of the military regime in Brazil. Captured and tortured, he was released the next year in exchange for the West German ambassador. In exile until the 1979 amnesty, he has become famous as a writer of memoirs. His first book, *O que é isso, companheiro?* (What's Up, Comrade?) (1979), recounting his experiences in the 1960s, was very successful and was controversial again in 1997 when Bruno **Barreto** adapted it to the screen as *Four Days in September*. He is one of the leaders of the Green Party, and supports the legalization of cannabis and gay marriage.

JOHN GLEDSON

Gabilondo Soler, Francisco

b. 1907, Orizaba, Mexico; d. 1990, Texcoco, Mexico

Musician

Gabilondo was a popular singer and composer specializing in songs and stories for children, which he performed under his stage name of 'Cri-Crí, el grillito cantor' (The Singing Cricket) on Mexico City's Radio XEW between 1934 and 1961. These broadcasts made him famous in Mexico and throughout Latin America. His songs, in which animals behaved like humans or children spoke directly, were based on fairy tales, traditional Mexican stories and his own childhood memories. Musically they used the popular rhythms of the day – polkas, waltzes, tangos (see **tango**), rumbas (see **rumba**) and so on, and parodies of Chinese and Russian music. He composed over 200 songs.

EDUARDO CONTRERAS SOTO

Gabriela

Gabriela is a TV **Globo** *telenovela* (see ***telenovelas***) adapted by Walter George Durst from Jorge **Amado**'s novel *Gabriela, cravo e canela* (Gabriela, Clove and Cinammon), which first aired in 1975. The story takes place in Ilheus, in the interior of Bahia province, where the cocoa plantation owners hold absolute power. Two events transform the city: the arrival of Dr Mundinho Falcao (José Wilker) with his reforming ideas, and the love affair between the Turk Nacib (Armando Bogus) and the retiring Gabriela (Sonia **Braga**). The sound track included Gal **Costa**'s 'Modinha para Gabriela' and 'Alegre Menina' (Cheerful Girl) with words by Amado and music by Dori **Caymmi**, sung by Djavan.

ANTONIO CARLOS MARTINS VAZ

Gaceta de Cuba, La

The official alternative to the controversial ***Lunes de revolución***, this cultural journal reflected the complex shifts in Cuban cultural life, from open debate to institutional centralism. Founded in 1962 by **UNEAC** (Union of Cuban Writers and Artists) after its first Congress, it was edited by Nicolás **Guillén**. At first published fortnightly, it became monthly from issue 42 onwards until ceasing publication in 1991 because of the economic crisis. With the support of European publishers like Italy's Arci Nova, it resumed in January 1993. In the 1990s, though with reduced circulation, it became an important space for new currents in Cuban art and ideas.

WILFREDO CANCIO ISLA

Gadea, Norma Elena

b. 1949, Managua, Nicaragua

Singer

Gadea's lyrical soprano voice, vibrant style and commitment to the cause of the poor have made her the most important female musical performer of contemporary Nicaragua. Together with the **Mejía Godoy** brothers, she represented Nicaragua at popular festivities internationally during the Sandinista (see **Sandinista Revolution**) administration. Her most famous interpretation is 'El jilguero pregunta por Arlen' (The Hummingbird asks for Arlen), a song dedicated to Arlen Siu, an Asian Latin American Sandinista (see **Sandinista Revolution**) militant singer killed by the Somoza regime (see **Somoza dynasty**).

ESTEBAN E. LOUSTAUNAU AND ILEANA RODRÍGUEZ

Gaijin

Made during the last years of the Brazilian military dictatorship, *Gaijin* (Foreigner), directed by Tizuka **Yamasaki** (1980) depicts the arrival in Brazil around 1908 of a group of Japanese workers contracted by a coffee plantation where they join others from Italy, Spain and other parts of Brazil. In contrast to the myth of racial integration, the film shows their brutal incorporation into the local capitalist system. In realist tones, the film portrays the hard labour and privation to which these exploited people are subjected, the cultural and emotional contacts made in their rare moments of rest and their gradual loss of hope of ever returning to their homelands.

ISMAIL XAVIER AND THE USP GROUP

Gairy, Eric M.

b. 1922, Paradise, Grenada; d. 1997, Grand Anse, Grenada

Politician and dictator

A trade unionist, Gairy eventually headed the United Labor Party, which defeated the Grenada National Party in 1967. He became the island's first prime minister, and quickly established himself as a dictator with the assistance of his notorious Mongoose Gang. In 1979, with huge popular support, Maurice **Bishop**, leader of the **New Jewel Movement**, overthrew him peacefully. Apart from his corruption and brutality, Gairy is remembered for recommending, during a speech at the UN sometime in the 1970s, that a special organization be set up to investigate UFOs.

KEITH JARDIM

Gaitán, Jorge Eliecer *see* Violencia, La

Gaitán Durán, Jorge

b. 1925, Pamplona, Colombia; d. 1962, Guadaloupe, French Antilles

Poet, essayist and literary critic

The son of a well-off family, in the 1950s Gaitán lived in Paris, where he studied cinematography. In 1955, he founded ***Mito***, a magazine and intellectual movement which also included Eduardo **Cote Lamus**, Hernando Valencia Goelkel and Jorge Eliécer Ruiz. Gaitán's poetry has a predominantly tragic tone, with reflections on life, death and love. His collections of poems include *Insistencia en la tristeza* (Insistence on Sadness) (1946), *Asombro* (Amazement) (1951), *Amantes* (Lovers) (1954), *Si mañana despierto* (If I Wake Up Tomorrow) (1961). As a political activist, Gaitán fought against Rojas Pinilla's dictatorship.

MIGUEL A. CARDINALE

Galapagos Islands

The Galapagos archipelago, set in the Pacific Ocean approximately 570 miles west of the Ecuadorean coast, consists of thirteen major islands, six small islands and 40 to 50 islets, some no bigger than large rocks. Each island is unique; many are virtual deserts, others are mountainous with relatively lush vegetation. Spread over 30,000 square miles of ocean, all the islands are of volcanic origin, formed by the accumulation of lava from underwater eruptions. The islands thus are the 'heads' of various volcanoes, some still active, poking up 30,000 feet from the ocean floor. Though originally lifeless, today the islands are filled with bizarre plants and animals. Since the islands were never connected to the South American continent, fauna and flora had to travel across a 620-mile stretch of ocean. This explains the present-day predominance of sea birds, sea mammals and reptiles, which probably made the journey on vegetation-like rafts.

Historians contend that the islands were accidentally discovered in 1535 by the Spaniard Fray Tomas de Berlanga, Bishop of Panama, while en route to Peru. Pirates and explorers from different parts of the world visited the islands throughout the centuries. Ecuador claimed the islands in 1832. Charles Darwin reached the Galapagos in 1835 and was the first to observe how each arriving species had adapted over time to survive in their newfound environment; since the islands evolved in isolation, its wildlife was particularly interesting from the point of view of evolutionary history. In 1855, Darwin made the unique creatures of the islands the cornerstone of his theory of evolution by natural selection.

Despite having only two **seasons** – hot/wet or cold/dry – there are six vegetation zones, beginning with the shoreline and ending with the highlands. Vegetation is diverse, from cacti to ferns and orchids. The variety of land and sea birds is extraordinary, including finches, boobies, doves, hawks, albatrosses and lava gulls (said to be the rarest bird species in existence). Over 307 species of fish have been recorded. Giant tortoises (one of the most ancient and rarest of reptiles, weighing up to 550 pounds), penguins, dolphins, sea lions, black marine iguanas and giant green turtles live free and fearless of man. The name of the islands, 'galapagos', was taken from a Spanish word for tortoise, the giant creatures which astonished the first explorers and today are the most impressive attraction for more than 45,000 tourists who visit each year.

Further reading

Jackson, M.H. (1993) *Galápagos: A Natural History*, Calgary: University of Calgary Press.
Villasís Terán, M. (1990) *Galápagos: taller de Dios*, Quito: Banco Central del Ecuador.

MERCEDES M. ROBLES

Galarza, Ramona

b. 1937, Corrientes, Argentina

Singer

Galarza became famous in the 1960s as the first singer to popularize the **chamamé** and other musical genres of northeastern Argentina. In a period of growing popularity for popular music, her success ensured that the music of Corrientes would be included in the repertory of national folk music. As a singer she placed herself in the line of traditional musicians like Ernesto Montiel, Tránsito Cocomarola and Tarrago Ros (the older). She has recorded more than sixty albums and has won several awards and golden discs.

CRISTINA IGLESIA

Galeano, Eduardo Hughes

b. 1940, Montevideo, Uruguay

Writer

To call Eduardo Galeano a 'writer' merely hints at his prodigious talents, for he practises his craft with remarkable versatility as an essayist, journalist, novelist, historian and social and political commentator. He has even tried his hand at children's storytelling, publishing *La piedra arde* (The Hot Stone) in 1987. The dustjacket blurb of *Guatemala: país ocupado* (Guatemala: Occupied Country) (1967) credits Galeano, before deciding to become a writer, with having earned his keep among other activities, 'as a bill collector, commercial artist, caricaturist, stenographer, bank clerk and fashion page artist'. Periods working in Uruguay for the weeklies *El Sol* and **Marcha**, and the daily *La Época*, preceded his exile in 1973 in Argentina, where he founded and edited **Crisis**. After a second period of exile, this time in Spain (1977–85), Galeano returned to his native Montevideo.

His best known works, however, are *Las venas abiertas de América Latina* (Open Veins of Latin America) (1971), and the trilogy **Memoria del fuego** (Memory of Fire) (1982–5). The former is bold, assertive, sweeping in its scope, quick-paced and urgently written, the view of an agitated young man; the latter is nuanced, tender, contemplative in tone, slow-moving and meticulously wrought, the vision of a patient, mature mind. Both, however, are passionate and heartfelt, for Galeano wants nothing to do with the dry fabrications that purport to be objective and neutral about depicting a Latin American reality, which for him is as inspiring and dignified as it is demoralizing and tragic.

As a prose stylist, Galeano's mastery of the vignette is unparalleled in Latin American letters. He is economical with words, blessed with a keen ability to pare things down to the quick; the reader is left marvelling at how much can be said with so little text. Galeano's vignette style was well established by the time he published his second novel *Días y noches de amor y de guerra* (Days and Nights of Love and War) (1978), but it flourished and became his literary trademark with *Memoria del fuego*. Since then, Galeano has authored three books in which the vignette is the preferred, characteristic mode: *El libro de los abrazos* (The Book of Embraces) (1989), *Las palabras andantes* (Walking Words) (1993) and *El fútbol: a sol y sombra* (Football: Light and Shade) (1995), which he also illustrated himself. Two anthologies, *Nosotros decimos no* (We Say No) (1989) and *Ser como ellos y otros artículos* (To Be Like Them and Other Articles) (1992) showcase his journalism.

Further reading

Galeano, E. (1973) *Open Veins of Latin America*, trans. Cedric Belfrage. New York: Monthly Review Press.

—— (1985–8) *Memory of Fire*, 3 vols, New York: Pantheon Books.

Palaversich, D. (1995) *Silencio, voz y escritura en Eduardo Galeano*, Frankfurt-am-Main: Bibliotheca Ibero-Americana.

W. GEORGE LOVELL

Galich, Franz

b. 1951, Guatemala City

Writer

Primarily a short-fiction writer, Galich lives in Nicaragua where he also engages in committed editorial activity. His 1989 collection, *La princesa de ónix* (The Princess of Onyx), plays off references to modernist fantasy. Although referring to the conquest and to recent Guatemalan and Nicaraguan history, he breaks free of **Asturias** and **Cardoza y Aragón**'s influences and the themes of land and regionalism, instead being reminiscent of **Monterroso**. Galich's tone is playful, critical and ironic, but the violence in his stories points to the violence of his country.

MARC ZIMMERMAN

Galich, Manuel

b. 1913, Guatemala City; d. 1984, Havana, Cuba

Writer

The best known playwright of Guatemala's Generation of 1930, a student leader in 1944 and a political force in the 1944–54 period, Galich eventually went to Cuba where he helped establish the testimonial genre (see ***testimonio***) and where he lived until his death. His most famous testimonial book is *Del pánico al ataque* (From Panic to Attack) (1949), about the student uprising against the **Ubico** regime. He also wrote *Por qué lucha Guatemala. Arévalo y Arbenz: dos hombres contra un imperio* (Why Guatemala Struggles. Arévalo and Arbenz: Two Men Against an Empire) (1958), one of the best volumes about the revolutionary period.

MARC ZIMMERMAN AND LINDA CRAFT

Galindo, Alejandro

b. 1906, Monterrey, Mexico

Film-maker

Galindo learned his trade at Columbia Pictures in Hollywood. His first Mexican film was *Almas rebeldes* (Rebellious Souls) (1937); he later worked in other genres including melodrama, comedy, crime and even horror, with a preference for urban settings and stories based on actual events. *Campeón sin corona* (Uncrowned Champion) (1945) confirmed his place among the best directors of Mexico's 'Golden Age' and initiated a fruitful collaboration with actor David Silva. Galindo's work is characterized by its realism, visual directness, crowded urban scenes and his skilful direction of actors.

PATRICIA TORRES SAN MARTÍN

Galindo, Blas

b. 1910, Jalisco, Mexico; d. 1993

Composer and conductor

Blas Galindo (Carlos Blas Galindo Dimas) is composer of more than 150 symphonies, choral pieces, chamber works and ballet, theatre and film music, his most important compositions include *El zopilote mojado* (The Wet Vulture) and his ballet *Entre sombras anda el fuego* (Fire Moves Among the Shadows). He studied at the National Conservatory of Music with José **Rolón**, Candelario **Huízar** and Carlos **Chávez**, and with Aaron Copland in the United States. In 1934 he formed the Grupo de los Cuatro with Ayala, Contreras and Moncayo, and was director of the Conservatory from 1947 to 1961.

MARIANNA POOL WESTGAARD

Gallegos, Rómulo

b. 1884, Caracas, Venezuela; d. 1969, Caracas

Writer and politician

The best-known and most widely read Venezuelan twentieth-century writer, Gallegos's ethical and political concerns centred on the need to transform the country and overcome its backwardness. From his journalistic articles to novels which became emblematic of the confrontation between civilization and barbarism, like ***Doña Bárbara*** (1929), which brought him international fame, and *Cantaclaro* (1934) and *Canaima* (1935), Gallegos viewed writing as an instrument of social transformation. He moved logically into politics, founding the Acción Democrática party in 1936, becoming a deputy and finally President of the Republic in 1948, though he was deposed in November of that year by a military junta.

RAFAEL CASTILLO ZAPATA

Gallegos Lara, Joaquín

b. 1911, Guayaquil, Ecuador; d. 1947, Guayaquil

Writer

Gallegos Lara was a member of the **Guayaquil Group** and co-author of ***Los que se van***, *cuentos del cholo y del montuvio* (The Vanishing Ones: Stories about the Cholo and the Montuvio) (1930). An almost mythical figure, with severe physical disabilities, he was regarded as the ideologue and best critical mind of his generation. He advocated a literature in favour of the proletariat and downtrodden. His novel, *Las cruces sobre el agua* (Crosses on the Water) (1946), transcends his social realism and effectively depicts the city prior and during the 1922 labor uprising in Guayaquil.

HUMBERTO E. ROBLES

Gallet, Luciano

b. 1893, Rio de Janeiro, Brazil; d. 1931, Rio de Janeiro

Composer, musician, teacher and ethno-musicologist

Inspired by Glauco Velasquez, a composer he greatly admired, and by Darius Milhaud, with whom he studied composition in 1917, Gallet embarked on serious studies of Brazilian folk and popular music. His first two collections of songs, *Canções populares brasileiras* (Brazilian Popular Songs) were published in 1924; three additional collections were published in 1926 and 1928. These songs established his reputation as a serious composer. In 1930 Gallet campaigned for the creation of an Associação Brasileira de Música and in the same year was appointed Director of the Instituto Nacional de Música. Despite his early death at the age of thirty-eight, he had a pronounced influence on a younger generation of nationalist composers, including **Villa-Lobos**. His compositions were characterized by an intense concentration on national themes, and include works for orchestra and chamber music as well as the songs for which he is perhaps best known.

DAVID P. APPLEBY

Gallo, María Rosa

b. 1921, Buenos Aires, Argentina

Actress

One of Argentina's outstanding actresses, Gallo's performance in the play *The Trojan Women* won her the National Arts Foundation Prize in 1972, and her interpretation of Eleanor Duse and Phaedra brought her further awards. During a seven-year exile in Italy in the 1950s she worked with theatre companies in Rome and Milan. She worked in film with Manuel **Antín** (in *La cifra impar* (The Odd Number) (1961)) and Leopoldo **Torre Nilsson** (*La mano en la trampa* (Hand in the Trap) (1960)) among others. In the 1990s, she made a successful transition to **telenovelas**, a genre she vigorously defended.

ALEJANDRA LAERA

Galpón, El

One of the most important theatre companies in Latin America, El Galpón (The Shed) was founded in 1949 by Atahualpa del **Cioppo**, Manuel Domínguez Santamaría, Nelly Goitiño, César Campodónico and Roberto Fontana, among others. Part of the independent theatre movement that pervaded the region in the 1940s, El Galpón was committed to engaging with its community artistically and politically, even going so far in its early days as to pass the hat from door to door for funding. Its stated goal was, and continues to be, to develop its audience as both its base and objective. Non-profit and dedicated to low production costs to avoid turning to big business for financial support, El Galpón also conceived of art as democratically created in collaboration with the community. To that end, El Galpón created an extensive repertoire of productions of plays by both national and international playwrights that, due to historical, aesthetic or thematic values, simultaneously reflected the temper of its time and served to fortify the culture. Eschewing dogmatism, the company sought to combine Brecht's social engagment with Stanislaviski's stress upon emotional realism creating in the process a performance style that, at its best, combined a clear ideological content with coherent characterization in theatrically resonant productions.

Such a politically engaged artistic thrust led the company into direct conflict with the military government that took over after the 1973 *coup d'état*. One of the most repressive dictatorships of the period in Latin America, the government imprisoned and tortured many members of the company. In 1976, El Galpón's legal rights were abolished and all of its holdings confiscated. Its smaller theatre space, the Sala Mercedes, was destroyed and its larger theatre taken over by the state. The company went into exile in Mexico where it remained for nearly ten years, adapting itself by creating children's theatre for Mexican audiences and adult productions drawing upon Uruguayan literature, history, and culture such as *Puro cuento* (Tall Tales) and *Artigas, general del pueblo* (Artigas, The People's General). Among the El Galpón artists persecuted by the dictatorship was the playwright and journalist Mauricio **Rosencof**, a founder and key ideological force in the Tupamaro guerrilla movement (see **Tupamaros**) whose activities were a justification for the 1973 military *coup*.

See also: Brechtian theatre; Teatro independiente

Further reading

El Galpón: un teatro independiente uruguayo y su función en el exilio (1983) Mexico City: Cuadernos de Difusión Cultural, El Galpón.

ADAM VERSÉNYI

Galvão, Patricia

b. 1910, Sao João da Boa Vista, Brazil; d. 1962, Santos, Brazil

Writer

Joining the movement led by Oswald de **Andrade** in 1929, Galvão became the muse of anthropophagy. In 1931 she joined the Communist Party, but due to political differences she used the pseudonym Mara Lobo when writing her first 'proletarian novel' *Parque Industrial* (Industrial Park) (1933). She was also Pagú, the mysterious poet Solange Sohl, and Ariel when writing social chronicles. In 1945 she co-founded the anti-Stalinist journal *Vanguarda Socialista* (Socialist Vanguard). From 1952 she devoted herself to theatre. She was the first female political prisoner in the country. Hers were also the first translations into Portuguese of Ionesco, Beckett and poems by Valéry and Apollinaire, and a translation of *Ulysees* by Joyce.

ADRIANA AMANTE

Gálvez, Manuel

b. 1882, Paraná, Argentina; d. 1962, Buenos Aires, Argentina

Writer

Gálvez is a Catholic and nationalist writer who, despite his ideology, wrote some of the most ambiguous social novels of Argentina, even publishing one of them – *Nacha Regules* (1919) – in the socialist newspaper *La Vanguardia*. The intense ambiguity of his social novels has led critics to include him in the movement known as critical realism. With Ricardo Olivera he founded the journal *Ideas*, which promoted the nationalist credo of the turn of the century. Many of his texts deal with the newly visible **tango** world. He fought with fervour for the institutional organization of **intellectuals**.

FLORENCIA GARRAMUÑO

Gamarra, José

b. 1934, Tacuarembó, Uruguay

Painter

Gamarra studied in Uruguay and then travelled through South America until moving to France in 1963. His work of the 1960s and 1970s used cartoon-like techniques to comment on political issues. In the 1980s he began to paint in a style reminiscent of nineteenth-century traveller–artists to South America, incorporating humorous anachronisms in rich tropical scenes and commenting on the issues raised by the discovery of America.

GABRIEL PEREZ-BARREIRO

Gambaro, Griselda

b. 1928, Buenos Aires, Argentina

Playwright, novelist and short story writer

Perhaps the most important contemporary woman playwright in Latin America, Gambaro's plays are forceful investigations of the physical and psychological violence that have historically characterized

Argentinian political and daily life. Her early plays such as *Los siameses* (Siamese Twins) (1967) and *El campo* (The Camp) (1968) have frequently been analysed in terms of Artaud's 'Theatre of Cruelty' or Martin Esslin's definition of the 'Theatre of the Absurd'. In its depiction of socially, psychologically and physically deformed characters, however, Gambaro's work is directly rooted in the Argentinian *grotesco criollo* (creole grotesque) pioneered by Armando **Discépolo** (1887–1971) and **Defillipis Novoa** (1889–1930). Intricately constructed, Gambaro's plays confront the myriad ways in which the forces of daily existence can serve to delimit and destroy our dreams and aspirations.

In 1977 during the 'Dirty War', Gambaro's novel *Ganarse la muerte* (To Win One's Death) was banned by then president Jorge Rafael **Videla**. Equivalent to a death threat, the extraordinary decree forced Gambaro to flee to Spain where she remained until 1980. Her plays from the 1980s, such as *Decir sí* (Say Yes), *La malasangre* (Bitter Blood) (1982) and *Antígona furiosa* (Furious Antigone) (1986), increasingly investigate the repercussions of complicity with repressive regimes and the terror they engender. The manner in which they do so is diverse. *La malasangre* draws upon the iconography of nineteenth-century dictator Juan Manuel de Rosas, and *Antígona furiosa* upon classical material to critique the military junta of the 1970s. Some of her plays, such as *Información para extranjeros* (Information for Foreigners) (1972), have yet to be performed in Argentina. Her plays of the 1990s, *Penas sin importancia* (Unimportant Sorrows) (1991), *Atando cabos* (Loose Ends) (1991), *La casa sin sosiego* (House without Calm) (1991) and *Es necesario entender un poco* (A Little Understanding is Crucial) (1994), take her work in new directions reflecting the altered social and political context since the fall of the military junta.

Further reading

Gambaro, G. (1992) *Information for Foreigners: Three Plays by Griselda Gambaro*, trans. M. Feitlowitz, Evanston, IL: Northwestern University Press.

Mazziotti, N. (ed.) (1989) *Poder, deseo y marginación: aproximaciones a la obra de Griselda Gambaro*, Buenos Aires: Puntosur Editores.

Taylor, D. (1991) *Theatre of Crisis: Drama and Politics in Latin America*, Lexington, KY: University of Kentucky Press.

ADAM VERSÉNYI

Gandini, Gerardo

b. 1936, Buenos Aires, Argentina

Musician

Director of the Centro Experimental for opera and ballet at the **Teatro Colón** and a pianist as well as a composer, in 1996 Gandini presented his first opera, *La ciudad ausente* (Absent City), based on the novel of the same name by Ricardo **Piglia**. He studied piano with Roberto Caamaño and Ivonne Loriod, and composition with Alberto **Ginastera** in Buenos Aires and at the Santa Cecilia Academy in Rome with Goffredo Petrassi. He has also recorded his piano improvisations on **tango** themes.

RODRIGO PEIRETTI

Ganga bruta

A major work of Brazilian cinema, *Ganga bruta* (Brutal Gang) (1933) is distinguished by its exploration of the possibilities of silent cinema (see **silent film**), despite the fact that it had a partial soundtrack. It depicts the recovery of a man's passion after murdering his wife. Director Humberto **Mauro** creates a highly eroticized rural world whose sensuality was well ahead of its time. In the search for symbolic images and the psychological depth of its characters, the film became a cinematic milestone comparable to the greatest moments of silent film in the 1920s.

ISMAIL XAVIER AND THE USP GROUP

Gaona, Rodolfo

b. 1888, León, Mexico; d. 1975, Mexico City

Bullfighter

One of the most famous of bullfighters, Gaona first

entered the ring with a young *cuadrilla* at the age of nineteen, and had his first bull fight a month later (October 1907) in Mexico City. The following year he went to Spain, where he became one of the leading *toreros* at a time when there were many famous bullfighters. He had his last fight in April, 1925 and received a tremendous send-off. Among the numerous homages paid to him, a street in Mexico City carries his name.

ERIC WEIL

Gaos, José
b. 1900, Gijón, Spain; d. 1969, Mexico City

Philosopher

A member of the 'Madrid school' and a disciple of Manuel García Morente and José Ortega y Gasset, Gaos was Rector of the University of Madrid between October 1936 and the fall of the Spanish Republic in 1939. *Transterrado* (translanded) and *empatriado* (empatriated) – the neologisms were his own – in Mexico in 1939, he was a professor at the Casa de España, later the Colegio de Mexico, and the National University (**UNAM**). His main areas of interest and concern were Mexican philosophy, the history of Latin American ideas as a discipline, and promoting a philosophy of 'lo mexicano' (Mexicanness).

HORACIO CERUTTI-GULDBERG

Garay, Sindo
b. 1868, Havana, Cuba; d. 1968

Composer and musician

The outstanding exponent of the tradition of the cuban *trova*, and a symbol of the Bohemian lifestyle that every *trovador* should live. As a young singer he travelled through the Caribbean before settling in Havana. In 1928 he travelled to Paris with Rita **Montaner** and others to make programmes for Cuban radio stations. Although many of his songs were recorded, it is assumed that many others were lost, particularly those he improvised on the spot, since he could not transcribe them. His best known compositions include 'La tarde' (Evening), 'Perla marina' (Marine pearl), 'Adiós a la Habana' (Goodbye to Havana).

JOSÉ ANTONIO EVORA

García, Alan
b. 1950, Lima, Peru

Politician

President of Peru between 1985 and 1990, his initial measures were highly popular. By unilaterally reducing foreign debt payments, he created a temporary economic bonanza, although international pressures restricted investments and loans and inflation skyrocketed to unprecedented levels. His handling of the internal political situation in Peru, however, was disastrous. He was indirectly responsible for the genocide of 248 political prisoners in June 1996. He has since been found culpable of the embezzlement of at least 700 million dollars in unofficial operations. He currently lives abroad protected by international extradition treaties.

JOSé ANTONIO MAZZOTTI

García, Ana María
b. 1953, Havana, Cuba

Film-maker

Living in Puerto Rico from an early age, García became interested in film while studying in New York. Her commitment to socially-conscious filmmaking grew after her return to Cuba with the first Antonio Maceo brigades, an experience documented in Jesús **Díaz**'s *55 hermanos* (55 Brothers) (1978). After doing cinematography for a number of independent productions, García's *La operación* (The Operation) (1977–81) was a hard-hitting exposé of the Puerto Rican government's forced sterilization of women in the 1960s. Her second feature-length documentary *Cocolos & Rockeros* (1992), explores the significance of music for Puerto Rican identity in the shadow of the USA.

MARÍA CRISTINA RODRÍGUEZ

García, Charly

b. 1951, Buenos Aires, Argentina

Musician

Charly García is one of the mythical figures of Argentine **rock nacional**. With Nito Mestre, a school friend, he formed **Sui Géneris**, which became the most successful 'progressive' music group of the 1970s. The duo split in 1976, at the high point of their success, and Charly formed *La máquina de hacer pájaros* (The Machine for Making Birds), which radicalized the later work of Sui Generis in compositions close to the British symphonic rock in vogue at the time.

In 1978, with David Lebón, Pedro Aznar and Oscar Moro, he formed the group Serú Girán, 'the Argentine Beatles' as Aznar called them. In the four years that followed, the group beat every previous record for record sales and concert audiences (in 1980, 60,000 people attended a single concert). They produced memorable compositions like 'Canción de Alicia en el país' (Song of Alice in the Country), 'Seminare' and 'Peperina', and Charly's musical development took him far from the work of Sui Géneris. The piece 'Serú Girán', built on a pure signifier that can communicate nothing, in the highest tradition of the artistic avant-garde (see **avant-garde in Latin America**), can be read as an emblematic theme of a moment when words were inadequate to give voice to anguish, repression and murder.

After the break up of Serú Girán, Charly began a solo career. The double album *Yendo de la cama al living/Pubis angelical* (Going from Bed to the Living Room/Angelic Pubis) (1982) included music for a film based on Manuel **Puig**'s novel of the same name. *Clics modernos* (1983) initiated a new phase in García's work; the 'pop' phase, of 'crazy new hairstyles' and a sceptical and ironic modernity.

The record's cynical lyrics and new sound met some resistance at first. The albums *Piano bar* and *Parte de la religión* (Part of Religion) and *Tango* (1986), made with Pedro Aznar, one of the most serious musicians of *rock nacional*, belong to the post-1983 current.

After *Cómo conseguir chicas* (How to Get Girls), García turned to the production of a rock opera *La hija de la lágrima* (Daughter of the Tear), which was enthusiastically received in Buenos Aires. At the height of his popularity, the much-loved father figure of *rock nacional*, key musical innovator for contemporary Argentine music, García participated in 1997 at the folk festival at Cosquín, where rock was traditionally forbidden (see **music festivals**), and cut a record, *Alta fidelidad* (High Fidelity) with Mercedes **Sosa**, another legend of Argentine music.

Further reading

Chirom, D. (1987) *Charly García*, Buenos Aires: El Juglar.

Enciclopedia rock nacional: 30 años de la A a la Z (1996) Buenos Aires: Ed. Mordisco.

DIEGO BENTIVEGNA

García, Federico

b. 1937, Cusco, Peru

Film director

García began his career as a State functionary making documentaries in support of the **Velasco** government's social reforms. His subsequent work was still political in nature, for example in his full-length films, *Kuntur wachana* (Where the Condors are Born) (1977), *Laulico* (1980) and *El caso huayanay* (The Huayanay Case) (1981), with peasant actors. He made several historical films – *Melgar* (1982), *Tupac amaru* (1984) and *El socio de Dios* (God's Partner) (1986–7) before entering the comedy genre with *La manzanita del diablo* (The Devil's Little Apple) (1989). One of Peru's most prolific directors, García's work is sometimes technically deficient and uneven in quality.

CESAR SALAS

García, Germán Leopoldo

b. 1944, Junín, Buenos Aires, Argentina

Writer and psychoanalyst

In 1968, García published his successful novel *Nanina*, which was followed by several more. Having trained as a psychoanalyst with Oscar **Masotta**, he was a co-founder in 1974 of the Freudian School of Buenos Aires. His publications in the field of psychoanalysis include *La entrada del psicoanálisis en la Argentina* (The Arrival of Psychoanalysis in Argentina) (1978), *Psicoanálisis, una política del síntoma* (Psychoanalysis, a Politics of the Symptom) (1980) and *Psicoanálisis dicho de otra manera* (Psychoanalysis Put Another Way) (1983). He is president of the Descartes Foundation of Buenos Aires and a council member of the Escuela de Orientación Lacaniana (the Lacanian School) of Argentina.

See also: psychology in Latin America

GRACIELA MUSACHI

García, Juan Francisco

b. 1892, Santiago, Dominican Republic; d. 1974, Santo Domingo, Dominican Republic

Composer

Better known as don Pancho García, García studied music and cornet with José Oviedo García and was self-taught in piano and violoncello. He composed the *Quartets* no. 1 and no. 2, *Quisqueyana Symphony*, *Dominican Rhapsody* and *Indian Fantasia*. He was also author of three zarzuelas (a type of Spanish opera), and several boleros (see **bolero**) and criollas (Dominican creole songs), such as 'El espejo' (The Mirror) with lyrics by Nicolás **Guillén**. Don Pancho García was one of the first Dominican musicians interested in adapting folkloric rhythms for symphony orchestra.

FERNANDO VALERIO-HOLGUÍN

García, Ricardo

b. 1928, Puerto Montt, Chile; d. 1990, Havana, Cuba

Cultural promoter

Osvaldo Larrea García took the name Ricardo García in the 1950s when he became a **radio** announcer in Chile. His activities in radio included pioneering work with Violeta **Parra** in broadcasting Chilean folklore. He was a founder of the Viña del Mar song festival (see **song festivals**), and later of the Festival of Chilean *nueva canción*. When the **Pinochet** dictatorship took power in Chile in 1973, García was among the many blacklisted. Unable to work in radio, he created the **Alerce Records** label to disseminate the music of the exiled *nueva canción* artists and to showcase the new generation of *canto nuevo* musicians.

NANCY MORRIS

García, Santiago

b. 1928, Bogotá, Colombia

Playwright

García studied architecture in Bogotá, Paris, and Venice. In 1957 he participated in courses with Japanese director Seki Sano, who was invited by the Colombian government to professionalize television. García furthered his preparation in Prague and Vincennes, France, and attended the Actors Studio and the Berliner Ensemble. In 1958, he founded the theatre group El Buho, which later failed. In 1962 he founded the Casa de la Cultura, subsequently known as the Teatro La **Candelaria**, one of Colombia's most successful theatre institutions, renowned for its collective style of work, and a key participant in the unionization of thespians. He has written extensively, dramaturgy as well as dramatic theory.

HÉCTOR D. FERNÁNDEZ L'HOESTE

García, Sara

b. 1895, Orizaba, Veracruz, Mexico; d. 1980, Mexico City

Actress

García was the cinematic embodiment first of the selfless Mexican mother and later of the perfect grandmother. She first played a mother at the age of twenty in the theatre, and from then on became the prototypical mother of several genres including melodramas, musicals and *comedias rancheras* (see **rancheras, comedias**). She became a grandmother in Rafael J. Sevilla's *La abuelita* (Grandma) (1942) and Juan **Bustillo Oro**'s *Cuando los hijos se van* (When the Children Leave Home) (1941), where the family was represented in its most traditional, conservative and melodramatic form.

PATRICIA TORRES SAN MARTÍN

García Agraz, José Luis

b. 1952, Mexico City

Film-maker

García worked as assistant to Arturo **Ripstein** and José Estrada before directing his own films. His short *Patricio* (1981) won an Ariel prize, and his first feature, *Nocaut* (Knockout) (1982) was well received by critics and public alike. Like many contemporary directors, García Agraz alternates film and video. His television work includes *Biografías del poder* (Biographies of Power) and 42 episodes of the series *Tony Tijuana*. More recent work, like *Desiertos mares* (Deserted Seas) (1993) and *Salón México* (1995), suggests a promising director still in search of his own style.

PATRICIA TORRES SAN MARTÍN

García Arancibia, Fernando

b. 1930, Santiago, Chile

Composer and musicologist

García Arancibia is a key composer who combines a modern musical language with social and political concerns. In the late 1970s he worked at the Instituto Nacional de Cultura in Peru, moving to Cuba in the 1980s to work with the **Ballet Nacional de Cuba** (Cuban National Ballet). In 1989 he returned to the University of Chile and became assistant editor of the *Revista musical chilena*. He has written important works on colonial music and Peruvian organ music. As a composer, he adopted the twelve-tone system from the outset, absorbing random techniques and serialism at a later stage. Outstanding among his works are his *Firmamento sumergido* (Submerged Firmament) and *Temblor del cielo* (Tremor in the Sky) for orchestra, *América insurrecta* (America in Insurrection) for narrator, chorus and orchestra, with text by **Neruda**, his ballet *Urania, Bestiario* for soprano and piano, with a text by Nicolás **Guillén** and *Tierras ofendidas* (Offended Lands) for flute, oboe and clarinet.

ALFONSO PADILLA

García Ascot, Jomi

b. 1927, Tunis, Tunisia; d. 1986, Mexico City

Film-maker

A Spanish national, García Ascot worked in Mexico on the famous newsreels *Cine-Verdad* (Cinema of Truth) with Manuel **Barbachano Ponce**. Film critic for the *Revista de la Universidad*, he belonged to the Nuevo Cine (New Cinema) group, which advocated a new direction in Mexican film-making in the 1960s. In 1962 he directed and produced independently *En el balcón vacío* (On the Empty Balcony), a poetic expression of nostalgia for a lost childhood and nation. In 1976 he directed his first and only commercial film, *El viaje* (The Journey).

PATRICIA TORRES SAN MARTÍN

García Calderón, Ventura

b. 1887, Lima, Peru; d. 1959, Paris, France

Writer

Best known as a short story writer, García's first

book of short stories, *Dolorosa y desnuda realidad* (Painful and Naked Reality) (1914) was shaped by *modernismo* (see **modernismo, Spanish American**). His greatest success was a short story collection of neo-realist inspiration, *La venganza del cóndor* (The Condor's Revenge) (1924), which directly addressed the status of Peruvian Indians in the republican era. He wrote literary criticism and also published *Cuentos peruanos* (Peruvian Short Stories) (1952) and several volumes in French, including *Danger de mort* (Danger of Death) (1926) and *Couleur du sang* (Colour of Blood) (1931).

JOSÉ ANTONIO MAZZOTTI

García Canclini, Néstor

b. 1939, La Plata, Argentina

Philosopher and social researcher

García Canclini's theses are very influential in current debates on Latin American culture and societies and in cultural studies. His thesis that Latin American cultures and societies are hybrid, and his complex analysis of modernity (see **cultural theory**) and its cultural configurations – the cult, the popular and the massive – are useful tools with which to analyse Latin American reality. His critical analysis of cultural policies and globalization have also been important and influential.

There are two main trends in García Canclini's thought. The first is the elaboration of a theory of symbolic (cultural) production. Influenced by Bourdieu and Gramsci, García Canclini sees symbolic production as a social process of production. This implies taking into account (a) cultural products as social reality, as well as ideal representations, (b) the material processes which produce them, and (c) their production, circulation and consumption (reception) as parts of a complex but unified process.

The second trend – especially developed in *Culturas Híbridas* (Hybrid Cultures) (1995) but already evident in his earlier writings – is the analysis of the field of symbolic production in order to illuminate the characteristics and contradictions of Latin American culture and its historical development. In his view, the indigenous traditions (especially in Central America and the Andean region), the Hispanic-Catholic colonial traditions, and modern education, communication and politics produce a multitemporal and multicultural heterogeneity that is a basic feature of Latin American societies. The concept of **hybridity** emerges at this point as the key to understanding these complex settings.

Having studied in Buenos Aires and later in Paris, since 1976 Canclini has lived in Mexico City where he chairs the Program of Urban Culture Studies at the Metropolitan Autonomous University. He has also taught at the universities of Texas, Barcelona, Buenos Aires, São Paulo and Stanford, among others. A Guggenheim Fellow (1982) and adviser to **UNESCO**, OAS (see **Organization of American States**), and other international institutions, he was awarded the Premio **Casa de las Américas** for *Las culturas populares en el capitalismo* (Transforming Modernity: Popular Culture in Mexico) (1992) and the Book Award of the **Latin American Studies Association** for *Culturas Híbridas*.

Further reading

Travesia 1(2) (1992); number devoted to hybrid culture, with articles by J. Franco, G. Martin, J. Martín-Barbero and others.

FERNANDO RABOSSI

García Caturla, Alejandro

b. 1906, Remedios, Cuba; d. 1940, Remedios

Composer

García Caturla was a lawyer and judge as well as a composer, and one of the central figures of the *afrocubanismo* movement and of musical modernism. He studied with Pedro Sanjuán in Havana (1926–7) and Nadia Boulanger in Paris (1928). Although he co-founded the *Orquesta de Cámara de Conciertos de Caibarién* (Caibarien Concert Chamber Orchestra), which presented modern music from Europe, North America and Cuba, he did not play a very important role in Havana's musical life. He was a magistrate working in the smaller provincial towns, and was murdered by a criminal on the eve of a trial.

While in Paris he studied the work of Milhaud, Satie and Stravinsky, and his early work shows their influence; but he soon began to develop his own distinctive style, using elements of the Afro-Cuban tradition as well as **mestizo** and rural Cuban forms, though setting them within a language even more modern, dissonant and unexpected than Amadeo **Roldán**. According to Alejo **Carpentier**, 'García Caturla achieved a synthesis of all the musical genres on the island within an expression that embraced modern European techniques'. His principal works include *Obertura cubana* (Cuban Overture) and *Tres danzas cubanas* (Three Cuban Dances) for orchestra, *Yamba-O* for chorus and orchestra with text by **Carpentier**, *Canto de los cafetales* (Plantation Song) for chorus, with traditional text, *Bembé* for fourteen instruments, *Yambambó* for soprano and piano, with text by Nicolás **Guillén**, *Danza lucumí*, *Comparsa*, *Son* and *Berceuse campesina*, all for piano.

Further reading

Carpentier, A. (1988) *La música en Cuba*, Havana: Editorial Letras Cubanas.

ALFONSO PADILLA

García Espinosa, Julio

b. 1926, Havana, Cuba

Film-maker

Film-maker, critic and theorist of film practice, García Espinosa studied film in Rome in the early 1950s and in 1954 made *El Megano* (The Charcoal Worker) (1954), a documentary on the charcoal burners of the Cienaga de Zapata. In 1959 he was made director of the Film Unit of the Rebel Army, later transformed into the Cuban Film Institute (**ICAIC**), which he founded with Alfredo **Guevara** and Tomás **Gutiérrez Alea**. His 'Por un **cine imperfecto**' (For an Imperfect Cinema) (1973) is a key essay. He was also director of *El joven rebelde* (The Young Rebel) (1961), *Son...y no son* (They Are and Are Not) (1980) and *Mi socio Manolo* (My Partner Manolo) (1990) among others.

JOSÉ ANTONIO EVORA

García Herreros, Padre Rafael

b. 1909, Cúcuta, Colombia; d. 1988, Bogotá, Colombia

Religious figure

Founder of 'El minuto de Dios' (God's Minute), a widely respected and successful Christian philanthropic corporation, García Herreros was ordained a priest in the Eudista community in 1934. A teacher, evangelical, short-story writer and editor of ecclesiastical publications, he made his reputation as an honest Christian devoted to helping the poor through radio and television nightly addresses appealing to evangelical notions of social justice. His high moral stature enabled him to become a mediator between the Colombian government and the Medellín cartel in the early 1990s; his role is described in Gabriel **García Márquez**'s *Noticia de un secuestro* (1996).

ÁLVARO FÉLIX BOLAÑOS

García Joya, Mario

b. 1938, Havana, Cuba

Cinematographer

Considered one of Cuban cinema's most important figures, García Joya has made more than sixty films including, with Tomás **Gutiérrez Alea**, *Una pelea cubana contra los demonios* (A Cuban Struggle against Demons) (1971), *La **última cena*** (The Last Supper) (1971) and ***Fresa y chocolate*** (Strawberry and Chocolate) (1993). A painter and designer, he contributed to ***Lunes de revolución*** and became a professional photographer and book illustrator. He began his film career in 1961 as a cameraman for **ICAIC**, the Cuban Film Institute, and from 1971 as director of photography. He has also written studies of photography and film, and was a founder member of the Fototeca de Cuba. Since 1995 he has lived in the USA.

WILFREDO CANCIO ISLA

Garcí Manuel see Manuel, Víctor

García Márquez, Gabriel
b. 1927, Aracataca, Colombia

Novelist

Gabriel García Márquez was born in 1927 (not 1928, as is usually believed) in a small town in northern Colombia surrounded by US-owned banana plantations. From this humble and conflictive background he rose in due course to become the most admired and widely read novelist from Latin America, and perhaps the most universally celebrated literary figure from the Hispanic world since Cervantes.

Immediately after his birth, the young García Márquez was placed with his grandparents and brought up by them until the age of nine. He lived in a household full of women, with the exception of his grandfather, who had been a colonel in the army of the Liberal Party during Colombia's catastrophic War of the Thousand Days (1898–1901). This historical background, together with a notorious massacre of fruit company workers by the Colombian army near Aracataca in 1928, inspired much of what García Márquez would come to write in later decades; all of it framed by the experience of life in a household criss-crossed by the conflicting narratives of history, folklore and superstition.

After the death of his grandfather in 1937 ('nothing of importance ever happened to me after his death'), the young García Márquez was sent away to school in Barranquilla and then to Zipaquirá, near the capital Bogotá. Here he first became aware of the vast cultural difference between the tropical Caribbean coastlands where he was born and the stiff, chilly culture of the Andean regions from which the country was governed. By 1948 he was an unenthusiastic law student in Bogotá – one who had already published a couple of well-reviewed stories – when the 'Bogotazo' took place: Jorge Eliecer Gaitán was murdered and his enraged supporters set fire to the centre of the city, setting off La **Violencia**. García Márquez abandoned his studies, fled to Cartagena and became a journalist. By 1955 he had worked not only in Cartagena but also in Barranquilla – as a member of the so-called **Grupo de Barranquilla** of artists and intellectuals – and Bogotá, had written literally hundreds of essays and articles, and had become one of his country's most admired newspapermen. He had also published his first novel, *La hojarasca* (Leafstorm) (1955), based on childhood memories of Aracataca filtered through the influence of William Faulkner. His home town had lost its name, however, and taken on a name that would resonate through world literature: Macondo.

García Márquez travelled to Europe in 1955 to study cinema – a lifelong obsession – in Italy and then moved to Paris, where he wrote one of the most perfect short novels by a Latin American, *El coronel no tiene quien le escriba* (No One Writes to the Colonel), not published until 1961. From Paris he moved to Venezuela in 1958, the year he married his childhood sweetheart, and from there to New York where he worked as a press officer for the new Cuban Revolution (see **revolutions**). In 1961 he took up residence in Mexico and worked in advertising and film, scripting, among others, *Tiempo de morir* (Time to Die) (1965) and Arturo **Ripstein**'s *Opera prima*, and appearing in Alberto **Isaac**'s *En este pueblo no hay ladrones* (In This Town There Are No Thieves) (1964). Finally, in 1965, he began work on the novel that would make him both famous and rich, **Cien años de soledad** (One Hundred Years of Solitude). When published in Buenos Aires in 1967, this unique novel caused a sensation which gave García Márquez the kind of fame and glamour only usually associated with matinee idols, sporting heroes or bullfighters. He became known by his nickname, Gabo, moved to Barcelona and settled down, despite the uproar, to write again. The result, in 1975, was *El otoño del patriarca* (The Autumn of the Patriarch), a quite different kind of novel but another startling success. It was about the rise and fall of a brutal Caribbean dictator and staged two of the writer's fundamental obsessions: love and power. That same year he published his first book of collected stories, featuring particularly the ones from his best collection, *Funerales de la Mamá Grande* (Big Mother's Funeral), which had appeared without much fanfare in 1962.

In the later 1970s García Márquez took up residence in Mexico again, and devoted himself to political writing. By now he was the best-known Latin American celebrity supporting the Cuban Revolution, and he became a personal friend of Fidel **Castro**. In 1981 he eventually published another short novel, *Crónica de una muerte anunciada* (Chronicle of a Death Foretold), and in 1982 became one of the most popularly acclaimed winners of the Nobel Prize (see **Nobel Prizes**), thus emulating two of his most admired models, Faulkner and Hemingway.

Nothing, however, could dent García Márquez's extraordinary concentration. 1986 saw the appearance of *El amor en los tiempos del cólera* (Love in the Time of Cholera), one of the most popular of all his books, and in 1989 he published *El general en su laberinto* (The General in his Labyrinth), his astonishingly audacious interpretation of the last months in the life of the great Simón Bolívar. In the 1990s his creativity was undimmed: *Del amor y otros demonios* (Of Love and Other Demons) appeared in 1994 and the scintillating *Noticia de un secuestro* (Report of a Kidnapping) in 1996, a documentary narrative surveying Colombia's horrific contemporary situation.

No Latin American writer in the twentieth century has ever combined critical and popular success in the way that García Márquez has succeeded in doing. The unique status of *Cien años de soledad* has tended to associate him with the 'magical realist' label (see **magical realism**), but his work is in fact marked by an extraordinary commitment to the everyday lives and beliefs of quite ordinary Colombians. Similarly, those who expect that a writer who is a socialist will write tub-thumping novels are invariably surprised by these wise, humorous but somewhat pessimistic, albeit life-enhancing narratives. The explanation lies partly in the history of Colombia, partly in his memories of his grandfather and partly in a still more ancient influence: that of Sophocles, who gives a hint perhaps that García Márquez, despite his celebrity status, was always searching for some more timeless, classical profile.

See also: Escuela de Tres Mundos; Espectador, El

Further reading

Bell-Villada, G. (1990) *García Márquez: The Man and his Work*, Chapel Hill, NC: University of North Carolina Press.

Martin, G. (1989) *Journeys through the Labyrinth: Latin American Fiction in the Twentieth Century*, London: Verso.

McGuirk, B. and Cardwell, R. (1987) *Gabriel García Márquez: New Readings*, Cambridge: Cambridge University Press.

Minta, S. (1987) *García Márquez: Writer of Colombia*, New York: Harper & Row.

GERALD MARTIN

García Marruz, Fina

b. 1923, Havana, Cuba

Poet and literary critic

An early member of the literary group **Orígenes**, together with her husband, the poet and critic Cintio **Vitier**, García has not received much critical attention, due perhaps to her diffidence and the overshadowing presence of other Orígenes poets. Her poetry is nevertheless first-rate, combining attention to worldly detail with metaphysical (at times religious) investigation. After the Revolution, she combined Christian and socialist values in her poetry and solid and perceptive critical essays. She is especially noted for her research into the works of José Martí, much of it undertaken in collaboration with Vitier.

BEN A. HELLER

García Monge, Joaquín

b. 1881, Desamparados, Costa Rica; d. 1958, San José, Costa Rica

Writer

García was editor throughout most of his life (1919–58) of the important cultural review *Re-*

pertorio *Americano*. He published his first novel, *El Moto*, in 1900; others followed in the 1910s and 1920s. Part of the anti-imperialist intelligentsia, in 1913 he founded a cultural centre with the *Arielist* idea of educating workers. After retiring from his post as director of the National Library in 1936 for political reasons, he devoted himself to his editing work.

JUSSI PAKKASVIRTA

García Ponce, Juan

b. 1932, Mérida, Mexico

Writer

García Ponce's work incorporates various genres, including novel, short story and theatre. He is also a prolific art and literary critic. He has made an enormous contribution to Mexican literary culture through his teaching in the Universidad Nacional Autónoma de México (**UNAM**) and his editorial involvement with numerous literary magazines, including ***Revista mexicana de literatura***. Ponce's fiction is primarily concerned with the evocation of the female, and his 1963 collection of short stories, *La noche* (Night), is a haunting exploration of the destructive nature of relationships. His work has received many prestigious prizes, including the Premio Nacional de Literatura in 1990.

NUALA FINNEGAN

García Riera, Emilio

b. 1931, Ibiza, Spain

Film historian

García is a film critic and historian, founder of several film journals including *Nuevo Cine* (New Cinema) and *DICINE*, and later Director of the Centre for Film Studies and Research at the University of Guadalajara. His major work is the monumental *Historia documental del cine mexicano* (Documentary History of Mexican Film). First published in nine volumes in 1973, its new and definitive 1994 edition contains eighteen volumes of exhaustive research into the development of Mexican cinema from the beginnings of sound in the late 1920s up to the mid-1970s. His autobiography, *El cine es mejor que la vida* (Cinema is Better Than Life) (1990) won the Villaurrutia Prize.

PATRICIA TORRES SAN MARTÍN

García Romero, Rafael

b. 1957, Santo Domingo, Dominican Republic

Writer

Like many others from the Generation of the 1980s, García Romero was a member of the César Vallejo Literary Workshop. He started publishing poetry in the Literary Section of the *La noticia* newspaper. In 1991 he won Third Prize in the **Casa de Teatro** Literary Contest for the short story, 'Y así llegaste tú, Aurora' (And You Arrived Like That, Aurora) written in collaboration with René Rodríguez Soriano and Ramón **Tejada Holguín**. Besides his 1983 short story volume *Fisión* (Fission), this prolific writer has published three other books.

FERNANDO VALERIO-HOLGUÍN

García Uriburu, Nicolás

b. 1937, Buenos Aires, Argentina

Painter

A self-taught artist, García Uriburu was influenced by Mexican arts and crafts. His approach to painting followed the informalist school of the 1960s, but he later experimented with a system of simulated hieroglyphs. His pictorial language included human forms, plants and animals that underwent remarkable transformations. He later experimented with a variety of media to create interior and exterior choreographies. *Prototipos para un jardín artificial* (Prototype Artificial Gardens) (1967–8), exhibited in Paris, for example, included a fashion show. He caused an international outrage when he colour-stained Venice's Grand Canal (1968) and New York's Hudson River (1970).

MAGDALENA GARCÍA PINTO

Gardea, Jesús

b. 1939, Ciudad Delicias, Mexico

Writer

A prolific novelist and short story writer, Gardea is self-taught and one of the very few Mexican writers whose literary world is outside the urban environment. He withdrew from his dentistry practice in 1983 in order to pursue his true vocation, having won the 1980 Xavier Villaurrutia Award for his short story collection *Septiembre y los otros días* (September and Other Days). Two recurrent themes in Gardea's prose are death and solitude, and they often occur in the imaginary and ironically named town of Placeres (Pleasures), where an atmosphere of existential crisis prevails (see **existentialism**).

EDUARDO SANTA CRUZ

Gardel, Carlos (Charles Romuald Gardés)

b. 1890, Toulouse, France; d. 1935, Medellín, Colombia

Singer

The best known of all **tango** singers, both within Argentina and internationally, Gardel's recordings remain popular over sixty years after his death. By around 1910, 'El Morocho' (as Gardel was known) could be found singing at political gatherings in the Balvanera district of Buenos Aires, intoning sentimental ballads in a market, and presenting rural folk songs at some stud farm celebrating the success of its newest racehorse. The older singers were impressed by the young man. In 1913, the new Gardel–Razzano duo had its debut in a club on Corrientes Street; the ovation they received was echoed in all their subsequent performances. Words had still not been added to tango; it was only when Contursi added words to the tango 'Lita' that the duo decided to perform it as 'Mi noche triste' (My Sad Night). Here, for the first time, the love, joy and pain of city life found authentic expression. At about the same time, Gardel began to record for film and photo promoter Max Glucksmann's record company, and it was these discs and the impact of his voice and image on the cinema screen, which carried tango beyond national frontiers. He was the first 'star' of Hollywood's Spanish-language cinema, with films like *Luces de Buenos Aires* (Lights of Buenos Aires) (1930), shot in New York. In 1935 Gardel embarked on a Latin American tour that was to culminate in his 'beloved Buenos Aires', but he never completed the journey. His plane crashed at Medellín on 24 June 1935.

His vital voice, neither nostalgic nor melancholy, has served to sustain what can be called 'the living myth of Gardel', which persists even sixty years after his death; it is said that 'his singing just gets better and better'. It is the voice that keeps alive the myth, of his time in Paris, the fortune he lost at the racecourse, his tragic death in Medellín. His body was so badly burned after the accident that it was unrecognizable, fostering the popular legend that he was still singing, his face burned and disfigured, in some Buenos Aires cafe. It is the register of his singing that ensures the persistence of the myth: typically, his voice is sombre, its 'r' stretched. He does not dramatize the song so much as interpret the feeling of each individual and each situation evoked by the song. Its high point is in 'Anoche a las dos' (Last Night at Two), when he uses three different registers to interpret the three protagonists of the tango, one of whom is a woman. His voice never drowns the orchestra or the guitars, yet it comes from the heart. As Horacio **Ferrer** has said, it is not that Gardel is the voice of tango, it is that tango emerged from his voice.

Further reading

Collier, S. (1986) *The Life, Music and Times of Carlos Gardel*, Pittsburgh, PA: University of Pittsburgh Press.

Eichelbaum, E. (1985) *Carlos Gardel*, Buenos Aires: Javier Vergara.

LUIS GUSMAN

Garibay Kintana, Angél María

b. 1892, Toluca, Mexico; d. 1967, Mexico City

Priest and philologist

Catholic priest, poet and philologist, Angél Garibay Kintana is a seminal figure in Náhuatl studies. He translated numerous works of Aztec poetry, theatre and other genres making them accessible to millions of Spanish readers. Also the translator of Classical Greek works by Sophocles, Euripides and others, Garibay was deeply interested philosophical issues, most particularly Aztec thought. A much beloved commentator on language, Garibay wrote regular columns on language use in Mexico City dailies, often defending the language of his country. His enthusiasm for Náhuatl literature coincided with a renaissance of interest in that language in Mexico, tied in turn to a national reevaluation of the centrality of Aztec culture to Mexican national consciousness.

See also: Náhuatl and Aztec languagues

CHRISTOPHER VON NAGY

Garifuna see Garinagu

Garinagu

The Garinagu (also known as Garifuna or Black Caribs) are an Afro-indigenous ethnic group living in villages along the Caribbean coast of Central America in Belize, Guatemala, Honduras and Nicaragua. They are originally from the Caribbean island of St Vincent, where escaped African slaves (**maroons**) mixed with the native Carib population in the 1600s, forming a syncretic Afro-indigenous culture. In 1797, after a prolonged war with the British, the surviving Garinagu population was exiled to the Central American coast where they established the villages they inhabit today.

Garinagu are considered to be ethnic minorities in all of the countries within which they are found, with a distinctive language and culture. The Garifuna language is based on the grammar of the language spoken by the Island Carib at the time of contact, but with vocabulary and phonetics later borrowed from African languages, French, English and Spanish. Their traditional economic activities include the cultivation of cassava for the production of bread (*ereba*) and fishing; however they also migrate in large numbers to find work in the major cities of Central America, and to the United States (mainly Los Angeles and New York City). Garifuna culture is primarily known for its strong tradition of music and dance which is based on drumming and call-and-response singing such as that performed at wakes (punta), at ancestor rituals and at village festivals (fedu, parranda and wanaragua). Many of these dances are choreographed and performed throughout the world by Garifuna dance troupes such as the Honduran Folkloric Ballet and the Wanichigu Dance Company of New York City. Due to the commercialization and popularity of punta rock, Garifuna music and culture have come to be symbols of national culture and identity in both Belize and Honduras. On 12 April 1997 they celebrated the first bicentennial of their arrival in Central America. This anniversary and the anniversary of the arrival of the Garinagu to Belize (Settlement Day, on 19 November) are celebrated by most Garifuna communities in Central America and the United States with music and dance performances.

Further reading

Cayetano, R. (1993) *The People's Garifuna Dictionary*, Belmopan: National Garifuna Council.

Gonzalez, N. (1988) *Sojourners of the Caribbean*, Urbana, IL: University of Illinois Press.

Kerns, V. (1983) *Women and the Ancestors*, Urbana, IL: University of Illinois Press.

Suazo, S. (1994) *Conversemos en garifuna*, Tegucigalpa: Editorial Guaymuras.

SARAH ENGLAND

Garmendia, Salvador

b. 1928, Barquisimeto, Venezuela

Short story writer, novelist and scriptwriter

Co-founder in the 1950s of the literary group and journal **Sardio**, Garmendia then split from it to form, with others, the **Techo de la Ballena** group. He won the National Prize for Literature in 1973. From *Los pequeños seres* (Little People) (1959) onwards, Garmendia continued to cast his sharp, existential and hyperrealist eye on the city of Caracas and its inhabitants. He was also the writer of one of Venezuela's best soap operas (*culebrón*), *La hija de Juana Crespo* (Juana Crespo's Daughter), and of adaptations of two novels by Rómulo **Gallegos**, *Doña Bárbara* and *Pobre negro* (Poor Black).

JORGE ROMERO LEÓN

Garota de Ipanema

Composed by Antônio Carlos **Jobim** and Vinícius de **Moraes**, 'Garota de Ipanema' (The Girl from Ipanema) is the most famous Brazilian song of all time. It was inspired by Heloísa Eneida de Pinto, a tanned blonde who caught the attention of the two composers as she passed by Veloso's Bar, their hang-out near Ipanema beach. The song first gained international fame in 1964 when Astrud **Gilberto** recorded an English version written by Norman Gimbel, which reached number five on the Billboard charts and won a Grammy as the year's best song. After countless schmaltzy renditions, most Brazilian singers only perform it with considerable ironic distance.

CHRISTOPHER DUNN

Garrincha

b. 1933, Rio de Janeiro, Brazil; d. 1983, Rio de Janeiro

Footballer

Manuel dos Santos, known as Garrincha, the 'little bird', became one of Brazil's most famous footballers. His small frame and crooked legs did not suggest an athletic career, but he was signed by Botafogo and his speed and bewildering dribbling skills propelled him into the national team in 1956. His inventive attacks led to spectacular goals in the **World Cup** victories of 1958 and 1962. He was seen as a *malandro*, a gifted underdog whose talent could surprise opponents. Life after football was difficult. When he died prematurely, his body lay in state at the Maracana Stadium while thousands filed past; many more lined the funeral route. Joaquim Pedro de **Andrade** paid homage to his skills in the short film *Garrincha, alegría do povo* (Garrincha, the People's Joy) (1963).

TONY MASON

Garro, Elena

b. 1920, Puebla, Mexico; d. 1998, Cuernavaca

Writer

By the early 1960s, on the basis of two plays, a novel and a short-story collection, Elena Garro had established herself as one of the leading Mexican women writers of the twentieth century. After studying humanities briefly at the **UNAM** in 1936, Elena Garro studied dance and worked as an actress and choreographer in the Teatro de la Universidad, under the direction of Julio **Bracho**. In 1937 she married the poet Octavio **Paz** and together they worked with the International Brigades in the Spanish Civil War (see **Spanish Civil War, impact of**). Garro began writing journalism and theatre upon their return to Mexico in 1938 and during their sojourns in New York and Paris. She wrote her classic short-story collection, *La semana de colores* (The Week in Colours) (1960), and her most famous novel, *Los recuerdos del porvenir* (Recollection of Things To Come) (1963), while she was hospitalized in a sanatorium in Berne, southern France. The novel went on to win the Xavier Villaurrutia Prize, and was adapted for the screen by Arturo **Ripstein**. A saga of the Cristero Wars told by an entire community, the novel's stories revolve around the loves of the Cristero generals and their mistresses. The novel has recently been the subject of criticism by Jean Franco and Debra Castillo.

La semana de colores was an equally original book of short stories, which included the masterpiece, 'La culpa es de los tlaxcaltecas' (It's the Fault of the Tlaxcaltecas). Here Garro again explores female subjectivity, as a neglected bourgeois wife, circa 1960, finds happiness by running off with an Aztec warrior, with the complicity of her maid. As this plot suggests, Garro was among the first Mexican authors to make extensive use of **magical realism**, through the fantasy life of imaginative little girls, alienated housewives and resourceful prostitutes and *campesinos*: all marginal characters.

During her years in Paris, Garro had a monthlong affair with the Argentine writer Adolfo **Bioy Casares**, followed by an intimate correspondence that lasted two decades. Shortly after Paz and Garro returned to Mexico City in 1948, their daughter Helene was born; the two women would be inseparable for five decades. In 1951–8 the family lived in Japan, and in New York from 1959–63. Back in Mexico again, Garro wrote the play, *Felipe Angeles* (1979), on the life of the revolutionary general, as well as several film scripts and the trilogy, *Un hogar sólido* (A Solid Home) (1958). These works earned her a reputation as a major playwright, as well as a writer of fiction.

Ever the strong-willed individualist, Elena Garro made herself a *persona non grata* in Mexican intellectual circles beginning in 1968, when she and her daughter Helena, taken to a student meeting by Carlos **Monsiváis**, publicly accused leaders of the movement of collusion with the government. Subsequently she was accused of naming names to government officials (a charge that she steadfastly denied). When they began receiving anonymous death threats, she and her daughter went into self-imposed exile, first in New York; then, from 1974 to 1984, in Madrid and Paris. During this period Garro published her memoirs of the Spanish Civil War, *Memorias de España*, and the novel, *Andamos huyendo Lola* (Let's Make a Run for It, Lola) (1980), revolving around the themes of persecution and the mother–daughter bond.

Garro finally returned to Mexico twenty years later, and in 1994 she settled, with her daughter and five cats, in a cramped apartment in Cuernavaca. She died of a heart attack, brought on by emphysema, four years later, in poverty and relative obscurity.

During the final years of her life Garro published a series of minor novels written during the 1960s: *Un corazon en un bote de basura* (A Heart in a Garbage Can) (1996), *Un traje rojo para un duelo* (A Red Dress for a Duel) (1996) and others. The year 1999 saw the appearance of the posthumous novel, *Mi hermanita Magdalena* (My Little Sister Magdalena) (1999); still other unpublished manuscripts may well follow.

Scandal has always trailed Garro, from her denunciation of the student leaders in 1968, to her daughter's current conflict with University of New Mexico Professor Patricia Rosas, over intellectual property rights to Garro's unpublished manuscripts and personal photograph collection. As Carlos Monsiváis wrote shortly after her death, Garro was controversial, contradictory and a great writer.

Selected bibliography

Garro, E. (1997) *First Love and Look for My Obituary: Two Novellas*, trans. David Unger, Willamantic, CT: Curbstone Press.
—— (1979) *Recollections of Things to Come*, trans. Ruth L.C. Simms, Austin: University of Texas Press.

Further reading

Bradu, F. (1987) *Señas particulares, escritora: Ensayos sobre escritoras Mexicanas del siglo XX*, Mexico City: Fondo de Cultura Economica.
Castillo, D. (1999) *Easy Women. Sex and Gender in Modern Mexican Fiction*, Minneapolis: University of Minnesota Press.
Franco, J. (1989) *Plotting Women. Gender and Representation in Mexico*, New York: Columbia University Press.
Stoll, A.K. (ed.) (1990) *A Different Reality: Studies on the Work of Elena Garro*, Lewisburg: Bucknell University Press.
Winkler, J. (2000) *Light into Shadow: Marginality and*

Alienation in the Work of Elena Garro, New York: Peter Lang.

CYNTHIA STEELE

Garvey, Marcus Mosiah

b. 1887, Saint Ann's Bay, Jamaica; d. 1940, London, England

Pan-Africanist leader

Founder in 1914 of the **Universal Negro Improvement Association** (UNIA) in Jamaica, which won considerable influence in the USA during the 1920s, Garvey was born in rural Jamaica, and moved to Kingston as a young man. After working for a short time as a printer he made visits to Central America and also lived briefly in England between 1913 and 1914. The decision to found the UNIA was based on his observations of the negative political and economic circumstances faced by people of African descent around the world. At first, the organization had difficulty winning wider popular support. Then, in 1916, Garvey travelled to the USA where he settled in New York, giving public lectures and promoting his political ideas. He advocated the founding of black businesses and civic organizations and also criticized the political and economic disabilities faced by black populations under colonialism in Africa and the Caribbean and under discriminatory laws or practices elsewhere. He advocated various commercial and political ties between black people in the Americas and on the African continent; however, scholars still debate the extent to which he envisioned large scale emigration to Africa. Garvey founded a branch of the UNIA in New York in 1918 and from the USA the organization grew into an international movement with tens of thousands of members. Partly in response to this organizing success, Garvey was arrested on mail fraud charges in 1922. He was convicted, imprisoned and eventually deported from the USA in 1927. He spent most of the remainder of his life in Jamaica and in England, continuing UNIA activities but never again with the mass success of the early 1920s. He died in England in 1940, survived by his second wife, Amy Jacques Garvey, and two sons. In 1964 he was declared Jamaica's first national hero and his remains were sent back to Jamaica and interred at a Marcus Garvey memorial site in Kingston.

ROSANNE ADDERLEY

Garzón y Collazos

One of Colombia's best-known singing duos, Darío Garzón and Ángel Collazos achieved national and international recognition for their *bambuco*s; hence their status as heroes of Colombian folk music. Their first album appeared in 1949, and they have recorded over 200 songs, including Los cisnes (The Swans), Espumas (Foam), Flor del campo (Flower of the Countryside) and Me llevarás en ti (You'll Carry Me within You). They continued to sing together until 1976.

ALEJANDRA JARAMILLO

Gasalla, Antonio

b. 1941, Buenos Aires, Argentina

Comedian

Gasalla's satirical, witty humour led him towards the café-concerts. A graduate of the National Conservatory of Drama, his first appearance was in a show called *Chin-Chin* in 1964. By 1978 he had become highly successful with his show *El Maipo es el Maipo y Gasalla es Gasalla*, but his greatest triumph was his role as the grandmother in Alejandro Doria's film *Esperando la carroza* (Waiting for the Hearse) (1985). In the 1990s, Gasalla worked in television, where he effectively combined his fine humour with social commentary.

RODRIGO PEIRETTI

Gaspar Ilóm

b. 1939, Guatemala City

Guerrilla leader

Born Rodrigo Asturias Amado, he joined a

revolutionary group in 1961 and was twice arrested and exiled to Mexico. Rejoining the guerrillas in Guatemala in 1973, he adopted the name of Gaspar Ilóm, protagonist of a novel written by his father, Nobel Prize-winning novelist Miguel Angel **Asturias**. Ilóm later formed the ORPA (Organizacíon Revolucíonaria del Pueblo en Armas – Revolutionary Organization of the People in Arms) which became active in 1979. As its commander, Ilóm participated in the formation in 1982 of the **URNG** (Guatemalan National Revolutionary Unity), which brought together all Guatemala's revolutionary organizations. He was its chief negotiator in peace negotiations beginning in 1987, which led finally to a treaty signed in 1996.

ARTURO ARIAS

Gasparini, Graziano

b. 1924, Venice, Italy

Architect

A specialist in restoration, Gasparini has organized the restoration of a number of colonial civic and military constructions in Venezuela and has directed architectural research throughout Latin America. As Professor of Architectural History at the Universidad Central in Caracas, and director of the Centre for Historical and Aesthetic Research there, he has written widely on colonial architecture and the baroque in Latin America. Gasparini has always rejected the term 'mestizo architecture' to designate what was built during the period of Spanish colonial domination, arguing that it represents a process of acculturation rather than mixing.

GUILLERMO GREGORIO

Gatica, José María

b. 1925, San Luis, Argentina; d. 1963, Buenos Aires

Boxer

Gatica, nicknamed 'El Mono' (the Monkey), dominated Argentine boxing in the 1940s and 1950s (though he was never national champion). Born into a poor provincial family, he was a shoeshine boy and bottle collector before turning professional in 1945. He won eighty-five of his ninety-five fights and lost seven. In the heyday of **Peronism** he evoked as much adoration as resentment, professing admiration and loyalty for both Evita (see **Perón, María Eva Duarte de**) and **Perón**. He earned a fortune and died penniless. His life was fictionalized by novelist Enrique **Medina** (*Gatica* (1991)) and film director Leonardo **Favio** (*Gatica el mono* (1993)).

CLAUDIA TORRE

Gatica, Lucho

b. 1928, Rancagua, Chile

Singer

Born Luis Enrique Gatica Silva, Gatica was the epitome of the **bolero** singer and made his first recording in 1949. With the support of influential disc jockey Raúl Matas, Gatica performed with great success on Santiago's Radio Minería. Early hits included 'En nosotros' (In us) and 'Amor que malo eres' (Love you're so bad) and his series of recordings with the group Los Peregrinos, producing classics like 'Contigo en la distancia' (With you in the distance) and 'Sinceridad' (Sincerity). His album with Roberto Inglez' orchestra, which included 'Bésame mucho' (Many kisses) and 'Las muchachas de la plaza España' (The girls of España Square) was an international hit. He now lives in Mexico City.

OSCAR HAHN

Gattorno, Antonio

b. 1904, Havana, Cuba; d. 1980, New York, USA

Painter

A painter within the *criollista* (peasant) current, Gattorno nevertheless developed a style characterized by langour, sober lines and warm colours, exemplified in canvases like *Mujeres junto al río*

(Women by the River) (1927). Though he studied in Havana, it was a period spent in Europe (1920–7) in contact with the Spanish and Italian Old Masters and the new French artistic trends that determined the direction of his work. In the late 1930s he moved to the United States and abandoned his rural, peasant themes for surrealism.

WILFREDO CANCIO ISLA

gaucho

The gaucho is an ethnic and cultural type, emblematic of Argentine culture. According to **Borges**:

> It is the gauchos of Buenos Aires province who dominate, paradoxically because it is the area closest to the great city of Buenos Aires which produced several prominent 'gauchesque' writers. If instead of questioning literature, we were to look into history, we would find that these much glorified gauchos have played little or no role in the history of their own province or the country as a whole.

This comment brings to an end a debate that began in Argentine culture in the late nineteenth century concerning the origin and nature of the gaucho, and whose resolution was sought in both literature and history.

From the beginning of the nineteenth century, the gaucho, inhabitant of the temperate zones around the River Plate, was a literary character, the protagonist of 'gauchesque' literature. In a historical context, he was an agricultural labourer or a peasant farmer from the provinces of Corrientes, Entre Rios, Santa Fe and Uruguay between the mid-eighteenth and the late nineteenth century. He was a soldier in the wars of independence and later, since his existence was nomadic, a fighter in the various guerrilla armies. He is associated exclusively with the uninhabited lands at the margins of the ***pampa***, and he is never to be found in the city.

In literature, by contrast, the gaucho is associated with Buenos Aires province, and continues to appear well into the twentieth century (Ricardo **Güiraldes**' *Don Segundo Sombra* was published in 1926). Since his disappearance coincided with the consolidation of the nation-state and the constitution of cultural nationalism, the gaucho became, thanks to several intellectuals linked to the state power, the emblem of 'lo argentino' – the Argentine character – an identity that privileged the elites just as they felt threatened by the arrival of large numbers of European immigrants. An example are the lectures read by Leopoldo **Lugones** before the President of the Republic in 1913 and published as *El payador*, or the work of Ricardo **Rojas**, in whose history of Argentine literature (1917) the gaucho and his principal poetic expression *Martín Fierro* (1872–9) is placed at the centre of the epic story of Argentina. In 1948, Ezequiel **Martínez Estrada**, taking for granted the 'representativity' of the gaucho in Argentine life, wrote 'The gaucho poems, the accounts of the English travellers and the works of W.H. Hudson together form a great literature, a great marginal literature outside the list of texts we normally like to read'. The national classics, *Martín Fierro* and *Don Segundo Sombra* have a gaucho as their hero and the countryside as their setting. The gaucho dimension has also come to be identified with popular culture, especially outside Argentina. In the 1920s, for example, Carlos **Gardel** sang tangos in Europe and North America wearing gaucho dress; even today in international sporting competitions, the Argentine team tend to be called 'the gauchos'.

The origin of the term gaucho is unclear, as so often with terms that in the first instance define an oppressed group, but in Argentine culture it has both negative and positive connotations. On the one hand it is synonymous with an individual outside the law, marginal, lazy, corrupt; on the other it has come to signify nobility, industry and loyalty. Calling someone 'gauchito/a' is a term of endearment and 'hacer una gauchada' (behaving like a gaucho) means doing someone a favour. It is rarely used in the feminine except as an adjective.

Further reading

Ludmer, J. (ed.) (1987) *El género gauchesco. Un tratado sobre la patria*, Buenos Aires: Ediciones Sudamericana.

Montaldo, G. (1993) *De pronto al campo. Literatura argentina y tradición rural*, Rosario: Beatriz Viterbo.

Slatta, R.W. (1983) *Gauchos and the Vanishing Frontier*, Lincoln: University of Nebraska Press.

GRACIELA MONTALDO

gaúcho culture

Rio Grande do Sul, the southernmost state of Brazil, has a complex history owing to its geographical position at the frontier of the former Spanish and Portuguese empires (a frontier that was unstable in colonial times and well into the nineteenth century). The plains area in the western part of the state is a continuation of the pastoral region of Uruguay and northeastern Argentina, and its culture is marked by linguistic and cultural crossings of many kinds; indeed, it is widely believed that the Spanish word **gaucho** originated with the Portuguese gaúcho, and the speech of the border region between Uruguay and Brazil has fascinated linguists for some time (see **borders**).

Out of this complex history came the gaúcho traditionalist movement, which began in the 1940s and currently counts some two million adherents. Perhaps the largest folk movement of its kind in the world, the thousands of *Centros de Tradição Gaúcha* (Centres of Gaúcho Tradition), or CTGs, organize folk song festivals, poetry competitions, commemorative public events, dance and other performance, and many other activities. There are CTGs not only in the southern states of Rio Grande do Sul and Santa Catarina but also in São Paulo (where there are some forty centres) and in the other major cities of the centre and north, with others as far afield as Tokyo and Los Angeles. Major figures associated with the CTGs include Luiz Carlos Barbosa Lessa, Antonio Augusto Fagundes and Jayme Caetano Brum. Fagundes's writings include a fascinating *Curso de Tradicionalismo Gaúcho* (Course in Gaúcho Traditionalism) (1997), which includes instructions on how to found a CTG, and byzantine instructions on how to determine what is and what is not authentic gaúcho culture.

The movement began with a group of high school students in Porto Alegre in 1948 who, dissatisfied with the Comtean positivism that prevailed in their city, sought to find (or invent) roots in rural life. They founded the "35 CTG', with the number '35 referring to the date of the Farroupilha Revolution of 1835. (The rustic lodge of the '35 is now dwarfed by the mosque-like dome of the adjacent shopping mall.) Inspired in part by the 'nativist' movement in neighbouring Uruguay, their group led to a vast network of traditionalist centres, better organized, and politically and culturally more powerful, than anything that currently exists in Uruguay and Argentina. Ruben Oliven, in a controversial study of the traditionalist movement, argues that its urban roots are essential to the movement: the young students invented a past that they did not know and had not experienced. The nostalgic impulse, according to Oliven, is not at ease with the modernity of the entire enterprise, which depends on mass communications (these days including many hours of live broadcasts on the weekends from traditionalist centres) and the support of the state government. In 1999 some leftist intellectuals expressed their discomfort with the **PT** (Labour Party) majority in the Rio Grande state government for lending its support to what they consider a reactionary movement. Meanwhile, Renato **Borghetti**, the accordeonist who had been a rather heterodox figure in the music of Rio Grande, has come out with an album of traditionalist music entitled *Gaúcho* (1999).

Further reading

Antologia da Estância da Poesia Crioula (1987) Porto Alegre: Editora Sulina, 2nd edn.

Fagundes, A.A. (1997) *Curso de Tradicionalismo Gaúcho*, Porto Alegre: Martins Livreiro Editor, 3rd edn.

Lessa, L.C.B. (1987) *As Mais Belas Poesias Gauchescas*, Porto Alegre: Editora Sulina.

Oliven, R. (1996) *Tradition Matters: Modern Gaúcho Identity in Brazil*, trans. C. Chaves Tesser, New York: Columbia University Press.

DANIEL BALDERSTON

Gavaldón, Roberto

b. 1909, Chihuahua, Mexico; d. 1986, Mexico City

Film-maker

A master of the melodrama, Gavaldón worked with some of the outstanding figures of forties Mexican cinema including cinematographers Gabriel **Figueroa** and Alex Phillips, scriptwriter José **Revueltas** and designer Gunther **Gersz0**. After training as assistant director, his first film was *La barraca* (The Hut) (1944), a faithful version of Blasco Ibáñez's original novel. Forty-seven films followed, outstanding among them *La otra* (The Other) (1946) with Dolores **Del Rio**, *El rebozo de Soledad* (Soledad's Shawl) (1952), *Macario* (1959) and *La Rosa blanca* (The White Rose) (1961). His work, previously overshadowed by better-known contemporaries, has recently been positively re-evaluated.

PATRICIA TORRES SAN MARTÍN

Gaviria, Victor

b. 1955, Medellín, Colombia

Writer and film-maker

Gaviria began producing amateur films with a strong documentary impulse, experimenting with Super 8 and later video, as an extension of his literary work. His first feature film, ***Rodrigo D: no futuro*** (Rodrigo D: No Future) (1990), continued this trajectory and was a national and international revelation of his talent. Featuring real street kids, the film depicts the chaotic and rootless gangs of teenagers that roam Medellín's working-class *barrios*. Four of the boys who acted in this film had been killed in the streets of Medellín by the time the film was released. Also set in Medellín, his next film, *La vendedora de rosas* (The Rose Seller) (1997), focused on another kind of street character, a thirteen-year-old rose vendor who sets out into the night on Christmas Eve to sell enough flowers for a new dress and a nice time with her drug-dealer boyfriend. Shot in eighteen weeks on night-time locations and again with non-professional street kids (but this time set up in special housing, complete with an adoptive father, a psychologist and cleaning women to keep things stable), Gaviria's compassionate film has been well-received internationally.

ANA M. LÓPEZ

gay and lesbian cultures

Gay and lesbian cultures have been an integral part of Latin American culture. Lesbians and gays have participated and assumed positions of relative power in historical and contemporary cultural debates. At times, these debates have used homosexuality – under the guise of 'effeminacy' or 'decadence' – as the point of departure for exclusionary acts. At other times, the very participation of homosexuals has produced a 'homosexual panic' underlying those debates. An example of the former in the late nineteenth and early twentieth century read the 'decadent' Latin American *modernismo* (see **modernismo, Spanish American**) as a pan-Hispanist patriarchal construct. Exemplary of the latter were the debates about the 'virility' of Mexican literature after the Mexican Revolution (see **revolutions**), those taking place in relation to cosmopolitanism or 'nationalism' throughout Latin America in the 1940s, or discussions about aesthetics and social commitment in the 1960s: all were marked by a homosexual panic produced because some gays and lesbians occupied instrumental positions of power. Nevertheless, if it is clear that homosexuality has been the named or unnamed panic involved in many Latin American cultural disputes, it is also clear that this panic has consistently involved gay men, for the patriarchal nature of cultural institutions has always resisted considering lesbians equal participants in national discourses. Because the more recent interest in gay and lesbian studies (at least in the USA) – with its correlative 'outing' of important figures of the past and present – is no guarantee that networks of power will not once again conspire to erase homosexuality as an unnamed source of intellectual debate, it is important to include within the very notion of gay and lesbian cultures the wide array of cultural subjects and objects that in some way or another we claim as our own. What we can consider 'gay and lesbian cultures' in Latin America runs the gamut from the popular milieu of the farándula to the abstract figurations of poetics, and it has produced documentary films and realist novels, biting satire and agonized laments, political manifestoes and dense, allusive poems: all of which are always questioning the very sense of contradiction that the culture at large sees in these terms.

Although many authors have openly dealt with issues of homosexuality (José **Donoso** in *El lugar sin límites* (1966), Octavio **Paz** in *El **laberinto de la soledad*** (1950) among others) and there have been interesting, homosocial studies on many canonical Latin American writers (José Martí, Jorge Luis **Borges** and others), it is useful to distinguish between those authors and others whose complex subject positions open them up for a poetics of suspicion, as is the case with the seventeenth-century Mexican writer Sor Juana Inés de la Cruz, Venezuelan novelist Teresa **de la Parra**, Cuban anthropologist Lydia **Cabrera**, Nobel Prize-winner Gabriela **Mistral** and Argentine poet Alejandra **Pizarnik**. In historical terms, it is perhaps more accurate to start the inevitable roster of names with nineteenth-century literary *modernismo*, since the figure of the alienated poet and artistic dissident gave rise to a number of voices collapsing a vision of art and homosexuality. This accounts for the exquisite orientalism of Julián del Casal in Cuba, for example. In Brazil, particular mention should be made of Adolfo Caminha (1867–97), whose *Bom-crioulo* (1895) is innovative for embedding not only homosexuality but also an interracial love story within its narrative. More homosexual, and strictly in the twentieth century, the Guatemalan Rafael **Arévalo Martínez** needs to be included since his short story, 'El hombre que parecía un caballo' (The Man Who Looked Like a Horse), revolves around the friendship between two poets who have generally been taken to be Arévalo himself and the Colombian Porfirio **Barba-Jacob** (pseudonym of Miguel Angel Osorio, 1883–1942). Similarly, Augusto **D'Halmar** in *La pasión y muerte del cura Deusto* (The Passion and Death of the Priest Deusto) (1924), and *Nirvana* (1920), talks about homosexual relationships between older and younger men.

Perhaps the more important nuclei of openly gay writers after Latin American *modernismo* were the poets and artists grouped around the magazine *Contemporáneos* in Mexico, who were openly identified as 'effeminate' or 'queer' and spawned a polemic over the 'virility' of Mexican literature. The list includes Salvador **Novo** and Xavier **Villaurrutia**, the latter the author of one of the most important book of Mexican poetry, *Nostalgia de la muerte* (Nostalgia of Death) (1938). In Cuba, the tortured poetry of Emilio **Ballagas** was whitewashed for its homosexuality by official critics until Virgilio **Piñera** wrote a long article in **Ciclón** on its homosexual themes. Piñera's homosexuality in turn was an open secret, as was that of José **Lezama Lima** and José Rodríguez Feo, the publisher of the two most important literary journals of twentieth century Cuba, **Orígenes** and *Ciclón*. Although Piñera did not openly write about homosexual themes, they do appear in his best novel, *La carne de René* (René's Flesh) (1953). José Lezama Lima's masterpiece **Paradiso** (1966) contains accounts of homosexual sex, rendered in his difficult **neo-baroque** prose. *Contemporáneos* and *Orígenes* signal the collective appearance of a group of (particularly) gay men at the centre of a literary and cultural polemic during a period of intense self-questioning in Latin American culture.

Although these writers were part of a 'first generation' of Latin American gay and lesbian authors in the twentieth century, there were other figures who worked in different contexts and knew of these developments. The Argentine Manuel **Mujica Laínez** included homosexual characters in his early fiction, although his first 'openly' homosexual text was the novel *Sergio* (1976); so did the Argentine José **Bianco** (1909–86), author of such works as *Las ratas* (1943) (Rats), and René **Marqués**, from Puerto Rico, author of *La mirada* (The Gaze) (1975). At least two other South American writers were particularly open about their homosexuality: Peruvian poet César **Moro** and Argentine Juan Rodolfo **Wilcock** (1919–78).

The generation of Cuban writers who came of age during the 1960s was also directly affected by the revolution's attitude towards homosexuality. Writers like Calvert Casey, Reinaldo **Arenas** and Severo **Sarduy** left Cuba and died in exile, the last two openly talking about their homosexuality in

New York and Paris. Beyond literature, we should include cinematographers like Néstor **Almendros**, who co-directed *¿Conducta impropia?* (Improper Conduct?) (1984), an account of the Cuban Revolution's (see **revolutions**) treatment of homosexuals, that became a *cause célèbre* in the early 1980s and spawned a belated response from Cuba in **Gutiérrez Alea**'s *Fresa y chocolate* (Strawberry and Chocolate) (1993), based on a story with homosexual themes by Senel **Paz**. Perhaps the only member of the literary '**Boom**' in the 1960s who was gay and openly identified with homosexuality was Manuel **Puig**, particularly in *El beso de la mujer araña* (The Kiss of the Spider Woman) (1976), a novel that is still unsurpassed in its treatment of the intellectual and personal dispute between the left and homosexuality.

In chronological terms, the next generation was more open about its homosexuality, including Luis Rafael **Sánchez** (Puerto Rico), Sylvia **Molloy** (Argentina), Cristina **Peri Rossi** (Uruguay), particularly in her book of poems *Evohé* (1971), Manuel **Ramos Otero** (Puerto Rico), Néstor **Perlongher** (Argentina) and Luis **Zapata** (Mexico). More recent figures include Diana **Bellessi** (Argentina), Silviano **Santiago** (Brazil) and João Silvério **Trevisan** (Brazil), along with film-maker Jaime Humberto **Hermosillo** (Mexico). This work has also been complemented by a roster of brilliant lesbian and gay Latino writers in the United States, who can only be barely mentioned here: John Rechy, Cherrie Moraga, Achy Obejas, Luz María Umpierre, Frances Negrón and Elías Miguel Muñoz.

See also: gay and lesbian movements

Further reading

Balderston, D. and Guy, D. (eds) (1997) *Sex and Sexuality in Latin America*, New York: New York University Press.

Bergmann, E. and Smith, P.J. (1995) *¿Entiendes? Queer Readings, Hispanic Writings*, Durham, NC: Duke University Press.

Foster, D.W. (1994) *Latin American Gay Literature: A Biographical and Critical Sourcebook*, Westport, CT: Greenwood Press.

Molloy, S. (ed.) (1997) *Hispanisms and Homosexualities*, Durham, NC: Duke University Press.

JOSÉ QUIROGA

gay and lesbian movements

In the same year as the Stonewall riot in the United States, 1969, the first homosexual group in Latin America, Nuestro Mundo (Our World) was formed in Argentina. Through the 1970s, a dozen or so gay and lesbian groups were formed in three of the region's forty-one countries. By the early 1980s there were over one hundred groups organized around the defence of the rights of homosexuals. This was a reflection of the prevailing national and regional politico-economic instability; yet the end of the decade was marked by a dramatic decline in the levels of mobilization of sexual minorities. This coincided with a period of grave violations of the rights of gays, lesbians and transsexuals, and with the spread of **AIDS**, which predominantly affected male homosexuals. The 1990s witnessed a significant resurgence of these minority movements, borne out by the formation of pioneer groups in countries where no homosexual organizations had previously existed, by the significant growth of more militant groups, by the first legal victories in some countries, and by the successful organization of continent-wide meetings of the leaders of these groups. The prospects for the future are optimistic, and today Latin American homosexuals can be heard chanting at meetings and demonstrations the slogan of the international movement: 'We are millions, we are everywhere and the future is ours!'

The *Spartacus Gay Guide* indicates the existence of cruising areas, bars and commercial establishments sympathetic to or openly favouring this population in all forty-one countries of Latin America and the Caribbean. Yet only half of those countries register the occasional existence of groups in defence of homosexual rights. Four of these countries – Chile, Ecuador, Cuba and Nicaragua – had till recently penal codes criminalizing homoerotic acts, although there is no evidence that these statutes have been applied during the last decade.

A typology of the homosexual movement in Latin America could begin by gathering countries into four groups or tendencies: (1) those countries in which, since the 1970s, there has been consistent mobilization of a variety of organized groups, in particular Argentina, Brazil, Mexico, Peru, Colombia and Venezuela; (2) countries where small homosexual groupings have emerged, albeit intermittently, through the 1980s, like Chile, Uruguay, Jamaica, the Dominican Republic and Puerto Rico; (3) countries which have seen the emergence of embryonic homosexual movements, with one or two small groups arising in the nineties, like Bolivia, Ecuador, Costa Rica and Nicaragua; and (4) the rest, countries where no homosexual movement exists.

Latin American countries are culturally diverse, some with a strong indigenous presence, others influenced by African culture, and some with pronounced Hispanic traditions. Yet all these countries are characterized by virulent *machismo* (see **machismo, Mexican**) and homophobia, reinforced by the omnipresence of the **family** and the difficulty for young people of attaining economic independence, all of which inhibits the willingness of young people to come out; and in turn explains the small size and short life of militant gay groups. Social rejection, public humiliation and police persecution are the daily diet of Latin American homosexuals, to such a degree that it is often said 'you have to be really macho to be gay in Latin America'. The term 'marica' (queer) and its variants are still regularly used everywhere in Latin America.

Despite such barriers and restrictions, the gay and lesbian movement has consolidated its presence in some countries as an important agent in the struggle for democratic freedoms and in defence of the human rights of sexual minorities, in particular in Argentina, Brazil, Mexico and Peru.

Argentina

It was during the military dictatorship (1966–72) that Argentina, the most European country in South America, saw the emergence in November 1969 of its first homosexual politico-sexual group, Nuestro Mundo, which in 1971 changed its name to the Homosexual Liberation Front (FLH), absorbing several similar small organizations like Eros, Safo and Bandera Negra (Black Flag). The FLH described itself as an anti-capitalist, anti-imperialist and anti-authoritarian movement defending the need for homosexuals to struggle against the oppression of 'mariquitas', 'maricones' (queers) and 'tortilleras' (lesbians). In 1973 it began to produce the magazine *Somos* (We Are), which ran to eight issues. The FLH was dissolved in 1976, when another military *coup* ushered in a decade of strong police repression, repeated raids of places frequented by gays and the murder of homosexuals. In 1984, when this second military regime was overthrown, the struggle for the defence of the human rights of homosexuals began again, producing the most persistent and dynamic national organization, **Comunidad Homosexual Argentina** (CHA, Argentine Homosexual Community) devoted to defending the right to freedom of sexual expression, the exposure of homophobic abuses and the support of victims of oppression and authoritarianism. Carlos Jáuregui (d. 1996) and Alejandro Zalazar, both university-educated, have been among its most prominent leaders. In 1986, the International Day of Homosexual Dignity was celebrated for the first time with a rally in the Parque Centenario. The 1990s were marked by a rising level of homosexual organization, the formation of specific lesbian and transsexual groups, among them the Sociedad de Integración Gay Lesbiana de Argentina (Argentine Society for Gay Lesbian Integration), Centro Argentino de Estudios y Documentación Lésbicos-Homosexuales (Argentine Centre for Lesbian-Homosexual Studies and Documentation), **Gays por los Derechos Civiles** (Gays for Civil Rights), Investigación en Sexualidad e Integración Social (Research into Sexuality and Social Integration), Convocatoria Lesbiana (Lesbian Convocation), Las lunas y las otras (Moons and Others), Comunidad de la Iglesia Metropolitana (Metropolitan Community Church) and Transexuales por el derecho a la vida y a la identidad (Transsexuals for the Right to Life and Identity). In 1996, Buenos Aires became the first Hispanic American city to outlaw discrimination on the grounds of sexual orientation.

Brazil

Brazil was the second country in Latin America to witness the formation of a gay organization, but it is undoubtedly in this huge country, with more than 160 million inhabitants, that the gay and lesbian movement has developed furthest both in terms of the number of militant groups and of the importance of its political victories. Unlike Spanish America, Brazil did not suffer the terrifying presence of the Inquisition that executed twenty or more sodomites. In 1823, when the first Imperial Constitution was written under the influence of the Napoleonic Code, sodomy ceased to be a crime (see **sodomy laws**). The age of consent in Brazil is eighteen.

Despite **carnival**, androgyny and the much-vaunted sensuality of Brazilians, homosexuals are the most persecuted minority in the country; the degree of rejection reaches 80 per cent in opinion polls. One homosexual is murdered every three days, the victim of homophobia. The first gay column in the Brazilian press, the first national gay journal and the first gay liberation groups all appeared during the military dictatorship (1964–83). 1977 can be considered the founding year for the Brazilian homosexual movement, for it was then that the editor of *Gay Sunshine*, Winston Leyland, was invited to Brazil by lawyer João Antonio Mascarenhas; he was prevented from speaking at the University of São Paulo, but the visit was widely publicized in the national press. The first and most important homosexual journal, *O Lampião*, was founded the following year, and a year later the pioneering militant Brazilian gay group – Somos – was established, taking its name from the review published by the FLH in Argentina. Eight more groups were rapidly formed across the country and in 1980 the First Conference of Brazilian Homosexuals was held in São Paulo. In the same year anthropologist Luiz **Mott** formed the **Grupo Gay da Bahia**, the oldest such group in continuous existence in Latin America and responsible for a number of fundamental victories: it was the first to be officially incorporated and to be declared a municipal public service organization; it led the campaign to remove homosexuality from the category of diseases in the Brazilian health code, which happened in 1985; and it was responsible for the passage of seventy-three laws prohibiting discrimination on grounds of sexual orientation in Brazilian states and municipalities. In 1995 the Associação Brasileira de Gays, Lésbicas e Travestis (Brazilian Association of Gays, Lesbians and Transsexuals) was formed.

Mexico

The **Frente Homosexual de Acción Revolucionaria** (Homosexual Revolutionary Action Front) is considered the first militant organization in Mexico. It was formed out of the fusion of three anarchist (see **anarchism**) and socialist (see **socialism**) groups and made its public appearance in July 1978 at a meeting in solidarity with the Cuban Revolution (see **revolutions**). In the following year FHAR headed the first national gay march, which led to the formation of new organizations including Grupo Orgullo Homosexual de Liberación (Homosexual Pride Liberation Group), Nueva Batalla (New Battle), Grupo de Jóvenes Homosexuales y Lesbianas de Tijuana (Young Gay and Lesbian Group of Tijuana) and Coordinadora Nacional de Lesbianas (National Lesbian Coordination). As in Argentina and Brazil, the second half of the 1980s saw a decline in the level of mobilization of sexual minorities as a result of police violence, illegal detentions or invasions of gay establishments, and the murder of some gay leaders. The AIDS crisis produced new groups dedicated to its prevention among them Colectivo Sol (Sun Collective) led by Juan Jacobo Hernández, the Grupo Homosexual de Acción Revolucionaria and El Closet de Sor Juana (Sor Juana's Closet).The cultural supplement *Letra S* appears monthly in *La Jornada*, and a **Semana Cultura Gay** (Gay Cultural Week) is held every June in Mexico City.

Peru

The Movimiento Homosexual de Lima (**MHOL**, Homosexual Movement of Lima), founded in 1983, has sustained a tireless resistance in defence of gay, lesbian and transsexual rights in Peru, and pursued two main objectives: raising the confidence and consciousness of homosexuals in defence of their civil rights and disseminating correct information on sexuality to the population in general. Unlike Argentina and Mexico, where a number of short-lived groups emerged, in Peru MHOL continued to be active and remained almost alone, apart from the Grupo de Autoconciencia de Lesbianas Feministas (Lesbian Feminist Self-Awareness), and the Asociación Peruana de Liberación Homosexual (Peruvian Homosexual Liberation Movement) and Contramano (The Other Hand). 1991–2 were key years in the development of sexual politics in Peru, marking the first celebration of Gay Pride and the first publication of two journals, *Déjà Vu Gay* and *Conducta Impropia* (Improper Conduct). Rebeca Sevilla, President of MHOL, was the first Latin American to be elected General Secretary of the International Gay and Lesbian Association.

In general terms, it can be said that the gay and lesbian movement in Latin America has the following features. Its leaders are young, middle class and university-educated, while the majority of its members are from the poorer sectors of society. The first organizations included gays, lesbians and transsexuals, but more recently each group has tended to organize separately, while maintaining friendly and cooperative relations. Homosexual groups are usually small, poorly resourced, and rarely have a stable base or systematic contributions from their membership. Many groups emerged at moments of deep political crisis and in response to violence against homosexuals, receiving support from other civil and human rights organizations, left-wing parties or groups and individuals living abroad. Their activities are usually widely covered in the national media. In both quantitative and qualitative terms the movement of gays, lesbians and transsexuals in Latin America is growing as new groups are formed, the older groups become more sophisticated and begin to receive institutional support, homosexuality itself becomes more visible and more respectable, organizations are meeting at the continental level, and Latin American gay and lesbian leaders are increasingly participating in international organizations.

Further reading

Balderston, D. and Guy, D. (eds) (1997) *Sex and Sexuality in Latin America*, New York: New York University Press.

Carrier, J. (1995) *De los otros: Intimacy and Homosexuality among Mexican Men*, New York: Columbia University Press.

Comité de Servicio Chileno-Cuáquero (1993) *Abriendo Puertas: Una aproximación a la realidad lésbico-homosexual de América del Sur*, Santiago: CSCHC.

Green, J.N. (2000) *Beyond Carnival: Male Homosexuality in Twentieth-Century Brazil*, Chicago: University of Chicago Press.

Howes, R. (1987) 'The Literature of Outsiders: The Literature of the Gay Community in Latin America', in *Latin American Masses and Minorities: Their Images and Realities*, Madison, WI: University of Wisconsin Press.

Lumsden, I. (1996) *Machos, Maricones, and Gays: Cuba and Homosexuality*, Philadelphia: Temple University Press.

—— (1991)*Society and the State in Mexico*, Toronto: Canadian Gay Archives and Solediciones.

Mott, L. (1996) *Homophobia: Violation of Human Rights of Gays, Lesbians and Transvestites in Brazil*, San Francisco: International Gay and Lesbian Human Rights Commission.

Murray, S. (1995) *Latin American Male Homosexualities*, Albuquerque, NM: University of New Mexico Press.

Trevisan, J.S. (1986) *Perverts in Paradise*, trans. M. Foreman, London: Gay Men's Press.

LUIZ MOTT

gay male literature

The 1990s witnessed a concerted effort, primarily by Euro-American scholars, to track a gay male literary heritage. The differences in sexual systems within and among Latin American countries make the application of Euro-American gay identity politics problematic and uneven because the social construction of male homosexuality in Latin America differs from US and European counterparts. Few Latin American countries can claim a gay liberation movement like the US model. In Mexico, for example, men who exclusively play the role of penetrator with other men do not necessarily lose their heterosexual identity. Luis **Zapata**, Mexico's most prominent gay novelist, refuses the ghettoized classification of his novels as gay literature.

Despite these differences and tensions, the category of gay male literature in Latin America exists, on a minor scale, as a marketing category and as an object of inquiry. The pioneer text addressing male homosexual practices is Adolfo Caminha's Brazilian naturalist novel *Bom-Crioulo* (Bom-Crioulo: The Black Man and the Cabin Boy) (1895), where male–male sexuality is racialized as a psycho-sexual aberration since the emancipated seaman slave is the tragic victim of his uncontrollable desires for the nubile blonde cabin boy. Other early texts belonging to the tragic homosexual genre include Chile's Augusto **D'Halmar**'s *La pasión y muerte del cura Deústo* (The Passion and Death of Father Deusto) (1924) and Mexico's *El diario de José Toledo* (The Diary of José Toledo) (1964) by Manuel **Barbachano Ponce**. Both conclude with the lead character's suicide, the first due to the priest's unreconcilable and unarticulated erotic attachment to his younger protégé, while in the latter, unrequited love leads to the tragic denouement. In José **Donoso**'s *El lugar sin límites* (Hell Has No Limits) (1966), socioeconomic power relations are played out through gender and sexual roles, where the transvestite brothel owner La Manuela and her sadistic, hyper-masculine suitor Pancho are in varying degrees both victims of compulsory heterosexuality. Authoritarian dictorships give rise to texts which link political repression to questions of sexual choice and liberation as are the cases with Cuba's Senel **Paz**'s *El lobo, el bosque y el hombre nuevo* (The Wolf, the Forest, and the New Man) (1991), adapted to the screen as **Fresa y chocolate** (Strawberry and Chocolate) (1993), and Manuel **Puig**'s *El beso de la mujer araña* (Kiss of the Spider Woman) (1976). Politically less repressive than the aforementioned national contexts, Luis Zapata's *Las aventuras, desventuras y sueños de Adonis García, el vampiro de la colonia Roma* (The Adventures, Misadventures and Dreams of Adonis Garcia: Vampire of the Roma District) (1979) celebrates male homosexual urban subcultures through the figure of a Mexico City hustler.

See also: gay and lesbian culture; gay and lesbian movements

Further reading

Balderston, D. (1999) *El deseo, enorme cicatriz luminosa*, Caracas: ExCultura.

Bergman, E. and Smith, P.J. (eds) (1995) *¿Entiendes? Queer Readings, Hispanic Writings*, Durham, NC: Duke University Press.

Foster, D.W. (1991) *Gay and Lesbian Themes in Latin American Writing*, Austin, TX: University of Texas Press.

—— (ed.) (1994) *Latin American Writers on Gay and Lesbian Themes: A Bio-Critical Sourcebook*, Westport, CT: Greenwood Press.

Molloy, S. and Irwin, R.M. (1998) *Hispanisms and Homosexualities*, Durham: Duke University Press.

SERGIO DE LA MORA

Gayoso, Milia

b. 1962, Villa Hayes, Paraguay

Writer

A regular contributor to newspapers like *El Día*, Gayoso's first published journalism appeared in the university journal *Turú*. She has published four short story collections: *Ronda en las olas* (Serenade in the Waves) (1990), *Un sueño en la ventana* (A Dream in the Window) (1991), *El peldaño gris* (The Grey

Stair) (1993), and *Cuentos para tres mariposas* (Stories for Three Butterflies) (1996).

TERESA MÉNDEZ-FAITH

Gays por los Derechos Civiles

Gays por los Derechos Civiles (Gays DC) was founded in October 1991 by Carlos Jáuregui and Marcelo Feldman. It is an organization which fights 'against discrimination on grounds of sexual orientation and for the right to be different'. It provides legal services and psychological counselling without charge. It created the first twenty-four-hour anti-discrimination telephone help line in Argentina. It has presented three draft laws to Congress, one of which, the Law for a Contract of Civil Union between people of the same sex, has gained some support in Congress.

RODRIGO PEIRETTI

Gazitúa, Francisco

b. 1944, Santiago, Chile

Sculptor

A strong believer in the duty of culture to appropriate public spaces, Gazitúa has spent much of his career creating monumental sculptures of wood, stone and, in the 1990s, steel. He designed the doors to the **Congress Building** in Valparaíso, and a twenty-five-foot stylized navigational instrument pointing to the future for the **Santiago Airport, International Terminal**. His abstract and human figures always contain strong references to pre-Hispanic and colonial sculptural styles, expressed in baroque forms. In the 1990s Gazitúa explored the problematic relationship between Chile's natural geography and Santiago's urban growth, in works like a steel version of the central valley's weeping willow.

CELIA LANGDEAU CUSSEN

Gebara, Ivone

b. 1944, São Paulo, Brazil

Philosopher and theologian

A Catholic religious, her pastoral and theological work has evolved among the Christian communities of the northeast of Brazil, the poorest region in the country. A member of the Congregación de Nuestra Señora, Canónicas de San Agustín, her theological reflections seek to contribute to the liberation of women and the reorganization of society along egalitarian lines. Gebara has adopted the ecofeminist view in offering a critical and holistic understanding of the central questions faced by Christianity.

See also: Catholicism; feminist liberation theology; liberation theology

MARÍA PILAR AQUINO

GECU

In 1972, the Grupo Experimental de Cine Universitario (Experimental University Cinema Group), or GECU, was founded in Panama as part of the progressive cultural measures taken by **Torrijos**. The group, headed by Pedro Rivera, worked to create a filmic nationalist history of Panama. Their first short dealt with a bloody incident in 1964 when Panamanian students attempted to fly the flag in the **Canal Zone**. Over the next five years they produced more than thirty short documentaries. The group's theoretical journal, *Formato 16*, became despite its irregular publishing schedule one of the most serious film publications in Latin America. GECU began to lose momentum when it lost state funding in 1977.

NORMAN S. HOLLAND

Gego

b. 1912, Hamburg, Germany; d. 1994, Caracas, Venezuela

Artist

Although part of the neoconstructivist tradition, Gego (Gertrudis Goldschmidt) also distinguished herself from that movement and was admired and imitated by younger, contemporary artists and critics. Gego's work is marked by the presence of reticular patterns woven in metal thread, some in monumental and environmental proportions (like the *Gran reticulárea* in the collection of the National Gallery of Art, Caracas). She deconstructs the rigid constructivist forms by integrating disposable materials into 'rizomas' by successive insertions and aleatory additions. Going beyond kineticism (see **kinetic art**), Gego opened new directions in modern Venezuelan art.

LUIS PÉREZ ORAMAS

Gelman, Juan

b. 1930, Buenos Aires, Argentina

Poet

Gelman's poetry has a quality of exalted speech, touching directly on events of this world, public and private, yet speaking of them with passion and (sometimes) rage. In eloquent poems like 'Bellezas' (Beauties) and 'Arte poética' (The Art of Poetry) (1973) he attacks the static ideas of poetry that he associates with the work of Octavio **Paz**, José **Lezama Lima** and Alberto **Girri**. For Gelman, poetry is 'como un martillo la realidad/ bate/ las telitas del alma o corazon' (like a hammer reality/ beats/ on the tissues of the soul or the heart.) His work includes ardent poems on the Cuban Revolution (see **revolutions**), beautiful love lyrics, translations from imaginary English and Japanese works, lyrics in Ladino (the language of Sephardic Jewry after the expulsion from Spain in 1492), and a moving letter to his late mother. A central figure in the **Montoneros**, Gelman was exiled to Italy and then to Mexico, where he still resides, after members of his family were killed by the military.

In 1988, in a book-length series of interviews with Roberto Mero, he was frank in his self-critique and in a review of the errors of the Argentine left of the 1970s. The Ladino poems of *Dibaxu* (Below) (1985) are very popular, and have been set to music. An extraordinary poet, a complex man, Gelman (who won the Juan Rulfo prize in 2000) is revered and widely read in a country where he has chosen not to live.

DANIEL BALDERSTON

gender

Gender is a cultural construct which changes according to place and time. In Latin America, the culture that imposes distinct gender roles on the population can be traced back to the Conquest and the ensuing patterns of expected gendered behavior; it only began to be challenged with the postwar processes of **urbanization** and industrialization. The dominant gender ideology, based on the cultural and symbolic value system of *machismo*/**marianismo**, circumscribes what is deemed 'appropriate behaviour' for both sexes. **Machismo**, which stresses male dominance and virility, relies on a dual sexual morality that expects promiscuity of men and chastity of women. Its roots lie in Old World culture; concepts of honour and shame associated with manliness can be found in many of the cultures of southern Europe. While these concepts of behaviour seem to be in decline in Spain, they seem to have flourished and become more aggressive in Latin America. *Machismo*'s counterpart, *marianismo*, requires submissiveness from women, involving qualities such as gentleness, humility, kindness, self-sacrifice, patience and moral strength. This contrast of roles is symbolically enacted in the lyrics of tangos (see **tango**) and boleros (see **bolero**), which in their turn become the source through which writers like Manuel **Puig** and José **Donoso** address the unspoken prescriptions that bear down on their protagonists.

Gender roles are spatially depicted in terms of a dichotomy of separate spheres in which the 'public' world of the street (*la calle*) symbolizes the world of the male and the 'private' world of the home (*la casa*) stands for the world of the female. The implication of this social ordering of space is that women tend to be primarily concerned with home and family, that is the personal, and therefore are less likely to participate in the public arena of employment and politics. In the postwar years, demographic changes in the urban/rural composition of the population and economic crises have undermined the material bases of gender relations. The growing need for all adult members of the family to contribute earnings has blurred the boundaries between private and public spheres, and among the poorer sections of society a majority of households are economically dependent on women. And yet, underpinned by legal and **kinship** systems, and reinforced in many areas of popular and mass culture, the emphasis on male dominance has maintained a firm grasp on Latin American culture at an ideological level.

Further reading

Cubitt, T. and Greenslade, T. (1997) 'Public and private spheres: The end of the dichotomy', in E. Dave (ed.) *Gender Politics in Latin America*.

Jelin, E. (1991) *Family, Household and Gender Relations in Latin America*, London: Kegan Paul/UNESCO.

MacEwan, S. (1994) *Divisions and Solidarities: Gender, Class and Employment in Latin America*, London: Routledge.

TESSA CUBITT

Gené, Juan Carlos

b. 1928, Buenos Aires, Argentina

Playwright, theatre director and actor

Gené is the author of *El herrero y el diablo* (The Blacksmith and the Devil) (1955), an Argentine recreation of the Faust legend, *El inglés* (The Englishman) (1974), a cantata set during the English invasions of 1806, and *Memorial del cordero asesinado* (Memoir of the Sacrificial Lamb) (1990). In the 1950s he worked as an actor and director in theatre and television. During the military government, he went into exile in Venezuela where he worked intensively with groups like **Rajatabla**. He served as president of the Argentine Actors' Association and director of the **Teatro San Martín**.

NORA MAZZIOTTI

Generación del 60

The intense cultural renewal that prevailed in Argentina in the late 1950s in literature, theatre and humour produced a similar movement in cinema. The growth of **cine clubs**, the emergence of specialized journals and legislative and financial incentives for short film production encouraged a group of new film-makers, including Rodolfo **Kuhn**, Manuel **Antín**, David **Kohón**, Lautaro **Murúa** and Simón **Feldman**, to experiment with new forms of expression. Stylistically heterogenous, the group nevertheless acknowledged common influences and antecedents in neo-realism and the French New Wave, and in the work of Argentine directors like Leopoldo **Torre Nilsson**, Fernando **Ayala** and Fernando **Birri**.

DIANA PALLADINO

General, El

b. 1970, Rio Abajo, Panama

Musician

El General (Edgardo Franco) first struck it big in the US market with 'Tu Pun Pun' in 1991. He had begun to write and perform much earlier, at the age of twelve. Asked to write a campaign song for a mayoral candidate, his successful patron then arranged a scholarship for him to study business administration in the USA. 'Muévelo' (Move it), his video directed by Rolando Hudson, marked his return to music and earned him an MTV award. *Es Mundial* (It's Worldwide) (1995) won Best Rap Album at the 1995 Latin Music Awards, and included 'Latinos a ganar' (Latinos Let's Win), a song adapted by Spanish-speaking soccer (see **football**) fans at the 1994 **World Cup** as their anthem.

NORMAN HOLLAND

Gerbasi, Vicente

b. 1913, Canoabo, Venezuela; d. 1992, Caracas, Venezuela

Poet

In Gerbasi's exceptional poetry, the magnificent flora and fauna of his home region in northern Venezuela merge with the twilight world of the poetry of Novalis and others. His poetry is at once sensual and meditative, portraying through word and rhythm a real or imaginary landscape reconstructed from memory and dream. His 1945 volume *Mi padre el inmigrante* (My Father the Immigrant) was the first in a series of fine works including *Los espacios cálidos* (Warm Spaces) (1952), *Edades perdidas* (Lost Ages) (1981) and *Iniciación en la intemperie* (Initiation in the Storm) (1990).

RAFAEL CASTILLO ZAPATA

Gerchman, Rubens

b. 1942, Rio de Janeiro

Painter and printmaker

In the 1960s, Gerchman was influenced by the general return to figuration in Brazilian art. From 1968 to 1971 he was in the USA, making a living from commercial art. When he returned, Brazilians were re-evaluating the importance of **neo-concretism**. Gerchman combined a knowledge of and interest in **pop art** with the more abstract explorations of language and form of the neo-concretists.

GABRIEL PEREZ-BARREIRO

Gerchunoff, Alberto

b. 1883, Proscuroff, Ukraine; d. 1949, Buenos Aires, Argentina

Fiction writer, essayist, poet and journalist

Born in a *shtetl* (small town with mainly Jewish population) in the Ukraine, Gerchunoff emigrated in 1890 with his family to Argentina, settling first in the Jewish colony of Moisés Ville, Santa Fe, and later in Rajil, Entre Ríos. The memory of his early rural experiences formed the basis of his most famous work, *Los gauchos judíos* (The Jewish Gauchos), published in 1910 in commemoration of the Centenary of Independence. This series of stories offers an elegiac vision of life on the *pampas*, showing immigrants and *criollos* in harmonious coexistence in spite of the occasional hint of underlying prejudices. Gerchunoff's wide range of interests is reflected in his novels and approximately two thousand essays dealing with such topics as love, nationality, politics, literature and **Judaism**. His fictional writings include evocative studies of Heine and Spinoza. His admiration for Cervantes led to the publication of *Nuestro señor Don Quijote* (Our Lord Don Quixote) (1913), *La jofaina maravillosa* (The Enchanted Pitcher) (1922) and the posthumous *Retorno a Don Quijote* (Return to Don Quixote, prologue by Borges) (1951). There is also an autobiographical account in *Entre Ríos, mi país* (Entre Rios, My Country) (1950) and *El hombre importante* (The Important Man) (1934) offers a humorously critical portrayal of the nascent democratic politics of his day.

Gerchunoff became one of Argentina's leading cultural figures, making accessible through his essays and lectures some of Europe's most important writers as well as the poetry of Darío and other modernist (see **modernismo, Spanish American**) poets. He was remembered, by Borges among others, for his elegant turn of phrase both as conversationalist and as a prose writer. Gerchunoff combined his literary activities with being a prolific journalist: he wrote for a variety of newspapers but is identified mainly with **La Nación** for which he was an easily recognizable leader writer, and where he wrote justly famous obituaries over a period of forty years. Gerchunoff exemplifies the immigrant who became totally assimilated into and accepted by his adoptive country while maintaining a faithful interest in his own cultural past.

See also: Jewish writing

Further reading

Gover de Nasatsky, M.E. (1976) *Bibliografía de Alberto Gerchunoff*, Buenos Aires: Fondo Nacional de las Artes.

Jaroslavsky de Lowy, S. (1957) *Alberto Gerchunoff: Vida y obra – Bibliografía – Antología*, New York: Hispanic Institute.

EVELYN FISHBURN

Gerszo, Gunther

b. 1915, Mexico City

Painter and set designer

Gerzso studied theatrical set design in the USA and began to paint. Upon returning to Mexico, he began his career as a film set designer on the third version of *Santa* (Norman Foster, 1943) and went on to work with all the principal directors of the Mexican cinema while continuing to paint. His earliest paintings reflect the influence of the European surrealists (see **surrealism in Latin American art**), but by the 1960s Gerzso developed his mature style: brightly-coloured geometric abstractions with architectural and archeological connotations, based on carefully delineated grids. He is one of Mexico's principal exponents of postwar internationalism.

JAMES OLES

Gesta Bárbara

Gesta Bárbara was a journal which provided a platform for two generations of Bolivian writers. Founded in 1918, its first ten issues were published in Potosí. Twenty years later in 1948, the second series began publication, though it only ran to four issues. Both series published poetry of group members as well as essays and articles by contemporary writers, among them Carlos Medinaceli, Gamaliel **Churata** and Armando Alba, who could be described as the founders of Bolivian literary criticism.

J.M. DE LA VEGA RODRÍGUEZ

Ghabiang

Ghabiang are a Surinamese band that played an important role in the popularization of **maroon music** in Suriname and the Netherlands. In the early 1980s lead singer Iwan Esseboom, an Afro-Surinamer from the coastal region, joined with Saramaka and Ndjuka maroon musicians from the interior and helped launch a new 'roots-muziek' trend drawing on traditional maroon styles. In 1989 he formed Ghabiang, along with the influential Saramaka maroon musicians Ernie Seedo and Errol Burger. Whether performing pan-Caribbean genres such as **reggae** and **soca** or local Surinamese styles such as kaseko or winti-poku, Ghabiang seamlessly blends the maroon musical heritage into their mix.

KEN BILBY

Giardinelli, Mempo (Oscar)

b. 1947, Resistencia, Chaco, Argentina

Writer

A journalist and commentator, Giardinelli's first creative writings were poetry and short stories – but he is best known as a novelist. He was awarded the Rómulo Gallegos literary prize in 1993 for his novel, *Santo oficio de la memoria* (The Holy Office of Memory), and the Mexican National Award in 1983 for *Luna caliente*, published in English as *Sultry Moon* (1998). He founded the short-story magazine, **Puro cuento**, in 1986 and was its editor until it closed in 1992. In 1976, Giardinelli went into exile in Mexico after his novel, *Toño tuerto rey de ciegos* (One-Eyed Tony, King of the Blind), was pulped by the publishing house for political reasons. He returned in 1990 to live in his home town of Resistencia. Giardinelli has published articles, essays and stories in newspapers and magazines throughout the world, and his works have been translated into a dozen languages.

ANDREW GRAHAM-YOOLL

Gieco, León

b. 1951, Cañada Cosquín, Argentina

Singer and songwriter

Considered the Bob Dylan of Argentina, and influenced principally by folk music, Gieco achieved from his earliest recordings a combination of the rhythms of progressive music and Argentine popular and **folk music**. In this sense, his most ambitious musical project was undoubtedly *De Ushuaia a La Quiaca*, which set out to offer a panorama of Argentine music from one extreme of the country to the other, including styles as different as the 'cuartetazo' of Córdoba and the Andean 'vidala'. The project, which included video, was never completed for lack of funds, though three albums did appear in 1985–6.

DIEGO BENTIVEGNA

Gil Gilbert, Enrique

b. 1912, Guayaquil, Ecuador; d. 1973

Writer

Member of the **Guayaquil Group** and co-author of *Los que se van*, *cuentos del cholo y el montuvio* (The Vanishing ones. Stories about the Cholo and the Montuvio) (1930). He saw literature as a vehicle for social protest, but this does not detract from his considerable lyrical powers. Nuestro pan (Our Daily Bread) (1943) his most famous novel, was first runner up to the Farrar & Reinehart prize won in 1940 by **Ciro Alegría**'s *El mundo es ancho y ajeno* (Broad and Alien is the World). Other works include *Yunga* (Jungle) (1933) and *Relatos de Emmanuel* (Emmanuel's stories) (1939).

HUMBERTO ROBLES

Gil, Gilberto

b. 1942, Salvador, Bahia

Singer and songwriter

Gilberto Gil (Gilberto Passos Gil Moreira) ranks with his contemporaries Caetano **Veloso** and Chico **Buarque** as a composer and lyricist of rare beauty and insight. A master guitarist with a marvellous voice, he is perhaps the most spectacular performer of his generation. Since the mid-1960s, Gil has also distinguished himself as a committed activist on behalf of social and racial equality, democratization and, most recently, the environment. Like Veloso, Gil has consistently explored the intersection of cosmopolitan eclecticism and the tradition of Brazilian popular song.

Raised in the small town of Ituaçu in the Bahian outback, Gil's early musical influences included the regional stars of the *baião* (a rural northeastern dance music), especially Luiz **Gonzaga**, who inspired him to learn the accordion following his move to Salvador in 1951. By the end of the decade, deeply impressed by João **Gilberto** and **bossa nova**, he would begin to learn the guitar. In the early 1960s he studied business administration at the Federal University of Bahia, and began to compose songs, record promotional jingles, and perform on television. In 1965, following a pair of successful concerts in Salvador with Caetano **Veloso**, **Maria Bethânia**, Gal **Costa**, and Tom **Zé** (the Bahian group), he moved to São Paulo where he became active in the left-wing artistic milieu which was beginning to protest the recently installed military regime. Together with the Bahian group, he performed in two musical theatre productions directed by Augusto **Boal**, *Arena canta Bahia* (Arena Sings Bahia) and *Tempo de Guerra* (Time of War) and made frequent appearances on Elis **Regina**'s televised musical showcase *O fino da bossa* (The Best of Bossa). His early compositions, featured on the 1967 album *Louvação*, are marked by politically-engaged populism with particular concern for the plight of rural peasants.

At the Third Festival of Brazilian Popular Music aired by TV Record in November 1967, Gil performed Domingo no Parque (Sunday in the Park), rhythmically based on Afro-Brazilian **capoeira** music and accompanied by the experimentalist rock group, Os **Mutantes**. Gil's composition won second prize and was hailed as an important innovation of **MPB** together with Veloso's 'Alegria, Alegria'. These two performances initiated the musical experience of *tropicalismo*, a broad cultural movement manifest in several artistic fields. During this period he composed important songs with poet Torquato **Neto**, including Marginália II, a poetic statement on Brazil's peripheral global position, and Geléia Geral (General Jelly), a jocular critique of Brazilian modernity which was a key song-manifesto of the tropicalist movement (see **Tropicália**). At the end of that year, Gil and Veloso were arrested by military authorities who were alarmed by their increasingly brazen irreverence toward the authoritarian regime and the conservative values it promoted. On the eve of his exile to London, Gil recorded the hit Aquele Abraço (That Embrace), an exultant celebration of Rio de Janeiro, popular culture, and the Brazilian masses.

By this time, he had already begun to explore new creative directions driven by spiritual and technological concerns evidenced on his third solo album from 1969 and by his musical production overseas. During the post-tropicalist phase he also began appropriating elements of African-American soul which anticipated later forays into **reggae**, funk, rap (see **rap music**), and other musical forms of the African diaspora. Throughout the 1970s, Gil evidenced increasing awareness of his own position as an Afro-Brazilian artist. In 1977, following his participation in the Second International Black Arts and Culture Festival in Lagos, Nigeria, Gil recorded his most consciously black-identified album, *Refavela*, featuring songs by Afro-Bahian carnival organizations, **Filhos de Gandhi** and **Ilê Aiyê**. Two years later Gil recorded his biggest hit ever, Não chore mais, a Portuguese version of Bob **Marley**'s No Woman, No Cry which expressed an irrepressible faith in the incipient redemocratization process and became the hymn for the amnesty of political exiles.

Since the political opening in Brazil, Gil himself has become increasingly involved in the civic and political life of Brazil. As president of the Gregório de Matos Foundation, a municipal organ of Salvador, he strengthened cultural ties with West Africa and organized early plans to restore the city's historic centre **Pelourinho**. After an unsuccessful bid for the mayor's office in 1988, he was elected to the municipal council where he focused on protecting the environment and combating racial discrimination. He would later found a private foundation, *Onda Azul* (Blue Wave), dedicated to the protection of Brazilian inland and coastal waters.

In the 1990s, Gil retreated from party politics, pursued non-governmental action on behalf of the environment, and continued to compose, record, and perform internationally. His 1994 live recording *Gilberto Gil: Unplugged* featured acoustic versions of many of his best songs from the last thirty years. During this time he also developed a fascination with the internet and has maintained an informative web-site which updates his activities as a musician, environmentalist, and public intellectual. Gil has explored technologies of mass communication since the beginning of his career and the internet is just the latest vehicle for his expansive intellect and globally-aware artistic imagination.

Further reading

Gil, G. (1982) *Gilberto Gil: Expresso 2222*, ed. A. Risério, Salvador: Corrúpio.

Gil, G. and Risério, A. (1988) *O poético e o político*, Rio de Janeiro: Paz e Terra.

—— (1992) *Songbook*, 2 vols, Rio de Janeiro: Lumiar.

—— (1996) *Todas as letras*, São Paulo: Companhia das letras.

Perrone, C. (1989) *Masters of Contemporary Brazilian Song: MPB 1965–1985*, Austin: University of Texas Press.

CHRISTOPHER DUNN

Gilberto, Astrud

b. 1940, Salvador, Bahia, Brazil

Singer

Astrud Gilberto began singing **bossa nova** in casual gatherings and parties in the south zone of Rio de Janeiro. Her professional career began serendipitously in 1963 when she accompanied her husband, João **Gilberto**, to a recording session with Stan Getz for the Grammy award winning album *Getz/Gilberto*. At the session, Getz insisted that she record an English version of two songs, including '**Garota de Ipanema**' (The Girl from Ipanema), which became a massive hit in the United States. After the couple divorced in 1965, she pursued a successful solo career in the USA and Brazil.

CHRISTOPHER DUNN

Gilberto, João

b. 1931, Juazeiro, Bahia, Brazil

Musician

The principal innovator of **bossa nova** in the late 1950s, João Gilberto (João Gilberto do Prado Pereira de Oliveira) is one of the most exalted interpreters of twentieth-century Brazilian popular music. He has recorded relatively little and his public performances are rare. An exacting and meticulous musician, he can spend months perfecting one song. In a musical culture which values novelty and change, Gilberto has steadfastly devoted himself to the original stylistic innovations he made in the 1950s.

Born and raised in a rural Bahian town, he was a great admirer of the romantic crooners, Lúcio Alves and Orlando **Silva**. Gilberto moved to Rio de Janeiro in 1949 where he joined a popular vocal group, Garotos da Lua, and circulated within a young artistic milieu which was beginning to absorb North American bebop and cool **jazz**. In 1955, after several frustrating years singing in nightclubs, he left Rio and spent the next two years in different cities, relying on the support of his friends. During this hiatus, he experimented incessantly with new rhythms and harmonies on his acoustic guitar which would revolutionize Brazilian popular music.

He returned to Rio in 1957, and there met young composer-musicians like Antônio Carlos **Jobim**, Ronaldo Bôscoli, Roberto Menescal and Newton Mendonça, who would form the core of the emergent bossa nova movement. In 1958, he recorded a 78 rpm of Jobim's '**Chega de saudade**', a song which has been called 'the minute and 59 seconds which changed everything'. It was later released on his first LP album, *Chega de saudade* (No More Blues), which also featured Jobim's 'Desafinado' (Off Key), the musical manifesto of bossa nova which coyly replied to conservative critics of the new style. After releasing two more highly successful albums, *O amor, o sorriso e a flor* (Love, a Smile and a Flower) and *João Gilberto*, he performed in the historic 1962 Carnegie Hall concert which introduced bossa nova to the American public. He later collaborated with tenor saxophonist Stan Getz, a luminary of West Coast jazz, on *Getz/Gilberto*, which also featured his wife, Astrud **Gilberto**, singing 'The Girl from Ipanema' and 'Quiet Nights of Quiet Stars' in English. The album reached the top of the *Billboard* pop charts, achieved gold status, and won six Grammys in 1964.

In the 1960s and 1970s, Gilberto lived outside Brazil and released several acclaimed albums including his 1973 *João Gilberto*, which is perhaps the purest, most distilled bossa nova sound ever recorded. Since his definitive return to Brazil in 1980, he has recorded little and performed even less, yet continues to fascinate music critics and the public with his reclusive existence, mysterious habits, and tireless dedication to perfecting the style he invented decades ago.

Further reading

Campos, A. et al. (1974) *O balanço da bossa e outras bossas*, São Paulo: Perspectiva.

Castro, R. (1990) *Chega de saudade*, São Paulo: Companhia das Letras.

Treece, D. (1996) 'Guns and Roses: Bossa Nova and Brazil's Music of Popular Protest, 1958–68' in *Popular Music* 15(1): 1–29.

CHRISTOPHER DUNN

Gilkes, Michael

b. 1933, Georgetown, Guyana

Playwright

Gilkes's plays typically combine realism and surrealism, dance and music, to explore the multi-racial identity of the Guyanese peoples. *Couvade* is based on an Amerindian ritual associated with birth, and was chosen to represent Guyana at the first **CARIFESTA** of 1972. He is also an actor and producer. As an academic, Gilkes has lectured in Britain, the United States, Guyana and in Barbados, his adopted home. He is a leading interpreter of Guyanese writers Wilson **Harris** and Edgar **Mittelholzer**.

LOUIS JAMES

Gilroy, Beryl

b. 1924, Berbice, Guyana

Writer, educator and clinical psychologist

Gilroy went to England in 1951 and became the first black headmistress in her North London borough. Taking a Ph.D. in psychology, she opened a private counselling clinic in London for black women. Her many-faceted experience underlies her writing, including the autobiographical *Black Teacher* (1976), poetry and short stories, and fiction, of which *Frangipani House* (1986) won a GLC prize for Black Literature. *Stedman and Joanna – a Love in Bondage* (1991) and *Inkle and Yarico* (1996) are historical fiction.

LOUIS JAMES

Giménez, Carlos

b. 1948, Buenos Aires, Argentina; d. 1991, Caracas, Venezuela

Playwright and theatre director

Giménez directed the El Juglar theatre in Buenos Aires and founded and directed the Fundación **Rajatabla** in Caracas, where he worked until his death. Giménez arrived in Venezuela in 1968 on his way to exile in Europe. He stayed in Caracas instead, and established the theatrical company Rajatabla in 1972 with the staging of Antonio Miranda's *Tu país está feliz* (Your Country is Happy). Giménez's dramaturgy was based upon an understanding of theatre as an all-encompassing spectacle. It was also characterized by his preoccupation with the aesthetic effects of visual elements in plays.

JACINTO FOMBONA

Ginastera, Alberto

b. 1916, Buenos Aires, Argentina; d. 1983, Geneva, Switzerland

Composer

While Ginastera is rightly celebrated as the most powerful voice in Argentine musical nationalism, his deepest wish was to be identified as a 'craftsman' (or 'architect') of 'America', rather than 'Latin America'. To this end, the national elements characterizing his earliest works, notably the ballets *Panambi* and *Estancia* (Ranch) became gradually stylized, transformed and (in Ginastera's own phrase) subjective, leading finally to a compositional phase where dramatic structure, serial and aleatoric techniques, and neo-expressionistic writing (in the opera **Bomarzo**, for example) all but obscured the exuberant colours of his early folklorism.

Ginastera trained at the Williams Conservatory in Buenos Aires before entering the National Conservatory in 1936. In 1937 he produced two works which immediately proclaimed his nationalist leaning: the ballet *Panambi* and the piano suite *Danzas argentinas* (Argentine Dances). In Argentina, Juan José **Castro** and Luis Gianneo in particular had pioneered the use of folkloric elements in a 'classical' music context, but Ginastera, in these and other works, brought this synthesis to the boil, and drew international attention. Already, in his 1934 *Impresiones de la Puna* (Impressions of the Puna) for flute and string quartet, Ginastera had evoked the windswept Andean altiplano and its ancient Incan culture. In *Panambi*, indigenous music and mythology of the Río de la Plata received evocative, neo-impressionistic treatment. The vital *Danzas argentinas* drew sinewy, fleeting thumbnail sketches of typical country characters, a subject developed in the ballet *Estancia* (1941) which traces a simple love story unfolding during one day on a pampean *estancia*. The distant horizons, waving grasses and corn, and rugged country life all receive affectionate treatment. The American composer Aaron Copland (whose ballet *Appalachian Spring* deals with similar themes) was so impressed by Ginastera's output when they met in 1941 that he arranged a Guggenheim Fellowship, allowing Ginastera to travel (after the war) to the USA, where he attended the important Tanglewood Festival.

Estancia employed spoken texts from the epic poem *Martín Fierro*, and focused on Ginastera's preoccupation with the symmetries of time passing, horizon, seasons and landscape on the *pampas* (see **pampa**). The song cycle *Las horas de*

una estancia (1943), based on poems by Silvina **Ocampo**, and the three *Pampeanas* (1947–54) (no. 1, violin and piano; no. 2, cello and piano; no. 3, orchestra) develop this interest, and in particular demonstrate the structural use of a chord based on the guitar's open strings, a symbol for Ginastera of the *pampas* itself. The driving rhythms of the malambo are also important. A predilection for moving music from and to silence through a vast arch of sound characterizes these works, reflecting landscape itself, bounded by dusty blue horizons.

Ginastera's distinguished teaching career was interrupted several times under **Perón**. In 1945 he was removed from his post at the National Military Academy for signing a civil liberties petition, and in 1952 he was dismissed from his own Conservatory of Music and Dramatic Arts in La Plata, but was reinstated in 1956. In 1958 he founded the Music Faculty at the Catholic University of Argentina. He continued to teach until 1971, when he married the cellist Aurora Natola and moved to Switzerland to concentrate fully on composition. His Piano Sonata no. 1 (1952) had been a huge success, and throughout the 1950s Ginastera was in demand as a film composer in Argentina.

Increasingly, the USA became Ginastera's compositional centre of gravity. Two almost simultaneously composed works from 1960–1 resulted from American funding, and were first performed at the 1961 Interamerican Music Festival in Washington DC: Piano Concerto no. 1 and *Cantata para América mágica* (Cantata for Magical America). Both works opened a door on intense and dramatic expression, virtuoso vocal or instrumental technique, and on taut, finely controlled micro- and macro-structures; both also revelled in hitherto untried magnificent and sonorous spatial effects. The *Cantata*, for soprano and vast percussion orchestra, celebrates the magical, primitive origins of the entire American continent, and is written in language suffused with archaic, gritty ritual, yet firmly grasping modern compositional technique. Its symmetrical structure is emphasized by an exactly palindromic central 'Scherzo fantastico', a compositional *tour de force*.

Ginastera's operas (see **opera**) *Don Rodrigo* (1963–4), *Bomarzo* (1966–7), and *Beatrix Cenci* (1971) further develop his skills as dramatist and lyricist: each dwells on cruelty, sex, power and corruption. His marriage to Natola prompted several fine cello works: *Serenata* (1971), *Puneña* no. 2 (1976) and *Sonata* (1979). In his last (and incomplete) composition, *Popul Vuh*, for orchestra (1975–83), Ginastera turned once again to his roots and the creation mythologies of Latin America.

Further reading

Kuss, M. (ed.) (1986) *Alberto Ginastera: A Complete Catalogue*, New York: Boosey & Hawkes.
—— (ed.) (1990) *Alberto Ginastera: Musikmanuskripte*, Winterthur: Amadeus.

SIMON WRIGHT

Giorgi, Bruno

b. 1905, São Paulo, Brazil; d. 1993, Rio de Janeiro, Brazil

Plastic artist

One of Brazil's major monumental artists, Giorgi studied in Europe before returning to Brazil in 1939. In 1941 he executed the *Monumento a Juventude* (Monument to Youth) at the Ministry of Health and Education (**Ministério da Educação e Saúde**) in Rio de Janeiro. In the 1950s he moved away from figurative work, though the human body remained a dominant motif. His *Monumento aos Candangos* (Monument to the Candangos) (1960) commemorated the founding of **Brasília**. By 1967 his works in bronze and marble had become wholly non-objective. In 1985, a major exhibition in São Paulo marked his eightieth year.

ANTONIO CARLOS MARTINS VAZ

Giral, Sergio

b. 1937, Havana, Cuba

Film-maker

To date one of the Cuban Film Institute's (**ICAIC**) few Afro-Cuban film-makers and the director of a formally and thematically coherent filmic *œuvre*, Giral spent his childhood travelling back and forth between the USA (where his father had emigrated) and his native Cuba; from 1953–9 he studied painting at the Art Students' League in New York. When the revolution triumphed in 1959 he was in Cuba and decided to stay. Although he had no film-making experience, he joined ICAIC in 1961 and began making documentary shorts under the mentorship of Tomás **Gutiérrez Alea**. His first fiction feature, the very original *El otro Francisco* (The Other Francisco) (1974) was the first of a trilogy of films [with *Rancheador* (Bounty Hunter) (1976) and *Maluala* (1979)] about the history of slavery in Cuba, which, given its extensive dissection of the topic, Cuban audiences dubbed *negrometrajes* (a pun on the Spanish for feature-length, *largometraje*). His next film, *Techo de vidrio* (Glass Ceiling) (1982), addressed the continuing existence of class- and race-based privileges in socialist Cuba; it was censored and only obtained a very limited release six years later. By that time, Giral had already returned to more politically comfortable themes with *Plácido* (1986), the real story of a turn of the century mulatto poet executed by the Spanish for treason. His *María Antonia* (1990), an adaptation of a classic Cuban play, was, therefore, a resounding surprise. Although this story of a poor inner-city woman who seeks help with her love problems from **Santería** was set in the 1940–50s, the film concludes with a stunning epilogue in which the action is suddenly transferred to a very unsettling contemporary *mise en scène*. After this success and at the height of his creativity, Giral decided to seek exile, first in Paris and later in Miami, where he resided through the 1990s. Beyond the production of some documentary video work, he has not been able to continue film-making and teaches at local colleges.

ANA M. LÓPEZ

Girigorie, Jean

b. 1948, Willemsted, Curaçao

Painter

With ateliers in Santo Domingo and Curaçao, Girigorie is a truly Caribbean painter who began her career in the Combo Studio in Haiti. Her paintings combine Haitian and expressionist styles (see **expressionism**). Women, crying children, roosters, but also crowds of people are her themes. She is a passionate and fast painter who always refers to the social problems of the Caribbean in her work.

NEL CASIMIRI

Girondo, Oliverio

b. 1891, Buenos Aires, Argentina; d. 1967, Buenos Aires

Poet

Girondo was the most daring and experimental poet of his generation. A typical 1920s cosmopolitan dandy, his commitment to the artistic avant-garde (see **avant-garde in Latin America**) was expressed through the journal ***Martín Fierro***, which he co-edited. In its fourth issue, his 'Martin Fierro Manifesto' defined the contours of this most representative avant-garde journal, and Girondo himself became its central figure. His first two volumes, *Veinte poemas para ser leídos en el tranvía* (Twenty Poems to Read on the Tram) (1922) and *Calcomanías* (Transfers) (1925) reveal the cosmopolitan gaze of the poet moving through the shifting space and time of a traveller's guide. The first book moves between the cities of Europe and America; the second is devoted to Spain, but in both the poetry portrays an alienated, fragmented and grotesque society. His writings are marked by corrosive humour, reinforced by the accompanying coloured cartoons drawn by the author himself.

The 1930s mark the end of the aestheticizing experimentalism of a whole generation. *Espantapájaros (al alcance de todos)* (Scarecrow Within Everybody's Reach) (1932) opens with a two-coloured calligram of the scarecrow of the title. The volume consists of twenty-four prose-poem vignettes, an inner exploration mixing elements of surrealism (see **surrealism in Latin American art**) with expressionist despair. Girondo abandons the Cubo-futurism of his early work and combines word games with a wild, highly sexual imagination. *Interlunio* (Interlune) (1937), dedicated to the writer who later became his wife, Norah **Lange**, is more sombre. The *feísmo* (ugliness) of his previous work is further accentuated here through the terrifying engravings of Lino **Spilimbergo**. Europe and urban culture are now called into question and rejected, to the detriment of both the ***pampa*** and the Argentine *arrabal*. The cow, now one of the totems of Girondo's poetry, appears here for the first time. The 'there' of Europe, now old and broken, yields to a 'here' that is Argentina, rural and infinite.

The last of Girondo's poetic revolutions began with *Persuasión de los días* (Persuasion of Days) (1942), and ran through to one of the finest works of poetry in Spanish, *En la masmédula* (Into the Moremarrow) (1954). The radicalism of this work located him within the tradition of Vicente **Huidobro**, César **Vallejo** and **concrete poetry**. The explosion and estrangement of the word, the immersion in the materiality of language, make this final work one of the key works of Argentine poetry.

Further reading

Girondo, O. (1999) *Obra Completa*, Madrid: Archivos.
—— (1968) *Obras completas*, Buenos Aires: Losada.
Nóbile, B. de (1972) *El acto experimental*, Buenos Aires: Losada.
Pellegrini, A. (1964) *Oliverio Girondo*, Buenos Aires: Eds Culturales Argentinas.
Pío del Corro, G. (1976) *Oliverio Girondo: los límites del signo*, Buenos Aires: Fernando García Cambeiro.
Schwartz, J. (1993) *Vanguardia y cosmopolitismo en la década del veinte*, Rosario: Beatriz Viterbo.

JORGE SCHWARTZ

Gironella, Alberto

b. 1929, Mexico City

Visual artist

Gironella's work transforms the work of others by imitation or parody, a type of art which he initiated with *La Condesa de Uta* (The Countess of Uta) (1952) based on an eighteenth-century sculpture by Naumbrog. His later paintings take as their starting point the work of Velázquez, Goya and the films of Luis **Buñuel**, drawing on the sinister and grotesque aspects of the Spanish tradition. In these acts of transformation, Gironella works with the painting but also with the frame, with woods, and fragments of dolls, tins and pieces of machinery.

GONZALO AGUILAR

Girri, Alberto

b. 1919, Buenos Aires, Argentina; d. 1991, Buenos Aires

Poet

An outstanding poet and translator (of Wallace Stevens and John Donne, among others), Girri's considerable body of work begins with *Playa sola* (Lonely Beach) (1946). His poetry is a constant reflection upon the poetic act itself, a concern further explored in his critical essays (particularly in his important *Notas sobre la experiencia poética* (Notes on the Poetic Experience) (1983)) and his regular contributions to **Sur**, ***La Nación*** and *Correo Literario*. His poetry explores the various dimensions of experience, artistic as well as everyday, with a sharp eye and a laconic tone.

ENRIQUE FOFFANI

Gisbert, Teresa

b. 1926, La Paz, Bolivia

Historian

Professionally trained as an architect, Gisbert and her husband José de Mesa have published some seventy works on architecture and arts (painting, sculpture, silverwork and festivals) in the Peruvian and Bolivian Andes. Her individual work has been more concerned with indigenous and mestizo culture, as in *Iconografía y mitos indígenas en el arte* (Indigenous Myths and Iconography in art) (1980) and her most celebrated work, *Arte textil y mundo andino* (Textile Arts and the Andean world) (1987), written with two of her students. Another influential article (1987) suggested that **Aymara** migrations from the south had destroyed the Tihuanaco culture.

XIMENA MEDINACELI

Gismonti, Egberto

b. 1947, Carmo, Rio de Janeiro, Brazil

Musician and composer

Internationally recognized as a brilliant guitarist and highly innovative composer, Gismonti's eclectic music combines avant-garde experimentalism and modern **jazz** with traditional Brazilian rhythms such as **samba**, baião and **frevo**. He is best known for his mastery of the eight-string and ten-string guitars, but also plays electric keyboards and dozens of exotic instruments. His 1977 collaboration with fellow Brazilian experimentalist Naná Vasconcelos, *Dança das cabeças* (Dance of the Heads), set a new standard for ambient jazz-fusion. His best work is featured on the Oslo-based ECM label.

CHRISTOPHER DUNN

Gitana Tropical

Oil on wood (46.5 × 38 centimetres), painted in 1929 by Victor **Manuel**, *Gitana Tropical* (Tropical Gipsy) symbolizes and encapsulates a specifically Cuban quality and establishes the presence of the language of modern art in Cuban painting. It represents the torso of a woman, with a tender and melancholy expression on her face, against the background of a simply painted landscape in soft colours. For Víctor Manuel, it was an archetype from which arose a range of variations on the face of women. The canvas is today in the National Museum of Fine Arts in Havana.

WILFREDO CANCIO ISLA

Gladwell, Joyce

b. 1939, St Catherine's, Jamaica

Writer

Gladwell's ground-breaking autobiography *Brown Face Big Master* (1969) exposes her struggle to maintain Christian faith within the stifling colonial atmosphere of a Jamaican boarding school and traces the psychological implications of moving from rural Jamaica to London University and her mixed marriage. Gladwell's second autobiography is unpublished. She works as a family therapist and freelance journalist in Canada.

SANDRA COURTMAN

Glantz, Margo

b. 1930, Mexico City

Critic and novelist

The most eminent literary critic of her generation and a highly original novelist, Glantz has also given public service in the National Institute of Fine Arts (**INBA**) (1983–6) and as Cultural Attaché to the Mexican Embassy in London (1986–8). In her autobiographical novel, *Las genealogías* (*The Geneologies*) (1981), Glantz recounts her experiences growing up in an intellectual and artistic Jewish immigrant family in Mexico City during the 1940s. In *Síndrome de naufragios* (Shipwreck Syndrome) (1984) Glantz draws on her incisive readings of chronicles of the Conquest, and in *Apariciones* (Apparitions) (1996) she explores the mystical raptures of a colonial nun. Much of her early criticism of Mexican literature focused on nineteenth- and twentieth-century Mexican narrative, but in recent years she has published important collections of essays and editions on the Conquest, La Malinche and colonial nuns. She was awarded the Magda Donato Prize in 1982 and the Xavier Villaurrutia Prize in 1984. Glantz received her Ph.D. in Literature from the Sorbonne in 1958, and from 1959 to 1995 she held an **UNAM** chair in Mexican Literature. Drawing on her remarkable erudition in Mexican and European cultural history, much of Glantz's criticism has been influenced by contemporary French philosophers, including Barthes, Bachelard and Bataille, in their reflections on eroticism, the body, gender and society.

CYNTHIA STEELE

Glissant, Edouard

b. 1928, Sainte Marie, Martinique

Writer

It is because of the reputation of writers like Edouard Glissant that Martinique is called the island of intellectuals. He and his contemporary Frantz **Fanon** are the best known of the generation that came after Aimé **Césaire**. Like Fanon, he was educated at the Lycée Schoelcher and later left for Paris after participating in Césaire's electoral campaign. His early poems were dense meditations on landscape that were remarkably different from work by his contemporaries. His first book of essays, *Soleil de la conscience* (Sun of Consciousness) (1956), set out his definition of the Caribbean as diverse and constantly changing, as opposed to the more ideologically static picture derived from **négritude** and Marxism. *La **Lézarde*** (The Ripening), which won the Prix Renaudot in 1958, and *Le quatrième siècle* (The Fourth Century) (1965) brought him to prominence because of their original treatments of Martinican space and history and their refusal to be restrained by generic conventions.

After spending nineteen years in Paris, during which he produced enthusiastic reviews of the work of writers as diverse as St John **Perse**, Victor Segalen, William Faulkner and Alejo **Carpentier**, and became involved in anti-colonial politics through the Front Antillo-Guyanais formed with Paul Niger, he returned to Martinique in 1965 and founded the Institut Martiniquais d'Etudes. By inviting artists such as **Matta** from Chile and Cárdenas from Cuba, and with the publication of the magazine *Acoma*, Glissant tried to counter the rapid Europeanization of Martinique, which had become a French Department in 1946. His bleak view of Martinique's future as a Department is recorded in the 1975 novel, significantly entitled *Malemort* (Undead). In 1980 he left Martinique to become the editor of the *UNESCO Courier* in Paris. In the following year he published his well-known and influential *Le **Discours Antillais*** (Caribbean Discourse) and the novel *La case du commandeur* (The Driver's Cabin). By this time, he had established himself as the major Caribbean theorist of the post-négritude period. His most recent novels, with the untranslatable titles *Mahagony* (1987) and *Tout monde* (1993), continue to explore the themes and characters of the early fiction. Similarly, his theoretical work *Poétique de la Relation* (Poetics of Relating) in 1990 and *Faulkner, Mississippi* (1996) further develop his theories of a Caribbean and New World identity.

Further reading

Baudot, A. (1993) *Bibliographie annotée d'Edouard Glissant*, Toronto: Ed. du Gref.

Dash, J.M. (1995) *Edouard Glissant*, Cambridge: Cambridge University Press.

Glissant, E. (1989) *Caribbean Discourse*, trans. J.M. Dash, Charlottesville, VA: University Press of Virginia.

J. MICHAEL DASH

Glissant, Gabriel

b. 195?, Guadaloupe

Film-maker

Trained at the Institut de Hautes Etudes Cinématographiques (IDHEC) in Paris, Glissant believes in creating films with wide appeal. His projects include the twenty-minute *Le Pion* (The Pawn) (1972) which focuses on the experience of exile; *La Machette et le Marteau* (The Machete and the Hammer) (1975) which documents a series of strikes by Guadaloupean agricultural labourers in 1974; and *Chiba Ti Mal-La*, (1976) which has been described by Mbye Cham in *Ex-Iles* (Cham, M. (ed.) (1992), Trenton, NJ: Africa World Press) as a 'Creole dubbed kung fu film'.

ANN MARIE STOCK

Globo

The history of the Globo group begins with the first number of the newspaper *O Globo*, founded by Irineu Marinho in 1925. It had twelve pages and a print run of 33,435. When Marinho died twenty-three days later, his son Roberto, at age twenty, became its editor. From then on the newspaper held the forefront of technological innovation; in 1996 the newspaper was entirely computerized, printed 258,191 copies daily, and had 180,000 subscribers.

Radio Globo went on the air in 1945, combining news and entertainment, and it provided the foundation for the launch in 1965 of TV Globo, channel 4. After a productive alliance with Time–Life which aided its professionalization, Globo became Latin America's largest television network (fourth largest in the world), embracing four other stations and ninety affiliates. Its viewing audience of more than 37 million daily is the largest in the country, and is assiduously tracked by the national ratings marketing firm Ibope; its broadcasts reach 4,400 out of 4,425 municipalities in Brazil. Its broad scope has meant that TV Globo has become an extraordinarily powerful economic force (and a great innovator in advertising) as well as the voice of modern Brazil, uniting the vastly diverse and farflung national territory. Its contributions to the production of a modern national identity were especially significant during the military dictatorship, when Globo's alignment with the state helped shape a hegemonic public sphere.

TV Globo produces 78 per cent of its own programming. Among its most popular programmes are the daily news broadcast 'Jornal Nacional', the news and entertainment Sunday variety show 'Fantastico', and its daytime children's shows. But TV Globo is best known for the high quality of its dramas, including **telenovelas** and mini-series that are exported internationally. By emphasizing the role and contribution of writers, Globo has been at the forefront of TV drama innovation. Writers such as Alfredo Dias **Gomes** (*Roque Santeiro*) and Doc **Comparato** proved that the *telenovela*, beyond melodramatic excess, could be an effective genre for reflecting upon contemporary Brazilian life. The careers of the best known and most popular Brazilian entertainers and actors – **Xuxa**, Sonia **Braga**, José Wilker and many others – were launched by Globo programmes. In production, TV Globo's extraordinary attention to quality and technology – its *padrão de qualidade* (standard of quality) – has become the standard against which all other Brazilian audio-visual production is measured.

Always at the forefront of technological innovation, in 1996 the enterprise inaugurated the PROJAC production centre, the biggest in Latin America at 1.3 million square metres in size, in Jacarepaguá, Rio de Janeiro. Globosat, a satellite channel, and Globonews, a cable system, complete the Globo enterprise.

Editora Globo, the publishing arm of the group, produces magazines, encyclopedias and books. Its recording company, Som Livre, founded in 1969, distributes records, cassettes and CDs and specializes in the soundtracks of TV Globo's own *telenovelas*, which have launched many musical careers. The Globovideo company, formed in 1981, markets VHS videos. The group is run by Roberto **Marinho** and his sons.

Further reading

Mattelart, M. and Mattelart, A. (1989) *O carnaval das imagens: a ficção na TV,* São Paulo: Editora Brasiliense.

Simpson, A.S. (1993) *Xuxa: The Mega-Marketing of Gender, Race and Modernity,* Philadelphia: Temple University Press.

Vink, N. (1988) *The Telenovela and Emancipation: A Study of Television and Social Change in Brazil,* Amsterdam: Royal Tropical Institute.

ANTONIO CARLOS VAZ

Glusberg, Jorge

b. 1930, Buenos Aires, Argentina

Art critic

Glusberg is one of the most controversial and important figures in Argentine artistic life, as an art critic and curator. He founded and directed the Art and Communication Center of Buenos Aires (CAYC) at the **Instituto Di Tella**. He belonged to the CAYC Group, an interdisciplinary art group. His principal works are *The Group of Thirteen at the XIV Biennal of São Paulo* (1977) and *Arte en la Argentina: Del Pop-Art a la Nueva Imagen* (Art in Argentina: From Pop-Art to the New Image) (1985). He has directed the National Museum of Art since 1994.

FERNANDO RABOSSI

Gnatalli, Radamés

b. 1906, Porto Alegre, Brazil; d. 1988, Rio de Janeiro, Brazil

Composer and conductor

Gnatalli's success as conductor of the popular Radio Nacional orchestra and his many arrangements and light compositions tended to overshadow his serious career as art music composer. His assimilation of national and popular idioms, however, informs works like *Rapsódia brasileira* for piano (1931), and the series of *Brasilanas* for various media (1944–62). After 1955 Gnatalli moved away from nationalism, turning to neo-classical and **jazz** styles. Later works reveal a fresh appraisal of his nationalist roots: for example, the Violin Concerto no. 2 (1962), which is influenced by **bossa nova**.

SIMON WRIGHT

Godoy, Arturo

b. 1913, Iquique, Chile; d. 1987, Santiago, Chile

Boxer

Godoy fought twice for the world heavyweight boxing title. After becoming national champion, Godoy fought in Buenos Aires, Havana and Barcelona before going on to the United States, the most competitive boxing environment of the time. In his ten years in North American rings between 1937 and 1947, Godoy came to rank among the ten best boxers in the world. He twice fought the legendary Joe Louis in New York on 9 February 1940, and again on 20 June 1940. Although these fights did not bring him the world title, Godoy is widely remembered for his powerful punch and his tenacity.

LUIS E. CÁRCAMO-HUECHANTE

Goeritz, Mathias

b. 1915, Danzig, Germany; d. 1990, Mexico City

Visual artist

Sculptor, architect and concrete poet (see **concrete poetry**), Goeritz's best known works are the five giant concrete pylons at the entrance to **Ciudad Satélite** on the outskirts of Mexico's Federal District. Exiled from Germany in 1941, he was invited to teach in Guadalajara, Mexico, in 1949. In 1952 the El Eco Museum provided him with an area in which he could freely experiment with massive sculptured metal and concrete forms within created urban spaces. Goeritz's abstract modernism was harshly criticized by **Siqueiros** and **Rivera**, but he remained an influential teacher whose work punctuates Mexico's urban space.

MIKE GONZALEZ

Goldenberg, Jorge

b. 1941, Buenos Aires, Argentina

Playwright

Goldenberg's play *Relevo 1923* (Changing of the Guard, 1923) (1975), about a political assassination by a foreign anarchist during a period of strikes in **Patagonia**, raised a difficult topic during the military dictatorship. Goldenberg's theme responded to an official rhetoric which blamed 'foreign infiltrators' for alleged subversion. With the return to institutional democracy, Goldenberg wrote *Knepp* (1983), which addressed the issue of state terror and the disappearance of dissidents during the dictatorship. He has written extensively for film, including for María Luisa **Bemberg**'s last film, *De eso no se habla* (We Don't Talk about Such

Things) (1983) and Sergio Cabrera's *Ilona llega con la lluvia* (Ilona Comes with the Rain) (1996).

DAVID WILLIAM FOSTER

Gomes, Alfredo Dias

b. 1922, Salvador, Bahia, Brazil; d. 1999, Sao Pãulo

Playwright

A key figure in modern Brazilian theatre, Gomes's work is inspired by conflicts between idyllic rural life and corrupt urban life. His most famous play, *O pagador de promessas* (Journey to Bahia) (1962) was adapted for the screen by Anselmo **Duarte** and won Brazil's first Golden Palm Award at the Cannes Film Festival. Much of his work in the 1960s and 1970s was satirical, inspired by the severe political repression during the military dictatorship. *O santo inquérito* (The Holy Inquisition) (1966) and *O bem-amado* (The Beloved) (1977) are most often viewed as contemporary allegorical and morality plays. Dias Gomes has also written many important ***telenovelas*** for TV **Globo**, among them ***Roque Santeiro*** (1986).

SUSAN CANTY QUINLAN

Gomes, Paulo Emílio Salles

b. 1916, São Paulo, Brazil; d. 1977, São Paulo

Film critic and novelist

Born into a rich São Paulo family, Salles Gomes was early committed to the Left. After the Second Worold War, he spent almost a decade in Paris, and there the cinema became his leading passion. He was committed to the idea of a Brazilian cinema, and was friends with the major figures of the **Cinema Novo**: his article 'Cinema and Underdevelopment' was highly influential. He was married to the writer Lygia Fagundes **Telles**. Towards the end of his life, he published a brilliant satirical novel about the São Paulo bourgeoisie, *Três mulheres de três pppês* (1977) (Three P's Three Women).

JOHN GLEDSON

Gómez, Ana Ilce

b. 1945, Masaya, Nicaragua

Poet

One of the most refined and polished lyrical poetic voices of Nicaraguan poetry, Ana Ilce Gómez's perfection in form is highly praised by her peers. Because she is not a member of the ruling elite, Gómez is rarely included in public events. She studied journalism at the National Autonomous University of Managua, and worked for the National Bank for many years. Her work concentrates on the repressive effect of Roman Catholicism, capitalism and patriarchy created in 1970s Nicaragua. A single mother, she resides in her home town and commutes to work every day. Only two books of her poems have been published, and she has literally burned her lesser works rather than see them in print.

SILVIA CHAVES AND ILEANA RODRÍGUEZ

Gómez, Andrés

b. 1960, Guayaquil, Ecuador

Tennis player

One of Ecuador's greatest sportsmen, Gómez won many Davis Cup and Marlboro Caribbean Cup matches as well as thirty-eight grand prix titles for doubles play. He won twenty-one individual titles, including the French Open in 1990. For Ecuadorean youth and the national press, he was an idol who could stand beside great tennis players like Lendl, Connors and **Vilas**. His victories in Florence, Bordeaux, Dallas, Nice and Hong Kong, among others, helped to make tennis more popular in Ecuador. He remains a major figure on the veterans circuit.

FERNANDO BALSECA

Gómez, Juan Vicente

b. 1857, La Mulera, Táchira, Venezuela;
d. 1935, Maracay, Venezuela

Politician

Gómez was the dominant figure in Venezuelan political life from 1908 to 1935, either ruling directly as president, or indirectly via puppet presidents. Born into a cattle-ranching family, he entered politics in the early 1890s, eventually seizing the presidency in 1908. Absolute power and unlimited personal wealth were his main objectives; all dissent was crushed, and his regime became infamous for its torture, imprisonment or elimination of opponents. The oil industry (see **oil in Latin America**), opened up to foreign interests, developed rapidly during his regime, but social spending remained negligible. The beneficiaries were the wealthy elite and the military, whose loyalty sustained him in power until his death, at the age of seventy nine.

MARK DINNEEN

Gómez, Manuel Octavio

b. 1934, Havana, Cuba; d. 1988, Havana

Film-maker

In 1959 Gómez joined the film unit of the Cultural Section of the Rebel Army as an assistant director and later became a founder member of the new Cuban Film Institute (**ICAIC**). He wrote film criticism for the journal **Cine cubano** and headed the Cinema, Radio and Television section of the Cuban Writers and Artists Union (**UNEAC**). His most important films include *La primera carga al machete* (The First Machete Charge) (1969), *Patakin* (1982), *El señor Presidente* (The President) (1983) and *Gallego* (Galician) (1987).

JOSÉ ANTONIO EVORA

Gómez, Norberto

b. 1941, Buenos Aires, Argentina

Sculptor

Gómez is one of the most significant Argentine sculptors of the end of the dictatorship in the late 1970s/early 1980s. His first works date from 1967 under the generic title of *Objetos y dibujos* (Objects and Drawings), in which strict geometrical objects appear to disintegrate into organic forms. In 1981 he exhibited works in polyester based on intestines and teeth. These sculptures were understood to be loosely-veiled references to torture (**torture and disappearance, reports of**) and political repression. Gómez, together with Alberto **Heredia** and Juan Carlos **Distéfano**, exemplifies a tendency to represent violence through a metaphorical expressionism.

GABRIEL PEREZ-BARREIRO

Gómez, Sara

b. 1943, Havana, Cuba; d. 1974, Havana

Film-maker

Cuba's first woman film director, Gómez joined the Cuban Film Institute (**ICAIC**) in 1961 as an assistant director, working with Tomás **Gutiérrez Alea**, Jorge Fraga and the French director Agnes Varda, who was then working as a guest director with ICAIC. Gómez made a number of documentary shorts for the *Enciclopedia Popular* (People's Encyclopedia) series. At the time of her death she had completed the filming of her first full-length feature film, *De cierta manera* (One Way or Another), which was later edited by Gutiérrez Alea and Manuel Octavio **Gómez**.

JOSÉ ANTONIO EVORA

Gómez, Wilfredo

b. 1958, Santurce, Puerto Rico

Boxer

Amateur world champion in 1975, Gómez began

his professional career a year later. He was world flyweight and world featherweight champion. In 1985 he won the world junior lightweight title, his third world crown. He lost his third title in 1986 and retired from the ring; three years later he attempted a comeback. He ended his career with 43 victories (40 by knockout) and 3 defeats.

JUAN CARLOS QUINTERO HERENCIA

Gómez Hurtado, Álvaro

b. Sta Fe de Bogotá, Colombia; 1919; d. 1994, Santafé de Bogotá, Colombia

Political leader

Gómez Hurtado was the son of Colombian president Laureano Gómez Castro (1950–3) and owner and director in chief of the newspaper *El Siglo*. He was actively involved in politics from 1940 when he was elected representative. He was elected six times to the Senate (1950s through 1980s) and ran for president in 1974, 1986 and 1990. In 1994, he was assassinated when running for the fourth time for president. He was a firm supporter of conservative social values, as established by Catholic doctrine.

MIGUEL A. CARDINALE

Gómez-Peña, Guillermo

b. 1955, Mexico City

Performance artist

Since moving to the United States in 1979, Gómez-Peña has achieved acclaim as a leading 'border' artist, combining Mexican elite and popular culture with conceptual art in outrageous hybrid characters like the 'Border Brujo' and the 'Warrior for Gringostroika'. His performances shock audiences into reflecting on political issues like cultural and linguistic diversity, racism, and immigrants' rights. During the mid-1980s Gómez-Peña collaborated with other US, Mexican and Chicano artists in the Border Arts Workshop in San Diego. Since 1989 he has performed on both coasts, either alone or with the Puerto Rican performance artist Coco Fusco.

Gonçalves, Milton

b. 1935, Monte Santos, Minas Gerais, Brazil

Actor

Extraordinarily talented and versatile, Gonçalves was the first Afro-Brazilian to secure serious theatrical dramatic roles, first with the Teatro Arena in São Paulo (see **Arena Theatre Group**), later with the **Cinema Novo** film-makers and in TV **Globo** productions. Gonçalves credits his experiences with Teatro Arena (see **Arena Theatre Group**) for his acting success: 'Arena was my work-place but also a school', he claims. In addition to dozens of appearances in Arena plays, including Augusto **Boal**'s *Arena contra Zumbi* (which he restaged as director with an all-black cast in 1966), Gonçalves has had a prolific career in the media. He has appeared in more than a hundred films, including Leon **Hirszman**'s *Eles não usam black tie* (They Don't Wear Black Tie) (1981) and *Quilombo* (Carlos **Diegues**, 1984). However, his biggest claim to fame has been his work in *telenovelas*, in which he has become a ubiquitous face (from *Irmãos couragem* (Courageous Brothers) (1970) to *O rei do gado* (The King of Cattle) (1996)).

ANA M. LÓPEZ

Gonzaga, Adhemar

b. 1901, Rio de Janeiro, Brazil; d. 1978, Rio de Janeiro

Film-maker and critic

Gonzaga, who directed *Barro humano* (Human Clay) in 1929, was an influential producer, editor of the magazine **Cinearte** and founder of **Cinédia** Studios. An admirer of Hollywood, he tried at first to transfer its methods to Brazil. He produced dozens of films, including **Mauro**'s *Ganga bruta* (Brutal Gang) (1930) and wrote scripts for **chan-**

chada stars like **Oscarito** and **Grande Otelo**. Unlike many producers of his generation, he adapted to the realities of Brazilian underdevelopment, distancing himself from a market dominated by foreign films. He researched and co-wrote (with Paulo Emílio Salles **Gomes**) *70 Anos de Cinema Brasileiro* (70 Years of Brazilian Cinema) (1966).

ISMAIL XAVIER AND THE USP GROUP

Gonzaga, Chiquinha

b. 1847, Rio de Janeiro, Brazil; d. 1935, Rio de Janeiro

Musician

Gonzaga broke with a comfortable bourgeois upbringing to become Brazil's most important female popular composer. Separated from the rich landowner she had married at sixteen, she joined Rio's bohemian community of **choro** musicians. Her real breakthrough came in 1885, when she began composing the theatre scores that launched her reputation as a prolific inventor of modinhas and choros. In 1899 her 'O Abre-Alas' was the first marcha expressly composed for Rio's **carnival**. At her death, aged eighty-seven, she left an incomparable legacy of seventy-seven stage scores and some 2,000 shorter compositions including the choro 'Corta-jaca' and the modinha 'Lua Branca' (White Moon).

Gonzaga, Luiz

b. 1912, Exu, Pernambuco, Brazil; d. 1989, Rio de Janeiro, Brazil

Musician and composer

The most celebrated avatar of northeastern Brazilian music, such as baião, xaxado and **forro**, Gonzaga chronicled life in the arid backlands and migrants to the industrial south. In the 1940s he had a string of hits, including 'Vire e Mexe' (Turn Around and Shake), 'Baião', 'Asa Branca' and 'Paraíba,' which popularized northeastern dance music. Although by the late 1950s his popularity had waned, in the 1970s his career got a boost when stars such as Caetano **Veloso** and Gilberto **Gil** recorded his songs. During performances, he always donned the ornate triangle hat and leather chaps worn by *cangaceiros*, the bandits of the northeastern backlands.

CHRISTOPHER DUNN

Gonzalez, Anson

b. 1934, Mayo, Trinidad

Writer

Gonzalez was editor and publisher of *The New Voices* (1973–93), a journal of creative writing and essays which he financed almost entirely himself. He anthologized poems and stories by other writers, inaugurated World Poetry Day in 1979 in the Caribbean, and taught at primary, secondary and university levels in Trinidad and the region. His publications include *Collected Poems 1964–1979* (1979), *Moksha: Poems of Light and Sound* (1988) and *Merry-Go-Round and Other Poems* (1992). In 1996, the University of Miami Caribbean Writers' Institute honoured him with a lifetime achievement award for contributions to Caribbean art and culture.

KEITH JARDIM

González, Celina

b. 1929, Jovellanos, Cuba

Singer

The foremost exponent of Cuban *guajira* (rural/peasant) music, González began to sing traditional Cuban songs with Rutilio, on the Cadena Oriental radio station in Santiago de Cuba at the age of sixteen. In 1948 the duo, now married, were contracted by a Havana radio station. They appeared in films like *Rincón criollo* (Creole Corner) (1950), directed by Raúl Medina, and *Bella, la salvaje* (Beauty, the Beast) (1952), by Medina and Roberto Rey. In 1964 Celina began her solo career – seven years before the death of her husband – with her appearances on the Sunday television programme *Palmas y cañas*, which brought and continue to bring her enormous success.

JOSÉ ANTONIO EVORA

González, Elián

b. 1994, Cárdenas, Cuba

Child pawn in international human rights dispute

The little rafter ('balserito'), Elián was rescued at sea in November 1999 after a failed attempt to reach the USA by his mother, her boyfriend and several others. The Protestant minister-cum-fisherman who rescued him claimed that dolphins protected him and that a divine radiance was visible. After Elián was given temporary asylum in Miami's Little Havana by his great-uncle, Lázaro González, his case became an international tug-of-war between Fidel **Castro**'s government and the Cuban exile community. The US government under Attorney General Janet Reno took the position that little Elián should be reunited with his father, Juan Miguel González, who eventually came to the USA and took custody of the boy after a raid on the great-uncle's house by armed Immigration and Naturalization Service agents. The boy returned to Cuba with his father in June 2000.

DANIEL BALDERSTON

González, José Luis

b. 1926, Santo Domingo, Dominican Republic; d. 1996, Mexico City

Writer

Emblematic contemporary writer whose concern with exile reflects a common Caribbean experience. Born to a Puerto Rican father and a Dominican mother, he began his journey into exile when the family moved to Puerto Rico, fleeing from hurricane Zenón and the **Trujillo** dictatorship. He completed his university studies on the island, where he met the Dominican *émigré* Juan **Bosch** who encouraged him to write. By the time he moved on, in 1946, he had already published two volumes of short stories, *En la sombra* (In the Shadows) (1943) and *Cinco cuentos de sangre* (Five Stories of Blood) (1945). His writing was concise in style and tense in narrative; his rural themes and concern for the social suffering of the peasantry suggested a link with the work of Emilio S. **Belaval**.

He travelled widely in North America and Europe, pursued postgraduate studies in political science in New York and lived in Prague. *El hombre de la calle* (Man in the Street) (1948) marked the first representation of urban conflicts in Puerto Rican literature. The brief story, 'La carta' (The Letter), for example, addresses the issue of Puerto Rican heteroglossia, exploring in its two paragraphs the class and cultural gulfs that divide this US colony. In 1954, while residing in Guanajuato, Mexico, he published *En este lado* (On this Side), a collection of stories including 'En el fondo del caño hay un negrito' (There's a Black Boy at the Bottom of the Pipe). The setting of his writing was now the marginal communities around the great cities of Latin America, and his theme the tragic consequences of the move from rural to urban worlds.

His open commitment to Marxism precipitated his decision to renounce US citizenship; in solidarity, Mexico made him a citizen of that country. The US government's refusal to allow him into Puerto Rico confirmed his exile status. He remained a participant, albeit at a distance, in the political life of the island. He continued to write stories, novels and essays, developing new themes and concerns: the peasant who becomes a marginal worker in *La galería* (The Gallery) (1972); the involvement of young men in the Korean and Vietnam Wars in *Mambrú se fue a la guerra* (Mambru has Gone to War) (1973); the changes in the nature of agricultural production on the coast and in the mountains in *La balada de otro tiempo* (Ballad of Another Time) (1978); the US occupation of Puerto Rico in 1898 in *La llegada* (The Arrival) (1978). The question of Puerto Rican cultural identity is explored in two volumes of essays, *El país de cuatro pisos* (The Four-Storey Country) (1980) and *Una visita al cuarto piso* (A Visit to the Fourth Floor) (1986). No bureaucratic obstacle could deny José Luis González his citizenship, for he has established his identity as a writer.

Further reading:

Díaz Quiñones, A. (1977) *Conversación con José Luis González*, second edn, Santa Rita, Rio Piedras, P.R.: Ediciones Huracan.

González, J.L. (1993) *Puerto Rico: The Four-Storeyed Country and Other Essays*, Princeton: M. Wiener.

MARÍA JULIA DAROQUI

González, Otto Raul

b. 1921, Guatemala City

Writer

A founding member of Grupo Acento and director of its journal, González was a key literary voice in the 1944 Revolution and the years that followed. With the intervention of 1954, he fled to Mexico where he wrote political poetry with strong Nerudean inflections (see **Neruda**), even as he turned toward erotic poetry, fiction and other forms. He won the Miguel Angel Asturias national prize for literature in 1990, and has been able to visit his native country in recent years. Among his many works are his 1943 landmark collection, *Voz y voto del geranio* (Voice and Vote of the Geranium), reprinted in his *Poesía fundamental* (Fundamental Poetry) (1967).

MARC ZIMMERMAN

González Casanova, Pablo

b. 1922, Toluca, Mexico

Social scientist

A pioneering analyst and interpreter of Latin American society, González Casanova's *La democracia en Mexico* (Democracy in Mexico) (1965) opened a public debate on the corporate nature of the Mexican State and the limited nature of Mexican democracy. As president of **FLACSO** (Latin American Faculty of Social Science) based in Santiago from 1959–65, he played a key role in establishing social science faculties in Latin American universities. As rector of the **UNAM** (1970–2), he introduced a series of 'modernizing' academic reforms during the early part of the **Echeverría** presidency. Throughout the 1970s and 1980s his work represented an accumulating analytical response to the growth of the global market and the developing modes of resistance it evoked, culminating in the co-authored volumes, *La nueva organización capitalista vista desde el sur* (The New Organization of Capital Seen from the South) (1995, 1996).

MIKE GONZALEZ

González Dávila, Jesús

b. 1942, Mexico City

Playwright

A member of the late 1970s Mexican movement Nueva Dramaturgia (New Drama), his dramas are nihilistic tragedies which starkly represent the plight of outcasts such as street youth and homosexuals. His first important work to be staged was *El jardín de las delicias* (The Garden of Delights) in 1984, about father–son incest in rural Mexico. González Dávila's most successful play was *De la calle* (Of the Street), directed in 1987 by Julio **Castillo**; written in brief, almost cinematographic scenes it tells the tragic story of a streetbound youth searching for his father.

ANTONIO PRIETO-STAMBAUGH

González de Alba, Luis

b. 1944, Charcas, San Luis Potosí, Mexico

Writer and activist

While a student and professor of psychology at **UNAM**, González de Alba became a leader of the 1968 student movement; he was arrested after the massacre of students by the army at **Tlatelolco** Square in Mexico City on 2 October. After several months in **Lecumberri** Prison he was exiled to Chile, experiences he recounts in *Los días y los años*

(The Days and the Years) (1971). Returning to Mexico, he published a weekly newspaper column on scientific and political issues in *La Jornada* and became a leading advocate for gay rights. He has published short stories, fiction, essays, poetry and drama.

CYNTHIA STEELE

González de León, Teodoro

b. 1926, Mexico City

Architect

Le Corbusier, with whom he worked briefly in Paris, was a decisive influence on González León. After working with prefabricated units in the construction of the Casa Catán in Mexico City in 1951, he demonstrated a mature style in the Law School of the University of Tamaulipas (1966). Here, within the framework of the international style, he used the patio as a distributive core, extended the building on a horizontal plane and employed visible concrete. As his work developed the concrete began to take on the appearance that would be his unique mark, the result of combining the concrete with other materials so that it took on a very particular texture and colour.

In his early career in Mexico he worked with outstanding architects like Carlos Obregón, Carlos **Lazo** and Mario **Pani**; from 1953 he tended to work independently. In 1968 he began a series of collaborations with Abraham **Zabludovsky**, a relationship which produced a number of important buildings in the history of contemporary Mexican architecture. These include the residential complexes Lomas de Plateros (1971), La Patera (1973) and the Ex-hacienda de Enmedio (1976), all in Mexico City; among their public buildings there were the Delegación Cuauhtémoc (the Municipal Town Hall) (1972–3), INFONAVIT (Institute of Workers' Housing) (1973–5) and the Colegio de México (1974–5), where the use of an asymmetrical patio covered by pergolas and the interplay of several levels, among other elements, produced a building that was both respectful of its surroundings and full of movement.

His works in the city of Villahermosa, Tabasco, in collaboration with Francisco Serrano have won considerable recognition. Among these the Parque Tomás Garrido Canabal (1985), the Administrative Centre (1986) and the State Library (1987). The Palacio de Justicia Federal (Federal Courthouse) in Mexico City (1987–92) is also remarkable for its proportions. His construction for the state publishing house **Fondo de Cultura Económica** (1990–2), with its combinations of curved and straight lines, is one of his most masterly works.

Further reading

Noelle, L. (1994) *Teodoro González de León: la voluntad del creador*, Bogotá: Escala.

LOURDES CRUZ GONZÁLEZ FRANCO

González Delvalle, Alcibiades

b. 1936, Ñemby, Paraguay

Writer

A polemical writer and playwright, González Delvalle has explored elements of **Guarani** folklore and Paraguayan history in plays such as *El grito del luisón* (The Cry of the Werewolf) (1972) and *Perú Rimá* (1987). His *San Fernando*, based on the 1865–70 War of the Triple Alliance, was banned on the eve of its premiere in 1975 and again in 1989. He also wrote *Nuestros años grises* (Our Grey Years) (1985) and *Función Patronal* (Patron Saint Function) (1980), a *costumbrista* (see **costumbrismo**) novel.

TERESA MÉNDEZ-FAITH

González Tuñón, Raúl

b. 1905, Buenos Aires, Argentina; d. 1974, Buenos Aires

Poet

Poet of the city of Buenos Aires, González Tuñón shared with Jorge Luis **Borges** a preoccupation with the literary representation of the suburbs. Although at first associated with the group

Florida, his political commitments distanced him from the group's purely aesthetic concerns and he became aligned with a more politicized international avant-garde. With their fractured and miscellaneous structure, his poems show an immigrant Buenos Aires in rapid transformation. They were rediscovered by the politicized poets of the 1970s (like Juan **Gelman**), were made into tangos (sung by the **Cuarteto Cedrón**) and were celebrated by Beatriz **Sarlo** in her book, *Buenos Aires, una modernidad periférica* (1988).

FLORENCIA GARRAMUÑO

Goodison, Lorna

b. 1947, Kingston, Jamaica

Poet

The best-known woman poet of the Anglophone Caribbean, her poetry is concerned with personal space, freedom and spirituality as well as social justice. Goodison has a remarkably fluid and sensuous poetic voice developed through *Tamarind Season* (1980), *I Am Becoming My Mother* (1986), *Heartease* (1988), *Selected Poems* (1992) and *To Us, All Flowers Are Roses* (1995). She writes in a range of registers from Jamaican Creole (see **creole languages**) to international English; her work, like Derek **Walcott**'s is both Caribbean-centred and international. Her short stories, *Baby Mother and the King of Swords* (1990), depict gender relations in Jamaican culture.

ELAINE SAVORY

goombay

Musical term of West African origin used to describe a style of music and the dancing and drumming related to it. The word presumably originated during the years of slavery between the seventeenth and nineteenth centuries; by the twentieth century the term was most commonly used in the Bahamas. Some scholars argue that the term most properly applies to a particular set of rhythms played on a goatskin drum, accompanied by a stringed instrument (such as a guitar) and perhaps other percussion instruments, along with the singing of Bahamian versions of calypso-like satire. The word 'goombay' however is often used with much less specificity; for example as an adjective to describe particular goatskin drums as 'goombay drums'. During the 1970s and 1980s, government-sponsored summer evening celebrations of Bahamian music and culture (aimed heavily at tourists) were referred to as 'Goombay Summer'.

ROSANNE ADDERLEY

Gorodischer, Angélica

b. 1928, Buenos Aires, Aregntina

Writer

Something of a cult writer among **science fiction** enthusiasts, her novels have won prizes in Argentina and abroad. Gorodischer's writing is characterized by its subtle play with gender, particularly as it is embedded in language, and by its concern with women's domestic worlds and their relationship to men. The stories of *Bajo las jubeas en flor* (Under the Flowering Jubea Trees) (1973) and novels like *Trafalgar* (1979), *Kalpa Imperial* (1983) and *Prodigios* (Prodigies) (1994) combine humour with great narrative skill.

SANDRA GASPARINI

Gorostiza, Carlos

b. 1920, Buenos Aires, Argentina

Playwright and theatre director

Gorostiza began his careeer with **Teatro Independiente**, where his play *El puente* (The Bridge) (1949) renewed theatrical discourse, presenting class conflicts in a convincing colloquial language and influenced the new realist playwrights of the 1960s. Later works exhibited a more mature realism, symbolic language and some elements of the grotesque. His plays *El pan de la locura* (Bread of Madness) (1958), *Los prójimos* (Fellow Men) (1966), *Los hermanos queridos* (Dear Brothers) (1978), *El acompañamiento* (The Accompaniment) (1981) and *Aeroplanos* (Aeroplanes)

(1990) reflect on Argentine identity and the complexity of human relationships. He participated in **Teatro Abierto**.

STELLA MARTINI

Gorostiza, José

b. 1901, San Juan Bautista (hoy Villahermosa), Tabasco, Mexico; d. 1973, Mexico City

Poet

Gorostiza is the author of one of the classic works of Mexican poetry, *Muerte sin fin* (Endless Death) (1935). A member of the generation of **Contemporáneos**, his early poems were published in *Contemporáneos* and the *Revista de la Universidad Nacional*. He also wrote other remarkable poems, essays and 'synthetic dramas' like *Ventana a la calle* (Window on the Street) (1924). During **Vasconcelos**'s tenure at the Education Ministry, Gorostiza edited the magazine *El Maestro* (The Teacher) and contributed to *Lecturas clásicas para niños* (Classic Readings for Children). A career diplomat from 1935 to 1965, he was awarded the National Literature Prize in 1968.

LILIANA WEINBERG

Goulart, João ('Jango')

b. 1919, São Borja, Rio Grande do Sul, Brazil; d. 1976, Corrientes, Argentina

Politician

President of Brazil from 1961 to 1964 (when he was overthrown by a military *coup*), Goulart, known commonly by his nickname 'Jango', was an erratic and unsuccessful politician but has nevertheless attained the status of myth. A protégé of Getulio **Vargas** (and minister of labour under Vargas in 1953–4), Goulart led the Brazilian Labour Party (PTB) and was close to Juscelino **Kubitschek** and Jânio Quadros, becoming vice-president under Quadros in 1960. Quadros's resignation in 1961 led to threats by the military to prevent Goulart's presidency. With the help of his brother-in-law,

Leonel Brizola, who organized against a possible military *coup*, Goulart succeeded. Goulart's presidency was marked by conflict with the business community and with the USA (especially over the nationalization of a subsidiary of a US phone company), economic depression and political difficulties. Overthrown by a military *coup* on 1 April 1964, Goulart lived out the rest of his life in **exile** in Uruguay and Argentina.

DANIEL BALDERSTON

gourds

The use of gourds (*jícaras*) as water containers and bowls dates back to 6500 BC. In today's Indian markets in Mexico, *cacao* is still served in decorated gourds. The gourds are dried in the sun and then lacquered and decorated, a process involving the application of a layer of seed oil then a layer of commercial pigments and mineral pastes. A special decorative relief technique known as *rayado* has been developed in Mexico and Peru. Gourds are also used as percussion instruments like maracas, the Afro-Cuban chekeré – a gourd strung with cowrie shells – and the güiro, a dried hollowed-out gourd with a grooved surface.

JAN NIMMO

Gout, Alberto

b. 1931, Mexico City; d. 1966, Mexico City

Film-maker

He worked in several genres, but was best known for his **Cabaretera films**, starring the most famous singers and dancers of the 1940s and 1950s: Meche Barba, María Antonieta **Pons** and Ninón **Sevilla**. His collaboration with scriptwriter Alvaro Custodio and cinematographer Alex Phillips produced some of the classics of the genre, like *Aventurera* (Adventuress) (1949), *Sensualidad* (Sensuality) (1950) and *Mujeres sacrificadas* (Selfless Women) (1951) all starring Ninón Sevilla. Later he directed vehicles for actress Silvia **Pinal**, such as *La sospechosa* (Suspicious Woman) (1954). His 1956 version of Genesis, *Adán y Eva*, was a great if unexpected box office hit.

PATRICIA TORRES SAN MARTÍN

Gouverneurs de la rosée

Published posthumously in 1944, *Gouverneurs de la rosée* (Masters of the Dew) the masterpiece of Haitian ***indigenisme***, has been translated into a dozen languages and filmed twice (as *Cumbite* (1964) by Tomás Gutiérrez Alea). Written while **Roumain** was chargé d'affaires in Mexico, it is a political parable that treats the hardships of rural Haiti and an anthropologically accurate picture of peasant culture. The novel offers a **Utopian vision** of peasant solidarity and a renewal of culture through collective labour which is preached by the protagonist Manuel who returns from cutting cane in Cuba to his drought-stricken village.

J. MICHAEL DASH

Goveia, Elsa Vesta

b. 1925, British Guyana; d. 1980, Kingston, Jamaica

Historian

Goveia's influence on West Indian intellectual life belies her small academic output. She received her doctorate from the London Institute of Historical Research there with her thesis *A Study of the Historiography of the British West Indies*. Her *Slave Society in the British Leeward Islands* (1965) challenges the 'plural society' thesis, arguing that Caribbean societies are unified by the belief, held by *both* blacks and whites, that whites are superior. Appointed Professor of West Indian History at the **University of the West Indies** in 1961, she became at once its first woman professor and the first West Indian to hold the Chair in History.

PAT DUNN AND PAMELA MORDECAI

Goyeneche, Roberto

b. 1926, Buenos Aires, Argentina; d. 1994, Buenos Aires

Singer

One of **tango**'s outstanding singers, he was nicknamed 'el polaco' (the Pole), because of his European appearance. Formed in the **Gardel** and **Rivero** school, his baritone voice later lent itself to subtle interpretations of the lyrics of Expósito, **Manzi** and **Discépolo**. He had a particular way of phrasing songs, 'word by word', respecting and sometimes adding meaning to capricious punctuation. This made him the 'voice of tango' in Buenos Aires, where his version of songs like 'Sur', 'Malena', and 'Cafetín de Buenos Aires' are particularly remembered.

LUIS GUSMAN

Gracias a la vida

'Gracias a la vida' (Thanks to Life) was Violeta **Parra**'s most famous song, composed in 1966 and recorded on her 1967 album *Las últimas composiciones de Violeta Parra* (Violeta's Last Compositions), launched just a few days before her suicide. The ideas of the song – an ode to all that is beautiful, profound and mysterious in life – are contained in a letter written to her mother from Paris in 1965. The song has been subsequently recorded by artists in many countries and several languages, the best of which include, apart from versions by Violeta herself and her daughter Isabel Parra, recordings by Joan Baez, Mercedes **Sosa**, Omara **Portuondo** and Plácido Domingo.

ALFONSO PADILLA

Graef-Marino, Gustavo

b. 1955, Santiago, Chile

Film-maker

Important new contributor to the contemporary Chilean cinema, Graef-Marino began his university career in the earliest days of the **Pinochet** dictatorship, not an auspicious time for the national cinema. He went to West Germany in 1976, where he studied film-making in Munich, worked with various television corporations and directed his first fiction feature in 1983. After returning to Chile in the early 1990s, he wrote and directed *Johnny cien pesos* (Johnny One Hundred Bucks), a Chilean–Mexican co-production about a much publicized hold-up of an illegal currency exchange house in Santiago. The film – stylishly filmed, edited in a quick MTV-like pace and featuring new, handsome, young actors – was extremely well-received by critics and national and international audiences, and heralded the beginnings of a 'new' Chilean cinema. Graef-Marino has a promising future, but has not yet been able to complete another film despite the success of *Johnny cien pesos*.

ANA M. LÓPEZ

graffiti

Graffiti is a popular means of artistic expression across Latin America and the Caribbean. There are two apparent principal sources of inspiration: politics and humour, with social subversion the frequent message of both. There are as many ways of creating graffiti as of using paint, from the chalk-on-slate originally employed by dockers and marketeers to the aerosols commonly used by the younger generation.

In Paris, where many practising Latin American artists took refuge in the first half of this century, the great Hungarian artist and photographer Brassaï issued a graffiti artist's manifesto in 1949, which insisted on the inseparability of graffiti and writing. The anti-establishment nature of graffiti art tends toward this kind of disjunction, much of its writing taking the form of anagrams, in-jokes and pithy witticisms. At the same time, they are intended to agitate, at least subliminally. In Argentina, under the military dictatorships of 1976–84, graffiti not only inveighed (most usually with the Peronist Youth (see **Peronism**) or the **Montoneros** guerrilla movement) against the regime's 'dirty war', but under the rubric Voces de la Calle (Street Voices) claimed that 'lo poético es lo político' (the poetic is political) while asserting that 'las paredes limpias no dicen nada' (clean walls tell us nothing).

In Uruguay, at the height of the Tupamaro guerrilla movement (see **Tupamaros**) in the 1970s, there was a group of activist artists who called themselves *Así dicen los muros* (So the Walls Say). More recently, after the defeat of the Sandinistas in Nicaragua, public murals gave way to spontaneous individualism as part of a campaign to keep the revolutionary message alive, called *Los muros de Managua* (The Walls of Managua). In Peru, those disaffected both with the government's and the **Sendero Luminoso**'s (Shining Path) militaristic adventurism, looked to reclaim the *Muros, Esquinas, Calles y Callejones de Lima* (Walls, Corners, Turnings and Alleyways of Lima) and the Internet logs a fresh manifesto from the *latino* 'Graffiti Aerosol Sharpshooters' claiming graffiti as 'writing in spaces, traces, features, surfaces, textures, colours, images, paints, phrases, aerosols, jokes, prohibitions, signs, all this graffiti'.

Some contemporary graffiti artists claim pre-Columbian ancestors. In Mexico, particularly in the capital where repeated excavations attempt to shore up the colonial buildings sinking into the lake on which they were raised, ancient walls are again coated with contemporary anonymous art works reminiscent of the earliest murals. Since many pictogram codes of even the ancient and widespread Maya people have been lost, new graffiti now daub Aztec remains with crude copies of the glyphs at nearby Tetitla and Tepantitla, or distant Tulum and Bonampak. Signed off as 'the revenge of the indigenous', they are a clear illumination of the arbitrary boundary between graffiti and murals, or between popular and professional, or low and high art.

Possibly the best-know graffiti artist of the last decade was Jean-Michel Basquiat, who signed his doors and walls 'SAMO'. Of mixed race and Haitian origin, he grew up and worked in New York. Although he later adapted his cartoon characters and deliberately primitivist style to canvases and friezes, he never abandoned delivering his cryptic messages written in chalk or spraypainted in public places. He denied any politically satirical content to his caricatures, yet when asked why he drew people so crudely answered that most people were crude. He died of a heroin overdose in 1988, at least partly destroyed by the people he depicted tearing him and his work apart in the attempt to maximize their own profits.

AMANDA HOPKINSON

Graham-Yooll, Andrew

b. 1944; Buenos Aires, Argentina

Journalist

An English-speaking writer, Graham-Yooll spoke out from the pages of the *Buenos Aires Herald* to denounce the violation of human rights and the assassinations taking place throughout the Southern Cone during the government of Isabel Perón and the military dictatorships (1976–83). In exile in Britain, he published several books including *The Forgotten Colony* (1981), *Small Wars You May Have Missed* (1983), *A State of Fear: Memories of Argentina's Nightmares* (1986), *De Perón a Videla: Argentina 1955–1976* (1989) and *After the Despots: Latin American Views and Interview* (1991). Returning to Argentina, he became editor-in-chief of the *Buenos Aires Herald* in 1994.

JORGE ELBAUM

Gramatges, Harold

b. 1918, Santiago de Cuba

Musician and composer

Gramatges is the composer of more than 100 works which combine elements of the universal musical heritage and the Cuban tradition. A pupil of Amadeo **Roldán** and José **Ardevol** at the Havana Conservatory, he studied in the United States before returning to found the Orchestra of the Conservatorio Municipal de La Habana (Havana Municipal Conservatory) in 1944. In the 1950s he led the Sociedad Cultural Nuestro Tiempo, which drew together all the avant-garde intelligentsia. After the Cuban Revolution of 1959 (see **revolutions**) he organized the reform of musical education and created the National Symphony Orchestra.

WILFREDO CANCIO ISLA

Gramcko, Ida

b. 1924, Puerto Cabello, Venezuela; d. 1994, Caracas, Venezuela

Poet, playwright, essayist and journalist

Together with Enriqueta **Arvelo Larriva** and Ana Enriqueta **Terán**, Gramcko may be considered a pioneer of modern women's poetry in Venezuela. Her considerable poetic and dramatic work embraces symbolic, psychological and even folkloric themes; in short, the whole range of archetypes of Venezuelan imaginary. A graduate of the Universidad Central of Venezuela, where she subsequently taught, Ida Gramcko contributed to a number of important journals and newspapers including *El **Nacional*** (she was its first leader writer, from 1943–6), *El **Universal**, **Revista Nacional de Cultura**, Cultura universitaria* and ***Repertorio Americano*** (Costa Rica).

JORGE ROMERO LEÓN

Gran Circo Teatro

Gran Circo Teatro is a Chilean theatre company of the 1980s and 1990s, directed by Andrés **Pérez**, which borrowed elements and techniques from Latin American popular and religious festivals, circus and commedia dell'arte to recover theatre's origins in public rituals. In 1988 the company staged *La Negra Ester* (Black Esther), a play set in a lowlife brothel in the small port of San Antonio, based on a work by Roberto Parra. It became one of the most successful plays in Chilean history, and began a renewal of Chilean theatre by attracting theatregoers with live music, dance, sounds, special effects, elaborate costumes and make-up.

AMALIA PEREIRA

Gran fiesta, La

Directed by Marcos **Zurinaga** and written by Zurinaga and Ana Lydia **Vega**, *La gran fiesta* (1986) (The Big Party) marked Puerto Rico's entry into international film circuits. The story takes place in 1942, during the last ball celebrated at Puerto Rico's Grand Casino prior to its takeover by the US government as a military base. During the ball, José Manuel, the son of a Spanish merchant, must choose between his fiancée, the daughter of a wealthy landowner, and his true love, a politically conscious co-worker. Both the Casino and José Manuel's love triangle work as symbols of Puerto Rican politics and society. Raúl **Juliá** makes a cameo appearance as an *independentista* poet.

ROBERTO CARLOS ORTIZ

Granda, Chabuca (Isabel)

b. 1920, Cotabamba (Abancay), Peru; d. 1983, Miami, USA

Musician

The best-known composer of the 'vals limeño' (Lima waltz), Chabuca Granda's compositions include 'La flor de la canela' (The Cinnamon Flower), 'Fina estampa' (Fine Figure), 'María Landó and Ese arar en el mar' (Ploughing the Sea). Her music evokes a bygone era, yet it also defines the musical identity of modern Lima. Her songs have been recorded by singers as diverse as Susana **Baca** (Peru), Caetano **Veloso** (Brazil) and María Dolores Pradera (Spain). Though not a great singer herself, her own recordings have a fresh, somewhat breathless sound. Her statue adorns a park above the Pacific in Barranco, the Bohemian Lima neighbourhood still noted for its music scene.

See also: waltz

DANIEL BALDERSTON

Grande Otelo

b. 1915, Uberlândia, Brazil; d. 1994, Paris, France

Actor

One of the best actors in the world, according to Orson Welles, Grande Otelo (real name Sebastião Bernardes de Souza Prata) decided to become a performer when he saw Chaplin's *The Kid* at age eight. At nine he joined the black revue company Companhia Negra de Revistas, which included **Pixinguinha**. His enormous, precocious talent helped him to overcome the difficulties faced by a black artist in a racist country like Brazil. His adopted family in São Paulo wanted him to be a lawyer, but Otelo went on acting on radio and in theatre groups like Jardel Jércolis, where he was given the name he was to use for the rest of his life: The Great Othello.

His first film appearance was in the successful *Noites cariocas* (Rio Nights) (1935). In the early 1940s he participated in the **carnival** depicted in *It's All True*, the film that Orson Welles was making for RKO. His performance in the autobiographical *Moleque Tião* (directed y José Carlos **Burle**) (1943) consolidated his reputation as one of Brazil's best dramatic actors and, while continuing his theatrical career, he went on to form with **Oscarito** a comic duo that lasted for two decades. He made several musical comedies and *chanchadas* for **Atlântida**. In films like Watson Macedo's *Aviso aos Navegantes* (Warning to Sailors) (1951) and Brule's *Carnaval Atlântida* (1953), he portrayed the typical *malandro* (scoundrels) of Rio de Janeiro. One of his outstanding roles was the **samba** musician Espírito in Nelson Pereira dos **Santos**'s *Rio Zona Norte* (1957), displaying a dramatic skill which he revealed again in Roberto **Farias**'s *O Assalto ao Trem Pagador* (The Great Train Robbery) (1962). His most intense and self-reflective work came with his performance in Joaquim Pedro de **Andrade**'s *Macunaíma* (1969), at once comic and dramatic, popular and powerful. In the years that followed, the many films and plays in which he worked built on his fame and often used the facts of his own life as their theme.

Further reading

Grande Otelo (1985) Rio de Janeiro: Embrafilme/Funarte.

Moura, R. (1996) *Grande Otelo*, Rio de Janeiro: Relume.

Stam, R. (1997) 'Carmen Miranda, Grande Otelo and the *chanchada*', in *Tropical Multiculturalism*, Durham, NC: Duke University Press, pp. 79–106.

ISMAIL XAVIER AND THE USP GROUP

Grande sertão: veredas

Grande sertão: veredas (The Devil to Pay in the Backlands) (1956), by João Guimarães **Rosa**, is recognized as one of the high points of contemporary Latin American fiction. It has been translated into several languages, but its verbal experimentation and wealth of neologisms have stimulated a number of new versions, most recently a new French translation.

The plot of the novel addresses struggles between *jagunços* (north eastern bandits), vengeance and the love affair between Riobaldo and Diadorim. Riobaldo, the novel's narrator-protagonist, is a man who seeks in memory and reflection a way to deny the existence of the Devil, with whom he makes a pact when he is looking for ways of overcoming Hermógenes, 'lord of all cruelty'. The work is inspired by chivalric novels and feudal epics, where the sacred and the profane, and good and evil, coexist.

Underpinning the epic is the conflict between the Narrator-Hero and the ***sertão*** (northeastern backlands), between the I and the World. For Guimarães Rosa's narrator, the *sertão* is a metaphor for the wider world with all its moral, religious and philosophical conflicts. 'The *sertão* is everywhere' or 'The *sertão* is the size of the world', the author says. This huge area, which embraces the interior of several Brazilian states, becomes in this novel the scenario of a complex literary construction where poetry and myth fuse to both veil and reveal a global vision of existence. The contradictions and contrasts between the primitive rustic world of the *sertão* and the urban-industrial world can be sensed in Riobaldo's references to the people who will hear his stories. According to Alfredo **Bosi**, the conflict between hero and world does not disappear in this novel; it is resolved by a pact between men and the origin of these tensions – the Other, the Reverse Side of the world. The dialectics of the plot are not processed through an analysis of psychic fractures nor through the mimesis of local groups and types, but rather through the assiduous interaction of the character with an omnipresent natural-cultural Whole – the *sertão*.

Further reading

Bosi, A. (1988) *Céu, inferno*, São Paulo: Ediciones Atica.

Campos, H. (1967) *Metalinguagem de outras metas*, São Paulo: Ediciones Vozes.

Candido, A. (1964) *Tese e ántitese*, São Paulo: Cia Ed Nacional.

Galvão, W. (1972) *As formas do falso*, São Paulo: Ediciones Perspectiva.

Schwarz, R. (1981) *A Seréia e a Desconfiado*, Rio de Janeiro: Ediciones Paz e Terra.

MILTON HATOUM

Granma

Granma is the official organ of the Cuban Communist Party, founded by Fidel **Castro** in October 1965 after a strategic reorganization of the communications media in Cuba. The product of a fusion of the newspapers ***Revolución*** (organ of the 26th July Movement) and *Hoy* (organ of the Popular Socialist Party, as the Communist Party was previously called), *Granma* became the most important newspaper in the country. Its initial circulation was 498,784, one of the highest in Cuban history, although it later reached 680,000; in its early phase it also published a cultural supplement called the *Revista del Granma*.

The name of the newspaper refers to the motor yacht which, in 1956, carried 82 revolutionaries under Castro's leadership from Mexico to Cuba. Its first editor was Isidoro Malmierca; he was succeeded by Jorge Enrique Mendoza, a close collaborator of Castro's since the armed insurrection in the Sierra Maestra, who continued to edit the paper for some twenty years.

From the outset, the newspaper faithfully reflected the instrumental conception of the role of the media put in place by the revolutionary government. Its trajectory over more than three decades expresses the propaganda purposes of a press system which has conditioned the information needs of the population to the manoeuvres of the political leadership. Defined as ideological workers, its journalists have been required to fulfil their tasks under an iron regime of party instructions, which in practice shaped both the professional ethos and the forms of expression of the paper. Castro has called *Granma*'s workers 'capable and experienced fighters who will not be defeated on any battlefront'. The newspaper's editorials have had an important role in mobilizing the population at key moments in Cuba's socio-political life. It is *Granma* that publishes the official versions of speeches by Castro and other leading government figures.

Technical changes transformed the newspaper from a broadsheet to a tabloid at the end of the eighties. As the economic crisis deepened early in the 1990s, it became the country's only newspaper, currently printing 400,000 copies from Tuesday to Saturday. *Granma Internacional* is published weekly in several languages, and since 1996 it has also been accessible via the Internet. The website for the daily edition is www.granma.cubaweb.cu.

Further reading

Ferrera, A. (1990) *El Granma: la aventura del siglo*, Ciudad de La Habana: Editorial Capitán San Luis.

Laino, R. (1994) *Cuba: Martí, Granma y todavia*, Buenos Aires: Ediciones Que haces Maldad (y después).

WILFREDO CANCIO ISLA

graphic art

Since the middle of the nineteenth century, the graphic arts in Latin America have developed through the political cartoon in newspapers like the Mexican *El calavera*, *El hijo del Ahuizote* and *La orquesta*, *Don Junípero* in Cuba and *Caras y caretas* in Argentina. In Mexico, José Guadalupe **Posada** was one of its principal exponents; his lithographs and zinc etchings that appeared in various anti-Porfirista publications and the broadsheets edited by Vanegas Arroyo and featuring his skeletons (***calaveras***) and ballads (see **corrido**) on topical events, reveal a highly expressive draftmanship full of significant detail and eloquent expressive deformations.

The Mexican muralists (see **muralism**) of the 1920s found in Posada a crucial source in their search for a national-popular imagery of the Mexican Revolution (see **revolutions**). **Rivera**, **Siqueiros** and **Orozco** developed their graphic work in *El Machete*, newspaper of the Union of Workers, Technicians, Painters and Sculptors founded after the revolution. Their drawings and illustrations clearly show the influence of German expressionist graphics (see **expressionism**), and Dadaist and constructivist applications of photomontage. Social and political graphics were centrally significant in post-revolutionary Mexico. In 1935 the Liga de Escritores y Artistas Revolucionarios (League of Revolutionary Writers and Artists) set up a mural and graphics workshop. When the League was dissolved, the director of its Arts section, Leopoldo **Méndez**, together with Luis Arenas and Pablo O'Higgins, founded the **Taller de Gráfica Popular** (Popular Graphics Workshop), teaching techniques and producing lino cuts, lithographs and xilographs on national themes (like the portfolios devoted to the life, myths and rituals of the Mexican Indians).

In 1930 the Exhibition of Books and Graphic Arts held in Rio de Janeiro, São Paulo, Montevideo and Buenos Aires brought the artists of those countries into contact with the work of the great German expressionists, Köllwitz, Beckman, Grosz, Kokoschka and Schmidt-Rottluff. Their influence is clearly present in the work of Livio Abramo, who continued in the great Brazilian graphic tradition inaugurated by Oswaldo Goeli. In the 1940s Brazilian artists like Vasco Prado, **Scliar** and Danubio evolved political graphics of resistance to the dictatorship of Getulio **Vargas**. The Mexican experience encouraged the foundation of a number of leftist clubs, such as the Clube de Gravura de

Porto Alegre (1950) and Baje (1950), for example. *Gravura Gaúcha* (1952) collected the traditional **literatura de cordel** pamphlets with their popular verses and stories illustrated by engravings. In Argentina, political engraving began to develop with the work of the Artistas del Pueblo (Artists of the People) group, including José Arato, Adolfo Bellocq, Guillermo Facio Hebecquer, Agustín Riganelli and Abraham Vigo, whose theme was the life and struggles of the popular sectors. These artists worked in opposition to the hegemonic culture of Argentina, exhibiting their work in the Salón de los Recusados in 1914 and the Salón de Artistas Independientes in 1918. They published comments in the anarchist newspaper *La montaña* and in *La protesta*, and illustrated works by members of the Boedo group published by the Claridad publishing house (founded in 1926) (see **Boedo vs Florida**). The direction taken by these artists, and encouraged by the Mexican example, would later be continued by Pompeyo Audivert, Lino Enea **Spilimbergo** and Antonio **Berni**, who regularly published their engravings and drawings in the journal of the Agrupación de Intelectuales, Artistas, Periodistas y Escritores (Intellectuals', Artists', Journalists' and Writers' Group), founded in 1936, *Unidad por la Defensa de la Cultura*. Spilimbergo's 'Breve historia de Emma' (Brief History of Emma), a series of black and white drawings telling the story of an impoverished young woman who becomes a prostitute and finally kills herself, proposed the series of engraving as a visual narrative. Berni continued this current into the 1960s, with his series on the life of the prostitute Ramona Montiel and of Juanito Laguna, a young boy living in a shanty town. The work of Carlos Alonso and Ricardo Carpani, founder of the Espartaco group in 1959, continued the line of Berni's work; Alonso sometimes opted for crude realism, sometimes for brutal satire like the 'El ganado y lo perdido' (Won and Lost) series (1972–76), with its play on the word *ganado* (meaning cattle and won) to ridicule the landowning oligarchy. Carpani's work was more directly political, centring on the vindication of figures like Juan **Perón**, Evita (see **Perón, María Eva Duarte de**) and Che **Guevara**, and on the defence of workers' struggles.

In Cuba, graphics was one of the most highly developed areas in the period after the 1959 Cuban Revolution (see **revolutions**). In an atmosphere of learning and experimentation, the Taller Experimental de Gráfica (Experimental Graphics Workshop) was founded in Havana in the early 1960s. Its first high quality posters advertised the activities of the Cuban Film Institute (**ICAIC**), the Unión de Escritores y Artistas de Cuba (**UNEAC**, Cuban Writers' and Artists' Union) and **Casa de las Américas**. By the mid-1960s, Cuban graphics were more uniformly devoted to producing large posters for public spaces addressing a variety of issues – civil defence, women's participation in the revolution, agriculture, military service, commemorations, and so on – in a range of styles. René Maderos and Raúl **Martínez** employed pop imagery while Umberto Peña preferred op art; Muñoz Banchs based his work on cartoons, while Kiko combined simple forms with typography and Félix Beltrán exploited the schematic language of urban street signs. The movement as a whole represented a synthesis of plastic arts and conceptual communication.

The Bienales of Latin American Graphics organized in Puerto Rico have been extremely important in seeking an artistic autonomy for this technique. Lorenzo **Homar** led this movement for autonomy, later taken up and continued by Antonio **Martorell**, Myrna Báez, José Rosa, Consuelo Gotay and Joaquín Reyes.

Further reading

Arte en Iberoamérica (1990) Madrid: Turner.

Bayon, D. (1984) *Arte moderno en América Latina*, Madrid: Taurus.

Chase, G. (1970) *Contemporary Art in Latin America: Painting, Graphic Art, Sculpture, Architecture*, London: The Free Press/Macmillan.

De Juan, A. (1980) *Pintura cubana, temas y variaciones*, Mexico City: UNAM.

El grabado social y político en la Argentina del siglo XX (1992) Buenos Aires: Museo de Arte Moderno.

MARÍA ALBA BOVISIO

Grau, Enrique

b. 1920, Cartagena, Colombia

Visual artist

Considered one of Colombia's leading artists, Grau's work can loosely be described as realist. He has painted murals in several Colombian cities, designed theatrical sets and also directed two films. The bulk of his work, however, has been oil on canvas, drawings and engravings, and his work has been much influenced by the Renaissance.

ALEJANDRA JARAMILLO

Grau San Martín, Ramón

b. 1881, La Palma, Pinar del Río, Cuba; d. 1969, Havana, Cuba

Politician and physician

Grau San Martín was President of the Republic on two occasions, 1933–4 and 1944–8. Leader of the student opposition to the government of Gerardo **Machado**, he was jailed and persecuted. After becoming president in 1933 he established a Labour Ministry, new labour laws and university autonomy. He was founder of the Partido Auténtico and creator of its 'decalogue', whose precepts included 'sugar for all' and 'women to the fore'. He presided over the Assembly which drew up the extremely progressive 1940 Constitution. He was the only ex-president to remain in Cuba after the Cuban Revolution of 1959 (see **revolutions**); when he died, on government orders he was buried quietly and without ceremony.

JOSÉ ANTONIO EVORA

Greater Antilles

Term used to describe the four largest islands in and around the Caribbean Sea: Cuba, Jamaica, Puerto Rico and the island of Hispaniola which includes the two countries, Haiti and the Dominican Republic. With a surface area of over 1800 square miles, Trinidad is the fifth largest Caribbean island, and is significantly larger than most of its smaller neighbours, but is nevertheless not included as one of the Greater Antilles.

ROSANNE ADDERLEY

Greco, Alberto

b. 1931, Buenos Aires, Argentina; d. 1965, Barcelona, Spain

Artist

A legendary artist of the 1960s in Argentina, Greco participated in the informalist movement in 1959 and then, in 1962, embarked on his exploration of living art. His 'vivo-ditos' are actions that consist in showing and signing people and objects, actions intended to bring art close to life and to expose the death of the work of art. In 1965, in Ibiza, he wrote *Besos brujos* (Magical Kisses), an autobiographical work that bore witness to his final months of life. He committed suicide in Barcelona on 12 October 1965, writing the word 'fin' (the end) on his hand.

CECILIA RABOSSI

green activism

The environmental movement boomed in many Latin American countries in the late 1980s and early 1990s, but in many countries the level of activism subsequently settled down. Whether environmentalists can reverse some of the ecologically devastating patterns of economic development in the region depends on their strategies and organization, but also on the depth and extent of public support for the cause.

Opinion surveys on Latin American environmental concerns and participation in environmental groups have been scarce, but sociologist Riley Dunlap and the Gallup Institute conducted a poll in 1992 called the 'Health of the Planet Survey'. The survey asked a series of questions of representative national samples in twenty-two nations around the world, including Mexico, Brazil, Chile and Uruguay. The World Values Survey was conducted over the 1990–93 period in forty-three nations, including the same Latin American countries with the exception that it examined

Argentina in place of Uruguay. A 1997 poll called the International Environmental Monitor sampled Mexico, Chile and Peru. All three studies therefore were biased to the larger and wealthier countries in Latin America, but they provide the only existing cross-national look at environmental concern among citizens.

The prior two surveys show extremely high levels of approval of the environmental movement and levels of concern about the environment, in some places higher than in North America and Europe. People in these Latin American countries are worried about local environmental issues such as air and water pollution (see **water resources in Latin America**). The most serious local issue for respondents in all four countries was inadequate sewage treatment. Concern over global issues such as the ozone layer and the greenhouse effect was at a level similar to that for Northern countries (Europe and the USA).

There is even some evidence that a majority of citizens in these Latin American countries might value environmental protection over economic gain. Given the choice which forces respondents to place priority on *either* protecting the environment *or* economic growth, 64 per cent of Chileans and Uruguayans and 71 per cent of Mexicans and Brazilians chose protecting the environment (levels higher than those of the United States). Over half of respondents in each country said they were 'willing to pay higher prices to protect the environment'. The World Values Survey found similar results for Argentina (about 50 per cent). Rates of reported 'green consumerism' (avoiding certain products that harm the environment) were low in the region, however, and the percentage of the population saying they were active in environmental groups varied from 4 per cent in Brazil to 10 per cent in Chile (one of the world's highest). While these polls must be taken extremely cautiously, they do show why environmental non-governmental organizations (NGOs) in Brazil have gone from just two groups in 1971 and about 40 in 1980 to over one thousand in 1992. Other nations have seen substantial if not such extreme rates of growth: Costa Rica, Venezuela, and Ecuador have especially strong environmental movements.

Environmental movements in Latin America have the potential to bridge social strata; research in Brazil, for example, suggests that environmental activists there tend to be urban professionals. The groups are well connected with universities, government agencies, policy circles and international financial sources. A class of highly educated technicians and administrators are heading these advocacy and research organizations, making the movement increasingly a professional one. Supporting this view are two recent polls in Brazil which showed that the degree of interest in the environment 'increases proportionally to education and family income'. However, the Brazilian polling agency IBOPE found that overall levels of interest in environmental issues did not vary significantly by class or education. They report that lower education respondents were more practical and interested in conservation of local resources, while higher education people 'were more idealistic' and interested in national and international environmental issues. It is important to remember that the background of public supporters and environmental activists and staff people differ substantially.

These differences in types of issues of concern to different social classes in Latin America are reflected in the number and diversity of environmental organizations. Some grassroots groups such as those made up of Amazon rubbertappers (once led by Chico **Mendes**), chicle (see **chewing gum**) gum gatherers in Central American forests, small farmers and shanty town (see **shanty towns and slums**) dwellers, have taken up environmental causes. These groups differ in their approaches and interests from mainstream environmental groups: they tend to be interested more in human health, social justice and/or livelihoods rather than habitat preservation, and they often prefer direct action such as protests and education campaigns rather than lobbying and legal work.

Environmental NGOs in Latin America, however, share a common problem. In North America and Europe, hundreds of thousands of dues-paying members provide independence, power and legitimacy for their environmental leaders. Because civil society in Latin America is historically weaker, there is a smaller potential constituency of dues-paying members. While the World Wildlife Fund in Britain has 1.2 million members, donating varying amounts, after a nationwide publicity campaign Brazil's largest group, S.O.S. Mata Atlântica, only grew from 1,000 to 2,000 members. The World Wildlife Fund in Brazil itself has virtually no dues-paying members, in the sense of US or European groups.

Thus these NGOs are forced to look for other sources of funding, primarily either from international groups, from corporate sponsors or from government contracts. Each option opens new doors at the cost of a certain amount of the group's autonomy. An undeniable result of the UNCED conference in Rio de Janeiro in 1992 was the massive presence of NGOs at official and non-official parallel events. In some cases when these links involved money, the NGOs have pushed Latin American groups to focus on issues far from their own priorities, namely species or habitat preservation instead of urban pollution and the environmental effects of poverty. That is, greater dependence on overseas funding may have forced some Latin American environmental groups to focus on preserving large, 'charismatic' species which sell calendars and bring in pledge money in the US and Europe.

'The whole world is watching' is a common cry of protest movements, and with the expansion of electronic networks on the Internet this is increasingly true. Internet groups such as Econet and the Environment in Latin America Network link Latin American and Northern environmentalists, academics, journalists and citizens. Action alerts on pressing environmental issues from the Ecuadorian Amazon and the Galapagos, from Mexico's south and north border regions, from Guatemala, Costa Rica, Venezuela and Brazil have been disseminated through these networks. Usually these alerts call for letter-writing, phone calls and other forms of outside pressure on corporations, funders and Latin American states to protect the environment. Their success at generating this pressure has not been studied, but the flow of information may often inhibit the state from committing environmentally and socially degrading actions.

The effect of the flow of information to North American and European environmentalists is seen in two examples from the Brazilian Amazon which were pivotal in redirecting the lending strategy of the World Bank. First, a photograph of the western Amazon taken one evening from the US space shuttle showed over 5,000 fires. That photo covered an area of the state of Rondonia where a huge World Bank and Interamerican Development Bank funded colonization project called Polonoroeste was under way. After a public outcry and a campaign by environmentalists to stop the project, in 1985 the World Bank halted money for the project, the first time it had ever done so for environmental reasons. Second, with the help of the World Bank the Brazilian state planned how to turn the massive Carajás iron deposits in the eastern Amazon into a regional development project. The most controversial part of the plan was twenty-two pig-iron factories which were proposed to run on charcoal from the native rainforest.

In fighting the projects, international environmentalists, working with local groups, such as peasant leagues and indigenous peoples, have focused attention on the international press, the United States Congress, and other lenders such as the European Union and the **Inter-American Development Bank**. Hearing of the potential devastation through pressure from environmentalists, who dubbed the Carajás project potentially one of the world's worst five ever, the EU boycotted Carajás iron and the World Bank issued warnings about future funding for Brazil. Later, after the struggles with Chico Mendes's group of rubber-tappers and peasant farmers, funds for the paving of a critical highway in Acre were also suspended several times. Battles over a number of projects still continue, but since 1985 the environmental evaluation components of these loans have pressured Latin American states to enforce *some* environmental laws more actively and even to expand their areas under preservation. Referring to his country's Amazon region, Brazil's president Fernando Henrique **Cardoso** stated in 1995 that the nation could not get low-cost loans from such sources as the World Bank, 'if we don't have a sense that we are responsible before the rest of mankind for preserving nature, for preserving indigenous culture'.

Outside pressure over environmental issues has also brought a sometimes strident nationalist backlash in Latin America. These backlashes typically come from the political right, business interests and militaries of Latin America, but they often gain the support of much wider segments of the population. The backlashes appeal to sentiments of national sovereignty and reveal a weakness in externally imposed and top-down environmental regulations and activism, such as external cash dependency and their heavy reliance on and pressure from outside of funding and regulatory agencies.

In sum, then, public opinion appears to have 'greened' significantly in the Latin American nations for which we have survey results. The region's many groups have made significant advances, but many remain tied to and dependent upon Northern environmental groups. These links, however, have provided them with some leverage to use in their battles with the major forces they see as responsible for the worst environmental atrocities: their governments and transnational corporations.

See also: Aridjis, Homero; environmental issues

Further reading

Dunlap, R.E., Gallup Jr., G.H. and Gallup, A.M. (1993) *Health of the Planet: Results of a 1992 International Environmental Opinion Survey of Citizens in 24 Nations*, Princeton, NJ: George H. Gallup International Institute.

Inglehart, R. (1995) 'Political Support for Environmental Protection: Objective Problems and Subjective Values in 43 Societies', *PS: Political Science and Politics* 23 (1): 57–72.

Keck, M.E. (1995) 'Parks, People and Power: The Shifting Terrain of Environmentalism', *NACLA Report on the Americas* 28 (5): 36–41.

Leff, E. (1986) 'Notas para un Análisis Sociológico de los Movimientos Ambientalistas', in M. Cárdenas, *Política Ambiental y Desarrollo: Un Debate para América Latina*, Bogota: FESCOL/INDERENA, 115–26.

Viola, E.J. (1992) 'O movimento ambientalista no Brasil (1979–1991): da denúncia e conscientização pública para a institucionalização e o desenvolvimento sustentável', in M. Goldenberg (ed.) *Ecologia, Ciência e Política*, Rio de Janeiro: Editora Revan, 49–75.

J. TIMMONS ROBERTS

Green Revolution

Initially developed in the post-war period in the USA, Green Revolution technologies were exported to Latin America in the 1960s and 1970s in order to increase and diversify crop yields. Seed varieties, fertilizers, pesticides, irrigation and mechanization developed at North American land grant universities and by large multi-national petrochemical corporations were introduced into the region without much regard for the effect that new technologies would have on farmers and the environment. The costly new technologies proved to be unviable for small- and medium-scale farmers, and caused environmental problems such as soil erosion, contamination of ground water resources, the appearance of pesticide residues in food crops, the reduction of genetic diversity and an increased vulnerability of crops to pests and environmental changes.

During the 1970s and 1980s, much of Latin American agriculture focused on export crops to the detriment of producing food crops for the local population. For example, research efforts in Central and South America focused on export and luxury crops. Another major problem in Latin America is the weak link between universities and the private sector, which makes the introduction and commercialization of new biotechnologies difficult. One exception is Mexico's Universidad Autónoma de México (**UNAM**), which founded the Centre for Technological Innovation in 1984 to market their scientific and technological findings.

Two basic positions have been advocated in the assessment of the Green Revolution's impact in Latin America. On one hand, there are those who see it as a panacea to the world's food problems. Large photochemical companies like Monsanto represent this position. On the other hand, there are those who see biotechnology as a First-World phenomenon that will foster the dependency of developing countries on advanced capitalist countries and further aggravate underdevelopment and poverty.

Ecological and public health concerns have prompted **green activism** in Latin America, but there is great diversity among the different organizations. In countries like Brazil and Mexico, green parties have presented candidates in public elections and have won representation at various levels while in countries like Ecuador, Guatemala and Colombia, green parties are still in the process of gestation. In 1997, seventy representatives from European, North American and Latin American green parties and movements met in Mexico City for the Green Horizons meeting and established the Federation of Green Parties of the Americas, a network of international green parties. They also discussed free-trade agreements like the European Union, **MERCOSUR** and **NAFTA**, and called for the inclusion of clauses that would protect labour and the environment.

Further reading

Pan American Health Organization (1996) *Biodiversity, Biotechnology, and Sustainable Development in Health and Agriculture: Emerging Connections*, Washington, DC: Pan American Sanitary Bureau, Regional Office of the World Health Organization.

Peritore, N. and Galve-Peritore, A. (eds) (1995) *Biotechnology in Latin America: Politics, Impacts and Risks*, Wilmington, DE: SR Books.

Thiesenhusen, W. (1972) *Green Revolution in Latin America: Income Effects, Policy Decisions*, Madison: University of Wisconsin–Madison, Land Tenure Center.

MARCIE D. RINKA

Grenada

The small Caribbean country of Grenada has 94,000 inhabitants in its 344 square kilometres of land area. Its long history of intervention ranges from the eighteenth-century extermination of the island's **Caribs** by the French to the 1983 US invasion designed to destroy Grenada's socialist experiment just nine years after it had removed the yoke of British imperialism. The growth of **tourism** since then has not resolved Grenada's most pressing problem, unemployment.

Grenada's three islands (Grenada, Carricou and Petit Martinique) contain three ethnic groups (African, East Indian and European in origin) and two languages (English and patois). Known as 'spice island', Grenada's principal product is nutmeg. Grenadan literature since the 1970s has produced writers like Paul **Keens-Douglas**, Francis Bain, David Simon and Merle **Collins**. Grenadan **calypso** and **soca** have an important place in Caribbean music.

See also: Bishop, Maurice; New Jewel Movement

Further reading

Heine, J. (ed.) (1991) *A Revolution Aborted: The Lessons of Grenada*, Pittsburgh, PA: Latin American Series.

Grenada: Revolution in Reverse (1990) New York: Monthly Review Press.

Thorndike, T. (1985) *Grenada: Politics, Economics and Society*, London: St Martins Press.

LUIS L. ESPARZA

Griffero, Ramón

b. 1955, Santiago, Chile

Playwright

Griffero founded the Teatro de Fin de Siglo in 1984 in an abandoned warehouse. In his plays performed in the late 1980s – *Historias de un Galpón Abandonado* (Stories of an Abandoned Warehouse), *Cinema Utoppia, 99 La Morgue* – he creatively responded to the limitations of working as an artist within an oppressive military regime. To work around censorship, his plays de-emphasized the text and instead experimented with performance spaces, sets and presentation styles. His 1995 play *Río Abajo* (Downriver), with sets by Herbert **Jonckers**, gives an irreverent yet sensitive view of the world of Santiago's tenement dwellers.

AMALIA PEREIRA

Grinbank, Daniel

b. Buenos Aires, Argentina

Entrepreneur

Known for his involvement in the rock industry, Grinbank began by representing Argentine artists and groups like Serú Girán, León **Gieco** and Charly **García**. In the mid-1980s he founded the famous Rock and Pop, the first Argentine radio station devoted entirely to ***rock nacional***. The monthly magazine of the same name, edited by Grinbank, was a second component of his enterprise, to which were added a short-lived television programme and a concert promotions organization. In later years, Grinbank organized Argentine tours for artists like the Rolling Stones, Michael Jackson, Madonna and David Bowie.

DIEGO BENTIVEGNA

Grippo, Víctor

b. 1936, Junín, Argentina

Conceptual artist

Víctor Grippo's first training was as a chemist, and an interest in science and natural processes is evident in his artistic work. In the early 1970s he joined the *Grupo de los trece* (Group of the Thirteen) centred around Jorge **Glusberg**'s *Centro de Arte y Comunicación* (Centre for Art and Communication) in Buenos Aires. His most important works of the 1970s are the *Analogías* (Analogies), in which potatoes connected to electrodes are used as metaphors of growth, decay and even torture (**torture and disappearance, reports of**). Grippo is considered one of Latin America's most significant conceptual artists (see **conceptual art**) for his ability to combine 'pure' experimentation with social concerns.

GABRIEL PEREZ-BARREIRO

grotesco criollo

Grotesco criollo is a dramatic form derived from the *sainete* typical of Argentine drama since the nineteenth century. Its tragic, despairing vision of the world is simultaneously expressed in dramatic and comic situations full of absurd characters and deep ironies. Metaphorically, it decries the few possibilities open to newly-arrived immigrants. In 1923 Armando **Discépolo** described his own play *Mateo* as '*grotesco*'. In the 1930s, 'the infamous decade', the grotesque permeates the lyrics of tangos (see **tango**), films and literature. In the 1970s it returns again, particularly in the work of Roberto **Cossa**, in acerbic descriptions of everyday life and its uncertainties, which in their turn produce immorality, despair and madness.

NORA MAZZIOTTI

Grove, Marmaduke

b. 1878, Copiapó, Chile; d. 1954, Santiago, Chile

Politician

Charismatic leader of Chile's 1932 twelve-day socialist republic, Grove played a key role in the creation of Chile's Socialist Party in 1933; he was largely responsible for its radical nationalism. Prominent in the young officers' revolutionary movement of 1925, he became Air Force chief before retiring from the armed forces for political reasons in 1928. He was imprisoned on Easter Island (**Rapa Nui**) in 1931 and again after the fall of the short-lived republic. He became a senator and the party's presidential candidate, though he withdrew from the 1938 elections in favour of victorious Popular Front candidate, Pedro Aguirre Cerda.

PHILIP O'BRIEN

Grupo Cine de la Base

Led by film-maker Raymundo Gleyzer, this grassroots Argentine cinema group formed in 1969 promoted the use of film to develop a revolutionary political consciousness among Latin American workers and peasants. Its most important films were *México, la revolución congelada* (Mexico, the Frozen Revolution) (1970) and *Los traidores* (The

Traitors) (1973), a fictional feature about the corruption of the Argentine trade union leadership. In the early 1970s, Cine de la Base developed a series of affiliated organizations throughout the country. The military *coup* of 1976 forced many of its members into exile, Gleyzer was '**disappeared**', and the Group effectively disbanded.

See also: New Latin American cinema

DIANA PALLADINO

Grupo Cine Independiente

Formed in the late 1960s by Felipe **Cazals**, Arturo **Ripstein**, Jaime Humberto **Hermosillo**, Paul **Leduc** and others, this short-lived group had a significant influence on the marginal, committed cinema of the 1970s and was one of the few links between Mexican cinema and the **New Latin American Cinema**. The 1968 student movement in Mexico and radical parties directly affected their films as well as others like *El grito* (The Cry) (1968) by Leobardo López Arteche. Under Rodolfo Echeverría, the Banco Cinematográfico Mexicano (Mexican Film Foundation) absorbed many of these previously independent film-makers into the industry.

PATRICIA TORRES SAN MARTÍN

Grupo Cine Liberación

Grupo Cine Liberación was a film-making collective of left-wing Peronists (see **Peronism**) including Fernando **Solanas**, Edgardo Pallero and Gerardo Vallejo. It arose between 1966 and 1968 through the filming of *La hora de los hornos* (Hour of the Furnaces), which proposed the need for an aesthetically and politically alternative film-making practice. It gave rise to the *tercer cine* (third cinema) group founded in 1969. In 1971, Cine Liberación produced two documentaries in which Getino and Solanas interviewed **Perón** in exile in Madrid, and collaborated with Vallejo for *El camino hacia la muerte del viejo Reales* (Old Man Reales's Road to Death) (1971), before disappearing.

DIANA PALLADINO

Grupo Convite

Grupo Convite is a vocal-musical group founded in 1976 in Santo Domingo and influenced by the *nueva canción latinoamericana*. Convite, which means 'invitation to work together in the fields', had as its main objective to research, compose and interpret folkloric and popular Dominican songs. Its members were university students, intellectuals, sociologists and musicians. They combined traditional musical instruments with typical Dominican instruments such as atabale drums, **marimba**, güira scrapers and maracas rattles to perform meringues (see **merengue**), salves, mangulinas, palos and peasant tonadas. One of its most important members was Luis **Días**, a well-known **bachata** composer.

FERNANDO VALERIO-HOLGUÍN

Grupo Corpo

An avant-garde dance group founded in Belo Horizonte, Brazil in the mid-1970s, Grupo Corpo has represented Latin American dance throughout the world. Innovative and experimental, its creative choreography reveals an aesthetic combining the popular and the erudite, Milton **Nascimento** and the avant-garde sounds of Uakti and Tom **Zé**, with classical, computer and minimalist sounds. It uses traditional themes, like the *sertão*, a recurrent topic of Brazilian **Cinema Novo** and literature, to reveal a concept of Brazilian identity which is never folkloric or clichéd. In presenting Brazilian experience as universal, Grupo Corpo has brought to fruition the aesthetic proposal of the *Antropofagia* movement.

Grupo de Barranquilla

The Grupo de Barranquilla (Barranquilla Group) was a group of intellectuals – Álvaro Cepeda Samudio, Alfonso and José Félix Fuenmayor, Germán Vargas, Bernardo Restrepo Maya, Gabriel **García Márquez** and Alejandro Obregón – which emerged in 1940 with the arrival of Ramón

Vinyes, an erudite Catalan, to the Colombian port of Barranquilla and lasted into the late 1950s. Their written production, issued in *Crónica* (Chronicle), the group's publication, and other media, is made up mostly of journalistic articles. In these, they harshly chastise the literary establishment of Bogotá, the Colombian capital, for its isolation, conventionalism and lack of acceptance of international literary influences. The group and its leader are gently caricatured in Garcia Marquez's **Cien años de soledad** (One Hundred Years of Solitude) (1967).

HÉCTOR D. FERNÁNDEZ L'HOESTE

Grupo de Guayaquil   see   *Guayaquil Group*

Grupo de los Cuatro

A group of four Mexican composers – Daniel **Ayala**, Salvador **Contreras**, Blas **Galindo** and José Pablo **Moncayo**, they were given the name by music critic José Barros Sierra in 1935, when they presented a joint concert in Mexico City. All four studied with Carlos **Chávez** as well as Candelario **Huízar**, Silvestre **Revueltas** (particularly Ayala and Contreras) and Aaron Copland (Galindo and Moncayo).

EDUARDO CONTRERAS SOTO

Grupo de Renovación Musical

Group of art music composers founded and organized by José **Ardevol**, a Catalan composer who settled in Havana, Cuba in the 1930s, creating a unique school of composition. The Renovación group gave great impetus to Cuban composing and included many composers now considered luminaries of Cuban art music, among them Edgardo Martín (b. 1915), Harold **Gramatges**, Gisela Hernández (1912–71), Hilario González (b. 1920) and Argeliers **León**, who became an important Cuban musicologist and researcher.

ANA M. LÓPEZ

Grupo Escambray

A Cuban post-revolutionary theatre group started in 1968, Grupo Escambray became a model for collective theatrr production in Latin America. The group sought to extend theatre productions beyond Havana playhouses, and settled in Escambray, an underdeveloped northern region which had been the site of most of the contra-revolutionary (*bandido*) activity in the early 1960s. Once eradicated, the revolutionary government began investing in the area's economic and cultural development. Their plays stem from collective ethnographic investigations and are characterized by a socialist-realist style seeking to portray and critique the historically conditioned personal and political assumptions obstructing the development of the new socialist society.

BARBARA D. RIESS

Grupo Gay da Bahia

Founded 29 February 1980 in Salvador, Grupo Gay de Bahia is the oldest continuously active gay rights group in Brazil and one of the most active in Latin America. The group's activism has included denunciation of police brutality, publicizing Brazil's high murder rate for gays and lesbians, and the development of a law project for civil registry of same-sex domestic partners. Allied closely with black (see **black movements**) and the **women's movements**, the GGB also sponsors groups for lesbians, transvestites and Afro-Brazilian gays and operates the Centro Baiano Anti-Aids (Bahian Anti-**AIDS** Centre).

See also: gay and lesbian movements; Mott, Luiz

SCOTT A. COOPER

Grupo Minorista

An intellectual movement emerging out of improvised gatherings in Havana in the early twenties, Grupo Minorista rapidly became the cultural and political epicentre of the epoch. Led by young left wing intellectuals, its 1927 manifesto – the Declaración Minorista – expressed a spirit of rebellion against distortions of the Cuban cultural heritage and demanded changes in national political life. It had no organ of its own, but its members wrote regularly in journals like *Social*, *Carteles* and the cultural supplement of the *Diario de la marina*. Internal political and ideological tensions led to its collapse at the end of the decade.

WILFREDO CANCIO ISLA

Grupo Ukamau

Film-making collective organized in 1968 in Bolivia by Jorge **Sanjinés**, with Antonio Eguino, Oscar Soria (a scriptwriter for Bolivian film-maker pioneer, Jorge Ruiz) and Ricardo Rada, named after Sanjinés's first film *Ukamau* (That's the Way it is) (1966). Working with non-professional actors and focusing on stories based on real events that revealed the problems and cultural and political oppression suffered by the indigenous **Quechua** and **Aymara** populations, the collective developed a unique and compelling politically engaged aesthetics.

Their first film, *Yawar malku* (Blood of the Condor) (1969), and its indictment of the US presence in Bolivia brought them great national and international acclaim. Yet the experience of making this film in collaboration with the indigenous Kaata community, and self-distributing the film among peasant and working-class audiences, led the collective to rethink their approach to film-making, eschewing the convention of mainstream narrative film (such as flashbacks and close-ups, for example) to develop a more communicative aesthetics that could allow the people to relay their own history, with protagonists enacting their own experiences.

The negatives for their second film, *Los caminos de la muerte* (The Roads of Death) were lost in a German laboratory, but their third project, *El coraje del pueblo* (The Courage of the People) brilliantly illustrated their methodology. Based on the story of a miners' massacre in 1967, the film incorporated some of the miners who had survived the massacre and allowed them to re-enact and retell the story, emphasizing the resistance function of collective address in Andean culture.

Ukamau finished shooting the film only days before Hugo Banzer's military *coup*; most of the collective (except Eguino) went into exile. After *Fuera de aquí* (Get Out of Here), a semi-documentary filmed in Ecuador in 1977, the group dissolved and Sanjinés followed a solo career.

ANA M. LÓPEZ

Guadalupe años cincuenta

Written and produced in 1975 by the La **Candelaria** company and El Nuevo Teatro Colombiano, *Guadalupe años cincuenta* (Guadalupe in the 1950s) is an incisive exploration of the political events that took place during the period of La **Violencia** (1948–62) in Colombia. The play's main character, Guadalupe Salcedo Unda, was a commander of the Liberal guerrilla forces of the eastern *llanos* of Colombia, who later betrayed the movement. The subtitle of the play, 'La historia sin contar de los años cincuenta' (The Untold Story of the1950s), pointed out the difficulties Colombians have in facing the facts of the civil war.

ALEJANDRA JARAMILLO

Guadeloupe

Guadeloupe is the largest of the two French island Departments, and includes several outlying islands. Half of the island is dominated by a volcano, La Soufrière (as is the case with its sister Department, Martinique), and the rest is an undulating plain covered by **sugar** cane and **banana** estates. The island has a distinctive shape with two land areas, Grande Terre and Basse Terre, that appear like the open wings of a butterfly. Its capital, Pointe à Pitre, is in Grande Terre, separated by a canal from Basse Terre, where the administrative centre is located. Traditionally uneasy with its neo-colonial status, Guadeloupe has produced several writers, including distinguished women writers like Maryse **Condé** and Simone **Schwarz Bart**.

J. MICHAEL DASH

guaguancó

One of the varieties of **rumba** (the other is yambu), guaguancó begins with an extended song whose denouement usually produces a repeated chorus. Melodically, it has a very simple form, little more than a basic rhythm to link the improvisations of the percussionists. The verse forms may vary – indeed sometimes the singer may simply recite a piece of prose. The rhythm of the guaguancó is usually faster than the yambu; the dance steps are much freer, as the pair initiates a ritual of attraction and rejection, of surrender and evasion, until the man finally dominates her with a series of pelvic bumps.

JOSÉ ANTONIO EVORA

Guantanamera

A Cuban guajira-**son** tune often used by Cuban folk singers to improvise couplets. The popular singer Joseíto Fernández claims to be the composer of the song, which he began to sing in 1928 and transcribed in 1941, when the radio station CMQ launched its programme, 'La Guantanamera', where Fernández improvised verses about the gossip of the day with the backing of this familiar tune. The programme enjoyed huge popularity until the advent of television. In the 1960s US singer Pete Seeger set verses from José Martí's *Versos sencillos* to the tune, which has since become a standard – more than 120 versions of the song have been recorded. Guantanamera was a leitmotif in Tomés **Gutiérrez Alea**'s film of the same name

WILFREDO CANCIO ISLA

Guantánamo

Famous outside Cuba for two reasons: the US military base, founded in 1903 and still functioning on Guantánamo Bay; and its associations with the internationally renowned song, La **Guantanamera**.

In the extreme southeast of the island of Cuba, the town was founded in the late seventeenth century, but not officially designated a city until 1870. Since 1976, it has been the capital of the province of the same name. The area around Guantánamo Bay and the Guaso river were important areas of pre-Columbian settlement. Today, the province produces **coffee** as well as **cocoa**, **bananas** and coconuts. It remains one of the country's most backward areas, for its agriculture has suffered badly because of the salination of the soil. In the nineteenth century, it experienced a boom in sugar production; by 1860 it possessed some twenty sugar mills, most of which were destroyed during the war of independence (1868–78). Coffee was grown in the mountainous areas, having been introduced by French colonists from Haiti. Indeed, the French influence and the black population brought as slave labour has given the regional dances and music a very particular character, with the so called 'tumba francesa' and musical genres like changüí, nengón and kiribá, considered predecessors of **son**. The historical isolation of the region from the rest of the country, however, inhibited its artistic development, though it has produced important figures in popular music and literature, like the poet Regino Boti (1878–1958).

Guantánamo Bay, eleven square miles in extent, is one of the largest in Cuba. The US naval base on the external part of the bay has been a focus of tensions since the victory of the Cuban Revolution in 1959, and a number of Cuban border guards have died there. It has also been used by many Cubans as a departure point for emigration to the USA. In 1994, during the so called '*balseros*' (rafters) crisis, it became a camp for many thousands of refugees trying to escape the island. The Cuban government considers the base land stolen from the nation. The province also contains Nuestra Señora de la Asunción de Baracoa, first city of the new Cuba founded by Diego Velázquez in 1512. The region boasts a zoological park, built around a series of stone sculptures by Angel Iñigo.

WILFREDO CANCIO ISLA

guaracha

Some researchers consider the guaracha the first authentically Cuban music, fusing Spanish musical forms and African rhythms. The oldest known guaracha, 'La guabina', dates from the late eighteenth century, but the genre became popular in the 1850s as the musical accompaniment to early Cuban theatre, when local scenes and characters began to replace the traditional Spanish ones and the guaracha took the place of the Spanish tonadilla. The contemporary guaracha is a descendant of the original, but influenced by dance and songs which have changed its traditional verse and chorus shape. Its best-known exponents, like Nico Saquito and Pedro Luis **Ferrer**, have retained its satirical tone.

JOSÉ ANTONIO EVORA

Guaracha del Macho Camacho, La

La Guaracha del Macho Camacho (Macho Camacho's Beat) is a novel by the Puerto Rican Luis Rafael **Sánchez**, first published in Buenos Aires in 1976. Its title came from a popular song which is heard blasting out in the background throughout the novel. It was significant that this text should first have found acceptance outside its natural context, and equally significant the fact that in the same year René **Marqués**, the most authoritative voice in Puerto Rican culture, published his novel *La mirada* (The Look) in Puerto Rico. Sánchez's novel had to wait for recognition until the early 1980s, when it coincided with the discursive break with the 'pessimist' canon.

A prostitute, a corrupt politician, a retarded hydrocephalic child, a poor woman and a frustrated society lady meet in *La guaracha* for the purpose of creating the national saga of Puerto Rican *guachafita* (disorder). It is as if uninhibited sexuality, disorder and muddle are merely simulations whose purpose is to avoid confronting the existential problem; Sánchez's metafictional proposal seeks to find in humour and parody a secure refuge not only for these miserable beings, but also for the readers, who are as impotent and defenceless as the characters of the novel, and perhaps as the narrator himself, who invites his audience to join him in watching this grotesque tragicomedy.

Voices that intercept and quote one another, people in danger, popular culture, bourgeois clichés, intertextualities, slogans and warnings all meet in the space of orality. For what finds expression in each chapter of *La guaracha* is the project of speaking in Puerto Rican, all of whose voices and accents find a place in its fictional heterogeneity. Luis Rafael Sánchez constructs a metafictional cultural artefact, in which the coexistence of multiple languages permits him to develop a theory of Caribbean linguistic hybridism. Ana Lydia **Vega**, Juan Antonio Ramos and Edgardo **Rodríguez**, among others, have shared Sánchez's aesthetic project to set in train a new narrative.

These oppressed sectors who take the pages of the novel by storm are not the stereotypical figures of pre-industrial tradition but serve to throw into relief the inequalities that have arisen within society itself. Faced with the impossibility of creating a new order, however, all that is left is laughter, carnival and the affirmation that 'life's great'.

Further reading

Barradas, E. (1981) *Para leer en puertorriqueño: acercamiento a la obra de Luis Rafael Sánchez*, Rio Piedras: Ed. Cultural.

Gelpi, J.G. (1993) *Literatura y paternalismo en Puerto Rico*, Rio Piedras: Editorial de la Universidad de Puerto Rico.

Ramos, J. (1982) 'La guaracha del macho Camacho: texto de cultura puertorriqueña', *Texto crítico* 8(24–5): 171–83.

MARIA JULIA DAROQUI

Guarani

Alone among the indigenous tongues of the Western Hemisphere, the Guarani language of Paraguay enjoys stature as a national medium of communication and artistic expression. Though other Native American tongues, notably **Quechua**, **Aymara**, various Mayan languages and

Náhuatl (see **Náhuatl and Aztecan languages**), retain substantial speaker populations in their respective countries, only Guarani actually surpasses Spanish as an oral medium in the principal country where it is extant. Approximately 80 per cent of Paraguayans speak Guarani, as opposed to only 50 to 55 per cent who speak Spanish, and while these figures reveal a high degree of bilingualism, Guarani remains the preferred tongue of most, particularly in rural areas. Enclaves of Guarani speakers, moreover, can be found in neighbouring regions of Bolivia, Argentina and Brazil.

Modern Guarani is an agglutinating language of the Tupi-Guarani stock once dominant in much of central and northern South America. Current dialects include those of the Pai Tavyterã Indians of Paraguay and the Chiriguano Indians of Bolivia and Argentina. The vast majority of speakers, however, are persons of European or mestizo ancestry who use the variant known simply as 'Paraguayan Guarani'.

After more than four and a half centuries of contact, the two principal languages of Paraguay have quite naturally influenced each other. Paraguayan Spanish contains numerous words of Guarani origin, particularly items which denote the natural world and the daily life of the people. Guarani has also effected certain changes in the structure of spoken Spanish, though this influence is less pervasive. Much more profound have been the changes wrought by Spanish on Guarani. Typically, between one-fifth and one-third of the words in any substantial sample of colloquial Guarani will be of Spanish origin. So extensive is this linguistic mix or *yopará* that purists disdain it as a separate language. Many Guarani scholars, however, consider *yopará* as essentially Guarani, for it retains in the main its indigenous morphology, and even its many Spanish loan words are often altered phonetically to fit native patterns.

The survival of Guarani is a matter of concern for most Paraguayans, who regard the language as a potent symbol of national identity. Educators and legislators have promoted its use in schools and government, and the language has an extensive written literature, particularly in the genres of poetry, song, theatre and folk narrative. Poets Carlos F. Abente, Zenón Bogado Rolón, Narciso R. Colmán, Susy **Delgado**, Pedro Encina Ramos, Félix de Guarania, Juan Maidana, Carlos Martínez Gamba, Miguelángel Meza, Teodoro Mongelós and Rudi **Torga**, the dramatist Julio Correa, the songwriter-poets Emiliano R. Fernández and Darío Gómez Serrato, the dramatist and poet Félix Fernández, and the folk anthologist Rubén Rolandi are only a few of the many contributors to Guarani literature in the middle and late twentieth century.

Despite these efforts, and despite recognition in the Paraguayan constitutions of 1967 and 1992, Guarani is primarily an oral tongue. Home, street and farmer's field are the scenes of its ascendancy over Spanish. Spanish, however, remains the primary language of political and commercial discourse, especially in Asunción, Paraguay's capital. It dominates where written communication is required, and where decisions of national or international consequence are made. Guarani is the primary tongue of daily life, but Spanish is the language of power.

Oddly marginalized in a country where it is both the majority language and an emblem of fierce nationalism, Paraguayan Guarani is thus subject to a certain fundamental irony. Such statements, however, should not obscure the extraordinary demography, singular in the Americas and perhaps in the world, of an indigenous language which has thrived in a non-indigenous population.

Further reading

Guasch, A. (1983) *El idioma guaraní: gramática y antología de prosa y verso*, Asunción: Ediciones Loyola.

Guasch, A. and Ortiz, D. (1992) *Diccionario castellano-guaraní, guaraní-castellano*, Asunción: Centro de Estudios Paraguayos 'Antonio Guasch'.

Meliá, B., Farré, L. and Pérez, A. (1992) *El guaraní a su alcance*, Asunción: Centro de Estudios Paraguayos 'Antonio Guasch'.

Méndez-Faith, T. (1994) *Breve antología de la literatura paraguaya*, Asunción: El Lector.

—— (1994) *Breve diccionario de la literatura paraguaya*, Asunción: El Lector.

TRACY K. LEWIS

guarania

The guarania is a traditional Paraguayan musical form created by composer José Asunción Flores (1904–72) in 1925, when he arranged the polka 'Maerãpareikuaase' by Rogelio Recalde. It is slower than the polka and often accompanied by words in **Guarani**. The first written guarania was 'Jejúi' (1928), but the best-known is 'India', with text by poet Manuel Ortiz Guerrero (1894–1933). Flores also arranged guaranias for symphony orchestra. Originally written in 2/4 time, Flores changed the metre to 6/8, closer to Paraguayan rhythms. The guarania is played on the **harp** and often accompanied by **guitar**. Other well-known guaranias include 'Mi dicha lejana' (My Distant Joy), 'Recuerdos de Ypacaraí' (Memories of Ypacaraí) and 'Pájaro campana' (Bell Bird).

BETSY PARTYKA

Guarany, Horacio

b. 1925, Las Garzas, Argentina

Musician

An extremely popular singer and television star, Guarany (real name Eraclio Catalino Rodríguez) began singing with orchestra leader Herminio Giménez in 1943. Later he began to compose 'Guitarra de medianoche' (Midnight Guitar) and 'La litoreña', working with his quartet Los Amerindios, and he made his first recording in 1950. He sang at an International Youth Festival in Moscow, toured the Soviet Union and made musical soundtracks for films. Guarany appears regularly at folklore festivals (such as Cosquín, 1997) and on television.

FERNANDA A. ZULLO

Guardia, Gloria

b. 1940, Panama City

Writer

An important Panamanian writer, Guardia's *El último juego* (The Final Game) (1997) is a complicated experimental novel, critical of Panamanian dependency on the United States and political corruption. The plot deals with the terrorist kidnapping of a group of politicians by a guerrilla commando. Through several narrative voices, Guardia portrays the alienation and solitude of her characters in a world inundated by propaganda, consumerism and money. She has also published an important critical work on Pablo Antonio **Cuadra**, and numerous articles. She lives in Colombia.

NICASIO URBINA

Guarnieri, (Mozart) Camargo

b. 1907, Tieté, São Paulo, Brazil; d. 1993, São Paulo

Composer and conductor

One of the most important composers of the Brazilian nationalist school, as well as a successful conductor and teacher, Guarnieri's life's ambition was 'to be a Brazilian composer'. His orchestral song cycle *Quatro poemas de Macunaíma* (1931) and opera *Pedro Malazarte* (1932) both employ texts by Mário de **Andrade**, and his many solo songs, some featuring Amerindian texts and melodies, are as significant as those by **Villa-Lobos**. Guarnieri's *Homenagem a Villa-Lobos* for orchestra (1966) demonstrates his debt to and respect for his older compatriot.

SIMON WRIGHT

Guarnieri, Gianfrancesco

b. 1934, Milan, Italy

Playwright and actor

One of Brazil's most important playwrights and an extraordinary actor, Guarnieri was born into a family of talented classical musicians who emigrated to Brazil in 1936. He began his professional career as an actor in São Paulo, at the newly founded Teatro de Arena (see **Arena Theatre Group**) (1953) in 1956. In 1958 he premièred his first play there, the realist political thriller, *Eles não* usam black tie (They Don't Wear Black Tie). When Leon **Hirszman** adapted Guarnieri's play to the screen in 1981, Guarnieri co-wrote the script, updating the story into the politically turbulent 1970s. He also gave a fine performance as one of the protagonists, Otávio, a long-time leftist disturbed by the rising militancy of a new generation of activists including his own son (his wife was played by the brilliant Fernanda **Montenegro**). Guarnieri has continued writing for the stage and television, most recently (in 1999) starring in his own play, *Anjo na contramão* (Angel Going the Wrong Way) (co-written with his son, Cacau Guarnieri) in São Paulo.

ANA M. LÓPEZ

Guastavino, Carlos

b. 1914, Santa Fe, Argentina

Composer

Argentina's leading composer of art songs, Guastavino studied with Athos Palma in Buenos Aires. Songs such as *La rosa y el sauce* (The Rose and the Willow) and *Se equivocó la paloma* (The Dove was Wrong) were popularized during the 1980s in recordings by José Carreras. Although he works most effectively as a miniaturist (the Christmas carol *Canción de Navidad* is a gem), large-scale works include a ballet *Once Upon a Time* (1942), a piano sonata (1946) and a violin sonata (1952).

SIMON WRIGHT

Guatemala

Located south of Mexico, with coasts on both the Pacific Ocean and the Caribbean, it borders El Salvador and Honduras. Guatemala is the most populated country in Central America, with nearly 10 million people, half of whom are descendants of the Mayas. Antigua, the colonial capital of southern Mexico and Central America (known as the Captaincy General of Guatemala) and one of the best preserved eighteenth-century cities on the continent, is today a World Heritage Site (see **World Heritage Sites**).

Guatemalan culture has been marked by the continuity of Mayan resistance, best exemplified by the *Popol Vuh*, written in Quiché by anonymous Maya intellectuals in the 1540s (translated into Spanish by Fray Francisco Ximénez, it was published in 1752). The culture has been torn by a need to find justice for the dead, the tortured and the **disappeared**, a need that has crossed all boundaries of cultural production. Examples include symbolic codes framing Guatemalan painting, topics set to music and motifs appearing in popular craft work (see **crafts**).

Guatemala became independent from Spain in 1821. It briefly attempted to unite the Central Americans into a federal entity, but the failure of the project was sealed by a regional civil war that lasted a decade. It was ruled by conservative dictatorships until a liberal revolution toppled them in 1871. During the nineteenth century, artists and writers played a crucial role in framing political issues. The lack of social scientists, and the dearth of liberal professionals and technicians until the 1960s, left them trying to fulfil those social needs.

Literature as social commentary began in colonial times. Both the conquering soldier Bernal Díaz (1495–1584), author of *La verdadera y notable relación de la conquista de México y Guatemala* (True History of the Conquest of Mexico and Guatemala) (1568, published 1632), and land-owner Francisco Antonio de Fuentes (?1642–?1700), author of *Recordación Florida* (1685, published 1932) saw their works as means of justifying their deeds or claims to the Spanish Crown. A century later Jesuit Rafael Landívar's (1731–93) poem in Latin, *Rusticatio Mexicana* (1781), published in exile in Bologna, was a step in the direction of conscripting literature to the service of nationalism. Literature was used in this way because of its capacity to promote identification with a certain national territory and history, as well as its ability to plant national symbols in everyday practices.

During the colonial period, Mayans altered Spanish-imposed clothing; new signs and symbols were woven into sixteenth-century patterns, which represented a counter-statement to official colonial discourse, as well as re-articulating the Mayans' own symbolic and spiritual needs. From this period date famous examples of weaving, considered nowadays to be some of the finest handicrafts in the world. A similar phenomenon occurred in the same period with Church sculptures and paintings. Usually given a free rein to express their 'faith', anonymous Mayan artists recast Roman Catholic lore in their image, to great visual effect. Popular Mayan dances like '*El baile de la Conquista*' (Dance of the Conquest), '*Moros y cristianos*' (Moors and Christians), '*el torito*' (The Little Bull) and '*El venado*' (Dance of the Deer) borrowed Spanish motifs but reversed discursive positioning, presenting Mayans as vanquished, yet morally victorious subjects. Mayan artistic genius is also visible in seventeenth- and eighteenth-century ceramics.

After independence from Spain, intellectuals and artists imagined themselves in the role of military leaders and prophets, who would redeem their people from barbarism. Their work was didactic, often linked to political considerations. Antonio José de Irrisari (1786–1868), for example, published *El cristiano errantre* (The Wandering Christian) in 1846, a hybrid text mixing fictive memoirs, a travelogue and a diary.

Between 1871 and 1884 the country was ruled by liberal Justo Rufino Barrios; though authoritarian, his regime introduced modernity and saw the emergence of a romanticized history of its origins as a foundational discourse for '*ladino*' (mixed Spanish and Mayan) hegemony. Notable in this group were José Milla (1822–82), with novels like *La hija del adelantado* (The Governor's Daughter) (1866) and *Los nazarenos* (The Nazarenes) (1867).

The first half of the twentieth century was dominated by a series of dictatorships sponsored by US banana companies that ruled virtually non-stop from 1898 to 1944. During this period, the phrase 'banana republic', coined by the US short story writer O. Henry, came into public use. Modernist writer Rafael **Arévalo Martínez** produced his famous story, 'El hombre que parecía un caballo' (The Man Who Looked Like a Horse) in 1915, and went on to publish two novels – *La oficina de paz de Orolandia* (Orolandia's Peace Office) (1925), a forerunner of carnivalesque anti-imperialist discourse full of irony, and *Noches en el palacio de la Nunciatura* (Nights in the Nuncio's Palace) (1927), noted for its avant-garde style and surrealist influences.

Carlos **Mérida** inaugurated pictorial modernism, blending avant-garde techniques with themes from folklore rooted in Mayan motifs. In the 1930s, he developed the abstract and plastic-surrealist style for which he is best known. Playing with form and colour, and working with geometric abstraction, he rediscovered pre-Hispanic Mayan muralism.

Also during the 1930s, the turn in the novel to **regionalismo** or '**criolismo**' novel was exemplified by Flavio Herrera (1895–1968), Carlos Wyld Ospina (1891–1956) and Carlos Samayoa Chinchilla, whose works defended an oligarchic world. Wyld Ospina's *La gringa* (1935) was racist and defended the interests of the coffee growers, while Herrera's *La tempestad* (The Storm) (1935) celebrated plantation-building.

The long night of dictatorship came to a dramatic end with the popular insurrection of 20 October 1944. Ten years of democratic, progressive and nationalist governments with a social democratic orientation followed although they were perceived as communist by the USA. A **CIA**-led invasion in June 1954 overthrew the elected government of Jacobo **Arbenz** and brought the period to a sad and abrupt end. The overlapping role of writer and politician is well illustrated by members of Guatemala's governments between 1944 and 1954. Arévalo, Vice-President Mario **Monteforte Toledo**, Private Secretary to the President Carlos **Illescas** and Foreign Secretary Manuel **Galich** were all leading contemporary writers.

This period represents a 'golden age' of twentieth-century Guatemalan culture. Besides supporting public education and initiating the publication of school textbooks that dealt with the country's specific reality, institutions like the National Ballet and Symphony Orchestra were also created in these years. Similarly, new education centres were established, like the College of Humanities at the University of San Carlos, which opened in 1947. Cinema also received official support and a few feature films were made during this time.

A group of painters who hoped to pictorially blend the Maya and *ladino* visions of the world, appeared around mid-century; outstanding among them were Juan Antonio Franco, Dagoberto Vásquez, Guillermo Grajeda Mena and Roberto González Goyri, who won a prize in a sculpture contest sponsored by the London Institute of Contemporary Arts in 1951.

In literature, Monteforte Toledo's work of the late 1940s constitutes a crucial transmission of narrative forms between the 1930s and the modernization initiated in the 1950s. *Entre la piedra y la cruz* (Between the Stone and the Cross) (1948) is his outstanding work, which proposes a racial mix of Maya and *ladino* peoples as the basis of a modernized Guatemala.

A contemporary of Monteforte's, Miguel Angel **Asturias**, winner of the 1967 Nobel Prize for Literature (see **Nobel Prizes**), merged surrealist and ethical concerns in the genre of **magical realism**. His masterpiece, *Hombres de maíz* (Men of Maize) (1949), is one of Latin America's greatest prose works. Using mythical elements of the *Popol Vuh*, according to which corn (maize) (see **corn and corncakes**) is defined both as a staple food and symbolically as the base of the dough from which the first peoples were created, he aesthetically shapes the great divide between *ladinos* and Mayas, merging both world-views in a single symbolic framework. His other outstanding texts include *Leyendas de Guatemala* (Legends of Guatemala) (1930), a surrealist *tour de force* of Guatemalan popular culture, *El **señor presidente*** (The President) (1930, published 1948), a classic depiction of authoritarian regimes, *Mulata de tal* (Mulatta) (1963) and *Maladrón* (1969).

Luis **Cardoza y Aragón** – poet, essayist and art critic – was Asturias's contemporary. An iconoclastic surrealist and early believer in irrationality, Cardoza evolved from French symbolism and the Latin American avant-garde to become the *enfant terrible* of Guatemalan letters, while befriending personalities like Diego **Rivera**, Frida **Kahlo** and Antonin Artaud. His major works included *Luna Park* (1923) (poetry); *La nube y el reloj* (The Cloud and the Clock) (1940) (art criticism); *Guatemala, las líneas de su mano* (Guatemala, the Lines of its Hand) (1955) (essays); and *El río, novelas de caballería* (The River: Novels of Chivalry) (1986) (an autobiography). Cardoza inspired young writers who had lived through the 1944–54 period as student militants. They formed the group *Saker-Ti* (meaning 'dawn' in K'akchikel) in 1947. Other writers, including Carlos Navarrete (1931–) and Huberto Alvarado (1927–74) were more closely linked to **socialist realism**.

From 1954 to 1986, Guatemala was ruled by a succession of military governments and became a byword for military repression. **Guerrilla warfare** began in 1960, triggering a long political crisis that led to civil war from 1979 to 1984 between various governments and the united **URNG** front. A civilian government elected in 1986 initiated prolonged negotiation with the guerrillas, which culminated in agreement, ten years later, in 1996.

After the overthrow of Arbenz in 1954, most writers and artists went into exile and cultural production declined. The Grupo Acento blossomed in Mexico and produced a major short-story writer in Augusto (Tito) **Monterroso**, whose work included collections of stories like *Movimiento perpetuo* (Perpetuum Mobile) (1972) and an early postmodern novel, *Lo demás es silencio* (All Else is Silence) (1976). Two major poets also emerged from the group: Carlos Illescas (whose works included *El mar es una llaga* (The Sea is a Wound) (1980) and Raúl Leiva.

A handful of younger writers fled to El Salvador after 1954, led by Otto René **Castillo** and Roberto **Obregón**, both of whom blossomed into revolutionary activists and poets in the 1960s. Captured by the army, Castillo was tortured to death; his posthumous poem, 'Vámonos patria a caminar' (Walk with Me My Country), became an anthem of the struggle for freedom for years thereafter. Obregón too was **disappeared** by the army in 1970.

Nuevo Signo was founded in 1968 and included Francisco Morales Santos (1940–), Delia Quiñonez (1946–), José Luis Villatoro (1932–), Julio Fausto Aguilera (1929–) and Luis Alfredo Arango (1935–), who produced two outstanding volumes in *Papel y tusa* (Paper and Chalk) and *El zopilote biónico* (The Bionic Buzzard) (1979). Independently of Nuevo Signo, poet and playwright Manuel José Arce (1935–85) surfaced as a dominant figure during the same period with two splendid books of poetry, *Los epsiodios del vagón de carga* (Episodes on a Freight Car) (1971) and *Palabras alusivas al acto* (Words Alluding to the Act) (1978), as well as plays including *Sebastián sale de compras* (Sebastian Goes Shopping) (1969) and *Delito, condena y ejecución de una gallina* (Crime, Sentence and Execution of a Chicken)

(1971). They introduced modern techniques and agility into Guatemala's otherwise lacklustre and didactic theatre writing.

In painting, the Vertebra group was founded in 1969 by Roberto Cabrera, Marco Augusto Quiroa and Elmer Rojas, who emphasized forms of popular art with geometric shapes and employed aggressive colours and dream-like images aspiring towards sensuality and peace. Monstrous images reminded the viewer of the violence that had crept into the fabric of society. Independently of this group, Luis Díaz also became an outstanding artist during these years, pioneering art installations in the 1970s.

In prose, younger writers influenced by the beat generation in the USA and their Mexican counterparts of 'La **Onda**' materialized in the early 1970s. They included Mario Roberto **Morales**, Dante **Liano**, Arturo **Arias**, Luis de Lión (1939–84) and Luis Enrique Sam Colop (1955–). The latter two were the first Mayans, albeit writing in Spanish, to appear on the literary scene. De Lión was disappeared by the army in 1984. His posthumous novel, *El mundo principia en Xibalbá* (The World Begins in Xibalbá) (1985), became the basis for the subsequent emergence of literature in various Maya languages. Other important texts from this group include Arias's *Después de las bombas* (After the Bombs) (1979) and *Jaguar en llamas* (Jaguar in Flames) (1989), Morales's *Los demonios salvajes* (The Savage Demons) (1978) and Liano's *El hombre de Montserrat* (The Man from Montserrat) (1984) and *El misterio de San Andrés* (The Mystery of San Andrés) (1996).

The 1970s also saw the emergence of feminist poetry, inaugurated by Alaíde **Foppa**, Luz Méndez de la Vega (1919–) and Margarita Carrera (1929–). Outstanding for its transformation of domestic space and the body are Foppa's *Los dedos de mi mano* (The Fingers of my Hand) (1958), *Elogio de mi cuerpo* (In Praise of my Body) (1970) and *Las palabras y el tiempo* (Words and Time) (1979). Noted for the vibrancy and directness of her attacks on male phallocratic behaviour is Ana María Rodas, whose major work is *Poemas de la izquierda erótica* (Poems from the Erotic Left) (1973). Dina Posada (1946–) followed in her footsteps with the lyrical eroticism of *Fuego sobre el madero* (Fire on Wood) (1996).

The 1980s saw the rise of the Imaginaria group, working in photography (Luis González Palma), sculpture (Pablo Swezey) and painting (Moisés Barrios, Isabel Ruiz and Erwin Guillermo). They had a major impact after exhibitions in Mexico City (Spring 1988 and Summer 1996), London (Spring 1995) and Madrid's International Art Fair in Winter 1997. Their works transform the traumatic daily life of violence into an affirmation of the human condition, mixing sensual, ironic and tragic elements against a carnivalesque backdrop that is humorous because of its very grotesqueness.

In the 1980s, literary *testimonios* (see **testimonio**) operated as a new foundational discourse that promoted identification with the revolutionary struggle against military dictatorship. *Días de la selva* (Days in the Jungle) by Mario Payeras (1940–95) and Rigoberta **Menchú**'s life story as recorded by Elizabeth Burgos-Debray, *Me llamo Rigoberta y así me nació la conciencia* (1983) stand out. Her trajectory as a human-rights activist won Menchú the Nobel Peace Prize in 1992 – though some controversy surrounded her work in later years. It is not yet clear whether *testimonio* will continue, or whether it was a momentary trend in the closure of the political crisis with the signing of a peace treaty between guerrillas and government on 19 December 1996.

Further reading

Anleu Díaz, E. (1991) *Historia crítica de la música en Guatemala*, Guatemala: Artemis.

Dosal, Paul J. (1995) *Power in Transition: The Rise of Guatemala's Industrial Oligarchy*, Westport: Praeger.

McLintock, M. (1987) *The American Connection: State Terror and Popular Resistance in Guatemala*, London: Zed Books.

Schelinger, S. and Kinzer, S. (1983) *Bitter Fruit*, New York: Anchor/Doubleday.

Warren, Kay B. (1998) *Indigenous Movements and their Critics: Pan Mayan Activism in Guatemala*, Princeton: Princeton University Press.

Wilson, R. (1995) *Maya Resurgence in Guatemala*, Norman/London: University of Oklahoma Press.

Zimmerman, M. (1995) *Literature and Resistance in Guatemala*, Athens: Ohio University Press.

ARTURO ARIAS

guayabera

Amply-cut, lightweight cotton shirt, with front pockets, vertical pleating and fancy embroidering worn untucked by men. Its origins are uncertain, but known to be in Cuba, where a wealthy *hacendado* fell in love with his wife's lightweight cotton fabric called *batista* (batiste) and asked her to make him a shirt with multiple pockets. His workers also liked it and copied the style; they called it the *yayabera*, after the nearby Yayabo river. The name turned into *guayabera* for the *guayaba* or guava trees, where workers sat for lunch to avoid the midday sun. Once worn only by *campesinos* – for various occasions that required dressing up, from playing a game of dominoes to attending church on Sundays – the *guayabera* has again become chic, not only in the Caribbean and Central America, but in the USA as well. The June 1999 issue of the magazine, *Cigar Aficionado*, dubbed it the 'historical apparel piece of Cuba'.

ANA M. LÓPEZ

Guayaquil Group

A literary group consisting of Demetrio **Aguilera Malta**, José de la **Cuadra**, Joaquín **Gallegos** Lara, Enrique Gil Gilbert, and Alfredo **Pareja Diezcanseco**. Its defining features were: a socialist-inspired exposé of socio-economic abuses; a literature rooted in popular culture; Freudianism; a grotesque vision of the world; and a concern with orality, anthropology and indigenous culture. The Guayaquil Group is considered a forerunner of the magical realist current (see **magical realism**).

See also: *Los que se van*

HUMBERTO E. ROBLES

Guayasamín, Oswaldo
b. 1919, Quito, Ecuador

Visual artist

Guayasamín is certainly Ecuador's most famous painter, if not necessarily its most accomplished. Born into a large poor family, he became one of Ecuador's wealthiest people; though some critics have suggested that his art became excessively consumer-oriented and commercialized. His ventures into the realm of design and his substantial production of jewellery as well as other objects bearing his signature might seem to confirm the suggestion. In any event, this does not invalidate Guayasamín's importance and originality as a painter. His social and economic background, his identification with the marginal and downtrodden independent of party affiliation, and his training as a painter and muralist contributed to his unique and distinctive style. There are other influences present as well: there are traces of El Greco in his use of colour and movement and in his depiction of Quito, of Van Gogh's brilliant colours and arrangements in his depiction of flowers, and of Picasso's cubist techniques in more than one of his paintings.

The most prominent feature of his work, however, is the depiction of a world of anxiety, constrained suffering, wrath about to explode, and human beings subjected to extreme pain and sorrow. Guayasamín's expressionistic brush moves quickly on the canvas, capturing the essential. Visually he recalls Jorge **Icaza**'s prose with its abrupt and almost angry juxtaposition of quick images; he also echoes that writer's social and political concerns in his use of his art to depict an unacceptable social and historical reality. His monumental undertakings, such as *Huancayñan* – which translated from **Quechua** into Spanish means *Camino del llanto* (Path of Tears) – and 'La edad de la ira' (The Age of Wrath), fit into that mould. 'La edad de la ira' consists of some 250 large oils, while 'Huancayñan' includes 103 paintings and a movable mural, the product of time spent in Mexico learning and working with the great muralist (see **muralism**) José Clemente **Orozco**. All these works are statements about Latin American history. Many of them, now dispersed all over the world, are symbolic expressions of the struggle between oppressor and oppressed that Ecuador and Latin America have endured since colonial times. Guayasamín's list of connections is cosmopolitan, if we are to judge by his friendship with Pablo **Neruda**, the support he received from Nelson Rockefeller, and his portraits of Gabriel **García Márquez**, François Mitterrand and Fidel **Castro**, among others.

Further reading:

Camón Aznar, J. (1981) *Oswaldo Guayasamín*, Barcelona: Polígrafa.
(1991) *Guayasamín: una vida dedicada por entero a la creatividad*, Quito: Génesis.

HUMBERTO E. ROBLES

Guebel, Daniel

b. 1956, Buenos Aires, Argentina

Writer

Guebel's first novel was *Arnulfo o los infortunios de un príncipe* (The Misadventures of a Prince) (1987), but recognition as an accomplished and imaginative writer came with the Emecé Prize for *La perla del emperador* (The Emperor's Pearl) in 1990. Many have compared his work to that of César **Aira**. Guebel is also a journalist and a dramatist. His several collaborations with Sergio **Bizzio** are important and innovative contributions to Argentine theatre, including *El amor* (Love), for example, in which different love situations are resolved in sudden and dramatic scenes.

DANIEL LINK

Guedes, Lino

b. 1897, Campinas, São Paulo, Brazil; d. 1951, Campinas

Writer

Lino Guedes was a leading figure in black literary circles in Campinas and São Paulo during the 1920s and 1930s. He was editor-in-chief of the Afro-Brazilian newspaper in Campinas, *Getulino* (1923–4), and a frequent contributor to São Paulo's *Clarim d'Alvorada* (1924–35), which was an important vehicle for black social and political mobilization. He published eight volumes of poetry which dramatized the historical and contemporary tribulations of Afro-Brazilians. His poems about black communities of the *cortiços* (urban slums) in São Paulo register an early attempt to versify the colloquial speech of Afro-Brazilians.

CHRISTOPHER DUNN

Guelier Tejada, Lidia

b. 1921, Cochabamba, Bolivia

Politician

Guelier Tejada began to figure prominently in popular struggles against the governments of the oligarchy during the 1940s, when she joined the Movimiento Nacionalista Revolucionario (Nationalist Revolutionary Movement), or MNR. After the **Bolivian Revolution** of 1952 she was the first woman leader of the Congreso Obrero Boliviano (Bolivian Workers Congress), or **COB**. In November 1980 she became the first woman elected to the Presidency as the result of a Congressional vote, but she was overthrown by the *coup* of 17 July 1981.

MAGDALENA CAJÍAS DE LA VEGA

Guerra, Jorge

b. Peru, 1953

Director and teacher

Internationally recognized for his accomplishments in the theatre, Guerra is also well-known for his studies on actor training, the director's function, and the presence of tragedy in the modern world. In 1983 Guerra, Alberto Isola, and Luis Peirano were the driving force behind the creation of **Ensayo**, an association dedicated to theatrical research and director training. Ensayo's many productions enthusiastically brought together participants from different generations of the Peruvian theatre and helped to reinvigorate the Peruvian stage. Guerra is currently Dean of Theater at the New World School of the Arts in Miami.

ADAM VERSÉNYI

Guerra, Juan Luis
b. 1956, Santo Domingo, Dominican Republic

Musician and composer

At the end of the 1980s, Juan Luis Guerra became the Dominican Republic's most famous musician and composer with an international reputation. His meringues (see **merengue**), bachatas (see **bachata**) and ballads found an audience in Europe and the United States as well as throughout Latin America. Guerra studied music at the National Conservatory of Music and in 1980 won a grant to study at Berklee College of Music in Massachusetts. It was there that he extended his musical knowledge to embrace **jazz**, bebop and swing, as well as other rhythms.

Returning to the Dominican Republic, Guerra formed the group 4.40 and began to experiment with jazz. In *Soplando* (Blowing) (1984), his first CD with the group, traditional meringues like 'Feliciana' and 'Juana Mecho' were combined with jazz and traditional Dominican folk rhythms. It was only with the appearance of his second CD, *Mudanza y acarreo* (Moving and Freight) (1986) that Juan Luis Guerra and 4.40 became known in Santo Domingo. The next album, *Mientras más lo pienso...tú* (The More I Think About It...You) (1988), showed the increasing influence of the Cuban **nueva trova** (New Song) movement, and a break with the paradigmatic merengue of Johnny **Ventura** and his Combo Show, Wilfrido **Vargas** and Los Beduinos and Fernandito Villalona and his Orchestra. For four years running, Guerra's new merengues were chosen as the 'Merengue of the Year'.

His 1988 album *Ojalá que llueva café* (I Hope it Rains Coffee) (1989) brought Guerra to the peak of popularity in Latin America, Europe and the United States. Merengues like 'Visa para un sueño' (Visa for a dream) and 'Ojalá que llueva café' were more sophisticated in style, but also contained social comment about the living conditions that many Dominicans had to suffer at home and in economic exile in the United States.

With *Bachata Rosa* (Pink bachata) (1990), Guerra began to use the popular form of the bachata as a basis for a new type of song that some consider poetic. The album *Areíto* (1992), with its forceful political tone, was received with some ambivalence by the public and was less successful than his previous work. But his CD *Fogaraté*, with its recreations of the peasant merengues called *perico ripiao*, has won him back his public.

Juan Luis Guerra's reputation is due not only to his indisputable musical talent but also to the fact that, more than any other contemporary musician, he succeeded in modernizing popular rhythms and transforming them into sophisticated musical forms.

Further reading

Manuel, P. (1995) *Caribbean Currents: Caribbean Music from Rumba to Reggae*, Philadelphia: Temple University Press.

Pacini Hernandez, D. (1995) *Bachata: A Social History of a Dominican Popular Music*, Philadelphia: Temple University Press.

FERNANDO VALERIO-HOLGUÍN

Guerra, Lucía
b. 1942, Santiago, Chile

Writer and critic

Guerra's work builds upon early Chilean feminist discourses. Her novel *Más allá de las máscaras* (Beyond the Masks) (1984) looks at women in history, and explores the hardships faced by women in a culture where even language is inherited from men. In her fiction and criticism, Guerra warns against feminist discourses centred on women's perspectives alone, particularly where, as in Latin America, men have also been subjected to colonization. Her *La mujer fragmentada: historias de un signo* (The Fragmented Woman: Stories of a Sign) won the 1994 **Casa de las Américas** prize.

Her critical work on María Luisa **Bombal** is of great importance.

SANDRA GARABANO

Guerra, Ruy

b. 1931, Lourenço Marques, Mozambique

Film-maker

Guerra was the first Brazilian **Cinema Novo** director to achieve recognition, with the French New Wave-inspired *Os **Cafajestes*** (The Hustlers) (1961), an innovative chronicle of two decadent **Copacabana** hustler-playboys and the women they victimized. *Os Cafajestes* scandalized audiences with the first frontal nudity – Norma **Bengell**'s – in Brazilian cinema. More in line with the first phase of Cinema Novo, his subsequent *Os **Fuzis*** (The Guns) (1964) mixed documentary and fictional modes to focus on the complex interface between urban and rural proletariat. This was one of the most political and anti-militarist films of the early Cinema Novo, and it won the Silver Bear at Berlin.

Guerra left Mozambique at age nineteeen, studied film at the IDHEC (Paris) and, after working with several European directors, moved to Brazil in 1958, where he formed an uneasy alliance with the future Cinema Novo directors. Back in Europe from 1967, he made *Sweet Hunters* (1969) in Brittany with an international cast, before returning to Brazil to shoot *Os deuses e os mortos* (The Gods and the Dead) (1971), a complex allegorical exploration set in the 1920s of the social and economic conflicts of the *cacao* region in Bahia, brilliantly photographed by Dib Lufti. After seven years of 'magnificent silence' – during which he acted in European films, co-wrote the play *Calabar* with Chico **Buarque**, and directed theatre – Guerra directed the long-awaited sequel to *Os Fuzis*, *A Queda* (The Fall) (1977), possibly the first Brazilian film to seriously address the urban proletariat as an oppressed class. A formally innovative work, *A Queda* harked back to the earlier aesthetic precepts of Cinema Novo, yet pushed them into new aesthetic territories. One of the few films of the period produced without **Embrafilme** support, it was originally banned but was approved after it won the Silver Bear at Berlin in 1978.

Between 1977 and 1980 Guerra returned to now independent Mozambique to organize the National Film Institute. He directed the country's first feature film, *Mueda Memória Massacre* (Coin, Memory, Massacre) (1978). Back in Brazil in the 1980s, he filmed three somewhat insipid literary adaptations: *Eréndira* (1982), a Mexican production, and *A Fábula da bela palomeira* (The Fable of the Beautiful Pigeon Keeper) (1986), both based on texts by **García Márquez**, and the Brazilian epic *Quarup* (1989), based on the **Callado** novel. Only in *A Opera do malandro* (The Beggar's Opera) (1985), from a Chico **Buarque** play, do we see glimpses of his former stylistic brilliance and political concerns.

Further reading

Johnson, R. (1984) 'Ruy Guerra', in *Cinema Novo X 5* Austin, TX: University of Texas Press.

ISMAIL XAVIER AND THE USP GROUP

Guerra Sánchez, Ramiro

b. 1880, Batabanó, Cuba; d. 1970, Havana, Cuba

Historian and educator

Guerra Sánchez played a key role in educational and curriculum reform of the Cuban school system in the 1920s. He was at different times general superintendent of schools, director of the Havana Teachers College and founder of the country's first business school, in Havana. Editor of the *Heraldo de Cuba* (1930–2) and ***Diario de la marina*** (1943–6), he was also an outstanding historian, whose works included *Manual de historia de Cuba* (Handbook of Cuban History) (1938) and the seminal work *Azúcar y población en las Antillas* (Sugar and Population in the Caribbean) (1927).

WILFREDO CANCIO ISLA

guerrillas

The theory and practice of guerrilla warfare is principally associated with Latin American political struggles in the 1960s and 1970s, although its first manifestations occurred during the Spanish resistance to French occupation early in the nineteenth century. Though there are examples of this form of armed resistance in Latin America in the 1930s, particularly in Nicaragua under **Sandino**, the theory and practice of guerrilla war became generalized through Latin America after the success of the Cuban Revolution of 1959 (see **revolutions**). The theory was encapsulated by one of the Cuban revolutionary leaders, Ernesto Che **Guevara**, in a speech delivered in late 1959. He argued then, and later restated in his important book *La guerra de guerrillas* (Guerrilla Warfare) (1961), that the experience of the Cuban Revolution had shown that a determined and well-organized group of revolutionaries engaging in armed struggle with the state could precipitate a revolutionary crisis without waiting for the objective conditions to mature first. This idea resonated with a generation of young people who were sceptical of the Latin American **communist parties**, many of which seemed to have compromised with questionable regimes, and inspired by the Cuban events which had put revolution back on the historical agenda. Both inside and outside Cuba, the orthodox Communist parties were deeply suspicious of what they saw as a dangerous adventurism among largely middle-class youth who saw their role as substituting for a mass movement.

Nevertheless, for a whole generation this method of political warfare seemed proven by Guevara's descriptions of the Cuban experience. It seemed to them that the creation of small armed cells (*focos* – see ***foco***), based in rural areas and protected by the local population, would set in motion an irresistible process of social change. The first such groups, in Paraguay and in Nicaragua, were quickly identified and destroyed, in Paraguay with the tragic loss of some eighty young idealists. Thereafter, more careful preparations were made. The first sustained guerrilla organization, the 13th of November Movement in Guatemala, was led by two young army officers, Yon Sosa and Luis Turcios Lima, who took to hills in 1961. At about the same time, a small rural cell was established in Nicaragua under the leadership of Carlos **Fonseca**, Tomás **Borge** and Silvio Mayorga. Two years later it adopted the name Sandinista National Liberation Front (**FSLN**). In only three other Latin American countries were rural guerrillas successfully founded in the early 1960s: Venezuela, under Douglas Bravo, and Peru, where the MIR (Revolutionary Movement of the Left), led by Luis de la Puente among others, was effectively crushed in its first major confrontation with the Peruvian state in 1965.

By this time the Sino-Soviet division in the world communist parties had produced a new strategic approach to armed revolutionary struggle, the so-called 'prolonged popular war' strategy, based on the Chinese experience during the 1940s. In many ways it was a mechanical transposition of Chinese experience into Latin America, just as the guerrilla warfare method represented a direct imitation of what was represented as the Cuban experience in the struggle against **Batista**. Where the two strategies differed was in their understanding of the political relationship between the revolutionaries and the mass movement. In the Maoist version, the fighters must be part of the self-defence of the rural population, encircling and ultimately taking the cities. The guerrilla warfare strategy, on the other hand, saw the growing mass movement as a product of armed struggle and the resulting social crisis; the military thus took priority over the political. The resulting isolation of the guerrilla organizations arose for two reasons. First, the rulers of Latin America also learned their lesson from Cuba and, in conjunction with United States military advisers, developed sophisticated anti-guerrilla strategies, one victim of which would be Guevara himself, in Bolivia in 1967. Second, the rural (and in some cases indigenous) population were distrustful of groups of mainly middle-class revolutionaries who were largely marginal to their experience and organizations (again, Bolivia was a crucial case in point). Indeed, in some cases the revolutionaries arrived physically from outside the country, often after training in Cuba.

While it waxed and waned in the early part of the decade, between 1965 and 1967 the Fidel **Castro** regime threw its weight behind the guerrilla warfare strategy. After Guevara's death, and given the obvious failure of the strategy to take root anywhere, the Cubans distanced themselves from those it had inspired by its example (as the Venezuelan Douglas Bravo complained bitterly in a letter to Fidel in 1970) and began to seek a definitive rapprochement with the Soviet Union and, consequently, with Latin America's orthodox communist parties, who remained deeply opposed to armed struggle strategies, particularly since the Sino-Soviet split. Cuba's new relations with **Torrijos** in Panama, **Velasco** in Peru and later with **Allende** in Chile pointed in a political direction very different from the creation of 'one, two, three, many Vietnams' advocated by Guevara. Yet there were groups devoted to guerrilla strategies in each of these countries.

A different conception of guerrilla war, which employed the language of rural armed struggle but applied it in an urban context, had been put forward in Brazil in 1966 by Carlos **Marighela**, ex-central committee member of the Brazilian Communist Party and author of the *Minimanual del guerrilhero* (Minimanual of the Guerrillero) (1964). Marighela was killed in 1969 and the strategy he suggested was almost entirely unsuccessful, especially after the post-1968 intensification of military repression. The concept of urban guerrilla warfare was applied with far greater success in Uruguay by the **Tupamaros**, led by Raúl **Sendic**, in a country whose lack of mountains or jungle made this adaptation of guerrilla warfare strategies an inevitability. Sendic's legendary capacity to escape and a series of spectacular acts of armed propaganda in the poorest areas of Montevideo won the Tupamaros a Robin Hood reputation, and they certainly enjoyed a widespread network of support. The imposition of a peculiarly barbarous form of military rule in 1973 effectively meant the end of the organization.

In Central America, new armed struggle organizations grew up through the 1970s in response to repressive government and increasing desperation in the countryside. In El Salvador, their successful combination of mass rural and urban organizations brought the country to a point of authentic revolutionary crisis early in 1980; for the next ten years their unified organization, the **FMLN** (Frente Farabundo **Martí** para la Liberación Nacional) waged a war of position and manoeuvre against a state absorbing huge amounts of US military aid for what was described as a 'low intensity' war. In Guatemala, genocidal assaults on the indigenous population produced many forms of resistance, and a continuous armed confrontation throughout the 1980s led by the coalition URNG (National Revolutionary Union of Guatemala). Other organizations emerged in the same period: **Sendero Luminoso** and the MRTA (**Movimiento Revolucionario Tupac Amaru** – Tupac Amaru Revolutionary Movement) in Peru; the Colombian guerrilla organizations that continued the civil war begun in the late 1940s after the murder of Gaitán; the ERP and **Montoneros** organizations in Argentina, each emerged in response to intensified repression. While each called themselves guerrilla armies, they differed widely in ideology – from the extreme orthodox Maoism of Sendero to the neo-Peronist (see **Peronism**) nationalism of the Montoneros – and indeed in their understanding of the conduct of armed struggle and the relationship between the revolutionary organizations and the urban and/or rural masses. In a strict sense, they had departed from the guerrilla warfare strategy, and the concept of the armed revolution, that Guevara had advocated. For the issue of arms is not what distinguishes the guerrillas from other advocates of revolutionary change; it is the question of whether arms are subject to political control or whether political change is deemed to be the consequence of a successful armed struggle conducted by a small and dedicated group of professional revolutionaries. Thus the great resistance movements of the 1980s and 1990s – and in particular the mass rising in Chiapas, Mexico in 1994, under the leadership of the EZLN, the Zapatista National Liberation Army (see **Zapatistas**) – belongs to the history of armed popular insurrection rather than to the record of guerrilla war.

Further reading

Aguilar, L.E. (ed.) (1968) *Marxism in Latin America*, New York: Alfred Knopf.

Castañeda, J. (1994) *Utopia Unarmed: The Latin American Left after the Cold War*, New York: Alfred Knopf.

Gott, R. (1970) *Rural Guerrillas in Latin America*, Harmondsworth: Penguin.

Guevara, C. (1985) *Guerrilla Warfare*, Lincoln and London: University of Nebraska Press.

Wickham-Crowley, T. (1992) *Guerrillas and Revolution in Latin America*, Princeton, NJ: Princeton University Press.

MIKE GONZALEZ

Guevara, Alfredo

b. 1925, Havana, Cuba

Intellectual and administrator

Founder of the Cuban Film Institute (**ICAIC**) and of the journal, *Cine cubano*, Guevara was one of the principal architects of Cuban cultural policy after the revolution of 1959. A Marxist from his youth, he became a close friend of Fidel **Castro** and participated in the underground struggle against **Batista** in the late 1950s. In 1955, together with Tomás **Gutiérrez Alea** and Julio **García Espinosa**, he made *El Mégano* (The Charcoal Worker), considered a precursor of the new Cuban cinema. Guevara's close collaboration with Castro has ensured ICAIC's prominent role in the cultural life of the country and in Latin America, through the Havana International Film Festival (see **Festival Internacional del Nuevo Cine Latinoamericano**). Guevara directed ICAIC from 1960–81 and again from 1991–2000, when he was personally called in by Castro to resolve the problems caused by the satirical film, *Alicia en el país de las maravillas* (Alice in Wonderland) (1991). In the intervening years, he had been Cuba's representative to UNESCO. *Revolución es lucidez* (Revolution is Clarity) (1998) is a collection of his articles, speeches and interviews.

WILFREDO CANCIO ISLA

Guevara, Ernesto (Che)

b. 1929, Rosario, Argentina; d. 1968, La Higuera, Bolivia

Revolutionary

Although he was killed in 1968, the face of Che Guevara remains the recognized symbol of the revolutionary guerrilla, icon for successive generations of rebellious youth in both First and Third World. His reputation rests on his involvement in the Cuban Revolution of 1959 (see **revolutions**), the government that followed it, and in the attempt to generate guerrilla warfare (see **guerrillas**) throughout Latin America which ended tragically in Bolivia.

Ernesto Che Guevara was born to a middle-class family, which moved around frequently in search of the climate least likely to affect young Ernesto's crippling asthma. Despite his illness, Ernesto lived an extremely active life at home and later as a medical student. In 1951 he travelled across Latin America on a motorcycle with a friend, returning to complete his medical studies before travelling northwards again in 1953. In 1954, he found himself in Guatemala when a US-backed military *coup* overthrew the reforming government of Jacobo **Arbenz**. He fled to Mexico, where he made his first contact with a group of Cuban exiles belonging to the July 26th Movement led by Fidel **Castro**. In training, his characteristic enthusiasm and commitment won him a leading role in the armed expedition that set out in the motorboat *Granma* in November 1956 to establish Cuba's first guerrilla cell. The boat was ambushed on arrival and only eighteen survived, including the wounded Guevara. Within two years, however, the **Batista** dictatorship had fallen, and it was Guevara who led the first revolutionary column into Havana on 2 January 1959.

Guevara's interpretation of the intervening two years became the standard history as well as the model for subsequent guerrilla organization in Latin America warfare. His conclusion was that the revolutionaries themselves must lead the struggle, with the urban or workers movements in a supporting role. Though he described himself as a Marxist, Guevara shared with Castro two key concepts: that the mountains should prevail politically over the town, and that rather than waiting for the objective conditions for revolution to exist the revolutionary group itself could precipitate those conditions. A generation of young Latin American revolutionaries took their inspiration from Guevara's *Guerrilla Warfare* (1963). Their experience, however, was tragically negative; revolution (see **revolutions**) proved to involve rather more than the willpower of dedicated revolutionaries acting on behalf of the masses.

Guevara occupied a number of key government roles after 1959. Charged with organizing state security, he then became Director of the National Bank and later Minister for Industry. He frequently represented Castro on foreign delegations. Che's conviction that rapid industrialization was the only way for Cuba to escape economic dependency, however, clashed with advice given by increasingly influential Soviet economists. His admiration for China's Great Leap Forward translated voluntarism from the political into the economic arena, as he argued in his seminal essay 'Man and Socialism in Cuba', published in 1965, shortly before Guevara's sudden departure from Cuba. His final letter announced his return to the guerrilla struggle, because Cuba's survival depended on ending her isolation and creating a series of revolutionary fronts ('one, two, three, many Vietnams') to undermine the USA's single-minded economic and political assault. But that was not the only reason for his departure; there were increasing disagreements between himself and Castro on political strategy. Too disciplined a revolutionary to dissent openly, Guevara instead left Cuba. The first attempt, in the Congo, was failure. Later, having returned briefly to Cuba in disguise, he moved to Bolivia in 1967 to establish a guerrilla *foco* (cell) there. His choice of Bolivia stemmed partly from assurances that he would have the support of the Communist Party there – which proved empty – and partly because Bolivia's central location would allow him to organize guerrilla warfare in Argentina. He clearly assumed that the local population would support the guerrillas, but in fact they were suspicious of the guerrillas and had recently benefited from an agrarian reform. After an unsuccessful year, recorded in his *Bolivian Diary*, Che and his companions became separated and an extensive military search operation, supported by CIA operatives, discovered and captured him. He was shot as he lay wounded.

But Guevara's significance did not end there. His picture, the thin bearded man with naked torso lying on a table, was reproduced around the world. For a rebellious 1960s generation he became the symbol of resistance; in Cuba itself, his face decorated every public platform just as the Cuban government was distancing itself from the strategy of international armed struggle. Since then Che's face has appeared on T-shirts, posters and badges and on walls and hoardings from South Africa to Mexico, wherever revolutionaries have taken up arms again.

Further reading

Anderson, J.L. (1997) *Che: A Revolutionary Life*, London: Bantam.

Castañeda, J. (1997) *Compañero: The Life and Death of Che Guevara*, London: Bloomsbury.

Gerassi, J. (ed.) (1968) *Venceremos: The Speeches and Writings of Che Guevara*, New York: Monthly Review Press.

Guevara, C. (1969) *Obra revolucionaria*, Mexico City: ERA.

Taibo, P.I. (1996) *El Che*, Mexico City: Joaquin Mortiz.

MIKE GONZALEZ

Guevara Arce, Walter

b. 1912, Cochabamba, Bolivia; d. 1996,

Politician

Guevara Arce was a founding member and principal ideologue of the Movimiento Nacionalista Revolucionario (MNR, Nationalist Revolutionary Movement) in Bolivia. In 1944 he occupied a ministerial post under President Gualberto Villarroel (1944–6). After the **Bolivian Revolution** of 1952 he served as Foreign Minister, Minister of Government, Deputy and Senator. In 1960 he founded the Partido Auténtico Revolucionario (PAR, Authentic Revolutionary Party). He was elected by Congress to the Presidency in

August 1979, and overthrown by a military *coup* in November of that same year.

MAGDALENA CAJÍAS DE LA VEGA

Guido, Beatriz

b. 1922, Rosario, Argentina; d. 1988, Madrid, Spain

Writer

Guido's fiction focuses obsessively on the decline of the Argentine upper classes and oligarchy. She summarized the relationship between history and fiction in her work with the formula 'to lie the truth'. Private, claustrophobic spaces such as home are her preferred locations, in which young people struggle through violent sexual rites of passage. Her husband, film-maker Leopoldo **Torre Nilsson**, adapted several of her works to the screen, for example *La **casa del ángel*** (The House of the Angel) (1957) and *La caída* (The Fall) (1959).

SILVANA DASZUK

Guignard, Alberto da Veiga

b. 1896, Nova Friburgo, Brazil; d. 1962, Belo Horizonte, Brazil

Painter

One of the most important Brazilian portraitists and landscape artists, Guignard produced timeless and deceptively naive canvasses in which a magical light highlights buildings, historical figures and contemporary faces. A consistent and hardworking teacher, Guignard was instrumental in establishing modernism (see **Brazilian modernism**) in art through his own work and that of distinguished disciples. Having studied in Europe, Guignard first showed in Brazil at the Rio de Janeiro Fine Arts Exhibit (1924) and then settled in Belo Horizonte. He exhibited almost annually in Brazil and abroad.

M.A. GUIMARÃES LOPES

Guillén, Nicolás

b. 1902, Camagüey, Cuba; d. 1989, Havana, Cuba

Poet

Often considered the 'national poet' of Revolutionary Cuba, Guillén is one of the most important poets of the African Diaspora, and a central figure in the Latin American poetic canon. His poetry belongs to two traditions, ***negrismo*** or 'poesía negra', and social poetry, while also drawing on the rich tradition of Spanish verse.

Born in the year Cuba was officially declared independent, Guillén came from a relatively well-to-do family of Afro-Cuban ancestry, but his father, a high-ranking politician and newspaper editor, was assassinated in 1917 in a political reprisal, and Guillén was forced to take over financial responsibility for the family. His early poetry was primarily within the *modernista* vein. Later he was influenced by the avant-garde (see **avant-garde in Latin America**) aesthetics of poets such as Federico García Lorca and Langston Hughes, who explored popular traditions and colloquial diction. Guillén's first book of poems, *Motivos del son* (1930), represents Afro-Cuban speech while capturing the rhythmic form of the '**son**', a popular music form combining African and Spanish elements. By his second collection, *Sóngoro cosongo* (1931), he called this 'mulatto poetry', emphasizing the transculturation (see **cultural theory**) central to the formation of a new Cuban culture. Guillén continued to write in this form throughout the 1930s and 1940s, giving voice to the under-represented and mounting an anti-imperialist critique in *West Indies, Ltd.* (1934), *Cantos para soldados y sones para turistas* (Songs for Soldiers and Suns for tourists) (1937), and *El son entero: Suma poética, 1929–1946* (1947). He also embraced leftist politics, becoming a member of the Communist Party of Cuba, supporting the Republicans in the Spanish Civil War (see **Spanish Civil War, impact of**) and attending the anti-fascist Second International Conference of Writers for the Defense of Culture in Madrid in 1937, with fellow Latin American poets César **Vallejo**, Pablo **Neruda**, Octavio **Paz** and others. Like Vallejo and Neruda, he published a collection of poems about the conflict, *Poema en cuatro angustias* *y una esperanza* (Poem in Four Anguishes and a Hope) (1937). In the next two decades Guillén adopted an increasingly critical stance toward the Cuban government (dominated by the dictator Fulgencio **Batista**), which resulted in his exile in 1953. He returned in 1959, three weeks after the triumph of the Revolution.

Guillén played a leading role in the cultural politics of the Cuban Revolution as president of the newly-formed Union of Writers and Artists of Cuba (**UNEAC**); his full endorsement of the Utopian urge of the Revolution is evident in his 1964, *Tengo* (I Have). Guillén's later work, especially *Diario que a diario* (daily diary) (1972), shows his always mordant sense of humour and ardent anti-imperialism, while also bringing poetry into critical contact with the discourse of history, through the integration of snippets of newspaper articles, advertisements and official documents.

Further reading

Ellis, K. (1983) *Cuba's Nicolás Guillén: Poetry and Ideology*, Toronto: University of Toronto Press.

Kubayanda, J. (1990) *The Poet's Africa: Africanness in the Poetry of Nicolás Guillén and Aimé Césaire*, New York: Greenwood Press.

Williams, L.V. (1982) *Self and Society in the Poetry of Nicolás Guillén*, Baltimore, MD: Johns Hopkins University Press.

BEN A. HELLER

Guillén, Sebastián Vicente *see* Subcomandante Marcos

Guillot, Olga

b. Santiago de Cuba

Singer

Guillot's sensual and serious voice, with its broad register and rare capacity for modulation, marks the high point of the development of the **bolero** as the musical expression par excellence of Latin American popular culture. She began her career singing with her sister Ana Luisa as Las Hermanas Guillot (The Guillot Sisters). Having won a radio competition for amateur singers, she went on to study at the Havana Conservatory and joined the group Siboney, with singer and composer Isolina **Carrillo**. Her solo career began in 1945 with her first success, 'Lluvia gris' (Grey Rain). Two years later a visit to Mexico set in train an international career.

RAFAEL CASTILLO ZAPATA

Güiraldes, Ricardo

b. 1886, Buenos Aires, Argentina; d. 1927, Paris, France

Writer

Devoted to literature with an almost romantic religiosity and a prolific writer in his own right, Ricardo Güiraldes's claim to fame is based on one novel – *Don Segundo Sombra* (Don Segundo Sombra: Shadows on the *Pampa*), published a year before his unexpected and untimely death. Regarded as one of the classic *novelas de la tierra* (novels of the land) of the 1920s, it is, in fact, a complex and highly symbolic *Bildungsroman*. The story of Fabio Cáceres – an illegitimate child who is initiated into the life of the gauchos and eventually settles down when, unexpectedly, he inherits a cattle ranch – is a symbolic plea for a conciliation between **Sarmiento**'s *barbarie* (the gaucho; native traditions) and *civilización* (the Eurocentric elite; modernity: see **cultural theory**). According to Güiraldes, true progress can only be based on a syncretic national identity.

MAARTEN STEENMEIJER

guitar

The guitar is one of Latin America's most popular instruments, incorporated into most forms of popular music across the continent; there are a large number of guitarists, and its presence in cultural life is expressed in a variety of forms, sounds and materials.

Like horses and wheat, guitars arrived with the Spaniards, for at the time of the Conquest the instrument was already widely played in Italy and Spain, to which it had been introduced in an earlier form by the Arabs. It was rapidly and widely accepted across the social spectrum; in Argentina, for example, the *gauchos* accompanied themselves on the guitar during their song duels called *payadas*. Elsewhere in the continent the guitar underwent some changes; in Venezuela, Cuba and Chile the small four-stringed cuatro was widely used, whereas in Colombia the triple, an entirely Latin American variant, was the favoured accompanying instrument. In Mexico the classic guitarrón (the big guitar) has a large number of strings, whereas in the Andes it is the **charango**, a small, high-pitched mandolin made from an armadillo shell that prevails. Brazil has the high, four-stringed cavaquinho (also called cavaço or machete) based on a Portuguese guitar.

The most significant transformation in recent years has been the technological advances that have brought the electric guitar and the introduction of electronic music. The relatively low resonance of the guitar compared with other orchestral instruments, like trumpets, violins or drums, required that its sound be amplified, and that in turn produced a change in the instrument, beginning with the incorporation of a microphone into an acoustic guitar and ending with the development of an electric guitar requiring no sound box but which can make no sound without amplification. This allowed an almost limitless range of sounds with the addition of synthesizers. At first, the electric guitar was limited to certain genres, like jazz and rock, and to Britain and the USA, but later spread across the world. It was these genres that popularized the electric instrument in Latin America.

Further reading

Olsen, D.A. and Sheehy, D.E. (1998) *Garland Encyclopedia of World Music: Vol. 2: South America, Mexico, Central America and the Caribbean*, New York/London: Garland Publishing.

PABLO JAVIER ANSOLABEHERE

Guiteras, Antonio

b. 1906, Montgomery, Pennsylvania, USA; d. 1935, El Morrillo, Matanzas, Cuba

Political leader

Leader of the underground resistance to government of Gerardo **Machado**, Guiteras was arrested and jailed in 1931. When Machado fell in 1933, the new President **Grau San Martín** invited him to join his government as Secretary for War. Guiteras was still only twenty-seven. The new government's popular nationalist measures included the creation of a workers' pension scheme and nationalization of the US-owned Cuban Electricity Company. When Grau resigned in January 1934, Guiteras returned to the underground struggle, founding an organization later called 'Joven Cuba' (Young Cuba). He was already a legend when he died in a shootout with police while trying to escape to Mexico by boat.

JOSÉ ANTONIO EVORA

Gullar, (José Ribamar) Ferreira

b. 1930, Sao Luis do Maranhão, Brazil

Poet

A member of the Generation of 45, Gullar published *A Luta Corporal* (The Corporal Struggle) in 1954. Two years later he participated in the first exposition of **concrete poetry** in São Paulo. However, the abstract notion of the visual soon gave way to the sensuality of the word, and Gullar went on to found the neo-concrete movement (see **neo-concretism**). Gullar's interest in popular culture and the social function of poetry was sparked in the 1960s when he directed the Fundação Cultural (Cultural Foundation). Always polemical, he has contributed to the social, political and historical reintegration of Brazilian culture as poet, playwright, art critic and president of **FUNARTE** during José Sarney's presidency.

PEGGY SHARPE

Gurrola, Juan José

b. 1935, Mexico City

Actor and director

A key figure in Mexico's avant-garde (see **avant-garde in Latin America**) theatre and film, Gurrola has adapted and directed many plays of contemporary Euro-American and Latin American playwrights. In 1970, he produced his own *Los buenos estragos* (The Good Injuries), which at twenty seconds is considered the world's shortest play. In the field of experimental performance, he developed several projects in the spirit of the situationist movement. In the mid-1960s he directed experimental documentaries on the work of artists such as José Luis **Cuevas** and Vicente Rojo. He played Diego **Rivera** in Paul Leduc's *Frida, naturaleza viva*. His present *nom de plume* is j.j.gurrolaiturriaga.

ANTONIO PRIETO-STAMBAUGH

Gusman, Luis

b. 1944, Buenos Aires, Argentina

Writer

Gusman was a founding member of the artistic avant-garde of the 1970s, grouped around the journal **Literal**. In 1973 he published 'El frasquito' (The Little Bottle), a story rightly acclaimed for the power of its writing and which many have associated with the work of Osvaldo **Lamborghini**. His ten published works include *En el corazón de junio* (In the Heart of June) (1983), his autobiography *La rueda de Virgilio* (Virgil's Wheel) (1988) and *La música de Frankie* (Frankie's Music) (1993).

DANIEL LINK

Guterro, Alfredo

b. 1882, Buenos Aires, Argentina; d. 1932, Buenos Aires

Painter

From 1904 to 1927 Guterro studied, like many of his generation, in Europe. In 1927 he returned to Argentina and was involved in setting up the Nuevo Salón (1929–32). In 1932 he co-organized the first artistic Cursos Libres (Open Schools). His paintings are symbolic and fresco-like, recalling his training with Maurice Denis in Paris. His neoclassical style concentrated mostly on figure compositions, but also on some industrial landscapes.

GABRIEL PEREZ-BARREIRO

Gutiérrez Heras, Joaquín.

b. 1927, Tehuacán, Puebla, Mexico

Composer and musician

Music critic and journalist, Gutiérrez Heras is also the composer of award-winning film scores for *Naufragio* (Shipwreck) (1978) and *El corazón de la noche* (Heart of the Night) (1984). Although he works in a free atonal style, he is not averse to experimenting with other styles, as in *Variaciones sobre una Canción Francesa* (Variations on a French song) (1960), for harpsichord. The symphonic sketch *Los cazadores* (The Hunters) (1962) is clearly influenced by Mexican folk music. Other pieces include *Dos Piezas para Tres Metales* (1967), for trumpet, horn and trombone, and *Trío de Cuerdas* (Trio for Strings) (1968). Director of Radio UNAM (1966–70) he also taught musical analysis and composition.

EDUARDO GUÍZAR-ALVAREZ

Gutiérrez, Gustavo

b. 1928, Lima, Peru

Theologian

Often considered 'the founding father of **liberation theology**', Gutiérrez's *Teología de la liberación*

(A Theology of Liberation) was the first systematic treatise on the issue. Internationally, he is probably the best-known liberation theologian. Having studied and graduated in medicine at San Marcos University in Lima, he received degrees in theology (Santiago, Chile) and philosophy and psychology (Louvain, Belgium), and a doctorate in theology in 1959 (Lyon, France). Ordained in the latter year, he returned to Peru in the early 1960s. He lives and works in Rimac, a slum neighbourhood of Lima, dividing his time between pastoral work and teaching at the Catholic University of Lima, where he has been professor of theology since 1960. He is the founder of Instituto Bartolomé de las Cassa, and was a close friend of 'guerrilla-priest' Camilo **Torres**.

Gutiérrez defined theology as 'a critical reflection on praxis in the light of the Word of God'. He first called this kind of theology 'liberation theology' at a meeting of Latin American theologians in Chimbote, Peru, in July 1968. A month later he served as a theological adviser at the **Medellín Conference** of Latin American Catholic bishops. His influence is noticeable in the final document of the conference.

Although his theology has been subject to official investigation, Gutiérrez has never been silenced nor his theology declared unorthodox by the Vatican; it is deeply rooted in classical Christian theology and spirituality, and he has always been keen to open up a dialogue with the Church hierarchy. He sees a vital connection between contemplation and action, between theology and spirituality, thus joining an old tradition in the Catholic Church.

Gutiérrez emphasizes the unity of history: there are not two histories, one profane, the other sacred, but only one human happening. Human history and salvation history are united and brought together in the person and life of Jesus Christ. Thus, historicizing of salvation is one of the backbones of his thinking. Central for the biblical roots of this thought is the concept of the Kingdom of God: more than processes of liberation in human history, it is an eschatology for the concrete human struggles for liberation.

According to Gutiérrez, liberation has three dimensions, not parallel or chronological, but simultaneous and mutually inclusive. First, there is the economic, social and political liberation of the oppressed, historical praxis (the realm of politics and the social sciences). Second, there is personal and cultural transformation, the construction of the 'new human being' in a qualitatively different society (ethical and philosophical order, the realm of Utopia). Finally, there is liberation from sin, which is the ultimate root of all injustice, and reconciliation with God and other human beings (theological order, the realm of faith). For a Christian, this last dimension is the 'orientating pole' of the global process of liberation. Gutiérrez aims at overcoming deeply-rooted dualisms in Christian theology, such as temporal versus eternal (spiritual) and sacred versus profane.

Gutiérrez has been strongly influenced by such Peruvian thinkers as the novelist José María **Arguedas** and the political philosopher José Carlos **Mariátegui**, in whom he found an essential expression of his own search for a specifically Latin American intellectual tradition. The former expressed a Latin American experience of Christian faith in the form of literature; the latter formulated an indigenous Latin American socialism, based on the history and traditions of the continent. Gutiérrez himself has aimed to give a voice to the impoverished masses, who are simultaneously poor and Christian. His new introduction to the latest editions of *A Theology of Liberation* speaks of the necessity of seeing the poor not only in economic terms; the most impoverished face oppression not only as lack of material goods and basic necessities, but in the form of racism and sexism too. This shift in his thinking is the result of growing dialogue with other theologies of liberation, such as black theology and feminist theology (see **feminist liberation theology**).

For Gutiérrez, 'the irruption of the poor into history' is a major fact of our times. Liberation theology, including his own version of it, is the religious expression of this irruption, reflecting the change of emphasis of Christianity from the First to the Third World.

Further reading

Ellis, M. and Maduro, O. (eds) (1989) *The Future of Liberation Theology: Essays in Honor of Gustavo Gutiérrez*, New York: Orbis Books.

Gutiérrez, G. (1973) *A Theology of Liberation: History, Politics, and Salvation*, New York: Orbis Books.
—— (1983) *The Power of the Poor in History*, New York: Orbis Books.
—— (1984) *We Drink from Our Own Wells: The Spiritual Journey of a People*, New York: Orbis Books.

ELINA VUOLA

Gutiérrez, Miguel

b. 1940, Peru

Writer

In the 1960s and 1970s, Gutiérrez was the principal ideologue of a Marxist-oriented group of Peruvian writers linked to the magazine *Narración*. He advocated a new type of social narrative which would ally the artistic sophistication of the new novel to a popular perspective. In 1991 he put these ideas into practice in *La violencia del tiempo* (The Violence of Time), the major Peruvian novel of the post-Boom period.

JAMES HIGGINS

Gutiérrez Alea, Tomás

b. 1928, Havana, Cuba; d. 1996, Havana

Film-maker

The most important film-maker in Cuban history, the films of Titón (as he was known to his friends) demonstrate that it is possible to make political films that are not mere propaganda and which are fully aesthetic achievements when they are in the hands of a genuine artist. As a law student at the University of Havana, he began to make his own 16 mm films, one of them, *Una confusión cotidiana* (An Everyday Confusion), based on a Kafka story and made in collaboration with Néstor **Almendros**. In 1951, he went to Rome to study at the Centro Sperimentale da Cinematorgrafía, graduating in 1953 with a short film, *Il sogno di Giovanni Bassain* (Giovianni Bassain's Dream). Two years later, he began directing advertisements and humorous shorts shown before the main feature in Cuban cinemas. In 1959 he was a joint founder (with Alfredo **Guevara** and Julio **García Espinosa**) of **ICAIC**, the Cuban Film Institute. Its first feature (of the twelve it produced), *Historia de una revolución* (Stories of a Revolution) (1960) was directed by Gutiérrez Alea.

An uncompromising supporter of the Cuban Revolution, Gutiérrez Alea nevertheless always held to the principle that it had to be open to 'internal criticism' if it was to develop. His body of work, some successful (like **Memorias del subdesarrollo** (Memories of Underdevelopment) (1968)), some unsuccessful (*Una pelea cubana contra los demonios* (A Cuban Struggle against Demons) (1971)), is testimony to his determination to defy censorship and party lines. In 1991 he was diagnosed with lung cancer, but this did not prevent him from directing, with Juan Carlos **Tabio**, the two films that were most widely exhibited outside Cuba – **Fresa y chocolate** (Strawberry and Chocolate) and *Guantanamera* (1995).

Further reading

Chanan, M. (1985) *The Cuban Image*, London: BFI.
Evora, J.A. (1996) *Tomás Gutiérrez Alea*, Madrid: Cátedra.

JOSÉ ANTONIO EVORA

Guy, Rosa

b. 1928, Diego Martin, Trinidad

Novelist

Taken as a child to Harlem in 1932, Rosa Guy (Rosa Cuthbert) grew up there and participated in the Harlem Renaissance. She writes primarily for children and young adults, and has published thirteen major works of fiction and a play, and edited a collection of writings by young African-Americans of the 1960s. In the 1940s, she worked with the American Negro Theater and was influenced by the revolutionary politics of Black **Garvey**ites, Martin Luther King, Jr, and Malcolm X. In 1951 she became the founding president of the Harlem Writers' Guild and began writing seriously. Her first novel, *Birds at My Window*, was published in 1966.

FUNSO AIYEJINA

Guyana

The largest of the three **Guyanas**, with 215,000 square kilometres and 764,000 inhabitants, Guyana was the first cooperative republic in the world and enjoys a high level of literacy. Just two years after obtaining its independence from Britain (in 1968), **CARICOM**, the Caribbean Community, was formed on the initiative of Guyana with a permanent headquarters in Georgetown, the capital. Two years later it became the second country in the region (after Cuba) to join the Non-Aligned Movement, to which it still belongs. A desperate situation of economic stagnation and chronic debt, however, forced the government of Guyana in 1989 to radically change its strategy and open its frontiers to foreign investment. Its frontier conflicts with Suriname and Venezuela (which claims two-thirds of its territory) prevented it from joining the **Organization of American States** (OAS) until 1990.

Guyana's most difficult challenge was to find ways to overcome the divisions and social polarization inherited from the colonial past. Despite its many efforts, Guyanese political life remains dominated by ethnic antagonisms, particularly between Guyanese of East Indian and African origin, descendants of the two major groups of workers brought into the country during the colonial period. Today the **East Indians**, who comprise more than half the total population, are involved primarily in rice farming, while the population of African origin (just over 30 per cent of the total) live mainly in the cities. The rest of the population is made up of Portuguese, Chinese, mestizos (see **mestizo**) and Amerindians. In marked contrast to the coastal belt, where 90 per cent of Guyanese live, the rainforests of the interior are only sparsely populated by Amerindians and **maroons**.

But not everything in Guyana is disunity; the whole population participates in national festivals like *Mashramani* (23 February) 'in celebration of a job well done'. A number of young painters have found inspiration in the Amerindian cultural tradition and the natural beauties of the country, which has generated a new symbolic language. Guyana's outstanding literary tradition has opened new channels of expression both within and outside the country through the work of writers like Grace **Nichols**, Wilson **Harris**, Harry **Narain** and Denis **Williams**. In the field of social science, Walter **Rodney**, founder of one of the country's principal political parties, made an outstanding contribution.

See also: Burnham, Forbes; Jagan, Cheddi

LUIS L. ESPARZA

Guyana Chronicle

The *Guyana Chronicle* is a newspaper with a stormy history, first launched in 1880 as the daily *The Chronicle*. In the 1970s, now called the *Guyana Chronicle*, it merged with the competing *Citizen* and was taken over by Guyana National Newspapers Limited, under the premise of 'development communication within the paramountcy of party', claimed by President Forbes **Burnham** in 1974. Through the 1980s and early 1990s, the *Chronicle* and its supplement the *Sunday Chronicle* were denounced as instruments of government 'paramountcy' by former prime minister and opposition leader Cheddi **Jagan**. With Jagan's re-election in 1992, however, press freedom began to improve.

JILL E. ALBADA JELGERSMA

Guyanas

Enclosed by the ocean and the Amazon and Orinoco Basins, *Guiana* (land between waters) was the frontier of both Spanish and Portuguese empires. It was easily taken by other European colonial powers (France, the Netherlands and Britain) seeking a bridgehead from which to challenge Iberian dominion of the New World. The region's plantations absorbed waves of forced labourers from other continents. Guyana, Suriname and Guyane (known as French Guyana) represent, like Belize, cultural enclaves in Iberoamerica. Their multi-ethnic populations, born of colonial demographic transfers, are now facing the challenge of nation-building, having finally won their independence (except for French Guyana).

LUIS L. ESPARZA

Guzmán, Abimael

b. 1936, Arequipa, Peru

Politician

Guzmán is the founder and leader of **Sendero Luminoso** (Shining Path). After writing a dissertation on Hegel, he became a philosophy professor in Ayacucho. In 1970 he founded the political movement that, ten years later, became the bloodiest in contemporary Peruvian history. His orthodox Maoism inspired a military strategy that destabilized successive democratic governments during the 1980s. Called 'Presidente Gonzalo' and living clandestinely since 1980, he was finally captured in Lima in September 1992. Thereafter, he called for a peace agreement that has helped the relative pacification of the country. He is now held in a maximum security military prison in Lima.

JOSÉ ANTONIO MAZZOTTI

Guzmán, Augusto

b. 1903, Cochabamba, Bolivia; d. 1994, Cochabamba

Writer

Productive in almost every literary genre, Guzmán wrote novels, essays, criticism and biography. *La sima fecunda* (The Fruitful Abyss) (1933), a novel set in the valleys of Cochabamba, and *Prisionero de guerra* (Prisoner of War) (1937), which addresses the problems of prisoners during the **Chaco War**, are his best-known works. He is also the author of a number of critical approaches to Bolivian literature. His essays often address religious issues, a topic rarely discussed in Bolivia, as in his *El Cristo viviente* (The Living Christ) (1981).

MARÍA DORA VILLA GÓMEZ

Guzmán, Delfina

b. 1930, Santiago, Chile

Actress

Guzmán has won a national and international reputation for her theatre, film and television work. Starting out with the University of Chile's Teatro Experimental (1955) and the Universidad Católica's Teatro de Ensayo (1957), she later co-founded the theatre group **ICTUS**. She directed *Diálogos de fin de siglo* (End of Century Dialogues) by ICTUS with Isidora **Aguirre** and Michel Tremblay's *Albertina en 5 tiempos* (Albertina in Five Ages); she appeared on television in *La manivela*, and in film in Raúl **Ruiz**'s *La expropiación* (The Expropriation) (1972), Silvio **Caiozzi**'s *Julio comienza en julio* (July Begins in July) (1979) and Tatiana Gaviola's *Angeles* (1988).

ELIANA ORTEGA

Guzmán, Martín Luis

b. 1887, Chihuahua, Mexico; d. 1976, Mexico City

Writer

A participant in the Mexican Revolution (1910–17), he was also one of its principal chroniclers. He worked with the Madero government, but resigned his post when it was overthrown by Victoriano Huerta in 1913. From his youth, Guzmán was an active political journalist, and was personally acquainted with most of the leading actors in the revolution – including Venustiano Carranza (whom he criticized bitterly) and Pancho Villa, who appear in his novels. He spent several periods in political exile in the USA (1916–20) and Spain (1915–16, 1925–36). While in Spain he contributed to several Madrid newspapers and later joined the editorial board of *El Sol* and *La Voz*. On returning to Mexico he played an important role as the founder of a publishing house and as editor of the journals, *Romance* and *Tiempo*.

Guzmán's first book, published in 1915 in New York, was *La querella de Mexico* (The Mexico Debate), a powerful reflection on the lack of direction in the Mexican Revolution after the fall of Diaz. His two major novels, *El águila y la serpiente* (The Eagle and the Serpent) (1926) and *La sombra del caudillo* (The Shadow of the Chief) (1928–9) were originally published in instalments in Mexican and foreign newspapers – and gained him a wide audience. In the first novel, Guzmán chronicles the events of the period 1913–15 in Mexican history, when various political factions were disputing the control of the nation. The second work, a bitter drama based on real events, exposed the bloody power struggle between the politicians who had inherited the revolutionary mantle but not its democratic and revolutionary ideals. It was Pancho **Villa** who fascinated Guzmán, and who provided the inspiration for his most ambitious work, *Memorias de Pancho Villa* (Pancho Villa's Memoirs), published in four volumes between 1936 and 1951. But, despite his dedication, Guzmán never successfully found the form or the language that could express the particular characteristics of this elusive historical figure.

Further reading

Abreu Gómez, E. (1968) *Martín Luis Guzmán*, Mexico City: Empresas Editoriales.

Portal, M. (1977) *Proceso narrativo de la revolución mexicana*, Madrid: Ed. Cultura Hispánica.

Rutherford, J. (1971) *Mexican Society during the Revolution: A Literary Approach*, Oxford: Clarendon Press.

RAFAEL OLEA FRANCO

Guzmán, Patricio

b. 1941, Santiago, Chile

Film-maker

Having studied philosophy and cinema in Chile and Spain, Guzmán returned to Chile in 1970 just in time for the **Popular Unity** victory. Although he had studied fiction film-making, on returning to **Allende**'s Chile he found 'reality' more compelling and in 1971 made his first documentary, *El primer año* (The First Year), chronicling the first twelve months of Allende's government. His three-part record of the escalation of the class struggle from the February elections in 1973 to the military *coup* of September, *La* **batalla de Chile**, stands as his most important work and took five years to complete in exile in Cuba. His most recent work is *Chile, la memoria obstinada* (Chile, Obstinate Memory) (1997).

DOLORES TIERNEY

Guzman, Rudy *see* Santo, El

Gyula Kosice

b. 1924, Kosice, Hungary

Visual artist

Known for his articulated sculptures and use of light and water, Kosice (born F. Fallik) moved to Buenos Aires with his family at age four. In 1940 he met Carmelo **Arden Quin**, who was a major influence on his own work. In 1944 he became a member of the editorial board of the journal, *Arturo*, edited by Arden Quin together with Edgar **Bayley** and Rhod Rothfuss; his first articulated sculpture dates from the same year. In 1945 he became a member of the Movimiento Arte Concreto-Invención, and in 1946 was one of the founders of the Movimiento Madi, together with Arden Quin, Rothfuss and others. His first light sculptures were presented in 1946, and Kosice's first solo exhibition in Buenos Aires the following year. He began to produce using light and moving water while in Paris (1957–63) and in 1972 presented his *La ciudad hidroespacial* (The Hydro-Space City), a manifesto followed by several works in plexiglass. He has created a number of aqua-kinetic works for public spaces, particularly in Buenos Aires.

GUILLERMO GREGORIO

hacienda

Hacienda is the name given to large landed estates in Latin America. They generally combine livestock and cereal production. *Haciendas* are also sometimes referred to as *latifundios* (see **latifundio**). In Argentina, the term ***estancia*** is used to refer to large cattle or sheep ranches; in Brazil the term used is ***fazenda***. *Haciendas* vary in size from a few hundred to more than a hundred thousand hectares. The *hacienda*'s origins lie in the colonial period, and the oppressive and exploitative labour relations which prevailed on these estates have often been characterized as feudal; nevertheless, the *hacienda* is also a hallowed, nostalgic realm in the Latin American imagination (for example, the *comedia ranchera* genre in Mexico – see **rancheras, comedias**). *Haciendas* are less common since the 1950s, as many were expropriated during the wave of **agrarian reform** in Latin America and/or were subdivided into smaller farms.

CRISTÓBAL KAY

Hadad, Astrid

b. 1954, Chetumal, Quintana Roo, Mexico

Singer and actress

Hadad is known as 'The Diva of Heavy Nopal' because of her highly personal fusion of rock and Mexican popular music. She was a member of the Divas company that presented Jesusa **Rodríguez**'s *Donna Giovanni*, her version of Mozart's *Don Giovanni*, and appeared at international festivals with the group 'Los Tarzanes'. Her solo work includes her homage to Lucha **Reyes**, *La occisa...o Luz levántate y lucha* (Light/Luz Get Up and Fight/Lucha), *Nostalgia arrabalera* (Slum Memories), *Del rancho a la ciudad* (From the Farm to the City), *Apocalipsis ranchera*, *Pecadora* (Sinner) and the CD *Corazón sangrante* (Bleeding Heart).

TITO VASCONCELOS

Hahn, Oscar

b. 1938, Iquique, Chile

Poet

Hahn combines the literary language of the classic Spanish tradition with colloquial expressions and elements of contemporary lyric poetry in poetic and philosophical explorations of love and death. His works include *Mal de amor* (Love Breaks) (1981), *Imágenes nucleares* (Nuclear Images) (1983), *Estrellas fijas en un cielo blanco* (Fixed Stars in an Open Sky) (1989) and *Versos robados* (Stolen Verses) (1995). His work has been translated by James Hoggard as *The Art of Dying* (1987) and *Love Breaks* (1991). He teaches at the University of Iowa.

ELIANA ORTEGA

Haiti

Haiti occupies the western third of the Caribbean island of Hispaniola, which it shares with the Dominican Republic. Its land is mountainous and main towns are situated on the coast. Haiti was the first Caribbean or Latin American colony to achieve independence in 1804 after a war in which the slaves defeated the French. The population is estimated at seven million and mostly of African descent. The French language is spoken by approximately 10 per cent of the population and the rest are largely monolingual creole speakers (see **Haitian creole**). Haiti's creolophone peasantry forms the majority of the population and is distinct from the small, Francophone urban elite. Haiti's population has been marked by migration because of political and economic upheaval and, at present, approximately one million Haitians live abroad, particularly in New York, Montreal and southern Florida.

Despite its glorious beginnings, Haiti has had a troubled history. The protracted war of independence left the once prosperous colony of St Domingue devastated. The period from 1804 to the American Occupation in 1915 is marked by civil strife as one military strongman after another seized power. Haiti ultimately lost its precarious independence when its capital, Port-au-Prince, was seized by the US marines after a period of violent and chronic instability. Haiti was governed by puppet presidents until the withdrawal of American troops in 1934 but the end of armed occupation did not produce stability as militarism quickly reasserted itself in public life. In 1957 Dr Francois **Duvalier**, also known as Papa Doc, was elected president in army-controlled elections, thereby ushering in a twenty-nine year dynasty that ended in 1986 with the fall of his son, Jean Claude **Duvalier**, known as Baby Doc.

The Duvaliers ruled through terror, brutally enforced by their militia, the **Tontons Macoutes**, and the manipulation of Haiti's popular culture. Francois Duvalier died in 1971 leaving his son as the head of state. By the 1980s, government inefficiency, state corruption and Haiti's image abroad further aggravated economic decline which became evident to the outside world in the increasing number of boat people. By 1986 mounting protests, fomented by the grassroots Catholic Church and small radio stations like *Radio Soleil*, forced Baby Doc to flee to France, leaving behind an empty treasury and an army notoriously hostile to democratic reform. The ensuing period was one of much turbulence and Haiti's first democratic elections were held in December 1990 under United Nations supervision. A young militant Catholic priest, Jean-Bertrand **Aristide**, was elected by an overwhelming majority. He was overthrown in 1991 and after three years in exile and a UN-imposed embargo on Haiti, he was returned to power by an American-led, UN-sanctioned multinational force.

One of the paradoxes of Haitian culture is that despite political failure and economic disaster, Haiti's achievement in the arts is an enviable one. Much of modern Haiti's success in this area is ironically related to the American Occupation. After the initial shock created by the loss of sovereignty, Haitian writers and intellectuals, spurred on by an intense nationalism in the 1920s, launched the literary movement, ***indigenisme***, which sought inspiration in local culture. Led by the the Haitian ethnologist Jean **Price-Mars**, young writers such as Jacques **Roumain**, Philippe **Thoby-Marcelin**, Emile Roumer and Carl **Brouard** declared that their forebears had sold the nation short and turned to the peasantry as a source of authentic inspiration. *Indigenisme* soon gave way to other movements, such as ***noirisme*** which sought to promote Haiti's African heritage and Haitian Marxism, with the formation of the Haitian Communist Party in 1934.

In the mid-1940s a younger generation of Haitian writers was influenced by the visits of Aimé **Césaire**, Andre Breton and Alejo **Carpentier**. Surrealism and **magical realism** led to major poetic and fictional achievements by René **Depestre** and Jacques Stephen **Alexis** respectively. The excesses of Duvalierism forced many writers into exile. Writing within Haiti became increasingly difficult with Franck Etienne's short-lived *Spiralisme* representing the only real attempt at a literary movement. Writing by Haitians on the outside flourished. Initially anti-Duvalierist in intent, they soon called into question many of the populist and nationalist beliefs of their literary antecedents. Writers such as Jean Claude Charles,

Anthony Phelps, Dany **Laferriere**, Emile Olivier and the cinematographer Raoul **Peck** as well as Edwidge Danticat who writes in English, represent the best of this recent phase of artistic activity.

Haitian culture is equally well known because of the popular religion, **Vodun**, and the visual arts over which it has a strong influence. The Duvalier regime's sustained attack on the Catholic Church since the 1960s and the promotion of Vodun as a national religion has given it greater visibility. This system of beliefs, often the object of lurid sensationalism by foreigners, is deeply related to the survival of Haiti's peasantry and is a syncretic fusion of gods from Dahomey and Catholic saints. Vodun has a profound influence on the Haitian folk imagination and is the source of creative pictography in Haitian painting. The success of Haiti's visual arts goes back to the 1940s and the promotion of Haiti's folk arts of that time. The *Centre d'Art* was founded by an American, Dewitt Peters in 1944 and brought world-wide recognition to such self-taught artists as Philomé **Obin**, Wilson **Bigaud** and Hector **Hippolyte** very much at the same time that Catherine Dunham was introducing Haiti's folk dances and rhythms to the USA.

Haitian painting and sculpture subsequently fell prey to rampant commercialism but saw a revival in the 1970s with the painters of Saint Soleil. This expressionist school of Haitian painting attracted the attention of André Malraux who played a role similar to that of André Breton in the 1940s in championing Haiti's naive artists. Though less recognised internationally, Haitian music, closely tied to the annual carnival, is a vital element in popular culture. This music ranges from the traditional meringue to the melodic compas. In recent times, this music has become politicized in the Vodun rhythms of the group Boukman Eksperyans and the songs of protest of the former mayor of Port-au-Prince, Manno **Charlemagne**. This music along with a number of small radio stations played a major role in dismantling the vestiges of the Duvalierist state since 1986.

Further reading

Courlander, H. (1960) *The Drum and the Hoe*, Berkeley: University of California Press.

Dash, J.M. (1981) *Literature and Ideology in Haiti 1915–1961*, London: Macmillan.

Metraux, A. (1972) *Voodoo in Haiti*, New York: Schocken.

Nicholls, D. (1979) *From Dessalines to Duvalier, Race, Colour and National Independence in Haiti*, Cambridge: Cambridge University Press.

Rodman, S. (1988) *Where Art is Joy*, New York: Ruggles Delatour.

Wilentz, A. (1989) *The Rainy Season: Haiti Since Duvalier*, New York: Simon & Schuster.

J. MICHAEL DASH

Haitian creole

Haitian creole, or kreyòl, as it is commonly known, is the only language spoken by nearly 85 per cent of the Republic of Haiti's 7,000,000 inhabitants. The remaining 15 per cent, who represent the educated segment of the population, are bilingual in creole and French. As is common in societies where a creole remains in contact with the European language from which it derives most of its lexicon, Haitian creole has traditionally been stigmatized in relation to French, which continues to function as a language of prestige. For creole/French bilinguals, this has led to a situation of diglossia in which each language is associated with specific domains of use: creole tends to be used in intimate or informal contexts such as with friends and family, while French is reserved for formal or official contexts.

Despite the low prestige from which creole continues to suffer, especially among the educated elite, its status was raised to that of official language (alongside French) by the Haitian Constitution of 1987. As the sole language of the poor masses, creole also functions as a powerful symbol of national identity. An especially effective practitioner of the language is President **Aristide**, who eschewed the highly Frenchified register of creole typical among Haitian politicians and affected instead a simple, direct style that eloquently expressed his solidarity with the masses.

Creole is widely used in the print and broadcast media, and there is a modest but growing literary production in the language. The use of creole in writing is facilitated by the existence of an officially recognized orthography (that of the Institut Pédagogique National), although it is not universally employed in creole publications. While for many years French served as the only language of instruction in Haitian schools, today creole is used as well, reflecting both the growing acceptance of creole as a legitimate language and the reality that almost no Haitian children arrive in school with proficiency in French.

In contrast to a number of other **French-based creoles** which are threatened with extinction, Haitian creole is a thriving language with growing numbers of speakers. Thanks to the Haitian diaspora, the language is also extending its geographic spread. Today Haitian creole may commonly be heard in several major cities of North America and Europe, including Miami, New York, Montreal, and Paris.

Further reading

d'Ans, A.M. (1968) *Le créole français d'Haïti*, The Hague: Mouton.

Holm, J. (1989) *Pidgins and Creoles*, vol. 2, Cambridge: Cambridge University Press.

Valdman, A. (1984) 'The linguistic situation of Haiti', in C.R. Foster and A. Valdman (eds), *Haiti – Today and Tomorrow*, Lanham, MD: University Press of America, pp. 77–99.

THOMAS KLINGLER

Halac, Ricardo

b. 1935, Buenos Aires, Argentina

Playwright

Halac's plays *Soledad para cuatro* (Solitude for Four) (1961), *Estela de madrugada* (Dawn Trail) (1965) and *Fin de diciembre* (End of December) (1965) are within the critical realist tradition, nourished by the discontent, solitude and frustration of the middle class. Later he adopted a style akin to the ***grotesco criollo*** to explore the crisis of a couple (in *Segundo tiempo* (Second Half) (1976)) or of a family (*Un trabajo fabuloso* (A Great Job) (1980)) through parody and humour. He has also written scripts for television series like *Compromiso* and the investigative programme *Yo fui testigo* (I Was a Witness).

NORA MAZZIOTTI

Halffter, Rodolfo

b. 1900, Madrid, Spain; d. 1987, Mexico City

Composer

Halffter's music follows in the melodic and tonal traditions of his idol Falla, although in the *Tres hojas de álbum* for piano (Three Album Pages) (1953) he became the first Mexican composer to employ serialism. Often confused with his brother Ernesto and nephew Cristóbal, both composers, he fled to Mexico after the Spanish Civil War (see **Spanish Civil War, impact of**) and became naturalized in 1939. He taught composition at Mexico's National Conservatory, founded the music journal *Nuestra música* (1946–53), and managed the publishing house Ediciones Mexicanas de Música.

SIMON WRIGHT

Hall, Stuart

b. 1932, Kingston, Jamaica

Cultural theorist

Hall's extremely influential body of work on cultural theory grew out of the British 1950s 'new left', whose search for a materialist understanding of culture free of Stalinist determinism was expressed in *Universities and Left Review* which Hall edited (1958–61). Under his direction (1968–79) the Birmingham Centre for Cultural Studies married Marxism and other theories of discourse in an imaginative exploration of popular cultural practices. By 1980, as cultural studies moved towards the USA leaving behind much of its Marxist heritage, Hall's ideas converged with those of Ernesto **Laclau** around a concept of new (postmodern) times which stressed the disengagement between cultural practices and objective material circumstances. In the 1990s, Hall's concerns increasingly turned towards a post-colonial experience closer to his own trajectory as a 'diasporic intellectual'.

MIKE GONZALEZ

Halley Mora, Mario

b. 1926, Coronel Oviedo, Paraguay

Writer

Author of more than fifteen published plays including the two volumes of *Teatro Paraguayo* (Paraguayan Theatre), Halley is the most prolific Paraguayan playwright of the twentieth century. He was also chief editor of the newspaper *Patria* during the **Stroessner** regime, **radio** librettist during the 1950s, script writer (as Alex) of the first Paraguayan **Guarani** comic strips, and editor of the newspaper *La Unión* (1990s). Among his many novels, *Ocho mujeres y las demás* (Eight Women and the Rest), was hailed as the most widely read novel of 1994.

TERESA MÉNDEZ-FAITH

Halperin Donghi, Tulio

b. 1926, Buenos Aires

Historian

Halperin is one of Latin America's most respected historians. His main research area is nineteenth-century Argentine history, and *Una nación para el desierto argentino* (1982), the culmination of several decades of investigation on the process of nation-building, his most relevant publication. His *Contemporary History of Latin America* (1993) is also a classic in the field. One of Halperin's main contributions has been to situate Argentine history in a Latin American context, drawing comparative approaches as in *El espejo de la historia* (1987). This comparative approach is an unusual perspective in Argentina, a country proud of its 'uniqueness' in respect to its Latin American neighbours. Another area of interest is intellectual history, to which belong works such as *José Hernández y sus mundos* (1985), where he discussed some populist readings of the author Martín Fierro.

After abandoning chemistry to study history at the University of Buenos Aires, Halperin studied in Turin and Paris where he met Fernand Braudel, who deeply influenced him. His first book, *El pensamiento de Echeverría* (1951), discloses an enduring interest for the nineteenth century and the formation of the Argentine elite, particularly the figure of Domingo F. Sarmiento (1811–88). He later taught at University of the Littoral, University of the Republic (Uruguay) and the University of Buenos Aires until 1967, when he left Argentina. He continued teaching at different institutions, among them Harvard and Oxford, until he accepted a permanent position at the University of California, Berkeley in 1972.

Halperin's interest in contemporary history led him to write about **Peronism**. His attraction to Peronism has much to do with his desire to explain Argentina's decline in the last fifty years, and has provocative parallels with Sarmiento's fascination with barbarism. Halperin's formidable influence over Latin American historical studies demonstrates his ability to oversee research production in two worlds, Latin America and the United States, whose academic universities seem to be becoming more connected.

A. FERNÁNDEZ-BRAVO

Hamilton, Judith

b. 1952, Spanish Town, St Catherine, Jamaica

Poet

Belonging to the 'new' generation of Caribbean poets, Hamilton claims Mervyn **Morris** and the late poets Anthony **McNeill** and Dennis **Scott** as influences. Morris's legacy is economy and craft: Hamilton's poems are brief, recalling haiku. Scott's gift is careful lineation and the occasional surreal image, and McNeill's is whimsy, the spare power of images, Jamaica-talk as 'noise in the street'. Hamilton's work has appeared in anthologies like *Focus 1983*, *From Our Yard* and *Caribbean New Voices I*. *Rain Carvers* (1992) was her first collection.

PAT DUNN AND PAMELA MORDECAI

Handler, Mario

b. 1935, Montevideo, Uruguay

Film-maker

Founder of the Cinemateca del Tercer Mundo (Third World Cinematheque), he was three times awarded the annual prize for the Best Uruguayan Film for *Carlos* (1965), *Elecciones* (Choices) (1967), codirected with Ugo **Ulive** and *Me gustan los estudiantes* (I Like Students) (1968). In 1973 he moved to Venezuela where he made *Tiempo colonial* (Colonial Times) (1977), which won a prize for the best Latin American film at the Bilbao Festival of Short Films. His *Mestizo* (1989) won prizes for photography and sound at the Caracas Film Festival of that year.

MARCO MAGGI

happenings

An artistic event of a theatrical nature, but usually improvised spontaneously without the framework of a plot, happenings develop in a succession of moments in which all the senses are stimulated. Action and personal involvement are the classic elements of a happening. The term originated with the creation and performance in 1959 of Allan Kaprow's *18 Happenings in 6 Parts*, a work that emphasized various sorts of performance and experience, including slide projection, dance, and taste and odour sensations. Many examples of the genre required audience participation and the aesthetic effect produced was a result of the combination of events experienced. Celebrated happenings include: Claes Oldenburg's *Store* (1961), *Autobodies* (1963) and *Washes* (1965); Robert Rauschenberg's *Map Room II* (1965); Robert Whitman's *The American Moon* (1960); and Kaprow's *Calling* (1965).

The late 1960s was a period of great politicization in Latin America, particularly among, but not limited to, younger artists. New left politics and ideas spread throughout Latin American and common cause was sometimes made with the older social realists (see **socialist realism**). The 1960s was also the era of avant-garde exploration in the areas of pop, conceptual, performance, happenings and mail art. The **Southern Cone** countries, particularly Argentina, were at the forefront of experimental art in which local artists no longer incorporated foreign codes into their work. In 1963 the Neo-Figurative art movement – la Nueva Figuración (see **otra figuración**) – was disbanded and in August of that year the Visual Arts Centre of the **Di Tella Institute** was inaugurated in Buenos Aires; Jorge Romero Brest was its director. The Centre was the setting for environments, avant-garde events, theatre, music, happenings and pop art events, until its closure in 1969. In 1964 D. Puzzovio, Santatonín, Ciorda, Delia Cancela, Pablo Mansejeón, Carlos Squirru, Edgardo Giménez and Antonio **Berni** staged *La muerte* (Death), the first happening in Buenos Aires. In March of 1965 the group, La Siempre Viva, was presented by Puzzovio, Squirru, Giménez, Marilú Marini, A. Rodríguez Arias, Juan Stoppani and Miguel A. Redondo in the series of happenings entitled *Microsucesos* (Micro-Events). Two months later Marta **Minujín** staged *La menesunda*, in which she presented the same kind of experiments she created in France.

In the 1970s, happenings developed as a collaborative art form from a fusion of several artistic media, such as painting, film, video, music, drama and dance, and deriving in part from the 1960s performance happenings.

Further reading

Glusberg, J. (1986) *Art in Argentina*, Milan, Italy: Giancarlo Politi Editore.

Goldman, S.M. (1994) *Dimensions of the Americas*, Chicago: University of Chicago Press.

Ramírez, M.C. (1997) *Re-Aligning Vision*, Austin: Archer M. Huntington Art Gallery, University of Texas

ISABEL BARBUZZA

Harder They Come, The

In *The Harder They Come* (1973), a Jamaican film directed by Perry **Henzel**, **reggae** star Jimmy **Cliff** plays Ivan, a young singer from the country who travels to Kingston in hopes of becoming a recording star, but must grapple with a racially polarized Kingston in which employment opportunities are scarce. After days of rebuffs in the gardens of the affluent and nights of proving his mettle in the shanty towns, Ivan becomes a handyman for a local preacher. When an argument with a co-worker over a bicycle turns into a bloody knife fight, Ivan is sent to jail. Upon his release he doggedly courts Jamaica's biggest record producer, Hilton, who eventually allows Ivan to record the song 'The Harder They Come', but offers him a mere $20 for the recording. When Ivan proudly refuses the offer, Hilton releases the record with no promotion, promising its swift demise in the cutthroat Jamaican music scene. Ivan finds a similar politics at play when economic desperation forces him to work in the *ganja* (marijuana) trade in which the island's police and local government exploit the Rastafarian (see **Rastafarianism**) growers and capitalize on their lucrative crop. Desperate and fed-up, Ivan takes to a life of crime, fashioning himself as a Robin Hood-like character in accordance with the lyrics to the song for which the film is named. Ivan becomes a cult figure in the shanty towns and by popular demand his recording begins to dominate the radio waves. Ivan's celebrity is doomed, however, as he falls in a hail of police and army bullets in the highly-stylized, quasi cowboy-western final sequences of the film.

The Harder They Come represents Jamaican cultural and musical movements which would later agglutinate as 'reggae' with the later work of Bob **Marley**: the emergent rastafarian culture, **ska** style, the sound system scene, the politics of the 1960s Jamaican record industry, and the emergent 'toasting' culture in the early 1960s where, as in contemporary **rap music**, DJs fashioned themselves as gangsters. Ivan's gangster persona also references mid-1960s 'rude boy' culture, referring to the angry youths of the Jamaican slums who took to carrying German ratchet knives and pistols, turning to lives of crime rather than performing menial labour. The music of *The Harder They Come* provides a panoramic view of the Jamaican musical styles of the 1960s, including performances by Cliff, Desmond Dekker and The Slickers.

Further reading

Henzell, P. (1997) *Power Game*, Kingston: Hastings House Publishing.
Thelwell, M. (1980) *The Harder They Come: A Novel*, New York: Grove Press.

JOHN HARVEY

Hardoy, Jorge Enrique

b. 1926, Buenos Aires, Argentina; d. 1993, Buenos Aires

Historian and city planner

Starting with issues of urban development, Hardoy explored questions of the environment, child poverty and the role of NGOs. Founder in 1962 of the Instituto de Planeamiento Regional y Urbano (Institute of Regional and Urban Planning) at the Universidad del Litoral, he has actively campaigned to protect historic urban sites. Editor of the journal *Medio ambiente y urbanización*, his writings include *Las ciudades de América Latina* (The Cities of Latin America) (1971), and *Repensando la ciudad en América Latina* (Rethinking the Latin American City) (1992), with Richard Morse.

GONZALO AGUILAR

Harnecker, Marta

b. Chile

Political analyst

Harnecker's most important work has been her interpretation and elucidation of Marxism for Latin America. Her first work, *Conceptos elementales del materialismo histórico* (Basic Concepts in Historical Materialism) (1975) sold over a million copies in its fifty-one editions; it was followed by *El Capital: conceptos fundamentales* (Marx's Capital: Basic Concepts) (1971). An active member of the Chilean Socialist Party, she played a key role during the period of the **Popular Unity** government (1970-3), editing the influential Socialist Party journal, *Chile hoy*. After the **Pinochet** *coup* in 1973, Harnecker was exiled to Cuba, where she married Manuel Piñeiro, head of the Cuban government's security services. She currently directs the Centro de Investigaciones Memoria Popular Latinoamericana in Havana, devoted to the recuperation of the popular historical memory, under whose rubric she produced the edited volume, *La izquierda latinoamericana en el umbral del siglo XXI* (The Latin American Left on the Threshold of the 21st Century) (1998). Other works include *Cuba ¿democracia o dictadura?* (Cuba, Democracy or Dictatorship?) (1975).

MIKE GONZALEZ

Haro, David

b. Veracruz, Mexico

Composer and singer

David Haro, a Mexican composer of trova music, or canto nuevo (new song), was influenced by a wide number of sources, including the Beatles, Brazilian music, Cuban ***nueva trova*** and whatever he heard on the radio. In a repertoire of some 250 songs, Haro expresses his feelings and ideas on a wide range of topics, including urban life, love, eroticism, God, and hope, in original, spontaneous concerts that usually have no pre-planned programme, but rather are left open to requests from the audience. The trova, he has stated, is not a musical genre, but rather a tradition that originated with the Provençal poets, with Spanish and Arabic influences, and which found fertile ground in the port of Veracruz, where he was raised. He collaborated with Armando **Chacha** for the album *Matamba* (1999).

EDUARDO GUÍZAR-ALVAREZ

harp

The harp is unrivalled amongst musical instruments in Latin America in terms of the broad and sustained role it has played since its introduction by Jesuit missionaries in the sixteenth century. The diatonic harp (diatonic refers to a single row of strings) constituted a crucial element in the Jesuits' evangelization process as they travelled to remote regions teaching the indigenous communities how to play the instrument. Today, four Latin American regions have significant and influential modern harp traditions: Paraguay, Mexico, Venezuela and Peru.

Paraguay probably has the most dynamic tradition; the harp is officially designated the national instrument. Asunción, the capital, has several renowned harpmakers and its players and makers play an important part in contemporary Paraguayan folklore. In Mexico there are two very distinct indigenous harp traditions in Sonora and Chiapas, and one major mestizo harp tradition in Veracruz. The so-called 'Kennedy' corridos (see **corrido**), narrative ballads popular in early 1960s Texas, are evidence of the far-reaching influence of the Veracruz harp. Venezuela has two separate harp traditions: the *arpa llanera* (harp from the plains), which is generally carried by the harpist from place to place in a manner reminiscent of the medieval troubadours and the *arpa aragueña* (from the Aragua region) which is also popular in Colombia. Peruvian writer José María **Arguedas** attests to the vibrant indigenous Peruvian harp tradition, noting that 'every Andean village, however small, has at least one Indian violinist or harpist'. Currently, the Peruvian *arpa indígena* (indigenous harp) is routinely used in processions.

Styles of playing and performance practices differ widely throughout the continent. In some regions, it is customary to play using only the fingernails (Chiapas), whereas in others harpists use the pads of their fingers. A very interesting feature of harp playing in Latin America is the *golpeador* function, where the box of the harp is directly struck and used as complementary percussion for dramatic musical effect. The harp is central to much ritual practice throughout the continent – whether played upside down as part of a colourful procession or seated for rituals like weddings or a child's wake. The harp is a potent symbol of Latin American history and plays a vital role in the distinct regional musical cultures that flourish today.

Further reading

Schechter J. (1992) *The Indispensable Harp: Historical Development, Modern Roles, Configurations and Performance Practices in Ecuador and Latin America*, Kent, OH: Kent State University Press.

NUALA FINNEGAN

Harris, Claire

b. 1937, Port-of-Spain, Trinidad

Poet

Claire Harris's major preoccupations in her generally experimental poetry include racism, minority rights, and expatriation. Author of five collections of poetry; her *Fables from the Women's Quarters* (1984) won the Americas' regional award of the Commonwealth Poetry Prize (1985). Her writing has been influenced by a wide range of writers, especially European surrealists and prose poem writers. Harris studied at University College, Dublin, Ireland; the University of the West Indies, Jamaica; and the University of Nigeria, Nsukka. She emigrated to Calgary, Alberta, Canada in 1966 to teach. She has travelled extensively and participated in community literary activities in Canada.

FUNSO AIYEJINA

Harris, Wilson

b. 1921, New Amsterdam, British Guiana

Writer

A visionary and original novelist, Harris left school at seventeen to become a land surveyor and led a number of expeditions into the jungle of British Guiana between 1941 and 1953. These jungle expeditions were extremely important to Harris and his later work. So profound were his experiences that conventional forms of fiction proved inadequate to their expression; so too did poetry, which seemed too limited to fully render a fantastical Amerindian culture. He turned, therefore, to poetic prose to present the spirit of Amerindian mythology in conflict with the European conquerors.

Indeed, Harris seems to suggest that we cannot become truly civilized until we examine thoroughly, and with empathy, the nature of existence in the pre-Columbian world and the tragedies inflicted on its humanity and natural history. The result is a narrative that is sometimes difficult but at the same time a testimony to the possibility of a universal spiritual revival. His twenty novels include *Heartland* (1964), *Age of the Rainmakers* (1971), *Resurrection at Sorrow Hill* (1993) and *Jonestown* (1997).

Further reading

Maes-Jelinek, H. (ed.) (1991) *Wilson Harris: The Uncompromising Imagination*, Sydney, NSW: Dangaroo Press.

KEITH JARDIM

Haseth, Carel P. de

b. 1950, Curaçao, Netherlands Antilles

Writer and politician

A chemist by profession, de Haseth has written both in Dutch and in **Papiamentu**. In his poetry collection in the native creole language, *Poesia venená* (Venomous Poetry) (1985), and a short novel, *Katibu di shon* (A Master's Slave) (1988), he depicted Curaçao society as ethnically mixed. This involved him in serious debates with those who tended to privilege Afro-Caribbean people and their sociocultural aspects as more authentically Curaçaoan. Since 1994 he has been a full-time politician.

AART G. BROEK

Hasta no verte Jesús mío

Elena **Poniatowska**'s second book, *Hasta no verte Jesús mío* (Until I See You, My Lord) (1969) is a testimonial narrative tracing the long, hard life of Jesusa Palancares, a slightly fictionalized version of Josefina Bórquez, a feisty washer-woman and former *soldadera* living in a Mexico City shanty town during the 1960s. (For a photograph of Josefina Bórquez and the youthful Poniatowska in 1963, see Steele p. 29.)

The contours of Jesusa's life mirror those of the modern Mexican peasantry and subproletariat, from the impoverished, violent patriarchal countryside of the Porfiriato, to the alienated individuals of the Mexican Revolution (see **revolutions**), and on to the ranks of survivors, mainly women and children, who flooded into Mexico City's slums after the revolution. Jesusa's lingering sense of betrayal and disappointment, and her unsatisfying professional and family life, echo the failures of the revolution to meet the needs of the country's impoverished masses.

This is the first of many texts in which Poniatowska fashions a unique narrative voice, combining the ideolects of a multitude of poor Mexicans she has known, from every region of the country. On the surface this use of popular dialect, to address progressive sociopolitical themes, by a daughter of the European nobility, seems highly contradictory. In fact this contradiction constitutes the core of the hybrid originality of this text and of testimonial narrative in general (see **testimonio**). As she describes in an autobiographical essay originally published in **Vuelta** in 1978, 'And here's to you, Jesusa', Poniatowska has always managed to negotiate, if at some personal cost, between her mother's world and that of Jesusa Palancares; between a cocktail party at the French Embassy and a hovel in one of Mexico City's most wretched slums (see **shanty towns and slums**). Poniatowska again wrote eloquently about this poignant and difficult balancing act, that of the committed intellectual woman in a developing country, in an essay on the death of Jesusa Palancares that is included in her collection of essays on Mexican women, *Luz y luna, las lunitas* (Light and the Moon, Little Moons) (1994).

Selected bibliography

Poniatowska, E. (1994) *Luz y luna, las lunitas*, Mexico City: Ediciones Era.

—— (1978). 'Hasta no verte Jesús mío: Jesusa Palancares', *Vuelta* 24: 7–9. (English translation in Meyer, Doris (ed.) (1988) *Lives on the Line*, Berkeley: University of California Press).

—— (1969) *Hasta no verte Jesús mío*, Mexico City: Ediciones Era.

Further reading

Jorgensen, B. (1994.) *The Writing of Elena Poniatowska*, Austin: University of Texas Press.

Kerr, L. (1992). 'Gestures of authorship: Lying to tell the truth in Elena Poniatowska's *Hasta no verte Jesús mío*', in *Reclaiming the Author: Figures and Fictions from Spanish America*, Durham: Duke University Press.

Sommer, D. (1999) *Proceed with Caution, When Engaged by Minority Writing in the Americas*, Cambridge: Harvard University Press.

Steele, C. (1992) 'Gender, genre and authority', in *Politics, Gender, and the Mexican Novel, 1968–1988: Beyond the Pyramid*, Austin: University of Texas Press.

CYNTHIA STEELE

Hatoum, Milton

b. 1952, Manaus, Brazil

Novelist

Few Brazilian writers have explored the intersections and disjunctions between the locally and ethnically specific and the national and global dimension as has Milton Hatoum in his two novels, *Relato de um Certo Oriente* (The Tree of the Seventh Heaven) (1989), which received the 1989 Jabuti Prize, and *Amazonas, palavras e imagens de um rio entre ruínas* (Amazonia, Words and Images of a River among Ruins) (1979). Without relying on facile notions of *mestizaje* or **syncretism**, Hatoum recreates his Arabic background in a dense and multi-layered chronicle of the 1920s Christian and Muslim Lebanese immigration to the Amazonian city of Manaus.

CÉSAR BRAGA-PINTO

Havana Film Festival *see* Festival Internacional del Nuevo Cine Latinoamericano

Havelange, Jean

b. 1916, Rio de Janeiro, Brazil

Sports official and businessman

President of the International Football Federation (FIFA) from 1974 to 1998, 'João' Havelange is now reputed to be Brazil's richest man, with interests including transport, chemicals and insurance. Graduating as a lawyer at twenty-one, he was a national and South American swimming and water polo champion, and represented Brazil in both sports at the Olympics of 1936 (swimming) and 1952 (water polo). He was President of the Brazilian Sports Federation from 1958 to 1973, before becoming FIFA president, where he increased the game's popularity and its finances during his twenty-four-year tenure.

ERIC WEIL

Haya de la Torre, Víctor Raúl

b. 1895, Trujillo, Peru; d. 1978, Lima, Peru

Politician

A leading force in Peruvian political life from the 1920s onwards, Haya did not live to see the party he founded, APRA, finally achieve power under Alan **García** in 1986; nor its departure four years later amid allegations of corruption. Born into a provincial aristocratic family, he became a leader of the Student Federation at Lima's San Marcos University, and was one of the leaders of massive strikes in favour of an eight-hour day in 1918. In 1923 he headed demonstrations against Augusto B. Leguía's dictatorship, and was arrested and exiled. He went on to found a continental and anti-imperialist political movement, **APRA** (Alianza Popular Revolucionaria Americana, or American Popular Revolutionary Alliance). At an international Anti-Imperialist Congress in Brussels in 1927, he set APRA apart from international communism and began to develop his own political philosophy for Latin America.

Haya returned to Peru in 1931 as presidential candidate of the Peruvian Aprista Party (PAP), losing in fraudulent elections in 1932. He went underground after a violent Aprista revolt in Trujillo in the same year. He and his movement were persecuted for several years; the Trujillo revolt left an open wound between the Peruvian army and the Aprista party which was not healed until 1985, when APRA formed a Peruvian government for the first time. Between 1933 and 1945, APRA was officially illegal, though it participated in elections under different names. Haya was always the strongman of the movement.

In 1949 Haya took refuge in the Colombian Embassy in Lima. He remained there until 1954, when he was finally allowed to leave and go into exile, where he worked as a freelance journalist in Europe. He returned to Peru in 1957, less radical and more inclined to advocate reformist policies; he tried, for example, to apply the Northern European social democratic welfare state experience to Peru. Haya was again his party's presidential candidate in 1962, where he was defeated by a military *coup*, and in 1963, when Fernando **Belaúnde Terry** won. He died in August 1978 without achieving his lifelong dream of an economically independent Peru.

Haya was an active writer and journalist. His first attempt to explain his political and social theory was *Antimperialismo y el APRA* (1927). Later he developed his controversial ideas applying Einstein's theory of relativity to the social and historical sciences, introducing the concept of 'historical space-time' as an instrument of Latin American political unity, and analysing imperialism as the first phase of capitalism in Latin America.

Further reading

Alexander, R. (1973) *Aprismo: The Ideas and Doctrines of Víctor Raúl Haya de la Torre*, Kent, OH: Kent State University Press.

Haya de la Torre, V. (1982) *Obras completas*, Lima: Editora Siglo XXI.

Sánchez, L.A. (1979) *Haya de la Torre o el político, Crónica de una vida sin tregua*, Lima: Editora Atlántida.

JUSSI PAKKASVIRTA

Hearne, John

b. 1926, Montreal, Canada; d. 1994, Kingston, Jamaica

Writer

Hearne is a significant, if atypical, figure in the postwar development of the West Indian novel. Living mainly in London and Paris, he published five novels of which *Voices under the Window* (1954) and *Land of the Living* (1961) remain the finest. In these, Hearne explored the role of the middle-class liberal on the imaginary island of Cayuna, based on Jamaica. In 1962 he returned to Jamaica and became Head of the Creative Arts Centre at Mona. His fine last novel, *The Sure Salvation* (1981), set on a slave ship, explores the historical roots of conflict in the Caribbean.

LOUIS JAMES

Heath, Roy

b. 1926, Georgetown, Guyana

Novelist

Roy Heath grew up in Georgetown, Guyana, where all his novels are set, although in 1951 he settled in London. His first novel, *A Man Come Home* (1974), revealed a disturbing vision in which detailed realism thinly masks the tensions of a claustrophobic Guyanese society, which develops into violence in *The Murderer* (1978), a *Guardian* fiction prize-winner. *From the Heat of the Day* (1979) began a three-part saga of a Georgetown family. *Kwaku* (1982), a tragi-comedy with a trickster hero, reflects a Guyana in social disintegration. *Shadows Round the Moon* (1990) is his autobiography.

LOUIS JAMES

Helman, Albert (Lou Lichtveld)

b. 1903, Paramaribo, Suriname; d. 1996, Hilversum, Netherlands

Writer, historian and diplomat

The first and most prolific writer from Suriname to publish in Dutch, he went to the Netherlands in his teens, but later worked in Suriname, represented the Netherlands at the United Nations in New York, travelled widely and spent his final years in the Netherlands. His writing reflects his wide travels, but he is best remembered for the novels and short stories from Suriname. He was awarded an honorary doctorate from the University of Amsterdam for his literary and scholarly achievements, among which his 1983 critical historiography of the Guyanas, *De foltering van Eldorado* (The Torturing of El Dorado) is outstanding.

ART BROEK

Hendriks, Arthur Lemiére

b. 1922, Kingston, Jamaica

Poet and broadcaster

In 1950, Hendricks began a career developing broadcast services in the Caribbean. From 1961 he was General Manager of the Jamaican Broadcasting Corporation, and in the 1960s he was director of Thompson Television in Bermuda, before finally settling in England. A writer of both short stories and verse, he is best known for his volumes of poetry, *On this Mountain* (1965), *These Green Islands* (1971) and *Muet – Poems* (1972). Elegant, precise and objective, his poems are marked by a simple clarity and reflect an inner peace uncharacteristic of most contemporary Jamaican verse.

LOUIS JAMES

Henfil

b. 1944, Bocaiúva, Brazil; d. 1988, Rio de Janeiro, Brazil

Cartoonist and writer

Part of the 1960s generation of mordant cartoonists, Henfil (real name Henrique de Souza Filho) used his art to comment on Brazilian social life and politics. During the military dictatorships, cartooning became an important vehicle for expressing opposing views, if only in highly oblique ways.

Henfil's aggressive, black humour underscored issues of authoritarianism, social disarray, urban alienation, violence as a reflex of the lack of communitarian solidarity and the deadly arbitrariness of the social contract. His cartoons for the Rio magazine *O **pasquim*** were most important. He also wrote a play, movie scripts and prose texts such as *Cartas de mãe* (Mother's Letters) (1980).

DAVID WILLIAM FOSTER

Henríquez, Graciela

b. 1932, Barquisimeto, Venezuela

Dancer, choreographer and anthropologist

One of Latin America's most innovative choreographers, Henríquez's work challenges both traditional ballet, in which she was trained, and the canons of modern dance. She danced in Europe before becoming prima ballerina for the Venezuelan National Ballet. Later she worked in Mexico with the **Ballet Folklórico de México** and the Ballet Independiente, where her abstract choreography for *Gymnopedias* and *Invenciones* was extremely successful. Developing the concept of dance theatre, she produced *Topicanas* and *Recuerdos de Juan Perdido* (Lost John's Memoirs), based on the daily life of ordinary Latin Americans. She studied anthropology and popular culture, and now specializes in historical research.

TERESA ALVARENGA

Henriquez, May

b. 1915, Curaçao, Netherlands Antilles

Writer and sculptor

A poet and short story writer in **Papiamentu** as well as the author of two studies about the idiomatic contributions of the Sephardic Jews to Papiamentu, May Henriquez (née Alvarez-Correa) has also translated works by Molière, Shakespeare, Shaw and Sartre into Papiamentu, thus contributing substantially to the development of the dramatic arts in Curaçao. After studying in Paris with Zadkine, she also distinguished herself as a sculptor. As a member of the Board of Supervisory Directors of the Maduro & Curiel's Bank, she was instrumental in the bank's extensive support for local arts.

AART G. BROEK

Henríquez Ureña, Camila

b. 1894, Santo Domingo, Dominican Republic; d. 1973, Santo Domingo

Writer

Like her brother Pedro **Henríquez Ureña**, Camila spent most of her life outside the Dominican Republic. She obtained her Ph.D. in Cuba, where she founded the Lyceum and the Instituto Hispano-Cubano de Cultura. She taught literature in Cuba and in the USA. As a feminist, Camila participated actively in conferences and associations. Her works, such as *Feminismo y otros temas sobre las mujeres en la sociedad* (Feminism and Other Subjects on Women in Society), were published posthumously in the 1980s.

FERNANDO VALERIO-HOLGUÍN

Henríquez Ureña, Max

b. 1885, Santo Domingo, Dominican Republic; d. 1968, Santo Domingo

Writer

Like his brother Pedro **Henríquez Ureña**, Max was a fiction writer, historian, literary critic and professor. Among his most important books are *Panorama histórico de la literatura dominicana* (Historical Overview of Dominican Literature) (1945) and his *Breve historia del modernismo* (Brief History of Modernismo) (1954). He lived in Cuba, Mexico and Puerto Rico for many years, was a minister and diplomat during **Trujillo**'s dictatorship, and taught literature at the Universidad Autónoma de Santo Domingo and Universidad Nacional Pedro Henríquez Ureña.

FERNANDO VALERIO-HOLGUÍN

Henríquez Ureña, Pedro

b. 1884, Santo Domingo, Dominican Republic; d. 1946, Buenos Aires, Argentina

Writer

Poet, literary critic, linguist and professor, Henríquez Ureña came from an intellectual family: his maternal grandfather and his mother were poets. His father, Francisco Henríquez y Carvajal, was an educator and President of the Dominican Republic. His brother Max **Henríquez Ureña** and his sister Camila **Henríquez Ureña** were also important writers.

From 1900 on, Pedro Henríquez Ureña lived in the USA, Spain, Cuba, Mexico and Argentina. A friend of Alfonso **Reyes** and José **Vasconcelos**, he influenced an entire generation of young intellectuals and promoted the foundation of the Escuela de Altos Estudios at the Universidad de México. He founded the Centro de Estudios Históricos (Center for Historical Studies) with Ramón Menéndez Pidal in Spain. He taught at the Universidad de La Plata in Argentina, where he became friends with Jorge Luis **Borges** and Ernesto **Sabato**.

Henríquez Ureña started his career writing poetry, which he abandoned in order to focus on criticism. His early poems were collected in the 1946 book *Poesías Juveniles* (Juvenile Poems). In the early twentieth century, Henríquez Ureña published *Ensayos críticos* (Critical Essays) (1905), *Horas de Estudio* (Study Hours) (1910), and *La enseñanza de la literatura* (The Teaching of Literature) (1913). As an *americanista*, his most important books are *La utopía de América* (The Utopia of Hispanic America) (1925) and *Seis ensayos en busca de nuestra expresión* (Six Essays in Search of Our Expression) (1928). In these books, Henríquez Ureña assesses diverse aspects of Latin American cultural identity.

Henríquez Ureña also contributed to the study of Latin American Spanish with his book *El español en Santo Domingo* (Spanish Language of Hispanic America) (1940) and *Observaciones sobre el español de América* (Observations on Hispanic American Spanish) (1921). His book *Gramática castellana* (Castillian Grammar) (1938–9), published with Dámaso Alonso, was used in Latin American schools for many decades.

Further reading

Alvarez, S. (1981) *La magna patria de Pedro Henríquez Ureña. Una interpretación de su americanismo*, Santo Domingo: Editora Taller.

Borges, J.L. (1960) 'Prologue', in P. Henríquez Ureña, *Obra crítica*, Mexico: Fondo de Cultura Económica.

Céspedes, D. (1983) 'Pedro Henríquez Ureña: lingüística y poesía', in *Seis ensayos sobre poética latinoamericana*, Santo Domingo: Biblioteca Taller.

Henríquez Ureña, M. (1950) *Pedro Henríquez Ureña*, Ciudad Trujillo: Librería Dominicana.

Sabato, E. (1979) 'Pedro Henríquez Ureña', in *Apologías y rechazos*, Barcelona: Editorial Seix y Barral.

FERNANDO VALERIO-HOLGUÍN

Henzel, Perry

b. 1937, Port Maria, St Mary, Jamaica

Film-maker

Henzel's international fame rests almost solely on his 1973 cult favourite *The **Harder They Come***. Technically crude and low budget, it possesses considerable political power, as it chronicles Jimmy **Cliff**'s turn to crime to become a famous **reggae** singer in Kingston, Jamaica. The film was planned as the first part of a trilogy, followed by *No Place Like Home* (1985), a study of Jamaican rural life that was ten years in the making. His films are committed to world solidarity, but his legacy will no doubt be to have introduced the world to **reggae**.

DOLORES TIERNEY

Heraud, Javier

b. 1942, Lima, Peru; d. 1963, Puerto Maldonado, Peru

Poet

Killed in a confrontation between a guerrilla group

(see **guerrillas**) and the Peruvian army, Heraud left behind him a small but very promising body of lyric poetry (published in Cuba in 1967 as *Poemas*); by his life and example he also shared in the mythology of the 'guerrilla poets'. Those who joined the guerrilla groupings in Latin America in the 1960s were almost all from educated, middle-class backgrounds; Heraud with others of his generation, like Guatemalan Otto René **Castillo**, wrote of their conviction and idealism. In Heraud's case, his poetry was set in emblematic landscapes, unsullied and open to transformation.

MIKE GONZALEZ

Herbert, Cecil

b. 1924, Belmont, Trinidad

Poet, teacher and land surveyor

Although he has published very little recently, in the past Herbert contributed many poems to major journals such as ***Bim***, *Tamarack Review*, ***Caribbean Quarterly***, and a number of anthologies. His output continues to stand up to rigorous critical scrutiny and has been collected as *The Poems of Cecil Herbert* (1981), edited by Danille Gianetti. Herbert's poetry is distinguished by a sensuous and celebratory approach to the landscape. He attended Queen's Royal College, Port-of-Spain before training with the Royal Air Force in Moncton, Canada. After the war, he became a land surveyor, returning to Trinidad to practise.

FUNSO AIYEJINA

Hercules, Frank Elton Mervyn

b. 1917, San Fernando, Trinidad; d. 1996, Roosevelt Island, New York, USA

Novelist

Hercules has published three novels and one book of non-fiction, a study of racism in the USA – *American Society and Black Revolution* (1972). Both *Where the Humming Bird Flies* (1961) and *On Leaving Paradise* (1980) focus on colonialism and Caribbean reactions to it. As with his non-fiction, his third novel, *I Want a Black Doll* (1967), also examines racism in the USA. Educated in Trinidad and England where he read law at Middle Temple, London, during the Second World War, he emigrated to the USA where he engaged in business, becoming a US citizen in 1959.

FUNSO AIYEJINA

Heredia, Alberto

b.1924, Buenos Aires, Argentina

Sculptor

Heredia studied ceramics and fine art in Buenos Aires. During the 1950s he came under the influence of Tomás **Maldonado** and produced abstract, geometrical works. In 1960 he moved to Madrid and came into contact with the Spanish informalist avant-garde and in Amsterdam with artists of the CoBrA group. His sculptures tend to use discarded materials and often contain sardonic and ironic references to political repression and national idols.

GABRIEL PEREZ-BARREIRO

Hermosilla Alvarez, Carlos

b. 1905, Valparaíso, Chile; d. 1991, Viña del Mar, Chile

Artist

Recognized as the founder of modern Chilean engraving, Hermosilla also taught lithography and drawing. In 1939 he founded the Taller de Artes Gráficas of the Escuela de Bellas Artes in Viña del Mar, where he taught engraving for forty-three years. Despite his handicap – he lost an arm and a leg in an accident – he created an impressive body of work, particularly a series of lithographic portraits of Chilean politicians, artists and writers. Widely exhibited, his work has also illustrated books by Chilean writers, including Pablo de **Rokha** and Pablo **Neruda**.

JUAN ARMANDO EPPLE

Hermosillo, Jaime Humberto

b. 1942, Aguascalientes, Mexico

Film-maker

A leading member of the new generation of directors that in the 1970s gave new impetus to the Mexican film industry. His initial films, made while he was still a student at Mexico's first film school, already expressed the concerns marking his later work: the breakdown of the middle class family, sexuality and morality. His first film, *Los nuestros* (Our People) (1969) was well received by the critics; his first feature was the comedy *La verdadera vocación de Magdalena* (Magdalena's True Vocation) (1971). *La pasión según Bernice* (The Passion According to Bernice) (1975) and *María de mi corazón* (Maria of my Heart) (1979) brought him recognition as an outstanding representative of Mexico's 'New Cinema Movement' promoted by Rodolfo Echeverría. From 1977 he made both commercial and independent films.

In 1984 Hermosillo moved to Guadalajara and made **Doña Herlinda y su hijo** (Herlinda and her Son) and *La tarea* (Homework) (1991), films that marked a new direction in his work. The latter was an ingenious and original narrative under sixty minutes, made on a single plane and in one long take which rejects montage and its fragmentation of time and space.

Hermosillo then moved to placing the camera as an extension of the spectator's eye. In *Intimidades de un cuarto de baño* (Bathroom Intimacies) (1989), it is the mirror reflecting the problems of four characters and the optimism of the fifth. In *La tarea* it is the all-seeing eye of the voyeur in the room. Camera and spectator are witnesses, authors and also characters in the film, since without them there could be no film. Through this new practice, Hermosillo proposed not just a new style but also an alternative method of low-cost production with minimal resources and short production schedules – a response to the limitations that the bureaucratic economic situation had begun to impose in the course of the 1980s.

Hermosillo's films betray the influence of playwright Eugene O'Neill and the pure and elliptical style of director George Cukor. Within Mexico, his work has provoked arguments and debates, notwithstanding its impact and recognition abroad. His most recent film, based on a work by Elena **Poniatowska**, is *De noche vienes* (You Come at Night) (1998).

Further reading

Noriega, C. and Ricci, S. (eds) (1994) *The Mexican Cinema Project*, Los Angeles: UCLA Film and Television Archive.

PATRICIA TORRES SAN MARTÍN

Hernández, Amalia

b. 1917, Mexico City

Choreographer

Mexico's most famous choreographer, teacher and promoter of folk dance, Hernández created the Ballet Moderno de México in 1952, now known as the **Ballet Folklórico de México**. It performs at Mexico City's Palacio de Bellas Artes (Palace of Fine Arts) and tours constantly. Hernández has choreographed over thirty pieces, each of which attempts to showcase examples of folk dances from Mexico's regions and indigenous cultures. Rather than stage authentic folk dances, she creates new artistic spectacles based on folklore. The theatrical aspect of her work was influenced by her studies with Seki Sano.

ANTONIO PRIETO-STAMBAUGH

Hernández, Carlos 'Morocho'

b. 1940, Caracas, Venezuela.

Boxer

Hernández was the first Venezuelan boxer to win a world title. Turning professional in 1959, he became renowned for his hard punch and won many of his contests by knockout. He became world junior welterweight champion in Caracas in January 1965, when he defeated the American Eddie Perkins on points. It made him a national idol, though he lost the title the following year. Although regarded by many as Venezuela's most accomplished and exciting boxer, his tempestuous lifestyle shortened his career. It ended in 1971, when he was defeated in London by Scotland's Ken Buchanan.

MARK DINNEEN

Hernández, Felisberto

b. 1902, Montevideo, Uruguay; d. 1964, Montevideo

Writer

Hernández has a unique place in Latin American fiction and his work defies categorization. His first two books bore titles that made a point of their anonymity: *Fulano de tal* (So and So) (1925) and *Libro sin tapas* (Book Without Covers) (1928). Hernández always enjoyed the admiration of a small and select group, thus sometimes he saw himself as an impostor; at other times he was bitterly ironic about the world's refusal to recognize him. This ambivalence was reflected in his themes. For many years, Hernández was read as the memorialist of a bucolic Montevideo, yet he was only really interested in memory as a mode of consciousness, alongside madness (a distracted consciousness) and identity (experiential consciousness). His style was distracted and concentrated and his syntax peculiar and idiosyncratic. A solitary pioneer, like the Argentine novelist with whom he is often compared, Roberto **Arlt**, recognition came only posthumously. Both writers exemplified the self-taught, struggling individual, incarnating the rising middle class, and shared an air of illusion and failure.

For more than a decade, Hernández was a concert pianist touring small rural towns, accompanying silent films and giving school recitals; sometimes he would follow the concert with talks on subjects like 'What artists do with feelings'. When he occasionally ran out of money on a tour he would sell the piano to get home. Hunger was an obsessive topic in his work; he wrote as if feeding on the past, with a hedonsim that invades memory and evokes the past. There are echoes in his work of the ideas of Carlos **Vaz Ferreira**, a Socratic figure whose discussion circles Hernández attended. Jules **Supervielle** stimulated, advised and admired him, helping him to find his own register somewhere between the symbolic and the allegorical. Hernández often visited his friend Alfredo Cáceres at Montevideo's Pilardevó psychiatric hospital, where he observed with aesthetic interest various cases of madness, which enabled him to use his writing to explore deviant behaviour. In this respect, as in his view of hunger, poverty and marginality, Hernández was a kind of residual positivist, although he only addressed questions of individual identity.

In his fifties, Hernández became a devotee of Western films. He lived on a meagre municipal wage earned doing trivial tasks, perfected his own shorthand system and participated in a virulent anti-communist radio campaign.

See also: Hortensias, Las

Further reading

Girladi del dei Cas, N. (1975) *Felisberto Hernández, del creador al hombre*, Montevideo: Ediciones Banda Oriental.

Hernández, F. (1967–74) *Obras completas*, Montevideo: Ed Arca, 6 vols.

Sicard, Alain (ed.) (1977) *Felisberto Hernández ante la crítica actual*, Caracas: Monte Avila.

SERGIO CHEFJEC

Hernández, José Gregorio

b. 1864, Isnotú, Venezuela; d. 1919, Caracas, Venezuela

Doctor and religious figure

Hernández's popular reputation in early twentieth-century Venezuela derived from his declared religious vocation and his devotion to practising medicine among the poor. His early death in a traffic accident in Caracas did not prevent him from becoming the object of popular devotion; he came to be seen as a saint protecting the poor and the sick, and his tomb became a place of popular pilgrimage. He is currently a candidate for canonization. Popular images of him depict him in a black suit and bowler hat or in his white medicine gown.

RAFAEL CASTILLO ZAPATA

Hernández, Juan José

b. 1932, Tucumán, Argentina

Writer

Hernández's writing includes poetry and prose, but his best work has been in the short story: *El inocente* (The Innocent) (1965), *La favorita* (The Favored Woman) (1977), and *La señorita Estrella y otros cuentos* (Miss Star and Other Stories) (1982). In 1971 he published his novel *La ciudad de los sueños* (The City of the Dreams). Unifying elements in his structurally complex fictions are provincial culture and the ambiguities of childhood. Hernández has won many prizes and has been recognized by the best writers of Latin American.

CRISTINA GUZZO

Hernández, Luisa Josefina

b. 1928, Mexico City

Playwright and novelist

A teacher and translator as well as a writer, Hernández has taught at the Theatre School of the Mexican Institute of Fine Arts and the National University of Mexico (**UNAM**). Her plays include *Aguardiente de caña* (Cane Liquor) (1951), *Los frutos caídos* (Fallen Fruit) (1955), *Los huéspedes reales* (The Royal Guests) (1958), *Los duendes* (The Spirits) (1963), *La paz ficticia* (The Fictional Peace), *Apócrifa* (Apocrypha) (1980) as well as translations of Shakespeare, Christopher Fry, Dylan Thomas and Jerzy Kawalerowicz. She has written novels, among them *La noche exquisita* (Exquisite Night) (1965) and *Nostalgia de Troya* (Nostalgia for Troy) (1970).

TITO VASCONCELOS

Hernández, Rafael

b. 1893, Aguadilla, Puerto Rico; d. 1965, San Juan, Puerto Rico

Musician and composer

Known as 'el jibarito' (the little peasant), Hernández was perhaps the greatest composer of popular music on Puerto Rico and a key figure in the development of popular music in Latin America. He founded and led the Trío Borinquen, later the Victoria Quartet. He lived in Cuba, Mexico and New York, but it was in Mexico that he and his group achieved the greatest success. He worked in various musical genres and his successes include 'Lamento borincano' (Puerto Rican Lament), '**Preciosa**' (Beautiful), 'Campanitas de cristal' (Glass Bells), 'Silencio' (Silence), 'Perfume de gardenias' and 'Cumbanchero'.

JUAN CARLOS QUINTERO HERENCIA

Hernández Moncada, Eduardo

b. 1899, Jalapa, Mexico; d. 1995, Mexico City

Musician

Conductor and composer of music for ballet, theatre and films including Emilio **Fernández**'s *Enamorada* (In Love) (1946), Hernández Moncada was invited in 1929 by Carlos **Chávez** to join the Mexico Symphony Orchestra and the National Conservatory. He directed the Opera Academy from 1947 to 1956, premiering works by Darius Milhaud and Debussy; he translated the librettos of Chávez's *Los visitadores* and Poulenc's *Dialogue des Carmélites*, conducting the latter's Mexican premiere in 1959. His compositions include an innovative First Symphony, an opera *Elena*, the piano piece 'Costeña' and a number of songs, including 'Tres sonetos de Sor Juana' (Three Sonnets by Sor Juana).

EDUARDO CONTRERAS SOTO

Hernández Núñez, Angela

b. 1960, Jarabacoa, Dominican Republic

Writer

Hernández Núñez appeared on the Dominican cultural scene with her 1980 essay *Emergencia del silencio* (Emerging from the Silence), which revealed her sympathy with the Pluralismo group's call for a literature distanced from its social function. Her poetry in *Tizne y Cristal* (Soot and Glass) (1987) and *Arce espejada* (1994) sustained that idea. *Masticar una rosa* (Chewing a Rose) (1993) completed her aesthetic project; this consists of brief stories paying homage to little people overwhelmed by the bustle of urban life and the hectic pace of modernization.

MARIA JULIA DAROQUI

Herrera, Carolina (María Carolina Josefina Pacanins y Niño)

b. 1941, Caracas, Venezuela

Fashion designer

A leading figure in the world of design, Carolina Herrera is known for her feminine, sophisticated and simple designs. Daughter of an old Venezuelan family, she was educated by a Hungarian governess at home; as part of her education her grandmother took the young Carolina to Parisian Couture shows. In 1981, she made her entry into the world of fashion; slowly, and conservatively, she built up her empire, helped tremendously by the success of her original fragrance, Carolina Herrera. Married at eighteen, she divorced seven years later and in 1968 married Reinaldo Herrera, special projects editor for *Vanity Fair*.

ISABEL BARBUZZA

Herrera, Darío

b. 1870, Panama City; d. 1914, Valparaiso, Chile

Writer

Herrera travelled to Buenos Aires in 1898 to associate with the great Modernist poet, Rubén Darío. He published work in *La nación* and *El Mercurio de América*. Poet, storyteller, essayist, chronicler, and literary critic, he is the best known modernist of Panama outside his native country, combining cosmopolitan flair with the modernist aesthetic. His work is known for its moderation, modesty, and a melancholy that avoids the overly dark and desperate. His best short stories were collected in *Horas lejanas* (Distant Hours) (1903), but most of his work remained unpublished.

NORMAN S. HOLLAND

Herrera Luque, Francisco

b. 1927, Caracas, Venezuela; d. 1990, Caracas

Psychiatrist, novelist, historian and essayist

In the early 1960s the first of his controversial writings on the psychology of the Venezuelan – *Los viajeros de Indias* (The Travellers to the Indies) – appeared, and from then on his essays and historical novels have figured consistently among the best selling works of national literature. A graduate in medicine from the Central University of Venezuela in 1953, he went on to study neuropsychiatry in Madrid. He taught for many years at the Central University, where he set up the School of Psychiatry. Later he was Venezuelan ambassador to Mexico.

JORGE ROMERO LEÓN

Hidalgo, Alberto

b. 1897, Arequipa, Peru; d. 1967, Buenos Aires, Argentina

Poet

Hidalgo was a pioneer of avant-garde (see **avant-garde in Latin America**) poetry, first in his native Peru and then in Buenos Aires, where he settled in 1919. His artistic credo, defined as *simplismo* (simplism) and expounded in the 1925 book of the same name, involved the reduction of poetry to its essentials. He was particularly innovative in his experiments in typographical arrangement, notably in the 1928 collection, *Descripción del cielo* (Description of Heaven).

JAMES HIGGINS

higher education

Public universities in Latin America have their roots in the colonial period, particularly in the Spanish colonial model of the Jesuit university. At the time of independence in the nineteenth century, the French Napoleonic model of the secular and modern university was the most influential. Later, the 1918 Córdoba (Argentina) Student Reform focused on university governance and autonomy, and this rapidly spread throughout Latin America. One of the main elements of this model of governance involved the representation of three key groups (professors, students and alumni) on the decision-making bodies of universities. Despite this change, Latin American public universities remained predominantly professional schools until the 1950s, with students choosing liberal professions, especially **law**, engineering and medicine, as their avenue to social, economic and political mobility.

Until the early 1970s, universities were small in size, the teaching staff was stable and the majority of the professors were part-time liberal professionals. With the exceptions of the University of Buenos Aires, the University of São Paulo, the National University (**UNAM**) in Mexico and the University of Chile, research was not one of the central missions of public universities. Among the most visible pressures that changed Latin American universities in the 1960s and 1970s were student movements actively involved in confrontations with military governments. In many cases these conflicts evolved into violent repression from military governments and **guerrilla warfare**.

Educational expansion in Latin America between 1960–70 accounts for the highest rates of educational growth in the world. During that decade, the rate of growth was 167.5 per cent for primary education, 247.9 per cent for secondary education and 258.3 per cent for higher education. Systems of higher education underwent a particularly accelerated expansion between the early 1950s and the economic crisis of the 1980s. Enrolments grew from approximately 270,000 students to more than 7 million; hence increasing the net enrolment rate for 18–24 year olds from less than 2 per cent in 1950 to almost 18 per cent in 1990. In 1950, the higher education enrolment rates for Argentina, Colombia, Chile and Mexico were 5.2 per cent, 1.0 per cent, 1.7 per cent and 1.5 per cent, respectively. By 1990, the rates had increased to 39.9 per cent in Argentina, 14.2 per cent in Colombia, 2.2 per cent in Chile and 14 per cent in Mexico. Among the reasons for this expansion were high rates of population growth, **urbanization**, the expansion of the middle classes, and the participation of women in the labour market and education. This creation of huge universities that gave access to a broader social spectrum has led to several notable trends: the growing participation of middle and lower classes (*mesocratización*), the feminization and terciarization of enrolments (more than 50 per cent of female enrolments concentrated in social sciences, education, nursing and so on), regionalization (institutions of higher education established outside metropolitan areas), and privatization (enrolment in private institutions is typically one-third of total enrolments).

During the early 1990s, the traditional social contract between public universities and the state was broken. Not surprisingly, public universities have suffered in the context of **structural adjustment** and neoliberal (see **neoliberalism**) economic frameworks. The autonomy of higher education has been affected by the process of globalization and changes in the institutional culture of universities which have been promoted by regulatory international institutions such as the World Bank. Recent debates about the role of higher education in Latin America centre on the problem of autonomy and the role of the state. Two state-induced models have emerged. On one hand, there is a model of governmental control by an interventionist state in which higher education is an homogeneous enterprise and governments have the responsibility of regulating and controlling all elements of the system, including admissions, curriculum, requirements for certification, personnel recruitment and quality of education. This model does not recognize that the organizational culture of higher education is loosely coordinated and multidimensional. In contrast, there is a model of state supervision that sets up evaluatory mechanisms for tighter control of higher education. This model recognizes the need for the state to establish basic functional parameters, but fundamental academic decision-making remains the responsibility of the individual institutions. Even so, there are still incentives which are used to control the effectiveness of resource allocation, research agendas and faculty productivity. Both of these models have encountered serious roadblocks because of the organizational culture of public universities and the long legacy of university autonomy in Latin America.

Higher education reforms in the region show strong parallels with the political–economic changes brought about by processes of economic restructuring and neoliberalism. Several attempts at democratic reform in higher education have been introduced, although they either suffer from over-reliance on market orientations or languish away without public funding. Worse yet, in some cases, universities have been subject to zealous government regulations which try to usurp university autonomy; in some cases too, universities have suffered systematic repression. All in all, no agenda for higher education reform has been advanced with the coherence, cost effectiveness, efficacy and political legitimacy necessary to overcome contemporary financial restraints, or with the essential elements which would allow universities to fulfil their mission of seriously addressing political democratization, social issues and concerns. Dilemmas, paradoxes and contradictions besiege the uncertain future of higher education in the region.

Further reading

Brunner, J.J. (1990) *Educación superior y ciencia: Chile en perspectiva internacional comparada*, Santiago, Chile: FLACSO, Documento de Trabajo 447.

Torres, C.A. (1990) *The Politics of Nonformal Education in Latin America*, New York: Praeger.

—— (1996) *Las Secretas Aventuras del Orden. Estado y Educación*, Buenos Aires: Miño y Davila Editores.

Torres, C.A. and Puiggrós, A. (eds) (1997) *Latin American Education: Comparative Perspectives*, Boulder, CO: Westview.

MARCELA MOLLIS AND CARLOS ALBERTO TORRES

Higuita, José René

b. 1966, Medellín, Colombia

Soccer player

A spectacular goalkeeper, and one of the first to play the ball outside the penalty area – which cost Colombia a goal and elimination from the 1990 World Cup. Born into a poor Medellín family, Higuita joined the town's Club Nacional in 1985; a year later he joined the national team. From childhood he had admired drug baron Pablo **Escobar**, though he claimed never to have been involved in the business. In 1994, he spent seven months in jail after he had negotiated the release of a kidnapped girl – which is against Colombian law. This kept him out of the 1994 World Cup finals.

ERIC WEIL

Hijo de hombre

Published in Buenos Aires in 1960 (rev. 1982), Augusto Roa Bastos's first novel, *Hijo de hombre* (Son of Man) won the **Losada** novel prize for the previous year. It has since become a recognized classic of Latin American literature. As in subsequent novels, in *Hijo de hombre* Roa Bastos scrutinizes intellectual (see **intellectuals**) commitment. The text of the novel is a found manuscript in which the military man Miguel Vera, its narrator and central character, tests himself as both storyteller and man of action; finding himself wanting in both respects he, apparently, commits suicide. The story he tells is thus one of betrayal. He fails as a narrator, for example, in comparison to Macario, the old **Guarani**-speaking peasant storyteller of his youthful days in the countryside. Having left the community for Asunción and become a man of the State, his representational skills betray him and his narrative becomes, he feels, inauthentic. Subsequently as a committed man of action, he cannot betray the State and class he now serves. Instead, in a drunken moment, he betrays his peasant companions. Through Vera the novel thus stages the relation of misunderstanding and conflict between State institutions — such as the Church and the military — and the '*pueblo*'. Indeed, the heroic acts of the latter serve as a critical counterpoint to the former. In this way the novel becomes a dense network of stories representing the violent effects of capitalist modernization (Macario, for example, dies with the arrival of the railway) as well as of cultures of resistance. Culminating with the **Chaco War** — in which all participate, nearly all die and from which very few benefit — *Hijo de hombre* also addresses the contradictory logics of sacrifice.

JOHN KRANIAUSKAS

Hijo Pródigo, El

El Hijo Pródigo appeared from 1943 to 1956. Its founding editor was Octavio Barreda, with Xavier **Villaurrutia** and Octavio **Paz** playing leading roles. A polemical publication in the tradition of *Contemporáneos*, it sought to bring current international ideas on literature and the arts to Mexico. Those writing for *El Hijo Pródigo* often felt that Mexico had become too isolated culturally after the revolution, and that its cultural development was thwarted by socialist realism and **populism**. (For instance, the art of Rufino **Tamayo** was defended in its pages against the charge that it was not as Mexican as the work of **Rivera**, **Orozco** and **Siqueiros**.) The magazine published translations of works by T.S. Eliot, Jean Giraudoux and many others, and works by Mexican writers including Rodolfo **Usigli**, Samuel **Ramos**, Ermilo Abreu Gómez, Antonio Castro Leal and Leopoldo **Zea**.

DANIEL BALDERSTON

Hill, Errol

b. 1922, Port of Spain, Trinidad

Dramatist

For Hill, theatre had a central role to play in the development of a national culture — and, in the case of Trinidad, that necessarily implied a marriage between theatre and **carnival**, the most important of indigenous performing arts. Hence his work with calypsonian **Mighty Sparrow** and choreographer Beryl **McBurnie**. His *Man Better Man* (1964) is built around the ritual of stick-fighting; its language, as in most of his plays, evokes the **calypso** form. His critical writings and essays express a lifelong dedication to the creation of a Caribbean theatrical tradition.

MIKE GONZALEZ

Hinduism

Trade with Asia and the exchange of missionaries ensured that Hinduism was known, and often persecuted, in New Spain. After 1838, the inter-colonial migration policy of the British Empire brought the first Hindu communities to the Caribbean. Rather than spreading their ideas or competing with other religious groups, Hinduism remained within these communities, adapting to local conditions and assimilating elements of other religions. Western versions of Hinduism gained acceptance in North America, where Indian communities have been growing since 1890. The extension of these currents into Latin America is evidenced in the proliferation of Hindu-inspired temples and religious sects throughout the continent from the 1970s onwards.

LUIS ESPARZA

Hinkson, 'Jackie' Donald

b.1942, Port-of-Spain, Trinidad

Painter

Hinkson's paintings are informed by a fascination with rural landscape, the architectural designs of the Port-of-Spain of the 1940s/50s, and the desire to combine realistic and impressionistic traditions. He advocates the impressionistic notion that objects seen in the open cease to have individual colours and become a series of tonal masses optically blended together. Having studied art in France and Canada, he taught art at his Alma Mater, Queen's Royal College, Port-of-Spain, until he retired to become a full-time artist in 1986.

FUNSO AIYEJINA

Hippolyte, Kendel

b. 1952, St Lucia

Writer and theatre director

Considered one of the outstanding popular Caribbean poets of his generation, Hippolyte's writings have appeared frequently in anthologies. Much of his early work employed the once-fashionable **nation language**. A graduate of the **University of the West Indies**, Hippolyte teaches literature and drama in Castries, St. Lucia. He has edited *Confluence: Nine Saint Lucian Poets* (1988) and *So Much Poetry in We People* (1990) – an anthology of performance poetry from the Eastern Caribbean. His own collections of poems include: *Island in the Sun – Side Two* (1980), *Bearings* (1986) and *The Labyrinth* (1993). In 1984 he co-founded The Lighthouse Theatre Company with his wife Jane **King**.

KEITH JARDIM

Hirszman, Leon

b. 1937, Rio de Janeiro, Brazil; d. 1987, Rio de Janeiro

Film-maker

A founder of Brazilian **Cinema Novo**, Hirszman came to film via the university film club circuit, theatre (he worked with Gianfrancesco **Guarnieri** and Oduvaldo **Vianna Filho** in the Teatro de Arena – see **Arena Theatre Group**) and the Center of Popular Culture (**CPC**). His first directing experience was the Pedreira de São Diogo episode of *Cinco vezes favela* (Five Times Shanty Town) (1962), a film produced by the CPC which also gave Carlos **Diegues** and Joaquim Pedro de **Andrade** their first directing opportunity. Hirszman's first feature film, *A Falecida* (The Dead Woman) (1965), was a powerful social criticism based on the eponymous work by Nelson **Rodrigues**. The script was co-written with Eduardo **Coutinho**, with whom he later formed Saga Filmes and planned his next film *Garota de Ipanema* (Girl from Ipanema) (1967) with Vinícius de **Moraes** and Glauber **Rocha**. His adaptation of Graciliano **Ramos**'s *São Bernardo* (1972) was a classic example of Brazilian critical realism. *Eles não usam black tie* (They Don't Wear Black Tie) (1979), winner of the Golden Lion at Venice, was adapted from a work by Guarnieri, written and set in 1958. In Hirszman's version, the action was transferred to the industrial suburbs of São Paulo known as ABC, where the strikes that marked the beginning of the end of the military dictatorship occurred. Hirszman tried to reconcile his characteristic harsh social realism with the conventions of mainstream cinema to make his work more accessible to popular audiences, an example of an articulation between documentary and narrative films. His work in documentary includes the documentary *ABC da greve* (ABC on Strike) (1998), one of several he made including musical documentary shorts like *Nelson Cavaquinho* (1969), *Partido alto* (1976) and *Imagens do inconsciente* (Images of the Unconscious) (1983/86), a three-film series recording and dramatizing the art work and therapeutic process of Fernando Diniz, Adelina Gomes and Carlos Pertius, three patients of the psychoanalyst Nise da Silveira at the Centro Psiquiátrico Dom Pedro II in Rio de Janeiro.

Further reading

Hirszman, L. (1995) *É bom falar*, Rio de Janeiro: Centro Cultural Banco do Brasil.

Salem, H. (1997) *Leon Hirszman: o navegador das estrelas*, Rio de Janeiro: Rocco.

ISMAIL XAVIER AND THE USP GROUP

Hispamérica: revista de literatura

Hispamérica: revista de literatura is an academic journal founded in 1972 by Saúl **Sosnowski**. It appears three times per year. *Hispamérica* took advantage of the enormous interest in Latin American literature in the 1960s and the early 1970s to establish a dialogue between North American Latin Americanists and Latin American intellectuals. The journal focuses primarily upon twentieth-century literature, and each issue also contains poetry and fiction, occasional dramatic texts by well-known writers, interviews with important figures and reviews. Although the content is heavily Argentine–Uruguayan, the journal continues to be one of the best in the field of Latin American literary and cultural studies.

DAVID WILLIAM FOSTER

Hispanic American Historical Review

The oldest US journal focusing on Latin American history, published regularly since 1918 except for a two-year hiatus between 1923 and 1925. Thematic and bibliographical essays are followed by book reviews, professional reports, interviews, and obituaries. It includes articles in English and Spanish. It is indexed in *Hispanic American Periodicals Index*.

PAUL BARY

Hispanic cinema in Hollywood

After the coming of sound (*c.* 1927) the Hollywood industry had to deal with the problem of the sudden linguistic unintelligibility of its films in order to retain its dominance in foreign markets, among which the Spanish-language one was the most financially significant. Because at first dubbing was technically impossible and subtitling was cumbersome, the majors established a system to produce what were called 'multiple language versions' – different production teams would use the same sets and stages to film different versions in various languages – which was implemented roughly until 1931. Paramount even went so far as to establish a special studio in Joinville, outside Paris, with six sound stages, a $10 million annual budget and the goal of producing sixty films in fourteen languages annually.

In Latin America, neither audiences nor critics received these Hollywood 'Hispanic' films favourably. Exhibiting a total lack of cultural sensitivity, the films typically combined actors from throughout the Spanish-speaking world, mixing accents indiscriminately and appealing to bastardized forms of national folklore. Furthermore, audiences were interested in watching 'real' Hollywood stars, rather than Latin American or peninsular unknowns.

However, the Hispanic film experience did have a significant impact upon Latin American cinema at various levels. First of all, it served as a training ground for a number of future directors, producers and actors, who, upon returning to Latin America, played important roles in the establishment of national cinemas. For example, many important figures in the Mexican cinema had Hispanic experience, among them, Emilio **Fernández**, Julián Soler, Arcady **Boytler**, José **Bohr**, Tito **Davison** and even Luis **Buñuel**. Furthermore, because of their generally negative reception, the Hispanic films also inaugurated a significant public debate about the relationship between Latin American and national cultures, and the alleged universality of the Hollywood cinema. This debate eventually culminated in the conclusion that each nation should have its own national cinema in order to guarantee the authenticity of its representation; a belief that legitimized the efforts of many to do so throughout the 1930s. Lastly, although the actors of the Hispanic films could not compete with the Hollywood star system, it did produce and/or exploit several memorable stars, whose appeal seemed to extend beyond national borders: the Mexican actress Rosita Moreno, the Argentine Mona Maris and above all, Carlos **Gardel**, whose eight films for Paramount in

Joinville and New York were extraordinarily successful worldwide.

Further reading

Curubeto, D. (1993) *Babilonia Gaucha*, Buenos Aires: Sudamericana.

Durovicova, N. (1992) 'Translating America: The Hollywood multilinguals 1929–1933', in R. Altman (ed.), *Sound Theory, Sound Practice*, New York: Routledge, pp. 138–53.

García Riera, E. (1987–90) *Mexico visto por el cine extranjero*, 6 vols, Mexico City/Guadalajara: Era/CIEC.

Woll, A. (1980) *The Latin Image in American Film*, Los Angeles: UCLA Latin American Series.

ANA M. LÓPEZ

historia oficial, La

Directed by Luis **Puenzo**, written by Aída **Bortnik**, and starring Norma **Aleandro**, Héctor **Alterio**, Chunchuna Villafañe, María Luisa Robledo and Jorge Petraglia, *La historia oficial* (The Official Version) (1985) is the only Argentine film to win an Oscar for best foreign film. *La historia oficial* is the paradigmatic film of the first period of democracy in Argentina, concerned to reflect upon the military dictatorship not so much as a fierce repressive machine but in terms of the effects that this machine produced in people. It tells the story of Alicia (Aleandro), an uncommitted and elegant teacher of Argentine history who passes from ignorance and indifference to an understanding that the daughter she thought was adopted is in fact a child of **disappeared** parents; so that she too is a victim of repression. As the film progresses, she also discovers that her husband (Alterio), a man of influence about whom she knows very little, has been an active participant in the repression.

Constructed in a slow crescendo, the story develops through a process of investigation that leads the protagonist from ignorance to knowledge. Employing her skill as a historical researcher, the respectable teacher who at the beginning is disconcerted by the fragments of reality that her pupils' newspaper cuttings bring her, explores files and hospital wards, inspects the girl's clothes and eventually deconstructs the official version of history presented by her husband. In the course of the narrative, the iconography of Alicia changes like the story she is taking apart; the elegant bourgeois lady becomes a combative woman, uncovering identities and rediscovering origins, a process underscored by continual close-ups.

Camila, the other major film of this period, rested on the genres of tragedy and melodrama to sustain its narrative; *La historia oficial* refers back to the thriller, and the hermeneutics of searching and discovery. In the films, it is women who conduct the search, breaking with the hegemonic order which expects them to be passive, inert and silent. The icon of *Camila* is the suffering body, repressed and sacrificed; in *La historia oficial* it is the mothers and grandmothers who continue as the incarnation of resistance, denunciation and the struggle for memory and truth.

In addition to the 1986 Oscar, the film received prizes at Cartagena, Cannes and Havana in 1985.

DIEGO BENTIVEGNA

historic centres

Historic centres depict original city locations, their development, and testify to their architectural past. Historic centres are located in metropolitan areas such as Mexico, Santo Domingo, Havana, Quito or San Juan in Puerto Rico; or in regional cities such as Santiago de Cuba, Cartagena, Arequipa, Puebla, Salta and Salvador. They are either national or state capitals, and comprise administrative, political, cultural and commercial activities. Historic centres include cities that were also relevant centres of the past. Such cities include, among many others, Guanajato and Querétaro (Mexico), Cajamarca (Peru), Potosí (Bolivia), Antigua (Guatemala), Portobelo (Panama) and Ouro Preto (Brazil). Additionally, smaller cities are also included such as: Tiradentes and São João del Rei in Brazil; Ollantaytambo and Chinchero in Peru; and the urban and architectural patrimonies of Mompox in Colombia, and Jajo in Venezuela.

Because the conquerors settled near indigenous populations, these cities often reflected the history and memory of pre-Hispanic culture. Historic centres are relevant due to the organizational grid typology of the Spanish colonial settlement which designated the Plaza Mayor or central square as a nucleus for administrative and religious architecture. Consequently, street patterns emphasized the power which radiated from these centres; they still reflect the original settlement, and offer a sense of identity to regional inhabitants.

Mexico City and Cuzco in Peru illustrate the pragmatic and symbolic reasoning which guided the Spanish. They followed the original urban schemes and land use patterns of the existing Aztec and Inca settlements. Although many pre-Hispanic ceremonial centres were destroyed, major road patterns and urban contours were preserved. After the 1950s, cities such as Buenos Aires, Bogotá, Caracas, Mexico and Rio de Janeiro were radically transformed, yet still retained isolated colonial buildings, groupings of nineteenth-century structures, and areas with early twentieth-century urban characteristics. Many historic centres still maintain institutional buildings like the *cabildo* (town council), major religious monuments, and governmental and private palaces. Private use patterns, which now devote the ground floors to commerce and upper levels to offices, have changed, while the affluent society has relocated. The combination of changing urban patterns and attempts to solve transportation problems have resulted in the alteration and destruction of areas of urban fabric and architectural patrimonies. A few cities, such as Puebla, Salvador and Arequipa, have maintained their rich urban heritage, while smaller cities, such as Ouro Preto or Pátzcuaro, have seemingly remained frozen in time. Most historic centres have been affected by twentieth-century transformations. San Juan, Puerto Rico, represents one of the first successful attempts to restore a historic centre. Since the 1980s, the importance of urban and architectural heritage has prompted recommendations and actions which preserve and revitalize historic centres.

Most specialists agree that interventions into the historic centre should focus on preserving architecture which represents urban evolution and transformation instead of interventions targeting only select historical periods; preserving the entire centre rather than just isolated buildings; involving the public and private sector, not only to restore facades and interiors, but also to integrate operational, cultural, economical and environmental aspects of the entire centre; considering, not only **tourism**, but the inhabitants' overall quality of life; and finally, controlling unsupervised construction of new materials, while promoting knowledge of cultural patrimony.

Salvador in Bahia, Brazil, exemplifies the problems confronting historic centres. It was founded by the Portuguese in 1549 on the Bay of All Saints. A myriad of narrow sweeping streets created a unique network of monuments, block houses and open spaces which offer spectacular vistas of the bay. Salvador was the colony's capital from 1554 to 1763. Although the capital was relocated to Rio de Janeiro, the city remained prosperous. The historic centre exhibits a blend of Portuguese, African and indigenous flavour and local houses accented by elaborate mouldings and homogeneous stucco finishes. The centre is also enriched by the presence of monasteries and churches renowned for their seventeenth-century gold engravings and forceful baroque sculptures. During the twentieth century, the affluent society relocated to the urban periphery. Population migration and the city centre's growing numbers of poor created a desire to move the administrative core outside the traditional centre. Since the 1960s, a series of measures have been implemented to promote tourism; however, no attention was given to supporting services for the existing population. Salvador typifies problems which result from restoration policies that isolate historic centres for purposes of tourism only.

The rehabilitation of the historic centre of Córdoba, Argentina, implemented in 1979–80 by Miguel Angel **Roca**, was continued by subsequent administrations and is ongoing today. It exemplifies a policy which utilizes the centre's multi-functional capacity while creating a dynamic, complementary relationship to the city's periphery. This strategy emphasizes a need to preserve and restore existing monuments, buildings and zones, while developing health, educational and cultural facilities. The design team responsible for revitalizing the historic centre purposely wanted to mirror their time. Instead of reviving the past, they employed available modern technology, materials and a contemporary architectural language.

Further reading

'Latin American cities' (1997) *OWHC (Organization of World Heritage Cities) Newsletter* 9 (January).
World Heritage List (1999) New York: UNESCO.

See also: urbanization

JOSÉ BERNARDI

historiography

A history is a constructed narrative that seeks to illuminate the unfolding and interdependence of events; historiography is the study and criticism of the sources and their analysis, and the development of history as a branch of knowledge. Historiography questions the role of the historian, the methodology and interpretative frameworks utilized by the historians and analyses contemporary schools of thought or conflicting views of historians regarding central events. Historiography tracks additions and progress in the overall field.

Contemporary Latin American historiography dates from the nineteenth century. The new independent republics sought to define their identity and shape the future course of their nations by analysing the social and economic impact and legacy of 250 years of colonial status. In addition, during this period, major collections of documents were selected, organized and indexed. For most of the first half of the twentieth century, historiography was characterized by political and institutional histories. These works laid the foundation for inquiry in the field. Generally they were broad in scope and heavily dependent upon official State and ecclesiastical records. Beginning in the 1970s, influenced by trends in European history, especially the French Annales school, historians of Latin America became more interested in social, demographic, labour and economic history, especially regional and microstudies. These works can be seen as an attempt to flesh out or colour in the broad lines drawn by the previous generation of political historians.

Also during this same era, ethnohistory established a secure foothold in the historiography as scholars, trained in native languages and influenced by anthropology, turned to indigenous sources to counter and/or enhance histories that had been based upon traditional Spanish ones. This would spearhead inquiry into the lives and contributions of other ethnic minorities such as Africans. The growth in ethnohistory and social history has also generated scholarly interest in gender issues and family life. Latin American cultural history, first on the scene in the late 1980s, is a natural outgrowth of Latin American social and ethnohistory as it attempts to analyse such issues as identity, nationalism, ethnic and power relations, etc. through cultural forms and production, and their evolution through time.

See also: Galeano, Eduardo Hughes; Halperin Donghi, Tulio; Buarque de Holanda, Sérgio; Rama, Carlos; Picón Salas, Mariano; Zea, Leopoldo

LINDA A. CURCIO-NAGY

Hlito, Alfredo

b. 1923, Buenos Aires, Argentina; d. 1993, Buenos Aires

Painter

Hlito's friendship with Tomás **Maldonado** led them to co-found in 1945–6 the Asociación de Arte Concreto-Invención. Hlito trained at the Escuela Nacional de Bellas Artes in Buenos Aires from 1938 to 1942 and his first works (*c.*1940) show a stylistic debt to Joaquín **Torres García**. The paintings of his Concrete Art period (1945–54) are composed according to strict geometrical rules. From the mid-1950s to his death, his style was lyrical and painterly, leaving behind the austere geometry of his earlier work.

GABRIEL PEREZ-BARREIRO

Hodge, Merle

b. 1944, Calcutta Settlement, Trinidad

Fiction writer and essayist

One of the Caribbean's best known Anglophone

women writers, her first novel *Crick, Crack Monkey* (1970), explores the clash of cultural values in the upbringing of young girl in Trinidad; her second, *The Life of Laetitia* (1993), presents these conflicts through the eyes of Laetitia and her Indian friend Anjanee. Hodge is well known for her essays on the condition of the Caribbean, especially in relation to women's roles, and for her extensive writing on the importance of **creole** for the Caribbean person. Widely travelled, she always returns to Trinidad to write and teach.

GAY WILENTZ

Hogar, El

A family magazine founded in Buenos Aires in 1904, *El Hogar* (The Home) included helpful information for housewives, copious advertisements on fashion and style, and articles on famous people, literature, sports, etc. Moralizing in tone, the editorial comments were quite out of synch with the contents of the magazine. In the 1920s, Horacio **Quiroga** published some of his most famous texts there, including his 'Decálogo del perfecto cuentista' (Ten Commandments for the Perfect Short Story Writer) (1927). Roberto **Arlt**, Ezequiel **Martínez Estrada**, José **Bianco** and Enrique **Amorim** frequently published work in the magazine (Amorim with a column on cinema). **Borges** published a whole page every two weeks (every other issue) from 1936 to 1939 on foreign literatures; these columns have been partially collected in *Textos cautivos* (Captive Texts) (1986) by Emir **Rodríguez Monegal** and Enrique Sacerio-Garí, with an ample selection in Eliot Weinberger's edition of Borges's *Selected Non-Fiction* (1999).

DANIEL BALDERSTON

Hogar Obrero, El

One of the landmarks of the co-operative movement in Latin America, founded by the Socialist Party in Argentina on 30 July 1905, under the leadership of Juan B. **Justo**, a physician, writer, member of parliament and founder of the socialist movement in Argentina. El Hogar Obrero was the second foundation of socialism after the newspaper *La vanguardia*, founded in 1894. The co-operative provided low-cost housing and co-operative supermarket facilities. The organization grew as a popular savings bank through the twentieth century, in spite of military regimes. It foundered during a constitutional government when, in 1988, hyperinflation forced its collapse. In spite of tax office and judicial investigations, El Hogar Obrero's failure was not attributed to fraud but to mismanagement in conditions of raging inflation. The sale of its properties during bankruptcy proceedings allowed the management to refund its more than 100,000 account holders.

ANDREW GRAHAM-YOOLL

Holder, Boscoe

b. 1922, Port-of-Spain, Trinidad

Visual artist and dancer

The versatile Holder has made multifaceted contributions to the culture of Trinidad and Tobago. In the 1940s he researched into Caribbean dance forms, forming a dance group, originally with Beryl **McBurnie**, producing shows in which he was choreographer, costume designer, dancer and pianist. His internationally acclaimed painting, in both oils and acrylic, focuses on the Caribbean. While his interest in depicting the landscape revived in the 1990s, Holder's dynamic representations of West Indian people reveal explicitly his love of dance in their exuberant grace and beauty.

JILL E. ALBADA-JELGERSMA

Holder, Geoffrey

b. 1930, Port-of-Spain, Trinidad

Actor, dancer and choreographer

Probably most recognized as the 7-Up 'Uncola man', Holder has had a long and varied career as an actor, appearing in movies from *Dr Dolittle* (1967) to the Bond film, *Live and Let Die* (1973), to the Eddie Murphy film, *Boomerang* (1992). He won two 1975 Tony awards as director and costume designer for the Broadway musical, *The Wiz*. His deep, distinctive voice has won him Clio Awards for his work in television commercials, and he performed a song from the animated film, *The Little Mermaid* (1989), at the 1990 Academy Awards. Along with his wife, Carmen de Lavallade, Holder has also had a distinguished career as a dancer and choreographer, having worked with the noted Alvin Ailey American Dance Theater, the Dance Theater of Harlem and the Metropolitan Opera of New York. In addition, he is an artist and recipient of a prestigious Guggenheim Fellowship in art.

CAROL J. WALLACE

Holguín, Grishka

b. 1922, Mexico City

Dancer and choreographer

Holguín introduced the principles of modern dance to Venezuela. He trained in the US and Mexico, where he worked under eminent teachers like Guillermina Bravo and met Conchita Crededio, who became his companion in both art and life. Together they formed the Venezuelan School of Contemporary Dance. Although not well understood at the time, their work was supported by intellectuals and by 1959 they had choreographed seventeen new pieces. After separating from Crededio, Holguín established the Fundación de Danza Contemporánea (Contemporary Dance Foundation) with Sonia **Sanoja** in 1961. This lasted for eight years until the National Cultural Institute decided to fuse classical and modern dance in the Compañía Nacional de Danza under Holguín. In 1981, the Central University of Venezuela named him Director of its Dance Workshop and he created the Pisorrojo company. His choreography is marked by its theatricality and its concern for the ethnic as in his versions of *Medea*, *Hiroshima* and *Blancos inquietantes* (Disturbing Whites) among others. He retired to a town in the Venezuelan Andes.

TERESA ALVARENGA

Hollywood's impact on Latin American cinema

Hollywood acquired its hegemony over international markets, including Latin America, before and during the First World War; having saturated its domestic market, which more than amortized production costs, it sought international markets with a vengeance, tailoring its pricing structure and establishing new distribution practices. During the First World War, the major studios took advantage of the temporary halt in European production to take over the markets that Europeans had previously dominated, including Latin America. The sudden arrival of Hollywood subsidiaries in Brazil, for example, is cited as the principal reason for the demise of indigenous production known as the Bela Epoca.

The presence of Hollywood in Latin America was keenly felt throughout the 1920s, especially in the **film exhibition** and **film distribution** sectors. Beyond purely financial and importation deals (including many Latin American actors and actresses, like Dolores **Del Rio** and, later, Pedro **Armendáriz**, Arturo de Córdova and many others), the Hollywood studios also established a firm connection with the US State Department that allowed it to wield extraordinary diplomatic clout. In 1922, the US studios established the Motion Pictures Producers and Distributors of America (MPPDA), a trade association representing the industry's trade interests abroad. The MPPDA and its offshoot since the Second World War, the Motion Picture Export Association of America (MPEAA), act as a legal cartel for foreign trade and have successfully negotiated with foreign governments to fight quota legislations curtailing the presence of Hollywood films. Furthermore, the US government has fully backed their endeavours, either via the Motion Picture Division of the Department of Commerce (established in 1929) or directly via the State Department. Jack Valente, head of the MPEAA since the 1940s, endearingly dubbed the agency 'the little State Department' because of its close alliances with US policy and ideology.

These alliances were more than strengthened during and after the Second World War, when the government saw Hollywood films as propaganda for democracy and 'the American way of life', and facilitated film exports. The Hollywood cinema was then perceived as an extraordinarily valuable weapon to maintain the political alliances of the USA's South American 'neighbours' and their profitable markets. Reviving the dormant 'Good Neighbour Policy', the State Department created the Office of the Co-ordinator of Inter-American Affairs (OCIAA) with a $20 million budget in 1940 to combat pro-Axis sentiment in Latin America, and its Motion Picture division worked with Hollywood producers to ensure the production of films with Latin American themes, locations, rhythms and talent.

This was also the first time that Hollywood interests were able to interfere directly in Latin American film production. The first move was to manipulate raw film stock quota allowances, thus shifting the balance of power between the suddenly cursed Argentine industry (which, as a non-aligned nation suspected of pro-Axis sentiments, was allotted only enough raw film stock for twenty-four films, less than half of what it had previously been able to produce) and a blessed Mexican one. A second initiative was to offer technical and financial assistance to certain regional interests, like RKO's participation in the founding of the **Churubusco Studios** in Mexico City. A third involved facilitating the distribution of US **newsreels** to compete with regional products, in many cases the only regular cinematographic activity in smaller nations. Finally, OCIAA was also systematically opposed to any kind of protective legislation like screen quotas and the development of alternative distribution networks in 16 mm.

Exaltations of Pan-Americanism proliferated in both Latin American and US films: in Mexico, *La liga de las canciones* (The League of Songs, Chano Urueta, 1941); in Argentina, *Melodías de América* (American Melodies, Eduardo Morera, 1942); and, in the USA, the series of extraordinary films featuring Carmen **Miranda**, the Disney cartoon characters, Panchito and Zé Carioca in *Saludos Amigos* (1943) and *The Three Caballeros* (1944); and Orson Welles's aborted docu-drama, *It's All True*.

Although in the 1950s Hollywood's interest shifted back to Europe, the alliance between the MPEAA and the State Department continues to date. For example, in 1970–1, the MPEAA collaborated with the USA's efforts to undermine **Allende**'s **Popular Unity** government by participating in an 'invisible blockade'. The majors stopped shipping prints and demanded advance payments on rentals, which effectively eliminated Hollywood films from Chilean screens, further discredited the regime and increased popular dissatisfaction. However, **ICAIC** in Cuba, which cannot legally import US films because of the trade embargo, has systematically exploited donated and black-market prints despite MPEAA protests.

In the late 1990s globalized climate, Hollywood is far more interested in co-opting Latin American talent than interfering with the halting advances of national cinematographies. As always, Mexico has proven a fertile field, providing Hollywood with the ripe talents of, among many others, actress Selma Hayek and directors Guillermo **del Toro** and Alfonso **Arau**. With shooting typically taking place further and further away from 'Hollywood' and financial interest in production becoming increasingly global it has become very difficult to pinpoint 'Hollywood' in terms other than budget size; this may become, in the 2000s, the ultimate discriminating factor between 'Hollywood' and other national cinemas.

Further reading

De Usabel, G.S. (1982) *The High Noon of American Films in Latin America*, Ann Arbor, MI: UMI Research Press.

Fein, S. (1998) 'Transnationalization and cultural collaboration: Mexican film propaganda during World War II', in A. López (ed.), *Popular Cinemas/Popular Cultures, Studies in Latin American Popular Culture* 17: 105–28.

López, A. (1994) 'A cinema for the continent', in C. Noriega and S. Ricci (eds), *The Mexican Cinema Project*, Los Angeles: UCLA Film Archives, pp. 7–12.

Thompson, K. (1985) *Exporting Entertainment: America in the World Film Market, 1907–1934*, London: BFI.

ANA M. LÓPEZ

Holst, Gilda

b. 1952, Guayaquil, Ecuador

Writer

Holst was one of an outstanding group of women writers appearing on Guayaquil's literary scene in the 1980s, many of them the product of the literary workshop directed by Miguel **Donoso Pareja**. Collectively, their work emphasized the conflicts between reality and desire, a sense of alienation and the plight of being female in a society intolerant of deviations from expected behavioural norms. Holst's stories are illustrative, exploring the question of literal and metaphorical power, authority and transgression, gender inequality and the lack of tenderness. Holst has published *Más sin nombre que nunca* (More Nameless Than Ever) (1989), and *Turba de signos* (A Mass of Signs) (1995).

MERCEDES ROBLES

Holy Week

Holy Week or *Semana Santa* celebrates the Christian holiday of Easter. It is Latin America's second most important holiday after Christmas and runs from Palm Sunday to Easter Sunday. Traditional Easter observances date back to the time of the Spanish Conquest or early colonial period when live representations and dramatizations were used to instruct Christian doctrine. In some regions, these practices have mixed with traditions from the pre-Columbian era, demonstrating the synthesis of indigenous and European cultures in Latin America.

Each Latin American community celebrates the holiday with its own regional flavour, but the majority of Latin Americans attend mass on Good Friday and Easter Sunday. During Easter Week, the entire Passion Play is re-enacted, beginning with the Last Supper, through the Betrayal, Crucifixion and Resurrection. Some re-enactments even include flagellation. The Passion Play is sponsored by religious or community groups called **cofradías** (confraternities) and includes large processions of *penitentes* (penitents). In many cities, important religious images from the Church are displayed, and traditional altars, flower decorations and palm crosses can be found in homes and in the streets. On Holy Saturday (the day before Easter Sunday), after evening mass, brightly coloured *papier mâché* figures representing Judas Iscariot, the devil or even unpopular politicians are ignited and destroyed with fireworks, representing the triumph of good over evil.

Throughout Latin America, Easter traditions combine with pre-Hispanic indigenous cultures. In Mexico, the Tarahumara (an indigenous people of the Sierra Madre Occidental) erect arches of flowers and branches, and the *pascola* dancer performs traditional dances to the music of flutes and drums while prayers are chanted and copal incense burned. In San Cristóbal de las Casas (state of Chiapas, Mexico), Indians of Mayan descent hold celebrations with parades and processions. The old silver town of Taxco has a famous procession that winds its way up its steep streets. Most of Latin America celebrates *Semana Santa*, but certain cities and villages are better known for celebrating the holiday, including Ixtapalapa, San Cristóbal de las Casas and Taxco in Mexico, Popayán in Colombia, and Cusco and Tarma in Peru.

Further reading

Damen, F. and Zanon, E. (eds) (1992) *Cristo crucificado en los pueblos de América Latina: Antología de la religión popular*, Quito, Ecuador: Ediciones Abya-Yala.

Kennedy, J. (1981) *Semana Santa in the Sierra Tarahumara: A Comparative Study in Three Communities*, Los Angeles: Museum of Cultural History, University of California.

MARCIE D. RINKA

Holzmann, Rodolfo

b. 1910, Breslau, Germany; d. 1992, Lima, Peru

Ethnomusicologist and composer

Holzmann's dedication to the study of Peruvian music has strongly influenced composers of that country. His wide-ranging scholarly work includes the folk melody collection, *Panorama de la Música Tradicional del Perú* (1966), one of the most important publications of this type, and the preparation of systematic catalogues of the works of six twentieth-century Peruvian composers. Holzmann's work as a composer also reflects a dominant interest in Peru, as evidenced in his orchestral suites embedded with Peruvian melodies, like *Suite arequipeña* (Arequipa Suite) (1945) and *Pequeña Suite Peruana* (Little Peruvian Suite) (1948). Among his most noteworthy compositions is the powerful *Dodedicata* (1966), a stark, serial piece.

EDUARDO GUÍZAR-ALVAREZ

Homar, Lorenzo

b. 1913, San Juan, Puerto Rico

Graphic artist

Considered the father of the Puerto Rican poster, Homar's vast and varied work also includes drawings, murals, engravings, illustrations and set designs. When he was fifteen, his family moved to New York in search of prosperity. Unable to study engineering because of the Depression, he began working at a colour-printed textiles warehouse to help his family. In 1937, he joined Cartier as an apprentice under the guidance of French designer Maurice Daudier, learning engraving and design. Eventually, he worked as a jewellery designer.

During the Second World War, Homar served in the US Army. Many of his war-themed drawings and caricatures appeared in US publications and in the Puerto Rican newspaper **El Mundo**. After the war he went back to work as jewellery designer for Cartier, and studied at the Brooklyn Museum's School of Art. He returned to Puerto Rico in 1950, after several exhibitions in US museums and galleries, and decided to dedicate himself principally to the graphic arts.

Homar was appointed director of the Taller de Gráfica (Graphic Arts Workshop) of the Division of Community Education, a governmental agency annexed to Puerto Rico's Department of Public Instruction. In 1956, he moved to New York with a scholarship from the Guggenheim Foundation. Upon his return to Puerto Rico in 1957, he organized and directed the Graphic Arts Workshop of the Institute of Puerto Rican Culture until 1973, when he started his own workshop.

Homar has participated in innumerable expositions and has taught renowned Puerto Rican artists such as Myrna Báez, Antonio Martorell and Francisco **Rodón**. His works are featured in many museums including New York's Museum of Modern Art, the Metropolitan Museum and the Library of Congress. Homar's work expresses a genuine concern for the preservation of Puerto Rican folklore and historical values and also tackles the island's social problems. Among Homar's most significant contributions to the poster arts are his harmonic integration of text and image, his treatment of the poster as having the same artistic value as a canvas, and his experimentation with new materials that do not deteriorate as quickly as paper.

Further reading

Cupeles, J. (1992) *Lorenzo Homar. Artista ejemplar de la gráfica contemporánea de Puerto Rico*, San Juan: J.D. Cupeles.

ROBERTO CARLOS ORTIZ

Homines

Homines is a journal published by Inter-American University of Puerto Rico. Founded in 1977, it was initially devoted exclusively to the social sciences but later developed into a multidisciplinary journal. It enjoys a solid reputation, ranking among the best and most enduring journals published in Puerto Rico. Under the guidance of its director and editor, Aline Frambes-Buxeda, it has provided a forum for scholarly discussion, focusing primarily on Puerto Rican and Caribbean issues and creative arts. Its collaborators have included the island's most distinguished scholars and artists as well as intellectuals from Latin America and the Caribbean.

VÍCTOR F. TORRES ORTIZ

Honduras

Honduras has lived out its modern history under the shadow of a contemptuous sobriquet – as the original 'banana republic'; but its real meaning points not to comic-opera stereotypes, but to tragedy. As the twentieth century unfolded, Honduras found itself increasingly at the mercy of foreign banana companies; as the century came to its close, once again external forces have played out their conflicts and ambitions at the expense of its population. Honduras reached the millennium with 70 per cent of its population living in poverty, and 50 per cent surviving in what the United Nations acknowledge as the direst misery. In late 1997, a column of Lencas, the indigenous Indian peoples of Honduras, marched to the capital Tegucigalpa to protest the invasion of ancestral lands. Nearly 500 years earlier they had fought the colonizing Spaniards under their leader, Lempira (whose name is now commemorated in the national currency).

The late nineteenth-century coffee boom transformed the rest of Central America, but in Honduras a weak State and entrenched regional interests inhibited development and it was unable to resist the encroachment of the United Fruit Company twenty years later. By 1910, 80 per cent of banana land was in the hands of US companies whose surrogates in government ensured relief from taxes and the provision of cheap labour. When the banana workers organized to resist, the dictator Carias worked with the companies to break the strike. When a more successful action in 1954 led to union recognition, the union leaders were given free access to the companies' purse. Yet the early 1960s saw the beginnings of a modernizing agrarian reform and the growth of militant peasant organization. The López Arellano government crushed the movement, but carried forward a programme of industrialization under US guidance. The failures of reform led to the 'football war' of 1969 in which that failure was blamed on the neighbouring El Salvador – though both processes were moved by forces external to the region. Discontent and unrest deepened into the 1970s and reform measures were an attempt to behead the movement. But events in Nicaragua after 1979 would shape Honduran social life through the last twenty years of the century. For the USA organized its military assault on Sandinista (see **Sandinista Revolution**) Nicaragua from Honduran territory; arms poured in and corruption spread through a military now under Washington's protection. There was resistance – but it was easily crushed. In the aftermath of the contra war (see **contras**), the impact of its role in US regional strategy may be seen in the destruction of agricultural land, the growth of the drug and prostitution trades, and the sabotage of an incomplete project for reform that left Honduras so weak and vulnerable that Hurricane Mitch completed in 1999 what a century of external involvement had already begun.

The historical experience of exploitation has informed a body of socialist realist writing represented by the work of Ramón Amaya Amador, whose famous *Prisión verde* (Green Prison) (1950) drew on his own experiences of fighting the banana companies. More recent prose writers, like Julio Escoto for example, have offered their view in more oblique ways, often influenced by the techniques of **magical realism**. Among the recent generations of poets, Roberto **Sosa** is outstanding; his *Obras* (Works) (1993) are imbued with a sense of injustice and sorrow. An earlier and neglected writer, Clementina **Suárez** (1902–91), was ahead of her time in form and her themes of liberated desire.

Further reading

Lapper, R. and Painter, J. (1985) *Honduras: State for Sale*, London: Latin America Bureau.

Norsworthy, K. and Barry, T. (1993) *Honduras*, Albuquerque, NM; Interhemispheric Education Resource Center.

Schulz, D.E. and Sundloff Schulz, D. (1994) *The United States, Honduras and the Crisis in Central America*, Boulder, CO: Westview Press.

Valle, R.H. (1981) *Historia de la cultura hondureña*, Tegucigalpa: Universidad Nacional Autónoma de Honduras.

MIKE GONZALEZ

Hoogesteijn, Solveig

b. 1943, Stockholm, Sweden

Film-maker

Raised in Venezuela, Hoogesteijn studied cinema production in Germany in the mid-1970s, before returning to Venezuela to begin her career as a film director at the end of the decade. Her films highlight women's issues, as in *Macu, la mujer del policial* (1987), which was a major box office success, and the search for identity in Venezuelan society, seen in *Manoa* (1979), and *Santera* (1997), both of which bring together characters of different race and class embarked on voyages of self discovery. By the end of the 1990s, Hoogesteijn had established herself as one of the most prominent figures of Venezuelan cinema.

MARK DINNEEN

Hopenhayn, Martín

b. 1955, New York city

Philosopher

Hopenhayn left Chile after the 1973 *coup d'état*, moving first to Buenos Aires and then Paris, where he had the opportunity to broaden his intellectual horizons working with the philosopher Gilles Deleuze at the University of the Sorbonne. In *Escritos sin futuro* (Writings Without a Future) (1984), Hopenhayn explores the fragmentary style of the aphorism as a mode of writing and thinking. In *Ni apocalípticos ni integrados: Aventuras de la modernidad en América Latina* (Neither Apocalyptics nor Assimilated: Adventures of Modernity in Latin America) (1994), he approached questions such as subjectivity, culture and modernity (see **cultural theory**) from a Latin American perspective.

LUIS E. CÁRCAMO-HUECHANTE

Hopkinson, Slade

b. 1934, New Amsterdam, Guyana

Poet, playwright, actor and teacher

An actor of remarkable versatility, Hopkinson has worked with the leading playwrights of the region. He founded the Caribbean Theatre Guild Company in Trinidad in 1970. He embraced the Muslim faith and took the name Baakoo Abdul-Rahman. He has published both plays and collections of poetry including, *The Onliest Fisherman* (1957), *A Spawning of Eels* (premiered, 1968), and *The Friend* (1976). Educated in Guyana, Barbados, and Jamaica, Hopkinson has lived and worked across the Caribbean region and now resides in Toronto, Canada.

FUNSO AIYEJINA

hora da estrela, A

Suzana **Amaral**'s first feature film, based on Clarice **Lispector**'s eponymous novel, *A hora da estrela* (Hour of the Star) (1985) presents scenes from the daily life of Macabeia, a migrant from the northeast living in São Paulo. Her apathetic existence unfolds between her shared room in a poor hotel, the mean office where she works, and her meetings, always in public spaces in the city, with her lover Olímpico, another migrant. Macabeia seems locked in an almost philosophical perplexity, unable to fight the cruel social mechanisms that entrap her. Actress Marcelia Catarxo won the Golden Bear award at Berlin in 1985 for her role as Macabeia.

ISMAIL XAVIER AND THE USP GROUP

hora de los hornos, La

Produced collectively in 1966–8 by the **Grupo Cine Liberación** and distributed clandestinely, the militant and formally experimental three-part film-essay *La hora de los hornos* (The Hour of the Furnaces) articulated the most radical aspirations of the **New Latin American Cinema**. As the members of the collective – Fernando **Solanas**,

Octavio Getino, Gerardo Vallejo and Juan Carlos DeSanzo – explained a year later in the much-circulated manifesto 'Hacia un tercer cine' (Toward a Third Cinema) (see **manifestos**), it was an example of 'guerrilla cinema' which broke with the conventions of Hollywood and European auteur cinemas by demanding politically active spectatorship and reverberated with the revolutionary rhetoric of Frantz **Fanon** and Ernesto 'Che' **Guevara**.

Totalling over four hours, the film is divided into three parts. The first, 'Neocolonialism and Violence' (the most formally experimental), is a call for tri-continental revolution dedicated to Che Guevara. Analysing political repression and the prospects of revolutionary liberation in Argentina and the rest of the developing world, Part One makes effective use of avant-garde techniques, ranging from collage, graphically bold intertitles, citations, satire, dialectical editing and even kitsch. It is a politically biting essay as well as a modernist work of art. Perhaps most complex are its sound–image relations, especially the use of music to counterpoint images, as in the juxtaposition of opera with images of the rural poor. The other two parts – 'An Act for Liberation' and 'Violence and Liberation' – chronicle the history of **Peronism** and its future prospects; exemplary of the film-makers' own radical Peronism of the time (on the eve of Perón's 1973 return), they did not have the international repercussions of Part One and have not aged well.

Adopting as their motto the Fanon slogan prominently cited in Part One – 'all spectators are cowards or traitors' – the film-makers set out to abolish passive spectatorship in favor of revolutionary action, textually, but also in terms of distribution and exhibition. Censored by the Onganía regime, the film was distributed clandestinely, primarily through Peronist trade unions, and exhibited in union halls and community centres, places where discussions and political debates could take place. Most famously, it was shown at the **Viña del Mar Festival** in Chile in 1969, where the screen was festooned with a banner bearing Fanon's quote. After Perón's return the film was released commercially in Buenos Aires, although re-edited with a prologue hailing the Peronist victory and without the famous five-minute silent freeze frame close-up of the dead Che Guevara that had previously ended Part One.

A masterpiece of political modernist film-making, *La Hora* is exhilarating, formally complex and politically single-minded, and one of the most influential films of the New Latin American Cinema.

Further reading

Stam, R. (1990) '*The Hour of the Furnaces* and the Two Avant Gardes', in J. Burton (ed.), *Cinema and Social Change in Latin America*, Pittsburgh, PA: University of Pittsburgh Press, 250–66.

DIANA PALADINO

horse racing

Contests of speed and distance between men on horseback date from the days of the Conquest, and remain popular in Latin America. In Europe, horses symbolized elite military prowess and played a central role in the invasions of the Americas; although unknown there, they multiplied quickly. Thus until the nineteenth century horse racing was popular mostly with the upper classes (landowners and cavalrymen) and working classes, who in regions such as La Plata, New Granada and northern Mexico were expert horsemen and had a cheap and almost unlimited supply of horses. The racing of horses entered into Latin American popular culture as a rough and informal contest between horse owners, in contrast to Europe, where the 'sport of kings' remained an upper-class pastime.

In the late nineteenth century, however, the sport was transformed by modernizing elites, who by the 1880s had adopted British style races on circular tracks, organized **Jockey Clubs** and started stud books in an effort to standardize the sport and bring gambling under their control. Horse races also became important socially, as the upper class promenaded in the latest Parisian fashions across luxurious stands and vied for membership in the exclusive Jockey Clubs. In separate stands, the middle and lower classes participated in the sport as passive spectators, or stadium employees and jockeys.

This transformation from a folk cultural event to an elite-dominated spectator sport did not necessarily dampen the appeal of horse racing. By one estimate, Argentines wagered half a billion pesos in the 1890s, or one-fifth of that nation's total export earnings, on horse racing. The sport continued to enjoy an incredible level of popularity in the first half of the twentieth century, when celebrities such as tango singer Carlos **Gardel** owned race horses and the jockey Irineo **Leguisamo** became a national hero in Argentina and Uruguay. High society's control of horse racing, however, conflicted with nationalist and populist regimes and the desire of governments to control gambling after 1930. Juan **Perón**, for instance, nationalized the sport and a group of his supporters attacked and set fire to the Buenos Aires Jockey Club in the 1950s. Soccer has since displaced horse racing as the great sporting passion of the region. Today, horse racing is waning in quality and popularity in Latin America due to the modest purses awarded to winners and the enormous expense of maintaining thoroughbreds.

Further reading

González, A. (1971) *Historia del Turf*, Buenos Aires: Centro Editor de America Latina.

Zatti, R. (1990) *Gardel, su gran pasión: El turf*, Buenos Aires: Corregidor.

THOMAS EDSALL

Hortensias, Las

Las Hortensias is a novella by the Uruguayan writer Felisberto **Hernández**, first published in 1949. Narrated in the third person (unusually for Hernández), it tells the story of Horacio, a married man who collects slightly larger than life-size rubber dolls. The dolls, displayed in glass cases or arranged in various scenarios, are initially integrated into the life of the couple. Horacio encourages the manufacturer to perfect one of these dolls – Hortensia, a replica of his wife – to the point where it reproduces human skin and body temperature. Unexpected passions are evoked by the dolls, which produce marital conflict and later lead Horacio into madness.

LILIANA ZUCCOTTI

Hosein, Clyde

b. 1940, Couva, Trinidad

Short-story writer

Hosein's collection of stories, *The Killing of Nelson John* (1980) offer a panorama of Caribbean life and characters which is at once socially conscious and deeply ironic. His short story 'Crow' is included in *The Penguin Book of Caribbean Short Stories* (1996). Having studied in London, Hosein worked for Radio Trinidad and the ***Trinidad Guardian*** before emigrating to Toronto, where he has remained to study film direction and to work with the Canadian Broadcasting Company.

KEITH JARDIM

House for Mr Biswas, A

Acclaimed novel by Trinidad-born V.S. **Naipaul** published in 1961. Mr Biswas, loosely based on the author's father, is a Trinidadian Indian, a descendant of indentured labourers who came from the sub-continent after the abolition of slavery. A man with aspirations to greater things, he is a failed writer who ends up devising lurid stories for a local tabloid before being put in charge of the paper's 'Deserving Destitutes' fund, which brings him into daily contact with the misery of the poor of colonial Trinidad. Mr Biswas's own poverty is a central concern of the novel, and he is frequently forced to rely on the largess of his wife's large and all-controlling family, the Tulsis. As part of this feuding and over-crowded household, Mr Biswas struggles to maintain his sense of manhood, waging his own small war against the Tulsis, winning small victories and suffering daily humiliations.

The first half of the novel is set in the sugar-cane fields of rural Trinidad, a luxuriant and unforgiving environment in which Mr Biswas's constant existential questioning leads to a mental breakdown. The question of individual and social identity in an island colonized first by the Spanish, then by the British, to which migrants came from Europe, Africa, India and China is often articulated in racial terms in Naipaul's work. His colonial subjects experience profound feelings of rootlessness and find themselves at the mercy of arbitrary swings of history.

The second half takes place in the capital city to which Mr Biswas comes by accident. Port-of-Spain represents the hope of a more fluid society, in which Mr Biswas can get a day's work sign-painting at a newspaper's office and end up a journalist. However, fate repeatedly frustrates ambition and, by middle age, Mr Biswas transfers this ambition on to the education of his son. In fact, two of Mr Biswas's children manage to win scholarships to London, part of a new generation that will play a crucial part in the nation-building after independence. It is the success guaranteed by a metropolitan education that saves the family from penury and allows Mr Biswas to keep the ridiculously flawed house he had at last managed to buy and which represents his own solution to the issue of inheritance in a post-colonial society.

Further reading

Celestin, R. (1996) *From Cannibals to Radicals: Figures and Limits of Exoticism in V.S. Naipaul*, Minneapolis: University of Minnesota Press.
Levy, J. (1995) *V.S. Naipaul: Displacement and Autobiography*, New York/London: Garland.
Thieme, J. (1987) *The Web of Tradition: The Uses of Allusion in V.S. Naipaul's Fiction*, London.
Weiss, Timothy (1992) *On the Margins: The Art of Exile in V.S. Naipaul*, Amherst: University of Massachusetts Press.

LORRAINE LEU

housing

Latin American housing represents all the gross inequalities of the social and economic situation. Even in a country as relatively rich as Brazil, over half the population lives in absolute poverty and the great majority live in low-income, often illegal, housing. In rural areas, homeless often also means landless; in urban areas, a large and growing number of people, including families and children, live on the streets.

The wealthy and middle class live in substantial houses and apartments, sometimes cheek-by-jowl with low-income housing, and there is generally a thriving construction and building industry for new dwellings and condominia. For the poor, the alternatives are: to live with members of the extended family who have housing; to rent a room(s) in slums, tenements, shanty towns (see **shanty towns and slums**) or other rental accommodation; to squat on unoccupied or unused land; or to buy housing in an existing low-income settlement.

The majority of low-income settlements are self-built. Many were originally established by the occupation of private or public land and squatting. They have a variety of names: *pueblos jóvenes* in Peru, *barriadas* in Ecuador, *favelas* in Brazil, *ranchos* in Venezuela and so on. By 1991, some 30 per cent of the population of Rio de Janeiro lived in shanty towns, 40 per cent in Recife, 37 per cent in Lima, 10 per cent in Buenos Aires and 61 per cent in Caracas.

Materials for construction vary: in the initial stages buildings may be quite flimsy, while longer established settlements may use sophisticated building materials typical of many housing estates and city developments. Some settlements of this latter kind are very large: one *favela* in Rio de Janeiro, for example, has between 150–200,000 residents and is, in reality, a small town. In many cities, such as São Paulo, there are large numbers of smaller settlements.

Official attitudes have changed from indifference to hostility in the 1950s and 1960s, when migration to the main cities of the region increased dramatically. Then, the plight of the inhabitants was either ignored or drastic policies of demolition, particularly under military governments, were employed to free land for middle-class developments. Subsequent schemes were more tolerant. Programmes for sites and services were developed in the late 1960s and 1970s, often with international funding from agencies such as the World Bank. Today, countries have policies for upgrading existing shanty towns, partly through changed attitudes to the residents (who now elect the government) and partly due to the fact that demolition and relocation are impractical because of the huge numbers of people, and the logistics and resources involved.

Further reading

Allen, E. (1988) *Housing Programmes, Opposition Government, and the Move Towards Democracy in Brazil: 1983–1986*, Glasgow: University of Glasgow Institute of Latin American Studies.

Gilbert, A. (1994) *The Latin American City*, London: Latin American Bureau.

Gilbert, A. and Ward, P. (1985) *Housing, the State and the Poor: Policy and Practice in Three Latin American Cities*, Cambridge: Cambridge University Press.

Perlman, J. (1976) *The Myth of Marginality: Urban Poverty and Politics in Rio de Janeiro*, Berkeley: University of California Press.

ELIZABETH ALLEN

Houssay, Bernardo

b. 1887, Buenos Aires, Argentina; d. 1971, Buenos Aires

Scientist

A physician by training, Dr Bernardo Houssay began his research in physiology at the University of Buenos Aires. His work on the pituitary gland earned him the Nobel Prize for Medicine in 1947. He was expelled from the University between 1945 and 1955 by the government of **Perón**, at which time he founded the Institute of Biology and Experimental Medicine (IBYME). Considered the father of Argentine biomedical research, in 1958 he was elected President of the recently formed National Research Council for Science and Technology (**CONICET**), a post he held until his death.

PABLO KREIMER

Houwen, Ria

b. 1947, Horst, the Netherlands

Painter

Houwen has lived and worked in Curaçao since 1973, where her art lessons have inspired many local artists. Her figurative paintings depict her surroundings: the Curaçao landscape, its people and architecture; she is especially fascinated by rocks, sand and sea. Although she started to paint figuratively, she also adds abstract feelings, so that her work also depicts a struggle between these two sides of her own personality.

NEL CASIMIRI

How to Read Donald Duck *see* Para leer el Pato Donald

Howell Aguilar, Patricia

b. 1952, Costa Rica

Film-maker

Howell sees film as a medium for empowering women, for teaching them 'not to dominate, but to exist': *Dos veces mujer* (Twice Woman) (1983) shows the difficulties faced by poor women in Costa Rica who work long days outside the home and spend much of the night caring for children and the home. *Fuerza de los siglos* (Strength of Centuries) (1994) describes the feminization of poverty in Central America; and *Más que palabras* (More Than Words) (1996) documents the efforts to advance human rights issues at the Fourth International Conference of Women held in Beijing. Although now a resident in Holland, she insists that she will continue making films about Central American women.

ANN MARIE STOCK

Hoy

Hoy is a daily newspaper in Quito, Ecuador, formed in 1982 as an independent, pluralist alternative source of news. Fundamentally, *Hoy* is a journal of opinion with editorials addressing cultural, political, social, ecological, journalistic and urban questions. The newspaper also published the 'Periolibros' series, reprinting key works of Latin American literature. Its first fifteen years of existence were recorded in the 1997 volume *15 años, 1982–1997: Hoy testigo de la historia* (*Hoy*, a Witness to History).

ALICIA ORTEGA

Hoyos, Ramón

b. 1936, Marinilla, Colombia

Racing cyclist

A road race specialist known as 'El escarabajo' (The climber) because of his strength in mountain races. He is an idol in his country, having won the Tour of Colombia, the leading South American road race, five times (from 1952–4, in 1956 and in 1958). He was a regular participant in this race from his first appearance in 1952 until his retirement in 1974. He took part in the Olympic road race event in 1956 and 1960. Since retirement he has been a businessman in Medellín.

ERIC WEIL

huaso

The cowboy of Chile's Central Valley, the *huaso* is distinguished from the Argentine **gaucho**, the Mexican **charro** or the Colombian *llanero* by his distinctive traditional clothing, consisting of a flat-brimmed hat, woven cloak, pin-striped wool pants and long-rowelled spurs. The *huaso*'s saddle and riding style are derived from the colonial Spanish military seat. As rural migrants moved to the cities from the 1920s onwards, the *huaso* became a symbol of an idealized rural past epitomized by the cowboy quartets like Los Cuatro Huasos and Los Huasos Quincheros who sang versions of the traditional tonadas. In the aftermath of the military *coup* of 1973, there was a clear attempt to restore the *huaso* as a central emblem of a conservative, rural-based national culture.

SCOTT A. COOPER

huasteca music (son huasteco)

Son huasteco ('huastec sound'), also known as huapango, is the name given to a musical style found in the region around the Gulf of Mexico comprising parts of the states of Hidalgo, Tamaulipas, Puebla, Querétaro and Veracruz. It is typically performed by a trio of musicians playing a violin, a huapanguera or guitarra quinta (a deep-bodied eight-string guitar) and a jarana (a small five-string guitar). The violinist plays the melody with a strummed guitar backing. The accompanying song, often delivered in a high falsetto, is improvised and delivered in couplets. Among the best known are Cielito lindo (Little Heaven), El toro Sacamandú (Sacamandu, the Bull) and La huasanga (Frolics).

EDUARDO GUÍZAR-ALVAREZ

huayno

The huayno is a recreational dance of prehispanic origin for couples or larger groups. *Huayno* is the Quechua word for 'dance'; *wayñu* or *huayñu* are also used. It is particularly associated with the Andean regions of Ecuador, Peru, Bolivia and northern Chile and Argentina. Among its variants are the huainito and carnavalito in Argentina, huaylas in Peru, the Bolivian saya and the Chilean trote. Traditionally, huaynos are played by a pan pipe (sicuri or zampoña) or flute (quena or pinquillo), solo or in ensemble, with percussion. Its more sophisticated versions include **guitar**, **harp**, charango, mandolin, violin, indigenous and European wind instruments, and percussion.

ALFONSO PADILLA

Huerta, Efraín

b. 1914, Guanajuato, Mexico; d. 1982, Mexico City

Poet

From his first volume of poetry *Absoluto amor* (Absolute Love) (1935), Huerta focused on the many faces of love. Many of his poems were inspired by his passionate love-hate relationship with Mexico City. He translated into poetic language the sordid reality of everyday life and the anonymous voices of the city's streets. The 'poemínimos' or 'minimal poems' of his later years were full of wit and irony. In his poetry and his public activity, he expressed his solidarity with the oppressed and all those fighting for national liberation.

EDITH NEGRÍN

Huidobro, Vicente

b. 1893, Santiago, Chile; d. 1948, Cartagena, Chile

Poet

The polemical Huidobro was Latin America's foremost avant-garde (see **avant-garde in Latin America**) poet. He wrote in both Spanish and French, experimented in poetry, theatre and film, founded his own literary movement (creationism) and was not only Latin America's roving cultural ambassador to Paris but also perhaps its first performance artist (see **performance art**). He apparently staged his own kidnapping in Paris at the hand of British imperialist agents. Even if Huidobro's life should not obscure the dazzling metaphors of his poetry, a cursory reading is in order here, for language as well as the staging of authenticity was one of Huidobro's most important themes.

Born to an aristocratic Chilean family, Vicente García Huidobro Fernández realized early on the importance of juicy polemics. One of his first books, *Pasando y pasando* (Going On and On) (1914) – confiscated by the authorities and burned by members of his family – opened with a much too premature autobiographical essay titled 'Yo', in which he proceeded to systematically debunk Jesuit schools, despotic priests, the Catholic Church, Spanish poetry and prominent critics. In Santiago, Huidobro was already making fun of futurism, writing caligrammatic poems and planting the seeds of future manifestos. In 1917, he took his young wife and children to Paris. He collaborated with the review *Nord–Sud* – the most important cubist journal – and wrote a number of his books in French: *Horizon Carré* (Squared Horizon) (1917), *Hallali* (1918), *Tour Eiffel* (1918) and *Saisons choisies* (Chosen Seasons) (1921). Juan Gris helped him with the language, Pablo Picasso drew his portrait and Tristan Tzara published his poetry. From Paris to Madrid, from Santiago to Zurich, Huidobro edited magazines, gave interviews and announced collaborations – which never materialized – with friends Stravinsky, Pound, Picasso, Tzara, Nijinsky and the Ballets Russes. The increasing power and prestige of his polemical darts – against André Breton and Pablo **Neruda**, among many others – prematurely took him out of the picture, and he returned to Chile, was a candidate for President on a reformist platform, lost the election, and finally settled into a kind of dejected discontent.

Through it all, he left what is perhaps one of the most baffling and interesting poems in the Spanish language: ***Altazor*** (1919–31), in which language is a transparent piece of clockwork allowing the reader to peer into its own mechanisms. It is a final epitaph for the heroic avant-garde.

Further reading

Camurati, M. (1980) *Poesía y poética de Vicente Huidobro*, Madrid: Cambeiro.

Concha, J. (1980) *Vicente Huidobro*, Madrid: Júcar.

De Costa, R. (1975) *Vicente Huidobro y el creacionismo*, Madrid: Taurus.

—— (1984) *Vicente Huidobro: The Careers of a Poet*, Oxford: Clarendon Press and New York: Oxford University Press.

Schwartz, J. (1978) 'Vicente Huidobro o la cosmópolis textualizada', *Eco* 202:1.

Yúdice, G. (1978) *Vicente Huidobro y la motivación del llenguaje*, Buenos Aires: Galerna.

JOSÉ QUIROGA

Huillca family

Born in 1942 in the Indian community of Queromarka in the district of Tinta, Antonio Huillca Huallpa trained at the Escuela Superior de Bellas Artes (1963–9) in Cusco. He experimented for several years before creating the 'Naif Peru' (Peruvian Naive) style of primitive painting (see **primitivism in art**) in 1974. His brightly coloured detailed images of Inca civilization and daily events and festivals in Cusco, which at times are condensed in one canvas, celebrate the history and richness of Andean culture. It is a view of the Andean universe from within. Taught by Huillca, his sons Anthoni (b. 1966), who specializes in Amazonian scenes, Angeles (b. 1963) and Salvador Dalí (b. 1972) also paint in a naive manner and exhibit jointly with their father as a family. Antonio likes to include his wife Barbara Tunque de Huillca (b. 1944, Tinta), and his daughters Rina (b. 1969) and Yone (b. 1975), who were both born in Cusco, in his 'family of painters', but they rarely exhibit.

PAULINE ANTROBUS

Huízar, Candelario

b. 1883, Jerez, Mexico; d. 1970, Mexico City

Musician

A composer and horn player, Huízar's musical career began when he arrived in Mexico City in 1917 with the brass band of a revolutionary army. He studied composition and joined the National Conservatory, where he taught musical analysis. He played horn with the Mexico Symphony Orchestra, which premiered most of his works; they characteristically combined romantic forms with indigenous and mestizo rhythms. His descriptive qualities and his orchestrations were outstanding. He wrote five symphonies, the best known of which is the Fourth, *Cora*, and several symphonic poems, including 'Imágenes' (Images), 'Pueblerinas' (Country Girls) and 'Surco' (Furrow). He won the National Prize of Arts in 1952.

EDUARDO CONTRERAS SOTO

human rights

Human rights are freedoms that people claim by virtue of their humanity and as citizens of states. Although most Latin American republics have recognized such rights since gaining independence, it was not until the second half of the twentieth century that these rights were systematically protected throughout the region.

The idea of 'human rights' first appeared in 1215, when King John of England signed the Magna Carta, guaranteeing his citizens rights such as equality and due process before the law. The idea gained momentum in the eighteenth and nineteenth centuries when European philosophers developed the idea of 'natural rights', which were rights belonging to each person by nature. In the late 1700s, the US Declaration of Independence and the French Declaration of the Rights of Man enshrined 'human rights' into national law for the first time. Nearly all Latin American constitutions included such guarantees, such as the freedom of expression and the inviolability of the home. But during the first hundred years of independence, as in the colonial era, the rights of most individuals and groups in society were not respected. Indigenous peoples, slaves, and peasants had few rights, and suffered mass and persistent patterns of killings and persecution. Aside from a small urban elite, few people in Latin America enjoyed political rights such as the freedom of association.

With political change, economic development, and the gradual introduction of democratic mechanisms in the early 1900s, some human rights protections in Latin America were strengthened, such as labour codes and land rights. Rights began to be conceived as 'positive' as well as 'negative' – that is, requiring the active protection of the state and not just a prohibition of interference in individual actions. A range of internationally-recognized human rights were set out in the Universal Declaration of Human Rights of 1948, the International Covenant on Civil and Political Rights and the International Covenant on Economic, Social and Cultural Rights of 1967.

Although most of Latin America signed these covenants, most of its twentieth-century regimes conducted violations of basic rights on a wide scale. Some of these regimes were long-term dictatorships, such as of the Duvaliers in Haiti from 1964 to 1986, Alfredo **Stroessner** in Paraguay from 1954 to 1989, the Somozas (see **Somoza dynasty**) in Nicaragua from 1936 to 1979, and Rafael **Trujillo** in the Dominican Republic from 1930 to 1961. Other egregious rights violators were the military regimes in Guatemala, Honduras, El Salvador, Bolivia, Uruguay, Peru, Ecuador, Brazil, Suriname, and Chile at various times between the 1950s and the 1980s. The 1976–83 military regime in Argentina carried out a national campaign of 'disappearances', in which it detained, tortured, and killed up to 30,000 persons without trial (see **disappeared, the**).

But with widespread democratization in Latin America and the Caribbean since the 1980s, most countries have established institutions designed to protect human rights. Along with the judiciary, the Fiscal General (Attorney General) is responsible for ensuring state agencies' respect for constitutional rights. Some countries have an ombudsperson or Human Rights Defender, an independent official who receives and follows up on specific rights complaints. Guyana, Trinidad and Tobago, Argentina, and Guatemala have national ombudspersons, and there are ombudspersons in certain states and municipalities in Mexico, Brazil, and Argentina. Treaties such as the 1969 Inter-American Convention on Human Rights have procedures to resolve rights issues, while local, national, and international non-governmental organizations throughout the hemisphere monitor and pressure governments on rights problems.

Even with such institutions, however, the protection of human rights continues to face many challenges. Killings and other rights violations are carried out by vigilante squads, paramilitary units and police forces in much of Latin America. Some claim, for example, that more people are killed every year in questionable circumstances by the police in São Paulo, Brazil than by the military junta between 1964 and 1985. In addition, emergency decrees and suspensions of the constitution can lead to rights violations by state officials. Venezuela suspended basic constitutional guarantees five times between 1989 and 1995, while rights have been suspended indefinitely in many areas of Colombia. Other contemporary human rights challenges include the development of new areas of rights protections, such as land rights, language rights, consumer rights, and the right to a clean environment (see **environmental issues**), which are guaranteed in many countries' constitutions.

Further reading

Claude, R. and Weston, B. (1989) *Human Rights in the World Community*, Philadelphia: University of Pennsylvania Press.

Interamerican Institution of Human Rights (1984) *Penal Systems and Human Rights in Latin America*, Buenos Aires: Depalma.

Melden, A.I. (ed.) (1970) *Human Rights*, Belmont, CA: Wadsworth Press.

Timerman, Jacobo (1981) *Prisoner Without a Name, Cell Without a Number*, New York: Knopf.

MARK UNGAR

Humor

Edited by Andrés Cascioli and successor to *Rico Tipo*, *Hortensia* (published in Córdoba) and *Satiricón*, the fortnightly *Humor* (1978–99) was a breath of fresh air for a whole layer of middle-class youth through the dark years of the **Proceso**, the military dictatorship of 1976–1983. *Humor* evaded the censors and gave a platform to some of the best cartoonists and humourists of the time. During the period of 'democratic transition' it accepted Raúl Alfonsín's version of that process, and in some of its interviews whitewashed individuals who had made a suspiciously rapid transition from collaboration with the military to the advocacy of a new democracy.

JULIO SCHVARTZMAN

hurricanes

Hurricanes are tropical cyclones which, at a rate of about eight per year, between May and November, visit the coasts of Yucatan and the Caribbean islands, bringing rain, sudden weather changes and often disaster. In the *Popul Vuh*, one of the few extant classic Maya texts, Huracán, god of wind, who gave the hurricane its name, takes part in the act of creation. In the Pacific region of Mexico, around six tropical cyclones known as 'cordonazos' occur annually. In 1988 Hurricane Gilbert, the most violent hurricane of the century, with winds of 350 kilometres per hour, wreaked havoc in Jamaica and the Yucatan coast.

LUIS ESPARZA

Hurtado, Padre Alberto

b. 1901, Viña del Mar, Chile; d. 1973, Santiago, Chile

Priest

Hurtado was a Jesuit who devoted his life to the education and protection of the poor. In 1944 he founded 'El Hogar de Cristo' (Christ's hearth), a children's refuge; by the late 1990s it had become Chile's largest and most successful charitable organization. In 1948 he founded ASICH (Asociación Sindical Chilena, or Chilean Syndicalist Association). An educator and adviser to Acción Católica (Catholic Action), he founded the journal *Mensaje* in 1951. Loved and respected throughout Chile, he was beatified in Rome on 16 October 1994.

ELIANA ORTEGA

Hutchinson, Lionel

b. 1923, St Michael, Barbados

Writer

A novelist who spent much of his working life in government service, Hutchinson is known primarily for two novels. *Man from the People* (1969) is a bluntly comic portrayal of politics during the 1960s after the Barbados Labour Party of Grantley **Adams** was swept from office in favour of the Democratic Labour Party. *One Touch of Nature* (1971) is a commentary on race relations and on the people known in Barbados as 'Red Legs', descendants of the white slaves and indentured servants displaced by black slavery. Long considered failures and degenerates, they were not even offered the paternalistic sympathy sometimes offered to blacks.

The novel's central character, Harriet Jivenot, believes that she is entitled to a better life and scorns East Indians, blacks, and her own 'Red Legs' community.

CAROL J. WALLACE

Hyatt, Charles

b. 1931, Kingston, Jamaica

Writer

Hyatt's early career unfolded in theatre and, above all, in radio, where he worked with the BBC in the development of a vernacular theatre, based largely on the oral storytelling tradition in which Hyatt was a consummate performer, as in his portrayal of Pa Ben in Trevor Rhone's play, *Old Story Time* (1981). His own stories and memories are collected in his volume of tales, *When Me Was a Boy* (1989).

MIKE GONZALEZ

hybridity

Utilized in different contexts, the concept of hybridity is related to concepts like **syncretism**, *mestizaje*, half-breed or **creole**, which trade with the idea of cultural crossings, interrelations and mixtures. As used by Néstor **García Canclini** in his *Culturas Híbridas*, hybridization is the principal characteristic of contemporary Latin American societies. It focuses on the heterogeneity that emerges from their multitemporal and multicultural background. To understand the process of hybridization, it is crucial to consider the relations between tradition and modernity, the popular, the cult and the mass-mediated.

See also: cultural theory

FERNANDO RABOSSI

Hyde, Eugene

b. 1931, Cooper's Hill, Portland, Jamaica; d. 1980, Portland (unconfirmed), Jamaica

Painter, ceramist and muralist

A major exhibition in Jamaica in 1963 first launched Hyde's career as painter, ceramist, and muralist. Stylistically expressionistic, Hyde's vibrant colours and bold, fluid drawing blend elements of commercial and fine art in representations of socio-political turmoil within Jamaican society. In 1964, Hyde co-founded the broad-based Contemporary Jamaican Artists Association, together with Karl **Parboosingh** and Barrington Watson. Intrigued by the dynamics of the human figure and involved in the **National Dance Theatre Company of Jamaica**, Hyde produced a series of abstract works in 1966, titled *The Dance*. His murals adorn many buildings in Jamaica, including the **University of the West Indies**.

JILL E. ALBADA-JELGERSMA

Hyppolite, Hector

b. 1894, St Marc, Haiti; d. 1948, Port-au-Prince, Haiti

Artist

Long before there was any formal recognition of Haitian art there were painters in Haiti, among them Hyppolite. In contrast to his contemporary, **Obin**, his paintings are inspirational. Described as the priest who occasionally painted and the painter who occasionally conducted rites, Hyppolite was a *houngan* or **Vodun** priest, a role he inherited from his father and grandfather.

On a visit to Montrouis in 1943, DeWitt Peters was intrigued by the decorated doors of Hyppolite's house topped by the phrase '*Ici la renaissance*' (Here the renaissance), and he invited him to the Centre d'Art in Port-au-Prince. Hyppolite preferred to work in a very basic hut on the outskirts of the city. Within a week he finished sixteen paintings. His work opened Peters's eyes to the possibility of a popular movement and the Centre d'Art became its rallying point.

Hyppolite was among the muralists who decorated the Centre d'Art but died before the Cathedral project began. Hyppolite and André Pierre were among the most explicit in their depiction of the *loas* (Vodun gods). However, Hyppolite's technique was never wholly adequate to translate his visions into effective plastic images. He introduced Wilson **Bigaud** to the Centre d'Art, but unlike the latter, **Vodun** informed his art but did not consume it.

After the First World War, Hyppolite cut cane in Cuba before sailing to Equatorial Africa. He visited Dahomey and Ethiopia, earning a living decorating chamber pots. There is some suggestion, however, that this was no more than a journey of the mind.

In 1920 he returned to Haiti, and until the early 1940s he wandered from village to village trying to earn a living. By 1946 he enjoyed a fame no other Haitian artist had ever experienced, with a one-man show in the USA; in 1947 his paintings in a UNESCO exhibit created a sensation. He lived to see one of his religious canvases carried through the streets by a cheering crowd. He dreamed of sailing the world in a boat decorated with birds, women and the *loas*, on whose mast would be pinned a notice reading 'Hyppolite the Haitian Painter'.

Further reading

Alexis, G. *et al.* (1995) *50 années de peinture en Haiti 1930–1980: Tome 1: 1930–1959*, Port-au-Prince: Fondation Culture Création.

Rodman, S. (1948) *Renaissance in Haiti: Popular Painters in the Black Republic*, New York: Pellegrini and Cudahy.

Williams, S. (1969) *Voodoo and the Art of Haiti*, Nottingham: Morland Lee.

MARY BOLEY

Ibáñez, Roberto

b. 1907, Montevideo, Uruguay; d. 1978, Montevideo

Writer

An elegant and musical poet, Ibáñez's central concerns were the human tragedy, lost childhood, love and death, and the solitude of the poet. He won the first **Casa de las Américas** Poetry Prize in 1961. Ibáñez was a scholar with a large unpublished bibliography and a controversial critic, who famously engaged in public debate with Emir **Rodríguez Monegal**. He was responsible for many years for the literature programmes studies in his country's schools; he was also Uruguay's first Socialist deputy. One famous poem, 'Balada de tu nombre' (Ballad of Your Name), was written for his wife Sara de **Ibáñez**.

NORAH GIRALDI DEI CAS

Ibáñez, Sara de

b. 1909, Chamberlain, Uruguay; d. 1971, Montevideo, Uruguay

Poet

Sara de Ibáñez combined national historical themes, often of an epic cast – 'Canto a Montevideo' (Hymn to Montevideo) (1941), 'Artigas' (1952) – with intensely lyrical poetry on topics of universal importance, such as war, the apocalypse, death, nature, and love – 'Canto' (1940), 'Pastoral' (1948), 'Apocalípsis' (1970). She often used traditional verse forms, like the sonnet, as well as freer verse forms. Her *Poemas escogidos* (Selected Poems) (1974) contains selections from all her works. De Ibáñez is part of an outstanding generation of Uruguayan female poets including Juana de **Ibarbourou**, Dora Isella Russell, Esther de Cáceres, Selva Márquez, Clara Silva, Concepción Silva, and Susana Soca.

GWEN KIRKPATRICK

Ibarbourou, Juana de

b. 1892, Melo, Uruguay; d. 1979, Montevideo, Uruguay

Poet

Crowned in 1929 as 'Juana of America', this young poet began her work within the avant-garde (see **avant-garde in Latin America**). However, her voice is very distinct: seductive, spontaneous, fresh and modest. In a reaction to modernism, she glorifies everyday objects while giving them a marvellous and mysterious air. In her first book, *Las lenguas de diamante* (Diamond Tongues) (1919), she demonstrated this tendency to sentimental and innovative expression. However, by 1950, with the appearance of collections such as *Perdida* (Lost), she took on a more sombre and melancholic voice.

VICTORIA RUÉTALO

Ibarra, Federico

b. 1946, Mexico City

Composer and pianist

A highly original composer, Ibarra (born Federico Ibarra Groth), unlike many of his contemporaries, does not reflect the dominant influence of seriality in his work. Outstanding among his compositions, which often include poetic or dramatic texts, are *Canta VI. Del Unicornio* (On Unicorns) (1972), for mixed chorus, male and female narrator, piano, clavichord, organ and three percussion instruments; *Cantata VII, Nocturno Muerto* (Dead Nocturne) (1973), a dramatic and poetic piece featuring poetry by José Ramón Enríquez and Xavier **Villaurrutia**; and *El Proceso de la Metamorfosis* (1970), for narrator and symphonic orchestra, with texts by Kafka and André Breton. Also well known as a concert pianist, his musical originality led him to premiere piano compositions by Cage, Cowell, De Castro and other contemporary composers in Mexico.

EDUARDO GUÍZAR-ALVAREZ

Ibero-Amerikanisches Archiv

The Iberoamerican Institute was formed in 1930 with 120,000 volumes from three sources: donations from Argentine scholars Vicente and Ernesto Quesada, the 'Mexican Library' donated by the Mexican government and the library of the University of Bonn's Instituto de Investigaciones Iberoamericanas (Iberoamerican Research Institute). 40,000 volumes as well as Ernesto Quesada's manuscript collection disappeared during the war. Reconstructed and transferred to its own building in Berlin, it is now Europe's largest specialist archive, containing some 700,000 volumes, 4,300 journals, 57,000 maps, photographic, musical and video archives. It organizes conferences and exhibitions and publishes specialist monographs and publishes a journal of the same name.

CELINA MANZONI

Iberoamerica

The term Iberoamerica alludes to the twenty countries that emerged from the Iberian empires of Latin America, nineteen of them Spanish-speaking and one, Brazil, whose language is Portuguese. The unity of the Iberoamerican peoples was a central idea during the struggles for independence, and there were many attempts to create confederations during the nineteenth century. Today the term refers to the cultural relations that these countries maintain with Spain and Portugal, especially in the literary field.

See also: Instituto de Cooperación Iberoamericana; Instituto Internacional de Literatura Iberoamericana

LUIS L. ESPARZA

ICAIC

ICAIC (Instituto Cubano del Arte e Industria Cinematográficos) (Cuban Institute of Cinematic Arts and Industry) was established in 1959 by Law no. 169 of the newly established Cuban revolutionary government, and placed under the directorship of Alfredo **Guevara**. The law states that cinema is an art form, which did not prevent it from being used for blatantly propagandistic purposes by the new socialist system (see **socialism**). By 1965, ICAIC controlled all film-making and distribution in the country. By the late sixties, Cuban cinema – and especially documentary film – enjoyed great prestige internationally through the work of Tomás **Gutiérrez Alea**, Santiago **Alvarez** and Humberto **Solas** among others. From 1979 the Institute organized the International Festival of **New Latin American Cinema**, which became a Third World alternative to Cannes and Venice. In 1980 Solas's film *Cecilia* overran its budget many times over, leading to a purge which resulted in Guevara's replacement by Julio **García Espinosa**. In the 1980s, the first generation of film-makers trained by ICAIC, many of whom were originally documentary makers, began to make feature films – they included Jesús **Díaz**, Juan Carlos **Tabio**, Fernando Pérez and Daniel Díaz Torres whose film *Alicia en el país de las* *maravillas* (Alice in Wonderland) (1990) provoked the fury of the government, and the eventual return of Guevara to the presidency of the Institute. In 1988 the film-makers had combined into three groups, led respectively by Gutiérez Alea, Solas and Manuel Pérez, with the aim of decentralizing decision making procedures, but with the return of Guevara they ceased to function. The economic crisis of the 1990s drastically reduced the Institute's resources, forcing many film-makers to seek foreign producers to back their projects or to go into exile.

JOSÉ ANTONIO EVORA

Icaza, Jorge

b. 1906, Quito, Ecuador; d. 1978, Quito

Writer

Icaza's controversial *Huasipungo* (The Villagers) (1934), his first novel, exposed the terrible living conditions of Indians and the complicity of church and government. His characteristically shocking style used images of the grotesque, popular speech, and a tone of protest. Icaza is usually located within the ***indigenista*** trend in Latin American literature, but he was more interested in the psychological and social complexes of the mestizo; his novel *El chulla Romero y Flores* (The Half-Breed Romero y Flores) (1958), for example, is a penetrating study of the concerns with **race**, appearance and culture that haunt the Ecuadorean experience.

HUMBERTO ROBLES

ICRT

The Instituto Cubano de Radio y Televisión (Cuban Institute of Radio and Television, or ICRT), formed under its present name in 1976, organizes all broadcasting in Cuba. It includes five national, seventeen provincial and thirty local **radio** stations and Radio Habana Cuba, for external transmission, as well as two **television** stations, nine regional transmitters and the Cubavisión satellite transmitter. It is based in central Havana, in the ex-headquarters of **CMQ-TV**. The 1976 Constitution (amended in 1992) states that radio and television are the property of the state and cannot be passed into private ownership, giving the state absolute centralized control over the mass media.

WILFREDO CANCIO ISLA

ICTUS

Independent theatre group that denounced and exposed the barbarities of the military dictatorship in Chile throughout the 1980s, in works like *Lindo país esquina con vista al mar* (Desirable Country on the Corner with a Sea View). Formed in 1956 by a group of independent artists – Delfina **Guzmán** and Claudio Celedón among them – it has presented works ranging from Ionesco to Jorge **Díaz**. It developed its own production style, *creación colectiva* (collective creation), in works like the TV programme, *La* ***manivela*** (The Handle), which was taken off the air after the military *coup* of 1973. It has its own video production and distribution company.

ELIANA ORTEGA

Ilê Aiyê

Dissatisfied with the options available to Afro-Brazilians during **carnival**, a group of young black petroleum workers from the working class neighbourhood of Curuzu/Liberdade organized the first *bloco afro* (see ***blocos afro***), Ilê Aiyê (Yoruba for 'House of Life') for the 1975 carnival. At first denounced by the local press for introducing racial protest into Salvador's carnival, the group soon became enormously popular, initiating what Antônio Risério called the 'reafricanization of Bahian life' in his study, *Carnaval Ijexá* (1982). By the 1980s, the group had emerged as a primary reference for Afro-Brazilians committed to political, cultural, and aesthetic affirmation. Ilê Aiyê has made numerous recordings and their songs have been covered by pop stars.

CHRISTOPHER DUNN

Illapu

Illapu is a musical group formed in 1970 in Antofagasta, northern Chile, and belonging to the **nueva canción** movement. Its nucleus was the Márquez brothers, with Roberto as musical director. After the military *coup* of September 1973, Illapu (which means 'a flash of lightning' in **Quechua**) was the only member of the movement that remained in Chile, until its expulsion from the country in 1980. Thereafter the group lived in Paris and Mexico, returning to Chile in 1987. Illapu remains one of the best and most popular Chilean music groups; it has recorded over twenty discs.

ALFONSO PADILLA

Illescas, Carlos

b. 1919, Guatemala City

Writer

One of the most talented poets of the Generation of 1940, Illescas joined the opposition against **Ubico** and participated in the 1944 uprising and the ten years of social agitation which followed, often working on an ad hoc basis with members of writer groups Acento and Saker-ti, without joining one group or the other. After the intervention of 1954, he lived in exile in Mexico, where he wrote several books and film scripts, working for various years in the **UNAM**, and contributing to Mexico's intellectual life.

MARC ZIMMERMAN

Imagen

The military coup in Chile in 1973 brought censorship and financial difficulties to the theatre community, as well as threats to personal safety. This caused many of Chile's once-flourishing theatre groups to collapse. Imagen, directed by Gustavo Meza (b. 1938), was one of the strongest of the independent theatre companies that survived during the **Pinochet** regime. Under conditions of repression, Imagen produced a Theater of Testimony which included *Te llamabas Rosicler* (Your Name Was Rosicler, 1976) and *El último tren* (The Last Train) (1978.) Imagen's work has continued with contempory theatre productions, among them the outstanding *Lo Crudo, lo cocido, lo podrido* (The Raw, The Cooked, The Rotten) by **De la Parra**.

RUTH DOMINGUEZ

Images Caraïbes

Created in 1985 by Suzy Landau and Viviane Duvigneau, the Martinique-based association Images Caraïbes (Caribbean Images) is devoted to promoting Caribbean cinema, the development of films made about the region by its inhabitants. To that end, the non-profit Images Caraïbes sponsors a biennial festival in Fort-de-France showcasing films and videos of the Caribbean diaspora. While festival topics vary from one year to the next (examples have included Plantation Movies, African Images and An Outside Look at Caribbean Existence), all are designed to promote dialogue between regional and international filmmakers and scholars, and to facilitate the dissemination of Caribbean production.

ANN MARIE STOCK

Imaná, Gil

b. 1933, Sucre, Bolivia

Visual artist

In the debates among artists that followed the Bolivian Revolution of 1952, Imaná argued for a social commitment that would be reflected both in the themes and the forms of his work. Like many of his contemporaries, he chose a symbolic language that referred to the landscapes of Bolivia and the historic cultures of the **altiplano** as vehicles for his message about social solidarity. They inform his mural at the Sucre Telephone Company (1955) and inspire the working women who are so often the subjects of his paintings – *Su soledad horada, gota a gota, la piedra* (Her Solitude Pierces the Stone).

DANIEL BALDERSTON

Imber, Sofía

b. 1926, Besarabia, Romania

Journalist, museum director and television presenter

The principal founder in 1973 of the Museum of Contemporary Art in Caracas, which now bears her name. Under her directorship, it became established as one of the best art galleries of its kind in Latin America. Sofia Imber emigrated to Venezuela with her family when aged four. Settled in Caracas, she abandoned her degree in medicine at the Central University there to dedicate herself to the arts, and she became well known as a writer for the cultural pages of such papers as *Ultimas Noticias* and *El **Universal***. For many years she also presented a programme of debate and interviews on Venezuelan television.

MARK DINNEEN

immigration to Latin America

There is an old Argentine joke that facetiously points out that while Mexicans descended from the Aztecs, Argentines descend from ships. The quip grossly over-simplifies the complex history of Latin American immigration, yet it does recognize the major difference between immigration flows to northern Latin America and to the Southern Cone. Southern Cone nations all experienced unprecedented levels of European immigration from the 1850s until the great Depression in 1930. More recently, the Southern Cone has joined Mexico and the Caribbean Basin to become an area of net out-migration.

Unprecedented growth in Europe's population during the nineteenth century coincided with innovations in transportation that made long-distance travel much cheaper and faster, allowing new levels of emigration from Europe. In the Americas, successful independence struggles throughout Latin America in the early nineteenth century created the need for an industrial and agricultural workforce. Many of these newly independent nations made deliberate efforts to encourage European immigration. That some of these countries were home to significant indigenous and ex-slave populations did not prevent their governments from encouraging immigration by providing newcomers with preferential access to education, jobs and property. Also important in the formation of the Southern Cone's working class was the common anarchist (see **anarchism**) and socialist (see **socialism**) background of many of these turn-of-the-century immigrants.

Between 1830 and 1930 roughly 50 million Europeans emigrated; 11 million of this total opted for Latin America, pulled there by its familiar cultural and linguistic characteristics. During the seventy-year period from 1854 until 1924 European arrivals to Latin America were led by Italians (38 per cent), Spaniards (28 per cent) and Portuguese (11 per cent), while French, German and Russian immigrants each accounted for three per cent of the total. Easily the most popular destination was Argentina, which received almost half (46 per cent) of all Latin American immigration during this period. Brazil (33 per cent) and Cuba (14 per cent) opened their doors to many of these immigrants, while Uruguay (4 per cent), Mexico (3 per cent) and Chile (2 per cent) were other major destinations.

Immigration to Latin America since 1930 has been much less significant numerically. During the 1930s Depression all the Southern Cone nations moved to restrict immigration and various countries saw anti-immigrant backlashes. By the 1960s out-migration came to predominate even in Argentina and Uruguay, which now produced refugees themselves. While there has been relatively little European immigration in the second half of the twentieth century, a surge in Asian immigration has occurred recently, coming largely from Korea and earlier from Japan.

Further reading

Marshall, O. (1991) *European Immigration and*

Ethnicity in Latin America: A Bibliography, London: Institute of Latin American Studies.

TED HENKEN

import substitution industrialization

With the Second World War, Latin America's exported raw materials and agricultural products reached increasingly high prices on the world market. At the same time, metropolitan industries were largely redirected to war production. This encouraged a strategy of creating a local manufacturing industry, with State subsidy, capable of producing goods no longer available as imports. There was considerable debate at the time as to whether this might represent an opportunity to break the circle of **dependency** and lay the foundation for national economic development. The reality, however, was that the substitute industries concentrated on highly produced consumer goods that often required inputs – machinery, basic raw materials, etc. – which had to be imported. By the late 1950s it was already becoming clear that the strategy in some ways increased dependence on the international economy, and that in any event they could not compete with corporations with access to advanced technologies, bigger markets and the possibility of effecting economies of scale. Protectionist measures were often undermined by foreign capital's ability to associate with domestic finance behind tariff walls. The attempts at widening the market through regional economic agreements (**CACOM** or the **Andean Pact**, for example) quickly failed and the Latin American economies were again fully integrated into the global market – a process known as 'liberalization' – by the 1980s.

MIKE GONZALEZ

In the Castle of My Skin

Published in 1953, *In the Castle of My Skin* established the reputation of its author George **Lamming**, and was a landmark text in the emergence of West Indian literature in the 1950s. The novel was based on Lamming's own experience of life in a Barbadian village between 1927 and 1950, when he emigrated to England. At the centre is the story of 'G', his early relationship with his mother, his schooling, his discussions with his friends, and his growing away from his roots as he enters secondary school. From early boyhood, G's sensitive and artistic individuality is in conflict with the intimacy of the village, and the story objectifies the tensions common to **intellectuals** in a colonized society who gain Western education at the cost of losing their communal roots. The novel ends with G leaving the island for further education abroad.

Yet the work is not a conventional autobiography. Lamming has written that it is not about an individual but a community, and this is mediated through a loose, open-ended narrative form that moves across a range of styles, from poetic prose to dramatic speech and reportage. Opening with G's seventh birthday, his experience merges with that of the village as a whole, which itself finds a voice in two elder figures, 'Ma' and 'Pa', whose long dialogues explore in poetic prose its history and concerns. The limestone island itself is vividly recreated with its landscape, weather, customs, food, and speech. Because the novel takes place across the formative period when Barbados moved from traditional rural life to an individualistic materialism and towards political independence, G's coming of age coincides with similar changes on the island.

The novel begins with a scathing analysis of British colonialism as mediated through education, where the school children are regimented in squads and taught only English history, and the remains of the plantation society are embodied in the landowner Creighton in his house on the hill. The activities of Mr Slime, a schoolmaster dismissed for sexual misconduct, introduce the land sales which deprive the villagers of their traditional rights, and towards the end of the novel, the political riots of the 1940s anticipate national independence.

The work was a revelation to contemporary West Indian writers. Edward Kamau **Brathwaite**, also from Barbados, was one whom it enabled to find his native idiom. Its penetrating critique of colonialism was recognized by the Kenyan author Ngũgũ wa Th'iongo, who called it 'one of the great political novels in modern "colonial" literature'. Jean-Paul Sartre republished it in his series *Les Temps Modernes*.

Further reading

Munro, I. (1971) 'The Theme of Exile in George Lamming's *In the Castle of my Skin*', *World Literature Written in English* 20: 51–60.

Nair, S. (1996) *Caliban's curse. George Lamming and the revisioning of history*, Ann Arbor, MI: University of Michigan Press.

LOUIS JAMES

INAH

Part national park service and part research organization, INAH (Instituto Nacional de Antropología e Historia – Mexican National Institute of Anthropology and History) is the organization responsible for the protection and investigation of Mexico's national past. INAH undertakes these duties as part of the Federal Department of Education (SEP) overseeing the restoration, maintenance and public presentation of key federal historical properties ranging from churches and convents to entire pre-Hispanic cities such as Teotihuacán and Chichen Itzá. Created in 1939 during the waning years of Lázaro **Cárdenas**'s tenure as president, INAH is the institutional reflection of both modern Mexico's public commitment to its pre-Hispanic past as an integral portion of the national story and its commitment to develop a national understanding of indigenous Mexico as a prelude to just development.

CHRIS VON NAGY

INBA

The Mexican Instituto Nacional de Bellas Artes y Literatura (INBA) was created in 1947 as a branch of the Secretaría de Educación Pública (Ministry of Education) to protect and foment Mexican and foreign arts and literature throughout the country. Under its care are a number of **museums** located both in Mexico City and in other areas throughout the country, many of which are ancient buildings and former convents, of value in themselves for their architecture and history, as well as theatres and other public forums. INBA's various departments support many artistic and cultural centres including dance, theatre and opera companies, eight orchestral and choral groups, and twenty-nine schools or academies where students receive training in various artistic disciplines, among them the Academia de la Danza Mexicana, the Centro de Educación Artística, and the Conservatorio Nacional de Música. Also under INBA's regis are the Centros de Investigación Nacional housed in the **Centro Nacional de las Artes** building in Mexico City, in which research is carried out to document, disseminate and preserve Mexico's legacy in music, dance, theater and the plastic arts. Of particular note among the buildings under INBA's direction is the Palacio de Bellas Artes (The Palace of Fine Arts) in Mexico City, an imposing structure begun at the turn of the century and whose interior contains work by **Rivera**, **Siqueiros**, **Orozco** and **Tamayo** among others. Of special note is the theatre's famous *cortina de cristal*, or glass curtain, a mosaic of more than a million pieces of opal crystals on a background of steel, constructed by Tiffany's of New York and depicting a view of the Valley of Mexico. The building's façade is almost entirely of Carrara marble, and, since its construction covered a span of more than thirty years, its architecture embodies a range of styles, with the exterior noteworthy for its art nouveau forms and the interior a combination of art deco styles juxtaposed with prehispanic motifs. It has hosted a wide range of cultural events, including art exhibitions and concerts by world-renowned artists and elaborately staged performances by the highly acclaimed **Ballet Folklórico de México**.

EDUARDO GUÍZAR ALVAREZ

INCAP

Founded in 1949 under the auspices of the **Pan American Health Organization** (PAHO), with partial funding from the Kellogg Foundation, INCAP (Institute of Nutrition of Central America and Panama) has done important research work on questions of nutrition and health. Studies of goitre and other nutritional deficiencies resulted in practical solutions like the widespread use of iodized salt (to combat goitre) and of a protein supplement for children, Incaparina. INCAP's extraordinary longitudinal data were studied by Judith Balderston, Maria E. Freire, Alan Wilson and Mari Simonen, and published as *Malnourished Children of the Rural Poor* (1981).

DANIEL BALDERSTON

INCINE

A dependency of the Sandinista Ministry of Culture under Ernesto **Cardenal**, the main purpose of INCINE (Instituto Nicaragüense de Cine – Nicaraguan Film Institute) was to foment the production of films on and about Nicaragua. Under its auspices a **cinematheque** was created to bring the best foreign productions to Nicaragua and an intellectual group created to judge international works. Early in the **Sandinista Revolution**, INCINE produced a series of excellent newsreels, invited foreign directors to collaborate with them and sent students to Eastern Europe to study cinema. Amongst its co-productions are *Alsino y el condor* (Alsino and the Condor) (1983) and *Sandino* (1989) with Kris Kristofferson, both directed by Miguel **Littín**.

ESTEBAN E. LOUSTAUNAU AND ILEANA RODRÍGUEZ

independent film producers

Producers can be 'independent' from a studio's corporative structure – i.e. not salaried – yet remain bound by studio-based imperatives. A truly 'independent' producer is the one that is not linked to studios and sustains a certain practical/ideological independence or embarks upon a search for alternative methods and/or styles. Under either definition, however, it is difficult to speak of independent productions in Latin America; given the comparative instability of many local studios, most productions seem haphazard when compared to those of fully industrialized systems like Hollywood. Yet, historically, there has been a qualitative difference between films produced within studios or by independent production companies aligned with the studios (no matter how under-capitalized) and those produced by 'independents' on the margins.

One of the pioneers of independent production in Latin America was the Mexican actress, Adela 'Perlita' **Sequeyro**. Unable to find a studio willing to produce the projects she wanted to direct, she organized her own fledgling production company (capitalized by all her family's savings) for *La mujer de nadie* (Nobody's Woman) (1937), an audacious and well-received film and the first feature film directed by a Mexican woman. However, her second film, *Diablillos del arrabal* (Imps of the Ghetto) (1938), shot under great financial constraints, was barely distributed, was a box-office failure and bankrupted the company. Perlita never directed again.

Perlita's experiences point to the great stumbling blocks faced by independent producers to this day: the difficulties of securing access to mainstream **film distribution** channels and to theatres multiply exponentially the risks of under-capitalized production.

Conscious of these difficulties, Manuel **Barbachano Ponce**, who has been called the 'first' real independent producer in Mexico, based his business upon the production of **newsreels**, from which he derived a steady enough source of income to venture into producing the kinds of films that the studios were not interested in. These were, at first, Benito Alazraki's *Raíces* (Roots) (1953) and Luis **Buñuel**'s *Nazarín* (1958); later most of Jaime Humberto **Hermosillo**'s iconoclastic films through the 1980s and Marisa Sistach's *Anoche soñé contigo* (Last Night I Dreamt of You) (1991), among many others.

Since the late 1970s, the work of independent producers has been increasingly focused on fund-raising from State film institutes (like **Embrafilme** in Brazil) and agencies, and arranging co-production deals (see **co-productions**). The independent production company headed by Luiz Carlos **Barreto** and his wife Lucy Barreto in Brazil is a case in point. After working as a journalist and a cinematographer, Barreto moved into production as **Cinema Novo** blossomed, with Nelson Pereira dos **Santos**'s *Vidas secas* (Barren Lives) (1963). As he became aware of the difficulties of obtaining access to theatres and to box-office receipts, he organized the co-operative Difilm in 1964 to distribute films and to reinvest the proceeds in productions; the company distributed most Cinema Novo films and produced key films by Glauber **Rocha**, Joaquim Pedro de **Andrade**, and dos Santos. By 1971, Barreto had established his own company, L.C. Barreto, which profited greatly from **Embrafilme** as well as from the international success of the films directed by Barreto's two sons, Bruno **Barreto** and Fábio **Barreto**, which guaranteed access to international financing.

In Argentina, Lita **Stantic** has been an extraordinary independent producer, responsible for organizing the complex financial deals that enabled Maria Luísa **Bemberg** to direct such extraordinary films as *Camila* (1984) and *Yo la peor de todas* (I, Worst of All) (1990). In Mexico, another contemporary independent producer of note is Jorge Sánchez, who, through his production–distribution company Zafra has been able to produce a series of films, ranging from María **Novaro**'s (his wife) films, to Nicolas **Echevarría**'s *Cabeza de vaca* (1991) and Guillermo **del Toro**'s *Cronos* (1993).

In order to survive in the late 1990s, Latin American independent producers must be global, seeking not only international sources of financing through co-productions and national distribution, but international distribution as well.

ANA M. LÓPEZ

Indian

The term 'Indian' (and its cognates in Spanish and Portuguese) refers to indigenous peoples of the Americas, commemorating the misapprehension of Columbus upon happening onto the Americas and the West 'Indies'. In much of Latin America, the term soon took on opprobrious connotations, as the native peoples became an undercaste. Fighting to receive equal treatment under the law, protect their lands, and maintain their lifeways, some groups have adopted the label *indio* defiantly; other groups eschew the term and use more specific group designations (such as language affiliations), or more euphemistic ones (such as cognates of indigene, native or natural).

JUDITH MAXWELL

Indianismo

Indianismo is a representation produced by non-Indians in which the Indian appears as an exotic motif or as a source of nostalgia. When Christopher Columbus wrote his Diary (1492–3) he became the first Indianista by default. Believing that they had landed in India, Columbus and his crew gave the name 'Indians' to the human beings they saw and captured in the Caribbean. Indianista representations abounded during the Colonial period; however, Indianismo refers specifically to texts written by non-Indian authors especially during the nineteenth century. This literature exploited Indian themes while ignoring the injustices suffered by the real Indian populations; indeed, its development is related to the reception of European Romanticism in Latin America represented by Chateaubriand's novel *Atala* (1801). Latin American Romantic novelists wrote interracial love stories in which Indians and their environments were represented exotically and located in a remote past. On the one hand, most Indian characters were depicted as savages who practised strange customs and rituals; on the other hand, a few isolated Indians were configured as 'noble savages' who lived in idyllic landscapes. Several of the *bons savages* at the end of the novels turned out to be mestizos or even white *criollos*, who only looked Indian because they had been raised by Indians.

It is not coincidental that Indianismo was most prevalent in the nineteenth century, when national states were just established in Latin America. In the new national orders, the remaining Indian populations had two options: noble savages could be integrated into the new nation by becoming civilized, while the untameable savages would be eliminated. The canon of Indianista works includes *Cumandá* (1879) by the Ecuadorean Juan León Mera, *Enriquillo* (1882) by the Dominican Manuel de Jesús Galván and *Tabaré* (1888) by the Uruguayan José Zorrilla de San Martín. In this century there are still some residues of Indianista perspective, but it is almost impossible to find a significant Indianista text (see for example **Saer**'s *El **entenado***).

Indianismo is almost always confused with ***indigenismo***. The latter term derives from *indígena* (indigenous) and was coined in order to avoid the wrong use of the term Indian. Unlike Indianismo, the most important feature of *indigenismo* is its desire to offer political representation in favour of the contemporary indigenous population of the Americas.

Further reading

Melendez, C. (1934) *La novela indianista en Hispanoamérica*, Madrid: Hermando.

Sommer, D. (1991) *Foundational Fictions*, Berkeley, CA: University of California Press.

JUAN ZEVALLOS AGUILAR

indigenisme

A radical literary movement in the 1920s, Haitian *indigenisme* was provoked by the nationalist backlash against the US occupation. Influenced by Charles Maurras and ethnologist Jean **Price-Mars**, the *indigenistes* criticized Haiti's Francophile elite and demanded that literature be grounded in an identifiably national reality. Their literary organ was the shortlived *La revue indigène* (1927–8), edited by Emile **Roumer** with the collaboration of poets Jacques **Roumain**, Carl **Brouard**, Philippe **Thoby-Marcelin** and Normil Sylvain. *Indigenisme* was similar to other movements in the Americas like the Harlem Renaissance, Afro-Cuban writing and ***indigenismo***.

J. MICHAEL DASH

indigenismo

Indigenismo is an artistic movement that seeks to represent and emphasize the marginalized and exploited position of Indian peoples throughout Latin American history. *Indigenismo* was most influential in the Andean region, Central America and in Mexico. Although the commitment of artists to Indian cultures extends beyond the flourishing of *indigenismo* proper, the label is more usually assigned to the wave of revolutionary and egalitarian ideologies during the first half of the twentieth century.

It was the Peruvian essayist José Carlos **Mariátegui** who in his ***Siete ensayos de interpretación de la realidad peruana*** (Seven Interpretive Essays on Peruvian Reality) (1928) established the scope of literary *indigenismo*. While so-called '**Indianismo**' is more related to an exotic, folkloric or sentimental depiction of the Indians, *indigenismo*, according to Mariátegui, is committed to the representation of the social and economic forces which intervene in their exploitation and subjection. An *indígena* literature, Mariátegui adds, one produced and consumed by the Indians themselves, has not yet been written. Mariátegui's classification reveals the paradoxes of *indigenismo*, since it constructs the split between the usually urban, educated and Spanish-speaking artists and the subjects they intend to represent. Most of this early *indigenista* literature is inscribed within Western narrative conventions, written in a non-Indian language and abounding with didactic passages and lexical explanations for the uninformed reader; this literature can be conceived of as alien to Indian cultures and as responding to the assimilative interests of the modern nation.

The precursor of the *indigenista* novel is *Aves sin nido* (Birds Without a Nest) (1889) by Peruvian writer Clorinda Matto de Turner. *Raza de Bronce* (People of the Sun) (1916), by the Bolivian Alcides **Arguedas**, *Huasipungo* (The Villagers) (1931), by the Ecuadorian Jorge **Icaza**, and *El mundo es ancho y ajeno* (Broad and Alien is the World) (1941), by the Peruvian Ciro **Alegría**, are among the most important works of the movement. The novels combine the depiction of scenes and characters in the vein of ***costumbrismo*** with naturalist and realist narrative causality. The inclusion of novels influenced by European modernism within the scope of *indigenismo* has been a subject of disagreement. The novels of José María **Arguedas**, Rosario **Castellanos**, Miguel Angel **Asturias** and Manuel **Scorza** are good examples of this trend, which has been called *neo-indigenismo*. These novels abandon representational or mimetic paradigms and an emphasis on social inequality in favour of a more general inquiry into Latin American identities through the filter of an Indian cosmovision.

Although a reaction against ornamentalism and academicism in pictorial art, *indigenismo* has become stagnated, particularly in the Andean region, as a purely folkloric and representational form, without taking into consideration new artistic trends. The most acclaimed artist of this tendency was the Peruvian José **Sabogal**, who dominated *indigenista* painting during the 1920s and 1930s. He also contributed to *Amauta*, the magazine that José Carlos Mariátegui directed. Other Peruvians who followed the same trend were Enrique Camino Brent, Camilo Blas, Julia Codesido, Jorge Segura and Mario Urteaga. The Ecuadorian Camilo **Egas** was also a recognized *indigenista*, achieving a certain success in the United States. In Mexico, the tendency cannot be understood without taking into account the 1910 Mexican Revolution (see **revolutions**), which transformed *indigenismo* into official cultural policy. Diego **Rivera**, David Alfaro **Siqueiros** and José Clemente **Orozco** were commissioned by the state to create monumental murals which can be considered both nationalist and *indigenista*. Without rejecting their modernist artistic sensibilities and education, they depicted the Indian past and present as the very essence of the Mexican soul.

Latin American music has been widely influenced by Indian tunes, rhythms, scales and instruments since the early twentieth century, and particularly during the various nationalist movements. The development of these trends in music runs parallel to the collections and the research undertaken by folklorists and ethno-musicologists. Theorist and composer Carlos **Chávez** is the most important figure of a Mexican cultured musical trend called Aztec Renaissance. The Brazilian Heitor **Villa-Lobos** incorporated anthropological research into Indian themes in order to create his symphonic compositions. *Indigenismo* in music cannot be easily delimited, since the scope of any kind of music that makes use of Indian elements exceeds any possible classification.

The Mexican cinema was profoundly marked by *indigenismo*, which was especially important for director Emilio **Fernández**, as in his *María Candelaria* (1943). A number of films with Indian motifs were also made in Bolivia and Peru, particularly after the 1950s. A major figure of an anti-imperialist and social revolutionary trend among these initiatives is Bolivian Jorge **Sanjinés**. His *Ukamau* (That's How It Is) (1966) was filmed in **Aymara**. This and his other films explicitly address Aymara and **Quechua** audiences, taking an indigenous point of view and critically reworking cinematic conventions. In Peru, the collective Cine Club Cuzco made documentaries about the Indians during the 1950s, an enterprise subsequently taken up by Eulogio **Nishiyama** and César Villanueva, who mixed documentary and fictional forms.

Further reading

Favre, H. (1998) *El indigenismo*, Mexico: Fondo de Cultura Económica.

Kaliman, R.J. (1994) 'Unseen systems: Avant-garde indigenism in the central Andes', in D. Jordan (ed.), *Regionalism Reconsidered: New Approaches to the Field*, New York: Garland, pp. 159–83.

Masferrer, K.E. (1981) *Indice general de boletin indigenista y noticias indigenistas de America, 1940–1980*, Mexico: Instituto Indigenista Interamericano.

Morana, M. (ed.) (1998) *Indigenismo hacia el fin del milenio: homenaje a Antonio-Conejo Polar*, Pittsbugh, PA: Instituto Internacional de Literatura Iberoamerica.

Prieto, R. (1996) 'The literature of Indigenismo', in R. Gonzalez Echevarria and E. Pupo-Walker (eds), *The Cambridge History of Latin American Literature, II: The Twentieth Century*, Cambridge: Cambridge University Press, pp. 138–63.

FERNANDO J. ROSENBERG

indigenous cultures

The term 'culture' refers to a contingent mix of elements; yet there is no essential feature of culture such as religion, language, land, economics, an institution, or customs. However, certain broad categories of cultural boundaries can be recognized. For instance, we speak of 'the Maya' or the 'Incas' as a cultural entity, while at the same time we are conscious that such labelling is complex. Although many books have been written defining the Mayas or the Incas, these cultural categorical terms do not reflect the many dialects spoken by these peoples and the many differing lifestyles of indigenous rural and urban communities.

Many indigenous peoples retain and value the legacy of their ancestors in regard to religion, agricultural practices, kinship affinities, indigenous economic systems, and appreciation of cultural artefacts. Often cultural knowledge is passed down from generation to generation despite the distractions of scientific and technological innovations. To be **Indian** formerly was thought to mean belonging to an indigenous community, to have a rich communal and ceremonial understanding of life, to reject western logic. Yet, Indian peoples actively acculturate and combine influences from external sources in their cultural *mélange*. Now indigenous pilots fly patients to hospitals to be diagnosed by indigenous doctors, native historians use laptops to research Indian history, and Indian politicians speak in sophisticated soundbites to excitable television reporters. Thus, the practice of culture is not an end in itself, but at the centre of economic and political struggle. Defining culture and cultural boundaries promotes indigenous self-determination, which allows for development along alternative patterns of a world view expressed in ancient rituals as well as communal land-holding and labour practices.

A focus on a number of specific cultural practices in Latin American regions carries us beyond faulty stereotypes of isolated villages and traditional crafts: the cause of cultural autonomy among the Miskitu (see **Miskitus**) (Nicaragua), coca culture among the Andean Indians, cultural-political alliances to settle land disputes in Ecuador, modern preservation of culture among the Mayans, and multi-media acculturation in Brazil.

The case of the Sandinistas (see **Sandinista Revolution**), who waged a long war and gained political hegemony in Nicaragua, illustrates the complexity of social change. The Miskitu peoples objected to the presence of troops in their villages and the restrictions on farming and fishing imposed by the Sandinistas on the Atlantic coast. The Miskitu's struggle for land rights, control of natural resources, self-government and respect for Miskitu culture brought them into conflict with Sandinista policies until 1987 when Nicaragua was the first in the Americas to enact an autonomy law which guaranteed cultural, religious, and linguistic rights. Despite this legislation, in February 1990, with the Sandinistas receiving a mere 10 to 20 per cent of the Miskitu vote, Violeta **Chamorro** was elected to the Presidency. With her victory, an Institute for Development of the Autonomous Regions was established and Brooklyn Rivera, a popular Miskitu leader, serves as the central government's representative. The Sandinistas, for their part, acknowledged their mistakes among the Miskitu: 'We arrived with no understanding of coast people's culture ... We tried to impose models from the Pacific' (Hale, p. 26).

Similar problems exist for Andean Indians in Bolivia and Peru who confront government attempts to curb mastication of a mild stimulant, the coca leaf. The use of coca is a cultural statement in the Andes: a medium of exchange, a means of communicating with the supernatural world, and a bonding mechanism for the promotion of kinship ties and cultural loyalties. Since the passage of international decrees on the control of coca (the Single Convention on Narcotic Drugs, 1961) as well as national decrees (Peruvian Legal Decree 22926, in 1976), peasants have mobilized in Cuzco (Peru) and Chaparé (Bolivia) to protest the coca leaf eradication programmes, heavily funded by the USA. Indians sought acceptance of coca leaf for 40 different health remedies and some 87 per cent of inhabitants in the small towns use the leaf daily. Furthermore, Indians seek the right to freely market the crop; in April 1983, Indians in three Bolivian cities mobilized a week-long road block.

The retention of Mayan culture is the occasion for considerable discussion among Mayan nationalists, who challenge both progressive and conservative positions on the topic. While one quarter of the nine million Mayans wear traditional clothing, at the same time university-educated Mayans are advocates for increased cultural freedom, the right to change according to self-determined guidelines. A blending of 'modern' science with traditional medicine and know-how may then develop new forms of Mayan knowledge. Concern about the significant decline in Mayan language use in Guatemala contributed to the founding of the Academy of Mayan Languages (1986). An autonomous state entity in 1990, the Academy promotes the knowledge and use of Mayan languages and research of linguistic and literary materials.

Negotiations between the Indians and the Ecuadorian state were spurred on after the 1990 uprising and a later march of protest in 1992. In both instances, land titles were a major issue. **CONAIE** (the Confederation of Indigenous Nationalities in Ecuador) demanded the return of land confiscated over the centuries and supported a regional proposal by CONFENAIE (Confederation of Indigenous Amazonians) to allocate and title 90 per cent of Pastaza province lands and sub-soil rights to four resident Indian ethnic groups. This plan, seen as creating a 'parallel state' within Ecuador's borders by many Ecuadorian citizens, was promoted by the Confederation as a model of development using ecological equilibrium in the extraction of oil from the tropical forest.

For the Kayapó (Brazil), preserving their culture led to active political confrontation with authorities. On 14 October 1988, 400 Kayapó warriors, painted in war colours of red and black and armed with clubs, arrived at a federal courthouse in Belém. When the first chief strode forward to testify to the government's disrespect for Indian rights, lands, and natural resources, the judge refused to hear the testimony. The Kayapó chief was told to dress in a 'respectable manner', not 'semi-nude'. When the incident was televised, media attention engulfed the tribe struggling for its rights. The Kayapó were willing participants in the media blitz. As of 1987, they have their own video cameras, VCRs, monitors, and videotapes in exchange for their participation in a documentary filmed by Granada Television. The Kayapó use their equipment to film their traditions as well as their negotiation sessions with government officials. Video has served as a legal transcript to record their lobbying of delegates regarding changes in the Brazilian constitution. As an anthropologist asserts, video for the Kayapó is 'as a means of getting other groups to speak *about* them... in giving political support and in furthering... projects of cultural mediation' (Turner, p. 106).

Further reading

Hale, C.(1991) 'Miskitu: Revolution in the revolution', *NACLA* 25(3): 24–9.
Pacini, D. and Franquemont, C. (eds.) (1986) *Coca and Cocaine: Effects on People and Policy in Latin America*, Cambridge, MA: Cultural Survival and Latin American Studies Programme, Cornell University.
Turner, T. (1995) 'Representation, collaboration and mediation in contemporary ethnographic and indigenous media', *Visual Anthropology Review* 11(2): 102–6.
Van Cott, D. (ed.) (1994) *Indigenous Peoples and Democracy in Latin America*, New York: St Martin's.
Wearne, P. (1996) *Return of the Indian: Conquest and Revival in the Americas*, Philadelphia: Temple University Press.

REGINA HARRISON

indigenous languages of highland South America

For the past 500 years there have been two major indigenous languages spoken in highland South America: Kichwa (**Quechua**/Quichua) and **Aymara** (Aimara). Kichwa was the language of the Incan court. While it was not widely imposed on subject communities during the Incan rule, Spanish friars and *encomenderos* found it expedient to use as a lingua franca during the early colonial period, and spread Kichwa rapidly. Colonial sources list some other languages in the highlands, the next most populous being Puquina, also thought possibly to have been the language of the cultural centre of Tiawanaku. Jesuits proselytizing during the early colonial period were required to learn Puquina, Kichwa and Aymara; however, as the latter two spread other languages, including Puquina died out. The Cuzco variety of Kichwa was chosen as the variety to disseminate. Reasoning at the time claimed it to be the purest form, the most correct or the most ancient. Glottochronological studies suggest, however, that the Cuzco dialect underwent the most innovation, perhaps from the necessity of administrating a far-flung empire. Today Kichwa is the largest native American language, having between eight and 12 million speakers. Aymara is the second most widely spoken language of South America, having between 2 and 2.5 million speakers. Kichwa and Aymara have been in contact for centuries; core vocabulary lists reveal many shared terms. Rather than prove derivation from a single mother tongue however, the patterns of interconnections suggest a long history of trade and cultural interchange. Today both languages are being used locally in written form; signs appear in the language of the region. Popular music is recorded and distributed in Kichwa. **Bilingual education** is becoming more generally available. The 1993 constitution of Peru makes Quechua (*sic*), Aimara, and other indigenous languages of the country co-official with Spanish in the regions in which they predominate. Other languages still spoken in some areas of the highlands include: Kawki and Jaqaru (of the Aymaran family) in Peru, Uru (a language isolate) in Bolivia, near Lake Titicaca and Chipaya (another isolate) spoken in Bolivia.

Further reading

Manelis Kline, H.E. and Stark, L.R. (eds) (1985) *South American Indian Languages: Retrospect and Prospect*, Austin: University of Texas Press.

Sherzer, J. and Urban, G. (eds) (1986) *Native South American Discourse*, Berlin: Mouton de Gruyter.

JUDITH M. MAXWELL

indigenous languages of lowland South America

Lowland South America is linguistically diverse. In the Amazonian basin the major language groups are Arawakan, Tupian, Yanomama, Saliban, Peba-Yaguan, Tacanan, Tukanoan, Zaparoan, Ge (or Jê), Carib, and Panoan. Tucanoan (Tukanoan), Zaparoan and Jivaroan as well as a number of isolates are also spoken in the lowland interior of Ecuador. Kichwa (**Quechua**/Quichua) is also spoken in the Ecuadorian lowlands. Numbers of Kichwa speakers are increasing both with immigration from the highlands and from spread as a lingua franca. Other lowland groups inhabit portions of Argentina: Guyakuruans, Matacoan, Jaqi (**Aymara**), Lule-Vilelans, Mapuche (Araucanians) (see **Mapuches**), Yagan, and Chon. Populations of Kichwa speakers also live this far south. Tupi-Guarani speakers in Argentina in recent years have established cross-national contact with speakers in Bolivia for mutual aid in **bilingual education** and community development. Paraguay is home to five language families: Zamuco, Mascoi, Matacoan, Guaykuru, and Tupi-Guarani. Guarani is co-official with Spanish in Paraguay. Louisa Stark estimates that Ecuadorian languages are becoming extinct at the rate of one every 25 years; Ernest Migliazza gives even higher language shift figures for Amazonia. Many of these languages are underdocumented, have only short word lists or sketch grammars recorded. Others, particularly, Guarani, Kichwa, Aymara, Yanomama, Arawakan, and Mapuche are well documented. Many communities have active bilingual education programmes, though some Guarani communities of Bolivia have opted to keep out western education, including bilingual classes.

The northwest Amazonian basin presents a marvellously complex linguistic picture. Indigenous communities are structured around linguistic exogamy. One must marry out of one's language group. A man must take a wife who speaks a different tongue. Extended families live together in long houses. Within a single house eleven or twelve different languages may be spoken. Children learn their father's tongue and their mother's tongue. Adults are multi-lingual. In addition to languages of the home, many people also speak Tukano as a lingua franca and Spanish or Portuguese for trade and politics.

Further reading

Derbyshire, D.C. and Pullum, G.K. (eds) (1986) *Handbook of Amazonian Languages*, vol. 1, Berlin: Mouton de Gruyter.

Jackson, J.E. (1983) *The Fish People: Linguistic Exogamy and Tukanoan Identity in Northwest Amazonia*, Cambridge: Cambridge University Press.

Manelis Klein, H.E. and Stark, L.R. (eds) (1985) *South American Indian Languages: Retrospect and Prospect*, Austin: University of Texas Press.

JUDITH M. MAXWELL

indigenous literature

The concept of indigenous literature was created by literary historians and historiographers in order to integrate Indian cultural production into both national and Latin American literatures. The most important collections of indigenous literature contain texts in languages of the most developed pre-Columbian civilizations and their successors. In other words, indigenous literatures are the collections of recorded compositions created by Aztecs, Incas, Mayans. The forms of recording include alphabetic writing, non-alphabetic writing, and devices of human memory in Indian, European and a mixture of European and Indian languages. The studies of indigenous literatures acknowledge the following periods: pre-Columbian, colonial, republican, and contemporary. The main sources of the pre-Columbian period are mesoamerican codices and inscriptions in Náhuatl and Mayan languages (see **Náhuatl and Aztecan languages**. The codices and the inscriptions include hieroglyphic and visual systems to register knowledge on paper and other materials. The reconstruction of the pre-Columbian period was also based on texts written during colonial times. The texts of the colonial and republican periods include documents written by Indians in Amerindian Languages, but using the Roman alphabet such as Fernando Alvarez Tezozómoc who wrote his *Crónica Mexicayotl* (*c.* 1609) in Náhuatl, or Guamán Poma de Ayala who wrote *Nueva Corónica y buen gobierno* (1613) (translated as Letter to a King) in a mixture of Spanish and **Quechua**. There are texts written by mestizos such as Inca Garcilaso de la Vega who translated Quechua oral tradition into Spanish in his *Comentarios Reales* (Royal Commentaries) (1609), and Europeans like Fray Fernandino de Sahagún who together with a group of Indian specialists wrote the earliest ethnography about Aztec culture in Náhuatl, Latin and Spanish from 1545 to 1580, or the Spanish priest Francisco de Avila who led an Indian group to compile Quechua oral tradition during the Catholic Campaign of *extirpación de idolatrías* (extirpation of ideolatries) later collected in *Dioses y hombres de Huarochiri* (Gods and Men of Huarochiri) (*c.* 1598).

In addition to collaborative/testimonial texts and transcriptions of oral tradition, both the republican and the contemporary period include textual production in Spanish and indigenous languages by indigenous authors. In the nineteenth century, production in indigenous languages includes letters, proclamations, and communiqués, but in the twentieth century, and especially during the last thirty years of it, the textual corpus by indigenous authors has grown to include genres more immediately recognizable as literary, including dramas, short-stories, poetry, and at least one novel (*El tiempo principia en Xibalbá* (Time Begins in Xibalbá) (1985), by the Guatemalan writer Luis de Lión). A significant amount of this literature has been produced in writing workshops with non-Indian writers as facilitators (see **workshop poetry**).

In addition to linguistic issues, these works raise significant questions of genre. The most important work produced by indigenous authors in indigenous languages has been in genres associated with oral tradition, especially drama and poetry. For example, the members of the Maya theatre company in Chiapas, Mexico, **Sna Jtz'ibajom** (and its feminist offshoot, Fomma) work within a tradition established by Mexico's National Indigenous Institute, which, in the 1950s promoted a Maya puppet troupe performing works written in collaboration with the well known intellectual Rosario **Castellanos**. However, granted that poetry is the genre most closely aligned with oral tradition, it is not surprising that the most prominent Indian writers are poets, such as the renowned Quiché poet Humberto **Ak'abal** (Guatemala) and the Mapuche (see **Mapuches**) poet Elicura **Chihuailaf** (Chile). Works by Ak'abal and other Indian poets are often published in bilingual editions which are accessible to a wider reading public, and together with other trends, such as testimonial narratives and auto-ethnographic writings, these texts by indigenous authors are extending a counter-tradition of Indian writings which draws from the dominant, Hispanic literary history while profoundly questioning its ability to express national or cultural identity.

Further reading

Bareiro Saguer, R. (1980) *Literatura Guaraní del Paraguay*, Caracas: Editorial Ayacucho.

Bendezú, E. (1993) *Literatura Quechua*, Caracas: Biblioteca Ayacucho, 2nd edn.

Segala, A. (1990) *Literatura náhuatl. Fuentes, identidades, representaciones*, Mexico DF: Grijalbo.

Sodi, D. (1990) *La literatura de los Mayas*, Mexico, DF: Joaquín Mortoz.

Vázquez, J.A. (1977) 'The field of Latin American Indian Literatures', *Latin American Indian Literatures* 1: 1–33.

JUAN ZEVALLOS AGUILAR AND BRIAN GOLLNICK

indigenous movements

The rise of indigenous movements throughout Latin America has had dramatic consequences for politics and culture across the continent. Twenty-five years ago, the predominant cultural model for the Latin-American nation-state was *mestizaje*, the blending of different cultural traditions into a new and specifically Latin American type of individual. Today, indigenous groups have reappeared where many people thought they no longer existed, for example in Argentina, demanding the right to be recognized as distinct peoples within the nation (and sometimes across national boundaries). They have called for changes in national **Constitutions**, improvements in legal and human rights, recognition of customary law and the implementation of bilingual intercultural education (see **bilingualism and biculturalism**). And Latin American indigenous leaders have achieved international recognition. Two Guatemalan Mayan women, Rigoberta **Menchú** and Rosalina Tuyuc, have come to prominence respectively as the youngest ever Nobel Peace Prize laureate and vice-president of the Guatemalan Congress. The Brazilian Kayapo leader Paulinho Paiakan received a UN prize for his work to protect the tropical forest environment. In Bolivia an indigenous Aymara, Víctor Hugo Cárdenas, was elected vice-president of the country in 1993.

In the mid-1990s there were around 40 million indigenous people in Latin America, 6 per cent of the total population, and their numbers are growing. In Bolivia and Guatemala they are in a majority. Until recently, the general assumption was that Latin American indigenous populations would disappear. With greater economic prosperity and cultural development, indigenous people would be absorbed into the 'national' culture and lose their distinctive identities. Their colourful costumes would be confined to museums and folkloric festivals, their languages replaced by Spanish or Portuguese, their communities dissolved into a more entrepreneurial individualism, their pagan religious practices giving way to more restrained forms of Christian worship.

In the early twentieth century, *indigenista* movements in many Latin American countries arose out of concern at the economic exploitation and lack of legal rights of rural indigenous populations, and sought to celebrate indigenous culture in writing and the plastic arts. But the *indigenistas* were mainly urban intellectuals. Many of them did not speak indigenous languages fluently, since only in Paraguay does an indigenous language – **Guarani** – function as an effective second national language. The rise of indigenous movements in the 1960s–1990s is, then, an unprecedented phenomenon.

In the 1960s and 1970s, the spread of schooling meant that in some areas young indigenous people were well-educated, and hoping for professional careers. When they came up against well-established patterns of discrimination and racism (see **race**), they were no longer as prepared as their parents to deny their ethnic origins in order to get on in the urban mestizo world. Simultaneously, the increased presence in rural areas of NGOs and sympathetic religious leaders, especially from the liberal wing of the Catholic Church (see **Catholicism**), led to the founding of organizations with a strong indigenous presence, often peasant unions. The Shuar Federation, founded in Ecuador in 1964 to safeguard the collective landholdings of the Amazonian Shuar people, was perhaps the first of these. Land was, and remains, a crucial issue for indigenous peoples. Furthermore, as literacy requirements for the right to vote have given way to universal suffrage, the potential votes of formerly disenfranchised indigenous populations have become significant political capital over which aspiring politicians compete.

The decline of left-wing politics and the growth of **new social movements**, based more on shared identity and consumption than on class politics, have contributed to the growth of indigenous movements worldwide. The discourse of equality and liberation typical of revolutionary socialist movements ignored or suppressed the particular concerns of indigenous peoples, and denied the prevalence of racism. Examples of the growing divergence between the left and indigenous people abound. Peasant organizations were excluded altogether from the leftist Bolivian Popular Assembly of 1971. In Nicaragua in the early 1980s, Miskito Indians (see **Miskitus**) became vociferous opponents of the revolutionary Sandinista (see **Sandinista Revolution**) government. In Colombia, indigenous organizations such as CRIC (Indigenous Regional Council of the Cauca) have struggled against takeovers by revolutionary groups, and have continued to be victims of guerrilla violence.

These developments, and the burgeoning of indigenous organizations, were dramatically reinforced by the 1992 Quincentenary of Columbus's first voyage to the Americas (see **Columbian quincentenary**). In preparation, indigenous and leftist organizations across the continent planned their opposition to the official celebrations of the 'discovery' of the Americas. Their own slogan became '500 years of resistance by indigenous, black and mestizo people'. These meetings brought together organizations and groups for the first time, who gained strength by sharing and exchanging experiences, and by the sense of being part of an international movement. The 1989 ILO Convention 169 on Indigenous Peoples was in part inspired by the preparations for 1992, as was the indigenous uprising of 1990 in Ecuador. The awarding of the 1992 Nobel Peace Prize to Rigoberta Menchú Tum, a K'iche' activist from Guatemala, and the instatement of the 1993 Year of Indigenous Populations, followed by the 1994–2004 Decade of the Indigenous Populations of the World, were also direct consequences of 1992 and what it stood for.

While many indigenous movements have their origins in trade union or religious organizations, they have developed original and distinctive tactics for voicing their demands. For example, in Bolivia indigenous groups have repeatedly disrupted national communications and commerce through effective roadblocks. In Peru, indigenous peasants have developed effective vigilante organizations known as *rondas campesinas*, both as a response to political violence and as a means of promoting justice in their communities in the absence of any effective national judicial system in rural areas. The traditional hostility and suspicion between highland and tropical forest indigenous peoples has been transcended in some countries, most notably in Ecuador, where **CONAIE** (The Confederation of Indigenous Nationalities of Ecuador, founded in 1980) has proved an extremely effective organization because it is seen as representing indigenous groups in the country. There are now numerous umbrella organizations crossing national boundaries, of which the largest is **COICA** (Coordination of Indigenous Organizations of the Amazon Basin), founded in 1996.

Many indigenous organizations have become adept at exploiting the media. The Brazilian Kayapo hosted an international meeting in 1988 with the rock star Sting, to protest against proposed dams on the Xingu river. Footage and photos of them in their feathers and body-paint, making videos of the journalists, were headline news across the international media. In both Bolivia (1990) and Ecuador (1992), long marches from the distant Amazon lowlands to the highland capital captured the local media's attention. In Mexico the EZLN (**Zapatista** Army of National Liberation) used the Internet to draw world attention to the plight of the indigenous people of Chiapas, timing their initial action for 1 January 1994, the day the Free Trade Agreement (**NAFTA**) among Mexico, Canada and the USA came into force. They have succeeded in retaining a high profile ever since, in part through their skilled use of electronic communication.

Indigenous peoples have been caught up in the bloody confrontations between leftist guerrillas and government forces in several countries, notably in Peru and Guatemala in the 1980s. The ending of conflict has seen strikingly different outcomes for indigenous groups. In Guatemala, many indigenous people, faced by the unspeakable brutality of the counter-insurgency forces, ended up joining the guerrillas. Their interests were actively taken into account in the peace negotiations that began in 1991, leading to the signing of an Accord on Identity and Rights of the Indigenous People in 1994. However, they were not allowed to participate directly, an experience that reinforced their sense of permanent exclusion from national political life. As a result, Maya organizations and groups burgeoned during the 1990s.

By contrast, in Peru indigenous movements are confined to the Amazon lowlands. The peasants in the former Inca domains of the high Andes have not developed a consciously indigenous presence of any significance, even though they number over 8 million and belong to a single language group, Quechua. The reasons for this surprising contrast to other Latin American countries are hard to determine. In part they are certainly due to the consistent dismissal of indigenous issues by **Sendero Luminoso** (Shining Path), the most successful guerrilla organization. Perhaps another factor is the way that the populist (see **populism**) military government of General **Velasco** (1968–75) used and manipulated indigenous traditions and imagery in its attempt to win popular support, and so debased their currency. Whatever the reasons, in stark contrast to developments in other parts of the continent, the dominant political and cultural discourse in Peru of the late 1990s is that of national integration and security, and the most striking form of indigenous organization in the Andean region is the local vigilante groups.

The late modernist decline of universalist theories has led to a growth of interest in indigenous cultures and religions across the world. In the Americas, the shamanistic practices (see **shamanism**) of many indigenous groups, with their techniques for entering altered states of consciousness, have enjoyed a dramatic revival, encouraged by the enthusiasm of Westerners in search of an alternative spirituality. In many Latin American cities, devotees of indigenous spirits and deities are to be found, sometimes in trance, sometimes decked in colourful feather costumes dancing through the streets. A well-known example is the *concheros* of Mexico City, whose quest for an authentic Mexican identity has led them back to Aztec religion).

Land, and the staple foods of maize (see **corn and corncakes**), potatoes (see **potato**) or game, are the basis of indigenous identity. A strong attachment to nature is powerfully expressed in indigenous religions, which promote harmony and integration between human and natural worlds. In consequence, many people proclaim that indigenous cultures offer an example to the destructive West of how to live in harmony with nature and how to treat the environment with respect. On the other hand, many indigenous people adapt to modernity by abandoning their ancestral religion altogether, and joining one of the thousands of Protestant churches (see **Protestantism**) that have exploded across Latin America.

This example points to what is probably the major dilemma faced by indigenous people and organizations: how can they retain their distinctive identity while changing, modernizing, and engaging with all the complexity of life in the late twentieth and early twenty-first centuries? Indigenous culture is still identified primarily with a rural and subsistence-based way of life, and with 'tradition'. Opponents of indigenous movements often point out that today's indigenous cultures are not 'authentic' in the sense that their costumes may be adapted from colonial fashions and motifs. Their languages have incorporated Spanish and Portuguese loan words, their music is hybrid, and their whole way of life reflects their centuries-long association with European, African and other outside cultures. These arguments affect even the most isolated indigenous people in the depths of the forest.

Debates on how to retain a sense of their distinctive traditions while not remaining ossified in the past take different forms. Many groups strive to define distinctive indigenous development policies that draw on their own collective traditions and values, as well as on outside technologies and skills. Others focus on the need to rewrite history from an indigenous point of view, in order to demonstrate that indigenous people have always been changing and adapting to new circumstances, while resisting colonial and neo-colonial oppression. Others emphasize the importance of changing terminology. The term '**Indian**' underlines their status as colonized people. 'Peasant' emphasizes class affiliation rather than cultural identity. 'Indigenous' suggests that they are outside the mainstream of modern civilization. 'First people' (*pueblos originarios*) is growing in currency as a term which draws attention to their new legal demands.

In the late 1990s, indigenous peoples' concerns to end centuries of cultural, political and racial discrimination have led to the formulation of increasingly specific campaigns. The growing interest in bilingual intercultural education reflects the need to promote indigenous languages and cultures in the face of mass education. A number of Latin American countries have altered their constitutions to recognize the 'multicultural and plurilingual' status of their citizens. One of the first such reforms was that of Colombia in 1991, which includes a provision reserving two seats in the national Senate for indigenous representatives. Increasingly, indigenous movements are demanding the recognition of indigenous territories to safeguard what remains of their lands in the face of neoliberal policies (see **neoliberalism**), and to ensure a level of local autonomy. This has led in turn to demands for the recognition of customary law and traditional authorities.

These demands would have seemed inconceivable even in the 1970s. The speed with which certain entrenched positions have dissolved in the 1990s indicates that dramatic changes are occurring in Latin American political and cultural life. Opponents speak of the danger of 'yugoslavization', suggesting that national integrity is undermined by the upsurge in ethnic identities, and civilized values are destroyed by a return to the ways of savagery. But more optimistic voices argue that these developments can help to reformulate Latin American cultures in terms of a genuine pluralism, and that the recognition of indigenous rights will lead to a positive deepening of **democracy**.

Further reading

Albo, X. (1991) 'El retorno del indio', *Revista Andina* 18: 229–366.
Bonfil, G. (1981) *Utopía y revolución. El pensamiento político contemporáneo de los Indios de América Latina*, Eds Revolución.
Burgos Debray, E. (1983) *I, Rigoberta Menchú*, London: Verso.
Díaz Polanco, H. (1997) *Indigenous Peoples in Latin America: The Quest for Self-Determination*, California: Latin American Perspectives Publications, no.18.
Fischer, E. and McKenna Brown, R. (1996) *Maya Cultural Activism in Guatemala*, Austin, TX: University of Texas Press.
Rappaport, J. (1994) *Cumbe Reborn: An Andean Ethnography of History*, Chicago: Chicago University Press.
Van Cott, D.L. (1994) *Indigenous Peoples and Democracy in Latin America*, Basingstoke: Macmillan.
Wearne, P. (1996) *Return of the Indian. Conquest and Revival in the Americas*, London: Cassell and Latin American Bureau.

OLIVIA HARRIS

Indio ecuatoriano, El

Pío Jaramillo Alvarado's fundamental and pioneering book *El Indio Ecuatoriano* (The Indian in Ecuador), on the indigenous question in Ecuador, was first published in 1922 and reprinted repeatedly thereafter. Although its author considered it a matter of absolute necessity that the Indian should be incorporated into white–mestizo culture, the work is a dramatic denunciation of the continuing practice of *concertaje*, or imprisonment for debt, and of the unequal distribution of land which disregarded the rights of indigenous communities.

RAÚL VALLEJO

infant mortality

The overall rate of infant mortality was on the decline in the Latin American and Caribbean region during the 1990s, but the rate remains high in a number of countries. The highest infant mortality rates are found in the Caribbean countries of Haiti and the Dominican Republic, the Andean countries of Bolivia, Peru and Ecuador, and the Central American countries of El Salvador, Guatemala, Honduras and Nicaragua. The lowest are found in Chile, Cuba, Puerto Rico, and some of the smaller islands of the Caribbean. It is estimated that each year about 600,000 infants die before their first birthday in Latin America and the Caribbean.

Worldwide, Africa has the highest rate of infant mortality, at an average of 94 deaths per 1000 live births, with Sierra Leone topping the list at 170 per year for the period of 1995–2000 (source: United Nations Population Division). In comparison, Haiti's infant mortality rate was 109.5 for 1993, which dropped to 97.6 for 1998. Bolivia's rate was 76.7 for 1993 and 62.2 for 1998. Guatemala's rate was 55.6 for 1993 and 46.15 for 1998. Brazil showed the greatest drop in infant mortality for the period, with a rate of 61.7 for 1993 which dropped to 35.4 for 1998. Paraguay, Costa Rica and Panama showed increases for the period, with Paraguay having the greatest increase, from 26.4 for 1993 to 36.4 for 1998 (source: CIA Fact Book). Precise measurements of infant mortality are notoriously difficult to pinpoint, given the fact that both births and deaths of infants are often underregistered. The United Nations has set a goal of decreasing infant mortality rates in all countries to 35 or less by the year 2015.

The primary causes of infant mortality are intestinal infections, acute respiratory infections from pneumonia and influenza, perinatal congenital defects, nutritional deficiencies, and low birth weight. Social conditions such as extreme poverty, poor housing, lack of prenatal health care and lack of maternal education are major factors in the development of these health problems. Some of the most important steps that have contributed to lowering infant mortality rates in underdeveloped countries include improvements in sanitation campaigns, breastfeeding and literacy campaigns for women, promotion of oral rehydration therapy, immunization programmes and improved access to health care services.

Further reading

Bahr, J., and Werhahn, R. (1993) 'Life expectancy and infant mortality in Latin America', *Social Sciences Medicine* 36 (10): 1373–82.
Bucht, B. (1990) 'Child mortality in developing countries' in H.M. Wallace and K. Giri (eds), *Health Care of Women and Children in Developing Countries*, Oakland, CA: Third Party Publishing, pp. 279–91.

CAROL WALLACE

Infante, Pedro

b. 1917, Sinaloa, Mexico; d. 1957, Mérida, Yucatan, Mexico

Actor and singer

A Mexican cinema icon, Infante was a radio singer until winning a part in 1942 in *La feria de las flores* (The Flower Market). *La ametralladora* (The Machine Gun) and *Viva mi desgracia* (Long Live My Misery) followed a year later. His first box office hit was Ismael **Rodríguez**'s *Los tres García* (The Three Garcias) in 1946, but *Nosotros los pobres* (We the Poor) (1947) established their success as a team, working together continuously until the actor's death. Infante's career was tied to the urban comedy and ***ranchera*** melodrama genres.

PATRICIA TORRES SAN MARTÍN

inflation and hyperinflation

Inflation is commonly explained as 'too much money chasing too few goods'. Inflation occurs when prices are rising. This means that money loses value as the same amount of money buys fewer goods and services than in the past. The rate of inflation is calculated as the average rate of increase of consumer prices. In developed countries it generally fluctuates between 2 and 6 per cent per year while in developing countries inflation rates tend to be much higher and more erratic.

Hyperinflation or runaway inflation occurs when inflation increases rapidly and runs out of control. This is due to an excessive printing of money by the Central Bank in response to government budget deficits and balance of payments crises. A notorious example of hyperinflation in Latin America is Bolivia with an inflation rate of 11,750 per cent in 1985. Argentina and Peru experienced hyperinflation between 1989 and 1990, Brazil from 1989 to 1994, and Nicaragua from 1988 to 1991. Periods of hyperinflation are often associated with economic and social turmoil. After a period of hyperinflation a new currency replaces the old. In Brazil, the Minister of Finance, Fernando Henrique **Cardoso**, introduced a stabilization plan which he named after the new currency – the Plan Real. His success in taming Brazil's hyperinflation led to his election as President. In 1995 most Latin American countries had an inflation rate of between 5 and 25 per cent, reflecting a more normal situation.

During the 1950s and 1960s a group of Latin American economists challenged the conventional wisdom on the nature and cures of inflation, giving rise to a protracted debate between 'structuralists' and 'monetarists'. The structuralist position on inflation also emerged as a reaction to the stabilization policies pursued by some Latin American governments at the urging of the International Monetary Fund (IMF) based in Washington, DC. At the heart of the controversy were different economic philosophies. Structuralists give far greater weight to the social and political origins of inflation than monetarists or neoliberals. They also placed greater emphasis on the role of the State in promoting economic development, overcoming the deficiencies of the market and curing inflation. For structuralists, social and political reforms as well as structural changes in the economy are needed to achieve development and tackle the inflationary problem. While structuralists favoured an inward-oriented and, to some extent, a self-reliant development strategy, monetarists advocated an outward-oriented development strategy which relied more heavily on the international market.

What, then, are the cures for inflation? While monetarists stress monetary and fiscal measures to reduce demand, structuralists emphasize development measures which tackle specific supply bottlenecks. Structuralists do not disregard monetary and fiscal policies but subordinate these to their programme of structural change. The structuralist versus monetarist controversy had a major influence on government anti-inflationary or stabilization policy throughout Latin America. In the 1990s structuralist and monetarist positions have begun to converge.

Further reading

Cardoso, E. and Helwege, A. (1992) *Latin America's Economy: Diversity, Trends, and Conflicts*, Cambridge, MA: The MIT Press.

CRISTÓBAL KAY

Ingenieros, José

b. 1877, Palermo, Sicily; d. 1925, Buenos Aires, Argentina

Writer, sociologist and psychiatrist

Ingenieros is widely regarded as responsible for the introduction of positivism and utilitarianism into Argentina. Like his teacher Ramos Mejía, Ingenieros explored simulation, criminality and madness in his *La simulación en la lucha por la vida* (Simulation in the Struggle for Life) (1904). In 1908 he formed the first Argentine Psychological Association; he is regarded as the founder of criminology in Argentina, with his 1908 volume *Criminología*. Together with Horacio Piñero, he laid the groundwork for a natural and objective psychology. He also actively promoted the study of history.

GRACIELA MUSACHI

ingenio, El

A historical essay by Manuel **Moreno Fraginals**, its first volume was published in 1964 by the Cuban National Commission of UNESCO. Its second edition, in 1978, included all three volumes of the work, which analysed the historical development of the sugar industry and its connections to the political and social phenomena of the time. It is a key work in understanding the evolution of Cuban history. *El ingenio* brings together accounts of the industry, a dictionary of sugar-related terms and a full statistical survey. The 1964 edition was translated into English in 1976.

WILFREDO CANCIO ISLA

Ingram, Kenneth Everard Niven

b. 1921, St Ann, Jamaica

Bibliographer and poet

With poets like George Campbell, Una Marson and Vivian **Virtue**, Ingram helped indigenize Jamaican poetry. He attended Jamaica College and the University of London. His poems and short stories of the 1940–4 period formed part of the creative nationalistic surge influenced by Edna **Manley** and the 'Drumblair' circle; he has a small (unpublished) body of poetry from the post-1944 years. A librarian with strong research interests, his output is mainly in bibliography. Although his work appears in anthologies and serials (*Focus, Public Opinion, Life and Letters*), no collection of his poetry or fiction exists.

PAT DUNN AND PAMELA MORDECAI

INI

INI (Instituto Nacional Indigenista – National Indigenous Institute) is the organism of the Mexican State charged with overseeing government policy towards indigenous peoples. Formed in 1948, the INI replaced earlier government outreach programmes to indigenous communities and was initially based on a model of regional economic development, inspired in part by the success of the Tennessee Valley Authority in the USA. This model of integrated regional development was implemented through a series of regional co-ordinating centres, the first of which was formed in the Highlands of Chiapas in 1951. The INI and the Instituto Nacional de Antropología e Historia (**INAH**) have played a central role developing one of the strongest national traditions of ethnographic research in Latin America. Important writers of Mexico's *indigenista* literature, including Rosario **Castellanos** and Carlos Antonio Castro, worked on the INI's anthropological projects, and Juan **Rulfo** worked for many years as the INI's Director of Publications. However, the more explicitly political function of the INI *vis-à-vis* the INAH has been heavily criticized for maintaining a paternalistic approach to the implementation of the State's Indian cultural politics, and in recent years both the INAH and the Centro de Investigaciones y Estudios Superiores en Antropología Social (CIESAS) have eclipsed the INI as an academic institution.

BRIAN GOLLNICK

Inkarri

Inkarri is a mythical character of Peruvian popular culture. The name derives from 'Inka Rey' (King Inca), a conjunction of an Indian ruler with the universal power of a European monarch. The myth proclaims the return of an Inca who will turn the world upside down and liberate the Indian population from centuries of Western domination. This popular response to the trauma of the conquest started with the decapitation of the last surviving Inca, Tupac Amaru the First, in 1572. The myth has it that the Inca will return when the head (taken to Spain) is reunited again with his body (in Peru).

JOSÉ ANTONIO MAZZOTTI

Inodoro Pereyra

A cartoon character created in 1978 by Roberto **Fontanarrosa** and representing a folkloric, philosophical and offbeat view of Argentine life and customs. Named 'inodoro' (toilet bowl) 'because my father worked in the sanitation department', Pereyra's two interlocutors are his dog Mendieta, whose remarks on his master's actions and sayings are intended as the reflections of a sane observer, and his bedraggled wife Eulogia, who comes into the cartoon when crisis, failure and doom are imminent. Widely distributed as a cartoon strip, and published annually by Ediciones de la Flor in book form, Inodoro Pereyra became a national, much-quoted point of cultural reference.

ANDREW GRAHAM-YOOLL

Institute of Jamaica

Founded in 1879 as an intellectual, artistic and literary association, by the late twentieth century the Institute of Jamaica had become an umbrella organization encompassing the principal research and cultural institutions of the island nation. The organizations embraced under the Institute's authority include: the National Library of Jamaica, the Jamaica Folk Museum, the Arawak (Indian) Museum, a Natural History Division, the Maritime Museum, the African-Caribbean Institute/Jamaica Memory Bank and the National Gallery of Jamaica. Prior to 1983 the Institute was also responsible for the Jamaica National Trust Commission and the Port Royal Centre for Archaeology and Conservation Research, but these were placed under a separate new authority known as the Jamaica National Heritage Trust. Publications of the Institute include: the ***Jamaica Journal***, dealing largely with social science, humanities and cultural issues; a *Bulletin*, dealing with science; and also a separate series of occasional papers in natural history.

ROSANNE ADDERLEY

Instituto Caro y Cuervo

Founded in 1944 in Bogotá under the directorship of Father Félix Restrepo, the Instituto Caro y Cuervo's primary objectives were to prepare a scholarly Spanish-language dictionary and to collect the writings of the two nineteenth-century Colombian scholars after whom it was named. The *Diccionario de construcción y régimen de la lengua castellana* was completed and published in eight volumes in 1994. The institute had already published a number of other dictionaries of Latin American Spanish, and its journal, *Thesaurus*, has provided a forum for scholarly debate on issues of linguistics and philology since its initial publication in 1947. The institute now contains departments of cultural history and literature, and the Andrés Bello Centre devoted to training Latin American philologists and lexicographers. In May 1998 an exhibition commemorating the institute's work was organized at the **Casa de las Américas** in Havana.

MIKE GONZALEZ

Instituto de Cooperación Iberoamericana

The Instituto de Cooperación Iberoamericana, or ICI as it is widely known, is an organization funded by the Spanish government that has a network of cultural centres throughout Spanish America. Its headquarters in Madrid publishes *Cuadernos Hispanoamericanos* and sponsors many cultural activities. The branch offices, located in the capital cities of many Spanish American countries, have libraries and sponsor activities such as exhibits and book presentations. The directors of the centres are sent from Spain. The ICI branches, along with other institutions that had funding and government support from abroad, such as the Goethe Institutes, played important cultural roles during the difficult years of military dictatorship in the **Southern Cone** countries.

DANIEL BALDERSTON

Instituto de Cultura Puertorriqueña

The Instituto de Cultura Puertorriqueña (Institute of Puerto Rican Culture) is a government institution created by Law 89 of the Estado Libre Asociado de Puerto Rico (Free Associated State of Puerto Rico) of 21 June 1955, to encourage, develop and conserve every manifestation of island culture. Consisting of a Board of Directors and an executive director nominated by the governor of the island, the institution represented in its early years the state's emphasis on preserving what was called the 'cultural heritage of Puerto Rico'. Its first director was Dr Ricardo Alegría. It has its own publishing house, sponsors a number of artistic festivals and runs workshops in a variety of artistic media.

JUAN CARLOS QUINTERO HERENCIA

Instituto Di Tella

The Instituto Di Tella is a cultural institution established in Buenos Aires in 1958 by the Di Tella family, to promote the arts and social sciences. It was founded with the aim of opening up post-Peronist Argentina (see **Peronism**) and making Buenos Aires an international artistic capital. The Institute absorbed the vibrant cultural atmosphere of the 1960s, and gave special attention to the avant-garde and experimentation. It was organized in two areas, social sciences and the arts, the latter embracing three centres devoted to visual arts, music and theatre. The art centres were closed in the early 1970s because of mounting financial difficulties and growing hostility from the military government.

ALVARO FERNÁNDEZ-BRAVO

Instituto Internacional de Literatura Iberoamericana

The Instituto Internacional de Literatura Iberoamericana was founded in 1938 in Mexico City by a group of professors of Latin American literature that included Arturo **Torres-Ríoseco**, Concha Meléndez, John Englekirk and Francisco Monterde (with the backing of Alfonso **Reyes** and Pedro **Henríquez Ureña**), and began to publish the *Revista iberoamericana* in the following year; the first issue opened with obituaries for Leopoldo **Lugones** and Alfonsina **Storni**. Since then, the Instituto has regularly held international conferences and has published the journal, volumes of conference proceedings and other books, including in recent years compilations in honour of Angel **Rama** and Antonio **Cornejo Polar**. From 1955 until his death in 1991, the *Revista iberoamericana* was edited by the Argentine poet and critic, Alfredo Roggiano, and for almost all of that time (and in the years since) the Instituto has been based at the University of Pittsburgh. The journal and publication series are currently directed by Mabel Moraña. The *Revista* has published special issues on **Borges**, José María **Arguedas**, **Vallejo**, **Huidobro** and other major figures, as well as on the literature of individual countries and topics of current interest (women's writing, colonial literature, fin de siècle, literature and sexuality).

DANIEL BALDERSTON

Insularismo

Puerto Rican essayist Antonio S. Pedreira's *Insularismo* (Insularity) (1934) was part of a series of extended essays that purported to diagnose a national pathology, a tradition that was related to so-called ***arielismo***. A significant example from Spain was José Ortega y Gasset's *España invertebrada* (Invertebrate Spain) (1921); other examples include Alcides **Arguedas**'s *Pueblo enfermo* (Sick People) (1909) on Bolivia and Samuel **Ramos**'s *El perfil del hombre y de la cultura en México* (Profile of Man and Culture in Mexico) (1934). Pedreira's essay, as its title implies, took its guiding metaphor from geography; Puerto Rico's geography, as well as its continued colonial status (four hundred years under Spanish rule, and then US occupation), made it isolated and docile. (The idea of Puerto Rican docility was taken up in a later essay by René Marqués, 'El puertorriqueño dócil' (The Docile Puerto Rican) (1962).) Pedreira was a defender of Puerto Rico's Hispanic identity, which sometimes coloured his observations on the presence of black culture on the island, and on its lost indigenous culture, with an unmistakable racism (see **black cultures; indigenous cultures**). He was also rather dismissive of the island's popular culture. His essay has been in print since its publication, with many editions by the **Instituto de Cultura Puertorriqueña**, and is considered one of the central texts of the Puerto Rican canon; at the same time, Pedreira's analysis and conclusions have been questioned (or perhaps demolished) by critics such as Juan Flores and Juan Gelpí.

DANIEL BALDERSTON

Insurgentes Avenue

Mexico City's longest boulevard, Insurgentes, crosses the city from north to south for eighteen miles, reaching into the State of Mexico; it is crossed from west to east by Reforma. Insurgentes is a major highway, along with the network of *ejes viales* or 'lateral points'. There are countless landmarks along its path, from the central intersection marked by Cuauhtémoc Monument. South lie Plaza Insurgentes, the **Polyforum Cultural Siqueiros**, the Insurgentes Theatre, the Álvaro Obregón Monument, the national university, **UNAM** and beyond, its Cultural Centre. North lie the Monumento a la Raza and the Instituto Politécnico Nacional (The Polytechnic).

EDUARDO SANTA CRUZ

Integralismo

Integralismo is a Brazilian variant of fascism (see **fascism in Latin America**), founded in October 1932 by Plínio **Salgado**. Influenced by the neo-Indianist nationalism of Salgado's earlier project, ***verdeamarelismo***, its appeal was limited since it could not defend a theory of national racial purity in as ethnically diverse a country as Brazil. Its anti-semitism and anti-communism hastened the rightward drift of the **Vargas** regime. After a 42,000-strong Integralista congress in October 1935, and the bloody suppression of an insurrection in November, the fabrication of a communist conspiracy, the 'Cohen Plan', precipitated the implantation of the dictatorial **Estado Novo**. Ironically, the clampdown on political opposition hit the Integralistas themselves, who were banished to the political wilderness as Brazil entered the Second World War on the Allied side.

DAVID TREECE

intellectuals

The public intellectual has long played a prominent role in Latin American society. As analysed by the Uruguayan critic Angel **Rama** in *La ciudad letrada* (The Lettered City) (1984), the figure and role of the elite writer has been debated for a hundred years. The intense debates around issues of social justice of the last several decades have often been led by figures who are oppositional to governments and official cultural institutions. **Green activism**, **gay and lesbian movements**, indigenous rights movements (see **indigenous movements**), **liberation theology** and liberation philosophy as well as diverse **women's movements** have been organized by and centred around public intellectuals.

One example is the Mexican writer and social commentator Carlos **Monsiváis**, who has made cameo appearances as himself on Mexican television soap operas, has appeared in strip cartoons, and was even called 'a frumpy Mexican Woody Allen' in the *New York Times* account of the funeral of Octavio **Paz**. Latin America has a long tradition of politicians who are intellectuals, often writers, including such eminent figures as Domingo Faustino Sarmiento, José Martí, Rómulo **Gallegos**, Juan **Bosch**, Ernesto **Cardenal**, Sergio **Ramírez**, Rosario **Castellanos**, Luis Alberto **Sánchez** and Elena **Poniatowska**. The experience of Cardenal, Ramírez and others in contemporary Nicaragua suggests, however, that relations in what Angel Rama called 'the city of letters' between the intellectual and the state are often uneasy and being renegotiated. (This process continues with such figures as Subcomandante Marcos in Chiapas, but also just as uneasily with intellectuals in positions of power today like Fernando Henrique **Cardoso** in Brazil and José Joaquín **Brunner** in Chile.)

The intellectual, considered as an identity category, was first used as a noun in late nineteenth-century France, and circulated almost immediately in Spanish and Portuguese. Writers of the *modernista* group in Spanish America (see ***modernismo*, Spanish American**) clearly considered themselves an elite class whose function was to articulate social issues and to design the future of society. This tendency is most famously associated with José Enrique Rodó's essay *Ariel* (1900), which led to the tradition called ***arielismo***. The professionalization of the writer in the first three decades of the twentieth century, and the writer's dissociation from the patronage system and movement into journalism and/or diplomacy (the Mexican writer Carlos **Fuentes** is a prominent case in point), created a new social space in which the writer as public intellectual mediated between the national bourgeoisie and the aspiring middle classes. Prefiguring the political movements of the 1960s and 1970s, writers often wrote on behalf of the dispossessed, for example in the *indigenista* novel and *negrista* poetry (see **indigenismo; negrismo**). Similarly, the painters of the Mexican muralist (see **muralism**) and Andean *indigenista* groups cast themselves as spokespeople for the illiterate and undereducated masses, considered unable to speak for themselves. This notion appears forcefully in works such as José Carlos **Mariátegui**'s *Siete ensayos* (Seven Essays on Peruvian Reality) (1927) and Pablo **Neruda**'s '**Alturas de Macchu Picchu**' (Heights of Macchu Picchu) in the 1940s (published in *Canto General* (1950).

After the Cuban Revolution (see **revolutions**) artists and intellectuals, of whatever political stripe, were expected to take political positions of leadership on the social issues of the day. A famous example of this phenomenon was the **Casa de las Américas** debate including Mario **Benedetti**, Julio **Cortázar** and Mario **Vargas Llosa** on the role of the intellectual in the revolution, out of which emerged a hardline position from which Vargas Llosa and others quickly and loudly dissociated themselves, particularly after the **Padilla** case, arguing the necessity for the intellectual's independence from the state. By the time the Nicaraguan poet Ernesto Cardenal occupied the post of Minister of Culture in the Sandinista revolutionary government, the fractures in the traditional political movements had made clear that this established role was no longer sufficient. Emergent in the late 1970s, in a response both to authoritiarian leftist tendencies and the explicit repression of dictatorships, the **new social movements** of Latin America became the vital centre of political activity by the end of the next decade. New social movements (theorized by Ernesto **Laclau**) are distinguished from their predecessors not only by the content of their ideologies and world views, but also by the ways in which the ideas of the movements are materialized and disseminated – often sidelining the traditional intellectuals in favour of spokespersons whose qualifications included life experience and representativity.

Further reading

González, C. (ed.) (1979) *Cultura y creación intelectual en América Latina*, Mexico City: Siglo XXI.

Laclau, E., and Mouffe, C. (1985) *Hegemony and Socialist Strategy*, London: Verso.

Marichal, J. (1978) *Cuatro fases de la historia intelectual latinoamericana (1810–1970)*, Madrid: Fundación Juan March/Cátedra.

Miller, N. (1999) *In the Shadow of the State. Intellectuals and the Quest for National Identity in 20th Century Spanish America*, London: Verso.

Rama, A. (1984) *La ciudad letrada*, Hanover, New Hampshire: Ediciones del Norte. (English translation: *The Lettered City* (1996) Durham, NC: Duke University Press.)

Zea, L. (ed.) (1986) *América Latina en sus ideas*, Mexico City: Siglo XXI.

DANIEL BALDERSTON

Inter-American Court of Human Rights

The Inter-American Court of Human Rights is, according to the Court Statute, 'an autonomous judicial institution whose purpose is the application and interpretation' of the 1969 American Convention on Human Rights. Although first proposed in 1948, it was not created until 1979. Based in San José, Costa Rica, the court has adjudicatory jurisdiction over all cases submitted by countries that are party to the convention. It also has an advisory function: any member of the **Organization of American States** (OAS) may consult the Court on the interpretation of the convention, other human rights treaties in the Americas, or domestic laws.

MARK UNGAR

Inter-American Development Bank

The Inter-American Development Bank was established in 1959 to promote development by providing finance for public and private sector projects. Its members include all the Latin American and Caribbean countries. Since its headquarters are in Washington and the USA holds 35 per cent of the vote on its Board of Governors, its lending policies are heavily influenced by the USA.

Social projects receive fewer loans than energy, industry or transport. The Bank became one of the main lending agencies to Latin America; its publications, including the respected *Economic and Social Progress Report*, have wielded a powerful influence on Latin American development programmes and policies.

PHILIP O'BRIEN

Inter-American Music Review

This scholarly semi-annual journal has been edited since 1978 by Robert Stevenson, a UCLA musicology professor, and covers music in all of the western hemisphere, but the great majority of articles and reviews are on topics of Latin American interest. The journal occasionally contains extended musical scores. Most articles are in English; a very few are in Spanish. It is indexed in *Hispanic American Periodicals Index*.

PAUL BARY

internal migration

Though immigration (see **immigration to Latin America**) to Latin America and the Caribbean has slowed considerably from its highs early in the twentieth century, capital cities and major industrial centres have grown tremendously, thanks in large part to displacements of population within the countries. This movement from rural to urban areas, and from small towns to larger cities, has had a dramatic impact on the shape of the **city** throughout the region, contributing to the growth of shanty towns (see **shanty towns and slums**). Often consigned to menial labour or to the informal economy, these migrants are also victims of prejudice and discrimination.

In Argentina, for instance, the *cabecitas negras* (little black heads) or **mestizo** immigrants from the north-western part of the country to Buenos Aires and other major cities were important in the rise of Juan Domingo **Perón**; they are the subject of literary works like Germán **Rozenmacher**'s book of stories, *Cabecita negra* (1963). The migrants from the Brazilian northeast to São Paulo and the other industrial cities of the south, called *cabeça chata* or 'flat-head', are featured prominently in Brazilian **Cinema Novo** and in such literary works as Clarice Lispector's *A hora da estrela* (The Hour of the Star) (1985) – and in the film version by Susana **Amaral**. Mexico City, Lima and Santiago, Chile have large populations of displaced Indians and peasants; José María **Arguedas**'s *Todas las sangres* (All the Bloods) (1964) is one of many works that deals with their situation. Mexico also has the unusual situation that many smaller cities along its northern border (see **borders**) have mushroomed in size thanks to the work available (particularly for women) in the *maquiladoras* and from the floating population of those hoping to cross to the other side. Another magnet for floating populations of underemployed males are gold mines, called *garimpos* in Brazil; the photographer Sebastião **Salgado** became famous with his photographs of the miners of Serra Pelada. Post-revolutionary Cuba saw the departure of much of the urban middle class for the USA and the migration to Havana of poorer and often darker people from Oriente and other areas in the eastern part of the island, which has contributed to the city's complexities of **race** and **class**. A poignant work on the migration of an Amazonian Indian or mestizo girl to the city of Belém do Pará, where she drifts into **prostitution**, is Jorge Bodansky's *Iracema: uma transa amazônica* (Iracema, trans-Amazon/an Amazonic Fuck) (1974).

In the 1980s, a different impulse to internal migration was the regional conflict that swelled the population of the regional capitals with refugees from the war zones, and sent other refugees across frontiers, particularly from Guatemala into southern Mexico. There were also attempts at forced migration in the region, with the creation of 'safe villages' – in fact secure enclaves – for those same indigenous refugees. In the 1990s, the same phenomenon poignantly repeated itself in Peru, as the government's war with **Sendero Luminoso** reached its height, and in Colombia, where the control of the central State seemed to have collapsed by the end of the decade. In the 1970s, in Chile and elsewhere, the curiously brutal punishment of 'internal exile' sent political and trade union activists to the remotest regions, as portrayed, for example, in films like *La frontera* (1991, directed by Ricardo Larraín).

DANIEL BALDERSTON

International Style

The debate between the dominant neoclassical architectural style and the modern style advocated by the avant-garde (see **avant-garde in Latin America**) movements, began to develop in the 1920s. Le Corbusier's visit to Rio de Janeiro and Buenos Aires set in motion the development of a modern architecture labelled International Style after Russell Hitchcock's and Philip Johnson's exhibition at the New York Museum of Modern Art in 1932. Although the term International Style embraces different and contradictory expressions, it can be defined as a style preoccupied with functionality and the use of modern synthetic materials and inspired by engineering works like the great transatlantic liners (it has been called the 'ship style' because of its frequent use of porthole windows, ship's bridge-like balconies and circular rails).

According to Ramon Gutiérrez, the International Style prevailed in Latin America between 1930 and 1945. The most advanced projects in modern architecture were realized in Brazil, inspired by Le Corbusier and promoted by the Brazilian Lúcio **Costa** (later responsible for the pilot project for **Brasília**), the Russian *emigré* Gregori **Warchavchik** (named Latin American delegate to the CIAM, International Congress of Modern Architecture, by Le Corbusier) and the younger Oscar **Niemeyer**. There the modern style was characterized by its fusion of the modern with landscape and national elements. In Argentina, even before Le Corbusier's 1929 visit and the exhibition of Italian architecture in 1933, Alberto **Prebisch** challenged neoclassicism and eclecticism in the pages of the avant-garde journal ***Martín Fierro***.

The modern style did not arrive, however, until the construction of the Kavanagh Building (Sánchez, Lagos and de la Torre), **Prebisch**'s Gran Rex cinema, and the work of the Grupo Austral (Antonio Bonet and Le Corbusier's disciples Jorge Enrique **Hardoy** and Juan Kurchan). The work of Antonio Ubaldo **Vilar** was significant because it took the new style into the interior of the country through his network of gas stations. In Montevideo, the absence of a strong neoclassical tradition allowed the rapid development of International-Style-type projects by Mauricio Cravotto and Julio **Vilamajó** among others. In Mexico, the socialist architects Carlos Obregón Santalicia and Juan **O'Gorman** were outstanding; in Panama, Manuel Mújica Millán and in Venezuela, Carlos Raúl **Villanueva**. The triumph of the International Style came later in Chile and Colombia. In recent years, critics have abandoned the use of the term International Style because it is imprecise and simplistic.

Further reading

Gutiérrez, R. (1983) *Arquitectura y urbanismo en Iberoamérica*, Madrid: Cátedra.

Bullrich, F. (1969) *New Directions in Latin American architecture*, London: Studio Vista.

GONZALO AGUILAR

Inti-Illimani

Formed in 1967, the musical group Inti-Illimani is one of the most important participants in the Chilean ***nueva canción*** movement. From the beginning the group was distinguished by its versions of Andean and Latin American folk music and its fine musical arrangements. From the mid-1970s, Inti-Illimani developed its own creative direction under Horacio **Salinas**. In the 1970s too, they collaborated with composers Luis **Advis** and Sergio Ortega, and in the 1980s with John Williams, Paco Peña and Patricio **Manns**. From 1973 to 1987 the group lived in exile in Italy, where they were extremely popular. By the mid-1990s, Inti-Illimani had recorded over twenty albums.

ALFONSO PADILLA

Inti Raymi

An Inca festival to the Sun, enacted each 24 June in Cuzco, Peru in the fortress of Sacsayhuamán. Originally celebrated in June, month of the summer solstice, Inti Raymi was revived by the *indigenista* movement that began in the late 1920s, and it was the then president Augusto B. Leguía who created the 'Day of the Indian' to be celebrated annually on 24 June. In effect, Inti Raymi belongs to the set of symbolic activities and practices appropriated by the Creoles (see **creole**) to represent the Indian. In that sense it belongs to an 'invented tradition', that takes a past event (real or fictitious) and ritualizes it for political ends.

The pre-Columbian festival of Inti Raymi was initiated by Pachacuti to commemorate his victory over the Chancas and consisted of a dawn to dusk festival of solstitial bonfires, chanting and dancing. During Inca times the celebration of solstices and equinoxes was relevant, but in contemporary Andean communities the celebration has been syncretized with the Catholic festival of San Juan, 24 June.

In its current form, Inti Raymi was officially inaugurated in 1944 even though it had been staged before; the 1944 version included the four 'suyus' or territorial divisions of the Inca Empire. As the popularity of the enactment grew, intellectuals in Lima asked José María **Arguedas** to supervise the historical accuracy of the script and the representation of the Inca past. Arguedas pointed out some of the anachronisms in order to improve the ritual and a commission was appointed to write an official script in Quechua for the celebration. The 1952 script combines versions of the sixteenth- and seventeenth-century writings of Garcilaso de la Vega, Cristóbal de Molina y Cieza de León, and received Arguedas's approval. This script is now considered the 'official' one.

Further reading

De la Cadena, M. (2000) *Indigenous Mestizos: The Politics of Race and Culture in Cuzco, Peru, 1919–1991*, Durham and London: Duke University Press.

MERCEDES NIÑO-MURCIA

Inundados, Los

A film-manifesto by the **Escuela Documental de Santa Fe** and Fernando **Birri** (1961), *Los inundados* (The Flood Victims) is a gentle satire about a group of shanty town (see **shanty towns and slums**) dwellers on the banks of the Paraná river. Based on a short story by Santa Fe writer Mateo Booz, the power of its social commentary derives from its meticulous documentation of the social milieu, realist cinematography and brilliant acting. Although commercial theatre owners were not disposed to exhibit it and authorities at the National Cinema Institute attempted to block it from international competitions, it did win several international prizes, and is considered a key predecessor of the **New Latin American Cinema**.

DIANA PALLADINO

Invención de América, La

Edmundo **O'Gorman**'s 1958 book *La Invención de América* (The Invention of America) contributed to the debate about the impact of Spain's arrival in America. Rejecting the idea of 'conquest', 'creation' or 'discovery', O'Gorman argued that from an ontological perspective America was an invention of the Western mind. The arrival in the new continent destabilized European perceptions of the world, requiring the modification of existing paradigms of understanding and explanation. Other Latin American writers adopted this approach; Carlos **Fuentes**'s *Terra nostra* (1975) betrays O'Gorman's influence. Most Latin American intellectuals approached the 1992 **Columbian quincentenary**, however, with a new formulation: 'the encounter of two worlds'.

ALEJANDRA LAERA

Invisible

Invisible was an Argentine rock group formed in 1974 by Luis Alberto **Spinetta**, Carlos 'Machi' Rodríguez Rufino and Hector 'Pomo' Lorenzo. From the outset the group was conceived as an experimental band, an unusual idea in the context of ***rock nacional***. The group worked within the frame of 'tango-rock'; its compositions showed a clear jazz influence, and made a major contribution to the renewal of Argentine urban music. Before its breakup in 1976, the group recorded three albums: *Invisible* (1974), *Durazno sangrando* (Bleeding Peach) (1975) and *El jardín de los presentes* (The Garden of the Living) (1976).

DIEGO BENTIVEGNA

Iommi, Enio

b. 1926, Rosario, Argentina

Sculptor

Born into a family of sculptors and artisans, Iommi moved to Buenos Aires in 1939 and in 1945 joined the Asociación Arte Concreto-Invención led by Tomás **Maldonado**, Alfredo **Hlito** and others. His early works were in a severe constructivist language (see **constructivism**). By the 1950s he was working with rhythmic metallic forms. In 1977 he held an exhibition called *Adiós a una época* (Farewell to an Epoch) in Buenos Aires, which marked a clear break with his earlier work in favour of a more chaotic Arte Povera style.

GABRIEL PEREZ-BARREIRO

Irakere

Irakere is a Cuban band formed in 1973 by ex-members of the Orquesta Cubana de Música Moderna (Cuban Modern Music Orchestra). They were German Velazco and Carlos Averoff, saxophonists; Arturo **Sandoval** and Jorge Varona, trumpet; Carlos Emilio, electric guitar; Carlos del Puerto, electric bass; Enrique Plá, drums; Jorge Alfonso and Carlos Barbón, percussionists; Oscar Valdés, vocals and percussion; and Jesús (Chucho) Valdés, piano and organ. Paquito **D'Rivera** later joined the group but went into exile in the United States in 1988, followed later by Arturo Sandoval. The majority of the band's repertoire consists of compositions by its leader Chucho Valdés, which translate Cuban popular music into an orchestral format where the traditional percussion is strengthened by the addition of electric guitars.

JOSÉ ANTONIO EVORA

Irarrázabal, Mario

b. 1940, Santiago, Chile

Sculptor

Irarrázabal adheres to the notion of the artist as prophet of denunciation and change, and his work has consistently dealt with human emotions and social issues. Beginning in the 1970s, he created chains and groupings of small stylized human figures in bronze, portraying institutional repression and alluding to the artist's struggles with the Catholic hierarchy while studying for the priesthood, and to his later persecution by the **Pinochet** government. After a brief experiment with **conceptual art** in the 1980s, Irarrázabal returned to creating large and small representations of the human figure in quotidian expressions of intimacy. Among his best known work is a monumental concrete hand which seems to emerge out of Chile's Atacama desert, suggesting hope and redemption.

CELIA LANGDEAU CUSSEN

Isaac, Alberto

b. 1925, Colima, Mexico; d. 1997, Colima

Film-maker

Isaac's first film, *En este pueblo no hay ladrones* (There are No Thieves in this Town) (1964), based on a short story by **García Márquez**, won second prize in the Independent Film Competition organized by the Film Workers' Union. He directed the official documentaries for the 1968 Mexico Olympics and the 1970 soccer **World Cup**, and was the first Head of the Mexican Film Institute (1971–85). His feature films are largely set in his native Colima, and have a characteristic nostalgic air. Critical opinion on his work is divided; some recognize its merits while others see it as shallow and uninspired.

PATRICIA TORRES SAN MARTÍN

Isabel La Negra
b. 1901, San Antón de Ponce, Puerto Rico; d. 1974, San Antón de Ponce

Brothel-keeper and philanthropist

Isabel la Negra (real name Isabel Luberza Oppenheimer), was born in the same neighbourhood where she died of bullet wounds, in mysterious circumstances, seventy-three years later. Daughter of a construction worker and a maid, she became the proprietor of 'Elizabeth's Dancing Place', a renowned bar and brothel. A philanthropist, she donated generously to a number of charitable causes. Her name evokes admiration in some, contempt in others; but 13,000 people accompanied her funeral procession. Her life was fictionalized by Manuel **Ramos Otero** and Rosario **Ferré**.

JUAN CARLOS QUINTERO HERENCIA

ISEB

The ISEB (Instituto Superior de Estudos Brasileiros) was an influential late 1950s think-tank in Brazil. Although not an ideological mouthpiece of the Juscelino **Kubitschek** regime (1956–61), the developmentalist optimism of those years was reflected in ISEB's work. Its theoretical publications, such as Roland Corbisier's *Formação e Problema da Cultura Brasileira* (Formation and Problem of Brazilian Culture) (1959) and Álvaro Vieira Pinto's *Consciência e Realidade Nacional* (Consciousness and National Reality) (1960), came to define the nationalist-reformist thinking of the Brazilian left.

Earlier cultural theorists, like Gilberto **Freyre**, considered national identity to be constituted historically through race; the *isebianos* drew on Hegel and Mannheim, to address the dilemma of national culture within the context of colonialism as a process of 'becoming', the realization of a hitherto alienated Being. The *isebianos* found in Hegel's dialectic of the master–slave relationship, as revised by Marx, Balandier and Sartre, a model which could be adapted to their own experience of colonization. Whilst Balandier and Sartre focused on the alienation of the colonial oppressor, the *isebianos* shared with Frantz **Fanon** the perspective of a peripheral, oppressed Third World identity seeking to break the colonial complex of cultural and economic enslavement by recovering a consciousness of its authentic essence.

At the point of defining what sort of movement could achieve that end, Fanon and the *isebianos* parted company. Fanon argued for the self-liberation of the oppressed through the revolutionary violence of an anti-colonial war. The *isebianos* believed this role would be played by the struggle for national economic development within capitalism; the Brazilian 'people' had already constituted itself as a 'civil society', whose legitimate representatives were the progressive nationalist bourgeoisie and their intellectual expression, the ISEB. The realization of the national Being was a matter of the gradual achievement of economic autonomy through the 'option for development'; revealingly, the phrase was taken from an essay entitled 'Culture and Development' by Roberto **Campos**, the planning minister in the first phase of military rule (1964–6).

As well as substituting the process of national economic development for the political struggle against imperialism, the *isebianos*' analysis conflated the 'people' with the nation, collapsing together the interests of workers and peasants and those of their national bourgeoisie. This strategy of reformist developmentalism subsequently became the orthodoxy for the communist left within the popular culture movement of the early 1960s. The founder of the **CPC**, Carlos Estevam, and the educationalist Paulo **Freire** both had close links with the ISEB, whose concept of cultural alienation clearly informed the work of dramatists Augusto **Boal** and Gianfrancesco **Guarnieri**, and the theoretical writings of the **Cinema Novo** movement, such as Paulo Emílio **Salles Gomes**'s 'Uma situação colonial' (A Colonial Situation) and Glauber **Rocha**'s 'Uma estética da fome' (An **Aesthetics of Hunger**).

Further reading

Navarro Toledo, C. (1977) *ISEB: fábrica de ideologias*, São Paulo: Ática.

Ortiz, R. (1986) 'Alienação e cultura: o ISEB', *Cultura brasileira e identidade nacional*, São Paulo: Brasiliense, 45–67.

DAVID TREECE

Isella, César

b. 1928, Salta, Argentina

Composer and poet

A member of the famous Salta group Los Fronterizos, notable for disseminating the folk songs of northwestern Argentina, Isella is a gifted composer, an excellent guitarist and the author of beautiful and popular lyrics. Isella and Los Fronterizos recorded with major figures, such as Ariel **Ramírez** and Eduardo **Falú**. In the late 1970s he embarked on a solo carreer, performing with Silvio **Rodríguez**, Milton **Nascimento**, Mercedes **Sosa** and Víctor Heredia among others. His songs include 'Canción con todos' (Song for All).

MAGDALENA GARCÍA PINTO

Isidrón, Chanito

b. 1903, Calabazar de Sagua, Cuba

Singer

A singer of traditional songs and ballads, Isidrón was made famous by radio throughout Cuba. In 1931 he abandoned his work as a farmer to travel the villages of his home province of Las Villas singing his songs. His skill as a a *repentista* , an improviser of songs to the accompaniment of a traditional trio of guitars and claves, made him a key figure in the revival of the so-called 'punto cubano', the Cuban traditional ballad. He participated in hundreds of *controversias*, song duels between two *repentistas*. He has published poems and prose, principally about rural life, and characterized by the same humour that flavours so many of his songs.

JOSÉ ANTONIO EVORA

Isla 70

A huge canvas by Raúl Martínez (1927–1995), Cuba's best-known pop artist (see **pop art**), painted in 1970, the ostensible subject of *Isla 70* is the Committees for the Defence of the Revolution (CDR), the initials of which appear in the lower part of the centre next to the Cuban flag. Yet the painting is also a celebration of gay and lesbian lives: the butch lesbian has her arm around her femme companion, who holds their cat; the androgynous young man in the lower left is eating a very phallic looking ice cream cone (no doubt purchased at Coppelia, the gay meeting point in Havana that frames **Gutiérrez Alea**'s film *Fresa y chocolate*), while the young man eating some sort of sandwich in the centre of the painting (above the CDR symbol and the Cuban flag) is surrounded by a veritable forest of erect phallic vegetation. The tropical flowers, especially orchids, are there to remind us that flowers also speak of the polymorphous perverse of our sexuality. The butch-femme couple, the pinky ring, the fruit, the ice cream cone: these winks at the gay and lesbian visitor say that they too are the revolution. Martínez has populated the painting not only with a number of his friends of the time but also with Ho Chi Minh, Lenin, José Martí, Che **Guevara**, Fidel **Castro**, as if to say that all together they form a new and improved committee in defence of the revolution. The painting hangs in the National Museum of Fine Arts, near the Granma (the boat that took Castro's group of guerrillas from Mexico to Cuba to start the revolution), and next to the Museum of the Revolution. When Martínez painted *Isla 70*, the times were difficult: gays were being rounded up and sent to the **UMAP** (Military Units in Aid of Production) camps, which was surely the case with some of the young men and women pictured here. Martínez's painting is remarkable for the explicit and transgressive nature of its depiction of a tolerant and inclusive national revolution.

DANIEL BALDERSTON

Isla de la Juventud (Isle of Youth)

Columbus called this island, south of Cuba, Evangelista in 1494. As a pirate harbour, it became a legendary 'treasure island'. Later, as Isla de Pinos (Isle of Pines), it served as a protective residence for *independista* Cubans, most notably José Martí. Its Model Penitentiary (*presidio modelo*), built under the **Machado** dictatorship (1928–33), housed political prisoners, among them Fidel **Castro**. After 1959, the Isle of Youth became the site of the International Schools of the Third World, and a centre for recreation. The Penitentiary became the Revolution's Historical Museum.

BARBARA D. RIESS

Isla que se repite, La

La isla que se repite (The Repeating Island) is a key work of Latin American literary criticism by Antonio **Benítez Rojo**, published in the United States in 1989 and in a revised version in 1998 in Spain. From a postmodernist perspective (see **postmodernism**), the author proposes a new reading of the Caribbean world through its history, sociology, economics, anthropology and art. It is presented as a complex island bridge asymmetrically connecting South and North America and interwoven into the chronology of great moments in world history. Divided into three sections – Society, The Writer and The Book – the essay explores everything from the rich African religious and cultural traditions to the role of historical and literary figures.

WILFREDO CANCIO ISLA

Islam

Latin American Islam (Druze are included) is not comparable with that of the English or Dutch speaking countries of North America or the Caribbean. There are barely 612,000 Muslims in Latin America (though precise statistics are difficult to obtain). Besides, while North American and Caribbean Islam is mainly of African, Indian or Indonesian origin, Islam was brought to Latin America by Arab immigrants at the end of the nineteenth century. The proportion of Muslims among these immigrants was small, and many of them tended to lose or dissimulate their faith due to the hostility of the milieu and the social character of the Islamic cult. Only in Brazil did an Islamic communitarian life develop in the late nineteenth century with clubs, schools, hospitals and journals.

The situation changed in the second half of the twentieth century, especially due to the growing numbers of Muslim immigrants after the political unrest in Palestine and Lebanon (1947–79). The first mosques appeared (in São Paulo in 1958), and some Muslims reached important positions. The most salient case is the Argentine politician Carlos Saúl **Menem**, son of a Syrian immigrant. His political career led him to convert to Catholicism to reach the Presidency (a constitutional prerequisite when he first came to power in 1979).

In the late twentieth century, the largest communities are in Brazil (200,000), Argentina (66,000) and Venezuela (51,000). Latin American Muslims are mostly urban and middle class, ignorant of Arabic and thus of much of their faith. They read the Qur'an in Spanish or Portuguese translations, intermarry with Christian women (which is accepted in Islam) and even educate their children as Christians (which is forbidden). Differences between Sunni, Shia or Druze are little, if at all, known.

Traditionally despised for religious or cultural reasons, Islam now has a better status, partly due to the decision of the new generations to reassert their religion and because of the cooperation of the oil-rich Muslim states in the construction of mosques, and religious and linguistic education. Nevertheless, there is opposition against the Buenos Aires mosque led by the conservative Tradicion, Familia y Propiedad (Tradition–Family–Property) group; the frequent press mockery of Menem's 'turco' origin is also a contributory factor.

Further reading

Delval, R. (1992) *Les musulmans en Amerique Latine et au Caraibes*, Paris: L'Harmattan.

HERNAN G.H. TABOADA

Island Records

Established in the UK by white Jamaican expatriate Chris Blackwell in 1962, Island Records was responsible for the international breakthrough of Jamaican **reggae** musicians such as Jimmy **Cliff**, Toots and the Maytals, and Bob **Marley** and the Wailers. Blackwell had set up Island in Jamaica, but the UK parent company enabled him to finance and promote the leaders of Jamaica's reggae revolution. The Wailers' first international album *Catch a Fire* (1973) was funded by Island Records, recorded in Jamaica and then remixed in the UK. Reggae bands subsequently released on the Island label include **Third World** and Aswad. Island became part of the Polygram Group in 1988.

MICHAEL BURNETT

Isle, Ludwig de l'

b. 1949, Aruba

Painter

The modest painter Luti de l'Isle studied art in the Netherlands and is an art teacher at an Aruban high school. He produces abstract paintings with very special compositions of colours and lines, and has a very fine technique which other Aruban artists strive to emulate.

NEL CASIMIRI

IstoÉ

IstoÉ is a news magazine circulating throughout Brazil, published in São Paulo by Editora Tres. Founded in June 1976 as a monthly, its first director was Domingos Alzugaray and its first editor the journalist Mino Carta. In 1977 it became a weekly. The name 'IstoÉ' (That's It) affirms that it clarifies, explains and examines things in detail. It was the first weekly in Brazil to identify the authors of its articles. In 1988, it fused with the journal *Senhor*, published by the same company, and changed its name to *IstoÉSenhor*, but returned to its original name in 1992. Its best selling edition, number 1357, October 1995, sold 650,000 copies.

ANTONIO CARLOS VAZ

Iturbide, Graciela

b. 1942, Mexico City

Photographer

Iturbide is among the best-known Latin American photographers of the 1980s and 1990s. Her work is noteworthy for its lyrical eloquence and strong ritual overtones, involving the Amazon-like Zapotec women of Juchitán or the annual sacrifice of goats by the poverty-stricken Mixtecs in Oaxaca. Iturbide trained as a professional photographer in 1969, after her children were grown. In 1970 Manuel **Alvarez Bravo** invited her to be his assistant, and her second husband was the Mexican photographer Pedro **Meyer**. Since 1975 she has had more than sixty exhibitions in Latin America and elsewhere. Her photographs have been included in numerous books, and she has published five collections, including *En el nombre del Padre* (In the Name of the Father) (1993).

CYNTHIA STEELE

Ixtapalapa crucifixion

This simulated crucifixion of Jesus, Mexico's most famous and most impressive religious festival, is held on Good Friday on the slopes of the Ixtapalapa Hill in Mexico City. People come from all over the country to witness a young man bound tightly by the wrists and left to hang from a cross that he had previously dragged with great difficulty through the streets, accompanied by thirty gladiators and the police. Most of the crowd arrives the night before to see scenes of the Last Supper, Judas's betrayal, and Jesus's trial, portrayed by participants who have gladly paid a stipulated fee for the honour of depicting a primary figure or simply one of the 300 Nazarenes of all ages who make up the jeering crowd. The crucifixion occurs in a carnivalesque atmosphere of street merchants hawking all kinds of food and religious ware.

EDUARDO GUÍZAR-ALVAREZ

Izaguirre, Boris

b. 1965, Caracas, Venzuela

Writer

Writer, chronicler and *enfant terrible* of the 1980s, Izaguirre began publishing a weekly column, 'Animal de frivolidad' (Frivolous Animal) in *El Nacional* in 1982 under the direction of Tomás Eloy **Martínez**. Throughout the 1980s Izaguirre collaborated in José Ignacio **Cabrujas**'s *telenovelas*, *La dama de rosas* (Lady with the Rose) and *Señora*. Both productions were considered a turning point in the Venezuelan television industry. After his collaboration with Cabrujas, Izaguirre worked as a script-writer for co-productions in Argentina and Spain. Izaguirre's first novel, *El vuelo de los avestruces* (The Flight of the Ostriches) (1992) is a portrayal of the city's gay life. It was the second most widely sold book of the year. In the late 1990s Izaguirre was living in Spain and writing for TV and magazines.

JACINTO FOMBONA

J

Jabor, Arnaldo

b. 1940, Rio de Janeiro, Brazil

Film-maker

Jabor's first film, *Opinião pública* (Public Opinion) (1967), a cine-vérité documentary, explored the political aspects of private life. Subsequent films like **Toda nudez será castigada** (All Nudity will be Punished) (1972), *Tudo bem* (Everything's OK) (1978) and *Eu te amo* (I Love You) (1981) satirized the patriarchal morality that coexisted with conservative modernization. Later work portrayed the identity crisis among youths produced by modernization, reflected in the films' use of visual imagery derived from advertising. In the 1990s, Jabor continued his apocalyptic explorations of social life as a journalist through his fictionalized *crónicas* (see **crónica**) of political life in the press and on TV **Globo**.

ISMAIL XAVIER AND THE USP GROUP

Jackman, Oliver

b. 1929, Black Rock, St. Michael, Barbados

Writer

A successful lawyer and newspaper columnist, Jackman's literary reputation is based on one short story, 'A Poet of the People' (1970) and one novel *Saw the House in Half* (1974), in addition to a series of poems published in the literary magazine **Bim**. The novel is concerned with themes of the West Indian in exile. The story is a more concise, and often considered superior, version of the novel. Jackman studied law at Sir Hugh Wooding Law School in Trinidad and was a member of the diplomatic corps in Washington DC from 1967 to 1984.

CAROL J. WALLACE

Jagan, Cheddi

b. 1918, Guyana; d. 1997, Georgetown, Guyana

Dentist and politician

A dominant figure in the politics of British Guiana, Jagan, who entered politics as a communist, founded the People's Progressive Party in 1950. The PPP went on to win the first national elections held under universal suffrage in 1953, and to win again in 1957 and 1961. As independence approached, however, the British government made it clear that they would not allow Jagan to assume power and threw their weight behind Forbes **Burnham**, leader of the People's National Congress. In 1963, against a background of race riots, the CIA and the British Colonial Office conspired to sustain a general strike lasting seventy-nine days that effectively brought Jagan down. In the 1964 elections it was Burnham who emerged with the majority; two years later Guyana gained its independence and for the next sixteen years lived under a Burnham dictatorship that brought the economy to the edge of collapse. In 1992, Jagan returned to power at age seventy.

KEITH JARDIM

Jagger, Bianca

b. 1945, Managua, Nicaragua

Social activist

Growing up in a repressive Catholic aristocratic household, Jagger rejected Nicaraguan female roles, went to Paris to study political science, became a model and, in 1971, married the Rolling Stones's Mick Jagger. The marriage lasted eight years. After the 1972 Managua earthquake she took a stand against the Somoza dictatorship (see **Somoza dynasty**), foreign political intervention and economic exploitation. Her ardent criticism in 1983 of the Nicaraguan government's support of foreign **rainforest** exploitation brought her recognition from the Sumo and Miskito groups (see **Miskitus**). She has directed documentary films on Nicaragua and written for the *New York Times*.

ESTEBAN E. LOUSTAUNAU AND ILEANA RODRÍGUEZ

Jaimes, Julio

b. 1936, Tucumán, Argentina

Photographer

Jaimes's elegant and technically accomplished work is profoundly evocative of the mysteries of space, both urban and rural. Specializing in architectural facades and landscapes, he has worked and exhibited in Argentina, Mexico and the USA. His filmed interview with Juan Carlos **Onetti** (with Jorge Ruffinelli) is a brilliant portrait of the Uruguayan writer. He served as the official photographer of the **Ballet Folklórico de México** in their 1979 world tour, and has done still photography for films by Eduardo Mignogna. Rarely exhibited, his work is an intense, almost secret, exploration of places and their meanings.

DANIEL BALDERSTON

Jairas, Los

Los Jairas was a Bolivian folk group formed in 1965 by Edgar Yayo Joffré, Julio Godoy, Ernesto **Cavour**, Gilbert Favre (a Swiss) and, later, Alfredo Domínguez. First established in the 'Naira' Club, it was the group with the greatest influence through the 1960s. They introduced the **quena** and the **charango** into popular urban music. Sponsored by the Patiño Foundation, they toured Europe in 1969, and introduced Andean music to European audiences. They later settled in Geneva, leaving behind them a tradition that other groups have since followed.

BEATRIZ ROSSELLS

Jamaica

The twentieth century has brought Jamaica's transition from British colony to independent State; the process was fraught and difficult, and Jamaica faces the twenty-first century with full political independence, but economically subject to the global market forces that affect every other Nation-State in the region.

If nineteenth-century Jamaica was largely a single-product economy – **sugar** – its slave-owning past continued to haunt it through the nineteenth century. The concentration of power in a minority of (white) landowners and the division of the rest of the land among small peasant farmers on subsistence plots was a pattern surviving from the days of slavery. By the turn of the century, a growing population could no longer be sustained by the land, and an increasing flow of migrants gravitated towards the capital, Kingston, where they occupied the poor **shanty town** areas surrounding the city. In the first twenty years of the century, **bananas** became increasingly important to the economy – until Panama disease struck in the late 1920s and the crop was decimated.

The first **trade unions** on the island, and the first **strikes**, were registered in 1919; they were influenced in part by the increasing radicalization of labour throughout the region, and in part by the revivalism of Alexander Bedward, a black nationalist whose messianic rhetoric created a current then picked up by Marcus **Garvey**. Garvey's speaking tours in 1921, and his expulsion from the USA in 1927, generated a movement of black nationalism imbued with both a messianic religious idea and an impulse to achieve social justice through struggle. Its echoes may still be heard clearly in the Rastafarian movement (see **Rastafarianism**).

In the 1930s returning emigrants and unemployed workers experiencing the impact of the Depression organized in a growing wave of militancy between 1935 and 1937, which exploded in the national strike wave of mid-1938. In the course of those events, Alexander **Bustamante**, a recently returned migrant in his fifties became a dominant figure in the growing trade union movement. His bizarre mix of religious rhetoric, nationalism and allegiance to the British Crown seemed to work; in 1943 he founded the JLP (Jamaican Labour Party) and won a landslide victory in that year's elections against the PNP (People's National Party) under Norman **Manley**. From then on, Jamaican politics would be a contest between these two parties and these two names, and despite the sometimes radical rhetoric of the PNP, they would often agree on the major issues.

After 1950, the Jamaican economy grew as bauxite and **tourism** became its key industries; in the early 1960s, growing numbers left the Caribbean to enter the British labour market. It was these new migrants who cheered the Jamaican **cricket** team to its long awaited first victories over British teams as the island gained independence – but within the British Commonwealth – in 1962. However, unemployment on the island continued to rise and the British influence still prevailed. Trenchtown and the other shanty towns were swelling with rural migrants, some of whom had been involved with a rural Rastafarian commune destroyed by police in the late 1940s that continued the longer traditions of Pocomania and other millenarian groups of the past.

With its charge of black nationalism and anti-colonialism, the movement showed its influence when Haile Selassie (Ras Tafari – Emperor of Ethiopia) visited Jamaica in 1966 to a rapturous reception. It was quickly associated with a new music – a combination of the older mento with rock-steady dance beats that produced the new pulsating, home-produced **reggae** beat. By the mid-1970s, reggae was an international music, symbolized above all by Bob **Marley**, though less internationally known figures like Peter **Tosh** and Burning Spear had an equally devoted local following, and marketed by the enormously successful **Island Records**. Reggae spoke to and for a disaffected local youth that danced and smoked ganja, and who wore **dreadlocks** as a statement of rejection.

The 1960s were a turning point in many ways. Independence brought very little perceptible change, and Bustamante remained dominant until the 1970s electoral victories of Michael **Manley** – PNP leader whose public political positions were significantly to the left of his father's. Michael Manley opened relations with Cuba and identified Jamaica with the Non-Aligned Movement. Yet a deepening social conflict at home expressed itself in growing violence on the streets. Perhaps it was the contrast between the wealthy tourists visiting the new exclusive and foreign-owned resorts around the island (like Sandals) and the poverty and harshness of life for most ordinary Jamaicans, as powerfully portrayed in the film, *The **Harder They Come*** (1972), whose central protagonist was played by reggae artist, Jimmy **Cliff**. The violence exploded during the election campaign of 1978, when an ailing Bob Marley sang his famous 'One Love' at a concert attended by both Michael Manley and his conservative opponent, Edward **Seaga**.

Two years later Manley was dead and Seaga was Prime Minister; it was he who implemented the Caribbean Basin Initiative, the Antillean variant of **structural adjustment**. Although Manley returned to the post in the early 1990s, the hopes he once represented were largely abandoned.

Alongside reggae, Jamaica has produced other powerful expressions of popular culture. From the early 1960s there existed a literary movement with the intention of recuperating popular speech; and oral culture found expression in '**nation language**' and a poetry and narrative of popular speech. This was exemplified by Olive **Senior**, Louise **Bennett**, **Matabaruka** and Una Marson, editor of the extremely influential BBC radio programme, *Caribbean Voices*, which provided a platform for these new Caribbean voices for a decade and more.

The recuperation of popular culture was also taking place in the visual arts, in Eugene **Hyde**'s paintings of the people of Kingston, and in Osmond Watson's Rastafarian Christ in *Peace and Love*. There were precedents in Edna **Manley**'s great 1935 sculpture *Negro Aroused* and Alvin Marriott's *Banana Man* (1955). And that recovery of a hidden history was given added impetus by the central role played by the **University of the West Indies**, with its campuses on a number of islands, and publications like ***Callaloo*** and the more scholarly ***Jamaica Journal***.

Further reading

Senior, O. (1988) *A to Z of Jamaican Heritage*, Kingston, Jamaica: Heinemann Educational Books (Caribbean) Limited.

Sherlock, P.M. and Bennett, H. (1998) *The Story of the Jamaican People*, Princeton, NJ: Markus Weiner Publishers.

DANIEL BALDERSTON AND MIKE GONZALEZ

Jamaica Journal

Quarterly publication of the **Institute of Jamaica**, founded in 1967, and aiming to provide reliable and informative articles for the Jamaican public on a wide variety of local topics. Features on history, on language and literature, and the visual and performing arts, on scientific topics for the lay person, especially natural history, have maintained a high standard, testifying to the quality of work in progress in research and education. The journal is handsomely produced, with illustrations in colour and black and white, constituting a valuable source of reference on Jamaican art and iconography. Information and commentary cover the annual Jamaican festival competitions, and special numbers have commemorated twenty years of independence, the work of Marcus **Garvey**, Norman **Manley**, etc. The publication is indexed and available on microfilm.

MIKE GONZALEZ

James, Cyril Lionel Robert

b.1901, Tunapuna, Trinidad; d.1989, Brixton, England

Writer

C.L.R. James was one of the Caribbean's most creative intellectual, artistic, and political figures. A Marxist, he wrote fiction and drama, sports journalism, history, philosophy, literary and cultural criticism, and political pamphlets and was a tireless supporter of revolutionary causes throughout the world. Born of well-educated, black, bourgeois parents in the then-English colony of Trinidad, James began his career as a fiction writer and a **cricket** reporter; the game remained a lifelong love and the basis around which he organized his autobiographical reflections on sport, colonial politics, art, and society in *Beyond a Boundary* (1962). In often-neglected short stories like 'La Divina Pastora' and 'Triumph' and in his novel *Minty Alley* (1936), James brought the techniques of modern European narrative to bear on the gritty reality of West Indian slums, focusing particularly on the problems and resources of women.

In 1932, James embarked upon a quarter-century odyssey through Britain and the USA, during which he produced some of his most remarkable written work and established himself as one of the Marxist tradition's most original revolutionary thinkers. This period included *The **Black Jacobins*** (1938), a still classic study of the 1793 slave revolt in Saint Domingue which led to Haitian independence in 1804. Ten years later, James published *Notes on Dialectics*, a close, critical reading of Hegel grounded in, as James put it, a critical review of the 'labour movement from 1789', and focusing particularly on the theory and practice of Marx and Lenin. In 1950, James published *State Capitalism and World Revolution*. This work, critical of both Stalinism and the Fourth Trotskyist Fourth International, established James as a forceful and independent thinker in international Marxism. Yet James did not devote himself only to Marxist political theory and practice. While in jail facing deportation hearings on Ellis Island, he also wrote *Mariners, Renegades, and Castaways* (1953), a creative and succinct study of Herman Melville's *Moby Dick* analysing the relations between the novel's narrator, the ship's captain, and its expert 'Third World crew'. This work, in turn, grew out of notes and essays on American culture and politics that were only published, as *American Civilization*, five years after his death.

Mariners, with its focus on the Third World, also presaged James' active involvement in revolutionary decolonization in Africa, the Caribbean, and Latin America, as well as among African-Americans in the USA. During the 1950s and 1960s, James visited many Africa nations (he wrote a full-length study of the revolution in Ghana) and Cuba, as well as major inner-cities in the USA. He also returned to Trinidad for a brief period beginning in 1958, attempting to shape the future of the soon-to-be-independent nation. It was this work – political organization, lectures, pamphleteering on an international scale – which occupied James for most of the last quarter-century of his life.

Further reading

James, C.L.R. (1989) *The Black Jacobins: Toussaint L'Ouverture and the Santo Domingo Evolution*, New York: Vintage.
—— (1992) *The C.L.R. James Reader*, Oxford: Blackwell.
—— (1993) *Beyond a Boundary*, Durham: Duke University Press.
—— (1993) *American Civilization*, Oxford: Blackwell.
Buhle, P (ed.) (1986) *C.L.R. James: His Life and Work*, London and New York: Alison & Busby.
Farred, G. (ed.) (1996) *Rethinking C.L.R. James*, Oxford: Blackwell.

SANTIAGO COLÁS

Jara, Cronwell

b. 1950, Piura, Peru

Writer

Jara exemplifies a new development in the Peru of the 1970s and 1980s: the emergence of writers from lower-class backgrounds whose work seeks to give their class a voice and a history. His 1989 novel *Patíbulo para un caballo* (Scaffold for a Horse), the story of a **shanty town**'s fight against eviction, is a foundational myth of the marginalized masses' conquest of a space in national society.

JAMES HIGGINS

Jara, Víctor

b. 1935, Lonquén, Chile; d. 1973, Santiago, Chile

Singer

Víctor Jara was a singer and composer – not the most obvious candidate to be one of the first victims of the military government under **Pinochet**, which came to power in Chile on 11 September 1973. Yet the dictator's first decree banned the use of the indigenous musical instruments like the pan pipes and the flute, which were so identified with the song movement known as ***nueva canción*** to which Jara had belonged. Four days later Víctor Jara was murdered by the military in Santiago's national football stadium. His hands were broken first so that he could no longer play the songs that had become identified with the **Popular Unity** government under Salvador **Allende**, which the military had overthrown.

Allende once said, famously, that 'there can be no revolution without song'. It was certainly the case that the *nueva canción* movement had accompanied and reflected the political radicalization that led to Allende's election.

Víctor himself came from a poor rural background – many of his songs describe the harshness of peasant life. Having moved to Santiago after an accident hospitalized his older sister, Víctor entered a seminary in 1950; two years later he left to complete his compulsory military service. A period of work with a mime group led him to the University Theatre School in Santiago, where he started on a three-year course in 1956. In 1957 he met Violeta **Parra**, the singer and collector who was the driving force behind the new Chilean song movement; that same year he joined the folk group, Cuncumén, which two years later toured Eastern Europe with its songs and dances of Chile. Through the 1960s, Víctor worked as a theatre director; and he was among that outstanding generation of musicians who played and performed at the Peña de los Parra, the folk club that was the crucible of *nueva canción*.

In 1969, Victor appeared at the First Festival of New Chilean Song in Santiago; the song he performed there was among his most famous, and reflected the mood of the times. Plegaria de un labrador (A Worker's Prayer) called on Chile's workers to 'Rise up and look at your own hands – take now your brother's hand, and you will grow.' Víctor was also playing with a very popular rock group – Los Jaibas – though the social content of his songs was usually similar. Yet the other song for which Víctor is remembered is an emblematic, revolutionary love song – Te recuerdo Amanda (I Remember You, Amanda) is the song of a girl whose lover disappears into the mountains, presumably to continue the struggle there.

Jara's murder by the **Pinochet** regime became symbolic of the State terrorism that followed Allende's overthrow. Songs were written about him across the world and his words continued to be sung by exiled Chilean musicians, like the groups **Quilapayún** and **Inti-Illimani**. One of his last songs (Manifiesto) declared 'My song makes sense, because it flows through the veins/Of everyone who dies singing out the truth.'

Further reading

Jara, J. (1983, 1998) *Víctor: An Unfinished Song*, London: Bloomsbury

MIKE GONZALEZ

Jaramillo, Julio

b. 1935, Guayaquil, Ecuador; d. 1978, Guayaquil

Singer

Within Ecuadorean culture, Jaramillo is a popular hero, whose renditions of the **pasillo** are icons of the national imaginary. Throughout the continent his fans are legion, for he gave voice to the regional in the context of an assailing global culture. His origins and identification with the marginal and poor, as well as his iconoclastic, feisty, bohemian, womanizing, dissolute, extremely generous and charismatic personality catapulted him to the level of a myth. Nicknamed S. Juramento (Mr Oath), his funeral was marked by an unprecedented outpouring of grief.

HUMBERTO ROBLES

Jaramillo Agudelo, Darío

b. 1947, Santa Rosa de Osos, Colombia

Poet and novelist

A student of law and economics, Jaramillo began by writing intellectual and ironic poetry, but later switched to more intimate poems of love. Most of his poetry has been gathered in two volumes, both published in 1992: *Antología poética* (Poetic Anthology) and *Cuánto silencio debajo de esta luna* (So Much Silence under This Moon).

MIGUEL A. CARDINALE

Jaramillo Levi, Enrique

b. 1944, Colón, Panama

Writer

Although best known internationally for his short stories, including *Duplicaciones* (Duplications and Other Stories) (1973) and *The Shadow: Thirteen Stories in Opposition* (1996), Jaramillo is also a poet and essayist. He has also edited two anthologies, one in conjunction with Chambers entitled *Contemporary Short Stories from Central America* (1994) and the other being *When New Flowers Bloomed: Short Stories by Women Writers from Costa Rica and Panama* (1991). In addition, he founded and edited the influential Panamanian literary and cultural magazine *Maga*. He was educated at the local university, at the University of Iowa and at the Universidad Nacional Autónoma de México (**UNAM**).

NORMAN S. HOLLAND

Jaramillo Uribe, Jaime

b. 1917, Abejorral, Colombia

Historian

A pioneer in the modernization of the study of history in Colombia, Jaramillo Uribe's main contribution has been the introduction of an exhaustive scientific method relying on archival matter as the primary source of information. His work offers an alternative to the canonical interpretation sponsored by the Academia Colombiana de Historia, promoting a more up-to-date rendition of historiography based on rigorous analysis and abundant documentation. He studied in Bogotá and Paris and has taught at the Universidad Nacional and the Universidad de los Andes (receiving honorary doctorates from both), and at Hamburg, Vanderbilt, St Anthony's College, and Seville.

HÉCTOR D. FERNÁNDEZ L'HOESTE

jarocho music *see* son jarocho

Jarr, Alfredo

b. 1956, Santiago, Chile

Installation artist

Jarr trained as a film-maker and as an architect in Chile. In 1982 he moved to New York. Jarr came to international prominence in the late 1980s with a series of boxes in which videos or photographs are projected. These works, despite their 'cool' minimalist appearance, deal with political issues such as the exploitation of the Third World. He is seen as a major artist of political **conceptualism**.

GABRIEL PEREZ-BARREIRO

Jauretche, Arturo

b. 1901, Lincoln, Buenos Aires Province, Argentina; d. 1974, Buenos Aires

Writer

In 1935, Jauretche founded FORJA (the Radical Orientation Force of Argentine Youth) with Raúl **Scalabrini Ortiz** and Luis Dellepiane, launching him on a career as a nationalist intellectual. FORJA was virulently anti-imperialist and strongly critiqued the liberal basis of Argentina's state and intellectual formation. After the rise of **Perón** (1943–5), Jauretche became a prominent Peronist intellectual, publishing such works as *Libros y alpargatas: civilizados o bárbaros* (Books and Slippers: Civilized and Savages) (1983) and *El medio pelo en la sociedad argentina* (The Middle-Brow in Argentine society – or, as Nicolas Shumway has translated it, *Pretense and social climbing*) (1966) and the satirical *Manual de zonceras argentinas* (Guide to Argentine Follies) (1968).

DANIEL BALDERSTON

Javier, Adrián

b. 1967, Santo Domingo, Dominican Republic

Poet

One of the best poets from the younger generations in Santo Domingo, Javier is a former member of the Literary Circle Domingo Moreno Jimenes and the Franklin Mieses Burgos Poetry Workshop. He was only twenty-one years old when his book *El oscuro rito de la luz* (The Dark Rite of Light) (1989) won first prize in a contest. In *Bolero del esquizo* (The Bolero of the Schizoid) (1994), Javier returns to the simplicity of **bolero** lyrics to explore the split being of **postmodernism**.

FERNANDO VALERIO-HOLGUÍN

Javier, Francisco

b.1934

Theatre director

Working with the group Los Volatineros, which he founded, he directed works like *Qué porquería que es el glóbulo* (How Disgusting the Globule) by José María **Firpo** in 1976 and Claude de Marigny's *Cajamarca* in 1978, both incorporating pantomime, dance and acrobatics. With a doctorate in Theatre Studies from the Sorbonne, Javier worked simultaneously in theatrical research and experimental theatre, above all in the study of scenic space. He is author of *Notas para la historia científica de la puesta en escena* (Notes for a Scientific History of Direction) (1984).

NORA MAZZIOTTI

jazz

Musical genre arising in the southern USA in the second half of the nineteenth century and becoming popular in the twentieth. Originally restricted to the black population of the USA, it eventually expanded through the whole country without distinction of race or class. Jazz developed into a series of styles – from Dixieland, Chicago, New Orleans, Mainstream and Swing in the early part of the century through Bebop, progressive, West Coast and Cool in mid-century to the emergence of jazz-rock, latin-jazz, fusion, funk and acid jazz in more recent times.

The spread of jazz embraced Latin America too. The first jazz records reached Latin America in the 1920s, and some Argentine **tango** orchestras, like Francisco **Canaro** or Roberto Firpo's ensembles, included jazz tunes in their repertoire. In the same decade, the first exclusively jazz bands emerged, though their audiences were small. The first jazz recording in Latin America, by Eleuterio Iribarren's jazz group, was in 1925. Later, jazz became more popular, with the growth of cinema (the first talking picture was *The Jazz Singer*). From then on jazz was present in the music of every country, particularly in the cities; its impact was expressed in the creation of jazz bands that included prominent Latin Americans – the Argentine pianist Enrique 'Mono' Villegas, the Cuban saxophonist Paquito **D'Rivera** or the Peruvian drummer Alex Acuña, for example. On the other hand, indigenous music began to absorb jazz sounds, arrangements, harmonies and styles that greatly enriched their originals – this could be heard in the orchestral arrangements of the Argentine tango pianist Mariano Mores, in the work of the bandoneón player and composer Astor **Piazzola** (who made an important album in 1974 with North American saxophonist Gerry Mulligan), in the arrangements for the brass sections of Caribbean orchestras like Eddie Palmieri's, in the harmonies of Brazilian **bossa nova** and in the growing use of improvisation. The process also worked in reverse: jazz itself was reinvigorated by the assimilation of rhythms, instruments, sounds, compositions and instrumentalists from the music of Latin America and Brazil. This was already identifiable in the 1940s in the work of jazz giants like Dizzy Gillespie, and is the key to understanding the new twentieth-century jazz innovations that draw on the music of the southern continent.

Further reading

Marre, J. and Charlton, H. (1985) *Beats of the Heart: Popular Music of the World*, New York: Pantheon.

Roberts, John Storm (1979) *The Latin Tinge: The Impact of Latin American in the United States*, New York/Oxford: Oxford University Press.

The Rough Guide to Jazz (1995) London: Penguin Books.

PABLO JAVIER ANSOLABEHERE

Jeffers, Audrey

b. 1896, Woodbrook, Trinidad; d.1968, Port of Spain, Trinidad

Social worker

Returning from England to Trinidad in 1920 with a Diploma in Public Health, Jeffers embarked on a lifelong commitment to the education and welfare of women and the poor. She established a chain of breakfast sheds across the country, founded the Côterie of Social Workers (1921) as an organization for advocating women's rights, initiated the celebration of Mothers' Day in Trinidad and Tobago (1927), and made history when she became the first woman to run for, and win, elective office in the country (1936). In 1956, she spearheaded the formation of the Caribbean Women's Association.

FUNSO AIYEJINA

Jekyll, Walter

b. 1849, Sussex, England; d. 1929, Jamaica

Folklorist and translator

Educated at Harrow and Cambridge, Walter Jekyll was in succession priest and music teacher, before in 1892 settling in the Blue Mountain region of Jamaica, partly for health reasons. His musical training, and experience gained in travelling Europe and Scandinavia, fostered his interest in popular Jamaican music, dance and folklore, of which his collection *Jamaican Song and Story* (1907) is still a standard source. He was responsible for encouraging Claude **McKay** to write his groundbreaking verse in the Jamaican idiom, and appears, thinly disguised, in McKay's 1933 novel ***Banana Bottom***.

LOUIS JAMES

Jenkins, William

b. 1878?, USA; d. Mexico City

Businessman and film theatre owner

Jenkins moved to Mexico in 1901 and quickly amassed a fortune based on distributing alcoholic beverages, medicines and drugs; he was also a US vice-consul in Puebla and the central figure in a notorious political kidnapping in 1919. In the late 1930s he moved into the **film exhibition** business, first in Puebla, where most of his other businesses were based. By the 1940s his film interests expanded into Mexico City, where he established a monopoly through his company, Operadora de Teatros (Theatre Operators), by absorbing smaller competitors' circuits, including that of Emilio Azcárraga, with whom he would later co-operate to establish **Televisa**. Through political patronage, Jenkins became extraordinarily powerful during the Miguel Alemán presidency (1946–52), ostensibly controlling the Banco Cinematográfico (he was its principal stockholder) and being at the centre of the corrupt practices that then characterized the Mexican film industry – when writer José **Revueltas** publicly attacked Jenkins he was expelled from the film-makers' union (Sindicato de Trabajadores de la Producción Cinematográfica). Following the protests of film-maker Miguel **Contreras Torres** and other independent producers (and the publication of Contrera Torres's exposé, *El libro negro del cine Mexicano* (The Black Book of the Mexican Cinema) (1960)), the Mexican State purchased the Jenkins exhibition circuit and the **Churubusco Studios**, with which he was also allied, in 1960.

ANA M. LÓPEZ

Jesus, Clementina de

b. 1902, Valença, Rio de Janeiro, Brazil; d. 1987, Rio de Janeiro

Singer

With a deep, raspy voice and vast knowledge of traditional Afro-Brazilian songs, Clementina de Jesus revitalized genres such as samba-de-roda, lundu and jongo. She lived in Mangueira, home to the famous **samba** school, and worked as a maid for over twenty years. In 1965, she was invited by composer and impresario Hermínio Bello de Carvalho to perform in a musical showcase, *Rosa de Ouro* (Golden Rose), with **Paulinho da Viola** and others. She subsequently recorded several acclaimed albums, including *Gente da Antiga* (Old Timers) with two early innovators of samba, **Pixinguinha** and João da Baiana.

CHRISTOPHER DUNN

Jesús, Dionisio de

b. 1959, Cevicos, Dominican Republic

Poet

Dionisio de Jesús studied philosophy and letters at the Universidad Autónoma de Santo Domingo, and his first poems appeared in magazines and anthologies in the early 1980s. Among other books, he has published *Axiología de las sombras* (Axiology of the Shadows) (1984) and *Oráculo del suicida* (Oracle of the Suicide) (1985). Although he works in marketing and advertising, he has continued writing and trying to integrate his professional experience into his poetry. His book *Homus Advertiser* (1996) points to the existential struggle of modern men.

FERNANDO VALERIO-HOLGUÍN

Jesús, Maria Carolina de

b. 1914, Sacramento, Minas Gerais, Brazil; d. 1977, São Paulo

Writer

Granddaughter of slaves, illegitimate daughter who never knew her father, shanty dweller who made a precarious living gathering waste paper for sale, Maria Carolina de Jesús had a moment of great and unexpected fame when the journalist Aurélio Dantas edited the writings that she had put down in thirty-five notebooks and helped her publish *Quarto do despejo* (Trash Room, translated as *Child of the Dark*) (1960). The book went through numerous editions in Brazil and was translated into some thirty languages. She also published a novel, *Casa de alvenaria* (Brick House) (1961). A posthumous collection of her brief stories, *Diário de Bitita* (Bitita's Diary) (1986) was based on interviews with French journalists. Her writing was celebrated for her simple allegories, parables in the manner of St Francis of Assisi, which told the truth about oppression, **class** and political struggle.

DANIEL BALDERSTON

Jesús Paredes y Flores, Mariana de

b. 1616, Quito, Ecuador; d. 1645, Quito

Religious figure

An Ecuadorean saint, known commonly as Mariana de Jesús, she is popularly identified as the 'Azucena de Quito' (Quito's Lily), an allusion to her purity. She joined the Third Order of St Francis at the age of twenty-one. Never entering a convent, she spent most of her solitary life in an upper room of her sister's home. She developed a free clinic for the poor and a school for Indian children. A figure not without controversy, Mariana was subjected to criticism by the Jesuits. She has been worshipped for centuries, and miracles have been ascribed to her. Mariana was canonized in 1950 by Pope Pius XII; her feast day is celebrated on 26 May.

MERCEDES M. ROBLES

Jewish writing

In the first half of the twentieth century, Jewish writing in Latin America – of which Alberto Gerchunoff's *Los gauchos judíos* (The Jewish Gauchos of the *Pampas*) (1910) is the classic example – dealt mostly with the forging of a new identity combining Jewishness with various national identities. In recent decades, most Jewish writers have continued with the same basic subject, although the procedure has been reversed: starting from well-established national identities, they search for their Jewish roots and for the components shared by both. In some cases, this was a result of traumatic historical experiences such as dictatorship and repression in their native countries.

It is not sufficient to define Jewish writing by the explicit presence of Jewish themes, or by the writer's Jewish self-identification or origin. It seems more accurate to look for its specificity in the focus on experiences shared by both Jews and Latin Americans – **exile**, survival in a hostile environment, multiple allegiances, marginality, and a complex identity which should not be foregone in favour of cultural homogeneity: 'Jewish writers want to conjugate their own verb within the collective, polyphonic text of Latin American letters' (Senkman, 1983). S. Sosnowski (1987b) defines it as a 'hyphenated' literature which 'must be read on two fronts at once'; this very fact 'negates the homogeneity of the continent' and therefore 'contributes to the central debates of Latin American literature'.

Increasing consciousness of Jewish writing as a specific though integrated literary space within Latin American literature has produced many books and articles on the subject, and has led to the creation in 1985 of the International Association of Jewish Writers in Spanish and Portuguese, and its literary review *Noaj*. The Association is based in Jerusalem, with some 120 members living in the Americas, Europe and Israel. Several international conferences on Jewish writing in Latin America have taken place in various countries, and special sections have been devoted to it in conferences on general Latin American studies. Moacyr **Scliar** of Brazil, Margo **Glantz** of Mexico, Teresa **Porzencanski** of Uruguay, Luisa **Futoransky** and Sergio **Chejfec** of Argentina exemplify these trends.

See also: Judaism

Further reading

DiAntonio, R. and Glickman, N. (eds) (1993) *Tradition and Innovation. Reflections on Latin American Jewish Writing*, Albany: SUNY Press.

Kalechofsky, R. (ed.) (1980) *Echad: An Anthology of Latin American Jewish Writings*, Marblehead, MA: Micah Pub.

Landis, J.C. and Glickman, N. (eds) (1992) *Argentine Jewish Literature – A Selection*, Flushing and New York: Queens College Press.

Lindstrom, N. (1989) *Jewish Issues in Argentine Literature*, Columbia: University of Missouri Press.

Lockhart, D.B. (ed.) *Latin American Jewish Writers: A Critical Dictionary*, New York: Garland Publishing.

Senkman, L. (1983) *La identidad judía en la literatura argentina*, Buenos Aires: Pardés.

Senkman, L. and Goldberg, F.F. (eds) (1987–) *Noaj – Literary Review*, Jerusalem: International Association of Jewish Writers in Spanish and Portuguese.

Sosnowski, S. (1987a) *La orilla inminente. Escritores judíos argentinos*, Buenos Aires: Legasa.

—— (1987b) 'Latin American Jewish Literature: On Ethnic and National Boundaries', *Folio* 17: 1–8.

FLORINDAL .F. GOLDBERG

Jiménez, José Alfredo

b. 1926, Dolores Hidalgo, Guanajuato, Mexico; d. 1973, Mexico City

Singer and composer

A fairly conventional singer, Jiménez is the best-known popular composer in Mexico, with the exception of Agustín **Lara**. A self-taught musician, he sang on radio and in restaurants with the Trio Los Rebeldes. His first hits – 'Yo (I) and Ella (She)' – changed the direction of the **canción ranchera**, already an indispensable part of the education of any city dweller. He worked, though he did not need to, in **radio**, in farce, recordings and in films; his films, like *Guitarras de medianoche* (Midnight Guitars) and *Ni pobres ni ricos* (Neither Poor nor Rich), all of them terrible, used as many of his songs as they could fit in. His songs were sung by innumerable artists – including Jorge **Negrete**, Pedro **Infante**, Lola **Beltrán**, Amalia **Mendoza**, Chavela **Vargas** and, from 1990 onwards, by a number of flamenco singers. A legend in his own lifetime, Jiménez combined alcoholic self-destruction with an unending productivity – and as quickly as they were composed his songs would be absorbed into the 'Mexican repertoire' or the 'repertoire of deep emotion'.

José Alfredo's early songs exalted the *cantina*, the alcohol that is the liquid source of **machismo**, the confession, the sincerity that does not fear ridicule and the love that overcomes every obstacle if it is true. They include 'Corazón, corazón' (My heart, my heart), 'Paloma querida' (Beloved Dove), 'Cuatro caminos' (Four-Way Crossroad), 'Camino de Guanajuato' (Road to Guanajuato) and 'Un mundo raro' (Crazy World). If 'Mexicanness' before José Alfredo was festive, brilliant and challenging, his version is pained, sometimes cheerful, desperate – the story of someone who flies in the face of decent people and always ends in failure. His songs became collective anthems, *de rigueur* in any gathering, creators of imaginary communities, instant evocations of melancholy. And in his later songs, this dark tone becomes ever more emphatic – in 'Amanecí en tus brazos' (I Woke up in Your Arms), 'El último trago' (The Last Drink), 'Si nos dejan' (If They Leave Us) and in particular 'El rey' (The King), with its celebration of the highest ambitions of people on the margins of society.

CARLOS MONSIVÁIS

Jiménez Leal, Orlando

b. 1941, Havana, Cuba

Scriptwriter and film director

Jiménez Leal directed the controversial documentary ***PM***, in 1961, together with Sabá Cabrera Infante. Later the same year he left Cuba. In 1984 he and Nestor **Almendros** made *Conducta impropia* (Improper Conduct), a documentary about repression in Cuba that won a Grand Prix at the Human Rights Festival in Strasbourg and was selected as film of the year (1984) at the London Film Festival. *El Super* (1989), made with León Ichaso, is a portrait of an exiled Cuban family living in the USA. His other works include *8-A* (1992), a documentary exploring the trial and execution of Cuban general, Arnaldo Ochoa, in 1989.

WILFREDO CANCIO ISLA

Jiménez Mabarak, Carlos

b. 1916; d. 1994

Composer

Composer of over one hundred works, all based on popular music, Jiménez was a professor of music at various higher education institions from the 1940s onwards. His works include *Sinfonía en sí bemol* (Symphony in F Sharp), settings of works by various poets, ballet suites like *Recuerdo de Zapata* (Remembering Zapata) and *La maestra rural* (The Country Schoolmistress) as well as chamber music, **opera** and film music. His *Fanfarria* was used during the prizegiving ceremonies at the 1968 Olympic Games in Mexico City (see **Olympic Games, Mexico 1968**). He was awarded the National Prize for the Arts in 1993.

MARIANNA POOL WESTGAARD

jinetera

Jinetera is the name given to those Cuban women who have sexual relations with foreigners in order to earn US dollars or acquire consumer goods. The term comes from the verb *jinetear*, which means to ride a horse, particularly in public places, with arrogance and pride. The phenomenon of the *jineteras* proliferated in Cuba from the mid-1980s onwards, as the island attracted growing numbers of tourists and the economic crisis deepened. The term designates not only the act of prostitution; it can be used to refer to a whole range of illicit, personal relationships with foreigners.

WILFREDO CANCIO ISLA

jing ping

Jing ping is the folk music of Dominica, played by a band with four instruments: the accordion, or 'musique', the flat drum, or 'tambou', the 'gwage' or 'shiak', a sealed, grater-like metal tube filled with seeds or pebbles and scraped with wire, and the 'boom boom', a long wooden tube usually made from the 'bois cano' tree, played like an Australian didgeridoo. Instruments such as the fiddle, trumpet and steel triangle are sometimes added. The music is influenced by African and French **creole** rhythms and accompanies creole dances and folk songs, **carnival** 'paseos' and 'chanté mas', the latter based on a call, 'chanté', and the refrain, 'lavway'.

LENNOX HONEYCHURCH

Jitrik, Noé

b. 1928, Rivera, Province of Buenos Aires, Argentina

Critic and writer

Considered one of the most knowledgeable commentators on Latin American literature, Jitrik's critical writings are notable for their polemical quality, still in the spirit of his early work in **Contorno** (though he later broke with co-editor David **Viñas**). His best-known essays include studies of Domingo Faustino Sarmiento, **Lugones**, **Güiraldes**, **Arlt**, **Borges**, **García Márquez**, **Vallejo**, **Carpentier** and numerous others. His writings on literary theory focus on practices of reading. He has also written poetry, short stories and novels, notably *Mares del sur* (Southern Seas) (1997). He has taught in Argentina, France, Mexico and the USA. He currently heads the Instituto de Literatura Hispanoamericana at the University of Buenos Aires, and is directing a twenty volume critical history of Argentine literature.

DIEGO BENTIVEGNA

Joaquín Mortiz

Joaquín Mortiz is a Mexico City publishing house founded in 1962 by Spanish immigrant Joaquín Díez-Canedo, which specialized in works by Mexican authors (including Rosario **Castellanos**, Elena **Garro** and Carlos **Fuentes**), promoted cosmopolitan writings by authors associated with the *Revista mexicana de literatura*, and introduced young Mexican writers associated with La **Onda**. In 1983 the company joined **Planeta Chilena**, a Spanish transnational publishing group, and in 1995 the founder's daughter, Aurora Díez-Canedo Flores, left the firm and ended the family's tradition as the arbiters of taste at Joaquín Mortiz.

DANNY J. ANDERSON

Jobim, Antônio Carlos Brasileiro de Almeida (Tom)

b. 1927, Rio de Janeiro, Brazil; d. 1994, New York, USA

Musician

Perhaps Brazil's best-loved and most influential composer, Jobim wrote over 300 songs and was the principal creative spirit behind the **bossa nova** movement. He studied piano and composition as a child and enrolled in architecture school, but dropped out to play piano in Copacabana bars. His first hit came in 1954 with 'Teresa da Praia' (Teresa of the Beach), recorded by Dick Farney and Mauricio Alves. After recording 'Sinfonia de Rio de Janeiro', he was given his own television show, 'Bom Tom' (nice Tom/tone) and began to compose the manifesto-songs of the new bossa nova sound: 'Desafinado' (Out of Tune), 'Samba de uma nota só' (One-Note Samba), 'Meditaçao' (Meditation).

However, it was his association with poet/lyricist Vinícius de **Moraes** – beginning with the soundtrack for the film *Orfeu negro* (Black Orpheus) (1959) (adapted from Moraes's play *Orfeu da Conceição*) for which Jobim wrote the haunting 'A Felicidade') (Happiness) – that proved most productive. Combining almost erudite musical forms with romantic lyrics, they produced the biggest international hits of the Brazilian popular music movement **MPB**, ranging from 'Aquarela do Brasil' (Brasilian Watercolour), 'Só danço samba' (I Only Dance Samba) and 'Sinfonía da Alvorada' (for the inauguration of Brasília), to the most famous of all, 'A garota de Ipanema' (The Girl from Ipanema) (1962). Composed at the table of an Ipanema bar, 'A garota' has been recorded by hundreds of artists and is an international classic.

Jobim's international career was launched in 1962, the year Charlie Byrd and Stan Getz recorded his 'Desafinado', and he performed at Carnegie Hall and officially introduced the bossa nova sound solidified by his 1967 album with Frank Sinatra. His oeuvre did not end with bossa nova. Constantly experimenting with musical forms and complex harmonies, he collaborated with Chico

Buarque, produced in a constructivist style the brilliant 'Aguas de Março' (March Waters) (considered by critic Leonard Feather one of the most significant compositions of all time), developed a series of ecological motifs and experimented with songwriting in other languages.

Jobim influenced generations of musicians in Brazil and abroad, and his death from post-surgical complications in New York was widely mourned. In homage, during the fireworks at the 1994 New Year's eve celebrations in Copacabana, his image was electronically projected over Guanabara Bay while his music filled the air.

Further reading

Jobim, H. (1996) *Antonio Carlos Jobim: un homem iluminado*, Rio de Janeiro: Nova Frontera.

MARíA JOSÉ SOMERLATE BARBOSA

Jobson, Dickey

b. Jamaica

Film-maker

One of Jamaica's best-known film-makers, along with Perry **Henzel**. Jobson scripted and directed *Countryman* (1982), a Rasta movie popular with audiences at home and abroad. Ed Guerrero (in 'Jah no dead: Modes of resistance in *Rockers* and *Countryman*', in M. Cham (1992) Trenton, NJ: Africa World Press) explains the film's crossover appeal, noting that from the opening scene, 'the spectator/consumer is positioned to enjoy the stereotypical pleasures of an island paradise offered up by a friendly native *other* who asks for no greater reward for his services than the acceptance and satisfaction registered on his guests' faces' (107).

ANN MARIE STOCK

Jockey Clubs

At their peak from 1900 to 1945, these clubs functioned as centres of elite social life and culture and maintained active international social contacts between the upper classes of Latin American countries. Mostly founded between 1860 and 1890, they included a racecourse, betting concessions, social centre and country club, although governments gradually limited them to social functions. The Jockey Club of Buenos Aires is the richest and most famous. Racing clubs thus became symbolic of the cosmopolitan elite's social and economic dominance. In a nationalist backlash, the Buenos Aires Jockey Club was burned down by supporters of President Juan **Perón** in 1953.

See also: horse racing

THOMAS EDSALL

Jodorowsky, Alejandro

b. 1930, Iquique, Chile

Film and theatre director

Jodorowsky began his career in Mexico, making films that were irreverent, critical of Western values and institutions and imbued with Oriental philosophy. His first work, *Fando y Lis* (1967), based on work by Spain's Fernando Arrabal, caused a scandal at its premiere, and thereafter Jodorowsky was frequently censored. In 1968 his *El topo* (The Mole) became an instant cult movie. *La montaña sagrada* (The Sacred Mountain) (1972) is widely regarded as his best work. After a fourteen-year gap, during which he worked in literature, theatre and music, he returned to the cinema with the prizewinning *Santa sangre* (Holy Blood) (1989).

PATRICIA TORRES SAN MARTÍN

Jogo do Bicho

An illegal lottery in Brazil, the Jogo do Bicho was established in 1893 by Barão João Batista Vianna Drummond, founder and director of Rio de Janeiro's Zoological Gardens. Lacking funds for animal feed, he began to raise money by selling visitors numbered tickets which carried the picture of an animal. At the end of the day a draw was made, and the person whose ticket carried the image of the animal drawn won a prize of 20,000 reis. Gradually the game became popular throughout the country.

The game consists of twenty-five numbers, each corresponding to a specific animal or group – for example the ostrich (number 1), eagle (2), butterfly (4), calf (7), cobra (9), elephant (12), lion (16), pig (18), peacock (19), tiger (22), deer (24) and cow (25). A block of four tens corresponds to each animal's group: 1 to 4, to the ostrich; 5 to 8, to the eagle and so on up to 97 to 00 for the cow. Each group has its corresponding hundreds and thousands too, formed by adding a number between 0 and 9 to the animal's own number. So the elephant includes numbers 45, 46, 47, 48, the hundreds 045, 046, 047, 048 and the thousands 0045, 0046 and so on. The result of the game is based on the tens corresponding to the five numbers drawn by the official lotteries. Bets can be made against animal groups, which pay eighteen times the original bet if any ten of the original group was drawn; the tens pay sixty times the bet, the hundreds 600 times, and the thousands 4,000 times the original bet. The bets can be made in a variety of combinations, by number, group and several combinations.

Although it has been illegal since 1946, it is common to find in every Brazilian city a *ponto* (betting shop), a *cambista*, who notes down the bets and a *bicheiro*, who finances the lottery. These are the key elements of the game. In the 1980s the government began to lay siege to the game, suspecting that it was linked to organized crime, drugs and other illegal forms of gambling. Yet the game has passed from the economic field to take its place in the symbolic space of Brazilian culture where its manifestations embrace soccer (see **football**), the Rio **Carnival** and cinema, where it inspired Fábio **Barreto**'s *O Rei do Rio* (King of Rio) (1984) and the *telenovela* (see **telenovelas**) *Partido Alto*.

Further reading

Soares, F.F. (1993) *O Jogo do Bicho: A saga de um fato social brasileiro*, Rio de Janeiro: Bertrand Brasil S.A.

VNALDOS A. SANTOS

John, Errol

b. 1924, Port-of-Spain, Trinidad; d. 1988, London, England

Playwright and actor

John's lively, unflinching representations of the struggles of slum-dwellers are based on the city of his birth. A leading member of several amateur groups in the 1940s, his early, one-act plays, *How Then Tomorrow* (1947) and *The Tout* (1949) established his style as a playwright drawing on speech and song. Moving to London in 1951, disappointment with the minor roles offered to him as a black West Indian urged him to complete his major three-act work, *Moon on a Rainbow Shawl*, internationally recognized winner of the 1957 *Observer* playwriting award.

JILL E. ALBADA-JELGERSMA

Jonckers, Herbert

b. Belgium; d. 1997, Santiago, Chile

Designer

Jonckers came to Chile because of his ties to director and playwright, Ramón **Griffero**; Griffero had returned to Chile in the mid-1980s, having gone into exile in Europe to escape the threat imposed on the artistic community by the **Pinochet** regime. Jonckers worked closely with Griffero as part of the Fin de Siglo (End of the Century) theatre group. He was the principal designer for all of Griffero's plays produced in Chile, most notably *Historia de un galpón abandonado* (History of an Abandoned Warehouse) (1984) and *Cinema Utopia* (1985).

RUTH DOMINGUEZ

Jones, Marion (Marion Glean O'Callaghan)

b. 1934, Woodbrook, Trinidad

Novelist

The author of *Pan Beat* (1973), a novel about

steelband and the involvement of women in its development, and *J'Ouvert Morning* (1976), which examines middle-class predicaments in a society with a colonial heritage, Jones is preoccupied with issues of alienation and the claustrophobic ethos of island/colonial societies, race, and poverty. She was educated in Trinidad (one of the first two women to be admitted to the Tropical School of Agriculture, St. Augustine), the USA, and England, in library science and social anthropology.

FUNSO AIYEJINA

Jorge Alvarez, Editorial

One of Argentina's most important publishing houses between 1964 and 1972, when the country experienced a publishing boom led by the internal market, and the books of Argentine writers and the novelists of the **Boom** began to sell massively. Jorge Alvarez was one of the publishers who nourished this expanding market, producing, for example, the short stories of Rodolfo **Walsh**. It also published a number of very successful thematic anthologies and the *crónicas* (Reports) on the bourgeoisie, on communication, on Latin America, on Cuba etc., as well as some lighter, more trivial topics, like the Reports on Christmas. Alvarez later became a producer of rock concerts.

PABLO ALABARCES

Jorge Ben (Jorge Duílio Lima Meneses)

b. 1942, Rio de Janeiro, Brazil

Musician

An adroit negotiator of often conflicting national and international musical values of the 1960s, Jorge Ben created his own unique fusions of **samba**, **bossa nova**, rock, and soul. Ben composed and recorded classic pop hits such as 'Más que nada', (Oh, Come On), 'Qué Pena', (What a Shame) and 'País Tropical' (Tropical Country). His music was embraced by Caetano **Veloso** and Gilberto Gil, the leading artists of the **Tropicália** movement. In 1975, he recorded an acoustic album with Gilberto **Gil**, which explored Afro-Brazilian cultural themes. In the early 1990s, after years of scant commercial success, he enjoyed a massive comeback with his recording '23' under a new professional name, Jorge Benjor.

CHRISTOPHER DUNN

Jorge Cardoso, Onelio

b. 1914, Calabazar de Sagua, Cuba; d. 1992, Havana, Cuba

Writer

One of Cuba's most important short story writers, he worked for many years as a rural schoolteacher, journalist and scriptwriter for radio and television. Recognition came in 1945, when his story 'Los carboneros' (The Charcoal Burners) won the national literary prize. Later volumes – *El cuentero* (The storyteller) (1958) and *El caballo de coral* (The Coral Horse) (1960) confirmed his skilful use of popular language and culture, and the deep humanism characteristic of his work. He wrote a number of children's stories, and produced several more volumes of stories including *Caballito blanco* (Little White Horse) (1974).

MARÍA IRENE FORNÉS

Jornal do Brasil

The *Jornal do Brasil* is a daily newspaper founded in Rio de Janeiro in 1891 by Rodolfo de Souza Dantas and Joaquim Nabuco; its first edition consisted of five thousand copies. In its first declaration of principles, the *Jornal do Brazil* (as the masthead spelled it) announced that it would maintain good relations with the republican regime while reserving its right to criticize the government. In addition to its editorial team, the paper recruited correspondents from around the world, including Wilhelm Schimper, rector of Bonn University; Paul Leroy Beaulieu, in France; Emile de Laveleye, professor at the University of Liège, in Belgium; and W. Franklin in the United States. In

1893, Rui Barbosa became editor; his first act was to correct the paper's title to *Jornal do Brasil*.

Taken over by Mendes and Co in 1894, the newspaper returned to the streets in November 1895 under the editorship of Fernando Mendes de Almeida. In 1919, faced with economic difficulties at the end of the First World War, the Mendes brothers sold the paper to Count Ernesto Pereira Carneiro, who in 1935 founded Radio Jornal do Brasil. On his death in 1953 the editorship passed to his widow, Maurina Dunshee de Abranches Periera Carneiro. In 1956 the paper underwent a major transformation and gained a new management under M.F. Nascimento Brito and Anibal Freire, who invited journalist Odilo Costa Filho to reshape the *Jornal*. One year later, a picture appeared on the front page for the first time, and major changes in format and presentation followed under the direction of Amilcar de Castro.

In 1960 *Caderno B*, an arts supplement with special interest in cinema and theatre, appeared for the first time; at the same time, classified advertisements began to appear in another new supplement, *Caderno C*. The transformation of the paper was complete by the time Alberto Dines took it over in 1961. Among the those who have written for the paper are Carlos **Drummond de Andrade**, Carlos Castelo Branco, Barbosa Lima Sobrinho and Rubem Braga. In 1983, with the death of Countess Pereira Carneiro, M.F. Nascimento Brito took over as joint managing editor with his daughter Maria Regina do Nascimento Brito.

ANTONIO CARLOS VAZ

José José

b. 1948, Mexico City

Singer

A legend in his time, because of his turbulent life and his innovative style, his thirty-plus albums contain many 'standards'; in fact many of them have become 'standards' precisely as a result of his performance of them. His style is at once sensual and homely, the lyrics sometimes 'arranged' for his traditionalist audience. José José (born José Sosa) creates an intimate relationship with the **bolero** – not like the torch singers of 1930–50 who infused it with a tone of autobiography and the ravages of class and gender (like María Luisa Landón, Elvira Ríos or Chelo Silva), nor like the tropical singers who added a feeling of late night parties and dawn confessions (Daniel **Santos**, Alberto Beltrán, Celio González or Julio **Jaramillo**). Despite his musical training, José José does not follow the semi-operatic line of Pedro **Vargas** or Jorge **Negrete**, but opts instead for an open and direct emotionalism. That is his specific quality – the use of the voice to transmit clearly to the listener an old romance in new versions or a new romance with transgressive lyrics. In the 1970s, when rock and roll and **cumbia** were in the ascendant and bolero was regarded as an anachronism, José José gave it strength and credibility. His songs reveal a sensitivity now separated from unconditional surrender, secular but suspicious of the single night of passion. Here the singer both acknowledges the desolate life of the city and sings of couples who can find, for a time at least, some kind of permanence.

CARLOS MONSIVÁIS

José Olympio

José Olympio is the name of the Rio de Janeiro publishing house founded in 1931. The publisher of many classics of Brazilian literature, including João Guimarães **Rosa**, Graciliano **Ramos**, Clarice **Lispector** and Carlos **Drummond de Andrade**, José Olympio is perhaps best known in Portugal and Brazil for its compact editions of the complete works of the Portuguese writers Eça de Queiroz and Fernando Pessoa and of numerous Brazilians including Joaquim Maria Machado de Assis, the great late nineteenth-century novelist, Carlos Drummond, Manuel **Bandeira**, Cecília **Meireles** and numerous others.

DANIEL BALDERSTON

Journal of Latin American Studies

Published three times a year (in February, May and October), the *Journal*'s (May 1969–) editorial offices are located at the Institute of Latin American Studies, University of London. Its editorial board includes representatives of Latin American Centres or Institutes at the Universities of Cambridge, Essex, Glasgow, Liverpool, London and Oxford. It publishes recent research in the field of Latin American history, economic history, economics, geography, politics, international relations, sociology, social anthropology and cultural history. Regular features include articles on contemporary themes, specially commissioned 'commentaries' and an extensive section of book reviews. There is no commitment to any political viewpoint or ideology. Recent issues have covered prospects for democratization in a post-revolutionary setting in Central America; Europeanism and nativism in *Os Sertões*; and models of public-sector intervention in providing for the elderly in Argentina c. 1890–1993.

MIKE GONZALEZ

Journal of West Indian Literature

Twice-yearly journal of the Departments of English of the **University of the West Indies**, it began publication in 1986. During the 1960s, members of the University's Faculty of Education and English Departments began to devise courses centred on West Indian literature and to press for the teaching of work by West Indian authors in regional schools, where previously their work had been subsumed into the study of 'Black' or 'Commonwealth' literature. The Journal's emblem is Anancy, the folktale trickster, a character who epitomizes the ambivalences and ironies of West Indian identity.

LORRAINE LEU

Journalists' professional associations

SIP (Sociedad Interamericana de Prensa, or IAPA as it is called in English) was founded in 1943 in Havana and represents some 1,300 newspapers and journals in Latin America. Its objectives include the defence of press freedom, the protection of its members' interests, the promotion of high standards of journalistic professionalism, the exchange of information and the promotion of technical innovation. It also has two autonomous affiliated organizations – the Instituto de Prensa (Press Institute), which offers technical advice, and the Fondo de Becas (Grants Foundation), which provides funding for educational activities. It now has its headquarters in Miami, USA.

The Latin American Journalists' Association (FLP – Federación Latinoamericana de Periodistas) is an NGO linked to UNESCO and represents more than 80,000 journalists across the continent. It is also associated with over fifty organizations concerned with the study and practice of journalism, research centres, schools of journalism, libraries, bulletins, etc. Since its foundation in 1976, it has organized courses for journalists and, since 1991, has supported the Comisión de Investigación de Atentados a Periodistas (CIAP – Commission for the Investigation of Attacks on Journalists) as well as the OIP (Organzación Internacional de Periodistas – International Journalists' Organization).

The Federación Latinoamericana de Facultades de Comunicación (FELAFACS – Latin American Federation of Schools of Communication) is also an NGO that brings together 240 such schools in twenty Latin American countries. It also carries out and sponsors its own research, with technical and financial assistance from the Konrad Adenauer Foundation. Its headquarters are in Lima, Peru.

CIESPAL (Centro Internacional de Estudios Superiores de Comunicación para América Latina – International Centre for Advanced Studies in Communication in Latin America) is a non-profit making NGO founded in 1959. Its objectives are to work for the development and the democratization of the information and cultural media throughout the region. It has trained thousands of professionals in thirty countries or more in radio news production, the production of educational programmes and drama, as well as written and TV journalism. It has published 280 titles in collections that include the Cuadernos Chasqui and CIESPAL Monographs. It is based in Quito, Ecuador.

Periodistas de Investigación (Investigative Journalists), founded in Mexico in 1996 under the chairmanship of Pedro Enrique Almendares, is a network of investigative reporters and editors. It is an arm of the US organization, Investigative Reporters and Editors, whose aim is to train reporters and facilitate the exchange of information. Journalists with Frontiers and the International Press Federation also have regional branches.

WILFREDO CANCIO ISLA

Juan Gabriel

b. 1950, Parácuaro, Michoacán, Mexico

Singer

Born Alberto Aguilera Valadez, when he was still young, the singer's family moved to Ciudad Juárez and placed him in an orphanage where he discovered his passion for music – though he never studied music formally. His first performance was at the Noa Noa night-club in Ciudad Juarez; in 1971 he moved to Mexico where he recorded his first hit, No tengo dinero (I've Got No Money). His behaviour on stage, which broke with every show-business tradition, brought him criticism and scorn, but his public adored him. In 1977 he changed from teen songs to singing a combination of ranchera (see **canción ranchera**) and ballads. He fought with **Televisa** and the recording companies, and finally won the right to keep the royalties from his songs – an unprecedented situation in Latin America. His hits include Se me olvida otra vez (I've Forgotten Again), Querida (Darling), Amor eterno (Eternal Love) (a hymn to mothers) and La diferencia (The Difference).

CARLOS MONSIVÁIS

Juantorena, Alberto

b. 1950, Santiago de Cuba

Athlete

The first Cuban athlete to achieve world ranking in both the 400 and 800 metres, Juantorena was known for the elegance of his running style. At the 1976 Montreal Olympics he won gold with a time of 44.26 seconds in the 400 metres and 1:43.50 in the 800 metres, a world record which he broke again, with a time of 1:43.44, in 1977. He again won both races at the Helsinki World Championships. A graduate in economics, he retired in 1985; since then he has occupied important posts with the National Sports Institute and on Cuba's Olympic Committee.

WILFREDO CANCIO ISLA

Juarroz, Roberto

b. 1925, Coronel Dorrego, Argentina; d. 1995, Buenos Aires

Poet

The originality of Juarroz's poetry is suggested by *poesía vertical* (vertical poetry), the constant title of all his collections, from *Poesía vertical* (1958) to *Décimotercera poesía vertical* (Thirteenth Book) (1993). All his writing is an intermittent journey in one direction, its language wholly consistent with this developing exploration. He graduated from the University of Buenos Aires, where he remained as lecturer and head of department. Juarroz was a fine translator and critic, and from 1958 to 1965 edited the journal *Poesía=Poesía*.

ENRIQUE FOFFANI

Judaism

A monotheistic religion anchored in ancient practices and traditions, Judaism is based on an elaborate system of articles of faith in an abstract, non-representational and omnipotent God who has chosen His people to follow a series of elaborate precepts. The *Torah* (*Pentateuch* or 'Five

Books of Moses') codifies the creation of the universe and the historical origins and early history of the Hebrews, and organizes a pattern of behaviour that unites ethics with strict adherence to measures that express belief in God. The written *Torah* is supplemented by the 'Oral Torah': the *Mishnah*, a six-volume Hebrew-language code sealed in AD 200, which interprets the meaning of the *Torah*, and the *Talmud*, sealed in AD 500, which in turn, comments on the *Mishnah* tracts. In addition, precepts systematized in Rabbinic Responsa developed over the centuries join these basic texts to mould the foundation of traditional Jewish life.

Supported by core basic tenets, the practice of Judaism is inextricably linked to historical developments. The Babylonian exile that followed the destruction of Solomon's Temple in 586 BC; the broader dispersion that followed the destruction of the Second Temple by Roman legions in AD 70; and the 1492 expulsion from Spain, with its resulting impact on the Americas, shaped the traditions, customs and the languages in which Judaism was expressed.

Two general branches are recognized to date, each with its own subdivisions according to birthplace and concomitant religious and cultural experiences: *Ashkenazi* (from the Hebrew name for Germany, *Ashkenaz*) applies to Jews who descend from Central and Eastern European Jewry; *Sephardi* (from the Hebrew name for Spain, *Sepharad*) is commonly used for Jews from Iberia, North Africa and the Middle East. Over a millennium, two distinct Jewish languages developed for daily use – Yiddish and Ladino – while Hebrew remained the sacred language.

Branches from both *Sephardi* and *Ashkenazi* communities migrated to Latin America. The most intensive migration of Jews to Latin America took place from the latter part of the nineteenth century through to the first half of the twentieth century. Migrations resulted from various factors: the promise of safe havens in the Americas was an enticing option to anti-Semitism, pogroms, wars and, lastly, the Holocaust. Currently, there are approximately 500,000 Jews in the region, with Buenos Aires continuing to be a major centre of Jewish life and a training ground for teachers and rabbis for other Latin American nations.

A religion that shuns conversions, Judaism has survived through various degrees of adherence to strict laws and traditions, and through an inextricable link to the Land of Israel as the site of origin as well as of individual and communal destiny. Rabbinical academies in the Diaspora ordained guides and interpreters of Judaism, allowing Rabbis to teach and legislate on religious matters. In time, Jewish identification has adopted a number of practices, and Judaism is seen in both religious and cultural facets. Since the establishment of the State of Israel, Judaism is the defining factor that under the Law of Return conveys citizenship to any resident Jew.

A cohesive, but far from monolithic, Orthodoxy was once the sole marker of Judaism. It is increasingly accompanied and challenged by other, less strict, canonical interpretations of Jewish law. In addition to the Conservative, Reform and Reconstructionist movements that dispute Orthodoxy's pre-eminence, non-institutionalized communities also practise Judaism, while many who identify themselves as Jews deny any religious belief.

Jewish schools – which reflect political parties and/or religious leanings – span the gamut from anti-Zionist, Bundist programmes (where Yiddish and not Hebrew is taught), to Hasidic academies and Yeshivoth, where strict Orthodox training is the rule. A recent addition to Latin America, the growing Conservative movement continues to attract youth that had previously shied away from formal affiliations.

Judaism should not be identified solely with religious practices or synagogue membership. In the name of its ethical and egalitarian principles, non-religious Jews have erected political barricades, and have participated in and led socialist efforts and workers' unions. A percentage of Jews that exceeded many times over the Jewish population of their countries was counted among the imprisoned and disappeared during the last Southern Cone dictatorships; evidence, as government officials justified, of the high number of Jews involved in 'subversive activities'. That involvement – certainly not unanimous – signified the adoption of Judaism through its power of survival and claims for social justice, and the view that redemption is tied to historical workings, rather than exclusively to faith in a God-related event.

Judaism can be a clear-cut identity marker; it is also part of the 'religion or nationality' debate. An old issue that came to the fore under Napoleon, for instance, has oft-times surfaced in Latin American countries where a minority with its own religion and cultural history is viewed with suspicion. Identity based on the expressed will to be *at once* Jewish and Latin American (in the corresponding national definition) plays a central role in the intellectual map of many who find compatible their commitment to origins and to their found promised land.

Further reading

Elkin, J.L. and Merckx, G. (1987) *The Jewish Presence in Latin America*, Boston: Allen & Unwin.

Lindstrom, N. (1989) *Jewish Issues in Argentine Literature*, Columbia: University of Missouri Press

V Congreso Internacional de Investigadores sobre el Judaismo Latinoamericano (1990) *Ensayos sobre Judaismo en América Latina*, Buenos Aires: Mila.

SAÚL SOSNOWSKI

Juliá, Raúl

b. 1940, San Juan, Puerto Rico; d. 1994, New York, USA

Actor

Already distinguishing himself in acclaimed Latin American films such as *La **gran fiesta*** (The Big Party) in 1987 and *Tango Bar* in 1988, this versatile performer is best known for his Hollywood appearances, ranging from his Latin lover in **Coppola**'s 1981 *One From the Heart* and the bisexual revolutionary in *Kiss of the Spider Woman* (see ***Beso de la muyer oraña***), to the Paul Henreid character in *Havana*, a 1989 remake of *Casablanca* set in the Caribbean. His biggest commercial successes came starring alongside Anjelica Huston in the 1991 *Addams Family* and a 1992 sequel, where urbanity and romantic intensity informed his inspired portrayal of the Gothic patriarch Gómez, a cross between César Romero and Errol Flynn.

JOHN D. PERIVOLARIS

Juliana, Elis

b. 1927, Curaçao, Netherlands Antilles

Poet, short-story writer and artist

From the early 1950s, Juliana has contributed extensively to **Papiamentu** literature, with over a dozen collections of poetry and short stories (some for children) to his name, including the four volume *Organisashon Planifikashon Independensia* (Organisation Planning Independence) (1979, 1981, 1983, and 1989). He cultivated as no other the intrinsic rhythmic and tonal aspects of the language, while also developing his interest in the Afro-Caribbean life-styles of his people. In addition, Juliana distinguished himself in the visual arts, with various international exhibitions, and in ethnography, specializing in local folklore and the oral tradition.

AART G. BROEK

Junco, Pedro

b. 1920, Pinar del Río, Cuba; d. 1943, Havana, Cuba

Composer and pianist

Something of a child prodigy, Junco played piano from an early age in his home town. Although he died very young, at twenty-three, he left behind thirty-six songs including 'Soy como soy' (I Am What I Am), 'Ya te lo dije' (I Told You So) and the very popular 'Nosotros' (Us).

JOSÉ ANTONIO EVORA

jungla, La

La jungla (The Jungle) is a gouache (228 × 238 cms) painted by Wilfredo **Lam** in 1943. It depicts a recreated tropical landscape based on a symbolism of African origin, in which an exuberant vegetation mingles with the human. There is no border between the two. Using Cubist forms and combining earthy and vibrant colours, the artist achieves a fantastic atmosphere that condenses sensuality, mythology and the power of the Caribbean earth. Critics have placed this work among the hundred most important contemporary paintings. It now belongs to the permanent collection of the Museum of Modern Art in New York.

WILFREDO CANCIO ISLA

junkanoo

A parade festival of masquerade, music and dance, originally performed by African slaves and their descendants between the seventeenth and nineteenth centuries in various parts of the Caribbean (and North America), usually during the Christmas season. Its roots are in West African masquerade traditions, mixed with European influences like English mumming. It continued most elaborately in Jamaica and the Bahamas into the twentieth century; Bahamian junkanoo was revived in the late twentieth century to become the official national festival, performed twice annually on 1 January and 26 December and involving tens of thousands of participants and spectators. The origin of the name 'junkanoo' is variously ascribed to West African languages or to one John Canoe, who lived in the slave trade era.

ROSANNE ADDERLEY

Juruna, Mario

b. circa 1941, Aldeia Couto Magalhães, Mato Grosso, Brazil

Indian leader

In 1982, Mario Juruna of the Xavante (Shavante) people became the first Indian elected to Brazil's National Congress. He was elected on a PDT (Democratic Workers' Party) slate, from an urban district in the state of Rio de Janeiro. Famous for tape recording the false promises of high-ranking government officials and exposing them to the press, Juruna earned public acclaim for his denunciations of corruption in the military government during the late 1970s and early 1980s, a time when the dictatorship muted other opposition voices. Protected by his Indian status (a 'relatively incapable' ward of the State, a legal minor) Juruna articulated indigenous concerns that resonated with the civil and political frustrations of the general public. When the nation's political climate improved with the '*abertura*', Juruna was no longer useful to the political machine that propelled him into national office. His reputation degenerated into a caricature of a corrupt buffoon.

Prior to his election to Congress, Juruna was prominent in international human-rights circles. In 1980, Brazil denied him the right to a passport and the ability to officially participate in the Fourth Russell Tribunal on Crimes against Indians in the Americas. Juruna's case was argued in the Federal Appellate court, which decided in Juruna's favour. He attended the final sessions of the Tribunal, where he had been elected President of the Jury. The government's handling of Juruna's case served to focus critical attention on Brazil's unjust treatment of its indigenous peoples.

LAURA R. GRAHAM

Justiniano, Gonzalo

b. 1956, Santiago, Chile

Film-maker

Part of a new generation of Chilean film-makers who emerged during the **Pinochet** dictatorship, Justiniano wrote and directed the award-winning 1994 *Amnesia*, a film that addresses Chile's recent two decades of military government and concerns two men who meet again long after the end of a war where one was a prisoner of the other. Justiniano studied film in France, where he also produced several programmes for French television. Among his other films are *Los hijos de la Guerra Fría* (Children of the Cold War) (1985) and *Sussi* (1987). In 1997 he began his fifth feature, *Corazones fritos* (Fried Hearts).

AMALIA PEREIRA

Justo, Agustín P.

b. 1876, Concepción del Uruguay, Entre Ríos; d. 1943, Buenos Aires

President

Argentine General and President (1932–8) who dominated politics during the 'Infamous Decade' of the 1930s. He drew his political support from dissident Radicals, provincial conservatives, and members of the upper class. This coalition won him the Presidency in 1932 in a fraudulent election. His administration followed economically conservative, anti-labour and pro-British policies. Cultural and economic resistance to these policies fostered the growth of a strong nationalist movement and ulitimately led to the rise of Peronism after Justo's death.

THOMAS EDSALL

Justo, Juan B.

b. 1865, Buenos Aires, Argentina; d. 1928, Los Cardales, Pilar, Argentina

Physician and socialist leader

An innovative physician turned socialist leader, Justo's brand of conservative **socialism** and genteel behaviour won him the respect of the urban working class as well as many in the landowning elite. His conversion to orthodox socialism by immigrants inspired him to found *La Vanguardia*, one of the premier socialist journals of the time. Justo also wrote, translated, and edited numerous works relating to the socialist cause. Active in international conferences, he also served as a Socialist Party representative (1912–24) and senator (1924–8) in the national legislature. Two years prior to his death, Justo opened the Casa del Pueblo (The House of the People), a socialist centre with an extensive library, classrooms and meeting halls.

See also: Justo, Alicia Moreau de

THOMAS EDSALL

Juventud rebelde

The newspaper *Juventud rebelde* was founded on 21 October 1965 by Fidel **Castro** as part of a strategy for reorganizing the revolutionary government's press. Until 1987 it occupied the building previously belonging to the ***Diario de la marina***. The organ of the Cuban Young Communists (UJC), it became the country's second most important newspaper; and in 1966 it began to publish the cultural supplement ***El caimán barbudo*** (The Bearded Alligator). Among the government's publications, it stands out as the best in its standard of writing, use of graphics and treatment of new issues. In 1990 it became a weekly, but it resumed its daily circulation in 2000. Its website is www.jrebelde.cubaweb.cu.

WILFREDO CANCIO ISLA

Kagel, Mauricio Raúl

b. 1931, Buenos Aires, Argentina

Composer, conductor and film-maker

Kagel is one of the most important innovators in Argentine contemporary music. His work comprises some 150 pieces (twenty of them radiophonic) and eighteen films. In 1949 he became artistic adviser to the **Agrupación Nueva Música**, participated in the founding of the Cinemateca Argentina in 1950, and became Director of the Chamber Orchestra of the **Teatro Colón** in 1955.

In 1957 Kagel studied electronic music in Cologne, Germany, where he has lived ever since, conducting the Rheinisches Kammerorchester (1957–61) and forming the Kölner Ensemble für Neue Musik (1962–94). He has been awarded numerous distinctions and prizes including the Koussevitsky (1966), Mozart (1983) and Erasmus (1998) prizes.

His musical language ranges from an early expressionism and serialism to experimental musical theatre, passing through concrete and electronic music, a varied use of random techniques, collage and stylistic quotation. The roots of his music are a combination of expressionism and surrealism (see **surrealism in Latin American art**), parodic modernism and the spirit of the theatre of the absurd. Kagel has renewed modern music in a profound sense, introducing a note of refined and critical humour, a serious irony and a concert aesthetics that breaks dramatically with the past.

Oustanding among his works composed in Argentina are *Variaciones para cuarteto mixto* (Variations for Mixed Quartet) (1952) and *Sexteto de cuerdas* (String Sextet) (1953–7). In Cologne, he joined the European avant-garde. His *Anagrama* (1957) for soloist, spoken chorus and chamber group introduced a new form of choral music, of musical notation (a field in which he has been an important innovator) and the widest range of vocal resources. His *Sur scène* (1959) creates a modern instrumental theatre with precise instructions on the positions, gestures, movements, spoken parts and attitudes of the musicians, and even scenography, props and lighting. In this field his outstanding works include *Sonant* (1960), *Atem* (1970), the monumental *Staatstheater* (1970), *Aus Deutschland* (Out of Germany), a lieder opera (1980) and *L'art bruit* (Art of Noise) (1995).

Kagel reduced the histrionic elements and concentrated on musical syntax itself in more recent work like *Diez marchas para la pérdida de la victoria* (Ten Marches for the Loss of Victory) (1981), the radio fantasy *Rrrrrr...* (1982) and *Die Stucke der Windrose* (1989–91).

Kagel was also an experimental film-maker, mostly of films of musical works. His cinema shows the influence of **Buñuel** and of Dali's *Un chien andalou*, for which he composed a musical score in 1982. His principal films are *Antithèse* (1965), *Match* (1966), *Ludwig van* (1969) and *Blue's Blue* (1981).

Further reading

Kagel, M. *Tam-Tam*, Paris: Christian Bourgeois.

ALFONSO PADILLA

Kahlo, Frida

b. 1907, Mexico City; d. 1954, Mexico City

Artist

When the pop star Madonna let it be known she wanted to collect as many Kahlo originals as possible, and was prepared to pay record prices, the Mexican artist's work at last emerged from the shadow of her famous husband Diego **Rivera**. Until that point in the 1990s, a generation after her death, her critical success had never been matched by success in the auction room. Her quintessential narcissism, repeatedly using self-portraiture as the springboard for allegory, fantasy and oneiric self-analysis, coincidentally matched what audiences had come to regard as a woman's view, across the arts and across cultures.

Frida Kahlo was herself a consequence of **hybridity**. Her German father, an architectural and landscape photographer, built the house in Coyoacán (in 1904) that has come to be known as the Casa Azul. It remains a national monument to Frida and Diego's domestic and artistic sojourn there (off, as well as on, from 1929–54). Her mother was of Zapotec/Spanish origins and was responsible for directing her new husband (whom she had met working in a jeweller's shop) towards photography. It was arguably Guillermo Kahlo's medium that prompted his daughter's fascination with the literal image, and her parents certainly provided much of the subject matter for her repeated painted musings on heredity, identity, beauty and belonging.

A second formative aspect in her background was the trolley-bus accident which occurred when Frida was just eighteen years old. Forcefully impaled by a chrome pole, she was left crippled and sterile, feeling both her youth and her maturity blighted. While the trauma of the injury lent vivid material (and at times lurid colours) to her painting, it is also possible that defiance bred flamboyance in her refusal to give in to the apparent physical restrictions. Frida Kahlo became as much of an icon in her time for her politics as her art, and for the integration of both in her life, as she attended radical demonstrations – heading the Communist Party contingent with her husband – leaning on a cane or riding in a wheelchair.

Her artistic reputation rests primarily on her paintings. These owe much both to the brilliant colours and often two-dimensional aspect of the popular 'decorative' arts, particularly in Kahlo's depiction of still lives, birds and animals. Also to the major cultural and intellectual movements of the first half of the twentieth century, dada and surrealism (see **surrealism in Latin American art**) on the one hand, Freudian psychoanalysis and revolutionary Marxism on the other. André Breton described her art as a ribbon tied around a bomb, while she herself took as her chosen themes 'my sensations, my states of mind, my reactions to life'; to which she invariably joined a love of surprises, like that of 'finding lions on the bookshelf instead of books'.

Photographs of Frida indicate a phenomenal degree of high-powered gregariousness – parties at Tina Modotti's or Lupe **Marín**'s, welcoming the Trotskys to their Mexican exile, at a New York opening or a film launch or a political rally – but her paintings remained profoundly personal, obsessively related to her pain, her family, her country. Her background was a constant source of artistry in her everyday life, as she dressed in a luxuriant combination of traditional/indigenous and painterly avant-garde (see **avant-garde in Latin America**), hair tied around her head with ribbons like a Oaxacan and modern jewellery elaborated from Tasco silver and semi-precious stones. Even when in hospital with her final illness, after a lifetime of tortuous complaints mainly brought about by the damage caused both by the injuries of her accident and subsequent mishandled medical treatments, she used a hand mirror to paint her plaster corset with traditional flower designs. At her funeral, her hearse was accompanied not only by the most prominent artists and writers of the day but by former president Lázaro **Cárdenas** and a host of overseas luminaries joining in to applaud Carlos **Pellicer**'s specially-composed odes and the singing of the *Internationale*.

Her oils, however, and even her carefully-conserved costumes, are far from constituting her only legacy. In terms of public artworks, she assisted Rivera in his grand sweep of painting murals across the United States between 1930–4, and she created her own murals at the *pulquería* (bar) 'La Rosita', with her students, when made a professor of painting at La Esmeralda, the Ministry of Education's School of Fine Art in Coyoacán in 1943. Her illustrated journal of the last ten years of her turbulent life addresses the anti-fascist political activity of the War and the anti-imperialist struggles thereafter; the rigours of her last illness and the amputation of her leg; and above all her stormy relationship with her husband. Like a child's blotter crossed with William Blake, the sometimes simplistic, sometimes visionary record of a decade of a life nails it firmly to the art.

Further reading

Herrera, H. (1989) *Frida: A Biography of Frida Kahlo*, New York.

—— (1991) *Frida Kahlo: The Paintings*, London.

Lowe, S.M. (ed.) (1995) *The Diary of Frida Kahlo* London: Bloomsbury.

Rauda, J. (1985) *Frida Kahlo*, Paris.

AMANDA HOPKINSON

Kalenberg, Angel

b. 1936, Montevideo, Uruguay

Arts administrator

Kalenberg has been director of the Uruguayan National Museum of the Visual Arts since 1969, vice-president of the International Council of Modern Art Museums (CIMAM) and a council member of the International Association of Art Critics (AICA). He is in charge of the Latin American section of the Tenth Paris Biennale and a member of the international committee of the XVIIth **Bienale de São Paulo**. He is also a member of the jury at Biennales of Graphic Arts and Engraving in Japan, Colombia and Yugoslavia. His works include *Arte uruguayo y otros* (Uruguayan Art and Others) (1993) and *Damiani* (1993).

MARCO MAGGI

Kamenszain, Tamara

b. 1947, Buenos Aires, Argentina

Poet and essayist

Distinguished as a writer by her precision of poetic language and critical perception, she explores memory, childhood, literature, Argentine life and Jewish tradition in spare and stylized patterns. Her texts are described by Sylvia **Molloy** as 'spectacles, as ceremonies, dazzling yet not indecipherable'. Kamenszain studied philosophy at the University of Buenos Aires. Resident in Mexico during Argentina's military dictatorship, she published there a major study on Latin American poetry, *El texto silencioso* (1983). Her books of poetry include *De este lado del Mediterráneo* (On this side of the Mediterranean) (1973), *Los no* (The nos) (1977), *La casa grande* (The big house) (1986), *Vida de living* (Sitting room life) (1991), *La edad de la poesía* (The age of poetry) (1996), and *Tango Bar* (1998).

GWEN KIRKPATRICK

Karlik, Sara

b. 1935, Asunción, Paraguay

Writer

A resident of Chile and prolific short story writer and novelist, Karlik has published five collections of short stories and three novels. In the short story genre her books include *Entre ánimas y sueños* (Between Spirits and Dreams) (1987), *Demasiada historia* (Too Much History) (1988), and *Efectos especiales* (Special Effects) (1989). Her novels include *Los fantasmas no son como antes* (Ghosts Are Not Like Before) (1989), *Juicio a la memoria* (Judgment to Memory) (1990) – which won the 1990 Premio Planeta (Planeta Prize) and the 1991 Premio Sésamo – and *Desde cierta distancia* (From a Certain Distance) (1991).

TERESA MÉNDEZ-FAITH

Karsters, Ruben

b. 1941, Paramaribo, Suriname

Painter

Trained as a classical painter in the Netherlands, Karsters has lived in Suriname since 1968. Using paint, pencil, chalk and even ballpoint, he draws very meticulously in his efforts to achieve a faithful reproduction of nature. He has produced several symbolic works, but usually creates realistic portraits and still-lifes. Sometimes he works from photographs, but then adds the caption: 'commercial art'.

NEL CASIMIRI

Kartún, Mauricio

b. 1946, Buenos Aires, Argentina

Playwright

In his plays *Chau Misterix* (1980), *La casita de los viejos* (The Old People's House) (1982), *Cumbia morena cumbia* (Cumbia, Brown Girl, Cumbia) (1983), the latter presented by **Teatro Abierto**, Kartún explored the construction of fantasies through the recreation of the world of children and their relations with adults. He rediscovered elements and characters from the **sainete** and other popular cultural practices (**carnival**, dances and touring '*criollo*' actors) in *El partener* (1988). He has won a number of prizes and is well-known for his teaching of dramaturgy and script writing.

NORA MAZZIOTTI

Kassav'

Renowned as the band which created the French Antillean dance style **zouk**, Kassav' was formed in Paris in 1978 by Guadaloupian expatriate Jacob Desvarieux. An experienced rock guitarist, Desvarieux synthesized elements of African-American funk with popular and traditional Caribbean music. A dramatic innovation was the band's incorporation of the Guadaloupian gwo ka drum ensemble with **funk** electric guitars and riffs. The band's lead vocals are smoothly phrased and contrasted with riffs from a small backing group. Unusually, the band features solo violin. Kassav' broke up during the early 1990s, but was later re-formed and featured in Euzhan **Palcy**'s film *Siméon* (1992).

MICHAEL BURNETT

Kaulen, Patricio

b. 1921, Santiago, Chile; d. 1999, Santiago, Chile

Film-maker

He made his cinematic début at age twenty-one with *Nada más que amor* (No More than Love) (1942), and collaborated with José **Bohr** and Jorge Délano in the active decade of the 1940s, during which time he also directed another two feature films and several documentary shorts. Perhaps his best-known film was *Largo viaje* (Long Trip) (1966), which was awarded a special prize by UNESCO in 1986. He also worked actively to better the conditions of the national industry and the rights of film workers. While serving as director of **Chile Films** in the 1960s, he wrote and promoted a Film Law, approved in 1967 and in place until 1973, which provided tax exemptions for film stock imports, film-making equipment and theatres exhibiting national films. He stayed in Chile during the dictatorship but was unable to film. His last film, *Via crucis* (1997), was many years in the making and was released only shortly before his death.

ANA M. LÓPEZ

Keens-Douglas, Paul

b. 1942, Silver Mill, San Juan, Trinidad

Storyteller

Since 1974 in Trinidad, Keens-Douglas has concentrated on preserving, performing and developing Caribbean storytelling, poetry and oral traditions, with emphasis on Eastern Caribbean vernacular. He has created a host of memorable characters including Tanti Merle, Vibert, Slim, Sugar George, and Dr Ah-Ah who populate his seven volumes of stories, twelve albums and videos. He is founder/producer of Trinidad's Tim Tam Storytelling Show and the annual Carnival Talk Tent which gives a variety of Caribbean performers, including younger folk artists, an opportunity to enact oral traditions.

JOHN H. PATTON

Kellman, Anthony

b. 1958, Barbados

Writer and editor

Kellman is best known as a poet: his two collections *Watercourse* (1990) and *The Long Gap* (1996) were widely praised. His only novel, *The Coral Rooms* (1994), is a beautiful and disturbing examination of guilt, materialism and corruption on a postcolonial Caribbean island. As in his poems, his rendering of nature and landscape is profound. Editor of the first full-length US anthology of English speaking Caribbean poetry, *Crossing Water* (1992), in 1997 he edited a Caribbean section of *Atlanta Review*. Kellman is professor of English and creative writing at Augusta State University in Georgia, USA.

KEITH JARDIM

Kempadoo, Peter (Lauchmonen)

b. 1926, Port Mourant, Guyana

Writer

Kempadoo's innovative narrative is framed by his experience of rural Indo-Guyanese society. Though he has worked in publishing, journalism, broadcasting and teaching, Kempadoo is widely recognized for two major novels, both published in London under his pseudonym. In *Guiana Boy* (1960), the narrative voice of an Indo-Guyanese boy documents in simple detail the episodes of rural life which build his culture, engaging the reader by interweaving local and creole expressions. *Old Thom's Harvest* (1965) focuses on religious and ethnic practices in the life of a rural family.

JILL E. ALBADA-JELGERSMA

Khan, Ismith

b. 1925, Port-of-Spain, Trinidad

Writer

Like the character Jamini in his best known novel *The Jumbie Bird* (1961), Khan was greatly influenced by his grandfather, a leader of the 1884 Hosay Rebellion, in which Muslims clashed with colonial authorities over the annual parade to commemorate early martyrs of Islam. The novel examines questions of identity and nation confronted by Trinidadian Indians ranging from former indentured labourers who dream of repatriation and rely on memory to deal with the experience of their dislocation, to first and second generations born in the island, whose culture becomes inevitably more hybrid. Other works include *The Obeah Man* (1964) and *The Crucifixion* (1987).

LORRAINE LEU

Khana

Khana is a journal of Bolivian art and letters published in La Paz between 1953 and 1967, under the editorship of Jacobo Libermann Zelonka. It reappeared in 1976. The contents of both series are catalogued in Gregorio Calanis Quisbert's *Indice de Khana*, published in 1987. The journal published the work of Bolivian writers, but also brought to its readers' attention the work of writers like Thomas Mann and Arnold Toynbee.

J.M. DE LA VEGA RODRÍGUEZ

Khouri, Walter Hugo

b. 1929, São Paulo, Brazil

Film-maker

Khouri's first, low-budget film, *O gigante de pedra* (The Stone Giant) (1952–3) echoed contemporary European art cinema and established his characteristic personal style marked by beautiful images, philosophical dialogues and sensual actresses. For the next three decades he produced artistic auteur films paralleling the more politicized **Cinema Novo**. His *Noite vazia* (Empty Night) (1964) is a classic, portraying the existential anxiety of two bourgeois searching for the meaning of life in nighttime São Paulo; a theme developed through the psychologically complex characters of films like *Eros: O deus do amor* (Eros, God of Love) (1981).

ISMAIL XAVIER AND THE USP GROUP

Kid Chocolate

b. 1910, Havana, Cuba; d. 1988, Havana

Boxer

Born Eligio Sardiñas, in 1929 Kid Chocolate won the world featherweight title by knockout from Benny Bass. He successfully defended his crown several times, and was chosen by a European magazine as the world's best-dressed man. He was also photographed nude for the influential journal ***Social*** in the 1930s, the period when Nicolás **Guillén** also wrote his 'Oda (Ode) a Kid Chocolate'. In 1938 he retired because of health problems linked to childhood malnutrition and to his dissipated life while a champion, but he had already been elected to **boxing**'s Hall of Fame.

WILFREDO CANCIO ISLA

Kid Gavilán

b. 1926, Camagüey, Cuba

Boxer

Winner of the world welterweight championship in 1951, beating Johnny Bratton at New York's Madison Square Garden, Kid Gavilán (real name Gerardo González) retained his title until late 1954, when he lost it in a bout disgracefully fixed by his manager and **boxing**'s main promoters. He had 143 fights in his career, winning 106 (27 by knockout), drawing 6 and losing 30. Light and fast on his feet and capable of absorbing a great deal of punishment, he was never knocked out. He retired in 1958, and moved to the USA at the beginning of the 1960s.

WILFREDO CANCIO ISLA

Kincaid, Jamaica

b. 1949, St John's, Antigua

Writer

Born Elaine Potter Richardson, to an Antiguan father and a mother of half-Carib descent who was from Dominica, Kincaid left Antigua in 1966 to become an au pair in New York. She made contact with a major writer from the *New Yorker* and, in 1973, adopted her writing name. By 1976 she was a staff writer for the magazine. Her stories *At the Bottom of the River* (1983) establish her very clear, highly professional literary style. She received acclaim for her work, including *Annie John* (1985); in which she captured a laconic, feisty, unselfconscious and highly perceptive young female voice which signified the struggle of Caribbean women to transcend colonization and its constructions of race, class and gender.

Her polemical essay on Antigua, *A Small Place* (1988), and her novels *Lucy* (1991) and *Autobiography of My Mother* (1996), while admired for their literary polish, have received mixed reviews and critical responses. Like Jean **Rhys**, Kincaid is a fine stylist and an emotionally and politically disturbing writer, not easily summed up in terms of political affiliations, but often co-opted by critics to their own political constructions. Like V.S. **Naipaul** and Rhys, she left the Caribbean at a young age and made her mark in prominent literary circles in the metropolis. Like Naipaul again, to whom she has been compared, Kincaid in *A Small Place* turns a savagely critical gaze on her birthplace, focusing on **tourism** and **corruption**, and has thus provoked some resistance. *Autobiography of My Mother* was the first Kincaid text to receive a largely negative reception. In this text, the characteristic terseness of the Kincaid protagonist, young and female, carries no self-questioning and seems to dull, in its relentless note of anger, the compexities of other characters as well.

Further reading

Andrade, Susan Z. (1996) 'Jamaica Kincaid', in B. Lindfors and R. Sander (eds), *Twentieth Century Caribbean and African Writers*, Third Series, Vol. 157, Detroit: Gale Research, pp. 131–9.

Ferguson, M. (1994) *Jamaica Kincaid: Where the Land Meets the Body*, Charlottesville, VA: University Press of Virginia.

ELAINE SAVORY

kinetic art

Kinetic art was one of the dominant international tendencies during the 1960s, one of several abstract geometrical artistic currents which succeeded the constructivists of the avant-garde of the early 1920s (see **constructivism; avant-garde in Latin America**). The word kinetic, from the Greek *kinetica*, meaning movement, derives from physics, and its use acknowledges the appropriation of the knowledge of mathematics and physics in elaborating works which seek in various ways to give material form to the experience of movement by provoking the spectator's senses.

Latin American artists have made brilliant and original contributions to the development of this tendency, above all the Venezuelans Carlos **Cruz-Diez**, Jesús Rafael **Soto** and Alejandro **Otero** and the Argentines Julio **Le Parc**, Horacio García Rossi, Hugo Demarco, Luis Tomasello and Martha Boto. All of them participated in the first exhibition of kineticism *Lumière et mouvement* (Light and movement) in Paris in 1967. And for all of them the contact in Paris in the 1950s with the Hungarian Vasarely, father of kineticism, and Mondrian's neo-plasticity, was decisive. Cruz Diez began his explorations of the kinetic properties of colour which found expression in his series *Fisiocromías* (1960), ribbons of colour hung vertically across the surface of a reflecting square, so that the work changes according to the spectator's point of view. Soto developed his series *Vibración* (Vibration) (1963), where metal rods were superimposed on a surface painted in stripes; the resulting vibrating structure dissolved its constituent elements. His 'kinetic murals', using metal rods or nylon threads hanging from the ceiling and his 'penetrables', environments set in motion by the spectators as they entered a maze of hanging metal tubes, had the same 'dissolution' effect. Otero's pioneering *Colorritmos* (Colourhythm) (1995) series, wooden boards 2 metres long by 50 centimetres wide, spraypainted with linear structures of colour, created a permanent sense of ambiguity between figure and background. In Paris, Le Parc and García Rossi cofounded the Recherche d'Art Visuel (Visual Art Research) group in 1960, with the aim of exploring the use of light and movement to generate objects and environments; they proposed the necessity for an active spectator, stressing visual instability, the time of perception, the processes of collective creation, the possibility of creating multipliable works. The ultimate objective was to modify the relation between the artist and society, demystifying the notion of a unique immutable art work and the artist as creative genius.

Further reading

Dujovne, M. and Gil Solá, M. (1967) *Julio Le Parc*, Buenos Aires: Editorial Estuario.

Lucie-Smith, E. (1983) *Arte hoy*, Madrid: Cátedra.

Pellegrini, A. (1967) *Nuevas tendencias en la pintura*, Buenos Aires: Muchnik Editores.

Sullivan, E. (1992) 'Artistas del siglo XX en Latinoamérica: una perspectiva de fin de siglo', exhibition catalogue, MOMA, Madrid, Comisaría de la Ciudad de Sevilla.

MARÍA ALBA BOVISIO

King, Hugh B.N.

b. 1953?, Old Harbour, Jamaica

Playwright, producer, actor, director and screenwriter

King has produced his plays in North America and Europe, although their subject matter is firmly focused on the burning social issues in Jamaican life. His first play, *The Resurrection of Jonathan Digby*, first performed in Jamaica in 1977, examined the crisis of absentee fatherhood. Others, such as *Nightwork* (1978), deal with violent abuse and prostitution, topics often made palatable for the stage by comic situations and island humour, emerging from the wit and cadences of Jamaican speech. King also manages his own production and graphics companies.

JILL E. ALBADA-JELGERSMA

King, Jane

b. 1952, Castries, St Lucia

Writer

Jane King's prize-winning poetry has been published in several regional and international anthologies, for example the anthology, *Confluence: Nine Saint Lucian Poets* (1988). Her own collections include *Fellow Traveller* (1994), winner of the James Rodway Memorial Prize, and *In the Centre* (1993). She is also co-founder of the Lighthouse Theatre Company with her husband, Kendel **Hippolyte**. She is a lecturer in English at Sir Arthur Lewis Community College, Castries.

KEITH JARDIM

Kingman, Eduardo

b. 1913, Loja, Ecuador

Painter

A pioneer of twentieth-century Ecuadorean painting, Kingman has influenced several artists, including **Guayasamín**. Introspective and perfectionist, he searches constantly, sometimes even neurotically, for the right expression, colour, touch and line. His work exhibits different styles and themes: from social concerns to reflections on artistic form, from the specific representation of the Indian to the suffering of humankind to the metaphorical idiom of hands full of existential anxiety to religious themes. He was also influenced by Mexican **muralism**. His best-known work is *Camillas* (1941), an expression of the suffering of the indigenous people.

kinship

As a result of common Iberian heritage and of similarities of historical experience in the New World, kinship, which includes all relatives traced on maternal and paternal line as well as in-laws, plays an important part in peoples' lives across the region.

Kinship offers a source of security and permanence in a changing and insecure environment, and the recognition of a wide network of kinship ties is a feature of Latin American life. Expansion of the network is greatest among the rich, for whom family names are important. In some countries, names demonstrate aristocratic status and the elite may be referred to, as in Peru, as the 'forty families', signifying descent from the traditional Spanish families. But kinship for the wealthy is not only a source of prestige; it also has a very functional aspect, since family networks are manipulated in the course of politics and business. Some of the most modern industrial companies in Latin America are family businesses (for example, **Globo** in Brazil), with boards of directors of relatives and friends who can be trusted. Above all, the family is a property-owning unit, whether the property is business, estates, land or houses, so that these resources are controlled and acquired by succeeding generations through kinship.

For the poor, kinship is not a mechanism to control resources but an institution to turn to because of the scarcity of resources. The scope of their kinship networks is smaller but just as significant, as kin provide help in time of hardship. Peasants migrating to the city usually turn to relatives for help either in the form of shelter in the new and daunting environment or a loan.

Traditionally, kinship was patriarchal and authoritarian. In Brazil, for example, plantation owners not only exercised control over large numbers of family, servants and resources but their word was absolute. The dominant role of kinship has been undermined by the opportunities created by **urbanization** for young people to be independent and earn a living outside the family, and by conceptions of the North American family as portrayed by the media. Nevertheless, kinship remains patriarchal and a key institution in society.

Further reading

Cubitt, T. (1995) *Latin American Society*, New York: Longman.

Lomnitz, L. (1977) *Networks and Marginality*, New York: Academic Press.

Nutini, H., Carrasco, P. and Taggart, J. (1976) *Essays on Mexican Kinship*, Pittsburgh, PA: University of Pittsburgh Press.

TESSA CUBITT

Kirindongo, Yubi

b. 1946, Curaçao

Visual artist

Kirindongo, an autodidact, began as a painter in Germany but shifted to sculpture upon his return to Curaçao. His favourite media are auto parts, especially car bumpers which he shapes into birds, horses, human figures, abstracts, and even automobiles again. A shortage of shiny bumpers and personal demands for new directions led him to try other materials, especially scrap iron in big installations. He has participated in the Bienales of São Paulo (see **Bienale de São Paulo**), Cuba, Santo Domingo and South Africa and the Documenta in Kassel, Germany.

NEL CASIMIRI

Kirkwood, Julieta

b. 1936, Santiago, Chile; d. 1985, Santiago

Social scientist

Researcher at **FLACSO**-Chile (Latin American Faculty of Social Sciences) from 1972 to 1985, Kirkwood helped to found the journal *Furia*, the Chilean Movement for Women's Emancipation (MEMCH 83), the Movimiento Feminista (Feminist Movement) and the La **Morada** Women's Centre. After her death, friends and fellow feminists collected material from her classes (1981–4) into two volumes which are essential to an understanding of feminism in Latin America and specifically under the Chilean military dictatorship: *Ser política en Chile (Las feministas y los partidos)* (Being Political in Chile: Feminists and the Parties) (1986) and *Feminarios* (1987).

ELIANA ORTEGA

Kiss of the Spider Woman *see* Beso de la Mujer Araña, El

Kissoon, Freddie

b. *c.* 1928, Trinidad and Tobago

Actor, director and playwright

Founder and director of the Strolling Players, Kissoon has made over two hundred stage appearances and written more than fifteen plays, including *Zingay* and *God and Uriah Butler*, commissioned by the Oilfield Workers' Trade Union for its thirtieth anniversary. It is an epic drama, three hours long, with fifty-eight speaking parts and crowds of people. It chronicles twenty-two years of **Butler**'s life from 1928 to 1950. Kissoon was commissioned by Radio Trinidad to write a radio serial – *Calabash Alley* – whose seventy-eight episodes ran from 2 November 1970 to 17 February 1971.

KEITH JARDIM

kitsch

The word kitsch originated in Munich, during the late nineteenth century, from where it became universal during the early part of the twentieth century. The word *kitschen* from which kitsch is believed to have been derived means to spread, smear or scrape together. Today kitsch is understood as something of gaudy design, appearance or content created to appeal to popular or undiscriminating taste. Examples of kitsch in Latin America are seen in private as well as in the public arena and include small plastic covers imitating crochet knitting, artificial plants, flowers and fruit, bookends of baby shoes, car or bus accessories; laminated photos of Carlos **Gardel**, Oscar de la Hoya, or La Difunta Correa, pacifiers, or babies shoes, decorative displays of bronzed roses, miniature gnomes or ducks for the garden, plastic images of the Virgin Mary or baby Jesus.

ISABEL BARBUZZA

Kjarkas, Los

Los Kjarkas are a folk music group established in 1972, emphasizing the use of Andean instruments like the **quena** (flute), zampoña (pan pipe) and wankara (Andean drum). With simple lyrics, its songs mixed traditional rhythms like the **huayno**, chuntunqui, **cueca** and saya with mainly romantic subjects, bringing them closer to international romantic music. Los Kjarkas was the first of Bolivia's 'folk' groups to adopt the techniques of the contemporary cultural industry and modern methods of recording and distribution. The group broke every sales record in Bolivia and neighbouring countries, then moved to Mexico and changed its name to 'Pacha'. In 1986, part of the group reestablished Los Kjarkas, while the rest formed the group Tupay.

BEATRIZ ROSSELLS

Klas, Rinaldo

b. 1954, Moengo, Suriname

Painter

Originally a naturalist painter focused on Suriname scenes, Klas also experimented with form and colour, and although the figurative element did not disappear, it was transposed into an interplay of lines exemplified by his extensive series 'Yard Dwellings'. More recently he has taken up new themes, such as the tropical **rainforest** and inland cultures. He teaches at the **Nola Hatterman Institute** and has had exhibitions in Suriname and other Caribbean islands.

NEL CASIMIRI

Klimovsky, Gregorio

b. 1922, Buenos Aires, Argentina

Philosopher

Klimovsky is an important epistemologist who has been extremely influential as a university professor, although he has not written extensively. In *Las desventuras del conocimiento científico* (The Misadventures of Scientific Knowledge) (1994), Klimovsky argues that despite its shortcomings, science provides the best way to know reality because it has logical and empirical procedures to deal with data and assess hypotheses. In 1977, he co-founded the **human rights** group Asamblea Permanente por los Derechos Humanos. He also participated in the National Commission on Disappeared People (CONADEP) (see **disappeared, the**), set up in 1984 by Raúl Alfonsín's government.

FERNANDO RABOSSI

Klotz, Mathias

b. 1965, Santiago, Chile

Architect

One of Chile's leading young architects, Klotz

designs houses of simple, rectangular volumes constructed in wood, concrete, cinder block and metal which seem to float above their moorings. The minimalism and subtle Japanese inspiration of his building designs contrast with the elaborate interiors Klotz has created for several Santiago stores, restaurants and discotheques. These public spaces are meant to suggest avant-garde theatrical settings in which the client is at once spectator and participant. In 1996, Klotz designed the stage sets for *Cinco Sur*, Alberto **Fuguet**'s play about the lives of contemporary youth.

CELIA LANGDEAU CUSSEN

Klotzel, André

b. 1954, São Paulo, Brazil

Film-maker

In the 1980s Klotzel, together with cinematographer Pedro Farkas and producer Zita Carvalhosa, formed Superfilmes, which produced his *A marvada carne* (Evil Flesh) (1985), a film typical of the work of the young film-makers of São Paulo in its rejection of the **Cinema Novo** tradition and its pursuit of well-made narratives attractive to audiences. His second feature *Capitalismo selvagem* (Savage Capitalism) (1993) returned to the issues raised by Mário de **Andrade**'s *Macunaíma*, telling the story of an Indian boy who survives the massacre of his tribe and is adopted by the head of a mining company before rediscovering his identity as an adult.

ISMAIL XAVIER AND THE USP GROUP

Koellreutter, Hans Joachim

b. 1915, Freiburg, Germany.

Musician

Koellreutter influenced a generation of Brazilians as teacher, conductor, flautist, journalist and composer. He trained under Hindemith in Berlin before moving to Brazil in 1937, where he taught until 1963. After periods in Munich, Delhi and Tokyo, he returned again to Brazil. His journal and informal group of composers, Música Viva, founded in 1939, preached serialism and attracted such eminent composers as Cláudio **Santoro** and César Guerra **Peixe**. Música Viva breathed an anti-nationalist aesthetic, although Koellreutter in no way diminished the achievements of **Villa-Lobos**: he gave the première of *Bachianas brasileiras* no. 6.

SIMON WRIGHT

Koenders, Julius G.A.

b. 1886, Suriname; d. 1957, Suriname

Writer

An ardent defender of his native tongue Sranan Tongo and its cultural heritage, Koenders published the monthly *Foetoeboi* (Messengerboy) in Sranan Tongo and Dutch, which appeared for ten years between 1946 and 1956. Koenders was virtually the sole contributor, with numerous articles on education, Afro-Surinamese cultural heritage, politics and language. Koenders was a primary school teacher in Suriname and, as he used to emphasize, the grandson of slaves.

AART G. BROEK

Kogui

The Kogui (also spelt Kogi and Cogui) are an Amerindian tribe. Today, most of the Kogui population live in the Kogui Malayo reservation, on the western and northern slopes of the Sierra Nevada de Santa Marta (Department of Magdalena, Colombia). The Kogui language is part of the Chibchan linguistic family. Despite some contacts with explorers, priests, and anthropologists, Koguis have resisted Western acculturation.

MIGUEL A. CARDINALE

Kohón, David José

b. 1929, Buenos Aires, Argentina

Film-maker

The most formally gifted member of the **Generación del 60**, Kohón began writing criticism and fiction and later made award-winning shorts. His first two films – *Prisioneros de una noche* (Prisoners of One Night) (1960) and *Tres veces Ana* (Three Times Ana) (1961) – articulated his central preoccupations: portraying the melancholy of Buenos Aires residents and their chance encounters and short-lived urban loves. *¿Qué es el otoño?* (What is Autumn?) (1976), perhaps his most conventional film, was banned by the military government for its references to the **disappeared**. His last film was *El agujero en la pared* (The Hole in the Wall) (1981).

DIANA PALLADINO

Kom, Cornelius Gerard Anton de

b. 1898, Paramaribo, Suriname; d. 1945, Neuengamme, Hamburg, Germany

Political activist and writer

Influenced by international communist labour movements in the 1920s and 1930s, De Kom contributed substantially to the rise of nationalism in Suriname with the publication of *Wij slaven van Suriname* (We Slaves of Suriname) (1934) which details the atrocities of Dutch colonial administration since slavery. De Kom ends by claiming Suriname's right to self-determination. In the Netherlands, the book was first published in a censored edition; only in the 1980s would fragments of the original manuscript be included in new editions of the work. He died in a concentration camp in Germany.

AART G. BROEK

Korda, Alberto

b. 1928, Havana, Cuba

Photographer

A pioneer of fashion photography in Cuba with his Korda Studios, after the victory of the Cuban Revolution in 1959, Korda (born Alberto Diaz Gutiérrez) worked for the journal, *Revolución*, and was Fidel **Castro**'s personal photographer. His photo of Che **Guevara**, taken in 1960, is considered one of the world's ten best, and is one of the most widely reproduced photographs. From 1969 to 1981, he devoted himself to fashion and underwater photography, producing the *Atlas de corales cubanos* (Atlas of Cuban Coral Reefs) for the Academy of Sciences. His work is widely exhibited, including his most recent volume of photographs taken during Pope John Paul II's visit to Cuba in 1998.

WILFREDO CANCIO ISLA

Kordon, Bernardo

b. 1915, Buenos Aires, Argentina

Writer

A social realist writer best known for his short stories on the plight of marginal individuals, Kordon's material is drawn from the urban underbelly, and like most social realists, he writes in a direct and forceful manner. His cinematographic style (many of his narratives have been turned into films) and use of colloquialisms make his texts highly readable, especially as they are totally free of the omniscient preachiness of other social realists. Kordon has also published five books on China and an anthology of Chinese writing.

DAVID WILLIAM FOSTER

Korn, Alejandro

b. 1860, San Vicente, Argentina; d.1936, Buenos Aires, Argentina

Philosopher

Korn is one of the best-known Argentine philosophers. He subscribed to a native form of positivism, promoting human liberty and values. His major work, *La libertad creadora* (Creative Liberty) (1922), views liberty as a struggle against necessity, having, as such, an ethical purpose. Liberty is also a key to elaborating the distinction between objective and subjective orders and the concepts of consciousness and human value. In 1918, Korn was a strong supporter of the university reform movement, known as La Reforma Universitaria, which began in Argentina.

FERNANDO RABOSSI

Kovadloff, Santiago

b. 1942, Buenos Aires, Argentina

Writer

Though known mainly as an essayist and cultural journalist, Kovadloff has also written poetry, children's stories and is a distinguished poetry translator. *La nueva ignorancia* (New Ignorance) (1992), *El silencio primordial* (Primordial Silence) (1993) and *Lo irremediable* (Irreparable, Irretrievable) (1996), his three most important collections of essays, deal with subjects ranging from the topical to the metaphysical and reveal an original and polemical mind. He is a regular contributor to the newspapers *La **nación*** and *La prensa*, and also appears regularly on television. In 1992 he received Argentina's highest literary prize, the Premio Nacional de Literatura Argentina.

EVELYN FISHBURN

Krajcberg, Frans

b. 1921, Kozienice, Poland

Artist and photographer

Having studied in the Soviet Union and Germany, Krajcberg finally settled in Brazil in 1948 and became one of its best known and most versatile artists, whose work includes painting, print making, sculpture and photography. Plant-like forms are the focus for many of his sketches and paintings, and he has often worked with natural materials, producing sculptures in wood and reliefs in stone. The relationship between humans and nature, and the threats now facing the environment, are his major concern. Some of his most powerful work highlights environmental destruction, typified by his disturbing black and white photographs of burned rainforests. He participated in Walter Salles Jr's extraordinary documentary *Socorro Nobre* (1996).

MARK DINNEEN

Krieger, Armando

b. 1940, Buenos Aires, Argentina

Musician

One of the most important musicians of his generation, Krieger studied composition with **Ginastera** and at the Latin American Centre for Advanced Music Studies with Copland, Dallapiccola, Messiaen, Malipiero and Maderna. In 1959 he formed the Argupación Euphonia (Música Viva) and in the 1960s his own orchestra, Solistas de Música Contemporánea de Buenos Aires. His musical work ranges from rigorous serialism to the wide use of random techniques and includes his *Cuarteto de cuerdas no. 1* (String Quartet) (1960), *Tensiones II* (1961), *Metamorphose d'après une lecture de Kafka* (Metamorphosis: After a Text by Kafka) (1968) and *Cantata II* (1969 with text by Ernesto **Sabato**).

ALFONSO PADILLA

Krieger, Edino

b. 1928, Brusque, Santa Catarina, Brazil

Composer, conductor and critic

Edino Krieger began to study the violin with his father at an early age. In 1943 he won a scholarship to study in Rio de Janeiro, where he presently lives. There he became an active member of a new music movement, Música Viva, and studied composition with H.J. **Koellreutter**. During this period he wrote a number of works in a serial style of composition. Later studies in orchestration and composition with Aaron Copland, and a period of study at the Juilliard School in New York preceded a successful career as administrator and president of the Brazilian Society for Contemporary Music.

DAVID P. APPLEBY

Kroon, Willem Eligio

b. 1886, Curaçao, Netherlands Antilles; d. 1949, Curaçao

Writer and activist

Working as an independent commercial artist, in the 1920s Kroon was also one of the first novelists writing in the native creole **Papiamentu**. He strongly defended Roman Catholicism in his novels, poetry and local journalism. In the 1930s, however, he clashed severely with the local Roman Catholic mission. Although he never left the church, he stopped defending it in his writing. From the 1930s on he was also very active in the gradual rise of labour unions on the island.

AART G. BROEK

Kröpfl, Francisco

b. 1928, Szeged, Hungary

Composer

Kröpfl studied composition with Juan Carlos **Paz** and joined the **Agrupación Nueva Música** in 1950, becoming its director in 1956. In 1959 he organized the Musical Phonology Studio at the University of Buenos Aires and in 1962–3 founded the Electronic Music Laboratory, which he directed into the 1990s. His musical work employs a variety of compositional techniques. Works include *Música para 25 instrumentos* (Music for 25 Instruments) (1960), *Tres canciones* (Three Songs) (1954–6) with texts by Mario Porro, and *Diálogos I–III* (1964–8).

ALFONSO PADILLA

Kubitschek, Juscelino

b. 1902, Diamantina, Brazil; d. 1976, Rio de Janeiro, Brazil

Politician

A visionary politician, Kubitschek won the Brazilian presidential elections of 1956. **Brasília**, Brazil's new capital city, was his creation and a synthetic expression of his presidency. Son of a clerk and primary teacher, he studied medicine in Minas Gerais, specializing in urology, and in 1931 joined the military police of Minas as a colonel-physician. He entered politics in 1933, becoming a federal deputy, mayor of Belo Horizonte and eventually state governor. Despite attempts to prevent his assumption of the presidency, he completed his term of office, but his civil rights were suspended in 1964 by the military junta. He died in an automobile accident. His tomb is one of the monuments of **Brasília**.

ANTONIO CARLOS VAZ

Kuhn, Rodolfo

b. 1934, Buenos Aires, Argentina; d. 1987, Mexico City

Film-maker

A principal figure of the **Generación del 60**, Kuhn studied film-making in the USA and debuted with a series of award-winning shorts. *Los jóvenes viejos* (Aged Youth) (1961), his first feature, depicted the lack of communication and existential boredom of three young couples and was much praised for its representation of contemporary youth. Among his subsequent films, *Pajarito Gómez, una vida feliz* (Little Bird Gómez, A Happy Life) (1964), an ironic vision of the life of a rock singer, was the best received. Exiled in Europe in 1976, he worked for television until his return to Argentine cinema with *El señor Galíndez* (1984), his last film.

DIANA PALADINO

Kuiperi, Stan

b. 1954, Aruba

Painter

Kuiperi studied in the United States, Puerto Rico, the Netherlands and France, and is an art teacher at the Pedagogical Institute of Aruba. Always exploring Aruban landscapes and scenes, Kuiperi uses real sand, shells and archeological artefacts as media for his paintings. He often refers to prehistoric times and incorporates pre-Columbian symbols into his canvases.

NEL CASIMIRI

Kuitca, Guillermo

b. 1961, Buenos Aires, Argentina

Visual artist

Kuitca mounted his first exhibition at the age of thirteen. In 1982 he produced the series of paintings *Nadie olvida Nada* (No One Forgets Anything) and directed his first theatrical work under the same title. In 1985 he exhibited in Europe and participated in the **Bienale de São Paulo** for the first time, exhibiting regularly thereafter in both Europe and the United States. In 1992 he was selected to participate in Documenta IX at Kassel. He presented an installation of twenty beds whose mattresses were painted maps. Indeed, maps have dominated his more recent work.

DANIEL LINK

Kumina

African-derived religious system practised in Jamaica, most significantly in the eastern parish of Saint Thomas. The religion focuses heavily on maintaining good relationships between human beings and ancestor spirits who are believed to influence both success and misfortune. Ceremonies involve dancing, drumming and singing. The dancing has received most attention from outside observers because of its unique, dramatic style. The religion is believed to have its main origins in west-central Africa among Kongo peoples. Some historians surmise that the practice may have begun after emancipation in the mid-nineteenth century when hundreds of Kongo immigrants entered Jamaica as indentured labour after having been rescued from illegally operating slave ships by the British navy. It is also possible, however, that the practice began during the years of slavery and was simply revitalized by the nineteenth-century Kongo immigrants. Also known as 'cumina' and 'pocomania', although this latter term has often had derisive connotations.

ROSANNE ADDERLEY

Kusch, Rodolfo

b. 1922, Buenos Aires, Argentina; d. 1979, Buenos Aires

Writer

Writing in several genres, Kusch focused on Argentine reality and the question of the 'essence' of America. Through marginal characters and settings and appealing to popular ideas, he opposed liberal historiography with a celebration of 'barbarism'. Close to historical revisionism, in *La muerte del Chacho* (The Death of Chacho) (1960) he argued that 'civilization' was a false option. In *Credo rante*, a play first presented in 1958, and in *La leyenda de Juan Moreira* (The Legend of Juan Moreira) (1960), he mobilized elements of the popular imaginary.

SANDRA GASPARINI

Kyk-Over-Al

An annual literary magazine founded in 1945 in Guyana by A.J. **Seymour**, the name *Kyk-Over-Al* refers to a still existing Dutch fort (circa 1616) on the island of the same name. Under Ian **McDonald**'s directorship (1984–), it became one of the most distinguished literary publications of the Caribbean region, publishing writers such as Derek **Walcott**, Martin **Carter** and Wilson **Harris**. According to Seymour, it was meant to build an awareness of the Guyanese people's 'intellectual and spiritual possibilities', which it has done by giving voice to resident West Indian and exiled writers. A special fiftieth anniversary edition was edited by Ian McDonald in 1995.

KEITH JARDIM

Labarca, Amanda

b. 1886, Santiago, Chile; d. 1975, Santiago

Writer and activist

Undisputed leader of the struggle for women's emancipation and women's rights in Chile, Labarca was an active member of the Radical Party, UN delegate and the first woman to hold the Chair of Philosophy at the University of Chile. In 1915 she created the 'Women's Reading Circle', an organization for the study of feminism; she wrote widely on feminist issues, coedited the newspaper *Acción Feminina* (Feminine Action) and helped to create the Partido Cívico Feminino in 1922. Her works include *¿Adónde va la mujer?* (Where are Women Going?) (1934).

ELIANA ORTEGA

Laberinto de la soledad, El

Octavio **Paz**'s *El laberinto de la soledad* (The Labyrinth of Solitude) (1950) is an exploration of the inner and outer histories of Mexico. It is both a treatise on the myths that constitute 'the Mexican' as well as an intellectual history of the country itself; it explores Paz's own obsessions, and critiques the Mexican intellectual class. The project was grounded in Spanish philosopher Miguel de Unamuno's vision of an 'intrahistoria', and on Paz's readings of French philosopher Georges Bataille. In the book Paz defines the 'problem' of Mexico: it is a nation poised as an adult within the community of nations after its revolution, but at some level arrested in another state where solitude and introspection inhibit its free and open relationship with itself and the world. Paz's vision of Mexico is the result of very concrete biographical experiences when he himself, in the early 1940s, left Mexico for the United States. The book's first three essays have been much discussed and disputed, since many writers have taken issue with Paz's comments on the Mexican-American *pachucos*, on homosexuality, on '**Malinchismo**', and on women in general. In subsequent editions Paz broadened the book's scope, incorporating his vision of the Mexican state after the Massacre of **Tlatelolco** in 1968, and his most recent opinions on the Mexican government and its relations with the United States.

Further reading

Bartra, R. (1987) *La jaula de la melancolía: identidad y morfósis del mexicano*, Mexico City: Grijalbo.

Oclio, E.B. (1980) 'The "distaff" perspective in Paz's *El laberinto de la soledad*', *Publications of the Arkansas Philological Association* 6 (2).

Palazón, M.R. (1968) 'Sobre *El laberinto de la soledad*', *Punto de Partida II*.

Rangel-Guerrero, D. (1977) 'The Labyrinth of Solitude Revisited', *Proceedings of the Pacific Northwest Conference on Foreign Languages* 28 (2).

Toro, F. de (1979) '*El laberinto de la soledad* y la forma el ensayo', *Cuadernos Hispanoamericanos* 343–5.

JOSÉ QUIROGA

Laboratorios Alex

Founded in 1937 by Alejandro Connio, these laboratories allowed the photographic quality of Argentine films to attain international standards. His son, Carlos Connio Santini, studied at the research department of Eastman Kodak in Rochester, and returned with the knowledge required to ensure quality processing. He also imported a moviola, which ensured higher quality editing. The company's present building was opened in 1950; it provides a range of services and facilities which make it one of the world's leading film laboratories.

RODRIGO PEIRETTI

Labrador Ruiz, Enrique

b. 1902, Sagua La Grande, Cuba; d. 1991, Miami, USA

Writer

A poet, short-story writer, essayist and novelist, his '*gaseiforme*' (gasiform) fiction, as he called it, were fragmentary fictions whose innovative quality prefigures the **Boom** of the 1960s. A journalist and travelling salesman, his volumes of stories include *Trailer de sueños* (Dream Trailer) (1949) and *El gallo en el espejo* (The Rooster in the Mirror) (1953), considered by many as classics of the Cuban short story, and *Cuentos* (Stories) (1970). Among his novels are *El laberinto de sí mismo* (Labyrinth of Himself) (1933) and *La sangre hambrienta* (The Hungry Blood) (1950), which brought him the National Novel Prize. In 1976 he left Cuba for Miami and published his essays in *El pan de los muertos* (Bread of the Dead) (1988) and *Cartas a la carte* (Letters à la Carte) (1990).

WILFREDO CANCIO ISLA

Labuchin, Rassoul

b. 1939, Port-au-Prince, Haiti

Screenwriter

A noted writer of screenplays, especially for *Map Pale Net* (The Whole Story) (1976), one of the first creole-language films exploring the social and psychological reality of a typical urban Haitian family. Labuchin also wrote and directed the 16mm film drama *Anita* (1980) using actors from Evans **Paul**'s theatre troupe. *Anita* is one of the first Haitian films to assert a cinematic language rooted in the recurring themes of Haitian culture: the rural exodus, domestic life, class relations, and the significance of **Vodun**. In the 1990s Labuchin was director of the Haitian National Theatre.

CHARLES ARTHUR

Lacan in Latin America

Lacan's presence in Latin America owes much to the extraordinary Argentine Oscar **Masotta**, who came across Lacan's writings in 1959 and founded the first Freudian School outside Paris in Buenos Aires in 1974. In 1970 he translated and introduced two of Lacan's lectures – *Las formaciones del inconciente* (The Formations of the Unconscious) and *El deseo y su interpretación* (Desire and Its Interpretation) – and a year later directed the collection *Cuadernos Sigmund Freud*. Masotta's group then split and he formed, in Spain, the Escuela Freudiana de la Argentina. Most of that group, however, now belong to the Escuela de Orientación Lacaniana (formed in 1992), a member of the World Psychoanalytical Association (AMP), which defends Lacan's ideas against its detractors.

In the 1980s, apart from the many groups and schools formed after Masotta's death, the dispersal of his followers and the fashion for 'the Lacanian school', two important new journals appeared: **Conjetural** (1983), edited by J. Jinkis, and *Descartes* (1986), edited by Germán **García**. The publishing imprints Amorrortu, Atuel and Manantial also published Lacanian works.

In Brazil, the first Lacanian institute was established in 1970 (the Centro de Estudios Freudianos de São Paulo). In Rio de Janeiro, the Colégio Freudiano emerged in 1979. But it was Argentine exiles who really gave impetus to the Lacanian current, culminating in the founding in 1985 of the Escola Brasileira de Psicoanálise (Brazilian School of Psychoanalysis), a member of the AMP.

The political vicissitudes in Argentina and in psychoanalytical circles meant that Lacan elected Venezuela (where his ideas had been taken by Argentine exiles) as the site of his first Latin American trip, to address a seminar on 'Lacan's teachings and psychoanalysis in Latin America'. There he gave his last talk, on 'Misunderstanding'. The seminar laid the bases for the founding of Escuela del Campo Freudiano de Caracas, the Venezuelan branch of the AMP. Since the late 1980s, other Latin American countries have joined *Campo Freudiano* (the Freudian Camp), the most influential Lacanian network in the world.

Lacan's writings, published in Mexico in 1975, have gone through twenty editions. His lectures were published in 1981, and his writings appeared in Portuguese in the late 1970s.

Further reading

García, G.L. (1978) *La entrada del psicoanálisis en la Argentina*, Buenos Aires: Ed. Altazor.

Revista analítica del litoral, nos 5 and 6 (1995–6) 'La entrada del pensamiento de Jacques Lacan en lengua española', Santa Fe: Ed. Apeiron.

GABRIELA MUSACHI

Lacerda, Carlos

b. 1914, Rio de Janeiro, Brazil; d. 1977, Rio de Janeiro

Politician, journalist

After a brief spell in the Communist Party, Lacerda became a vigorous anti-communist and a prominent journalist, writing regularly in **Correio da Manhã** and elsewhere; in 1949 he founded his own *Tribunal da Imprensa*. A leading politician from the late **1940s**, in 1954 an attempt by people close to President Getúlio **Vargas** to kill him produced a political crisis that led to Vargas' suicide. Deprived of his civil rights in 1968 for ten years by the military, he withdrew from politics and dedicated himself to his business interests and writing.

ANTONIO CARLOS VAZ

Laclau, Ernesto

b. 1935, Buenos Aires, Argentina

Political philosopher

Laclau's theory of radical democracy, developed in conjunction with Chantal Mouffe in *Hegemony and Socialist Strategy: Towards a Radical Democratic Politics* (1980) has had a profound impact upon modern political theory. Laclau and Mouffe deconstruct the Marxist tradition, reinscribing it into a new political project for the Left. Laclau's radical historicization of the notion of the Enlightenment subject proposes a more pluralist definition of identity not exclusively limited by **class**, and receptive to particularisms such as gender and ethnicity. In Laclau's view, this opens up the possibility of building new forms of radical democracy.

See also: new social movements

ALVARO FERNÁNDEZ-BRAVO

Lacrosil, Michèle

b. 1915, Guadaloupe

Writer

Lacrosil's first two novels – *Sapotille et le serin d'argile* (Sapotille and the Clay Canary) (1960) and *Cajou* (1961) – are narrated by a female mulatto protagonist whose struggles in the face of persistent patriarchal discrimination recall the earlier work of Martinican Mayotte **Capécia**. Subjects of their discourse, but objects of men's violence, the protagonists seek flawed solutions in suicide and the predictable flight to Paris respectively. The multiple points of view of Lacrosil's third novel, *Demain Jab-Herma* (1967), offer a less bleak outcome of the racial and social tensions in Guadeloupe, as the title suggests: the black protagonist Jab-Herma will have his day.

JILL E. ALBADA-JELGERSMA

ladino

Term used in Guatemala to refer to the non-Indian population. In Moorish Spain it referred to members of outside ethnicities who used Spanish – first Moors/muslims, later Sephardic Jews – and was adapted in Guatemala to refer to Spanish-speaking Indians. But by the late seventeenth century, ladinos had emerged as a separate ethnicity, between Spanish and Indian in the caste/class system. Unlike Indians, ladinos had freedom of movement and were exempt from payment of tribute; they were prohibited from living in Indian towns, however, and could not hold tributary positions. Nonetheless they gradually emerged as the dominant political, cultural and economic force in the country.

JUDITH MAXWELL

Ladoo, Harold
b. 1945, Couva, Trinidad; d. 1973, Trinidad

Writer

An extraordinary and tragic figure, Ladoo (known as 'Sonny') emigrated to Canada in 1968, studying by day and working at night to support his family. In 1972, his graduation year, he published the uncompromising *No Pain Like This Body*, a novel following the trials of a rice growing family faced with a hostile Nature, alcoholism and extreme poverty. Their completely uncontrived, bare dialect reflects the limited possibilities of their lives. The novel is rarely studied – perhaps because it is genuinely distressing reading. Ladoo's own life was cut short during a research trip to Trinidad, where he was attacked and left for dead in a ditch. The novel *Yesterdays* (1974) was published posthumously.

LORRAINE LEU

Laferriere, Dany
b. 1953, Port au Prince, Haiti

Writer

A journalist under Francois **Duvalier**, Laferriere left for exile in Montreal in 1978 where he published his first bawdy, satirical novel *Comment faire l'amour avec un nègre sans se fatiguer* (How to Make Love to a Black Man without Getting Tired) (1985), a scandalous best-seller and major film. His next work, *Eroshima* (1987), was in the same vein. He later moved to Miami and published in 1991 a novel about growing up in Haiti, *L'odeur de café* (An Aroma of Coffee), followed by two more autobiographical novels. His most recent novel again returns to Haiti, *Pays sans chapeau* (Land without a Hat) (1996).

J. MICHAEL DASH

Lafourcade, Enrique
b. 1927, Santiago, Chile

Writer

Noted for his use of irony and black humour, Lafourcade wrote several novels, including *Frecuencia modulada* (Modulated Frequency) (1968) and *Palomita blanca* (Little White Dove) (1971), later filmed by Raúl **Ruiz**. He wrote regular *crónicas* (see **crónica**) in *El* **Mercurio**, one of which, *Salvador Allende* (1973), was published as a book. He remained in Chile until 1984, when he became a political **exile**. His other work includes *La fiesta del rey Acab* (King Acab's Party) (1959), a satire on Dominican dictator **Trujillo**, *El gran taimado* (Great Cunning) (1984), indirectly about **Pinochet**, and *Hoy está solo mi corazón* (Today My Heart Is Lonely) (1990). He is also a fixture on Chilean **television**.

CELINA MANZONI

Lagsner, Jacobo

b. 1927, Romania

Playwright

Since the 1950s and 1960s, Lagsner's plays and scripts have been characterized by their ingenuity and urbane and witty perspective on middle-class life. Like many Uruguayans, he has worked extensively in Argentina in theatre, film and television. *Esperando la carroza* (Waiting for the Hearse) is his most famous work; it explores the hypocritical attitudes of the middle class towards the elderly. It opened in Montevideo in 1974 and ran for seven years, making it the largest hit ever in Uruguayan theatre, and was made into a successful film in Argentina in 1985 by Alejandro Doria, starring the Uruguayan actress China **Zorrilla**.

DAVID WILLIAM FOSTER

Laird, Colin

b. 1924, North Shields, England

Architect

One of Trinidad's most important architects, his work and influence is evident in building projects throughout the eastern Caribbean. Laird has written widely on various aspects of Caribbean conservation, ecology, environmental issues and sustainable energy. A key figure in urban planning in the Caribbean, Laird's portfolio includes design and renovation of the St. Kitt's Legislative Council building, the CARICOM Secretariat, Guyana, and the Trinidad National Library. Laird is also at the forefront of restoration work on Trinidad's most important heritage buildings. The 1993 development of Port-of-Spain's Independence Square combines Laird's sense of history with contemporary landscaping and design.

LORRAINE LEU

Laleau, León

b. 1892, Port au Prince, Haiti; d. 1979, Petionville, Haiti

Writer

A writer and diplomat, Laleau was sympathetic to ***indigenisme*** even though he more conservatively clung to the techniques of French Parnassianism. His most prolific period was in the 1930s, when he published his best-known collection of poems *Musique nègre* (Black Music) (1931). He never belonged to any movement, but his reputation grew with the inclusion of some of his stylized evocations of national or racial themes in Leopold Senghor's 1948 anthology of black writing. He was also known in Haiti as a novelist for *Le Choc* (The Shock) (1932) which chronicled life during the Occupation.

J. MICHAEL DASH

Lam, Wifredo

b. 1902, Sagua La Grande, Cuba; d. 1982, Paris, France

Visual artist

One of Latin America's most universally recognized contemporary painters, Lam began his studies in Havana before spending two years at the San Fernando Fine Arts Academy in Madrid. In Spain he acquired a solid academic foundation and made a successful career as a portraitist. His contact with surrealism in Paris, where he arrived after the defeat of the Spanish Republic in 1939, however, set in motion the development of a visual style of his own. In Paris he met Picasso, André Breton, Benjamin Péret and Max Ernst, and it was there that Pierre Loeb mounted his first exhibition, which attracted the attention of galleries and artists across Europe.

When the Nazis occupied France, he returned to the Americas in the company of Breton, Lévi-Strauss and other artists and intellectuals; his route back to Havana passed through Martinique, where he met Aimé **Césaire** and began a lifelong friendship. His return to the Caribbean and to his homeland was to have a definitive impact on his artistic development. The encounter with nature, a suggestive tropical vegetation and the forms of black culture were a revelation to him. It may be said that his mature period began at this time, expressed in works like *La jungla*, *La silla* (The chair), *La presencia eterna* (The Eternal Presence) and *El rumor de la tierra* (The Rumbling of Earth). His work evolves through a symbiosis of themes taken from the natural world and magic-religious representations from black Caribbean culture. For Alejo **Carpentier**, Lam's paintings 'celebrate the transformation of the world into myth and solidarity'.

In 1943, the Pierre Matisse Gallery in New York presented an exhibition of his work, coinciding with an official exhibition of Cuban art in which Lam had refused to participate. He visited and worked in Haiti with Breton, with whom he shared a fascination with the rituals of **Vodun**, and travelled through Latin America, the USA and Europe, before settling in Paris once again in 1952. From 1954 onwards, he was a regular participant in the Salon de Mai, and his painting entered a phase of stylistic and thematic consolidation, as his reputation grew. In 1958 he was elected a member of the Graham Foundation for Advanced Studies in Fine Arts in Chicago.

In the 1960s, Lam visited Cuba frequently; on one trip he painted *El tercer mundo* (The Third World), a massive work mingling fantastic figures, human forms, elements of tropical flora and fauna, and African symbols. Later, in the 1970s, he added to his achievements in painting, drawing and illustration with an important body of work in ceramics, made for the most part at his workshop in Albisola Mare, in Italy.

Further reading

Blanc, G.V. et al. (1993) *Wifredo Lam and His Contemporaries*, New York: Abrams.

Fouchet, M.-P. (1989) *Wilfredo Lam*, Barcelona: Ediciones Polígrafa.

Martínez, Juan A. (1994) *Cuban Art and National Identity: The Vanguardia Painters 1927–1950*, Gainesville: University of Florida Press.

WILFREDO CANCIO ISLA

Lamarque, Libertad

b. 1909, Santa Fe, Argentina

Actress and singer

Already a well-recognized **tango** singer, Lamarque made her screen debut in Moglia Barth's *¡Tango!*, the first Argentine sound film. José Agustín **Ferreyra** made her a star in his **tango melodramas**, especially *Ayúdame a vivir* (Help Me to Live) (1936), *Besos brujos* (Bewitching Kisses) (1937) and *Madreselva* (Honeysuckle) (1938). Specializing in suffering but determined characters, Lamarque worked with important directors, including **Amadori**, **Saslavsky** and **Soffici**. After a squabble with Eva **Perón**, she moved in 1946 to Mexico, where she made more than thirty films and worked in television. In the 1970s she successfully returned to the Argentine stage in versions of *Hello Dolly* and *Applause*.

RODRIGO PEIRETTI

Lamas, Marta

b. 1947, Mexico City

Writer

Lamas is the founding director of the scholarly journal, **Debate feminista** (Feminist Debate, 1992–), a co-founder of DiVersa: Asociación Política Feminista (DiVerse: Feminist Political Association, 1997–) and a leading contemporary spokesperson and writer on women's rights in Mexico.

CYNTHIA STEELE

Lamata, Luis Alberto

b. 1959, Caracas, Venezuela

Film-maker

The most promising of all contemporary Venezuelan directors, Lamata began working in television at a very young age, writing and directing widely exported **telenovelas**, like *Topacio* and *Cristal* in the early 1980s. After making some **short films**, he also wrote and directed a series of direct-to-video features, a booming market in Venezuela in the 1980s. Finally, in 1986, he participated in Gabriel **García Márquez**'s screenwriting workshop held at the Escuela Internacional de Cine y Televisión in Cuba, where he polished the script of his first feature, the extraordinarily successful and much awarded historical epic, *Jericó* (1990). His second feature, another historical tale with elements of **magical realism**, *Desnudo con naranjas* (Nude with Oranges) (1995) was again a critical and popular success. But his most watched film, seen by more than 320,000 people in Venezuela alone, was his third, *Salserón, la primera vez* (Salserón, the First Time) (1997), featuring the popular band of the same name. In the late 1990s, Lamata became director of a TV production company, Marte-TV, and was working on another script for a feature.

ANA M. LÓPEZ

lambada

A Brazilian rhythm and dance, lambada started in the Brazilian Amazon region in the 1970s. Local musicians added elements of **merengue**, **salsa** and **reggae** to carimbó, producing a new beat. In the 1980s it reached northeast Brazil, where a dance was created from the rhythm. French music producers made it internationally known. Lambada's licentious choreography shares similarities with the libidinous movements of maxixe (Rio de Janeiro, 1870s and 1880s). Couples hold themselves in body-to-body contact, dancing in fast, synchronized steps, continuously circling their hips, moving as one. Lambada became known more for its eroticism than for its musical style. The most famous lambada song was borrowed from a Bolivian **huayno** by Los **Kjarkas**.

MARÍA JOSÉ SOMERLATE BARBOSA

Lamborghini, Osvaldo

b. 1940, Buenos Aires, Argentina; d. 1985, Barcelona, Spain

Writer

From his first text *El fiord* onwards, Lamborghini flew in the face of all the prevailing currents in an Argentine literature absorbed with the definition of identity. His writing is 'illegible' because of its obscenity, the violence of its scenes, its opposition to representation, and its foul language. It is illegible because of its destruction of the narrative and because its texts are a kind of collage of pieces of paper, scribblings and doodles. His poetics is one of the most original and innovative of the century; its lines of writing only began to be taken up at the end of the 1980s by writers like César **Aira** and Alan **Pauls**.

GRACIELA MONTALDO

Lamming, George

b. 1927, Carrington, Barbados

Writer

George Eric Lamming was a prominent figure in the London West Indian literary movement in the 1950s. His first work, ***In the Castle of My Skin*** (1953), has attracted a wide readership, and the seven novels he has written to date along with such critical work as *The Pleasures of Exile* (1992) have assured his place in the Caribbean 'canon'. Lamming taught in Trinidad, and emigrated in 1950 to Britain. This experience sharpened his awareness of his colonial upbringing, which was explored, evocatively and critically, in *In the Castle of my Skin*. While *Castle* ended with 'G.' leaving his home island, *The Emigrants* (1954) portrays West Indians from different areas voyaging to England on the ironically named 'Golden Image', for each is searching for the fulfilment denied him at home. They discover a new shared identity as 'West Indians', but in England they find only confusion and the novel, dominated by scenes of darkness, ends with a club brawl.

Set on the composite Caribbean island of San Cristobal immediately before independence, *Of Age and Innocence* (1958) is a political novel where 'age' is represented both by the reactionary forces surrounding the white chief of police and by Ma Shepherd, spokeswoman for the traditional black folk. The 'innocents' are boys, African, Indian and English, the multicultural society of the future. Between them stands Shephard, the popular leader who, although emotionally unstable, holds the key to the island's future. His mysterious murder leaves that future in the balance. *Season of Adventure* (1960) takes place immediately after independence, and concerns Fola, the coloured step-daughter of Piggott, the chief commissioner of police. Fola has a moment of vision in a **Vodun** ceremony which turns her away from her adoptive culture to search for her true father among common people of the Forest Reserve. Piggott's murder leads to their violent repression by the police, and the drums, the expression of their communal spirit, are smashed. This eventually provokes a rebellion, and the novel ends with qualified hope for the future.

Water with Berries (1971) returns to the immigrant scene some twenty years later. The title refers to Caliban's words in *The Tempest*, but the setting is Prospero's island, England, and the Calibans are three West Indian artists, working out their search for an independent identity amid increasing violence. In *Natives of My Person* (1971), set in the sixteenth century, a slave ship retraces the middle passage without slaves, hoping to create an ideal society, but the expedition is doomed by the moral failure of the captain and the crew. The women of the expedition, sent on ahead, express a qualified hope for redemption. A complex, poetic work, drawing on historical sources but creating a timeless exploration of the colonial dilemma, it is arguably Lamming's finest work to date.

Further reading

Jonas, J. (1990) *Anancy in the Great House*, New York: The Greenwood Press.

Pouchet Paquet, S. (1982) *The Novels of George Lamming*, London: Heinemann.

LOUIS JAMES

Lampião and Maria Bonita

Lampião was the nickname of Virgolino Ferreira da Silva, the most famous and feared of the bandits, or *cangaceiros*, who roamed the interior of north-east Brazil. Born in Pernambuco, into a family of cowhands and mule breeders, he entered banditry whilst still in his teens. For many, the conditions of existence in the rural interior were desperately harsh, due to the chronically unequal pattern of land ownership, the oppression by the powerful land-owning elite, endemic social injustice and deprivation caused by the periodic droughts. For some of those affected, banditry offered a viable living and even an attractive way of life. Lampião quickly established himself as the leader of his band, raiding ranches, pillaging towns and constantly eluding the police who pursued him.

Lampião's audacious exploits, together with his notorious violence and sadism, became legendary and were regularly recounted in popular songs and stories throughout the north-east from the mid-1920s onwards. He revelled in the publicity he increasingly attracted, whilst his relationship with Maria Bonita, his lover and companion, and his renowned love of music, song and dance, added to the aura that surrounded him. He was finally tracked down and killed by a battalion of military police in Sergipe in 1938. Maria Bonita and nine of his men died with him.

So strong had the legend become, that the corpses were decapitated and the heads put on public display, by way of proof of the band's annihilation. Lampião's story has continued to fire the popular imagination right up to the present. His familiar figure – dressed in leather garb and hat, wearing spectacles and carrying a rifle, and frequently with Maria Bonita alongside – has been reproduced in numerous popular engravings, drawings and carvings, and in the pottery of folk artists such as Mestre **Vitalino**. However, it is **literatura de cordel** that has done the most to ensure that Lampião remains a major theme in Brazilian popular art. Scores of *folhetos* (see **folheto**) on his adventures have been printed, presenting him as part demon, part avenger of the poor, and inventing new stories about him, both on earth and in the afterlife. This popularity has frequently inspired erudite artists in Brazil as well, seen in such work as Lima **Barreto**'s film *O cangaceiro* (1952), Raquel de **Queiroz**'s play, *Lampião* (1953), and Claudio Aguiar's novel, *Lampião e os meninos* (Lampião and the Boys) (1990).

Further reading

Chandler, B.J. (1978) *The Bandit King: Limpião of Brazil*, Texas: Texas A&M University Press.

Hobsbawm, Eric (1981) *Bandits*, New York: Pantheon Books.

Yong, A. (1994) *Lampion of Brazil*, London: Menard Press.

MARK DINNEEN

Landeta, Matilde

b. 1910, San Luis Potosí, Mexico

Film-maker

Landeta is the widely respected Mexican woman director of the trilogy *Lola Casanova* (1948), *La negra Angustias* (Black Angustias) (1949) and *Trotacalles* (Streetwalker) (1951), which challenged the conventions of mainstream cinema. Working first as a script girl and then as assistant (1938–43) to directors of the stature of Emilio 'El Indio' **Fernández**, Julio **Bracho** and Roberto **Gavaldón**, she learned her trade during the most productive era in the Mexican film industry. She went on to make 110 16mm cartoon shorts for US television, returning to the cinema only in 1991 with *Nocturno a Rosario* (Nocturne for Rosario).

PATRICIA TORRES SAN MARTÍN

Lange, Norah Berta

b. 1906, Buenos Aires, Argentina; d. 1972, Buenos Aires

Writer

An *ultraista* poet, Lange wrote for several Argentine avant-garde publications. Her first volume of poetry *La calle de la tarde* (Afternoon Street) (1925) was recommended by her friend Jorge Luis **Borges**. Lange's novels *Cuarenta y cinco días y treinta marineros* (Forty-five Days and Thirty Sailors), *Personas en la sala* (People in the Room) and *Los dos retratos* (Two Portraits) are the work of a solid and individual writer. Together with Oliverio **Girondo**, her partner since 1930, she was the point of contact between artists and intellectuals from Argentina and abroad. *Cuadernos de infancia* (Childhood Notebooks) (1937), her autobiography, is her best known work.

ADRIANA AMANTE

language loss

When an individual loses the capacity for speech, this is known as aphasia. When a community of speakers does so, this is known as language loss; a language may be 'lost' in a number of ways. The entire group of speakers may die off. Hemming estimates that the total indigenous population of the Amazon Basin dropped from a pre-1500s level of between 2 and 4 million to around 100,000 today. Diamond finds that North American Indians as well suffered 90 per cent fatality rates upon coming into contact with European settlers.

Figures for Mesoamerican populations do not suggest such massive depopulation, but chronicles such as the *Annals of the Kaqchikel* recount plague scourges decimating the cities. None the less, the more common means of language loss is for speakers of a language to shift from one language to another. The model for immigrant populations is three generations to language shift. The original immigrant generation speaks the native language of their place of origin. They learn the language of their new home, perhaps imperfectly; the original language remains the language of the home. The second generation learns the host community's language in school and possibly in their daily social interactions. They continue to speak in the place-of-origin language to their parents, but speak in the host language to their children. The third generation is host-language dominant. They have little fluency in the original language, knowing a few words, as emblems, but being basically speakers of the host community language. As long as the original community continues to speak the language, however, the language shift by emigrants does not affect the viability of the language *per se*, nor does the loss of a set of speakers decrease the store of the world's languages, with their gamut of possible human variations and potentials.

However, this is not the only language contact situation that can lead to language loss. In the last two decades of the twentieth century, the number of indigenous languages spoken in the Americas has been cut in half (see **indigenous languages of highland South America**; **indigenous languages of lowland South America**). The last elderly speakers of hundreds of languages have died and their descendants no longer speak their 'native' languages. In some cases, such as eastern Ecuador, local languages have been replaced by an indigenous tongue of wider currency, in this case Kichwa (**Quechua**). In most cases, the replacing language has been Spanish, Portuguese or English.

While stable bilingualism is possible (see **bilingualism and biculturalism**), differential access to power can privilege one code over another, leading to transitional bilingualism and an eventual language shift. When the population shifting their speech patterns is the sole repository of a language, the transition to another tongue results in the loss of a language from the human repertoire.

Further reading

Diamond, J. (1997) *Guns, Germs, and Steel: The Fates of Human Societies*, New York: W.W. Norton & Company.

Hemming, J. (1978) *Red Gold: The Conquest of the Brazilian Indians*, London: Macmillan.

Hernández Arana Xajilá, F. and Díaz Qeb'uta Quej, F. (1934) *Memorial de Tecpán-Atitlán (Anales de los Cakchiqueles sic)*, trans. J. Antonio Villacorta, Guatemala: Tipografía Nacional.

Wardhaugh, R. (1987) *Languages in Competition: Dominance, Diversity, and Decline*, New York: Blackwell.

Wolfson, N. and Manes, J. (eds) (1985) *Language of Inequality*, Berlin: Mouton

JUDITH M. MAXWELL

language policy in Latin America

Language policy in Spanish-speaking Latin America deals with challenges to the status of Spanish as the official language, a status inherited from the colonial administration of the New World. These challenges come from several sources: the assertion of the rights of indigenous groups; the 'danger' of fragmentation of Spanish into a multitude of local dialects; the growing prestige of English and influence of the USA; and, along the southern border of Brazil, contact with Portuguese.

In the initial phase of colonization, the Roman Catholic Monarchs and later Charles V required all of their new subjects to learn Spanish, just as their predecessors had imposed the learning of Castilian on the conquered Arab territories in order to bind them more closely together in the nation governed by Castile. However, it soon became clear that the linguistic diversity of the New World was too great to allow for the immediate implantation of Spanish, and some allowance had to be made for the usage of indigenous languages in teaching and evangelization. The resulting policies led to a separation of colonial society into a minority of Spanish/*criollo* Spanish-speakers governing an indigenous majority speaking one of many indigenous languages. The separation became so great that it all but halted the Hispanization of rural areas and created local indigenous elites with considerable autonomy from the central administration. After independence, the new nations maintained the official status of Spanish as a means of strengthening national unity and pursuing modernization through education. It is only since the Second World War that this policy has suffered any substantial change.

With respect to the status of Spanish among native speakers, independence led to the creation of national educational institutions and a desire to reform Spanish orthography so as to facilitate its learning by American speakers, as well as to foster a literary tradition independent of Spain. Such reforms came to little in the face of the turbulence created by independence, but a second round of standardization began as part of the modernization process initiated around 1870. Increasing immigration into Latin America (see **immigration to Latin America**) and the strengthening of trends towards democratization led to the fear among the intellectual elite that the linguistic unity of Latin America would collapse into a cacophony of local variants, much as the Latin of the Roman Empire fragmented into the variety of Romance languages.

The final threat to the official status of Spanish is the growing contact with other European languages: with English throughout Latin America, and with Portuguese along the southern border of Brazil. Contact with English arises through migration to the USA for economic or political reasons or sojourns for business or education. This contact is particularly acute in the case of Puerto Rico, where its administrative dependency on the USA has led to an extensive diffusion of English, as well as the threatened imposition of English as the official language should Puerto Rico ever gain statehood. This threat has sparked intellectual debates that echo the Spanish-vs-indigenous-language debates heard on the mainland: language is an expression of identity, perhaps the fundamental expression of identity, and it should not be given up lightly.

HARRY HOWARD

Lanz, Rigoberto

b. 1944, Upata, Edo. Bolívar, Venezuela

Sociologist

Lanz's academic career has been devoted to the promotion of social science research in Venezuela during a distinguished teaching career at the Universidad Central de Venezuela in Caracas, where he has been particularly concerned with postgraduate and postdoctoral studies. Having studied in Caracas and at the Sorbonne in Paris, he was the founder in 1988 of the Centre for Postdoctoral Research in the University's Social Science Faculty. As its director through the 1990s, he helped to develop its international reputation for innovative, high-quality research. His own numerous and wide-ranging publications have discussed such key concepts as ideology, democracy and postmodernity (see **postmodernism**).

MARK DINNEEN

Lanza, Alcides

b. 1929, Rosario, Argentina

Musician

A prolific composer and a leading innovator in the field of electronic music, Lanza studied piano and composition at the **Instituto Di Tella** with Messiaen, Maderna and **Ginastera**. Between 1959 and 1965 he was artistic director of the **Teatro Colón**, and from 1966 to 1970 taught at the Columbia Princeton Electronic Music Center and at New York Community College. His abundant musical production includes *Eidesis II* (1967) for thirteen instruments, *Eidesis III* (1971) for orchestra and tape recorder and *Plectros III* (1971) for piano and synthesizer.

ALFONSO PADILLA

Lara, Agustín

b. 1897, Mexico City; d. 1970, Mexico City

Singer and composer

Lara was one of the most prolific composers and the most unmistakable voice of twentieth-century Latin American popular music. He began his musical career as a pianist in a brothel at age thirteen, and later played piano in clubs and cabarets throughout Mexico. At Santa María la Redonda he was slashed in the face by a jealous woman; the scar left by this passionate assault no doubt contributed to his air of perversion and romance. His companions were always chorus girls or actresses, among them the famous María **Félix**, for whom he composed in 1945 the song 'María Bonita' (Beautiful Maria).

Lara's musical career really began in 1929 when he was discovered in the Bar Salambó in Mexico City by the tenor Juan Arvizu, who contracted him as his accompanist. Later he became associated with the radio station XEW, 'Voice of Latin America'; in the weekly programme 'La hora íntima' (The Intimate Hour), he played many of his songs for the first time. He was also playing in Mexico City theatres, and his name soon became nationally known as an imaginative pianist, composer and singer. He toured widely outside Mexico and was a great success everywhere. And as if that were not enough, he also appeared in several Mexican films, including *Perdida* (The Lost Woman) and *Coqueta* (Coquette), both issued in 1949, and *La mujer que yo amé* (The Woman I Loved) in 1950.

Lara is best known as a prolific and original composer. Though he had no formal training, he learned the secrets of the piano by playing Cuban **danzón**, and composed many of the best known boleros (see **bolero**) of the Latin American repertoire: 'Solamente una vez' (Just Once), 'Señora tentación' (Lady Temptation), 'Arráncame la vida' (Tear My Life Apart), 'Piensa en mí' (Think of Me), 'Humo en los ojos' (Smoke in My Eyes) and 'Noche de ronda' (Night Serenade) among many others. His compositions are characterized by their melodic cadences, with singer and pianist alternately occupying the centre of the song and by metaphorically sophisticated lyrics that would merit inclusion in any anthology of Latin American *modernismo* (see **modernismo, Spanish American**). He did not only compose boleros, however; Lara wrote in every form of Latin American popular music, and was particularly skilled in writing in the Spanish style, with songs like the famous 'Granada' and 'Sevilla'.

Further reading

Taibo, I. (1985) *Agustín Lara*, Mexico D.F: Júcar.
Martínez, G.A. (1993) *El flaco de oro*, Mexico D.F.: Planeta.

RAFAEL CASTILLO ZAPATA

Lara, Brian Charles

b. 1969, Trinidad

Cricketer

In 1994, at age twenty-five, Brian Lara made the highest individual score in Test cricket – 375 against England in Antigua – and then seven weeks later hit 501 for Warwickshire against Durham, the highest individual score in first-class cricket. Overnight he became a cult figure, nicknamed the Prince and a target for marketing men; his name was soon selling a range of products. Commercial demands plus year-round cricket produced their own forms of fatigue, and he withdrew from the West Indies tour of Australia in 1995. Charming and talented, he has often been accused of arrogance, and his appointment as captain of the West Indies in 1997 was controversial. He resigned the post in 1999.

TONY MASON

Lara, Christian

b. 1939, Guadeloupe

Film-maker

One of the most prolific Antillean film-makers, Lara maintains that cinema must be a mirror 'where we Antilleans can discover our differences as the "French of America"'. Lara sees cinema as 'an engine, a vehicle for the generation of ideas, of change'. His work includes a political trilogy – *Coco le Fleur Candidat* (Coco the Flower Candidate) (1978) – one of the first films to use creole (see **creole languages**), *Mamito* (1980), the television series *Yoka* (1988) and *Sucre amer* (Bitter Sugar) (1998) which explores the history of Guadeloupe through the legendary figure of Ignace. Lara's work has been criticized for replicating stereotypes about the Exotic Caribbean.

ANN MARIE STOCK

Lara, Jesús

b. 1898, Muela, Cochabamba, Bolivia; d. 1980, Cochabamba

Writer

A poet, novelist and essayist, Lara participated as a private soldier in the **Chaco War** (1932–3). His first language was **Quechua**, and he was a member of the Bolivian Communist Party – and its candidate for the vice presidency in 1956. An *indigenista* intellectual, he wrote prolifically from 1957 onwards, when his *Tragedia del fin de Atahuallpa*

(The Tragedy of Atahualpa's Death) was published. His twenty or so published works include a *Diccionario Quechua* (1978), writings on the Inca empire and Quechua literature, several novels set in the Cochabamba valley, the biography of the guerrillero Inti Peredo, who died beside Che **Guevara** in 1967, and *Repete* (1978) on the Indians in the Chaco War.

XIMENA MEDINACELI

Lara, Raúl

b. 1940, San José de Ororo, Bolivia

Painter

Lara's work, particularly that done after his return from several years in Argentina, explores Bolivian folklore and traditions. Some of his paintings are reminiscent of the colonial baroque, and of Bolivian **carnival**, in their fixation with the temptations of the flesh. His *Domingo de tentación* (Temptation Sunday) (1975), for instance, shows what seems to be a conversation between two businessmen and a prostitute, but the animal and primitive masks of the men and the almost bird-like costume of the woman suggest magical transformations.

DANIEL BALDERSTON

Laredo, Jaime

b. 1941, Cochabamba, Bolivia

Violinist

A child prodigy who played the violin from age four, Laredo is considered one of the best violinists in the world and has been a soloist with the most famous orchestras and conductors. He is a key figure in the Marlboro Music festival, the Lincoln Center Chamber Music Society, and directs the Scottish Chamber Orchestra. Among his many recordings, his Bach violin sonatas with Glenn Gould are outstanding.

CARLOS ROSSO OROZCO

Larreta, Antonio

b. 1922, Montevideo, Uruguay

Playwright and theatre director

Founder of the Teatro de la Ciudad de Montevideo (TCM) in 1960, which was at the centre of a brilliant period in theatre, Larreta was instrumental in bringing to Uruguay some of the best international plays, which he translated, adapted and directed.

His version of Lope de Vega's *Fuenteovejuna* was a particular milestone. In 1972 he won the coveted **Casa de las Américas** prize in theatre for his play, *Juan Palmieri*, but it was censored by the military dictatorship; however, it did première in Buenos Aires in 1973. Exiled in Spain, Larreta wrote a number of film and TV scripts, made a film, *Nunca estuve en Viena* (I was Never in Vienna) (1988) and published a novel, *Volavérunt* (1980), which won the Planeta prize in 1980. Currently he alternates his residence between Spain and Uruguay. In Montevideo he founded the Teatro del Sur where he has returned to directing and acting.

MARINA PIANCA

Laso, Margarita

b. 1963, Quito, Ecuador

Poet and singer

A talented popular singer with considerable interpretative skill, Laso is also gaining a reputation as a poet. Her works *Erosonera* (Erorhythms) (1991), *Queden en mi lengua mis deseos* (Let my Desires Remain on my Tongue) (1994) and *El trazo de las cobras* (The Cobras' Path) (1997) reveal rich erotic images and experimental rhythms. The exaltation of the body, nature and the recovery of the plenitude of fulfilled, unrestricted love underline the subversive and liberating force of the erotic in a repressive society. Her poetry combines the concrete and the cosmic, so that reality and desire can become one.

MERCEDES M. ROBLES

Lastra, Pedro

b. 1932, Quillota, Chile

Writer

Lastra is a university professor at State University of New York at Stony Brook (1972–95), literary scholar and poet. From 1966 to 1973 he directed the influential collection Letras de Américas (Letters of America) at Editorial Universitaria. He has studied rigorously the Spanish American short story from the nineteenth century and the most distinguished Latin American contemporary narrators. In *Noticias del extranjero* (Travel Notes) (1996), Lastra deploys a concise and incisive language to reveal the ghost-like existence of the poet and his immediate surroundings.

OSCAR D. SARMIENTO

latifundio

A *latifundio* is a very large traditional landholding, sometimes also known as a **hacienda**. The *latifundista* is often an absentee owner who belongs to the country's oligarchy or ruling class. A *latifundista* has considerable economic and political power and wields enormous control over the dependent rural population. Labour is secured through various tenancy relations, often described as servile, as well as through wage labour arrangements. *Latifundios* have become less important following the implementation of **agrarian reform** programmes and their transformation into modern, generally smaller, commercial farms.

See also: *minifundio*

CRISTÓBAL KAY

Latin America

The cultural and political region embracing the countries lying south of the Río Bravo, as distinct from North (or Anglo-Saxon) America. The diversity of these countries transcends the ethnolinguistic unity which the term suggests. Thinkers like José Martí therefore preferred the term 'Our America' which embraced the Iberian, the non-Iberian and the indigenous traditions.

The search for a Latin American identity has evolved against the background of ambivalent animosities towards the USA. During the Independence period in the early nineteenth century, admiration for the northern neighbour inspired a critique of the Spanish colonial inheritance; simultaneously, the threat of US expansionism underlined the necessity for a common defence. Concerned by what they saw as the inevitable triumph of the Anglo-Saxon civilizational project, the intellectuals of the new nations, referring to the old opposition between the Nordic and the Mediterranean, adopted the concept of 'Latinity' as the best means of resistance. By the end of the nineteenth century, the term Latin America began to be used in the same sense of continental unity that Bolívar had alluded to a century earlier.

Twentieth-century thinkers have affirmed that the concept of 'Latin' is more inclusive than exclusive, and that a Latin identity should not be sought in common attributes like a shared language or Roman legal system, but in the particularity of the American peoples, forged by a fusion of various ethnic groups – or as José **Vasconcelos** had described it, a *raza cósmica* (cosmic race) which could embrace everything. Others asserted that the Latinity of the American peoples derived from the Iberian peoples, reflecting a kind of conciliatory attitude towards difference and a search for affinities which is not unknown to Europe. The Latin American imagination has found representation in novels like Alejo **Carpentier**'s *Concierto barroco* (Baroque Concert) (1974). Nonetheless, a Latin '*mestizaje*' is inevitably Eurocentric and inhibited from recognizing indigenous or black cultures, reduced to the category of secondary elements.

The dangers for Latin America are now perceived differently in view of another cultural synthesis set in motion by contemporary migrations. Intellectuals like Leopoldo **Zea** have spoken of the fusion of the two Americas, whose complementarity is not just inevitable, but desirable.

Further reading

Stabb, M. (1967) *In Quest of Identity; Patterns in the Spanish American Essay of Ideas, 1890–1960*, Chapel Hill: University of North Carolina Press.
—— (1994) *The Dissenting Voice: The New Essay of Spanish America, 1960–1985*, Austin: University of Texas Press.
Zea, L. (ed.) (1986) *América Latina en sus ideas*, México, DF: Siglo Veintiuno Editores.

LUIS L. ESPARZA

Latin American Art

This quarterly publication, founded in 1989, includes articles on Latin American artists, individual works of art, and art movements. It includes regular sections on auctions and recent exhibitions; and book reviews. It is indexed in *Hispanic American Periodicals Index*.

PAUL BARY

Latin American Indian Literatures Journal

A multidisciplinary publication that includes bibliographies, translations of Latin American Indian texts and critical articles about ***indigenista*** literature and Indian languages, as well as creative writing. *Journal of the Latin American Indian Literature Association* (LAILA), the journal superseded in 1985 which had been *Latin American Indian Literatures*, founded and edited in 1977 by Juan Adolfo Vázquez. Published at the University of Pittsburgh, its current editor is Mary Preuss.

JUAN ZEVALLOS AGUILAR

Latin American Music Review

The Latin American Music Review (*Revista de música latinoamericana*), the preeminent, semiannual scholarly periodical on the music of Latin America, founded by Gerard Behague in 1980 at the University of Texas, covers ethnic music, classical music, and popular music. Most articles and reviews are in English; a few are in Spanish, and very occasional articles are in Portuguese. The journal contains articles, review articles, reviews, and necrologies. Articles include numerous short and occasional lengthy examples of the music scores mentioned in the text. Reviews cover books, musical scores, and recordings. It is indexed in *Hispanic American Periodicals Index*.

PAUL BARY

Latin American music, export of

It seems curious to speak of the export of Latin American music at the century's end, when Latin music has become incontestably a world music. **Salsa** is played and danced in every corner of the world – the success of crossover artist Ricky **Martin** is testimony to that. Yet it is not the first time that Latin American popular music has made its mark on the wider world – though, with some outstanding exceptions, the same could not be said of Latin America's **art music**.

In the early part of the century, the enormous popularity of **tango** evoked denunciations from the Vatican – though this did nothing to stop its proliferation before and after the First World War. Rudolph Valentino's dark, seductive eyes and sensual dancing defined an age. The post-First World War 'lost generation' of Europe and North America adopted **rumba** and **samba** rhythms with passionate enthusiasm, though the music was adapted to the dance salons of Europe, remoulded into a couple dance that would eventually evolve into the unrecognizably stiff and formalized ballroom varieties of what were once vibrant and sensual folk dances.

In the 1930s, rumba – which arose out of Cuban **son** – was carried to the USA by Cuban musicians. The feelgood movies of the 1930s drew on the exotic rhythms of the south, partly at least to divert attention from Depression USA. Rumba bands with flounced shirts and tropical backdrops played for Rogers and Astaire. Carmen **Miranda** came to exemplify an idealized image of Brazil that was carefully nurtured for its own purposes by **Vargas**'s **Estado Novo**.

The 1950s was a period when Cuban music and musicians played a key role, both in the evolution of jazz through figures like Dizzy Gillespie and in the growth of big band **mambo**, identified with musicians like **Pérez Prado**. The US response to the Cuban Revolution (see **revolutions**), however, severed the link. The new Latin craze – salsa – was not so much an export as the creation of Hispanic communities in the USA, a fusion of Puerto Rican, Dominican and Cuban rhythms. Indeed it could be said that salsa was exported *to* Latin America.

Simon and Garfunkel's El condor pasa had created an interest in **Andean music** that was then nourished by the exiled musicians of the Chilean ***nueva canción*** movement in the 1970s. And the growth of the world music movement in the 1980s brought new dance crazes – like the **lambada** from Brazil – and a resurgent interest in tango and salsa.

The latest musical arrival from Latin America to hit the world scene comes in the unlikely form of a group of retired Cuban musicians recorded by Ry Cooder in Havana in 1997. The resulting *Buena Vista Social Club* album broke all commercial records and introduced an entirely new audience to the sentimental ballads, sung to the rhythmic music of son, that was once called 'vieja trova' or 'feeling'.

Further reading

Figueroa, F. (1994) *Encyclopedia of Latin American Music in the United States*, St Petersburg, FL: Pillar Publications.
Manuel, P. (1995) *Caribbean Currents*, Philadelphia: Temple University Press.
—— (1988) *Popular Musics of the Western World: An Introductory Survey*, New York/Oxford: Oxford University Press.
Roberts, J.S. (1979) *The Latin Tinge: The Impact of Latin American Music on the United States*, NewYork/Oxford: Oxford University Press.

MIKE GONZALEZ

Latin American Perspectives

Subtitled 'a journal on capitalism and socialism', this important revisionist journal has been published quarterly since 1974. Each issue focuses on a theme generally relating to Latin American politics or economics, and sometimes includes documents and book reviews. It is indexed in *Hispanic American Periodicals Index*.

PAUL BARY

Latin American Research Review

This official publication of the Latin American Studies Association, issued three times a year since 1965, is one of the foremost sources for reviews of current research and methodologies in the field. The journal is committed to an interdisciplinary approach but recognizes the importance of the traditional disciplines. The journal provides a mix of scholarly articles, research notes and review essays. It is indexed in *Hispanic American Periodicals Index*.

PAUL BARY

Latin American Spanish dialectology

Latin America has just enough dialectal variation to identify a speaker's regional or national background, but not enough to impede understanding between speakers of different variants. It is traditional among linguists to draw a distinction between highland and lowland varieties. By 'highland' is meant the central plateau of Mexico, highland Guatemala and the Andes. By 'lowland' is meant the rest of Spanish-speaking Latin America: the Caribbean and Caribbean coast of Central and South America, the Río de la Plata and lowland Southern Cone, and the Pacific Coast from Chile to Mexico. Highland Spanish is characterized phonetically by 'strong consonantism': the retention of syllable-final /s/ and its voicing before a voiced consonant, the retention of intervocalic /b, d, g/ as fricatives and no vacillation between /r/ and /l/. Lowland Spanish is characterized phonetically by 'weak consonantism': the aspiration or loss of syllable-final /s/, the loss of intervocalic /b, d, g/ and vacillation between /r/ and /l/.

This contrast between the two macrolects of Latin American Spanish is generally attributed to the differential intensity of colonization of the two zones. After fifty years of consolidation in the Caribbean, the Spanish moved quickly from 1550 to 1600 to occupy the centres of mainland population and wealth, those of the Aztecs in central Mexico, the Maya in highland Guatemala and the Inca in the Andes. In the absence of any such rapid influx of population, some lowland areas took up to 200 more years to attain an equivalent level of urban development.

As an urban bureaucracy was established to attend to the functions of the Church, government and university, a local linguistic form coalesced from the speech of the colonists to serve as the standard. There was a strong skewing towards Andalusia among the colonists, given that at least half of the men and most of the women were from Andalusia, the sailors manning the ships during the long passage to the Americas were from this region and emigrants were required to complete the formalities of emigration in Seville – a process that could take up to a year. It follows that the standardization of a local, urban, prestige variant would reflect the mixture of Peninsular variants spoken at the time, but with a disproportionate representation of contemporary Andalusian. The Andalusian spoken during the first round of highland standardization was closer to Castilian in its preservation of consonants in weak positions, but as it evolved such preservation faltered, so that later rounds of lowland standardization incorporated subsequent phonological innovations. The global outcome is a pattern of change in which similar varieties are found at great geographic remove.

Further reading

Lipski, J.M. (1994) *Latin American Spanish*, London: Longman.

Steel, B. (1990) *Diccionario de americanismos/ABC of Latin American Spanish*, Madrid: Sociedad General Española de Librería.

HARRY HOWARD

Latin American Studies Association (LASA)

Scholarly association formed by the Latin American Research Board, the Joint Committee on Latin American Studies and the Hispanic Division in the Library of Congress in 1969. LASA's mission is to 'encourage more effective training, teaching and research in Latin American Studies and to provide a forum for dealing with matters of common interest' in different academic fields. It organizes congresses every eighteen months in different locations of the Americas, gathering Latin American specialists from all over the world. LASA publishes the newsletter *Forum* and a journal, ***Latin American Research Review***.

JUAN ZEVALLOS AGUILAR

Latin American Theatre Review

One of the longest-lived academic journals of Hispanic studies and the first devoted exclusively to theatre, the *Review* has been edited by George Woodyard, one of its founders, since 1967. Its two annual issues include historical and interpretative articles, performance and festival reviews, and book reviews. The *Review* has played a crucial role confirming the cultural importance of Latin American theatre and insisting on the importance of privileging the theatre as an integrated cultural phenomenon.

DAVID WILLIAM FOSTER

Lau, Hazel

b. 1958, Río Coco, Nicaragua

Politician

Lau assumed a leading role in the **Miskitu** community after the 1979 **Sandinista Revolution** in Nicaragua. The Sandinistas supported the establishment of mass-based organizations on the Atlantic Coast, but were unwilling to allow such organizations to be ethnically-based. Miskitu leaders refused to accept that the peasant organization (**ATC**) could represent their interests. Subsequent negotiations led to the establishment of **MISURASATA**, a Sandinista organization for indigenous peoples of the Atlantic Coast. In the 1980s one Miskitu group led by Stedman **Fagoth** joined the contra opposition (see **contras**), while another led by Lau and Brooklyn Rivera continued to negotiate with the government.

ANUPAMA MANDE AND ILEANA RODRÍGUEZ

Lauer, Mirko

b. 1947, Zatec, Czech Republic

Writer

Living in Peru from his early years, Lauer became known as a poet with his first collection, *En los cínicos brazos* (In the Cynical Arms) (1966). Later came *Ciudad de Lima* (City of Lima) (1968), *Santa Rosita y el péndulo proliferante* (Little Saint Rose and the Proliferating Pendulum) (1972), *Bajo continuo* (Basso continuo) (1975), and others. He is also a noted researcher on popular plastic arts and contemporary literature. His journalistic work appears in the editorial pages of the Lima social democratic newspaper *La República*.

JOSÉ ANTONIO MAZZOTTI

Lauffer, Minerva

b. 1957, Curaçao

Painter

Lauffer transforms her two-dimensional paintings into three-dimensional ones by putting them in motion, transforming them literally into pillars. Her energy is expressed through her choice of colours, which is one of her strengths. Oscillating between realism and expressionism, Lauffer often focuses on Caribbean women, the strong and powerful pillars of the community.

NEL CASIMIRI

Lauffer, Pierre A.

b. 1920, Curaçao, Netherlands Antilles; d. 1981, Curaçao

Writer

The best-known author writing in **Papiamentu**, Lauffer has a dozen collections of poetry and short stories to his name. He edited the first anthology of Papiamentu literature, *Di Nos* (Our Literary Heritage) (1971), and wrote essays on the history of Papiamentu writing. He focused on traditional social and cultural patterns of Curaçao society, while criticizing the industrialization and westernization of the island. He was a master at deploying the tonal and rhythmic patterns of Papiamentu and defended the use of archaic or little known words and phrases.

AART G. BROEK

Laurel

Laurel: antología de la poesía moderna en lengua española is an ambitious and controversial anthology of Spanish and Spanish American poetry, prepared by the Mexican poets Xavier **Villaurrutia** and Octavio **Paz** and the Spanish poets Emilio Prados and Juan Gil Albert, and published in 1941 by Editorial Séneca in Mexico City. Thirty-seven poets are included, with a portrait sketch, brief bio-bibliographical information and some dozen texts for each figure. León Felipe and Pablo **Neruda** refused to have their works included, apparently because of animosity toward José Bergamín of Séneca or other organizers.

MERLIN H. FORSTER

Lavelli, Jorge

b. 1934, Buenos Aires, Argentina

Theatre and opera director

Famous for his audacious and controversial interpretations, Lavelli has worked with famous writers, including Witold Gombrowicz (whose *Le mariage* he successfully directed in 1963), Fernando Arrabal

(*Pique-nique en campagne* (Picnic in the Country) (1966) and *La guerre de mil ans* (The Thousand Year War) (1974), and **Copi**. His versions of the latter's *La journee d'une reveuse* (Dreamer's Day) (1968) and *Le Homosexuel* were highly controversial. His staging of operas by Debussy, Mozart and Verdi attacked all the conventions of the genre. Between 1988 and 1996 he directed the famous Théatre National de la Colline, exclusively devoted to contemporary work.

GONZALO AGUILAR

Lavista (Camacho), Mario

b. 1943, Mexico City

Composer

A leading experimental musician, composer and teacher, Lavista created the musical group Quenata in 1967, after a period of study in Europe, and founded and directed *Pauta*, a journal dedicated to music theory and criticism. In 1972 he was invited to work in electronic musical laboratories in Japan, where he conducted research in new musical aesthetics. This is reflected in the aleatory and electronic elements present in many of his works. In 'Quotations', for example, written for violoncello and piano (1976), he experiments with a complex process of musical citations, while 'Jaula' (Cage) is a piano composition written for four hands. Other outstanding compositions include 'Diacronía' (1969) a string quartet, 'Pieza para un(a) Pianista y un Piano' (Piece for One Pianist and a Piano) (1970), 'Game', for one two, three or four flutes, (1970–2), and the opera *Aurat* (based on Carlos **Fuentes**'s short novel) (1989), as well as music for films. He has been a Professor at the Conservatorio Nacional in Mexico since 1969, and chaired the music department at the **UNAM** from 1974 to 1975. His works have been widely recorded.

EDUARDO GUÍZAR-ALVAREZ

law

The lawyer (*abogado* or *licenciado*) is one of the most controversial figures in Latin America. A prestigious profession, accompanied by an aura of power and the suspicion of moral duplicity, the law has been, and still is to some extent, one of the most popular choices of high school graduates of the region.

The Latin American legal system is, in most countries, based on the so-called Roman-Germanic system. Historically, it appeared in the thirteenth century with the renaissance of Roman law studies. In Spain, one of the most important documents related to the existence of this legal system is the *Siete Partidas* of Alfonso X 'The Wise' (*El Sabio*), considered one of the first codifications of the Spanish legal system. Unlike the Anglo-Saxon system of the United Kingdom and the United States, this system is solely based on written proofs. Testimonies, petitions and most of the other procedures of the litigation are carried on in writing, and many trials can be solved without the parties uttering a word in front of the judge. Consequently, the ability to write well is greatly appreciated in a lawyer.

Through years of litigation during and after the colonial period, lawyers became a necessity more than a commodity. Thus it is not surprising that we find lawyers in almost every important position in the political and also cultural history of the region. Increased demand for lawyers meant that law schools became virtual factories, saturating the market with lawyers. Nowadays it is not difficult to find lawyers driving taxis or selling candy on the streets of many Latin American countries. However, despite the situation of the profession, lawyers are still produced by the thousands in a market that already has many more that it can accommodate.

Despite the profession's loss of prestige among Latin Americans, its image is still current and parents are still driven by the hope their children will be *doctores* or *licenciados*. Among others, Carlos **Fuentes**, Nicolas **Guillén**, Fidel **Castro**, Gabriel **García Márquez**, Rubén **Blades**, César **Vallejo**, Juan **Rulfo** and Mario **Vargas Llosa** were driven to law school by pressures more related to their families and society than by vocation, and this is a phenomenon that still occurs and will probably occur for the coming decades.

Further reading

David, R. and Bowerly, J.E.C. (1978) *Major Legal Systems in the World Today*, New York: The Free Press.

IVÁN REYNA

Lazo, Agustín

b. 1898, Mexico City; d. 1971, Mexico City

Artist

Lazo was the only Mexican artist directly connected to the surrealist movement, introducing surrealist theories to Mexico. Affiliated with the **Contemporáneos** group, Lazo avoided political themes in his paintings, which combine post-impressionist brushwork with dreamlike scenes, at times absurd, at times melancholic. His collages, and his watercolours of 1930–2, are among the most important examples of Mexican surrealism. Lazo also designed sets and costumes for numerous theatrical productions, wrote several plays, and translated Shakespeare and Pirandello into Spanish. Lazo produced relatively little after the death of his dear friend Xavier **Villaurrutia** in 1950.

JAMES OLES

Lazo, Carlos

b. 1914, Mexico City; d. 1955, Mexico City

Architect

General manager of the construction of Mexico City's **Ciudad Universitaria** (University City) (1950–2), Lazo was also a prominent urban planner and a working architect. Graduating in 1938, he subsequently studied in North America. His design work was experimental, as in the Cuevas Civilizadas (Civilized Caves) at Belén de las Flores in Mexico City (1953), inspired by natural forms and constructed underground. He was also responsible for other outstanding examples of architecture in the international style, including the Banco de México in Veracruz (1950) which has become the symbol of this port city.

LOURDES CRUZ GONZÁLEZ FRANCO

Le Parc, Julio

b. 1928, Mendoza, Argentina

Artist

A key representative of the **kinetic art** movement, between 1960 and 1968, Le Parc worked with García Rossi, Morellet, **Sobrino**, Stein and Yvaral, in the *Groupe de Recherche d'Art Visuel* (GRAV – Visual Art Research Group) which proposed that the work should seek its resolution in the multiple possiblities of real space. The group worked with movement and light, recuperating the element of play and encouraging active spectator participation. In 1966, Le Parc won the International Painting Prize at the 33rd Venice Biennale. A year later he was made a Chevalier of the Order of Arts and Letters by the French government.

CECILIA RABOSSI

Le Pera, Alfredo

b. 1904, Buenos Aires, Argentina; d. 1935, Medellín, Colombia

Tango lyricist

A key figure in the intense renewal of **tango** in the 1930s, Le Pera wrote the lyrics of some of **Gardel**'s most famous tangos – *Mi Buenos Aires querido* (My Beloved Buenos Aires) and *Cuesta abajo* (Downward Slope) – and was his collaborator and friend until their death in a plane crash over Medellín. He also worked on the scripts and sets of Gardel's films, including *Melodía de arrabal* (Arrabal Melody). The Le Pera and Gardel collaborations created an international tango style, smoothing away local features such as the **lunfardo** slang.

FLORENCIA GARRAMUÑO

Leal, Fernando

b. 1900, Mexico City; d. 1964, Mexico City

Artist

Leal's earliest paintings, including an encaustic mural in the stairwell of the National Preparatory School (*La fiesta del Señor de Chalma* (Feast of the Lord of Chalma) (1922–3)), are among the first modern Mexican works with idealized folkloric themes. Later murals include cycles on heroes of Latin American independence (*La epopeya bolivariana* (The Bolivian Epic); National Preparatory School, 1930–3) and *El triunfo de la locomotora y la edad de la máguina* (The Triumph of the Locomotive and the Age of the Machine) (1943) in the train station of San Luis Potosi. An allegorical mural in Panama (*Neptuno encadenado* (Neptune in Chains) (1935)) criticizing American involvement in the Canal Zone, was destroyed by local authorities.

JAMES OLES

Leal, Rine

b. 1930, Havana, Cuba; d. 1996, Caracas, Venezuela

Theatre critic

Leal's career as journalist and critic began in the Havana daily *Pueblo* and the magazines **Carteles** and **Bohemia** in 1954. In 1959 he became theatre critic for **Revolución** and was a founder of its supplement **Lunes de revolución**. His critical essays and historical research included *En primera persona* (First Person) (1967) and the most thorough history of Cuban theatre from its origins until 1902, published in the two volumes of *La selva oscura* (The Dark Forest) (1975, 1982). In 1995 he edited *Cinco autores* (Five Authors), an anthology of Cuban exile drama.

WILFREDO CANCIO ISLA

Leal Spengler, Eusebio

b. 1942, Havana, Cuba

Historian

As director of the Museum of the City of Havana from 1967, Leal undertook the restoration of colonial buildings in the city. A close colleague of Fidel **Castro**, he has directed the restoration and recovery of the colonial centre of Havana, declared a UNESCO World Heritage Site (see **World Heritage Sites**), since 1980. He is historian of the city and a member of the National Assembly. His publications include *Detén el paso, caminante* (Stop a While, Traveller) (1987), *La Habana, ciudad antigua* (Havana, Ancient City) (1988) and *Regresar en el tiempo* (Returning in Time) (1995). He rediscovered the diary of the independence leader, Carlos Manuel de Céspedes, published in 1994.

WILFREDO CANCIO ISLA

Leão, Nara

b. 1942, Vitória, Espírito Santo, Brazil; d. 1989, Rio de Janeiro, Brazil

Singer

Leão was the teenage 'muse' of the post-**bossa nova** era and of its chief lyricist, Vinicius de **Moraes**. From 1963 she worked with the left-wing **CPC** and was introduced to Rio's grassroots *favela* sambistas (see **samba**), such as Zé Keti, with whom she collaborated on Oduvaldo **Vianna Filho**'s 1964 show protesting the recently installed military regime, *Opinião* (Opinion). Having turned from bossa nova to protest song, Leão won joint first prize in the 1966 TV Record Festival with Chico **Buarque**'s song 'A Banda', before making a further radical shift in style by appearing on the

Tropicália movement's experimental 1968 album.

DAVID TREECE

Lebacs, Diana

b.1947, Curaçao, Netherlands Antilles

Actress and writer

From the late 1960s Lebacs has been an actress in local theatre and film. From the early 1970s on she has written in **Papiamentu** for young children, while switching to Dutch for older youths. Her novels are invariably set in the Dutch Antilles and deal with present day problems with which youngsters have to learn to cope, such as *Suikerriet Rosy* (Sugarcane Rose) (1983), which was adapted to the screen in 1997.

AART G. BROEK

Lechín Oquendo, Juan

b. 1914, Corocoro, Bolivia

Lechín was permanent secretary of the Bolivian Miners' Federation (FSTMB) from its foundation in 1944 until 1987, a member of the revolutionary committee which led the 1952 **Bolivian Revolution**, executive secretary of the **COB** (Bolivian Trade Union Congress) from 1952–87 and Vice-President of the Republic (1960–64). Illegitimate son of a Lebanese immigrant, he was renowned for his oratory. In 1980, Lechín set up the Comité Nacional de Defensa de la Democracia (CONADE, Committee for the Defense of Democracy) to resist the brutal military *coup* in July. He returned from exile in 1987. Paradoxically, he backed his arch-enemy Hugo Bánzer's 1997 presidential campaign whilst vehemently criticizing the previous president for privatizing leading state enterprises.

ISABEL BASTOS

Lecumberri

Lecumberri is the Mexico City prison infamous for holding political prisoners from the railroad workers' movement of the 1950s, the student movement of 1968 and the guerrilla movements of the 1970s. José **Revueltas** was imprisoned there after 1968, and it was the setting for his novel *El **Apando***. It is also frequently mentioned by those who gave testimony to Elena **Poniatowska** for her narrative of the 2 October massacre in central Mexico City, *La noche de Tlatelolco* (1969). It has now been converted into the Mexican National Archives.

CYNTHIA STEELE

Lecuona, Ernesto

b. 1895, Guanabacoa, Havana, Cuba; d. 1963, Tenerife, Canary Islands

Musician

The best known of all Cuban composers and a piano virtuoso, his 850 compositions included 196 piano pieces and over 500 songs, including 'Siboney' and 'Aquella tarde' (That Evening). By the age of eleven he was playing to accompany silent films, and at twelve he composed his first work. At seventeen he gave his first public concert and triumphed with his composition, 'La comparsita', a classic of Cuban music. He was the first to transcribe the sound of the conga for piano. He made his US début in New York in 1917, and his performances in Spain and Latin America attracted the interest of Paderewsky and Ravel. His music combined popular Cuban rhythms with classical forms; he was among the first composers to compose in the Afro-Cuban idiom at a time when the African cultural inheritance remained unrecognized within Cuba. He transcribed the rumba, drum beats and other popular expressions into musical notation for works like 'Danza lucumí', 'Danza negra' and others.

Founder of the National Symphony Orchestra in 1922, he also composed within the Spanish tradition, with tunes like 'Ante el escorial' (Facing the Escorial) and 'La malagueña'. He was an early writer of musicals, with his *zarzuelas* (comic operas),

Niña Rita (1927) *El cafetal* (1928) and *María la O* (1930). Lecuona left Cuba in 1960 and, after a brief sojourn in the USA, moved to the Canary Islands.

Further reading

Díaz Ayala, C. (1981) *Música cubana: Del areyto a la nueva trova*, San Juan: Cubanacan.

León, C. de (1995) *Ernesto Lecuona, el maestro*, Havana: Música Mundana.

Martínez, O. (1989) *Ernesto Lecuona*, Havana: UNEAC.

Orovio, H. (1992) *Diccionario de la música cubana: biográfico y técnico*, second edn, Havana: Letras Cubanas.

WILFREDO CANCIO ISLA

Leduc, Paul

b. 1942, Mexico City

Film-maker

An independent film-maker of the 1970s, Leduc worked with Alberto **Isaac** on the official documentary of the 1968 Mexico Olympics (see **Olympic Games, Mexico 1968**). His own documentaries, *Reed México insurgente* (Reed, Insurgent Mexico) (1971) and *Etnocidio, notas sobre el Mezquital* (Ethnocide, Notes on Mezquital) (1976), were sober in tone. He made several shorts before directing his brilliantly austere 1983 film on Frida **Kahlo**, *Frida, naturaleza viva* (Frida, Moving Life), which won critical acclaim worldwide. His later work, *Barroco* (Baroque) (1989), *Latino Bar* (1990) and *Dollar Mambo* (1993) confirm him as one of Mexico's most idiosyncratic directors, especially because of his growing aversion to dialogue.

PATRICIA TORRES SAN MARTÍN

Lee, Easton

b. 1931, Trelawny, Jamaica

Playwright and poet

Lee's early plays are based on improvisations from the period when, as drama officer, he worked with groups across Jamaica. He has worked in radio and television, producing (live) and directing his plays, *Paid in Full* (1965) and *Born for the Sea* (1962–5). In 1988 he received the Institute of Jamaica's Silver Musgrave Medal. Also an actor and poet, Lee was educated in Jamaica, thereafter studying theatre in the USA and communications in the UK. His first book of poetry, *From Behind the Counter: poems from a rural Jamaican experience*, was published in 1998.

PAT DUNN AND PAMELA MORDECAI

Lee, John Robert

b. 1948, St Lucia

Poet and teacher

A graduate of the **University of the West Indies**, Jamaica, Lee worked for several years in theatre, radio and television. Since 1979 he has been active in the Christian Ministry, teaching, preaching and writing a weekly Christian column for the main local newspaper. His collections of poetry include: *Vocation*, 1975; *Dread Season*, 1978; *The Prodigal*, 1983; and *Possessions*, 1984, *Saint Lucian*, 1988 and *Clearing Ground*, 1991. Lee is also a drama critic and librarian; he has compiled a bibliography of Saint Lucian literature.

KEITH JARDIM

Lee, Rita (Rita Lee Jones)

b. 1947, São Paulo, Brazil

Singer and songwriter

A pioneer in Brazilian rock, Rita Lee, descended from Confederate inmigrants to Brazil, was the lead singer for the experimental rock group, Os **Mutantes**, which participated in the *tropicalista* movement of the late 1960s. Her high-pitched, ethereal voice, occasionally erupting into rock histrionics, was well-suited to the ironic surrealism of the band's lyrics. After leaving Os Mutantes in 1973, she developed a successful solo career with the pop rock band, Tutti Frutti, and later with Roberto de Carvalho. During the 1990s, she continued to compose and record popular rock songs which combined social criticism with upbeat humour.

CHRISTOPHER DUNN

Leeuwen, Willem Christiaan Jacobus van

b. 1922, Curaçao, Netherlands Antilles

Writer

A practising lawyer in Venezuela and Curaçao, in 1947 van Leeuwen (nicknamed Boeli) made his literary debut as a poet, but soon turned to prose writing in Dutch. He is the author of five novels, which address the position of white creole elites and interracial relationships in Antillean society, such as in *De rots der struikeling* (The Rock of Offence) (1959), which is also available in Spanish as *La piedra de la tropieza* (1964). His later novels, including *Het teken van Jona* (The Sign of Jonah) (1988), show a preoccupation with social outcasts and their struggles to survive.

AART G. BROEK

Leeward Islands

Term used for the eastern Caribbean islands lying between Puerto Rico and Guadeloupe, including the latter island but not including Puerto Rico. The US Virgin Islands are also excluded. The British Virgin Islands are included only sometimes. The term originated in the seventeenth century among British colonists who used it to describe certain eastern Caribbean islands in terms of prevailing winds and sailing patterns from the main British colony at Barbados. The term acquired political meaning in 1871 with the creation of the British colony of the Leeward Islands: Saint Kitts, Nevis, Anguilla, Antigua, Barbuda, Montserrat and Dominica, all administered by a single governor. This federation colony lasted until 1956. (Dominica was transferred out of the group in 1940.) In the late twentieth century, the term became principally a geographic one used, often vaguely, to describe the northern part of the arc of eastern Caribbean islands.

ROSANNE ADDERLEY

Legião Urbana

One of the few rock bands from the 1980s Brazilian new wave to remain faithful to British pop influences, Legião Urbana disbanded in 1996 after its lead singer and composer Renato Russo (Renato Manfredine, Jr) died of AIDS at the age of thirty-six. Unlike **Cazuza**'s angry, almost heroic struggle against the disease, Russo's last years were characterized by the media as depressed and suicidal. Russo's long, narrative lyrics reveal a dark and dispassionate approach to subjects as diverse as Brazilian politics and impossible love stories. His solo album, *The Stonewall Celebration Concert* (1993), listed national gay and lesbian organizations. The band's 1996 record *A Tempestade* (The Tempest) was its last.

CESAR BRAGA-PINTO

Legorreta, Ricardo

b. 1931, Mexico City

Architect

One of Mexico's most important architects, Legoretta has an international reputation. His work has been based on a study of traditional Mexican architecture, with its rich colours and use of varied materials. His technical skill and knowledge owe much to his early experience in the workshop of the pioneer of Mexican functionalism, José **Villagrán García**, with whom he worked between 1948 and 1960, first as a draughtsman, then as head of the studio and ultimately as a partner. An outstanding example of their work is the Hotel María Isabel in Mexico City, built in the international style in 1961–2 in collaboration with Villagrán and Juan Sordo. He also absorbed the influence of Luis **Barragán** and Mathias **Goeritz**, advocates of what was called 'emotional' architecture. His own distinguishing characteristics are a synthesis of these different elements in a unique formal expression expressed in both living spaces and large-scale buildings.

His early works, in the international style, include the Celanese Mexicana building (1966–8), with its daring technologies. A few years later, he developed a more personal style exemplified in the Hotel Camino Real in Mexico City, built in 1968. Legorreta went on to design a number of other hotels for the same chain in Cancún, Quintana Roo (1975) and the Ixtapa in Zihuatenejo (1981), both of which are in perfect harmony with their surroundings.

He has also made a major contribution to industrial architecture in Mexico, as in the IBM factory in Guadalajara, Jalisco (1975) and the Renault works in Gómez Palacio, Durango (1983). He also has several important office developments to his name, including the offices of Seguros América Banamex in Mexico City (1975–7), as well as the Museum of Contemporary Art in Monterrey (1971) and Managua Cathedral, Nicaragua (1992).

Legorreta's private practice, Legorreta Asociados, with Noé Castro and Carlos Vargas, also began in 1977 to design furniture and accessories, as all their work was conceived as an integral whole whose colour schemes and furnishings were incorporated into the whole scheme. These principles apply equally to private housing, commercial buildings and hotels, where Legoretta employs stone, clay, wood, leather and craft textiles and carpets.

Further reading

Noelle, L. (1989) *Ricardo Legorreta: tradición y modernidad*, Mexico City: Coordinación de Humanidades, Universidad Nacional Autónoma de México.

LOURDES CRUZ GONZÁLEZ FRANCO

Legrand, Mirtha

b. 1927, Villa Cañás, Argentina

Actress

Legrand (real name Rosa Martínez Suárez) had her first starring role was in 1941, in Francisco **Múgica**'s melodrama *Los martes orquídeas* (Orchids on Tuesdays). She became the prototypical ingenue of the expanding national film industry, and spurred the passions of millions throughout Latin America. Married in 1946 to director Daniel **Tinayre**, she became a star and appeared in many films spanning all genres. After retiring from the cinema Legrand became a fixture on television, presenting through most of the 1980s the classic lunchtime show *Almorzando con Mirtha Legrand* (Lunch with Mirtha Legrand), which remains the most coveted public platform for Argentina's artistic and political world.

DIEGO BENTIVEGNA

Leguisamo, Irineo

b. 1903, Salto, Uruguay; d. 1985, Buenos Aires, Argentina

Jockey

Uruguayan-born top jockey who won over 3,000 classic races at the peak of **horse racing**'s popularity in South America. Leguisamo's career began in Uruguay but culminated in Buenos Aires where his talent earned him the respect and affection of both elite landowners and the lower classes. The athlete's status as a friend and rider for the great tango singer Carlos **Gardel** reinforced his immense popularity among horse racing fans. Leguisamo is widely considered the best South American rider of the twentieth century.

THOMAS EDSALL

Leguizamon, (Gustavo) Cuchi

b. 1917, Salta, Argentina

Musician

An outstanding folk artist, Leguizamon was also a penal lawyer, a professor of literature and history in the Salta College, a congressman, journalist and playwright. Most importantly, he was a poet, a pianist and the director of a number of folk song groups. A leading figure in Argentine music, his works include classics like 'Zamba de Lozano', 'Zamba del laurel', 'Balderrama', 'Zamba de Anta' and 'Chacarera del Chaco'. He founded the Dúo Salteño, collaborated with composer Manuel **Castilla**, musician Jaime Dávalos and poet César Pedriguero, and with the poet's permission set Pablo **Neruda**'s poem 'La muerta' (The Dead Woman) to music.

CLAUDIA TORRE

Leirner, Jac

b. 1961, São Paulo, Brazil

Visual artist

One of the most promising of Brazil's contemporary artists, Leirner's work has already been exhibited in Brazil, Europe and the United States. Her work is rated for its originality; her final products are always novel, new and unexpected. She works with materials that are available in everyday life: disposable consumer objects like cigarette stubs (which she smokes), old banknotes, ashtrays taken from planes, envelopes and leaflets. Through an ingenious technique of montage, or what might be called cultural recycling, the objects are transformed into sculptures and works of art.

VIVALDO SANTOS

Leites, Víctor Manuel

b. 1933, Paysandú, Uruguay

Playwright

In the 1960s Leites wrote television scripts, before moving to theatre with *Informe para distraídos* (A Report for the Distracted) (1968). There followed *Historia de bien nacidos* (Story of the Well Born) (1972), *Quiroga* (1979), *Doña Ramona* (1982), a successful adaptation of José Pedro Bellán's novel of the same name, *El chalet de Gardel* (**Gardel**'s house) (1985), *El reformador* (The Reformer) (1990) and *El copamiento* (1996). He was Artistic Director of the **Comedia Nacional** on three different occasions.

MARCO MAGGI

Lejos del nido

Lejos del nido (Far from the Nest) was an exceedingly popular novel by Juan José Botero of low literary quality published in 1924, and made into radio and television soap operas (see **radionovelas** and **telenovelas**) between the 1960s and 1983. It tells the story of the abduction of a toddler, the daughter of rich, white, Roman Catholic land owners, by poor and repulsive Indians who lived nearby by virtue of a government land grant. Traditionally considered a '*costumbrista* novel' with an idyllic love story, the captive girl ends up marrying a white suitor of her own social class as opposed to the Indian one. It represents one of the louder voices against the deterioration of the rural, white, *criollo*, land-owner power of the old Spanish tradition and against the empowerment of peoples of non-European origin.

ÁLVARO FÉLIX BOLAÑOS

Leloir, Luis Federico

b. 1905, Paris, France; d. 1988, Buenos Aires, Argentina

Scientist

A student of Bernardo **Houssay**, Leloir studied medicine in Argentina and later in Cambridge, where he worked for two years in the biochemical laboratory. From then on, he specialized in research into the properties of sugar. In 1947, returning from the USA, he founded the Institute of Biochemical Research, the Campomar Foundation, with the support of industry. It became a leading centre of research excellence in biochemistry as well as molecular biology. His work on saccharides earned Leloir the Nobel Prize for Chemistry in 1970 (see **Nobel Prizes**).

PABLO KREIMER

Lemebel, Pedro

b. 1952, Santiago, Chile

Writer and performance artist

Lemebel set out to legitimize homosexuality in Chile through writing and public performances. In 1987 he and Francisco Casas formed Las **Yeguas del Apocalipsis**. His first book, *Incontables* (Tales Not to Be Told) (1986), presents writing as a transvestite act which displaces homosexual desire. In his urban *crónicas* (see **crónica**) *La esquina es mi corazón* (My Heart is the Street Corner) (1995), a postmodern *flâneur* walks the city, exposing the underlying poverty and social marginalization behind its neoliberal facade. Gay people from poor suburbs become tragic kitsch symbols of waste and injustice. *Loco afán* (Crazy Eagerness) (1996) depicts **AIDS** victims in Chile.

LUCÍA GUERRA

Lemoine, Bob

b. 1942, Port-au-Prince, Haiti

Film-maker

An important figure in the development of Haitian cinema, Lemoine was director and producer for Clairimage, the country's first production company with facilities for 35mm film-making. He directed the first Haitian-made 35mm feature film, *Olivia* (1977) which uses the story of a young girl's journey from the underdeveloped and isolated Haitian countryside to the capital, to explore social and cultural divisions. He also directed the 35mm feature film *Echec au Silence* (Silence, Checkmate) released in 1985, and eighty-two episodes of the soap opera *Gabel*, broadcast by the commercial Haitian television station, Télé Eclair.

CHARLES ARTHUR

Leñero, Vicente

b. 1933, Guadalajara, Mexico

Writer

Although a novelist and non-fiction wirter, Leñero is best known as a principal innovator in contemporary Mexican drama. He began a distinguished career as a writer in the late 1950s, and first won recognition in 1963 when Seix Barral Publishers (Barcelona) awarded the Biblioteca Breve Prize to his novel *Los albañiles* (The Construction Workers). The novel modified the conventions of detective fiction and portrayed class tensions among a group of construction workers, an architect and a police detective assigned to investigate the murder of a nightwatchman. Although his other 1960s novels were characterized by highly self-referential narrative games, in the 1970s two other central concerns became explicit: religion and non-fiction writing. In *El evangelio de Lucas Gavilán* (The Gospel Accroding to Luke Crow) (1979), Leñero created a Mexican version of the Gospel of Luke following the tenets of **liberation theology**. In *Los periodistas* (The Journalists) (1978), he recounted his experience during the government-orchestrated ouster of Julio **Scherer García** and other journalists from the daily **Excélsior** in 1976. He has published nine novels, both fictional and 'non-fictional'.

Leñero is also the author of more than sixteen plays, often adapting his own novels. His documentary drama, *El juicio* (The Trial) (1971) was based on court transcripts and represented the 1928 trial of two Catholics for the murder of President-elect Alvaro Obregón. A later play, *Martirio de Morelos* (Morelo's Martyrdom) (1981), explored historical interpretation through the biography of the nineteenth-century Independence War patriot. *Nadie sabe nada* (No One Knows Anything) (1988), subtitled a 'thriller', used simultaneous actions on a divided stage to address the problems of Mexican journalism and political corruption. Leñero's mastery of dialogue and dramatic structure also led to cinematic collaborations. He adapted a story by Guadalupe Loayza for Alejandro Pelayo's 1993 biographical film about actress Miroslava Stern, *Miroslava*, and he set a novel by Naguib Mahfouz in contemporary

Mexico City for Jorge **Fons**'s 1996 film *El callejón de los milagros* (The Alley of Miracles).

Also an active journalist, Leñero directed the women's magazine *Claudia* (1969–72), the weekly supplement of *Revista de Revistas* for *Excélsior* (1972–6) and, with Julio Scherer García, founded the weekly magazine **Proceso**, for which he has served as associate director or vice-president since 1976.

Further reading

Anderson, D. (1989) *Vicente Leñero: The Novelist as Critic*, New York: Peter Lang.

DANNY J. ANDERSON

León, Argeliers

b. 1918, Havana, Cuba

Musicologist and composer

Professor at the Havana Conservatory and of African Arts and Black Culture at the University of Havana, León has occupied a series of key posts in the fields of ethnology and musicology in a range of Cuban institutions. He studied composition with José **Ardevol** and with Nadia Boulanger in Paris before attending the University of Chile in 1951 to study folklore and music education. He travelled widely in Europe, Africa and America, before returning to Cuba in 1961 to take up his first post at the Cuban Institute of Ethnology and Folklore. His own compositions are profoundly influenced by the Afro-Cuban musical tradition.

JOSÉ ANTONIO EVORA

León, Eugenia

b. 1956, Mexico City

Singer

The warmth and power of her voice and her charismatic stage presence have made Eugenia León one of the best-known singers of recent years. Her varied repertoire includes popular songs, 'canto nuevo', tangos (see **tango**) and **danzóns**. Beginning as a member of the Víctor **Jara** group (1974) and of Sanampay (1980), she began her solo career in 1982, performing the work of composers like Marcial **Alejandro**, José Elorza, Jaime López and David **Haro**. She has released fifteen albums and has appeared at a number of music festivals including OTI International, Mexico's Cervantino, Varadero in Cuba and the Latino International Festival in New York.

EDUARDO CONTRERAS SOTO

León-Portilla, Miguel

b. 1926, Mexico City

Historian

Preeminent Náhuatl historian (see **Náhuatl and Aztecan languages**) and human rights advocate, Miguel León-Portilla has made a career of making the voices and thoughts of late pre-Hispanic and early colonial indigenous Mexico heard and felt. Continuing an emphasis on Aztec philosophy and thought pioneered by Angel María **Garibay**, León-Portilla has translated numerous key Náhuatl poetic and other texts – most famously in his *Visión de los vencidos* (translated as *The broken spears*) (1959). A 1956 doctoral thesis on Aztec thought began a series of works which explore the Aztec experience, including Aztec descriptions of the Spanish Conquest, culminating most recently in a 1995 study of the impact of the Mixtec Uprising in the formation of Spanish perceptions of the essential humanity of Native America. León-Portilla has long advocated the cultural and linguistic rights of Mexico's remaining indigenous peoples, favouring a pluricultural national vision.

CHRIS VON NAGY

Lerner, Elisa

b. 1932, Valencia, Venezuela

Writer

A member of the **Sardio** group, Lerner's prose is among the most elegant and caustic in contemporary Venezuelan literature. Writer of a number of successful plays, especially *Vida con mamá* (Life with Mother) (1975), Lerner is the most cultured and merciless chronicler of post-**Pérez Jiménez** Venezuela. Her reviews and *crónicas* (see **crónica**) use apparently trivial events and issues to draw a critical map of contemporary reality. *Una sonrisa detrás de la metáfora* (The Smile behind the Metaphor) (1969), *Yo amo a Columbo* (I Love Columbo) (1983) and *Cronicas ginecológicas* (Gynaecological Chronicles) (1984) are samples of her way of seeing and describing Venezuela.

RAFAEL CASTILLO ZAPATA

lesbian literature

Lesbian literature as a genre is a recent addition to literary studies, although its literary practice is not. Like most issues related to homosexuality, it had been forbidden or 'in the closet'; however, lesbian writing is coming out strongly through the publication of texts and the attention of contemporary readers and scholars. Partly as one of the many paradigmatic shifts spurred by feminist scholarship in the humanities, lesbian literature engages authors, readers, fictional characters and language itself in a discussion around homosexuality, whether the problematics are the inscription of ambiguity in suppressing sexual identity as dictated by cultural heterosexual norms, bringing out unexposed homosexual identities, or confronting sexual identities in the interaction of private and public spheres.

Still at the early stages of its development as a genre, lesbian literature has gained recognition as an important expressive system, mainly by the quality of the fiction and poetry abundantly produced and published in recent years. Excellent representative works of lesbian literature are *En breve cárcel* (Certificate of Absence) (1989) by Argentine novelist and critic Sylvia **Molloy**; the fiction and poetry of Cristina **Peri Rossi**, from Uruguay; the work of Puerto Rican poet and literary critic Luz María **Umpierre**; the writings of Alejandra **Pizarnik**; *La rompiente* (The Breakwater) (1987), and *Monte de Venus* (Mount of Venus) by Reina Roffé; the poetry of Magaly Alabau, Ana Cristina **César** and Nancy Cárdenas, and the novels of Rosamaría Roffiel. In addition to studies of lesbian literature published in the last quarter of the twentieth century, a new and important development in this field of inquiry is the rereading of canonical women of letters whose lesbianism was denied or never addressed. Two examples of the latter are recent critical writing on Gabriela **Mistral**, and Teresa **de la Parra**.

Among the issues that are of concern to lesbian literature are the construction of the lesbian body, the erotic function of the female gaze, the fear of dismemberment, lesbianism and exile, homosexuality and Latin American identity, cross-dressing, lesbian subjectivity and self-figuration, and lesbian representation.

Further reading

Balderston, D. and Guy, D. (ed.) (1997) *Sex and Sexuality in Latin America*, New York: New York University Press.

Bergmann, E.L. and Smith, P.J. (eds) (1995) *¿Entiendes? Queer Readings, Hispanic Writings*, Durham, NC: Duke University Press.

Foster, D.W. (1991) *Gay and Lesbian Themes in Latin American Writing*, Austin, TX: University of Texas Press.

Martínez, E.M. (1996) *Lesbian Voices from Latin America*, New York: Garland.

MAGDALENA GARCÍA PINTO

Lesser Antilles

Term used to describe the eastern Caribbean islands ranging from Puerto Rico to Trinidad and Tobago. The categorization does not include Puerto Rico, but does include the islands of Trinidad and Tobago. Also included are the islands of Aruba, Curaçao and Bonaire, located north of Venezuela's Caribbean coast. The term Lesser Antilles distinguishes this group from the **Greater Antilles** which are the four largest islands of the Caribbean region: Cuba, Jamaica, Hispaniola and Puerto Rico. The islands of the Bahamas and also Bermuda are usually considered a part of the Caribbean but are not included in either the Greater or Lesser Antilles designations.

ROSANNE ADDERLEY

Letelier Llona, Alfonso

b. 1912, Santiago, Chile; d. 1994, Santiago, Chile

Composer

With **Orrego-Salas** and others, he founded the Escuela Moderna de Música (Modern School of Music) in 1940. As a composer, his early work combined romantic and impressionist elements with Chilean folk music, while his work of the 1950s betrays the influence of German expressionism and neo-classicism. His more than seventy works range from his *Vida de campo* (Country Life) for piano and orchestra to the *Tres sonetos de la muerte* (Three Sonnets of Death), with texts by Gabriela **Mistral**, and to the *Fünf Anekdoten* for musical ensemble.

ALFONSO PADILLA

Levrero, Mario (Jorge Varlotta)

b. 1940, Montevideo, Uruguay

Writer

A writer educated in the marginal genres – **science fiction**, **crime fiction**, serials – Levrero was influenced by Lewis Carroll, the surrealists and Felisberto **Hernández**. His fictions centre around the permanent transformations of space and objects (as in 'Capítulo XXX' (Chapter XXX), winner of the 1984 Más Allá Prize or 'La máquina de pensar de Gladys' (Gladys's Thinking Machine) (1970)), and on non-linear time, as in the stories of *Todo el tiempo* (All The Time) (1982). *Nick Carter* (1975), a novel published under his own name, parodies serials and detective novels.

SANDRA GASPARINI

Lewis, W. Arthur

b. 1915, St Lucia; d. 1991, Barbados

Economist

Lewis is a much-cited economist responsible for original insights into rural-based economics. His *Theory of Economic Growth* (1955) was the first study to examine the developmental problems of post-colonial territories. Other works are *The Principles of Economic Planning* (1950) and *Economic Survey* (1949). Lewis studied in England, and in 1962 he became the first Vice Chancellor of the **University of the West Indies**. He held many international consultancies, and was knighted in 1963 for his ground-breaking work. Full recognition came in 1979 when he shared the Nobel Prize for Economics with Theodore Schultz (see **Nobel Prizes**).

KEITH JARDIM

Ley, La

The five-member Chilean rock band La Ley released its first record, *Desiertos* (Deserts), in 1989. Other records include *Doble Opuesto* (Double Opposite) (1991), *La Ley* (The Law) (1993), *Cara de Dios* (Face of God) (1994) and *Invisible* (1995). Lead singer and songwriter Alberto Cuevas grew up in Venezuela and Canada, and trained as a graphic designer. He is responsible for the group's sophisticated visual image, a principal component of its style and success. The band has performed extensively in Mexico, and has been located there for long periods, in its increasingly successful attempt to gain international recognition.

AMALIA PEREIRA

Lezama Lima, José

b. 1910, Havana, Cuba; d. 1976, Havana

Poet, novelist and essayist

A major poet and one of the most original thinkers Latin America has produced, Lezama is best known for his neo-baroque novel ***Paradiso*** (1966). His work, known for its ludic sensuality and allusive density, was also a model of hermeticism, influencing many younger writers such as Severo **Sarduy**. His analyses of Latin American culture, in the essays of *La **expresión americana*** (American Expression) (1957), are a fundamental contribution to the debate on Latin American identity, while his ideas on aesthetics, which he termed a 'poetic system of the world', comprise a complex if fragmentary philosophy.

Lezama Lima led a life of apparent tranquillity and simplicity, never straying far from his native Havana. His family was middle class; his father was a military man who rose to the rank of colonel in the Cuban army before his untimely death at the age of thirty-three. The young, asthmatic Lezama turned early to literature, and was a precocious reader. The loss of his father marked the young boy indelibly; much of his subsequent work, in particular *Paradiso*, can be seen as a creative response to the absence of the father. Lezama graduated with a law degree from the University of Havana and worked for some time at a Havana prison. After the Cuban Revolution he became vice president of the **UNEAC**, the Cuban Union of Writers and Artists, and later worked in a library. He lived with his mother until her death in 1964, then married a close family friend who cared for him until his death in 1976. Lezama was widely known to be homosexual; sexuality in general is central to his work, and the issue of homosexuality is the subject of several important passages of both *Paradiso* and its continuation, *Oppiano Licario* (1977).

Belying its calm exterior, Lezama's life was one of great intellectual activity and creation. Beginning in the late 1930s and continuing over the next twenty years, he edited a series of literary magazines culminating in ***Orígenes*** (1944–56), one of the most important journals of its time in the Spanish-speaking world. It published original contributions from authors worldwide, and was also a cohesive forum for an extended group of Cuban writers, musicians and artists, most of whom shared a certain belief – albeit unorthodox in the case of Lezama – in Catholicism. Lezama himself first burst upon the Cuban literary scene with *Muerte de Narciso* (Death of Narcissus) (1937), a long poem which startled readers with its lush images and Gongorist syntax. He followed with *Enemigo rumor* (Enemy Rumour) (1941), *Aventuras sigilosas* (Discreet Adventures) (1945) and *La Fijeza* (Fixity) (1949), this latter containing a series of important prose poems providing an early glimpse of the 'poetic system'. *Dador* (Giver) (1960) contains some of his most arcane and philosophical poems, influenced by his readings in world religion and mythology, while his posthumous *Fragmentos a su imán* (Fragments to His Magnet) (1977) includes his most direct and moving poetry. The publication of *Paradiso* – a semi-autobiographical *bildungsroman*, or novel of education – created a scandal in Cuba due to its baroque complexity and erotic passages, and earned Lezama a central place among the authors of the '**Boom**' in Latin American narrative. Lezama also published four books of essays, among them the important *La expresión americana*.

In the 1940s and 1950s, Lezama and the other writers and artists of *Orígenes* attempted to create an autonomous realm for art, seeing that cultural activity as a form of Utopian resistance to the dictatorial regime of Fulgencio **Batista**, under whom governmental corruption and political violence flourished. After the 1959 Revolution, however, many leftist critics accused the *Orígenes* writers of escapism. Lezama's own relationship with the Revolutionary government – problematic during the decade of the 1960s – took a turn for the worse after the **Padilla** Affair of 1971. Named for supposedly counter-revolutionary attitudes in Heberto Padilla's 'self-critique', Lezama was largely prohibited from publishing in the years leading to his death. He was only 'recuperated' officially by the Cuban government in the late 1980s and 1990s; one sign of this change in the official attitude is his treatment in the film ***Fresa y chocolate*** (Strawberry and Chocolate) (1993), where he figures as the gay protagonist's most important cultural hero.

Lezama Lima's 'poetic system', not a traditional philosophical system but a collection of ideas and quotations from diverse sources, views the world through the lens of aesthetics, privileging the irrational and the idea of a poetic causality. The most novel aspect of this system is Lezama's idea of the 'imaginary era', where he attempted to articulate a necessary relation between artistic creations and society, and to offer a new way of thinking about history. Lezama's poetic system is complemented by his reflection upon American cultural identity, what he called 'American expression', centring on his notion of the American Baroque as a hybrid product of a dialogue between European, African and New World cultures.

Further reading

Cruz-Malavé, A. (1994) *El primitivo implorante: el 'sistema poético del mundo' de José Lezama Lima*, Amsterdam: Rodopi.

Heller, B. (1997) *Assimilation/Generation/Resurrection: Contrapuntal Readings in the Poetry of José Lezama Lima*, Lewisburg, PA: Bucknell.

Levinson, B. (1996) *Secondary Moderns: Mimesis, History, and Revolution in Lezama Lima's 'American Expression'*, Lewisburg, PA: Bucknell.

Lezama Lima, J. (1975–7) *Obras completas*, Mexico: Aguilar.

—— (1974) *Paradiso*, trans. G. Rabassa, New York: Farrar, Straus and Giroux.

Pellón, G. (1989) *José Lezama Lima's Joyful Vision*, Austin, TX: University of Texas Press.

BEN A. HELLER

Lézarde, La

La lézarde (The Ripening) is the first novel by Edouard **Glissant**, previously known for his poetry, and winner of the Prix Renaudot in 1958. Written during the heyday of the *nouveau roman*, it is Glissant's most conventional novel and inaugurates a series of narratives with recurring characters and dealing with Martiniquan society, landscape and history. Based on Aimé **Césaire**'s 1945 election campaign, the plot centres on a group of political activists who hire a stranger to kill an assassin who threatens to upset their candidate's victory. Very much a poet's novel, it is less about politics than the group's self-discovery in a landscape dominated by the winding folds of the Lézarde river.

J. MICHAEL DASH

Liano, Dante

b. 1948, Chimaltenango, Guatemala

Writer and critic

A founding member of the writers' publishing group RIN-78, Liano has published an impressive collection of stories and two novels. The first, *El lugar de su quietud* (The Place of Quietness) (1989), is an experimental treatment of several events in Guatemalan history; the second, *L'uomo di Montserrat* (The Man from Monserrat) (1994), is the Italian version of Liano's only recently published Spanish-language novel dealing with military-guerrilla conflicts. Among his critical works, *La palabra y el sueño: Literatura y sociedad en Guatemala* (Word and Dream: Literature and Society in Guatemala) (1984) is a major study of national literature. He lives in Italy, where he teaches and edits the journal *Centroamericana*.

MARC ZIMMERMAN

Liautaud, Georges

b. 1899, Croix-des-Bouquets, Haiti; d. 1991, Croix-des-Bouquets

Metal sculptor

A blacksmith by trade, Liautaud also forged iron bells and pots for use in **Vodun** rituals, and decorative iron crosses for graves in the cemetery of Croix-des-Bouquets. In the early 1950s, he began producing free-standing metal sculptures for display in the Centre d'Art in Port-au-Prince. His sculptures portray moments from ceremonial **Vodun** and temple life, and depict representations of the *lwa* (Vodun spirits). The originator of Haitian metal sculpture, Liautaud's legacy lives on in his hometown where a flourishing community of sculptors create reliefs hammered from recycled metal oil drums.

CHARLES ARTHUR

liberation theology

Liberation theology stems from the conviction that giving priority to the poor and oppressed in theology and in the Church and the concrete defence of their rights in different societies is a central element of Christian faith. Liberation theology aims its critical analysis not only at society but at theology and the Church, in order to judge to what extent they are accomplices in maintaining the status quo, especially where it comes to basic human rights.

For centuries, the Catholic Church was one of the pillars of Spanish power in America. It was only in the twentieth century that the intimate connection between the church and the state began to crack. The circumstances that made liberation theology possible have long roots in history. Nevertheless, there are some more immediate secular and ecclesial causes.

The general conflictive atmosphere and the rise of authoritarian military dictatorships throughout Latin America in the 1960s and 1970s created extreme conditions in which the church could no longer remain indifferent to deepening poverty and violations of **human rights**. The Cuban Revolution of 1959 (see **revolutions**) was a source of inspiration for many who no longer believed in the postwar developmentalist populist project (see **development**). One of the earliest symbols for the new role of the church and theologians was Camilo **Torres**, the Colombian priest-guerrilla who died in combat in 1966. More moderate voices in the Catholic Church also started to question the political and economic situation in the continent. An influential theory behind liberation theology is **dependency theory**; early liberation theological jargon stressed that Latin America was dependent not only economically and politically but intellectually and theologically as well.

This belief was a partial result of global changes in the Catholic Church since the Second Vatican Council (1962–5). The 'opening' to the world, including social conflicts, was not only one of the focuses of the Council but of various papal encyclicals as well. New forms of theology were born which tried to respond to modern social questions; political theology, theology of hope and theology of revolution were among the most influential. Ecumenically, the World Council of Churches urged churches to take the lead on issues of social justice.

Liberation theology in Latin America has been ecumenical since its beginning, though the historical weight of Catholicism is of central importance. Institutionally, the second general meeting of Latin American Bishops' Conference (**CELAM**) in Medellín in 1968 (see **Medellín Conference**) was a key moment in the progress of the church towards becoming 'a church of the poor'. The first writings on liberation theology appeared soon after the Medellín Conference by authors such as Gustavo **Gutiérrez**, Leonardo **Boff**, Juan Luis **Segundo**, Enrique **Dussel**, Hugo Assmann and Pablo Richard, all from the Catholic tradition. The first Protestant liberation theologians included Rubem **Alves**, Julio de Santa Ana, José Míguel Bonino and Elsa **Tamez**.

At the grassroots level, priests, pastors, nuns and laypersons started to work with the poorest urban and rural people. In many regions, the ecclesiastical base communities (*comunidades eclesiales de base*, or CEBs) became the *primus motor* of the changes taking place in the church. Lay participation, Biblical interpretation and social activism went hand in hand. The local CEBs played an important role in the **Sandinista Revolution**, for example. In the 1990s, the influence of the CEBs was drastically diminished, as they lost members to the **Pentecostals** and other new non-Catholic churches and sects.

Theologically, what all liberation theologies have in common is a methodology that gives priority to practical issues over the classical 'over-metaphysical' Western theology. According to Gustavo Gutiérrez, liberation theology is 'a critical reflection on praxis in the light of the Word of God'. There is clear Marxist influence in liberation theologians' understanding of praxis, although the Vatican's fear that liberation theology is Marxism (see **Marxism in Latin America**) camouflaged as theology, a fear shared by the right in the USA, is exaggerated.

Liberation theologians use social science as the most accurate means of understanding society and its conflicts. Theology is the 'second step,' which addresses all the classical questions, such as God, Christ, sin and grace, and the church. New themes and issues began to arise during the 1990s, among them a growing dialogue between economics and theology, ecology and theology, the critique and reinterpretations of feminist liberation theologians (see **feminist liberation theology**), black liberation theology (especially in Brazil and the Caribbean) and the question of indigenous religions versus Christianity.

There are different phases and generations of liberation theology, as well as changes and internal disagreements. One of the major questions in the future will no doubt be the relation to the institutional church and its teaching, involving issues like sexual ethics, the hierarchical model of the church, the situation of women and papal authority.

The latest developments seem to point towards a crucial shift in the discourse and influence of liberation theology. On the one hand, the Catholic church as an institution moved onto a more traditional, conservative track. On the other hand, the political scene of the continent is drastically different from that of the 1970s, including the effects of post-Cold War political changes in international relations. Nevertheless, the ever deepening poverty and the globalization of the market economy raise both old and new questions. Liberation theologians will have to be both self-critical and attentive to these changes if they are to maintain their critical position towards the church and society. Because of the tremendous historical, cultural and moral importance of the Catholic Church in Latin America, the question of its future direction is of great importance. One concern that liberation theologians and the Vatican share is how to respond to the rapid growth of **Protestantism** and its appeal to the people in the continent.

Further reading

Boff, L. and Boff, C. (1987) *Introducing Liberation Theology*, New York: Orbis Books.

Ellacuría, I. and Sobrino, J. (eds) (1991) *Mysterium Liberationis. Conceptos fundamentales de la teología de la liberación*, San Salvador: UCA Editores.

Gutiérrez, G. (1973) *A Theology of Liberation: History, Politics, and Salvation*, New York: Orbis Books.

Keogh, D. (ed.) (1990) *Church and Politics in Latin America*, New York: St Martin's Press.

McGovern, A.F. (1989) *Liberation Theology and Its Critics: Toward an Assessment*, New York: Orbis Books.

Thistlethwaite, S.B. and Engel, M.P. (eds) (1990) *Lift Every Voice: Constructing Christian Theologies from the Underside*, San Francisco: Harper & Row.

ELINA VUOLA

libraries

There are three types of libraries in Latin America: national, university and private. Almost every country in Latin America has a national library, but the size of the collection and the quality of the facilities vary greatly from country to country. While Argentina and Mexico have the largest national libraries, which are open to the public, countries with lower literacy rates do not have such extensive collections. Initially established with government funds, national-library budgets have decreased in recent years and the collections have diminished due to excessive handling, loss and theft. Numerous university libraries exist in Latin America, but Argentina's Universidad de Buenos Aires (UAB) and Mexico's Universidad Autónoma de México (**UNAM**) are the largest and most well-established facilities. University libraries are often divided according to specialization and each university, school or college maintains its own library. Generally, university libraries are spread out geographically and do not exist in a centralized location.

One of the most unique phenomena in Latin America is the private library. Established by individual collectors or foundations, private collections are often closed to the public and available only through special invitation. Some have very limited hours. All are highly volatile and, if operating without State support, subject to sudden extinction due to economic constraints. While some private collections are donated either to national or university libraries, many private collections continue to be maintained autonomously. It is difficult to know the exact number of private libraries in Latin America since they are administered independently. Currently, many national and university libraries offer their catalogues via the Internet, but these efforts are individual and isolated. A global effort to link libraries and their catalogues has yet to be achieved.

MARCIE D. RINKA

libreta *see* ration book

Lier, Rudolf van

b. 1914, Suriname; d. 1987, Netherlands

Historian and poet

Author of a widely acclaimed social historical study of Suriname, *Samenleving in een grensgebied* (A Borderline Society) (1949), van Lier studied sociology and history in the Netherlands, Paris and the USA. From the 1930s on, he also wrote lyrical poetry, traditional in metre and imagery and meticulous in style, which was partly collected in the 1974 publication *Rupturen* (Ruptures).

AART G. BROEK

Liera, Oscar

b. 1946, Culiacán, Sinaloa, Mexico; d. 1990, Culiacán

Playwright

Liera's plays orchestrated rich theatrical tapestries involving many, complex characters and intricate plots; most revolved around controversial political and religious themes, incuding the corruption of the **PRI** and gay sexuality. In 1981, after right-wing protesters interrupted a Mexico City performance of *Cúcara y Mácara*, a play lampooning the legend of the Virgin of Guadalupe (see **Virgins, miraculous**), and brutally attacked cast and director, Liera left Mexico City for his native Culiacán. There he founded the TATUAS (Theatre Workshop of the Autonomous University of Sinaloa), transforming it into the best regional university theatre troupe of the 1980s. Liera's major plays include *Fábulas perversas* (Perverse Fables) (1984), *Etcétera* (1985), *El jinete de la Divina Providencia* (The Horseman of Divine Providence) (1988), and his most widely acclaimed production, *Dulces compañias* (Sweet Companions) (1988).

CYNTHIA STEELE

Lihn, Enrique

b. 1929, Santiago, Chile; d. 1988, Santiago, Chile

Writer

Known primarily as a poet, though he wrote narrative and drama as well, Lihn's work falls within a frame of '**antipoetry**': or at least what he himself called 'a poetry sceptical of itself'. His poem, 'Porque escribí' (Because I Wrote), from the collection, *Poesía de paso* (Poetry in Passing) (1966), is a sort of anti-manifesto, a gentle self-parody of the poet as hero. The conversational language adds to the irony of his writing – for his protagonists are fragile, vulnerable beings. An experimental artist, Lihn was often involved in performance poetry and organized encounters between different sorts of text. Remaining in Chile after the 1973 *coup*, his satire became far darker in the context of repression, as in *El Paseo Ahumada* (Ahumada Avenue) (1983) and the texts gathered posthumously in *Diario de muerte* (Death diary) (1989).

MIKE GONZALEZ

Lima, Attilio Correa

b. 1901, Rome, Italy; d. 1943, Rio de Janeiro, Brazil

Architect

A representative of Brazilian architectural modernism (see **Brazilian modernism**), in 1925 Lima won the scholarship awarded by the Escola Nacional de Belas Artes (National School of Fine Arts) to study at the Paris Institut d'Urbanisme headed by Donat-Alfred Agache. He developed the design for the city of Goiânia with Armando Godoy, and designed the Estação de Hidroaviões (the Seaplane Station) built in Rio de Janeiro in 1937–8.

MARÍA MARTA CAMISASSA

Lima, Jorge de

b. 1895, União, Alagoas, Brazil; d. 1953, Rio de Janeiro, Brazil

Writer

Although he also wrote novels, Lima is best known as a poet. His early verses were symbolist and parnassian, but in the 1920s he assimilated the innovations of **Brazilian modernism**. His major preoccupation was the search for spiritual values exemplified in his religious poetry, including *Tempo e eternidade* (Time and Eternity) (1935). His most popular work is the more accessible *negrista* poetry (see **negrismo**) celebrating the vivacity of Afro-Brazilian culture such as *Poemas negros* (Black Poems) (1947).

MARK DINNEEN

Lima Jr, Walter

b. 1938, Niterói, Brazil

Film-maker

Lima joined the **Cinema Novo** movement as assistant director on Glauber **Rocha**'s *Deus e o Diabo na terra do sol* (Black God, White Devil) (1964). His *Brasil Ano 2000* (1967–8) followed the allegorical precepts of *tropicalismo*; his subsequent films explored a range of aesthetic options. His more ambitious works addressed the Brazilian political and cultural context, while other films recreated fictional worlds drawn from legend and myth. He has adapted several literary works, including Lins do **Rego**'s *Menino do engenho* (Plantation Boy) (1965) and Moacir Lopes's *A ostra e o vento* (The Oyster and the Wind) (1996).

ISMAIL XAVIER AND THE USP GROUP

Limite

Limite (Limit) (1930) is a classic Brazilian experimental silent film about two women and a man cast adrift in a boat on the open sea, whose individual stories, told in flashbacks, show them to have been always adrift in endless misencounters. What is most amazing about *Limite* is its style, which pushed narrative film-making to its limits. Influenced by the French avant-garde of the 1920s, Mário **Peixoto** places the film's abstract characters in a symbolic landscape, lyrically evoking their states of mind through montage and photographic composition. *Limite* is an exploration of nature's indifference to human beings. The film acquired a mythical status as a great masterpiece, although few had seen it until its restoration fifty years later.

ISMAIL XAVIER AND THE USP GROUP

Limón, José

b. 1908, Culiacán, Mexico; d. 1972, New York, USA

Dancer and choreographer

Limón injected a new dynamism into male dancing and brought to his influential choreography a powerful sense of drama. Originally an art student in Los Angeles, he moved to New York where he was inspired to become a dancer by the German expressionists, Harald Kreutzberg and Yvonne Georgi. In 1946 he formed his own company, which almost immediately became one of the USA's leading dance ensembles. His most famous work, *The Moor's Pavane*, conveyed the powerful emotions of Shakespeare's Othello through the medium of a stately court dance. He later taught at the Juillard School of Dance and the Lincoln Center's American Dance Center. His ideas are continued through the Limón Dance Company, the Limón Institute in New York, who train young dancers, and the Limón West Dance Company, based in San José, California.

MIKE GONZALEZ

Linares, Omar

b. 1967, Pinar del Río, Cuba

Baseball player

One of the greatest Cuban batters of all time, Linares entered the major leagues at age sixteen, and in the following season made the national amateur team. Since then he has played in more than twenty internationals, four world championships and two Olympics. When **baseball** was included in the Olympic Games for the first time, at Barcelona in 1992, Linares was the highest home-run scorer (4) and second in batting average (500). In fifteen national series, he has accumulated 340 home runs. His lifetime average of 364 puts him second among all Cuban players.

WILFREDO CANCIO ISLA

Linares López, Pedro

b. 1906, Mexico City; d. 1992, Mexico City

Folk artist

After working from the age of six in the Carretones Glass Factory and at several odd jobs, at age fourteen Linares adopted his father's profession of *papier mâché* crafting or *cartonería* (see **paper art**). He became famous for his *piñatas* (see ***piñata***), Judases (for Easter celebrations), skeletons (for the **Day of the Dead**), and *alebrijes* (fantastic, macabre dragon-like monsters). Linares was the first recipient of the Mexican National Prize in Arts and Sciences in the area of Popular Arts and Traditions.

CYNTHIA STEELE

Lindo, Hugo

b. 1917, La Unión, El Salvador; d. 1985

Writer

A superb example of the Latin American *pensador*, a blend of thinker, writer and statesman, Lindo contributed to the cultural and political life of El Salvador as poet, writer, critic, journalist, diplomat and lawyer. His famous short story collection, *Guaro y champaña* (Moonshine and Champagne) (1957), presents a complex world in which the fantastic and the psychological play prominent roles. His only novel, *El anzuelo de Dios* (God's Hook) (1963), reveals religious and metaphysical concerns as well as *costumbrista* (see ***costumbrismo***) tendencies. His poetry is refined, idealistic and intellectual, in contrast to the more political texts of his Gruposéis contemporaries.

LINDA J. CRAFT

Lins, Ivan

b. 1945, Rio de Janeiro, Brazil

Musician and composer

Ivan Lins combines elements of **jazz**, **bossa nova**, and classical music to create work of great harmonic complexity. His first success came at the 1970 University Music Festival with his irresistible song *Madalena*, composed with Ronaldo Sousa and later recorded by Elis **Regina**. Soon after, he was contracted by TV **Globo** to host the popular musical showcase *Som Livre Exportação* (Free Sound Export). Since the late 1970s, several North American jazz luminaries such as Herbie Mann, Quincy Jones, and Ella Fitzgerald have recorded his songs. In 1996, he collaborated with New Orleans trumpeter, Terrence Blanchard, on the highly acclaimed recording *The Heart Speaks*.

CHRISTOPHER DUNN

Lins, Osman

b. 1924, Pernambuco, Brazil; d. 1978, São Paulo, Brazil

Writer

Lins's most innovative works, *Nove, Novena* (Nine, Novena) (1966) and *Avalovara* (1973), represent for the critic Antonio **Candido** key moments of modernity in contemporary Brazilian literature. His style fuses lyricism with rigour, or, as one character in his story 'Um ponto no Circulo' (A Point on the Circle) puts it, 'the balance between life and rigor, between disorder and geometry'. In São Paulo, he also taught literature and published journalistic chronicles. His first novel, *O visitante* (The Visitor) (1955), was followed by a volume of stories *Os gestos* (Gestures) (1957) and *O fiel e a pedra* (The Loyal Man and the Stone) (1961).

MILTON HATOUM

Lins, Paulo

b. 1958, Rio de Janeiro, Brazil

Novelist and poet

With the publication of his novel, *Cidade de Deus* (City of God) (1997), Paulo Lins was hailed as an important emerging voice in Brazilian literature. The novel is set in Cidade de Deus, a neighbourhood established on the urban periphery in the mid-1960s to house displaced communities after the demolition of several hillside shanty towns (see **shanty towns and slums**). It documents the sexual, racial, generational and cultural politics of this community in a context of abject cruelty and violence generated by the rise of the drug traffic in the 1970s, the emergence of heavily armed gangs vying for control of the trade and the actions of corrupt security forces motivated by vengeance and greed. Lins culled much of the material used in the novel when he worked as a research assistant for Alba Zaluar, an urban anthropologist who has worked extensively in the *favelas* of Rio de Janeiro.

CHRISTOPHER DUNN

Liscano, Juan

b. 1915, Caracas, Venezuela

Writer and folklorist

A profoundly spiritual writer, Liscano's sometimes controversial critical and artistic practices have occupied a central place in Venezuela's literary life, particularly through his editorship of the influential journal **Zona Franca** (1964–83) and his work with publishers **Monte Avila**. Early researches into the folk culture of the coastal regions of his country nourished a search for the pre-Hispanic sources of religious thought which is reflected in his early poetry. As director of the Servicio de Investigaciones Folclóricas, he was also closely identified with the nationalist ideas of Rómulo **Gallegos**, whose presidency ended in a military *coup* which led Liscano into exile for ten years. His work of that period, like the epic *Nuevo mundo Orinoco* (1959), returns to earlier cosmic themes but within a framework of existentialist concerns (see **existentialism**). Returning from exile in 1958 his poetry took a more lyrical and frequently erotic direction, while as a critic he became increasingly involved in both political and cultural debates with a new, more radical generation reflected, but only in a muted way, in *Zona Franca*. By the late 1960s, in both his critical essays and his poetry, it becomes clear that Liscano's central preoccupation is the spiritual bankruptcy of contemporary society, in Venezuela and beyond.

MIKE GONZALEZ

Lispector, Clarice

b. 1920, Tchetchelnik, Ukraine; d. 1977, Rio de Janeiro, Brazil

Writer

Lispector, who arrived in Brazil with her immigrant parents as an infant, often reflected on the consequences of having become a native speaker of Portuguese, rather than of another language more conducive to an international readership. Yet through other circumstances – the recent interest in **women's writing** and in the writing of the Jewish diaspora – she has become one of the better known and most translated Brazilian writers of this century.

After a difficult childhood, Lispector studied law and worked as a reporter for a Rio daily as one of the first women journalists in Brazil. In 1944 she published her first novel, *Perto do coração selvagem* (Near to the Wild Heart) (1990), which won a prize and attracted much critical attention. The title and epigraph are drawn from James Joyce, and the novel offers an introspective portrait of a headstrong and artistically inclined young woman. Soon after, Lispector, married by then to diplomat Maury Gurgel Valente, left Brazil to live abroad for most of the next fifteen years, mainly in Switzerland and the United States, with sojourns in Italy and England.

The two novels she published while living abroad, *O lustre* (The Lamp) (1949) and *A cidade sitiada* (The Besieged City) (1949), continue the introspective lyrical mode, where attention focuses on fluctuations of feeling and the course of perceptions rather than plot. While living in the United States (1952–9), Lispector published a collection of short stories (*Alguns contos*) (Some Stories) (1952), which includes some of her better known pieces (such as 'Love' and 'Family Ties') in the genre where she has written her most brilliant and influential work. In 1959 Lispector separated from her husband and returned to Rio de Janeiro with her two sons.

In the almost two decades until her death, Lispector became a well-known literary figure in Brazil, publishing five novels and five collections of short stories, although she did not lead a conventional literary life. Her fiction of the early 1960s, such as the short stories of *Laços de família* (Family Ties) (1960) and the novels *A maçã no escuro* (The Apple in the Dark) (1961) and *A paixão segundo G. H.* (The Passion According to G.H.) (1964), are among her most important works. They are written in an original, often strange language, dense with paradoxes, unusual phrases and abstract formulations that tease and elude the rational intelligence. The characters, mostly women, ponder metaphysical questions about their place in existence and in the universe as well as more immediate questions about their place in a constrictive social order.

During the 1960s and 1970s, Lispector also published four picture books for children and engaged in various journalistic activities: a newspaper column for women (published under a pseudonym), a series of interviews with writers and other intellectuals for a mass circulation weekly (later collected in *De corpo inteiro* (Full Length) (1975)), and, most significantly for her fiction, a weekly series of columns or *crônicas* (see **crónica**), this time in her own name, for an important Rio daily, the *Jornal do Brasil*, from 1967–73. A selection of these *crônicas* was published posthumously as *A descoberta do mundo* (1984) (Discovering the World) (1992). It could be argued that these newspaper columns and her imaginative engagement with writing for a more diverse readership contributed to the radical changes in her writing of her last eight years. In the novels and short stories published in the 1970s, Lispector's characters are no longer mainly middle class; she experiments with self-referential narrators and with farcical plots and parodies of her earlier introspective and well wrought fiction. *A **hora da estrela*** (1977)

(The Hour of the Star) (1986), the short novel she published a month before her death, has as its protagonist an impoverished young woman from the Northeast trying to make her way as a typist in the urban jungle of Rio de Janeiro. This novel, with its failed Cinderella plot, farcical humour and touches of lyrical gentleness, was the basis for a successful film directed by Suzana **Amaral** in 1986.

Although Lispector was acclaimed early on as an extraordinary writer, it was only twenty years after the publication of her first novel that a book-length study of her work appeared in Brazil. Several early critics read Lispector in the context of **existentialism**, tracing affinities between the philosophical ideas in her fiction and those of Heidegger, Kierkegaard, Camus and Sartre. Other critics analysed aspects of her style: her use of the epiphany and of rhetorical devices such as internal monologue. More recently, questions of gender, poststructuralism and **postmodernism** have been brought to bear upon her text. Lispector was singled out as one of the two Brazilian writers (with Guimarães **Rosa**) belonging to the so-called **Boom** of Latin American fiction in the 1960s. In the 1970s, 1980s and 1990s, she emerged as an object of more extensive international attention in the wake of feminist criticism and of the French writer Hélène Cixous's celebration of her work as a model of *écriture féminine*.

The many autobiographical and semi-autobiographical self figurations in Lispector's fiction and *crônicas* have given rise to a parallel critical interest in 'Lispector herself'. Praised by her contemporaries as a beautiful, strange and mysterious woman, she has become as compelling a figure as any of her fictional characters. Hélène Cixous, who did much to promote translations of her work in France, wrote critical texts haunted by an intense bond with Lispector. The first full-length biography of Lispector was published in Brazil in 1995, and in 1996 novelist Ana Miranda wrote a fictionalized biography in which fragments of her texts are made to appear as accounts of her life. Occupying a secure place among Lispector's gallery of characters that variously depict what it meant to be a woman, including a woman artist, in mid-twentieth-century Brazil – the constrictions one encountered, the vistas that could open up –

'Lispector herself' is perhaps Lispector's most fascinating creation.

See also: Jewish writing

Further reading

Cixous, H. (1990) *Reading with Clarice Lispector*, Minneapolis, MN: University of Minnesota Press.
Fitz, E. (1985) *Clarice Lispector*, Boston: Twayne.
Nunes, B. (1989) *O drama da linguagem: uma leitura de Clarice Lispector*, São Paulo: Ática.
Peixoto, M. (1994) *Passionate Fictions: Gender, Narrative and Violence in Clarice Lispector*, Minneapolis, MN: University of Minnesota Press.

MARTA PEIXOTO

Lisser, H.G. de

b. 1878, Falmouth, Jamaica; d. 1944, Kingston, Jamaica

Novelist

De Lisser was particularly well known for his novels of Jamaican politics, as well as his knowledge of West Indian history and understanding of the Jamaican dialect. His ten novels include *Jane's Career* (1914), *Susan Proudleigh* (1915), *The White Witch of Rose Hall* (1929), *The Arawak Girl* (1958), *The Cup and the Lip* (1956) and *Under the Sun* (1937). A journalist and a prominent figure in Jamaican society, he was editor of the Jamaica *Gleaner* for forty years, and also published a magazine called *Planter's Punch*.

KEITH JARDIM

List Arzubide, Germán

b. 1898, Puebla, Mexico; d. 1998, Mexico City

Writer

An important participant in Mexican **estridentismo**, List Arzubide contributed along with Manuel **Maples Arce** to many of the manifestos published in the early 1920s, and was listed as editor of *Horizonte* (1926–7), one of the group's principal journals. His early volumes, *Esquina* (Corner) (1923) and *El viajero en el vértice* (The Apex Traveler) (1926), were substantial contributions to the *estridentista* (see **estridentismo**) poetry style; *El movimiento estridentista* (The Estridentista Movement) (1926), a curious mix of prose and verse dedicated to Huitzilopoxtli, the Aztec god of war, proposed an idiosyncratic profile of the entire movement.

MERLIN H. FORSTER

literacy

Literacy is commonly understood as the ability to read and write at a level which allows people to function in society. While it is self-evidently intrinsically worthwhile, it is often also assumed that by increasing levels of literacy, national economic performance will improve. This concept of 'functional literacy' has flaws, however, for those who acquire literacy skills will not necessarily experience a change in their quality of life. A different view would hold that literacy serves no real purpose unless it helps people take control of their lives, especially those for whom poverty and hardship are an everyday reality. From this perspective, and particularly through the work of Paulo **Freire**, Latin American attempts to link literacy with the struggle for liberation have had a significant influence on the teaching of literacy throughout the world. In Cuba and Nicaragua, national campaigns to eradicate illiteracy have also attracted attention, both for their original ways of tackling the problem and the relative success they achieved.

In 1990, official statistics on literacy varied from 59 per cent (male) and 47 per cent (female) in Haiti, to 96 per cent in Argentina (by comparison, the UK and USA enjoy literacy levels of over 90 per cent). But statistics do not tell the whole story, and say little about *levels* of literacy – the baseline measurement is simply the ability to read and write a short statement – nor about the impact it might have on people's lives. Evidence that literacy helps eradicate poverty is also uncertain, a point brought out in a famous cartoon when a newly literate peasant declares 'I used to be miserably poor and couldn't even write my name – now I'm just miserably poor'. In fact, it can equally be argued that it is only when poverty has been overcome that literacy becomes an essential skill.

Within a liberatory view of education, it is not only reading words that matters but also, to quote Freire, the ability to 'read the world' and have a critical understanding of reality. Reading and writing are beneficial to the extent that they help people make sense of their world and do something to improve it. Where literacy (and numeracy) help people organize more effectively – to bypass profiteers or to run co-operatives, for example – it will be particularly useful. The concept of literacy for liberation raises a number of issues, however. With dominant ideologies reaching mass audiences through news reports or soap operas on **television**, many projects in **popular education** argue the need to work on 'visual literacy', to help people analyse images and become proficient in the use of video. For indigenous groups, the question of language can present a dilemma since learning literacy in their first language may strengthen cultural identity and promote self-esteem, but politically it may make more sense to learn the language of power, Spanish or Portuguese. Problems also arise if educators overemphasize the political aspects of literacy, as this can alienate those who merely wish to acquire technical skills. Whether in the context of functional or liberatory literacy, however, one thing remains clear: the social environment is crucial to success because once people have learned how to read and write, if they have no real need to do so on a regular basis, these newfound skills can quickly disappear.

Freire developed a method of teaching literacy which is now widely applied throughout Latin America (and beyond). Before doing any teaching at all, literacy workers spend time talking to learners and finding out what their concerns are, what it is that 'gets them talking'. Workers then draw up a list of key words which generate discussion but, coincidentally, also generate the range of sounds required to read and write the language. Classes start with a discussion of one of these words and learners then see it written down and broken into syllables. Once they know two or three words, learners are invited to cut and paste sounds and syllables to discover new words they might find of interest: from *chu-va* (rain) and *bi-ci-cle-ta*, for example, learners can produce *luta* (struggle) or *tela* (screen). From the beginning, then, literacy is focused on the reality of the learners and while liberatory educators might hope that action for social change will ensue, the same techniques can be adapted – or 'co-opted' – to a more functional approach.

Large-scale adult literacy campaigns have also been important in Latin America. In Brazil, Freire himself headed a national campaign which became a target of the *coup* of 1964. As only those who were literate had permission to vote, this campaign would have empowered large numbers of the disenfranchised poor and was thus considered a revolutionary threat. In Cuba in 1961, all schools closed while 250,000 teachers, students and literate schoolchildren went to live and work with peasants to eradicate illiteracy in the countryside. A similar 'crusade' took place in Nicaragua in 1980 involving over 50,000 volunteer 'brigadistas'. Both had considerable success in reducing levels of illiteracy and were awarded prizes by **UNESCO**. More importantly, perhaps, was the role they played in a post-revolutionary society, breaking down barriers between urban and rural communities and bringing marginalized groups into the revolutionary process. One Nicaraguan brigadista explained that 'my students learned how to write machete and I learned how to use one'. As both campaigns focused on their respective revolutions, however, there is some debate as to whether literacy had a genuinely liberatory function or whether it merely served as a form of revolutionary propaganda.

Further reading

Archer, D. and Costello, P. (1990) *Literacy and Power: The Latin American Background*, London: Earthscan.

Carnoy, M. and Samoff, J. (1989) *Education and Social Transition in the Third World*, Princeton, NJ: Princeton University Press.

LIAM KANE

Literal

Although only five numbers of this small format journal were published (1974–7), it remains an essential reference point in Argentine literary criticism. First published by a group dissenting from the direction of the journal *Los Libros* when it moved from structuralism towards politics, *Literal* continued to defend the autonomy of literature and a critical practice that reflected on the singularity of the literary text. Its editorial committee included Germán **García**, Luis **Gusman**, Osvaldo **Lamborghini** and Lorenzo Quinteros. It published the work of Cristina Forero and Oscar Steimberg, among others, and in a bilingual edition, printed the only poem by Lacan to have been published.

GRACIELA MUSACHI

literary criticism

The practice of literary criticism in Latin America is linked to the construction of cultural paradigms or models. It became an independent activity at the beginning of the twentieth century, coinciding with the emergence of professional intellectuals. It was their task to write the first national histories of literature and to organize the literary corpus of each country or region as the nation-states of the region and their attendant nationalisms began to consolidate. Thus education could be reorganized around a canon of literary works – the national classics. At the same time a small but active market for Latin American writing began to emerge in the context of expanding cities with a vigorous intellectual life. New journals and publishing houses were established, and the press made it possible to keep up to date with innovations in Europe and North America.

Against this background, critical texts which took literary works as their immediate object, quickly generalized the discussion to embrace the questions of the national and regional 'identity' whose values and nature were 'represented' in fiction. This was the role literary critics like Pedro **Henríquez Ureña**, for example.

During the 1960s, literary criticism became significant once again. As the work of Jorge Luis **Borges** won an international reputation and the writing of Julio **Cortázar**, Mario **Vargas Llosa**, Carlos **Fuentes**, Gabriel **García Márquez** and José **Donoso** began to make its impact, the literature and art of Latin America began to attract considerable international attention.

The new political situation in Latin America created by the Cuban Revolution of 1959 (see **revolutions**) and the left-wing liberation movements emerging in every country, made the region a focus for international expectations. In fact the politicized atmosphere of the 1960s throughout the Third World opened a space where, it was hoped, the questions that the traditional cultures (especially those which had engendered Nazism and Fascism) had proved incapable of articulating, still less of resolving, might finally be answered. The Latin American critics provided access to the new third world literature by offering creative critical writings which established the connection between the literary texts and the reality of their growing reading public.

Angel **Rama** stands out as a representative figure in this process. He began his career in the magazine ***Marcha***, published in Montevideo, which played a key role in stimulating the intellectual ambience by publishing debates, new readings from the past, launching collections of books, educating the young and engaging in a constant dialogue with writers, artists, musicians and cultural leaders. Of his vast body of work, it is probably his volume *La ciudad letrada* (The Literate City) (1984), a work still unfinished when he died, and his writings on modernism which are his most important legacy to subsequent generations.

Many of the major critics of the 1960s worked in similar ways, laying the basis for the critical and speculative writing of the generations that followed. Among them the work of David **Viñas** is fundamental, for he read culture through marginal texts, iconographies and documents and saw their connection to **law** and power. Antonio **Cornejo Polar** and Antonio **Candido** played equally important roles in politicizing and revising Latin American culture from a critical point of view, opening new areas of visibility. Their texts mark the culmination of one model of the literary critic, erudite and capable of producing a global vision of the continent. Later generations have chosen to work on specificities, on fragments of the cultural complex; many have abandoned militant activity in favour of another kind of political intervention – the deconstruction of cultural hegemonies.

See also: postmodernism

Further reading

Rama, A. (1984) *Las máscaras democráticas del Modernismo*, Montevideo: Fundación Internacional Angel Rama.

GRACIELA MONTALDO

literary histories

The beginning of the contemporary epoch coincides with a crisis that called into question the great totalizing literary histories of the nineteenth century. It is no coincidence that the most important surveys of national literature (like Sílvio **Romero**'s *Historia de la literatura brasileira*) belong to the last century, or that the last of them (like Ricardo Rojas's *Historia de la literatura Argentina*) appeared early in the twentieth. The crisis was engendered by the avant-garde (see **avant-garde in Latin America**)'s rejection of the totalizing, causal, nationalist and organic models in which a nation's greatness was reflected in its literature. The new approaches set out to go beyond the nationalistic and scientific schema of nineteenth-century literary histories. Pedro **Henríquez Ureña**'s *Seis ensayos en busca de nuestra expresión* (Six Essays in Search of Our Expression) (1928) and *Las corrientes literarias en la América Hispánica* (Literary Currents in Spanish America) (1945) were founding texts of this new criticism. In Brazil, Antonio **Candido**'s influential *A formação da literatura brasileira* (Formation of Brazilian Literature) (1959) presented a sociological vision of two periods in Brazilian letters: the Enlightenment and romanticism. A 1983 conference in Campinas, Brazil, addressed the redefinition of the genre according to the formulations suggested by Henríquez Ureña, Angel **Rama** and Antonio Cándido (the papers were published under the title, *La literatura latinoamericana como proceso* – Latin American Literature as Process). The co-ordinator of these discussions, Ana **Pizarro**, compiled *Palavra, literatura e culture* (Word, Literature and Culture), a three-volume history of literature that fell short of its declared purposes, as the editor herself recognized. None the less, the project was significant for its inclusion of Brazil and of minor literatures. The Chilean critic Cedomil Goic also proposed a renewal of the genre with his *Historia y crítica de la literatura Hispanoamericana* (History and Criticism of Hispanic American Literature) (1988), applying the ideas of Henríquez Ureña and the model developed by Francisco Rico in his history of Spanish literature. These works identified critical problems central in 1980s debates: the construction of traditions, the relationship between dominant and subaltern systems and the periodization criteria appropriate for the literature of Latin America and the Caribbean.

Further reading

Cándido, Antonio (1988) *O método crítico de Silvio Romero*, São Paulo: EdUSP.
González Echevarría, Roberto (1996) *Cambridge History of Latin American Literature*, vol. 1, Cambridge: Cambridge University Press.
Pizarro, Ana (ed.) (1985) *La literatura latinoamericana como proceso*, Buenos Aires: CEAL.

GONZALO AGUILAR

literatura de cordel

Like other Latin American countries, Brazil has a strong tradition of popular narrative poetry used by the rural and urban poor to communicate their vision of the world. For many centuries, this verse existed only in oral form, but in the late nineteenth century, some popular poets in Brazil started to produce small chapbooks or *folhetos* (see **folheto**) of their poems on simple hand presses (similar in format to earlier European pamphlet poetry) which they sold in the streets and markets. The poet would often display his *folhetos* on a length of string between two posts, and the poetry thus became known as *literatura de cordel*, 'literature on a string'.

The origins of Brazilian popular poetry can be traced back to the ballad or *romancero* tradition in the Iberian Peninsula. In the Brazilian Northeast – where socioeconomic structures and many aspects of traditional rural life associated with them were relatively slow to change – popular poetry proved to be most vigorous and enduring. Later, migrants from the Northeast disseminated the poetic tradition throughout the country, and the *folheto* began a new phase of its production and diffusion.

Cordel literature was at its most dynamic in the 1950s when it was created, produced and distributed by the rural and urban poor. Before the spread of radio and television, the *folheto* functioned as a type of popular journalism, reinterpreting regional, national and even international events according to the world view of those disadvantaged sectors. To the traditional themes inherited from the Iberian *romancero* tradition, such as the power of religious faith and the adventures of popular chivalric heroes, were added new topics of concern to the poet and his community, such as land struggles, government corruption, inflation and pollution. It is this capacity of *cordel* literature to respond to the problems affecting the poet's community that largely explains why it remained such a dynamic form of popular expression for so many decades.

The process of *folheto* production has declined since the 1960s, largely as a result of the gradual erosion of traditional patterns of life in the Northeast. The *literatura de cordel* printed today reveals significant changes both in content and format, but it continues to provide inspiration for many Brazilian writers, among them Jorge **Amado** and Ariano **Suassuna**, who perceive it as the embodiment of the experience and world-view of the population of the Northeast. The covers of *folhetos* have traditionally been illustrated with woodcuts by graphic artists like José Borges.

Further reading

Antologia da Literatura de Cordel (1978), 2 vols, Fortaleza: Secretaria Cultura.

Arantes, A. (1982) *O trabalho e a fala*, São Paulo: Kairós.

Dinneen, M. (1996) *Listening to the People's Voice*, London: Kegan Paul International.

Slater, C. (1982) *Stories on a String*, Berkeley CA: University of California Press.

MARK DINNEEN

literature

In Latin America, literature had a key role to play in the process/project of emancipation, revolution and resistance both to imperialism and to capitalism in general. Angel **Rama** and Antonio **Candido**, for example, saw literature as a liberating project; in the 1960s, the discussions that took place concerning the responsibility of the writer, committed writing and the relationship between literature and revolution took as their starting point a common anti-capitalist ethos already identified in earlier writers as different among themselves as Juan **Rulfo**, Graciliano **Ramos** and Miguel Angel **Asturias**. These different projects sometimes sought their legitimacy in *el pueblo*, the people, and sometimes in the 'nature' of Latin America. But whatever their point of view, all of these different narratives legitimized literature as an emancipatory practice.

One of the least studied factors contributing to the loss of legitimacy of this emancipatory narrative was the Cold War, and its surreptitious translation by both sides into the field of culture. On the one hand the promotion of 'cultural freedom' and the autonomy of art, on the other 'reality' and 'commitment' became the opposing banners under which the antagonists fought. East and West appropriated cultural values in the service of their cause – indeed both had successfully done so at an earlier stage. In the 1930s, the 'proletarian moment' in both North and South America, and Russian cultural criteria ('**socialist realism**', for example) prevailed. After the Second World War, the USA launched a powerful campaign to disseminate 'Western' values across the world. One of its instruments, the Congress for Cultural Freedom, constantly referred to the value of 'universality'; this tended to exclude any literature or art that was excessively local or regional, although in some cases, notably William Faulkner. João Guimarães **Rosa** and Gabriel **García Márquez**, this regionalism could be and was presented as a variant of universal themes already prefigured in classical mythology. The biographical, referential and contextual elements were simply disregarded. One critic, for example, argued that you could appreciate Jorge Luis **Borges** without knowing anything about Argentina. Beatriz **Sarlo** responded by noting that while Borges could be read as a universal writer from an aesthetic point of view, with the positive implication that it was a right of all Latin American artists to work within any and every tradition, what was lost was the connection to specifically Argentine traditions that Borges himself considered so important. The same argument was conducted in the visual arts, praising those Latin American artists who had adopted the 'international style'.

What is important here is not a conspiracy theory, but that Latin America was drawn into someone else's battles. While one side proposed an apolitical avant-garde, the other argued for an ill-defined realism and later, after the Cuban Revolution, for a vanguard whose logic led to guerrilla warfare (see **guerrillas**). From the 'Western' point of view, abstractionism quickly merged into a transnational market-place; on the other side, and despite the attempts by both Cuba and Nicaragua to democratize culture, neither country succeeded in its aesthetic project.

The shadow conflict was played out in the pages of **Mundo nuevo** on the one hand and **Casa de las Américas** on the other – and it allowed no middle ground. And yet the writing of the 1960s reveals an astonishing quantity and variety that escapes the parameters of the debate. Writers and artists were critics, teachers and creators, and they developed new theories that went beyond the East/West dichotomies in their defence of literature and literary values. With hindsight, the limitations of their proposals are obvious – the analogy between artistic freedom and national emancipation, a subject almost always constituted as masculine. Yet it was poets and novelists who offered the most interesting theoretical perspectives of the time, and who went furthest to overcome the manichaean character of politics. In *El arco y la lira* (The Bow and the Lyre) (1957), for example, Octavio **Paz** elaborated a theory of poetry and a critique of the avant-garde. The first exhaustive study of García Márquez is by Mario **Vargas Llosa**, and it is the Mexican novelist, Carlos **Fuentes**, who writes the first book on the new novel, *La nueva novela hispanoamericana* (The New Spanish American Novel) (1969). Julio **Cortázar** wrote important essays on the short story, painting, politics and writing, and a defence of surrealism (see **surrealism in Latin American art**). Fuentes and Vargas Llosa also wrote about Cervantes and Flaubert, respectively, exercising their right to intervene in discussions within the cultural metropolis. It was Paz who introduced the ideas of Lévi-Strauss and Oriental literature to Latin America, Augusto **Roa Bastos** and José María **Arguedas** who recuperated oral cultures, David **Viñas** who offered fundamental documentary research into the frontier wars and Severo **Sarduy** and José **Lezama Lima** who explained and defended the **neo-baroque**. There is no parallel anywhere else in the world for this new critical writing that broke free of the straitjacket of the Cold War to offer a range of ideas of literary value, from Lezama Lima's exaltation of poetry to Cortázar's Utopian project. What everyone agreed on was the value of literature: it is fire (Vargas Llosa), passion (Clarice **Lispector**), an alternative to the official language (Fuentes), revolutionary (Cortázar). What they all share, too, is their representation of Spanish America and Brazil in the global culture.

It is not my intention to idealize the **Boom** (with its alarming suggestion of marketing and sales), but rather to underline the fact that at least in the early 1960s a critical theory was to be found in literary texts and essays in literary criticism rather than in the academy. The situation changed in the 1970s, for several reasons. First, the national question that structured many of the novels of the Boom became compromised in many cases by military governments that imposed censorship and repression, and marginalized whole sectors of the population. Second, Cuba no longer represented Utopia and instead of developing a new aesthetics, it increasingly narrowed the limits of what was permissible within the revolution. Third, the development of the mass media meant that the printed word was no longer seen as the only means of gaining access to modernity (see **cultural theory**).

The Cold War in Latin America was not only conducted against communism, but also against any and every effort, however misguided, to seek regional solutions that might have compromised the process of globalization. Among the failures were numbered the many projects for the democratization of culture, from the writing workshops (see **workshop poetry**) to bilingualism (see **bilingualism and biculturalism**), from local theatre groups to national **cinema**. Yet, whatever the outcome, the 1960s saw a number of windows open, while the two decades that followed witnessed the triumph of military regimes in the **Southern Cone**, civil war in Central America and the advent of **neoliberalism**. In this period literature ceased to be 'relevant', and when the question of the value of literature is again addressed it is under more difficult and embattled conditions than during the 1960s. For while the Cold War destroyed and de-legitimized certain positions of opposition, neoliberalism has shown itself capable of an absorption so complete that it can destroy all opposition by embracing it.

The seduction of the market is nothing new; it was already an issue in nineteenth-century Europe. In 1958, Jorge **Amado**'s *Gabriela cravo e canela* (Gabriela Clove and Cinammon) was an instant best-seller. In 1966 Carlos Fuentes announced in an interview in *Mundo nuevo* that he had broken with the Cuban Revolution, and that 'we are now up to our necks in the rat race, as subject as any gringo or Frenchman to the world of competition and status symbols, of neon and Sears-Roebuck, washing machines, James Bond movies or tins of Campbell's Soup. The Graceful Epiphany of Art is dead.' This was an era that began with Fuentes's *Cambio de piel* (A Change of Skin) (1967), Vargas Llosa's *Pantaleón y las visitadoras* (Sergeant Pantoja's Special Service) (1973) and García Márquez's *telenovela* (see **telenovelas**) scripts. In Latin America, as elsewhere, cultural studies arose as the walls of the literary city collapsed. It had always had a strong interdisciplinary tradition: witness the links between literature and anthropology in the work of Asturias and Arguedas, for example; the theorization of mass culture starting from sociology, anthropology and communications but going far beyond the schema of cultural imperialism in important research projects by **García Canclini** in Mexico and Jesús **Martin Barbero** in Colombia. At the same time, literature was beginning to embrace mass culture as an essential component of the modern experience, as novels like José Emilio **Pacheco**'s *Las batallas en el desierto* (Battles in the Desert) (1981), the writings of La **Onda** in Mexico and the work of Manuel **Puig** were to demonstrate, our memories, our individual histories, our common points of reference are formed by comics, television programmes and popular music.

Mass culture is the culture of the majority; rap has brought poetry to millions and discussions about what goes on in soap operas are part of daily culture for millions, be they academics or workers. The impulse of European cultural studies to see mass culture and daily life as practices that were not wholly susceptible to control and manipulation, and could therefore become sites of resistance, yielded in the USA to their appropriation by academic institutions seeking novelty and publishing opportunities. The result was that the reasonable assertion that culture was not about literature alone led to a proliferation of studies and anthologies that discredited the original notion. A possible response came from a group of academics, many of them Latin American specialists, who have opposed the elitism of the institutions of literature by seeking the value of texts in the ethics of a responsibility towards the subjugated classes. Thus John Beverley in his *Against Literature* (1993) has suggested that it is not a question of destroying literature but of broadening its base so that it is more open to solidarity and love. In contrast to the novel of the Boom, the ***testimonio*** is a 'democratic and egalitarian narrative', although the genre provides an insufficient body of work to provide a paradigm. *Me llamo Rigoberta Menchú* (I, Rigoberta **Menchú**) (1984) is the work most often cited, and for Beverley it represents the possibility of a new relationship, of complicity and identification with popular causes, between reader and narrator. It calls into question the role of the writer and the function of literature itself, Beverley argues, and represents the beginning of a post-fictional literature that reflects an emerging popular-democratic culture. Others have argued that Rigoberta is the agent rather than the representative of the collective, and that *testimonio* is a practice rather than a representation. Whatever the conclusion, it is clear that literature's loss of legitimacy has provoked a search for new criteria outside the literary metropolis.

Some critics have called into question this approach to narrative. Beatriz Sarlo, for example, writing from Argentina, expresses the problem thus:

> Modernity combined the pedagogical ideal with a display of symbolic goods in the market that would have been unimaginable previously. One unexpected result was that the market and the cultural industry subverted the basis of authority on which it would have been possible to conceive an educative paradigm in the realm of aesthetics. The contradiction was rapidly identified by those who saw that 'industrialized art' spelled death for the refined values of the cultural elites. The market, inevitably, introduced quantitative criteria that often contradicted the aesthetic judgments of artists and critics, and suggested that the establishment of qualitative values was not the task of the market. Thus art loses its sanctified status as a perfectly logical result of modernization.

Sarlo herself maintains a nostalgia for the historical avant-garde and sees the present as evidence of decline. But I see the problem rather as a different crisis, which bears names like 'the collapse of paradigms' 'postmodernism', etc.

In Latin America the reaction to this pragmatism has generated among certain writers and artists a new concept of the aesthetic linked to marginality and exclusion. The new aesthetics shares the aversion to totalizing theories, plays with fragmentation and sometimes employs non-canonical forms like the *crónica*. In the recent *crónicas* of Carlos **Monsiváis** in Mexico and Pedro **Lemebel** in Chile, both very different from each other, there is an attempt to capture the multiple fleeting rituals through which people attempt to impose order on chaos (Monsiváis) or the archaeological traces of a recent past (Lemebel). What they represent is an aestheticizing of mass culture. Perhaps the strongest arguments in favour of a 'refractory' aesthetics are to be found in the Chilean journal, ***Revista de crítica cultural***, edited by Nelly **Richard**. The journal is unique in its insistence that art and literature transgress not simply by an inversion of terms, but through quotation, parody and exchange of categories and discourses. It is not a question of 'saving literature', but rather of valorizing documents, behaviours, art, texts, anything that calls into question from the periphery the narratives which continue to legitimate the centre.

See also: Poetry; Theatre

Further reading

Franco, J. (1969) *An Introduction to Spanish American Literature*, Cambridge: Cambridge University Press.

Gonzalez, M. and Treece, D. (1992) *A Gathering of Voices: The Poetry of Contemporary Latin America*, London: Verso.

Martin, G. (1990) *Journeys through the Labyrinth*, London: Verso.

Pupo-Walker, E. and Gonzalez Echeverría, R. (1996) *The Cambridge History of Latin American Literature*, Cambridge: Cambridge University Press.

JEAN FRANCO

Littín, Miguel

b. 1942, Palmilla, Chile

Film-maker

One of the most important directors of the **New Latin American Cinema**, Littín began his career in the cultural effervescence of the late 1960s as part of a generation of young Chilean film-makers. *El chacal de Nahueltoro* (The Jackal of Nahueltoro) (1969), his first feature, recreates the events surrounding the murder of a woman and her five children by a man depicted in the sensationalist press as a 'jackal'. The film articulates a radical social critique of a system which ignores the misery and deprivation that act as a breeding ground for criminals. 'El chacal' is rehabilitated to be aware of his crime and be penitent, but then the system executes him anyway. The film was seen by half a million people, and by subverting many claims of the Christian Democrat government, became an important element of popular mobilization. In recognition of his contribution to their election victory in 1970, **Allende**'s Popular Unity Government appointed him head of **Chile Films**, and he filmed the spectacular *La tierra prometida* (The Promised Land) (1973), completed in Cuba after the military *coup* that overthrew Allende and forced Littín into exile. Littín settled in Mexico, where he made a number of films: *Actas de Marusia* (Letters from Marusia) (1975), *El recurso del método* (Reasons of State) (1977), and *La viuda de Montiel* (Montiel's Widow) (1979). Apart from *Actas*, which was nominated for an Oscar for best foreign film, these films were less well received critically. His next film, *Alsino y el cóndor* (Alsino and the Condor) (1982), filmed in Nicaragua with the Instituto Nicaragüense de Cine (INCINE), was also nominated for the best foreign film Oscar.

While still officially in exile, Littín returned secretly to Chile in 1985 to film *Acta General de Chile* (General Act of Chile). An account of this experience has been written by Gabriel **García Márquez**, *Miguel Littín: Clandestino en Chile* (Miguel Littín: Clandestine in Chile) (1986). Disguised to avoid being recognized, he filmed throughout the country for six weeks, documenting the changes which had taken place in Chile since the installation of the military regime. Littín's multinational career embodies the continental nature of the New Latin American Cinema movement. In the 1990s he returned to Chile.

Further reading

García Márquez, G. (1987) *Clandestine in Chile: The Adventures of Miguel Littín*, New York: Holt.

DOLORES TIERNEY

Little Carib Theatre

Originally a simple structure with an open stage and poor lighting, the theatre was the brainchild of Beryl **McBurnie**, leader of the Little Carib Dance Company, whose performance of the pre-carnival show *Bele* opened the premises in February 1948 in Woodbrook, Port-of-Spain, Trinidad and Tobago. The City Council's Building Authority only permitted the makeshift structure the status of a temporary building. However, McBurnie's appeals for patronage at home and abroad have helped to rebuild it, while preserving the intimacy which makes it a popular cultural nucleus, not only for dance, but also for drama.

JILL E. ALBADA-JELGERSMA

little theatre movements and groups

Alternative drama in Latin America and the Caribbean has often been aimed at or produced by non-literate groups and always invites their creative participation. Derived from the ideas of Brecht (see **Brechtian theatre**) and inspired by the Cuban Revolution (see **revolutions**), the major pan-Latin American movement of this kind since the sixties has been the New Popular Theatre (Nuevo Teatro Popular). Anti-purist in outlook, the movement was frequently driven by collaborations between community and labour groups, theatre professionals and intellectuals, in the attempt to reconcile modernization with tradition by combining classical European, pre-Columbian, African and experimental theatre with vaudeville and slapstick. The movement set out to champion marginalized groups – Indians, women, street people, and blacks – through the use of their vernacular and recognition of their day-to-day resilience. Representatives of the movement have been, in the 1980s, Nicaragua's Sandinista-sponsored theatre collectives (see **Sandinista Revolution**), **Teyocoyani** and **Nixtayoleros**.

Post-revolutionary Cuba has been one of the Caribbean epicentres of this type of theatre. Hosting many international festivals which provided a meeting place for little theatre groups from around the world, generous government support enabled groups like **Teatro Escambray** to undertake their representation of popular culture, folk traditions and historical questions like slavery, revolution, colonialism and neocolonialism. Another group, Cabildo de Santiago, has explored African traditions and black themes.

Escambray's vernacular concerns are shared by popular theatre elsewhere in the Caribbean. The region's growing sense of its plurally independent cultural identity has generated a popular theatre in defiantly informal idioms and settings, which has blossomed with the support of key institutions like the **University of the West Indies** and the Eastern Caribbean Popular Theatre Organization.

In the Francophone Caribbean, the Haitian playwright Félix Morisseau-Leroy (1912–), drawing on a tradition of popular entertainment in Haiti, set the standard for serious drama in creole (see **French-based creoles**) as an alternative to mainstream theatre in French. Since his sensational 1953 creole version of Euripides's *Antigone*, performed under his direction by Haitian peasants, creole theatre has relied both on popular and classic traditions.

Further reading

Martin, R. (1994) *Socialist Ensembles: Theater and State in Cuba and Nicaragua*, Minneapolis, MN: University of Minnesota Press.

Weiss, J.A. et al. (eds) (1993) *Latin American Popular Theatre: The First Five Centuries*, Albuquerque, NM: University of New Mexico Press.

JOHN D. PERIVOLARIS

Little-White, Lennie

b. 1946, Montego Bay, St James, Jamaica

Film-maker

Trained in Canada, Little-White attempts to balance his interest in creating 'international emotional appeal' with his commitment to creating material about the people and traditions of his home country through his production company Mediamix, which also produces TV shows like the popular serial *Royal Palm Estate* (since 1989), and many others. In 1999, Mediamix inaugurated the 'Doctor Bird Awards' to recognize achievements by Jamaicans in film and television. After *Children of Babylon* (1980), a film he produced and directed, the Mutual Life Assurance Company sponsored *Way Back When* (1985). The broadcast of this film – which portrays two major figures in Jamaican history, Deacon Bogle and George William Gordon – was purportedly delayed for political reasons by the government-controlled Jamaican Broadcasting Corporation (JBC).

ANN MARIE STOCK

llano en llamas, El

El llano en llamas (The Burning Plain) (1953) by Mexican writer Juan **Rulfo** is a collection of stories written in a laconic, austere language inspired by the speech of Jalisco peasants but re-elaborated to both reveal and transcend its origins in a perfect balance of poetry and realism. The characters are overwhelmed by a religion shot through with fatalism and resignation, because, as Carlos **Monsiváis** explains, 'secular experience creates a collective capable only of seeing heaven and earth within the confines of their daily life – no longer the "beyond" but rather the "forever present"'. In the story 'Luvina', Rulfo presents a devastated village inhabited by women in mourning, an early version of the Comala of his novel ***Pedro Páramo***. The radical ambiguity of Rulfo's texts, full of silences and allusions, express the hermetic nature of these people and landscape, left barren by nature and history until it is no more 'than a lightning flash, a duststorm of the dead'.

MARGO GLANTZ

llapingacho

Llapingachos are deep-fried potato pancakes stuffed with cheese, commonly served in Ecuador with lettuce, coriander, chorizo, tomato, avocado and a fried egg. The term possibly derives from 'llapina', the **Quichua** word for 'to crush', and 'gacha', a dough made of flour, water and salt, because it is made with boiled potatoes fried with onions, pepper and cumin. It can also be written 'yapingacho' or 'shapingacho'.

FERNANDO BALSECA

Lloréns Torres, Luis

b. 1878, Collores, Puerto Rico; d. 1944, Puerto Rico

Poet

Champion of Pan-Latin Americanism (see **Pan-Americanism**) against burgeoning North American imperialism, Lloréns Torres was a leading poet of Puerto Rican *modernismo* (see ***modernismo*, Spanish American**), founder (1913) of an important Caribbean outlet for *modernista* writing, the *Revista de las Antillas* (Review of the Antilles). His poems, such as 'Canción de las Antillas' (Song of the Antilles) (1913) and 'Velas épicas' (Epic Sails, 1913) are imbued with a sensuous appreciation of the colours, smells and vernacular rhythms of the Caribbean he paradoxically claims both as an exotic outpost of Hispanic culture and as an independent homeland.

JOHN D. PERIVOLARIS

Loayza, Marcos

b. 1959, La Paz, Bolivia

Film-maker

One of the two key film-makers of the Bolivian film-making 'boom' of the 1990s, Loayza's first feature-length film, *Cuestión de fe* (A Matter of Faith) (1995), was the first project to benefit from the new national Cinema Law passed in 1991 and the creation of a State institution for the cinema, the Fondo de Fomento Cinematográfico. Widely awarded internationally, *Cuestión* is basically a road movie, the amusing chronicle of three friends travelling to deliver a statue of the Virgin commissioned by a local drug lord.

ANA M. LÓPEZ

Lobato, Monteiro

b. 1882, Tabauté, São Paulo State, Brazil; d. 1948, São Paulo

Writer

A major modernizing force in Brazilian literature, Lobato (born José Bento Monteiro Lobato) was tireless in founding presses and magazines, promoting regional and **children's literature**, writing cultural journalism and bridging the gaps between Brazil and Spanish America. Best known for his regionalist (see ***regionalismo***) stories about the coffee-producing area of São Paulo State, Lobato created a peasant character, Jeca Tatú, who has become one of the familiar archetypes in Brazilian popular culture. A founder and editor of the *Revista do Brasil* (1916–25), Lobato was later associated with the newspaper, ***O estado de São Paulo***. His children's literature is set on a coffee plantation, the 'Sítio do picapau amarelo' (Yellow Woodpecker Farm), which is inhabited by a series of memorable characters. Lobato was an enthusiastic supporter of Juan Domingo **Perón** and resided in Buenos Aires for part of his last years. His complete works were published in thirteen volumes in 1946–7.

DANIEL BALDERSTON

Lobo, Edu

b. 1943, Rio de Janeiro, Brazil

Songwriter, guitarist and singer

Lobo entered the **bossa nova** movement under the influence of Carlos Lyra and Baden **Powell**, collaborating with Vinicius de **Moraes** and the dramatists of the **CPC**. His songs for Ruy **Guerra**'s *Arena conta Zumbi* project, depicting the seventeenth-century slave rebellion of Palmares, combined the lyricism of bossa nova and Afro-Brazilian rhythms to dramatize themes of drought and landlessness. 'Reza' (Prayer) and 'Borandá' (Let's Away) lent themselves to theatrical performance as epitomized by Elis **Regina**'s award-winning 1965 rendition of 'Arrastão' (Dragnet). After two years of voluntary exile in the US (1969–

71), Lobo embarked on a less public but highly successful career as a composer.

DAVID TREECE

Lombardi, Francisco

b. 1949, Tacna, Peru

Film director

Peru's most important film director, Lombardi's work is narrative and dramatic in style, and presents a pessimistic view of the human condition. His films include *Muerte al amanecer* (Death at Dawn) (1977), *Los amigos* (The Friends) (1978), his contribution to *Cuentos inmorales* (Immoral Tales), *Muerte de un magnate* (Death of a Magnate) (1981), *La ciudad y los perros* (The City and the Dogs) (1985), based on a novel by Mario **Vargas Llosa**, *La boca del lobo* (The Wolf's Mouth) (1988), *Caidos del cielo* (Fallen from Heaven) (1994), *Sin compasión* (No Mercy) (1994) and *Bajo la piel* (Under the Skin) (1996). He has received several awards for best director.

CESAR SALAS

Lombardo Toledano, Vicente

b. 1894, Teziutlán, Puebla, Mexico; d. 1968, Mexico City

Political leader

The pre-eminent progressive Mexican labour leader of the twentieth century, Lombardo served in the Chamber of Deputies from 1924–8 and 1964–6. An organizer and secretary general of the country's major union, the Mexican Federation of Labor (CTM), he was ousted in the mid-1940s by Fidel **Velásquez**. In 1948 Lombardo became disillusioned with the possibility of reforming the government from within and left the PRI to found a leftist opposition party, the Partido Popular. He published widely in the popular press and became internationally renowned as an opposition leader and a Marxist thinker.

CYNTHIA STEELE

Lopes, Nei

b. 1942, Irajá, Rio de Janeiro, Brazil

Musician and writer

A leading proponent and practitioner of traditional **samba** and grass roots **pagode**, Nei Lopes has also distinguished himself as an advocate for the authorial rights of Brazilian musicians. He has produced several recordings with Wilson Moreira and two solo recordings including the 1996 *Canto Banto* which featured compositions relating to Afro-Brazilian history and culture. Lopes has published books on Afro-Brazilian music as well as several volumes of his own poetry. In 1996, he also published a dictionary of popular Brazilian vocabulary of Bantu origin.

CHRISTOPHER DUNN

López, Elvis

b. 1957, Aruba, Netherlands Antilles

Visual artist

A graduate of the Gerrit Rietveld Academy in Amsterdam, Lopez became director of the Visual Art Academy Aruba – Atelier 89, a local experiment in the area of art education. He makes drawings, paintings and sculptures, that can be read individually, but seen in changing contexts become towering installations. The earlier pieces dissolve indelibly into a whole new world. and the uniformity of shapes, the sterile arrangements, and the corporality create a distance that is deceptive as well as enchanting.

NEL CASIMIRI

López, Israel ('Cachao')

b. 1918, Havana, Cuba

Musician and composer

One of the musicians who most influenced the development of **salsa**, Cachao was the first musician to make the double bass a solo instrument with his jazz interpretations of traditional Cuban music. In the 1930s, working with his brother, Orestes, he composed twenty-five innovative danzóns (see **danzón**) every week for the dance band (*charanga*), Arcano y sus Maravillas. One of them, Mambo, inspired the famous rhythm that **Pérez Prado** made famous some years later. In 1957 he recorded the classic album, *Cuban Jam Sessions in Miniature*. In 1961 he went into self-imposed exile in the USA, where he played with Hubert Laws and Dave Pike, and brought his famous original up to date with the new album, *Descarga 77*. The actor Andy García directed the documentary, *Cachao, como tu música no hay dos* (There's no Music Like Yours) in 1989, which brought Cachao back to the stage in 1990 after several years of silence. He began to record again, with albums like *40 years of Cuban Jam sessions* (1993). He has composed over 2,000 danzones.

WILFREDO CANCIO ISLA

López, Luis Carlos

b. 1879, Cartagena, Colombia; d. 1950, Cartagena

Poet

López seldom left Cartagena, where he is considered a local treasure; he visited Bogotá once and served twice as consul, in Munich in 1928 and Baltimore in 1937. His work bears his pictorial bent; his poems are finely crafted vignettes, portraits of life in Cartagena spiced with sarcasm and ironic humour. Although López exercised free verse, thematically, he is considered beyond the influence of Spanish American modernism (***modernismo*, Spanish American**). Nicknamed *El Tuerto* (One-Eyed) and the oldest of eleven brothers, his days at medical school were interrupted by civil war, and he soon turned to management of the family business.

HÉCTOR D. FERNÁNDEZ L'HOESTE

López Albújar, Enrique

b. 1872, Chiclayo, Peru; d. 1966, Lima, Peru

Writer

López Albújar made a significant contribution to the development of Peruvian narrative with two works produced in the 1920s. *Cuentos andinos* (Andean Tales) (1920), though limited by Western preconceptions, prepared the way for later ***indigenista*** fiction by its realistic portrayal of the Indian peasantry. *Matalaché* (1928), a historical novel depicting slave-owning society on the eve of independence, is consciously traditional in manner and form but echoes **Mariátegui** by using history to question the foundations on which modern Peru is built.

JAMES HIGGINS

López Antay, Joaquín

b. 1897, Huamanga, Peru; d. 1981, Huamanga

Sculptor

One of the most renowned names in Peruvian popular art, Joaquín López Antay made *retablos* (see ***retablos* and *ex votos***), portable altars with doors which contain scenes with painted plaster figures organized on two levels. Traditionally, he reserved the upper level of the *retablo* or *sanmarco* for patron saints and the lower for events in the agricultural calendar. After José **Sabogal** and Alicia Bustamante discovered him in the early 1940s, he received commissions for *retablos* representing different Andean themes. In 1975 López Antay was awarded the Premio Nacional de Cultura (National Prize for Culture).

PAULINE ANTROBUS

López de Mesa, Luis

b. 1884, Don Matías, Colombia; d. 1967, Santafé de Bogotá, Colombia

Essayist

Having studied medicine in Colombia, and later psychiatry and psychology at Harvard, López de Mesa's writings constitute an exploration of the social and cultural development of his country within a frame of biological and geographical determinism. Thus he favoured the idea of 'improving' the native population to overcome underdevelopment. Consequently, in 1938, as the Minister of Foreign Affairs, he opposed Jewish immigration, but promoted the immigration of Europeans. His works include *Cómo se ha formado la nación colombiana* (How Colombian National Identity Developed) (1934).

MIGUEL A. CARDINALE

López Rangel, Rafael

b. 1929, Mexico City

Architect and historian

López Rangel's work on architecture, town planning and planning in Latin America in its relation to politics and society is widely known. He has also researched the relationship between architecture and the plastic arts. A graduate of the National Autonomous University of Mexico (**UNAM**) and the Autonomous Metropolitan University, both in Mexico City, he has received a number of international awards for his writings, including *La modernidad arquitectónica mexicana* (Modern Architecture in Mexico) (1989) and, with others, *Más allá del postmodernismo: crítica a la arquitectura reciente* (Beyond Postmodernism: A Critique of Recent Architecture) (1986).

LOURDES CRUZ GONZÁLEZ FRANCO

López Rega, José

b. 1916, Buenos Aires, Argentina; d. 1989, Buenos Aires

Politician

López Rega was a retired police corporal, whose role as bodyguard and spiritual confidant to Isabelita Perón in 1960s Madrid led him to a position of power as leader of right-wing **Peronism** (1973–1976) in Argentina. As Minister of Welfare, he launched an assassination campaign against political opponents through his Triple A (Argentine Anti-Communist Alliance) death squads. When Isabelita became president, following Perón's death, López Rega briefly became Argentina's most powerful political figure, until his failed hard-line labour policies and unpopularity led to his resignation in July 1975. The 'Brujo' (witch doctor) appears in novels by Luisa **Valenzuela** and Tomás Eloy **Martínez**.

THOMAS EDSALL

López Tarso, Ignacio

b. 1925, Mexico City

Actor

One of Mexico's foremost theatre and film actors, López Tarso played leading theatrical roles in plays like *La Celestina* (for which he won the 'best new actor' award in 1953), *Macbeth*, *Juan Pérez Jolote* and *The Dresser*. In 1992 he directed Valle Inclán's *Tirano Banderas*. Notable cinema appearances include his supporting role in **Buñuel**'s 1958 *Nazarín*, and his lead role in Roberto **Gavaldón**'s 1959 *Macario*, for which he won the best lead actor award at the San Francisco Film Festival. López Tarso has served as President and General Secretary of two of Mexico's actors' unions since 1978.

ANTONIO PRIETO-STAMBAUGH

López Trujillo, Alfonso

b. 1935, Villahermosa, Colombia

Priest

López has been one of the most powerful critics of **liberation theology**, for its supposed Marxist tendencies and politicization of the Church. Archbishop of Medellín from 1979–91 and cardinal since 1983, his nomination as secretary general (1972–8) and then president (1979–83) of the Latin American Bishops' Conference (**CELAM**) marked a return from the radicalism of Medellín in 1968 to more conservative positions, encouraged by the Vatican. He was co-founder of the journal *Tierra Nueva* in 1972, a central voice in the restoration of the Latin American Church.

ELINA VUOLA

Lora, Silvano

b. 1931, Santo Domingo, Dominican Republic

Painter

Due to the political conditions during Rafael Leonidas **Trujillo**'s dictatorship, Lora started his career as an abstract and symbolist painter in the 1950s to avoid censorship and persecution. After the dictator was overthrown, Lora joined the 1962 artistic movement *Arte y Liberación* (Art and Liberation). During the April Revolution, he was leader of an intellectual cultural movement that supported the Revolution. Using murals, collages and posters, Lora's painting evolved towards a testimonial representation of Dominican social conflicts during the 1960s and 1970s.

FERNANDO VALERIO-HOLGUÍN

Lord Kitchener

b. 1922, Arima, Trinidad

Musician

Lord Kitchener (born Aldwyn Roberts), also known as the Grandmaster, won the Road March and composed the winning steel-band **Panorama** song more times than any other calypsonian. Hired to entertain employees of the Arima Water Works in 1936, by 1946 he had three big hits that enabled him to open his own **calypso** tent, the 'Young Brigade'. His first Panorama win followed in 1964 with the calypso, Mama Dis Is Mas; he had his eighteenth win in 1997 with The Guitar Pan. Kitch is also a master storyteller famed for witty narratives that comment on politics and race and gender relations in Trinidadian society.

LORRAINE LEU

Los que se van

Los que se van, cuentos del cholo y del montuvio (The Vanishing Ones: Stories About the Cholo and the Montuvio) was the full title of a collection of short stories published in 1930 by Demetrio **Aguilera Malta**, Joaquín **Gallegos Lara** and Enrique Gil Gilbert. It is agreed by critics that the volume marked the emergence of a new style in Ecuadorean literature, a movement that came to be called the **Guayaquil Group** and included José de la **Cuadra** and Alfredo **Pareja Diezcanseco**.

HUMBERTO ROBLES

Losada, Alejandro

b. 1936, Buenos Aires, Argentina; d. 1985, Havana, Cuba

Critic

Losada's intense and fertile research into Latin American culture was cut short by his death in an aeroplane accident while flying from Havana to Managua; he was then directing a social history of Latin American literature. Until his death he was Director of Latin American Institute of the Free University of Berlin, where he was Professor of Languages and Literature and leader of a research team. His many publications include *La literatura en la sociedad de América Latina I: Los modos de producción entre 1750–1980* (Literature in Latin American

Society: Modes of Production between 1750 and 1980) (1980).

CELINA M. MANZONI

Losada, Editorial

Editorial Losada is the publishing house founded in Buenos Aires by a Spanish exile, Gonzalo Losada, in 1940. It soon established itself as the prime publishing house for writers associated at once with regionalist concerns and with international solidarity (see *regionalismo*). Its list included the emerging work of Miguel Angel **Asturias**, José María **Arguedas**, Ciro **Alegría** and others associated with *indigenismo*. It was also the publisher for decades of the works of Pablo **Neruda** and of the great Spanish poet (exiled for many years in Buenos Aires), Rafael Alberti. It also published Estela Canto, Olga **Orozco**, Silvina **Ocampo**, Virgilio **Piñera** and others. Still going today, years after the death of its founder, Losada is still a significant publisher (with a beautiful bookstore in Buenos Aires), though largely due to the prestige of its older list.

DANIEL BALDERSTON

lotteries

An omnipresent feature of daily life in most Latin American and Caribbean countries, lotteries derive their popular appeal from the promise of sudden riches, while governments favour the possibility of steady income that can be used for favoured projects, often cultural and educational. Already in nineteenth-century Mexico, a lottery helped support the Academia de San Carlos, the art academy where José María Velasco taught and where Diego **Rivera** and countless others studied. The old headquarters of the national lottery in Mexico City is an art deco masterpiece, but the offices have moved across **Reforma** to a modern skyscraper, suggesting that at least some of the funds derived from the lottery are spent on lavish buildings for the institution itself. The lottery ticket seller is a fixture of major intersections in most cities and towns; in total, many hundreds of thousands must work in this way as part of the so-called informal economy.

DANIEL BALDERSTON

Lovelace, Earl

b. 1935, Toco, Trinidad and Tobago

Writer

One of the Anglophone Caribbean's foremost writers, Lovelace belongs to the generation that came of age with Trinidadian independence in 1962. The lyrical realism of his novels, short stories, and plays portrays the cultural forms and the struggles for personhood of Trinidad's folk as they negotiate the pressures of colonial education, the law, political opportunism, poverty, and modernization. His 1979 novel *The Dragon Can't Dance* is a Caribbean classic. A critical tribute to Trinidad's lumpen proletariat, it uses **carnival** as a motif for exploring conflicting processes of self-creation, cultural co-optation, and Utopian resistance to capitalist values of ownership. In 1997 Lovelace received the Commonwealth Writers Prize for his novel *Salt*, a multi-generational novel which continues his poignant and sometimes gently humorous explorations of the Trinidadian people's struggles for a freedom that remains elusive.

SHALINI PURI

Loynaz, Dulce María

b. 1903, Havana, Cuba; d. 1997, Havana

Poet

A prolific writer, Loynaz has published over eight volumes of poetry, a novel, *Jardín* (Garden) (1951) and a collection of travel pieces, *Viaje a Tenerife* (A Trip to Tenerife) (1958). Daughter of a general in the Cuban Liberating Army against the Spanish and sister of the poet Enrique Loynaz Muñoz, her poems were first published in the Cuban newspaper *La Nación* in 1920, and later in journals as diverse as **Social**, *Grafos*, *Revista Bimestre Cubana* and **Orígenes**. She was president of the Academia Cubana de la Lengua (Cuban Academy of

Language) and won Cuba's National Literary Award in 1987 and the 1992 Premio Miguel de Cervantes in Spain.

LÁZARO LIMA

Lucía

Lucía (1968) is a full-length Cuban feature film directed by Humberto **Solas**. It tells three stories set at different moments of Cuban history: the late nineteenth century, the 1920s and the early 1960s, after the triumph of the Cuban Revolution of 1959 (see **revolutions**). The protagonists are three women with the same name – Lucía – whose experiences differ as their role in society changes. Originally produced by **ICAIC**, the Cuban Film Institute, for the centenary celebrations of the wars of independence, it quite rightly came to be seen as one of the classics of Cuban cinema.

JOSÉ ANTONIO EVORA

Ludmer, Josefina

b. Argentina

Literary critic

A university professor in the USA, Ludmer's writings are indispensable for any student of Latin American literature – *Cien años de soledad, una interpretación* (One Hundred Years of Solitude, an Interpretation) (1972); *Onetti, Los procesos de construcción del relato* (Processes of Construction of the Short Story) (1977). Her most important work, *El género gauchesco. Un tratado sobre la patria* (The Gaucho Genre. A Treatise on the Nation) (1988), draws on literary criticism, anthropology, history and psychoanalysis to analyse the constitution of a canon of Argentine literature that stretches from Hidalgo to **Lamborghini**. This work is a key innovative text in Argentine cultural criticism.

DIEGO BENTIVEGNA

Lugar sin límites, El

José **Donoso**'s novel *El lugar sin límites* (Hell Has No Limits), published in 1966, introduces into Latin American literature a groundbreaking narrative about how male homosociality, (homo)sexuality, homophobia, and misogyny function in relation to complex traditional patriarchal structures. Set in a forgotten rural town in Chile, the novel focuses on the erotically shared power relations between the male transvestite brothel owner La Manuela, the prostitute La Japonesa, their daughter, La Japonesita, Pancho, a hypervirile worker who desires both father and daughter, and don Alejo, the local large-scale landholder.

The brothel and the transvestite's body are the privileged spaces for examining social and political structures as well as the limits of gender and sexual categories. *El lugar sin límites* was adapted to the screen in 1977 by Mexican director Arturo **Ripstein** with a screenplay co-written by Manuel **Puig** (not credited). A critical and commercial success, Ripstein's representation of the dilemmas of homoerotic desire is a cult classic, especially for the sympathetic portrayal of La Manuela, played by Roberto Cobo, who made his film debut in Luis **Buñuel**'s *Los olvidados* (1950) as the adolescent delinquent el Jaibo. The deadly kiss between La Manuela, dressed in a red with white polka dot flamenco dress, and Pancho, stands as an ironic landmark in relation to the spectacle of Mexico's virile heterosexual national image.

SERGIO DE LA MORA

Lugo Filippi, Carmen

b. 1940, Ponce, Puerto Rico

Writer

Part of a group of intellectuals who in 1970 discarded the 'literary pessimism' and 'linguistic Hispanism' characteristic of Puerto Rican nationalist rhetoric, Lugo Filippi's writing displays humour and sharp wit, a distancing parody and a clear acknowledgement of the island's heteroglossic reality. Written with Ana Lydia **Vega**, *Vírgenes y* *mártires* (Virgins and Martyrs) (1981) is her most important short story collection.

MARÍA JULIA DAROQUÍ

Lugones, Leopoldo

b. 1874, Villa de Santa María del Río Seco, Argentina; d. 1938, El Tigre, Argentina

Writer

A good friend of Rubén Darío in Nicaragua, Lugones was to be Argentina's most important *modernista* poet. In his *magnum opus*, *Lunario sentimental* (Sentimental Calendar) (1909), however, he would transgress many assumptions and principles of *modernismo* (see **modernismo, Spanish American**) and write in an experimental vein that anticipated the work of the avant-garde writers of **Martín Fierro** and **Proa**, who admired his handling of metaphor but repudiated his pronounced deference to rhyme. In the next decades, Lugones's poetry evolved towards more traditional forms and themes, an evolution running parallel with the development of his ideological position: sympathizing with **anarchism** and **socialism** in his younger days, he was to end as an ultraconservative if not fascistic nationalist, who did not hesitate to participate in the conspiracy that led to the military *putsch* of 1930. Alienated and isolated, he committed suicide in a secluded hotel in the delta of El Tigre (near Buenos Aires). Lugones was an extremely prolific and versatile writer. Besides poetry he wrote various volumes of short stories (mostly in the fantastical mode) and countless articles, essays and studies on a great variety of political, historical, biographical, educational, religious, literary and cultural subjects. His universal knowledge, his conversion to tradition and his independent nature are only a few of many links with **Borges**, the co-author with Betina Edelberg of *Leopoldo Lugones* (1955). And yet, Lugones's work lacks the sophisticated irony and the subdued melancholy of Borges's and is, in the end, more virtuosic than penetrating.

Further reading

Jitrik, N. (1960) *Leopoldo Lugones: mito nacional*, Buenos Aires: Ediciones Palestra.

Kirkpatrick, G. (1989) *The Dissonant Legacy of Modernism: Lugones, Herrera y Reising, and the Voices of Modern Spanish American Poetry*, Berkeley: University of California Press.

Martinez Estrada, E. (1968) *Leopoldo Lugones: retrato sin tocar*, Buenos Aires: Emecé.

MAARTEN STEENMEIJER

Luis Miguel

b. 1970, Puerto Rico

Singer

Luis Miguel (born Luis Miguel Gallego Bastery) is a hugely successful singer who has moved from rock to **bolero**, and who cut his first disc, '1 + 1 = dos enamorados' (1 + 1 = Two Lovers), at age twelve. In the early part of his career his repertoire of ballads and soft rock won him a huge adolescent following and innumerable gold and platinum discs. In 1991 he recorded the album, *Romance*, produced by Armando Manzanero, a collection of 'classic' boleros that sold 8 million copies and won seventy platinum discs as well as a World Music Award. The two subsequent albums, *Segundo Romance* (1994) and *Romances* (1997), both huge sellers, have confirmed the strength of the bolero tradition and its popularity with the young.

CARLOS MONSIVÁIS

Lula

b. 1945, Garanhuns, Pernambuco, Brazil

Political leader

Born Luis Inácio da Silva, Lula came to public attention as the leader of the extraordinary strikes in the metallurgical industries around São Paulo in 1978–9. A key figure in the formation of the **PT** (Workers' Party), he became the party's presidential candidate in 1994 and seemed on the verge of winning power – but for an eleventh hour win by Fernando Henrique **Cardoso**. None the less, Lula's vote represented almost half the national total – an incredible achievement for a man from an impoverished background who was a shop-floor worker and union activist until the strikes of 1978. The São Paulo strikes did not end in victory, but in a compromise that left many participants dissatisfied. Lula's conclusion was that a new political party had to be formed that drew on the rising resistance to the military regime and posed a direct challenge by the workers to State power. When it was formed PT was a broad and open organization of the left – it has been described as a kind of 'rainbow coalition', though only in the sense that it brought together so many diverse groups. Internal splits and visions threatened PT – but all pulled together for the 1994 campaign. Thereafter, the divisions reappeared and Lula's vote in the 1998 elections was lower than the peak of 1994. Lula, none the less, remains a figure of enormous political stature.

MIKE GONZALEZ

Lumitón

The coming of sound led radio pioneers Cesar José Guerrico, Enrique Telémaco Susini, and Luis Romero Carranza to build Lumitón, well-equipped film studios in the Buenos Aires district of Munro, in 1932. After the success of *Los tres berretines* (The Three Whims) (1933), they produced a series of popular themed films with typical *porteño* characters and settings (exemplified by Manuel **Romero**) and developed great stars (Niní **Marshall**, Luis **Sandrini**, Mecha **Ortiz**). Francisco **Múgica** inaugurated a second tendency, sophisticated bourgeois comedies and melodramas attractive to middle-class audiences. Finally, in the 1940s Carlos Hugo **Christensen** adapted Argentine classics and introduced explicit sexuality. Conflicts with **Peronism** forced Lumitón to close in 1952. It is now a cultural centre and designated historical monument.

RODRIGO PEIRETTI

Luna, Alejandra

b. 1939, Mexico City

Stage designer

Luna is one of the most important stage designers of contemporary Mexican theatre, opera and television. From the mid-1960s, Luna has worked with directors like Ludwik Margules, Marta Luna, Juan José **Gurrola**, Julio **Castillo**, Héctor **Mendoza** and Nicolás Núñez in such productions as Marlowe's *Doctor Faustus*, *Los hijos de Sánchez* (Vicente **Leñero**'s 1972 adaptation of Oscar Lewis's *The Children of Sánchez*), *Miss Julie*, *The Threepenny Opera*, *A Streetcar Named Desire* and, in 1995, *Roberto Zucco* and Leonora **Carrington**'s *Penelope*. Luna has also directed architectural projects in several theatres around Mexico.

ANTONIO PRIETO-STAMBAUGH

Luna, Felix

b. 1925, La Rioja, Argentina

Historian and poet

A graduate in law, Felix Luna wrote a number of studies of **Peronism**, outstanding among them *El 45* (1969) and *Perón y su tiempo* (Perón and his Time) (1984), chronicling Perón's rise to power. Other writings include *Buenos Aires y el país* (Buenos Aires and the Country), and *Soy Roca* (I am Roca) (1989), a fictionalized autobiography of Argentine President Julio Roca (1847–1914). From 1967 he edited the journal *Todo es historia*. Some poems from his *Mujeres argentinas* (Argentine Women) (1965) were set to music by Ariel **Ramírez**. During Raúl Alfonsín's Presidency he was Secretary of Culture for Buenos Aires.

PABLO KREIMER

Lunes de Revolución

Lunes de Revolución was a weekly cultural supplement of the newspaper ***Revolución***, published in tabloid form between March 1959 and November 1961. Its 129 issues covered every area of cultural, artistic and political life in Cuba and internationally. Its impact on national life was demonstrated by its circulation of over 500,000 per issue, a success unequalled before or since in the Cuban media.

It was as innovative and polemical as the period in which it was produced, providing a space where free discussion on cultural identity could be conducted, a process marked by contingency and a constant struggle between different tendencies and currents of ideas. From issue 23 it was edited by Guillermo **Cabrera Infante**, assisted by Pablo Armando **Fernández**. Raúl **Martínez** was responsible for its design from the outset, becoming art editor from issue 74. Contributors included Virgilio **Piñera**, Antón **Arrufat**, Rine **Leal**, Calvert **Casey**, José A. Baragaño and Heberto **Padilla**.

The wide range of positions and opinions held by both its editorial team and its team of contributors symbolized the network of ideological and generational contradictions which coexisted during the first three years of the **Castro** regime. Its first editorial defined the eclectic and contestatory spirit in which the project was conceived: 'We are not a literary group; we are just friends of a similar age. We have no political ideology in common, though we do not reject some ways of interpreting reality – we are referring, for example, to dialectical materialism, psychoanalysis or **existentialism**.'

The work of *Lunes* embraced a terrain much wider than journalism, becoming the focus of other confrontations in Cuban cultural life. It promoted a number of important projects, like the Ediciones R publishing house, the 'Lunes en TV' programme and visits to Cuba by many international figures. However, Fidel Castro's 1961 speech '**Palabras a los intelectuales**' (Words to the Intellectuals) pointed to the publication's imminent closure.

The topics most frequently addressed were literature and politics; 543 people wrote for *Lunes*, of whom more than thirty were Cuban. It published poems, stories and extracts from novels and essays, as well as devoting a large amount of space to Cuban theatre, reproducing one-act plays and fragments of other works. It also produced several monographs on Third World countries, events in history and prominent artists and writers.

Its final number (in November 1961) was a special number devoted to Pablo Picasso.

Further reading

Cabrera Infante, G. (*c*. 1999) *Assays, Essays and Other Arts*, New York: Twayne Publishers.

WILFREDO CANCIO ISLA

Lunfardo

Lunfardo, the popular language of the River Plate Basin, originated as a popular slang. Loathed at first by the upper and middle classes, it later came to be considered an expression of the national identity of Argentina and Uruguay. As with **tango**, the vehicle of its popularization, the origins of Lunfardo have been much debated. But the question seems to be not whether Lunfardo was originally an argot – the language of the thieves – or a slang – a popular language spoken by the masses – but how an originally popular form, disdained by the upper classes and even censored by a dictatorial government as late as 1943, came to be regarded as a form of national identity.

In 1917 Pascual Contursi wrote the first tango canción to be recorded, Mi noche triste (My Sad Night), in which he used some Lunfardo words. Through recorded music, radio and the street barrel organ, tango and Lunfardo initiated a process of popularization that the **tango melodramas** would consummate by the 1930s.

Unlike some European argots and slangs, Lunfardo combined a considerable number of foreign words, mostly from the different Italian dialects but also from French argot and Spanish *caló*. Lunfardo thus displays the intense impact that **immigration** had in the formation of modern Argentina and Uruguay.

In 1962 interest in Lunfardo as an expression of Argentine culture led to the founding of the Academia Porteña del Lunfardo, and there are extensive dictionaries of Lunfardo by José Gobello and others. Even as late as the 1970s there was still much debate as to whether Lunfardo is just the language that tango popularized or the more popular language spoken by *porteños* and *montevidea-*

nos in general. What is clear is that all these changes and displacements, and all the controversy they have aroused, confirm that Lunfardo's evolution parallels the process of negotiation and the articulation of cultural differences that constitutes a cultural identity in its ever fluctuating and dislocating movement.

Further reading

Castro, D. (1987) 'Lunfardo, the language of the tango as a source for Argentine social history', *Proceedings of Pacific Coast Council on Latin American Studies* 14(2).

Salessi, J. (1995) 'Maleantes', in *Médicos maleantes y maricas*, Rosario: Beatriz Viterbo, pp. 115–76.

Zlotchew, C. (1989) 'Tango, Lunfardo and the popular culture of Buenos Aires: Interview with José Gobello', *Studies in Latin American Popular Culture* 8: 271–85.

FLORENCIA GARRAMUÑO

Lupe, La

b. 1932, Oriente Province, Cuba; d. 1992, New York, USA

Singer

The witty and passionate performances of La Lupe (born Guadalupe Victoria Voli Raymond) brought a new element to typical forms, from boleros (see **bolero**) to guarachas (see **guaracha**), ballads and rap (see **rap music**). She studied to be a teacher in Havana, but instead entered the world of music at a very young age. She won an amateur competition imitating Olga **Guillot**, and began singing with the Trio Los Tropicuba. Her star then rose continuously; she appeared with Mongo **Santamaría** and Tito **Puente** and toured widely in Latin America, singing songs such as 'Puro teatro' (Pure Theatre), 'Qué te pedí' (What did I ask for?) and 'Adiós' (Farewell).

RAFAEL CASTILLO ZAPATA

Luppi, Federico

b. 1934, Buenos Aires province, Argentina

Actor

Luppi's stellar acting career began in 1960s *telenovelas*, but took off with his prize-winning role in *El romance de Aniceto y la Francisca* (The Ballad of Aniceto and Francisca) (1967), directed by Leonardo **Favio**. A taciturn yet naturalistic actor, he appeared in many important films and stage productions. His work with director Adolfo **Aristaráin** is especially noteworthy, among them *Tiempo de revancha* (Time for Revenge) (1982) and *Un lugar en el mundo* (A Place in the World) (1991). Luppi has worked on more than fifty films, including productions in Mexico (*Cronos* (1992), directed by Guillermo **del Toro**), Peru and Spain as well as with John Sayles on *Men with Guns* (1997).

DIANA PALADINO

Luso-Brazilian Review

A biannual publication of the University of Wisconsin Press, the *Luso-Brazilian Review* was founded in 1964 and is sponsored by the Latin-American and Iberian Studies Program. The journal is also funded in part by a grant from the Cyril W. Nave Fund of the University of Wisconsin Foundation. Its editorial advisory board includes many famous scholars of Brazil, Lusophone Africa and Portugal. The *Luso-Brazilian Review* is committed to interdisciplinarity in area studies and publishes essays in English, Portuguese and Spanish on history, language, literature and sociology. It is one of the foremost academic journals in Portuguese studies.

SUSAN CANTY QUINLAN

Luthiers, Les

Les Luthiers is an Argentine musical group presenting comic shows featuring their own compositions, including quotations and parodies of both classical and popular music. In addition to normal instruments, the group also employ 'informal instruments', built by the members and others using a variety of waste materials. Formed in 1967 by Gerardo Massana (who died in 1973), Carlos López Puccio, Jorge Maronna, Marcos Mundstock, Carlos Núñez Cortés, Daniel Rabinovich and Ernesto Acher (1973–87), the group attributes most of its compositions to a fictional figure, Johann Sebastian Mastropiero. They have toured worldwide and produced eight albums, including the live album *Mastropiero que nunca* (1978).

EDUARDO CONTRERAS SOTO

luxury tourism

Luxury tourism, popularized in the 1950s and 1960s with the development of enormous luxury chain hotels, resorts and package vacations, is still very popular. 1950s Havana was perhaps the perfect emblem of these practices, with luxury hotels, beaches, casinos and nightclubs only ninety miles from Key West. The development of Acapulco (and later Cancún) in Mexico followed a similar model. Many luxury tourist scenarios tend to de-emphasize the natural and cultural specificity of their locations, their walls and gates offering not only a resort from the quotidian march of Europe and North America, but from the daily struggles of local people in some of Latin America's most desperate economies as well. The most obvious at this have been the Club Med type resorts throughout the region, especially the Caribbean.

Package vacation tourism often works within this paradigm, offering pre-planned holidays to Latin American countries in which every detail of the itinerary has been planned so as to minimize contact with the culture outside of the resort compound. Some package vacation and resort tourism scenarios offer natural and human sightseeing expeditions outside the compound, though the tourist and the object of his or her gaze are carefully mediated by a variety of different kinds of barriers, from glass windows to savvy tour guides. Other luxury resorts offer simulacral representations of the countries in which they are located, while assuaging their visitor's apprehensions of any true intercultural contact with the help of formidable borders and barriers. These walls demonstrate an oddly determined permeability: neither tourists nor their currency seem to cross these barriers, but local indigenous inhabitants often make this border run each day, incorporated into a wage-based service economy which often replaces local agricultural economies in rural areas.

'Big house' tourism, though far lacking the economic and developmental dimensions of luxury hotel and resort tourism, is another popular form of luxury tourism in Latin America. Lavish plantation estates and enormous ranch houses, painstakingly preserved in the apex of their historical splendour, are opened to a few who, for a high price, can indulge in a nostalgia for an era whose passing has provided more than a modicum of relief for many.

JOHN HARVEY

Lynch, Marta

b. 1925, Buenos Aires, Argentina; d. 1985, Buenos Aires, Argentina

Writer

Marta Lynch wrote seven novels and nine collections of short prose before her suicide. *La alfombra roja* (The Red Rug) (1962) is a jaundiced view of a presidential campaign, which drew on her experience with Argentine president Arturo Frondizi. *Al vencedor* (To the Victor) (1965) is a bleak look at the lives of two young men returning from military service. *La senora Ordonez* (Mrs Ordonez) (1967) chronicles the empty life of a working-class girl who marries into the bourgeoisie. *El cruce del río* (River Crossing) (1972) tells the story of a *guerrillero* and his politically active mother. *Un árbol lleno de manzanas* (A Tree Filled with Apples) (1974) is a love story about politics, or vice versa. *La penultima version de la Colorado Villanueva* (The Penultimate Version of Red Villanueva) (1978) is another chronicle of middle-class family life and its disintegration during times of political crisis. *Informe bajo llave* (Report under Lock and Key) (1983) tells of a woman's sexual obsession. Lynch's short stories, like her novels, are stylistically sophisticated variations on the themes of loneliness, sex and politics.

AMY KAMINSKY

Lyra, Carmen

b. 1888, San José, Costa Rica; d. 1949, Mexico

Writer

The first major Costa Rican female writer, Lyra lost her position as a school teacher when her writing turned from sentimental *modernismo* to political denunciation. In 1930 she joined the Communist Party. Lyra came to view literature as an instrument of social protest and revolution, and was one of the earliest writers to criticize the fruit companies in her *Bananos y hombres* (Banana Trees and Men) (1931). Costa Ricans best remember her for her children's narratives, *Los cuentos de mi Tía Panchita* (Stories from Aunt Panchita) (1920), which blended popular stories with 'universal' folktales.

LINDA J. CRAFT

M-19

Formed in Colombia in 1972 to build a mass-based armed-struggle movement; unlike many of the earlier guerrilla organizations in Colombia (see **guerrillas**), M-19 did not emerge from a left or socialist tradition. Its founders included members of ANAPO, the movement founded in 1964 by the military dictator, Rojas Pinilla, and dissident members of the Fuerzas Armadas Revolucionarias de Colombia (FARC – Revolutionary Armed Forces of Colombia), among them Jaime Bateman and Carlos Pizarro. Its spectacular theft of arms from an army barracks in 1977 earned it the bitter enmity of the military. Under Turbay Ayala's presidency (1978–82), M-19 were relentlessly persecuted. In 1984 an amnesty was agreed with the Betancur government, but as it began to win political support through 1985, the army launched renewed attacks on the group and systematically murdered its leaders. In November 1985 the organization seized the Palace of Justice; the army stormed the building killing all forty guerrillas and dozens of civilians. Though M-19 was severely weakened, the armed movement as a whole grew in the face of deepening military repression and government corruption. In October 1988, M-19 agreed to lay down their arms and prepare for the 1990 elections, with Carlos Pizarro as its presidential candidate. When he was murdered in his turn, his successor Navarro Wolf went on to accept a seat in the Cabinet, causing a deep rift in the organization.

MIKE GONZALEZ

Mabe, Manabu

b. 1924, Kumamoto, Japan; d. 1997, São Paulo, Brazil

Painter

Considered one of the most outstanding painters in Latin America in the late 1950s and 1960s, and a master of colours and stains resembling ideograms, Mabe moved to Brazil at age ten and settled with his family on a coffee plantation in the interior of São Paulo. An autodidact, he began painting in the middle of the coffee fields on breaks from his labours; when he had no canvasses, he substituted coffee sacks. In 1956 he began his abstract phase, which earned him great respect and admiration. When he won the Grand Prize at the fifth **Bienale de São Paulo** in 1959, he had to rush to get his Brazilian citizenship in order to accept the award. Mabe received more than eighty international awards and left an archive of some 3,000 paintings, among them some of the highest prized contemporary Brazilian canvasses.

ANA M. LÓPEZ

Macalé (Jards Anet da Silva)

b. 1943, Rio de Janeiro, Brazil

Musician and composer

Macalé is an irreverent composer associated with the Brazilian counterculture since the late 1960s. In the mid-1960s, he worked as musical director for several productions of the **Opinião** and Arena theatre groups (see **Arena Theatre Group**) and later wrote soundtracks for important films, including Joaquim Pedro de **Andrade**'s *Macunaíma* and Nelson Pereira dos **Santos**'s *Amuleto de Ogum* in which he also acted. In the early 1970s, he composed underground classics such as Gotham City, Anjo Exterminado, Go Back, and Vapor Barato.

CHRISTOPHER DUNN

Machu Picchu

Inca city whose existence was unknown during the colonial period; it was brought to public attention in 1911 by an expedition from the University of Yale led by the archaeologist, Hiram Bingham. Machu Picchu (its **Quechua** name means 'ancient peak') lies 110 kilometres northeast of the city of Cusco. It is one of the most complete pre-Hispanic urban sites in Latin America, and embraces an urban and a rural zone. It is not only the most famous archaeological monument in the Americas, but has inspired many artists, including Pablo **Neruda**.

CESAR SALAS

Macció, Rómulo

b. 1931, Buenos Aires, Argentina

Artist

Seeking to go beyond the abstraction/figuration dichotomy, Macció formed the Neo-figuración group in 1961 with Ernesto Deira, Luis Felipe **Noé** and Jorge de la **Vega**. Reacting against geometric abstraction, they turned to informalism. Taking their surroundings as a reference point, they rediscovered expressionist abstract language (see **expressionism**). After the group disbanded in 1965, Macció employed various languages to address the theme of the city in his Paris, New York and Buenos Aires series. In 1983, he settled in Buenos Aires' La **Boca** district, which provided much of the inspiration for his 1990s work.

GONZALO AGUILAR

Macera, Pablo

b. 1929, Huacho, Peru

Historian

Regarded as one of Peru's most critical and challenging intellectuals, Macera's work recast Peruvian historiography and in its turn greatly influenced the social sciences. His early work explored the history of ideas in pre-independence Peru; he later turned to writing economic history within a Marxist framework. He is a professor at the University of San Marcos, where he had been a student of history and law, and director since 1966 of its Andean Rural History Seminar. His works include *Trabajos de historia* (Historical Works) (1977) and *Las furias y las penas* (The Rage and the Sorrow) (1983).

CESAR SALAS

Machado y Morales, Gerardo

b. 1871, Santa Clara, Cuba; d. 1939, Miami Beach, USA

Politician

Fifth president of Cuba, Machado had fought as a general in the last war of independence against Spain (1895–98). He assumed the Presidency in 1925 under the slogan 'Water, roads and schools'; his period in government oversaw an expanding public works programme which included the building of the Capitolio Nacional (the Capitol building in Havana), the extension of the Malecón (the Sea Wall along Havana harbour) and the central highway. He introduced tariff reforms to encourage national industry. His enforced reelection in 1929 produced major social discontent, particularly among students; by 1933 a series of protests reached the dimensions of a popular rising. After attempting to reimpose order by terror, Machado was forced to leave the Presidency on

12 August 1933 and to flee the country. He is buried in the Woodlawn cemetery in Miami.

JOSÉ ANTONIO EVORA

machismo, Mexican

It is only when the ideas of Freud begin to spread in Mexico that the term *machismo* comes to be used in the same sense as its current usage. In the years of the Mexican Revolution, there was nothing special about 'being *macho*' – everyone was, or at least was supposed to be. But with the explorations into the power of the phallus and the theatrical reinvention of the revolution, the term disengaged from the simple male/female (*macho/hembra*) dichotomy to become a badge of pride signifying courage in the face of death, imposition of the self over others and scorn for the weakness of women and effeminacy in men. In the beginning, criticisms were few and highly Freudian (for example Samuel **Ramos** in his *Perfil del hombre y de la cultura en México* (Profile of Man and Culture in Mexico) (1934)). If US films saw the 'Aztec *macho*' as a symbol of ferocity and cruelty, the Mexican cinema took enormous pride in the *macho* exemplified and personified by Jorge **Negrete**, '*macho* of *machos*': manly, fearless, seductive and monogamous.

What is picturesque on screen becomes in reality the butt of opprobrium, an inability to acknowledge the rights of women, a cult of barbarism, contempt for the environment, a belief that rape is a phallic right and the production of homophobic hate crimes. The *macho* – and many take pride in being one even if large groups of people distance themselves verbally from this behaviour – owes no one any explanations; his attitude says it all.

The opposition to *machismo* arises out of a combination of factors: the feminization of the economy, the cultural internationalization of Mexico, feminist demands and legislative changes regarding rape, the disappearance of the terms bastard and *hijo natural* (Illegitimate child) from the Civil Code and an element of fashion – *macho* is outmoded.

More and more households rely on working women, the number of male and female students in universities is now more or less equal, in the working-class districts rapists are paraded through the streets by women, the term 'homophobia' enters the journalistic vocabulary and there is a growing environmental awareness. All of these factors reduce the space for *machismo*, though there are still last redoubts of patriarchy – but as a term it has now become ridiculous and as a behaviour its room for action is increasingly limited.

See also: masculinity

Further reading

Gutmann, M. (1996) *The Meanings of Macho: Being a Man in Mexico City*, Berkely: University of California Press.

CARLOS MONSIVÁIS

Machito

b. 1909, Havana, Cuba; d. 1984, New York, USA

Musician

A percussionist and singer, Machito (Frank Grillo) performed with the great Maria Teresa **Vera** in Havana before his brother-in-law Mario Bauza convinced him to move to New York in 1936. He recorded several albums there with Xavier Cugat, among others. In 1940 he formed his own orchestra, Machito and his Afro-Cubans, widely regarded as the creator of Afro-Cuban jazz. Its first *timbales* player was Tito **Puente**, and some of the greatest jazz musicians of the day played with the band. In the 1950s, as **mambo** grew more popular, his reputation declined, though he continued playing until his death.

JOSÉ ANTONIO EVORA

Macías, Raúl 'El Ratón'

b. 1934, Tepito, Mexico City

Boxer

His country's most famous boxer, 'El Ratón' (the Mouse) Macías was the first of a dynasty of

Mexican bantamweight champions. After a good amateur campaign – he fought in the 1952 Olympics – he made a winning professional debut in April 1953 and won the National Boxing Association (NBA) world title in March 1955, knocking out Thailand's Chamrem Songkitrat. But he lost his attempt to unify titles, losing on points to Algeria's Alphonse Halimi in November 1957. He retired in October 1962 with a professional record of 41 wins (25 by KO) and two defeats.

See also: boxing

ERIC WEIL

Macumba

Throughout the centuries of slavery (1558–1888), the captive black population of Brazil gradually created a syncretic (see **syncretism**), religious cosmos in which they could develop a sense of identity. Forced to convert to **Catholicism** upon arrival, the slaves blended Christian religious teachings with their lifelong beliefs and rituals (which invariably included dancing, singing, drumming, the cult of the dead and respect for their ancestors). Many African religious practices also found counterparts in native Brazilian religions. Thus, Macumba originated from a mixture of elements from various African religions, indigenous Brazilian traditions, and popular Catholicism. In the early twentieth century, the rituals and values of *espiritismo* (see **New Age**) and Kardecism (doctrine based on the teachings of Alain Kardec) were incorporated into Macumba's belief system. While Macumba was never an organized cult, its religious syncretism gave rise to **Umbanda** in the 1930s in Rio de Janeiro, where the terms Macumba and Umbanda are used interchangeably.

In Kimbundu (an Angolan language), the word 'macumba' refers to a musical instrument and dance, but in Brazil the word has acquired several meanings. It can signify offerings and/or sacrifices to the ***orixás*** (African deities); it can refer to a place of worship; it can also mean religious belief. Most frequently, Macumba is used as a generic term to refer to various Afro-Brazilian religions (**Candomblé**, Umbanda, Xangô, Catimbó); indeed it has become such a vague term that it refers to any ceremony which courts the spirits. It often carries a derogatory meaning, used to indicate **Vodun** or fetishism. What most characterizes Macumba is not the cult of African deities (as in Candomblé), but the guidance and intervention of the spirits of the dead which can return to earth to coach mediums (people who, when in trance, establish communication with the dead, receive messages for the living, and prescribe guidance on how to cure and comfort). Macumba is popular partially because it has become a trusted, viable alternative to costly medical and psychological care, and a highly interactive and dynamic form of spirituality.

Further reading

Bastide, R. (1978) *The African Religions of Brazil: Toward a Sociology of the Interpretation of Civilizations*, Baltimore, MD: The Johns Hopkins University Press.

Bramly, S. (1994) *Macumba: The Teachings of Maria José, Mother of the Gods*, San Francisco: City Lights Books.

MARÍA JOSÉ SOMERLATE BARBOSA

Macunaíma

Mário de **Andrade**'s prose 'rhapsody' *Macunaíma* (1928) was published amid a critical debate within the modernist movement (see **Brazilian modernism**) regarding the country's cultural identity and development. Andrade's fantastical narrative, recounting the 'primitive' anti-hero's odyssey from the Amazon to São Paulo and back, is testimony to Brazil's wealth of popular and regional cultures, as well as a complex and sober commentary on the dilemmas of modernity and **development** and the prospects for survival of traditional identities and ways of life.

Andrade drew on many sources, but owed much to German traveller Theodor Koch-Grünberg's *Myths and Legends of the Taulipange and Arekúna Indians* (1916). Koch-Grünberg's Makunaima ('the great wicked one') supplied Andrade with the crucial paradox of the book's subtitle, 'the hero without any character'. While debates raged about 'national character', often using the language of scientific racism, Andrade celebrated the exploits of an ethnic chameleon, black, indigenous, blonde and blue-eyed, whose moral, psychological and even linguistic inconsistency mocked Brazil's official Order and Progress ideology. An enemy of Order, like his real-life urban counterpart, the Brazilian 'hustler' or **malandro**, Macunaíma is infuriatingly irresponsible, yet irresistibly subversive.

Andrade saw identity not as a stable category but as an open-ended process of becoming, hybrid (see **hybridity**) and transcultural. He appeared to share this dialectical perspective with Oswald de **Andrade**, who seized on the book as the masterpiece of his cannibalist movement, **Antropofagia**; the subsequent rift between the two, however, suggested profound differences in their prognosis for Brazil's cultural development. The overwhelming defeatism with which *Macunaíma* concludes suggests, not the revolutionary cannibalist synthesis envisaged by Oswald, but a more pessimistic scenario in which the Brazilian capacity for adaptation also renders him vulnerable to marginalization and acculturation, and to being devoured by the world around him.

This was the perspective of Joaquim Pedro de **Andrade**'s 1969 film adaptation which, in updating the setting to reflect the atmosphere of the **economic miracle**, foregrounded the theme of consumer capitalism. A product of the **Tropicália** movement and of the third phase of **Cinema Novo**, Andrade's film captured this carnivalesque atmosphere using the resources of the commercial cinema – colour, elaborate sets and a large cast – together with elements of Brazil's genre of musical comedy, the **chanchada**. In a further adaptation in 1978, this time for the stage, experimental dramatist **Antunes Filho** made ingenious use of actors and stage choreography to convey the narrative's rhapsodic flux. Its success on repeated international tours over the following decade suggests that Andrade's text and its popular trickster hero will remain a crucial and enduring source of reflection on Brazil's cultural development.

Further reading

Andrade, M. de (1978) *Macunaíma: o herói sem sem nenhum caráter*, São Paulo: SCCT.

—— (1988) *Macunaíma*, trans. R. Goodland, London: Carcanet.

Johnson, R. (1978) 'Macunaíma as Brazilian Hero', *Latin American Literary Review*: 38–44.

Proença, M.C. (1969) *Roteiro de Macunaíma*, Rio de Janeiro: Civilização Brasileira.

DAVID TREECE

Madariaga, Francisco

b. 1927, Buenos Aires, Argentina

Poet

Madariaga might well be considered one of the most important poets of the late twentieth century, were his work to be more widely known. In 1987, the **Fondo de Cultura Económica** published his complete works under the suggestive title *El tren casi fluvial* (The Almost Riverborne Train); it included ten volumes, from *El pequeño patíbulo* (The Little Scaffold) of 1954 to *Resplandor de mis bárbaras* (Light of My Barbarians) of 1985. The setting of his work is the province of Corrientes; its central theme is the tension between urban and rural, expressed through bilingualism. **Guarani** scans its rhythms and its world view, producing a strange everyday experience.

ENRIQUE FOFFANI

Madres de Plaza de Mayo

One of the most enduring of the Latin American mothers' movements, the Mothers of Plaza de Mayo defied the dictatorship from almost the beginnings of the Argentine **Proceso** (1976–83). They organized to demand information about their **disappeared** children and, frustrated by the lack of information and judicial delay, began marching in the Plaza de Mayo, becoming the conscience of Argentina. They wore white scarves symbolizing diapers and motherhood, and marched bearing photos of their children on Thursday afternoons. Several of these brave women were also disappeared or were threatened during their campaign. As a result of the mothers' protests, the public space of the Plaza de Mayo, claimed by patriots and politicians, underwent a complete transformation which went with a redefinition of the figure of the mother and of motherhood in Argentina.

Initially dubbed the Mad Women (*Las Locas*) of Plaza de Mayo by the dictatorship, they were considered intransigent even by democratic governments because of their commitment to the judgment and punishment of all culprits. While their discourse was appropriated by the extreme left, they persevered as a group united by the simple but often unrealizable slogan *Aparición con vida* (Bring Them Back Alive), which acknowledged their pledge not to mourn their children but to bring the assassins to justice. With the advent of democracy, however, the Mothers split and some difficulties arose with other human rights groups.

When President Alfonsín formed the National Commission on the Disappeared (CONADEP) – not a parliamentary commission with substantive powers but an advisory panel to merely review and send criminal cases to the courts – he appointed ten prominent citizens to it, none of whom was a member of the Mothers. Nobel Peace Prize winner Adolfo **Pérez Esquivel** refused to join the Commission in protest at this neglect. While the 1985 trials of the members of the Junta (the military government) under Alfonsín's government became an important historical event, the leniency of the sentences and the subsequent pardon (*indulto*) by President **Menem** provoked serious disappointment among the Mothers. By the late 1990s, their demands remained largely unfulfilled. Though they are heroines to the Europeans, some Argentines have found the obstinate and painful struggle of the Mothers difficult to tolerate even in a democratic regime.

See also: Bonafini, Hebe de

Further reading

Fisher, J. (1989) *Mothers of the Disappeared*, Boston, MA: South End Press.
Guzmán Bouvard, M. (1994) *Revolutionizing Motherhood: The Mothers of the Plaza de Mayo*, Wilmington, DE: Scholarly Resources.

FLORENCIA GARRAMUÑO

Mãe Menininha

b. 1894; d. 1986, Salvador, Bahia, Brazil

Candomblé priestess

As the most celebrated **Candomblé** priestess of the twentieth century, Mãe Menininha (born Escolástica Maria da Conceição Nazaré) was instrumental in establishing the legitimacy and dignity of her religion in a society that was often intolerant and fearful of Afro-Brazilian culture. For over fifty years, she was the head priestess of Ilê Iyá Omin Axé Iyamassé, a temple popularly known as Gantois. She maintained close relationships with intellectuals, bourgeois patrons and local politicians, who courted her support. In 1971, Dorival **Caymmi** composed 'Oração de Mãe Menininha', a praise song that spread her fame throughout Brazil.

CHRISTOPHER DUNN

Mãe Stella

b. 1925, Salvador, Bahia, Brazil

Candomblé priestess

Since 1976, Mãe Stella (Maria Stella de Azevedo Santos) has been the supreme priestess, or *iyalorixá* of Ilê Axé Opô Afonjá, currently the most prestigious **Candomblé** temple in Brazil. She has distinguished herself as a guardian of Afro-Brazilian religious orthodoxy and a wise advocate on behalf of her temple. At the Second World Conference of the Orixá Tradition in 1983 (see ***orixás***), Stella positioned herself at the forefront of an ongoing movement to re-Africanize Candomblé by publicly repudiating its syncretic association with Catholicism. In 1993 she published her memoirs, *Meu Tempo é Agora* (My Time is Now).

CHRISTOPHER DUNN

Mafalda

Mafalda first appeared in a comic strip, but she is much more than a cartoon character. Umberto Eco, Julio **Cortázar** and Gabriel **García Márquez**, among others, have written about her, for Mafalda is a unique icon. In 1963, the humourist

Quino was contracted to write a comic strip which would indirectly promote a new line of kitchen equipment. Mafalda was born, and although the products never appeared on the market, the comic strip did survive and on 29 September 1964 appeared for the first time in the magazine *Primera plana*. A young girl (Mafalda) pressures her parents with continuous questions about freedom, equality, dignity, politics, the role of women, tenderness, God, justice and so on. In the following year a new friend, Felipe, appeared to help her. In 1965 Mafalda moved to the newspaper *El Mundo*, where Susanita and Manolito joined the two friends. Mafalda's success was incontestable; strips cut out of the newspaper appeared in windows, in people's diaries and on notice boards. In Christmas 1966 the first annual appeared, published by Editorial Jorge Alvarez, who went on to publish four more. When *El mundo* closed, Mafalda moved to the weekly *Siete días*, where Mafalda's brother Guille was born and Libertad arrived.

In 1968 the cartoon was published in Italy when thirty strips were included in the anthology *Libro dei bambini terribili per adulti masochisti* (Book of Terrible Children for Masochistic Adults) and the compilation *Mafalda la contestataria* (Mafalda the Rebel). In 1970 Mafalda was taken over by Ediciones de la Flor for the sixth annual, and she made her first appearance in Spain, where the Franco government insisted that the books carry the injunction 'for adults only' on the cover. By 1971 Mafalda had been translated into over seven languages and published in books, journals and newspapers across the world. In 1973 Mafalda and her friends bid farewell to *Siete Dias* and to the cartoon strip. Thereafter Mafalda was used in public information campaigns, and in 1977 UNICEF asked Quino to illustrate their world campaign for the Declaration of the Rights of the Child. In 1981 Mafalda appeared in her own full-length feature, and in 1988 was awarded the 'Max and Moritz' prize at the the Third International Festival of the Comic in Germany.

Further reading

Quino (1997) *10 años con Mafalda*, Buenos Aires: Ediciones de la Flor.

RODRIGO PEIRETTI

Maga, La

Argentine cultural weekly which began publication in September 1991 under the editorship of Carlos Ares. It specializes in reports and information on cinema, theatre, books, visual arts, serials, psychology, television, radio, ecology, photography, architecture, humour, language, music, dance, education, fashion, and social customs. Its tone is light, and its primary function is to provide a calendar of events, though it also contains investigative reports. It is a forty-eight-page tabloid in black and white, with a print run of 20,000. It also publishes monthly issues dedicated to radio, television, football, theatre, **tango**, humour and special issues on Julio **Cortázar** and Pablo **Neruda**.

LAURA SIRI

Magaña, Sergio

b. 1924, Tepalcatepec, Mexico; d. 1990, Mexico City

Playwright

A major figure in twentieth-century Mexican theatre, Magaña wrote a small number of carefully crafted and profound plays exploring the themes of liberty, power and despair in the modern world.

Magaña learned his dramatic skills from Salvador **Novo**, Fernando Wagner, Seki Sano and Rodolfo **Usigli** (though he later distanced himself from Usigli) and worked with outstanding dramatists like Luisa Josefina **Hernández** and Emilio **Carballido**, who was also a member of the Filosofía y Letras Theatre Group at **UNAM** which first performed Magaña's *La noche transfigurada* (The Transfigured Night) in 1947. Recognition came in 1951 with the première of *Los signos del Zodíaco* (The Signs of the Zodiac), directed by Salvador Novo.

The central theme of Magaña's work is liberty. His protagonists face dilemmas in their struggle to overcome fear and repression, sometimes succeeding and sometimes failing. He examines the power relations between individuals in a microcosm representative of more complex social and historical realities.

Schooled in the realist mould, only half his work is written in that way. He also wrote pieces involving many individuals in a kind of mural, as well as intense and concentrated monologues, such as *El reloj y la cuna* (The Clock and the Cradle) (1952). He worked in all dramatic forms, from tragedy to political commentary, and pioneered musical theatre in Mexico – in the US style – with *Rentas congeladas* (Frozen Rents) (1960), *El mundo que tú heredas* (The World You Inherit) (1970) and *Santísima* (1980). He composed the music for all these works, as well as a number of songs.

Magaña's work can be grouped in several cycles: his urban cycle embraces *Los signos de Zodíaco* (The Signs of the Zodiac) (1951), *El pequeño caso de Jorge Lívido* (The Little Case of Jorge Lívido) (1958) and *Los motivos del lobo* (Motives of the Wolf) (1965); another cycle is set in Pre-Columbian and Conquest times – *Moctezuma II* (1953), *Cortés y la Malinche* (better known as *Los argonautas* (The Argonauts)) (1967) and *Los enemigos* (The Enemies) (1984). Magaña also wrote theatre for children, including *El viaje de Nocresida* (Nocresida's Travels) (1952), written with Carballido, and *El anillo de oro* (The Golden Ring) (1960). Other important works include *Ensayando a Molière* (Rehearsing Molière) (1966), *El que vino a hacer la guerra* (The Man who Came to Make War) (1972) and *La última diana* (The Last Reveille) (1984).

Magaña combined writing with theatre criticism and classes at the Theatre School of Mexico's National Institute of Fine Arts. He also wrote film scripts, a book of stories *El ángel roto* (Broken Angel) (1946) and a novel, *El molino del aire* (The Windmill) (1953). In later years he began to create an archive of his own work at the Rodolfo Usigli Centre for Theatre Research and Documentation. His work has yet to be collected in a complete works; most of it remains dispersed in journals.

Further reading

Magaña, S. (1985) *Moctezuma II, Cortés y la Malinche*, Mexico: Mexicanos Unidos.

—— (1990) *Los enemigos*, Mexico: Mexicanos Unidos.

EDUARDO CONTRERAS SOTO

Magdaleno, Mauricio

b. 1906, Zacatecas, Mexico; d. 1986, Mexico City

Writer

Several years spent living in one of Mexico's poorest regions provided rich material for Magdaleno's novels, notably *El resplandor* (Sunburst) (1937). He organized the avant-garde (see **avant-garde in Latin America**) group Teatro Ahora with **Bustillo Oro** and became an exceptional screenwriter, working closely with the director Emilio 'El Indio' **Fernández**, cinematographer Gabriel **Figueroa** and stars like Dolores **Del Rio**, María **Félix** and Pedro **Armendáriz**. Magdaleno wrote numerous novels, short story collections, biographies and essays. During the administration of Adolfo López Mateos, he played a prominent role as senator and Undersecretary for Cultural Affairs.

CYNTHIA STEELE

Maggi, Carlos

b. 1922, Montevideo, Uruguay

Playwright

Considered the most important playwright of 'the generation of '45', Maggi is also a respected essayist and fiction writer. His major plays include *La trastienda* (The Back Store) (1958), *La noche de los ángeles inciertos* (The Night of the Uncertain Angels) (1960), *La gran viuda* (The Great Widow) (1961), *El baile del cangrejo* (The Crab's Dance) (1971), *Frutos* (Fruit) (1985) and *Un cuervo en la madrugada* (A Blackbird at Dawn) (1989). He has also ventured into film and television, and won, in 1962, the Brussels Film Festival grand prize for his film, *La raya amarilla* (The Yellow Line) (1962). His essays include *Gardel, Onetti y algo más* (Gardel, Onetti, and More) (1964) and *Los militares, la televisión y otras razones de uso interno* (The Military, Television and Other Matters for Internal Use) (1986).

MARINA PIANCA

magic, white/black

The term magic covers a wide range of acts and phenomena, from simple illusion and prestidigitation, usually performed for amusement, to invocation of supernatural powers to effect changes in the natural world. As amusement, magic can be simple (card tricks, making coins appear behind children's ears) or elaborate, (with many props, smoke and mirrors). In Latin America the most frequently seen prestidigitators are circus clowns. Small, usually one-ring circuses, circulate throughout the cities of Latin America, often timing appearances to coincide with patronal festivities.

As manipulation of supernatural powers, magic is typically divided into two classes: 'white' magic, which seeks to bring about positive changes, and 'black' magic, which typically is maleficient. When applied to manipulation of supernatural powers, the term 'magic' is usually an out-group label, applied by non-believers to another group's exercise of part of a belief system, religious or allo-religious. During Spanish colonial times, many indigenous rites were condemned by the Church for idolatry and paganism; religious practitioners were labelled witches and persecuted. In the highland regions of Chiapas and Guatemala, the term *brujo* is used to refer to those who transform themselves into moths or other spirit-pair animals and can send illness and misfortune; periodically, communities purge themselves of witches by enclosing them in their houses and burning the structures.

Some magics do not require religious specialists. Lay people may manipulate simple good-luck charms (lucky coins or divinatory beans), ward off evils with talismans (pouches of *asafoetida* or garlic) or make signs in the air (the habit of crossing oneself before setting out on a journey in a vehicle), or practise sympathetic magic that depends on metaphoric associations: using small images of game animals in preparation for the hunt; drinking milky saps by women wanting to increase lactation. These simple magics rely on immanent relationships or spiritual bonds.

Some indigenous groups of Mexico, the Amazon and highland South America divine through the interpretation of the patterns seen in visions induced with plant substances, such as native **tobacco**, mushrooms, coca leaves and tree barks. Mayan religious specialists may divine with the use of locust beans, crystals or visual and auditory properties of sacred fires. Omens present themselves to Mayan laity as well, who recognize the crackling of household fire as signals that guests are coming, interpret the appearance of moths in the home, coyotes in town and owl cries as harbingers of death, and credit being remembered by someone as the cause of sneezing. To ward off evil, many Latin Americans wear crosses, or relic bundles, around their necks. Garlands or twists of garlic heads protect thresholds against witches. Babies are protected from the evil eye by covering their faces in public, and burning chile peppers over them or in their rooms. Sympathetic magics are induced by eating hot foods to become potent, by rubbing milky saps on breasts or drinking such gruels for lactation, or by planting crops or spermatazoa during the full moon.

More potent supernatural powers must usually be invoked by forms of prayer. Once invoked, they may be bartered with or cajoled into helping the supplicant. If such help brings no harm to others, the magic is classified as 'white'; if it involves sending illness or death to others, then it is 'black'. Some magico-religious systems do not separate these functions; in others, different spirits must be invoked to cause harm. In some systems, the same practitioner may work for 'good' or 'evil' depending on the needs of her client; in others, specialists handle the invocation of 'evil'. Whereas in many systems, such as **Candomblé**, **Santería** and Choloq'ij, the powers, ***orishás*** or *ruwaq'ijs*, invoked are bivalent, having both positive and negative attributes; the recent popularization of these belief systems and their export to non-traditional practitioners has resulted in more unidimensional stereotyping of the nature of the spirits, some coming to be invoked for good and others being considered powerful agents of evil. Practitioners find that rendering proper homage to these spirits can result in aid in their daily lives: curing of illness, success in business, romantic gratification and revenge. Non-practitioners either find no basis for the supposed efficacy of these practices or attribute experienced success to the strength of the belief – a spiritual placebo effect.

Further reading

Bastien, J.W. (1978) *Mountain of the Condor: Metaphor and Ritual in an Andean Ayllu*, St Paul: West Publishing Company.

Coelho, V.C. (1998) *Ritos encantatórios: os signos que serpenteiam as chamadas bruxas*, São Paulo: R. Annablume.

Davis, W. (1985) *The Serpent and the Rainbow*, New York: Simon & Schuster.

Tedlock, B. (1992) *Time and the Highland Maya*, Albuquerque: University of New Mexico Press.

JUDITH MAXWELL

magical realism

Coined by art critic Franz Roh in 1925 to describe German post-expressionist painting, this term was adopted and popularized by Latin American fiction writers and critics after it declined in Europe. Its literary meaning has changed radically and is still debated. Since the mid-1970s, it has been widely associated with the style or narrative mode of novels like Alejo **Carpentier**'s 1949 *El reino de este mundo* (The Kingdom of This World), Miguel Angel **Asturias**'s 1949 *Hombres de maíz* (Men of Maize), Juan **Rulfo**'s 1955 *Pedro Páramo*, and Gabriel **García Márquez**'s 1967 *Cien años de soledad* (One Hundred Years of Solitude). Similar authors of this period include Ecuadorian Demetrio **Aguilera Malta** and Brazilian João Guimarães **Rosa**. The style is characterized by storytelling from a primitivist viewpoint that challenges modern western norms. The authors draw from the worldview of tribal societies of Indian, African or archaic Christian origin, as well as their fusion known as **syncretism**. Myth, magic, and superstition are presented as normal everyday realities in Latin America, while common aspects of technology, modernity, and western rationality are naively regarded with suspicion and disbelief. Due in part to the recent international influence of Latin American fiction, magical realism is now considered a worldwide phenomenon.

Its meaning within Latin American criticism has undergone three major stages. It was first adopted by dramatist Rodolfo **Usigli** (1940) and critics Alvaro Lins (1944) and José Antonio **Portuondo** (1952) to signify the opening of traditional realism to new poetic, psychological, and existential tendencies then in vogue – particularly among writers of the southern cone (Argentina, Uruguay, and Chile). A second stage began with Angel Flores' influential article (1955) which defined the term as a 'mixture of reality and fantasy', citing Kafka as precursor and **Borges** as initiator. This broad definition, including any deviation from traditional realism, gave rise to a debate never fully resolved. Yet in the 1970s, French criticism distinguished 'the fantastic' as a genre (see **fantastic literature**), indirectly narrowing the scope for magical realism. No longer confused with the fantastic, and with psycho-existentialist literature out of vogue, magical realism came to be regarded as modernist anthropological fiction sympathetically portraying the surviving magical worldview of 'primitive' folk – particularly in the Caribbean and the larger 'Afro-Indian zone'. The enormous success of *Cien años de soledad* reinforced that conception, as this novel became a sort of model and trademark for magical realism internationally.

The primitivist conception of magical realism originates, however, with Italian writer Massimo Bontempelli, who proposed since 1926 a 'realistic precision and magical atmosphere', claiming the dawn of a new era where modern artists must be 'primitives with a past' and discover the surreal in reality itself. His friend, Venezuelan writer and diplomat Arturo **Uslar Pietri**, defined magical realism in Venezuelan fiction as a 'realism of primitives' (1948). Uslar, who befriended Asturias and Carpentier in 1920s Paris, must have been the link whereby the concept passed to Latin America. The three participated in Surrealism's cult of primitive art. After returning home, Asturias, inspired by Mayan myths of his native Guatemala, would refer to his own work as magical realism. In turn, Carpentier would coin his own related term: *lo real maravilloso americano* (the marvellous American real). Carpentier criticized French Surrealism for invoking the marvellous in disbelief by means of artificial recipes such as the 'chance encounter' of objects never to be found together in reality. He considered European primitivism false in comparison to the primitive realities of Latin America, where the marvellous was found daily and throughout history in a natural 'authentic' state, by virtue of the chance encounter of disparate cultures and the syncretism of Indian, African, and Christian beliefs. He concluded that 'the sensation of marvellous presupposes a faith'. Carpentier's 'marvellous real' has been immensely influential, not just as a literary concept, but as a matter of Latin American identity and expression.

The marvellous real, however, is not quite synonymous with magical realism, nor with the concoction 'marvellous realism' proposed by some. Carpentier could not admit an 'ism' at all, because he claimed the marvellous was in Latin American reality itself, not in the technique of storytelling. Yet, his concept served to justify magical realism as a form of expression rooted in regional identity; therefore claiming to be 'authentically' Latin American, not another imitation of western (or northern) models. Carpentier and Asturias have been criticized for claiming a mystical connection with the primitive essence of Latin American reality. As faith in their foundational literary myth eroded, authors like Rulfo and García Márquez engaged magical realism frankly as an artful distortion of reality, bordering on parody and caricature. There is no pretence that the supernatural events in their novels should be taken at face value; rather, they suggest an allegorical interpretation of Latin American history and culture. This movement toward greater artificiality underscores more recent novels like Isabel **Allende**'s 1982 *La casa de los espíritus* (The House of the Spirits), Mario **Vargas Llosa**'s 1987 *El hablador* (The Storyteller), and Laura Esquivel's 1990 ***Como agua para chocolate*** (Like Water for Chocolate). Film versions of Allende's and Esquivel's novels have further popularized the style.

See also: *real maravilloso, lo*; fantastic literature

Further reading

Angulo, M.-E. (1995) *Magic Realism: Social Context and Discourse*, New York and London: Garland.

Parkinson Zamora, L. and Faris, W. (eds) (1995) *Magical Realism: Theory, History, Community*, Durham and London: Duke University Press.

ERIK CAMAYD-FREIXAS

Maia, Éolo

b. 1942, Ouro Preto, Brazil

Architect

Maia's work is infused with a revolutionary spirit. He is a graduate of the Federal University of Minas Gerais in Belo Horizonte, the city where he still lives and works, organizing with other architects a series of social residential and restoration projects. Irreverence and eclecticism, founded on a creative subjectivity, mark his work in a reaction against the dogmatism of earlier schools of architecture. His style fuses traditional and modern, seeks a reconciliation of the aesthetic and the social, and sets out to adjust his disturbing buildings to local conditions, people and environment. His aim always is to give architecture a more human dimension.

VIVALDO SANTOS

Mais, Roger

b. 1905, Jamaica; d. 1955, Jamaica

Writer

Called 'the spokesman of emergent Jamaica' by Jean **D'Costa** in a critical 1978 essay, Mais was arrested and imprisoned for six months in 1947 for an essay called 'Now We Know' – an attack on British colonialism. He started writing his first novel in prison; it was published nine years later. His subsequent writings included *And Most of All Man* (short stories and verse), 1939; *Face and Other Stories* (short stories and verse), 1942; *The Hills Were Joyful Together* (novel), 1953; *Brother Man* (novel), 1954 and *Black Lightning* (novel), 1955. Mais died of cancer in Jamaica after travelling for three years in Europe. He left a fourth, incomplete novel.

KEITH JARDIM

Maison de l'Amérique Latine

French institution based in two historic town houses in Paris's Faubourg Saint Germain. Founded in 1946, the Maison de l'Amérique

Latine is supported by the French and several Latin American governments, whose ambassadors occupy by turn the post of director of the institution. The Maison organizes diplomatic activities, cultural events (concerts, round tables, lectures, exhibitions, literary and painting competitions) and economic projects (establishing relationships between French and Latin American enterprises and commercial institutions). It is financed by government subsidies and income from the use of its premises.

JULIO PREMAT

maize *see* corn and corncakes

Malagueña, La

In 1938 Pedro Galindo Galarza, a member of Los Trovadores Chicanos, a Yucatecan musical group formed in 1932, composed the lyrics to one of Mexico's most popular love songs, 'La Malagueña'; the music had been written by another member of the troupe, Elpidio Ramírez ('el Viejo'). In La Malagueña, a soulful lament, a male suitor praises the beauty of a young woman who has bewitched and deceived him, and whom he accuses of rejecting him because of his poverty. There is another version of the song, with similar words but a different melody, by Cuban composer Ernesto **Lecuona**.

CYNTHIA STEELE

malandro

The *malandro* is an urban Brazilian social type regarded as a shiftless and crafty hustler or rogue, who avoids work and lives on the margins of conventional society. The figure of the *malandro* has been famously portrayed in Manuel Antônio de Almeida's 1855 novel *Memórias de um sargento de milícias* (Memoirs of a Militia Sergeant) and Chico **Buarque**'s musical drama of 1978, *Ópera do malandro*, which was subsequently made into a film by Ruy **Guerra**. Countless samba songs, such as those sung by Bezerra da Silva, exalt the malandro as a subversive figure in an unjust society.

CHRISTOPHER DUNN

malaria

Malaria, the most prevalent of all serious infectious diseases, occurs throughout tropical and subtropical regions, and the so-called malaria belt includes portions of Mexico, Haiti, the Dominican Republic, Honduras and Ecuador, where climactic conditions are favourable to the anopheles mosquito that transmits the disease. Symptoms of the disease include repeated attacks of shaking, chills, high fever, headache and profuse sweating. In some types of malaria blood vessels may be blocked, affecting the brain and resulting in coma and even death. Although it is not known with certainty when malaria first appeared in the Americas, it is believed to have been introduced in this area by European explorers in the late fifteenth century. It is estimated that more than 100 million cases occur each year, about 10 per cent of which are fatal. In some places nearly the entire population is infected, with many people developing only mild cases because of partial immunity, due to repeated infections. An early effective treatment used to alleviate malarial fevers from 1700 until the Second World War, was the administration of quinine, a substance extracted from the bark of the cinchona tree, an evergreen native to the South American Andes and found as far north as Costa Rica. The tree is now extensively cultivated in Latin America as an important source not only of quinine but also of quinidine, used in certain disorders of heart rate and rhythm. Attempts to control malaria depend primarily on eradicating the mosquitoes that carry the disease. The use of insecticides may be very effective, as is draining marshy areas where mosquitoes breed. Advances in eradicating the mosquitoes were made with the introduction of DDT, used in a major antimalaria campaign launched by the United Nations World Health Organization in 1955. Although this programme succeeded in reducing the incidence of malaria in many areas, scientists believe that complete eradication of the disease may not be possible.

Before visiting a region in which malaria is common, travellers can use preventive drugs presently available, although a chloraquine-resistance version of the disease currently spreading around the world is making this drug less effective. In the early 1990s, a Colombian scientist, Dr Manuel **Patarroyo** developed a new vaccine which he donated to the WHO; his discovery is still the subject of controversy.

Further reading

Desowitz, R.S. (1991) *The Malaria Capers: More Tales of Parasites and People*, Norton: Research and Reality.
Knell, A.J. (1991) *Malaria*, Oxford: Oxford University Press.

EDUARDO GUÍZAR-ALVAREZ

Malavoi

Malavoi is an eclectic band of Western classically-trained musicians prominent in the French Antilles since the 1960s. The band combines Cuban-influenced rhythms with ideas drawn from traditional dance forms such as quadrille and ensembles such as the Guadaloupian gwo ka drums. It also features large-scale string arrangements related to the use of violins in Cuban charanga groups, combining these with material stemming from French Antillean traditional melodies. Malavoi has also assimilated elements of the region's popular **zouk** style. Essential to the band's 1990s success was the contribution of the talented lead singer Pipo Gertrude.

MICHAEL BURNETT

Maldonado, Eduardo

b. 1941, Mexico City

Film-maker

Maldonado is an outstanding **documentary** film-maker, working in a genre which is underdeveloped in Mexico. His early short films focused attention on the problems of rural Mexico. In the early 1970s he formed the Cine Testimonio (Testimonial Cinema) group, whose pioneering films included his *Atencingo, cacicazgo y corrupción* (Landlords and Corruption) (1973), *Una y otra vez* (Over and Over Again) (1975) and *Jornaleros* (Day Labourers) (1977), innovative documentaries of social and political analysis. Maldonado also conducted research on agricultural projects for Mexico's National University, and from 1983 to the late 1980s directed the Centro de Capacitación Cinematográfica (Film Training Centre).

PATRICIA TORRES SAN MARTÍN

Maldonado, Rocío

b. 1951, Tepic, Nayarit, Mexico

Artist

In the late 1980s and early 1990s, Maldonado was a leading figure in the so-called 'neo-Mexicanist' movement, in which artists adopted representational modes and incorporated images from traditional folk culture. Her paintings and prints frequently include images of the Virgin of Guadelope (see **Virgins, miraculous**), hearts, and papier-mâché dolls, along with fragmented classical and baroque sculptures. Other works are more meditative and delicate depictions of natural forms (plants, shells and stones). Her first one-person exhibition was in 1980, and she has since participated in numerous exhibitions, including *Women in Mexico* at the National Academy of Design in New York in 1990. She lives and works in Mexico City.

JAMES OLES

Maldonado, Tomás

b. 1922, Buenos Aires, Argentina

Painter, designer and theorist

Tomás Maldonado studied at the Academia Nacional de Bellas Artes in Buenos Aires to 1938. In 1944 he contributed to *Arturo* magazine. In 1945, he and his poet brother Edgar **Bayley** formed the Asociación Arte Concreto-Invención in

Buenos Aires. Many of the most important texts of the group were written by Maldonado. He left Argentina in 1955 for a distinguished international career in industrial design, having abandoned painting in the early 1950s.

GABRIEL PEREZ-BARREIRO

Maldoror

Maldoror is a literary journal named after the book by Uruguayan-French writer Isidore Ducasse. It was founded in 1967 by Paul Fleury, Lucien Mercier, Amanda Berenguer and José Pedro Díaz, to promote bilingual (French and Spanish) culture in Uruguay. The magazine identified with the left but did not limit itself to realist works, publishing writings which exalted all spheres of the imagination. During the dictatorship of 1973–85, Paul Fleury fled the country and the French faction started diminishing. By 1975, when Carlos Pellegrino became editor, *Maldoror* had lost its cosmopolitan bilingualism; by its final issue in 1992, its focus had become solely Spanish.

VICTORIA RUÉTALO

Maldoror, Sarah

b. 1929, France

Film-maker

Documenting black culture and struggle, especially that of women, Maldoror's first short, *Monangambée* (1969), concerns a black Algerian woman whose husband is unjustly imprisoned; in *Des Fusils pour Banta* (Guns for Banta) (1971) Algerian resistance fighters represent themselves, while *Sambizanga* (1972) traces an Angolan woman's participation in her country's political struggles. Two among the nearly twenty films she made in the 1970s and 1980s pay homage to the influential Caribbean intellectual and resistance leader, *Aimé* **Cesaire**: *Un Homme, une terre* (A Man, A Country) (1977) and *Aimé Césaire, le masque des mots* (The Mask of Words)

(1987). Maldoror remains a fervent advocate of African cinema.

ANN MARIE STOCK

Malecón, El

El Malecón is a seven-kilometre promenade and sea wall along Havana harbour, and a symbol of the capital. It begins at two docks in the bay and extends to the mouth of the river Almendares, integrating a series of colonial forts into the city. Building began in 1901–2 and was completed during the 1930s, although it found its definitive form only in the 1950s. It is central to Havana's social life, and is frequently referred to in literature, cinema, the visual arts and popular music. Havana carnival has often been held there, and it remains a meeting place for the urban population.

WILFREDO CANCIO ISLA

Malfatti, Anita

b. 1896, São Paulo, Brazil; d. 1964, São Paulo

Painter

Malfatti's expressionistic style and bold, subjective colours depicting Brazilian imagery created shock waves that propelled **Brazilian modernism** into public consciousness, creating a furious and eventually fruitful debate. Her first art teacher was her mother. Technically aware and eager to experiment, Malfatti trained in Europe (1910–14) and the USA (1915), encountering expressionism in Germany and cubism in France, where she was acquainted with Léger, Matisse and Fujita. Returning to São Paulo, she became an art teacher. She was recognized in the 1933 São Paulo Fine Arts Show with a silver medal.

MARIA ANGELICA GUIMARÃES LOPES

Malinchismo

Malinchismo is a cultural pattern in which an individual devalues his national identity and culture in favour of a foreign, imported culture. A *Malinchista* (someone who practises *Malinchismo*) sells out his own nation. The term has its roots in Malinche, the name of the Indian woman who aided Hernán Cortés in the conquest of the Aztec empire. Very little is known about her life; in many respects, she is a literary construct because what is known is based upon short descriptions provided by Native and Spanish writers from the period. Also called Doña Marina by the Spanish, her original name was probably Malinalli Tenepal and she was born in 1502 or 1505, making her a teenager when she met Cortés. She apparently was born into nobility and then sold into slavery, after her mother had married a second time and produced a male heir to the throne. Along with nineteen other slaves, she was given to Cortés as gift from a Tabascan native ruler. Whatever her social status, Malinalli appeared to be highly educated for a slave and had a great facility with languages. She spoke both Yucatec Maya and Náhuatl and very quickly learned Spanish. Consequently, she became the primary linguistic and cultural interpreter for the European invaders. She was present at all major meetings between the Spanish and the native leadership including those with the emperor Montezuma. Considering the fact that Cortés could not have succeeded without hundreds of thousands of native allies, her linguistic abilities and cultural insights made Spanish victory possible. Malinche became the concubine of Cortés and bore him a son, Martín Cortés, in 1522. A year later, Cortés arranged her marriage to Juan Jaramillo, a fellow Spaniard. After that point, Malinche disappears from the historical record. After Independence from Spain, she was resurrected as an anti-Spanish symbol in Mexico. She is viewed as the first Eve, a symbol of national betrayal because she assisted, cohabited, married and bore the children of the invaders, rejecting her native people and especially native males. She has become the Mexican archetype of the whore and the traitor. Yet, she is considered the first mother of Mexico, a culturally and racially mixed nation, because she gave birth to the first mestizo. Today, feminist (and) Chicana scholars and writers are leading the way in an effort to redefine the real Malinche and reevaluate her role in Mexican history.

Further reading

Alarcón, N. (1983) 'Chicana's Feminist Literature: A Revision through Malintzin/or Malintzin: Putting Flesh Back on the Object', in C. Moraga and G. Anzaldúa (eds), *This Bridge Called My Back*, New York: Kitchen Table Press.

Cypress, S.M. (1991) *La Malinche in Mexican Literature: From History to Myth*, Austin: University of Texas Press.

Del Castillo, A.R. (1977) 'Malintzin Tenépal: A Preliminary Look into a New Perspective', in R. Sánchez and R. Martínez Cruz (eds), *Essays on La Mujer*, Los Angeles: Chicano Studies Centre.

LINDA A. CURCIO-NAGY

Mallea, Eduardo

b. 1904, Bahía Blanca, Argentina; d. 1982, Buenos Aires, Argentina

Writer

Mallea's works exude a chauvinistic nationalism and a fervent search for the Hispanic roots of Argentine society. He devoted many of his writings – *La Bahía del silencio* (The Bay of Silence) (1940), *Historia de una pasión argentina* (History of an Argentine Passion) (1937) and *La ciudad junto al río inmóvil* (The City by the Unmoving River) – to analysing the 'essence' of Argentine nationality. He was on the editorial board of the influential journal *Sur*, and also directed the literary supplement of the conservative newspaper *La **Nación***.

FLORENCIA GARRAMUÑO

Malvinas

The Malvinas (Falkland) Islands lie in the South Atlantic, some 800 kilometres from the Argentine coast and 12,500 kilometres from Britain. They are currently home to some 2,000 inhabitants, locally governed by their own legislative council, but ultimately under the direct colonial rule of Britain. There is also a large British armed garrison of a similar size to the local population. The capital, Port Stanley, is located on the eastern island and houses over half the population in mainly wood-built houses. Scattered sheep farm settlements and isolated farm houses cover the remainder of the islands, though farming is now in decline. This unlikely site of big power rivalry has been disputed territory between Britain and Argentina since the late eighteenth century.

Possibly first colonized by Breton sailors, the Malvinas were claimed by Spain in 1767 and, after independence from Spain in 1810, by Argentina. The British took over the islands in 1833 and claimed non-negotiable sovereignty over them from 1841. While the British and Argentine governments co-operated economically – as occurred throughout the nineteenth and early twentieth century – the question of sovereignty was hardly raised. With the withering of the special relationship, the growth of nationalist sentiment and the move towards decolonization in the mid-twentieth century, the Malvinas became a constant issue in inter-governmental talks and international fora. Little energy was expended, especially in Britain, on resolving the complexities of the dispute. In the early 1980s, British Foreign Minister Lord Carrington stated that the islands were foreign-policy priority Number 242 for Her Majesty's Government – not so for the Argentines, for whom they were priority Number 1.

It was a tragic irony that just while the British Foreign Office thought languidly about how to get out of the islands through lease-back, the military junta in Argentina decided to take them by force, in an attempt to bolster its waning internal control. They did not expect the decisive response of Margaret Thatcher, herself a nationalist warrior. The incomprehension and tragic mistakes led to a brief war of two months in which over a thousand died. As Reagan's UN adviser Jeanne Kirkpatrick put it: 'In Act One, the Argentines occupied the Falkland Islands, in Act Two, the British reoccupied them. Act Three has not yet been written.' In the aftermath of war, the British built up the islands' economy, installed a large garrison and the islanders became experienced political lobbyists.

Britain and Argentina restored diplomatic relations in 1990, agreeing to pursue bilateral relations, with the issue of sovereignty kept separate. That policy has held: there are now many areas of co-operation between Britain and Argentina, but the question of sovereignty over the islands remains as intractable as ever.

Further reading

Latin American Bureau (1982) *Falklands/Malvinas, Whose Crisis?*, London: Latin America Bureau.

Barnett, A (1982) *Iron Britannia: War over the Falklands*, special issue of *New Left Review* 134, July–August.

JOHN KING

mambo

The mambo is a Cuban dance music of uncertain origin. Some have suggested that Cuban bassist Cachao (see **López, Israel**) invented the term; he played in 1937 with the orchestra of Antonio Arcano, who added the conga drum to his line up to vary the rhythms and attract dancers. Cachao's brother Orestes, a cellist, wrote a dance piece called 'Mambo' in 1938, and the term became more widely used. But it was Cuban pianist **Pérez Prado** who made it popular; he formed an orchestra in Mexico in 1949 in the US style, with an expanded brass section, and composed pieces all containing the word 'mambo'.

JOSÉ ANTONIO EVORA

Mañach, Jorge

b. 1898, Sagua la Grande, Cuba; d. 1961, San Juan, Puerto Rico

Writer

A leading member of Cuba's **Grupo Minorista** and founder of the ***Revista de avance***, Mañach was a central figure in Cuba's cultural life through the 1930s. He was a journalist and editor of *Acción* (1934–5). In 1940 he returned to Cuba from five years of exile in the USA and was elected to the

Constituent Assembly. He taught at Havana University and presented the influential television programme *Ante la prensa* (Meet the Press). His many writings include the highly-praised biography *Martí el apóstol* (Martí the Apostle) and *Teoría de la frontera* (Theory of the Frontier) (1970), a posthumous collection of his lectures.

WILFREDO CANCIO ISLA

Manchete

A weekly magazine produced in Rio de Janeiro, *Manchete* originated with the design group Ucrania, founded by the Bloch brothers, refugees from the Russian revolution who arrived in Brazil in 1925. Launched in 1952, *Manchete* was modelled on European journals like *Epoca*, *Paris Match* and the US photo magazine *Life* in its extensive use of photography and its concern with **television**. Its collaborators included famous names like Carlos Heitor Cony, João Ubaldo **Ribeiro**, Carlos Chagas and Ziraldo. The Bloch group publishes several other titles, and its presses, located in the Parada de Lucas suburb of Rio de Janeiro, have the capacity to produce one million copies daily.

Radio Manchete AM began broadcasting in July 1971, and was followed by four FM transmitters in Rio, São Paulo, Brasília and Salvador. TV Manchete went on air in 1983 in Rio, and later became a national network with five stations of its own and 39 affiliates. Its opening programme was 'O Mundo Mágico', directed by film-maker Nelson Pereira dos **Santos**; that night it ran Steven Spielberg's *Close Encounters of the Third Kind*. The station later became known for its coverage of Rio's **carnival** processions and dances, for its ***telenovelas*** (particularly *Pantanal* (Swampland) (1989) set in the central region of Brazil known as the Pantanal do Matto Grosso), for its news programmes *Jornal da Manchete*, *Conexão Internacional* (International Connection) and its specials *Xingú*, on the indigenous peoples of Brazil, and *Japão* (Japan).

The headquarters of the Manchete organization are on a site designed by Oscar **Niemeyer** at **Aterro do Flamengo** which also houses the Adolfo Bloch theatre. After the death of the Bloch brothers, the directorship of the group was assumed in 1995 by Pedro Jack Kapeller.

ANTONIO CARLOS VAZ

Manga, Carlos

b. 1928, Rio de Janeiro, Brazil

Film-maker

Manga was principal director of *chanchada* films for the **Atlântida** studios until their closure in 1962. He was fascinated by Hollywood, and during his long collaboration with the comic actor **Oscarito** made a series of Hollywood parodies, like *Matar ou correr* (Kill or Run) (1954) where, in a clear allusion to Fred Zinneman's *High Noon*, he plays a Western gunman. *O homem do Sputnik* (Sputnik Man) (1959), was a satire on the Cold War and his most daring and personal statement. Later Manga moved into television, working for TV **Globo** as a producer, writer, director and publicist.

ISMAIL XAVIER AND THE USP GROUP

mangue beat

A Brazilian pop music movement of the early 1990s, mangue beat (the beat of the mangrove) emerged in the northeastern city of Recife. Its most important exponents include Jorge Cabeleira, who mixes punk rock with the traditional rhythms of Luiz **Gonzaga**'s accordion, the band Mundo Livre S/A, which combines Jorge Benjor's samba-funk with punk rock, and **Chico Science** and Nação Zumbi, whose lead singer died in a car accident at the age of thirty in 1997. Chico Science's two albums, the 1994 *Da Lama aos Caos* (From Mud to Chaos), and the 1996 *Afrociberdélia*, refer to *tropicalismo* as their inspiration.

CÉSAR BRAGA-PINTO

manifestos

Taken most broadly, a manifesto is a public declaration of principles or beliefs, and its often aggressive presentation can bear on politics, religion, philosophy or the arts. Most commonly associated with literary schools or periods, literary manifestos abounded in the twentieth century, perhaps because of the political and cultural turbulence surrounding the First World War. Rubén Darío's well-turned introduction to his seminal *Prosas profanas* (Profane Songs) (1896), representative of the refined language and ivory tower escapism typical of turn-of-the-century Spanish American modernism, was a predecessor.

A glance at the compilations of texts by Hugo Verani (1986), Nelson **Osorio** (1988), and Jorge **Schwartz** (1991) reveals that some forty literary manifestos or manifesto-like pronouncements appeared in the 1920s. Avant-garde figures and groups were in evidence in almost all nations, but the most significant manifestos were produced in the larger cultural centres. For example, the Chilean Vicente **Huidobro** and his *creacionismo* provided the earliest Latin American examples of avant-garde position-taking; his verse manifesto 'Arte poética' (Ars Poetica) (1916) and the multiple texts included in *Manifestes* (1925) are important representations of Huidobro's ideas. In Argentina, the most significant examples are the *Prisma* mural broadsides, written in 1921 and 1922 by Jorge Luis **Borges** and others, and the declamatory ***Martín Fierro*** manifesto, written by Oliverio **Girondo** and published in 1924. In Brazil, the argumentative tone was even more marked. Mário de **Andrade**'s 'Prefácio Interesantíssimo' (Most Interesting Preface) (1922) was a manifesto-like introduction to a long experimental poem; Oswald de **Andrade**'s 'Manifesto Pau-Brasil' (Brazilwood Manifesto) (1924) made a noisy case for new poetry in local terms. The most unusual such pronouncement in Brazil, and perhaps in all of Latin America, was Oswald de Andrade's 'Manifesto Antropófago' (Cannibalist Manifesto) (1928). Organized in fifty numbered segments and dated the '374th Year of the Swallowing of Bishop Sardinha', Andrade poked fun at antiquated European traditions (for example, the third section reads 'Tupi or not tupi, that is the question', a clever parody of Hamlet's words), which needed to be devoured and used as an energy source for new creations. Finally, Mexican ***estridentismo*** produced several aggressive manifesto texts during the 1920s. The first – 'Actual, Núm. 1' (Current, No. 1, 1921), written by Manuel **Maples Arce** and pasted on downtown walls in the city of Puebla – recommended drastic action: 'Chopin to the electric chair!' A second proclamation by Maples Arce and others was entitled 'Manifiesto estridentista núm. 2' (Second Stridentist Manifesto, 1923) and equated the movement with manhood and strength: 'To be a stridentist is to be a man. Only the eunuchs are not with us. We'll put out the sun with a single sweep of our hats!'

Manifestos of the visual arts are included in an appendix to Dawn Ades's *Art of Latin America* (1989), the most famous being Siqueiros's manifesto of the Mexican muralist movement. Of note in the 1960s and 1970s were the film manifestos associated with the **New Latin American Cinema**, especially those by **Grupo Cine Liberación**, Julio **García Espinosa** and Jorge **Sanjinés**.

Further reading

Schwartz, J. (1991) *Las vanguardias latinoamericanas*, Madrid: Cátedra.

Unruh, V. (1994) *Latin American Vanguards: The Art of Contentious Encounters*, Berkeley: University of California Press.

MERLIN H. FORSTER

manioc

A tuber, also known as cassava, which can be sweet (*Manioc palmata*) or bitter (*Manioc utilissima*). It is cultivated throughout the tropical world and used to produce flours, breads, tapioca, laundry starch and even alcoholic beverages. It is believed that it was first cultivated by the Maya in Yucatán.

In its sweet form, known as *yuca* in Spanish and *aipim* or *macaxeira* in Portuguese, it is a popular vegetable accompaniment – akin to potatoes – when boiled (for a long time) till tender and accompanied by a savoury sauce, as in the Cuban *mojo* of olive oil, lemon and garlic. It is also often simply fried and served as a snack in many Brazilian bars, and, when mixed with pork cracklings, throughout Central America; it is also the basis for the Jamaican *bami mush*. The bitter variety is most utilized in Brazil, where the tubers are pressed and roasted (to expel the poisonous hydrocyanic acid, once used for deadly darts and arrows), and then finely ground into *farinha de mandioca*, a gritty flour-like powder that is a food staple throughout the country. Traditionally a job performed by women (as seen at the beginning of Glauber **Rocha**'s *Deus e o diabo na terra do sol* (Black God, White Devil) (1964)), the grinding is a back-breaking process; today it is done industrially and *farinhas* are purchased in supermarkets, although the artisanal ones are highly-valued. *Farinha* is a 'must' with black beans and ***feijoada***, but is also always present on the table in special containers called *farinheiras* to be sprinkled atop any dish. This basic food staple is also the base for other accompaniments, like *pirão*, where it is mixed with coconut milk or other liquids (and often accompanies ***moqueca***), or *farofa*, where it is mixed with vegetables or eggs and fried in butter to resemble stuffing.

ANA M. LÓPEZ

Manisero, El

El Manisero (The Peanut Vendor) is the classic Cuban song, written by Moisés Simón (1889–1945) in 1928, popularized by the soprano Rita **Montaner**, and recorded by countless artists since, is an elaboration of the *pregón*, the cry of a street vendor advertising his wares. Typically, rather than being stationed at a kiosk or booth, the vendor makes his way around the neighbourhood on foot, alerting potential customers with his cry. The *pregón*, perceived as musical by many artists, inspired formal compositions, such as Nicolás **Guillén**'s poem 'Pregón' or Félix **Caignet**'s song 'Frutas del Caney'. In Moisés Simón's composition the singer addresses one young woman in particular, the 'muchachita', enticing her with his paper cones full of peanuts.

JAMES BUCKWALTER-ARIAS

Manivela, La

La manivela was a weekly Chilean television programme, shown on Channel 7 (1970), Channel 13 of the Catholic University (1971) and the University of Chile's channel (1972). Produced by the theatre group **ICTUS**, it included dramatic sketches, collectively created, which took a critical look at daily life or political events through the forms of the theatre of the absurd and black humour. A programme of great importance, combining critical ideas, entertainment and comedy, it was presented by Delfina **Guzmán**, Nissim **Sharim**, Julio Jung, Elena Devauchelle and Jaime Celedón. It was produced again in 1985 for the University of Valparaiso's television channel and in 1990 for the national channel.

ELIANA ORTEGA

Manley, Edna

b. 1900, Bournemouth, England; d. 1987, Jamaica

Sculptor

Edna Manley married her cousin, the future prime minister of Jamaica Norman **Manley**, in 1921 and moved to the island. Although she made multiple contributions to Jamaican art and culture as a dedicated patron of the arts, and was founding editor of the literary journal *Focus* in 1943, she is renowned for her sculpture, which captures the diverse and turbulent events of twentieth-century Jamaican history. The most acclaimed of her works is the 1935 *Negro Aroused*, a figure whose defiant gesture represents the Jamaican struggle for social and racial equality in the era of repressive British colonialism.

JILL E. ALBADA-JELGERSMA

Manley, Michael Norman

b. 1924, Kingston, Jamaica; d. 1997, Kingston

Politician

Son of political leader Norman Manley and sculptress Edna Manley, Michael Manley was born into one of the most prominent Jamaican families of the twentieth century. After receiving secondary education in Jamaica, Manley joined the Royal Canadian Air Force in 1943. After the Second World War, he received his college education in England. He graduated from the prestigious London School of Economics and worked for a year with the BBC before returning to Jamaica in 1952.

In Jamaica, Manley quickly became involved in the Peoples' National Party (PNP), the political party founded and led by his father. He worked first as a labour organizer with unions closely allied with the PNP. After a narrow PNP electoral defeat in 1962, Manley received a seat in Jamaica's appointed senate. In the 1967 elections he won his own elected seat in the House of Representatives, but the PNP remained the minority opposition party. In 1969, on the eve of his father's death, the younger Manley became the party leader. Thus, in 1972 when the PNP emerged victorious in general elections Michael Manley became Prime Minister. The PNP since its founding in 1938 had identified itself as a nationalist party and a party that favoured a strong government role in shaping social and economic development for the benefit of the majority working population. During two successive PNP governments between 1972 and 1980, Manley led efforts to carry out such policies and ultimately labelled PNP philosophy as democratic socialism.

While the decade did see much social and infrastructural progress, Jamaica also experienced severe economic difficulties caused by numerous factors including: government policies themselves; struggles with the IMF; and global economic troubles related to high oil prices and foreign policy conflicts with the USA. Manley and his government earned criticism from the US government for their professed socialist policies and also for the close relationships developed with international socialist and communist leaders, most notably Cuba's Fidel **Castro**. During this era Manley emerged as a well-respected statesman in the developing world and particularly within the Non-Aligned Movement, consisting of nations seeking to ally themselves with neither the USA nor the Soviet Union in the Cold War context.

In 1980, faced with continuing economic problems and rising crime and violence (fomented according to some observers by **CIA** intervention), the PNP was defeated in general elections. Manley was succeeded as Prime Minister by Edward Seaga, leader of the Jamaica Labour Party (JLP). The political rivalry between Seaga and Michael Manley in many ways continued that which had existed between Norman **Manley** and JLP founder Alexander **Bustamante**. The PNP was returned to power in 1989 elections and Manley served another term as Prime Minister until health problems forced him to step down in 1992. During this latter term he did not seek to fully reincarnate the democratic socialism of the 1970s, often explaining that such policies would always be constrained by the domination of the USA and other Western capitalist nations in the global economy. He addressed this problem at length in his book *Up the Down Escalator: Development and the International Economy. A Jamaican Case Study* (1987).

Manley was author of numerous other books and essays including *The Politics of Change: A Jamaican Testament* (1974) and *A History of West Indies Cricket* (1989). Despite the controversy that many of his policies generated he remains respected as one of the most distinguished and significant leaders of the twentieth-century Caribbean. Manley is still referred to by many Jamaicans according to the biblical nickname, 'Joshua', which he acquired as a labour leader in the 1960s.

Further reading

Levi, D. (1990) *Michael Manley: The Making of a Leader*, Athens: University of Georgia Press.

ROSANNE ADDERLEY

Manley, Norman Washington

b. 1893, Roxborough, Manchester, Jamaica; d. 1969, Kingston, Jamaica

Politician

An early activist on behalf of Jamaica's black majority, Manley founded the People's National Party (PNP) in 1938. The PNP and its rival, the Jamaica Labour Party (JLP), contested all Jamaican elections through the 1940s and 1950s. When Jamaica was granted increasing self government by the British in the mid-1950s Manley, as leader of the majority party, became the first Chief Minister and later the first Premier. However the PNP was the losing party in the general elections of 1962, the year of Jamaican independence. It was Manley's chief political rival Alexander **Bustamante**, leader of the JLP, who became the first Prime Minster of an independent Jamaica, while Manley served as leader of the opposition almost until his death. A lawyer, Manley completed his law degree as a Rhodes Scholar at Oxford University in England, although he interrupted his studies for two years to serve in the First World War, returning to Jamaica in 1922 where he practised law with distinction. He was married to noted Jamaican sculptress Edna **Manley**. Their second son Michael **Manley** inherited the leadership of the PNP and had a distinguished political career of his own.

ROSANNE ADDERLEY

Manns, Patricio

b. 1937, Bío Bío province, Chile

Writer and musician

Best known as a composer and singer, Manns' songs reflect his own lifelong political commitment; but they are far from 'pamphlet songs' – their lyrics are poetic and dense. Some, notably 'Cuando me acuerdo de mi país' (When I Remember my Country), have become unofficial anthems of the dispersed Chilean **exile** community. He is also poet, novelist, essayist, playwright and screenwriter and the biographer of the musical mentor of his generation, *Violeta* **Parra** (1986). His book of poems *Memorias de Bonampak* (Memories of Bonampak) (1995) is a neo-*indigenista* work that seeks to speak for the oppressed Maya people (see ***indigenismo***). The novel, *El corazón a contraluz* (The Heart in Silhouette) (1996), is about a historical figure, Julio Popper, a Jewish adventurer in southern Chile who links up with an Ona Indian girl in Tierra del Fuego. He has lived in France since 1973.

DANIEL BALDERSTON

Mano a mano

Like Contursi's Mi noche triste (My Sad Night) (1917), the first tango with lyrics, Mano a mano (Hand to Hand) (1920) was a new kind of tango with a more literary and poetic character. Written by Celedonio **Flores**, the song was inspired by the singer Nunziatta, who sat in a Buenos Aires cafe musing about past loves while dying of tuberculosis. 'Absorbed in my own sadness, I call you back to mind and I see that in my poor marginal life you were a good woman to me.' Carlos **Gardel** and Razzano added the music and it became a key song in Gardel's repertoire.

LUIS GUSMAN

Manos del Uruguay

Founded in 1968 to employ women of the interior of the country within their own surroundings, Manos del Uruguay (Uruguayan hands) was sponsored by established oligarchical families in the interior of the country. The participation of the upper class facilitated access to places, materials and people, and thus ensured the group's connection to the CCU, Centro Cooperativista Uruguayo (Uruguayan Center for Cooperatives).

The development of the organization brought rapid growth and its sales increased. At first, all work was done manually, from the spinning of the wool to the knitting of ponchos, sweaters, capes, scarves and the weaving of rugs. However, increased exports to the United States and Europe produced a change in the organization. There was a need for standardization, so Manos adopted a common practice and stitch and the process became more mechanical. This mechanization allowed for cost reductions and adaptation to an ever-changing market. The resulting restructuring brought reductions in personnel and wages. Furthermore, mechanization made participation more difficult due to the high skills expected of its workers.

From a collective volunteer effort, Manos grew to eighteen cooperatives scattered throughout the country and one central location in charge of creating and developing sources of employment. In 1995 there were five hundred women workers. Although participation was not limited to women, work at home and in central locations offered an ideal alternative for women burdened with family-based traditions that made it impossible to take on a regular job. Manos has recently become affiliated with other organizations such as PLEMU (Plenario de mujeres del Uruguay) (Uruguayan Women's Organization) and AUPFYRH (Asociación uruguaya de planificación familiar y reproducción humana) (Uruguayan Family Planning and Human Reproduction Association), two planned parenthood organizations that educate women about sexuality, the family and children, making these workers conscious of their role as women.

Further reading

Rostagnol, S. (1989) *Las artesanas hablan*, Montevideo: CIEDUR.

VICTORIA RUÉTALO

Manuel, Víctor

b. 1897, Havana, Cuba; d. 1969, Havana

Painter

Born Víctor Manuel González, he led Cuban painting into the modern age. Dissatisfied with his courses at the San Alejandro school in Havana, he travelled to France in 1925 and returned two years later, inspired by the European avant-garde. His first exhibition in Havana in 1927 presented a group of paintings announcing a new pictorial language and the irruption of the Cuban avant-garde (see **avant-garde in Latin America**). The serene, melancholic atmosphere that prevails in his landscapes and his variations on the female face, like ***Gitana tropical*** (Tropical Gipsy), were essential marks of his work.

WILFREDO CANCIO ISLA

Manual del perfecto idiota latinoamericano

Under the title of the *Manual del perfecto idiota latinoamericano* (Manual of the Perfect Latin American Idiot) (1996), Plinio Apuleyo Mendoza, Carlos Alberto Montaner and Alvaro Vargas Llosa collected, classified and parodied the idiocies advanced by **intellectuals** during revolutionary processes in their societies. The prologue by Mario **Vargas Llosa** defines ideological, political and sociological idiocy as the incapacity to think for oneself or to challenge a rhetoric that supplants thought. If it universalizes an idiocy that does seem to affect every political current, the 'manual' concentrates on gaffes and clichés and caricatures them in a fairly predictable way.

CELINA MANZONI

Manzanero, Armando

b. 1935, Mérida, Mexico

Musician

A singer and composer, Manzanero's songs mark the transition in popular music from the **bolero** to the US-influenced ballad. He began as accompanist to singers like Luis Demetrio and Angélica María. From 1960 he began to succeed with his own songs such as 'Adoro' (I Adore), 'Voy a apagar la luz' (I'm Going to Turn Out the light), 'Esta tarde vi llover' (I Saw it Rain this Afternoon) and 'Me vuelves loco' (You Drive Me Crazy). Elis **Regina**, Eugenia **León** and Tania Libertad have recorded his songs. Manzanero is a major record producer and a leading member of the musicians union.

EDUARDO CONTRERAS SOTO

Manzi, Homero

b. 1907, Santiago del Estero, Argentina; d. 1951, Buenos Aires, Argentina

Writer

A poet who wrote tangos instead of sonnets, Manzi grew up in Santiago de Estero's Boedo district (see **Boedo vs Florida**). He belonged to the generation of Celedonio **Flores** and Pascual Contursi, although he was equally influenced by García Lorca and Evaristo Carriego. He experienced the misery and longings expressed in songs like 'Malena', 'Barrio del tango' (Tango District) and 'Sur', subsequently featured in Fernando Solana's *Sur* (1988), his finest work. He also scripted *La guerra gaucha* (War of the Gauchos) (1942) and directed *El último payador* (The Last Balladeer) (1950), both of which are important Argentine films.

LUIS GUSMAN

Maples Arce, Manuel

b. 1900, Papantla, Veracruz, Mexico; d. 1981, Mexico City

Poet and diplomat

The central figure in Mexican ***estridentismo***, Maples Arce wrote most of the group's manifestoes and was the moving force behind its principal journals, *Irradiador* (1923) and *Horizonte* (1926–7). His own *estridentista* poetry collections, *Andamios interiores* (Interior Scaffolding) (1922), *Urbe* (Metropolis) (1924), and *Poemas interdictos* (Prohibited Poems) (1927), reveal strong ties to the futurist and cubist avant-garde (see **avant-garde in Latin America**). *Memorial de la sangre* (Blood Memorial) (1947) gathers his more mature poetry. Maples Arce entered Mexico's foreign service in 1935, and held consular and ambassadorial posts in Europe, Latin America and elsewhere.

MERLIN H. FORSTER

Mapuches

The Mapuche people (mapu: land; che: people), or Araucanians, fiercely resisted both Inca and Spanish conquests. Grouped in small communities, they live today in southern Chile, between the Bío-Bío river in Arauco province and Chiloé Island. Their language is Mapundungun (tongue of the land). In 1992, the Chilean census registered 928,060 self-identified Mapuches who have continued to maintain their indigenous cultural values such as language, religion and communal lifestyle. Mapuche communities trade their agricultural products in nearby urban areas, such as Temuco and Osorno. Since 1992, they have reactivated their struggle for the recovery of the lands they lost to the Spaniards in the colonial period and in the late nineteenth century.

LUIS E. CÁRCAMO-HUECHANTE

maquiladoras

A blanket term for assembly plants along Mexico's northern border that put together parts manufactured in the USA or elsewhere and which export the finished product. The word derives from *maquila*, which in colonial Spanish referred to the portion of grain retained by a miller for the use of the mill. Thus, the term *maquiladora* refers to the profit retained for the use of an assembly plant in processing materials belonging to foreign companies.

Following careful investigation of ways to increase foreign trade, the Mexican government initiated *maquiladora* production in 1965 through the Border Industrialization Programme (BIP). The BIP built on free-trade zones that the Mexican government had established in the 1930s along the most isolated parts of its northern border: areas such as Baja California, where illegal trade in basic commodities from the USA flourished. From 1942 to 1964, the *bracero* programme recruited Mexican agricultural workers to make up for US labour shortages and further formalized long-standing practices of legal and illegal economic activity across the border. As early as the 1950s, small-scale export assembly plants were operating under the auspices of the free-trade zone around Tijuana. In 1965, the Mexican Ministry of Industry created an official programme for the duty-free import of parts and export of finished products, to offset unemployment after the cancellation of the *bracero* programme. The *maquiladora* programme was in many ways an extension of processes already in motion, but the BIP emphasized developing large-scale assembly plants associated with major foreign industries tied to global markets, rather than small-scale operations functioning in regional economies.

The *maquiladora* programme began slowly, but grew rapidly from the late 1960s until 1974, when economic stagnation in the USA and labour militancy in Mexico sent the programme into a decline that lasted until 1979. Since that time, the programme has continued sporadic and sometimes explosive growth. In its initial formulation, the *maquiladora* programme was conceived as a means of jump-starting the regional economy of northern Mexico, and the programme was restricted to operations within twenty kilometres of the border. However, as successive Mexican governments have adopted a neoliberal economic agenda (see **neoliberalism**), the *maquiladora* system has become a cornerstone of national economic development and the programme has been extended to include cities further from the border, such as Chiuhuahua. As of 1983, *maquiladoras* were also allowed to sell a portion of their assembled products to the internal market of Mexico, thus initiating the displacement of some national industries. The effects of the *maquiladoras* have also extended to the north, which, with the exception of the the Los Angeles–San Diego corridor, was one of the most economically underdeveloped regions in the USA prior to 1965.

Although commodity assembly in dispersed locations has been a part of the global capitalist system for some time, Mexico's *maquiladoras* are of the most sustained and systematic efforts to base regional and now national development on such a programme. However, the massive devaluation of the peso *vis-à-vis* the dollar since 1982 has introduced a contradiction into the formula: as an ever-stronger dollar buys more labour and pays for more raw materials and processing costs, the profit margins and foreign exchange brought in by *maquiladoras* becomes less and less viable as the engine of development.

Many other problems plague *maquiladora*-style production. *Maquiladoras* are often used for production processes that require hazardous materials, and environmental activists on both sides of the border have decried their ecological impact. *Maquiladoras* also employ a high percentage of young women, who in some cases are specifically targeted for repetitive tasks involving fine motor-skills. This gender-inflected workforce has codified a new international division of labour that rearticulates existing forms of patriarchal oppression. Finally, as economic globalization continues, the threat that foreign investors will move their *maquiladora* lines to even cheaper labour markets means that local and national sovereignty have been deeply eroded through reliance on export-assembly production plants.

Despite these and other problems, the *maquiladora* programme in Mexico is increasingly taken as a model by neoliberalizing regimes. Across Latin America and the Caribbean, the poorest countries are opening up free-trade zones (*zonas francas*) to offer foreign investors incentives to build *maquiladora*-style factories. The *maquiladora* programme in Mexico has in this sense become a hallmark of the global capitalist economy.

Further reading

Cravey, A.J. (1998) *Women and Work in Mexico's Maquiladoras*, Lanham, Maryland: Rowman & Littlefield.

Fatemi, K. (ed.) (1990) *The Maquiladora Industry: Economic Solution or Problem?*, Westport, CT: Praeger.

Sklair, L. (1989) *Assembling for Development*, Boston: Unwin Hyman.

Peña, D.G. (1997) *The Terror of the Machine. Technology, Work, Gender, and Ecology on the US–Mexico Border*, Austin: University of Texas Press.

Peterson, K. (1992) *The Maquiladora Revolution in Guatemala*, New Haven, CT: Orvill H Schell Center for International Law–Yale University Law School.

BRIAN GOLLNICK

maracatú

The maracatú is thought to derive from an early form of the congo or congado, an Afro-Catholic processional dance with figures dressed as European royalty. Unlike the **Bumba-meu-boi**, the chegança and other Brazilian folkloric dances, the maracatú does not have a narrative theme, revolving instead around the dancing *dama-do-paço* (lady of the palace) who carries a black rag doll known as a *calunga*. Performed primarily in Recife, Pernambuco, during carnival, the maracatú is danced to percussion-based groups. Its rhythm has been used to great effect in pop songs like Jorge Mautner's 'Maracatú Atômico', recently recorded by **Chico Science** and Nação Zumbi.

CHRISTOPHER DUNN

Maradona, Diego Armando

b. 1960, Buenos Aires

Football player

The greatest footballer of his generation, Maradona was yet another example of the role of football as a passport from the back streets to the mansion. Born the fifth of eight children, his rare skills had persuaded Argentinos Juniors to sign him by the age of twelve. He was not quite sixteen when he played his first league match for them in 1976. He captained the Argentine team which won the World Youth Championship in 1979. He was the world's most wanted player, being transferred to Boca Juniors in 1981 and then to Barcelona on a then world record fee of three million pounds. He never settled there, and suffered a serious leg injury. In 1984 another world record fee of around five million pounds moved him to Napoli, where he achieved his greatest triumphs. Maradona led the underachievers of the Italian South to their only two championships in 1987 and 1990 and the UEFA Cup in 1989. Boys were named after him, academics wrote learned paeans of praise, Maradonian became a superlative and Neapolitans looked forward to Sunday afternoons.

Maradona was at the heart of Argentina's World Cup win in 1986, scoring decisive individual goals in the quarter and semi-finals. President **Menem** named him as special ambassador for sport in 1990. He was at the height of his fame, a hero in many countries, the creator of luck, intrepid, strong as a bull, fast as a missile, the star of the century. However, his decline from sporting hero to negative role model was even more rapid than his rise. In April 1991 he was suspended by the Italian Football Federation after failing a drug test. The 1990s were punctuated by failed comebacks and more failed drug tests, most disastrously in the World Cup of 1994.

As a player, Maradona was not graceful but electrically effective. He is short, 5′ 6″ tall, but thickset with powerful legs which gave him the ability to twist and turn while still able to control the ball. The dribble at speed like the slalom, or 'gambetta', was his hallmark together with a strong left foot. His craftiness was admired in Argentina and Naples, symbolized by his 'hand of God' goal against England in 1986. He was a cult figure in Naples, a champion and virtuoso, a symbol of how many Neapolitans saw themselves and wanted others to see them. He may have lost his reputation elsewhere but not there; and perhaps both there and in Buenos Aires, he was admired as much for his vices as for his virtues.

Further reading

Bernstein, G. (1997) *Maradona, iconografía de la patria*, Buenos Aires: Editorial Biblos.
Besa i Camprubi, R. (1998) *Maradona, historia de un desencuentro*, Barcelona: Barcanova.
Burns, J. (1996) *Hand of God: The Life of Diego Maradona*, London: Bloomsbury.
Levinski, S. (1996) *Maradona, rebelde con causa*, Buenos Aires: Corregidor.

TONY MASON

Maran, René

b. 1887, Fort-de-France, Martinique; d. 1960, Paris, France

Novelist

Born of French Guyanese parents in Martinique,

René Maran is considered an important precursor to ***négritude*** and the first major writer from French Guyana. He spent little time in his homeland, however, and was educated in Bordeaux, France. He later spent thirteen years as a colonial administrator in Bangui in Central Africa, where he wrote his most famous novel, *Batouala*, which won the Prix Goncourt in 1921. It was a vigorous critique of French colonialism in Africa and eventually hostile reaction to the novel caused Maran to leave the French colonial service. He was celebrated as the father of *négritude*, but was also criticized as a deeply ambivalent *assimilée* by Frantz **Fanon** for a later novel, *Un homme pareil aux autres* (A Man like Any Other) in 1947.

J. MICHAEL DASH

Marcha

Uruguayan weekly magazine founded in 1939 by journalist Carlos Quijano, it is regarded as one of Latin America's most important independent publications and has subscribers throughout Latin America, the USA and Europe. With an explicitly socialist orientation, it spoke out against imperialism and in favour of social democracy and independence from any social or economic forces. In its thirty-five years of existence, the journal was closed fourteen times and several members of its editorial board were imprisoned during the military dictatorships that governed Uruguay through the 1970s and early 1980s. Its contributors included Juan Carlos **Onetti**, Hugo Alfaro, Eduardo **Galeano**, Angel **Rama**, Mario **Benedetti**, Carlos María Gutiérrez and Ernesto González Bermejo.

In 1967, Quijano began to produce other publications that complemented the journal's work: the *Cuadernos de Marcha*, for example, were a collection of essays on the history, politics and culture of Uruguay and Latin America, while the *Biblioteca de Marcha* published the work of a range of authors from Proust and Kafka to **Borges** and **Quiroga**. The effect of both was to extend *Marcha*'s cultural and political influence.

The journal also encouraged debate between readers and journalists, proposing weekly topics for discussion and stimulating investigative writing. Some of its contributors, particularly Benedetti and Gutiérrez, later criticized the journal for its failure to express a commitment to direct political action. Carlos Quijano's reply was that his view of his political task was 'a modest duty to educate'. *Marcha* organized literary competitions and supported film festivals where the most important and avant-garde films of the day were shown. They provided a space where Latin American alternative cinema could be seen; it was *Marcha* that brought Santiago **Alvarez**, Joris Ivens and Glauber **Rocha** among others to the notice of a Uruguayan public. And the showings were not limited to Montevideo; every week the films were shown in locations in the interior of the country. The magazine even, briefly, produced its own short films.

Although it did not have a party allegiance, *Marcha* adopted a critical posture, particularly towards the military dictatorships. In 1974, after its publication of Nelson Winston Marra's short story, 'El guardaespaldas' (The Bodyguard), it was closed down and its editorial board imprisoned; it proved impossible to recover from closures, and the imprisonment and exile of its main contributors, and it closed for the last time in November 1974.

Further reading

Alfaro, H. (1994) *Por la vereda del sol*, Montevideo: Ediciones de Brecha.

WILFREDO CANCIO ISLA

Marchena, Pedro Pablo Medardo de

b. 1899, Curaçao, Netherlands Antilles; d. 1968, Bonaire, Netherlands Antilles

Political activist

Influenced by the Jamaican activist Marcus **Garvey**, De Marchena sharply criticized the Dutch presence in the Netherlands Antilles. The Roman Catholic missionaries and their alleged discrimination against Afro-Caribbean people were a major target for his attacks, especially in his 1929 pamphlet *Ignorancia ó educando un pueblo* (Ignorance or Educating a People). At the outbreak of the Second World War he was sent to an internment camp on Bonaire as a prisoner dangerous to the state. After the war, he gave up public life.

AART G. BROEK

Marcial *see* Salvador, Cayetano Carpio

Marcos, Juan Manuel

b. 1950, Asunción, Paraguay

Writer and literary critic

The prolific Marcos has published sixteen books and more than fifty articles in journals around the world. Founder of the international journal ***Discurso literario*** (1983), he has been awarded several international literary prizes and honours. His published works include *Poemas* (Poems), *Roa Bastos, precursor del postboom* (Roa Bastos, Precursor of the Post-Boom), *El invierno de Gunter* (The Winter of Gunter), his first novel, and *Así como por la honra, Selección de textos sobre la libertad* (Such as for Honour, Selection of Texts on Freedom). Marcos also participated very actively in the politics of his country, especially after the fall of the **Stroessner** dictatorship in 1989.

TERESA MÉNDEZ-FAITH

Marechal, Leopoldo

b. 1900, Buenos Aires, Argentina; d. 1970, Buenos Aires

Writer

Marechal's most important novel, *Adán Buenosayres* (1948), anticipated many of the formal innovations introduced years later. *Megafón o la guerra* (Megaphone or War) (1970) and *El banquete de Severo Arcángel* (1965) completed the trilogy. Marechal was also a poet, essayist and playwright. The extraordinary coherence of his work is not solely due to a poetics which turns to symbolism and to a myth in which man is seen as transcendence and religion as restitution, he also deploys generic significations:

theatricality in the novel, the epic in poetry, the intrinsic correspondence between fiction and essay, the nationalization of epic figures like 'Adam' Buenosayres and 'Antígone' Vélez. In the 1940s and 1950s, Marechal was a prominent Peronist (see **Peronism**) intellectual.

ENRIQUE FOFFANI

marginal poets

The marginal poets were a group of young underground Brazilian poets of the mid-1970s. Their colloquial informality and epigrammatic representation of a fragmented, subjectivized world is reminiscent of the 1920s modernists (see **Brazilian modernism**). However, the marginals' grimly ironic tone spoke of a different social atmosphere, the violence, alienation and anonymity of the darkest years of military rule following the collapse of the **economic miracle**. Struggling to operate outside the constraints of commercial publishing and state censorship, the 'mimeograph' poets, as they were also known, sought out their readers directly, distributing their work in cinema queues, bars and bookshops. While much of the generation's output was ephemeral, it did produce some of the most distinctive and original voices of the 1970s and 1980s, such as Francisco Alvim, Cacaso, Chacal and Ana Cristina **César**.

DAVID TREECE

Maria Bethânia

b. 1946, Santo Amaro, Bahia, Brazil

Singer

A famously passionate and dramatic vocalist with a husky alto voice, Maria Bethânia (Maria Bethânia Viana Teles Veloso) began singing professionally with her brother, Caetano **Veloso**, in the early 1960s. In 1965, she was invited to replace Nara **Leão** as lead vocalist in the musical drama ***Opinião***, an early manifestation of protest culture against the recently installed military regime. Her fervent rendition of João do Vale's 'Carcará' (Vulture) was a constitutive event of post-*coup* cultural production. Although she did not participate in *tropicalismo* with her brother, she recorded its key songs. Since the 1970s, she has been the premiere female interpreter of Brazilian romantic music.

CHRISTOPHER DUNN

María Candelaria

María Candelaria (1943) marked the beginning of Emilio 'El Indio' **Fernández**'s most creative and successful period as a director. María, a simple Indian girl, is shunned by her fellow villagers and is eventually stoned to death because of their ignorance. *María Candelaria* established the folkloric and nationalistic motifs of his work influenced by ***indigenismo***, and its characteristic stylistic and narrative qualities: the beauty of Indian faces, clouds caught by the powerful camerawork of Gabriel **Figueroa**, and the tragic couple, represented here by two key figures of Mexican cinema, Dolores **Del Rio** and Pedro **Armendáriz**. The film won the best film award at Cannes in 1946.

PATRICIA TORRES SAN MARTÍN

María Lionza Monument

One of the most dramatic emblems of Venezuela's attempt to construct a modernity that was linked to earlier traditions is a statue in the middle of a highway in central Caracas depicting a naked woman riding a tapir, her hands holding a crown or wreath. The statue, like the highway where it was erected and the nearby **Ciudad Universitaria**, was built during the dictatorship of Marcos **Pérez Jiménez**. It represents an Indian princess who is still revered for her magical powers, particularly in the area around Sorte in Yaracuy, a remote coastal area west of Caracas. The Caracas statue is similarly revered, often at risk of life and limb, by pilgrims who leave wreaths of flowers and other offerings on and around it.

DANIEL BALDERSTON

mariachi

The characteristic mariachi ensemble of two trumpets, two violins, the bass guitarrón, the guitar or vihuela and a singer, all dressed in silver-studded narrow trousers and short jacket with high-heeled boots and wide decorated hat, has come to be emblematic of Mexico and its music. The standard explanation for many years of the origins of mariachi was that it derived from the French *mariage* – used during the French occupation of Mexico (1862–7); but that picturesque etymology has now been called into question.

Mariachi came to prominence as the national music of Mexico *par excellence* (though it is popular in Central America too) in the post-revolutionary environment of the 1930s, particularly through the cinema and radio. The original *mariachi conjunto* was smaller and bore little resemblance to its contemporary image; the more familiar extended band developed in response to the commercial music industry in association with film, and adopted the lyrical ranchera ballads (see **canción ranchera**) of rural nostalgia and lost love as their favoured melodies.

The most famous of them all has been the Mariachi Vargas de Tecalitlán, dominant since the 1940s. Composer-arranger Rubén Fuentes, who joined them in 1945, introduced modern harmonies and instrumentation into mariachi while maintaining its musical conventions.

MIKE GONZALEZ

Mariani, Roberto

b. 1892, Buenos Aires, Argentina; d. 1946, Buenos Aires

Writer

Mariani's *Cuentos de la oficina* (Stories from the Office) (1925) achieved a literary balance between a purist position and the idea of social responsibility which separated the Boedo and Florida literary groups in Argentina (see **Boedo vs Florida**). His posthumously published novel *La cruz nuestra de cada día* (The Cross We Bear Every Day) (1955) revealed narrative qualities and formal concerns which set him apart from other writers of the Boedo school. In July 1924, in an open letter to the magazine **Martín Fierro** called 'Martín Fierro y yo', he criticized those poets who failed to honour the name in the journal's title.

CELINA M. MANZONI

marianismo

Marianismo is a social and cultural phenomenon prevalent in Latin American society that posits certain expectations regarding the behaviour of women. Its roots are in Iberian and Mediterranean culture, and its basic foundational precepts crossed the Atlantic with the European colonists. It is connected to the Virgin Mary, the primary image of traditional popular veneration in Latin America. Historically, she has served as a model of comportment and a limiting factor regarding possible roles of women in Latin America. Based upon the Catholic faith's most saintly female figure (see **Catholicism**), there developed a stereotype of the ideal woman. Marianismo assigns moral superiority, spiritual strength and piety to women, along with humility and a willingness to sacrifice and suffer on behalf of their families. This strong element of self-denial is linked to submissive behaviour especially towards the men of the family (husbands, older brothers and fathers). This submissiveness translates into a patient and almost resigned attitude regarding the foibles and infidelities of husbands. Under *marianismo*, women remain virgins until marriage and remain loyal to their spouses even when they have a mistress. Additionally, women should not particularly enjoy sexual relations; sex constitutes a duty, the specific goal of which is to procreate. Consequently, women define their roles primarily as mothers, responsible for the care and education of their children. The domestic sphere, the home, is her domain, while the public sphere is that of the males in the family.

However, the moral and spiritual authority attributed to women has allowed them to act politically in the public sphere in the name of the welfare of their children and families. A fine case in point is the **Madres de Plaza de Mayo** in Argentina, who protested effectively against the military regime that committed atrocious human rights violations. These women were able partially to counter the regime because of their status as mothers and grandmothers. Countering *marianismo*, middle-class women may select a career outside of the home, usually in education or some other traditonal 'female' field. However, the primary duty is to their families, and employers are theoretically expected to respect that duty. Nonetheless, it should be pointed out that their careers are dependent upon domestic servants who are hired to tend to the children and the house.

Further reading

Chaney, E. (1979) *Supermadre: Women in Politics in Latin America*, Austin, TX: University of Texas Press.
Jelin, E. (ed.) (1991) *Family, Household and Gender Relations in Latin America*, London: Kegan Paul International (UNESCO).
Pescatello, A. (1976) *Power and Pawn: The Female in Iberian Families, Societies, and Cultures*, Westport, CT: Greenwood.

LINDA A. CURCIO-NAGY

Mariátegui, José Carlos

b. 1894, Moquegua, Peru; d. 1930, Lima, Peru

Writer and journalist

One of the most original and creative Marxists of Latin America, Mariátegui's writings cover a vast array of topics from world politics and sociology to surrealism and literary criticism. His book **Siete ensayos de interpretación de la realidad peruana** (Seven Interpretative Essays on Peruvian Reality) (1928) is one of the most widely read and translated works of Latin American sociology.

Born in southern Peru, he spent his childhood in Lima and Huacho. A bone disease kept him from school, but he educated himself. Because of his family's deteriorating economic situation, he started working in a Lima printing house at the age of fourteen. He worked as linotypist for the newspaper *La Prensa*, and between 1912 and 1914, wrote articles as 'Juan Croniqueur'. He moved in Peruvian intellectual circles, and in 1916 began to write about poetry, literature, theatre and general cultural issues for other newspapers.

In 1919 Mariátegui founded the newspaper *La Razón* with César Falcón, and also the short-lived weekly *Nuestra Epoca*. After the Russian Revolution of 1917 he took a growing interest in socialist ideas, and these new publications showed him moving more clearly towards Marxism. During the social agitation of 1918–19 in Peru he, like Víctor Raúl **Haya de la Torre**, called for ideological co-operation among intellectuals, workers and students.

La Razón and its editors fiercely attacked Augusto B. Leguía's government, and in late 1919 Mariátegui was forced to accept Leguía's travel grant for Europe. He worked in Italy as a journalist, where he also had the status of cultural attaché. In Europe he became a convinced Marxist, and started to develop his own socialist interpretations for Peru and Latin America. Among those who influenced him were Italian Marxists and leftist intellectuals like Labriola and the syndicalist ideas of Georges Sorel. Some even claim that Mariátegui represents a 'Nietzschean Marxism', because of his unorthodox southern European socialist contacts. His three years in Europe also affected Mariátegui in a different sense, as his medical condition improved in the southern Italian climate.

Returning to Peru in early 1923, Mariátegui devoted himself to journalism and also, increasingly, to political activity. He lectured in the Popular Universities, and became the leading young intellectual of Lima's Marxist circles. In 1924 his illness worsened and his left leg was amputated. This did not, however, prevent his search for new kind of solutions to the social and economic problems of Latin America. On the contrary, it seemed that after the amputation, Mariátegui became even more determined to develop his ideas for a socialist Peru. Mariátegui founded with his brother a new printing house, Minerva, while he simultaneously prepared the publication of a new monthly magazine, ***Amauta***.

The years 1926–30 were very productive for Mariátegui, who was editing *Amauta* and contributing to many Peruvian and Latin American magazines and journals. In 1928 he completed his famous *Seven Essays*, which presented Mariátegui's original Marxist interpretations of a range of issues, most famously the Indian problem and land reform. Mariátegui's political involvement began in the labor movement. When Haya de la Torre founded APRA in Mexico in 1924, Mariátegui sympathized with the idea of a continental anti-imperialist movement, but from 1927 on, the two young political leaders chose different ideological paths. Haya's united front theory was problematic for Mariátegui; he sought a more class-based political movement. In 1928 they disagreed openly: Haya accused Mariátegui of 'European thinking' (Marxism) as unsuitable for Latin America, while Mariátegui began to organize a class-conscious socialist party. In many respects, the ideological dispute between Haya and Mariátegui symbolizes the divisions within the Latin American left at the end of the 1920s.

In 1928, Mariátegui founded the Confederación General de Trabajadores del Perú (General Confederation of Peruvian Workers), which later became the most important centralizing force in the Peruvian labour movement. That same year Mariátegui began to publish a bimonthly newspaper *Labor* which, unlike *Amauta*, was directed at Peruvian workers.

In 1930, the shadow of Mariátegui's life, the malignant tumour in his left thigh, took its toll. He died on 16 April. Although his life was short, Mariátegui's legacy was considerable. Mariátegui's Marxism was always free of one-dimensional extremisms and dogmatism. He studied pre-Columbian cultures seriously and developed with Luis **Valcárcel**, for the first time in Peru, what might be called a 'non-paternalistic ***indigenismo***'. Indeed, Mariátegui was one of the first Latin American intellectuals to criticize the elitist Eurocentrism of Latin American thinking, challenging Arielist idealism in his famous essay '¿Existe un pensamiento latinoamericano?' (Is There a Latin American Thought?).

Mariátegui's revolutionary thinking has subsequently been used for many political purposes. The modern Peruvian guerrilla movement **Sendero Luminoso** (Shining Path) took its name from Mariátegui's sentence 'Marxism–Leninism will open the shining path for the future', although

Mariátegui would hardly have supported its ideology or violent actions.

Further reading

Flores Galindo, A. (1989) *La agonía de Mariátegui*, Lima: Instituo de Apoyo Agrario.

Mariátegui, J.C. (1989) *Seven Interpretative Essays on Peruvian Reality*, Austin, TX: University of Texas Press.

—— (1981) *Obras completas*, Lima: Editorial Minerva.

Quijano, A. (1991) *José Carlos Mariátegui: textos básicos*, Lima: Fondo de Cultura Económica.

Vanden, H. (1986) *National Marxism in Latin America: José Carlos Mariátegui's Thought and Politics*, Boulder, CO: Lynne Rienner Publications.

JUSSI PAKKASVIRTA

Marichal, Juan

b. 1937, Montecristi, Dominican Republic

Baseball player

Also known as the 'Dominican Dandy', Marichal was the first Latin American **baseball** player to be inducted into the Hall of Fame, in 1983. In his lifetime he won 243 games and lost 142 with an average of 2.89 ERA. Marichal won the title as 'Best Pitcher of His Era'. From 1960 until 1971 he played with the San Francisco Giants, then later with the Red Sox and Dodgers. He was an All Star for nine years consecutively, and was one of the finest pitchers in baseball history.

FERNANDO VALERIO-HOLGUÍN

Marighela, Carlos

b. 1911, Bahia, Brazil; d. 1969, São Paulo, Brazil

Political activist

A Central Committee member of the Brazilian Communist Party (PCB), Marighela joined the dissident Revolutionary Brazilian Communist Party in 1967 and launched the manifesto *Ação Libertadora Nacional* (Action for National Liberation), calling for armed struggle against the military dictatorship. Marighela's adoption of the strategy of **guerrilla warfare** (fictionalized in Antonio **Callado**'s 1971 novel *Bar Don Juan*) expressed the frustration of many at the PCB's failure to mobilize against the regime. The handful of ALN spectacular actions, however, simply underlined its isolation from the masses they hoped to lead. Marighela was killed in 1969; by late 1971, the urban guerrilla movement was likewise dead.

DAVID TREECE

marimba

The marimba, a wooden-keyed xylophone, was originally introduced into several parts of the Americas by Africans who recreated some of the various forms of the instrument found throughout sub-Saharan Africa. While the instrument has virtually disappeared from some areas, such as Brazil, it is currently still found in two broad geographical zones: (1) from southern Mexico, especially the states of Oaxaca and Chiapas, through western Central America to the *meseta central* of Costa Rica; and (2) the Pacific coast of Colombia, Ecuador and northern Peru. In the latter area, marimbas are still used by the Afrocoastal population, although a few neighbouring indigenous groups have also adopted the instrument. These marimbas are on legs or suspended by ropes and are usually large enough to accommodate two to four musicians. The folk-rooted repertoire conserves a strong African musical foundation, especially the music of the famous Afro-Colombian **currulao**. Marimba music from the largely African-American Esmeraldas province has gained some national exposure in Ecuador in recent years.

The substantial African colonial population (since subsumed into the general population) introduced the marimba into Mesoamerica, though no records exist as to exactly where or when this took place. The indigenous population soon adopted and adapted the instrument, partially because of its similarity to the slit drum (*teponatzli* in

Náhuatl; *tun tun* in Mayan) in use before European and African contact. Specious claims to a Mayan origin by some Guatemalan cultural nationalists in the 1960s and 1970s reflect the importance of the instrument in that country, where it has been declared the 'national instrument'. All Latin American marimbas retain the *miltron*, or buzzing sound produced by a membrane attached to each resonator, common to African marimbas (a feature eliminated in the contemporary concert marimba used in classical music and jazz). The earliest marimbas also had a hoop, or wooden arc attached to the frame, a feature of African marimbas still found on the Guatemalan *marimba de tecomates* (marimba with gourds) and the Nicaraguan *marimba de arco* (marimba with an arc). In the late 1800s, Guatemalan and Mexican musicians mounted the keyboard on legs and extended the single (diatonic) keyboard several octaves. The creation of the first chromatic, *marimba doble* (two-row marimba) is attributed to Sebastián Hurtado of Quetzaltenango in 1894 and Corazón Borraz Moreno of Chiapas in 1897. New *marimba doble* duos successfully reproduced the European-based repertoire of the growing *ladino*/mestizo population. Marimba bands became extremely popular throughout southern Mexico and Central America and each nation boasted several major ensembles. In the 1920s and 1930s, Guatemalan and Mexican marimba ensembles toured and recorded in the USA and Europe and achieved a level of novelty success. The advent of inexpensive sound equipment and the popularity of North American styles that do not translate well onto the marimba led to its steep decline throughout the region, though it still conserves an important place as a localized marker of traditional music.

See also: Música Grande

Further reading

Chenoweth, V. (1964) *The Marimbas of Guatemala*, Lexington: University of Kentucky Press.

Jackson, I.V. (1985) *More than Drumming: Essays on African and Afro-Latin American Music and Musicians*, Westport: Greenwood Press.

Kaptain, L. (1992) *The Wood that Sings: The Marimba in Chiapas, Mexico*, Everett, Pennsylvania: Honey Rock.

Scruggs, T.M. (1999) *La Marimba: estudio sobre el instrumento nacional*, Guatemala: Ministerio de Educacíon Pública.

T.M. SCRUGGS

Marín, Lupe

b. 1896, Jalisco, Mexico; d. 1982, Mexico City

Actress

Marín was an olive-skinned, green-eyed beauty who was the model for the fertility goddess in Diego **Rivera**'s early murals, and was also his wife (1922–7). Unlike his other wives, Lupe retaliated with scandalous public scenes against Diego's flagrant infidelities and frequent absences. When he had an affair with Tina Modotti, she divorced him and married poet and critic Jorge Cuesta, whose personality and politics were the opposite of Diego's. When she was affected by post-natal depression, Cuesta had her institutionalized and soon afterwards they divorced. She devoted the remainder of her life to sewing and cultivating friends, and produced two autobiographical novels.

CYNTHIA STEELE

Marinello, Juan

b. 1898, Jicotea, Las Villas, Cuba; d. 1977, Havana, Cuba

Writer

A leading critic, in the 1920s Marinello was a member of both the political and the artistic vanguard as a member of the **Grupo Minorista** and founder of the ***Revista de avance***. In 1934 he edited *Masas*, organ of the Cuban Anti-Imperialist League, and Communist journals *La palabra* and *Mediodía*. Jailed for political reasons in the 1930s, he went into exile in Mexico. In 1948 he was presidential candidate for the PSP (Popular Socialist Party), becoming Rector of Havana University in 1962. His writings include several studies on José Martí, the product of a lifetime of research.

WILFREDO CANCIO ISLA

marinera

A mainly Peruvian dance that evolved around 1900 from earlier dance forms like the zamacueca and the resbalosa. In fact the zamacueca came to be known in the latter part of the nineteenth century as the cueca chilena. Peruvians were unhappy that their national dance was named after their enemies in the Pacific War of 1879 and renamed it the marinera. There are several variants of the marinera – the marinera limeña is accompanied by guitar and a cajón, or wooden box, as percussion. The dance often accompanies a song duel, improvised in three-line stanzas. The finest interpreters of marinera were usually Afro-Peruvians.

MIKE GONZALEZ

Marinho, Roberto

b. 1904, Rio de Janeiro, Brazil; d. 1998, Rio de Janeiro

Media magnate

Director General of TV **Globo**, Globo Radio and a number of other enterprises, Marinho joined his father's newspaper *O Globo* in 1925 as a journalist, and then began to create what is acknowledged, alongside Mexico's **Televisa**, as Latin America's most important communications network. He also created the Roberto Marinho Foundation, which sponsors cultural and educational activities. Brazil's delegate to the United Nations in 1952, he was named Man of the Year in 1990 by the Rio de Janeiro Stock Exchange and in 1993 was elected to Brazil's Academy of Letters. Despite his advanced age, he was until his death one of Brazil's most powerful men.

ANTONIO CARLOS VAZ

Marins, José Mojica

b. 1931, São Paulo, Brazil

Film-maker and actor

Founder of the tropical horror genre, Marins' experimental films are now internationally recognized as masterpieces of third world trash. The logic of nightmares, the erotic, the absurd and the tragicomic dominate his work. Closely linked to 1970s experimental Brazilian cinema, Marins popularized his character Zé do Caixão (Coffin Joe) in Brazil, fusing with him in public appearances and creating a mythology around his work. Outstanding among his films are early works like *A Meia Noite Levarei sua Alma* (At Midnight I Will Take Your Soul) (1963). In recent years he has presented horror films on television.

ISMAIL XAVIER AND THE USP GROUP

Marisol

b. 1930, Paris, France

Sculptor

Educated in Caracas with regular travel to Europe and the USA, Marisol (Marisol Escobar) studied art in France and the USA. Her most famous works are the wooden constructions of the 1960s, which parody contemporary political figures. In the 1970s, she used forms from her own body in a series of prints and drawings, and in the 1980s she concentrated on portraits of artists.

GABRIEL PEREZ-BARREIRO

Marley, Bob

b. 1945, Rhoden Hall, Jamaica; d. 1981, Miami, USA

Musician

The son of a black woman and a middle-aged white British army officer, Marley was the world's greatest **reggae** musician. As a young man he moved to the slums of Kingston, where he began making music with friends Bunny Wailer and Peter

Tosh. His first record, in 1962, included the controversial 'Judge not'. In 1963 The Wailin Wailers (Marley, Bunny and Peter) recorded their first disc on the Coxsone label. The dominant music then was **ska**, a dance rhythm incorporating elements of rhythm and blues and the sounds of the Kingston ghetto.

In 1966 Emperor Haile Selassie of Ethiopia, revered by the Ras Tafari movement, visited Jamaica. From then on, **Rastafarianism** gained influence on the island, and it impressed Marley deeply. In 1967 he reformed his band, now called The Wailers, though his beliefs brought him into increasing conflict with his record company. Marley's ideological transformation brought a change in his music, taking him from ska to the reggae form that The Wailers would express at its most brilliant, adding elements of rock, soul, blues and funk. In 1972 the group signed with **Island Records**, and Marley began to achieve international success. His first album, *Catch a Fire*, had an immediate impact, reinforced by tours of Britain and the USA. *Burnin'* followed in 1973 and included the track 'I Shot the Sheriff', subsequently recorded by Eric Clapton; the 1974 *Natty Dread* included the famous 'No Woman No Cry'. The band, now relaunched as Bob Marley and the Wailers without Wailer and Tosh, launched *Rastaman Vibrations* in 1976, including the song 'War' based on a speech by Haile Selassie.

Marley's music had made him an international star and an influence on Jamaican youth as a Rastafarian. In 1976 he organized a Peace Concert in Jamaica against the background of increasingly violent political conflict on the island. Just before the concert Marley was shot and wounded, but he still performed; later he left the country. 1977 brought the *Exodus* and *Kaya* albums. He returned to Jamaica in 1978 to play at the One Love Peace Concert in front of Prime Minister **Manley** and opposition leader Seaga, and was awarded the United Nations Peace Medal. Two years later, his famous Zimbabwe concert coincided with a new Pan-African feeling expressed in his 1979 album *Survival*. Marley recorded his last album, *Uprising*, in 1980, a few months before the cancer was diagnosed that was to take his life. He was thirty-six years old.

Further reading

Gilfoyle, M. (2000) *Bob Marley*, Philadelphia: Chelsea House.
Lazell, B. (1994) *Marley, 1945–1981*, London: Hamlyn.
McCann, I. (c. 1994) *The Complete Guide to the Music of Bob Marley*, London: Omnibus Press.
Sheridan, M. (1999) *Bob Marley: The Wailing Soul: The Story behind Every Song*, London: Carlton.

PABLO JAVIER ANSOLABEHERE

Mármol, José

b. 1960, Santo Domingo, Dominican Republic

Poet

A celebrated young poet, Mármol has been the centripetal force for the 1980s postmodern generation, which opposed the aesthetics and the political programme of the generation of 1965. Mármol has won the following prizes: the National Prize of Poetry for *La invención del día* (The Invention of the Day) (1989), the Pedro **Henríquez Ureña** Prize for *Lengua del paraíso* (Language of Paradise) (1992), and the **Casa de Teatro** Prize for *Deus ex machina* (1994). Informed by the philosophy of Nietzsche and the poetry of Octavio **Paz**, Mármol's poetry points to a conceptual reflection on mankind.

FERNANDO VALERIO-HOLGUÍN

Mármol, Miguel

b. 1905, Ilopongo, El Salvador; d. 1993, San Salvador, El Salvador

Trade union leader

Union leader and founding member of the Communist Party of El Salvador (PCS), Mármol participated in the organization of the peasant revolt in El Salvador in 1932 which resulted in the systematic capture and murder of large groups of Salvadoran peasants; the estimated numbers range from 10,000 to 30,000. At that time, Mármol was captured and sentenced to execution by the government of the dictator Maximiliano Hernández Martínez. Taken for dead, he survived the firing squad and lived to tell his story. Salvadoran writer Roque **Dalton** collected his testimony in a text titled *Miguel Mármol* (1983).

BEATRIZ CORTEZ

maroon music

Maroon communities (see **maroons**) in Latin America and the Caribbean have long been recognized by ethnomusicologists and other scholars as repositories of rich and distinctive African-based musical traditions. Broader audiences, however, have seldom been exposed to maroon music. This started to change in the 1980s, as migrant musicians from these communities began to have a significant impact on the urban popular musics of their countries.

From the sixteenth through the nineteenth centuries, escaped slaves, known as maroons (*cimarrones*), banded together and attempted to form viable societies in inaccessible areas across plantation America. Some of these groups waged highly successful guerrilla wars (see **guerrillas**) against the European colonists, eventually forcing them to sign treaties recognizing their freedom. A few such maroon societies survive as distinct ethnic groups today. The best-known present-day maroon peoples live in Suriname, French Guiana, Jamaica, Colombia and Mexico. In each of these countries, music has played an important part in the maintenance of separate maroon cultural identities.

The country with the largest and most conspicuous contemporary maroon presence is Suriname (formerly Dutch Guiana). The five main maroon ethnic groups there (Saramaka, Ndjuka, Paramaka, Matawai and Kwinti) possess a wealth of distinctive drum-based music and dance genres such as sékéti, susa, songe, papa, kumanti, awasa and aleke. In neighbouring French Guiana, the Aluku (also known as Boni) maroons boast a similar variety of African-based styles. In Colombia, the maroons of Palenque de San Basilio, known as Palenqueros, are likewise known for a strongly African musical tradition, including a unique Kongo-influenced funerary music called lumbalé.

During the 1980s, maroons in each of these countries began migrating to urban areas in large numbers, bringing with them their African-derived musical traditions. Young maroon musicians rapidly inserted themselves into burgeoning local recording industries. By the early 1990s, especially in Suriname, they were exerting an influence way out of proportion to their relatively small numbers, launching new stylistic trends and changing the face of urban pop music. Among the dozens of maroon bands that have contributed to the new 'roots' trend in Suriname are Cosmo Stars, **Ghabiang**, **Excos**, Aphiong Boyz and Yakki Famiri. In French Guiana, maroon groups such as **Wailing Roots** and Local Song have done the same, and in Colombia, the leading maroon band, **Anne Zwing**, has paved the way for numerous others, such as Kusima and Caribe Stars.

As proud descendants of enslaved Africans who seized their own freedom, these maroon popular musicians enjoy an ideologically privileged position. Because of the symbolic potency of the maroon epic, they have come to play an important role in expressing and mediating tensions between local and globalizing conceptions of 'blackness' in the new urban contexts in which they operate.

Further reading

Price, R. (ed.) (1996) *Maroon Societies*, 3rd edn, Baltimore: Johns Hopkins University Press.
Price, R. and Price, S. (1999) *Cultural Vitality in the African Diaspora*, Boston: Beacon Press.

KENNETH BILBY

maroons

Groups of escaped slaves who successfully maintained runaway communities, usually located in mountains, dense forests or other poorly accessible locations. These communities ranged from ten people or fewer to as large as twenty thousand in the case of the seventeenth-century community of Palmares in northeastern Brazil. Large maroon communities also existed in Jamaica and Dutch

Guiana (later Suriname). Maroon communities were able to survive because their difficult locations and their use of guerrilla tactics made it almost impossible to eradicate them by conventional repressive methods. Relatively isolated from local slave societies, maroon communities developed their own distinct cultures, some of which survived into the late twentieth century, most notably in the case of Suriname.

See also: maroon music; *Biografía de un cimarrón*

ROSANNE ADDERLEY

Marqués, René

b. 1919, Arecibo, Puerto Rico; d. 1979, San Juan, Puerto Rico

Writer and playwright

A prolific writer, Marqués's literary work is dominated by moralizing allegories which tend to separate the logic of social processes and the subjectivities he represents. A sometimes strident *telurismo* (integrated vision of man and nature) dominates his literary discourse, through which Marqués often expressed his clear anti-imperialism.

He graduated from the Agricultural College at Mayagüez in 1942, and worked for two years in Puerto Rico's Department of Agriculture. In 1946 he studied literature at the Universidad Central de Madrid, and sent a series of articles called 'Chronicles of Spain' to the newspaper *El Mundo*. Returning to Puerto Rico in 1947, he continued to write newspaper articles and won a Journalism Prize awarded by the **Instituto de Cultura Puertorriqueña** (Puerto Rican Institute of Culture). In 1948 he became editor and leader writer of the *Diario de Puerto Rico* and published his play *El hombre y sus sueños* (Man and His Dreams) in the journal *Asomante*. A Rockefeller Foundation Fellowship allowed him to go to New York to study theatre at Columbia University and Piscator's Dramatic Workshop.

Returning to Puerto Rico in 1950, he began to work in the Education Ministry and directed its publishing operations. In 1951, with the encouragement of Nilita **Vientós Gastón**, he founded the Teatro Experimental del **Ateneo Puertorriqueño**. A Guggenheim grant enabled him to write his first novel. His reputation was established with his plays *La carreta* (The Cart) (1953) and *Los soles truncos* (Cut-Down Suns) (1958), a volume of short stories, *En una ciudad llamada San Juan* (In a City Called San Juan) (1960) and his novel *La víspera del hombre* (The Eve of Man) (1958), which won the Ateneo Puertorriqueño Prize for 1958 and the William Faulkner Foundation prize in 1962. His essays were collected in *El puertorriqueño dócil* (The Docile Puerto Rican) in 1962 and *Ensayos 1955–1966* (Essays) in 1966. His last novel, *La mirada* (The Look) (1976), was not as well received by critics as his earlier work, but is of interest for its exploration of homoeroticism.

Further reading

Díaz Quiñones, A. (1982) *El almuerzo en la hierba*, Río Piedras: Ed. Huracán.

Gelpí, J. (1993) *Literatura y paternalismo en Puerto Rico*, Río Piedras: Universidad de Puerto Rico.

JUAN CARLOS QUINTERO HERENCIA

Márquez Rodríguez, Alexis

b. 1931, Barinas, Venezuela

Literary critic

Márquez Rodríguez has devoted his life to critical writing on Venezuelan and Latin American writers like Alberto Arvelo Torrealba, Rómulo **Gallegos**, Miguel **Otero Silva** and above all Alejo **Carpentier**. He wrote for many years in *El nacional*, and was a director of the **Monte Avila** publishing house from 1994 onwards. In 1966 he won the Caracas Municipal Prose Prize for his *Aquellos mundos tersos* (Those Terse Worlds). A graduate of the Pedagogical Institute of Caracas in Spanish and Literature, he later became professor in the School of Communications at the Universidad Central de Venezuela.

JORGE ROMERO LEÓN

Marrero, José Luis (Chavito)

b. 1926, Río Piedras, Puerto Rico

Actor and director

Marrero is one of Puerto Rico's most versatile performers, and has acted in and directed for radio, television and theatre. He has received several acting awards for bravura performances ranging from strictly dramatic roles, such as Ignacio in **Méndez Ballester**'s *Tiempo muerto* (Dead Time), to comedy (Albin in *La cage aux folles*). He is also an accomplished director, particularly successful in staging comedies and Spanish zarzuelas since the 1960s.

ViCTOR F. TORRES

Marshall, Niní

b. 1903, Buenos Aires, Argentina; d. 1996, Buenos Aires

Performer

Marshall (born María Esther Traveso) was the most brilliant comedienne of Spanish-language cinema. Although she began working and became very popular in **radio** – first as a singer and later as an ironic commentarist of current events named 'Mitzy' – she became internationally known for her film work. Manuel **Romero** brought her to the screen in *Mujeres que trabajan* (Women Who Work) (1938), where she introduced 'Catita', perhaps the most famous of the many typical Argentine figures she created throughout her prolific career. She was the subject of 'Niní,' a popular 1996 theatre review.

RODRIGO PEIRETTI

Marshall, Paule

b. 1929, New York City, USA

Writer

Marshall's finely crafted stories are important contributions to the collective narrative of pan-African peoples, and especially women, in their post-colonial journey towards repairing the damage wrought by colonialism, racism (see **race**), sexism and class divisions. Her first novel, *Browngirl, Brownstones*, (1959) is a young Barbadian-American girl's journey to self-discovery. *Soul Clap Hands and Sing* (1961) contains four pieces of short fiction, 'Barbados', 'Brazil', 'Brooklyn' and 'British Guiana', connected by their sensitive portraits of ageing men as well as by the alliterative titles of the stories and their pan-African milieu. *Reena and Other Stories* (1983, 1985) includes Marshall's very important essay 'From the Poets in the Kitchen', about the inheritance of verbal skills from her mother's circle. In the novels *The Chosen Place, The Timeless People* (1969) and *Praisesong for the Widow* (1983) Marshall develops a major theme in her work, the spiritual survival of African peoples in the Americas through their rituals, especially dance.

Further reading

Boyce Davies, C. (1996) 'Paule Marshall', in Lindfors and Sander (eds), *Twentieth Century Caribbean and Black African Writers*, Third Series, Detroit: Gale Research, pp. 192–202.

ELAINE SAVORY

Martí, (Augustín) Farabundo

b. 1898, Teotepeque, El Salvador; d. 1932, San Salvador, El Salvador

Revolutionary

Martí was leader of the Salvadorean Communist Party (PCS) and principal organizer of the failed insurrection of January 1932. The rising was betrayed before the appointed date and Martí was arrested; he was executed ten days later. The repression that followed, known as 'La Matanza' (the massacre), left 30,000 dead. In the 1920s, Martí was a trade union and political organizer. Repeatedly jailed and exiled for political agitation, he was twice released after a hunger strike. He was secretary to the Nicaraguan revolutionary **Sandino** before they separated in 1929 over Sandino's refusal to accept Martí's revolutionary communist ideas.

MIKE GONZALEZ

martial law

Martial law, also known as 'state of siege' (*estado de sitio* in Spanish), is the suspension of constitutional guarantees and the assumption by the State of emergency powers; it is often written into the legal code as the prerogative of the legislative branch. Frequently invoked by military governments (but also too often by civilian ones), the measure is unhappily and quite rightly remembered as one of the features of times of repression in Latin America. Often accompanied by curfews and by people being arrested without charges being filed, martial law has often served to cover the activities of **death squads** and **paramilitary organizations**. The Costa-Gavros film, *State of Siege* (1973), based on the **Tupamaros** kidnapping of CIA bureau chief Dan Mitrione in Montevideo, Uruguay, and of the subsequent bloodbath of repression, is eloquent in denouncing the ways in which martial law is part of the mechanism of terror.

DANIEL BALDERSTON

Martin, Ricky

b. 1971, San Juan, Puerto Rico

Singer and actor

A Puerto Rican pop singer very popular in the Hispanic world, Ricky Martin (Enrique Martin Morales) became a huge star in the English-speaking world with his 1999 English-language salsa album *Livin' la Vida Loca*. This followed two extremely popular 1998 international salsa hits – María and La Copa de la Vida (The Cup of Life), the latter with phrases in several languages. Martin's career began in 1984, when, at age twelve, he joined the boy-band **Menudo**, which he left five years later to begin a successful career as a pop ballad singer. He has appeared in several soap operas, including *Muñecos de Papel* (Paper Dolls) in Mexico, and *General Hospital* in the USA, and on Broadway in the role of Marius in *Les Miserables*. Particularly proud of his Hispanic heritage, Martin often refers to a strong personal wish to make people everywhere more appreciative of Hispanic culture.

EDUARDO GUÍZAR-ALVAREZ

Martin Barbero, Jesús

b. 1953, Avila, Spain

Cultural theorist

One of a small group of important social and cultural theorists (see **cultural theory**) who have explored the implications of globalization for Latin American culture, Barbero's *De los medios a las mediaciones* (From the Media to Mediations) (1987) is a key work in the developing debate in and with **postmodernism**. While there is general agreement, descriptively, that the growth of a global market and its attendant neoliberal economic policies (see **neoliberalism**) have produced both the cultural domination of new electronic media dominated by massive, transnational corporations, Barbero's concern is to identify the fractures and tensions that result from this process. In that sense his ideas counter some of the cultural pessimism that flows from a model of mass manipulation of vulnerable minds by a pervasive and all-powerful machine.

Indeed what Barbero centrally affirms is that when the process is viewed from the perspective of popular culture (rather than from the point of view of the intentions of the global TV executives) the new cultural spaces produce, in some cases at least, new practices of adaptation and negotiation – new hybridities (to use the term coined by Néstor **García Canclini**), which on the one hand blur all the traditional cultural boundaries (high/low, elite/popular, traditional/modern), and on the other generate new expressions and new identities (see **hybridity**).

Historically, **radio** was a medium of mass communication that both served a burgeoning State and responded to the particular experience of new migrants to the city, who found in popular music and the *radionovela* (see **radionovelas**) some reflection of their own yearnings. The *telenovela* (see **telenovelas**), for Barbero, is an authentically Latin American cultural product whose origins lie in a different urban experience – of fragmentation, and loss.

In the 1980s and 1990s, according to Barbero, neither the nation nor the city can offer a meaningful community. Television offers what he calls a 'simulacrum' – a virtual experience that is rapid, instant and transient. Restless movement is the prevailing dynamic.

Yet Barbero finds in that very process a new, and possibly emancipatory, phenomenon – the creation, within this virtual universe of atomized people, of new kinds of popular culture and popular identity. Youth groups, identities in music, the game-playing world that takes images and remakes them with video or on the Internet.

Barbero's work has continued and has developed a new vocabulary and new analytical tools with which to address a new Latin American reality. Much of this work has evolved at the Universidad del Valle (Colombia) where Barbero is full professor and founder of the School of Communication. His writings on media and the politics of culture have appeared in such journals as *Intermedia*, *Contratexto*, *telos* and *Diálogos de la comunicación*.

Further reading

Martín Barbero, J. (1987) *De los medios a las mediaciones*, Bogotá: Ed. S. Gili; translated into English (1993) as *Communication, Culture and Hegemony: From the Media to Mediations*, London: Sage Publications.

MIKE GONZALEZ

Martín-Baró, Ignacio

b. 1942, Valladolid, Spain; d. 1989, San Salvador, El Salvador

Jesuit priest

Martín-Baró lived in El Salvador from the 1960s and was a psychology professor at the Central American Catholic University (**UCA**), where he also held several high administration positions. In 1986 he founded the University Institute of Public Opinion (IUDOP), which published information about the political situation in El Salvador as an alternative to the limited offical information disseminated by the Salvadoran government. On 16 November 1989 Martín-Baró, five other Jesuits and two women were murdered by members of the Salvadoran army.

BEATRIZ CORTEZ

Martín Fierro

Martín Fierro was a cultural and literary magazine published between 1923 and 1927 dedicated to promoting European avant-garde ideas, in an effort to regenerate and modernize Argentina's cultural and social life. The magazine took its name from José Hernández's poem *Martín Fierro* (1872, 1879). It included essays on the plastic arts, architecture, and literary movements and debates about the future of Argentine civilization. The eclectic Florida group of intellectuals were its principal contributors (see **Boedo vs Florida**). The magazine never resolved the inherent contradiction between promoting a national cultural movement and dedication to a 'universalized' art.

THOMAS EDSALL

Martina, Harold

b. 1935, Curaçao, Netherlands Antilles

Pianist

An internationally renowned pianist, Martina studied at the Academia de Bellas Artes in Medellín, Colombia, and at the Akademie für Musik und Darstellende Kunst in Vienna, Austria. He has performed throughout Europe and the New World. His repertoire is varied and includes work by Albéniz, Bach, Bartok, Beethoven, Brahms, Debussy, Grieg and Scarlatti. He lives in Colombia, and virtually every year he returns to his native island for piano recitals, which include compositions from the Dutch Antilles.

AART G. BROEK

Martínez, Berta

b. 1931, Yaguajay, Cuba

Actress and theatre director

Leading roles in **Teatro Estudio** productions like **Estorino**'s *La casa vieja* (The Old House) and Brecht's *Mother Courage*, and her direction of Lorca's *Bodas de sangre* (Blood Weddings) and *La casa de Bernarda Alba* (The House of Bernarda Alba), ensured Martínez' central place in post-1959 Cuban theatre. Having worked on radio and television she began to be recognized for her work with the Prometeo theatre in the 1950s. Her own productions are visually and rhythmically rich. In the 1980s, her acclaimed adaptations of Spanish zarzuelas rediscovered a popular theatre tradition.

WILFREDO CANCIO ISLA

Martínez, Dennis

b. 1955, Granada, Nicaragua

Baseball player

The first Nicaraguan to play in the Major Leagues, Martínez is the leading active pitcher in victories (231), innings (3,748) and starts (528). His professional career began in 1973 with the Baltimore Orioles; he later played six seasons for the Montreal Expos. After a ten-year battle against alcoholism, on 28 July 1991 he pitched a perfect game and dedicated it to his people. Nicaragua proclaimed the day a national holiday. Since the late 1980s he has helped Nicaraguan expatriates in Miami, and in January 1992 raised money for a cathedral in Managua. In 1993 he joined the Cleveland Indians.

See also: baseball

ESTEBAN E. LOUSTAUNAU AND ILEANA RODRÍGUEZ

Martínez, Odaline de la

b. 1949, Matanzas, Cuba

Conductor and composer

One of only a handful of women who have had major international careers as conductors, de la Martínez is also a brilliant composer with a simple, minimalist quality influenced by George Crumb, electronic music and her Latin American heritage. De la Martínez emigrated to the USA with her family in 1961, where she attended Tulane University. After obtaining a scholarship to study composition with Paul Patterson at the Royal Academy of Music in London in 1972, she settled permanently there. At the University of Surrey she studied composition with Reginald Smith Brindle and obtained her Ph.D. in 1980. In Europe, she is well known as the conductor of Lontano, a chamber music ensemble she helped found in 1976 to perform and record contemporary music. She also founded and conducted the London Chamber Symphony and the European Women's Orchestra.

ANA M. LÓPEZ

Martínez, Raúl

b. 1927, Ciego de Avila, Cuba; d. 1995, Havana, Cuba

Visual artist and designer

A central figure in post-revolutionary Cuban culture, Martínez was a member of the *Los Once* group who cultivated abstract **expressionism** through the 1950s. After 1959 he became art director of the cultural magazine ***Lunes de revolución***. His 1964 series *Homenaje* (Tribute) broke with abstraction, introducing elements of **pop art** and graphic design (see **graphic art**). From then on his paintings and murals, like ***Isla 70***, portrayed Cuban reality and the key symbolic representatives of the Cuban Revolution (see **revolutions**). In the late 1980s he produced one of his most important series of works, on the Conquest of America.

WILFREDO CANCIO ISLA

Martínez, Tomás Eloy

b. 1934, Tucumán, Argentina

Writer and critic

Martínez won international recognition with the publication in 1996 of the English translation of his novel, *Santa Evita* (1995), which coincided with the controversies surrounding the production and release of the film, *Evita* (1996), Alan Parker's adaptation of the musical written by Andrew Lloyd Weber and Tim Rice and starring international superstar Madonna in the title role. The novel was important in momentarily internationalizing the political and sexual fascination for Eva **Perón** that until the mid-1990s had been an Argentine cultural phenomenon. Indeed, *Santa Evita* is in many ways a compilation of the many myths that have fed and reproduced that national obsession.

Santa Evita may be best read as a companion piece to Martínez's earlier and better work, *La novela de Perón* (The Peron Novel), published in 1985. Both novels combine aspects of meta-historical fiction (as practised, for example, by his one-time screenplay writer colleague, Augusto **Roa Bastos**) and the journalistic narration of real political events (as exemplified, in Argentina, by Rodolfo **Walsh**). This compositional combination is then inflected thematically in the texts in the form of an exploration of the processes whereby figures of political authority become the organizing principles of private fantasy. This is what the author means when he says that he writes 'intimate history'.

Martínez has also written *La pasión según Trelew* (The Trelew Passion) (1973) and *La mano del amo* (The Master's Hand) (1991). In 1974, after a bomb explosion in the offices of the newspaper, *La opinión*, where he worked, Martínez left Argentina for exile in Venezuela. Since the mid-1980s he has worked as a university professor in the USA.

JOHN KRANIAUSKAS

Martínez Estrada, Ezequiel

b. 1895, Santa Fe, Argentina; d. 1964, Bahia Blanca, Argentina

Writer

A completely original figure in Argentine culture, Martínez Estrada developed a manner of writing interpellated by its context but resistant to all the clichés of his time. His two major books of essays ***Radiografía de la pampa*** (X-ray of the *Pampa*) (1933) and *Muerte y transfiguración de Martín Fierro* (Death and Transformation of Martin Fierro) (1948) explore the question of national identity conceived as displacement and failure to adapt; for him it is the external view – W.H. Hudson, **gaucho** literature and the writings of the English travellers – that constructs Argentine literature, yet the reality is quite different. At a time when the crisis of political institutions of the 1930s and the irruption of **Peronism** in the 1940s required a positive national response, Martínez Estrada approached politics as a way of thinking culture, combining it with arguments from social psychology to form a highly polemical discourse.

GRACIELA MONTALDO

Martínez Gil, Hermanos

Composers and singers, the brothers Carlos Martínez Gil (b. 1907, Misantla, Mexico; d. 1972, Mexico City) and Pablo Martínez Gil (b. 1910, Misantla, Mexico; d. 1987, Mexico City) pioneered the **bolero** with guitar trio and were the main influence on all the groups that succeeded them, above all the **Trío Los Panchos**. Arriving in Mexico in 1929, they joined the capital's XEW radio station and in 1930 they formed a trio with their cousin Octavio Gil Barradas and later a quartet with cousins Alfredo and Jesús Bojalil Gil. They played with great success in New York and Buenos Aires. The brothers' compositions include 'Chacha linda' (Lovely Chacha), 'Relámpago' (Lightning), 'La novia blanca' (The Bride in White) and 'No salgas niña a la calle' (Don't Go Out into the Street, Girl).

EDUARDO CONTRERAS SOTO

Martínez Peláez, Severo

b. Guatemala

Historian

While working at the Universidad Autónoma de Puebla, Mexico, Martínez published *Patria del criollo* (Creole Fatherland) (1971), one of the great works of Guatemalan national history. He argues that the existence of Indian groups was largely a survival of Spanish colonial feudal arrangements reinforced by the developing agro-export economy. Attacked for failing to recognize how the colony helped to preserve as well as transform Indian identity, and criticized for underplaying Indian resistance, Martínez is nevertheless a major Guatemalan historian. In 1992, he received an honorary doctorate from the University of San Carlos.

MARC ZIMMERMAN

Martínez Solares, Gilberto

b. 1906, Mexico City; d. 1997, Mexico City

Film-maker

Starting as a Hollywood extra, Martínez Solares's first film was *El señor alcalde* (Mr Mayor) (1938). He went on to direct 140 films, of which he wrote 60. In 1948 he began a long and fruitful relationship with the comic actor **Tin Tan** (Germán Valdez) with *Calabacitas tiernas* (Tender Zucchini), a highly successful and representative film comedy. He worked in several genres, but comedy was always his main interest with *Internado para señoritas* (Young Ladies Academy) (1943), *Mi querido capitán* (My Dear Captain) (1950) and *Yo bailé con don Porfirio* (I Danced with Porfirio Díaz) (1942), among others.

PATRICIA TORRES SAN MARTÍN

Martinho da Vila

b. 1938, Duas Barras, Rio de Janeiro, Brazil

Musician

A celebrity of contemporary **samba**, Martinho da Vila (Martinho José Ferreira) has produced a steady stream of hits since his debut with the Unidos de Vila Isabel samba school in 1965. For that year's carnival he launched 'Carnaval de Ilusões' (Carnival of Illusions), an innovative fusion of samba-enredo (a samba composition with a set narrated theme) and partido-alto (a samba with short refrains and improvised verses), which revolutionized both genres. In the early 1970s he broke into the mainstream pop market with 'Canta, canta minha gente' (Sing, Sing my People) and 'Disritmia'. Since the 1980s, he has turned to exploring the Afro-Brazilian cultural heritage of Rio.

CHRISTOPHER DUNN

Martinique

The most developed of the Overseas French Departments, Martinique has a reputation for being the island of intellectuals. Its population is concentrated in Fort de France, which developed after the destruction of Saint Pierre by the explosion of Mt Pelée in 1902. The development of modern Martinique has been deeply influenced by the poet-politician and founder of **négritude**, Aimé **Césaire**, who was mayor of Fort de France from 1945 and deputy from 1946. Césaire's success has laid a foundation for a sophisticated literary tradition that includes writers such as Frantz **Fanon** and Edouard **Glissant**. In the 1990s Martinique has the only literary movement in the French Caribbean, **Créolité**, which extends to include the creole performance artist, Joby Bernabé, and the music of the group **Kassav'**.

J. MICHAEL DASH

Martins, Wilson

b. 1921, São Paulo, Brazil

Literary critic

While Martins admits that sociohistorical background may play a role in literature, he does not believe that this information has any place in the evaluation of a specific work. He insists on judging a work of literature solely and exclusively by its paramount literary merit, its aesthetic quality. Martins lived for over twenty-five years outside Brazil until he retired from his professorship at New York University and returned to Curitiba, Paraná. He is best known for his work on **Brazilian modernism** and his extensive history of the Brazilian intellectual class.

SUSAN CANTY QUINLAN

Martinus (Arion), Frank E.

b. 1936, Curaçao, Netherlands Antilles

Writer

Martinus founded and edited the socio-literary magazine *Ruku* (1969–71) and has written poetry in Dutch and **Papiamentu** as well as four lengthy novels in Dutch, including *Dubbelspel* (Double Play) (1973) and *De laatste vrijheid* (The Final Freedom) (1995). A linguist, he specialized in **creole languages** and became a fervent defender of Papiamentu. In his literary work and essays, Martinus Arion has been critical of the continuing political, economic and cultural dependence of the Dutch Antilles on the Netherlands.

AART G. BROEK

Martorell, Antonio

b. 1939, Santurce, Puerto Rico

Graphic artist

Onoe of Puerto Rico's leading graphic artists, Martorell studies wood engraving and silk-screening with Lorenzo **Homar** before founding his own Taller Alacrán (Scorpion Workshops) in Santurce in 1968, producing illustrations and designs and a deck of political playing cards called Juego de Manos (Sleight of Hand). Martorell has made frequent incursions into journalism, often in collaboration with Rosa Luisa **Márquez**, worked with Teatreros Ambuylantes de Cayey (Cayey Travelling Theatre) and painted the mural devoted to Julia de **Burgos** at Puerto Rico's Centro de Bellas Artes (Fine Arts Centre). His 1991 memoirs *Le piel de la memoria* (The Skin of Memory) include poetic reflections and his own illustrations.

ROBERTO CARLOS ORTIZ

Marugg, Silvio Alberto

b. 1923, Curaçao, Netherlands Antilles

Writer

Marugg is the author of three novels in Dutch, including *De morgen loeit weer aan* (Again the Roar of Dawn) (1988), in which solitude, death, alcohol and sexuality are given pivotal roles. He published his first poetry in the literary magazine *De* **Stoep**, and later, the collection *Afschuw van Licht* (Abhorrence of Light) (1976). Marugg is also the author of a dictionary of erotic words and phrases in Papiamentu. Marugg worked in public relations at a large refinery on the island, from which he retired at an early age.

AART G. BROEK

Marut, Ret *see* Traven, B.

marvellous realism *see* real maravilloso, lo

Marx, Roberto Burle

b. 1909, São Paulo, Brazil; d. 1994, Rio de Janeiro

Landscape architect

The pioneer of a modern landscape aesthetic, Burle Marx left a powerful mark on public spaces and private gardens in Brazil, Venezuela and elsewhere in the world. Sima Eliovson has written: 'His is the greatest single influence in contemporary garden design'. The designer of some three thousand gardens (though not all the projects were realized, or survive today), Burle Marx's work made bold use of Brazilian native flora. His aquatic gardens, such as that at Fazenda Vargem Grande in São Paulo State (1979–90), are justly famous, as are his projects with the major modernist architects of the day. From the 1930s until the 1990s, Burle Marx defined a new field, was its most powerful exponent, and created works in which millions of people take delight every day.

Burle Marx discovered the Brazilian native flora during a trip to Germany in 1928, where he had gone to study painting and music, in a greenhouse at the Dahlem Botanic Garden. When he returned to Brazil, enrolling in the National School of Fine Arts in 1930, he studied architecture, painting and landscape design. Friends in the 1930s included the modernist architects Gregori **Warchavchik**, Marcelo and Milton Roberto (see **Roberto family**), Oscar **Niemeyer** and Lúcio **Costa**. He was also strongly influenced by the botanist Henrique Lahmeyer de Mello Barreto, head of Rio's famous botanical garden (see **botanical gardens**), and travelled with him throughout Brazil finding plants that could be used in horticulture. In 1932 he obtained his first commission, a roof garden for the Alfredo Schwartz House designed by Costa and Warchavchik. In 1936–38 he designed the roof garden for the famous **Ministério da Educacão e Saúde** (Ministry of Education and Health) building in Rio, designed by a team of Brazilian architects working in consultation with Le Corbusier. A bold mature design (1948) was for the Rio house of Odette Monteiro, designed by Wladimir Alves de Souza; for which Burle Marx made spectacular use of curve, contour and colour.

Burle Marx's most famous public projects were bold designs for the giant landfill project of the **Aterro do Flamengo** in Rio and the adjacent **Museu de Arte Moderna** (1954), the stunning design of the Parque del Este in Caracas, Venezuela (1956–61), and the abstract mosaic walkway that runs for several miles on both sides of the Avenida Atlántica along the beach in Copacabana, Rio (1970). He worked with Niemeyer on the design of the Hospital da Lagoa in Rio (1955), and on a design of Ibirapuera Park in São Paulo that was never realized. He designed gardens for the **Brasília** buildings of the Ministry of Foreign Affairs (1965), the Ministry of the Army (1970) and the Tribunal de Contas da União (1972). The design for the army was a particularly bold, sculptural use of blocks of stone, pools, and plantings, set to spectacular effect against the big sky of the arid plateau around Brasília.

Many of Burle Marx's finest projects were gardens for houses designed by his friend Rino Levi, whose elegant modern designs worked in brilliant counterpoint to the Burle Marx gardens. A fine example of their collaboration is the Olivo Gomes house in São José dos Campos, São Paulo (1950, with later modifications). He also designed the garden for the Gustavo Cisneros House in Caracas designed by James Alcock (1980). (Earlier, while working on the Parque del Este, Burle Marx had designed fourteen residential gardens in Caracas.) A fascinating residential design was for his own house, the Sitio Santo Antônio da Bica in Campo Grande south of Rio de Janeiro; from the time he purchased this property in 1949 until his death, the gardens were constantly modified in keeping with their owner's spirit of improvisation. This house also features his paintings, lithographs, sculpture, mosaics and tablecloths. The house includes extensive nurseries, and features an important collection of palms, bromeliads and orchids, as well as of the aquatic plants that Burle Marx so loved.

Later works include the gardens for the Safra Bank in São Paulo (1982). For this project Burle Marx chose to work largely with pebbles of different colours, what William Howard Adams has called 'a twentieth-century version of a Zen monastery garden'. He also did bold designs for the Manchete Building in Rio (1969), for the **Petrobrás Building** in Rio (1969, 1972) and for the atrium of the Xerox Building in Rio (1980). He also designed gardens for factories, hotels, universities, embassies, churches, aquaria, parks, schools and playgrounds.

Burle Marx was also a painter throughout his career, and was involved in all fields of artistic endeavour. In 1959 he did the wardrobe and stage design for a production of the ballet *Zuimaluti* with music by **Villa-Lobos** and libretto by Mário de **Andrade**. In fact, claiming a connection between his landscape design and his interest in painting, he stated: 'I paint my gardens'. Lisa Ponti quotes him in an obituary as having said to her in Rome in 1991: 'Paradise was a garden. Eden was a garden.

The garden came "before architecture" in the history of man. It was man's first home, an unbuilt home. And architecture never reached the condition of Paradise'.

Further reading

Adams, W.H. (1991) *Roberto Burle Marx: The Unnatural Art of the Garden*, New York: Museum of Modern Art.

Eliovson, S. (1991) *The Gardens of Roberto Burle Marx*, New York: Harry N. Abrams.

Ponti, L. (1994) 'Ricordo di Burle Marx/A memory of Burle Marx', *Domus* 764.

DANIEL BALDERSTON

Marxism in Latin America

The revolutionary ideas of Karl Marx have been claimed as a basis for many different political practices in twentieth-century Latin America, from the **Prestes** column to the Bolivian and the Cuban Revolutions (see **revolutions**), and each produced debates that centred on a redefinition of the core ideas of Marxism.

Juan B. **Justo**, the translator of Marx's *Capital* in 1895, was a social democrat – an inheritor of those European currents that endeavoured to separate Marx's searching analysis of capitalism from revolutionary practice by arguing that capitalism would collapse under the weight of its own contradictions.

The October Revolution in Russia, however, redeemed the idea of revolution. The immediate result was a division within Marxism between those who identified with a reformist road and those for whom Russia had vindicated the necessity of revolution as a conscious and organized action led by the working class. The polemic produced Latin America's first **communist parties** – in Argentina (1918), Mexico (1919), Uruguay (1920), Brazil and Chile (in 1922), though the precedent had perhaps been established by Luis Emilio **Recabarren**'s Partido Socialista Obrero, formed in Chile in 1912. Recabarren's role in the growth of the Chilean workers' movement was central, and the Chilean Communist Party he founded was the largest in Latin America; his suicide in 1924 robbed Latin American Marxism of perhaps its most important mass leader.

The major debate in Latin America was whether the lessons that Marx had drawn from the experience of an advanced capitalism set in the framework of Nation States were applicable in countries where the State was still weak and the economies yet to be developed. Was Marxism a European idea, and what should be its relationship to national movements? It was a central issue for the Third Communist International (Comintern) formed in 1919 to establish the international authority of the Russian Revolution. In Latin America the debate was most clearly exemplified in the debate between **Haya de la Torre**, founder of the populist-nationalist organization, **APRA**, and José Carlos **Mariátegui**, leading Marxist intellectual and founder of both the Peruvian Trade Union Congress and the Peruvian Socialist Party, forerunner of the Peruvian Communist Party. Julio Antonio **Mella**, Cuba's young communist leader, joined the attack on APRA with his famous polemic '¿Qué es el Arpa?'(1928). Mella played a key part in building a communist current in Cuba until his murder in 1929 in Mexico (described in Elena **Poniatowska**'s novelized life of Tina Modotti, *Tinísima* (1992)). Mariátegui's *Siete ensayos de interpretación de la realidad peruana* (Seven Interpretive Essays on Peruvian Reality) (1928) was the most original and compelling Marxist writing of the period, and remains an extraordinarily profound Marxist analysis of the specificity of Latin America. Although he too died young, within two years of the publication of *Siete ensayos*, his writings affirmed the revolutionary role of the working class but recognized that, faced with the weakness of the Peruvian bourgeosie, the 'bourgeois' tasks – industrialization and modernization, land reform, democratization – would also have to be carried out by a revolutionary movement embracing workers and peasants under working-class leadership. The contrary current, exemplified by APRA and adopted by **Sandino** in Nicaragua among others, insisted that imperialism was the enemy, and the 'nation' as a whole its antagonist; this was what Mariátegui described in documents sent to the 1929 Conference of Communist Parties in Montevideo as 'the anti-imperialist perspective'.

But by then things were already changing; the 1929 meeting of communist parties reflected Stalin's rise to power in Russia. Mariátegui's ideas were seen as suspiciously close to **Trotskyism**; and in any event the Peruvian's subtle fusing of national aspirations and revolutionary internationalism did not fit the new Moscow-led 'third-period' doctrine, which refused any politics of alliances. New communist leaders emerged, like the Argentine Vittorio Codovila (1894–1970), whose loyalty to Stalin led them to slavishly defend Moscow's policy shifts, from third-period sectarianism to the formation of popular fronts after 1934, which led the Cuban Communist Party to follow its US counterpart and 'dissolve' into patriotic alliances. The Brazilian experience, personified in Luis Carlos Prestes, dramatized the implications of these twists and turns – as his 'Prestes column' unsuccessfully attempted to marry a strategy of insurrection against **Vargas**'s **Estado Novo** with a policy of broad alliance with 'progressive forces'.

The theoretical products of Latin American Marxism under the dominance of Stalinism tended to be *post hoc* justifications of policy shifts. The politics of alliances produced common platforms with the Radicals in Chile, Somoza in Nicaragua, Batista in Cuba among others. When Cold War policies produced bans on communist parties in several countries, there was a moment of radicalization – strike waves in Colombia and Brazil in the early 1950s, and the central role of the PGT in the **Arbenz** government in Guatemala, overthrown in 1954 (see **Cold War, impact of**).

A new generation of social and economic analysts were again turning to Marxism – Caio Prado Jr, Sergio Bagú, André Gunder **Frank**, Silvio Frondizi among others, but the new generation of revolutionary activists, like the group around Fidel **Castro** in Cuba, emerged from different currents. The victory of the Cuban Revolution in 1959 inspired the creation of guerrilla (see **guerrillas**) *focos* (see *foco*) throughout Latin America. Their members were for the most part students and intellectuals alienated from populist and Christian democratic organizations, with few roots in the Marxist tradition and a deep scepticism about what they saw as hopelessly compromised communist parties. Their politico-military strategies reflected their isolation in strategies that replaced mass organization with individual will-power. The generalization of the Cuban experience into a body of theory fell largely to Ernesto 'Che' **Guevara**, who began to develop both economic and philosophical positions that rested on the Marxist tradition.

The revolutionary ideas of Trotsky, and the continuation of his critique of Stalinism after his murder in Mexico in 1940, were the foundation for a number of mainly small organizations in the region. The exception was Bolivia, where Trotskyism was firmly rooted in the working-class movements, and particularly among the miners, and played a key role in the 1952 Revolution. It was influential too in Peru and Chile where Marxist ideas informed an important body of, particularly, historical writing like that of Luis Vitale.

The Sino–Soviet split of 1962 produced a range of organizations calling themselves 'Marxist–Leninist' – the most influential of them in Peru, where one such group evolved into **Sendero Luminoso**. Their version of Marxism was rarely original, but repeated the words and ideas of Mao Tse-tung. Sendero did form its own 'revolutionary international' in the wake of changes in China itself – but argued that it represented a continuation of an 'authentic Mao Tse-tung thought'.

It could be argued that Latin America's most important contribution to the Marxist debate was the fusion of Marxism and radical Roman Catholicism in **liberation theology**. The ideas and categories of Marxism have continued to inform much writing in the fields of social science and political analysis. Whether 'Guevarism', for example, or the experience of Nicaragua under the Sandinistas (see **Sandinista Revolution**) have contributed significantly to Marxist thought is a matter of debate; they have certainly added to the range of practices and experiences that continue to inform the debate around Marxism as revolutionary praxis – a theory and practice of revolution.

Further reading

Alba, V. (1968) *Politics and the Labour Movement in Latin America*, Stanford: Stanford University Press.

Lowy, M. (ed.) (1992) *Marxism in Latin America from*

1909 to the Present: An Anthology, New York: Humanities Press.

Mariátegui, J.C. (1928) *Siete ensayos de interpretación de la realidad peruana*, Lima: Amauta.

Sánchez Vázquez, A. (1967) *Filosofía de la praxis*, Mexico City: Grijalbo.

—— (1929) *El movimiento revolucionario latinoamericano: Versiones de la Primera Conferencia Comunista Latinoamericana*, Buenos Aires: Correspondencia Latinoamericana.

MIKE GONZALEZ

mas

The Trinidadian term for its **carnival**, 'mas' derives from the pre-Lenten *bal masqués* held by members of the French plantocracy who settled in Trinidad from 1783. Pre-emancipation carnival was a strictly elite affair; after 1834, however, freed slaves brought their drum dances and songs onto the streets of east Port-of-Spain, where they had settled in appalling barrack housing after emancipation. Mas became a unique opportunity for a marginalized sector of society to make itself visible. The 1860s saw the emergence of the jamet carnival (the patois term translates as 'underworld'). Jamet mas focused on the **canboulay** processions, appalling the colonial authorities with its nudity and transvestism, and the widespread violence between masqueraders, much of which centred on the rival *calinda* groups led by male stickfighters, though women were involved too, continuing rivalries from former slave dancing associations. Indeed, today in Trinidad parlance the word *jamet* is applied almost exclusively to aggressive women.

In 1884 the banning of canboulay spelled the end of jamet mas and the emergence of carnival dominated by Trinidad's incipient middle class. It was the rise of the modern steelbands (see **steelband**) in the mid-1930s which brought the working classes back into the mas, and they remain (together with costumed bands) a central aspect of today's carnival, with the addition of the 'big trucks', massive mobile sound systems. The carnival season begins after Christmas with fetes, huge parties which provide an important space for live and recorded performance of that season's calypsos (see **calypso**). During January and February, preliminary competitions take place for the **Panorama** steelband competition and the King and Queen of Carnival, and judges visit calypso tents to select finalists for the Calypso Monarch competition. These contests represent key moments of Carnival celebrations. The last two are held the day after Panorama, known as the Dimanche Gras, the last Sunday of feasting before Lent. Masquerading begins before dawn on the Monday with *J'Ouvert*, or 'dirty mas', the vestiges of jamet carnival, with assorted characters from carnival's history; devils who 'terrorize' onlookers by threatening to rub their painted bodies against them if their demands for money are not met, and Midnight Robbers, who traditionally earned money with poetic renditions of their exploits. This is followed by the parading of Kings and Queens leading their bands, which can be up to ten thousand strong, on their way to a stage in the Queen's Park Savannah, where they are judged for the prestigious Band of the Year Award. This has been won on several occasions by one of Trinidad's outstanding artists, Peter **Minshall**, who uses the mas as his medium for breathtaking 'mobile sculptures'.

Further reading

Bailey, D. (1990) *Carnival in Trinidad*, Austin, TX: Steck-Vaughn.

Koningsbruggen, P.H. (1997) *Trinidad Carnival: A Question of National Identity*, London: Caribbean.

Mason, P. (1998) *Bacchanal!: Carnival, Calypso and the Popular Culture of Trinidad*, Montreal: Black Rose Books.

LORRAINE LEU

masculinity

The term *macho*, and its derivatives **machismo** and *machista*, are native concepts associated with the masculine make-up in Latin America that have been and are used by the actors themselves and by the social scientists. It has been assumed that the value of being *macho* reflects power, domination and superiority, which equals virility or masculinity. The ethos of masculinity is thus reduced to virility. This explains why the *macho* protects himself from any perceived attack on his masculinity. Without denying this important cultural dimension, it is important to focus on the various meanings of masculinity because not all of them are grounded in the term *macho* itself. For example, recent research has shown that performing men in sports are seen as carefree, irresponsible and everything that 'the father' as an authoritative figure is not. The image of the playing-man is not coincidental with authority, power, order, responsibility and discipline, values usually related to a supposed dominant meaning of masculinity and the military male. It is an arena for 'boys' to whom the 'men' attach themselves as representing lost youth and freedom.

Masculinity has been seen as a political discourse. Notions of masculinity like courage, honour or responsibility have always played a central role in the production of political legitimacy in Latin America. However, even in the political arena the prevailing notions of masculinity construct differences between men that feed into notions of the political. It has been demonstrated that the main tension between men is either that of the responsible father/husband and the *mujeriego* (womanizer), or between the honest public figure and the corrupt politician. This basic ambiguity evokes the notion of a 'trickster', a *piola*, **malandro** or *tiguere*, men who emerge well from every situation and not necessarily using violence. The image of the hegemonic masculine practice is very difficult to shape fully as constituting 'political order'.

The other field where new meanings are continuously created is sexuality. Masculinity is articulated through cross-sex sexuality. It is accepted that male sexuality in Latin America reflects a dual categorization of women between the decent mother and the whore. This is not the case. Popular music texts, tangos (see **tango**), **samba** or boleros (see **bolero**), and recent research show the powerful presence of a third category of women: the potential partner who is able to provide love and pleasure. The labels used to categorize women are symbols for men's projections of their complex sexual desires.

Against accepted images of heterosexuality, same-sex sexual relations are also an important dimension in the construction of masculinities. To be engaged in homosexual relations does not imply being feminine, nor does it negate the existence between femininity and masculinity. Bisexuality is not automatically opposed to masculinity. Hence hegemonic discourses and practices of masculinity in Latin America are continually contested through different sexual practices.

Further reading

Balderston, D. and Guy, D. (eds) (1997) *Sex and Sexuality in Latin America*, New York: New York University Press.

Gutmann, Matthew C. (1996) *The Meanings of Macho: Being a Man in Mexico City*, Berkeley/ London: University of California Press.

Lancaster, Roger N. (1992) *Life is Hard: Machismo, Danger, and the Intimacy of Power in Nicaragua*, Berkeley/ Oxford: University of California Press.

Melhuus, M. and Stølen, K.A. (eds) (1996) *Machos, Mistresses, Madonnas. Contesting the Power of Latin American Gender Imagery*, London: Verso.

EDUARDO P. ARCHETTI

Masotta, Oscar

b. 1930, Buenos Aires, Argentina; d. 1979, Barcelona, Spain

Psychoanalyst

Responsible for introducing **Lacan** into Argentina, Masotta moved from philosophy and linguistics to psychoanalysis. He published *Introducción a la obra de Jacques Lacan* (Introduction to the Work of Lacan) (1970) and *Cuadernos Sigmund Freud* (Freud Notebooks) (1971), and founded the Freudian School of Buenos Aires (1974).

BEATRIZ CASTILLO

Mastretta, Angeles

b. 1949, Puebla, Mexico

Novelist

Mastretta has created a publishing sensation with her novels and short stories about the loves of aristocratic provincial women in the early twentieth century. Her first novel, *Arráncame la vida* (Tear Out of My Life) (1985) (translated as *Mexican Bolero*), broke social taboo by telling the story of a revolutionary general's spunky wife and her extra-marital affair. It was followed by the short story collection *Mujeres de ojos grandes* (Big-Eyed Women) (1990), loosely based on the stories of Mastretta's great aunts; the essay collection *Puerto libre* (Free Port) (1993), in which Mastretta discusses her ambivalent relationship to feminism; and the well-received novel *Mal de amores* (Love Sickness) (1996).

CYNTHIA STEELE

Mata, Eduardo

b. 1947, Mexico City; d. 1995, Cuernavaca, Mexico

Conductor

Eduardo Mata's tragic death piloting his own light aircraft ended the career of the most gifted Mexican conductor of his generation. Although he studied composition at Mexico's Conservatorio Nacional de Música with **Chávez**, Julián Orbón and Rodolfo **Halffter**, it was his work as conductor, particularly in Latin American repertoire, which brought international acclaim. Recordings include Silvestre **Revueltas**'s complete orchestral output and works by **Ginastera** and Orbón. Mata was Music Director of the Dallas Symphony from 1977 until 1993. His own compositions include three symphonies (1962, 1963, 1967).

SIMON WRIGHT

Mata Gil, Milagros

b. 1951, Caracas, Venezuela

Writer

One of the most successful of Venezuela's women writers, both in terms of sales and of critical recognition, Mata Gil is also among the most frequent winners of literary prizes. She, together with Ana Teresa **Torres** and Laura Antillano, represents an important current of renewal in contemporary Venezuelan writing. She is a journalist and professor and has filled an important cultural role, particularly in the south of the country.

ALICIA RÍOS

Matarazzo family

Of Italian origin, the Matarazzos settled in São Paulo and accumulated one of the world's largest fortunes. Francesco Matarazzo arrived with his family in 1882 and began to manufacture lard, previously imported from the USA. He began to sell flour and candles in São Paulo, later opening a bank to administer his import business, which eventually comprised 365 factories. The business was passed to his son Chiquinho. André, another son, was briefly married to the singer **Maysa**. In the 1960s, the firm began to show signs of fatigue. Its São Paulo headquarters were sold in 1972; the Matarazzo Bank followed in 1977. After Chiquinho's death, the business continued to decline and ceased trading in 1983.

ANTONIO CARLOS VAZ

Mateo, Andrés L.

b. 1946, Santo Domingo, Dominican Republic

Writer

Like many **intellectuals** of his generation, Mateo was profoundly affected by the US invasion of the Dominican Republic in 1965 and its social and cultural repercussions. One result was the creation of a series of literary and intellectual groupings, including La Isla (The Island), founded by Mateo among others. Its ideas informed Mateo's first novel *Pisar los dedos de Dios* (Stepping on God's Fingers) (1979), where he represents two kinds of existence, one indifferent to the creation of a dictatorship, the other besieged by violence. He has also published *Mito y cultura en la Era de Trujillo* (Myth and Culture during Trujillo's Era) (1993), a cultural studies analysis of intellectuals during **Trujillo**'s dictatorship.

FERNANDO VALERIO-HOLGUÍN

Matogrosso, Ney

b. 1942, Bela Vista, Mato Grosso, Brazil

Singer

One of Brazil's greatest showmen, Matogrosso started his career as the lead singer of the irreverent group *Secos e Molhados* (Dry and Wet) in 1973. The group conquered Brazilian audiences of all ages with the androgynous look of its members, and Matogrosso's painted face, half-naked body, fluttering feathers and odd, unmistakable high-pitched voice. Some of the group's songs, such as 'Rosa de Hiroshima' (Hiroshima Rose) by Vinicius de **Moraes** and Gerson Conrad, and 'Sangue Latino' (Latin Blood), by João Ricardo and João Apolinário, are milestones in the history of Brazilian popular music. After two albums Matogrosso broke with the group, attaining comparable success only with his second solo album, *Bandido* (1976). Since then he has continued to incite Brazilian audiences with the sway of his hips, androgynous look, frequent stripteases and impersonations. In the 1980s he recorded songs by emerging young composers of the new wave generation, such as **Cazuza**'s 'Pro Dia Nascer Feliz' (For a Happy Sunrise).

Although Matogrosso has avoided revealing his sexual orientation publicly, he is often seen as a gay icon. Some of his popular songs, such as 'Homem com H' (Man with an 'M') in which he repeatedly claims to be a 'real man,' or 'Telma', in which he sings 'Telma, I am not gay/what they say about me is all calumny/baby, I've changed!', mock heterosexual anxieties and closeted identities, and further represent his own apparent homosexuality.

In his most recent albums, Matogrosso has dedicated greater attention to the technical performance of his voice and has paid homage to great traditional singers and composers of Brazilian popular music. In *Pescador de Pérolas* (Pearl Fisherman) (1987) he is accompanied by the acoustic guitar player Rafael Rebello in songs by notable Brazilian composers such as **Cartola**, Noel **Rosa** and Ary **Barroso**. In *Estava Escrito* (It Was Written) (1995), he performs songs made famous by Angela Maria, one of the greatest Brazilian singers of the 1950s. *Um Brasileiro* (1996) is devoted entirely to Matogrosso's interpretations of compositions by Chico **Buarque**.

Further reading

Vaz, D.P. (1992) *Ney Matogrosso, um cara meio estranho*, Rio de Janeiro: Rio Fundo.

CÉSAR BRAGA-PINTO

Matta

b. 1911, Santiago, Chile

Painter

Matta (Roberto Matta Echaurren) is the major Chilean visual artist of the twentieth century and one of the most important Latin American painters. Often identified as a late surrealist (see **surrealism in Latin American art**), he exhibited in surrealist shows as early as 1938 in Paris and 1940 in Mexico City. Matta's international career was also involved early with abstract expressionism; though he worked for a long period in Paris, he spent much of the 1940s in New York where he was close to artists such as Robert Motherwell and Jackson Pollock. And, although much of his professional career has taken place in New York, London, Paris and Rome, his thematics often reflect Latin American politics and culture.

Born in Santiago to a patrician family of Basque origin, he attended Jesuit schools and completed a degree in architecture at the Catholic University of Chile in 1931. He pursued his career as an architect for a couple of years in Le Corbusier's studio in Paris. After writing a play on the death of Federico García Lorca, he started to read on Latin America culture, especially the writings of the late-nineteenth-century Cuban poet José Martí, while under the tutelage of Gabriela **Mistral**. His career as a painter began suddenly in 1938. His newly found medium freed him from the material constraints of the architectural profession, and allowed him to explore both the new and the primitive, for a time represented for him by the conjunction of surrealism and the New World. He became close to Breton and Tanguy by 1939 and participated in various surrealist group shows in Paris and, after the outbreak of the Second World War, in Mexico and the USA. He spent the period from 1939 to 1948 mostly in New York, where he had his first solo exhibition in 1940 and received critical acclaim from important figures such as Meyer Schapiro. Expelled from the surrealist movement in 1948 due to personal differences, he was influential on the New York abstract expressionists and action painters. In Rome (1950–4) and Paris (1954–69) he gradually drew away from the anti-figural tenets of abstract expressionism and gave his painting ever stronger political messages. After involvement in the events of May 1968 in Paris, he moved to Italy where he has lived for the most part since 1969. He returned to Chile during **Popular Unity** in late 1971, meeting Fidel **Castro** and the muralist group **Brigada Ramona Parra**, as well as visiting **Neruda**.

Matta is best known for large, brightly coloured canvases with many squiggles that often suggest human or animal forms. His *Odisseano* (1971), done just after his visit to **Allende**'s Chile, is a vast canvas (3 by almost 10 metres) with rapidly moving figures in white, green and yellow against a blue background, perhaps the Mediterranean of Odysseus's voyages. *Coïgitum* (1972, 4 by 10 metres), set against a bright blue background, celebrates sex, technology and the cosmos. The 1973 protest painting on the assault on the Moneda, the *Passage from Death to Life*, recalls Picasso's *Guernica*, with dismembered body parts rising up against a tank-like dark mass to the right.

Matta also designed posters, such as one celebrating Cuban–Chilean friendship in 1971, but his drawings are a more important and continuous part of his artistic output. Erotic drawings such as *Bisous* (Kisses) (1980) and political ones like *United Snakes of America* (1973) are complemented by more abstract, often untitled drawings. Matta's titles for his paintings and drawings are inventive and multilingual, often using verbal puns to call attention to the visual play in the works.

Major retrospectives of Matta have taken place in the Museum of Modern Art, New York (1957), the National Gallery of Berlin (1970), and the Pompidou Centre in Paris (1985). The Paris exhibition resulted in a catalogue that gives the fullest account of Matta's career, including his occasional writings, which include poetry, theatrical works and artistic manifestos; numerous excerpts from interviews are also included. Matta's Utopian esthetics include calls to the imagination, to new ways of seeing, and for the rejection of lying, blindness, and conventional vision. He advocates a *Yo vivo* (a living self), in contrast to dead or conventional selves. In his poster on Chilean–Cuban friendship, he transforms the cry of the day, *Venceremos* (We shall triumph) into an aesthetic statement: *Ven Seremos* (Come/They see [and] we shall be). Similarly in a poem that celebrates Allende's electoral victory of 1970 he transforms the name of the Chilean revolutionary movement MIR into a call for a new way of seeing (MIRar = to look). Working mostly in Europe, Matta has drawn on New World Utopian visions and the grandeur of the Chilean landscape to proclaim a new way of seeing, preferring to call himself not a *pintor* (painter) but a *vertor* (a seer).

Further reading

Lippard, L.R. (1970) *Surrealists on Art*, Englewood Cliffs, NJ: Prentice Hall, 167–71.

Matta (1985) Paris: Centre Georges Pompidou.

Matta – A Totemic World: Paintings, Drawings, Sculpture (1974) New York: Andrew Crispo Gallery.

Roberto Matta, Paintings and Drawings 1971–1979 (1980) La Jolla, CA: Tasende Gallery.

DANIEL BALDERSTON AND AMALIA PEREIRA

Matthews, Marc

b. 1937, Georgetown, Guyana

Poet and actor

Matthews resides in London, where he has been active in groups like the **Caribbean Artists Movement** (CAM), which disseminates West Indian theatre, literature and culture. Matthews's experience in radio and on the stage, particularly on Carribbean tours with fellow actor Ken Corsbie as 'Dem Two' and, as the group expanded, 'All-Ah-We', have lent the vibrancy and rhythms of spoken creole to his two collections of poetry, *Guyana My Altar* (1987) and *Season of Sometimes* (1992), rich in allusions to Guyanese folklore and cultural practices. He also appeared in **Roopnaraine**'s documentary *Land Wall, Sea Wall* (1991).

JILL E. ALBADA-JELGERSMA

Mattos, Tomás de

b. 1947, Montevideo, Uruguay

Writer

Although trained as a lawyer and born in Montevideo, Mattos lives in northern Uruguay, which also provides the setting for his fiction. His many short stories have appeared in three collections, and his first novel *Bernabé, Bernabé* (1988) was a best-seller. Combining epistolary and manuscript forms, it describes the foundation of Tacuarembó by Colonel Don Bernabé Rivera and the subsequent massacre of the Charrúa Indians. The central character, a nineteenth-century female historian, gives voice to another silenced sector, women in science. The problems of national identity, aristocratic Uruguayan society, and the civilization–barbarism dichotomy are all addressed in this historical tale.

VICTORIA RUÉTALO

Maturana, Humberto

b. 1928, Santiago, Chile

Biologist

Maturana's research interests focus on understanding the organization of living organisms, and the functioning of the nervous system, as well as the implications of biological structure on human social conduct and organization. Maturana received his Ph.D in Biology from Harvard University (USA) in 1958, and has taught at the University of Chile since 1960. His principal publications include *Biology of Cognition* (1969–70). He was awarded Chile's National Science Prize in 1995.

AMALIA PEREIRA

Mauro, Humberto

b. 1897, Volta Grande, Minas Gerais, Brazil; d. 1983, Volta Grande

Film-maker

One of the most important figures in the history of Brazilian cinema, Mauro approached both documentary and fiction film-making with a refined realist sensibility modulated by expressionism. He began making films in the mining town of Cataguases in the silent period, generating one of the regional cycles that characterized this period of Brazilian cinema. Influenced by Hollywood films yet conscious of the need for a specifically Brazilian cinema, Mauro directed films like *Na primaveira da vida* (In the Springtime of Life) (1926), *Braza dormida* (Sleeping Log) (1929), and *Sangue Mineiro* (Minas Blood) (1930), which represents a transition between his work in Minas and his subsequent work in Rio de Janeiro (with scenes shot in both places). In Rio de Janeiro, Adhemar **Gonzaga**, founder of **Cinearte**, invited him to work at his newly established **Cinédia** studio, where Mauro filmed his first sound feature, the magisterial *Ganga bruta* (Brutal Gang) (1933). A lurid melodrama set in the tropics, *Ganga bruta*'s combination of subjective lyricism, naturalism, and expressionism did not convince contemporary audiences, but deeply impressed the future **Cinema Novo** directors when screened at a 1961 retrospective, especially Glauber **Rocha**, who argued that Mauro was the real 'father' of Brazilian cinema.

After *Ganga bruta*, Mauro made the semi-documentary *A voz do carnaval* (The Voice of Carnival) (1933), featuring popular singers and comedians like Carmen **Miranda** and **Oscarito**, then went to work with Carmen **Santos** at Brasil Vita Films, where he filmed a series of documentary shorts and fiction features, including *Favela dos meus amores* (Beloved Shanty Town) (1935), *Cidade mulher* (City Woman) (1936), and *Argila* (Clay) (1940).

From 1937 on, however, Mauro concentrated on documentary film production; that year he joined the Instituto Nacional de Cinema Educativo (INCE) (National Institute of Educational Cinema) established by Getulio **Vargas** and directed by anthropologist Edgar Roquette-Pinto, who believed that the cinema could valorize Brazilian culture and fulfil an educational mission, 'a school for those without'. In addition to agreeing with Roquette-Pinto's philosophy, INCE also provided Mauro with much needed financial stability, and he produced more than 300 short and medium-length films during his tenure there (1936–64), most notably *Os bandelrantes* (The Pioneers) (1940) and the series *Brasilianas* (1945–56). In 1936 he was also invited to direct a big budget superproduction funded by the Instituto de Cacau da Bahia, *O descobrimento do Brasil* (The Discovery of Brazil), which included a specially written soundtrack by Heitor **Villa-Lobos** (his only work for film). He produced his last feature film, *O Canto da saudade* (The Song of Nostalgia) (1952) in his home town Volta Grande.

'Rediscovered' by Rocha, Paulo Emílio Salles **Gomes** and Alex **Viany** in the 1960s, Mauro contributed to the new Cinema Novo movement: he wrote the Tupi dialogue for dos **Santos**'s *Como era gostoso o meu francés* (How Tasty was My Little Frenchman) (1971) and **Saraceni**'s *Achieta José do Brasil* (1978), appeared in **Neves**'s *Memórias de Helena* (Memories of Helen) (1969), co-wrote and acted in Viany's *A noiva da cidade* (The City Girlfriend) (1978) alongside **Grande Otelo**. His last film was the colour short *Carro de bois* (Donkey Cart) (1978), produced by his granddaughter Valéria Mauro and photographed by a young Murillo **Salles**.

Further reading

Gomes, P.E.S. (1974) *Humberto Mauro, Cataguases, Cinearte*, São Paulo: Perspectiva.

Mauro, A.F. (1997) *Humberto Mauro: O pai do cinema brasileiro*, Rio de Janeiro: IMF Editora.

Rocha, G. (1979) 'Humberto Mauro and the Historical Position of Brazilian Cinema', *Framework* 11: 7–8.

ISMAIL XAVIER AND THE USP GROUP

Maya, Rafael

b. 1897, Popayán, Colombia; d. 1980, Bogotá, Colombia

Poet

Raised in western Colombia, Maya attended law school in Bogotá and frequented the capital's intellectual (see **intellectuals**) circles. In the early 1920s he worked for the magazine *Cromos* (Prints), and in 1925 formed part of Los Nuevos (The New Ones), a group opposing the cultural predominance of the previous literary generation. He held various public offices, including the position of house representative for the Conservative party, president of the Universidad Pedagógica, and in 1956, UNESCO representative in Paris. His poetry is best described as neoclassical, proudly evincing its affinity to Virgil.

HÉCTOR D. FERNÁNDEZ L'HOESTE

Mayan Revitalization Movement

The Maya are the majority population in highland Guatemala, highland Chiapas and in the Yucatán Peninsula in Mexico. Most ethnically identifying Maya speak a Mayan language and practise some traditional lifeways. State-level political agendas long ago split the Mayan peoples. The modern states of Mexico, Guatemala, Belize, Honduras and El Salvador each administer lands once held by Mayas. In Honduras and El Salvador, no autonomously organized Mayan communities remain; in Belize, small remnant populations from pre-Contact times have been augmented by Q'eqchi' settlers from Guatemala forming to become the third largest population group after mestizos (see **mestizo**) and creoles; in Mexico and in Guatemala, indigenous communities remain largely intact, though out-migration to urban centres is common. Since the 1970s Maya in the last two countries have mobilized, identifying themselves as indigenous, with languages and cultural values that are unique and which are not subsumed by the State's political agenda.

These Maya have begun not only to reject assimilation into a mestizo/**ladino** society as a goal, but also to disseminate a common understanding of shared heritage, practice and cosmology. The trajectories of these projects have differed somewhat by country. Initial attempts in the mid-1970s to co-ordinate educational and scholarly programmes to promote Mayan identity, Mayan languages and Mayan constructs proved difficult; Guatemalan leaders explicitly decided to set their own 'house' in order first, before trying again to reach across national borders.

In Mexico, much initial education and conscientization was carried out through a writer's co-operative, **Sna Jtz'ibajom**, the House of the Writer. This group writes pamphlets and story books, writes and produces dramas that centre on Indian life, lifeways, problems and issues, makes a series of radio programmes on cultural and ecological themes, and sponsors a women's co-operative. They also write puppet plays (see **puppet theatre**), which they perform in towns within the Tzeltal and Tzotzil areas of Chiapas. The Zapatista movement (see **Zapatistas**) of the 1990s added an armed dimension to the ethnic tensions dramatized, recorded and denounced by the writers. The militarization of the conflict has led to rapid shifts in cultural paradigms. Women have been active participants both as bearers of arms, but also as unarmed opponents blocking town entrances with their bodies, driving off the government troops with dirt clods. The conflict has disrupted planting cycles, realigned labour division, altered the flow of economic wealth and political position. But indigenous values, the rights to land, to education in culturally appropriate terms, and the maintenance of language have been central to the political agenda of the movement.

In Guatemala, the revitalization movement has gone forth without a dedicated armed force, though the **URNG** (Unidad Revolucionaria Nacional Guatemalteca – Guatemalan National Revolutionary Unity) espoused indigenous issues, and dedicated point three of the Accords for a Firm and Lasting Peace, signed in March 1995, to guaranteeing the rights of the Maya to their languages and consuetudinary law. The revitalization movement in Guatemala has radiated from a linguistic core. In 1984 the Second National Congress on the Alphabet was convened to standardize and regulate writing practice for the Mayan languages of Guatemala. During this assembly linguists of all nationalities and trainings had a right to the floor, but only the indigenous peoples could vote. As a result of this assembly a unified orthography was adopted for the Mayan languages, reflecting the principle that Mayan languages should be represented in their own right and not tailored to ease transition to Spanish. A core group from this congress set about establishing a permanent body to oversee, promote and promulgate Mayan languages. This group won official recognition from the government in 1987 as the Academy of Mayan Languages of Guatemala. Carefully eschewing non-linguistic issues, this group travelled throughout indigenous areas, promulgating the positive values of Mayan languages and the cultural concepts they embody, building a sense of community that would be linguistically based, tracing descent from a common ancestral tongue, Proto-Maya.

Other groups rapidly sprang up to address issues not directly concerned with language. These groups range from textile and agricultural co-ops to grassroots political organizations to Maya schools. The Maya have sought access to radio time through secular and religious transmitters; they have started their own presses and worked out co-operative publishing arrangements with non-Maya newspapers. As is almost definitional in 'revitalization' movements, the Mayan identities forged in Mexico and Guatemala and disseminated through active programmes of education and conscientization are not isomorphic with any cultural snapshot from ethnographic accounts, be they sixteenth-century Spanish chronicles, nineteenth-century German scholars or twentieth-century anthropologists. The Maya who are actively promoting Maya-ness reject trait lists that essentialize them. They rejoice in those practices and products that provide an unbroken link with their past, such as pooling of food resources by co-workers, tokens of respect, woven designs and use of the ritual calendar; yet they refuse to be relegated to the past, claiming the right and the ability to invent and create, and continue to become Maya. Gaspar Pedro González, a Q'anjob'al author, writes: 'The word Indian, my son, can't be explained and there's nothing we can compare it to. Rather, it is a feeling that grows inside of you.'

Further reading

Fischer, E.F. and Mckenna Brown, R. (eds) (1996) *Maya Cultural Activism in Guatemala*, Austin, TX: University of Texas Press/Institute of Latin American Studies.

González, G.P. (1995) *A Mayan Life*, trans. Elaine Elliot, Palos Verdes, CA: Yax Te' Rancho.

Raxche' (Demetrio Rodríguez Guaján) (ed.) (1992) *Cultura Maya y Políticas de Desarrollo*, Guatemala: Cholsamaj.

Waqi' Q'anil (Demetrio Cojtí Cuxil) (1997) *Ri Maya' Moloj pa Iximulew (El Movimiento Maya en Guatemala)*, Guatemala: Cholsamaj.

Warren, K.B. (1998) *Indigenous Movements and Their Critics: Pan-Maya Activism in Guatemala*, Princeton, NJ: Princeton University Press.

JUDITH M. MAXWELL

Mayer, Franz

b. 1882, Mannheim, Germany; d. 1975, Mexico City

Photographer

A German financier and art collector, Mayer emigrated to Mexico in 1905 and devoted two decades, 1926–46, to photographing Mexican rural landscapes and archaeological sites. Like his compatriot, Hugo Brehme, Mayer initially worked squarely within the tradition of pictorial **photography**, attempting to evoke the Mexican national spirit through a succession of character types and dreamy landscapes. In his later works, however, the influence of Edward Weston and Tina Modotti's straight photography, featuring clear, geometric composition of objects, begins to be evident. Mayer's photographs were never exhibited during his lifetime. Rather, until recently he has been known almost exclusively for his exquisite collection of Mexican applied arts – ceramics, silver work, textiles and furniture – which is now housed in the Museo Franz Mayer in Mexico City, along with Mayer's photography collection.

CYNTHIA STEELE

Mayo, Hugo

b. 1898, Manta, Ecuador; d. 1988, Guayaquil, Ecuador

Poet

Hugo Mayo (Miguel Augusto Egas) was a leading avant-garde (see **avant-garde in Latin America**) poet who digested and promoted all the 'isms', from dadaism and *creacionismo* to *ultraísmo* and *estridentismo*. He edited several important avant-garde magazines including, *Síngulus* (1921), *Proteo* (1922) and *Motocicleta* (1924). Mayo's poetry has still to be collected; it is scattered in local newspapers and prestigious international journals, such as *Ultra* and **Amauta**. *El zaguán de aluminio* (The Aluminum Threshold) (1981), an incomplete and imprecise collection of some of his avant-garde poems, is the only text that he allowed to be published. In the late 1920s, Mayo was drawn towards **indigenismo**, but his later work became increasingly personal.

MERCEDES ROBLES

Mayolo, Carlos

b. 1945, Cali, Colombia

Film-maker

Part of the **New Latin American Cinema**, Mayolo's early documentaries criticize Colombia's political and economic situation. With Luis **Ospina**, he made polemical works like *Oiga vea* (Hear, See) (1971), an analysis of political and class antagonisms camouflaged by the 1971 **Pan-American Games** in Cali. *Agarrando pueblo* (Ripping People Off) (1977), a narrative about documentarists in Bogotá who stage misery when they cannot find it, satirizes state-sponsored *pornomiseria* film-making. Mayolo showed his promise as a feature film-maker in 1983 with *Carne de tu carne* (Flesh of Your Flesh), a highly successful fantastic tale of incest and vampirism.

ILENE GOLDMAN

Maysa

b. 1936, São Paulo, Brazil; d. 1977, Rio de Janeiro, Brazil

Singer

Maysa (born Maysa Figueira Monjardim Matarazzo) was the tragic diva of the fossa, a gushy, melodramatic song style of the 1950s and 1960s that dealt with unrequited love, personal failure, betrayal and other existential dilemmas. She left school in 1954 to marry André Matarazzo (see **Matarazzo family**), the young scion of Brazil's wealthiest industrialist, who disapproved of her career. In 1956, she recorded her first album featuring Meu mundo caiu (My World has Fallen), Adeus (Goodbye) and Ouça (Listen). After a complicated divorce, she began drinking heavily and gained the reputation as an aggressive and emotionally unstable performer.

CHRISTOPHER DUNN

Mayz Vallenilla, Ernesto

b. 1925, Maracaibo, Venezuela

Philosopher

An academic philosopher by conviction and a politician by circumstance, Mayz Vallenilla is one of Venezuela's most respected and important **intellectuals**, despite his often highly polemic views. Founder and first president of the prestigious experimental technological university, the Universidad Simón Bolívar (1969–79), he expressed increasing concern about the crisis into which Venezuela appeared to be entering as the twentieth century ended. He became an active member of the civic organization Fundapatria, which argued for a vigorous defence of national assets against foreign penetration and for a halt to the ills that had corrupted and undermined Venezuelan democracy.

ALICIA RÍOS

Mazza, Valeria Raquel

b. 1972, Rosario, Argentina

Model

Blonde, blue-eyed, 5′ 10″ tall and weighing one hundred and twenty-five pounds, this Claudia Schiffer look-alike is one of the few Latin American models ever to gain international recognition. In 1992, Mazza was the 'Caro Cuore' underwear girl and the September *Cosmopolitan* covergirl, and appeared on the catwalk in Milan for the Versace haute couture line. These successes were followed by her crowning achievement, the 'Guess Jeans' account in 1995. Never one to rest on her laurels, Mazza hosted the 1995–6 programme 'Fashion MTV', and shared the coveted *Sports Illustrated* 1996 swimsuit edition cover with Tyra Banks.

FERNANDA A. ZULLO

Mazzaropi, Amácio

b. 1912, São Paulo, Brazil; d. 1981, São Paulo

Film-maker and actor

Popular Brazilian comic actor Mazzaropi began his career with a travelling circus. He then worked in radio and quickly moved into cinema, playing his first role in *Sai da Frente* (Out of the Way) (1951) for **Vera Cruz Studios**. Through the 1950s, he came to represent the sentimental hillbilly (*caipira*), apparently naive and disaster-prone in urban contexts yet always persevering. He played the same character, Jeca, for thirty years. From 1960 onwards he began to produce and direct his own films, including *O Jeca e a Freira* (Jeca and the Nun) (1967), *Jeca contra O Capeta* (Jeca Against the Smart-Alec) (1976) and *O jeca e a Egua Milagrosa* (Jeca and the Miraculous Mare) (1980).

ISMAIL XAVIER AND THE USP GROUP

McAndrew, Wordsworth

b. 1936, Georgetown, Guyana

Poet

Beginning as a radio announcer, broadcaster and producer, McAndrew interwove elements of both Afro-Guyanese and Indo-Guyanese folklore, myth and the creole language in his broadcasts, which he later assembled in the 1979 folklore manual *OOIY*. While acclaimed poems such as 'Ole Higue' (Old Hag, a skinless vampire), are steeped in superstition and written for performance, McAndrew's poetry also makes an easy shift to standard English and traditional lyrical forms. His poems have appeared in several anthologies; his major collections are *Blue*

Gaulding (1958), *Selected Poems* (1968) and *More Poems* (1970).

JILL E. ALBADA-JELGERSMA

McBurnie, Beryl

b. 1915, Woodbrook, Trinidad; d. 1999, Port of Spain, Trinidad

Dancer and choreographer

The young McBurnie was intrigued by rural dance forms. In 1938, after training as a teacher and forming a dance troupe with Boscoe **Holder**, McBurnie moved to New York, where she studied choreography under Martha Graham. Returning to Trinidad in 1945, she launched both her Little Carib Dance Company and the **Little Carib Theatre** in Woodbrook with a performance of the pre-carnival show *Bele* in 1948. Her commitment to folklore and dance in Trinidad and Tobago earned McBurnie the Order of the British Empire (OBE) in 1959, the Humming Bird Gold Medal (1969) and an Honorary Doctorate from the **University of the West Indies** (1976).

JILL E. ALBADA-JELGERSMA

McDonald, Ian

b. 1933, St Augustine, Trinidad

Writer

His only novel, *The Hummingbird Tree* (1969), won the Royal Society of Literature Prize for best regional novel and was adapted to television by the BBC in 1992. The novel explores friendship, youth, class and race in colonial Trinidad and evidences the poet he later became: his love of landscape and mood, his interest in history and the lives of people who live close to the land.

Mercy Ward (1988), his first collection of poems, is humane yet disturbing in its examination of death. The terminally ill patients are like landscapes we all hope to avoid. But we rejoice in the events of their lives: loves, friendships, accomplishments, hopes and desires. His second collection of poems, *Essequibo*, was published in 1992 and won the Guyana Prize for Poetry that year. Most of the poems deal with some aspect of the natural history of Guyana. It is obvious McDonald knows and loves the flora, fauna and people of these forests and riverscapes. He is always gentle and deeply respectful, seeing beauty in a grain of river sand and the gleam of a toucan's eye. He is the humble priest without religion, who understands how and why, in a place where creation let its imagination flourish unhindered, even death can be beautiful.

In 1984 McDonald was instrumental in reviving ***Kyk-Over-Al***, the Guyanese literary journal. *Jaffo the Calypsonian*, his third collection of poems, appeared in 1994. McDonald has co-edited anthologies of poetry, is a columnist with *Stabroek News*, and was regional chairman (Canada and the Caribbean) on the panel of judges for the 1991 Commonwealth Writers' Prize. In 1986 he received Guyana's National Honour, the Golden Arrow of Achievement. In 1997, for his contribution to Caribbean literature, the **University of the West Indies** awarded him an honorary doctorate.

One of the Caribbean's most accomplished poets and citizens, McDonald was educated at Queen's Royal College in Port of Spain, Trinidad, and at Cambridge University, England, but has lived and worked in Guyana since 1955. He holds directorships in several companies, and is administrative director of the Guyana Sugar Corporation.

Further reading

Rohlehr, G. (1974) 'Introduction', in I. McDonald, *The Hummingbird Tree*, London: Heinemann.

KEITH JARDIM

McFarlane, Basil

b. 1922, St Andrew Parish, Jamaica

Poet and critic

Son of J.E. Clare **McFarlane** and brother of R.L.C. **McFarlane**, Basil McFarlane spent his life in Jamaica except for two years in the Royal Air Force (1944–6). After returning to Jamaica he joined the civil service. He was a sub-editor at *The Daily Gleaner* in 1955, and worked as a journalist with Radio Jamaica in the early 1960s. He has written art and film criticism. *Jacob and the Angel and Other Poems* appeared in the Miniature Poets Series (Georgetown, Guyana) in 1952.

PAT DUNN AND PAMELA MORDECAI

McFarlane, John Ebenezer Clare

b. 1894, Spanish Town, Jamaica; d. 1962, Kingston, Jamaica

Poet and politician

Founder of the Poetry League of Jamaica in 1923, McFarlane compiled anthologies such as *Voices from Summerland* (1929) and *A Treasury of Jamaican Poetry* (1950), published five collections between 1918 and 1957, and became Jamaica's Poet Laureate in 1952. McFarlane's poetry is not particularly noteworthy except perhaps for 'The Black Peril,' a 1920s poem defending Ethiopians and blacks from a British journalist's racist vituperation. A distinguished civil servant, McFarlane was the first Jamaican financial secretary. His sons, Basil and R.L.C. **McFarlane**, are also poets.

PAT DUNN AND PAMELA MORDECAI

McFarlane, R.L. Clare

b. 1925, Kingston, Jamaica

Poet

McFarlane was a member of a generation of poets, including his brother Basil, George Campbell, Una Marson, Ken **Ingram** and Vivian **Virtue**, which helped to indigenize Jamaican poetry. Brother of Basil **McFarlane** and son of J.E. Clare **McFarlane**, he was educated in Jamaica, going abroad to the University of London and Howard University. Returning to Jamaica, he joined the civil service, later turning to teaching. He has published several collections of poetry, the earliest being *Selected Poems 1943–1952* (1953), and the most recent, *A Gift of Black Mangoes (Poems 1989–95)* (1995).

PAT DUNN AND PAMELA MORDECAI

McKay, Claude

b. 1890, Clarendon Parish, Jamaica; d. 1948, Chicago, USA

Writer

A Jamaican writer closely associated with the Harlem Renaissance, McKay had already published his poetry, especially two volumes of 'dialect' verse, before leaving for America in 1912. Always hard-up, he travelled widely, using his experiences to portray black and cosmopolitan low-life with zest and sympathetic intelligence in novels like *Home to Harlem* (1928) and short stories. He wrote for the radical press in the USA and in London, and was fêted when he visited the Soviet Union in 1922–3, but always retained an independent stance towards racial and political dogmatism. A poignant nostalgia for rural Jamaica emerges in his 1933 novel, **Banana Bottom**, but his militant poetry and celebration of black working-class values have had the widest impact, notably on the **négritude** movements.

BRIDGET JONES

McKay, Tony

b. 1942, Tea Bay, Cat Island, Bahamas; d. 1997, Nassau, Bahamas

Musician

McKay sang and played guitar in a distinctive style that combined Bahamian **goombay**, **calypso** and **junkanoo** along with influences from other Caribbean forms and also from North America. He emigrated to the USA in his late teens, spending twenty years in New York City and another twelve based in New Orleans. McKay began his career in clubs in Greenwich Village in the early 1960s, ultimately receiving a recording contract and producing two successful albums under his identity of 'Exuma, the Obeah Man' –

'Exuma' referring to an island in the central Bahamas, and '**Obeah**' referring to a Caribbean system of folk beliefs. The two albums achieved some international success in the Americas and in Europe, and McKay continued recording through the 1970s, eventually under his own label, 'Nassau Records'. In the mid-1970s McKay also wrote and directed a musical called *Junkanoo Drums*, which was performed at the Lincoln Center in New York. He returned permanently to the Bahamas in the early 1990s where he performed for both Bahamians and tourists. He also took up painting, exhibiting his artwork in southern Florida and the Bahamas. McKay's songs often treated themes related to Bahamian folklore and popular culture. Although he continued recording in the 1980s and 1990s, many of his most enduring works came from his earlier years, including the songs 'Reincarnation', 'Cat Island' and 'Rake and Scrape' – a tune celebrating a particular form of Bahamian music.

ROSANNE ADDERLEY

McKenley, Herb

b. 1922, Clarendon, Jamaica

Runner

The first man to run 400 metres under 46 seconds (45.9 in 1948), McKenley had set his first world record (46.2 for 440 yards) while attending the University of Illinois in 1946. He won the silver medal in the Olympic 100 metres in 1952 and twice in Olympic 400 metres competition, and ran a 44.6-second leg on Jamaica's gold medal 4 × 400 relay team at the 1952 Olympics, which won in a world record time of 3 minutes 03.9 seconds. After retiring from competition he became Jamaica's national coach, representative to the IAAF and president of the Jamaican Athletic Federation.

RICHARD V. McGEHEE

McNeill, Anthony

b. 1941, Kingston, Jamaica; d. 1995, Jamaica

Poet

One of the finest and most original poets of his generation, McNeill's early collections *Hello Ungod* (1971), *Reel from 'The Life Movie'* (1975) and *Credences at the Altar of Cloud* (1979) explored existential (see **existentialism**) and religious questions. Born into a family of Jamaican politicians, McNeill's work addressed a variety of other subjects, from the Rasta cult (see **Rastafarianism**) to the writing of poetry itself, as his thematically arranged volume *Reel from 'The Life Movie'* (1975) makes clear. He was joint editor, with Neville Dawes, of the anthology *The Caribbean Poem* (1976).

KEITH JARDIM

McTair, Dionyse

b. 1950, Port-of-Spain, Trinidad

Teacher and poet

McTair has published one collection of poetry, *Notes Towards an Escape from Death* (1987). Her poetry explores interpersonal relationships, intense private emotions, the sense of innocence and experience, and the startling possibilities of island landscape. It attempts to capture the magic of special moments in as reflective and cryptic a manner as possible. Her poems give the impression that she has pared away at them, in the manner of minimalists, until she is left with nothing but the kernel of meaning. Educated in Trinidad and Jamaica, McTair has a degree in sociology and a diploma in education.

FUNSO AIYEJINA

McWatt, Mark

b. 1947, Georgetown, Guyana

Poet and critic

A poet whose work has been published in various journals and anthologies, as well well as in *Interiors*

(1988), much of McWatt's poetry describes the people and places of the Guyanese interior where he grew up. He received his doctorate from Leeds University in England and is senior lecturer in literature at the Barbados campus of the **University of the West Indies**, where he teaches and researches West Indian literature and postcolonial literature in English. In addition to contributing critical articles to journals such as the *Journal of West Indian Literature*, he has edited a critical volume, *West Indian Literature and Its Social Context* (1985).

CAROL J. WALLACE

meat in Argentina

There is general agreement that the founding work of Argentine literature is Esteban Echeverría's *El matadero* (The Slaughterhouse) (1816), a work that crystallizes the romantic sensibilities of the River Plate region and prefigures a body of writing concerned with the physical extermination of enemies, particularly enemies of the State. There is another reading of the same work, however, that is rarely addressed – perhaps because it seems too innocuous and obvious. The work is set in the abattoirs of old Buenos Aires where cattle were slaughtered. Since all tradition is retrospective, perhaps *El matadero* sets out, among other political and literary motifs, the importance of meat in the life of the nation. Another Argentine writer, Ezequiel Martínez Estrada, was convinced that cattle were the real instrument of Argentine colonization, relegating the European conqueror to a second or third level of responsibility for the gradual descent of the country into barbarism. A few cattle abandoned on the banks of the River Plate in the sixteenth century became millions of animals as the centuries passed.

Meat was the basic food of the archetypal Argentine nomad, the **gaucho**, and his methods of preparing it were the very simplest. Benevolent versions suggest that the gaucho roasted his meat in the camp fire, but it seems more likely that, at least in the first centuries after colonization, they ate it raw and without salt, given the scarcity of firewood on the *pampas* (see **pampa**) where the gaucho and the cattle roamed. Trees reached Argentina only in the nineteenth century, brought by ranchers bent on transforming the landscape. Just as the gaucho is seen as a natural man, so beef is seen as nature's food – occupying the place taken by corn, yucca or potatoes in other parts of Latin America. For over a century it has been suggested that Argentines exceeded their protein needs.

This may explain the general love in that region of barbecued beef (*carne a la parrilla*); few Argentines see any problem in this cult of the most primitive and basic form of cooking. On the other hand, all sorts of rituals and nuances have been introduced into the roasting of meat. There are a variety of cuts of beef, each requiring different cooking times and levels of heat. The internal organs of the animal, called *achuras* in Argentina, and a delicacy, also require different methods of cooking.

The culture of cooking normally requires 'a struggle to overcome', that is, to distance the cooked food as far as possible from its original state. In the case of Argentine cuisine, however, the opposite is true – all the protocols of preparation and cooking are designed to emphasize the origins of the food. Among the urban population barbecueing is a male prerogative. The Argentine man at the barbecue becomes the leader of his tribe, surrounded by others, including other men, who render him obedience. It is usually beef that is cooked this way, but it can also be chicken, fish, goat, suckling pig or veal – but never horsemeat. As far as the fire is concerned, it is almost apostasy to introduce gas or electricity – the fire should be of wood or coal. Unless the meat is set vertically, there should be no flames.

Around the barbecue gather several families or friends and relatives. The meat and *achuras* are eaten with a simple salad of lettuce, tomato and onion, and accompanied by red wine. Within the limits of modern life, the barbecue is a social occasion that can last all day; preparation begins mid-morning (some barbecue purists insist on several hours of preparation) and the meat is eaten after midday – and again after a siesta or a stroll, later in the afternoon. At night the remains are eaten cold.

This cultural relationship between man and meat has produced its own values and meanings. The aesthetic canon, which also embraces the gastronomic, insists that fat is part of the meat, salts it long before cooking, rejects too bloody a flesh and demands that each cut of meat has its own integrity – a piece weighing four or five kilos, however thick, must be cooked whole. Any suggestion that the meat be cut to accelerate the cooking is viewed with disdain by the craftsman at the grill who is also the 'man who serves', the host and the chief.

Argentina is one of the few countries where meat is never eaten rare – the barbecue is an archetypal occasion that always approaches, but never reaches, the same ideal. One proof is the sensation of being excessively full after eating the meat – as if they had consumed some part of themselves. Bones and fat are kept for the dogs.

SERGIO CHEFJEC

Medellín Conference

The second general meeting of the Latin American Bishops' Conference (**CELAM**), held at Medellín, Colombia, in August–September 1968, became a landmark in the recent history of the Catholic Church in Latin America (see **Catholicism**). The conference denounced poverty as a structural sin, and urged the Church to adopt a 'preferential option for the poor', and to defend justice and human rights. Often considered the starting point of **liberation theology**, in fact Medellín represented a Latin American interpretation of a movement started by Vatican II. Depending on perspective, Medellín represented either the Church's final break with a dependent, colonial role or an embarrassing deviation, to be corrected later.

ELINA VUOLA

media enterprises

In the 1990s climate of deregulation and globalization, Latin American media enterprises flourished. The region's governments no longer considered it a priority to protect their national cultures through powerful media monopolies. As a consequence, large television companies such as Venezuela's **Venevisión**, Mexican **Televisa** and Brazilian Rede **Globo** became major players in the global market.

At the beginning of this century, however, newspapers (see **press and mass media**) were the main vehicle for defining national culture in Latin America. Society's leaders were the literary intelligentsia. The combination of serial fiction, literary figures and advertising boosted the newspaper business. As newspaper companies ventured into the book, magazine and sound recording industries, and eventually into **radio** and **television**, journalistic empires began to arise. Cinema had its heyday in Mexico and Argentina in the late 1940s. The region's movie industry today, however, is not as strong as its television industry.

Television turned into an independent and pivotal commercial enterprise only after the mid-1980s. In the previous decade, state protectionism developed the necessary communication infrastructure and media entrepreneurs created new consumer markets. Satellite and cable technologies made broadcasting available to even the most isolated regions, as *telenovelas* found their niche in the international market.

As television accelerated the formation of cultural geographies, the US Spanish language media became an extension of that of Latin America. The economic crisis and political upheavals of the 1980s intensified the northward movement of Latin American immigrants making the USA one of the countries with the biggest groups of Spanish speakers in the world. The US Spanish television networks now produce a good portion of their own programmes, although the content of these is is mostly Latin American.

Joint ventures between US and Latin American partners abound, as private companies rush to secure a share of the global Spanish-speaking market. USA network, for example, teamed up with three Latin American cable operators to provide services to one million subscribers in several countries. Argentine and Venezuelan cable companies joined Hollywood studios in creating *Cine Canal*, a pan-American movie channel. Spain, Argentina and Mexico established a news service, and Peru brought its *Canal Sur* cable service into the United States.

Following global trends, Latin American newspapers have watered down their contents to expand circulation and attract advertisers. Magazines and radio now cater to special niche markets. Literature, on the other hand, now courts rather than rejects mass culture as in, for example, Mexican novelist Laura **Esquivel**'s *Como agua para chocolate* (Like Water for Chocolate) (1991).

TOMÁS LÓPEZ-PUMAREJO

media personalities

It has been said that we live in 'the age of showbusiness', meaning that entertainment produces society's leaders through the visual media. In other words, media personalities become our leaders and vice versa. Ratings decide news content, public relations agents connect presidents to media, and politicians recruit sports heroes, celebrity singers and movie stars to endorse their candidacies. As entertainment proves to be the most persuasive frame for public address, politicians adapt to it. At the same time, entertainers often use their popularity to launch political careers. Thus Fernando **Collor** de Mello in Brazil, Irene **Sáez** in Venezuela and Irma **Serrano** in Mexico came to politics via the mass media.

As **salsa** became a global beat, celebrity singers like Celia **Cruz** and Rubén **Blades**, involved in their own countries' politics, achieved the status of Latin America's ambassadors. According to Jean Franco, the noted US literary and cultural studies critic, it is the *salsera* Cruz, not José Enrique Rodó or Simón Bolivar, who is the contemporary apostle of Latinity. In 'Pasaporte Latinoamericano' (Latin American Passport), she sings of a 'single Latin people' driven by the work ethic and self-help: 'If we don't do it ourselves, who will help us?'. Celebrities like Blades, who ran for Panama's presidency, Brazilian Caetano **Veloso** and Dominican Juan Luis **Guerra** take up the cause of social justice.

The 'age of show business' is also the 'age of television'. If we think of media as an ecosystem, **television** is at its core. Television has become the intersection of all media, and as such the ultimate site of celebrity production. Within this star-making machinery, the Hispanic world consecrates media personalities through two agencies: ***telenovelas*** and high-society gossip magazines. *Telenovelas* work in tandem with the music industry by turning new releases into soundtrack and musical themes, by launching their actors' singing or film careers (Verónica **Castro** in Mexico, **Xuxa** in Brazil), and by casting celebrity singers. Uncommon in American soaps, this latter tactic is common in *telenovelas*. Celia Cruz, for example, played central roles in two Mexican soaps in 1992 and 1997. On the other hand, high-society gossip magazines – most notably Spain's widely-distributed *Hola!* – recruit media personalities into the 'jet-set' when they achieve celebrity status. These magazines focus on the European royalty. When aristocrats appear with presidents, sports champions, celebrity singers and movie stars in galas and ceremonies, it implies that these media personalities have reached the highest possible rank.

TOMÁS A. LÓPEZ-PUMAREJO

Medina, Enrique

b. 1937, Buenos Aires, Argentina

Writer

With almost two dozen books to his credit, including novels, chronicles, short stories and a play, Medina is Argentina's leading proponent of dirty realism. His first work, *Las tumbas* (The Tombs) (1973), remains his most famous; it has been widely translated and was adapted to the screen by Javier Torre, Leopoldo **Torre Nilsson**'s son, in 1991. *Las tumbas* uses the setting of a boy's reformatory to explore the construction of violent social subjects in the context of Argentine society. Medina was heavily censored by the dictatorships between 1976 and 1983. More recently, he is best known for his columns in the daily ***Página 12*** and his *El escritor, el amor y la muerte* (1998) (The Writer, Love and Death).

DAVID WILLIAM FOSTER

Medina, Ofelia

b. 1950, Mérida, Mexico

Actress

Along with Verónica **Castro**, the star of ***telenovelas*** and talk shows, Ofelia Medina (Torres) is Mexico's leading popular actress of the 1980s and 1990s. She has also been a prominent human rights activist on behalf of Mexico's Indian population. In the course of her career she has specialized in portraying strong women artists and activists, including Gertrudis Bocanegra (an Independence heroine from Michoacán), Sor Juana Inés de la Cruz in **Bemberg**'s *Yo la peor de todas* (I, Worst of All) (1990) and Frida **Kahlo** in **Leduc**'s ***Frida, naturaleza viva*** (1984).

CYNTHIA STEELE

Meiling

b. Trinidad

Fashion designer

One of the Caribbean's premier designers, she literally grew up in her dressmaker mother's sewing room. Meiling's work is inspired by the diversity of life in Trinidad, particularly the climate, vibrant colours, music, human movement and **carnival**. She has successfully realized her designs despite the fact that Trinidad imports most of the textiles it needs. Meiling has recently launched a secondary line inspired by streetwear aimed at the under-thirty age group. Bold and highly individualistic, its effect relies strongly on black and silver, juxtaposed with strong colours such as fuchsia, cobalt and lime.

LORRAINE LEU

Meireles, Cecília

b. 1901, Rio de Janeiro, Brazil; d. 1964, Rio de Janeiro

Poet

Considered the most important woman poet in Brazil, Meireles was greatly influenced by the symbolist poet Cruz e Sousa and created a uniquely personal and spiritual adaptation of symbolism's techniques, themes and forms. Meireles considered her work to be free of modernist (see **Brazilian modernism**) or nationalistic influences, yet she absorbed much from her contacts with the Catholic poets of the review *Festa* and with Indian and oriental spiritualism. Seldom recognized is the fact that she was one of the pioneers of Brazilian folklore studies and produced gifted ethnographic drawings.

SUSAN CANTY QUINLAN

Meireles, Cildo

b. 1948, Rio de Janeiro, Brazil

Visual artist

Meireles takes art away from its institutional surroundings and uses alternative materials such as telephone tokens, recycled bottles and even currency. He was first influenced by **neo-concretism** and co-founded the Experimental Unit of the Museum of Modern Art in Rio in 1969. He became a more socially and politically engaged artist, adhering to the principles of **conceptual art**. He set up the exhibition 'Do Corpo à Terra' in 1970, and co-founded the alternative art journal *Malasartes* with José Resende and Waltercio **Caldas**. His most recent work focuses on the destruction of indigenous populations by capitalism and the Catholic Church.

RUDI BLEYS

Mejía, Alvaro

b. 1940, Medellín, Colombia

Runner

In the 1960s and the early 1970s, Mejía was Colombia's foremost athlete. In 1965 he was champion in the 1,500, 5,000 and 10,000 metre races in the Juegos Bolivarianos (Bolivarian Games) in Quito, Ecuador. On 31 December 1996, he won the famous San Silvestre Marathon in São Paulo, Brazil, and in 1971 he won the Boston Marathon.

MIGUEL A. CARDINALE

Mejía Godoy, Carlos

b. 1943, Somoto, Nicaragua

Composer and musician

Established from the early 1970s as the nation's pre-eminent composer of music rooted in folk styles, and identified closely with the 1979 **Sandinista Revolution**, Carlos Mejía Godoy has been Nicaragua's most influential singer-songwriter in the latter half of the century. Son of a **marimba** maker and musician, he began his career creating radio dramas, until repression from the Somoza dictatorship forced him into a new career. His melodies creatively and subtly reinforce lyrics drawn from local experience and Nicaragua's unique vernacular speech. The compositions contained on the album *Canto al Flor de Pueblo* (Song to the Flower of the People), released after the 1972 earthquake, marked the beginning of the Nicaraguan New Song movement, which became one of the most vibrant in Latin America. In collaboration with other musicians, he set to music **liberation theology** writings by peasants from Ernesto **Cardenal**'s Solentiname collective as the *Misa Campesina* (Peasant Mass). Since its first attempted celebration in Managua in 1976, it has been widely translated and recorded, serving as a model for the creation of other masses based upon local musical material. Its innovative use of different folk-related styles for separate sections of the service coincided with the orientation of Vatican II, but also engendered some controversy.

Mejía Godoy's songs won international recognition, and his ironic celebration of street children, 'Quincho Barrilete', won the 1977 international OTI song competition. Together with his younger brother Luis Enrique **Mejía Godoy**, he made a singular contribution in 1978 to the success of the military insurrection that eventually toppled the Somoza regime a year later, with an album of didactic songs, *Guitarra Armada*. He briefly held a post in the Sandinista government in the nation's first Ministry of Culture, before leaving to resume his performing career. He sang and played accordion and chromatic marimba with his group, Los de Palacagüina, on several albums that featured his own material. He collaborated with his brother again on his largest work, the *Canto Épico al FSLN* (1981), an historical cantata with instrumental accompaniment.

Mejía Godoy conducted extensive research into the folk music of Nicaragua. He was the first Nicaraguan musician to set lyrics to the *mazurca segoviana*, the most representative musical form of his native northern region. He re-established the genre of songs with critical socio-political content after decades of successful government intimidation of the country's musical community. Through his musical and lyrical synthesis of peasant and popular urban culture, he became a leading cultural spokesman for the popular classes in the 1970s and 1980s.

T.M. SCRUGGS

Mejía Godoy, Luis Enrique

b. 1942, Somoto, Nicaragua

Musician

Together with his brother Carlos **Mejía Godoy**, Luis Enrique brought together socially critical lyrics and traditional Nicaraguan folk rhythms to lay the basis for the Nicaraguan New Song movement. Their joint album of directly political songs, *Guitarra Armada* (Armed Guitar) (1978) helped to promote the Sandinista (see **Sandinista Revolution**) cause. After the overthrow of Somoza in 1979, the brothers continued to argue the Sandinista case through music, as, for example, in *Canto Epico al FSLN* (Epic Song to **FSLN**) (1981). With his groups **Volcanto** and Mancotal, Luis Enrique toured the world and broadened the range of Nicaraguan new song, introducing elements of tropical music and jazz as well as classical instruments.

ESTEBAN E. LOUSTAUNAU AND ILEANA RODRÍGUEZ

Mejía Vallejo, Manuel

b. 1923, Jericó, Colombia

Writer

Mejía Vallejo is best known for his fiction dealing with the 1950s 'La **Violencia**', for example the stories of *Tiempo de sequía* (Drought Time) (1957) and his most recognized novel, *El día señalado* (The Appointed Day) (1964). The rural area of Antioquía is the setting for many of his novels. He has published twenty books of fiction as well as essays, and was awarded the Rómulo **Gallegos** Prize in 1989. His later novels include *Aire de tango* (Tango Tune) (1973), a work structured around tangos (see **tango**), as popular in Medellín as in Buenos Aires, and *La casa de las dos palmas* (The House with Two Palm Trees) (1989).

RAYMOND L. WILLIAMS

Melaan, C.

b. 1953, Bonaire, Netherlands Antilles; d. 1997, Bonaire

Painter

Melaan (nicknamed 'Papa') was an autodidact who painted classic figurative Bonairian scenes but also experimented with abstraction and airbrushing. He has several murals in Bonaire and has had exhibitions in Bonaire, Curaçao and the Netherlands. He has also designed sets for the theatre and for official meetings.

NEL CASIMIRI

Mele, Juan

b. 1923, Buenos Aires, Argentina

Painter

Juan Mele studied at the Academia Nacional de Bellas Artes in Buenos Aires, where he met Tomás **Maldonado**, Alfredo **Hlito** and other avant-garde artists. He joined the Asociación Arte Concreto-Invención in 1946, shortly after its foundation. His paintings are in a strictly constructivist language (see **constructivism**). In 1971 he moved to New York and continued to paint in a geometrical style. In the 1990s, he exhibited with the revived **Arte Madí** group led by Carmelo **Arden Quin**.

GABRIEL PEREZ-BARREIRO

Meléndez, Agliberto

b. 1942, Altamira, Dominican Republic

Film director

Meléndez has been director of **Radio Televisión Dominicana**, director of the National Cinematheque and a university professor. His first film, *Pasaje de ida* (One-Way Ticket) (1988), was well received and won many awards, such as the 'Gran Premio' at the San Juan Film Festival and two others at Biarritz in 1988. A low-budget film, self-financed by its director, *Pasaje de ida* is based on the true story of stowaways who died in the boat, Regina Express. Politically committed, Meléndez's film denounces the suffering of Dominicans trying to escape poverty by emigrating to New York. In 1996 he produced Pericles Meíja's *Cuatro hombres y un ataud* (Four Men and a Coffin), a comedy.

FERNANDO VALERIO-HOLGUÍN

Melià, Bartomeu

b. 1932, Palma de Mallorca, Spain

Anthropologist, ethnologist and linguist

Father Melià received his doctorate from the University of Strasbourg. His thesis, 'The Creation of a Christian Language in the Guarani Reductions of Paraguay', was researched in Paraguay under ethnologist León Cadogan. Melià continued to study the four **Guarani** subcultures of eastern Paraguay (guayakí, mbyá, chiripá and pãi) even after his exile in 1976. He was director of the journal *Acción* (now defunct) from 1969 to 1975, and a founding member and first director of *Estudios paraguayos*. His essays are published in *Una nación, dos culturas* (One Nation, Two Cultures) which discusses the linguistic complexities of contemporary Paraguay, and *El guaraní conquistado y reducido* (Guarani, Conquered and Reduced) which traces the ethnohistory of the Guarani.

BETSY PARTYKA

Mella, Julio Antonio

b. 1903, Havana, Cuba; d. 1929, Mexico City

Political leader

Leader of the opposition to the **Machado** dictatorship, Mella (born Nicanor McPartland) founded the Cuban Federation of University Students (FEU) in 1923, which organized the first national student congress and established the José Martí Popular University. In 1925, with worker Carlos Baliño, he formed the Cuban Communist Party and became its first general secretary. Exiled to Mexico, he made contact with the international communist movement but was asassinated by **Machado**'s agents. At the time of his death he had a relationship with the photographer Tina Modotti, whose intimate portraits of Mella are well known.

WILFREDO CANCIO ISLA

Melo, Jorge Orlando

b. 1942, Medellín, Colombia

Historian

Melo was a key contributor to the Nueva Historia (New History) movement, promoting the renovation of Colombian historiography. His 1977 text *Historia de Colombia: El establecimiento de la dominación española* (History of Colombia: The Establishment of Spanish Domination) is considered a canonical representative of this school of thought. An established Social Democrat, in the early 1990s Melo served as presidential adviser for human rights and for programmes of social development in Medellín. Melo studied philosophy and literature in Bogotá and history at Chapel Hill and Oxford. He has taught at various universities, including Uniandes, Univalle and Duke.

HÉCTOR D. FERNÁNDEZ L'HOESTE

Melo Neto, João Cabral de

b. 1920, Recife, Brazil; d. 1999, Rio de Janeiro, Brazil

Poet

João Cabral was brought up on sugar plantations in the Brazilian Northeast, and often took the landscape and society of the area as the subject of his poetry. He moved to Rio de Janeiro in 1942, and in 1947 began a diplomatic career which took him to many parts of the world, notably Spain in the 1950s. In the landscapes of Andalusia and Castile he found an analogue for the hard, rocky terrain of his native Brazilian interior, and in the work of medieval and modern poets, the kind of concreteness and solid realism he admires. He stands out from the generally mediocre formalism of the so-called 'Generation of 1945', and has been lionized by the concretists (see **concrete poetry**), though his poetic project has very little to do with theirs. After retirement he lived in Rio de Janeiro.

His poetry began with a problematic exploration of his subconscious, in which images float in a vacuum, out of interpretive reach. However, from the mid-1940s onward he turned to a rigorously objective style, in long poems centring on the river Capibaribe, which reaches the sea at Recife. The culmination of this series was the verse play ***Morte e vida severina*** (The Death and Life of a Severino) (1955), subtitled 'A Pernambucan Christmas play'. His most popular work, it became a resounding success in the 1960s when it was set to music by Chico **Buarque**, and made into a film. Its central character is a *retirante* (refugee), in flight from drought in the interior, who follows the river to its mouth in search of a decent life, only to encounter various types of death in the areas – the ***sertão***, the sugar plantations and the city – he passes through. It is a sharp denunciation of repressive social conditions, though it does end with a kind of celebration of new birth in the riverside slums. Cabral was always discreetly left-wing in his politics.

His objectivism continued in the 1960s, enclosed now in tight, short lyrics in *Educação pela pedra* (Education by Stone) (1966). More recently, he wrote a play about the early nineteenth-century rebel, Frei Caneca.

Further reading

Melo Neto, J.C. de (1975) *Poesias Completas*, Rio de Janeiro: José Olympio.

—— (1980) *A Knife All Blade or Usefulness of Fixed Ideas*, trans. K.S. Keys, Camp Hill, PA: Pine Press.

—— (1994) *Selected Poetry 1937–1990*, ed. D. Kadir, trans. E. Bishop, Hanover, NH: University Press of New England.

Peixoto, M. (1983) *Poesia com coisas*, São Paulo: Perspectiva.

Reckert, S. (1986) 'João Cabral: from *Pedra* to *Pedra*', *Portuguese Studies* 2: 166–84.

JOHN GLEDSON

Melodia, Luiz

b. 1951, Rio de Janeiro, Brazil

Musician

Discovered by Gal **Costa**, who recorded his song 'Pérola negra' (Black Pearl) in her 1971 album *Fatal*, Melodia released his own record, also entitled *Pérola Negra*, which became a classic. Even though he has since recorded relatively few albums, Melodia's anguished voice and often strange lyrics have put him among the most important artists of the generation of Caetano **Veloso** and Gilberto **Gil**. His 1976 song 'Juventude transviada' (Deviant Youth) from *Maravilhas contemporâneas* (Contemporary Marvels), became a national hit after it was included in the soundtrack of the popular *telenovela* (see **telenovelas**) *Pecado capital* (Mortal Sin).

CÉSAR BRAGA-PINTO

Melville, Pauline

b. 1948, Guyana

Actress and writer

Melville grew up in England, and worked as an actress while writing her accomplished prize-winning first collection of short stories, *Shape Shifter* (1990). She has a keen ear for accent and nuance of voice in characters from Britain and the Caribbean. She utilizes the supernatural in clever, contemporary ways which draw on Caribbean traditions, and has a sure comic touch. Her second novel, *The Ventriloquist's Tale* (1998), deals with Amerindian culture in Guyana.

ELAINE SAVORY

Memoria del fuego

Memoria del fuego is the title of a trilogy by the Uruguayan writer Eduardo **Galeano** comprising *Los nacimientos* (Genesis), *Las caras y las máscaras* (Faces and Masks) and *El siglo del viento* (Century of Wind), written during his exile in Spain (1977–85). It renders the history of the Americas from the pre-Columbian beginnings until 1984, in classic Galeano vignettes that collapse myriad events and circumstances into skilfully crafted evocations of time and place. The author's poetic eye catches larger cultural meanings by paying careful attention to detail. The narrative effect of Galeano's 1,164 vignettes is cumulative and sustained, offering a rich appreciation of the diverse land and life of the Americas past and present. The English-language version of the trilogy, superbly translated by Cedric Belfrage, won Galeano the American Book Award in 1989.

W. GEORGE LOVELL

Memorial de América Latina

This memorial in the centre of São Paulo expresses in architectural space a bold and original initiative – the achievement of cultural integration. In the words of Oscar **Niemeyer**, who designed the 25,000 square metre complex, 'it represents an act of faith and continental solidarity' (*Nossa América/ Nuestra América*, p. 30).

Inaugurated in March 1989, it gives form to a cultural project directed by anthropologist and writer Darcy **Ribeiro**, who conceived a series of actions to strengthen cultural, political, economic and social relations between the countries of Latin America. 'Our aim in promoting Lain American cultural integration in Brazil, in São Paulo', he said, 'is to widen the frame of reference of our youth by expanding the information available to them, so that they can opt more consciously for cultural alternatives within their own reality'.

The Latin America Library houses more than 30,000 volumes on the literature, history and thought of the continent. The Memorial also has an art gallery, a videothèque and an audio library containing thousands of hours of music. It publishes the journal *Nossa América* in Portuguese and *Nuestra America* in Spanish with contributions from writers, critics and artists. At the level of presentation it maintains the high intellectual and graphic standards established by Ribeiro and the journalist Eric Nepomuceno.

Every space in the Memorial, whether covered or open, incorporates works of art; in the library there is a ceramic panel by Mario Gruber and a glass panel by Marianne Peretti; in the Civic Square, panels and sculptures by Sérgio Ferro, Franz Weissman, Vera Torres, **Sebastián** and Vitorio Camacho – outstanding among them is the hand of Niemeyer, an emblem for the complex as a whole. In the Conference Room is Cândido **Portinari**'s most important work, the 1948 Tiradentes panel measuring eighteen metres long by three metres high. Also included in the complex are the Pavilion of Popular Creativity, the Permanent Headquarters of the Latin American Parliament and the Brazilian Centre for Latin American Studies (the cultural nucleus of the complex), a space for exchanges between institutions of Europe and the Americas and a centre for the dissemination of Latin America's creativity in the arts, humanities, science and letters.

Further reading

Nossa América/Nuestra América (1988) Número Zero, São Paulo: Memorial da América Latina.

CELINA MANZONI

Memorias del subdesarrollo

Tomás **Gutiérrez Alea**'s *Memorias del subdesarrollo* (Memories of Underdevelopment) (1968) is based on a short novel of the same name by Edmundo Desnoes, published in 1965. Set in Havana, its protagonist is Sergio, a young man from a wealthy Havana family, the rest of whose members chose exile in Miami after the Cuban Revolution of 1959 (see **revolutions**). Sergio's monologue through the film examines the effects of the revolution – the collapse of traditional institutions, the enshrining of a new way of thinking which judges everything that 'the rich' produce as pernicious, even if it is simply common sense, and as correct everything that comes from 'the poor', even if it is an attitude of scorn and insolence. The artistic daring of the director is underlined by his admirable mixing of documentary and drama, and its political courage in the fact that its director realized the project at the time of 'a revolutionary offensive' launched by the government to 'eliminate the debris of the past'. The *New York Times* included the film in its list of the ten best films shown in the USA in 1973, and in 1985 the International Federation of Film Clubs included it among its 150 most important films of all time.

JOSÉ ANTONIO EVORA

Menchú Tum, Rigoberta

b. 1959, Chimel, El Quiché, Guatemala

Political activist

A K'iche' Maya, she became the first Native American to win the Nobel Peace Prize in 1992 for her work in improving the lives of indigenous peoples of Guatemala and for her struggles for social justice, ethno-cultural respect and mutual reconciliation.

In her first book of memoirs, *Me llamó Rigoberta, y así me nació la conciencia* (I, Rigoberta: An Indian Woman in Guatemala) (1984), edited by Elisabeth Burgos-Dubray, Rigoberta describes her life as the sixth of nine children of Vicente Menchú and Juana Tum. The entire family was profoundly marked by the struggle for social justice; two of her brothers died as children due to living conditions on coffee plantations. Her father participated in the January 1980 occupation of the Spanish embassy in Guatemala City; he and thirty-eight compatriots died in the ensuing retaliation by the army. In April 1980 her mother, a midwife and herbalist, was abducted and held captive for several weeks; she was repeatedly violated and abused and then left exposed on a hillside, where wild animals fed on her corpse.

While working as a wage labourer in coffee fields and as a household servant in the capital, Rigoberta had also served as a catechist and Indian leader with her father and siblings. She fled death threats and found refuge in Mexico with the Guatemalan Church in Exile and Don Samuel **Rúiz**, Bishop of San Cristóbal de las Casas, Chiapas. The second instalment of her autobiography, *Crossing Borders*, was published in 1998.

In 1998 David Stoll's *Rigoberta Menchu and the Story of All Poor Guatemalans* produced a major controversy over the veracity of some of the events recounted in her memoirs, Stoll claiming that she had 'folded' the stories of others into her own life narrative.

Using the $1.2 million Nobel Prize, Menchú established the Fundación Rigoberta Menchú Tum to promote the cause of indigenous peoples around the world. In 1993, she organized the First International Indian Summit Meeting in Chinaltenango, Guatemala, which took place despite the suspension of civil liberties and dissolution of Congress by President Jorge Serrano. Also in 1993, Menchú became the United Nations' Goodwill Ambassador for the International Year of the Indigenous Peoples. She is the adviser to the Director General of UNESCO, a UN General Assembly-designated organizer of the International Decade of Indigenous Peoples and presides over the Indigenous Peace Initiative.

Since 1994 Menchú, her husband and her son, have lived in Guatemala City.

Further reading

Nelson, D.M. (1998) *A Finger in the Wound: Body Politics in Quincentennial Guatemala*, Berkeley: University of California Press.

Rus, J. (ed.) (1999) 'If truth be told: A forum on David Stoll's *Rigoberta Menchú and the Story of All Poor Guatemalans*', *Latin American Perspectives* 26(6), November: 5–88.

Stoll, D. (1999) *Rigoberta Menchú and the Story of All Poor Guatemalans*, Boulder, CO: Westview Press.

Warren, K.B. (1998) *Indigenous Movements and Their Critics: Maya Activism in Guatemala*, Princeton: University of Princeton Press.

JUDITH MAXWELL

Mendes, Chico

b. 1944, Xapuri, Acre, Brazil; d. 1988, Xapuri, Acre

Rubber tapper, environmental activist and union leader

A rubber tapper since the age of nine, Mendes (born Francisco Alves Mendes Filho) became internationally known as an environmental activist and union leader, dedicated to the preservation of the Amazonian rainforests (see **rainforest**) in the mid-1980s. When land speculators and cattle ranchers, aided by the Brazilian government's land redistribution programme, began to encroach on traditional rubber-tapping grounds, Mendes organized the Conselho Nacional dos Seringueiros (National Council of Rubber Tappers) and led the group's passive resistance demonstrations. Mendes promoted the idea of sustainable harvests and proposed the creation of extractive reserves, areas which local communities could continue to inhabit and harvest without destroying the environment or the ecosystem.

In 1987, Mendes was invited to Washington, DC and Miami by the Environmental Defense Fund and the National Wildlife Federation to discuss the Inter-American Development Bank's road-paving project with US policy makers and bank officials. Mendes cited the environmental consequences of development and the bank suspended project funding. Later, Mendes was awarded the United Nations' Global 500 Environmental Prize and Ted Turner's Better World Society Prize in recognition of his environmental efforts.

In 1988, after years of struggle, the Brazilian government established the first extractive reserve. Currently, a total of twenty-one extractive reserves and settlements have been established in seven states in Brazil, covering approximately 8.2 million acres.

In December 1988, Mendes was assassinated by neighbouring cattle ranchers. In 1990, land-owners Darly and Darcy Alves da Silva were found guilty of Mendes's murder and sentenced to nineteen years in prison. In 1993, they escaped only to be recaptured again three years later.

Mendes's story has been the subject of several books and films, notably the made-for-cable movie, *The Burning Season* (1994), directed by John Frankenheimer and starring Raúl **Juliá**, Sonia **Braga** and Edward James Olmos. Mendes has become a symbol of social justice and environmental protection for many environmental organizations. The Comité Chico Mendes markets a CD whose profits fund efforts to preserve the rainforest and aid the rubber tappers in their land struggle, and the Sierra Club annually confers the 'Chico Mendes' award to individuals or grassroots organizations who strive to protect the environment.

Further reading

Mendes, C. (1989) *Fight for the Forest: Chico Mendes in His Own Words*, London: Latin American Bureau.

Revkin, A. (1990) *The Burning Season: The Murder of Chico Mendes and the Fight for the Amazon Rain Forest*, Boston: Houghton Mifflin.

Rone, J. (1992) *The Struggle for Land in Brazil: Rural Violence Continues*, New York: Human Rights Watch.

MARCIE D. RINKA

Mendes, Gilberto (Ambrósio Garcia)

b. 1922, Santos, Brazil

Composer

A pioneer in electronic, aleatory, and concrete music in Brazil, Gilberto Mendes is the most prolific member of the **Música Nova** group of São Paulo. Throughout the 1960s, he attended summer workshops in Darmstadt, Germany where he studied composition with vanguard composers Henri Posseur, Pierre Boulez, and Karlheinz Stockhausen. His music shares deep affinities with **concrete poetry**. In 1966 he composed music for Décio **Pignatari**'s poem 'Beba Coca-Cola', a frenetic choral piece which humorously critiques mass advertising and unbridled consumption. A leader in the experimental music community, Mendes has taught music at the Musical Conservatory of Santos and served on the São Paulo State Commission of Music.

CHRISTOPHER DUNN

Mendes da Rocha, Paulo (Archias)

b. 1928, Vitória, Espírito Santo, Brazil

Architect

An ingenious mind combined with a poetic sensibility in the use of reinforced and exposed concrete made Mendes da Rocha a master of Brutalism of the São Paulo School. His views of architecture as infrastructure and denial of construction as 'object' were strongly influenced by his readings of Barthes and anthropology, balanced with the irreverence of Bakhtin's *Rabelais* and Hannah Arendt's *The Human Condition*. Particularly after designing the Sculpture Museum (São Paulo, 1988–91), his work has been labelled 'minimalist'. He is one of the few Brazilian modern architects to become an undeniable reference for current design.

SOPHIA DA SILVA TELLES

Mendes, Alfred Hubert

b. 1897, Port of Spain, Trinidad; d. 1981, Bridgetown, Barbados

Writer

Born of middle-class Portuguese parents and educated in England, Mendes fought in Flanders during the First World War and returned to Trinidad in 1920, inspired with socialist ideals by the Russian Revolution. In the 1930s he became a prominent member of the group associated with *The Beacon* (1931–5), a radical journal advocating Trinidad's cultural independence. He wrote some fifty short stories as well as two novels, *Pitch Lake* (1934), concerning the rise and fall of an ambitious young Portuguese man in Trinidad society, and *Black Fauns* (1935), an account of life among the island's yard folk.

LOUIS JAMES

Méndez, José Antonio

b. 1927, Havana, Cuba; d. 1989, Havana

Singer and composer

A towering figure of the Cuban musical genre known as **feeling** – essentially the Cuban version of **bolero** – Méndez was already an accomplished guitarist by age of thirteen and often played in his Havana high school. His first hit was 'Novia mía' (My girl) which he composed and performed for the first time in 1946. A year later he recorded 'La gloria eres tú' (You're the Glory) followed by 'Si me comprendieras' (If You Understood Me), 'Quiéreme y verás' (Love Me and You'll See) and 'Decídete' (Make Up Your Mind). From 1949 to 1959 he worked in Mexico, where he recorded five albums. Back in Havana, he appeared regularly at the 'Rincón del feeling' in the St. John's Hotel. Returning home around dawn on 10 June 1989 he was knocked down by a bus; he died some hours later, ten days before his sixty-second birthday.

JOSÉ ANTONIO EVORA

Méndez, Leopoldo

b. 1902, Mexico City; d. 1969, Mexico City

Printmaker

Mexico's leading printmaker of the mid-twentieth century, Méndez was initially affiliated with the ***estridentismo*** movement. Méndez strove to combine political militancy with art making: he joined the Mexican Communist Party (1929) and was a founding member of Lucha Intelectual Proletaria (1931) and other radical groups. His best prints (woodcuts, linocuts, lithographs) are highly didactic yet compelling attacks on contemporary injustice. Major projects include *En nombre de Cristo* (In the Name of Christ) (1939, a portfolio of lithographs); illustrations to Juan de la Cabada's *Incidentes melódicos del mundo irracional* (Melodic Incidents in an Irrational World) (1944); and linocuts for the title sequence of Emilio **Fernández**'s film *Río Escondido* (1947).

JAMES OLES

Méndez, Lucía

b. 1955, Guanajuato, Mexico

Actress and singer

Lucía Méndez launched her acting career in the 1970s, after the Mexican newspaper *El Heraldo* chose her as the most beautiful face in Mexico. She has performed in the theatre and had several significant film roles, but it has been through her parts in ***telenovelas***, television soap operas, that she has made her name. Starring roles in such popular soaps as *Viviana* (1976), *Vanessa* (1982) and *Tú o nadie* (You or Nobody) (1985) have made her well known in many Latin American countries as well as the USA. She has also enjoyed a successful singing career, with a string of high selling recordings of rancheras (see **canción ranchera**) and ballads.

MARK DINNEEN

Méndez Arceo, Sergio

b. 1907; d. Cuernavaca, Morelos, Mexico

Liberation theologian

Until he was forced to step down in 1983, Méndez Arceo, bishop of Cuernavaca, Mexico, was an outspoken proponent of **liberation theology**. He was among the Latin American bishops most profoundly influenced by Vatican II and the **CELAM** (Conference of the Latin American Bishops in Medellín) in 1968. From his pulpit he called for the Mexican government to release the political prisoners of the 1968 student movement. He championed the cause of post-revolutionary Cuba and Nicaragua and the popular struggles in El Salvador and Guatemala, shocking many conservative Catholics by his adherence to a democratic socialist theology, non-violent activism and Ivan Illich's controversial religious pedagogy based on principles of psychoanalysis.

CYNTHIA STEELE

Méndez Ballester, Manuel

b. 1909, Aguadilla, Puerto Rico

Writer

Méndez's first published work was the historical novel *Isla cerrera* (1937), but he is best known as a playwright who has played a major role in shaping twentieth-century Puerto Rican drama. His initial plays, *El clamor de los surcos* (The Noise from the Ditches) (1940) and *Tiempo muerto* (Dead Time) (1940) exemplify the social realism of the 1930s. After experimenting formally and thematically in subsequent plays, he returned to Puerto Rican themes with *Encrucijada* (Crossroads) (1958). In later plays – *Bienvenido, Don Goyito* (Welcome, Don Goyito) (1966), *Los cocorocos* (1977) – and in his regular columns in the island's press, he satirizes contemporary Puerto Rican society.

ViCTOR F. TORRES

Méndez Fleitas, Epifanio

b. 1917, San Pedro del Paraná, Paraguay; d. 1985, Buenos Aires, Argentina

Politician, writer and composer

Director of the newspaper *Patria* for several years, popular leader of the democratic wing of the Colorado Party and ardent fighter in the opposition to the dictatorship of General Alfredo **Stroessner**, Méndez Fleitas was forced to live the last half of his life in exile. Two of his works in particular are fundamental to the interpretation of modern day Paraguay: *Diagnosis paraguaya* (Paraguayan Diagnosis) (1965) and *Lo histórico y lo antihistórico en el Paraguay* (The Historical and the Anti-Historical in Paraguay) (1976). He wrote two early books of poetry and set to music various poems by Paraguayan writers.

TERESA MÉNDEZ-FAITH

Mendieta, Ana

b. 1948, Havana, Cuba; d. 1985, New York City, USA

Artist

A complex Cuban-American artist, whose life often eclipsed her art. In the downtown New York art world of the 1970s and 1980s, she was one of the first Latin American woman artists and the only Cuban to achieve prominence. Within Cuba, she was one of the first exiles to renew her ties to the island, expressing in her work the pain of exilic rupture. For many others, Mendieta was the victim in an infamous and unsolved death that resulted from a fall from a thirty-fourth floor window in the home of her husband, the minimalist sculptor Carl Andre.

Born into a wealthy, well-connected family, Mendieta lived a comfortable early childhood unsettled by the Cuban Revolution (see **revolutions**); afraid of communism, her family sent her and her sister to the USA in 1961 through Operation Peter Pan. The girls were resettled in an orphanage in Iowa and not reunited with their family until 1967; the experience of dislocation, separation and resettlement would permanently mark her life and art.

Mendieta studied art and multimedia and video art at the University of Iowa, then very anti-gallery, anti-art-as-commodity in spirit. She explored performance, body art, and site-specific sculpture through her feminist concerns and her own search for roots in Afro-Cuban ritual and music. Also appropriating from **Santería**, Mendieta formed her own figure into various landscapes in Iowa and Mexico, expressing her desire to establish her place in the world by retracing an elemental connection with nature.

After she moved to New York in the late 1970s, Mendieta moved among feminist and other exile cultures; she also joined Cuban Americans involved in talks to promote a *rapprochement* with Cuba. Finally, after nineteen years, she returned to Cuba, proposed some artwork and returned in 1981 to carve her figures into caves on the outskirts of Havana. The return to Cuba profoundly marked her and Cuban artists: her works, titled in Taino, self-consciously blurred the lines between art and archaeological artefacts, between cave painting, iconic glyph and sculpture. To this day she is the only Cuban-American artist to have been allowed to create and/or 'show' on the island. Her haunting poetics speak to many with histories shaped by forced migration, expropriation and loss.

Her husband's trial and murder acquittal divided the New York art world; now she is often invoked as a symbol of female victimization in the arts, according to one critic as 'a contemporary New York version of Frida **Kahlo**'.

Further reading

Blocker, J. (1999) *Where is Ana Mendieta?: Identity, Performativity, and Exile*, Durham: Duke University Press.

Clearwater, B. (ed.) (1993) *Ana Mendieta: A Book of Works*, Miami Beach: Grassfield Press.

ANA M. LÓPEZ

Mendive, Manuel

b. 1944, Havana, Cuba

Artist

From the outset, Mendive developed his own style of working, carving and painting wood based upon the tradition of decorated roof beams. The idea was that the home would be blessed by a pantheon of Roman Catholic (see **Catholicism**) and **Santería** saints looking down from on high. These *loas* (spirits) also appear in his masks and costumes for theatre and dance productions, and in body decorations and face paintings. Among his many awards, he won the Adam Montparnasse prize in the Salon de Mai (Paris, 1968) and represented Cuba at the 1988 Venice Biennale.

AMANDA HOPKINSON

Mendoza, Alberto de

b. 1921, Buenos Aires, Argentina

Actor

A prolific actor, Mendoza began in theatre but became famous with a supporting role in *Filomena Marturano* (1949) with Tita **Merello**. He has made more than 150 films since then, including *El infierno tan temido* (Hell Most Feared) (Raúl de la **Torre**, 1981), which cast him against the Buenos Aires macho role that made him famous in *El jefe* (The Boss) (Fernando **Ayala**, 1951) and *Barrio Gris* (Grey District) (Mario **Soffici**, 1954). Since 1961 he has lived in Spain, and he returns only sporadically to Argentina to work in film, theatre or television.

PAULA RODRÍGUEZ MARINO

Mendoza, Amalia ('La Tariácuri')

b. 1923, San Juan Huetamo, Michoacán, Mexico

Singer

Mendoza's solo career began in 1954 on Radio XEW and in the variety theatre, specializing in the songs of José Alfredo **Jiménez** (like Amarga

Navidad (Bitter Christmas)), Tomás Méndez and José Angel Espinoza Ferrusquilla. At first Amalia Mendoza fitted the mould of the run-of-the-mill ranchera singer who rounds off the Fiesta (the celebration of the family, or a local saint or a party for someone) with a song. Later her temperament led her to outbursts of emotion and she became the first performer to unearth the despair that sometimes lies behind a genre that is characteristically cheerful in the best and the worst of times. When Mendoza sings, it is suffering and the desire for expiation that you hear – exposing as never before the melodramatic quality of ranchera music – Qué sea tu cruel adiós mi Navidad (My Christmas Gift is Your Cruel Farewell). Ranchera is now no longer about an isolated rural world, nor yet a music of celebration, but the place where ill fortune is transformed into a 'philosophy of life' – 'since bad luck follows me everywhere, then I will speak of suffering'.

CARLOS MONSIVÁIS

Mendoza, Celeste

b. 1930, Santiago de Cuba; d. 1998, Havana, Cuba

Singer

A virtuoso singer and dancer, Mendoza was given the title 'Queen of **guaguancó**'. She began her career as a chorus girl at the Tropicana cabaret in Havana in the early 1950s; her singing debut came soon after on a programme on **CMQ-TV**; she distinguished herself then and later with the passion of her singing and the exuberance of her costumes and hairstyles. Her best known recordings include 'Soy tan feliz' (I'm so happy), 'Que me castigue Dios' (May God punish me) and 'Juan Pampiro'.

JOSÉ ANTONIO EVORA

Mendoza, Héctor

b. 1932, Apaseo, Guanajuato, Mexico

Theatre director and playwright

Called 'the first modern Mexican director' by his peer Luis de **Tavira**, Mendoza is certainly one of the most respected. He began as an actor, later becoming a playwright with his successful 1953 comedy *Las cosas simples* (Simple Things). Between 1956 and 1957 he directed *Poesía en Voz Alta* (Poetry Aloud), which initiated experimental theatre in Mexico under the direction of Octavio **Paz** and Juan José **Arreola**. He wrote and directed **Televisa**'s acclaimed TV-series *Toda una vida* (A Whole Life) (1981–2). In 1986 he co-founded the Núcleo de Estudios Teatrales, a drama school.

ANTONIO PRIETO-STAMBAUGH

Mendoza Leiton, Gunnar

b. Potosi, Bolivia; d. 1994, Sucre, Bolivia

Historian

Director of the Bolivian National Archive from 1944 until his death, Mendoza Leitón's professional career is an example of the importance of sources for historical research. Numerous researchers have acknowledged their debt to him. Apart from important prologues to works like *Diario de un comandante de la independencia americana 1814–1825* (Diary of a Commander in the Independence Wars) (1982), the bulk of his publications are guides to archival sources in the Bolivian National Archive and writings on the problems of documentation and cataloguing. He was given honorary doctorates by two of Bolivia's universities.

XIMENA MEDINACELI

Menem, Carlos Saúl

b. 1930, Anillaco, Argentina

Politician

Menem became the Peronist provincial governor of La Rioja in 1973, the year of **Perón**'s triumphant return after eighteen years of exile. Ousted by the military *coup* of March 1976, he was imprisoned for several years. In 1983, with the restoration of democracy, Menem was again elected to his previous post, and reelected in 1987. In 1989 he was elected President of the Republic, and immediately moved away from the traditional populist policies of his party and towards an alliance with the liberal right. By reforming the Constitution, he was able to stand successfully for reelection in 1995, although his Presidency had become notorious by then for its corruption and nepotism.

PABLO KREIMER

Meneses, Guillermo

b. 1911, Caracas, Venezuela; d. 1978, Margarita, Venezuela

Writer

Chronicler of the city of Caracas, Meneses was a contributor to the journal *Elite*, the *Papel Literario* (Literary Supplement) of *El **Nacional*** and the ***Revista nacional de cultura***, and in the 1960s he was a founder of the journal *CAL*. His work is marked by existentialist (see **existentialism**) introspection and the exploration of memory. Several of his works have been adapted for cinema, including *La balandra Isabel*, *La mano junto al muro* (The Hand by the Wall) and *El mestizo José Vargas*. He also occupied a number of important civic and diplomatic posts.

JORGE ROMERO LEÓN

Meneses, Vidaluz

b. 1944, Matagalpa, Nicaragua

Writer

A major poet whose work often deals with the simple realities of everyday living, Meneses maintained her revolutionary commitment to the **FSLN** without losing her Christian faith. Before the **Sandinista Revolution** of 1979, she was secretly involved with the Sandinistas when her father, a general in Somoza's (see **Somoza dynasty**) National Guard and Nicaraguan ambassador to Guatemala, was executed by the Sandinistas. She responded by reaffirming her staunch solidarity with the poor while refusing to renounce her father. After 1979, she became National Librarian and Vice Minister of Culture, working closely with Ernesto **Cardenal**. She is currently Dean of Humanities at the Central American University (**UCA**).

SILVIA CHAVES AND ILEANA RODRIGUEZ

Menudo

The Puerto Rican teen pop group Menudo is one of the greatest popular phenomena of Latin America. Created in 1977 by Edgardo Díaz, the group's original concept consisted of replacing its members after they reached a certain age to retain a juvenile and cleancut sound and image. In the late 1970s and early 1980s Menudo was extraordinarily successful in Latin America and the USA, breaking world records for concert audiences. By the late 1980s the group's popularity diminished and Díaz was later accused of child molestation. During the 1990s Menudo reorganized with English-speaking teenagers and moved its artistic base to Florida. One of its members, Ricky **Martin**, later pursued a highly successful solo career.

ROBERTO CARLOS ORTIZ

Mercado, Walter

b. 1931, San Juan, Puerto Rico

Astrologer

A pharmacist by training and an actor by choice, Mercado is a popular astrologer in Latin America and among Latinos in the United States. After a not very successful career as a dancer and actor, he created a new persona as a television psychic. With extravagant capes and flamboyant gestures, he combines Catholic beliefs with vague principles and images taken from **Santería**, Buddhism, Hinduism and **New Age** philosophy. In countries where *machismo* is dominant, it is amazing to see the popularity of Mercado, who challenges the dominant ideology through astrology and camp.

EFRAÍN BARRADAS

Mercosur (Mercado Común del Sur)

Mercosur (Mercado Común del Sur) is a project for the economic, industrial, financial and commercial integration of Argentina, Brazil, Paraguay and Uruguay, as well as their Pacific neighbour Chile, a region with a combined population of over 200 million people and an area of 13 million square kilometres. It has considerable economic weight and major development potential, and includes one of the world's largest industrial regions as well as rich agricultural areas whose gross product and levels of consumption are (with the exception of Paraguay) comparable with Europe. The great challenge is to develop initiatives which can bring cultural integration closer. In this, the **Memorial de América Latina** has a key role to play. Mercosur's headquarters are in Montevideo.

CELINA MANZONI

mercurio, El

The Chilean newspaper, *El mercurio*, is one of Latin America's most prestigious journals; it was founded in 1900 by the Edwards family, who have remained its proprietors throughout the century. Originally four pages, the newspaper now has between 70 and 200 pages daily. By 1902 it already had three editions: *El mercurio* (in the morning), *Las últimas noticias* (at midday) and *La segunda* (in the evening); the last two are still published in Santiago, but under independent ownership.

El mercurio has retained a traditional, conservative format. During the government of Salvador **Allende** (1970–3) *El mercurio*'s position was one of veiled hostility; its relationship with the **Pinochet** dictatorship established after the overthrow of Allende by a military *coup*, however, was friendly. Since the return to democracy in 1989, *El mercurio* distanced itself from the subsequent Christian democratic governments (see **Christian Democracy**), but generally supports the transition to democracy and the free-market policies of each of these governments.

Between 1982 and 1992, the newspaper was modernized, introducing new management systems and revitalizing its publicity department, with the object of making the paper one of the most profitable in the region.

A typical edition of *El mercurio* will begin with three pages of news and editorial comment, followed by several pages of social activities and gossip. International news, mainly taken from agency reports, appears only towards the end of the first section. Information is shared with other members of the Grupo de Diarios América whose activities are co-ordinated by *El mercurio*.

The newspaper publishes business, news, arts and literature, property, classified advertisements and sports supplements as well as *El país*, which gathers national news. It also publishes a series of magazines on different days of the week – *Ya*, on fashion and style; *Revista del domingo*, on travel and tourism; *Revista del campo*, on agriculture; *Zona de contacto*, for young people; and *Timón*, for children; *Siglo XXI*, on new technology; *Wiken*, on entertainment; *Casa y barrios*, on homes; *Vivienda y decoración*, on home decorating; and *Revista de libros*, with book reviews.

El mercurio is Chile's most important news medium; it also owns sixteen regional newspapers and its international edition has subscribers from seventy countries. Since 1996 it has had its own Internet website – www.elmercurio.cl.

WILFREDO CANCIO ISLA

Merello, Tita

b. 1904, Buenos Aires, Argentina

Actress and singer

Tita Merello (born Ana Laura Merello) was known as 'the vedette of **tango**'. Her first recordings in 1929 presented a gritty urban repertoire characteristic of her persona. After several earlier screen performances, she triumphed in the 1950s playing devoted powerful women willing to fight men to protect their children. Among her many stellar roles were the single mother of *Arrabalera* (Girl from the Slums) (1950) and the tricky mother-in-law of *Los isleros* (The Islanders) (1950). One of Argentina's most popular entertainers, she also worked in **television** and **radio**, wrote tango lyrics and published her memoirs, *La calle y yo* (The Street and I) (1972).

DIANA PALADINO

merengue

Merengue is the national music of the Dominican Republic. It originated during the nineteenth century from the Spanish *contradanza*, influenced by African rhythms. The merengue from the countryside, called *perico ripiao* (literally 'torn sparrow'), is played with güira scraper, tambora drum, **marimba** (a wooden box with plucked metal keys) and button accordion (see **accordion and bandoneón**). During the nineteenth century the merengue was considered vulgar and low class, but the dictator Rafael Leónidas **Trujillo** introduced it into the dance halls and used it for political propaganda. Played with electronic musical instruments, the modern merengue became international in the 1970s. Among its best-known interpreters are Johnny **Ventura**, Wilfrido **Vargas** and Juan Luis **Guerra**.

FERNANDO VALERIO-HOLGUÍN

Mérida, Carlos

b. 1891, Guatemala City; d. 1984, Mexico City

Painter

Mérida is considered Guatemala's greatest twentieth-century painter, and one of Latin America's major exponents of modernism. Closely associated with both Picasso and Modigliani in Paris, he held his first exhibition in Guatemala in 1915. He exhibited in Mexico in 1920, earning the admiration of the emerging Mexican muralists (see **muralism**), **Rivera**, **Siqueiros** and **Orozco**. He was commissioned to paint two murals at the Ministry of Education in Mexico City in 1921. In the 1930s he began to develop his characteristic abstract, plastic surrealist style (see **surrealism in Latin American art**). His best known work includes murals at the Benito Juárez housing complex in Mexico City and the City Hall in Guatemala City.

ARTURO ARIAS

méringue

Dance music of Haiti, related to Dominican **merengue** (though the French name of the latter probably implies that the Haitian version came first). Sung in **Haitian creole** in a call and response pattern, the music has a lyrical, lilting quality much closer to the Dominican rural merengue style called *perico ripiado* (stripped parrot) than to the commercial version. One or several voices are backed by a small orchestra of four to six musicians (petits ensembles or ti bands) that include a banjo or six string guitar, a manouva (something like a **marimba**), several drums, maracas and an empty rum bottle that is tapped with a coin or stone. The form was adapted by Nemours Jean Baptiste in the 1960s from earlier styles, probably derived ultimately from French *contredanse*. Contemporary bands include Tabou Combo, Missile 727 and Ti band L'Avenir. A famous méringue is Haïti chérie (Beautiful Haiti) composed by Othello Bayard, an unofficial second national anthem of the country.

DANIEL BALDERSTON

Merquior, José Guilherme

b. 1941, Rio de Janeiro, Brazil; d. 1991, Boston, USA

Literary critic

A prolific critic, Merquior spent much of his career as a diplomat, in Europe and Spanish America. As well as producing a useful short history of Brazilian literature to the end of the nineteenth century, and a book on **Drummond de Andrade**, he published numerous collections of essays. His position (set out most completely in a book on Rousseau and Weber) was determinedly liberal, and he often became involved in polemics with those to the left of him. He was a determined opponent of many modern theorists, including the Western Marxists, Foucault and Lacan.

JOHN GLEDSON

mescal   *see*   tequila and mezcal

Mesquita family

An old São Paulo family, proprietors of the newspaper ***O estado de São Paulo***, their long involvement with the newspaper began in 1888, when Julio Mesquita began to write for *A Província de São Paulo*, emerging as one of the most important political commentators of the time. Its name changed with the proclamation of the republic in 1889, and two years later Julio became its editor. In the wake of the 1924 revolution the paper was closed and its editor imprisoned. After his death in 1927, the editorship of the newspaper passed to successive generations of the family.

ANTONIO CARLOS VAZ

mestizo

While anthropology has rejected **race** as a valid classificatory system, notions of common ancestry, blood and genetic heritage have long been prevalent. In the sixteenth through eighteenth centuries, Spain and its colonies ranked subject peoples by 'biological' criteria along a scale from darker to lighter, from black or Indian to white or Spanish. Details of the scale varied from country to country. One such classification included mestizo, 'offspring of a Spaniard and an Indian woman'; *castizo*, offspring of an Indian man and a Spanish woman; *torna atrás*, 'offspring of a Spaniard and a light-skinned black woman'; and *lobo* 'offspring of an Indian man and a torna atrás'. However, the term mestizo has been generalized to mean anyone of 'mixed' racial, ethnic or cultural descent. Mexico promotes the idea of universal *mestizaje*, claiming the benefits of biological and social hybridization as one of the strengths of the nation. The term mestizo, while recognized in all of Latin America, is locally replaced with other terms, which vary slightly connotatively and denotatively. These terms include ***ladino***, *cholo*, *pardo*, *chino* and *mameluco*.

JUDITH MAXWELL

Mestre, Goar

b. 1912, Santiago de Cuba, Cuba; d. 1994, Buenos Aires, Argentina

Media entrepreneur

Mestre went to Argentina in 1937 representing Union Carbide. The following year, in Cuba, he founded a media empire embracing seven radio stations and seven television channels. After the Cuban Revolution of 1959 (see **revolutions**), which he supported financially, his relations with the communist government rapidly deteriorated and in 1960 he moved to Buenos Aires. There he set up Channel 13, whose programmes led the field. When the station was nationalized, Mestre moved into real estate. In 1981, he created the Teleinde film and television studios. His biographer, Pablo Sirvén, described him as the 'King of TV'.

CLAUDIA TORRE

Mestre Vitalino   *see*   Vitalino, Mestre

Mexican and Central American indigenous languages

There are approximately 350 indigenous languages still spoken in Mexico and Central America. These languages range from moribund tongues spoken by ageing enclaves of speakers whose children are speaking the hegemonic language, be it Spanish or English, to robust communities with hundreds of thousands of speakers, indigenous education systems, creative writers, and both traditional and technological media of language dissemination and reinforcement. These languages belong to twenty-one major families from fifteen independent stocks: Uto-Aztecan, Otomanguean, Hokan, Huave, Totonacan, Mixe-Zoquean, Mayan, Tarascan, Cuitlatec, Xincan, Lencan, Paya, Misumalpan, Naolan, and Arahuacan, with a scattering of unclassified remnants and extinct languages. Glottochronological estimates of the time depths of these groupings range between twenty and fifty-one minimum centuries of divergence.

The Uto-Aztecan family is the northernmost, ranging into the Western United States. While Náhuat(l) outposts may once have reached as far as south as the Incan empire, the southernmost modern populations now live in El Salvador. There is a robust literature in Náhuatl (see **Náhuatl and Aztecan languages**), the most widely spoken of the Uto-Aztecan languages. This language was used as a lingua franca during the early Spanish contact period and in the subsequent colonial goverments of New Spain and Guatemala. It was an 'official' language for court petitions and records. In the early independent periods of Mexico, Guatemala and El Salvador, Náhuatl was dropped from use as an official language. In Mexico, it has experienced an intellectual renaissance, literature, both prose and poetry, is again created and published in Náhuatl; nonetheless, its use in rural indigenous communities retreats in the face of Spanish as the language of the economic and political spheres.

Otomanguean is spoken from Central Mexico through the Isthmus of Tehuantepec. It is made up of twenty-three languages, three of which are moribund or extinct. This family includes Mixtec, a language which boasts fine painted codices from the early contact period. Several languages in this family are tonal. Two, Usila Chinantec and Chicahuaxtla Trique, have five tones, the record for languages of this area. Others in the Popolocan and Mixtecan groups have four tones; while some in these same groups have simplified the systems to three tones. Hokan also includes languages of California and the Great Basin in the USA. In some classifications these languages in Middle America are referred to as Tequistlatecan or Jicaquean. A set of the Tequistlatecan languages are called 'Chontal'; a term for 'enemy speakers', this group of Chontals is completely unrelated by the more famous and numerous Chontal of the Mayan family. One Jicaquean language is already extinct; the other is reduced to remnant communties in Honduras.

Huave, spoken in Oaxaca, Mexico, is a linguistic isolate; no languages can be shown to be related. There are four distinctive variants still spoken, but these are similar enough to be classified as dialects of a single language. Totonacan is split into two sets of languages Totonacan Proper and Tepehuan, separated by about twenty-six minimum centuries. Some archaeological data suggest that Totonacan peoples could have been the prime movers in the construction of Teotihuacan, an early Pre-Columbian urban centre from which innovations in political and economic organization spread through Mesoamerica. Mixe-Zoquean also splits into two main language groups: Mixe and Zoque, the latter being the prime candidate for the language of the Olmec civilization. Loanwords. from Zoquean name culturally central elements of horticulture and calendrics throughout Mesoamerica.

The Mayan family contains twenty-nine currently spoken languages. Pre-contact, a logo-syllabic writing system was in use. Writings have been discovered on stone monuments, in architectural elements (risers in staircases, lintels, built-in benches, door panels), on pottery, and on bark-paper codices. The earliest dated monument known (292 AD) is Stela 29 of Tikal. Tarascan, Cuitlatec, and Paya are language isolates. Xincan and Lencan are practically extinct languages, though descendants of Xinca-Lenca speakers maintain cultural identity as indigenes. Misumalpan contains two still viable languages: Miskito and Sumu spoken in Honduras and Nicaragua. In recent years the Miskito (see **Miskitus**) have become politically active, defining themselves, their language and their territory more distinctly. Arahuacan, also spelled Arawakan, is a language family chiefly spoken in South America.

The **Garifuna** (see **Garinagu**) of Guatemala and Belize represent a northern outlier. Deported from St Vincent in the British West Indies in 1797, they were invited into their current locations to help stabilize the area. A mix of Carib language forms in the speech of invading island men with the Arawakan speech of women led to the labelling of Garifuna as Black Carib; however, most of the Carib forms have been levelled out.

Despite the number of different languages and language families, Mexico and Central America form a *Sprachbund* with areal features of similarity, including (a) inalienable possession of some body parts and relatives; (b) base twenty; (c) absolutive noun suffixes; (d) aspect (rather than tense) as the dominant feature of verbs; (e) directional complements for verbs; (f) restricted use of copula; (g) restricted use of plural inflection of nouns; (h) three verb classes: intransitive, transitive, and stative. Couplets are a feature of semantic compounding and of rhetoric.

Further reading

Campbell, L. and Kaufman, T. (1976) 'A Linguistic Look at the Olmecs' in *American Antiquity* 4: 80–9.

Campbell, L. and Mithun, M. (eds) (1979) *The Languages of Native America: Historical and Comparative Assessment*, Austin: University of Texas Press.

Suárez, J.A. (1983) *The Mesoamerican Indian Languages*, Cambridge: Cambridge University Press.

JUDITH M. MAXWELL

Mexican cookery

Mexican cuisine is based on ingredients whose origins lie in pre-Columbian America – corn (maize) (see **corn and corncakes**), chile peppers, **beans**, tomatoes, courgettes – and to which other elements, like **cacao** or vanilla, also native to the region, are added. The diversity of the cuisine reflects the diversity of climate and of flora and fauna within the territory of Mexico. In the dry regions, for example, it is squirrels, rabbits, *yucca* flowers, prickly pears and *agave* leaves that provide the basis of local foods; on the coasts it is seafood – *huachinango* (red snapper), crabs, lobster, clams, etc. – that is the main source of nourishment.

Temperate zones produce the avocado (*aguacate*) and other native fruits and plants; the rivers yield a variety of fish. For hundreds of years crickets, ant eggs, maguey worms and so on have also been eaten. There is also an abundance of mushrooms across the country.

Cooking techniques vary widely: food may be boiled, steamed (like *tamales*), cooked *al pibil* (smoked underground wrapped in banana leaves), barbecued or cooked *en mixiotes* (meat wrapped in cactus leaves and placed in a hole in the ground previously heated with red-hot stones). Corncakes (*tortillas*) (see **corn and corncakes**) and chiles are usually toasted on a griddle (*comal*). On the Pacific coast the *tapesco* is a typical way of cooking fish over a mesh of sticks. **Ceviche**, raw fish marinated over a period in lemon and chile, is as common in Mexico as elsewhere in the region. And while it was the Spaniards who brought the method of frying, the Aztecs already fried their seeds in hot oil or fat.

Food preservation was traditionally done by salting, drying, preserving in chiles or smoking; Spain added pickling in vinegar and spices to the repertoire. Fruit may be crystallized or boiled in spiced syrups. The range of native spices is considerable, but the use of marjoram, thyme, bay, pepper, cloves, sesame and garlic derives from Arab cuisine.

Chile peppers are a key feature of Mexican cookery – there are nearly a hundred varieties used as an accompaniment or in sauces thickened with maize flour, peanuts, sesame seeds or almonds. They may be chopped or crushed with tomatoes or pimentos. The range of sauces includes *mole*, (the Náhuatl word for sauce) as in *guacamole*, sauce with avocado.

Implements characteristic of Mexican kitchens include the *metate*, a flat mortar made from volcanic rock; the mortar and pestle; clay and pottery dishes and pans; the *comal* griddle for making *tortillas* and wooden whisks for whipping chocolate.

Drinks include the various distillations from the maguey cactus – *pulque* (see **pulque and pulquerías**), **tequila and *mezcal***, as well as Mexican **beer**. In the indigenous communities, it is usual to prepare drinks of fermented maize, palms and other plants for ceremonial purposes.

It was the Spaniards who introduced the pig, sheep and cow to Mexico. These are now widely used, as are the cheeses and egg-based desserts to which Mexicans are devoted. The *tortilla* continues to be used in a multiplicity of forms, but traditional baking still prospers and for festivals like All Saints Day bakers traditionally produce sculpted bread masterpieces. However, Mexican cookery is also changing, in response to external adaptations and to the growth of a **fast food** culture. But, in every case, Mexican cooks have made them their own, adding chile to the hot dogs, avocado to the sushi, *mole* to the pizza.

See also: food and drink; eating out

Further reading

Kennedy, D. (1991) *The Tortilla Book*, New York: Harper & Row.
—— (1972) *The Cuisines of Mexico*, New York: Harper & Row.
Quintana, P. (1995) *The Taste of Mexico*, New York: Tabori & Clay.

CRISTINA BARROS AND MARCO BUENROSTRO

Mexicanidad, Movimiento de la *see* concheros

Mexico

Modern Mexico begins with a revolution that officially began on 20 November 1910, when Francisco Madero called for a political movement against the dictatorship of Porfirio Díaz in his Plan de San Luis Potosí; three months later, in February 1911, Emiliano **Zapata**'s manifesto, the Plan de Ayala, gave the revolution its social content. From then until the revolution's official end in 1917, Mexico was caught up in a civil conflict that displaced a million people. Political power passed out of the hands of the old land-owning classes and the new financiers whose interests Don Porfirio had protected. The revolutionary generals came from very different backgrounds – they were peasants, workers, sons of shopkeepers, though Carranza was a wealthy landowner. After 1917 it was they who built a new State, the so-called 'revolutionary family', in the name of a Mexican Revolution that they had first to transform into a symbolic language, an ideology for the new Nation-State.

Don Porfirio had complained that 'poor Mexico was so far from God and so near to the United States'; while the distance to heaven was never calculated, the shared border with the USA – what Carlos **Fuentes** called 'the glass frontier' – was and remains a conditioning element for Mexico's history since independence from Spain in 1810. If the revolution was fundamentally a movement for democracy and political modernization, Madero would be its symbolic figurehead; if it was a peasant insurrection whose central demand '*tierra y libertad*' (land and freedom) was definitive, then Zapata was emblematic; if it was a movement of protest and resistance by land workers in the north then Pancho **Villa** was the true leader. And when Villa and Zapata briefly occupied the capital city in November 1913, it might have seemed that this was a workers' and peasants' revolution. When they withdrew, and ceded effective leadership to Carranza, it became a bourgeois revolution of a kind and its purpose the creation of a strong, independent State.

As the new apparatus was created through the 1920s, first under Obregón and later under Calles, the task of creating a culture of consent was paramount, and José **Vasconcelos**, at the Ministry of Education, key to its achievement. The Mexican muralist movement (see **muralism**) was part of an ideological and educational strategy; new school textbooks (for a now compulsory educational system) retold Mexican history from the perspective of a nation constructed out of a Spanish *and* Aztec/Maya past, an example of the *mestizaje* (see **mestizo**), which Vasconcelos had defined (in his *La raza cósmica* (The Cosmic Race) (1928)) as the foundation of a new universal culture. That recuperation and reconstruction was exemplified by a new public space framed and defined by the symbolic language of nationhood – the indigenous figures painted by Diego **Rivera** in the Court of Miracles in the Ministry of Education, for example. Carlos **Chávez** and Silvestre **Revueltas**, among others, worked on a new musical idiom whose sources lay in a popular music ignored by the Europeanized cultured elite of the dictatorship. And in literature the '*novela de la Revolución Mexicana*', whose precursor was Mariano **Azuela**'s *Los de abajo* (The Underdogs) (1916) created an epic of the revolution, a new literature of foundation, characterized by an intense narrative pace, an episodic structure and a sense of a world of order forming out of violent and barbaric matter.

All this cemented a new identity – radical and national, and suspicious of the colonial past. The Cristero wars (see **Cristero War**), a counter-revolution led by a Roman Catholic Church under siege beginning in 1926, were a reaction of a vigorous rhetorical anti-clericalism, in which the Church was defined above all by its link to foreign powers and the colonial past. Yet even by the late 1920s, Calles was re-establishing economic relationships with the USA through Ambassador Henry Lane Wilson. While the new State was formed and established by the late 1920s, the revolution's promises of reform had yet to be realized: **agrarian reform** was proceeding at a snail's pace, the indigenous peoples remained oppressed (though lionized in theory) and workers' rights to trade union organization were in fact compromised by the entirely State-controlled national union federation under Luis Morones (whose deputy Fidel Velázquez would later break every known record for longevity by holding the same post for close to sixty years). Gregorio López y Fuentes's novels of the time, like *Tierra* (1930) recalled those early hopes. Outside the schools of socialist realism, the avant-garde (see **avant-garde in Latin America**) movements of the era found their expression in Mexico, taking a lead from the daring of José Juan Tablada. **Estridentismo** was Mexico's Futurism, with its exaltation of urban noise and modernity. **Contemporáneos** drew together a disparate group of poets including Xavier **Villaurrutia** and José **Gorostiza** among others. A young Octavio **Paz** was exploring the dilemmas of the poet's role early in the 1930s; his presence during the Spanish Civil War (see **Spanish Civil War, impact of**) drew him briefly into a world of political writing, but his essential view of culture as an alternative realm of existence to the unreliable and disagreeable world of politics would become the central idea in his critical and poetic writing thereafter. His *El **laberinto de la soledad*** (Labyrinth of Solitude), published in 1950, continued a debate on the nature of Mexican identity, but also found in national history a tragic and cyclical destructive force – as he would note in a *Posdata* (Postscript) (1969) to the book published after the terrible events of **Tlatelolco** in 1968.

The advent of Lázaro **Cárdenas** was a watershed. Not only did Cárdenas embark on a major agrarian reform programme and enshrine trade union rights into a reorganization of the Mexican State, he also revived the original State-building project. The Muralists returned and produced some of their best-known work – including Rivera's murals at the National Palace in Mexico City. Mexican cinema, somewhat arrested since the extraordinary documentary tradition during the revolution, which had culminated in *El automóvil gris* (The Grey Automobile) (1919), was in the midst of a burst of experimentation to adapt to the new technology of sound. And it received an unexpected boost from the State via direct support that enabled, among others, the survival of the floundering **CLASA** studios and the production of Fernando de **Fuentes**'s iconoclastic *El compadre Mendoza* (Godfather Mendoza) (1934). But more importantly than that, the consolidation of the Mexican State again required a symbolic language of shared past and present. That common emblem was supplied by the *comedias rancheras* (see **rancheras, comedias**), set in rural communities where men were men and women wives, mothers or whores – but never confused their roles! It was a curiously conservative vision to accompany such a key turning point in Mexican history; as educators moved into rural areas, the State expropriated foreign oil interests in 1938 and new government institutions drew each sector of the society into a fixed and established relationship with the executive. The new political organization he created – the PRM – was the immediate forerunner of the **PRI**, the system of patronage and control that sustained the Mexican political system for the next five decades.

In music, the era was defined by the whispering voice of Agustín **Lara** and the **bolero**, which he, more than any other single composer, had created with songs like 'Ella' (Her). While the Golden Age of Mexican cinema continued into the 1940s, and produced a generation of superstars like María **Félix**, Jorge **Negrete** and Pedro **Infante**, Mexico itself was moving away from the model of development based on agriculture. New industries began to grow around Monterrey and in the valley of Mexico, drawing growing numbers towards the capital. Juan **Rulfo**'s magnificent short novel, *Pedro Páramo* (1955), was an elegy for a provincial world represented as a kind of limbo; three years later

Carlos Fuentes's first novel, *La región más transparente* (Where the Air is Clear) (1958) provided a vast populous panorama of the city, whose population now exceeded 4 million. From then on the city's population would grow exponentially – by the century's end the Federal District was the largest urban concentration in the world.

The universities expanded as a new provincial lower middle class moved towards the centre of the country. These were the readers of the new youthful writers of **La Onda**, and they were the section of society most moved and excited by the Cuban Revolution of 1959 (see **revolutions**). Indeed Lázaro Cárdenas left retirement to lead a new organization in its support. Carlos **Fuentes**'s *La muerte de Artemio Cruz* (The Death of Artemio Cruz) (1962) was a withering critique of the failure of the revolution – or rather of its corruption. The critical expression began to gather force, while the Mexican ruling elite laid hold of the expanding medium of television to impose its views and values, turned on critical journalism (like the magazine, *Política*) and either incorporated or repressed its putative enemies. Even the national cinema industry, which had been stagnant and closed off to innovation since the mid-1950s, with the same group of old directors repeating the same tired formulas and genres, began to evidence signs of change. On the margins of the industry, a new generation of critics gathered around their publication, *Nuevo Cine*, and their film manifesto, Jomi **García Ascot**'s *En el balcón vacío* (On the Empty Balcony) (1962). Independent producers (see **independent film producers**) like **Barbachano Ponce** tried to direct the ambitions of young filmmakers unable to gain access to the industry. By 1964, the industry and its labour union recognized their own insularity and called for an **experimental film** contest, a first version of which was held in 1965 and a second in 1967. The contests were perhaps of greater symbolic than practical value, although the rhetoric of 'new values' allowed new careers to take off like those of Alejandro **Jodorowsky**, Felipe **Cazals** and Arturo **Ripstein**.

The conflicts could not be buried, and the student movement beginning early in 1968 began to gather momentum and support, just as the Díaz Ordaz government prepared for the 1968 Olympic Games (see **Olympic Games, Mexico 1968**), which had been intended as a showcase for a modern and developing Mexican economy. As the date for the opening ceremony grew near, the government responded with mounting repression, culminating in the massacre of hundreds of people in **Tlatelolco** Square in the city centre. In the event, the Games were most memorable for the Black Power demonstration by three US sprinters on the medal rostrum. Heavy censorship was subsequently imposed – at least until the 1970 **World Cup** competition brought foreign journalists back to Mexico; then the trauma of Tlatelolco could be examined in works like Elena **Poniatowska**'s *La noche de Tlatelolco* (1971), Luis González de Alba's *Los días y los años* (The Days and the Years) (1970) and Carlos **Monsiváis**'s *Días de guardar* (Days to Remember) (1970). Leobardo López Aretche's radical documentary, *El grito* (The Shout) (1969), earned him a jail sentence.

Luis **Echeverría Alvarez**, who had been Interior Minster in 1968, occupied the presidency in 1970, and appeared to take a different, more radical, line, identifying more with the Third World in foreign policy and winning the active support of some important intellectual figures, like Pablo **González Casanova**, who became rector of **UNAM**, and Carlos Fuentes, who became Mexico's ambassador in Paris after Echeverría announced an amnesty for the movement's leaders. However, another mass killing of student demonstrators in June 1971 remained unexplained, and after boasting of his regime's liberalization of Mexican society in 1976 Echeverría Alvarez closed down the newspaper, *Excélsior*, which had become an important (and rare) independent voice. When he left power, the Mexican State had expanded vastly and the foreign debt was rising alarmingly. It fell to his successor, López Portillo, to oversee the economic crisis that followed the oil boom of the mid-1970s and the vast speculative investment that followed it. The result, as his critics like Gabriel Zaid and Heberto Castillo predicted, was a disaster – the catastrophic devaluation of 1982 and bankruptcy by August.

This sequence of events changed the political landscape of Mexico, calling into question for the first time the absolute hegemony of the PRI; the Roman Catholic PAN (National Action Party) began to make serious gains in the north of the country and in Yucatán province in the south. And dissident factions within the PRI were beginning to coalesce with other groups outside the party around Cuauhtémoc **Cárdenas**, son of the previous president, and a small group still within the PRI. The whole process of change found its commentators and shrewd observers in the searing iconoclasm of Carlos Monsiváis, and the *crónicas* (see **crónica**) of ordinary life by Vicente **Leñero**, Cristina **Pacheco** and Poniatowska. The delicate irony of José Emilio **Pacheco** also betrayed a sense of crisis – his 1969 *No me preguntes cómo pasa el tiempo* (Don't Ask Me How the Time Goes By) sets out themes picked up again in his 1984 *Fin de siglo y otros poemas* (Century's End and Other Poems).

On 19 September 1985 Mexico was struck by a devastating earthquake (see **earthquakes**) – the worst in its history. Many died because the pervasive corruption throughout the Mexican political system had permitted the falsification of building permits – and many modern buildings collapsed into heaps of dust. Most revealing for ordinary Mexicans was the incompetence of the authorities and their primary concern to stop looting – the result was the much-publicized and heart-rending death of a group of seamstresses working in a basement sweatshop, who died because the building's owners refused to allow the destruction of machines in the floors above. Meanwhile the rescue was left to a huge, spontaneous movement of solidarity. The memory would remain with ordinary Mexicans long after the moment had passed; in 1986 elections provided an opportunity for them to support non-PRI candidates and break the party's monopoly, and its cynical control of social and political life. This the PRI could not permit; the barefaced fixing of elections put PRI candidates in again – and in the 1988 presidential elections only an unexplained national computer failure prevented the younger Cárdenas from becoming president.

The de la Madrid presidency (1982–8) had accelerated the privatization begun under his predecessor; despite the creation of the Instituto Mexicano de la Cinematografía (IMCINE), in 1983 film-makers had to begin looking for non-State sources of financing and assuming the role of co-producers. The *auteur* cinema of Paul **Leduc**, Jaime Humberto **Hermosillo** and Busi Cortes was one result. In Mexico's capital environmental activism (see **environmental issues**) was now growing apace, as the city seemed to come ever closer to ecological collapse. Along the border with the USA some 200,000 Mexicans (mainly women) now assembled goods in ***maquiladoras*** on the Mexican side for resale in the USA or Europe; in the southern state of Chiapas an expanding market for beef (*pace* McDonalds) was provoking a massive seizure of indigenous lands. The market was making inroads everywhere.

The 1988–94 presidency of Carlos **Salinas de Gortari** was not only one of the most corrupt among many corrupt regimes, it was also increasingly influenced by the growing drug trafficking in the north of the country and prone to deepening repression as political and economic crisis provoked swelling resistance movements – among students, bus drivers, small farmers, agricultural workers and many others. The political theatre movement exemplified by Jesusa **Rodríguez** and Tito **Vasconcelos** spoke through a mounting culture of dissent, satire and parody, like **Juan Gabriel**'s version of *ranchera* (see ***rancheras, comedias***) and Astrid **Hadad**'s extravagant stage pastiches. **Café Tacuba** and Eugenia León created a new music for the new times.

But no movement had as great an impact as the **Zapatistas** (EZLN), who seized several towns in the southern Chiapas in January 1994, coinciding exactly with the official inauguration of the North American Free Trade Area (**NAFTA**) that effectively integrated the Mexican economy with those of the USA and Canada. US finance and insurance companies had already moved into Mexico in force in anticipation of the profits to come – the Chiapas rising, however, made it impossible to conceal its real impact and repercussions. The confrontation between the government and the Zapatistas continued into 2000; the leader of the movement, Subcomandante Marcos (see **Subcomandante Marcos**) became for some a symbol of a 'postmodern revolution' – indigenous dress plus the Internet – and for others a kind of folklore. But for many Mexicans it was a hopeful sign of the longevity of rebellion. At the millennium, an occupation of the UNAM was close to its first anniversary – and armed groups of guerrillas had begun to emerge in a number of provinces. A new political landscape beckons as the first President who is not a member of the PRI, Vincente Fox, prepares to assume power.

Further reading

Córdova, A. (1973) *La ideología de la Revolución Mexicana*, Mexico: ERA.
Duncan, J.A. (1986) *Voices, Visions and a New Reality: Mexican Fiction since 1970*, Pittsburgh: University of Pittsburgh Press.
Gilly, A. (1983) *The Mexican Revolution*, London: Verso.
Krauze, E. (1997) *Mexico: Biography of Power*, New York/London: Harper & Row.
Monsiváis, C. (1997) *Mexican Postcards*, ed. and trans. John Kraniauskas, London: Verso.
Paranagua, P.A. (ed.) (1995) *Mexican Cinema*, trans. Ana M. López, London: British Film Institute.
Paz, O. et al. (1966) *Poesía en movimiento*, Mexico: Siglo XXI.

MIKE GONZALEZ

Meyer, Pedro

b. 1935, Madrid, Spain

Photographer

An internationally renowned Mexican photographer, Meyer was the founding President of the Mexican Council of Photography in the 1970s. The Council was responsible for creating the Latin American Colloquia on Photography, which are still continuing twenty-five years later. All major photographic institutions in Mexico today stem from this initial Council. Olivier Debroise has compared Meyer's jarring portraits to Diane Arbus's 'everyday monsters'. During the 1970s Meyer created ironic images of his own social class, the Mexican bourgeoisie, and of anonymous urban office workers. In 1978–9 he chronicled the Nicaraguan Revolution. After moving to Los Angeles in the 1980s, he began to lampoon the vulgarity, consumerism and racism of the US middle classes, and to celebrate the magical dimension of Oaxacan rural life. Throughout the 1990s Meyer has taken a controversial stand at the vanguard of digital photography; he also created and maintains an award-winning photography website, Zone Zero (www.zonezero.com). He has published, among other books: *Los cohetes duraron todo el día* (The Rockets Went on All Day) (1988) on the Mexican oil workers; *Espejo de espinas* (Mirror of Thorns) (1986), an overview of Meyer's work from 1965–85; and *Truth and Fictions. A Journey from Documentary to Digital Photography* (1995). The latter also appeared as a CD-ROM, as did *I Photograph to Remember* (1990), Meyer's poignant photographic document of the last year of his parents' lives. This was the first CD-ROM of its kind (with pictures and sound) made anywhere in the world.

CYNTHIA STEELE

mescal see tequila and mezcal

MHOL

MHOL (Movimiento Homosexual de Lima) (Homosexual Movement of Lima) is a non-profit-making organization dedicated to the elimination of oppression, injustice and discrimination against homosexual and bisexual men and women on the basis of their sexual orientation. Founded in Lima in 1982, it was the first institution of its kind in Peru. Its activities include education programmes on **human rights** and campaigns for the prevention of **AIDS**. It also offers legal advice, information and counselling, safe sex workshops, lifestyle workshops, information on Aids and sexuality, and so on. MHOL is led by the Peruvian economist Oscar Ugarteche.

See also: gay and lesbian movements

CÉSAR SALAS

Michelena, Bernabé

b. 1888, Durazno, Uruguay; d. 1963

Sculptor

A member of the Teseo group, Michelena studied drawing in Montevideo before travelling to Europe in 1913. Returning in 1928 with a grant from Uruguay's Ministry of Education, he studied with the sculptor Bourdelle at the Chaumiere Academy, exhibiting his work in 1930 at the Zak Gallery. He was awarded the major sculpture prize at the Uruguayan pavilion at the Paris International Exhibition of 1937.

MARCO MAGGI

Mickey, Fanny
b. 1931, Cali, Colombia

Actress

Mickey has lived and worked in Colombia for many years, starting her career with the **Teatro Experimental de Cali** (Cali Experimental Theatre) before transferring to the Teatro Popular de Bogotá (Bogota People's Theatre). In 1975 she set up the first Café Concierto in Colombia; its first presentation was *La gata caliente* (Hot Cat). She helped to form the Teatro Nacional in 1981 and became its director, a post she still holds. She has also been active in organizing Bogotá's Festival of Latin American Theatre.

ALEJANDRA JARAMILLO

Mighty Chalkdust, The
b. 1940, Trinidad & Tobago

Calypsonian and writer

In 1968, Chalkdust (born Hollis Liverpool) came to public attention with 'Brain Drain', a **calypso** about those fleeing the island for better employment. Winner of the Calypso Crown in 1976 and 1977, Chalkdust focuses on serious social comment. His research into calypso history, which he continues, has helped calypso achieve the respect it deserves as an art form. Recognized as Calypso Monarch of the World in 1993, Chalkdust has a Ph.D. in history/ethnomusicology. He is the author of *Kaiso and Society* (1986), *Calypsonians to Remember* (1987) and *Culture and Education: Carnival in Trinidad and Tobago* (1990).

KEITH JARDIM

Mighty Shadow, The
b. 1941, Tobago

Calypsonian

Born Winston Bailey, the Mighty Shadow's recent hit 'Poverty is Hell' again demonstrated his talent and sensitivity. By the mid-1970s his music was winning a wider North American audience than any other calypsonian. Yet judges in Trinidad, preferring the popular party calypsos (see **calypso**), most of which have consistently degraded women, sex, and other cultures and races, continue to ignore his abilities as a musician and writer. Shadow, like his fans, knows that to sing with a social conscience is to confront the (corrupt) powers that be. In 1974, on Dimanche Gras night in Trinidad, he sang 'Something is mad, here in Trinidad/They take it for fun, pushin' me around/ I want to catch those judges in Hell.'

KEITH JARDIM

Mighty Sparrow, The
b. 1935, Gouyave, Grenada

Musician

Slinger Francisco, known as the Mighty Sparrow, first won Trinidad's prestigious Calypso King competition in 1956; he has won this and other competitions so many times since then, that he is now known as the Calypso King of the World. In 1956 he also won that year's Road March competition (the most popular song with the public during the two days of Carnival), with the now legendary Jean and Dinah (originally called Yankees Gone), a song celebrating the departure of the Americans who had remained stationed on the island after the Second World War. Sparrow trained with The Original Young Brigade tent (early venues for the performance of **calypso** were tents fashioned from palm leaves) and what he calls the 'mouthband', a group of friends who got together to practise vocal imitations of the sounds of different steel pans (see **steelband**). He credits his discovery of the importance of gesture and mime to two Guyanese comedians he met while touring there. Among Sparrow's innovations to calypso are the use of microphones and band accompaniment. He has campaigned on behalf of calypsonians, challenging local music stations to give more time to calypso and championing the need for a Copyright Act to protect musicians. Master of the social commentary and double entendre forms of calypso, some of Sparrow's most memorable hits are Ten to One is Murder (1960), Federation (1962), Dan is the Man (1963) and School Days (1973).

LORRAINE LEU

Migliorisi, Ricardo

b. 1948, Asunción, Paraguay

Artist, architect and stage designer

Basically self-taught in the arts, Migliorisi's formative experience was as designer of theatre costumes and scenery. He represented the Neofiguración movement in Paraguay in the late 1960s with his satirical and humorous images and his absurd eclectic imagery related to pop and psychedelic art, rock music, **happenings**, audiovisual work and montages. His early work is biting and irreverent in style. He created a stir in Paraguay's artistic community for his audacity in the use of unrealistic hybrid characters, animals and objects from classical mythology, popular subjects, kitsch opera, circus, cabaret, television, gossip columns and body art.

BETSY PARTYKA

Mignone, Francisco

b. 1897, São Paulo, Brazil; d. 1986, São Paulo

Composer

Like Camargo **Guarnieri**, Francisco Mignone was of Italian descent and much influenced by the urban music of his native São Paulo. His many waltzes and tangos are poignant reminders of early times spent playing piano in cafés, under the pseudonym Chico Bororó. His friend Mário de **Andrade** criticized Mignone's Italianate leanings, persuading him to turn to Brazilian subjects; hence the ballets *Babaloxá* and *Batucajé* (both 1936), inspired by **Candomblé**, and the *Quadras Amazónicas* for orchestra (1939–42). Respighi, Stokowski and **Villa-Lobos** all championed Mignone's music, which significantly contributed to Brazil's nationalist movement.

SIMON WRIGHT

Mihanovich, Sandra

b. 1957, Buenos Aires, Argentina

Singer

In 1975 Mihanovich produced a solo album, *Pienso en vos* (I Think of You), and then did some acting and singing in pubs and clubs. In 1982 her second album, *Sandra Mihanovich*, won her considerable success. She reached number one with her version of 'Es la vida que me alcanza' (It's Life That Gets to Me) by Celeste **Carballo**, with whom she later recorded two albums, *Somos mucho más que dos* (Many More Than Two) (1988) and *Mujer contra mujer* (Woman Against Woman) (1990). A campaigner for gay rights (see **gay and lesbian movements**), she is one of the most unmistakable voices in Argentine music.

RODRIGO PEIRETTI

Milanés, Pablo

b. 1943, Bayamo, Cuba

Musician

A professional musician at the age of sixteen, his first compositions were influenced by Cuban forms like **son** and **feeling**. After completing his obligatory military service in the notorious **UMAP**s, he joined Silvio **Rodríguez** in the creation of a political song movement later called *nueva trova*. In 1969 he joined the Grupo de Experimentación Sonora de la ICAIC, directed by Leo **Brouwer**. Recognized as one of the most important figures in Cuban *nueva canción* (new song) in the 1970s and 1980s, he set up his own foundation in 1993 to encourage young Cuban musicians. Bureaucratic resistance led to its collapse in 1996. His best known songs include 'La vida no vale nada' (Life's Worth Nothing), 'Yolanda' and 'El breve espacio en que no estás' (The Brief Interlude when You're not There).

JOSÉ ANTONIO EVORA

military cultures

Outside the Caribbean areas subordinated directly to the United States, the Latin American military still define themselves by reference to the Prussian or French tradition which shaped their professionalization after 1900. That tradition and its discourse presumed the possibility of mobilizing all the resources of a modern society and was organized around compulsory military service; it was taken up by dependent states as they began to structure their territorial, financial and military sovereignty and consolidate the nation. Henceforth war would no longer be a conflict between armies but the process that gave birth to nations. The Prussian Marshal Friedrich von der Goltz optimistically predicted as much after the defeat of France in 1871. His book *The Nation Under Arms* was widely read by Latin American military officers, intensely aware of their colonial situation and searching for the secret of that distant and painful victory.

Only rarely was the army able to mobilize the enormous material, technical or human resources that this process of modernization through the national state would have required; but the army did forge relationships and links with civil society which transformed their warlike preparations into a transcendental, civilizing and moral mission. In practice, this necessarily shifting and conflictive process encouraged the voracity of a military whose internal rationalization was more complete than other bureaucracies. The republican discourse which underpinned the national project allowed the translation of these comparative differences into a notion of their superior role in the 'fulfilment of civic duties' and 'the destiny of the *patria* and its citizens'. In the risky business of defence, their corporate isolation became 'disinterest' and 'sacrifice' opposed to the 'public representation of private interests'. Discipline and the normative controls over career and command structures become 'order', 'self-sacrifice', 'integrity', 'regeneration' and 'salvation', set against 'civil liberties' and 'corruption'. Professional training and military access to technology became a duty of 'development', 'education' and 'progress', given society's general lack of technology and low levels of educational provision. The most stoical, organic and transcendental republican virtues – 'purity', 'moderation' and 'dedication' – easily linked to the dominant **Catholicism**, were not manifest in the course of this conflictive process of modernization. In the necessity and tendency of Latin American military cultures to dominate their surroundings, 'duty and rights' were not linked to 'freedom and equality'.

From 1945 onwards, US hegemony throughout the area reinforced the traditionalism of those cultures. Anti-Communism as a faith increased colonial dependency and promoted US involvement in national economic development and the struggle against international materialist subversion. The constitutional limits on US military culture were forgotten in their crusading zeal; few parliaments seemed to see the necessity of giving the training of the Latin American military a legitimate legal framework. The class differences between officers and men, members of the poorer classes of country and city who lacked the resources to avoid conscription, were reinforced on a daily basis within the cultural and material reality of superiority and inferiority within the military. Gender differences are also reinforced in language and attitudes; the primitive models of military conduct, for example, continue to impose a 'virile heroism' linked to 'discipline', 'courage' and 'virtue'; sex is thus linked to the body, the body to the soul, the soul to *esprit de corps* and the 'corps' to civilization itself. In behavioural terms, the only expression of this cult of sex and virility in exclusively masculine circles at the lower end of the institution, is violence. Mario **Vargas Llosa**'s *La ciudad y los perros* (Time of the Hero) (1962) is a powerful illustration of the intimate connection between the cult of *machismo* (see **machismo, Mexican**), violence and sexual repression; a repression dealt with in writings as diverse as Nelson Werneck **Sodré**'s memoirs *Do Tenentismo ao Estado Novo: Memórias de um soldado* (From Lieutenancy to the New State: Memories of a Soldier) (1986) and Reinaldo **Arenas**'s autobiography *Antes que anochezca* (Before Night Falls) (1992).

That cultural discourse is reinforced by the physical presence of major barracks in the centre of most capital cities, and by the visibility of the military in all civic ceremonials where even the most professionalized armies (in Mexico for example) are visibly the arbiters and guardians of the state. Between the mid-1970s and the late 1980s, of course, the military assumed power directly in much of the continent at one time or another, in the name of a crusade against subversion which legitimated the suppression of almost all democratic practices. This assumption of power and the repression that followed were invariably accompanied by sombre martial music and parades in which the ubiquitous dark glasses were the signifiers of a kind of an anonymous power in which the individuals were merely representatives of the corps. Reality often gave the lie to that aspiration, however, as the wilful pursuit of power by Chile's Augusto **Pinochet** serves to exemplify.

Further reading

Castro, C. (1990) *O Espíritu Militar. Um Estudo de Antropologia Social na Academia Militar das Agulhas Negras*, Rio de Janeiro: Jorge Zahar Editor.

Rouquié, A. (1982) *L'état militaire en Amérique Latine*, Paris: Editions du Seuil.

Vergara, M. (1997) *Silence, Order, Obedience and Discipline: The Educational Discourse of the Argentinian Military Regime*, Lund: Lund University Press.

ROBERTO MADERO

Millor Fernandes

b. 1924, Rio de Janeiro, Brazil

Graphic artist

Millor's first drawing appeared in *O Jornal* when he was eleven. Throughout the 1940s his satirical drawings appeared in Brazil's most important magazines. Their political content often brought him into conflict with the censors, particularly when the military came to power in 1964. A founder of the satirical magazine *O pasquim*, he also wrote a number of theatre pieces, including *Liberdade, Liberdade*, which was banned across the nation in 1966. He drew for *Veja*, *IstoÉ* and later in the *Jornal do Brasil*, where he began to use computer graphics.

ANTONIO CARLOS VAZ

milonga

The milonga is an Argentine and Uruguayan musical genre derived from the habanera. Born in the late nineteenth century in Buenos Aires and Montevideo, it later extended to the countryside. There are two currents within the milonga, urban and rural. The first, a dance form in four-four time, a rapid tempo and in a major key, has now become part of the repertoire of **tango** bands, for tango too derived from the urban milonga. The rural variant, a sung form, is slower, in minor keys and usually accompanied by a guitar. The milonga is also known in Chile and Paraguay.

ALFONSO PADILLA

mimeograph poets see marginal poets

Mindlin, Henrique

b. 1911, São Paulo, Brazil; d. 1971, Rio de Janeiro

Architect

Mindlin produced his major works and established one of the country's most important architectural practices in Rio de Janeiro. Initially his work followed the dictates of the 'Brazilian style', juxtaposing curves and straight lines and incorporating elements of traditional architecture. Later, he flirted with the iron and glass structures pioneered by Mies van der Rohe, before cultivating rationalism with structures in reinforced concrete. In his writings, he positioned his adaptation of rationalism to the prevailing environmental conditions of Brazil as a reinterpretation of colonial architecture.

ROBERTO CONDURU

minifundio

A *minifundio* is a small farm owned by the *minifundista* (smallholder) and worked with unpaid family labour. It is the most common type of family farm in Latin America. Most *minifundistas* are unable to make a subsistence living from the farm, and rural poverty is concentrated in the *minifundia* areas. Family members thus have to seek an outside source of income, often working as seasonal wage labourers or as sharecroppers on *latifundios* (see **latifundio**). *Minifundistas* are often characterized as semi-proletarians rather than as peasants. Latin America's highly unequal agrarian structure is often referred to as the '*latifundio–minifundio* complex'.

See also: agrarian reform; hacienda; plantations

CRISTÓBAL KAY

mining

Mining has provided a source of wealth in Latin America since pre-Encounter times. Although gold and silver are still mined, copper (Mexico, Peru and Chile), tin (Bolivia), bauxite (Jamaica, Venezuela and Guyana), iron (Brazil) and other minerals are also important. By the twentieth century, mining became dominated by US and European multinational firms with the technical capacity and capital investment needed for large-scale operations.

Multinational control of mining operations and profits became a focus of economic nationalism after the Second World War. After unsuccessful attempts to stimulate multinational production while controlling more of the profits, Chile's President Eduardo **Frei** (1964–70) initiated a policy of 'Chileanization', gradually giving the government a controlling interest in foreign enterprises by the 1960s. President Salvador **Allende** nationalized the larger mines in 1970.

In Peru, conflicts over contract negotiations with multinationals provoked nationalist sentiment that led to the establishment of a revolutionary military government in 1968. General Juan **Velasco Alvarado**'s government enacted mining laws in 1970 and 1971 that gave the State-run *Mineroperú* a monopoly on refining and exporting minerals. In both Chile and Peru, foreign capital retaliated by limiting investment and abandoning mining operations. A decline in world market prices further contributed to a weakening of these mining sectors in the 1970s.

Foreign capital also figured large in mining investment in Bolivia, although over 50 per cent of tin production was in the hands of the **Patiño** corporation until 1952. Bolivia's tin miners have a history of union activism dating to just after the First World War. The miners responded to attempts to control labour with a series of major strikes in the late 1940s. They joined forces with the Movimiento Nacional Revolucionario (MNR), a reformist political party. In April 1952, the military declared a state of siege following an MNR victory in national elections. A rebellion ensued, and armed assistance from the miners helped bring MNR leader Víctor **Paz Estenssoro** to the Presidency.

Mining leaders, such as Juan **Lechín**, were important in the early phases of the Bolivian Revolution. Under their influence, Paz nationalized the mines of the three largest companies in October 1952, establishing a State-run mining company, COMIBOL. Miners' support for the MNR declined after 1956, when the government adopted stabilization policies detrimental to labour interests. Mining unions were severely repressed during the Barrientos and Banzer governments.

In the 1980s and 1990s, government attempts to reinvigorate private investment brought new hardships to miners. Victor Paz Estenssoro, elected President of Bolivia again in 1985, issued decrees to close mines he had nationalized in 1952. Over 20 thousand miners were laid off. Peru and Chile also began denationalization programmes.

Further reading

Becker, D. (1983) *The New Bourgeoisie and the Limits of Dependency*, Princeton: Princeton University Press.

Moran, T.H. (1974) *Multinational Corporations and the Politics of Dependence*, Princeton: Princeton University Press.

Nash, J. (1993) *We Eat the Mines and the Mines Eat Us*, reprint, New York: Columbia University Press.

E. BROOKE HARLOWE

Ministério da Educacão e Saúde

In 1930, President Getulio **Vargas** created several new ministries, among them MES (Ministério da Educacão e Saúde), the Ministry of Education and Health. Its newly appointed head, Gustavo Capanema, was given the opportunity to modernize the education system and launched a competition for a new building. Since none of the entries fulfilled his expectations, he asked Lúcio **Costa** to develop a new design that reflected his modern ideas. Two studies by Le Corbusier, who had been called in as a consultant, were transformed into an innovative design, built between 1936 and 1945 in Rio de Janeiro, which is now considered a reference point for all modern Brazilian architecture.

MARIA MARTA CAMISASSA

minority languages (European and Asian)

Minority languages of European and Asian origin, meaning languages other than Spanish or Portuguese in Latin America and languages other than Dutch, English, French or Spanish in and around the Caribbean, are spoken wherever an ethnic community is large enough for the language and culture to remain viable. The Italian-speaking communities of Argentina and Chile, for example, numbering almost a million in each case, are even large enough to support schools in Buenos Aires and Santiago where instruction is in Italian. Similarly, there are English-language schools in Buenos Aires, Bogotá and other large cities of Latin America, and in São Paulo, the Japanese Culture Centre offers instruction in Japanese for Brazil's Japanese-speaking population. Other languages with large numbers of speakers in Brazil and the Southern Cone are Dutch, German, Ukrainian and Polish.

Cohesive ethnic communities in rural areas also exist, such as the 120,000 Plattdeutsch (Low German) speaking Mennonites in Mexico, Central America, Brazil and the Southern Cone, and the 100,000 semi-nomadic speakers of Romany, the Indo-Iranian language of Argentine, Brazilian and Colombian gypsies.

Some minority-language communities date to colonial times. Vernacular English is the first language of 11,000 Bay Island Hondurans and 15,000 inhabitants of the Netherland Antilles, and is extensively used in Suriname for commerce. English is the official language of Guyana, Belize, Jamaica, and numerous small island nations of the Caribbean (Trinidad, Tobago, Antigua, Grenada, St Kitts, and so on), but is spoken by only a minority of the populations; the majority speak English-, French- or Portuguese-based Creoles (see **creole languages**). A similar situation exists in Haiti, French Guiana and the many officially Francophone islands of the Caribbean (Guadeloupe, Martinique and others). Spanish, spoken by about 50,000 in Belize, is a minority language in this largely English creole-speaking nation, and is also spoken by about 4,500 US Virgin Islanders. (Spanish is also technically a minority language in **Guarani**-speaking Paraguay, where it is the first language of only about 5 per cent of the population.)

Several minority Asian languages are spoken in and around the Caribbean. As many as 250,000 inhabitants of Suriname, French Guiana, Guyana, Trinidad and Tobago speak Hindi, the 150,000 speakers in Suriname comprising 38 per cent of the population. Another 60,000 Surinamers speak Javanese. 6,000 speakers of Hakka Chinese reside in Suriname, Guyana and French Guiana, and an additional 6,000 in Panama. Costa Rica is home to 4,500 speakers of Hakka, Yue and Mandarin Chinese.

Finally, not all minority languages are oral. Many of Mexico's 1.3 million deaf use Mexican Sign Language (*el lenguaje de señas mexicanas*), a signed language with influence from French Sign Language and unrelated to Spanish.

Bibliography

Gunnemark, Erik V. (1992) *Countries, Peoples and Their Languages: The Geolinguistic Handbook*, Gothenburg: Länstryckeriet.

ROGER L. PARKS

Minorista *see* Grupo Minorista

Miñoso, Minnie

b. 1922, Havana, Cuba

Baseball player

Miñoso (real name Saturnino Orestes Arrieta Armas) played professionally in Cuba, Mexico, the US Negro Leagues and, after their integration, the US major leagues. He became known in Cuba by the surname of his ballplaying half-brothers, Miñoso, and in the US as 'Minnie'. The racial policies of US **baseball** prevented him from beginning his major league career until the relatively advanced age of twenty-nine; yet he was a top performer throughout the 1950s, nicknamed the 'Cuban Comet' for his speed and aggressive playing style. In 1976, at fifty-four, he became the oldest player to get a hit in a major league game.

DOUGLAS W. VICK

Minshall, Peter

b. Port-of-Spain, Trinidad

Visual and performance artist

At age fifteen Minshall became the youngest painter to have work shown at the Trinidad Art Society's Annual Exhibition, but the adult Minshall turned away from two-dmensional art in his search for a particularly Trinidadian medium. He found a dynamic form for his work in **carnival** and has elaborated a **mas** aesthetic based on costume art that is given life by the masquerader's body. Minshall creates art to be performed, drawing on the music and spontaneous dance of carnival, but also enacting allegorical narratives through choreographed movement and mime. Minshall's mas seeks to challenge the still commonly held view of 'art' in Trinidad as conventional painting and sculpture. His 'dancing mobile sculptures' also question monumentalism and permanence in artistic creation, as the art only exists while worn and a costume can never be used in more than one carnival.

Minshall's early concept bands flew in the face of the emphasis on detail and riotous colour, characteristic of traditional carnival costuming. Instead, bands like *Danse Macabre* and *Papillon* experimented with clean, striking forms and pure colour, climaxing in the trilogy enacting the changes brought by modernization to a riverside community. This began with the 1983 band, *River*, in which masqueraders in white, clad in the dress of the Shouter Baptists for whom the river is an important focus of worship, danced under a floating canopy of white fabric. In his 1990 band, *Tantana*, Minshall brought art out of the studios and on to the street by inviting some of Trinidad's leading painters to create on fabric, which was then used in carnival costumes.

Minshall won the prestigious Band of the Year title in 1995 and 1996 with *Song of the Earth* and *Hallelujah*, and in 1997 *Tapestry* won him the award again. *Tapestry* returns to traditional costume design, in particular the work of the late George Bailey, involving the use of large amounts of different fabrics. Minshall has staged theatrical events in diverse contexts world-wide, including at an American anti-nuclear march and at the opening ceremonies of the last two Olympic Games. Minshall's Callaloo Company, a group of artists, craftsmen and performers, in addition to working on his annual carnival band, also focuses on exploring the relationship between mas and theatre, and its implications for performance.

Further reading

Minshall, P. (1995) 'The place of carnival in Caribbean art and culture', in exhibition catalogue *Caribbean Visions: Painting and Sculpture*, Miami Center for the Fine Arts: Art Services International.

LORRAINE LEU

Minujín, Marta

b. 1943, Buenos Aires, Argentina

Artist

Marta Minujín studied in Paris between 1960 and 1963 with a grant from the French Embassy. In 1964 Minujín won the **Instituto Di Tella**'s Major National Prize for her work *Revuélquese y viva* (Roll About and Live), made from painted mattresses and pillows, which actively encouraged the spectator's involvement. In 1965 she produced the environmental work *La Menesunda* with Raúl Santantonín, and *El Batacazo* (Hammer Blow) a construction described as an 'object-happening'. Since 1966 Minujín has principally expressed herself through **happenings**. In *Simultaneidad en simultaneidad* (Simultaneity Within Simultaneity) (1966), realized with Allan Kaprow in New York and Wolf Vostell in Berlin, she used mass media. Later she created a series of symbolic monuments, ephemeral installations like *El obelisco de Pan Dulce* (Obelisk of Sweet Bread) (1979) and *El Partenón de Libros* (Parthenon of Books) (1983), which celebrated the end of **censorship**.

CECILIA RABOSSI

Mir, Pedro

b. 1913, San Pedro de Macorís, Dominican Republic; d. 2000, Santo Domingo, Dominican Republic

Poet

While exiled in Cuba during **Trujillo**'s dictatorship, Mir published his 1949 poem 'Hay un país en el mundo' (There is a Country in the World) which delineates the history of the Dominican Republic. In the early 1950s, Mir published another extensive poem 'Contracanto a Walt Whitman' (Countersong to Walt Whitman), in which he tries to respond to Whitman with the collective 'we' of exploited workers. Also important is his 1978 novel *Cuando amaban las tierras comuneras* (When Communal Lands were Loved), depicting the period between the two US invasions of the Dominican Republic (1916 and 1965).

FERNANDO VALERIO-HOLGUÍN

Miranda, Carmen

b. 1909, Marco de Canaveses, Portugal; d. 1955, Beverly Hills, California, USA

Entertainer

The status of Carmen Miranda (full name Maria do Carmo Miranda da Cunha) as one of Brazil's top entertainers of the 1930s is often overshadowed by her controversial role in the 1940s and 1950s as a Hollywood-created icon of 'Latin-ness' that, for many Brazilians, represented a betrayal of national identity and culture. Miranda grew up in Rio de Janeiro in a working-class environment. She began performing popular music such as **tango** and **samba** in her teens, and in 1929 made her **radio** debut and recorded her first record. Throughout the 1930s, Miranda's performances on radio, stage and in five Brazilian feature-length films (precursors of the *chanchada*) rendered her a national celebrity. Her interpretations of Brazilian popular music were broadcast nationwide by a radio industry that served state interests and formed part of a nationalist discourse promoted by populist President Getulio **Vargas**.

In 1939, Miranda accepted an invitation to perform on Broadway. Her departure was heralded as an opportunity to promote Brazilian culture abroad. An immediate hit in New York, Miranda soon moved to California where she appeared in fourteen Hollywood films between 1941 and 1953. She invariably played the role of the 'Brazilian bombshell', representing a 'Latin-ness' that was enormously engaging in part because it did not need to be taken seriously. Miranda became an asset of the US government for her roles in movies produced to promote the Good Neighbour Policy.

When Miranda returned to Brazil briefly in 1940 after her first year in the USA, she was booed by an elite audience in Rio de Janeiro and charged with having become 'Americanized'. Although her extraordinary success in the USA is a source of pride for many Brazilians, she is an ambivalent figure who is also regarded as embodying a facile, demeaning and inauthentic version of Brazilian culture. Miranda's importance as a critical and complex emblem of Brazilian-ness is underlined by the frequency with which her image continues to surface in cultural expressions ranging from **carnival** school themes to the **Tropicália** manifesto.

Further reading

Barsante, C. (1994) *Carmen Miranda*, Rio de Janeiro: ELFOS.

López, A.M. (1993) 'Are All Latins from Manhattan?: Hollywood, Ethnography and Cultural Colonialism', in J. King, A.M. López and M. Alvarado (eds), *Mediating Two Worlds: Cinematic Encounters in the Americas*, London: British Film Institute.

Saia, L. (1984) *Carmen Miranda*, São Paulo: Brasiliense.

Solberg, H. (1995) *Bananas Is My Business*, film.

Veloso, C. (1991) 'Caricature and Conqueror, Pride and Shame', trans. R. Myers, *New York Times*, 20 October 1991, 34, 41.

AMELIA SIMPSON

Miró, Chris

b. 1969, Buenos Aires, Argentina

Performer

The arrival in Argentina of one of Pedro Almodóvar's girls, Bibi Andersen, which caused great excitement in Buenos Aires, marked the moment chosen by agent Pepe Parada to launch the Argentine transvestite Chris Miró. While continuing his dental studies, Miró became a star of the Argentine review stage. He began his career presenting shows in clubs and discos, but quickly became famous for his great beauty; he needed no make-up to become a beautiful woman. He has a telephone line where callers can ask him questions about himself.

RODRIGO PEIRETTI

Miró, Ricardo

b. 1883, Panama City; d. 1940, Panama City

Poet

Born while Panama was still part of Colombia, Miró studied painting in Bogotá, Colombia before political events there forced him to interrupt his studies and return to his homeland. With the creation of the republic, a new literary era began to which he contributed actively. His poems served to unify national feelings; in 'Patria' (Homeland) he speaks in a late romantic voice of his country and its scenery. He became the national poet, and the annual Panamanian literary prize bears his name. On his centenary (1983), the National Institute of Culture published his complete works in two volumes: *Poesía* (Poetry) and *Novela y cuento* (Novels and Stories).

NORMAN S. HOLLAND

Miró Quesada Cantuarias, Francisco

b. 1918, Lima, Peru

Philosopher

A prolific writer, Miró's works include philosophical and scientific textbooks, works on the theory of reason, on logic and on the philosophy of mathematics. Founder of the Peruvian Philosophical Society in 1940 and Minister of Education (1963–4), he studied philosophy at the Catholic University and the University of San Marcos in Lima. He was professor of philosophy at San Marcos between 1940 and 1970 and in 1980 became Director of the Institute of Philosophical Research at the University of Lima.

CÉSAR SALAS

Miró Quesada, Aurelio

b. 1907, Lima, Peru

Historian and writer

Miró is director of the newspaper *El Comercio* (the oldest in Peru), ex-President of the University of San Marcos, and author of essays on Peruvian themes. The most important are *Veinte temas peruanos* (Twenty Peruvian Themes) (1966), *Nuevos temas peruanos* (New Peruvian Themes) (1982), and his major contribution, *El Inca Garcilaso de la Vega* (1948), expanded in 1971 and 1994, one of the best documented biographies of the colonial mestizo writer. He has also been Director of the Peruvian Academy of the Spanish Language and of the National Academy of History.

JOSÉ ANTONIO MAZZOTTI

Misa Criolla

The *Misa Criolla* is a major work by Ariel **Ramírez** for soloists, chorus and instrumental group, first performed in 1964. Its choral parts were arranged by Father J.G. Segade. One of several 'vernacular masses' composed in the 1960s (like the *Missa Luba*), it has been performed in many countries and recorded several times. The work follows the structure of the traditional Catholic mass, but uses Latin American folk music. Thus the 'Kyrie' has a tripartite structure in the sequence *vidala-baguala-vidala*; the 'Gloria' is a cheerful *carnavalito* and the 'Credo' a *chacarera trunca*. The rhythmic base of the 'Sanctus' is a *carnaval cochabambino* while the 'Agnus Dei' is an *estilo pampeano*.

ALFONSO PADILLA

Miskitus

An indigenous population of about 85,000 persons, the Miskitus comprise the majority population of eastern Nicaragua and Honduras (the Mosquito Coast). Their cultural identity has been shaped by British colonialism, US neo-colonialism and Nicaraguan state formation. In the early colonial period, Miskitus exchanged slaves, **cacao**, animal skins, turtleshells and balsam for British weapons, tools and jewellery. This commercial exchange helped the Miskitus establish their hegemony over other coastal indigenous groups.

In 1786, the British evacuated the Atlantic Coast after having strongly influenced many aspects of Miskitu culture. Subsequently the Miskitu Kingdom declined, and Central American independence from Spain in 1821 and the emergence of the Nicaraguan Republic in 1838 made it clear that political and economic power would pass to the mestizos and the modernizing elites of western Nicaragua. The Atlantic Coast was crucial for British commercial interests, however, and in 1847 Britain reoccupied it and established a protectorate from Cape Honduras to San Juan del Norte in the south. The British consul invited Moravian missionaries to set up schools and churches there. By the end of the nineteenth century, membership in the Moravian Church was part of Miskitu identity. However, the United States viewed British control of eastern Nicaragua as an affront to the Monroe Doctrine. The 1860 Treaty of Managua settled the dispute, ended the British protectorate and placed Mosquitia under the sovereignty of the Republic of Nicaragua.

Economic activity on the Atlantic Coast reached its zenith between 1880 and 1930. US and Canadian companies set up banana plantations (see **bananas**) and lumber and mining companies, and established their control over the Miskitu labour force through a system of company stores. However, the 1929 Depression and the rise of an anti-US guerrilla movement in Nicaragua under General **Sandino** led to the closure of many companies. Miskitu attitudes toward Sandino and later toward the Sandinistas (see **Sandinista Revolution**), however, remained ambivalent.

This history of the Atlantic Coast created a Miskitu identity in opposition to the mestizos of the Pacific region. The anti-imperialist elements that formed a significant part of the political identity of the mestizos were absent from Miskitu identity. Consequently, they opposed Sandinista government policies and demanded autonomy, which was granted in 1985.

See also: MISURASATA; Fagoth, Stedman

Further reading

Bourgois, P. (1981) 'Class, Ethnicity and the State among the Miskitu Amerindians of Northeastern Nicaragua', *Latin American Perspectives* 8(2): 23–9.

García, C. (1996) *The Making of the Miskitu People of Nicaragua: The Social Construction of Ethnic Identity*, Upsala: Acta Universitatis Upsaliensis.

Hale, C. (1994) *Resistance and Contradiction: Miskitu Indians and the Nicaraguan State, 1894–1987*, Stanford, CA: Stanford University Press.

ANUPAMA MANDE AND ILEANA RODRÍGUEZ

missionaries

Missionaries are members of religious organizations sent to carry out spiritual or humanitarian tasks, such as converting, training or lending assistance to the unconverted, the newly converted or a disadvantaged group. In Latin America the prominent sending agencies have historically been (1) the Roman Catholic Church (see **Catholicism**); (2) later, mainstream Protestant Churches (see **Protestantism**) comprising a number of Methodist, Presbyterian, Baptist and Evangelical denominations; (3) interdenominational Bible societies and mission boards; and, (4) more recently, sects which hold to non-traditional Christian doctrines. Of the latter, growth among Pentecostal groups (see **Pentecostals**) and the Church of Jesus Christ of Latter Day Saints (see **Mormonism**) has been particularly notable.

The first missionaries to Latin America were Roman Catholic: Jesuit, Dominican, Franciscans and Capuchin monks and priests dispatched during the colonial era to Spanish and Portuguese holdings in the Americas with royal patronage and military backing. The task of these early missionaries was to present the Gospel on behalf of the Catholic Church and to promote European culture and civilization on behalf of the king. Ostensibly, this would make the native populace productive members of Catholic society. In practice, however, it led to their subjugation and exploitation.

The independence movements of the early nineteenth century disrupted Roman Catholic missionary activity as newly autonomous nations renegotiated their relationship to the Church. This period of uncertainty paved the way for an era of Protestant missionary activity in Latin America. At first, the Protestant effort was directed towards non-Catholic immigrants. Although efforts by British and American Bible societies to encourage scripture reading were initially well received, later attempts to proselytize the nominally Catholic population met with harassment and persecution. Only towards the end of the nineteenth century did Protestant missionaries achieve meagre success in winning converts in Latin America. The most significant achievements of the historic Protestant missionary enterprise in Latin America have been the establishment of schools, clinics, hospitals and other charitable works.

Historically, Roman Catholic and mainline Protestant missionaries alike have chiefly been committed to transplanting existing ecclesiastical models to the New World. However, beginning in the first half of the twentieth century, missionary agencies have increasingly promoted indigenous expression of Christianity.

Further reading

Dussel, E.D. (ed.) (1992) *The Church in Latin America, 1492–1992*, Tunbridge Wells: Oates & Burnes, and Maryknoll, NY: Orbis Books.

Miller, D.R. (ed.) (1994) *Coming of Age: Protestantism in Contemporary Latin America*, Lanham, MD: University Press of America.

ROGER L. PARKS

misti

Misti is a social and racial term used by the Bolivian, Ecuadorian and Peruvian Indians to refer to a white person or a **mestizo** who is in a higher economic and social position. The term has a negative connotation for the Indians. It describes a person who exploits the Indians and carries out political, social, and sexual violence against them. The owners of *haciendas* (see **hacienda**), priests and government functionaries who have exploited and subjugated the Indians in the Andean highlands are labelled mistis. However, some Indians could also be called mistis if they assume misti attitudes.

JUAN ZEVALLOS-AGUILAR

Mistral, Gabriela

b. 1889, Vicuña, Chile; d. 1957, New York, USA

Poet

The first Latin American Nobel Prize winner for Literature (1945), Mistral's (real name Lucila Godoy Alcayaga) great contribution to poetry derives from her care and skill with the word. She signed her early work with her own name, until she won the highest award at the Juegos Florales (Floral Games) in Santiago with her 'Sonetos a la muerte' (Sonnets to Death) (1914), and began to use the pseudonym Gabriela Mistral. In 1920 she began a career in education which took her around Chile and all of the Americas. In 1922 she was invited by the then Education Secretary José **Vasconcelos** to participate in Mexico's educational reform. Her *Lecturas de mujeres* (Readings for Women), published in Mexico in 1923, was a key text for the artistic, social and spiritual education of young Latin American women, whom she saw as her 'spiritual family'. The publication of *Desolación* (Desolation) (1922) in New York brought her international recognition. Travelling to Europe for the first time in 1924, she published in Madrid a small volume of poems, *Ternura* (Tenderness), which included her cradle songs, folkloric poems, games and riddles.

Returning to Chile in 1925, she was named secretary of one of the League of Nations' American sections in the following year, beginning a diplomatic career that culminated in 1935 when she was named consul for life. Her travels were interrupted briefly in 1938 when she returned to Chile, and her volume *Tala* was published in Buenos Aires. This was Mistral's own favourite, because it contained 'the root of her Indoamericanism'. One poem in the volume, 'La flor del aire' (Flower of the Air) she described as a manifesto of her key concerns: the link between creation and passion, nature and mother earth, the centrality of the feminine; deep religiosity and a devotion to all living beings; the tensions in creativity; and the nature of poetry itself.

The Nobel Prize was followed by others in recognition of her humanitarian and literary activities. *Lagar*, published in Santiago in 1954, further developed her constant concerns; the search for a poetic language adequate to a complex Latin American identity expressed through the body and sensibility of a woman. Her language is rooted in the classics, in Spanish and Latin American baroque and the writing of Martí; as she said 'old language, new ideas'. She tested each of the experimental schools and moved on, but her preoccupation with the language of her country and of her childhood was constant. When she died after a long illness, she named the companion of her later life, Doris Dana, as her executor and donated all her royalties to the children of Monte Grande, the village where she grew up.

Further reading

Arrigoitia, L. de (1989) *Pensamiento y forma en la prosa de Gabriela Mistral*, San Juan: Ed. de la Universidad de Puerto Rico.

Dana, D. (ed. and trans.) (1961) *Selected Poems of Gabriela Mistral*, Baltimore, MD: The Johns Hopkins Press.

Fariña, S. and Olea, R. (eds) (1990) *Una palabra cómplice: encuentro con Gabriela Mistral*, Santiago, Chile: Isis Internacional/Casa de la Mujer La Morada.

Rubio, P. (1995) *Gabriela Mistral ante la crítica; bibliografía anotada*, Santiago, Chile: Dirección de Archivos y Museos.

ELIANA ORTEGA

MISURASATA

A grassroots organization of indigenous people from the Atlantic Coast of Nicaragua, MISURASATA (Miskitu, Sumu, Rama, Sandinistas Unidos) was created by the Sandinista (see **Sandinista Revolution**) government in 1979 to facilitate the integration of the indigenous peoples into the revolution. In 1980 it developed its own ethnopolitical agenda which conflicted with the revolutionary objectives of national unity and popular participation, and began to receive substantial financial aid from the US government. MISURASATA then split into three conflicting factions: one allied with the **contras** in Honduras, one linked to the contras in Costa Rica, and one which stayed with Nicaragua. In 1984, the Sandinista government granted autonomy to the Atlantic Coast, but its relationship with the MISURASATA remained a conflictual one.

ANUPAMA MANDE AND ILEANA RODRÍGUEZ

Mita

Mita is a religious figure and congregation founded in Puerto Rico in 1940. The 'goddess' Mita, Juanita García Peraza (1897–1970), brought up a Catholic, broke with her adoptive Pentecostalism (see **Pentecostals**) after revelations that she was the Holy Spirit's chosen incarnation. 'Mita' ('Spirit of Life') was God's newly revealed name. After creation by Jehovah the Father, and redemption by Christ the Son, the era of Mita, God the Mother, marks the final 'gathering' of the dispersed children of God. Aarón (Teófilo Vargas Seín) became Mita's heir and prophet in 1970. Strong among the working class, the cult has organized socioeconomically into an Utopian urban community around Congregación Mita Inc., a diversified cooperative business with headquarters in San Juan's Duarte Street and chapters in several Latin American countries and major cities in the United States.

See also: popular saints and popular religion; virgins, miraculous

ERIK CAMAYD-FREIXAS

Mitre family

The Mitres were a patriarchal Buenos Aires family. In 1862 Bartolomé Mitre (1824–1906) became President of the Republic and founded the newspaper *La nación*. The family produced soldiers, engineers, lawyers, poets and journalists who edited the daily. Mitre family members were elected to Congress, helped to found the Republican party, the **Unión Cívica Radical** (UCR or Radical Party) and the National Academy of History. The family home and first office of the newspaper is now the Mitre museum, a historical monument containing a library with important collections on San Martín, Belgrano and Latin American culture. The family still owns *La nación*.

VICTOR PAVÓN

Mittelholzer, Edgar Austin

b. 1909, New Amsterdam, British Guyana; d. 1965, London, England

Writer

Of his twenty-three novels and two nonfiction books, the novels *A Morning at the Office* (1950), which looks carefully at five hours of race and class in Trinidad; *My Bones and My Flute* (1955), probably one of the best ghost stories ever written; and *The Life and Death of Sylvia* or *Sylvia* (1953), show Mittelholzer's descriptive powers at their best. He had an obsessive interest in Oriental occultism and psychical research. His mental deterioration became obvious in later novels like *The Wounded and the Worried* (1962) and *The Harrowing of Hubertus* (1954). He eventually committed suicide by setting himself on fire.

KEITH JARDIM

Modern Art Week

An art exhibition in São Paulo in 1922, Modern Art Week (Semana de Arte Moderno) challenged academic language and artistic pretensions and advocated change. Most of the organizers (the fauvist painter Anita **Malfatti** and the cubist di **Cavalcanti**, the sculptor **Brecheret**, and the musician **Villa-Lobos**) had spent years in Europe and were influenced by the Parisian avant-garde. Oswald de **Andrade**, a journalist and poet from São Paulo, met Marinetti in Italy; shortly thereafter he began to argue for an art of renewal that would express Brazilian reality and not simply mimic

European models: 'tupi or not tupi' - an ironic rewriting of Shakespeare's 'to be or not to be' referencing the indigenous Brazialian **Tupi** language and ethnic group. Some nationalist writers, like Monteiro **Lobato**, attacked the show.

RAUL ANTELO

modernism, Brazilian *see* Brazilian modernism

modernismo, Spanish American

Spanish American *modernismo* refers primarily to a late nineteenth- and early twentieth-century literary movement incorporating elements of French symbolism and decadence with highly elaborated language. As such, it is sharply differentiated from later Anglo-American and Brazilian modernisms (see **modernism, Brazilian**). Nonetheless, its dynamism is based on a convergence of cultural and social factors which reshaped the role of the writer in Spanish America. The first generation of professional writers, many of them *modernistas* like José Martí, Rubén Darío, Julián del Casal and Manuel Gutiérrez Nájera were journalists, and many lacked aristocratic antecedents. Connected through an international network of periodicals and heightened cultural exchange, they helped to forge a new Spanish American literary unity. Often criticized for their exotic themes and highly wrought language, their openness to cosmopolitan trends reshaped the contours of writing in the continent, from Mexico to the **Southern Cone**, as well as influencing poetry in Spain. Particularly important were their contributions to newspapers and literary magazines, products of an expanded continental reading public. *Modernista* style includes both fiction and poetry, yet its most enduring legacy is associated with a certain style of poetry. *Modernismo*'s primary exponent, the Nicaraguan Rubén Darío (1867–1916), exemplifies the heterogeneous nature of the movement's impulses and achievements. Darío, while exalting the European (especially French) legacy in his poetry – *Azul* (Blue) (1888) and *Prosas profanas* (Profane prose) (1896) – revitalized poetic language in Spanish by exploring musicality, archaic forms and formal innovation. His *Cantos de vida y esperanza* (Songs of Life and Hope) (1905) includes a focus on New World cultures, with a sharp critique of the emerging materialist culture of the USA (an echo of José Enrique Rodó's 1900 essay *Ariel*).

Another direction of *modernismo* was initiated by the Cuban Jose Martí (1853–95), whose *Ismaelillo* (1882) and *Versos sencillos* (Simple Verses) (1891) incorporated popular poetic forms into literary modernity. Independence hero and cultural leader, Martí combined the roles of statesman, orator, journalist, novelist and poet in his prolific but brief career. In contrast to many *modernistas*, Martí's spare poetic style has had an enduring resonance in Latin American letters.

As readership expanded dramatically due to public education, journalism became increasingly important. Periodicals offered employment to writers and a medium for their creative works. Especially important in the period was the **crónica**, an essay form which included social and cultural commentary in an individualistic style, published in major newspapers and specialized magazines. Notable *cronistas* were Martí, Darío, Manuel Gutiérrez Nájera, and José Asunción Silva. The two most important, though short-lived, *modernista* magazines were the *Revista Azul* (Mexico) and *Revista de América* (Buenos Aires, founded by Darío and Jaimes Freyre).

Modernista prose fiction is more difficult to define, for its densely figured and ornate language was used in the service of novels and short stories of very different kinds. Inspiration drawn from symbolist and decadent movements can be seen in fictions ranging from regionalist emphasis (see **regionalismo**) to **science fiction** to prose poems. It is in prose that *modernismo* and naturalism cross paths, for naturalism's emphasis on physicality merged with the luxuriance of *modernista* style. The short story (Martí, Darío, Silva, Leopoldo **Lugones**) was more important than the novel.

Modernismo is most remembered for its expansion and elaboration of poetic forms in Spanish. Here Spanish America led Spain in the revitalization of literature. Martí's inclusion of the popular octosyllable, Darío's renewal of the alexandrine and medieval forms as well as his adaptations of French poetics, and an almost religious attention to form in general display the innovative impulse of the *modernistas*. Yet their adherence to elaborate form was precisely the element that later generations, most famously González Martínez in Mexico and **Borges** in the 1920s, rejected as overwrought 'rubendarismo'. Even *modernista* contemporaries had their doubts about the preoccupation with baroque language, physicality, and sometimes slavish attention to French culture. In particular, José Enrique Rodó was suspicious of Darío's early publications for their inattention to local concern and insistence on distant times and lands. Such criticisms were noted, especially by Darío, whose later poetry warns against the encroachment of the USA in Latin American territories and cultures. Later *modernista* poetry, particularly Leopoldo Lugones's *Lunario sentimental* (1909) and poetry by Uruguay's Julio Herrera y Reissig, carried *modernista* style to the breaking point through mockery and exaggeration, setting the stage for the rebellion of the following generation.

Overt eroticism is a major component of *modernismo*, particularly in its portrayal of the female through the evocation of the femme fatale, and this legacy has been as important as the renewal of poetic language. Because sexuality was centred on the female as object of the male gaze, the disruption of this axis created consternation. Uruguay's Delmira Agustini (1886–1914) entered the poetic scene when *modernismo* was in full force. Her poetry, open in its expression of female sexuality, turns around *modernista* iconology and reverses the gaze, often with violent imagery.

Modernismo has been critically reevaluated, after decades of dismissal, by figures like Octavio **Paz** and Angel **Rama**. Viewing *modernismo* in the context of modernization in Latin America, they signal the complexities of its innovations and legacies. Paz, in particular, sees Darío as initiator of a movement to insert Latin American aesthetics into international dynamics; Rama studies the movement as an elaborate baroque edifice constructed against the onslaught of the popular which accompanies modernization. These views have made the study of *modernismo* an indispensable element for the debates on modernity within Latin American throughout the twentieth century.

See also: arielismo

Further reading

Aching, G. (1997) *The Politics of Spanish American Modernismo, By Exquisite Design*, Cambridge: Cambride University Press.

Gonzalez, A. (1993) *Journalism and the Development of Spanish American Narrative*, Cambridge: Cambridge University Press.

Jiménez, J.O. (1985) *Antología de la poesía modernista*, Madrid: Hiperión.

Jrade, C. (1983) *Rubén Darío and the Romantic Search for Unity. The Modernist Recourse to Esoteric Tradition*, Austin, TX: University of Texas Press.

Kirkpatrick, G. (1989) *The Dissonant Legacy of Modernismo. Lugones, Herrera y Reissig and the Voices of Modern Spanish American Poetry*, Berkeley: University of California Press.

Paz, O. (1969) *Cuadrivio*, Mexico City: Joaquín Mortiz.

Rama, A. (1985) *Las máscaras democráticas del modernismo*, Montevideo: Fundación Angel Rama.

GWEN KIRKPATRICK

modernity *see* cultural theory

molas

Molas were originally highly decorated blouses worn by the Kuna women of the San Blas islands, Panama. At first, the designs were borrowed from flora, fauna and abstract designs similar to those used previously in body painting. After the Second World War, traditional designs underwent a process of acculturation. To satisfy growing tourist demand, the Kunas adapted and merchandized the blouses into framable wall hangings. As an art form, molas consists of different coloured fabrics cut away to make designs. Since the 1960s, molas have become a primary source of income for the entire San Blas region.

NORMAN S. HOLLAND

Moliendo Café

One of Venezuela's best known popular songs, 'Moliendo café' (Grinding Coffee) was written in 1959 by the Caracas-born musician Hugo Blanco. It was his first composition, and it achieved immense popularity in the 1960s, both in Venezuela and abroad. It is a song with traditional roots, but composed in a new rhythm, which Blanco labeled *ritmo orquídea* (orchid rhythm). The lyrics tell of a black worker who sings about his frustrated love whilst he works at night, grinding coffee. Over two hundred versions of the song have been recorded, involving such artists as **Pérez Prado**, Ray Coniff and Plácido Domingo.

MARK DINNEEN

Molina, Enrique

b. 1910, Buenos Aires, Argentina; d. 1997, Buenos Aires

Poet

An older member of the 1940 generation influenced by surrealism (see **surrealism in Latin American art**), Molina's poetry evoked the world of childhood and daily life, respecting the capacity of simple domestic objects to preserve traces of human history. In the 1950s he edited *A partir de 0. Revista de poesía y antipoesía* (Starting from Zero: Review of Poetry and Antipoetry) reviving the surrealist strand earlier espoused by Aldo **Pellegrini**. His first novel, *Una sombra donde sueña Camila O' Gorman* (A Shadow Where Camila O' Gorman Dreams) (1984) narrates the tragic love story of Camila and Ladislao Gutiérrez.

MAGDALENA GARCÍA PINTO

Molina, Horacio

b. 1935, Buenos Aires, Argentina

Musician

A self-taught guitarist, Molina debuted with an album of ballads and boleros (see **bolero**) with Sergio Mihanovich and Oscar López Ruiz. In 1970 he moved to Spain; returning to Buenos Aires in 1975 he recorded an album called *Por los amigos* (For My Friends). A composer and singer of boleros, jazz and **bossa nova**, he became known on the Argentine musical scene for his interpretation of tangos (see **tango**). He has performed with the Brazilian musician Vinicius de **Moraes**. He has recorded some 200 songs, many of them his own.

CLAUDIA TORRE

Molina, Miguel de

b. 1907, Málaga, Spain; d. 1993, Buenos Aires, Argentina

Singer and dancer

Already a successful singer and dancer when he went into exile from Franco's Spain in 1942, in Argentina Molina found an enthusiastic audience for his interpretation of songs like 'La bien pagá' (The Well-Paid Woman) and 'Ojos verdes' (Green Eyes), but was imprisoned for homosexuality in 1943. He appeared in several films, including *Esta es mi vida* (This is My Life) (1952), directed by Román Viñoly Barreto. The central character of the 1989 Spanish film *Las cosas del querer* (Things of Love), directed by Jaime Chávarri was based on him, but Molina himself, by then in retirement, never acknowledged the similarity.

LAURA SIRI

Molina, Uriel

b. 1930, Matagalpa, Nicaragua

Catholic priest

Nicaragua's leading Biblical scholar, Molina preached against social injustice and oppression from his humble Managua parish of Fátima. In 1973 he and Fernando Cardenal founded the Movimento Cristiano Revolucionario (MCR). Despite mutual distrust, the MCR provided the Sandinistas (see **Sandinista Revolution**) with safe houses and recruitment at the request of Tomás **Borge**, a Sandinista leader and former schoolfriend of Molina. After the 1979 Sandinista triumph, Molina and Baptist minister José Miguel Torres organized the Centro Antonio Valdivieso (CAV) to maintain the revolutionary spirit among Christians. Today it documents the history of Christian involvement in Latin America's liberation struggles.

ESTEBAN LOUSTAUNAU AND ILEANA RODRÍGUEZ

Molinari, Ricardo

b. 1898, Buenos Aires, Argentina; d. 1996, Buenos Aires

Poet

Molinari belonged to the Argentine avant-garde (see **avant-garde in Latin America**) group represented by the magazine *Martín Fierro*. His writings are informed not only by *ultraísmo* and surrealism (see **surrealism in Latin American art**) but also by the classical Hispanic tradition. His poetry frequently combines metaphysical concerns with an interrogation of the American condition. The landscape of the *pampas* (see ***pampa***) is presented in some of his poems as a lyrical space. He was awarded, among other distinctions, the Premio Nacional de Literatura in 1958. The collection of poems, *Las sombras del pájaro tostado* (The Shadows of the Brown Bird) (1974), encompasses his numerous books.

FERNANDO J. ROSENBERG

Molloy, Sylvia

b. 1939, Buenos Aires, Argentina

Writer

Molloy is one of the most insightful contemporary Latin American literary critics, and a creative writer of remarkable originality. Educated in Buenos Aires and at the Sorbonne in Paris, she later emigrated to the USA where she has taught at Princeton, Yale and is currently the Albert Schweitzer Professor of the Humanities at New York University.

Her critical career began with *La Diffusion de la littérature hispanoaméricaine en France* (The Dissemination of Spanish American Literature in France) (1972), written for her doctoral degree. A great admirer of Jorge Luis **Borges**, her *Las letras de Borges* (Signs of Borges) (1979) deals with the uncanny in Borges, exploring the fragile nuances and fragmentations in Borges's speaking subject. Her study *At Face Value: Autobiographical Writing in Spanish America* (1991) looks at the paradoxical nature of narratives that attempt the impossible task of telling their own story and has had considerable impact on how **autobiography** is understood in contemporary culture. She co-edited a valuable anthology, *Women's Writing in Latin America* (1991) with Sara Castro-Klarén and Beatriz **Sarlo**, including, among others, authors like Gabriela **Mistral**, Raquel de **Queiroz**, Norah **Lange**, Blanca **Varela**, Nancy **Morejón**, Hebe de **Bonafini** and Lourdes Arizpe.

As a writer of fiction, she first experimented with short stories published in the literary journals of Buenos Aires. While writing her study on Borges, she also began *En breve cárcel* (Certificate of Absence) (1981), a third-person novel exploring the narrator's confinement in the prison house of love and language. Its protagonist and narrator unveils a love triangle among three women that brings to the protagonist despair and a deep sense of emptiness. It is a narrative search for self and the recovered memories of childhood that haunt the character in her most vulnerable moments of uncertainty. The craft of the novel and the thematics of lesbian love have elicited a long list of critical studies that have hailed it as 'the most notable lesbian novel to date in Latin American literature'.

Further reading

Foster, D.W. (1991) *Gay and Lesbian Latin American Writing*, Austin, TX: University of Texas Press.

Kaminsky, A. (1993) 'Sylvia Molloy's Lesbian Cartographies: Body, Text and Geography', *Reading the Body Politic: Feminist Criticism and Latin American Women Writers*, Minneapolis, MN: University of Minnesota Press, 96–114.

Martínez, E. (1996) 'Lesbian Eroticism and the Act of Writing: Sylvia Molloy's *Certificate of Absence*', *Lesbian Voices from Latin America*, New York: Garland, pp. 143–66.

MAGDALENA GARCÍA PINTO

Monar, Rooplall

b. 1945, Lusignan Estate, East Coast Demerara, British Guiana

Writer

One of the few Guyanese writers permanently resident there, his novel, *Janjhat* (Peepal Tree) (1989) and three collections of short stories, *Backdam People* (1985), *Estate People* (1994) and *High House and Radio* (1992), are considered to be some of the best stories on Guyanese Indian life. His collection of poems, *Koker*, was published in 1987 and won the Guyana Prize for poetry that year, one of several prizes he has won. Monar has been a teacher, an estate book-keeper, a journalist and healer.

KEITH JARDIM

Moncayo, José Pablo

b. 1912, Guadalajara, Mexico; d. 1958, Mexico City

Musician

First conductor of the Mexican National Symphony Orchestra (1949–54), composer, pianist and percussionist, Moncayo studied with Carlos **Chávez** and Candelario **Huízar** in Mexico and Aaron Copland in the United States. His work expresses the impressionistic and neoclassical currents of his period. His best known symphonic pieces, like *Huapango* (which is the most popular Mexican symphonic work), *Tierra de temporal* (Land of Storms), *Sinfonietta* and *Bosques* (Forests), display his particular skill in orchestration. He wrote works for piano (like *Muros verdes* (Green Walls)) and an opera, *La mulata de Córdoba*, with libretto by Xavier **Villaurrutia** and Agustín **Lazo**, which is the most frequently performed Mexican **opera**.

EDUARDO CONTRERAS SOTO

Mondolfo, Rodolfo

b. 1877, Senigallia, Italy; d. 1976, Buenos Aires, Argentina

Philosopher

A brilliant scholar who specialized in Plato and ancient philosophy, Mondolfo was also an expert on Marxism (see **Marxism in Latin America**). He studied in Florence and taught in Padua, Turin and Bologna. In 1938, fascist racial laws drove him from Italy and he moved to Argentina, lecturing at several universities. He rejected linearity and non-contextualization of the history of philosophy, emphasizing the plurality of forces operating in any given period and their historical determination in *La comprensión del sujeto humano en la cultura antigua* (The Understanding of the Human Subject in Ancient Culture) (1969).

FERNANDO RABOSSI

Monsiváis, Carlos

b. 1938, Mexico City

Writer

One of the foremost authorities on Mexican literature and popular culture in the last third of the twentieth century, Carlos Monsiváis is the most important cultural critic and humourist in a generation of Mexican intellectuals which includes José Emilio **Pacheco**, Sergio **Pitol**, and Elena **Poniatowska**. Monsiváis rose to prominence through cultural journalism, directing the Mexico City weekly *La Cultura en México* (the supplement to *Siempre*) from 1972–87. A truly public figure, he publishes essays in all of Mexico City's major newspapers and magazines, including the column, 'A mi madre, bohemios' (To my Mother, Bohemians), in the newspaper *La Jornada*. He is also a regular television commentator.

Monsiváis's writings encompass the entire range of Mexican art and culture, and include major contributions on literary history, popular culture, the politics of nationalism, film, sexuality, and the visual and plastic arts. Within this broad field of study, he is perhaps best known as the premier chronicler of daily life in Mexico City. As early as 1966, Emanuel Carballo noted that Monsiváis was destined to inherit this role from Salvador **Novo**. However, where Novo chronicled the rise of Mexico City to become the centre of a major industrial economy, Monsiváis has chronicled the capital's struggles through a long series of political, economic, and ecological crises. Beginning with the student movement in 1968, Monsiváis has written on diverse social phenomena, including the 1985 earthquake which devastated Mexico City (see **earthquakes**), the celebrations of Mexican **football**/soccer fans, the struggles for indigenous self-determination in Juchitán, Oaxaca, and efforts to reform Mexico's labour movement.

Despite the difficult history Monsiváis has chronicled, his work is far from pessimistic. A highly synthetic thinker, Monsiváis's writings are always in touch with the latest trends in cultural theory but simultaneously engaged with the quotidian experience of popular culture. He never loses sight of the larger structures of power which overdetermine many aspects of commercial culture, but Monsiváis developed as an intellectual in the 1970s, when the leftist intelligentsia of Latin America began to absorb the writings of Antonio Gramsci. In keeping with a generally Gramscian approach to cultural history, Monsiváis has always defended popular culture as a powerful reservoir for alternative nationalist sentiments corrosive to the chauvinistic or authoritarian forms of nationalism promoted by Mexico's single-party state. A central feature of Monsiváis's engagement with popular culture on this level is his own acerbic sense of humour, which celebrates the liberating elements of **kitsch** while maintaining an ironic distance from the rapid-fire world of fashion, consumption, and changing style. His broad-ranging analyses have included foundational essays on personalities across the spectrum of Mexican culture, ranging from politics (Fidel **Velásquez**), humour (**Cantinflas**, Jis y Trino), literature (Salvador Novo, Juan **Rulfo**, José **Revueltas**), music (Agustín **Lara**, José Alfredo **Jiménez**, **Luis Miguel**, Gloria **Trevi**), art (David Alfaro **Siqueiros**, Jesús Helguera), film (Irma **Serrano**, María **Félix**, Dolores **Del Rio**) and boxing (Julio César **Chávez**).

Like other prominent intellectuals of his generation, Monsiváis has maintained an independent position as a professional writer and has never worked in any state-run institution.

Further reading

Monsiváis, C. (1966) *Carlos Monsiváis*, with introduction by E. Carballo, Mexico City: Empresas Editoriales.
—— (1997) *Mexican Postcards* trans. with introduction by J. Kraniauskas, London: Verso.
Mudrovcic, M.E. (1998) 'Cultura nacionalista v cultura nacional: Carlos Monsiváis ante la sociedad de masas' in *Hispamérica* 79: 29–39.

BRIAN GOLLNICK

Montaner, Rita

b. 1900, Guanabacoa, Cuba; d. 1958, Havana

Singer

In 1927 Montaner was included by Ernesto **Lecuona** in the cast of the zarzuela *Niña Rita*; her song 'Mama Inés' caused a sensation in Cuba and the United States. A singer clearly rooted in the black music of Cuba, she began making films in 1938 and appeared in vernacular theatre to packed houses. She performed with **Bola de Nieve** before moving to the Tropicana, where she sang for nine years. In 1950, when the first Cuban **television** channel was launched, she appeared with Guillermo Alvarez Guedes in 'Rita y Willy'. She continued to act on screen and stage; her last performance in 1957 came shortly before her death of cancer.

JOSÉ ANTONIO EVORA

Monte, Marisa

b. 1967, Rio de Janeiro, Brazil

Singer

Marisa Monte emerged in the 1990s as the most acclaimed female interpreter of **MPB**. Following a period in Italy studying opera, Monte returned to Brazil determined to pursue a career in popular music. She recorded an eponymous live album in 1989, followed by *Mais* in 1992, *Rose and Charcoal* in 1994 and *Good Sound* in 1996, which all included her own compositions. She has collaborated with key Brazilian composer-musicians of her generation, including Carlinhos **Brown**, Arnaldo **Antunes** and Nando Reis. In tune with Brazilian musical tradition and international pop trends, Monte is noted for assembling eclectic repertoires of songs and styles.

CHRISTOPHER DUNN

Monte Avila

A state-owned company founded in 1968, Monte Avila is Venezuela's largest publisher, and one of the biggest in Latin America. It is run without a profit-making objective, and the prices of its publications have always been kept low in order to make them as accessible as possible. That policy, and the quality of its publications, account for its high reputation throughout Latin America. It has played a valuable role in the mass production of educational texts for all levels, but its vast output covers a wide range of disciplines, including literature and the arts, philosophy, history and the social sciences. Its current director is Alexis **Márquez Rodríguez**.

MARK DINNEEN

Montealegre, Jorge

b. 1954, Santiago, Chile

Poet

Montealegre's poetic itinerary starts with the paradoxical circumstances of Chilean exile life during the 1970s in Europe in *Exilios* (Exiles) (1983), continues with the excruciating life conditions of Santiago shanty town (see **shanty towns and slums**) dwellers after **Pinochet**'s 1973 *coup d'état* in *Título de Dominio* (Certificate of Entitlement) (1980), and becomes a sharp critical view of the social and ideological transformations produced by the return to democracy in *Bien común* (Common Share) (1995). His keen eye for cultural contradictions reveals itself constantly as punning and wordplay.

OSCAR D. SARMIENTO

Montecino, Sonia

b. 1954, Santiago, Chile

Writer and anthropologist

Montecino's work is focused on issues of Chilean feminine identity, ranging from the essays *Mujeres de la tierra* (Women of the Earth) (1984) and *Madres y huachos: alegorías del mestizaje chileno* (Mothers and Chileans: Allegories of Chilean Mestizaje) (1991), to the novel *La revuelta* (The Revolt) (1988), which focuses on the conflictive situation of women and their responses to dictatorial political oppression. She directs the Women's Studies Programme at the University of Chile.

ELIANA ORTEGA

Monteforte Toledo, Mario

b. 1911, Guatemala City

Writer, politician and sociologist

Monteforte made a significant contribution to Guatemalan fiction by representing indigenous and **ladino** perspectives. Expelled from the University of San Carlos for his opposition to **Ubico**, he studied in Paris in the 1930s and then returned to live in the countryside to experience Indian culture. His psychological, populist and social realist narratives avoid the romanticizing and posturing of picturesque *indigenismo*. His two 1948 novels, *Anaite* and *Entre la piedra y la cruz* (Between the Rock and the Cross), are among his best written and richest. Monteforte was Vice President under Arévalo in the 1940s, but resigned, anticipating future dissent within the left.

MARC ZIMMERMAN AND LINDA CRAFT

Monteiro, Vicente do Rego

b. 1899, Recife, Brazil; d. 1970, Recife

Painter

Monteiro was a pioneer in finding inspiration for his work in the indigenous cultures of his country. He uniquely combined their geometrism with his personal interpretation of the modernist currents, particularly cubism, that he encountered during his long years in Paris. Monteiro's bold geometric figures, monumental in quality, are carefully organized against a simplified background of subtle tonal variations. His iconography includes South American motifs like the jaguar and scenes of Christian inspiration, reflecting his connections with the cultural life of both Brazil and France.

TANIA COSTA TRIBE

Montejo, Eugenio

b. 1938, Caracas, Venezuela

Poet

Montejo's first volume, *Elegos* (1967), won him an immediate reputation as a poet of landscape and of experience. His most emblematic book, *Terredad* (1978), brilliantly reflects his capacity to embrace the world through the simplest of language and the most serene of images. Montejo resists any temptation to exuberance and offers images of rural and urban landscapes whose constitutive essence reveals itself to the poet's penetrating glance. The core of his poetry, therefore, is temperate, colloquial, almost philosophical, as is obvious in other works like *Trópico absoluto* (Absolute Tropics) (1982), *Alfabeto del mundo* (Alphabet of the World) (1986), *Adiós al siglo XX* (Farewell to the 20th Century) (1992), now collected in a single *Antología* (1996). Montejo also wrote under a number of heteronyms a range of other volumes including *La guitarra del horizonte* (The Guitar of the Horizon) (1991) and *El hacha de seda* (The Silk Axe) (1995). *La ventana oblicua* (The Oblique Window) (1974) and *El taller blanco* (The White Workshop) (1996) include the bulk of his essays.

RAFAEL CASTILLO ZAPATA

Montenegro, Carlos

b. 1900, Puebla del Caraminal, Spain; d. 1981, Miami, USA

Writer

Montenegro was a merchant seaman and itinerant worker throughout Central America and the USA, before spending twelve years in jail (1919–31) in Havana. There he began to write and became a communist. Through the 1930s he edited several socialist newspapers, including *La Palabra* and *Hoy*. He went into exile in 1959. He wrote short stories, but his finest literary achievement is *Hombres sin mujer* (Men without Women) (1938), a brutal novel about Cuban prison life and an early approach to the theme of homosexuality. The novel was only republished in Cuba in 1995.

WILFREDO CANCIO ISLA

Montenegro, Fernanda

b. 1929, Minas Gerais, Brazil

Actress

A self-made woman, Montenegro (born Arlette Pinheiro Esteves da Silva) began her extraordinary career as a teenager in radio soap operas and made her stage début in 1950 appearing with Fernando Torres, who later became her husband. In the 1960s she became a fixture on TV **Globo** mini-series and ***telenovelas***. She made her filmic début in Leon **Hirszman**'s *A falecida* (The Deceased) (1964), a Nelson **Rodrigues** adaptation, and has appeared in dozens of films since, although the theatre continues to be her first and most constant passion. Her most famous screen appearance was her role in Walter Salles's *Central do Brasil* (1998), which earned her an Academy Award nomination for best actress. Described as a Brazilian Judi Dench, she has been acclaimed for her 'rubber face' – her uncanny ability to change expression and portray her character's emotions.

ANA M. LÓPEZ

Montero, Mayra

b. 1952, Havana, Cuba

Writer

Montero's fiction is sustained by the Afro-Caribbean world. The suffocating magical world of **Vodun** is the setting for her first story collection, *Veintitrés y una tortuga* (Twenty-Three and a Turtle) (1981). Her first novel, *La trenza de la hermosa luna* (The Plait of the Beautiful Moon) (1987), retains the Haitian setting and follows the crisis of an individual returning to his land and beliefs. In *Tú, la oscuridad* (You, Darkness) (1995), the work of a herpes specialist in Haiti is interrupted by the shadow of death and violence. *Como un mensajero tujo* (The Messager) (1998) is set during Enrico Caruso's visit to Havana in 1920 and set against a background of **Santería** rites.

MARIA JULIA DAROQUI

Monterroso Bonilla, Augusto

b. 1921, Guatemala City

Writer

Guatemala's most famous living author, and one of the many writers exiled after the fall of the **Arbenz** government in 1954, Augusto 'Tito' Monterroso spent his mature life in Mexico. He wrote several collections of fables which broke with the realistic dimensions of the Guatemalan prose tradition and won him an international reputation. Monterroso's stories are characterized by whimsy, irony, allegory and intellectual probing with little overt social content, although there are some obvious and famous exceptions: for example, in his story of multinational, imperialist and **CIA** intervention in Latin America, 'Mister Taylor'.

MARC ZIMMERMAN AND LINDA CRAFT

Montes, Amparo

b. 1924, Tapachula, Chiapas, Mexico

Singer

In 1970, Amparo Montes (Amparo Meza Cruz) opened her club La Cueva de Amparo (Amparo's Cave), where she has sung, performed and acted as master of ceremonies ever since. Having gone to Mexico City to study accountancy in 1938, her single appearance on radio station XEQ's programme 'Quiero trabajar' (I Want to Work) brought an invitation to sing on the same station with pianist Gonzalo Cervera. In 1944 she moved to XEW, and began to tour the whole of Mexico.

MARIANNA POOL WESTGAARD

Monti, Ricardo

b. 1944, Buenos Aires, Argentina

Playwright

Monti's productions in the 1970s were expressly political and synonymous with rupture and the search for a new theatrical language. *Una noche con el Sr. Magnus e Hijos* (One Night with Mr Magnus and Sons) (1970) and *Historia tendenciosa de la clase media argentina* (Tendentious History of the Argentine Middle Class) (1971) set out to unmask social hypocrisies. From *Visita* (Visit) (1977) to *Una pasión sudamericana* (A South American Passion) (1989), he continued to comment upon society, though less vehemently. Reelaborating **grotesco criollo** and the theatre of the absurd, his poetic plays were staged in sinister sets often employing masks and found objects.

STELLA MARTINI

Montoneros

Ultra-nationalist Peronist (see **Peronism**) faction emerging from Argentina's Catholic corporativist tradition to become an active guerrilla army from 1969 to 1977. The movement opposed foreign influence, wrapping itself in nationalist symbols. The political front of the Montoneros, the Peronist Youth, promoted a **socialism** loosely based on the ideas of **liberation theology** and the example of Evita **Perón**. Initially encouraged by Juan **Perón** while in exile but rejected in 1974, the Montoneros (led by Mario **Firmenich**) engaged in a spectacular series of kidnappings, assassinations, robberies and guerrilla operations. The armed forces defeated them, destroying their support base within Argentina in a vicious offensive known as the Dirty War.

THOMAS EDSALL

Montoya, Juan Pablo

b. 1975, Bogotá, Colombia

Racing-car driver

Montoya's international-celebrity status was guaranteed by his victory at the Indianapolis 500 in May 2000. However, he had already found fame in Colombia as a child go-cart champion in the years 1981–4. After this, he went on to win the junior championship in autoracing in France in 1992, then studied with Skip Barber, and picked up various national and international prizes in the following years. His triumph at Indianapolis (a previous winner was Emerson **Fittipaldi**) was decisive, and promises a brilliant future in the sport.

DANIEL BALDERSTON

Montoya, María Teresa

b. 1900, Mexico City; d. 1970, Mexico City

Actress

One of the foremost tragic actresses in Mexican theatre, Montoya began her career during the Mexican Revolution (see **revolutions**), and at age seventeen founded her own touring company under the auspices of General Pablo González. She played leading roles in plays by European, Russian, North American and South American playwrights, receiving numerous awards during her career. She is likewise credited with being one of the first supporters of Mexican playwrights, including the little-known theatrical work of politician and essayist José **Vasconcelos** (she starred in his *Mariana la mancornadora* in 1935). Her last performance was in a 1963 production of Brecht's *Mother Courage*.

ANTONIO PRIETO-STAMBAUGH

Montuvio ecuatoriano, El

An essay by José de la **Cuadra**, *El montuvio ecuatoriano* (The Montuvio of Ecuador) (1937) is a study of the *montuvio*, the archetypical inhabitant of the costal area of Ecuador, and the inspiration for much of the literature produced by the members of the **Guayaquil Group**, particularly de la Cuadra himself. The book presents geographical, sociological, anthropological, and ethnic information about the *montuvio*, the product of a mixture of three races: 60 per cent Indian, 30 per cent black and 10 per cent white. The essay interprets the *montuvio*'s literary history, as well as his criminal, political and mythical tendencies.

HUMBERTO E. ROBLES

Monumento a la Revolución

Porfirio Diaz's project for a Legislative Palace, designed by French architect Emile Bénard in 1900, was suspended at the onset of the Mexican Revolution (see **revolutions**). By 1912, only the steel frame of the central hall and dome had been completed. Winning a 1933 competition to transform this skeleton into a Monument to the Revolution, architect Carlos Obregón Santacilia produced a modified triumphal arch faced in limestone with a copper-covered dome. Situated on a raised esplanade, the 65-metre-high monument is decorated with four sculptural groups by Oliverio Martínez (1901–38). Completed in 1938, the austere, modernist monument houses the tombs of revolutionary heroes and serves as a site for official government rallies.

JAMES OLES

Monumento aos Bandeirantes

On 20 June 1920, Víctor **Brecheret** won a competition sponsored by the Brazilian government, to sculpt a monument honoring the *bandeirantes*, members of armed expeditions of Portuguese explorers in the colonial period who explored the interior seeking precious stones and expanding Brazilian territory. Simultaneously, Portuguese immigrants in São Paulo commissioned Teixeira Lopes to sculpt a similar monument. Because of the resulting disagreements and protests, both projects were shelved. In 1936, Brecheret finally began working on an immense granite block from which he sculpted thirty-seven figures. *Monumento aos Bandeirantes*, Brecheret's most famous sculpture, was unveiled in Parque Ibirapuera, São Paulo in 1953.

MARIA JOSÉ SOMERLATE BARBOSA

Monumento Cósmico

Built in 1937 in Montevideo's Parque Rodó, in front of the city's National Museum of Visual Arts, the Monumento Cósmico was the first monument of its kind created in Latin America by Joaquín **Torres García**. It was made out of individual blocks of pink granite on which were carved, in bas relief, universal microcosmic symbols representing the vocabulary of constructivism. On the stone wall parapet, Torres García placed a cube, a sphere and a pyramid, pure forms representing respectively wisdom, perfection and creation. From the work's base there emerge a fountain and a seat.

MARCO MAGGI

Monzón, Carlos

b. 1942, Santa Fe, Argentina; d. 1995, Buenos Aires, Argentina

Boxer

Monzón's life story could be entitled 'the rise and fall of an idol'. His sporting career was crowned with success; he retired without injuries in 1977, having won two world middleweight titles (the first in 1969). He belonged to the jet set and appeared in films. His fall began one drunken night in 1988 when he threw his wife from the balcony of their summer house. She died instantly and Monzón spent the rest of his life in jail, dying in an auto accident while on parole shortly before the end of his term.

GONZALO AGUILAR

moqueca

A popular Brazilian dish, which, according to Gilberto **Freyre**, was adapted by African slaves in the northeast from the indigenous Pokekas in the kitchens of the plantation *casas grandes* (big owners' houses). Originally it was a ragout of fish or shellfish cooked in **dendé oil** and pepper, and then wrapped in banana leaves and roasted in coals. Nowadays, it is cooked in black clay casseroles on regular stoves and, although the presentation may be less picturesque, it remains an excellent dish when prepared by the skilled cooks known as *quituteiras*, who zealously guard their recipes. The stew, which now typically includes a rich broth of fish stock, coconut milk and *dendé*, is served steaming and sputtering, accompanied by *pirão*, a mulled creamy paste of fish bits, *farinha* (ground **manioc** flour), broth and *dendé*. There are also many regional variations, such as the *moqueca capixaba* typical of the state of Paraíba.

ANA M. LÓPEZ

Mora, Lola

b. 1867, Trancas, Tucumán, Argentina; d. 1936, Buenos Aires, Argentina

Sculptor

Of Indian and Spanish descent, Dolores ('Lola') Mora was the first woman sculptor in Argentina. As a young artist, she studied in Rome with sculptors Barbella and Monteverde, and became acquainted with other European artists. She returned to Argentina in 1900, and was commissioned to realize two remarkable works: a fountain featuring the Birth of Venus for the city of Buenos Aires, today in the Avenida Costanera, and the bas-reliefs for the restoration of the Casa de Tucumán, the site of Argentina's declaration of independence. She lived a tragic life and died forgotten by all in a street accident.

MAGDALENA GARCÍA PINTO

Morada, La

Founded in 1983 in the context of the Chilean military dictatorship, the Casa de la Mujer La Morada (La Morada Women's Centre) was formed as a feminist collective with the object of 'exposing the subordination and discrimination suffered by women, and contributing to the development of a critical gender consciousness in the face of an oppression deepened by military dictatorship'. Its founders – Julieta **Kirkwood**, Margarita **Pisano**, Antonieta Saa and Eliana Largo – represented the most activist group within a Chilean feminist (see **feminism**) movement re-emerging in 1979 and constituted as the Círculo de Estudios de la Mujer (Women's Studies Circle). The Circle embraced two currents: researchers, who set up the Centro de Estudios de la Mujer (CEM), and the group dedicated to militant activity organized in the Casa de la Mujer La Morada. La Morada brought together women of different ages and social backgrounds both for internal activities (such as workshops) and external mobilizations in defence of the rights of women and the struggle for democracy. Their slogan 'democracia en el país y en la casa' (democracy in society and at home)
became the banner of the whole movement. Under Julieta Kirkwood, and, after her death, Margarita Pisano, La Morada offered audacious and effective leadership and became a focus for both Chilean and Latin American women. It created an autonomous space in which women worked together and with organized and non-organized popular movements; and it developed a series of gender-specific methodologies in areas of support, health, education and communication, one result of which was the **Radio Tierra** project, set up in 1991.

From 1992, Raquel **Olea** took over as director. The new Corporación de Desarrollo de la Mujer La Morada (Women's Development Corporation) distinguished institutional activity from political activism in response to the political consequences for feminists of the government's free market policies which privileged efficiency and specialization. Its new mission was 'to create a feminist institution supporting the transformations necessary for the construction of a fully democratic society, free of discrimination by reason of race, class or gender'. It developed strategies of political intervention in education, health and culture and published research on gender issues, and disseminated feminist ideas through cultural activities and Radio Tierra.

ELIANA ORTEGA

Moraes, Vinicius de

b. 1913, Rio de Janeiro, Brazil; d. 1980, Rio de Janeiro

Film critic, newspaper columnist, playwright, poet, song lyricist

One of Brazil's best loved public figures, Vinicius de Moraes famously combined the careers of diplomat, poet, songwriter, lover of women and professional drinker, with a bohemian *joie de vivre* whose popular instincts made of him a distinctive voice of democratic opposition to the post-1964 military regime. His early poetry, influenced by the neo-Catholicism of the 1930s modernists (see **Brazilian modernism**), shared Manuel **Bandeira**'s preoccupation with the tensions between the worldly and the divine, the erotic and the spiritual. But with his 1943 volume, *Elegias*, that balance had shifted definitively towards the blend of sensuality and simple colloquialism for which Moraes is known today.

By now, though, he had also begun a successful career as a film critic, writing over a hundred reviews and columns for Rio de Janeiro newspapers between 1941 and 1952, and unleashing a public debate about the industry on the occasion of Orson Welles's visit to Brazil in 1942. A period of residence as vice-consul in Los Angeles between 1946 and 1950 enriched his contact with the worlds of cinema and popular music, particularly **jazz**, and following his return to Brazil these experiences took him along a new creative path.

In 1956 he met the young composer Tom **Jobim** and collaborated with him on the musical score for the stage-play *Orfeu da Conceição*, the story of which he had already sold to the French film producer Sacha Gordine. Following the success of the play, in 1957 Gordine and director Marcel Camus finally went ahead with the film version, *Black Orpheus*, for which Moraes and Jobim added new songs, such as 'A Felicidade' (Happiness). With the release of a further Jobim–Moraes collaboration, '**Chega de saudade**' (No More Longing) by singer-guitarist João **Gilberto** in 1958, the arrival of the new wave in Brazilian popular music, **bossa nova**, was assured, along with Moraes's role as its leading lyricist.

While Moraes's partnership with Jobim produced many of the classic gems of the movement, such as 'Insensatez' (Foolishness), 'O Grande Amor' (The Great Love) and '**Garota de Ipanema**' (The Girl from Ipanema), many of his two hundred or more compositions were the fruit of other collaborations, with Carlos Lyra, Edu **Lobo**, **Toquinho** and Baden **Powell**, for instance. The partnership with Baden Powell marked Moraes's commitment to the politicized protest song movement of the early 1960s, before the military *coup*, and to its counterpart in the field of poetry, *Violão de Rua* (Street Guitar). More perhaps than any other artist of the period, it was Moraes who exemplified how the composer's art could shape the literary language of the lyric tradition to the rhythms of popular speech and music whilst avoiding either crude condescension or doctrinaire artificiality. In that sense, he set a demandingly high standard for the subsequent **MPB** generation of popular songwriters, having guaranteed them an unprecedented level of respect and prestige as artists as well as entertainers.

Further reading

Moraes, V. de (1991) *Livro de letras*, São Paulo: Companhia das Letras.
——(1982) *The Girl from Ipanema*, Merrick, NY: Cross Cultural Communications.

DAVID TREECE

Moraes Moreira

b. 1948, Ituaçu, Bahia

Musician and composer

A founder of the group Os Novos Baianos (The New Bahians), Moraes Moreira (Antônio Carlos Morais Pires) and his cohort followed in the wake of the radical pop movement, **Tropicália**, with a fresh take on Brazilian music and the international counterculture. After the band split up in 1976, Moreira established a successful solo career with hits such as 'Festa do interior', 'Assim pintou Moçambique' and 'Pombo-correia'. During carnival in Salvador he invariably appears on top of a *trio elétrico* to perform his unique style of **axé** music to enthusiastic revellers.

CHRISTOPHER DUNN

Morales, Armando

b. 1927, Granada, Nicaragua

Visual artist

A critically acclaimed painter and muralist, Morales is both an accomplished student of Western modernist painting and a central figure in Latin American contemporary art. His earlier works reflect the influence of Mexican muralist José Clemente **Orozco** and later of Joan Miró. His later work was more socially grounded, though still what Morales calls 'magical realist' in style (see

magical realism). His most famous paintings are *Mujer Sentada* (Seated Woman) and *Adiós a Sandino* (Good-bye to **Sandino**), in which the bodies of Sandino and his compatriots consume the majority of the foreground, floating darkly and returning the viewer's gaze.

DEREK PETREY AND ILEANA RODRÍGUEZ

Morales, Jacobo

b. 1934, Lajas, Puerto Rico

Film-maker and actor

A popular television and stage actor since the 1950s, Morales is also a poet, playwright and co-founder of the musical revue *Los rayos gamma* (The Gamma Rays). After appearing in several local and Hollywood productions, his first feature film was the brilliant comedy *Dios los cría* (Birds of a Feather) (1980). He has since written, produced and directed several films, among them the social satire *Nicolás y los demás* (Nicolas and the Others) (1984) and the very successful *Lo que le pasó a Santiago* (What Happened to Santiago) (1989).

VÍCTOR F. TORRES

Morales Benítez, Otto

b. 1920, Riosucio, Colombia

Essayist

One of Colombia's foremost essayists, Morales Benítez has published over thirty books. He appeared on the cultural scene in 1940s Medellín as director of the cultural magazine *Generación*, one of the earliest to promote modern international authors. His essays since the 1950s address *mestizaje* as the essence of Latin American identity, participatory democracy as the solution for Colombian political crises, and the importance of political, labour and agricultural reform. He has been one of the most vigorous and effective voices for liberal humanism in Colombia.

RAYMOND L. WILLIAMS

Morales Obregón, Mario Roberto

b. 1947, Santa Lucía Cotzumalguapa, Escuintla, Guatemala

Novelist and critic

Morales began as one of Guatemala's 'irreverent writers' (comparable to Mexico's post-1968 **Onda**) of the 1960s. Affiliated with the left, he was exiled in Nicaragua and Costa Rica and returned in 1989 to teach at the Universidad de San Carlos, while writing polemical articles in *Crónica* and *Siglo XI*. His works include four novels, a major 1994 study, *La ideología y la lírica de la lucha armada* (Ideology and Poetry of the Armed Struggle) and recent books of **testimonio** critique.

MARC ZIMMERMAN AND LINDA CRAFT

Morales Santos, Francisco

b. 1940, Ciudad Vieja, Sacatepéquez, Guatemala

Poet

Founding member of the group Nuevo Signo (New Sign), Morales has also been the group's organizer, promoter and meta-commentarist. Also a founding member and first president of the Comunidad de Escritores Guatemaltecos (Community of Guatemalan Writers), he has anthologized national poetry and published several of his own books of poetry. Throughout his work, Morales has sought forms with a specifically Guatemalan flavour, has concentrated on social as well as erotic and sentimental themes, and always alludes to Guatemala's multiple problems and identities.

MARC ZIMMERMAN AND LINDA CRAFT

Mordecai, Pamela Claire

b. 1942, Kingston, Jamaica

Writer

Mordecai is a poet (producing both adult and prizewinning children's poetry), editor, publisher and academic. *Journey Poem* (1989) demonstrated a strong poetic voice, sensuous, achieved in form, written largely in Jamaican-accented English. *de Man* (1995) portrays in Jamaican Creole (see **creole languages**) the witnessing of the Crucifixion by two Jamaicans, one a middle-aged maid in the service of Pontius Pilate's wife and one an old carpenter, taught by Joseph. Mordecai's academic work and publishing have contributed greatly to the development of Caribbean women's writing.

Further reading

Savory, E. (1996) 'En/gendering spaces: The poetry of Marlene Nourbese Philip and Pamela Mordecai', in Colville (ed.) *Other Women's Voices, Other Americas*, Mellon Press, pp. 192–211.

ELAINE SAVORY

Moré, Beny

b. 1919, Santa Isabel de las Lajas, Cuba; d. 1963, Havana, Cuba

Singer

The most highly regarded of Cuban singers, he was known as the 'the barbarian of rhythm'. As a child he often attended the family celebrations of the families of Congo and Lucumí origin living in his home town. In 1940, he went to seek his fortune in Havana and for several years earned a living as a singer in the capital's open air cafes and bars. Miguel Matamoros invited him to join his band (see **Trío Matamoros**), with which he performed on the Mil Diez radio station. In 1945, he toured Mexico with the Matamoros orchestra and remained there after their return, recording with the orchestras of Arturo Núñez, Rafael de Paz, Mariano Mercerón and **Pérez Prado**. Returning to Cuba in 1953, he played with Bebo Valdés before forming his own big band. He led it with great success but with very little technical understanding of conducting; he would 'dictate' his arrangements to musicians like Generoso Jiménez for them to transcribe, since he understood very little of musical notation. In this way he composed sones, guarachas, guaguancós (see **guaguancó**) and boleros (see **bolero**). He was frequently late or failed to appear at performances at all, which only inflated his superhuman reputation, since his style of life often took him from morning rehearsals or recording sessions to afternoon radio shows to evening theatre performances and all night cabarets (particularly at the Ali Bar) and dances. His funeral in Havana attracted unprecedented numbers of mourners.

JOSÉ ANTONIO EVORA

Moreau de Justo, Alicia

b. 1885, London, England; d. 1985, Buenos Aires, Argentina

Writer, political activist and physician

Moreau de Justo dedicated her life to social and political activism. Founder of the Socialist Women's Centre at age fifteen, she later practised medicine in working-class neighbourhoods. The second wife of noted socialist leader Juan B. **Justo**, in the 1930s, amid the decline of the Socialist Party, she led the women's movement with Victoria **Ocampo**, despite their obvious political differences. Editor of *La Vanguardia* (1956–62), she was also author of numerous influential books on feminist and socialist topics. A consistent critic of **Peronism**, she decried Argentina's excessive nationalism.

THOMAS EDSALL

Moreira, Jorge Machado

b. 1904, Paris, France; d. 1992, Rio de Janeiro, Brazil

Architect and engineer

Moreira was a member of the design teams responsible for the **Ministério da Educação e Saúde** (MES), based on sketches by Le Corbusier, and the campus of the UFRJ university, of which he was the chief architect. Both are located in Rio de Janeiro, and are key signposts in the history of architecture. His simplicity, gravity and eloquence were born of Le Corbusier's rationalism and the classical tradition. His sense of civic responsibility and professionalism led him to fight for the modernization of architectural education, and to defend the natural and architectural heritage of his country.

ROBERTO CONDURU

Morejón, Nancy

b. 1944, Havana, Cuba

Poet

One of the most important poets of post-revolutionary Cuba, Morejón was born in Los Sitios, a poor neighbourhood of Havana. Her poetry deals with issues of **race** and gender, as well as evoking the scenery, rhythms and people of her island. Her first volume of poetry, *Mutismos* (Silences) was published in 1962 and she has published more than a dozen collections of poems since, as well as volumes of essays and criticism. Her best known English translation is *Where the Island Sleeps Like a Wing* (1985). She is the niece of Cuban poet Nicolás **Guillén**.

CAROL WALLACE

Morel, Isabel Margarita

b. 1932, Santiago, Chile

Human rights activist

Morel was active in defence of human rights in Chile, and in the resistance to the dictatorship of Augusto **Pinochet**, who ordered the murder of her husband Orlando Letelier. She became a Fellow of the Washington Institute of Policy Studies in the Women's Human Rights project called 'Let the Other Half Speak' (later 'Third World Women Project'). Subsequently, she toured widely with an exhibition of Chilean patchworks (see **patchwork**), photographs and texts entitled 'Chilean Women Look at an Authoritarian Government', and she established the 'Letelier–Moffitt Memorial Award', given annually to a Latin American for outstanding human rights work.

ELIANA ORTEGA

Moreno, Gladys

b. 1933, Santa Cruz de la Sierra, Bolivia

Singer

From an early age, Moreno stood out for the power and expressive intensity of her singing and for the quality of her interpretations. She sang mainly the traditional songs of her own (eastern) region – takiraris, carnavales, valses – although she also sang the cuecas (see **cueca**) of Bolivia's western provinces. Her ability to captivate audiences throughout Bolivia transformed her into a symbol of national integration and in 1962, at a time of intense nationalism, won her the soubriquet 'Ambassador of Bolivian song'.

BEATRIZ ROSSELLS

Moreno, Marvel Luz

b. 1939, Barranquilla, Colombia

Novelist

In the 1950s and early 1960s, Moreno had some contacts with members of the Barranquilla Group (**García Márquez**, Alvaro Cepeda Samudio). In the 1960s, she moved to Paris where she started writing. Her best known novel is *Algo muy feo en la vida de una señora bien* (Something Very Ugly in the Life of an Aristocratic Lady) (1980). Her other works include *En diciembre llegaban las brisas* (The Winds Used to Come in December) (1987), a novel, and *El encuentro y otros relatos* (The Encounter and Other Stories) (1992).

MIGUEL A. CARDINALE

Moreno, Zully

b. 1920, Buenos Aires, Argentina

Actress

Zully Moreno (born Zulema González Borbón) was one of the great divas of Argentine cinema. From 1943 onwards she became iconic of the **Argentina Sono Film** style: with her long blonde hair and glamorous costumes, she perfectly matched the studio's predilection for elegant and grandiose sets. **Dios se lo pague** (May God Reward You) (directed by Luis César **Amadori**, 1948) was her greatest success, followed by *Nacha Regules* (directed by Amadori, 1950), *La mujer de las camelias* (Lady of the Camelias) (directed by Ernesto Arancibia, 1952) and *La dama del mar* (Lady of the Sea) (directed by Mario **Soffici**, 1953). She lived in exile in Spain with her husband, Amadori, from 1955 and retired after his death in 1960.

DIANA PALADINO

Moreno-Durán, R.H.

b. 1946, Tunja, Colombia

Writer

One of the most talented Colombian writers of the 1970s, Moreno-Durán is an urban and urbane novelist. After the hermetic modernist trilogy *Femina Suite – Juego de damas* (Checkers) (1977), *El toque de diana* (Reveille) (1981) and *Finale capriccioso con Madonna* (1983) – he published *Los felinos del Canciller* (The Chancellor's Cats) (1985), an accessible chronicle of an aristocratic Colombian family. He is also the author of essays on Latin American literature, *De la barbarie a la imaginación* (From Barbarism to Imagination) (1976) and memoirs of Latin American writers, *Como el halcón peregrino* (Like the Peregrine Falcon) (1995).

RAYMOND L. WILLIAMS

Moreno Fraginals, Manuel

b. 1920, Havana, Cuba

Historian

Considered one of Cuba's most important historians, Manuel Moreno Fraginals occupied a series of important economic advisory posts in the Ministry of Commerce and several state enterprises. While a graduate student in history at the Colegio de Mexico (1947–9) he researched in the Archivos de Indias in Seville and Simancas in Spain. Assistant director of Cuba's National Library (1949–50) and professor of history at the Universidad de Oriente (1950–1), he moved to Venezuela in 1954. There he occupied a range of posts – director of the brewery Cervecería Caracas, head of production for **Televisa** and owner of Radio Junín, while directing economic research projects on several Latin American countries before returning to Cuba in September 1959. Since 1994 he has lived in the USA.

JOSÉ ANTONIO EVORA

Morillo, Lila

b. 1943, Zulia province, Venezuela

Singer and actress

One of the most representative figures of Venezuelan mass culture from the 1960s onwards, she began her professional career in 1965 with Mario Suárez, a well-known Venezuelan folk singer. Her success enabled her to launch a solo career. In 1966 she married the singer and actor José Luis **Rodríguez** (El Puma), whom she later divorced. She has recorded more than fifty LPs and appeared in two of Venezuela's most celebrated television soaps, *Maria Mercé la Chinita* and ***Simplemente María***. Her record successes include 'El cocotero' (The Coconut Tree), 'La jaula de oro' (The Golden Cage) and more recently 'El Moñongo'.

JORGE ROMERO LEÓN

Moris

b. 1942, Buenos Aires, Argentina

Musician

Moris (Mauricio Birabent) is one of the founders of Argentine *rock nacional*, and one of the first to translate rock into Spanish. His first album, *30 minutos de vida* (30 Minutes of Life) (1970) included classic tracks like 'Ayer no más' (Just Yesterday) and 'De nada sirve' (It's No Use), perhaps the first nihilistic Argentine rap (see **rap music**) song. This first album articulated *rock nacional* with the **tango** tradition of Buenos Aires, giving Moris a particular and unique place within Argentine rock music.

Between 1974 and the mid-1980s he lived in Spain. The album *Sur y después* (South and After) (1995), marked a return to the style of the 1970s.

DIEGO BENTIVEGNA

Mormonism

The Mormon religion, founded in the 1830s in the USA by Joseph Smith, is today one of the most widespread and fastest growing religious groups in the Western World. The largest Mormon denomination, the Church of Jesus Christ of Latter-day Saints, has more than 7 million members, 40 per cent of whom live outside the USA. Latin America has been one region of outstanding growth; there may be between 1 and 2 million in Latin America and the Caribbean, though the Church itself claims more than 3 million.

In Latin America, Mormonism has expanded mainly in areas where modernization (see **cultural theory**) has advanced enough to create a religious vacuum, though instability and social decay in countries like Peru have also provided conditions for the growth of the Mormons. Mormonism has particularly attracted people who are prosperous economically but may still see themselves as outsiders. As elsewhere, Mormons in Latin America have not co-operated with other churches or participated in the ecumenical movement. The church is very hierarchical and the local congregations are highly dependent on the headquarters at Salt Lake City, Utah. Mormons have not adapted well to local cultures and only very recently have opened their missionary work to blacks. In that sense they differ notably from **Pentecostals**, the major Protestant movement in Latin America. However, they consider American indigenous groups to be part of the 'Lost Tribes Of Israel' and have concentrated part of their efforts among indigenous people.

The moral codes of the Mormons correlate closely with the norms of some conservative evangelical churches: abstinence from alcohol, tobacco, tea and coffee; strict dress norms; and adherence to a strict code of sexual morality. On the other hand, they have favoured sports, recreation and education. Despite their millennialism, Mormons have engaged widely in secular activities like business and politics. In most Latin American countries, however, their political participation has been less visible than in the USA.

Although Mormonism has been labelled an antimodern movement, in Latin America it can be seen as a modernizing force, due to its promotion of 'the American way of life'. Because of its 'North American' outlook and close relations to the church in the USA, the Mormons in Latin America have been suspected and accused of working for the US government and the **CIA**.

Further reading

Amorim, N.F. de (1986) *Os mormons em Alagoas: religião e relações raciais*, São Paulo: FFLCH/USP-CER.

Tullis, F. (1987) *Mormons in Mexico: The Dynamics of Faith and Culture*, Logan, UT: Utah State University Press.

JOUNI PIRTTIJÄRVI

Moro, César

b. 1903, Lima, Peru; d. 1956, Lima

Writer

As a surrealist poet and painter (see **surrealism in Latin American art**), Moro (born Alfredo Quíspez Asín) found his native Lima hostile to his aspirations as a gay artist; it was he who first described the city as 'Lima, the horrible'. In Paris in 1925 he joined the surrealists and published his first poems. Returning to Lima in 1934, he provoked new hostilities by espousing a surrealism that advocated total freedom of body and soul. In 1938 he left for Mexico City, where he met Xavier **Villaurrutia** and Agustín **Lazo**, and co-organized the First Exhibition of Surrealist Art in Mexico City (1940). His writing has recently been rediscovered by students of gay literature.

MAGDALENA GARCÍA PINTO

Morris, Mervyn

b. 1937, Kingston, Jamaica

Poet

The poems of Morris's first volume of poetry, *The Pond* (1973) range in subject from love and family to race politics and the colonial past. Awarded the 1976 Silver Musgrave Medal for poetry from the Institute of Jamaica, his subsequent volumes of poetry include *On Holy Week* (1976), *Shadowboxing* (1979), and *Examination centre* (1992). Morris's critical writings include the essays published as *Is English We Speaking and Other Essays* (1999). He currently teaches English at the Mona, Jamaica campus of the **University of the West Indies** and has edited several collections, including *Voiceprint: An Anthology of Oral and Related Poetry from the Caribbean* (1989), and *The Faber Book of Contemporary Caribbean Short Stories* (1990).

CAROL J. WALLACE

Morte e vida severina

Written by the Brazilian poet João Cabral de **Melo Neto** and published in 1956, *Morte e vida severina* (Death and Life of a Severino) is subtitled *auto de natal*, recalling the popular, originally medieval Iberian tradition of one-act nativity plays in verse. However, Melo Neto critically reworked this dramatic structure in order to reflect on the oppressed condition of a Northeastern peasantry marginalized by Brazil's postwar drive for industrialization, something anticipated in the title's inversion of the customary sequence of life and death (is death to precede, or prevail over, the hope of a better life?).

The everyman Severino's cultural and linguistic universe combines the elemental figures of the hostile landscape of the semi-feudal rural interior (stone, drought, violence and death) with the stoic religiosity of a popular **Catholicism** rooted in the promise of salvation beyond the grave. Contrary to the didactic, propagandistic approach of much of the protest art from the 1960s which it predates, Melo Neto instead submits the language of this universe to a dialectical process of interrogation, uncovering successive layers of meaning to arrive at an enriched and transformed consciousness of both word and world. By fusing in a single dramatic structure the biblical pilgrimage towards the miracle of Jesus's birth with the migrant's grim journey towards the coast in search of water, work and redemption, Melo Neto is able to expose in parodic form how the illusory faith in divine salvation is mirrored by the false secular promises of economic development.

Thus the 'rosary' of Severino's journey, the fragile thread of a dried-up riverbed punctuated by a succession of lifeless towns and villages, leads unremittingly through a litany of deaths (the arbitrary murders of peasants at the hands of greedy land barons, the slow grind of exploitation which swallows the plantation worker into the soil denied to him in life) that convince Severino that his pilgrimage to the city is nothing less than the road to his own funeral. Yet as he despairingly contemplates his suicide, the 'miraculous' birth of a sickly child in a riverside slum confronts him with the spectacle of man's stubborn resistance, the creative possibilities born out of his continual struggle to wrest life from seemingly exhausted material conditions.

Given this grimly materialist approach to the human struggle for survival and its deconstruction of the language of false promise employed by state and religion, it is not hard to understand the success of *Morte e vida severina* in the stage version performed across Brazil in the early years of the military dictatorship, with the musical settings composed by songwriter Chico **Buarque**. Walter Avancini's powerful 1980s screen adaptation for TV **Globo**, filmed on location in the states of Bahia and Pernambuco, further exploited the text's contemporary resonances by combining a professional cast with actors drawn from the local communities, and intercutting scenes from the drama with documentary footage of rural and urban poverty.

Further reading

Gonzalez, M. and Treece, D. (1992) *The Gathering of Voices: The Twentieth-Century Poetry of Latin America*, London: Verso: 253–8.

Kadir, D. (1994) *João Cabral de Melo Neto, Selected*

Poetry 1937–1990, Middletown, CN: Wesleyan University Press, 84–97.

Melo Neto, J.C. de (1980) *Morte e vida severina e outros poemas em voz alta*, Rio de Janeiro: José Olympio.

DAVID TREECE

Mortiz, Joaquín *see* Joaquín Mortiz

Mosquera, Gustavo

b. 1959, Buenos Aires, Argentina

Film-maker

Like others of his generation who struggled to make films in difficult political and economic constraints, Mosquera's career began making shorts (see **short films**), commissioned documentaries and even music videos (most notably, *Buscando un símbolo de paz* (Looking for a Symbol of Peace) by Charly **García**). His first feature, *Lo que vendrá* (What will Come) (1987) also starred García and, despite its extraordinary and sometimes excessive stylization, was very successful. In collaboration with students from the University of Buenos Aires, where he taught film-making, he directed the also highly stylized *Moebius* (1996), a fantastic tale of great ambition. Subsequently he moved to Los Angeles, with the hopes of breaking into Hollywood.

ANA M. LÓPEZ

motels, casas de citas, amuebladas

Urban centres in Latin America have traditionally had small hotels that rent rooms by the hour. Called by a great variety of names, including 'casa de citas' (house for dates), 'amuebladas' (furnished rooms) and 'albergues transitorios' (transit refuges), they figure large in popular culture, from the tango 'Cuartito azul' (Little blue room) to the opening scene of Tomás **Gutiérrez Alea**'s film ***Fresa y chocolate*** (Strawberry and Chocolate) (1993).

In recent years, however, these have been replaced by lavish newer establishments on the outskirts of cities, often near highways. Called motels after the US coinage for 'motor hotel', these feature discreet entrances, curtains that can be drawn to screen the car (and the identities of its occupants) from other clients. These establishments do a lot of business not only at night but also at lunchtime. The Brazilian auto club Guia Quatro Rodas (Four Wheel Guide) series gives them a rating from five red hearts (de luxe) to one red heart (some degree of comfort). The same source lists motels with names like: Tropical, Triángulo (Triangle), Love House, Swing, Opium, My Flowers, Frenesi (Frenzy), Harmony, Vip's (from V.I.P.), Alibi, Black Stallion, Labirinthe, Snob, Status, Champagne and – intriguingly – Skylab. Managua, Nicaragua is said to have the highest concentration of motels per capita in the region.

Guidebooks like the ***South American Handbook*** take pains to point out that these establishments are not to be confused with the somewhat tamer motels of the US, and do not recommend them for travellers with families.

DANIEL BALDERSTON

motor racing *see* auto racing

Mott, Luiz

b. 1946, São Paulo, Brazil

Anthropologist, historian and gay activist

Luiz Mott is Brazil's most prominent gay activist. The group he founded in Salvador, Bahia, the **Grupo Gay da Bahia**, has the distinction of being the longest running gay and lesbian organization in the region. A professor of anthropology at the Federal University of Bahia, he is the author of works such as *O lesbianismo no Brasil* (Lesbianism in Brazil) (1987), *Escravidão, homossexualidade e demonologia* (Slavery, Homosexuality and Demonology) (1988) and *O sexo proibido: Virgens, gays e escravos nas garras da inquisição* (Forbidden Sex: Virgins, Gays and Slaves in the Claws of the Inquisition) (1989). His most recent work is a biographical dictionary,

Homossexuais da Bahia (Homosexuals of Bahia) (1999), which provides fascinating life stories from the sixteenth to the nineteenth century.

DANIEL BALDERSTON

Motta, Zezé

b. 1944, Campos, Rio de Janeiro, Brazil

Actress and singer

One of the premier black entertainers of Brazil, Zezé Motta is an acclaimed actress and vocalist who began her career in 1967 in **Teatro Oficina**'s controversial play, *Roda viva*. She achieved national and international fame in 1976 in the starring role of Carlos **Diegues**'s film, ***Xica da Silva***, about a sultry and savvy slave woman who became the mistress of a wealthy Portuguese diamond merchant in eighteenth-century Minas Gerais. She has starred in over twenty films, including Diegues's 1984 film, ***Quilombo***, about a famous seventeenth-century runaway slave community led by Zumbi (see **Zumbi dos Palmares**) and his 1996 film adaptation of Jorge **Amado**'s novel, *Tiete do agreste*. Zezé Motta has also developed a successful musical career, recording several albums that celebrate Afro-Brazilian culture.

CHRISTOPHER DUNN

Moura, Clovis Steiger de Assis

b. 1925, Almarante, Piaui, Brazil

Poet, historian and sociologist

Moura pioneered the application of Marxism to the study of Brazilian slave rebellions, denounced racism (see **race**) in *Brasil: raízes do protesto negro* (Brazil: Roots of the Black Protest) (1983), and defended a militant **sociology** that links scientific practice with social change in *Sociologia do negro brasileiro* (Sociology of the Afro-Brazilian) (1988). He also examined the presence of racial prejudice in popular literature, founded the literary magazine *Jacuba* in Juazeiro, Bahia, edited the newspaper *O Momento* in Salvador, wrote for São Paulo newspapers and contributed in 1954 to the literary magazine *Fundamentos*, founded by writer and publisher Monteiro **Lobato**.

PEGGY SHARPE

Moura, Paulo

b. 1932, São José do Rio Preto, São Paulo, Brazil

Musician

A masterful clarinetist and saxophonist, Paulo Moura shifts easily from classical music to jazz, **bossa nova** and **choro**. In the early 1950s, he began playing professionally in the *gafieras* (samba dance halls) of Rio de Janeiro and was soon invited to play with touring bands. Between 1960 and 1977, he played solo clarinet in the Symphonic Orchestra of the Municipal Theater. In the 1980s, he made several acclaimed recordings of the work of **Pixinguinha**, Radamés **Gnattali** and **Villa-Lobos**. In 1992, Moura collaborated with guitarist Raphael Rabello on an exquisite duet recording, *Dois Irmãos*.

CHRISTOPHER DUNN

Movimento Armorial

The aim of the Movimento Armorial, founded by Ariano **Suassuna** in Recife in 1970, was to create erudite art forms inspired by the traditions of popular music, songs, poetry and engravings of the rural northeast of Brazil. Suassuna chose the word 'Armorial', referring to the book used to record the coat of arms of aristocratic families, to symbolize an ideal traditional and unified *sertão* culture. By evoking the wide range of heraldry, insignia and emblems created by popular artists, it linked the aristocratic with the popular, and the past with the present.

At its height in the mid-1970s, the Movement included some eighty artists practising literature, music and graphic art. All those involved shared an interest in the popular culture of the backlands (or *sertão*), and the belief that, through the assimilation of its cultural forms, a truly national high art could be produced which would represent a Brazilian world view, and would be resistant to the degrading and standardizing effect of mass culture. The differences between Armorial art and the popular art upon which it was based are immediately evident. More refined and polished, the work of the Armorial artists did not aim to reproduce popular art forms, but to recreate them for a different public. The centrepiece of the Movement was the Armorial orchestra, which remodelled traditional rhythms of the *sertão* into more sophisticated melodies, while writers such as Maximiano Campos, Janice Japiassu and Suassuna himself used the themes, characters, tone and imagery characteristic of **literatura de cordel** as the essential ingredients of their work.

The participants in the movement avoided any political implications and emphasized instead the fantastic and mystical qualities of regional popular expressions. A conservative approach to popular culture lay at the heart of Armorial art. Much of it was characterized by Arcadianism, exalting the simplicity of traditional rural life. The artists were selective in choosing their examples of popular culture, generally favouring more archaic forms and traditional themes like messianism, banditry and folkloric legends, whilst ignoring contemporary urban popular culture.

The use Armorial artists made of rich, popular material gave their work originality and vibrancy, but also produced contradictions. Despite their assertion that they were working with cultural values and expressions still existing in northeastern Brazil, the nature of their work made it difficult to avoid a tendency towards the picturesque, and a strong air of nostalgia for a way of life felt to be under threat of extinction. The popular material presented in Armorial art often appears as folklore linked to a past age, rather than a living, dynamic force.

Further reading

Dinneen, M. (1996) *Listening to the People's Voice*, London: Kegan Paul International.
Slater, C. (1976) 'Folklore and the Modern Artist: The North East Brazilian Movimento Armorial', *Luso-Brazilian Review* 16 (2).

MARK DINNEEN

Movimento de Educação de Base

Making innovative use of **radio** – and with financial help from the government – the Catholic Church in Brazil set up the the Movimento de Educação de Base (MEB, or Movement for Basic Education) in 1961 to bring literacy and Grassroots educational skills to the rural poor. The educators quickly became radicalized, adopted the educational methodology of Paulo **Freire** and encouraged peasants to think about the structural causes of poverty and take action to bring about change. The military *coup* of 1964 killed off this radicalism, though it surfaced elsewhere in the more independent Comunidades Eclesiásticas de Base (CEB, or Christian Base Communities).

LIAM KANE

Movimento Negro Unificado

The largest Afro-Brazilian political organization, the Movimento Negro Unificado (MNU) (Unified Black Movement), founded in São Paulo in 1978, seeks to raise consciousness of racial discrimination and inequality while promoting socioeconomic advancement, education, health care and legal rights for the black population. Founded following the death of a young black worker in police custody and the ejection of four black youths from a local sports club in São Paulo, the organization quickly spread to other Brazilian capitals as black activists took advantage of the gradual political opening (**abertura**) after years of hard-line military rule. The MNU has steadfastly resisted cooptation by political parties.

CHRISTOPHER DUNN

Movimiento Revolucionario Tupac Amaru

Movimiento Revolucionario Tupac Amaru (MRTA) is a Peruvian guerrilla organization born out of the fusion of two previous organizations, the Maoist PSR (M-L) (Revolutionary Socialist Party-Marxist-Leninist) and the Guevarist MIR-el militante (Revolutionary Movement of the Left – Militant). In 1984 the MRTA launched the armed struggle, though its early activities were limited to acts of propaganda, confrontations with the police and terrorist actions; it later moved to the phase of guerrilla war (see **guerrillas**). The MRTA characteristically launched spectacular actions like the occupation of the Japanese Ambassador's residence in Lima between December 1996 and April 1997; in fact, however, its numbers were already severely diminished before the occupation, and the crushing of the siege left most of its members dead or in prison.

CÉSAR SALAS

Moya, José Félix

b. 1944, Sánchez, Dominican Republic

Painter

Influenced by Salvador Dali's **surrealism**, Moya's paintings show desolated landscapes filled with bloody human organs and everyday life objects. A neosurrealist, Moya is a mystic painter who does not believe in the future of humanity. Born and raised in Sánchez, a small town on Samaná Bay, he later attended the School of Fine Arts at La Vega. In 1967 he presented his first individual exhibition at the Dominican-American Cultural Institute. He has participated in several biennials, and his paintings have been exhibited internationally.

FERNANDO VALERIO-HOLGUIN

Moya Pons, Frank

b. 1944, La Vega, Dominican Republic

Historian

Moya Pons is a history professor and author of the 1977 *Manual de historia dominicana* (Handbook of Dominican History), one of the most complete and rigorous studies of Dominican history. Other books include *Después de Colón* (After Columbus) (1987), *La española en el siglo XVI* (Hispaniola in the Sixteenth Century) (1971) and *The Spanish Caribbean in the Nineteenth Century* (1985). A widely travelled and well-published intellectual, Moya Pons's research and books on the colonial period in Santo Domingo and the Caribbean have contributed a great deal to knowledge of these areas.

FERNANDO VALERIO-HOLGUÍN

MPB

While the acronym stands for Música Popular Brasileira (Brazilian Popular Music), MPB refers more specifically to that extremely fertile current of songwriting which emerged out of three phenomena of the 1960s: **bossa nova**, the protest music of the song festivals, and the experimental movement known as **Tropicália**.

If its melodic inventiveness, harmonic richness, lyrical sophistication and stylistic eclecticism were the unmistakable legacies of those years, MPB also functioned under the dictatorship as an extension of the debate initiated by the shortlived **CPC** movement, as a kind of unofficial musical arena for rethinking the relationship between nationalism and internationalism, popular culture and politics. In a variety of ways, this movement – many of whose members were white, middle-class and university educated – has sustained an ongoing dialogue between a reflective and highly intellectualized literate culture and the popular rhythms and sensibility of collective experience.

For Chico **Buarque**, **samba** has been the perennial musical reference-point for the compositions which, during the 1970s, made him the leading voice of protest against the dictatorship, now in a more coded language than that used by Edu **Lobo**, Geraldo **Vandré** or Buarque himself in the mid-1960s. Another interpreter of the samba tradition is João Bosco who, with co-writer Aldir Blanc, also brought a dazzlingly inventive linguistic versatility to bear on his depictions of everyday working-class life, using African, Amerindian, French, English and Spanish vocabulary as well as an exuberantly colloquial Portuguese.

Many of these and other MPB songwriters' compositions have become familiar to audiences first and foremost through the recordings of a new generation of female vocalists, such as Elis **Regina**, Simone, Joyce, Maria Bethânia, Gal **Costa** and a revelation of the late 1980s, Marisa **Monte**. Bethânia and Costa initially made their names as part of the group of *Baianos*, who also included Caetano **Veloso** and Gilberto **Gil** and who, in the mid 1960s, descended on Rio and São Paulo from the Northeastern city of Salvador da Bahia to lay the foundations of the Tropicália movement. Veloso remains consistently the most audacious and surprising figure of the MPB songwriting tradition, who has woven an endless dialogue with Brazil's entire musical history, often championing unfashionable tastes and challenging listeners with the most experimental and 'literary' of lyrics.

Like Jorge Ben, since the early 1970s Gilberto Gil has explored the musical roots of his Afro-Brazilian identity, both in the light of visits to the African continent and the rediscovery of the black cultural movement of his native Salvador, which he has done much to promote. Other major black contributors to the MPB tradition include Djavan, Luis Melodia and Milton **Nascimento**, whose chief influences, along with jazz, bossa nova and Spanish American genres, are the baroque, classical and rural traditions of his native Minas Gerais.

Further reading

McGowan, C. and Pessanha, R. (1998) *The Brazilian Sound: Samba, Bossa Nova and the Popular Music of Brazil*, Philadelphia: Temple University Press.

Perrone, C.A. (1989) *Masters of Contemporary Brazilian Song: MPB 1965–1985*, Austin: University of Texas.

Discography

Various (1989) *Brazil Stars*, Vol. 3, Sigla. 600279.

DAVID TREECE

MST

Several of the poorest peasant organizations in Brazil united in 1984 to form the Movimento dos Trabalhadores Rurais Sem Terra (Landless People and Rural Workers' Movement), commonly known as the MST. With a membership of around 300,000 families, it is one of the largest social movements in Latin America.

Though some 32 million Brazilians are undernourished, the 1 per cent of land-owners who own almost half of Brazil leave much of their (fertile) land idle. Against this background, the MST has three main aims: 1) *land* – the expropriation of badly used land and its redistribution to those who are willing to live and work on it (the Brazilian constitution allows for the expropriation of land when it fails to 'fulfil its social function'); 2) ***agrarian reform*** – a piece of land is of limited value to peasant farmers without the support of, for example, access to affordable credit, technical training and national planning orientated towards need rather than profit; 3) *a just society* – without which there is little likelihood of meaningful agrarian reform. Accordingly, the MST struggles for wider political change, supports other marginalized groups and attempts to engage the public in dialogue about the future of Brazil.

Tactically, the MST's first step is to identify land not 'fulfilling its social function' and campaign for its redistribution. If conventional campaigning fails, hundreds of MST members then occupy this land and set up an 'encampment' to increase pressure on the government. Lasting anything up to four years, encampments offer a precarious existence to their inhabitants (land-owners often take violent reprisals), though they have proven a valuable experience in collective organization. Second, when the MST does acquire land, encampments become 'settlements' and the challenge is then to prove by example, in the co-operative way settlements are run, that alternative models of rural development are possible. The better settlements manage to do this – sometimes in spectacular fashion – but given the lack of wider agrarian reform it is a constant, uphill struggle. Third, the MST organizes major events, such as long marches through the whole of Brazil, in which thousands of members take their case to the wider public.

The MST's own, independent educational programme is an important case-study of **popular education** in Latin America.

Further reading

Kane, L. (2000) 'Popular education and the landless people's movement in Brazil', *Studies in the Education of Adults*, spring.

MST website at http://www.mstbrazil.org/.

LIAM KANE

Múgica, Francisco

b. 1907, Buenos Aires, Argentina; d. 1985, Buenos Aires

Film-maker

With no previous experience, Múgica joined the **Lumitón** studios in 1932 and worked his way up, assisting Manuel **Romero** (1935–8) and directing his first feature in 1939, *Margarita, Armando y su padre* (Margarita, Armando and Their Father). *Así es la vida* (That's Life) (1939), a comedy of manners, depicted three generations of an Argentine family. His now classic *Los martes orquídeas* (Orchids on Tuesdays) (1941) marked another new direction in national cinema – the 'white telephone' comedies. His twenty-five films, with their technical precision, carefully constructed dialogues and exquisite direction, are stellar examples of the classic Argentine cinema.

DIANA PALADINO

Mujica Láinez, Manuel

b. 1910, Buenos Aires, Argentina; d. 1984, Cruz Chica, Córdoba, Argentina

Writer

Mujica is an Argentine novelist and journalist. Some of his literary production explores European themes, as in **Bomarzo** (1962), a novel that served as text for the homonymous opera with music by **Ginastera**. It received the Kennedy Prize in 1964. He also wrote about Buenos Aires, mostly in historical novels. *Misteriosa Buenos Aires* (Mysterious Buenos Aires) (1971), a collection of short stories, is his most celebrated work about the city.

ALVARO FERNÁNDEZ-BRAVO

Mulata de Córdoba, La

According to a legend dating back to colonial Mexico, la Mulata de Córdoba was a beautiful young solitary woman who never grew old thanks to a pact she had made with the devil. Many men fell in love with her, but she rejected them all, devoting her supernatural energies to helping people in need. Incarcerated by the Inquisition, she is said to have drawn a ship on the wall of her cell in which she magically sailed away. The popular oral legend has been revived in the arts, most notably by Xavier **Villaurrutia** in a film and opera in the 1940s.

ROBERT M. IRWIN

Munchmeyer, Gloria

b. *c.* 1935, Chile

Actress

Munchmeyer joined the **ICTUS** group in 1975 and appeared in their *Tres noches de un sábado* (Saturday Night, Sunday Morning) (1972) and other productions. She worked with Teatro Lesigne in their version of O'Neill's *A Streetcar Named Desire* and with the Teatro de la Universidad Católica in Ibsen's *A Doll's House*. In the early 1990s she joined the Sombrero Verde company for Delaney's *A Taste of Honey*, among other works. Her film roles include a notable performance in Silvio **Caiozzi**'s *La luna en el espejo* (The Moon in the Mirror) (1990) a prizewinner at the Venice Film Festival.

CAROLA OYARZÚN

Mundo, El (Cuba)

El mundo is the newspaper that marked the beginning of the modern era, both technically and professionally, in Cuban journalism. Its first issue appeared on 11 April 1901. A new type of newspaper, it introduced daily sketches and social pages, an eight-column format and colour advertisements, and also pioneered the supplement, including the Sunday supplement *El mundo ilustrado* (Illustrated World), first published in 1904 and very popular with the Cuban public. It continued to publish until 1968 when a fire destroyed its presses.

WILFREDO CANCIO ISLA

Mundo, El (Puerto Rico)

From its founding in 1917 until the mid-1970s, *El mundo* was Puerto Rico's leading newspaper, characterized by its distinguished contributors of all political persuasions. In the 1970s the paper was crippled by a series of strikes, culminating in one that closed it for nearly a year. The strikes allowed its major competitor, *El **nuevo día*** to gain a stronger position in the daily newspaper market. *El mundo* ceased publication in 1991, but resumed publication under new ownership and with a new format in mid-1998.

NANCY MORRIS

Mundo nuevo

Mundo nuevo was a cultural journal, first edited by Emir **Rodríguez Monegal** and published in Paris (1966–8), and later by Horacio Daniel Rodríguez in Buenos Aires (1968–71). Considered the official journal of the **Boom**, *Mundo nuevo* created a space which overcame the marginality and isolation of previous Latin American generations by inserting Latin American culture into an international context and de-emphasizing national boundaries. The journal set out to affirm the creative freedom of each writer while highlighting the continent's unity.

Political controversy arose in 1967 when the *New York Times* exposed a link between the 'Congress for Cultural Freedom' and the **CIA**. *Mundo* was financed by the Ford Foundation through an organization called ILARI (Instituto Latinoamericano de Relaciones Internacionales), associated with the anti-Communist Congress. This link suggested that any organization receiving funding from the Congress was in fact receiving funding from the CIA and was consequently a puppet of its cultural imperialism.

Rodríguez Monegal, the overseeing and omnipotent editor, responded with a denunciation of the CIA and defended the independence of the journal, claiming that culture must be free of politics. In his defence, he asked that if such ideological boundaries were enforced, why was the magazine banned in such politically different environments such as Brazil, Argentina, Spain and Cuba? However, the political debate was not that simple. For example, an article criticizing Cuba's politics was published in the first issue while another favouring Cuba was rejected. This event sparked controversy and created enemies, especially in Cuba's **Casa de las Américas**. Nevertheless, this did not keep *Mundo* from publishing political artists such as Pablo **Neruda**, Nicanor **Parra**, Carlos **Fuentes** and Gabriel **García Márquez**.

According to Rodríguez Monegal, *Mundo* was based in Paris because it was a cultural capital of Latin America with many Latin American writers and it suited *Mundo*'s project of demarginalization. When the journal moved to Buenos Aires in 1968, Rodríguez Monegal resigned. Under the editorship of Horacio Daniel Rodríguez, the journal took a definite anti-communist stance. The quality and quantity of the writing deteriorated until its loss of funding and closure in 1971.

Further reading

Mudrovcic, M.E. (1997) *Mundo Nuevo: Cultura y Guerra Fría*, Rosario: Beatriz Viterbo.

VICTORIA RUÉTALO

mundonovismo

A literary term that was coined by the Chilean critic Francisco Contreras in 1917 to express his opposition to Spanish American *modernismo* (see ***modernismo*, Spanish American**) and his preference for an emphasis on the daily life of people in the New World. It has been used most frequently with regard to such works as José Eustacio **Rivera**'s *La vorágine* (The Vortex) (1924), Ricardo **Güiraldes**' *Don Segundo Sombra* (1926) and Rómulo **Gallegos**' *Doña Bárbara* (1929). These works have been designated as novelas de la tierra (novels of the earth) (see ***regionalismo***), by Arturo **Torres-Ríoseco**, and the latter term is favoured subsequently by critics like Jean Franco and Carlos **Alonso**. Cedomil Goic, however, prefers the term *mundonovismo*, because he uses it to categorize not only novels of rural life like those mentioned above, but also urban novels that emphasize local roots or regionalism (see *regionalismo*).

DANIEL BALDERSTON

Muñequitos de Matanzas, Los

Los Muñequitos de Matanzas, founded in 1952, are perhaps the greatest exponents of traditional Cuban **rumba** performed in the **guaguancó** style. Founded as Guaguancó Matancero by Florencio Calle, Angel Palladito and Juan Mesa, they quickly became a favourite act in Havana nightclubs. In the late 1950s they recorded the song 'Los Muñequitos' (The Little Dolls), based on a newspaper comic strip, which became so popular that it was adopted as the group's name. In the 1960s, Diosdado Ramos Cruz joined the group and later became its director. The group maintains traditional rumba format featuring complex polyrhythmic percussion, solo and chorus vocals, and dancers.

CHRISTOPHER DUNN

Muñiz, Angel

b. 1960, Santo Domingo, Dominican Republic

Film director

Producer, director and scriptwriter, Muñiz began as a comedian in the early 1980s with the group Los Tenorios, and later became a theatre actor. In 1995, he wrote, produced and directed *Nueba Yol* (New York), the first Dominican feature film nominated for an Academy Award. A low-budget modest film, *Nueba Yol* tells the story of Balbuena (Luisito Martí), a poor man from a Santo Domingo shanty town, who emigrates to the Big Apple looking for a better life. It was a box office hit and was especially well-received by the Dominican diaspora in New York.

FERNANDO VALERIO-HOLGUÍN

Muñoz, Gloria

b. 1949, Asunción, Paraguay

Playwright

Muñoz edited and published *Canto de poetas* (Poets' Song), a selection of poetry aimed at children, and *La prohibición de la Niña Francia* (The denial of the Little Girl Francia), a dramatic adaptation of the short story 'El romance de la Niña Francia' by Concepción Leyes de Chaves, performed in 1994. She is the author of *La Divina Comedia de Colón* (The Divine Comedy of Columbus), which premiered in 1992, and also adapted for the theatre *Yo el supremo* (I the Supreme), the novel by Augusto **Roa Bastos**, and *Vidas y Muerte de Chirito Aldama* (The Lives and Death of Chirito Aldama), a work by Juan Bautista Rivarola Matto; these premiered in Asunción in 1991 and 1993, respectively.

TERESA MÉNDEZ-FAITH

Muñoz Marín, Luis

b. 1898, Barranquitas, Puerto Rico; d. 1980, San Juan, Puerto Rico

Politician

Muñoz Marín was the populist leader of the Partido Popular Democrático (Popular Democratic Party), which he founded in 1938 and which dominated Puerto Rican politics until the 1960s. He was the prime modernizer in Puerto Rico's development from an agricultural to an industrial economy and a collaborator with the United States in transforming Puerto Rico into a commonwealth of the USA (Estado Libre Asociado, 1952), which he led as its first elected Governor (1948–64). He is a looming presence in contemporary Puerto Rican literature, personifying a paternalism continuing from a semi-feudal colonial past.

JOHN D. PERIVOLARIS

muralism, Mexican

Few artistic movements in Latin America have had the impact or the influence of the Mexican muralist movement and its three major figures – Diego **Rivera**, David Alfaro **Siqueiros** and José Clemente **Orozco**. Their work established a vocabulary for an aesthetic nationalism and a monumental **public art** that redefined public spaces. That language of public statement, symbolic or realist, has come to be a mark of moments of social transformation in Latin America. In Chile the **Brigada Ramona Parra** marked the period of **Popular Unity** government with anonymously painted murals on walls and fences throughout the country that incorporated words and monumental figures. Cândido **Portinari**'s work in Brazil echoes the pioneering expression of Mexico; and in Nicaragua, the appearance of sweeping wall paintings on often ruined walls was an early emblem of revolution – and testimony to the enduring influence of Mexican muralism.

The three major figures of the Mexican mural movement came from very different backgrounds and remained independent and distinct even within their common enterprise. José **Vasconcelos**, Minister of Education in the post-revolutionary government of Alvaro Obregón (1920–4), was charged with the task of creating a national cultural expression whose protagonist would be the Mexican 'people', identified as the symbolic foundation of the new Mexican State. He brought together the ex-Cubist Rivera, who returned to Mexico after a trip to Italy to study the Renaissance frescoes, Siqueiros, who had fought through the revolution in the armies of Pancho **Villa** and Orozco, an artist of anarchist (see **anarchism**) inclinations who had learned his craft from the great illustrator and satirical journalist, José Guadalupe **Posada**. Their task was to inscribe the rewritten history of Mexico on the walls of its public buildings.

From the beginning there was a degree of tension among the members of the movement, concerning politics as much as artistic method – or more precisely the relationship between the two. For Siqueiros's 1921 Manifesto of Muralism made clear not only that the movement would pursue a monumental art and employ the newest materials and techniques, but that the artists would themselves be workers engaged in a collective enterprise. Hence the involvement of the muralists in the Sindicato Revolucionario de Trabajadores Técnicos, Artistas y Escultores (The Revolutionary Union of Technical Workers, Artists and Sculptors), and in particular in its newspaper, *El machete*, whose brilliant front-page woodcuts and strident headlines brought together the Muralists and the members of the **Taller de Gráfica Popular** like Leopoldo **Méndez** and others. Rivera, at that time a leading member of the Communist Party (see **communist parties**), was engaged in the Court of Labour murals in the Ministry of Education – but he seemed uneasy with the collective project, and conflicts quickly developed between him and the other members, until Rivera effectively took personal control of the whole project. Siqueiros was at first more interested in the aesthetic revolution than the political, though he later became and remained an active communist; his growing conflicts with Rivera in the 1930s stemmed largely from Rivera's campaign to persuade the Mexican government to give asylum to Leon Trotsky. Orozco, on the other hand, remained sceptical of the post-revolutionary elite and their relentless pursuit of power, as was evidenced in his 1924 mural, *The Social and Political Junkheap*.

The muralists' work was in any event already under attack from conservative elements, who had smashed Orozco's *Christ Destroying His Own Cross* at the Escuela Preparatoria in the centre of Mexico in 1921, perhaps because it was one of the most powerfully iconoclastic and contemporary works of the era. As Rivera began to ensure that he became the undisputed leader of the muralists, Orozco's work of the mid- to late 1920s grew increasingly angry and sceptical of the revolutionary project and more prone to caricature and symbolism in its form. Rivera and Siqueiros, meanwhile, became more involved in their role as political activists; their art work, in turn, grew more didactic, in the mould of the **socialist realism** then becoming the official style of the communist movement.

Yet the reality is that the muralist movement as such functioned at its height for a maximum of six years; thereafter, the public art commissions were limited to Rivera and ceased when both Rivera and Siqueiros suffered political repression under the Calles government (1928–32). At that time, all three of the leading muralists were in the USA, where they painted memorable works at Dartmouth (Orozco), Los Angeles (Siqueiros) and San

Francisco, Detroit and finally New York (Rivera). It was his mural at the Rockefeller Centre in New York, where the Mexican placed Lenin next to Rockefeller, that caused the greatest scandal – and the Rockefellers eventually destroyed the wall when Rivera obstinately refused to change it.

The accession to the Mexican Presidency of Lázaro **Cárdenas** in Mexico brought the muralists back to Mexico (Siqueiros had been expelled from the USA in 1933 and was working in Chile and Argentina). Rivera's tempestuous relationship with his wife, Frida **Kahlo**, was now as much the focus of public interest as his work. In this period he completed what amounted to a new version of his Detroit mural in the Palacio de Bellas Artes in central Mexico City; at the same time he worked throughout the Cárdenas period on the hugely ambitious and magnificent panorama of Mexican history on the main stairway of the Palacio Nacional, the government building on Mexico's **Zócalo**, or central square. Early in 1937, Leon Trotsky arrived in Mexico at Rivera's invitation, and he stayed with Rivera and Kahlo until personal tensions led Trotsky to move to a house nearby, in the Coyoacan district of Mexico City, where he was murdered three years later. Siqueiros, meanwhile, was fighting in Spain as a volunteer. Returning to Mexico in 1939, he made the first attempt on Trotsky's life, on Stalin's instructions, later that year. He then fled Mexico, with the help of Pablo **Neruda**, then Chilean cultural attaché in Mexico. Rivera meanwhile re-entered the Communist Party.

Orozco was always the most individual and marginal of the group, as his *Autobiografía* (1983) made clear. His later murals, particularly in Guadalajara, like his *Man's Victory over Cancer* were extraordinary celebrations of human achievement, particularly those in science. Rivera died in 1947 at the height of his fame and was by then an icon of mural art, his work widely imitated, particularly in the USA, and acknowledged. Siqueiros devoted much of the latter part of his life to the creation of the extraordinary **Polyforum Cultural Siqueiros**, an environment rather than an art work that is huge and extravagant in its artistic intent and far more abstract than his earlier work. But his most famous works are probably those of the Museum of History (Chapultepec Castle) in Mexico City, where great columns of peasants marched across a room in *The Rebellion against Porfirio Díaz*. Rivera's monument, and almost his last painting, was the ***Sueño de una tarde dominical en la Alameda Central*** (Dream of an Afternoon on the Alameda), when the whole crowded panorama of Mexican history gather at the city centre Hotel del Prado. Though the building collapsed in the 1985 earthquake, Rivera's mural – like his reputation – survived.

Further reading

Charlot, J. (1962) *The Mexican Mural Renaissance*, Austin: University of Texas Press.

Diego Rivera: A Retrospective (1986) New York: Detroit Institute of Arts and W.W. Norton.

Gonzalez Melo, R. (1997) *José Clemente Orozco: La pintura mural mexicana*, Mexico: Ediciones Corunda.

Marnham, P. (1998) *Dreaming with his Eyes Open: A Life of Diego Rivera*, London: Bloomsbury.

Orozco, J.C. (1983) *Autobiografía*, Mexico: ERA.

Reed, A. (1956) *Orozco*, New York: Oxford University Press.

Rochfort, D. (1993) *Mexican Muralists*, London: L. King.

Siqueiros, D.A. (1975) *Art and Revolution*, London: Lawrence & Wishart.

MIKE GONZALEZ

Murena, Héctor A.

b. 1923, Buenos Aires, Argentina; d. 1975, Buenos Aires

Writer

It was through his essays that Murena's ideological propositions became well known; a disciple of Ezequiel **Martínez Estrada**, he wrote within the interpretative current concerned to define 'the national'. Polemical texts like *El pecado original de América* (America's Original Sin) (1954) presented his liberal cosmopolitanism and revealed his links to the journal *Sur*, for which he wrote. Set in a liberal humanist framework, his arguments were aimed at those intellectuals who radicalized their positions during the first Peronist governments (see **Peronism**).

SANDRA GASPARINI

Murga, La

'La murga' is a neighbourhood-based popular theatre form particular to Uruguay and Argentina. Although influenced by the Spanish zarzuelas, 'la murga' has developed into its own genre. Using only **percussion** instruments, large groups of elaborately costumed males comment on the year's political and social events during the **carnival** festivities. In recent years, women have also begun to participate. In Montevideo, during the longest carnival in the world, lasting forty days, murga performers compete for prize money, while in Buenos Aires they are considered a marginal group. During the dictatorships of the 1970s, performances were censured because of their satirical and highly critical political content.

VICTORIA RUÉTALO

Murillo, Rosario

b. 1951, Managua, Nicaragua

Poet

In her youth, Murillo was a leading member of the Grada group, which brought together avant-garde painters, poets and musicians. In the 1960s, she joined the Grupo Ventana founded by Sergio **Ramírez** and Fernando Gordillo. After the 1979 **Sandinista Revolution** she headed the Sandinista Association of Cultural Workers (**ASTC**) and edited *Ventana*, the cultural section of ***Barricada***, from where she criticized the popular **poetry** workshops led by Minister of Culture Ernesto **Cardenal**. A controversial presence in Nicaraguan politics, Rosario Murillo was married to Sandinista president Daniel **Ortega**.

SILVIA CHAVES AND ILEANA RODRÍGUEZ

Murúa, Lautaro

b. 1925, Tacna, Peru (now Chile); d. 1995, Madrid, Spain

Actor and film-maker

A member of the **Teatro de la Universidad de Chile**, Murúa worked in theatre and film in Chile before emigrating to Argentina in 1954. His sober, imposing style and distinctive voice quickly made him one of the favorite actors of Leopoldo **Torre Nilsson**, starring in *La casa del ángel* (House of the Angel) (1956). His career as a director began with the shockingly realist *Shunko* (1960) and the feature *Alias Gardelito* (1961). His *La Raulito* (1975) won several international prizes. Exiled to Spain after the 1976 military *coup*, he returned to Argentina in 1983 and resumed his acting career, working with Fernando **Solanas** and María Luisa **Bemberg**.

DIANA PALADINO

Museu de Arte de São Paulo

Opened on 2 October 1947, the Museu de Arte de São Paulo (MASP) was officially named after its founder **Assis Chateaubriand**, owner of a communications empire, who laid the basis of the Museum by purchasing from several collections that became available after the Second World War. Under the direction of Pietro Maria **Bardi**, the museum opened schools of industrial design, advertising, dance and a film seminar. In 1968 a new building designed by Lino **Bo Bardi** was added. MASP houses the most important collection in South America; it includes a Van Gogh, six canvasses by Modigliani and a Rembrandt self-portrait, as well as major works by Cândido **Portinari**.

ANTONIO CARLOS VAZ

Museu de Arte Moderna

The creation of the Museu de Arte Moderna (MAM) (Museum of Modern Art) in São Paulo in 1948 consolidated a modern movement that began in 1922 in Brazil with the Semana de Arte Moderna (see **Modern Art Week**). It opened on 8 March 1949 with the exhibition 'From Figurativism to Abstraction', a theme based both on modernist ideas and an evolutionary conception of art history. In 1951, MAM instituted the São Paulo Biennial of Modern Art, one of the most significant events in the modern art calendar. In 1961, the Biennial became independent of MAM. The Museum moved to the Parque Ibiripuera in 1969.

GONZALO AGUILAR

museums

When the visitor enters the Museo Nacional de Arqueología e Historia (National Museum of Archaeology and History) in Mexico City, the first sight is of a vast cement umbrella with cascading water and of a large International-Style building and courtyard beyond; then, perhaps, the visitor may notice in huge letters on the walls a number of poems about songs that have gone silent, about flowers that have died. The poems are translations from the Náhuatl (see **Náhuatl and Aztecan languages**), texts that Angel **Garibay** and Miguel **León-Portilla** claimed were post-Conquest written versions of older oral poems – although, as Amos Segala has shown, this may be the fantasy of scholars inventing a national past. Whatever the truth of that, the museum is clearly about the invention of the past, with its sequence (on the right side) of rooms on the history of the Valley of Mexico culminating in the large rooms on the Aztec empire across the back of the courtyard; on the left side are the 'other' pre-Columbian cultures of the Mexican national territory (Olmec, Maya, western Mexico, etc.), in a sequence made confusing by the desire to have the Aztec objects be the culmination of the story. Upstairs are rooms devoted to the contemporary indigenous cultures of Mexico, with dioramas of mannequins in indigenous garb. The museum stakes a claim for modern Mexico as the successor state to the Aztecs, and in a bold move erases the Spanish heritage of the country, as well as its African heritage, historical contacts with France and the USA. This national museum is certainly about the imagining of a community, in Benedict Anderson's famous phrase, or about the invention of the past.

Another museum of a different kind, the Museo Naval (Naval Museum) in Valparaíso, Chile, on a bluff at the southern end of the great port city, contains a variety of exhibits – on navigation around Cape Horn and through the Strait of Magellan, on the history of the Chilean navy – but the museum exists first and foremost as the keeper of objects sacred to the Chilean military's view of itself: the relics of Arturo Prat and of the other heroes of the War of the Pacific against Peru and Bolivia (1879–84). Prat, who died in the naval battle at Iquique in 1879, is something of a national saint in Chile, his heroic self-sacrifice and defiant last words appearing on the currency and on countless statues; the exhibit in the Naval Museum does not remember the pillage of Lima, it does not even really celebrate the Chilean victory in the war – instead, there is a muffled silence in the rooms devoted to Prat, who died in a hopeless stand of defiance in the early stages of the war.

Many of the national and municipal museums of Latin America and the Caribbean are didactic in the way that the Naval Museum and the Anthropology Museum certainly are: they are there to teach schoolchildren, adult citizens and foreign visitors some lessons about the ideology of the nation. Sometimes they are subtle in their strategies, but rarely do they exhibit art for art's sake (or, for that matter, old uniforms or boats or furniture or the spurs and gourds for ***yerba mate*** of bygone gauchos). School groups are led reverently through them, the children instructed to copy down in their notebooks the inscriptions by the objects. Many of these museums suffer because they present a static, not a dynamic, view of the past.

At the other extreme are some of the eccentric personal museums, often the houses of writers, artists or politicians. The 'blue house' in Coyoacán where Frida **Kahlo** grew up and where she lived with her sometimes husband, Diego **Rivera**, and with a variety of other lovers, preserves her collection of folk art, her body cast and an unfinished portrait of Joseph Stalin. The three houses where Pablo **Neruda** lived – in Santiago, Valparaíso and Isla Negra – are chock full of the objects he collected, from seashells to the figureheads of ships, from masks to old books. The house outside San Ignacio Miní, in the Misiones area of Argentina, where Horacio **Quiroga** lived in the last years of his life is largely empty, the objects stolen, but boasts a bench in the garden with an inscription stating that the writer went there in search of inspiration. The Museo Hemingway on a hill outside Havana preserves the writer's house as it was, and his boat was brought from the sea to the hilltop to form part of the display. The room in El Tropezón, an old hotel in the Paraná delta northwest of Buenos Aires, where Leopoldo **Lugones** committed suicide in 1938 has been preserved exactly as it was that day – though of course without the slumped body. And the fortress-like compound where Leon Trotsky sought refuge from **Siqueiros** and other emissaries of Stalin – and where he was assassinated in 1940 – has similarly been preserved as if in a bubble, an evocative place to reflect on **exile** and death (as Tununa Mercado has done in an evocative story about the place).

The bold Le Corbusier-inspired building of the **Museu de Arte de São Paulo** or MASP, a huge structure suspended between two columns, opens out on a vast panorama of the modern city of São Paulo (on one side) and a carefully preserved fragment of the native Atlantic forest (on the other). The gallery above displays Old Masters, impressionists, Picassos and Portinaris on clear plastic sheets, a bold innovation in the display of paintings but one that is not particularly welcoming to the visitor, as the explanations are on the back of the paintings. The building proclaims São Paulo's status as the industrial and financial powerhouse of modern Brazil.

Some of the most fascinating museums in Latin America are small and quirky. The Museo Larco Herrera in Lima is known above all for its room of erotic ceramics from the pre-Conquest cultures of Peru. The Museo de Oro, also in Lima, was created by a rival family, and some of its displays seem to argue with the interpretations of indigenous sexual practices in the Larco Herrera. The Carmen **Miranda** museum in the **Aterro do Flamengo** area of Rio de Janeiro contains disintegrating dresses and personal objects that belonged to the actress. The Padre Crespo museum in Cuenca, Ecuador, housed in a school where the late priest taught, is a bizarre collection of indigenous objects which Crespo believed proved that the Phoenicians and Egyptians had come up the Amazon in ancient times and influenced the cultures of the area.

But perhaps a favourite museum is one of the smallest: a public urinal in Florianópolis, Brazil, devoted to the history of public facilities.

DANIEL BALDERSTON

Música de feria

'Música de feria' is a composition by the Mexican composer Silvestre **Revueltas** for string quartet. Written in 1932, it was first performed on 7 November 1933 in Mexico City by the Cuarteto Clásico. It condenses in a single movement the structure and development of a traditional quartet, although it adds specific features like the simultaneous expression of autonomous melodic lines by each player with the rhythmic pattern as the only common reference point. It synthesizes the themes explored by Revueltas in earlier quartets, and is one of his most important works. In 1984 the **Cuarteto Latinoamericano** and Juan Arturo Brennan designated it Revueltas's String Quartet No. 4.

EDUARDO CONTRERAS SOTO

música de fusión

A current within Argentina's ***rock nacional***, *música de fusión* (fusion music) evolved in the late 1960s and set out to fuse typical folk rhythms and melodies with the sounds of rock and roll. Particularly notable in this area is the work of León **Gieco** and of groups like Arco Iris. Lito Vitale developed a more sophisticated version in the 1990s.

DANIEL LINK

Música Grande

Efraín **Recinos**'s striking wood sculpture *Música Grande* (Grand Music) from 1970 is at once a **marimba** and an armoured vehicle: the national musical instrument of Guatemala and the bane of its population. A large and imposing object (measuring 4.5 m in length), it is exhibited in the Museo de Arte Moderno in Guatemala City. Its feet and features have a human quality reminiscent of some of the squiggles in the painting of **Matta**, a disquieting experience for the viewer who cannot be sure whether they are soldiers or musicians. Recinos' later work includes paintings that are at once maps of Guatemala and images of its massacred population; the 1970 sculpture similarly represents the troubled nation (and seems prophetic of the terrible events to come).

DANIEL BALDERSTON

música norteña

A group of musical styles and genres, like the polka, chotis, and corrido, typical of northern Mexico and the southern USA, whose rhythmic and melodic influences come from early nineteenth-century Europe, from the medieval traditions of Spain, and the 'ranchero' style of northern Mexico. Played mainly by groups consisting of accordion, guitar and bass, clarinet, saxophone and redobla (a wooden block played as percussion) are sometimes added. The rhythm is simple and the song lyrics often risqué. Polka and chotis (a variant of the German 'schottische' or Scottish dance) are dances, but the corrido is a sung ballad form and the songs are usually romantic in content.

VICTOR MARTÍNEZ ESCAMILLA

Música Nova

In 1963, a group of young composers, including Rogério **Duprat**, Gilberto **Mendes**, Willy Correia de **Oliveira** and Damiano Cozzela, came together with the intention of reviving the avant-garde (see **avant-garde in Latin America**) tradition initiated by the Música Viva group under Hans Joachim **Koellreutter** in 1939. The group sought aesthetic orientation from the concrete poets (see **concrete poetry**), who published the founding manifesto of Música Nova in their literary review, *Invenção*. Calling for a 'total commitment to the contemporary world' with its expanding web of mass-media technologies, the Música Nova group rejected the pastoral nationalism of the erudite music establishment. Duprat and Cozzella composed and arranged extensively for film soundtracks, advertising jingles and popular music.

CHRISTOPHER DUNN

musical instruments *see* accordion and bandoneón; charango; guitar; harp; marimba; quena

musicology

The pioneers of the serious study of Latin American music include the Brazilian writer Mário de **Andrade**, USA-based scholars Gilbert Chase and Nicholas Slonimsky, and the Cuban novelist Alejo **Carpentier**. Major figures that followed include the Argentine musicologist Isabel Aretz, the Franco-Brazilian Gerard Béhague and the leading figure in the study of colonial Latin American music, Robert Stevenson. Aretz edited *América Latina en su música* (Latin America in its Music) (1977), part of a UNESCO-sponsored series of volumes on different arts and intellectual disciplines. Stevenson, now retired from UCLA, founded the *Inter-American Music Review*. Béhague, who has taught at the University of Texas for many years and trained many of the leading younger scholars (particularly those in **ethnomusicology**), is the editor of the *Latin American Music Review* and the author of important surveys of Latin American music for the *Grove Encyclopedia of Music and Musicians* and for *Music in Latin America: An Introduction*. Latin American and Caribbean centres for musical research include CENIDIM, part of the **Centro Nacional de las Artes** in Mexico City, and CIDMUC, the Centre for the Research and Development of Cuban Music in Havana. An important recent publication that brings together many leading figures in the field is Dale Olsen and Daniel Sheehy's *South America, Mexico, Central America, and the Caribbean*, the second volume of the *Garland Encyclopedia of World Music* (1998).

Further reading

Béhague, G. (1979) *Music in Latin America: An Introduction*, Englewood Cliffs: Prentice-Hall.

Chase, Gilbert (1962) *A Guide to the Music of Latin America*, Washington: Pan American Union.

Slonimsky, Nicholas (1946) *Music of Latin America*, London: Harrap.

DANIEL BALDERSTON

Mutabaruka

b. 1952, Kingston, Jamaica

Poet and dub performer

Born Allan Hope, Mutabaruka was raised a Catholic but became a Rastafarian (see **Rastafarianism**) in his teens. By the 1970s he was writing and performing, long before being associated with Mikey **Smith** and Oku Onoura. A tour-de-force on stage, Mutabaruka feeds off audience response, entertaining by his irreverent commentaries, as well as by his poetry. Early works include *Outcry* (1973), *Sun and Moon* (with Faybiene) (1976) and *Mutabaruka: The First Poems (1970–79)* (1980); his later work is mostly recordings, many of which include poetic texts. As with other dub poets (see **dub poetry**), his is a poetry of protest; but it is also introspective, romantic and exhortatory.

PAT DUNN AND PAMELA MORDECAI

Mutantes, Os

Celebrated as the first truly original Brazilian rock group, *Os Mutantes* (The Mutants) achieved a cult status comparable to the Velvet Underground or Captain Beefheart in the Anglo-American sphere. Founded in 1966, the band created unique fusions of psychedelic rock and a variety of Brazilian regional styles, often utilizing home-made electronic technologies. Led by vocalist Rita **Lee**, bassist Arnaldo Baptista and guitarist Sérgio Baptista, the group participated in several televized musical programmes and festivals both as headliners and accompaniment during the mid- to late 1960s. *Os Mutantes* was the premier rock band of the vanguardist cultural movement, *tropicalismo*. After forays into progressive rock, the band dissolved in the mid-1970s.

CHRISTOPHER DUNN

Mutis, Alvaro

b. 1923, Santafé de Bogotá, Colombia

Poet and novelist

As a child, Mutis lived in Belgium but returned frequently to his parents' *hacienda* in Colombia. Those childhood experiences are extensively reflected in his work. Mutis's fictional characters, especially those of European descent, suffer regular identity crises and have a desperate view of the world they live in. Among the most representative of his works are his poem *Un bel morir* (A Beautiful Death) (1989) and his novel *Maqroll el gaviero* (Maqroll the Topman). In 1997, Mutis was awarded the Premio de Príncipe Asturias literary prize. Since 1956, he has lived in Mexico.

MIGUEL A. CARDINALE

myalism

Myalism is a range of religious beliefs and rites of African origin that appeared in Jamaica in the mid-eighteenth century. Involving spirit possession, speaking in tongues, dancing, drumming, and millenarian elements, it believes in healing both physical and spiritual affliction, often to counter the effects of **Obeah**. Myalism assimilated Christian elements, and survives within Afro-Jamaican Christianity, especially amongst the **Baptists**. Many of Jamaica's contemporary religions, like Pukumina, **Kumina**, Revival and Revival Zion, are thought to have developed out of the encounter between myalism and Christianity. Instrumental in the emergence of a trans-ethnic African Jamaican identity, myalism has been an important means of cultural and political resistance, as in Erna **Brodber**'s novel *Myal* (1988).

SHALINI PURI

N

Na Bolom

Na Bolom, Tzotzil for 'the house of the Jaguar', is a Mayan studies centre, library and hotel in San Cristóbal de las Casas, Chiapas, founded in 1950 by archaeologist Frans Blom and his wife, the Swiss photographer and journalist Gertrude Duby Blom. Na Bolom is a mecca for Mayanists and a champion of the Lacandón Indians and the rainforest they inhabit. Following the deaths of Blom in 1963 and Duby in 1994, the museum is being renovated by Walter 'Chip' Morris, a scholar of contemporary highland Mayan textiles and author of *Living Maya* (1987).

CYNTHIA STEELE

nacatamal

All food products made from maize (see **corn and corncakes**) are part of the indigenous legacy, and nacatamal, one of the best-known of Nicaraguan dishes, is no exception. Its basic ingredients are ground corn cooked with bacon lard, onion, pepper, garlic and tomatoes. Portions of approximately one cooking spoon in size are then wrapped in banana leaves, to which a slice of potato and of tomato, a chunk of pork, some spearmint, hot chile pepper, olives and capers are added. Nacatamales are traditionally consumed on Sunday mornings.

ESTEBAN LOUSTAUNAU AND ILEANA RODRÍGUEZ

nación, La

One of Argentina's most important newspapers, *La nación* has a circulation of 290,000 for its daily edition and 365,000 on Sundays, when it includes a colour magazine and sports, cultural and children's supplements. It uses a wide range of international news agencies and has an international edition. Umberto Eco, Susan Sontag, Joseph Brodsky, Guy Sorman and Fernando Savater are among its regular contributors. Originally founded in 1870 and edited continuously by Bartolomé Mitre until 1906, the four succeeding generations of the **Mitre family** who have edited the newspaper have held to the liberal, constitutionalist and democratic criteria of its founder.

RODRIGO PEIRETTI

nacional, El

El nacional is one of Latin America's leading newspapers. Its foundation, in Caracas in 1943, represented a landmark in the development of the modern press (see **press and mass media**) in Venezuela, for it was innovative in its approach to presenting and discussing news items, and in its visual layout and organization. It was one of a number of newspapers created in response to the new era of democratic politics and press freedom that gradually emerged following the end of the dictatorship of Juan Vicente **Gómez** in 1936. Journalists began to organize themselves into new professional bodies, and entrepreneurs sought to produce papers and magazines that were in line with the most modern examples overseas, attractive in design and easy to read. It was against that background that the novelist and journalist Miguel **Otero Silva** launched *El nacional*, supported by his father, who provided the financial backing and imported the machinery required from the USA. In its early years it operated from a small office in the centre of Caracas, with Otero Silva himself as chief editor and Antonio Arráiz as overall manager.

The layout of *El nacional* immediately distinguished it from traditional Venezuelan newspapers. In order to facilitate reading and make it attractive to a wide public, larger lettering, clearer titles and bigger illustrations were used. Space was reorganized to create a less cluttered appearance, and the paper was divided into sections according to theme, with more pages devoted to political debate and cultural information. The editorial, which had long been established as a central feature of newspapers, was replaced by a briefer, more direct masthead. Many of these innovations eventually became standard among Venezuelan newspapers. Otero Silva was able to obtain the services of many experienced and able writers, and the paper quickly established a reputation for high quality journalism and debate. Of clear left-wing orientation, it supported many progressive movements within the country and beyond. It has come into conflict with central government on several occasions, and has been subjected to censorship as a result. It even faced brief periods of closure in 1949 and 1950, under the **Pérez Jiménez** regime, and again in February 1992 following the attempt to overthrow President Carlos Andrés **Pérez**, by which time the paper had moved to the political centre.

El nacional's quick response to new opportunities – taking advantage of new technology, for example, and introducing the popular weekend magazines *Feriado* and *Pandora* – have kept it in the forefront of developments in newspaper production.

Further reading

Díaz Rangel, E. (1987) *La información internacional en Venezuela, 1808–1985: desde la Gaceta de Caracas hasta nuestros días*, Caracas: Fondo Editorial de Humanidades y Educación, Universidad Central de Venezuela.

Los diarios de Caracas, 1837–1967 (1969) Caracas: Asociación Venezolana de Periodistas.

Las noticias del exterior en doce diarios latinoamericanos (1986) Caracas: Consejo de Desarrollo Científico y Humanístico, Universidad Central de Venezuela.

Villasmil, X. (1986) *Los contrastes informativos de la prensa: análisis de doce diarios venezolanos*, Maracaibo: Universidad del Zulia, Vice Rectorado Académico.

MARK DINNEEN

nacional de ahora, El

Founded in the Dominican Republic in 1966 by Rafael Molina Morillo, the newspaper *El nacional de ahora* (The National Now) was named after the magazine *Revista Ahora* (Now Magazine). Its first director was Freddy Gatón Arce, the famous poet of the **Poesía Sorprendida** (Surprised Poetry) movement. One of the leading afternoon newspapers, *El nacional* is a political tabloid. Its front page has gigantic headlines with graphic photographs of murdered people. Because of ideological differences, a group of journalists, led by Silvio Herasme Peña, left the newspaper and founded the left–centre tabloid *La Noticia*.

FERNANDO VALERIO-HOLGUÍN

NACLA

NACLA (North American Congress on Latin America) was founded in 1966 to provide information and analysis on Latin America to North American scholars and researchers. In particular it has provided a consistent account of US activities and interests in the region. Its main activity is the publication of the bi-monthly magazine, *NACLA Report on the Americas*, which offers insightful and carefully researched thematic analyses in an accessibly written and imaginative form, as well as regular news-briefs and updates. NACLA's collection of documents and other materials is now housed in the New School Library at Princeton University.

MIKE GONZALEZ

NAFTA

NAFTA (North American Free Trade Agreement) (known in Spanish as the Tratado de Libre Comercio (TLC)) is a treaty with a series of side-agreements designed to reduce or eliminate barriers to the movement of capital and goods between Canada, Mexico and the USA. NAFTA was implemented in 1994, but represents a formalization and extension of long-term economic developments such as the *maquiladora* (see **maquiladoras**) or *bracero* programmes.

NAFTA was strongly contested by non-governmental interests. Labour organizations in the USA and Canada saw low wages and highly controlled unions in Mexico as a major threat. Independent organizers in Mexico feared that NAFTA would increase the power of capital over workers. Environmentalists saw NAFTA as expanding the ecological damage associated with existing cross-border industry.

NAFTA also ignited nationalist sentiments. In the USA, Ross Perot, the mercurial millionaire-turned-presidential-candidate, referred to NAFTA during the 1992 elections as a 'giant sucking sound' coming from the south. Conservative business interests in Mexico also feared NAFTA would weaken the privileged position of State-protected industries. In that context, NAFTA was seen as the principal means for an emergent, neoliberal (see **neoliberalism**) political elite in Mexico to institutionalize its control over old-guard sectors of the ruling party.

The nationalist reaction to NAFTA included the cultural impact of free trade. Conservative politicians in the USA, such as presidential contender Pat Buchanan, articulated opposition to NAFTA within the context of a populist and racist discourse against immigrants. In Mexico, intellectuals from across the ideological spectrum feared the massive influx of US consumer goods and popular culture would erode national identity. More importantly, Mexican intellectuals saw NAFTA as part of a wider trend of concessions to the emergent global economic order, as represented by the International Monetary Fund. In that context, the future commitment of the Mexican State to cornerstone social programmes such as free education and health care were seen as threatened by NAFTA's economic opening.

At the time of implementation, NAFTA was presented by its proponents in the USA as an American answer to regional trading blocks in the global economy. The European Union (EU) was signalled as a particularly important example requiring an American response. In this light, many NAFTA opponents saw the treaty as the latest expression of US economic imperialism in the tradition of the Monroe Doctrine, a position that was only heightened when US president George Bush expressed his desire to see a NAFTA-like framework extending from Alaska to Tierra del Fuego. The choice of the Zapatista National Liberation Army (EZLN) (see **Zapatistas**) in Chiapas, Mexico, to begin its insurrection on 1 January 1994, the first day that NAFTA was to take effect, gave clearest expression to this view of the treaty as economic imperialism. In Mexico, NAFTA was touted by the government of Carlos **Salinas de Gortari** as signalling Mexico's entrance into the 'First World', but this image evaporated under the combined influence of the Zapatista rebellion, economic crisis, and disputes, assassination and revelations of massive corruption within the Salinas family and administration.

Despite the propaganda of its proponents, NAFTA is not comparable to the EU. The EU treaty was negotiated over decades, provides for representative multilateral political control and includes such provisions as economic aid from wealthier to poorer members, a common currency and, most importantly, the free movement of labourers alongside goods and capital. NAFTA was drafted in great haste, refers only to economic relations and, most problematically, includes no provisions for the movement of immigrants and labourers.

NAFTA has given rise to an immense bibliography that includes official government publications, handbooks on how businesses can negotiate their future within NAFTA and a series of highly critical studies of the impact of the treaty.

Further reading

Audley, J.J. (ed.) (1997) *Green Politics and Global Trade: NAFTA and the Future of Environmental Politics*, Washington, DC: Georgetown University Press.

Barndt, D. (ed.) (1999) *Women Working the NAFTA Food Chain: Women, Food & globalization*, Toronto: Second Story Press.

Guevara N., Gilberto and García Canclini, N. (eds) (1994) *La educación y la cultura ante el tratado de libre comercio*, Mexico, DF: Nueva Imagen.

McAnany, E.G. and Wilkinson, K.T. (eds) (1996) *Mass Media and Free Trade: NAFTA and the Cultural Industries*, Austin: University of Texas Press.

Metz, A. (ed.) (1996) *A NAFTA bibliography*, Westport, CT: Greenwood Press.

NAFTA Law and Policy Series, The Hague, Boston: Kluwer Law International. Multi-volume series discussing many aspects of the treaty.

Simmons, A.B. (ed.) (1996) *International Migration, Refugee Flows and Human Rights in North America: The Impact of Free Trade and Restructuring*, New York: Center for Migration Studies.

BRIAN GOLLNICK

Náhuatl and Aztecan languages

Náhuatl, Nahuat, and Nahua are names of languages which derive from the language spoken by the Aztecs and other groups in Mexico at the time of Spanish contact. These languages belong to the Uto-Aztecan family, which stretches from the central Great Basin Region of the USA to El Salvador. While Ute, the northern outlier, is quite different, Pipil (the variant spoken in El Salvador) and the Náhuatl of the Valley of Mexico are sufficiently similar to be mutually intelligible. Teachers trained in Mexico to work with local Náhuatl have been contracted for bilingual education classes by Salvadorean communities.

Náhuatl was the language of the Aztec empire. Aztec documents are recorded in pictographic writing with rebus elements. Upon contact, the *calmecac* (Aztec schools) began to teach alphabetic writing. Náhuatl documents from the early colonial period recorded land titles, disputes, wills, and catechisms. Fray Bernardino de Sahagún set his Nahuat pupils the task of recording their cultural practices, a massive work now known as the Florentine Codex. Spanish Friars provided grammars of Náhuatl and example texts to aid priests in learning the language for more effective proselytizing. A series of dialogues exemplifying courtly speech (now known as the Bancroft Dialogues) was presumably set down to aid this language learning policy.

Náhuatl speakers accompanied the Spanish armies as they pushed out from Tenochtitlán to subdue New Spain and Guatemala. They served as interpreters as well as soldiers; the place names they reported to the Spanish are often those that appear on modern maps, rather than the locally indigenous geonyms. Náhuatl was recognized by the court of Spain as an acceptable language for petitioning the crown. Many communities throughout New Spain and Guatemala employed Náhuatl scribes for this purpose until the Bourbon reforms delegitimized indigenous languages as legal instruments.

Modern Náhuatl speakers live in Durango, San Luís Potosí, Hidalgo, Veracruz, Puebla, Tlaxcala, Colima, Nayarit, Michoacan, Estado de México, the Districto Federal, Morelos, Guerrero, Oaxaca and Tabasco, and in El Salvador. Remnant communities existed in Guatemala until the late 1970s; Pipil has been re-introduced into Guatemala since the late 1980s, as refugee populations arrived from El Salvador.

The Mexican goverment supplies bilingual education materials and teachers to its populations and the Pipil peoples have contracted educators from Mexico using those same materials to teach in their communities.

Classical Náhuatl, the language recorded in alphabetic writing from the mid-1500s through the 1700s, is being revitalized as a literary language, used by the intelligentsia in Mexico for poetry and prose.

Further reading

Anderson, A.J.O. and Dibble, C.E. (1978) *Florentine Codex: General History of the Things of New Spain. Fray Bernardino de Sahagún*, Santa Fe, NM: School of American Research and the University of Utah.

Karttunen, F. and Lockhart, J. (eds) (1987) *The Art*

of *Náhuatl Speech. The Bancroft Dialogues*, Los Angeles: UCLA Latin American Center Publications.

JUDITH M. MAXWELL

Naipaul, Seepersad

b. 1906, Longdenville, Caroni, Trinidad; d. 1953, Port of Spain, Trinidad

Journalist and novelist

Seepersad Naipaul is best known as the father of V.S. **Naipaul** and the fictional model for the eponymous hero of latter's *A **House for Mr Biswas*** (1961). Although of the pundit caste, he began life as a sign-painter. In 1929 he became a reporter on the ***Trinidad Guardian***. In 1943 he published locally *The Adventures of Guruveda*, short stories which, as V.S. Naipaul noted, provide 'a unique record of the Indian or Hindu community in Trinidad in the first half of the twentieth century', pioneering creative writing in the area.

LOUIS JAMES

Naipaul, Shiva

b. 1945, Port-of-Spain, Trinidad; d. 1985, London, England

Writer

While still in his twenties, Naipaul won several literary prizes for *Fireflies* (1971), his first novel. In some of the most beautiful writing of his generation, Naipaul exposed the dishonesty and corruption he saw in political and religious leaders in works like *Black and White* (1980), which analyses the mass suicide of the Jim Jones community in Guyana. *Fireflies* and the later novel *A Hot Country* (1983) address themes of **exile** and alienation. An outstanding short story writer, as the collection *Beyond the Dragon's Mouth* (1984) clearly shows, he suffered in part from unfair comparisons with his brother V.S. **Naipaul**.

KEITH JARDIM

Naipaul, V.S. (Vidiadhar Surajprasad)

b. 1932, Chaguanas, Trinidad

Writer

Although Naipaul's first novels were criticized as imitative of English literary models, they were innovative works initiating a highly individual strand of West Indian writing. The grandson of a Brahmin immigrant from the Punjab, and son of Seepersad **Naipaul**, a journalist and writer, he found the intellectual world of Trinidad stifling. He won a scholarship to read English Literature at Oxford, and vowed not to return to Trinidad. Subsequently, freelancing for the BBC, recollections of his Trinidad childhood prompted the short stories collected in his first work (although it was his third work to be published), *Miguel Street* (1959), portraying a gallery of idiosyncratic characters in a poor area of Port of Spain through the affectionate humour of a growing boy.

The Mystic Masseur (1957) and *The Suffrage of Elvira* (1959) turned a satirical eye on his home island as it emerged into independence. The first work charts the rise of Ganesh Ramsumair from a village masseur with assumed magical power to 'G. Ramsay Muir', eminent politician, by playing on popular superstition. The second is a hilarious account of a village election manipulated by bribes, colour prejudice and rural gullibility. These and *The Middle Passage* (1961), a mordant account of a Caribbean tour, aroused hostile reactions in the West Indies. In the same year, however, he published *A **House for Mr Biswas*** (1961). Drawing on a thinly fictionalized account of his father's life, and charting two generations of an East Indian family (see **East Indians**), Naipaul created a tragicomic saga in which the eponymous hero surmounts poverty, exploitation and ill luck to achieve a precarious independence and self-respect. It remains his most sympathetic novel.

This work was followed by *Mr Stone and the Knight's Companion* (1963), the short stories of *A Flag on the Island* (1967) and his major novel, *The Mimic Men* (1967). Moving between England and an imaginary Caribbean island Isabella, Ralph Kripalsingh rises from island real estate to political power in the newly democratic island state. Within its interwoven stories and themes, Naipaul portrays the 'mimic' futility of West Indian society.

With the three novellas of *In a Free State* (1971), Naipaul looked outwards to Africa, the United States and Latin America. He also increasingly explored the interface between journalism and fiction. *Guerillas* (1979) was based on an actual rape and murder by revolutionaries that he had reported in an article. *A Bend in the River* (1979) paralleled *A Congo Diary* (1980), telling of an East Indian shopkeeper attempting to survive in a thinly disguised Zaire. Published seven years later, *The Enigma of Arrival* (1987) appeared to signal a retreat from narrative fiction. *A Way in the World* (1994) interwove Columbus's historical voyage to the Caribbean, revolutionary movements in Cuba and East Africa, and personal memories to further explore the interrelationship of factual and imaginative truth.

Naipaul's many honours include the Trinity Cross from Trinidad (1989), and an English knighthood (1990).

Further reading

Mustafa, F. (1995) *V.S. Naipaul*, Cambridge: Cambridge University Press.

LOUIS JAMES

Najlis, Michele

b. 1946, Granada, Nicaragua

Poet

A Sandinista (see **Sandinista Revolution**) militant during the Somoza regime (see **Somoza dynasty**), Najlis published her first book of political poetry, *El viento armado* (The Armed Wind), in 1969. It was followed by the poetry and fiction of *Augurios* (1980), the satirical, feminist short prose of *Ars combinatoria* (1989), and the collected journalism chronicling the Sandinista years of *Caminos de la estrella polar* (Roads to the Pole Star) (1990). Najlis's later poetry is a spiritual exploration of an individual deeply marked by the secular world, a Jewish poet who works in a profoundly Christian environment.

AMY KAMINSKY

Nalé Roxlo, Conrado

b. 1898, Buenos Aires, Argentina; d. 1971, Buenos Aires

Writer

Nalé Roxlo's eclectic writings are a unique fusion of poetry and humour. He was first recognized in 1923 for his poem *El grillo* (The Cricket); later for his contributions to the satirical literary magazine **Martín Fierro** and humorous sketches and articles signed 'Chamico' and 'Alguien' (Someone). Nalé Roxlo also contributed to the activities of the **teatro independiente** in Buenos Aires with such plays as the much-praised 1941 *La cola de la sirena* (The Mermaid's Tail).

FERNANDA ANALIA ZULLO

Namuncurá, Ceferino

b. 1886, Chimpay, Patagonia, Argentina; d. 1905, Rome, Italy

Popular saint

The first Argentine saint, though not recognized by the Catholic church, Namuncurá was the son of the Mapuche chief Manuel Namuncurá and the white captive Rosario Burgos. Ceferino's career served different interests. For his father, defeated by Argentine troops, his education was an opportunity to resist conquest by other means. The recently created Salesian Order of Don Bosco saw him as the emblem of its legitimate evangelizing mission. For the church and state he was an instrument of nationalization. Today, his image circulates on medals and he is a focus for religious **tourism**.

ROBERTO MADERO

Ñandutí

Ñandutí, 'spider web' in Guarani, is delicate cotton embroidery that may have originated in Arabia, but was brought from the Canary Islands to Paraguay. The decorative pattern corresponds to the 'Salamanca suns' motif common in Tenerife. Likened to the web spun by the *eperia socialis* spider, the more than 100 designs, drawn on cloth cut away when the weaving is finished, reflect rural traditions and customs: Paraguayan flora, fauna, domestic motifs and mythological scenes. Although *ñandutí* was first noted in the town of Tapu'a mi, near Asunción, in 1838, its centre of production is Itauguá where there is a four-day festival in early July for the crowning of Señorita Ñandutí. Popular legend says *ñandutí* was first made by an Indian woman who lost her lover in the forest and found him dead covered by a spider web. She returned home and in her sorrow found consolation imitating the web.

BETSY PARTYKA

Narain, Harry

b. 1950, Essequibo, Guyana

Writer

Narain's reputation as a writer of short stories is based on a single volume of stories, *Grass-Root People*, published in 1981 by the Cuban **Casa de las Américas** publishing house. Its thirteen stories portray the harsh everyday life of rural Guyana, capturing the creole dialect. Raised on a rice farm, Narain became a school teacher but returned to the farm in 1978. The first story of the collection is in the form of a letter to the 'Comrade Prime Minister' from 'Rice Farmer', describing the powerlessness of the small Indo-Guyanese farmer caught between senseless government policies and the wealthy landowners and is a barely veiled criticism of the autocratic government of Forbes **Burnham**. The ironic title of the volume suggests that the socialist propaganda of the Marxist government is at odds with its treatment of the 'grass-root people'.

CAROL J. WALLACE

Naranjo, Carmen

b. 1930, Cartago, Costa Rica

Writer

Costa Rica's most important contemporary novelist, Naranjo is also recognized for her poetry and essays. Her first book was *Canción de la ternura* (Song of Tenderness) (1964). *Diario de una multitud* (Diary of a Crowd) (1974) brought her international fame. Other important titles are: *Los perros no ladraron* (The Dogs Didn't Bark) (1966) and *Ondina* (1983), a collection of short stories dealing with gender representation, homosexual and heterosexual love, and power. She has been Costa Rican ambassador to Israel and director of **EDUCA**.

NICASIO URBINA

Naranjo, Rogelio

b. 1938, Morelia, Michoacán, Mexico

Graphic artist

An extraordinary and imaginative artist, the political effectiveness of Naranjo's drawing was recognized during the presidency of Luis **Echeverría Alvarez** – although his work is not humorous in an immediately amusing sense. His caricatures of writers and artists transform likenesses into symbols; in his political cartoons, although they may provoke laughter at hypocrisy and false pride, his main purpose is to create a visual paradox. For what is memorable about Naranjo's work is its perfection of line and its unexpected images, bringing together political satire and fantastic art. Naranjo's best political cartoons (the skeletal people sipping oil from a barrel through a straw, the drawings of a miniature Carlos **Salinas** that mocks his voice rather than his stature, the drawing in which Porfirio Díaz appears miraculously to Juan Diego – the Mexican peasant who saw a vision of the Virgin of Guadalupe) are characteristically acerbic politically and artistically phantasmagoric. There are echoes in them of Lewis Carroll, David Levine and others, as well as his own sardonic sense of humour.

Naranjo's central characters are always Mexican presidents – unavoidably so in a presidential system in which the executive is not only the central decision-maker but also the icon through which, for each six-year period, all ambitions are channelled. By denying them any qualities, Naranjo sends them into a space somewhere between the government and the people, a territory where all images are false.

His published works include *La escena política* (The Political Scene) (1976), *Me vale madre* (I Don't Give a Damn) (1978) and *Los presidentes en su tinta* (Presidents in Their Ink) (1998).

CARLOS MONSIVÁIS

Narváez, Francisco

b. 1905, Porlomar, Venezuela; d. 1982, Caracas

Sculptor

Venezuela's first modern sculptor, Narváez was the son of a renowned but modest cabinet-maker on the island of Margarita. In the 1920s he worked in an indigenous and '*criollista*' tradition, making monumental pieces for public spaces, and wood and stone carvings that fixed an iconography of the national *mestizaje* (racial mix). He then moved towards organic abstraction, akin to surrealism (see **surrealism in Latin American art**), using materials new to Venezuelan sculpture such as precious tropical woods and rough stones from the Caribbean. By the end of his life his work was wholly abstract, more constructivist than organic.

LUIS PÉREZ ORAMAS

Nascimento, Abdias do

b. 1914, Franca, São Paulo, Brazil

Artist, dramatist and political activist

The most prominent stalwart in the struggle for Afro-Brazilian rights of the twentieth century, Abdias do Nascimento has distinguished himself as a playwright, theatre director, painter and political activist. After participating in the **Frente Negra Brasileira** during the 1930s, he went on to found and direct the **Teatro Experimental do Negro**, a pioneering group in modern Afro-Brazilian dramaturgy and cultural activism. With the advent of military rule, Nascimento sought exile in the USA between 1968 and 1981. During this period, he taught at the State University of New York in Buffalo and participated in several major international black conferences. Upon his return to Brazil, he was elected to the federal House of Deputies, representing the Democratic Labor Party (PDT) of Rio de Janeiro. He was subsequently elected to the federal Senate. In conjunction with his political activities, he has published several volumes of essays, including *Brazil: Mixture or Massacre?* (1989) and *Africans in Brazil: A Pan-African Perspective* (1992). Nascimento has also produced a body of acclaimed paintings based largely on the mythology of the Afro-Brazilian religion, **Candomblé**.

CHRISTOPHER DUNN

Nascimento, Editorial

Editorial Nascimento is an influential Chilean publishing house. Having inherited the family bookstore, opened in 1875, Carlos George Nascimento (1885–1966) founded Editorial Nascimento in 1917. Its first volume was a 400-page anthology of Pedro Antonio González's poetry (1918). It then printed *Desolación* (Desolation) by Gabriela **Mistral**, followed by **Neruda**'s *Crepusculario* (1923) and his *Veinte poems de amor y una canción desesperada* (Twenty Love Poems and a Desperate Song) (1924) a highly controversial work in its time. By 1978, it had published over 6,000 titles. Having survived the crisis brought on by **Pinochet**'s regime, Nascimento remains important in Chilean publishing.

LUIS E. CÁRCAMO-HUECHANTE

Nascimento, Milton

b. 1942, Rio de Janeiro, Brazil

Musician

A central figure of Brazil's popular music movement **MPB** and a prolific and inventive singer and composer, Nascimento grew up in Três Pontas, Minas Gerais. Musically gifted, he received his first guitar at age fifteen and formed a band with his childhood friend, the pianist Wagner Tiso. He was also the crooner for the local group 'W's Boys', with whom he recorded one of his earliest compositions, 'Barulho de Trem' (Train Noise). In 1963 he moved to Belo Horizonte, capital of Minas Gerais, where he met a group of budding musicians who became his lifelong friends and collaborators: Fernando Brandt, Marcio Hilton Borges and his brother Ló Borges.

He participated in the First International Pop Song Festival in 1965, but came into national prominence after the second edition of the festival in 1967, in which his 'Travessia' (Crossing), with lyrics by Fernando Brandt, won second place. Singing his own lyrics, Milton also won the prize for best interpretation. Here too he met Creed Taylor, a US jazz producer who had introduced **bossa nova** to the USA. Milton's first LP came out in 1968, as he embarked on a tour of the USA and Mexico with João **Gilberto** and Airto Moreira. He recorded his first US LP, *Courage*, in 1969.

Nascimento became a national icon after his 1970 show in Rio's famous **Opinião** theatre. At a time of extreme repression when many artists were in exile, Milton's show became the focus of local cultural resistance. Shirtless, with an Afro-like hairdo under his perennial beret, Nascimento sent out a harsh message of protest with songs like 'Para Lennon & McCartney'. In 1971, Nascimento rented a beach house in Rio and gathered his friends and collaborators to record what would become his most popular LP, *Clube da Esquina* (Corner Club). They reunited in 1978 for the sequel, *Clube da Esquina 2*.

Nascimento's compositions blend a variety of musical influences, from traditional Minas Gerais music and church music (for example, his 'Sentinela', recorded in the 1980s with an orchestral arrangement in Notre Dame de Paris and a Benedictine choir) to technopop, jazz, folk and contemporary Latin American rhythms such as 'Canción por la unidad latinoamericana' (Song for Latin American Unity), and indigenous and Afro-Brazilian rhythms ('Yauareta', 'Missa dos Quilombos').

A natural tenor with a 'bronze' voice, Nascimento could have had an independent career as a vocalist. In addition to performing with all the principal voices of MPB, he has also performed at international festivals and Carnegie Hall and has recorded and/or performed with George Duke, Mercedes **Sosa**, Sarah Vaughan, Paul Simon, Quincy Jones, Pat Metheny, Hubert Laws, Sting, and others. Nascimento also wrote the film score for Ruy **Guerra**'s film *Os deuses e os mortos* (The Gods and the Dead) (1970), and his *Missa dos Quilombos* compositions provided the structure for Carlos **Diegues**' *Quilombo* in 1983.

Further reading

Borges, M. (1996) *Os sonhos nao envelhecem: historias do Clube da Esquina*, São Paulo: Geracao Editorial.

Delfino, Jean-Paul (1998) *Brasil, a musica: panorama des musiques populaires bresiliennes*, Marseilles: Parentheses.

MARÍA JOSÉ SOMERLATE BARBOSA

Nassar, Raduan

b. 1935, Pindorama, São Paulo, Brazil

Writer

Nassar is regarded as one of Brazil's most important contemporary writers, despite having published only three short volumes: *Lavoura arcaica* (Archaic Ploughing) (1975), *Um copo de cólera* (A Glass of Rage) (1978) and his story *Menina a caminho* (A Girl on the Road), published privately in 1994. The brief but intense novel *Um copo de cólera* narrates the breakdown and reconciliation of a married couple; the title refers to the enraged conversations of the protagonists. It offers a microcosm of the rural society of the interior of São Paulo province.

MILTON HATOUM

nation language

Nation language is an emergent Caribbean creole (see **creole languages**) blending European, African and other languages, developed after European conquest and the destruction of Amerindian cultures and languages. According to Edward Kamau **Brathwaite**, who coined the term, nation language derives from the submerged language used by slaves to inform the English imposed upon the Caribbean psyche. Its lexicon may be based in English, but its contours, rhythms and timbres are closely related to the African aspects of the Caribbean experience. Brathwaite comments that it is 'inconceivable' for any Caribbean author writing in English today to not be influenced by this 'submerged/emergent' linguistic structure.

GAY WILENTZ

national anthems

If national anthems were in any sense representative of the communities and ethnicities within a given national territory, then Latin American anthems would necessarily have to embrace a variety of rhythms and idioms to reflect their complex ethnicity. But that does not seem to be their purpose. Rather the *himno nacional* is an abstract expression of national pride in a language immediately recognizable to the nations of Europe and North America. Hence the resolutely Italian or German style of most Latin American anthems. Indeed the vast majority of them were written in the nineteenth century by non-nationals and their lyrics – with their frequent references to sacrifice, dying for the *patria* and so on – belong to an idiom closest to the military culture so often reflected in the military-style bands that are usually charged to play them. Even Mexico's watershed revolution (1910–17) is not reflected in its choice of national anthem – Mexicanos al grito de guerra (Mexicans to War) – which dates from the last century. The exceptions to the rule are few, and belong to moments of deeper social transformation – thus Nicaragua adopted a Sandinista (see **Sandinista Revolution**) anthem after 1979, which was abandoned as soon as the **Chamorro** government took office in 1990.

MIKE GONZALEZ

National Dance Theatre Company of Jamaica

The National Dance Theatre Company of Jamaica is a dance company formed by Rex **Nettleford** and Eddy Thomas, both dancers and choreographers, to celebrate Jamaican independence from Britain in 1962 and to 'experiment with dance forms and techniques ... helping to develop a style and form that faithfully reflect the movement patterns of Jamaica and the Caribbean area.' NDTC's first performance, *Roots and Rhythms* (1962), integrated traditional ballet and indigenous dance. *Court of Jah* (1975) highlighted Bob **Marley**'s **reggae** music and the Caribbean Rastafarian movement (see **Rastafarianism**). Catalyst for the Jamaica School of Dance, formed in 1970, NDTC broadened to include singers and musicians in disciplined performances representing Jamaica's unique historical and cultural experience.

JILL E. ALBADA-JELGERSMA

national parks

Parks and natural reserves have become a favourite response of governments to the century's ecological crisis, because of their good-intentioned image and the impact of accompanying government decrees. However, they exhibit serious socio-economic, ecological and cultural contradictions. Conceived within an aestheticist concept of a reified nature, the first national park was established in the United States in 1873 for purely recreational purposes. Later, this legal instrument inspired other models of conservation across the world.

In Latin America, where many of the tropical and subtropical rainforests which once covered the surface of the earth still survive, national parks began to appear in the second half of the twentieth century: examples include the Vicente Pérez Rosales in Chile, the Santa Teresa in Uruguay, the Isla de Guadalupe in Mexico and the Kaieteur in Guyana. The proliferation of the model through every country in the region in the decade following the Second World War caused serious conflicts with expanding industries and with local populations, especially the indigenous communities who, since time immemorial, had occupied areas of forest without disturbing the ecological balance.

The majority of parks and reserves in Latin America date from the 1970s, 1980s and 1990s, and reflect growing international pressure from environmental organizations. Many of these reserves incorporate legal obligations which on paper favour the interests of traditional communities and the local population. However, conflicts continue in Mexico, Brazil and elsewhere.

By 1997, the United Nations recognized 323 national parks and another 723 protected areas in thirty Latin American and Caribbean states. These areas vary considerably in title, size and physical characteristics, and also in their quality, function and degree of maintenance. In Venezuela and Costa Rica, such areas have come to occupy a large proportion of the national territory (46 per cent and 26 per cent respectively). For countries like Grenada and the majority of its Caribbean neighbours, which depend on **tourism**, the national parks are an important source of income.

The largest national park is Chile's Bernardo O'Higgins Park, with more than 3.5 million hectares (7.9 million acres) and the Parima-Tapirapecó in Venezuela, which is of comparable size. The largest reserve is the marine reserve of the **Galapagos Islands**, in Ecuador, which is almost 8 million hectares in extent.

See also: ecotourism; green movements

LUIS L. ESPARZA

national style

Generated by social and political events, national styles in Latin America searched for authentic cultural roots and political identity, and expressed a historicist view inspired by past styles. The search for a national style was the first attempt to examine archaeology and urban and architectural patrimony, and to systematically preserve local culture. Though often reduced to formal aspects, it generated a significant body of theoretical work that preserved a sense of identity in a culturally and historically diverse continent.

In Mexico, it originated during the late nineteenth century with the archaeological uncovering of monuments. Intensified during the crisis of policies of Porfirio Díaz and the influence of French ideology, it reached its peak during the Mexican Revolution (1910–1917). José **Vasconcelos** upheld regional culture in his book, *La raza cósmica* (The Cosmic Race) (1925), and championed the murals of Diego **Rivera**, David Alfaro **Siqueiros**, José **Orozco** and Roberto Montenegro. The masses easily identified with works that idealized peasants, Indians and pre-Hispanic myths. During the 1940s, artists and designers collaborated to produce murals for **UNAM**, the National Autonomous University in Mexico; it resulted in the pre-Hispanic styled library mural of Juan **O'Gorman**. The official position of ***Indigenismo*** promoted native values, and produced the Museum of Anthropology (1963) by Pedro Ramirez Vázquez and Jorge Campunzano, which housed Pre-Hispanic artefacts in symmetric volumes flanking a central court.

In Argentina, Chile and Uruguay, immigration produced a ferment sympathetic to indigenous culture. Essayist Ricardo Rojas maligned the cosmopolitan lifestyle in *La restauración nacionalista* (The Nationalist Revival) (1909) and called for a return to Indo-Hispanic traditions. Beginning in 1914, Martín Noel promoted the restoration of colonial monuments and adapted their style to his design for the Argentinean Embassy in Lima and his private residence, which is presently the Museo Fernández Blanco. Angel Guido generated city plans for Tucumán and Salta (1938). He proposed neo-colonial and California-style houses, and colonial arcades for commercial centres, and published his book, *Arqueología y estética de la arquitectura criolla* (Archaeology and Aesthetic of Creole Architecture) (1932).

In Peru, the plight of Indians and character of colonial architecture generated a movement to revitalize pre-Hispanic style. Several authentic buildings were destroyed in Lima in order to provide space for buildings of indigenous and neo-Hispanic 'style'. It was the first attempt to systematically explore design from within the local culture. Although the work of Jose Uriel García, Emilio Harth-Terré and Hector Velarde created a theoretical basis for neo-colonial architecture, most expressions ignored new technology and programmatic concerns, while merely producing stylized façades. A similar development in Guatemala City resulted in the cluster of neo-Maya museums, including the national museums of art and archaeology.

JOSÉ BERNARDI

Nationalist Party (of Puerto Rico) *see* Partido Nacionalista Puertorriqueño

Nazaré, Ernesto

b. 1863, Rio de Janeiro, Brazil; d. 1933, Rio de Janeiro

Musician

From his late teens, Nazaré began to associate with the **choro** bands of Rio, combining their rhythmic and melodic verve with the wistful romantic repertoire with which he entertained audiences in the foyer of the Odeon cinema from 1909 onwards. He made his name with the famous **tango** 'Odeon' (1909) and the *choro* standard 'Apanheite, Cavaquinho!' (I've Caught You, Cavaquinho!) (1915). He began to record his own compositions from 1930, but became deaf in one ear and died shortly afterwards in a psychiatric institute. Nazaré's 218 tangos, polkas and waltzes remain a cornerstone of the choro tradition.

DAVID TREECE

Ñe-ëngatú

Cultural magazine directed and founded in exile in Buenos Aires by Epifanio Méndez Vall in January 1983. *Ñe-ëngatú* began as a means of keeping Argentina's large Paraguayan community informed. It has appeared continuously since 1983; although it began as a bimonthly, since 1992 it has produced ten issues per year covering a range of topics – political, economic and social information, art, history, literature and music. Since March 1992 (No. 55), the magazine has included a 'Rincón Literario' (Literary Corner) directed by Dr Teresa Méndez-Faith devoted to Paraguayan literature.

TERESA MÉNDEZ-FAITH

Nebreda, Vicente

b. 1930, Caracas, Venezuela

Dancer and choreographer

The most influential of Venezuelan choreographers, Nebreda trained in Venezuela and later with the Alicia **Alonso** and Roland Petit Ballet companies. In 1957 he joined the Joffrey Ballet in New York as a soloist and toured widely with them; in 1964 he became ballet master and choreographer to the Harkness Ballet. He later became artistic director (1975–80) of the Ballet Internacional Caracas and of the Ballet Nacional de Caracas Teresa Carreño (1984–). His repertoire includes classical ballets and modern abstract works, including *Percusión para seis hombres* (Percussion for Six Men) and *Nuestros valses* (Our Waltzes) among many others.

TERESA ALVARENGA

Negra Angustias, La

Matilde **Landeta**'s acclaimed 1949 film *La Negra Angustias* was based on Francisco Rojas González's second novel and reworked the true story of the legendary leader 'Angustias Ferrara'. The film belongs to the prolific genre celebrating the events and characters of the Mexican Revolution (see **revolutions**), but with a feminist twist: Angustias joins the revolutionary army to escape male persecution. She breaks the stereotype of the 'soldaderas', the women who cooked for, tended and made love to the revolutionary soldiers. Angustias punishes male offences, defends the weak and imposes her will, pistol in hand, while also struggling against her own desire to be white, feminine and educated.

PATRICIA TORRES SAN MARTÍN

Negret, Edgar

b. 1920, Popayán, Colombia

Sculptor

Negret's sculptures are often made of sheet metal, painted in vibrant colours, and showing the nuts and bolts that hold them together. In the 1970s, his works frequently evoked futuristic architecture or space navigation, while in the 1980s and 1990s they demonstrated his evolving dialogue with natural forms and pre-Columbian art. He studied in Cali, but became acquainted with the work of Robert Indiana, Elsworth Kelly and Louise Nevelson while living in Europe and New York. His early *Aparatos mágicos* (Magical Machines) (1957) evoked machines, clocks and other mechanisms but revealed a growing inclination towards abstract sculpture.

RUDI BLEYS

Negrete, Jorge

b. 1911, Guanajuato, Mexico; d. 1953, Los Angeles, California, USA

Actor and singer

Negrete personified the prototypical 'singing cowboy' (***charro***), virile and romantic in appearance and brave and gallant in character. His breakthrough came with Fernando de **Fuentes**' *Así se quiere en Jalisco* (That's How They Love in Jalisco) (1942). Though highly versatile in front of the camera, it was in the *comedias rancheras* (see **rancheras, comedias**) that Negrete shone as both actor and singer. His fine baritone voice and arrogant bearing dominated the best *ranchera* films of the period: Joselito Rodríguez's *¡Ay Jalisco no te rajes!* (Jalisco, Don't Give Up!) (1941), Juan **Bustillo Oro**'s *Cuando quiere un mexicano* (When a Mexican Loves) (1944) and Ismael **Rodríguez**'s *Dos tipos de cuidado* (Two Kinds of Caution) (1944), which brought together the two most famous 'charros' in Mexican films, Negrete and Pedro **Infante**. In Miguel Zacarías' romantic drama *El peñón de las ánimas* (Rock of Dead Souls) (1942), Negrete played alongside another Mexican cinema icon, María **Félix**, who later became his second wife. The film made them the most highly paid actors in Mexico, and Negrete became an idol throughout Latin America.

Negrete originally wanted a career in classical music, auditioning for the Metropolitan Opera in New York. He still intended to pursue this career after playing his first film role in Ramón Peón's *La madrina del diablo* (The Devil's Stepmother) in 1937. Not itself particularly successful, it launched a series of seventeen films over sixteen years in which Negrete played opposite beautiful women (María Luisa Zea, Miroslava Stern and Gloria Marín, with whom he appeared in ten films). The list included two films made in Spain, one co-starring with Carmen Sevilla.

The 'immortal charro' of Mexican film knew how to move the masses. Having achieved success as a singer and actor, he devoted himself to labour union work through **STPC** (the National Actors' Association of Mexico), which he presided over from 1944 to 1947 and again just before his death in 1953. When he finally retired, he left behind a strong organization. He was due to give a number of concerts in Los Angeles, but his liver condition worsened and he died one month before the premiere of his last film, *Dos tipos de cuidado*.

Further reading

Negrete, D. (1987) *Jorge Negrete: biografía autorizada*, Mexico City, Diana.

PATRICIA TORRES SAN MARTÍN

negrismo

Negrismo is a Latin American movement that developed, mainly in poetry, between 1926 and 1940. Its purpose, in parallel to ***indigenismo***, was to recuperate the roots and traditions of countries with a large black population in order to redefine their national identity. Europe at the time was calling into question the hierarchical vision of a rational Western 'civilization' and a more intuitive and sensual 'primitive world'. In the arts, this questioning was reflected in avant-garde (see **avant-garde in Latin America**) movements and in a renewed search for identity.

Negrismo was not only racial; its concerns were also social, which is why it included white, mulatto and mestizo as well as black poets. In this sense it was quite different from its equivalents in the USA and West Indies (the Harlem Renaissance for example) or the French West Indies and some parts of Africa, which produced **négritude**. The starting point for the movement were the early works of Nicolás **Guillén**, *Motivos de son* (Son Motifs) (1930) and *Sóngoro Cosongo* (1931).

The main features of the poetry of *negrismo* were, at the thematic level, the re-evaluation of black (north and south) American customs and traditions, describing their rhythmic dances and their sensuality, the effect of music and drumming in producing religious ecstasy, and their integration into a tropical landscape not unlike that of Africa. But it was also concerned with protesting the exploitation and oppression to which peoples were subject, which they did by describing the daily life of the poorest sections of society.

These historical and sociopolitical issues were expressed through images that were highly original in their sensuality and synaesthesia, like the fusion of fruits, colours, textures, tastes, scents, climate, vegetation, the parts of the human body and the forms and sounds of musical instruments, all of them specific to Latin America. The rhythms, although they were basically the traditional metres of Spanish poetry, integrated the percussive elements of Afro-American music. The accents of traditional Castilian verse were modified to recreate the mulatto forms of popular music, **son**, **rumba**, guaguancó and others. Repetitition – of words, sounds, lines, accents – was a common device, as was the use of words of African origin and of nonsense words or *jitanjáforas* which onomatopeically reproduced the sounds of musical instruments while also alluding to religious rituals.

The protest extended from local issues to embrace the exploited throughout the world, and the opposition black/white was transformed into a unity of black and white. Many *negrista* poems have become part of the body of popular song, losing their author together with the solemnity which often accompanies poetry. Its chief exponents include Guillén, Emilio Ballagas, Luis **Palés Matos**, Ildefonso **Pereda Valdés** and Nicomedes Santa Cruz.

Further reading

González, J.L. and Mansour, M. (1976) *Poesía negra de América (antología general)*, Mexico City: ERA.

Mansour, M. (1973) *La poesía negrista*, Mexico: ERA.

MONICA MANSOUR

négritude

An international cultural and intellectual movement begun in Paris in the 1930s by scholars from French-speaking Africa and the Caribbean. In broadest terms, the idea of *négritude* rested on the notion that people of African descent, in Africa and throughout the world, possessed a shared cultural heritage. The movement acknowledged and criticized the fact that people of European descent either ignored, misunderstood or denigrated that unique heritage. The movement's founders argued that blacks themselves should embrace, promote and disseminate their culture. These leaders also linked the embrace of their African heritage with political and economic goals such as ending colonialism and racial discrimination, and securing opportunities for success and prosperity for black populations, especially in Africa and the Caribbean. The movement also criticized mulattoes (and blacks) of the middle and upper classes who rejected their common heritage with the black masses and embraced only European or Western culture.

However, as an artistic and social movement *négritude* by no means rejected all things European. On the contrary, the founders received significant influence from European thinkers and European ideas, most notably surrealism (see **surrealism in Latin American art**) and communism. The three main founders were Aimé **Césaire** of

Martinique, Leon **Damas** of French Guiana (Guyane) and Leopold Senghor of Senegal. Most scholars cite the beginning of the movement as the publication of *Légitime défense* by a group of students from Martinique, in Paris in 1932. This polemical essay criticized the Western capitalist world and the inferior place which that world assigned to non-white cultures. The founders of *négritude* took direct inspiration from this text. Other important publications included the *négritude* journal, *L'etudiant noir* (The Black Scholar), published in Paris and the magazine, *Tropiques*, published by Césaire in Martinique. Of all the voluminous literary works associated with the *négritude* movement, Césaire's epic poem, ***Cahier d'un retour au pays natal*** (Notebook of a Return to My Native Land), published in 1939, is probably the most famous. It was in this poem that the term '*négritude*' first appeared in print.

Although the height of the movement arguably occurred around the mid-twentieth century, the ideas of the movement continued to influence scholars and artists many decades later. Indeed, Lilyan Kesteloot, one of the foremost historians of the movement, even refers to different 'generations' of *négritude* writers. It is also important to note that some of the ideas expressed by *négritude* had appeared in the work of some black Francophone writers even before the 1930s. This is particularly true in the case of Haiti with publications such as the *Revue Indigene* and the work of scholar Jean **Price-Mars**. *Négritude* also shared common theories with the US Harlem Renaissance. In fact, some *négritude* scholars and artists communicated with writers of that North American movement.

Further reading

Kesteloot, Lilyan (1991) *Black Writers in French: A Literary History of Negritude*, trans. Ellen Conroy Kennedy, Cambridge, MA: Harvard University Press (first edition 1968).

ROSANNE ADDERLEY

neo-baroque

Neo-baroque (*neobarroco*) is a term used particularly with regard to the Cuban writers José **Lezama Lima** and Severo **Sarduy**, both of whom were fascinated by the baroque of the Spanish Golden Age and of colonial Spanish America. Beginning with his long poem 'Muerte de Narciso' (Death of Narcissus) (1937), Lezama sought to outdo the difficult seventeenth-century poet Luis de Góngora in density of allusion, tormented syntax and verbal obscurity. Sarduy, in his essay 'Barroco' (Baroque) (1974), studied the connections between the scientific revolution and the baroque. Another Cuban writer who showed an interest in the baroque was Alejo **Carpentier**, particularly in *Concierto barroco* (Baroque concerto) (1974). Néstor **Perlongher**, the Argentine poet, proposed to import the Caribbean neo-baroque to the River Plate region, and in honour of the muddy colour of that river-estuary proclaimed his adherence to the 'neobarroso' (neo-muddy). An anthology of neo-baroque poetry, featuring both the *neobarroco* and the *neobarroso*, is *Medusario* (Medusaur) (1996), edited by Roberto Echavarren, José Kozer and Jacobo Sefamí.

DANIEL BALDERSTON

neo-concretism

Neo-concretism is a Brazilian movement, launched in July 1959 with the 'Neo-Concrete Manifesto' published by the poet and critic Ferreira **Gullar** in the *Jornal do Brasil*. Neo-concretism was born of a dissatisfaction with the pure 'concrete' art which was developed in Brazil during the 1950s by artists associated with **constructivism**. Gullar postulated a freer non-mathematical art which would concentrate on the ability of art to transcend its traditional limits. The most significant artists of the movement were Hélio **Oiticica** and Lygia **Clark**.

GABRIEL PEREZ-BARREIRO

neoliberalism

Neoliberalism is a name given to the new generation of free market economists who currently dominate the economic policy establishment in Latin America. The neoliberals draw their inspiration from the great classical traditions of economic thought. The bible of classical economics is Adam Smith's *An Inquiry into the Nature and Causes of the Wealth of Nations* (1776). Refined in succeeding generations by economists such as David Ricardo, Thomas Malthus and John Stuart Mill, Smith's book endeavoured, in contemporary language, to explain the origins of economic growth in the unhindered operation of the market, which he memorably described as an 'invisible hand' working to maximize economic growth and human happiness. Smith and his followers fiercely criticized any government interference with the benign workings of the market as likely to damage the prospects for growth. Subsequently, Ricardo extended such ideas to trade between nations and wages.

The second strand of neoliberalism is monetarism, the theory that a change in the money supply leads to a corresponding change in the overall level of prices, but does not affect output or employment. The theory was formalized by Irving Fisher as the quantity theory of money, and was revived by Milton Friedman in the 1960s, following the successful challenge launched by Keynes's *General Theory* in 1936.

Classical economics provided the intellectual foundations for the *laissez-faire* capitalism of the Victorian age. The trauma of the great depression in the 1930s convinced many people that the untrammelled workings of the market were anything but benign, and the classical school suffered a temporary eclipse in favour of the ideas of its two greatest adversaries, Karl Marx, who challenged the supremacy of the market, and John Maynard Keynes, who challenged monetarism. Both men argued for a far more central role for the state in economic management, and their ideas won many adherents in Latin America. As the state-led models of these two thinkers ran into trouble in the 1960s, a new generation of economists and politicians were once again drawn to the attractive simplicity of Smith's view of the world; some, trained at the University of Chicago by Milton Friedman, became known as the **Chicago Boys**. The onset of the **debt crisis** provided them, along with powerful supporters in Northern governments and the international financial institutions, with an ideal opportunity to push through neoliberal reforms in much of Latin America.

See also: structural adjustment; dependency theory; import substitution

Further reading

George, S. (1988) *Fate Worse Than Debt*, London: Penguin.

Green, D. (1995) *Silent Revolution: The Rise of Market Economics in Latin America*, London: Latin America Bureau.

Roddick, J. (1988) *Dance of the Millions: Latin America and the Debt Crisis*, London: Latin America Bureau.

Taylor, L. (1988) *Varieties of Stabilization Experience: Towards a Sensible Macroeconomics in the Third World*, Oxford: Clarendon.

DUNCAN GREEN

neon art

In Latin America the use of neon, invented by Frenchman Georges Claude in 1910, as a medium for sculptures, pictures and objects, was linked to the development of concrete, kinetic and optical currents from the 1950s onwards (see **kinetic art**), advocating new forms of expression employing materials made available by technological advances. The emblem of energy in modern life and its corresponding aesthetics, neon was central to the **happenings** of the 1960s. **Gyula Kosice**, a Hungarian-Argentine concrete artist and a member of the MADI group, was among the first to realize sculptures using neon lights, in a series inaugurated in 1946 called 'Estructura lumínica madí'.

MARÍA ALBA BOVISIO

Nepomuceno, Alberto

b. 1864, Fortaleza, Brazil; d. 1920, Rio de Janeiro, Brazil

Composer and conductor

Called the 'father' of Brazilian music, Nepomuceno was one of the first composers to use elements of traditional music. He played a key role in the emerging nationalist current in Brazilian music. His many works, mostly neo-romantic, include two operas, theatre music, works for orchestra, four string quartets, choral pieces and more than eighty songs. Outstanding among them are the *Série brasileira*, one of the first nationalist symphonic works; *As Uyaras*, a choral work based on an Amazonian legend; and *Quatro peças lyricas* (Four Lyric Pieces) for piano.

ALFONSO PADILLA

Nepomuceno, Max

b. Curaçao (date unknown); d. 1975, Curaçao

Sculptor

An autodidact, Nepomuceno transformed all sorts of metals and tins into people, housing, interiors or wall decorations. With simple tools he shaped magical new worlds, maybe rusty, but always fascinating. Although first dismissed as handicraft, his works are now recognized and have become valuable collectibles.

NEL CASIMIRI

Neruda, Pablo

b. 1904, Temuco, Chile; d. 1973, Isla Negra

Poet

The embodiment of the poet as a public figure, Neruda (born Neftalí Reyes) is probably Latin America's best-known and most widely read poet – and one who has repeatedly found new audiences, the last a posthumous one rediscovering his writing through the international success of the film, *Il Postino*, based on Antonio **Skármeta**'s novel, *Ardiente paciencia* (Burning Patience) (1985).

Enormously prolific, Neruda's poetry embraces the most public forms and the most intimate of lyrics. His earliest work, however, was still deeply concerned with landscape – most famously in the *Veinte poemas de amor y una canción desesperada* (Twenty Love Poems and a Desperate Song) (1924) where the sexual encounter is also a journey into a landscape. Born the son of a railway worker, Neruda entered Chile's diplomatic service and in 1925 was sent to the Far East. His work over the next ten years was collected in the first two (of three) volumes of *Residencia en la tierra* (Residence on Earth). These poems are in stark contrast to his later work – private, intense and above all absorbed with the solitude of the poet in a world constantly on the verge of destruction. The poem, 'Walking around', is testimony to this crisis. A transfer to Barcelona in 1933 and, particularly, to Madrid in 1935 brought Neruda to a crossroads – aesthetic as well as political. It was impossible in the conflictive atmosphere of the Spanish Republic on the edge of Civil War (see **Spanish Civil War, impact of**) to deny politics – Neruda, after all, was a regular companion of García Lorca, Rafael Alberti, Luis **Buñuel** and others in these days – or the public responsibility of artists. The outbreak of the Civil War on 18 July 1936 produced an artistic decision that marked the rest of Neruda's life – the determination to assume the responsibilities of a public poet, to set experience and emotion in the context of history. 'Explico algunas cosas' (I Explain a Few Things) is almost a personal manifesto in these terms – 'You will ask/what happened to the lilies.... Come and see the blood in the streets.' The years that followed were a period of intense political activity that largely shaped his poetry of the time, like *España en el corazón* (Spain in My Heart) (1937) and the writings gathered in *Tercera residencia* (1947). 'Contingent', sometimes pamphleteering writings, they are products of the moment and rarely survive it; after all, these were moments of vigorous campaigning for the Chilean Popular Front (1938) and a time as consul in Mexico, one of whose more inglorious moments was Neruda's provision of diplomatic papers to the muralist **Siqueiros** after the latter's attempt on the life of Leon Trotsky.

Neruda joined the Communist Party officially in 1945, though he had for some years functioned as a close fellow traveller; elected a senator in the same year, the 1947 *ley maldita* (evil law) banning the party forced him (like many others) into hiding. It was during that period (1947–9) that Neruda wrote his great ***Canto general*** (General Song) (1950), a sweeping panorama of Latin America's history, geography and contemporary reality whose direction is set out in the first five cantos of the first part. Here Neruda embarks upon a 'rediscovery' of the continent, a renaming of its many parts and a rewriting of Latin America's history from the perspective of the nameless 'Juans' (John Stonecutter, John Railsplitter) whose labour forged both Indian and Spanish America. In that sense the 'song' of the title is an epic, a foundational narrative for a post-colonial Latin America.

From the sometimes rhetorical flavour and linguistic richness of the *Canto general* Neruda moved to a very different tone and language: the *Odas elementales* (Elementary Odes), published in three volumes from 1951 to 1957, addressed the simpler aspects of the daily life of ordinary people – 'Old socks', 'Tomato', 'Onions' – in which beauty and poetic power were also to be found. These were hugely popular in the public readings that Neruda offered in factories and stadia around Chile. But these were also the years of the the tender love poetry of *Los versos del capitán* (The Captain's Verses), privately published in 1952.

Neruda continued to write prolifically and in a range of moods – as his confidently titled 1962 volume, *Plenos poderes* (Fully Empowered), suggested. By now he was a prominent political figure as well as a major poet. In the run up to the 1970 elections he was nominated as the Communist Party's presidential candidate, though he withdrew when his party joined the Unidad Popular (see **Popular Unity**) coalition that supported the successful candidacy of Salvador **Allende**. Briefly Chilean ambassador to France, Neruda spent the last years of his life at Isla Negra, his home on the Pacific coast south of Santiago. The award of the Nobel Prize in 1971 produced a famous acceptance speech and the phrase that would haunt his final hours – 'we must wait with a burning patience'. He died a few weeks after the military *coup* that overthrew the Popular Unity government. Fearful that his funeral would provide an opportunity for protest demonstrations the government of **Pinochet** attempted to prevent his burial in Santiago. But they failed in the attempt, and it seemed fitting that the only public demonstration permitted by the military for many years should have been the funeral of this poet who had always tried to speak with the voice of the people.

Further reading

Neruda, P. (1974) *Confieso que he vivido: Memorias*, Buenos Aires: Losada.
—— (1974) *Five Decades: Poems*, trans. Ben Bellitt and Alastair Reid, New York: Grove Press.
—— (1973) *Obras completas*, 3 vols (fourth edn), Buenos Aires: Losada.
Duran, M. and Safir, M. (1981) *Earth Tones: The Poetry of Pablo Neruda*, Bloomington: Indiana University Press.
Rodríguez Monegal, E. (1966) *El viajero inmóvil*, Buenos Aires: Losada.
Santí, E.M. (1982) *Pablo Neruda: The Poetics of Prophecy*, New York: Cornell University Press.
Teitelboim, V. (1991) *Neruda: An Intimate Biography*, trans. Beverley J. deLong-Tonelli, Austin: University of Texas Press.

MIKE GONZALEZ

Nery, Ismael

b. 1900, Belém, Brazil; d. 1934, Rio de Janeiro, Brazil

Painter

A precursor of surrealism (see **surrealism in Latin American art**) in Brazil, Nery wrote poetry and philosophical essays, and led an influential modernist salon in Rio. His peculiarly lyrical, religious, erotic, and oneiric style is preoccupied with essentialism and cubism. Rebellious young Nery first studied at the traditional Rio Fine Arts Academy, then left for Paris where he frequented Chagall and the surrealists. A theoretician and perfectionist, Nery destroyed numerous pieces, but his friend, the poet Murilo Mendes succeeded in salvaging approximately 2,000 (today in the Chateaubriand collection). Nery's magnetic personality and early death from tuberculosis undoubtedly added to his prestige.

MARIA ANGELICA GUIMARÃES LOPES

Netherlands Antilles and Aruba

Hundreds of miles of Caribbean Sea separate the Dutch Windward islands – Saba, St Maarten and St Eustatius – and the Dutch Leeward islands, Aruba, Bonaire and Curaçao. The former constitute three of the numerous islands of the arch-shaped Caribbean archipelago, while the latter are situated just off the coast of Venezuela. In total, these islands have a population of some 260,000 spread across 1,000 square kilometres. Continual controversy over political and economic power between Curaçao and Aruba fed the desire of the latter to leave the constellation of Dutch Caribbean islands to form a relatively autonomous part within the Kingdom of the Netherlands. This was granted in 1986, leaving the other five islands – or rather four and a half islands: half of St Maarten is French territory – to form the Netherlands Antilles. Aruba, the Antilles and the Netherlands now constitute part of the Kingdom of the Netherlands. Until its independence in 1975, the territory of Suriname on the South American coast was also Dutch. Neither the Netherlands Antilles nor Aruba have strong movements for political independence.

Throughout post-Columbian history, the island of Curaçao has usually been the centre of the Dutch Caribbean island territories. In the 1970s and 1980s, both Aruba and St Maarten gained economic independence thanks to a boom in tourism, but in the 1990s bad government, money laundering and drug trafficking brought them under closer surveillance by the Netherlands. For these same reasons and because of its deteriorating economic situation, Curaçao also had to tighten its ties to the Netherlands. As a result, about 90,000 people of Antillean descent now live in the Netherlands.

Besides the political, economic and demographic bonds with the Netherlands, the official language, Dutch, emphatically and artificially creates the impression of unity. On the Windward Islands, English is the common language, while on the Leeward Islands the creole **Papiamentu** is the native language of 90 per cent of the population. Literary output in English is limited, but in Papiamentu it is substantial. The authors who write in Dutch have generally not moved to the Netherlands – in contrast to those from Suriname – but they do find their primary audience there. Literary production in all three languages, but especially Papiamentu, tends to highlight island-based topics, which some authors, especially those writing in Dutch, deploy creatively to reach a wider audience.

The visual arts in the decades after the Second World War have increasingly opened up to international developments and are comparatively less island-bound than literature. Many visual artists work as easily on the islands as elsewhere.

The dominant film-maker from the region is undoubtedly Felix de Rooy from Curaçao, who runs a production company in the Netherlands with Aruban film-maker Norman **De Palm**. Among his films, *Almacita di Desolato* (1986) and *Ava & Gabriel* (1990), both shot in Curaçao, have been much acclaimed.

AART G. BROEK

Neto, Torquato

b. 1944, Teresina, Piauí, Brazil; d. 1972, São Paulo, Brazil

Poet and lyricist

Anguished poet of the Brazilian counterculture, Torquato Neto (full name Torquato Pereira de Araújo Neto) became a cult figure following his suicide at a young age. After coming to Salvador in the early 1960s, he became acquainted with Caetano **Veloso** and Gilberto **Gil**, whom he later joined in São Paulo. He wrote the lyrics to several *tropicalista* songs including 'Geléia Geral' (General Jelly), 'Marginália II' and 'Domingou' (Sunday). Shortly before his death he played the vampire in Ivan Cardoso's underground film 'Nosferatu no

Brasil'. An excellent collection of his work is *Os últimos dias de Paupéria* (The Last Days of Poverty) (1973).

CHRISTOPHER DUNN

Nettleford, Rex

b. 1933, Falmouth, Jamaica

Writer, choreographer and dancer

Nettleford is one of the most significant Caribbean scholars of this century. Many of his writings deal with the problem of race, class, politics and education in Jamaica. They include *The Rastafari in Jamaica* (1960) (see **Rastafarianism**), with M.G. **Smith** and F.R. Augier, *Trade Union and Industrial Relations Terms* (1967) and *Caribbean Cultural Identity: The Case of Jamaica* (1978). Nettleford is also the founder and artistic director of the Jamaica National Dance Theatre Company and a recipient of the Order of Merit (Jamaica). He is now a dean at the **University of the West Indies**.

KEITH JARDIM

Neustadt, Bernardo

b. 1925, Romania

Journalist

Neustadt is a controversial Argentine journalist who has worked for a number of newspapers, including *El mundo*, *El Cronista Comercial* and *Ambito Financiero* and magazines like *Racing*, *Todo* and *La Semana*. In the 1960s he moved into television and radio journalism. From 1967 onwards he presented the influential weekly **television** programme *Tiempo Nuevo*, a programme which has uncritically presented the official views of whatever government was in power, including the military regimes.

JORGE ELBAUM

Neves, David

b. 1938, Rio de Janeiro, Brazil; d. 1996, Rio de Janeiro

Film-maker and critic

Founder and leading ideologue of Brazilian **Cinema Novo**, Neves had a leading role in CAIC, the state film-financing body which supported film-makers like Glauber **Rocha** and Roberto **Santos** through the 1960s. His poetic directing debut, *Memoria de Helena* (Remembering Helena) (1969), depicted the life of a young woman living in a small town in Minas Gerais. He went on to make several films set in the chic Zona Sul of Rio de Janeiro – his last in 1988 – exploring the social mores of the middle class. They include *Muito prazer* (With Great Pleasure) (1980) and *Fulaninha* (That Girl) (1985).

ISMAIL XAVIER AND THE USP GROUP

Neves, Tancredo

b. 1910, São João del Rei, Brazil; d. 1985, São Paulo

Politician

A town councillor in 1933, Neves joined the Social Democratic Party and became a federal deputy in 1950. Minister of Justice under **Vargas** in 1953, and Prime Minister under **Goulart**, he joined the Movimento Democrático Brasileiro (MDB) in 1966 and was elected to the House and later the Senate. In 1982 he was elected Governor of Minas Gerais. In 1985 he was the successful presidential candidate of the Aliança Democrática, but during a mass on the eve of his inauguration he suffered severe stomach pains, was hospitalized and died the next day.

ANTONIO CARLOS VAZ

New Age

Esoteric and occult beliefs and practices were first introduced to Latin America during the late nineteenth century. The writings of Helena Petrovna Blavatsky (1831–91), founder of the Theosophical Society, and the Spiritist doctrines of Allan Kardec (1804–69), exercised considerable influence, particularly among the *modernista* (see **modernismo, Spanish American**) poets and intellectuals of the era, such as Amado Nervo, José Asunción Silva and Julio Herrera y Reissig. In Brazil alone, where the Federaçao Espirita Brasileira ('Brazilian Spiritist Federation') was founded in 1884, there were an estimated 5,000 active Kardecist groups operating in 1980. In many cases, Spiritism melded with African religious traditions. The *misa espiritual* ('spiritual mass') practised among Palo Monte sects in Cuba, and the ceremonies of **Umbanda** practitioners in Brazil, depend upon contact with spirits from the Roman Catholic, African and National pantheons.

The New Age movement can be summarized by four guiding concepts: holism, or the belief in the interconnectedness of all phenomena; ecological awareness; individual transformation through an eclectic variety of Western and non-Western religious practices; and, finally, the search for material and emotional well-being. Continuity exists between certain tenets of the Spiritist tradition and the New Age, such as the 'channelling' of master spirits, and the importance of gurus. The spread of New Age beliefs has occurred primarily through the print medium and specialized bookshops, and therefore continues to be associated with the literate, upper middle classes. These bookshops are found throughout the region, from Mexico to Argentina, and generally provide reading material and transformational 'tools' such as crystals and tarot decks. Other centres of diffusion include vegetarian restaurants, yoga centres and Hare Krishna temples.

It is believed that certain geographical points, or 'power spots', radiate an energy conducive to healing. **Machu Picchu** and Marca Huasi in Peru, Valle de Elqui and San Pedro de Atacama in Chile, Chichén Itzá and Teotihuacán in Mexico have all become common sites for New Age revivals. Vale Dourado and Pirinópolis near **Brasília** have become virtual Meccas for the thriving Brazilian New Age movement. The Legião da Boa Vontade (Legion of Good Will), an ecumenical society founded in 1950 and steeped in New Age philosophy, currently claims 552 centres throughout the world. Its Temple of Good Faith, a space-age pyramid dedicated to the exposition of New Age beliefs, was inaugurated in Brasília in 1989 and is, according to the Tourism Ministry, the national site most visited by Brazilians. Other alternative religious groups abound throughout the country, such as **Santo Daime**, headquartered in **Amazonia**, and centred around the use of a powerful hallucinogenic of the same name.

A number of New Age writers have acquired guru status, although the best-known internationally is the Brazilian ex-rock star Paulo **Coelho**. Despite having been severely criticized as simplistic allegories composed of a mishmash of esoteric references, his first two books – *Diary of a Magus* (1987) and *The Alchemist* (1988) – have sold to date over 5 million copies in Brazil alone. In part due to Coelho's success and that of other New Age writers, references to alternative, holistic faiths have become commonplace in Brazilian popular culture.

Sects based on what are commonly known as Japanese New Religions have been experiencing steady growth since the 1960s, and the Rev. Sun Myung Moon has recently invested $30 million dollars building his New Hope East Garden in the Brazilian state of Mato Grosso do Sul, rumoured to be the future headquarters of his Unification Church.

Further reading

Carpenter, R. (1999) 'Esoteric literature as a microcosmic mirror of Brazil's religious marketplace', Christian Smith and Joshua Prokopy (eds) *Latin American Religion in Motion*, New York: Routledge, pp. 235–60.

Melton, J.G. (1990) *The New Age Encyclopedia*, Detroit: Gale Research, Inc.

Heelas, P. and Amaral, L. (1994) 'Notes on the "Nova Era": Rio de Janeiro and Environs', *Religion* 24: 173–80.

Rohter, L. (1999) 'Suspicion following Sun Myung Moon to Brazil', *New York Times*, 28 November: A3.

JAMES LÓPEZ

New Jewel Movement

Political organization formed in Grenada in 1973 in opposition to the government of Eric **Gairy**, which had become increasingly corrupt and repressive. The New Jewel Movement (NJM) led a military *coup* on 13 March 1979 and established a People's Revolutionary Government (PRG) headed by Maurice **Bishop**. While its policies and social programmes were both popular and successful, Grenada became an increasingly militarized one-party state facing great economic difficulties. In October 1983, the government split as a result of ideological disputes. Bishop and seven others were executed in a bloody internal *coup* and a so-called Revolutionary Military Council (RMC) became the new governing body. It lasted six days before being ousted by a US-led invasion force. The NJM effectively ceased to exist, and later attempts to revive it brought little success.

See also: US intervention in Latin America

ROSANNE ADDERLEY

New Latin American Cinema

Film movement that emerged in the late 1950s–1960s throughout Latin America, only retrospectively recognized as a movement of pan-national scope, which gathered the various 'new' cinemas of the continent – especially the work of Fernando **Birri** in Argentina, Brazil's **Cinema Novo** and the **ICAIC** cinema in Cuba – under a powerful and politicized umbrella that encompassed socially committed film-making throughout the continent.

Faced with the crisis of studio-based production in the 1950s – such as the failure of the **Vera Cruz Studios** in Brazil or the lack of success of **Chile Films** – and infused with the political radicalism and hope of the era, young film-makers throughout the continent searched for innovative ways to promote different kinds of national cinema. The most important influence was the success and social relevance of Italian Neorealism, which had shown international audiences that a national cinema committed to social concerns could arise from the ashes of the Second World War, with low budgets, location shooting and non-actors. A number of these young would-be film-makers had studied at the Centro Sperimentale della Cinematografia in Rome in the early 1950s (Tomás **Gutiérrez Alea**, Julio **García Espinosa**, Fernando Birri); others admired Neorealism's achievements and sought ways to transform them regionally (Nelson Pereira dos **Santos** in Brazil, for example). Also of great significance was the growth and development of film culture throughout the 1940s and 1950s, with the establishment of **cine clubs**, **cinematheques** and specialized publications that set the stage for a different awareness of the cultural significance of the cinema and shifted attention away from the Hollywood model to alternative practices. It was also, of course, an era of political effervescence, characterized by the rise of nationalism and militancy ranging from the Bogotazo in Colombia in 1948 (see La **Violencia**) and the 1952 Bolivian Revolution, to the suicide of Getulio **Vargas** in Brazil in 1954, the military *coup* against **Perón** in 1955 and the success of the Cuban Revolution in 1959 (see **revolutions**).

The new cinema movements that emerged in Argentina, Brazil and Cuba in the late 1950s and early 1960s established their own national identity against the commercial products that preceded them, against Hollywood cinema and in relation to the more progressive strands of European cinema. Then they began to turn towards the continent. At the time the existing Latin American **film festivals** were (with one exception, the **SODRE** in Uruguay) geared towards European art cinema. The first encounter of many of these Latin American film-makers took place in Italy, at a festival sponsored by a Jesuit organization in Sestri Levante in 1962, where Alfredo **Guevara** (head of ICAIC), Glauber **Rocha**, Rodolfo Kohn and others met and agreed to work to establish collaborative networks. Two years later that spirit was reinvoked at the festival organized by the Cine Club **Marcha** in Uruguay, but it was not made official until the momentous 1967 **Viña del Mar Festival** and the *Encuentro de Cineastas Latinoamericanos* (Meeting of Latin American Film-makers). By 1967 it was evident that this new cinema spirit exceeded the products of national movements and included the works of film-makers working in relative isolation in countries as diverse as Uruguay (Mario **Handler**) and Bolivia (Jorge **Sanjinés**). A continental unity was again displayed at the 1968 Second Meeting of Latin American Film-makers, which took place in Mérida, Venezuela under the auspices of the Centro Documental at the Universidad de los Andes, alongside a festival of Latin American documentaries that already included some of the most influential films of the movement: *La* **hora de los hornos** (The Hour of the Furnaces, **Grupo Cine Liberación**, 1968, Argentina), Handler's *Me gustan los estudiantes* (I Like Students, 1968, Uruguay), Marta **Rodríguez** and Jorge **Silva**'s *Chircales* (Brickmakers, 1968, Colombia) and Octavio **Cortázar**'s *Por primera vez* (For the First Time, 1967, Cuba). At this and several meetings held in subsequent years (Viña del Mar in 1969, Mérida in 1970 and 1977, Caracas in 1971 and 1974), the different projects of the New Latin American Cinema were consolidated and implemented, and the movement and its practitioners gained strength and solidarity.

In the late 1960s and early 1970s it was easy to discern the boundaries of the movement. The New Latin American Cinema encompassed revolutionary, explicitly political films that called for an end to underdevelopment, poverty and oppression. Many insisted on using the '**cinema as a gun**' in the struggle for the political and economic independence of Latin America. Others, in the realm of fiction, retained an entertainment function, but transformed and demystified its standard parameters, producing realist, historical and inventive films that subverted and deconstructed the traditional distinctions and categories of the dominant cinema to tell other stories and to show other facts: in Chile, Miguel **Littín**'s *El chacal de Nahueltoro* (The Jackal of Nahueltoro) (1969) and *La tierra prometida* (The Promised Land) (1973); in Brazil, Rocha's *O dragão da maldade contra o santo guerreiro* (Antonio das Mortes); in Cuba, **Solas**'s *Lucía* (1968), for example. Simultaneously, film-makers produced important manifestos theorizing the aesthetic and political parameters of their practices and coining new descriptive categories such as *tercer cine* and imperfect cinema (see **cine imperfecto**).

Above all, this cinema was not industrial. With the exception of Cuba, which was politically a case apart, the New Latin American Cinema did not include any films that relied on the structures and strategies of the dominant sector in their production methods, aesthetics or distribution. These were independent films, marginal cinemas on the fringes of existing industries (Argentina, Brazil, Mexico) or artisanal practices in nations without a developed national cinematic infrastructure (Chile, Uruguay, Bolivia, etc.). As the only socialist nation in the Americas, Cuban cinema, despite its official status, was always deemed part of the movement. In fact, ICAIC was instrumental in promoting the idea and – through extensive collaborative arrangements – the very existence of the New Latin American Cinema project. As waves of repressive regimes, military *coups* and failed socialist efforts spread throughout the continent in the 1970s, Cuba stepped in, assisting for example, many Chilean film-makers exiled by **Pinochet**. It was also instrumental in forging a Nicaraguan cinema after the Sandinista (see **Sandinista Revolution**) victory through co-production agreements. Most significantly, Cuba officialized the New Latin American Cinema by founding, in 1979, the **Festival Internacional del Nuevo Cine Latinoamericano**.

By then, however, it was clear that the original impetus driving the movement had shifted. Beyond the political challenges that forced many film-makers into exile and/or silence, the very nature of the New Latin American Cinema project was problematic. On the one hand, as a cinema designed to subvert, demystify and challenge the dominant cinema and political givens, it was marginal and anti-industrialization by definition. On the other hand, part of the New Latin American Cinema project was also strengthening national cinemas and encouraging sustained production – concerns that demanded discussion about State protectionist policies and the commercial and popular viability of films. Thus gradually, throughout the 1970s and into the 1980s, the various national branches of the movement saw themselves transformed by the lethal combination of politics and economics: in Brazil, the State enterprise for cinema, **Embrafilme**, co-opted many of the aspirations of the *cinemanovistas*; redemocratization in Argentina made possible the growth of a quite successful industrial sector; the Cuban cinema, ultimately, must be seen as a product of an official State apparatus and subject to rather different national imperatives. Even more damaging was technological evolution: the spread of easy and inexpensive video technology obviated the need to use the infinitely more expensive cinema for explicit political and/or didactic interventions and made video the preferred medium for grassroots groups and a new generation of audio-visual creators.

The New Latin American Cinema, despite the creation of the Fundación del Nuevo Cine Latinoamericano in Cuba in 1985 (spearheaded by another Centro Sperimentale graduate and film enthusiast, Gabriel **García Márquez**), has dissipated. Many of the film-makers who spearheaded the movement continue to be active, but their work is now more clearly ensconced either within the parameters of international art cinema **coproductions** or circumscribed by national concerns. No one any longer argues that the cinema should be a primary agent in the pursuit of social change; yet all still seem to hold on to the belief that the cinema that Latin Americans watch should promote their well-being and reflect their realities, a lasting legacy of the New Latin American Cinema movement.

Further reading

Burton, J. (1986) *Cinema and Social Change in Latin America*, Austin: University of Texas Press.

Martin, M.S. (1997) *New Latin American Cinema, vols 1 and 2*, Detroit: Wayne State University Press.

Pick, Z. (1993) *The New Latin American Cinema: A Continental Project*, Austin: University of Texas Press.

ANA M. LÓPEZ

new social movements

New social movements first appeared in Latin America and the Caribbean in the 1960s, and have grown and multiplied since that time. In contrast to traditional class-based movements like the labour and agrarian movements, the new movements comprised a range of different actors, including the urban poor, women (see **women's movements**), gays and lesbians (see **gay and lesbian movements**), students, teachers and indigenous groups (see **indigenous movements**). Over the years they have mobilized in defence of life and person (**human rights** movements), livelihood and living conditions (urban movements), identity (women's and ethnic movements), the environment and topical issues.

The emergence of these movements responded to two major developments that happened to coincide. First, there was the major 'lifeworld' shift from rural to urban and industrial society. The full demographic and social impact of this shift was not felt until the 1970s, when the great majority of Latin Americans were living in cities of more than 100,000 inhabitants. Second, there was the crisis of the populist and developmentalist state (and of the oligarchic state in Central America), and the advent of the repressive military and authoritarian regimes of the 1970s and 1980s. Linking the two developments was the massive increase of state intervention in social life in countries such as Brazil and Mexico.

The biggest change was the rise of urban social movements, a catch-all category of popular groups inspired by demands for public utilities, social services, or access to land and water (see **water resources in Latin America**). They were responding both to the precarious conditions of urban life in shanty towns (see **shanty towns and slums**) and elsewhere, and to the repressive policies of the state, at a time when political parties and trades unions were no longer free to act. This combination of urban expansion and repressive government also proved a fecund context for new demands for rights, which became characteristic of the movements in this period.

The urban movements attracted most attention, but all the new movements, especially ethnic movements and human rights movements in defense of the '**disappeared**' and exiled (see **exile**), began to make demands in the language of rights, including land rights, labour rights, educational rights and human rights. The adoption of this language was linked to the spread of the movements, and contributed to (re)create civil society and support the struggle for democracy. Following the subsequent transitions to **democracy** in many countries of the continent, social movement activity has appeared to decline. But this activity always tends to fluctuate, and new social movements continue to shape the continent's cultural and political landscape.

Further reading

Escobar, A. and Alvarez, S. (eds) (1992) *The Making of Social Movements in Latin America*, Boulder, CO: Westview Press.

Foweraker, J. (1995) *Theorizing Social Movements*, London: Pluto Press.

Foweraker, J. and Landman, T. (eds) (1977) *Citizenship Rights and Social Movements*, Oxford: Oxford University Press.

Haber, P. (1996) 'Identity and Political Process: Recent Trends in the Study of Latin American Social Movements', *Latin American Research Review* 31 (1): 171–87.

JOE FOWERAKER

New World

The preoccupation with perfection, and the tendency to search for it somewhere else, are two defining features of European thought. As Edmundo **O'Gorman** points out, America became for the Europeans a new world more in a sense of renewal than of novelty. Empty in the eyes of the colonists, and savage to conquistadors and the missionaries, America was from the outset subject to a massive transfer of people and culture with high expectations; as a result the native element was reduced to an inferior status and all things American robbed of originality. This problem has been interpreted differently by Anglo-American and Latin American thinkers.

LUIS L. ESPARZA SERRA

newspapers *see* press and mass media

newsreels

Perhaps the most consistent film genre in Latin America, newsreels evolved from the silent cinema (see **silent film**) 'views' and 'actualities' of current events. The silent newsreel, as Aurelio de los Reyes has argued in relation to Mexican Revolution (see **revolutions**) documentaries, was perhaps the Latin American silent cinema's greatest achievement and includes important practitioners in almost every nation: Federico Valle and Max Glucksman in Argentina, Alberto and Paulino Botelho in Rio de Janeiro, Gilberto Rossi in São Paulo, Arturo Acevedo e Hijos in Colombia, etc.

Although it functioned primarily as a means of survival for film-makers who really aspired to make feature fiction films but were often financially unable to do so, the newsreel was one of the few genres of Latin American film to obtain regular regional distribution. In its earliest stages, newsreels were often independently sponsored by commercial enterprises – like breweries and soap manufacturers, for example. Later they became part of the regular offerings of the bigger studios. In the 1930s and 1940s the Mexican newsreels, *Noticiero Clasa-Excelsior* and *Noticiero Mexicano*, were exported throughout Central America, while **Argentina Sono Film**'s *Sucesos Argentinos* and the *Noticiero Panamericano* were also shown in Chile and Paraguay. Unfortunately, Hollywood's inroads into Latin America (see **Hollywood's impact on Latin American cinema**), with US government support during the Second World War, included the importation of the far slicker and much more regular newsreels of the major studios (Fox Movietone News, for example) and put a dampener on regional distribution.

National newsreels survived the Second World War through State intervention, either by funding production, making their exhibition compulsory (Colombia in 1942, Peru in 1944, Argentina in 1944, Brazil in 1946) or both. In Brazil, for example, the weekly *Cine Jornal Brasileiro* was produced directly by the Getulio **Vargas** government through the **DIP**, while in Chile, *Chile al Día*, a bi-weekly, was produced by the Film Services of the President's Office. Other privately produced newsreels in Cuba (*Noticiero CMQ-El Crisol*), Mexico and Argentina were completely dependent upon commercial sponsorship, while Acevedo e Hijos's long-standing newsreel in Colombia (since 1923) was forced out of production in 1946.

Several noteworthy figures began their careers making newsreels, among them independent producer (see **independent film producers**) Manuel **Barbachano Ponce**, who produced Tele-Revista in 1950 and Cine-Verdad in 1953 and later provided important opportunities for amateur film-makers like Tomás **Gutiérrez Alea** to learn the craft.

Perhaps the most brilliant newsreel practitioner was Santiago **Alvarez**, whose extraordinarily creative work for the Cuban *Noticiero ICAIC Internacional*, which he initiated in 1960, is a high point in the newsreel's international history. Alvarez liberated the newsreel from the pressure of the topical and the prototypical voice-over commentary, and, approximating the documentary, used it to meditate upon contemporary social problems and issues. He dealt with the time pressure inherent to the medium and his own lack of resources with the greatest ingenuity, developing a collagist style and improvising provocative sound–image relations, especially with music as in *Now!* (1965) or *Hanoi, Martes 13* (1967).

Beyond Cuba, however, the newsreel waned in importance as television and its nightly news broadcasts gained currency. The effort to duplicate ICAIC's success with the newsreel in Sandinista (see **Sandinista Revolution**) Nicaragua's IN-CINE failed resoundingly, for example. Ultimately the newsreel's documentary achievements were absorbed into documentary practices and new video technologies.

ANA M. LÓPEZ

Nexos

Nexos is a scientific and literary monthly founded in 1977 by Mexican historians Enrique Florescano and Héctor Aguilar Camín. Thanks to its progressive analyses of political and cultural issues, *Nexos* is widely considered the centre-leftist counterpart of ***Vuelta***, a similar publication with a more conservative viewpoint. Nevertheless, its publishers' ties to President Carlos **Salinas de Gortari** and his administration in the early 1990s caused *Nexos* to lose credibility among many on the left. The magazine has an estimated circulation of 10,000 and is affiliated with Cal y Arena Publishers, which prints longer works by many *Nexos* contributors.

JUAN CARLOS GAMBOA

NG La Banda

Popular Cuban dance orchestra formed in 1988; the initials NG denote *Nueva Generación* (New Generation), for its members proposed to create 'a new Cuban music for the future'. Its founding leader was José Luis Cortés (1951–), known as 'El Tosco', an academically trained flautist. Its founding members included Isaac Delgado, who later formed his own orchestra. Its music is distinguished by its fusion of different rhythms – **son**, **guaracha**, **jazz** and rap (see **rap music**); the song lyrics give a critical view of Cuban society and try to use the street slang of ordinary Cubans. They achieved national success very quickly, with numbers like 'El baile del limón' (Dance of the Lemon) and 'Necesito una amiga' (I Need a Girlfriend). They have recorded more than twenty albums, both in Cuba and abroad; outstanding among them are *No se puede tapar el sol* (You Can't Hide the Sun) (1988), *En la calle* (In the Street) (1993) and *Veneno* (1998).

WILFREDO CANCIO ISLA

Nicaragua

Sandwiched between Honduras and Costa Rica, Nicaragua is the largest country in Central America with a population of 3.8 million (1990). More than 30 per cent of the country's population live in Managua, the capital city and the nation's commercial and administrative centre. The predominantly **mestizo** population of the western and central regions is concentrated in Granada, León and Masaya, while the Atlantic coast population is predominantly Miskitu (see **Miskitus**) with enclaves of Sumus, Ramas and creoles. Although most Nicaraguans speak Spanish and many are Roman Catholic, those on the Atlantic coast speak English and local indigenous languages.

Nicaragua's cultural and political history has been marked by its strategic geographical location and topography. It has three major geographical zones but the Pacific coast is the demographic and economic centre of the country.

Four nicknames have been applied to Nicaragua through time. It has been called the 'Brown Brothers Republic', referring to its attractions for foreign capital. The second, invented by avant-garde (see **avant-garde in Latin America**) poet José **Coronel Urtecho**, describes Nicaragua as a passageway or 'rapid transit', referring to the US perception of it as a bridge between the Atlantic and Pacific, and as the original site for the trans-oceanic canal eventually built in Panama. The third, the 'land of lakes and volcanoes' evokes Nicaragua's two large lakes – Managua and Nicaragua – and its chain of active volcanoes. It is also sometimes described as a 'Banana Republic', a name originally applied to Honduras, an allusion to the continuous US presence in Nicaraguan affairs, which provoked the armed resistance movement led by Augusto C. **Sandino** (1927–33). Thereafter the country was led for several decades by the Somoza family (see **Somoza dynasty**), who were content to represent US interests in exchange for power.

Nicaragua is one of the least industrialized countries in Latin America. Its agricultural exports include indigo, **coffee**, **bananas**, cotton, beef and **sugar**. Agricultural production has influenced politics and culture; two parties have vied for power, the conservative and the liberal, and two cultural movements for domination, modernism and vanguardism. Leon was the home of Latin America's outstanding turn of the century poet and leader of Latin American *modernismo* (see **modernismo, Spanish American**), Rubén Darío. Darío was the central figure in Nicaraguan culture under the liberal government of José Santos Zelaya and a member of its diplomatic service. In the first half of the twentieth century, Darío was followed by Santiago Arguello (prose, poetry and drama); Gustavo Aleman-Bolaños (novels, poetry and political tracts); and Salomón de la **Selva** (poetry). But in fact it was the anti-modernist *vanguardista* movement, based in the city of Granada, which dominated Nicaraguan culture for most of the twentieth century.

The **Sandinista Revolution** of 1979 removed the Somoza dynasty from power and embarked on a project to modernize the economy, improve education and transform the culture. It immediately faced a hostile US government, which from 1980, under the presidency of Ronald Reagan, attacked the Revolution directly, by financing the **contras**, an armed counter-revolutionary movement, and indirectly, by bringing US pressure to bear, particularly on international economic agencies. When the Sandinistas were defeated in the presidential elections of 1990, and replaced by a conservative coalition headed by Violeta **Chamorro**, the country was virtually in ruins. Fifty thousand died in a decade of civil war, and astronomical inflation figures had undermined the economic programme.

The *vanguardista* movement were divided over whether to support the 1979 revolution; the distinguished poet Pablo Antonio **Cuadra** opposed it; while Ernesto **Cardenal**, poet and ordained priest, actively supported the **FSLN** (the Sandinista front) and became Minister of Culture in its first government. Under his guardianship, the Ministry encouraged a range of cultural activities, including the *talleres*, art and poetry workshops, and the publication of poetry by a generation of younger writers. In music, post-1979 Nicaragua encouraged a new activity and inventiveness, led by the brothers Luis Enrique and Carlos **Mejía Godoy**. But clearly this 'cultural revolution', which included the 1980 **literacy** campaign led by Fernando Cardenal, was constrained by the extreme lack of resources within the country.

Nicaragua was and remains a deeply Roman Catholic country; **liberation theology** was a powerful influence on *Sandinismo*, and the government included several religious leaders. Religious festivals still figure large in popular culture, like the week-long celebrations of the Immaculate Conception, *La Purísima*, which end on 8 December. During this week, altars are erected in homes and workplaces, and children travel from one to the other singing, reciting prayers and collecting candies and toys. Other festivals have an indigenous origin, testimony to the cultural **hybridity** described in Nicaragua's most important colonial text, *El gueguense*.

Nicaragua has a unique cuisine. *Gallo pinto* (the red cockerel) combines refried beans and rice cooked in coconut milk; *nacatamales* are prepared by steaming corn dough, rice, tomatoes, cassava and some meat in banana leaf. Popular non-alcoholic beverages include *pinol*, *tibio* and *pinolillo*, made out of dry and ground corn, mixed with cocoa, and **chicha**, which is made out of fermented corn (see **corn and corncakes**). The favourite hard liquor is **rum**, of which Nicaragua has one of Latin America's very best brands, Flor de Caña.

There can be no doubt that between 1979 and 1990, Nicaragua's most important cultural icon was Sandino. The shape of his famous hat was sprayed on countless walls during those years, and it had come to symbolize the anti-imperialism and nationalism that were central to the philosophy of *Sandinismo*. Equally, this little known country became in the 1980s a symbol of a search for new, revolutionary directions throughout Central America, which earned the constant attention, and enmity, of successive US governments. Since 1990, Nicaragua's reintegration into a global economy has brought with it a deepening inequality, a rise in the use and distribution of drugs in the region, a dramatic rise in crime rates and continuing armed confrontations between remanants of both the contra and the Sandinista armies. The failure of the Sandinistas to win the 1996 elections suggested that internal divisions and revelations, and rumours of corruption within their ranks, had ensured their failure to win back the popular support they enjoyed in 1979.

Further reading

Rodríguez, I. (1996) *Women, Guerrillas, and Love: Understanding War in Central America*, Minneapolis: University of Minnesota Press.

Smith, H. (1993) *Nicaragua: Self-Determination and Survival*, London: Pluto Press.

Walker, T. (1991) *Nicaragua: The Land of Sandino*, Boulder: Westview.

Whisnant, D. (1995), *Rascally Signs in Sacred Places: The Politics of Culture in Nicaragua*, Chapel Hill: University of North Carolina Press.

ANUPAMA MANDE AND ILEANA RODRÍGUEZ

Nicaragua, Nicaragüita

Composed by Carlos **Mejía Godoy**, Nicaragua, Nicaragüita is one of the most popular Nicaraguan songs; the diminutives in the title suggest affection and sentimental attachment for Nicaragua. The song evokes Nicaragua's indigenous past and is sung on special occasions such as birthdays and funerals, or at welcome and farewell parties. During the Sandinista (see **Sandinista Revolution**) period, it became a kind of informal national anthem sung by Mejía Godoy and his group, Los de Palacaguina.

ESTEBAN E. LOUSTAUNAU AND ILEANA RODRÍGUEZ

Nicarauac

The bi-annual publication *Nicarauac* was the Sandinista (see **Sandinista Revolution**) Ministry of Culture's main journal. The name was taken from the indigenous word meaning, 'here are the Arahuacos'. The first issue, published in 1980, was dedicated to the revolution, insurrection, **agrarian reform**, heroes and martyrs. Other issues addressed special topics such as Christians and the Revolution, the Central American Atlantic Coast, solidarity with the Revolution and Nicaraguan literary production. Its editorial board members included Sergio **Ramírez**, Daisy **Zamora** and Lizandro **Chávez Alfaro**.

ESTEBAN E. LOUSTAUNAU AND ILEANA RODRÍGUEZ

Nichols, Grace

b. 1950, Georgetown, Guyana

Teacher, journalist, novelist and poet

In both her poetry and fiction, Grace Nichols focuses on women characters in an attempt to acknowledge women's, especially Caribbean women's, contribution to human civilization and struggle for survival. Her long poem *is a long memoried woman* (1983) won the Commonwealth Poetry Prize, has been adapted for film, and inspired a full-length radio drama on BBC. She has also published a semi-autobiographical novel, *Whole of a Morning Sky* (1986). A primary school teacher and journalist, Grace Nichols travelled extensively in the hinterland of Guyana before emigrating to England in 1977.

FUNSO AIYEJINA

Nicola, Isaac

b. 1916, Havana, Cuba

Guitarist

A professor at Cuba's Conservatory of Music from 1951, and later its director, Nicola taught many important guitarists, including Leo **Brouwer** and Pedro Luis Ferrer. He studied with his mother, Clara Romero, before continuing his musical education with Emilio Pujol in Paris. He researched the vihuela and the ancient guitar in Paris, London, Madrid, Barcelona and New York and gave concert performances and lectures in Cuba and elsewhere. Later he became President of the Consejo Científico Técnico de la Enseñanza Musical (Scientific Technical Council of Music Education).

JOSÉ ANTONIO EVORA

Nicola, Noel

b. 1946, Havana, Cuba

Singer songwriter

A co-founder of the Cuban *nueva trova* movement, together with Silvio **Rodríguez**, Pablo **Milanés** and Vicente Feliu, in 1969 he joined the Grupo de Experimentación Sonora del **ICAIC** (the Experimental Music Group of the Cuban Film Institute). In addition to his own verses, he composed children's songs as well as music for cinema and the theatre. He worked with Silvio Rodriguez in the latter's Ojalá recording studios, founded in the late 1980s to provide opportunities for younger Cuban musicians.

JOSÉ ANTONIO EVORA

Niemeyer (Soares Filho), Oscar

b. 1907, Rio de Janeiro, Brazil

Architect

In 1996 Niemeyer finished the Museum of Contemporary Art in Niterói, Brazil, and continued working on new designs at his Rio de Janeiro office, right on his cherished sea front. Architecture, he says, is a field like any other and nothing but life is of any real importance, which is quite a statement coming from an architect who designed the principal buildings of the capital city of **Brasília** (1960) and numerous public buildings in Brazil and abroad – and a citizen who, after joining the Brazilian Communist Party in 1945, has kept his political allegiance even after the crumbling of the Soviet Union. Niemeyer has mostly practised in Brazil, except when he sought self-exile in Paris (1965), for opposing the military dictatorship that ruled the country from 1964–84. In exile, he produced a series of designs that include the Mondadori headquarters (Milan, 1968), Constantine University (Algeria, 1969) and the Labour Exchange building in Bobigny (France, 1972). As the Brazilian dictatorship began to yield, Niemeyer returned to Rio de Janeiro (1980). He designed various public buildings such as **Memorial de América Latina** (São Paulo, 1988–92) and the Museum of Contemporary Art at Niterói (Rio de Janeiro, 1991). A man of highly independent personality, he has always supported the Communist social platform and remained a critic of poverty in Brazil, while at the same time defending architecture as an art form of moving, sheer beauty.

Niemeyer was educated in the 1930s, at the transition from a traditional rural society to a developing industrial society in Brazil, and he synthesizes the contradictions of the Brazilian modernization process. Included among twentieth-century masters because of his pioneering approach to modern architecture, Niemeyer did not identify in its programme the least chance to transform the dramatic social condition of his country. And, despite seeking political solutions, he abided by the elite patronage system deeply rooted in Brazil's colonial past. This attitude is common among intellectuals associated with **Brazilian**

modernism, who rely on this alliance to build a vigorous cultural identity. Niemeyer's position is in itself paradoxical in terms of the modern architecture that, as of the 1930s, had been identified with Brazil's **development** project, though founded on a prestigious, singular work.

>As a young and unknown architect, Oscar Niemeyer joined the office of Lúcio **Costa**, who had been commissioned to design the Ministry of Education and Health building (see **Ministério da Educacão e Saúde**) in Rio de Janeiro (1936–43), based on Le Corbusier's preliminary plans. At once Niemeyer grasped the ingenious, constructive mind of the Swiss architect, whose poetic vision and freedom of improvisation deeply impressed him. This project exposed the young Brazilian designer's undeniable talent, promptly recognized by Costa – himself an instrumental endorser of modern architecture and unfailing supporter of Niemeyer's work from then on. In 1938 Costa and Niemeyer entered an association to design the Brazilian pavilion for the 1939 New York World Fair. The building, bearing Niemeyer's unmistakable label, became a classical reference for Brazilian modern architecture as it combined a light structure and transparent, fluid spaces into a gently curved ground plan, upswinging ramp and undulating façade enhanced by Burle **Marx**'s tropical landscaping design. Even more than Baroque tradition, the appeal of Nature – the omnipresent landscape, the female figure and a strong confidence in his own intuition – drove Niemeyer out from a more strictly rationalistic pattern.

In the 1940s and 1950s, commissioned by Juscelino **Kubitschek**, then mayor of Belo Horizonte and later president of Brazil, Niemeyer designed a major project that earned him international renown. He juxtaposed, to his earlier Cartesian volumes, unique structural shapes such as V- or W-shaped pillars, and sinuous canopies, many of which were transformed into autonomous elements by the strength of their form, as for example at Casa do Baile (Belo Horizonte, 1942) or his own home in Tijuca (Rio de Janeiro, 1950). Particularly significant in the architect's work is the recurrent utilization of freely-shaped structural profiles – often drawing on the existing Brazilian tradition of innovative framework engineering – that he designed with the assistance of engineer and great master of reinforced concrete, Joaquim Cardozo. This initial phase of Niemeyer's work yielded a masterpiece, the church of St Francis (Belo Horizonte, 1942), featuring a concrete parabolic vault previously used in large spaces though unprecedented in such an intimate chapel decorated by Brazilian painter **Portinari**.

In the late 1950s, Niemeyer largely reviewed his design. Beginning with Brasília, he created more concise forms for programmes that comprised single volumes separated by ample spaces. The lyrical attribute of these sculptural forms is widely acknowledged. However, Niemeyer's sketches clearly show that the moving trace observes the ductile nature of reinforced concrete but the line promptly renders a geometric profile. These are not preliminary sketches: they are final project designs that, given their remarkable frontality, seem to dispense with the inside. This vigorous contour, which Cardozo described as 'geometric irradiation', creates a scale ambiguity as it isolates forms in space, while the structure appeals to its own materiality. His works bear a self-sufficient stability and often classical, even surreal appeal as they hover over the line of the horizon, distant from our everyday life. To some critics, this presents an unresolved dilemma to Brazil and Brazilian architecture.

See also: Pampulha; Brasília

Further reading

Botey, I., Gomez, J. and Dalman, M. (1996) *Oscar Niemeyer – obras y proyectos*, Barcelona: Gustavo Gili.

Niemeyer, O. (1975) *Oscar Niemeyer*, Milan: Mondadori.

Papadaki, S. (1960) *Oscar Niemeyer*, New York: Georges Braziller.

Petit, J. (1995) *Niemeyer – Poète d'Architecture*, Paris: Lugano.

Puppi, L. (1996) *Oscar Niemeyer, 1907*, Rome: Officina.

Underwood, D. (1994) *Oscar Niemeyer and the Brazilian Architecture*, New York: Georges Braziller.

SOPHIA DA SILVA TELLES

nightclubs *see* cabarets and nightclubs

Nik

b. 1970, Buenos Aires, Argentina

Cartoonist

Nik (Christian Dzwonik) published his first drawings in the magazine ***Patoruzú*** at age fourteen. As a professional, his work appeared in the magazine *Muy interesante*, the newspaper *El Cronista* and the news review *Noticias*. Since 1993, *La nación* has published his political cartoons, humorous photomontages and the comic strip *El Crucero de Noé, Gaturro y Flia* (Noah, Gaturro and Flia's Cruiser). He has published eight books and in 1995 was awarded first prize by the Interamerican Press Association. His work in *La nación* has earned him a place among the best caricaturists of his generation.

PABLO JAMILIS

Niño, El

Predicting the weather is for Peruvians a routine and necessary part of economic planning: if 'El Niño' (the boy), a warm ocean current, is strong, there will be heavy rains, though fishing will suffer; but if the currents are cold, 'El Viejo' (the old man) or 'La Niña' (the girl) will bring drought, though fishing will be good. 'El Niño' is associated with Christmas, for it is usually felt in December. Sometimes its effects are unexpected, and felt worldwide. In 1982–3, the heaviest rains in Peru's history made rivers overflow and caused several hundred deaths and economic losses running into millions.

LUIS L. ESPARZA SERRA

Nishiyama González, Eulogio

b. 1920, Cuzco, Peru; d. 1996, Cuzco

Photographer and film-maker

A photographer of daily life in the Andes, Nishiyama's archive of twenty-five thousand negatives depicts the Andean landscape, its inhabitants and their rituals and constumes. In the 1950s Nishiyama was one of the founders of 'Cine Club Cuzco', which produced several films and documentaries about the Peruvian Andes. Their most important films are *Kukuli* (1960), *Jarawi* (1966), and, as cinematographer, *Yawar fiesta* (1986) (based on José María **Arguedas**'s novel and directed by Luis **Figueroa**). This ***indigenista*** filmography was so coherent that film critics have named it 'Escuela Cuzqueña' (Cuzco School).

JUAN ZEVALLOS-AGUILAR

Nixtayoleros

Founded in the early 1980s by Nicaraguan playwright Alan **Bolt**, the Nixtayolero ('new dawn' in Náhuatl – see **Náhuatl and Aztecan languages**) theatre group reflects Bolt's strong advocacy of indigenous cultures. After Bolt's resignation as National Theatre Director, where he had worked with Ernesto **Cardenal** in the Ministry of Culture, the Sandinista (see **Sandinista Revolution**) government kept Bolt on its payroll, funding his theatre group. In 1984 he settled Nixtayolero in his thirty-acre La Praga agricultural/theatre community. Stylistically influenced by Brecht and Enrique **Buenaventura**, Nixtayolero productions addressed repression and governmental abuse of *campesinos* believed to be contra collaborators (see **contras**).

ESTEBAN LOUSTAUNAU AND ILEANA RODRÍGUEZ

Nobel Prizes

Nobel Prizes are awarded annually since 1901 from a fund established by the will of Alfred Bernhard Nobel to 'those who, during the preceding year, shall have conferred the greatest benefit on mankind'. Prizes are awarded in Physics, Chemistry, Medicine, Literature, Peace, and (since 1969) Economics.

It is telling that Latin Americans have featured prominently among the Nobel laureates in two principal categories, Peace and Literature. The first

Latin American award was the Peace prize granted in 1936 to the Argentine Carlos **Saavedra Lamas** (1878–1958), president of the League of Nations, for his role in mediating the conflict between Paraguay and Brazil. Other Peace prize winners were: Adolfo **Pérez Esquivel**, Argentine architect, sculptor, and human rights leader (in 1980); Alfonso García Robles, Mexican diplomat and United Nations delegate for the Commission on Disarmament (in 1982); Oscar **Arias** Sánchez (in 1987), Costa Rican President and initiator of peace negotitations in Central America (in 1987); and, most recently, Rigoberta **Menchú**, for her human rights campaigns in defence of indigenous peoples (in 1992).

The Literature prize has been awarded to five stellar figures in Latin American letters. The first to be honoured with a Literature award was the Chilean poet, Gabriela **Mistral** (in 1945). Until Menchu's Peace prize in 1992, she was the only Latin American woman to have been honoured with a Nobel. Miguel Angel **Asturias** received his award in 1967, 'for his vivid literary achievement, deep-rooted in the national traits and traditions of Indian peoples of Latin America'. Since then, Latin Americans have scored a Literature Nobel at the rate of one per decade: Pablo **Neruda** in 1971 for 'poetry that with the action of an elemental force brings alive a continent's destiny and dreams'; Gabriel **García Márquez** in 1982, for his novels and short stories 'in which the fantastic and the realistic are combined in a richly composed world of imagination, reflecting a continent's life and conflicts'; and Octavio **Paz** in 1980, for his 'impassioned writing with wide horizons'.

Less well represented in the sciences, Latin Americans have only received prizes in Chemistry and Medicine. Argentine Luis F. **Leloir** received the Chemistry Nobel in 1970 for his discovery of sugar nucleotides and their role in the biosynthesis of carbohydrates. Another two Argentines have been awarded the Nobel in Medicine: Bernardo Alberto **Houssay** in 1947, for his discovery of the part played by the hormone of the anterior pituitary lobe in the metabolism of sugar and César Milstein (1927–) in 1984 for research on the human immune system. Finally, Baruj **Benacerraf**, born in Venezuela but a US citizen since 1943, was awarded the Nobel Prize for Physiology in 1980 for research on the genetic basis of immunology.

ANA M. LÓPEZ

Noble, Roberto

b. 1902, Buenos Aires, Argentina; d. 1969, Buenos Aires

Newspaper proprietor and lawyer

As a Minister in the Provincial Government of Buenos Aires, Noble sponsored important laws during the 1930s and 1940s, among them the Ley de Justicia de Paz Letrada which prevents abuses of power by magistrates, and Law 11.723 concerning intellectual property and protecting the rights of writers and composers. In 1945 he founded the tabloid *Clarín*, with an editorial line favouring national industrial development and independence. In the early 1960s, Noble married Ernestina Herrera, who became the newspaper's director after his death. Today, *Clarín* is the highest circulation Spanish-language newspaper (600,000 copies daily).

JORGE HALPERÍN

Nobre, Marlos

b. 1938, Recife, Brazil

Composer

Nobre trained in Recife, and then in São Paulo under Camargo **Guarnieri**, and in Rio with **Koellreutter**. A Rockefeller Scholarship afforded him lessons with **Ginastera** and Messiaen. Amerindian culture, Ernesto **Nazaré** and **Villa-Lobos** were early influences. *Ukrinmakrinkrin* (1966) for wind, voice and piano employs modified serialism and the language of the Xucuru Indians: it was used in Glauber **Rocha**'s film *O Dragão da maldade contra o santo guerreiro* (entitled 'Antonio das Mortes' in English) (1968). Nobre delights in sonorous effect (*Sonâncias*, for piano and percussion, 1972) and neo-classical clarity (*Desafio VII*, for piano and strings, 1980). He has also worked as a pianist, broadcaster and **UNESCO** delegate.

SIMON WRIGHT

Noche de los Asesinos, La

La Noche de los Asesinos is a two-act play written in 1964 by José **Triana** and awarded the 1965 **Casa de las Américas Prize**. The play presents three characters who exchange roles and attitudes while acting out an imaginary parricide ritual. The single set is transformed into various locations, metaphors for the many contradictions within each individual. The piece enacts the tragedy of a purification through death that is also a liberating exorcism. The characters relive their family conflicts and rebel against their tyrannical parents. This complex and profound cry for freedom has found an echo across the world, having been staged in more than thirty countries.

WILFREDO CANCIO ISLA

Noche de ronda

'Noche de ronda' is a waltz composed by the Mexican Agustín **Lara**, which begins 'Noche de ronda, qué triste pasa...' (A night wandering the streets, how sad it is). It was first performed by its author on Radio XEW, Mexico City, where Lara broadcast regularly between 1930 and 1932. It was an immediate hit, and has been performed since then by countless artists in Mexico and elsewhere. Among the most famous versions are those by Pedro **Vargas** and **Toña la Negra**.

EDUARDO CONTRERAS SOTO

noche de Tlatelolco, La

Elena **Poniatowska**'s third book, a classic of Latin American testimonial literature, was published in Spanish in 1971, and Helen R. Lane's English translation appeared in 1975 and was reprinted in 1992. It is the definitive literary treatment of the Mexican student movement of 1968 and its brutal repression by the Mexican government in the Plaza of Three Cultures, or **Tlatelolco**, in Mexico City. On 2 October 1968, the Mexican army surrounded a peaceful meeting with tanks, ambushing the unarmed participants, killing some 300 and wounding countless others. Subsequently they attempted to cover up their actions, burning bodies and accusing the students of having instigated the assault. This all occurred immediately before the Olympic Games (see **Olympic Games, Mexico 1968**) were scheduled to open in the Mexican capital; the presence of international reporters helped to disseminate news of the massacre. Nevertheless, Secretary of State Luis **Echeverría**, who gave the order to open fire, became Mexico's next president.

At the time Poniatowska was a journalist and housewife with progressive sympathies but no history of political activism. After survivors of Tlatelolco came to her with their stories, Poniatowska's literary and political trajectory changed dramatically. Since then, she has adopted a passionately committed stance and addressed controversial issues in her work, including urban guerrillas, disappeared political prisoners, indigenous and feminist activists, victims of substandard housing and government corruption in the 1985 earthquake, the international brigades in the Spanish Civil War (see **Spanish Civil War, impact of**), etc.

Massacre in Mexico consists of a chorus of voices, ranging from students to soldiers to nurses, to the students' families, conveying the euphoria, anti-authoritarianism and democratic impetus of the mass mobilizations, as well as the bitter sense of betrayal and disillusionment following 2 October. Of particular poignancy are the testimonies of anguished mothers searching in vain for their children's bodies and finding, in their place, piles of bloody shoes. These descriptions anticipate the oral histories of the **Madres de Plaza de Mayo** in Argentina, and mothers of disappeared (see **disappeared, the**) political prisoners in Chile and Central America during the 1970s and 1980s.

After Tlatelolco, leaders of the student movement were imprisoned, then exiled from Mexico. In recent years, as the tenth, twentieth and thirtieth anniversaries of the Movement have approached, a number of important literary works and political analyses have appeared, as well as Jorge Fons's film. *Rojo amanecer* (Red Dawn) (1989), which draws heavily on dialogue from *Massacre in Mexico*. In 1998, in the midst of another, more prolonged student strike, the journalist and former student leader Luis **González de Alba**, author of the testimonial novel *Los días y los años* (The Days and the Years) (1971) and one of Poniatowska's key informants for her own book, publicly accused Poniatowska of plagiarism. This ignited a debate about the responsibilities of the testimonial writer, one that could not have occurred three decades earlier, when the genre was in its infancy.

Further reading

Campos, M.A. and Toledo, A. (ed.) (1996) *Poemas y narraciones sobre el movimiento estudiantil de 1968*, Mexico City: Universidad Nacional Autónoma de Mexico.

Jorgensen, B. (1994) *The Writing of Elena Poniatowska*, Austin: University of Texas Press.

Schaefer, C. (1992) *Textured Lives: Women, Art, and Representation in Mexico*, Tucson: the University of Arizona Press.

CYNTHIA STEELE

Noé, Luis Felipe

b. 1933, Buenos Aires, Argentina

Painter

Noé studied law in Buenos Aires but soon began to dedicate himself exclusively to painting and writing about art. In 1961 he founded the **Otra Figuración** (or Nueva Figuración) group with Ernesto Deira, Jorge de la **Vega** and Rómulo **Macció**. In 1965 he published an important book entitled *Antiestética*, which contains his ideas on art and society. His works of the 1980s are concerned with ecological themes, often expressed in terms of the Conquest of the Americas.

GABRIEL PEREZ-BARREIRO

Noguera, Héctor

b. 1937, Santiago de Chile

Actor and director

Noguera has been linked with the Chile's Teatro de la Universidad Católica for most of his professional career. He trained at the same university with outstanding directors like Eugenio **Dittborn**, Eugenio Guzmán and Pedro Mortheiru. His outstanding theatrical roles have included Shakespearean roles as well as Vodavonic's *Deja que los perros ladren* (Let the Dogs Bark) (1961). A founder of the Teatro Q and Teatro de los Comediantes, in 1989 he created his own company, Teatro Camino, con-ceived as a travelling theatre group. Its major presentations included *El contrabajo* (The Double Bass) (1986) and Calderón's *La vida es sueño* (Life is a Dream). He has appeared in several films including *El **chacal de Nahueltoro*** (1970) and *Archipiélago* (1992).

CAROLA OYARZÚN

Nogueras, Luis Rogelio

b. 1945, Havana, Cuba; d. 1986, Havana

Poet and novelist

One of a group of young writers linked to the journal, *El **caimán barbudo***, Nogueras's first volume of poetry, *Cabeza de zanahoria* (Carrot Head) (1967) announced an original and innovative poetic voice whose characteristic was a colloquial language unlike the previous generation of poets of the 1950s and the early years of the Cuban Revolution (see **revolutions**). His subsequent works, including *Imitación de la vida* (Imitation of Life), which won the 1981 **Casa de las Américas** prize, and *Las palabras vuelven* (Words Return) (1994) confirmed his skill and wit, and his often disconcerting poetic allusions. He was a pioneer of the crime novel in Cuba: his titles include *Y si muero mañana* (And if I Die Tomorrow) (1977) and *Nosotros los sobrevivientes* (We Survivors) (1983).

WILFREDO CANCIO ISLA

Noigandres group

A group of poets in São Paulo in the 1950s, the Noigandres group included Augusto de **Campos**, Haroldo de **Campos**, Décio **Pignatari** and other associates. Noigandres is a Provençal word whose meaning had baffled Romance philologists who studied the troubadors. It appears in *The Cantos of Ezra Pound*, where the Brazilian poets (working on a translation of Pound) discovered it. Noting both the scholarly mystery surrounding the word and the prestige of the US poet, they adopted 'noigandres' as an emblem of artistic adventure and made it the title of their own journal of experimental lyric and **concrete poetry** (published 1952–62).

CHARLES A. PERRONE

noirisme

Generally seen as a Haitian form of ***négritude***, this late 1930s movement proposed a racialist view of culture and politics. It was provoked by the racial resentment created during the American occupation, and initially inspired by the views on cultural authenticity propounded by Jean **Price-Mars** in his 1928 work *Ainsi parla l'oncle* (So Spoke the Uncle). Its views were promoted in the journal *Les Griots* (1938–40), started by Louis Diaquoi, Lorimer Denis and Francois **Duvalier**, and to which the writers Carl **Brouard** and Magloire St. Aude were frequent contributors. *Noirisme* was criticized by both Marxists and conservatives, but became the state ideology in 1957 when Francois Duvalier became president.

J. MICHAEL DASH

Nola Hatterman Institute

The Nola Hatterman Institute is an art academy in Suriname named after the painter Nola Hatterman, who moved to Suriname from Amsterdam in 1953, began teaching art classes and was appointed principal of the Art School of the Cultural Center in 1960. She was an inspiring personality, dedicated to fostering talent among the poorer creole community. Many now well-known Suriname artists started their career with drawing lessons with Hatterman.

NEL CASIMIRI

Noriega, Manuel

b. 1938, Panama

Soldier and politician

Noriega came to power in Panama after the unexplained death in an air crash of General Omar **Torrijos**. Accused of electoral fraud and political assassination by his own chief of staff, Noriega repressed the demonstrations that followed and refused to resign from his post when the accusations were taken up by the US government. President Reagan then imposed an economic blockade in an attempt to force him out. In May 1989 elections were held and then annulled by Noriega. In September an attempted *coup* was crushed, and in December Noriega, now appointed Head of State, declared war on the USA. The response of President Bush was a bombardment of Panama – called 'Operation Just Cause' – which left more than a thousand dead and thousands homeless. After taking refuge in the Papal Nunciature in Panama, Noriega finally surrendered to the US authorities on 3 January 1990 and was taken to Miami to answer charges of involvement in drug smuggling.

MIKE GONZALEZ

Norton, Noel

b. 1923, Woodbrook, Trinidad

Photographer

Largely self-taught, Norton is the English-speaking Caribbean's most important photographer. His career spans thirty-five years and numerous national and international awards. Norton's work originated in a realization of the fragility of life, born out of his experience as an RAF navigator during the Second World War. The driving force of his work is the transmission of memory, and his photographs document the most diverse aspects of social and cultural life in Trinidad and Tobago and the Caribbean. Norton is famed for his landscape photography, and has the largest archive of Trinidad **carnival** photographs in the world, charting the history of the **mas** from 1962 to the present.

LORRAINE LEU

Nosotros

Published in Buenos Aires from 1907 to 1934, *Nosotros* was edited by Alfredo Bianchi and Roberto Giusti. It was the most canonical of the influential literary and cultural reviews of the period. Its lasting influence was due in part to the presence of a new reading public concomitant with the rise of the middle classes. It brought together a group of mostly social realist writers and intellectuals associated with the Boedo literary group (see **Boedo vs Florida**). The influence of *Nosotros* was so great that it gave its name to a generation of writers – also called the 'Generación del Centenario' – that grouped some of the most important writers of the period, like Manuel **Gálvez**, Evaristo Carriego and Alfonsina **Storni**.

FLORENCIA GARRAMUÑO

Noticiero ICAIC Latinoamericano

Weekly cinema newsreel started by the Cuban Film Institute, **ICAIC**, in 1960. Its founding director was Santiago **Alvarez**, who brought to the genre a dynamic and creative conception of film reportage. The *Noticiero* caught the image of the social transformations that took place in the first few years of the Cuban Revolution (see **revolutions**) and provided much of the material for the documentary records of events in Cuba and the Third World generally. The newsreel was shown weekly in cinemas, preceding the feature film, and in the countryside in the *cines móviles* (see ***cine móvil***). Highly popular for thirty years, the newsreels were an important training school for documentary directors, many of whom went on to make features. In the 1980s it began to offer an incisive critique of the immediate problems the society was facing, producing vigorous debates in administrative and government circles. The newsreel ceased production in 1990 because of a lack of financial and technical resources. It had produced by then more than 1,500 weekly editions.

WILFREDO CANCIO ISLA

Novães, Guiomar

b. 1896, São João da Boa Vista, Brazil; d. 1979, São Paulo, Brazil

Pianist

Novães had already launched her career when she took the platform in São Paulo in February 1922 to give the Semana de Arte Moderna's (see **Modern Art Week**) only recital uninterrupted by audience hostility. Her interpretation of **Villa-Lobos** and Debussy won six curtain calls. A Paris Conservatoire scholarship (1909) had preceded triumphant debuts in Paris (1911), London (1912) and New York (1915). She maintained artistic links with Villa-Lobos (giving the Brazilian première of *Momoprecoce* in 1930), but was more famously associated with Chopin, Schumann and Mozart.

SIMON WRIGHT

Novaro, María

b. 1951, Mexico City

Film-maker

Novaro is among the most talented younger directors in Mexico. Beginning with fictional shorts and continuing with the features *Lola* (1989), **Danzón** (1990), and *El jardín del edén* (The Garden of Eden) (1995), Novaro explores female subjectivities in various social contexts, including rural Guerrero, post-earthquake Mexico City and the US–Mexican border. Her films often focus on the mother–daughter bond in increasingly fragmented societies, and are characterized by the predominance of poetic images over dialogue, powerful evocations of characters and settings, and a productive engagement with the Mexican melodramatic tradition.

CYNTHIA STEELE

Novás Calvo, Lino

b. 1905, La Coruña, Spain; d. 1983, Miami, USA

Writer

Novás Calvo's novel *Pedro Blanco, el negrero* (Peter White, the Slaver) (1933) is an acknowledged precursor of **magical realism**. His two volumes of stories, *La luna nona* (Grandma Moon) (1942) and *Cayo Canas* (1946), include some of the first **crime fiction** written in Cuba. His characters and plots are characteristically violent. Novás Calvo's family emigrated to Cuba when he was seven; as a young writer, he joined the **Grupo Minorista**. He was a correspondent in Spain during the Spanish Civil War (see **Spanish Civil War, impact of**), and editor of the magazine *Bohemia* until he left Cuba in 1960.

WILFREDO CANCIO ISLA

novel

The Latin American novel gets a relatively late start in the early nineteenth century, with important romantic works including Jorge Isaacs's *María* (1867) and José Alencar's *Iracema* (1865); Doris Sommer has argued that the novel of this period is centrally concerned with nation formation, though that is sometimes concealed as romance. The finest nineteenth-century novelist was Brazil's Joaquim Maria Machado de Assis (1839–1908), known for such psychological masterpieces as *Dom Casmurro* (1899). An important tradition in the novel from Clorinda Matto de Turner's *Aves sin nido* (Birds without a Nest) (1889) through the works of Alcides **Arguedas**, Jorge **Icaza**, Ciro **Alegría**, Miguel Angel **Asturias**, José María **Arguedas** and Rosario **Castellanos** was *indigenismo*, concerned with the representation of the oppressed indigenous population, particularly in the Andes and in Mexico and Guatemala. Another cycle of works was concerned with rural life: Ricardo Güiraldes's *Don Segundo Sombra* (1926) on the life of the **gaucho**, José Eustacio **Rivera**'s *La vorágine* (The Vortex) (1924) and numerous other works, sometimes called the *novela de la tierra* (novel of the earth). Brilliant Brazilian examples of this regionalist (see **regionalismo**) tendency are Graciliano **Ramos**'s *São Bernardo* (1934) and *Vidas secas* (Barren Lives) (1938), and João Guimarães **Rosa**'s monumental *Grande sertão: Veredas* (The Devil to Pay in the Backlands) (1956). The novel of modern urban life begins with Oswald de **Andrade**, Roberto **Arlt** and Juan Carlos **Onetti**. A special case, intensely experimental, oneiric and, at the same time, rooted in the particularities of place, is Juan **Rulfo**'s great novel *Pedro Páramo* (1955).

The Latin American novel in the 1960s came into vogue, thanks largely to the international success of Julio **Cortázar**'s *Rayuela* (Hopscotch) (1963) and, on a much greater scale, Gabriel **García Márquez**'s *Cien años de soledad* (One Hundred Years of Solitude) (1967). With José **Donoso**, Carlos **Fuentes** and Mario **Vargas Llosa**, these writers were considered to be part of an international **Boom** of Latin American writing; what they had in common was a taste for (sometimes rather pedestrian) experimentation in fiction. This Boom is generally not considered to include writing in Portuguese and the various languages of the Caribbean, but this period witnessed the emergence of Antonio **Callado**, V.S. **Naipaul**, Edouard **Glissant** and others. The experimental tradition came to its highest point in Augusto **Roa Bastos**'s *Yo el supremo* (I the Supreme) (1974), a spectacular monologue (mostly) by José Gaspar Rodríguez de Francia, the dictator who ruled Paraguay from 1814 to 1840.

Subsequent developments have included the novels of Manuel **Puig**, who played brilliantly with the conventions of the serial novel and the romantic film, Juan José **Saer**, known for his intense, knotty constructions, reminiscent of Onetti in their sustained concern with a group of characters and a particular place on the Paraná river, and Clarice **Lispector**, a famous novelist of introspection. Other notable novelists of recent years include Ricardo **Piglia**, Rubem **Fonseca**, Sergio **Pitol**, Roberto Bolaño, Cristina **Peri Rossi** and Patrick **Chamoiseau**.

Further reading

Alonso, Carlos (1990) *The Spanish American Regional Novel: Modernity and Autochthony*, Cambridge: Cambridge University Press.

Fuentes, Carlos (1969) *La nueva novela hispanoamericana*, Mexico City: Joaquín Mortiz.

Lafforgue, Jorge (ed.) (1972, 1974) *Nueva novela latinoamericana*, 2 vols, Buenos Aires: Editorial Paidós.

Martin, Gerald (1989) *Journeys through the Labyrinth: Latin American Fiction in the Twentieth Century*, London: Verso.

Sommer, Doris (1991) *Foundational Fictions: The National Romances of Latin America*, Berkeley: University of California Press.

DANIEL BALDERSTON

Novo, Salvador

b. 1904, Mexico City; d. 1974, Mexico City

Writer

Known for a small body of brilliant poetry and a vast corpus of *crónicas* (see **crónica**), Novo was one of Mexico's most prominent **intellectuals** of the post-revolutionary period. With Xavier **Villaurrutia**, a close friend from secondary school to the end of Villaurrutia's life, and a circle of other friends (Carlos **Pellicer**, Jaime **Torres Bodet**, Jorge Cuesta, Gilberto Owen and Bernardo Ortiz de Montellano), Novo published several magazines, including **Contemporáneos**, which gave the group its name. In association with Villaurrutia, Cuesta, Celestino Gorostiza and Antonieta **Rivas Mercado**, Novo founded the Teatro Ulises, the beginnings of modern theatre in Mexico City. After a tempestuous period in the civil service, during which he was persecuted by members of the *estridentista* group (see **estridentismo**) for his fairly public homosexuality, Novo became the unofficial *cronista* (chronicler) of Mexico for several decades, eventually being named official *cronista* of Mexico City.

Novo's poetry explores the themes of love and solitude, expressing homoerotic love without quite declaring it as such. (A collection of sonnets published almost secretly, however, celebrates adventures with policemen, taxi drivers and others.) The most memorable of his slim output of poems are the free-verse poems of *Nuevo amor* (New Love) (1933), of which one of the best known is 'Junto a tu cuerpo totalmente entregado al mío' (Next to Your Body Totally Surrendered to Mine). Novo was also the author of ferocious satirical poetry, most notably 'La Diegada', in which he calls Diego **Rivera** a 'Búfalo Vil' (Vile Buffalo, pronounced Buffalo Bill).

Novo's prose writings include **travel writing**, essays on literature, photography, boxing, Mexico City, politics and countless other topics, and a scandalous autobiography. *Return Ticket* (1928) is the record of travels in western Mexico (and a reflection on **tourism**), while *Continente vacío* (Empty Continent) (1935) tells of a trip to South America, which includes an important encounter with Federico García Lorca in Buenos Aires. *Nueva grandeza mexicana* (New Grandeur of Mexico) (1951) is presented as a gloss on a famous poem about Mexico City by Bernardo de Balbuena (written in 1599). *Las aves en la poesía castellana* (Birds in Spanish Poetry) (1952), written when he was invited to join the Mexican Academy of Letters, is a learned treatise from the time when Novo was fired from the government service. His posthumous autobiography, *La estatua de sal* (The Statue of Salt) (1998), is a memoir of his and Villaurrutia's scandalous youth, with hilarious incidents involving Pedro **Henríquez Ureña** and many others; it could not be published until all of those mentioned were dead, finally appearing with a brilliant preface by Carlos **Monsiváis**, which reflects on the importance of homosexuality to Novo's work.

Novo's *crónicas* have been collected by José Emilio **Pacheco** in three huge volumes, *La vida en México en el período presidencial de Lázaro Cardenas* (Life in Mexico during the Presidential Term of Lázaro Cárdenas) (1964) and identical titles for the terms of Manuel Avila Camacho and Miguel Alemán (1965 and 1967). Another work of interest is *Las locas, el sexo, los burdeles* (Queens, Sex, Brothels) (1972), which begins with the defiant sentence: 'Hubo siempre locas en México' (There were always queens in Mexico).

At the end of his life, Novo was a celebrity who played the role of the dandy to the hilt, and who expressed strong disapproval of the student movement that culminated in the massacre at **Tlatelolco** in September–October 1968. In the decades after his death, his importance as a writer has been recognized, and his works have been carefully collected and republished, though his output was so vast that some portions have yet to be brought together. A building he owned in Coyoacán is now the Teatro el Hábito, the premier venue for political theatre in Mexico City, run by Jesusa **Rodríguez** and Liliana **Felipe**; as he looks down from a portrait, one imagines his delight that the traditions of political satire and of audacious modern theatre are alive and well.

Further reading

Novo, S. (1998) *La estatua de sal*, intro. Carlos Monsiváis, Mexico City: Consejo Nacional para la Cultura y las Artes.
—— (1996) *Viajes y ensayos*, Mexico City: Fondo de Cultura Económica.
—— (1991) *Antología personal: Poesía, 1915–1974*, Mexico City: Consejo Nacional para la Cultura y las Artes.
Monsiváis, C. (1977) 'Salvador Novo: Los que tenemos unas manos que no nos pertenecen', in *Amor perdido*, Mexico City: Era, pp. 265–96.

DANIEL BALDERSTON

Novos estudos

Novos estudos is the quarterly journal of CEBRAP (Centro Brasileiro de Análise e Planejamento) (Brazilian Centre for Analysis and Planning). It addresses current issues in national and international culture from a sociological, economic, anthropological and aesthetic perspective. First published in 1981, in the context of the transition to **democracy** in Brazil, its first editorial proposed to offer a space for open, interdisciplinary discussion in a pluralist spirit, an imperative for the country if it was to return to democratic practices. Its contributors have included outstanding Brazilian intellectuals such as Antonio **Candido**, Roberto **Schwarz** and Fernando Henrique **Cardoso**.

ANA CECILIA OLMOS

NS

Canadian Journal of Latin American and Caribbean Studies/NS, Revue canadienne des études latino-américaines et caraïbes, formally *North/South*, is a biannual journal of interdisciplinary research and writing on Latin America and the Caribbean published by the Canadian Association of Latin American and Caribbean Studies (CALACS). CALACS was founded at York University (Toronto) in 1969 to provide a forum for Latin Americanists working in Canadian universities. The Association also publishes a newsletter as well as a directory of Canadian scholars interested in Latin American Studies.

CATHERINE DEN TANDT

Núcleo de Música Nueva

Founded in Montevideo, Uruguay in 1966 by Coríun Aharonián, Ariel Martínez, Conrado Silva and Daniel **Viglietti**, the Núcleo de Música Nueva (New Music Group) was dedicated to the dissemination of contemporary music and in particular of new Latin American composers. In 1968 the group expanded to include composers, instrumentalists and music scholars. Since 1975, the Núcleo has been under the direction of composer Héctor **Tosar**. It has organized over 450 events, including concerts, festivals, workshops, seminars and lectures, and has recorded five albums of music by Uruguayan composers.

MARCO MAGGI

nueva canción

Chile's most important twentieth century popular music movement, *nueva canción* (New Song) was officially born in July 1969 during the First Festival of New Song organized by the Catholic University of Santiago. In the 1950s and 1960s Margot Loyola, Violeta **Parra**, Héctor Pavez, Gabriela Pizarro, the Cuncumén group and others began to recuperate Chilean folk music. In the mid-1960s the neo-folklore movement was formed in Chile by musicians like Angel **Parra**, Isabel Parra, Patricio **Manns**, Rolando Alarcón and Víctor **Jara** as well as groups like Los Cuatro Cuartos. *Nueva canción* was born directly out of the group's work and of the radicalization of the creative work of singer-songwriters by groups like **Quilapayún**, **Inti-Illimani**, **Curacas**, Aparcoa and **Illapu**. As a result, a number of classically-trained musicians, including Sergio Ortega, Luis **Advis** and Gustavo Becerra began to work with popular musicians. The club known as 'La peña de los Parra' played a key role in the movement, and sparked the creation of similar clubs (***peñas***) throughout the country, particularly in university areas. The **DICAP** record label and several **radio** programmes also played an important part in disseminating *nueva canción*.

The movement was particularly significant during the period leading up to **Allende**'s victory in 1970, and throughout the three years of **Popular Unity** government. When it was brought down by the military *coup* of September 1973, many members of the movement were killed, among them Víctor Jara; others (like Angel Parra) were jailed and Inti-Illimani, Quilapayún, Patricio Manns and Isabel Parra, among others, were forced into exile. The movement continued during the subsequent **Pinochet** regime under the name **Canto Nuevo**, and spread through more than fifty countries. *Nueva canción* ceased to exist as a movement with specific politico-cultural goals in the mid-1980s, but its cultural and artistic influence continued. Artistically, the project had five aspects: the dissemination of Chilean and Latin American folk music; the creation of lyrical and poetic songs; the use of *canciones contingentes* (contingent songs) to carry clear political messages; the use of multiple musical instruments in the groups; and the development of the *cantata popular* form created by Luis Advis with the work *Santa María de Iquique*. It was these latter two aspects which distinguished *nueva canción* from similar Latin American movements.

Further reading

Carrasco, E. (1982) 'La nueva canción en América Latina', *Revista Internacional de Ciencias Sociales* (UNESCO) 34(4): 667–92.

González, J.P. (1991) 'Hegemony and Counter-Hegemony of Music in Latin America: The Chilean Pop', *Popular Music and Society* 15(2): 63–78.

Morris, N. (1986) '"Canto porque es necesario cantar": The New Song Movement in Chile 1979–83', *Latin American Research Review* 21(2): 117–36.

ALFONSO PADILLA

nueva figuración   *see*   Otra Figuración

Nueva Revista de Filología Hispánica

Nueva Revista de Filología Hispánica (New Review of Hispanic Philology) was founded in 1947 at the Colegio de México, with the support of Alfonso **Reyes** and Daniel Cosío Villegas. It continued the fruitful work of the original *Revista de Filología Hispánica*, edited at the Buenos Aires Instituto de Filología by Américo Castro and Amado Alonso, which had made an important contribution to the study of Hispanic languages and literature. Currently edited by Antonio Alatorre, it maintains its original philological perspective, enriched now by contributions on literary theory and the study of indigenous languages.

RAFAEL OLEA FRANCO

Nueva Sociedad

One of Latin America's most widely read social science journals, *Nueva Sociedad* (New Society) was founded in 1972. Initially it was published in Costa Rica, with Alberto Baeza Flores as its first editor, but in 1976 publication was transferred to Caracas, under new editorship. Since then, circulation has widened steadily. Produced bimonthly, numerous well-known writers have contributed to it over the years, and it has served as an important forum for debate on the major social, economic and political issues of Latin America, considered from a broad, left-of-centre political perspective.

MARK DINNEEN

nueva trova

The most original and enduring musical expression of the Cuban Revolution (see **revolutions**), *nueva trova* acknowledged in its name its debt to the Cuban tradition of improvised songs to guitar accompaniment – the ***trova tradicional***. At the same time it had other antecedents – in the political ballads of Carlos **Puebla**, in the musical activity of the Grupo de Experimentación Sonora (Sound Experimentation Group) at **ICAIC**, the Cuban National Film School, where many of the movement's participants first met and played together, and in the cool jazzy ballads of the 1950s that were called '**feeling**', where Pablo **Milanés**, one of the two major protagonists of the *nueva trova*, had his musical education. Milanés's very personal composition, Mis 22 años (My Twenty-Two Years), written in 1965, announced his abandonment of 'feeling' and his return to traditional Cuban musical forms. The new poetry of revolution, particularly the current known as *poesía conversacional*, provided a thematic source for the profoundly lyrical songs of Silvio **Rodríguez**, who in 1967 declared in a journal article that he had left behind the songs of personal emotion for a new kind of music. An early example, in July of that year, was La leyenda del águila (Legend of the Eagle), a song criticizing the US presence in Vietnam. The song reflected, perhaps, a growing awareness of other song movements developing elsewhere in Latin America, particularly the Chilean ***nueva canción*** movement, and in the USA, whose tradition of protest song was represented by Irwin Silber and Barbara Dane, among others, when the Cubans hosted the Primer Encuentro Internacional de la Canción Protesta (First International Festival of Protest Songs) in August 1967. The new movement found a medium of expression in the popular but short lived TV programme, *Mientras tanto* (named after one of Silvio's most famous songs).

By 1968, *nueva trova* had been defined and consecrated as the music of the Cuban Revolution, responding perhaps to the many articles and editorials that had appeared in preceding months in journals like ***El caimán barbudo*** and *Juventud rebelde* calling for a new music distinct from the commercial sounds produced in the USA. In that sense, it became the official – and the orthodox – style of the revolution. And yet the work of Pablo and Silvio, together with Vicente Feliú and Noel **Nicola** among others, was not limited to the explicitly political *canciones contingentes* – they also cautiously addressed areas of intimate and personal experience. By the mid-1970s, Pablo and Silvio in particular appeared regularly beside the other members of the new Latin American song current – Roy **Brown** from Puerto Rico, Daniel **Viglietti** from Uruguay, the Argentine Mercedes **Sosa**, Angel and Isabel Parra from Chile, among others. Many of the songs of the *nueva trova* became standards among the performers of that generation – Te doy una canción (I Give You a Song); La era está pariendo un corazón (The Times are Bringing Forth a Heart) by Silvio; or Pablo Milanés's El poeta eres tú (You are the Poet), dedicated to Ché **Guevara**; Pobre del cantor (Pity the Singer) and Yo pisaré las calles nuevamente (I Shall Walk the Streets Again), written after the military *coup* against **Allende** in Chile. Not all of the songs were political; the movement produced its great love songs too – Milanés's Yolanda, for example, and the enigmatic metaphors of songs like Silvio's El uncornio azul (Blue Unicorn). In the mid-1970s,

Cuban music turned towards groups rather than *cantautores* (see ***cantautor***) (singer-songwriters); Manguaré, Grupo Moncada and **Irakere** were outstanding among them. Their music rested more obviously on Afro-Cuban rhythms for dancing, though they also included the songs of the *nueva trova* in their repertoire. In the 1990s, the international success of the Buena Vista Social Club and other bands in the 'vieja trova' tradition, turned the attention of audiences back to '**feeling**' and the older music that had to some extent been marginalized. And new *trovadores* were emerging, like Carlos **Varela** and Pedro Luis **Ferrer**, but their critical commentary on the realities of life in Cuba ensured that they would never enjoy the State support their predecessors had received.

Further reading

Díaz Pérez, C. (1994) *Sobre la guitarra, la voz*, Havana: Letras Cubanas.

MIKE GONZALEZ

Nueva Visión

Founded in Buenos Aires on 2 January 1953 as a publisher of books on international art, architecture and world theatre. Its breakthrough came in 1961 with the purchase of translation rights of theatre by Bertolt Brecht. Its theatre catalogue included Harold Pinter, Edward Albee, Samuel Beckett and Luigi Pirandello among others. As from 1971, the catalogue expanded to cover contemporary psychology and related issues. Aníbal Víctor Giacone and Haydée Pérez Giacone became partners and directors of the company in 1964 and have run it since then. The company describes itself as aimed at developing awareness of social welfare as a foundation for the creation of a just society.

ANDREW GRAHAM-YOOLL

Nuevo Día, El

The oldest newspaper in Puerto Rico, *El nuevo día* began in Ponce in 1909 as *El Diario de Puerto Rico*, and was renamed *El Día* in 1911. *El Día* moved to the San Juan area and became *El nuevo día* in 1970. With the demise of ***El mundo*** in 1991, *El nuevo día* effectively became the paper of record for Puerto Rico. Owned by the family of former Puerto Rican governor Luis **Ferré**, it publishes writers of all political views in its daily and Sunday editions.

See also: *Claridad*; *San Juan Star*

NANCY MORRIS

Nuevo Texto Crítico

Building on the excellent record of *Texto Crítico*, Jorge Ruffinelli's move from the Universidad Veracruzana to Stanford University, prompted the launch of *Nuevo Texto Crítico* in 1988. This twice yearly publication includes an editorial board that grew over the years from a few Stanford colleagues to an international list of notable critics. *NTC* maintains the initial drive of *TC*; it has incorporated critical discourses and foci of the American academy and interest in feminism, music, film, Puerto Rican and Chicano literatures. Monographic issues (for example, on Rigoberta **Menchú** and Rodolfo **Walsh**) and the publication of major symposia frequently replace general issues.

SAúL SOSNOWSKI

Nuevos Horizontes

Nuevos Horizontes is a Bolivian theatre journal founded by Liber **Forti** and published between 1947 and 1962. When it ceased publication, the Argentine theatre magazine *Thalia* described it as the end of 'an adventure that lasted fifteen years'. The journal set out to introduce foreign plays to a Bolivian audience. Each issue contained a complete playscript, such as Arthur Miller's *View from the Bridge*, Lergevistk's *The Executioner*, Dürenmatt's *The Visit*, **Cuzzani**'s *Una libra de carne* (A Pound of Flesh) and **Figueredo**'s *La zorra y las uvas* (The Fox and the Grapes). It not only created a theatregoing public, but also helped to form key figures in Bolivian theatre like Hilde Ortiz, Leo Redin, Hugo

Roncel and Pepe Arrellano and the playwright Gaston Suárez Paredes.

J.M. DE LA VEGA RODRIGUEZ

Número

Número was a Uruguayan journal published in two series, 1949–55 and 1963–4, and acknowledged for its interests in contemporary art and ideas, its cosmopolitanism and its intellectual rigour. The founding group of Emir **Rodríguez Monegal**, Idea **Vilariño** and Manuel Claps was later joined by Mario **Benedetti**. The review published translations of Eliot, Pinter and Queneau among others, as well as unpublished writings by **Borges**, Manuel **Rojas**, **Sabato**, Alfonso **Reyes** and **Bioy Casares**. But it was only the second series that emphasized Latin America, when Martínez Moreno joined the editorial board. Vilariño, meanwhile, resigned over the journal's apolitical stance. There were severe disagreements over Rodríguez Monegal's opposition to the Cuban Revolution (see **revolutions**); many board members resigned, refusing the takeover offer from the Congress for Cultural Freedom.

NORAH GIRALDI DEI CAS

Nunes, Clara

b. 1943, Paraopeba, Minas Gerais, Brazil; d. 1983, Rio de Janeiro, Brazil

Singer

One of the great female vocalists of the 1970s, Clara Nunes achieved enormous success and critical recognition with her highly stylized interpretations of **samba** and ijéxá songs. Her 1974 album 'Alvorecer' (Dawn) sold over half million copies and secured her a preeminent position within the Brazilian music scene for the next decade. Some of her most famous songs, such as 'Conto de areia', 'A deusa dos orixás' and 'Ijexá', popularized the mythologies of the Afro-Brazilian religions. She died tragically after an operation on varicose veins, and has been the subject of a recent tribute album.

CHRISTOPHER DUNN

Nunes, Luiz

b. 1908, Rio de Janeiro, Brazil; d. 1937, Rio de Janeiro

Architect

Born Luiz Carlos Nunes de Souza, Nunes was a pioneer of modern architecture in Brazil. As a student in 1930, he argued against academicism and for the modernization of architectural education. He translated Russian constructivist ideas about new forms and methods of producing and using architectural works to Recife (1934–7), where a team comprising technicians, artists and artisans made public buildings, adapting the principles of functionalism to tropical conditions, developing new techniques and rescuing the region's traditional methods of construction. It was a unique experiment in Brazilian culture.

ROBERTO CONDURU

Núñez, Enrique Bernardo

b. 1895, Valencia, Venezuela; d. 1964, Caracas, Venezuela

Writer

Novelist, journalist and chronicler of Caracas, Núñez is today considered one of the key figures in modern Venezuelan literature and one of the most important innovators in the Venezuelan novel. A graduate in medicine and law from the Universidad Central of Venezuela, he was also a journalist, contributing to *El Nuevo Diario*, *La Esfera*, *El Universal* and **El nacional** as well as the important avant-garde (see **avant-garde in Latin America**) journals **Billiken**, *Actualidad* and **Elite**. His two novels, *Cubagua* and *Galera de Tiberio* (Tiberius's Galley), address the theme which obsesses him, the mythic and historic roots of memory and time.

JORGE ROMERO LEÓN

Núñez, Guillermo

b. 1930, Santiago, Chile

Painter

Núñez's painting expresses in images ideas he has also expressed in prose: 'Located within a beautiful geography, we forget that this image has been forged out of the pain of our ancestors, the struggle of civilizations, the merciless destruction of our roots and the cry against social injustice. It is a country born out of the eruption of the earth and the rage of men.' His paintings are in museums throughout the world. He has worked and exhibited extensively inside and outside Chile. Imprisoned by the **Pinochet** government, he went into exile in Paris in 1975. He now lives and works in Chile.

ELIANA ORTEGA

Núñez del Prado, Marina

b. 1910, La Paz, Bolivia; d. 1995, Lima, Peru

Sculptor

In a long and distinguished career, Núñez del Prado focused on Bolivia, and specifically the Andes. Her earliest works were starkly realist; in the mid-1930s, however, she turned her attention to finding ways of expressing the spirit of Andean culture. The result were works like *Pachamama* (Mother Earth) (1935). By the 1940s, however, she had moved into a more abstract or symbolic phase whose recurring theme was maternity and the enduring ancestral strength of the women of the **altiplano** in works like *Mujeres andinas al viento* (Andean Women in the Wind) (1960–70) and the powerful granite forms of *Mujeres andinas al vuelo* (Andean Women in Flight) (1985).

MIKE GONZALEZ

Núñez Talavera, Domicio Agustín

b. 1947, Villarrica, Paraguay

Actor, stage designer and director

In 1954, Núñez founded a puppet group (see **puppet theatre**) in Asunción, La Cachiporra, and later in 1969 a theatrical group, Tiempoovillo, which he directed until 1973. From 1975 to 1990 he taught and acted in Colombia; he then returned to Asunción and founded the Centro de Investigación y Divulgación Teatral (CIDT). He directed the Escuela Municipal de Arte Dramático in Asunción from 1990 to 1992. His productions include Juan **Rulfo**'s *Luvina* and Augusto **Roa Bastos**'s ***Yo el supremo***. In 1995 he published the book *Pasión de teatro, los primeros XXV años* (A Passion for the Theater: the First 25 Years).

BETSY PARTYKA

Bibliography

Ades, D. (ed.) (1989) *Art in Latin America*, New Haven, CT and London: Yale University Press.

Agosin, M. (ed.) (1995) *A Dream of Light & Shadow: portraits of Latin American women writers*, Albuquerque, NM: University of New Mexico Press.

Alexander, R.J. (1988) *Biographical dictionary of Latin American and Caribbean political leaders*, New York: Greenwood Press.

Arbena, J. (comp.) (1999) *Latin American Sport: an annotated bibliography, 1988–1998*, Westport, CT: Greenwood Press.

Arnold, A. J. (ed.) (1994-) *A History of Literature in the Caribbean*, Amsterdam and Philadelphia, PA: J. Benjamins.

Baddeley, O. and Fraser, V. (1989) *Drawing the Line: art and cultural identity in contemporary Latin America*, London and New York: Verso.

Beezley, W.H. and Curcio-Nagy, L.A. (2000) *Latin American Popular Culture*, Wilmington: Scholarly Resources.

Behague, G. (1979) *Music in Latin America. An Introduction*, Englewood Cliffs, NJ: Prentice-Hall.

Benson, E. and Conolly, L.W. (eds) (1994) *Encyclopedia of Post Colonial Literatures in English*, 2 vols, London and New York: Routledge.

Bethell, L. (1998) *A Cultural History of Latin America: literature, music, and the visual arts in the 19th and 20th centuries*, Cambridge and New York: Cambridge University Press.

—— (ed.) (1995–2000) *The Cambridge History of Latin America*, 11 vols, Cambridge: Cambridge University Press.

Blakemore, H., Collier, S. and Skidmore, T.E. (eds.) (1985) *The Cambridge Encyclopedia of Latin America and the Caribbean*, Cambridge: Cambridge University Press.

Burton, J. (1983) *The New Latin American Cinema: an annotated bibliography of sources in English, Spanish, and Portuguese, 1960–1980*, New York: Smyrna Press.

Castedo, L. (1969) *A History of Latin American Art and Architecture from Pre-Columbian Times to the Present*, New York: F.A. Praeger.

Cole, R.R., (ed.) (1996) *Communication in Latin America: journalism, mass media, and society*, Wilmington: Scholarly Resources.

Corke, B. (ed.) (1989) *Who is Who in Latin America: government, politics, banking and industry*, New York: Decade Media.

Ficher, M. (1996) *Latin American Classical Composers: a biographical dictionary*, Lanham, MD: Scarecrow Press.

Fox, E. (1997) *Latin American Broadcasting: from tango to telenovela*, Luton, Bedfordshire: John Libbey Media and University of Luton Press.

Franco, J. (1967) *The Modern Culture of Latin America. Society and the artist*, New York: F.A. Praeger.

Gonzalez, A. and Luis, W. (eds) (1994) *Modern Latin-American Fiction Writers. Second series*, Detroit, MI: Gale Research.

Gonzalez, M. and Treece, D. (1992) *The Gathering of Voices: the twentieth-century poetry of Latin America*, London and New York: Verso.

King, J. (1990) *Magical Reels: a history of cinema in Latin*, London and New York: Verso, in association with the Latin American Bureau.

Mainwaring, S. and Valenzuela, A. (1998) *Politics, Society, and Democracy. Latin America*, Boulder, CO: Westview Press.

Martin, G. (1989) *Journeys Through the Labyrinth: Latin American fiction in the twentieth century*, London and New York: Verso.

Martin, M.T. (1997) *New Latin American Cinema*, Detroit, MI: Wayne State University Press.

Molloy, M. (ed.) *Internet Resources for Latin America*, New Mexico State University Library. http://lib.nmsu.edu/subject/bord/laguia.

Navarro, M. and Sanchez Korrol, V. (1999) *Women in Latin America and the Caribbean: restoring women to history.* Bloomington, IN: Indiana University Press.

Olsen, D.A. and Sheehy, D.E. (eds) (1998) *The Garland Encyclopedia of World Music. Vol. 2: South America, Mexico, Central America and the Caribbean*, New York and London: Garland Publishing, Inc.

Osorio, N., (ed.) (1995) *Diccionario enciclopédico de las letras de América Latina*, 3 vols, Caracas: Monte Avila and Biblioteca Ayacucho.

Poupeye, V. (1998) *Caribbean Art*, London and New York: Thames & Hudson.

Roca, M.A. (ed.) (1995) *The Architecture of Latin America*, London: Academy Editions.

Rossi, E.E. (1992) *Latin America: a political dictionary*, Santa Barbara: ABC-CLIO.

Rubin, D. (ed.) (1995–2000) *The World Encyclopedia of Contemporary Theatre*, 6 vols, London and New York: Routledge.

Schechter, J.M. (ed.) (1999) *Music in Latin American Culture: regional traditions*, New York: Schirmer Books.

Scott, J.F. (1999) *Latin American Art: ancient to modern*, Gainesville, FL: University Press of Florida.

Smith, V. (ed.) (1997) *Encyclopedia of Latin American Literature*, London, Chicago, IL: Fitzroy Dearborn.

Standish, P. (ed.) (1995) *Hispanic Culture of South America*, Detroit, MI: Gale Research.

—— (ed.) (1996) *Hispanic Culture of Mexico, Central America, and the Caribbean*, Detroit, MI: Gale Research.

Sullivan, E. (ed.) (1996) *Latin American Art in the Twentieth Century*, London: Phaidon Press.

Tenenbaum, B.A. (ed.) (1996) *Encyclopedia of Latin American History and Culture*, 5 vols, New York: Charles Scribner's Sons; London: Simon & Schuster.

Versenyi, A. (1993) *Theatre in Latin America: religion, politics, and culture from Cortes to the 1980s*, Cambridge and New York: Cambridge University Press.

Williamson, E. (1992) *The Penguin History of Latin America*, London: Allen Lane.

WITHDRAWN